The Expanding Blaze

The Expanding Blaze

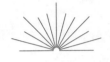

HOW THE AMERICAN REVOLUTION
IGNITED THE WORLD, 1775–1848

Jonathan Israel

Princeton University Press
Princeton & Oxford

Published by Princeton University Press, 41 William Street, Princeton, New Jersey 08540
In the United Kingdom: Princeton University Press, 6 Oxford Street, Woodstock, Oxfordshire OX20 1TR

press.princeton.edu

Jacket art courtesy of Manchester Libraries, Information and Archives, Manchester City Council

ISBN 978-0-691-17660-4

British Library Cataloging-in-Publication Data is available

This book has been composed in Ehrhardt MT Std

Printed on acid-free paper. ∞

Printed in the United States of America

10 9 8 7 6 5 4 3 2 1

From that bright spark which first illumed these lands,

See Europe kindling, as the blaze expands,

Each gloomy tyrant, sworn to chain the mind,

Presumes no more to trample on mankind:

Even potent Louis trembles on his throne,

The generous prince who made our cause his own, . . .

 —Philip Freneau, *On the Prospect of a Revolution in France* (March 1790)

Contents

Illustrations

The Expanding Blaze

The American Revolution and the Origins of Democratic Modernity

The Americans have taught us how to conquer liberty; it is from them also that we must learn the secret of how to conserve it.

—Condorcet, *Bibliothèque de l'Homme Public*, series II (1791), 5:250–51

The American Revolution (1774–83) ranks among the most written about episodes in history. It achieved independence and forged a great nation. But historians and readers have mostly approached it as an isolated American drama, the decisive formative episode in the history of the nation-state. That it also exerted an immense social, cultural, and ideological impact on the rest of the world that proved fundamental to the shaping of democratic modernity has since the mid-nineteenth century until very recently attracted little attention. The American Revolution, preceding the great French Revolution of 1789–99, was the first and one of the most momentous upheavals of a whole series of revolutionary events gripping the Atlantic world during the three-quarters of a century from 1775 to 1848–49. Like the French Revolution, these were all profoundly affected by, and impacted on, America in ways rarely examined and discussed in broad context.

The Thirteen Colonies seceded from Britain's empire, at the time by land and sea economically, politically, and militarily the world's most powerful entity, overthrowing the principle of monarchy in a vast territory where monarchy, long accepted, remained deeply rooted in culture and society. Challenging the three main pillars of Old World ancien régime society—monarchy, aristocracy, and religious authority—the Revolution altered, though not without extensive resistance, the character of religious authority and ecclesiastical involvement in politics, law, and institutions, and weakened, even if it did not overthrow, the principle of "aristocracy." Its political and institutional innovations grounded a wholly new kind of republic embodying a diametrically opposed social vision built on shared liberty and equal civil rights. The Revolution commenced the demolition of the early modern hierarchical world of kings, aristocracy, serfdom, slavery, and mercantilist colonial empires, initiating its slow, complex refashioning into the basic format of modernity. The wide repercussions of this American drama, the Revolution's world impact, accounts for the book's title, *The Expanding Blaze*, a phrase taken from Freneau's poem, and for its approach—presenting an overview of the revolutionary process in the Western and colonial worlds down to the 1850s viewed from the particular perspective of the American revolutionary example, experience, and ideas.

At the start of the American Revolution in 1774–75, hardly anyone intended to replace the highly elitist political systems in the Thirteen Colonies with more democratic and representative legislatures and constitutions, or make substantial alterations to the general frame of American culture and society. But amid the vast strain and effort involved, at a time when fundamentally new and disturbing ideas about politics, religion, and society radiated widely, it was inevitable that huge internal changes, intended and unintended, should ensue. The Revolution by no means ended the grip of the old elites on power or transformed the essentially hierarchical and deferential character of eighteenth-century American society, but it did exert an internationally democratizing and emancipating effect that proved—as many renowned reformers, project-formers, and political visionaries, male and female, acknowledged at the time—of immense consequence for America's future *and* the rest of the globe.

The Revolution affected and potentially, some thought and others feared, transformed all humanity, a few even claiming its external significance considerably outweighed the national. "The independence of America would have added but little to her own happiness, and been of no benefit to the world," contended the American Revolution's most forceful and internationally widely read publicist, Tom Paine (1737–1809), in 1805, "if her government had been formed on the corrupt models of the old world."[1] By "corrupt models," Paine, English by birth and upbringing, meant not just the absolutist and despotic monarchies dominating the European continent from Portugal to Russia, and the colonial empires then dominating Latin America, Africa, and Asia, but also "mixed government" systems, like Britain's constitutional monarchy, affording subjects more rights and freedoms than the absolutist monarchies but retaining appreciable influence for Crown and Church while transferring most power to the aristocracy. No country at that time resided under a more dominant and globally powerful aristocracy than Britain. Hence, radical detractors of "mixed government" expressly included England among the "corrupt models" presided over by kings, priests, and aristocrats. But only some Founding Fathers and parts of American society shared Paine's democratic republican standpoint; most revolutionary leaders and their followers rejected it.

Jefferson, Franklin, and their admirers, if sometimes less stridently than Paine, Price, Priestley, Barlow, Palmer, Freneau, Coram, Allen, and other Anglo-American democrats of the time, urged an American Revolution devoted not just to national independence but a much more expansive and ambitious goal: fundamental political, social, and educational reform within the United States and beyond. No doubt few adhered consistently to their publicly proclaimed emancipatory ideals. Many tailored their idealism in one way or another, compromising with the old order, including, when it came to slavery, America's foremost radical republican and declared opponent of "aristocracy," Jefferson himself. Nevertheless, in principle these democratizing republican writers and orators all demanded an American Revolution that adopted the powerful new concept of universal and equal human rights, emancipated every oppressed and exploited group, established full freedom of religion, expression, and the press, and removed religious control over society and education.

With the conclusion of the American War of Independence in 1783, there was much to celebrate, not only in America and countries allied to the nascent United States during the war—France, Spain, and the Dutch Republic—but, in the eyes of the progressive minded at least, also in Britain and beyond. In 1784, a year after the Peace of Versailles that set the seal on independence, the Welsh preacher and democrat Richard Price (1723–91), a leading political theorist of the age, delivered a stirring speech at an English banquet: "With heart-felt satisfaction, I see the revolution in favour of universal liberty which has taken place in America;—a revolution which opens a new prospect in human affairs, and begins a new era in the history of mankind;—a revolution by which Britons themselves will be the greatest gainers, if wise enough to improve properly the check that has been given to the despotism of their ministers, and to catch the flame of virtuous liberty which has saved their American brethren."[2] The American Revolution "did great good by disseminating just sentiments of the rights of mankind, and the nature of legitimate government; by exciting a spirit of resistance to tyranny which has emancipated one European country [the Netherlands], and is likely to emancipate others; and by occasioning the establishment in America of forms of government more equitable and more liberal than any that the world has yet known."[3]

In the Netherlands, American developments helped Europe's first avowedly democratic movement, the pro-American *Patriottenbeweging* (1780–87), to gain momentum and, during the 1780s, hold the attention of all European and American reformers. The Revolution's post-1780 consolidation, observed Price, afforded "still greater good by preserving the new governments . . . of the American States" from that "destruction in which they must have been involved had Britain conquered; by providing, in a sequestered continent possessed of many singular advantages, a place of refuge for opprest men in every region of the world; and by laying the foundation there of an empire which may be the seat of liberty, science and virtue, and from whence there is reason to hope these sacred blessings will spread, till they become universal, and the time arrives when kings and priests shall have no more power to oppress, and that ignominious slavery which has hitherto debased the world is exterminated."[4]

Both the American and French revolutions, and all the other supposedly "national" revolutions, were essentially tussles between rival "democratic" and "aristocratic" variants of a single Atlantic Revolution, just as all the alleged "national" enlightenments were in reality always battlegrounds between rival "moderate" and "radical" Enlightenment streams. Key themes of all the revolutions were democratic versus aristocratic republicanism, support for, versus rejection of, universal rights, citizenship for all versus limited suffrage, and disagreement over the place of religious authority in society. Where many late eighteenth-century contemporaries concurred with Adams and Hamilton in venerating Sidney, Locke, and Montesquieu, and in aligning American republicanism with existing aristocratic republics and "mixed government" systems, radical democrats like Paine loudly demurred, flatly denying such regimes—including the Netherlands, where the initial democratic upsurge was suppressed (with Prussian help) in 1787—were genuine republics at all. "It is true that certain countries, such as Holland, Berne, Genoa, Venice etc. call themselves Republics," affirmed Paine in June 1791, in a letter to the French revolutionary democrats Condorcet and Bonneville, "but these countries do not merit such a designation. All the principles upon which they are founded are in direct contradiction to every republican sentiment, and they are really in a condition of absolute servitude to an aristocracy."[5] In the Americas just as in Europe, the two kinds of republicanism, democratic and aristocratic, Paine rightly contended, were fundamentally divergent, at odds and irreconcilable.

Until 1848, "moderates" and democratizing radicals either side of the Atlantic not only argued their viewpoints drawing basic principles, examples, and precedents to a large extent from the American example and framework but appealed in conflicting ways to the two principal competing ideological trends, conservative and democratizing, within the American Revolution, to legitimate and justify their own moderate and radical perspectives and commitments. The architects of the radically reforming American Revolution—Franklin, Jefferson, and Paine—consequently became icons and sources of guidance for the Atlantic Revolution as a whole in its universalizing, secularizing, and egalitarian aspects. Correspondingly, those Founding Fathers—Adams, Hamilton, Morris, Jay, and to an extent Washington himself—associated with defending the pre-1776 American social status quo deploying Locke, Montesquieu, and the widely admired "mixed government" doctrine inherited from England served internationally, until the mid-nineteenth century, as standard-bearers of the "aristocratic" republicanism championing primacy of property and tenaciously resisting democracy by means of restricted suffrages, special qualifications for officeholders, and other oligarchic devices. In waging their ideological war, the rival groups of Founding Fathers inevitably construed the Revolution's founding documents divergently. The 1776 *Declaration of Independence*, more than any other American revolutionary document, strongly affirmed the everywhere bitterly divisive principle of universal and equal human rights, an aspect of the Revolution that proved of pivotal importance, becoming a particular hub of controversy in America and the entire sequence of Atlantic revolutions that followed, a controversy that powerfully surged up, once again, during the second half of the twentieth century following the 1948 Declaration of the United Nations and the African American civil rights movement.[6]

By an amazing coincidence, Adams and Jefferson died on the same day, 4 July 1826, the very day marking the fiftieth anniversary of the 1776 *Declaration of Independence*. The new republic of the United States, as Price, Priestley, Paine, and their British and European followers saw it, was not just unique but pressingly and universally relevant. For them, it was what Paine called the "opportunity of beginning the world anew" and "bringing forward a new system of government in which the rights of all men should be preserved that gave value" to American independence.[7] However, within and outside of America most of society prior to 1850 firmly rejected such perspectives, predominantly preferring to view Britain, the wealthiest, most powerful, and most industrially advanced nation, as the principal guide and inspiration for mankind's advancement, the best available model for political, economic, and social organization and reform. In Britain itself, all classes of the population except for certain dissenting elements nurtured an almost uncritical veneration for the "mixed government" constitution believed foundational to the country's unique world status. If not all English plebeians gloried in being "Protestant, flag-waving, foreigner-hating xenophobes,"[8] Britons predominantly shared the monarchical bias and politically and religiously reactionary leanings characterizing the late eighteenth- and early nineteenth-century British ruling elites and empire. Most people angrily denounced the homegrown movement of dissent that not only resented but dared to noisily deprecate monarchy, aristocracy, Anglicanism, and empire.

Yet adversaries of the "aristocratic" system in Britain, as in France, Holland, Ireland, Germany, and the United States, included much of the intellectual and literary elite. Indeed, England boasted an impressive number of radical enlighteners, progressive-minded thinkers, artists, writers, and poets, headed by Paine, Price, Jebb, Priestley, Godwin, Shelley, Millar, Erasmus Darwin, James Mill, John Stuart Mill, Catharine Macaulay, Mary Wollstonecraft, Mary Shelley, and later George Eliot, who all detested the antiquated legal system, restricted suffrage, "rotten borough" vestiges vitiating representation, lack of educational opportunity for most, and absence of full liberty of expression and religious freedom characterizing their country until the mid-nineteenth century, not to mention naval impressment (i.e., the "press gang" lasting until 1853), unequal marriage laws, and the obsolete penal code. In their eyes it seemed as plain as it was to Franklin, Jefferson, and Paine at the advent of the American Revolution that eighteenth- and early nineteenth-century England fell lamentably short of being the chief exemplum to the wider world. Together with many other Americans and European radicals they fervently hoped and expected that the nascent United States would assume this role.

Throughout the era from the 1760s to the 1850s, radicals rejecting the prevailing system in Britain and Europe faced a solid wall of disapproval and opprobrium. Some like Coleridge and Wordsworth abandoned the radicalism they espoused during their early years and later joined the intolerant conservative consensus. Equally, some post-1815 radicals designing the overthrow of British "mixed government" and aristocracy had earlier been firm supporters of the "corrupt" system they now unwaveringly assailed. The leading British philosopher of legal reform, Jeremy Bentham (1748–1832), in the 1770s a staunch critic of the American Revolution and of the proto-democratic ideas some contemporaries derived from its principles, after 1815 became an ardent advocate of democracy and the America he now considered modern representative democracy's prime vehicle. The consequent protracted, tortuous transatlantic ideological conflict reached its crescendo in the 1790s and opening years of the nineteenth century in Britain and America but dragged on disruptively for decades after throughout the Western world. In Britain, this social and cultural war waxed far more vehement during the first third of the nineteenth century than most Victorian Britons subsequently cared to recall. The rage and vitriol of an age in which the chief architect of modern political conservatism, Edmund Burke (1729–97), vilified Price for his "black heart" and "wicked principles" were later either watered down or, as with the great poet Shelley's unmitigated radicalism, altogether buried in oblivion.[9]

America's Revolution was the crucible of the United States, the "Atlantic Revolution" as a whole the crucible of modern representative democracy. It introduced universal and equal human rights, freedom of expression and the press, and republican liberty generally, as well as concerted efforts to end oppression of minority ethnic groups and establish an international code curtailing the curse of war. A sense of America's quest for liberty representing a new beginning socially, politically, and philosophically in a way the earlier Dutch Revolt against Spain (1567–1609) and the English seventeenth-century revolutions had not, and of great consequence for all men and worthy of close study, received widespread expression down to around 1850. So did acclaiming the Revolution's most renowned leaders—Washington, Franklin, Jefferson, Adams, and, more divisively, Paine—as heroes of all humanity. Yet the first modern historian to focus on this international aspect, R. R. Palmer, in his *The Age of the Democratic Revolution: A Political History of Europe and America, 1760–1800*, did so only in 1959. The American and French revolutions, Palmer reminded readers, "shared a good deal in common," and "what they shared was shared also at the same time by various people and movements in other countries," particularly, he suggested, Britain, Ireland, Holland, Belgium, and Switzerland but also Germany, Italy, and beyond.[10] This broad connection between the revolutions he presented as an overarching "Atlantic revolution." But Palmer's path-breaking idea never attracted as much consideration and discussion from Americanists or Europeanists (or Latin Americanists) as one might have expected.

Where the American Revolution's greatest impact in the 1770s and 1780s was on France, Holland, and Ireland (where the American example became especially closely linked to rising discontent), and among opponents of the British Crown and aristocracy, it was considerable also in southern Europe and Latin America. The most comprehensive work of political theory written during the Revolutionary War was actually composed in southern Italy by the Neapolitan political and legal theorist Gaetano Filangieri (1752–88) and much more widely diffused in Spain and Spanish America than in the English-speaking world. Banned outright by the papacy in December 1784, owing to its vehement declarations against the clergy and in favor of religious toleration, this multivolume work, *La Scienza della legislazione* (1780), a cornerstone of the late eighteenth-century "Radical Enlightenment,"[11] was "perus'd with great pleasure" by Franklin.[12] Inspired by the ideas of Raynal, Diderot, Helvétius, and Vico, Filangieri adopted the principle of equality of rights as proclaimed in America in 1776, viewing the American Revolution as the commencement of a generalized revolt against all despotism, oligarchy, and colonial oppression, and the hierarchical character of Old World society generally.[13] American revolutionary principles also permeated Filangieri's extended assault on the political ideas and geographical relativism of the most widely influential "moderate" political theorist of the age, the great French Enlightenment thinker Charles-Louis de Secondat, Baron de Montesquieu (1689–1755). Filangieri attacked Montesquieu for his promotion of the "mixed government" model bequeathing power in practice predominantly to aristocracies.[14]

Filangieri felt so uplifted by recent developments in America, he assured Franklin in 1782, he would have liked to settle permanently in Pennsylvania, America's "refuge of virtue," "country of heroes" and "brothers."[15] This was more than flowery courtesy. If the American Revolution exerted a democratizing effect, Pennsylvania, from 1776, surpassed the other colonies (except Vermont) by becoming the modern world's first near-democratic state, the first where government was formed by male society as a whole, electing the legislature and adopting a constitution granting universal adult male suffrage. Some contemporary observers eulogized Pennsylvania's new constitution and the inspiring part Pennsylvania's leaders played in ending state-supported institutionalized religious authority and in projecting black emancipation. The "immense populace that blesses your name," wrote Filangieri in his last letter to Franklin, dated 24 December 1785, endorsing his international, transatlantic renown, "is the only reward befitting the author of its liberty and avenger of its wrongs." In celebrating Pennsylvania's special character and the state's triumphs over royalty, aristocracy, slave owners, and ecclesiastical authority, Filangieri echoed a sentiment then common among radical *philosophes* and reformers that lingered for decades.[16] Philadelphia, which had around thirty thousand inhabitants when the Spanish American revolutionary Francisco de Miranda (1750–1816) arrived there in 1783, striking him as "one of the most pleasant and well-ordered cities in the world," was the heart of this extended, more democratic "American Revolution."[17] The French democratic republican Joseph Cérutti, in 1791, fully concurred: Philadelphia, "entirely populated with brothers and devoid of tyrants, slaves, priests, and without atheists, idle men or any poor, would deserve to be the capital of the world."[18]

The American Revolution's global impact was a matter of example and inspiration, providing a new ground-plan for human society. But this in turn raised issues of how far the Revolution had fulfilled its own promises at home and how far the United States should encourage and promote the wider process of transatlantic revolution abroad. In attributing to the new United States an especially exalted status in mankind's progress toward equality, liberty, and democratic republicanism, radical Enlightenment thinkers consciously assigned a global responsibility to America, a responsibility applying both within and outside the United States. "You free citizens of independent America," exhorted Filangieri in the fourth volume of *La Scienza*, in 1780, "you are too virtuous and too enlightened not to know that by winning the right to rule yourselves, you have accepted in the eyes of the entire world the sacred duty to be wiser, more moderate and happier than all other peoples! [agli occhi dell'universo il sacro dovere di esser più savi, più moderati e più felici de tutti gli altri popoli]. You must answer before the tribunal of mankind for all the sophisms your mistakes might produce contrary to liberty."[19] Price, Paine, and Condorcet too, besides others, were acutely conscious that the American Revolution's democratic aspect they and their allies cherished not only needed extending to Britain, Ireland, Europe, and the rest of the world but needed urgently to be consolidated, built on, and safeguarded within the United States themselves.

This part utopian, part realistic vision of the American Revolution stoked disaffection with the existing order in Europe and Latin America for three-quarters of a century. Where earlier revolutions rendering Switzerland and the United Provinces free republics, and seventeenth-century England a constitutional monarchy, were regarded virtually with "indifference" by the rest of humanity, remarked one of Filangieri's disciples, the Italian revolutionary Francesco Saverio Salfi (1759–1832), in 1821, and these upheavals had no truly lasting global effect, the American Revolution impacted far more widely and lastingly. The reason, contended Salfi, was that by the 1770s the Enlightenment had taken hold broadly, whereas before 1750 it had not yet pervaded society generally. Having first initiated a revolution of the mind "which soon became that of all Europe," the transatlantic intelligentsia, "les amis de la philosophie," priding themselves on having overthrown ecclesiastical intolerance and demolished the universities' obsolete science and scholasticism rooted in "the systems of Plato and Aristotle," entered on a new phase commencing in 1775, spurred by the American revolutionary experience, instigating a general assault on "political servitude." As a consequence of the new ideas and proliferation of the press the American Revolution was "forged in the crucible of the Enlightenment"; and it was this that made its message resonate as a truly universal event.[20] "The present is an age of philosophy; and America, the empire of reason,"[21] confidently averred Tom Paine's ally, the Connecticut revolutionary Joel Barlow (1754–1812), in 1787. Amid the optimism following the securing of American independence, he fully expected America to fulfill his radical vision of a world permanently transformed for the better. He later acknowledged having been wildly overoptimistic in his expectations of America *and* France.

By 1776, educated Pennsylvanians, New Englanders, and Virginians had changed appreciably in general culture, outlook, and religious beliefs—as had the societies of Europe and Latin America. Old-style piety had lost much of its hold at the elite level, and this was directly related to the advent of the innovative new political and social ideas. In New England, Enlightenment stress on reason and moral earnestness had displaced Calvinist dogmatism and stringency, though something of Puritan moral austerity still lingered. Gradual shedding of the old obsession with theology and denominational doctrinal disputes had engineered a fundamental shift toward toleration and secularization, trends common to all enlighteners. The United States' second president, John Adams (1735–1826), like Thomas Jefferson (1743–1826), the third president, was an outspoken champion of the Enlightenment, including freedom of conscience and worship. He disliked religious dogmatism, the clergy, and all talk of theological "mysteries." But suffused with New England earnestness, Adams did not push rejecting the claims of orthodoxy as far as the radical enlighteners. He was no atheist or "deist" but an austere Unitarian trusting in the ultimate reality and benign intent of divine providence, convinced organized religion, residually at least, remained necessary to society's well-being.[22]

Adams's moderate reformism in religion matched his moderate stance in political theory. His Enlightenment diverged from Jefferson's with respect to religion and, equally, the social and political spheres. Adams, admiring Sidney, Locke (no favorite of Jefferson's), and Montesquieu, upheld an older tradition of political theory, extolling "mixed government" and separation of powers, precisely the English gentry republicanism that until the mid-nineteenth century attracted ruling elites in Britain, France, Switzerland, and Holland as well as the United States. This type of republicanism, despised by Jefferson, Paine, and Condorcet, projected the aspirations of a landowner oligarchy venerating the Glorious Revolution of 1688 that first brought Britain and Ireland firmly under the political and economic domination of the aristocracy. A tradition mildly averse to commerce, cities, and the Dutch-Swiss commercial republican models, his was essentially an early Enlightenment thought-world, backward-looking socially but exerting a powerful enduring attraction for "moderates."[23] Few blended gentry republicanism with post-1750 mainstream Enlightenment constraint on religious authority more stereotypically than Adams.

Adams, consequently, never suffered anything like the public reprobation for irreligion that later dogged Paine and Jefferson.[24] His still more conservative son, John Quincy Adams (1767–1848), sixth president of the United States (1825–29), recalled these differences later, in 1831, rightly insisting on a considerable gap between his father's Enlightenment and that of Jefferson regarding politics, religion, and morality. As puritanical as his father but in later years tending more to religious orthodoxy, John Quincy had known Jefferson since childhood. It was the Enlightenment philosophy Jefferson imbibed in the 1760s from a certain teacher at William and Mary College in Virginia, he observed disparagingly, that led Jefferson to the "mysteries of freethinking and irreligion," "loose morals," and becoming if not an "absolute atheist" someone without "belief in a future existence." An avid reader, polymath, and convinced "deist," Jefferson, in fact, derived his philosophical outlook from a wide range of English and French writers, and unlike John and John Quincy Adams, grew more radical in outlook after 1775 down to around 1800. Jefferson, like Paine, combined his publicly more explicit animosity to religious authority with a more sweeping republican reformism and frequently declared hostility to "aristocracy."[25] As many realized, these various strands were closely linked practically and philosophically: Jefferson's radical reformism such as his abolishing the laws of primogeniture in Virginia and other anti-"aristocratic" reforms, noted John Quincy, arose from his "infidel philosophy."[26]

Adams and Jefferson were each iconic of a different type of Enlightenment. Each reflected, from opposite sides, the clash of revolutionary ideologies, moderate and radical, transforming political thought into a warring duality pervading the entire political and social arena—a struggle between "aristocratic" and democratic republicanism, partial and full rejection of religious authority, broad and narrow suffrages, and restricted and full freedom of thought and expression—all with vast implications for the late eighteenth-century world, the nineteenth century, and the future. Two irreconcilable tendencies within the American Revolution confronted each other, nationally and internationally, each working from a different philosophical base in league with closely related political movements abroad. American "moderates" exalted Locke, the legacy of the Glorious Revolution, and especially British "mixed government" as the proper ground-plan for America and all societies while Jeffersonians and Paineites embraced the philosophical democratic universalism and anti-aristocratic tendencies of Condorcet, Brissot, and the pre-Robespierre French Revolution, seeing Franco-American democratic republicanism as one body and the right path for mankind.

Until the 1970s historians, philosophers, and political scientists merely paid lip service to the fact that the Revolution, *Declaration of Independence*, and Constitution all stemmed from the "American Enlightenment."[27] Only with

Henry F. May's *The Enlightenment in America* (1976), still perhaps the best introduction among the remarkably few books devoted to the subject, did scholars begin investigating the Enlightenment's precise relation and relevance to the American Revolution. There was a serious problem with the historiography, May pointed out, regarding the Revolution's aspirations, rhetoric, political thought, and goals, a need to explore more fully the implications of attributing its special character to Enlightenment debates and ideas. May fully agreed that the Enlightenment in Europe and the Americas "tried to bring about," as one recent historian put it, through science, philosophical endeavor, critique of religion, educational reorganization, law reform, and studying political theory, "a new hopeful society."[28] The vast movement of intellectual and cultural reform and renewal comprehensively revolutionized philosophy, theology, historiography, the exact sciences, social science, literature, and moral thought and continued to strive for amelioration, he demonstrated, throughout the Napoleonic era (1799–1815) too. Historians and philosophers, May showed, therefore needed to appraise the American Revolution's ideas, rhetoric, and legislative terminology in a broader intellectual context than they had been accustomed to. But they also needed to sharpen their general categories. For the Western Enlightenment could never resolve its abiding internal split over whether Enlightenment meant reforming the existing social, legal, and institutional order while leaving the main structure intact, or whether correcting abuses meant replacing the old institutions, laws, and practices with an entirely new structure.[29] Only up to a point did enlighteners share a "common goal—the moralization and humanization of the world."

Disagreement over how far to retain the ancien régime built on monarchical, aristocratic, and ecclesiastical hegemony integrally connected developments and ideas either side of the Atlantic. The Atlantic revolutions were all intimately linked pragmatically and philosophically, rendering the rift between the competing Enlightenment moderate and radical streams universal and everywhere bitter and protracted. The first to step significantly beyond Palmer, May identified at the core of the American Revolution a struggle between two opposing transatlantic ideological wings, designating these "moderate Enlightenment" and "revolutionary Enlightenment" (or alternatively "radical Enlightenment"). These conflicting and irreconcilable ideological tendencies were rooted in divergent philosophical principles and systems of thought, extolling different thinkers, books, and intellectual trends. This dialectic between the American Revolution's rival dimensions, moderate and radical, along with the close affinities between the American and European revolutions, were for over six decades, down to around 1850, also widely understood and invoked by contemporaries.

Following May's seminal book it became more widely appreciated that while the American Enlightenment's intellectual content derived mostly from Europe (especially Britain and France), "America served European intellectuals as an example and even an inspiration of ideas at work, theories put into practice."[30] During the 1970s, the ensuing flurry of interest in America's Enlightenment as a deeply contested intellectual arena, a basic duality fundamentally shaping the essential character of American society and politics, proved, however, curiously brief. Distracted by the "cultural turn" of the 1970s, 1980s, and 1990s, scholars were soon again drawn away from the key intellectual and ideological issues, instead promoting the notion that the Enlightenment was chiefly a question of social practice and sociability rather than new principles, concepts, and thinking, as was always claimed by pre-1850 philosophers and revolutionaries. Scholars came to focus chiefly on general attitudes, changing modes, and culture, thereby reverting to the older pre-1970 conviction that Enlightenment intellectual and ideological debates and ideas were, after all, peripheral.[31]

The "cultural turn" hence obscured once again the main contours within the American and transatlantic Enlightenment that May identified as fundamental.[32] This is not to deny that the "cultural turn" opened up useful new fields of inquiry and yielded worthwhile results. But its historiographical one-sidedness, prioritizing popular and mass attitudes over intellectual debates, encouraged oversimplification by largely ignoring the role of conflicting philosophies and ideologies intellectually grounding and shaping, though not socially driving, the American Revolution and all the revolutions of the age. Clashing ideologies are, of course, to an extent socially driven; but their specific emphases, forms, rhetoric, and terminology are mainly determined not by sociability or social practice but by competing intellectual, ideological, educational, and religious agendas. Admittedly, the part played by the American people—then mainly farmers, artisans, and traders—as distinct from their leaders, who were mostly from a privileged background or aspiring to be part of the gentry elite, had been greatly understated by earlier historians. In terms of popular protest, group anger, mob behavior, broad civil disobedience, and rising exasperation, the American Revolution clearly began not in 1775 but with the Stamp Act of 1765 and the wide popular resentment it aroused.

But, as in France in 1787–99, social disaffection, unrest, and protest, no matter how powerful and turbulent, functioned mainly as a generator of social pressures and emotional reaction. Rising discontent, experience soon made abundantly obvious, just as present-day world events also show, could all too easily be shepherded in dramatically different directions. Anger and emotion, however furious, have no inherent connection with the claims promoted, propagated, and vaunted by the interminably changing, unstable, and shifting leadership vanguards of protest movements. Exactly as with Bolshevism, Fascism, Nazism, Stalinism, and Maoism later, all directing very different kinds of revolutionary upheaval, guiding ideologies, often fanatically championed and propagated by revolutionary leaders, far more often mold and exploit than derive from social or economic pressures.

Revolutions, then, are not shaped by sociability or general attitudes but by organized revolutionary vanguards marshaling their own distinctive political language and rhetoric, including apt slogans, as a means of capturing, taking charge of, and interpreting the discontent generated by social and economic pressures. In determining the actual direction and precise objectives of the revolutions of the 1775–1850 era, when justifying American (or Belgian, Greek, or Spanish American) independence, rewriting constitutions, reshaping institutions, drafting major new legislation, and formulating the "rights of mankind," it was invariably challenging new ideological frameworks opposing the status quo, not economic forces or culture, that were primary. As one of the Massachusetts delegates to the 1787 Constitutional Convention in Philadelphia recalled years later, revolutionary Americans were born the subjects of a king and until 1776 steeped in monarchical loyalty and thinking, initiating the "quarrel which ended in the Revolution not against the King, but against his parliament."[33] The Crown was nevertheless resoundingly eradicated despite the fact that practically no one wanted this earlier. Setting aside monarchy and instituting a republic in America, like abolition of the French monarchy in September 1792, in fact had very little to do with established or slowly changing general attitudes. The *Declaration of Independence*, the 1787 United States Constitution, and subsequent institutional framework, far from arising from sociability, contradicted everything the people were used to.

Bearing this is in mind, it has also seemed important to reverse the usual practice of historians discussing the nineteenth century who, anxious to separate the nineteenth from the eighteenth century, often employ the terms "nationalist" and "nationalism" and "liberal" and "liberalism" to lend the post-1815 era a distinctive cast, rendering these terms familiar to readers of nineteenth-century history but in the process erasing crucial continuities. European nationalism did indeed rear its head in the middle and later decades of the century but played little part during the first third despite the efforts of scholars, convinced the birth of the modern nation-state was the chief development of the age, to prove the contrary. And if the idea that nationalism was central has been greatly exaggerated for reasons that once mattered far more than they do now, regularly employing the term "liberalism" to characterize key early nineteenth-century trends is nothing less than a general historiographical disaster since this absurdly vague and elastic term equally accommodates anti-democratic moderates, heirs of the "moderate Enlightenment," and post-1800 philosophical radicals conserving the Radical Enlightenment legacy. These irreconcilably opposed trends figured among the principal ideological tendencies of the age; so it is almost as if some evil genius deliberately introduced these highly misleading and obfuscating labels to render the entire historiography of the period a fog of confusion. It is best assiduously to avoid them.

Reverting to the intellectual and ideological core of the America Revolution in recent years, historians such as Gary Nash, Seth Cotlar, Sean Wilentz, and Matthew Stewart revived and reworked May's basic dichotomy dividing the Revolution and Enlightenment into conflicting "moderate" and "radical" streams (albeit only in the last case actually using the key terms "radical Enlightenment" and "moderate Enlightenment" to designate these rival streams) as the most appropriate way to explain the American Revolution's inner dynamics and interaction with the wider world. This now firmly established theoretical framework has subsequently been developed further by others, including myself.[34] Such a schema implies that far from having "profoundly different social and political implications and consequences," the American Enlightenment's essential duality exactly paralleled the dual trajectory of the European Enlightenment.[35] Equally, the American and French revolutions, far from sharply diverging in character (as has frequently been claimed), actually ran parallel with no basic differences in principle or general tendencies discernible prior to the Montagnard takeover of June 1793, the change that dramatically (albeit only briefly) diverted the French Revolution from the basic and common transatlantic Enlightenment pattern.[36]

A major recent contribution to the study of transatlantic democratic thought and practice down to the nineteenth century resoundingly breaking with the old parochialism is James Kloppenberg's pathbreaking *Toward Democracy: The Struggle for Self-Rule in European and American Thought* (2016). There are significant points of convergence between his interpretation and this present study, notably a common impulse to place transatlantic intellectual debates, clashes, and theories at the center and sideline the "cultural turn." We both present the story as a complex mix of success and failure. But there are striking differences. Where we especially diverge is in his identifying as "partisans of democracy" key thinkers and statesmen such as John Locke and John Adams, supposedly drawing inspiration from religious faith (Kloppenberg assigns a major formative role to the Reformation and to the Judeo-Christian religious tradition), whom I classify as proponents of "mixed government" and the aristocratic republic clashing with the democratic tendency.[37] Our disagreement revolves at bottom around our different ways of defining "radical" and "moderate" Enlightenment: Kloppenberg characterizes "radical Enlightenment" rather narrowly as just atheism and materialism, excluding non-providential deists and democratic Unitarians like Price and Priestley, however opposed these were to the prevailing system of society and politics, while—confusingly as I see it—bracketing the Jeffersonian (democratic) and Hamiltonian (aristocratic) tendencies in post-Independence American ideological politics together as both being "moderate."

Despite the "hyperbolic rhetoric deployed by both sides from the 1790s through the War of 1812," holds Kloppenberg, both main American ideological factions should be deemed "moderate Enlightenment" not least because both "understood that a thoroughgoing democracy acknowledges the force of popular piety."[38] This approach reaffirms the wide gulf between the French Enlightenment and the Anglo-American Enlightenment that Hannah Arendt, Gertrude Himmelfarb, and many others have postulated. But the question whether Franklin, Jefferson, and Paine (who all professed to be deists) were really inspired by Christian piety remains highly debatable and anyway less decisive in this connection than whether a given enlightener held that a knowing, benevolent divinity governs the course of human affairs, sanctions the prevailing political, social, and educational norms, and revealed His purposes—or at least needs to be regarded as having so communicated his requirements—to religious leaders. If the answer is "yes" then ecclesiastical authority and theological rulings must necessarily be retained in the legislative process, policymaking and representation, education, and the accepted legal and moral order. By contrast, the "radical Enlightenment" built its "pursuit of happiness" exclusively on secular values, wholly eradicating religious authority. Hence, wherever an enlightener's views entail systematic elimination of theology, clergy, and state support for churches from the political sphere and education, demanding full secularization of public authority and comprehensive separation of church and state, he belongs to the "radical Enlightenment" whether he admitted to being an atheist and materialist or not.

Conversely, figures like Hume, Gibbon, Adams, Hamilton, and Morris whose Christian allegiance was just as dubious as that of a Franklin or Jefferson but who recommended limited suffrages, aristocratic political systems, and keeping a measure of ecclesiastical influence and privilege should be deemed "moderate Enlightenment" irrespective of whether they were personally irreligious or not. Differentiating between radical and moderate Enlightenment in a manner that locates Franklin and Jefferson among the "moderates" is especially problematic, I argue, in that it helps justify the longstanding and unfortunate historiographical tendency to understate America's protracted conflict between democratic and aristocratic republicanism, the central dynamic that became a major factor in 1776, grew intense during the 1790s, and subsequently remained central in America over the centuries.

Correctly characterizing "radical Enlightenment" as democratic republicanism combined with rejection of religious authority[39] shows at once that the relentless polemics dividing Federalists from Jeffersonians during the 1790s amounted to far more than just "hyperbolic rhetoric." Instead of presenting the French and American revolutions as standing in stark contrast, a great historical error, a viable classification must bring out the basic parallelism: demonstrating that the American and French revolutions share the same basic trajectory (until June 1793), both being equally a battleground for rival moderate and radical Enlightenment factions. The French Revolution, except during the Terror, was conceptually and rhetorically much the same kind of unremitting ideological arena as post-Independence America with "moderates" venerating Locke, Montesquieu, and British "mixed government" fighting democratic republicans championing secularism and universal and equal human rights, the latter consciously and explicitly aligning with Jefferson and his followers.[40] French republican revolutionaries like Condorcet, Bonneville, Desmoulins, Carra, Cérutti, and Brissot, and Italian radicals like Filangieri, Mazzei, and Gorani—no less than British "philosophical radicals"—pursued much the same goals of liberty, democracy, and equality with freedom of expression and the press, and security of person and property, as were promoted in America by Franklin, Paine, Freneau, Jefferson, Barlow, Coram, and Palmer. This wide international sweep continued throughout the revolutionary era down to 1848.[41]

The American Revolution, then, had a dual trajectory and in this respect formed part of a wider transatlantic revolutionary sequence, a series of revolutions in France, Italy, Holland, Switzerland, Germany, Ireland, Haiti, Poland, Spain, Greece, and Spanish America. In presenting the wider revolutionary context, I have striven to keep the comparative transatlantic dimension firmly in the foreground while maintaining a balance between American and non-American developments. Political narrative and recounting public controversies and ideological clashes are combined with a biographical component focusing on key Founding Fathers. Franklin, Adams, Jefferson, and Paine emerge not just as major figures in negotiating and harmonizing the dynamics of the American Revolution but equally as revolutionary icons and representatives inspiring, mobilizing, and cajoling competing forces within other revolutionary upheavals. The endeavors of the Founding Fathers and their followings abroad prove the deep interaction of the American Revolution and its principles with the other revolutions, substantiating the Revolution's global role less as a directly intervening force than inspirational motor, the primary model, for universal change.

During the 1790s, May pointed out, intellectuals everywhere were locked in a bitterly divisive debate about the French Revolution, and books by "intellectual representatives of the Revolutionary Enlightenment," the quantitative data show, "reached impressive heights of popularity in America."[42] Claiming basic ideological convergence between the American and French revolutions, strikingly, remained usual among the radicals themselves for decades. Stressing the affinities of the democratic wings of the two revolutions helped keep alive what true radicals deemed the authentic values of the American Revolution while continually reconnecting them with the democratic revolutionary consciousness of Europe, albeit after 1793 with only very sporadic success. Only during and especially after the Montagnard populist tyranny (1793–94) was there any plausible basis for the rival view, the potent myth that the American and French revolutions differed fundamentally. From 1795–96, however, a growing conservative pulpit and press campaign partly succeeded in introducing precisely this alleged basic divergence between the two great Atlantic revolutions, conjuring up a powerful new ideological device, anti-Jacobinism, afterward long utilized by American defenders of social hierarchy and checks and balances to tar the democratic tendency by denouncing Jeffersonians and Paineites as un-American "Jacobins."

An American writer who often invoked the consanguinity of the American and French revolutions and their common rootedness in the Enlightenment's radical tendency was the ex-Presbyterian minister Elihu Palmer (1764–1806), leader of the Deistical Society of New York in the 1790s. "The benevolent effects of reason, science and true philosophy," wrote this stalwart representative of democratic radicalism in 1797, would eventually triumph, overthrow political despotism and "despotism of the mind," and ground an age of peace and general "happiness." Philosophy would "extend over the face of the whole earth, and render happy the great family of mankind!" and then men would remember that "writings of the philosophers and philanthropists" had prepared the way. "Although superstition, from her dark and gloomy abodes, may hurl her envenomed darts, yet the names of Paine, Volney, Barlow, Condorcet, and Godwin will be revered by posterity, and these men will be ranked among the greatest benefactors of mankind."[43]

Radical literature diffused widely on both sides of the Atlantic, but many Americans abhorred the radicals and their ideas so that demand for books and pamphlets rejecting "radical Enlightenment" concepts escalated too, stoking up the rival impulses contesting the American Revolution's legacy in a manner vividly reflected in American bookselling and reading patterns. Writers like Condorcet, Raynal, Volney, Paine, Price, Priestley, Godwin, Beccaria, and Wollstonecraft abounded in American libraries and intellectual culture, but "anti-radical Americans," countering their conjoined democratic and irreligious claims, observed May, also penetrated the intellectual arena "in enormous volume." Moderates preferred Scottish Enlightenment religion-friendly books by writers like Kames, Smith, Beattie, and Blair, reconciling a rationalized conception of faith with science, philosophy, and nondemocratic forms of revolutionary politics. This divide, still perceptible long after 1800, arose, observed Donald Meyer—embracing May's findings—from majority American resolve to "tame the Enlightenment, dulling its radical and skeptical edge, and seeking accommodation between enlightened thinking and traditional moral and religious values."[44] The majority, led by the gentry elites, lawyers, and pastors, sought to restrain the Enlightenment and to an extent check the spirit of '76, the democratizing tendency itself.[45]

This profound rift in post-1783 American society caused some to consider the Revolution triumphantly complete while others judged it worryingly incomplete. The Revolution's deficiencies, held the radicals, lay partly in "defects" in the state constitutions, partly in the revival of religious authority, and partly in failing to abolish slavery and emancipate the blacks. America's state constitutions mostly left informal "aristocracy" intact while drastically restricting the right to vote even for adult white males—except, all too briefly, in Pennsylvania (until 1790) and Vermont. In 1784, Price had expected speedy improvement, his "heart-felt satisfaction" deriving in part from his trust that the "United States are entering into measures for discountenancing [the slave trade], and for abolishing the odious slavery which it has introduced." Until then, the American people would not "deserve the liberty for which they have been contending. For it is self-evident, that if there are any men whom they have a right to hold in slavery, there may be others who have a right to hold *them* in slavery."[46]

To restricted state constitutions, white resistance to black emancipation, and powerfully entrenched religious authority including compulsory taxes to fund churches and clergy was added the threat of strengthened oligarchy. In his 1784 speech exalting America's achievement Price expressed great optimism but also worried that he might have carried his expectations "too high, and deceived myself with visionary expectations." Independence only superficially ended "all their dangers," the greatest risk now being to "those virtuous and simple manners by which alone Republics can long subsist." With Independence, naked pursuit of wealth, complacency, and "clashing interests, subject to no strong control," so flourished as seemed likely to destabilize the Revolution and "break the federal union." Growing inequality spelled widespread loss of individual independence and economic and moral "self-direction," key principles for Price. The stakes were high for America and the world. Should America fail to build on her founding principles and promise, the "consequence will be that the fairest experiment ever tried in human affairs will miscarry; and that a Revolution which had revived the hopes of good men and promised an opening to better times, will become a discouragement to all future efforts in favor of liberty, and prove only an opening to a new scene of human degeneracy and misery."[47]

Despite the initially high expectations, America's revolutionary achievement was scarcely matched by comparable achievements elsewhere during the next three-quarters of a century. In fact, what followed American Independence disappointed even Enlightenment "moderates" and eventually all but shattered the hopes of radical democratic republican political thinkers. For all the apparent variety of political forms in the world and Montesquieu's relativism, radicals were convinced, there were ultimately only two kinds of political system: genuine democratic republics based on reason, natural rights, and the collective good, and those of the "intriguers," as Condorcet put it, that is, monarchies, dictatorships, and aristocratic republics entrenching vested interests, vitiating the common interest, and using religious authority, or what he deemed specious arguments, to dupe the great mass of the ignorant, confused, and "superstitious" deferring to monarchy, aristocracy, financial elites, and ecclesiastical control.[48] The American Revolution may have begun a process to make the world anew, but by the late 1790s "the intriguers" appeared to be winning.

A prominent "moderate" regretting the lack of successful follow-up to the American Revolution abroad was Adams. Beyond avid study of American developments, nothing lasting had emerged so far outside the United States, he agreed in 1814, writing to Jefferson, his former archrival in politics now a regular correspondent. Neither former president, surveying the scene in 1814, four decades after the Revolution's advent, underestimated what Adams called the "horrors we have experienced for the last forty years." In a world increasingly resistant to political reform and freedom of expression since 1793–94, all efforts to establish stable representative government had collapsed. What followed was an unrelieved story of failed revolutionary attempts, bitter ideological conflict, and war. Yet, Adams too, while unwilling to go so far as Jefferson, Paine, Price, or Filangieri in dismantling crowns, aristocracy, clergy, ecclesiastical authority, and colonial oligarchy, believed social, cultural, and political reform in emulation of America, correcting abuses and making substantial improvements, would eventually occur and benefit all humanity.

"Government has never been much studied by mankind," lamented Adams. "But [men's] attention has been drawn to it, in the latter part of the last century and the beginning of this, more than at any former period: and the vast variety of experiments that have been made of constitutions in America, in France, in Holland, in Geneva, in Switzerland, and even in Spain and South America, can never be forgotten." All these upheavals "will be studied and their immediate and remote effects, and final catastrophies noted. The result in time will be improvements."[49] This, however, was no preordained, inevitable progress. After Napoleon's downfall the world witnessed a powerful revival of absolutist monarchy, aristocratic dominance, and religious authority along with Counter-Enlightenment ideas, even perceptibly in the United States. After 1815, political and intellectual censorship, compared to pre-1789 levels, was significantly strengthened throughout Europe. To Adams it was clear that the "course of science and literature is obstructed and by so many causes discouraged that it is to be feared, their motions will be slow."[50] Slavery and serfdom were being reaffirmed and extended in the French, Spanish, and Brazilian empires, and also in the United States. Europe, the Americas, Africa, and Asia all experienced a general reversal of Enlightenment attitudes and institutions—a dramatic overall deterioration in rights, freedom of thought, and circumstances for the great bulk of humanity.

The root cause of the disheartening reverses, Adams and Jefferson agreed, was "superstition," ignorance, and defects in men's understanding of society, politics, and religion—in other words insufficient Enlightenment. When it came to battling Counter-Enlightenment attitudes, the basic split between radical and moderate Enlightenment receded into the background. Despite having long differed over political theory and the general principles of the American and French revolutions, in their last years Adams and Jefferson more and more converged in denouncing the reactionary surge. Republican liberty, free expression, religious toleration, spread of republican institutions, and just, orderly, constructive government for peoples everywhere remained for both, despite all the setbacks and opposition, desirable and possible.[51] The ferment convulsing the then world would "ultimately terminate in the advancement of civil and religious liberty and amelioration in the condition of mankind."[52]

After 1815, Adams and Jefferson hovered uneasily between optimism and pessimism. Adams had all along deplored Paine's excessive optimism and recalled this, writing to Jefferson in 1815. But Adams too had once been insufficiently cautious, replied Jefferson, and now, after Napoleon, was too pessimistic. The revolutions of 1789–1814 had indeed all disintegrated. "But altho' your prophecy has proved true so far," responded Jefferson, in January

1816, "I hope it does not preclude a better final result. That same light from our West seems to have spread and illuminated the very engines employed to extinguish it. It has given [Europeans] a glimmering of their rights and their power. The idea of representative government has taken root and growth among them. Their masters feel it, and are saving themselves by timely offers of this modification of their own powers. Belgium, Prussia, Poland, Lombardy etc., are now offered a representative organization: illusive probably at first, but it will grow into power in the end. Opinion is power, and that opinion will come. Even France will yet attain representative government."[53] Jefferson was probably right, replied Adams, but "all will depend on the progress of knowledge. But how shall knowledge advance?"[54]

Among those most intently pondering this continuing late eighteenth- and early nineteenth-century transatlantic drama was the novelist James Fenimore Cooper (1789–1851), who composed his historical novel *The Bravo* (Philadelphia, 1831) during a stay in Venice in the spring of 1830, shortly after the outbreak of the July Revolution in France. He intended it as a literary exposé of the injustice and perverseness of aristocratic republics in general (classifying Britain among the worst). By 1833 when he returned to America, Cooper had spent seven years in Europe and become convinced the post-1814 Restoration conservatism that so dismayed both Adams and Jefferson was an ideological curse blighting the Old World and the New alike. His own compatriots, he felt, were far too blind and unaware of the close intellectual and practical interaction between the American and European revolutions, and American and European counterrevolutionary tendencies, and how profoundly this complex interplay affected their own republic and America's social, cultural, and economic future.

No one, remarks Fenimore Cooper in the novel's preface, had yet authored a "history of the progress of political liberty, written purely in the interests of humanity"; but such a work was urgently needed. The old Venetian Republic, abolished by Napoleon in 1797 and incapable of protest, he adopted as his archetype of the corrupt, aristocratic republic. The Venetian Republic "though ambitious and tenacious of the name of republic, was in truth, a narrow, a vulgar, and an exceedingly heartless oligarchy."[55] His Venetian aristocrat was "equally opposed to the domination of one, or of the whole [that is, of monarchy and popular sovereignty]; being, as respects the first, a furious republican, and, in reference to the last, leaning to that singular sophism which calls the dominion of the majority the rule of many tyrants!" No one more diligently propagated "all the dogmas that were favorable to his caste," especially the notion that social hierarchy, and the subordination of the many, is a fact ordained by God.[56] Literary critics have noted the novel's relevance to both the French 1830 Revolution and contemporary American and British politics. Cooper's assault on the old Venetian oligarchy was actually a veiled attempt to discredit both the British ruling class *and* the American East Coast "aristocracy" of his day. Among the latter figured his own father, who had acquired land and a gentry lifestyle in Otsego County, New York.[57] Britain's aristocracy, though highly insidious according to Cooper, was at that time extolled by the East Coast social elite as the very epitome of political wisdom, probity, and good sense. A noteworthy contribution to the Radical Enlightenment as well as literature, Cooper's *The Bravo* was above all a timely admonition to his American fellow citizens.

It took decades for the American Revolution's broad global impact fully to recede in scholarly and general awareness and become a largely forgotten past. In the vastly changed intellectual milieu of the later nineteenth century, a post-Enlightenment era dominated by nationalism, imperialism, socialism, Marxism, and American isolationism, the American Revolution came to appear marginal to modern history outside America. It became standard to claim the American Revolution differed fundamentally from the French, and from all European and Latin American revolutions, and did not exert a broad impact. Untypical and highly perceptive in other ways, Hannah Arendt (1906–75), among the twentieth century's greatest political philosophers, wholly conformed to this curiously blinkered twentieth-century misapprehension. "That neither the spirit of [the American] Revolution nor the thoughtful and erudite political theories of the Founding Fathers had much noticeable impact upon the European continent," she stated in her book *On Revolution* (1963), "is a fact beyond dispute."[58] In this she could not have been more mistaken. Still more misguided, many scholars and readers today concur with the modishly dismissive stance that all this has ceased to be relevant and that "the eighteenth-century war of ideas is finally over."

Overly preoccupied with creating separate national stories, late nineteenth- and twentieth-century European and Latin American historians and philosophers shared their American colleagues' post-1850 disavowal of the Revolution's role in molding global modernity, refusing to see it as crucial to the wider Enlightenment movement and for shaping specific revolutions either side of the Atlantic between 1780 and 1848. If modern American historiography "remained remarkably insular,"[59] so equally did European historiography, both setting aside the broader picture and justifying a narrow approach by endorsing the myth of America's "exceptionalism." By its very nature, America's Revolution and post-revolutionary success was supposedly an experience others could not share, fully comprehend, or employ as a model. Accordingly, the Revolution remained familiar to readers almost exclusively as the harbinger of America's own independence, nationhood, and Constitution.[60]

Colonial rebellions against imperial governments have regularly occurred since the eighteenth century. National movements have often secured independence from the imperial power but only rarely succeeded in replacing it with a stable, manifestly better political and social order. In this respect, the American Revolution differed dramatically from the usual pattern. From 1775, America became the first albeit highly imperfect model of a new kind of society, laying the path by which the modern world stumbled more generally toward republicanism, human rights, equality, and democracy. Besides independence, it introduced egalitarian republican principles that impressed and appealed widely, forging an eventually democratic republic in principle even if in practice often not embracing equality before the law and equal treatment of citizens' interests. The American Revolution's global significance stemmed from its offering a new kind of polity starkly contrasting with the ancien régime monarchical-aristocratic political and social system dominating Europe, Latin America, Africa, and Asia between 1775 and 1850, and the vast, exploitative colonial empires that then, and long afterward, overshadowed the globe. It was the crucible of democratic modernity.

CHAPTER 1

First Rumblings

"What do we mean by the Revolution?" asked Adams, writing to Jefferson in August 1815. "The War? That was no part of the Revolution. It was only an effect and consequence of it. The Revolution was in the minds of the people, and this was effected, from 1760 to 1775, in the course of fifteen years before a drop of blood was drawn at Lexington." The real, meaningful Revolution, contended Adams (much like his radical opponent Paine), occurred in the vigorous, divisive deliberations of the colonial legislatures, in pamphlets and newspapers, prior to 1775, when the "steps by which the public opinion was enlightened and informed concerning the authority of Parliament over the colonies" were taken. For Adams, the crucial 1774 revolutionary Congress "resembled in some respects, tho' I hope not in many, the Counsell of Nice [i.e., Nicaea] in ecclesiastical history," the gathering of bishops and theologians for the first ecumenical council of the Church in 325 AD. Churchmen assembled from across the Roman Empire "compared notes, engaged in discussions and debates," and resolved numerous profound disagreements, sometimes by one or two votes, that subsequently went out "into the world as unanimous."[1]

The years 1760–74 prepared Americans for the Revolution. In the vast global contest for empire between 1756 and 1763—in America called the French and Indian War—Britain's victory over France and Spain had been overwhelming. But in the Thirteen Colonies the struggle had bequeathed a legacy of intransigent disputes and political difficulties that soon proved highly divisive. By 1763, Britain had triumphed on land and sea and become indisputably dominant in Asia, Africa, the South Seas, and the New World. With France almost wholly ejected from Canada and India, Spain stripped of the Floridas (including territory to the west of modern Florida), Britain, with her incomparable fleet, presided over the globe more entirely than any power previously in history. However, this unprecedented success accrued at the cost of considerable maritime and commercial disruption and massive financial outlay, saddling the British Crown and taxpayer with a gigantic national debt requiring the continuance of high taxation in England, Scotland, and Ireland and, as it seemed in London, a pressing need to exact greater resources on a regular basis from the American colonies (besides India and the East India Company).

The empire was thought to need a more coherent, robust imperial administration not only in Canada and the Floridas, and also the Caribbean where several valuable islands had been wrested from the French, but additionally over the sparsely populated Indian regions west of the Alleghenies, extending military and administrative control in the Ohio Valley and over the inhabitants of the borderlands between Nova Scotia and New England where the war accelerated an expansion that had begun earlier.[2] For the first time, protecting western frontier settlements and managing relations with the Indian peoples west was largely removed from the colonists' hands. In October 1763, an imperial decree fixed the new boundaries and provisionally forbade establishing new settlements, and assigning land, beyond the main ridge of the Allegheny mountain barrier. A standing army, based partly in Canada and the Floridas, and partly on the western edge of the Thirteen Colonies, settled in as a peacetime garrison, buttressing Britain's expanded global empire. In addition, British ministers sought to regulate shipping, imports, exports, and customs duties in North America and the Caribbean, especially by increasing import duties and excluding Dutch, French, and Spanish imports (a policy pursued under the Navigation Acts since 1651) in a tighter, more organized, imperially oriented fashion than in the past. Ministers aimed to tighten control over importing into the North American market so as to more strictly exclude competing European textiles and other goods and more systematically benefit England's manufacturers. To this end, the Crown strove to suppress the clandestine traffic (still largely in Dutch hands in the Middle Colonies and New England) and as far as possible "prevent intercourse of America with foreign nations."[3] Very popular with merchants and the public in England who felt the rules were not being imposed stringently enough, this restrictive policy worked to the clear disadvantage not only of European traders but also of merchants throughout the colonies and in Florida also the Creek Indians, who much preferred to continue their dealings with Cuba and with visiting vessels from other neighboring parts of Spanish America.[4] Whether the Thirteen Colonies still needed protecting or not, Florida, Canada, and the Mississippi Valley as well as the British Caribbean obviously did; and it was taken for granted in Parliament that the colonies must contribute more substantially to the cost of this burgeoning imperial umbrella.

The "Cow of British Commerce" being milked and dehorned right before Philadelphia by the Americans, Dutch, French, and Spanish while the British Lion sleeps (1775). Photo credit: Encyclopaedia Britannica/UIG/Bridgeman Images.

A measure that provoked a furious and unprecedented reaction was the 1765 Stamp Act, a substantial duty on all legal transactions, property purchases, royal licenses to practice law, and newspapers, designed to shift part of the imperial burden shouldered by the British taxpayer onto the Americans. Designed to extend imperial control as well as increase tax revenue, the Act met with an angry reception from New England's farmers and hugely antagonized local opinion in Boston, a town of some 15,500 inhabitants and North America's third largest city, but a port somewhat depressed since the 1750s and, for the first time, enduring economic distress and poverty. An agitation developed in August 1765 that was unparalleled in the colonies' history. Week after week the demonstrations continued, punctuated by burning of effigies, and soon stoning officials and the occasional demolishing of a royal official's house, culminating in five days of organized mass protest that paralyzed the entire city. The ferment transformed public affairs in New England and the city's character. Massachusetts's governor, Thomas Hutchinson, spoke of a "new model of government" gripping Boston with obstructive local committees and crowded, obstreperous town meetings hampering practically everything relating to port administration, customs and trade regulation, functioning of the law courts, and routine town affairs.[5] The street leader of the 1765 Boston Stamp Act protests, the people's "Masaniello" as Hutchinson dubbed him (alluding to the leader of the Neapolitan popular uprising of 1647), was an unruly Scots cobbler, Ebenezer Mackintosh (1727–1816), a rough populist. His role was symptomatic of how profoundly the agitation had penetrated Boston society's lower strata as well as infuriated the merchant elite, creating a peculiarly complex situation.

Those higher up the social scale deliberately fostered the growing rowdiness, which extended northward as far as the towns in Maine, instigating artisan crowd organizers like Mackintosh behind the scenes via a secret committee of elite citizens, the "Loyal Nine," formed in 1765 to fight the Stamp Act. The Loyal Nine was the conspiratorial predecessor of larger subversive local cliques that formed in Boston, and soon many other places, calling themselves the Sons of Liberty. The town's top merchants and ruling elite, with the brewer Sam Adams (1722–1803) well to the fore, remained in close touch with the artisan street activists;[6] but, at the same time, the insurgents' unruliness rendered them uneasy. Massachusetts's principal opposition figures—Sam Adams, John Adams, and John Hancock—were especially perturbed, indeed disgusted, by the pillaging and wrecking of several mansions in late August 1765, including that of Massachusetts's governor where everything was smashed up, the furniture destroyed, legal and administrative documents seized, and the cellars emptied.[7]

Violence against officials and their property erupted in various towns. Mackintosh, who led the 26 August nighttime foray that wrecked the governor's mansion, became known as the "Captain General of the Liberty Tree," alluding to a large elm in the Boston city center dubbed "the liberty tree." Protesters erected a liberty pole with a flag nearby, soon a popular symbol for revolt against "tyranny" to which slogans were affixed—among them "Vox populi, vox dei." The liberty tree ritual spread to Worcester and other disaffected Massachusetts towns, marking the initiation of revolutionary ceremonial surrounding the liberty tree, the most renowned emblem of late eighteenth-century transatlantic revolutionary insurgency, and an enduring reminder of how closely the American and other revolutions were interlinked.[8] Despite the reviled Stamp Act itself being hastily repealed to the glee of the colonies' citizens in 1766, resistance to imperial exactions, subtly prompted by the Massachusetts and Virginia legislatures and fed by widespread popular agitation, proved unrelenting. The crisis and profound distrust the Stamp Act excited subsided, moreover, only briefly being followed by other considerable, if less ambitious, revenue-raising measures.

Unrest and opposition to British fiscal and anti-smuggling measures seethed through the late 1760s, thoroughly souring relations between England and the colonies. But the disaffection also revealed deep fissures within American society. Among the principal modes of protest against the Stamp Act were localized nonimportation drives boycotting British imported manufactures and commodities, most notably at Boston. In 1768–70, renewed efforts to apply pressure to rescind import duties newly imposed under the Townshend Revenue Act of June 1767, again commencing in Boston, prompted further local boycotts. Housewives ceased buying British-imported tea, wines, paper, textiles, and other items, obstruction supported by numerous artisans but opposed by merchants and retailers. The latter, though, finding themselves loudly denounced at meetings and in newspapers, had to comply, first in Boston, then New York, and finally, after considerable delay, Philadelphia, where resistance to boycotting proved tenacious. Resented by some, boycotting appealed to many including staunch Calvinists averse to lavish consumption of wines and luxuries. That revolution and business often clash subsequently remained a familiar background theme. By early 1770, the boycott movement had permeated most colonies but, after a brief surge until October 1770, suddenly lost momentum and collapsed. Nonimportation was nevertheless crucial to the Revolution's history, the 1768–70 boycotts being the first generalized attempt to enforce a consensus of organized opposition to Britain's imperial system, coercing reluctant citizens into compliance, and the first revealing the true depth of division in American society.[9]

After briefly subsiding, a fresh surge of popular protest against Britain's imperial apparatus of control and trade regulation gripped town and country, now reaching even relatively remote places. By the early 1770s, the growing friction was sufficiently obvious to become a topic of international comment. Newspaper readers either side of the Atlantic began discussing America's increasingly troubled relationship with the British Crown. The philosopher David Hume (1711–76) took a gloomy view of the situation as early as March 1771 when he considered "our Union with America" something that "in the nature of things, cannot long subsist."[10] Hume was far from alone in already expecting an ugly and massive rupture. A close French observer convinced America would soon experience a "civil war" between rebels and loyalists was François-Jean, marquis de Chastellux (1734–88), an associate of the *philosophes* d'Holbach and Diderot, who from July 1780 served as a major-general in the French expeditionary force in Virginia under Rochambeau.[11] The brewer Sam Adams, a leading figure in the Massachusetts assembly, later assured the prominent Philadelphia physician Benjamin Rush (1746–1813) that independence was his dearest wish already "seven years before the war" began.[12]

The unrest culminated in the Boston Tea Party of 16 December 1773. This commotion arose from British efforts to tighten procedures for tea imports in response to the backlog of unsold tea in England caused by the boycotting campaign and by illegal Dutch tea imports to America, to strictly exclude foreign tea, strengthen the monopoly of the East India Company, and raise tea import duty—among the few colonial imports capable of yielding a substantial surplus to the royal treasury.[13] Intended to boost revenue, expand royal control, enhance monopoly at the expense of American merchants, and curb smuggling, this measure provoked furious resistance at Boston, New York, Philadelphia, and Charleston. Bostonians especially denounced the new rules for landing, checking, taxing, and distributing tea consignments from incoming vessels. When masked protestors boarded a newly arrived ship and hurled its East India cargo overboard, the episode had an unprecedented impact. "This is the most magnificent movement of all," recorded John Adams; "there is a dignity, a majesty, a sublimity, in this last effort of the Patriots, that I greatly admire. The people should never rise without doing something to be remembered, something notable and striking. This destruction of the tea is so bold, so daring, so firm, intrepid and inflexible, and it must have so important consequences, and so lasting, that I cannot but consider it as an epoch in history."[14] Royal ministers in London, unwisely losing patience and perhaps overly influenced by the outraged reaction of the British papers and in Parliament, responded with ill-advised severity. They enacted a batch of Coercive Acts, also known as the Intolerable Acts, aimed at bolstering royal authority and punishing Boston, among them the Boston Port Act closing the harbor until compensation for the destroyed cargo was paid. Still more resented was the Massachusetts Government Act outlawing unauthorized gatherings and town meetings and introducing royal appointees to replace the regular council elected by the legislature's lower house to appoint the colony's officials and judges.[15] Commencing in Boston where street, tavern, and public protest meetings boiled over, resistance to the Coercive Acts spread across the Thirteen Colonies.

Opposition was fomented especially by the Sons of Liberty committees, the clamor receiving support from many but not all segments of colonial society. Backing also came from sections of the main Protestant churches, especially those traditionally hostile to the Anglican (Episcopalian) Church given that the latter maintained especially close and longstanding ties with England and the Crown. Churches of Calvinist background, the Congregationalists and Presbyterians, were undoubtedly the most prone to sanction the growing resistance with John Witherspoon (1723–94), president of the College of New Jersey (today Princeton University), among the foremost in this respect, though it should be noted that even in these churches many preachers preferred to remain silent.[16] On 17 May 1774, the Dutch Reformed congregations of New York and New Jersey held a "Day of Fasting and Prayer" against the Coercive Acts.[17] At Albany, where many Dutch Reformed Church members joined, there was a noticeable overlap between lay members of church councils and the membership of Sons of Liberty committees.[18] Foremost was the Boston Committee of Correspondence, an organization created in 1772 by a group of highly literate, radical-minded professionals sworn to counter British imperial sway, which they denounced as despotic and oppressive. These individuals forged a network of communication linking Boston with Worcester and other Massachusetts backcountry towns, as well as neighboring colonies, designed to coordinate resistance and the opposition's methods and publicity effort. In this way, they brought quite remote places stretching into what is today upper New York State, Maine, and Vermont within the continuing agitation's orbit. Boston's success encouraged the spread of parallel "committees of correspondence" all over the colonies.[19]

Prominent on the Boston committee were Sam Adams, James Otis, a top Boston lawyer and powerful speaker, and Thomas Young (1731–77), a widely read, philosophically inclined New York physician and deist of Irish background fiercely critical of conventional religion and antagonistic to what he deemed spiritual as well as political tyranny. Readier than Otis to mobilize ordinary citizens in the fight for freedom against an imperial system and Parliament he detested, Young moved restlessly from Albany to Boston, Newport, and, finally, Philadelphia, deprecating the royal authorities but also seeking to loosen the grip of local oligarchies and the clergy. Young was the first wholly unambiguous spokesman within the American Revolution of radical rejectionism of the old order, abjuring all the institutions of ancien régime monarchy, aristocracy, and colonial government, including the church establishment.[20]

In June 1774, the Boston Committee took the crucial step of reorganizing the hitherto localized and sporadic nonimportation movement into a more systematic, closely supervised and enforced, and soon widely supported general embargo on British ships and goods, with women especially boycotting tea and British imported fabrics.[21] The resumed boycott movement was not just a form of retaliation punctuated by tea-burnings and burning copies of the offending laws but a means of reminding the public that Britain's New World colonies in no way enjoyed identical "common rights, the same privileges in commerce" as Britons, being "governed," as Benjamin Franklin expressed it in 1773, "by severer laws than the mother country."[22] Young's committee forged a "solemn league" of subscribers vowing to uphold the widening "nonintercourse" with Britain and freely import tea and all Asian, European, and African commodities from the only available alternative entrepôt for such supplies, namely Holland. The "Dutch model" in commerce—an open market in all commodities, including tea and gunpowder—was now more than ever a standing rebuttal of England's stringently closed mercantilist system in transatlantic trade, restricting all commerce in Old World colonial products to British sources of supply. It implied rejection of imperial regulation and subordination for an unrestricted global market.

Meanwhile, the Quebec Act, the widest-ranging, most enduring measure aimed at tightening Parliament's grip in North America, received royal assent on 22 June 1774. Denying Canada its own assembly and the jury system, this edict reaffirmed the governor's powers while retaining French civil law only for private and local matters. The Act antagonized American sentiment by acknowledging the Catholic jointly with Anglican Church as an established public church within Canada, promoting it above the nonconformist Protestant churches and enabling Catholics to participate in official functions under a new oath of allegiance tailored to their faith. Even though the Act carried no implication that Britain intended to extend toleration of Catholicism in North America further (and was actually fulfilling an undertaking given to the French Crown in 1763), its religious provisions deeply offended Protestant opinion in the Thirteen Colonies.[23] No less offensive to the protesting colonies, the Act vastly enlarged Canada at the expense of the older British colonies by rejoining Nova Scotia, Labrador, and the Labrador-Newfoundland Fisheries to the recently vanquished rump of New France and by reverting to older demarcation lines formerly separating French from British North America. This pushed Canada's boundaries—and hence the zone in which Catholicism was a state church—dramatically southward to the Great Lakes and the Mississippi and Ohio rivers, bringing the large, still mainly Indian-inhabited tracts covering most of what is today Illinois, Indiana, Michigan, Ohio, Wisconsin, and Minnesota back under the governor of Quebec's jurisdiction.[24]

Strengthening executive power at Quebec, and guaranteeing the Canadian Catholic Church an equivalent privileged legal status to the Anglican Church (the sole Protestant church patronized by the Crown), in effect promoting it above the other Protestant churches, the Quebec Act extended direct British control and infuriated Presbyterians and other Calvinists. The measure was deeply resented not just in New England and New York but throughout the Thirteen Colonies and was criticized also by Burke for separating constitutional entities in the south from absolutist government to the north, creating different systems of jurisdiction and legislation "where on one part the subject lived under Law, and on the other under Prerogative."[25] The preamble to South Carolina's revised constitution, approved following independence in March 1776, cites among justifications for terminating allegiance to Britain that "French laws are restored" in Canada and Catholicism established with

Canada's "limits extended through a vast tract of country" bordering on the "free Protestant English settlements," aligning a "whole people differing in religious principles from the neighboring colonies, and subject to arbitrary powers, as fit instruments to overawe and subdue the colonies."

As the ferment spread, it focused increasingly on Worcester, a town forty miles to the west of Boston. Crown officials in Worcester County, along with leading "Tories" and local magistrates loyal to Parliament, found themselves ousted from their positions by organized groups of "Patriots" mostly from lower social strata. The deep divisions the Revolution aggravated within American society from 1774 onward were to be one of the chief parallels between the American and French revolutions. Revolutionary politics gained traction well inland and had the effect of dividing and embittering a considerable region. Tempers flared. In Worcester County, the new governor of Massachusetts, Thomas Gage, reported to London in August 1774, "They openly threaten resistance by arms . . . and threaten to attack any troops who dare oppose them."[26] In September 1774, "several thousands of armed people drawn from the neighboring towns assembled at Worcester," noted a leading Tory, and drew up "a very treasonable league and covenant" stopping the royal courts of justice.[27]

To coordinate the mounting resistance to British policies, the colonies dispatched delegates to what became known as the First Continental Congress meeting at Philadelphia in the autumn of 1774. Only Pennsylvania and Rhode Island sent representatives chosen by their legislatures; the other delegations were co-opted. It was a distinguished gathering, including George Washington (1732–99), the two Adamses, and other prominent representatives of the colonial legislatures, among them unremitting conservatives such as John Jay (1745–1829) from New York and John Dickinson (1732–1808) from Pennsylvania. These men were to prove crucial to the Revolution. From the outset, their presence ensured a cautious approach and ample dispute about points of political theory and constitutional practice. The First Continental Congress, often much underestimated by historians, nevertheless reached agreement to defy the Coercive Acts by general adoption of the boycott on British goods, supplies, and ships, issuing a declaration refusing payment of royal taxes imposed without representation, and by ordering military preparedness.[28]

In *A Summary View of the Rights of British America*, a tract written in the July heat of 1774 at his plantation of Monticello, in Virginia, and anonymously published at Williamsburg, the still relatively unknown and inexperienced thirty-one-year-old Jefferson deprecated the "many unwarrantable encroachments and usurpations, attempted to be made by the legislature of one part of the empire, upon those rights which God and the laws have given equally and independently to all."[29] George III was "no more than the chief officer of the people, appointed by the laws."[30] Resort to armed resistance Jefferson justified by citing the "systematical plan of reducing us to slavery." Armed opposition was permissible under those "sacred and sovereign rights of punishment [of tyrannical kings] reserved in the hands of the people" that the English exercised in the Glorious Revolution of 1688–89, according to Americans and Englishmen alike the foundation of their modern liberties.[31] Another publication associated with the 1774 (First Continental) Congress was John Adams's *Novanglus*, twelve letters originally appearing in the *Boston Gazette*, later reissued many times. A young lawyer with strong "classical republican" as well as socially and politically conservative views, figuring among the Massachusetts delegation, Adams found the Congress's deliberations too timid.

For Adams, in 1774, the "Revolution" that chiefly mattered had occurred long before and was the achievement of such seventeenth-century English republican thinkers as Sidney and Harrington. The republicanism of Algernon Sidney (1622–83), although (or perhaps because) sufficiently vague and fragmentary to suit both "moderates" and "radicals"—and, indeed, even Loyalist opponents of the Revolution—played a notable part in strengthening the previously loose and undefined upsurge of republican sentiment in America during the 1770s.[32] *Novanglus*, the "New England man," eloquently sketched the ideology of what became the Revolution's moderate republican mainstream. Because the "nature of the encroachment upon the American constitution is, such as to grow every day more and more encroaching," vigorous steps were requisite.[33] Ardent for "mixed government" and the legacy of the 1688–89 Glorious Revolution, Adams's stance linked him to the later "moderate" stream in the Dutch and French revolutions. Americans' "attachment to their constitution," held Adams (long before there was a written American constitution), was unyielding. He clearly conceived of America as sharing in the existing "British constitution" under the king. "If we enjoy the British constitution in greater purity and perfection than they do in England, as is really the case, whose fault is this? Not ours."[34] If New Englanders like himself concerting the growing resistance were "rebels" and "traitors," as Parliament and local Tories alleged, then "the Lords and Commons, and the whole nation [of England and America], were traitors at the revolution [of 1688]."[35] Deeply venerating the existing "British constitution" and a firm Sidney enthusiast, Adams at the same time was a convinced anti-democrat.

In any case, Parliament was not Britain. That the "people of Great Britain are not united against us" mattered greatly to the young Adams of 1775. If king, ministry, Parliament, the army, and navy tyrannized over America, "we are assured by thousands of letters from persons of good intelligence, by the general strain of publications in public papers, pamphlets, and magazines,

and by some larger works written for posterity, that the body of the people
are friends to America, and wish us success in our struggle against the claims
of Parliament and administration."[36] Here he exaggerated but was not wholly
wrong. Even in Parliament there was dissent from the government's hard line.
The renowned parliamentary opposition leader Charles James Fox (1749–1806)
and the influential publicist and Irish MP Edmund Burke (1729–97), allies and
friends for the duration of the American struggle, headed those urging more
conciliatory tactics. Burke, who for a time was construed, albeit mistakenly, as
sympathizing with progressive views—he later became Britain's leading conservative theorist and opponent of the *philosophique* democratic revolution—
advised compromise and conciliation. It was in Britain's interest to reinforce
America's bonds with the empire, thereby keeping control of North America's
commerce with the rest of the world.[37] Burke did not support American independence and, like Adam Smith and Adam Ferguson, firmly rejected democracy in favor of "aristocracy," indeed detested the radical tendency penetrating
American political thought while dreading the incipient influence of American
egalitarian ideas in Britain and on English aristocratic culture. Burke opposed
the looming war, adopting an attitude apparently supportive of the American
cause, hoping to avoid a protracted conflict that would be hugely costly and in
his view damaging to liberty in England itself.[38] Burke and Fox, in any case,
were ignored.

Over the winter of 1774–75, Britain drifted into a state of angry, embittered
virtual warfare with a large portion of American society headed by a sizable
part of the American elite. The British Crown sought to overawe the resistance. Aware of the scale of the challenge, Governor Gage recommended massive military reinforcements; but only some four thousand additional troops
actually arrived, enough to further inflame American sentiment without offering much prospect of overpowering the burgeoning opposition. In February 1775, Parliament reaffirmed her supremacy over the American colonies
and introduced yet two more coercive measures: one imposing curbs on New
England's trade and shipping, the other extending these restrictions to all the
colonies except New York, Georgia, and North Carolina, which at this point
appeared less opposition-minded than the rest.

CHAPTER 2

A Republican Revolution

Early Stages (1774–76)

Britain was not trying to suppress American liberties or establish arbitrary government by force. The royal government did not intend the kind of imperial tyranny ruthlessly imposed earlier on Ireland and India. What royal ministers wanted was to extract more revenue and implement imperial authority in a more concerted, organized way in particular by cutting off America's trade, via the Dutch and French, with Europe and the outside world and regulating relations with the Indians, a tightening-up process that persuaded growing numbers of disgruntled Americans that London's intentions were more sweeping and sinister than they actually were.

Furthermore, despite the determined opposition and much talk of "rebellion," any notion that Americans would or should fight for their independence from Britain and abjure the monarchy was not yet palatable, or even plausible, to most Americans. With few exceptions, the colonists stayed residually faithful to Britain and the Crown throughout 1774–75, and a sizable portion of the elite, the "Tories," remained undeviatingly loyal. But the crisis was grave, a frequent topic of discussion in Europe, and pervaded every corner of the British empire in North America. Even in rocky Maine, then an outcrop of Massachusetts, a society bitterly divided between Anglicans and other Protestants where both landowning farmers and the landless poor (who represented practically half the population) stayed staunchly loyal to Britain until 1774, the Coercive Acts provoked general outrage eliciting mob violence against anyone opposing the boycott of British goods.[1]

In March 1775, ministers in London made the grave error of declaring Massachusetts to be in a state of "rebellion." This was a perfectly accurate description of the state of affairs in the colony where the local Patriot militia were openly exercising for armed action and Tory loyalists were being harassed and ejected from more and more districts. At this point, though, Massachusetts had edged ahead of the other colonies where, so far, resistance was largely confined to the boycott, civil disobedience, and the press war. New York's local political leadership—Jay, Gouverneur Morris, Robert R. Livingston, Philip Schuyler, and their allies—remained decidedly hesitant.[2] The landowning and mercantile gentry were principally concerned with preserving their primacy in local society, economy, and politics, and this inclined them to a particular approach—condoning resistance short of open rebellion while remaining cautious, flexible, and perennially vigilant against lower-class unruliness and presumption.[3] Leading Americans toying with the idea of open armed rebellion were aware that, if it came to it, much would depend on securing help—arms, munitions, funds, and supplies—from abroad, especially France and Holland, the only likely sources of large-scale military and naval supplies and other assistance. American ships returning from France's Atlantic seaports, reported the Boston papers, were receiving a rousing welcome, though, for now, the court at Versailles pursued a strictly correct and neutral attitude. Neither France nor the Dutch, the only potential allies against Britain possessing sufficient maritime reach, the organizers of resistance in New England knew, would interfere or could assist logistically, financially, or diplomatically without the colonists first breaking their allegiance and proclaiming open rebellion. As yet, there was widespread hesitation and no broad inclination to disavow British rule, or seek outside help, much less negotiate formal military alliances with foreign powers.[4]

On 19 April 1775, Governor Gage dispatched a column of troops from Boston to confiscate munitions the local militia had accumulated at Concord. This happened two nights after what became the official printing press of the emerging Massachusetts revolutionary government was smuggled from Boston to Worcester, an operation concerted by Timothy Bigelow (1739–90), a blacksmith leading the Worcester unrest and prominent member of the local Committee of Correspondence. Concord was a small town nearer and, Gage thought, easier to secure than now openly insurrectionary Worcester. But warnings had been sent ahead from Boston to affiliated groups over a large area, and the agitation had already proceeded too far to be so easily subdued.[5] In fact, Gage's initiative turned into a deeply humiliating fiasco for the Crown. Armed clashes erupted first at Lexington Green and then Concord, from where the redcoats were repulsed by a formidable assemblage of several thousand militia gathered from over an impressively wide area. Suffering seventy-three killed and two hundred wounded or missing, the cowed redcoats hurriedly turned and retreated, continually sniped at from behind hedges, back to Boston.

The New England colonies countered Gage's ill-advised effort at severity by gathering a considerable army with militia contingents from Connecticut, Rhode Island, and New Hampshire, and setting siege to the British garrison of six thousand, under Gage, quartered in Boston. Gage's disastrous further sallies, most famously his all-out assault on strategic Bunker Hill (17 June), north of the city, a battle in which his troops again suffered heavy casualties with over two hundred dead on the field, left his army trapped in what developed into a regular siege. Meanwhile, Concord had been the signal for the fighting to spread beyond Massachusetts. On 10 May, a force of Vermonters and insurgents from upper New York colony captured one of the principal British bases in the west, Fort Ticonderoga, a former French stronghold (Fort Carillon), constructed in 1755–58, commanding the southwestern side of Lake Champlain and guarding the mountainous passageway between New York colony and Canada's Saint Lawrence River valley. Over the next months, further clashes extended the armed conflict throughout the Thirteen Colonies, initiating a sporadic but bitter struggle also in the South.

Patriots secured wavering towns and ejected Tories from positions of local authority. Nevertheless, during the war's opening months, New Englanders and those taking up arms elsewhere resisted Parliament's decrees without the rebellious colonies developing any agreed political strategy for the struggle or defining their goals. In recent years, historians of the Revolution have become increasingly aware of the crucial role of "ordinary" lower-class leaders like Mackintosh and Bigelow in provoking local insurgency against royal officials and troops everywhere from Maine to Georgia. The Revolution's active initiators were often people of humble background, cobblers, blacksmiths, and tavern-keepers who in most cases had never heard of republicanism or writers like Sidney, Harrington, or Locke. The Enlightenment did not interest most people. However, just as in the French Revolution later, these semiliterate artisans taking the lead in 1765–66, and again in 1774–76, were not equipped to concert a wider strategy or draw up a political and constitutional plan. Their energy was crucial but also undirected, unruly, and potentially counterproductive. Most had little conception of the wider implications, so that during 1774–75 the growing armed rebellion conspicuously lacked any guiding concept as to what final political and social outcome was intended.

The Second Continental Congress, summoned to provide leadership and direction, gathered soon after the eruption of fighting, in May 1775. Besides coordinating resistance and deliberating how to secure satisfaction of the colonies' grievances, this body was again entrusted with negotiating and seeking reconciliation with the Crown. Among the sixty-five delegates representing the existing political elite, the leaders, except for the addition of Benjamin Franklin (1706–90), were much the same as in the First Congress. This second gathering again proved inconclusive regarding basic objectives. In June, Congress voted to raise troops in Pennsylvania, Virginia, and Maryland for service in the Boston area that throughout 1775 and the opening months of 1776 remained the principal theater of conflict. Congress also authorized the use of paper currency denominated in Spanish dollars, though British pounds sterling and pence remained everywhere acceptable throughout the revolutionary era. The commander chosen to lead the "Continental Army" in New England, Virginia's George Washington (1732–99), was among the colonies' most experienced militia officers. Appeals were dispatched in the name of Congress to Canada, Jamaica, and Ireland explaining American grievances.[6] But the armed rebellion remained strictly provisional, not indicative of a final break, as was demonstrated by the so-called Olive Branch Petition of 8 July 1775, adopted at the insistence of one of the principal conservative delegates, Pennsylvania's John Dickinson, who passionately believed America's stability and prosperity depended on remaining within the British empire and that America's oligarchs needed the Crown to ward off populist pressure.[7] Intended to keep all options open, this resolution affirmed the colonies' loyalty and intention to seek satisfaction of grievances and reconciliation on the basis of remaining firmly under the Crown.

Congress, anxious not to jeopardize their social status, families, or property, mostly preferred a tentative, finely calibrated, "moderate" stance. Few had any definite intention of pushing for a total break or persisting with armed resistance beyond a limited and so far vague set of goals. Time after time, though, British designs seemed poorly calculated to exploit American society's hesitation and profound divisions and rebuild trust or at least acquiescence among a majority who remained throughout 1774–75 indignant but disconcerted and predominantly willing to be reconciled. An especially atrocious blunder was the episode at Falmouth (today Portland, Maine) where the inhabitants were at odds with the interior towns and inclined to loyalism and maintaining trade links with England. Maine, like all the colonies, including Nova Scotia, was deeply divided, and Falmouth's citizens among the many New Englanders preferring to backtrack if possible. Urging compromise, not independence, they were reluctantly pushed into hostilities, first by militants from the surrounding countryside provoking strife in the town and seizing vessels carrying British army supplies, and next by town authorities refusing to surrender the munitions and insurgents to the naval squadron sent to overawe the town. Punishing such "unpardonable rebellion," on 18 October, four

British warships bombarded Falmouth for eight hours, reducing the town to ashes.[8]

Conflict escalated militarily and emotionally, and spread geographically. In November 1775, advancing from Fort Ticonderoga, a Patriot force crossed into Canada, appealing to the Canadians to join them, and captured Montreal, indeed seemed on the point of overrunning all of Quebec. Canada's governor, an Anglo-Irish general, Sir Guy Carleton (1724–1808), wounded in the capture of Quebec in 1759, found himself besieged in Quebec City. The United States had not yet been defined as an entity, and until 1774 nor had Canada, so that, initially, the Revolution conceived itself chiefly as wronged sections of the empire appealing to other segments to join their defiance of ministerial arrogance and imperial tyranny. Canada's French clergy and landowners, their social and legal preeminence, privileges, and tithes guaranteed by Parliament, stood solid for Britain. Ordinary French Canadians, tough and self-reliant but devout and barely literate, were hardly disposed to back a still utterly tentative revolutionary agenda rendered even vaguer, possibly menacing, and certainly more ambiguous by this early thrust into Canada. Canada, though, like the American colonies, was a divided society. A minority did sympathize with the inchoate insurgent message, especially among Nova Scotia Scots and those non-privileged able to read newspapers and books.[9]

Over the winter of 1775–76, Washington pressed the siege of Boston utilizing cannon transported from Ticonderoga. George III's ministers had blundered badly in presuming no viable alternative existed between bludgeoning the "rebels" into submission and watching them secede, and overrated the extent of American loyalism, in part because emphatic loyalism was so overwhelming in England itself. More than anything yet decided on the American side, overweening confidence and errors of judgment on the British side drove the sequence of mishaps and wrong moves pushing toward independence. Initial mistakes were compounded by the British ministry's grave overestimation of British military superiority. Caught in a strategic trap, on 17 March 1776, British commanders in Boston decided, despite such a withdrawal involving huge humiliation in terms of image and prestige, to evacuate New England's chief city. The commander, William Howe (1729–1814), a veteran of the Seven Years' War who had played key roles in the capture of Louisbourg, Quebec, and Havana, departed taking over 1,100 Loyalist émigrés with him; they were shipped to Halifax in Nova Scotia.[10]

Month by month the struggle widened inexorably in scope, intensity, and social complexity. In Virginia, the British governor, John Murray, Lord Dunmore (1730–1809), had dissolved the colony's assembly in May 1774 after it voted a Day of Fasting and Prayer against the Intolerable Acts. The assembly simply reconvened on its own and began concerting wider resistance.[11] The day after the encounters at Lexington and Concord, on 20 April 1775, Dunmore removed the gunpowder stores from Williamsburg, the colony's capital, marking the start of a tense standoff with local militia companies suspended somewhere between civil disobedience and armed rebellion. The Virginia militia called themselves "His Majesty's dutiful and loyal subjects" but were plainly mobilizing against the Crown and harassing royal officials, prompting Dunmore to threaten to "declare freedom to the slaves" should his officers and declared Loyalists continue to be victimized. He hoped threats would suffice to deter open armed resistance, assuring London that white Virginians "trembled" at the thought of a local slave revolt. But he also knew that a major slave revolt could be devastating. Well aware of the importance of the West Indies' slave-worked plantations to Britain's commerce and empire, he had no wish to desolate the colony. Mounting opposition, however, culminating in a Patriot march on Williamsburg, drove him first to retreat to offshore warships in June and, finally, to carry out his threat. On 14 November 1775, he proclaimed Virginia's black slaves free if they took up arms to assist his troops in "speedily reducing this colony to a proper sense of their duty."[12]

For various reasons the black response was neither massive nor wholehearted, especially not at first, while the British military and colonial authorities, for their part, only belatedly and patchily extended Dunmore's strategy to other colonies. Dunmore, in any case, was greatly weakened by his repulse from Great Bridge, near Norfolk, on the Virginia coast, a battle fought on 9 December 1775. Most Virginia blacks, moreover, like those of Haiti, and Europe's peasant rebels, were far from sharing in the revolutionary republican enthusiasm of a few literate and articulate revolutionaries. Rather, they believed their faraway monarch was indeed glorious and in intention their benevolent protector.[13] Nevertheless, by early 1776, around eight hundred runaway slaves had joined Dunmore's Loyalist force under the Union Jack, recruited into his "Royal Ethiopian Regiment" under white officers.[14] Other runaways, intercepted before they could join the British, were hanged or brutally flogged. Yet from Dunmore's viewpoint, the advantage redounding from fear of a general slave insurrection throughout the South (and the Caribbean) was scarcely worth the cost—though it did dampen support for the rebels in Jamaica and the other British West Indies. In Jamaica, where there was widespread sympathy for American protests among the white oligarchy, support evaporated from 1776.[15] If many Virginia Patriots were apprehensive lest Dunmore's slave emancipation cause slave owners to defect en masse (to protect their property), the actual effect was the reverse: fear and revulsion at Dunmore's action depleted what had been a large pool of Tory support, alienating a growing proportion of white Virginians from the Crown and making the war look distinctly more decisive and unavoidable than it had thus far.[16]

Further setbacks compelled Dunmore definitively to abandon Williamsburg. On 1 January 1776, warships under Dunmore's command began shelling the port of Norfolk after the town's large Tory following had fled and Patriot troops had occupied it. Although the fires that subsequently reduced the town to ashes began with the British bombardment, most of the destruction was apparently caused by retaliating Patriots sacking and torching Tory homes and properties. Even so, the mounting Patriot propaganda campaign in the *Virginia Gazette* and other papers redoubled denunciation of Dunmore's destruction of Norfolk and his emancipating slaves for the "express purpose of massacring their masters," eventually culminating in a print collection illustrating the war, assembled by Lafayette and Franklin for publication in Paris in 1779 denouncing British "atrocities," which presented as prime exhibits alongside the "bombardment of Falmouth" in Maine, Dunmore's "burning" of Norfolk and hiring of "negroes to murder their masters' families."[17]

Dunmore remained close by for many months, bombarding and sending ashore raiding parties along the coast, confronting General Charles Lee (1732–82), rebel commander in the South from early 1776. The conflict soon spread from Virginia southward. A fierce encounter in which a Loyalist force opposing the Revolution was beaten at Moore's Creek Bridge (17 February 1776), in North Carolina, ended the early partial Tory predominance in that colony. Loyalism remained exceptionally strong, though, in Georgia and South Carolina despite early reports that the British were encouraging slaves "to desert" their masters.[18] Understandably, both sides became increasingly embittered. Southern whites, moreover, became a more profoundly splintered society in two different senses: vertically, in allegiance, with Loyalists fighting Patriots, and horizontally, and more lastingly, in socioeconomic terms. Wealthy slave-owning landed gentry exempted themselves from militia duty while pressing hard, via their state legislatures, on their small tenant farmers and poor whites for rents and military service.[19] In South Carolina, one of the most aristocratic, socially unequal of the states, the planter elite divided roughly equally between Loyalists and Patriots, leaving four-fifths of the white population, mostly backcountry small farmers, severely underrepresented in the state legislature and sullen and reluctant to fight the British. To secure their social and political ascendancy, the Patriot slave-owning planter elite, when revising the state constitution in March 1776, felt obliged to increase white smallholder representation in the lower legislature from 6 to 38 percent. However, they continued excluding poor whites, the majority, entirely from voting for the upper house and from officeholding—while loudly repudiating the "abject slavery" the British Parliament designed to subject them to.[20]

Despite the tensions and difficulties, for the Americans the war began not just promisingly but sensationally well. By early 1776, before major reinforcements arrived, the British position had virtually disintegrated from Canada to the Carolinas; indeed, without the German hired regiments soon to appear there would hardly have been any contest at all. From the British standpoint, Adam Smith noted ruefully in June 1776, the "American campaign has begun awkwardly. I hope, I cannot say that I expect, that it will end better."[21] But the rebels had some thorny decisions to make. Like most rebel leaders, John Adams had not yet committed himself definitively to independence while Jefferson at this point still acknowledged the king, if not Parliament, as the "only mediatory power between the several states of the British empire."[22] To resolve the conflict, Britain needed to soften her demands while swiftly concentrating overwhelming force where it counted. Constrained by the Glorious Revolution's anti-military tradition, and the English gentry's aversion to any large standing army at home, which meant that there was no large pool of veteran troops to draw on, and the king's reluctance to raise fresh untried regiments given the urgent need to deploy trained men, Parliament solved the resulting strategic dilemma by hiring seventeen thousand (supposedly) trained and equipped troops in Hesse, Württemberg, and other German states (but not Prussia). These were to fight alongside the British under their own officers. In this way, a mercenary foreign army became integral to the British war machine in America and part of the complex interaction between the Revolution and the wider world.

Under a subsidy treaty, signed on 15 January 1776, Hesse-Cassel alone agreed to maintain 12,000 troops in America for the war's duration at a cost of £374,000 pounds sterling yearly, paid via the Dutch bankers to the ruling prince, the Landgrave Wilhelm. Hesse-Cassel's senior officers received some of the cash, but few others did. To raise the required numbers of able-bodied men, recruiting agents wielding princely authorizations swarmed over the Hessian countryside especially targeting farm helps and landless laborers. Between 1776 and 1783, keeping the Hessian contingents alone up to the agreed levels involved sending 18,970 landless men across the ocean locked into practically unlimited military servitude.[23] Wrangling over how long draftees must serve, deferments, and substitutions, and the criteria for differentiating between supposedly indispensable and "expendable" peasantry, not to mention the effect of reduced farm productivity on incomes and tax revenues, generated widespread ill feeling. To escape conscription, youths fled their villages, creating a vast tangle of disrupted apprenticeships, disused plots, deferred and broken marriages, and abandoned wives and children.

Leaving a sea of social dislocation behind, the hired regiments shipped to America fought the rebels with recruits often serving resentfully or half-heartedly. Many were killed or disabled, expired from disease, or deserted (often settling in America), before their terms elapsed, and needed replacing via further recruiting. Although Britain's monarch was probably cheated in his expectation that the hired men would be predominantly trained veterans, both the reliability and numbers of hired Germans sufficed to considerably bolster British strength in America. By September 1781, approximately 37 percent of total regular British soldiery fighting the rebels (i.e., excluding Loyalist volunteers and Indians) consisted of hired Germans.[24] In this way, the Revolution bore heavily on parts of Germany, provoking indignation in the diets of Hesse and Württemberg where local nobles and town dignitaries protested that British funds for the hired regiments arose from compulsory service of state subjects and should be deemed state revenue not private princely income. Princes and diets noisily disputed but both deemed remuneration for obligatory service to be exclusively for courtiers and nobles and obligatory military service exclusively for the poor and landless. Only a few dissidents disagreed. Controversy over how the British payments should be assigned dragged on for years, with noble disgruntlement aggravated by shortage of servants, coachmen, and valets for their own service caused by the relentless recruiting. The manifest injustice of it all inflamed local passions and helped form fresh cells of political subversion among professors, students, booksellers, and journalists with ties to the Illuminati, a secret underground sprouting everywhere in Germany in the mid-1770s.[25]

In southwestern Germany, as in France and Holland, and also the Electorate of Hanover where British recruiting was likewise stepped up to help man the big garrisons at Gibraltar and Menorca, thereby releasing more British troops for transfer to America, the Revolution thus became an intellectual and literary debating forum transforming the outlook of some and acting as a social and psychological lever generating resentment against princes, courts, and pervasive militarism. German critics of princely authority began speaking of a "sovereignty swindle," the deliberate confusing of princely "rights" with those of the state, to exploitatively transfer resources from the people. Among a literate few, indignation and intensification of grievances hardened into a more generalized and theorized anti-prince, anti-aristocratic, and anti-military stance laced by the growing renown of Franklin and Washington. To counter subversive talk expressing sympathy for the colonial rebellion, even relatively liberal German princes, like the duke of Brunswick, prohibited all public and group discussion of the American Revolution, whether at meetings or in the press, until the war's end. The split in intellectual society hence remained masked in the public sphere, as no princes, not even Frederick the Great (who was uninvolved in the war), would permit journals to write critically about royal "rights," courts, or princes.[26] With censorship tight, discussion of the Revolution in the press was sparse but became widespread in taverns, reading societies, student groups, and freemasonic lodges. In his dialogue *Ernst und Falk* (1778), the great playwright Gotthold Ephraim Lessing (1729–81) features a Freemason who "is one of those people who defend the American cause in Europe," believing the American Congress is a kind of Freemasons' lodge intent on spreading "their empire" by force of arms.[27]

The militarization of sections of German society and systematic squeezing of liberties to help buttress the British Crown and empire, and the "liberties" of Englishmen, thus became part of a gigantic transatlantic operation designed to repress American aspirations and opposition. Radical enlighteners in Germany drawing inspiration from the rebellion, like the deist Christian Wilhelm Dohm (1751–1820), the Huguenot professor Jakob Mauvillon (1743–94), and the military commander in Danish service Woldemar Hermann von Schmettau (1719–85), took to applying the apparent lessons to the German context, on occasion even publicly. Dohm was a leading publicist and advocate of Jewish emancipation, a republican critic of the British and Dutch imperial systems in Asia as well as the New World. In Germany, the Revolution resonated powerfully below the surface, he observed, in the journal *Deutsches Museum* in 1777, attracting "many important friends among our writers and poets" to the American side. American success, he noted in another article that year, in the *Deutscher Merkur*, would "give greater scope to the Enlightenment, a new edge to the thinking of peoples and fresh life to the spirit of liberty."[28] Von Schmettau, another deist adversary of existing institutions, laws, and attitudes (especially of Frederick the Great's militarism and wars), took a similar view. Pro-American sentiment surged behind the scenes, becoming integral to the clandestine radical political and intellectual underground. Enlightened minds contemplating the overthrow of princely despotism and oppressive religious authority began diffusing pro-revolutionary attitudes through their conversation, teaching, and writing.[29]

In France, Germany, and several other lands, sympathy for the rebels consequently generated an impressive opposing stream of recruits crossing the Atlantic, volunteers pledging to fight *for* the Revolution. Prominent among these was the Polish nobleman Tadeusz Kościuszko, later among Poland's greatest national heroes. Recommended by Franklin, he arrived in America in June 1776, joining Washington's command soon after.[30] Trained in military engineering at Paris and Warsaw, Kościuszko was a passionate abolitionist as well as a foe of Polish serfdom, an idealistic devotee of universal human rights as a result of reading French radical "philosophy," especially the *Histoire philosophique des Deux Indes* (1770). Another supporter was Goethe's friend the Count of Lindau (1754–76), a youth immersed in Enlightenment pedagogics. A later arrival was Friedrich Wilhelm von Steuben (1730–94), who became inspector-general of the "Continental Army." He reached America, after conferring with Franklin in Paris, in the autumn of 1777, volunteering for duty at Valley Forge the following March, albeit less out of idealism than chronic indebtedness. Prussian trained, he devised the "Continental Army's" drill and bayonet routines despite knowing practically no English, aided by his erudite French military secretary, another idealistic European recruit, Peter Steven Du Ponceau (1760–1844), later a famous expert in Native American languages.

The most renowned of the European volunteers was Gilbert du Motier, marquis de Lafayette (1757–1834), a high-minded young nobleman who arrived (landing in South Carolina), recommended by Franklin to Washington, in June 1777. Brave and competent, Lafayette soon figured as a senior officer among Washington's aides-de-camp. Filled with naïve enthusiasm for the equality and simplicity of manners he encountered, the "douce égalité" he thought reigned everywhere in the new United States, Lafayette emerged as one of the Revolution's most active proponents on both sides of the Atlantic. "In America," he wrote to his wife, "there are neither any poor nor what we call peasants": everyone supposedly shared in the same upright honesty and everyone "enjoyed the same rights as the most powerful landed proprietor."[31] Zealous for black emancipation and other progressive causes, again chiefly inspired by reading the *Histoire philosophique* (with which he was familiar before 1777), Lafayette became the iconic embodiment of pre-1789 *philosophique* French pro-Americanism.[32]

Philadelphia Radicalism

Nevertheless, the widening insurrection only slowly acquired a more defined and definite profile. In November 1775, answering inquiries for guidance from the New Hampshire and South Carolina conventions, Congress proposed adoption of constitutional reforms based on "a full and free representation of the people." In several colonies, the assemblies initiated steps to redraft their constitutions. Gradually, everywhere in the Thirteen Colonies, the general mood hardened. In early 1776, the shift was spurred by a radical undercurrent manifesting itself particularly at Philadelphia, now America's largest city with some twenty-five thousand inhabitants. This undercurrent found its most powerful expression in the most widely read, reprinted, and discussed of all the

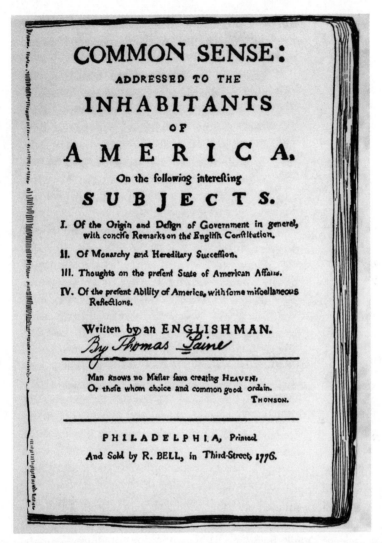

Title page of Thomas Paine's *Common Sense* (Philadelphia, 1776). Photo credit: JT Vintage / Art Resource, NY.

pamphlets of the Revolution: Tom Paine's *Common Sense, Addressed to the Inhabitants of America*, written late in 1775.[33]

Paine wrote the tract in collaboration with Benjamin Rush, one of America's leading enlighteners and medical men who, in the spring of 1777, was appointed physician general of the military hospitals. Rush encouraged Paine, made suggestions, and proposed his title—Paine had originally wanted to call

Thomas Paine (1737–1809), engraving from a painting by George Romney (c. 1792).
Photo credit: © Atlas Archive / The Image Works.

it *Plain Truth*. After Benjamin Franklin, "who held the same opinions," had examined and approved it, Rush helped find a sufficiently bold, challenge-prone, republican-minded publisher willing to print it. Robert Bell (1730–84), the bookseller engaged, was a Glasgow-born Scot in Philadelphia for some years since his Dublin bookshop had failed. A publisher of American editions of Beccaria and Voltaire and an Enlightenment enthusiast, he was the first large importer of the Scottish Enlightenment into America.[34]

Endorsed by Franklin, Rush, and Bell, Paine's celebrated text appeared anonymously at Philadelphia in January 1776.[35] Some attributed it to Franklin, others to Sam Adams;[36] hence, it did not immediately establish Paine's later renown. "The style, manner and language of this performance," observed a contemporary historian, David Ramsay, were "calculated to interest the passions, and to rouse all the active powers of human nature."[37] Subsequent editions of *Common Sense* appeared in 1776, at Philadelphia, Newport,

Salem, Hartford, Lancaster, New York, Albany, and Providence. "Not short of 150,000" copies, Paine later reckoned (perhaps exaggerating), were sold in America.[38] Before long, *Common Sense* also diffused widely in Britain and Ireland, with printings in London and more at Edinburgh, Newcastle, and Dublin. Notorious in Britain, Ireland, and the United States, *Common Sense* reappeared in French, at Rotterdam, and from 1776 was repeatedly reprinted on the Continent, later also in German.[39] In France, Holland, and Germany, it emerged as not just the Revolution's chief manifesto but, as the 1780 version of the *Histoire philosophique* affirms, its most dramatic rhetorical and intellectual intervention. In America, it decisively tilted the balance against hesitation and compromise. Revolutionary in intent and argument, the tract summoned Americans to fight for their independence, more equality, and new constitutional principles.[40] What better illustration could there be, demanded the *Histoire philosophique*, the premier European radical text of the day, of "philosophy" pointing the way.

For Paine, the veritable revolution of 1776 was an intellectual shift preceding the *Declaration of Independence*, a revolution in outlook that subsequently bifurcated pro-Independence American opinion.[41] In "A Serious Thought," an earlier article in the *Pennsylvania Journal; and the Weekly Advertizer* of 18 October 1775, Paine had already called for "independence" (which relatively few Americans yet contemplated) and a total break with Britain, drawing parallels between her alleged "tyranny" in America, with the "horrid cruelties exercised by Britain in the East Indies," and her despoiling the "hapless shores of Africa, robbing that continent of its unoffending inhabitants to cultivate her stolen dominions in the West."[42] That piece, and especially *Common Sense*, now powerfully infused the unfolding American drama; but their inspiration was patently not American or English. Rather, these texts propounded a rhetoric wholly alien to American debate thus far, echoing the radical "philosophical" denunciation of colonialism of Diderot, Raynal, and their circle in the *Histoire philosophique des Deux Indes*, an internationally vastly diffused work of far greater and more lastingly formative impact than Sidney or Harrington, circulating in numerous French and English-language (as well as German, Dutch, and Spanish) versions, a momentously subversive text thoroughly familiar and of special importance to Lafayette, Kościuszko, Franklin, Lee, Miranda, Condorcet, Mazzei, and many other internationally minded revolutionary leaders. Paine injected into the American scenario something fundamentally new to the American scene: radical, universalist revolutionary discourse already for some time familiar in France but rarely echoed in America or Britain that now profoundly influenced American sentiment.

Common Sense has been justifiably described as a "radical masterpiece." It was a work that "should be famous for ever," averred the commentator on the American Revolution and future French revolutionary Jean-Nicolas Démeunier (1751–1814), "because it contributed directly to the greatest revolution known in the annals of the world."[43] Prior to Paine's booklet, most Americans, held Démeunier, opposed the British ministry only tentatively, within respectable limits authorized by long customary constitutional and legal arguments. The same observation was made in Raynal's *The Revolution of America* (1781), a direct offshoot of the *Histoire philosophique*. Only after reading Paine's brochure, affirms the revised 1780 edition of the *Histoire philosophique*, had those privately contemplating full independence, headed by the two Adamses, Hancock, and Franklin, become empowered to mobilize the people to form a new republic.[44] Paine's pamphlet cleared the way for artisans, farmers, and shopkeepers, for elite and people alike, decisively impelling the move toward a total break, full independence, and a republican future.

Paine's pamphlet, vigorous in style, manner, and language, opened fresh perspectives at a juncture when American opinion was deeply divided, irresolution widespread, and loyalism rife. Many responded enthusiastically. Franklin insisted on its "prodigious" influence.[45] Lee styled *Common Sense* "a masterly, irresistible performance."[46] It was superbly timed, noted the Boston dissenting minister William Gordon (1728–1807), author of *The History of the Rise, Progress and Establishment of the Independence of the United States of America* (1788), the first general history of the Revolution. "It has produced most astonishing effects; and been received with vast applause; read by almost every American; and recommended as a work replete with truth."[47] But still more crucial than the pamphlet's unprecedented impact was its starkly radical character, causing the more conservative elements among the American Patriot social elite to react with revulsion and indignation.[48] For *Common Sense* was disturbingly innovative in declaring democratizing sentiments that even a year before could scarcely have been articulated with impunity, expression of which became possible in the colonies only due to the breakdown of royal authority, the widening rift between Patriots and Loyalists, and the mobilizing of the local militias. Roundly condemning those still urging negotiation and "reconciliation" with England, Paine equated willingness to forgive "oppression" and "tyranny" with wanting to "give prostitution its former innocence."[49]

Where the Virginia, Carolina, New York, and other landowners mostly remained wary of constitutional reform and cautious about declaring full independence, Paine's rejectionism appealed especially to men below the top elite level. So dramatically did its implications diverge from the "revolution principles" of the traditional colonial leadership that its wider message proved almost as disputed and divisive in Patriot circles as its call for independence was shocking and abominable to the British and Tories.[50] Among staunch Patriots appalled were Dickinson, John Adams, and John Witherspoon, all among the signatories of the pending *Declaration of Independence*. "Paineism" was repudiated with furious indignation by Loyalists and pro-Revolution oligarchs. Pro- and anti-revolutionary conservatives alike detested *Common Sense* for its anti-monarchism, revolt against English constitutional tradition and principles, stress on popular sovereignty and general democratic tendency, and undisguised hostility to "mixed government," Montesquieu, and Britain's empire and world hegemony.[51]

The Irish Tory assistant rector of Trinity Anglican Church in New York, Charles Inglis (1734–1816), who was later forced to emigrate and eventually settled in Nova Scotia, anonymously published one of the fiercest rebuttals, *The True Interest of America Impartially Stated, in certain Strictures on a Pamphlet entitled "Common Sense"* (1776), labeling Paine's tract "an outrageous insult on the common sense of Americans," an attempt to poison their minds and seduce them away from their true interest. Paine was an "avowed, violent republican, utterly averse and unfriendly to the English constitution." "Even Hobbes would blush to own the author for a disciple."[52] Another antagonist assailed him under the pseudonym "Candidus" in *Plain Truth: Addressed to the Inhabitants of America, containing Remarks on a late Pamphlet intitled "Common Sense."* British mixed government, "this beautiful system (according to Montesquieu), our constitution," a compound of monarchy, aristocracy, and democracy, was a system of ranks and empire that dominated the Atlantic, was cherished by the English of America and Britain alike, and had captured the commerce of the entire world. The "profound and elegant Hume" was among those abominating dangerous "demagogues" like the *Common Sense* author seeking to "seduce the people into their criminal designs" and foment rebellion.[53] Only someone rebelling against reason, retorted Paine, in January 1777, is a "rebel"; he who fights "tyranny" in defense of reason has a "better title to Defender of the Faith than George the Third."[54]

A number of revolutionary leaders were soon on the worst possible footing intellectually and personally with Paine and his circle.[55] While many Americans supported the rebellion, a great many preferred to negotiate or actively assist the British offensive, and in major areas of America the mood remained ambivalent, floating or fragmented by local social divisions and stresses. In the Hudson Valley, running the length of New York State, for example, most land was owned by aristocratic landowner dynasties such as the Livingstons, Philipses, Cortlandts, Beekmans, Van Rensselaers, and others who had acquired vast tracts during the seventeenth century and rented out farms to mostly poor and disgruntled tenants frequently on the basis of verbal rather than written leases.[56] Frederick Philipse owned two hundred thousand acres and possessed two large residences and thirty slaves. The nineteen-hundred-acre stretch forming the hub of Gouverneur Morris's holdings, though modest by comparison and away from the valley, facing Long Island Sound and hence closer to the British, likewise centered on a large manor house, Morrisania, serviced by (at one stage forty-six) black slaves.[57] In these socially hierarchical and potentially fraught areas, poor whites and blacks were as, or perhaps more, likely to resent and possibly resist local "aristocracy" as distant rulers of a global empire.

Some of the foremost leaders of the Revolution altogether repudiated Paineism. Shortly after *Common Sense* appeared, John Adams dismissed Paine's ideas as the most destructive influence at work on American shores, creating an impulse, he wrote, in May 1776, that "tends to confound and destroy all distinctions, and prostrate all ranks to one common level." His antipathy arose partly from Paine's rejecting separation of powers, and checks and balances, but chiefly from his advancing a scheme "so democratical, without any restraint or even an attempt at any equilibrium as counterpoise that it must produce confusion and every evil work."[58] Paine's tactical deployment of the Old Testament to back up his arguments Adams deemed scarcely "sincere." He strove to mitigate the tract's effect with his *Thoughts on Government* (April 1776), sternly repudiating Paine's call for a single democratic assembly, arguing for bicameralism with an upper chamber serving as "mediator" between the assembly "which represents the people and that which is vested with the executive power."[59] Ardently embracing the older republican legacy of "Sidney, Harrington, Locke, Milton, Nedham, Neville, Burnet and Hoadley," and the principles of Montesquieu, the most widely acclaimed political theorist in American political debate during the revolutionary era,[60] Adams demanded "aristocracy" and legislatures checked by a strong executive and separate "judicial power."[61]

"The so much boasted constitution of England" and cult of "balance of powers" surrounding it, averred Paine, might have been "noble for the dark and slavish times in which it was erected" when the "world was over-run with tyranny," but Britain's constitution had ever since been "imperfect, subject to convulsions, and incapable of producing what it seems to promise," namely "freedom and security"—the true purpose of government. Paine by no means agreed with Adams that the 1688 Glorious Revolution in Britain had delivered the essentials of what was needed in America. The "science of the politician," argued Paine, echoing Helvétius, Diderot, Raynal, d'Holbach, Priestley, and Dragonetti, "consists of fixing the true point of happiness and freedom" and devising "a mode of government that contained the greatest sum of individual happiness, with the least national expense."[62] By early 1776, very few among the American leadership went as far as Paine in insisting on eradicating traditional, inherited constitutional forms as well as monarchy, aristocracy, and empire from the future American Constitution or introducing comprehensive changes in the country's domestic political procedures. Besides a single legislature to preside over and above the states, "representation" should become far "more equal," urged Paine: all the colonies should elect their representatives to the future regular national Congress in the same way, dividing their territory into electoral "districts," "each district to send a proper number of delegates to Congress; so that each colony send at least thirty. Let the assemblies be annual," he recommended, foreshadowing the framers of the Constitution, "with a president only." The "whole number in Congress will be at least 390."[63]

It would be wrong to suppose that before *Common Sense* the Revolution lacked a radical "philosophical" dimension, as the example of the influential freethinking Irish physician Thomas Young shows. Democratic republicanism undoubtedly had substantial American as well as French, British, Italian, and other continental European roots. Charles Lee, Washington's British-born second-in-command during the early part of the Revolutionary War, also preceded Paine in this respect. Product of a highly untypical, partly continental European education, intensely cosmopolitan, speaking fluent Italian, German and Spanish as well as French, and far better read than most senior army officers of the day, Lee had proclaimed the American struggle's significance to be not local but universal in the *Pennsylvania Journal* two years earlier. In his *A Friendly Address to All Reasonable Americans* published in November 1774, in the *New York Gazetteer*, he summoned peoples everywhere to take up arms to resist monarchy and tyranny, claiming the Revolution made Americans the "champions and patrons of the human race." American success would have momentous implications, but if the Revolution failed, predicted Lee, "every vestige of liberty will be obliterated from the face of the globe."[64] Lee's universalist, "philosophique" radicalism was sketchier, though, and exerted nothing like the impact of Paine's pamphlet—any more than the rest of the roughly 250 controversial and polemical pamphlets debating the American crisis down to 1776.

Paine claimed never to have read Locke (whose influence on the American Revolution has often been greatly exaggerated)[65] and rarely resembles Locke in tone or stance, a divergence of itself setting him at odds with the gentry elite and pro-Revolution clergy. Aside from the *Histoire philosophique* with its uncompromisingly radical tone and ideology deriving principally from Diderot and the latter's circle, Paine drew on Priestley's *Essay on the First Principles of Government* (1768)[66] and the *Trattato delle virtue e de' premi* (1765), by Giacinto Dragonetti (1738–1818), a treatise that appeared in English in 1769.[67] Dragonetti, a "wise observer on governments" according to Paine, was—like Beccaria (after Montesquieu the second most quoted continental Enlightenment author in American revolutionary political literature)[68]—a disciple of Claude-Adrien Helvétius (1715–71), the founder of Utilitarianism and a declared critic of Montesquieu and Rousseau. The true goal of government, claimed Dragonetti—like Helvétius, Beccaria, and Filangieri, another great Italian devotee of the *Histoire philosophique*—is the "greatest sum of individual happiness" achieved for all with the least cost. Especially targeting monarchy and aristocracy, Dragonetti's work breathed a fierce anti-elite animus, denouncing the prevailing unjust distribution of rewards and wealth, arguments to which Adams remained allergic throughout his life.[69] Priestley too derived his arguments from Radical Enlightenment sources including Collins's one-substance determinism and materialism. Hence, in intellectual origin Paine's highly divisive stance—henceforth integral to the Revolution— was not part of the English classical republican legacy at all but rather a strand of the Radical Enlightenment legacy.[70]

Denouncing the British constitution and empire, as well as Parliament and the Crown, Paine's pamphlet brimmed with republican and democratic fervor, following Dragonetti in sweepingly rejecting all forms of monarchy and aristocracy.[71] Unlike Adams, Paine deemed the Revolution "universal, a Revolution through which the principles of all Lovers of Mankind are affected."[72] But what chiefly distinguishes Paine's discourse from "moderate Enlightenment" revolutionary ideology was its appeal to universal rights and values, and refusal to defer to or invoke English tradition, precedents, and history. His rhetoric, like that of Lee and the *Histoire philosophique*, projected an unyielding cosmopolitanism, his insistence that the "cause of America is in a great measure the cause of all mankind," pre-echoing Diderot's contention, in the 1780 edition of the *Histoire philosophique*, that the cause of the rebels is "celle du genre-humain tout entier."[73] Every part of the Old World is assumed, as in Diderot's segments of the *Histoire philosophique*, to languish, like America, under longstanding organized oppression.[74] "Britain, as a nation," had simply become too grasping and arrogant: "blessed with all the commerce she could wish for, and furnished by a vast extension of dominion with the means of civilizing both the eastern and western world, she has made no other use of both than proudly to idolize her own 'Thunder' and rip up the bowels of whole countries for what she could get." Britain "has made war her sport" like Alexander the Great and inflicted vast misery on the world:

the "blood of India is not yet repaid, nor the wretchedness of Africa yet re-
quited."[75] Paine was clearly suggesting that the newly expanded British imperial sway in America was part of a global system that comprised also the
fiercely invoked "corruption" and ruthlessness of British rule in India and
Africa.[76]

Like Franklin (since 1774), Paine thoroughly despised the appellation
"parent or mother country, applied to England only, as being false, selfish,
narrow and ungenerous."[77] "This new world hath been the asylum," he reminded readers, not just for the first settlers in New England fleeing from
Stuart despotism but "persecuted lovers of civil and religious liberty from
every part of Europe." Under a third of America's population were of "English descent." Men fled to America not from the "tender embraces of the
mother, but from the cruelty of the monster," namely monarchy, aristocracy,
empire, British law, and national prejudice. Mocking the American political elite's ingrained adulation of the British constitution, he advised further
"inquiry into the constitutional errors in the English form of government"
and the impossibility of just and satisfactory conclusions "while we continue
under the influence of some leading partiality." It was, he knew, "difficult to
get over local or long standing prejudices yet, if we will suffer ourselves to
examine the component parts of the English constitution, we shall find them
to be the base remains of two ancient tyrannies, compounded with some new
republican materials." The two negative components he identified as monarchy and the "remains of aristocratical tyranny in the persons of the peers."[78]

With Americans fighting for liberty, Paine denied all possibility of winning a secure freedom "while we remain fettered by an obstinate prejudice."
For as "a man who is attached to a prostitute, is unfitted to chuse or judge of
a wife, so any prepossession in favour of a rotten constitution of government
will disable us from discerning a good one." The unrelenting "prejudice of
Englishmen," he complained (exactly like the *Histoire philosophique*), "in favour of their own government by king, lords, and commons arises as much,
or more, from national pride than reason."[79] Neither Britain's empire nor its
mercantilist trading system, held Paine, was justified in itself or beneficial to
her colonies. Far better would be an open commerce with every country, an
argument again recalling the *Histoire philosophique* besides Helvétius, Dragonetti, Gorani, Mazzei, and Filangieri. Such a plan, held Paine, "will secure
us the peace and friendship of all Europe; because it is the interest of all Europe to have America as a free port."[80] Abhorring all notion of self-regulating
markets, he urged open commerce and free access to the world's markets
within a carefully crafted, overarching system of pro-public, pro-consumer
regulation of trade.

Much of America's gentry elite still held back from full independence and constitutional reform, not only in both major colonies still firmly resisting independence, New York and Pennsylvania, but in New Jersey, Maryland, Virginia, and North and South Carolina where Loyalism remained strong and where, as Washington noted in April 1775, there was much reluctance and hesitation.[81] In early May 1776, shortly before the long-planned British offensive threw the Americans onto the defensive, Congress reconvened and became the focus of a decisive drama in Philadelphia. With nearly all the colonies south of New England vacillating, Pennsylvania conservatives led the fight to block the demands for outright independence pushed by the Adams circle and the radicals forming a temporary tactical alliance. In the first ballot in Congress on whether state legislatures should proclaim it "necessary that the exercise of every kind of authority under the Crown should be totally suppressed" and all government powers placed under the authority of the people, the pro-independence coalition was narrowly defeated by two votes. When news of the defeat broke, Philadelphia's citizenry, realizing the Pennsylvania "aristocracy" had by a slither thwarted the will of most of their own colony's inhabitants, erupted in anger.

Philadelphia radicals reacted by inciting raucous public meetings, demonstrations, and soon also riots. May and June 1776 were the turning point of the Revolution, two months that decisively shaped the overall outcome. By early June, still only four colonies had definitely instructed their delegates to vote for independence. But pressure from below now tilted the balance. Prodded by angry crowds in the Philadelphia streets, Congress haltingly edged toward crucial resolutions. On 20 May, the greatest mass meeting thus far ever convened in North America—around four thousand people crowded into State House Yard, in driving rain—cheered speech after speech demanding "independence" and a new state government for Pennsylvania to oust those opposing independence.[82] The main petition was drafted by the radical leaders—Young, Rush, Matlack, Paine, and their friends. The Pennsylvania Assembly leadership, headed by Dickinson, resisted as long as they could. But with the Philadelphia militia refusing to back them, Pennsylvania's "aristocrats" were overwhelmed by a radical opposition in collusion with the Massachusetts delegates.[83] On 14 June, the sitting Pennsylvania Assembly, cowed by the crowds, adjourned, in effect dissolving itself and opening the way for a popularly elected convention to draw up a fresh state constitution. Dickinson, though, still headed the acting committees during the interim.

Returning to Philadelphia after the repulse from Canada, in June 1776, Franklin presided over the convention summoned to revise the Pennsylvania state constitution against the wishes of the colony's aristocratic governing elite. Until late May 1776, the predominance of the landowning gentry and of Anglicanism in the colony had, with Quaker support, been solidly and uninterruptedly maintained.[84] The old Pennsylvania legislature, like the assemblies of the other colonies, desired nothing more than to emulate the British "mixed government" constitutional model as a device for keeping power and authority in the hands of the "aristocratic" elite. Under the post-1688 English Constitution, voting rights in most constituencies were confined to a minority of property owners possessing a certain level of wealth, with most adult males altogether excluded from representation, participation, and the suffrage. This was fundamental to the "mixed government" concept and tradition, and the reason why Franklin and his radical British friends—Paine, Jebb, Price, Priestley, and their disciples—were so opposed to it.

"Europe, and not England, is the parent country!"

Challenging even the "warmest advocate for reconciliation to shew a single advantage, that this continent can reap, by being connected with Great Britain," Paine's rejectionist thesis that "Europe, and not England, is the parent country of America"[85] not only alarmed and antagonized the gentry elite but assumed a special significance given Pennsylvania's unusual cultural and linguistic character. Pennsylvania had long been more heterogeneous ethnically and religiously than other colonies, with sizable Quaker and Scots-Irish Presbyterian blocs; but it also hosted German, Alsatian, and Swiss Lutheran, Reformed, and Mennonite communities. The old order in Pennsylvania had been steadily crumbling since the withdrawal from active politics, since December 1774, of the previously influential Quaker bloc being unwilling to countenance the growing violence and resort to arms. Quakers, on principle rejecting rebellion, resented the Revolution and especially the Patriot local committees of "inspection and enforcement" along with the democratic tendency they represented. Then, in late June 1776, the presiding gentry elite with their strong Anglican affiliations lost their grip entirely due to the rowdy street and militia disaffection in Philadelphia.

Mobilizing and expanding the local militias in response to the eruption of fighting in Massachusetts guaranteed relentless continuing popular pressure against the old ruling gentry and the Quakers, opening the door to Pennsylvania's further radicalization.[86] Until late June, with the middle and most Southern colonies reluctant to seek independence and Dickinson still interim head of Pennsylvania's delegation to Congress, the outcome of America's independence debate still looked highly uncertain: it was the decisive weakening of the Pennsylvania oligarchy that precipitated the crucial shift at the top.[87] The culminating debate in Congress, on 1 July, continued interminably, pitting Dickinson against Adams in suffocating heat. Some Pennsylvania and other oligarchs afterward blamed Dickinson for mismanaging matters and, through miscalculation and intransigence, placing Pennsylvania's affairs into the "hands of men totally unequal to them."[88] Finally, on 2 July, after Pennsylvania, South Carolina, and Delaware switched from opposing to accepting Independence, and New York abstained, Congress voted "unanimously" in favor of independence and began preparing their public declaration, having earlier, on 11 June, asked a Commission of Five (including Adams, Livingston, and Franklin), to draw up a draft *Declaration*, on the presumption it would be needed.

Jefferson, who had now come round to a radical perspective, had been asked to write the original draft. His version avoided all reference to God and divine sanction, blamed American slavery on the British Crown, and stated that all men "are created equal and independent" and that from "that equal creation they derive rights inherent and inalienable." This original the committee then amended, toning down its Paineite tendency and inserting the reference to God; Congress then amended it further (much to Jefferson's chagrin).[89] The finalized *Declaration* was swiftly adopted, on 4 July. This justly famous text held "these truths to be self-evident, that all men are created equal, that they are endowed by their Creator with certain unalienable Rights, that among these are Life, Liberty and the pursuit of Happiness.— That to secure these rights, Governments are instituted among Men, deriving their just powers from the consent of the governed,—That whenever any Form of Government becomes destructive of these ends, it is the Right of the People to alter or to abolish it, and to institute new Government, laying its foundation on such principles and organizing its powers in such form, as to them shall seem most likely to effect their Safety and Happiness."

On these grounds George III's efforts to establish "an absolute Tyranny over these States" was forever repudiated and American independence declared. The *Declaration* was then diffused by the Philadelphia papers. On 8 July, the *Declaration* was formally read out at mass meetings in Philadelphia and Trenton, and on 9 July to Washington's troops in New York. In Philadelphia, "there were bonfires, ringing bells, with other great demonstrations of joy upon the unanimity and agreement of the Declaration."[90] In New York, the large equestrian statue of George III was pulled down by the troops and afterward melted and recast into musket balls. Everywhere, the royal arms were torn down from courtrooms and churches, and embossed and stone emblems of the British Crown shredded or pulverized.

In Pennsylvania major political developments followed immediately on Dickinson's resounding defeat. All members of the Pennsylvania militias were admitted to the vote in the ensuing state elections, and this expanded suffrage secured a wholly exceptional revolutionary outcome in just this one state. "The proprietary gentry have retired to their country seats," Rush advised Lee triumphantly, from Philadelphia, on 23 July 1776, "and honest men have taken the seats they abused so much in the government of our state."[91] For now, Dickinson and the conservatives, the Pennsylvania "aristocracy," were wholly ousted. But the radicals could be under no illusions as to the stiff opposition and difficulties that lay ahead for their democratic program. "The republican soil is broke up," noted Rush in late July 1776, "but we have still many monarchical and aristocratic weeds to pluck from it." "Time will meliorate us," he trusted at that juncture, albeit still uncomfortably aware that while the "substance" of royalty was overcome, "now and then we worship the shadow."[92]

Philadelphia radicalism before long resulted in Pennsylvania's transformation into the Union's then sole unicameral and near democratic state, thereby realizing what Brissot in 1786 called the "plan of a democracy as perfect as man can imagine."[93] Only Pennsylvania (and then Vermont) adopted a democratic course, in 1776, choosing a more emphatically republican constitutional format than was acceptable to the old Pennsylvania governing elite and all the elites of the other colonies. In this way, Pennsylvania defined, widened, and formalized the growing social and ideological rift at the heart of the Revolution during the summer of 1776. Many Founders besides John Adams grew alarmed lest more states should follow and adopt Pennsylvania's "spirit of leveling, as well as that of innovation," into their state constitutions. At length, however, the threat was deflected, leaving only Pennsylvania and Vermont adhering to a radical stance for the next fourteen years and openly championing (adult white male) democracy.[94]

The delegates to the Pennsylvania state convention, from July to September 1776, thus forged one of the Revolution's most significant achievements. Socially, they were quite distinct from the ejected old Pennsylvania governing body and differed also intellectually and in ideology. Besides some upcountry farmers and Franklin, who was chosen "president" of the drafting convention and who "alone is enough to confound with his presence a thousand such men as myself," noted Rush on 23 July, the new dominant faction represented the less affluent sections of the Philadelphia populace, principally Scots-Irish Presbyterians involved in manual trades.[95] The Irish also counted in the countryside outside Philadelphia, Rush estimating them at around 10 percent of Pennsylvania's total population of "about 350,000 souls."

In addition, "the Germans, who are an uninformed body of people," recalled
Rush disparagingly later, in 1784, "submitted to [the radicals'] usurpations
and formed a principal part of their strength."[96] Pennsylvania Germans,
Scots, and Irish were thus crucial to the American Revolution's radicalization; but some Pennsylvania German Lutherans and Calvinists were very
far from being "uninformed." The most notable of those who weighed in
post-1776 Pennsylvania politics was General Peter Muhlenberg (1746–1808),
one of Washington's top commanders who had studied theology at Halle
and whom Rush subsequently described as having "long been and still is the
most popular and powerful German in Pennsylvania," later crediting him
with swinging all Pennsylvania behind Jefferson, and against Adams and the
Republicans, in the hard-fought presidential election of 1800.[97]

Backed by a highly disparate, heterogeneous mix of minority social groups,
some markedly unrepresentative of the Thirteen Colonies as a whole, the
radical leaders, "Dr. Franklin," Paine, and those Rush initially called the "good
men," formed a phalanx of Philadelphia intellectuals all thoroughly attuned to
republican ideas. Chief among them were Young, Timothy Matlack (c. 1734–
1829), and the self-taught mathematician, astronomer, and inventor of German origin David Rittenhouse (1732–96), a scientific genius and energetic
radical,[98] all originally from humble backgrounds. Another of this remarkable
circle was James Cannon (1740–82), a Scots mathematician in Philadelphia
since 1765, first as a tutor and, from 1773, as a professor at the Philadelphia
College. Scientifically knowledgeable and philosophically inclined, Philadelphia's foremost Enlightenment enthusiasts, backed by farmers, Germans, and
religious dissenters, in May 1776 firmly assumed the leadership of the radical Revolution.

Nothing more clearly illustrates the transformed political situation than
Pennsylvania's constitutional drafting committee nominated by the state convention. Chaired by Franklin, it included Young, Cannon, Matlack, George
Bryan, and Robert Whitehill.[99] Though not formally a member, Rittenhouse
also participated. If George Bryan (1731–91) could be said to be a businessman and an active churchgoer, even he was an Irish Presbyterian, and the
rest of the Pennsylvania constitution drafters of 1776 were all far removed
from traditional American mainstream attitudes, business life, and religion.
Abhorred by Dickinson's conservatives and the oligarchies controlling the
legislatures of the other states, which understandably feared the spread of
radical ideas beyond Pennsylvania and Vermont,[100] these newcomers to political prominence were exactly the kind Franklin respected and whose company he sought. Cannon, a principal framer of the new Pennsylvania constitution in 1775–76, was a graduate of Edinburgh University and unrelenting

republican ideologue, among those most vehemently opposing the "aristocratical junto" in the name of the majority. It was precisely on this ground that Rush, after breaking with the radicals, reviled him as a "fanatical schoolmaster who had art enough to sanctify [the democratic constitution] with Dr. Franklin's name."[101]

Matlack was a brewer, long committed abolitionist, and rebel against his Quaker background, a militia colonel rebuking the main Quaker body for their political passivity, for their earlier support of the aristocracy, and for being too dilatory in advancing black emancipation. Paine "often visited in the families of Dr. Franklin, Mr. Rittenhouse, and Mr. George Clymer," Rush recorded later, "where he made himself acceptable by a turn he discovered for philosophical as well as political subjects." A respected merchant, George Clymer (1739–1813) was another ardent activist who had been a leader of the Patriot agitation in Philadelphia ever since 1765. He was prominent importer of Dutch goods (from St. Eustatius) and signatory of the *Declaration of Independence*. But unlike the others, Clymer, like Rush, came to oppose the 1776 unicameral Pennsylvania constitution.[102]

A physician, Young was a skilled linguist who taught himself French, German, Dutch, and Latin and was a disciple of the late seventeenth-century English "deist" Charles Blount, dubbed by modern scholars "the first of Spinoza's disciples in England."[103] Prominent in the Boston revolutionary ferment of the early 1770s and, in 1772, among the Boston Committee of Correspondence's founders, Young had fled to Philadelphia in 1774 when Massachusetts's governor tried to arrest him. A fervent enlightener steeped in Blount, Sidney, Gordon, Trenchard, Shaftesbury, and Bolingbroke, it was Young who, during their intense discussions in 1763–64, had converted the Vermont revolutionary leader Ethan Allen (1738–89) to militant freethinking and helped compose his book on the irrationality of supernaturalism and belief in miracles, *Reason the Only Oracle of Man*, later printed, in independent Vermont, in 1784. Young also instructed Allen (whose popularity in Vermont was immense) in republican political theory and encouraged his efforts, as leader of the Vermont Green Mountain Boys, to establish a Vermont free republic.[104] It was a harsh blow to the "democratical plans" of Allen, Paine, Cannon, Matlack, and the other Philadelphia and Vermont radicals when, in July 1777, only a year after the advent of the new Pennsylvania constitution, Young died from yellow fever contracted at the city hospital.[105]

The new Pennsylvania constitution of September 1776, published in the Philadelphia papers on 3 October, was indeed a landmark in the history of representative democracy, republicanism, and modernity. Abolishing all property and wealth qualifications for voting and officeholding, it stipulated that "every freeman of the full age of twenty-one years, having resided in this state for the space of one whole year next before the day of election for representatives, and paid public taxes during that time, shall enjoy the right of an elector."[106] This still excluded the very poorest who paid no taxes but, highly innovatively, included those free blacks who did.[107] The General Assembly of representatives was to be elected annually, every October. Rejecting the mixed-government concept central to the British constitution and Montesquieu's much-acclaimed eulogy of it, it eradicated every vestige of aristocracy and monarchy, providing for only one chamber that would be elected by the taxpayers without there being any higher body restricted to large property owners. A twelve-member Supreme Executive administered the state government. The executive was thus a committee, not an individual, and it possessed no veto, remaining subordinate to the legislature. It was elected jointly, in a two-stage process, by the citizenry and legislature.[108] Important too, and emulated later by a key French revolutionary reform in 1789, but not adopted into the United States Constitution, every citizen's vote was accorded equal weight by apportioning representation through the counties and towns so that each representative represented the same number of taxable inhabitants.[109] Those elected were supposed to be those "most noted for wisdom and virtue." A check to oversee, and if necessary overrule, any potentially deviating legislature or executive was also provided for: the Council of Censors, a review body and constitutional court, reelected every seven years, charged with evaluating the legislature's and executive's proceedings, to prevent legislature and executive ever deviating from the path of rectitude and the people's welfare. It was also the sole body, under the 1776 Pennsylvania constitution, empowered to summon a convention, should it think fit, to amend the constitution.[110] A constitutional appeal court of this kind reappeared in the French democratic constitution drafted by Condorcet, in February 1793.

Championed by Franklin, Cannon, Young, Paine, and Rittenhouse, the 1776 Pennsylvania constitution was reviled by Adams, for whom unicameral legislatures like Pennsylvania's and Vermont's were already a halfway house to despotism. From 1777, Rush too was a declared foe, rejecting the single legislature and the "new invented body of men called a council of censors" and the "many other newfangled experiments, absurd in their nature and dangerous to the liberties of the state." According to Rush, most of the "English" and Quakers in Pennsylvania were solidly against the new constitution. Its firmest supporters he identified as impecunious Irish, Scots, and German Calvinists.[111] Abroad, the new constitution was warmly eulogized by Diderot and Raynal in subsequent editions of the *Histoire philosophique*, turning this constitution into a focus of European as well as American debate and rendering

Pennsylvania more than ever an imagined utopia. Radical eulogies intensified the growing transatlantic controversy over the desirability or otherwise of democracy. The renowned French political thinker Mably, in his treatise on the nascent United States, published in 1783, perching on a fence, claimed the new Pennsylvania constitution was too democratic for a society lacking the austere morals necessary to allow such a system to function but that, from a purely theoretical standpoint, the new Pennsylvania state constitution did promote human equality and dignity, and the universal rights all men possess from nature, more uprightly and forcefully than any other known constitution.[112]

Too much for Mably, the 1776 Pennsylvania state constitution was nevertheless judged inadequate and defective in certain respects by the Philadelphia radicals and other radical democrats. In particular, it signally failed to abolish black slavery or remove race discrimination from the suffrage. It did nothing to safeguard the rights of Native Americans and little to guarantee press freedom and, despite removing the old anti-Catholic provisions, kept religious tests for officeholders. Candidates elected to the state legislature or a state office were obliged to swear to belief in One God, Creator and Governor of this universe, and acknowledge the divine inspiration of both the Old and New Testaments, a test plainly debarring Jews, deists, atheists, universalists, and Unitarians like Priestley and Price who condemned "religious tests" in principle.[113] The original first draft of the "oath of office"—published in the newspapers but never voted on by the public—required only belief in the "being of a God and a future state of rewards and punishments." But protesting clergy—on this point the Anglican, Calvinist, and German Lutheran pastors were all as one—secured enough farmers' votes to overturn it. Applying to all Pennsylvania officeholders, the amended oath injected a formalized intolerance rooted in the farmers' deference to theology and the preachers.[114]

Temporary conservative defeat by the Philadelphia radical caucus simultaneously opened the door to a more democratic Pennsylvania state constitution *and* American independence, which might well have been considerably delayed without the local drama.[115] Pennsylvania's business elite, landowners, and clergy, however, from the outset vowed to overturn the 1776 democratic constitution. Hostility to its provisions was pervasive within as well as outside the state, and since radical enlighteners had achieved their breakthrough only by default as it were, with the Anglicans and Quakers temporarily unseated by their opposition to Independence, leaving the Scots-Irish Presbyterians and German-speaking Lutherans and Calvinists briefly dominant when allied with the western farmers, all of whom shared the radicals' desire to exclude the old elites from power but not their antipathy to preachers and theology, the radical hold on Pennsylvania remained precarious. In March 1779, a conservative group, called the Republican Society, was established aiming to overthrow the 1776 constitution on behalf of institutionalized wealth privilege, social hierarchy, division of powers, and theology, and gained ground steadily with the support of many clergy.

Defeating the World's Greatest Seaborne Empire (1776–83)

If a long and bitter war was now inevitable, success in securing Independence was not. So powerful was imperial Britain in the 1760s and 1770s that many American "moderates" as well as out-and-out Loyalists beside Canadians, Native Americans, freed Virginia slaves, and Jamaican planters, expected and stayed hopeful, at least until deep into 1778, and often longer, that the American Revolution would be crushed or at least substantially checked. Excessively swayed by Loyalist reports, the London press was even more sanguine. There were also many in continental Europe who, for various reasons, hoped the Revolution would fail, rebuking those in Europe who had begun to speak of "the United States."[116] In Germany, where American Revolution principles directly challenged the principle that princely government derives from God and cannot be challenged by the people, conservative enlighteners and "moderates" insisted the Revolution was illegitimate and no basis for social and political improvement.

Immediately following Independence, during the summer of 1776, the war assumed an unpromising turn from the American standpoint, so much so that it seemed that the Revolution would either falter in a manner precluding a total break or collapse entirely. Following the arrival of sufficient warships and Hessians to give the British temporarily both the naval and military edge, royal forces captured the American shore batteries and emplacements on Manhattan, occupied New York and Long Island, and dominated much of the surrounding area. Suffering a series of defeats, a near-despairing Washington withdrew to the heights at the northern edge of Manhattan. American morale, it was jubilantly reported by Loyalists and in the London press, sank from euphoria to a low ebb. Following a decisive victory over the rebels in the battle on Long Island on 27 August 1776, an offer of peace talks was published by the British commanders, Admiral Howe and his brother, General Howe, to which many congressional leaders, headed by Dickinson and including Witherspoon, gladly responded. A significant portion of Washington's "Continental Army" had begun to desert or defect. The "military spirit of our countrymen seems to have subsided in that part of the continent," acknowledged Rush ruefully, and a "torpor seems likewise to have seized the citizens of America in general."[117] Inexplicably, though, as it seemed to many on both sides of the Atlantic, the Howes failed to press home their attack when it might well have succeeded in destroying the "Continental Army" entirely. Washington never forgot that New York was the place where the Revolution nearly died.[118]

Congress agreed to hear the British peace offer and, on 11 September, a delegation of three—Franklin, Adams, and Edward Rutledge (a South Carolina deputy allied to Dickinson and Jay in opposing independence)—met and conferred with the Howes, albeit refusing to be designated "British subjects" and with no definite result.[119] Fighting resumed in November when the British attacked and captured Fort Washington, controlling the northern tip of Manhattan, the encounter in which Lindau died. New York remained the chief bastion of the British occupation for the remainder of the war. By 1781, New York and its environs were still occupied by 20,000 "British" regulars, just over half of whom, 10,250, were actually hired Germans.[120] Substantial Loyalist support was at hand in New York City and State, and if all this proved insufficient to defeat the Revolution once the opportunity of the late summer of 1776 had passed, it converted New York into Loyalist activism's principal hub. Franklin's illegitimate son, the deposed governor of New Jersey, William Franklin, emerged as the leader of New York's armed "Associated Loyalists," a body that by 1780 regularly sallied forth to conduct raids against Patriots and their property in New Jersey and upstate New York.[121]

The military turning point of the war occurred between the small New Jersey battles of early 1777 and the escalating campaigns of the next summer and autumn. Washington's crossing of the River Delaware from New Jersey into Pennsylvania, and nighttime recrossing, in December 1776, surprising the Hessian garrison at Trenton, was followed by a hard-fought but crucial victory over the British garrison at Princeton on 3 January 1777, leaving Princeton College a heap of ruins but notably reviving sagging American morale and reversing the sobering effect of the second half of 1776. The most decisive phase of the war, though, ensued during the summer and autumn of 1777. On the northern fringes of New York State, a British army under the veteran commander General John Burgoyne, consisting of 8,000 regulars, British and Hessians, supplemented by around 2,000 Indians, French Canadians, and Tories, thrust southward from Canada, advancing from Fort St. John. Crossing by boat, the army reached the southern end of Lake Champlain on 1 July 1777. Fort Ticonderoga was retaken and the British began

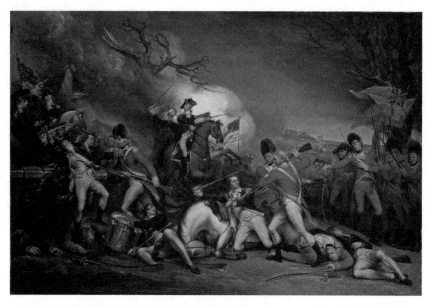

The Death of General Mercer at the Battle of Princeton, January 3, 1777 by John Trumbull. General Mercer was mortally wounded in the battle but did not die until several days later. Photo credit: Yale University Art Gallery.

their fateful march on Albany. But the original British strategic plan was not adhered to: because the Howes had come to believe Philadelphia was the key, most of the occupying army at New York, instead of marching up the Hudson Valley to join Burgoyne and cut New England off from the rest of the colonies as originally intended, was dispatched, 15,000-men strong, by sea from New York to the Pennsylvania coast, weakening Britain's entire strategic posture.[122]

Marching on Philadelphia, this force defeated (but failed to break) Washington's army at the Battle of Brandywine Creek (11 September 1777), where Lafayette was wounded, and occupied Philadelphia two weeks later. Patriot morale sagged anew. Britain seemed on the verge of victory. But in northern New York State General Burgoyne's army walked into a trap, a carefully concealed network of obstacles and intricate defenses at Saratoga designed by the Revolution's brilliant engineer, Kościuszko. Burgoyne's several determined efforts to break out were repulsed with heavy loss. Finally, on 17 October 1777, the beaten and dejected general gave up the struggle, surrendering his entire remaining force of 5,790 wounded, sick, and effectives.[123] Complete humiliation at Saratoga partly stemmed from the British command's astounding inability to mount a relief expedition from New York to rescue Burgoyne. News of this stunning American victory elated the United States, appalled

Britain, excited France, and shook Canada and the Caribbean. The United States had become a militarily successful transatlantic and global reality.

In their rapidly deteriorating situation following Saratoga and France's entry into the war (February 1778), British commanders reached the further disastrous conclusion, only nine months after occupying the rebel republic's capital, that they must now evacuate Philadelphia. Nothing could have been more detrimental to British prestige. As the British departed, Philadelphia's large Loyalist community was further unnerved by the Pennsylvania legislature's publishing a long list of persons designated "traitors." Some Loyalists marched out on 18 June with Sir Henry Clinton's troops; others fled by ship. All considered, the pull-out from Philadelphia and New Jersey proved ruinously costly in reputation, men, and equipment. Clinton abandoned all Pennsylvania to "the rebels" in June 1778, marching his men back across New Jersey to strengthen the defenses of New York City, now deemed vulnerable to a possible joint American-French attack. With New Jersey again the chief pivot of the war, the British rear was harried by Washington as they retreated until they turned and fought another major battle at Monmouth Courthouse (28 June 1778). A deadlock militarily, with neither side gaining an edge, this encounter meant further humiliation for England; it was the first time the "Continental Army" opted to fight in the open and stood its ground against trained professionals, emerging on even terms.

France's entry into the war rendered the struggle a global contest. Versailles was mainly seeking a means to weaken Britain and exact revenge for the humiliations of 1763. In negotiating with Congress, Louis XVI promised not to try to regain Canada; but at the same time French ministers had no wish to see the Americans wrest Canada from Britain. Being checked by a hostile neighbor would supposedly ensure America's continued dependence on France.[124] Louis's foreign minister, Vergennes, consequently instructed French commanders and the newly arrived French envoy at Philadelphia that the Americans should *not* be helped to acquire Canada. At the same time, French commanders were inciting Canada's French and Indian inhabitants to harass the British, and among French Canadians and French officers serving with the American army, notably Lafayette, enthusiasm lingered for restoring French rule in the former "New France." Britain's grip on Canada might disintegrate under the pressure of war, in which case France would have to intervene to prevent the Americans from absorbing the colony. On 28 October 1778, the French admiral, the comte d'Estaing, published a carefully worded declaration in the royal name, at Boston, avoiding all mention of a possible French reconquest but promising Canadians and Indians who fought the British the French Crown's "protection."[125] In the event, the substantial sea and land forces sent from France during the war were never deployed any nearer to Canada than Rhode Island while the Iroquois in northern New York and Vermont sided with the British.

Following the disastrous reverse at Saratoga and the French alliance, Britain seemed unlikely to reconquer the Thirteen Colonies. As the significance of this sank in, the effect in the Western world's capitals was extraordinary. Never before in humanity's history had liberty been established in a state comprising such a vast expanse of territory, remarked the contemporary French historian of the American Revolution and expert on American state constitutions, Jean-Nicholas Démeunier, and "never had it been established on such good principles." There was still a considerable delay, however, before peace negotiations could begin. England, where popular support for the war remained staunch, was politically and psychologically as yet wholly unprepared to countenance defeat despite the efforts of Burke and others to impress on the king and ministry that America was now effectively "independent" except in name and that the struggle had become pointless as well as extremely costly.[126]

With independence virtually a de facto reality, British forces nevertheless vigorously renewed the struggle in Virginia and the Carolinas. With only the loose Articles of Confederation holding the Union together, this prolongation of the conflict with no real remaining threat to the republic's major cities (aside from New York) was bound to test whether the unity and sense of purpose displayed during the desperate years of the struggle, from 1775 to 1778, would survive in less challenging and compelling circumstances. British efforts subsided only after the decisive and conclusive defeat in Virginia, at Yorktown, in October 1781. At Yorktown the Earl Cornwallis, who had earlier won the Battle of Camden (16 August 1780), strengthening the British grip on South Carolina, was forced to capitulate to a combined force of 16,000 French and Americans, surrendering what remained of his 9,000-strong army whose escape by sea, from the Virginia coast, the French had cut off. "The troops of every kind that surrendered as prisoners of war," recorded Ramsay, "exceeded 7,000 men, but so great was the number of sick and wounded, that there were only 3,800 capable of bearing arms."[127]

With the struggle winding down, the question was: Could the United States function effectively as a republic under their tenuous Articles of Confederation? From 1781, the various states took to collaborating less and less and increasingly diverged in their activities and goals.[128] Lacking the power to tax directly or regulate commerce, Congress was undoubtedly too weak a vessel, something that became ever more starkly obvious after the war officially ended in 1783. An increasingly pitiful spectacle, Congress mustered scarcely twenty-five representatives at most of its immediate postwar meetings. During 1784, attendance was too sparse to allow purposeful deliberation of measures and, at times, virtually all business ceased because too few states were represented. Georgia and Delaware, both impeccable in their cooperation with the rest during most of the war, attended only sporadically after Yorktown and were wholly absent throughout 1784. Except for Virginia and Pennsylvania, none of the states kept more than two representatives in Philadelphia.[129]

As America basked in the glow of victory, it seemed natural to most Americans to attribute the success of the revolutionary struggle and the dramatic transformation that had occurred to divine providence rather than Enlightenment concepts;[130] at the same time, the American Revolution became an increasingly controversial topic in Europe. Subversive, clandestine criticism of the German princes intensified, becoming part of a propaganda war between conservatives and radicals that continued uninterruptedly from 1775 for decades. Court propaganda, inspired by British diplomats in German capitals and at the stadholder's court at The Hague, but stiffened by German princely aversion to rebellion and democracy, pilloried the United States as a sink of anarchy doomed to failure. When the prominent South American revolutionary, the radical-minded Francisco de Miranda (1750–1816), who defected from the Spanish army in Cuba to the Americans toward the close of the Revolutionary War, visited Berlin, as a political exile, in 1785, he encountered emphatic claims from courtiers and preachers that "anarchy" and confusion reigned throughout the American states, independence having turned America into a "most distressing scene of carnage and desolation." Miranda strove to undeceive those "noted for their liberality of sentiment anxious about the situation of America" as to the "virtuous establishment of civil liberty which [the Americans] have so nobly commenced" and which German sympathizers "appear to have much at heart."[131] Only for radicals like Miranda, though, did the United States represent a prized and mighty step forward in the progress of humanity.

CHAPTER 3

Revolutionary Constitutionalism and the Federal Union (1776–90)

The State Constitutions under Critique

Most legislators desired to reform only at the edges. Yet, in the eyes of many, the Revolution had created the need, and greatly reinforced the rationale, for reforming America's constitutions and institutions along with her laws, education, and church-state relations. A basic defect of the Revolution, held radical critics, was that instead of grounding the new republic's laws and constitutional arrangements on "reason," philosophy, and the best authors, and comparing recommendations of leading authorities, most Americans had preferred to keep, or acquiesced in keeping, the pre-1776 framework, adhering as far as possible to their former colonial legal and constitutional systems. Revising their constitutions from 1776, most states retained much of their colonial past—with Connecticut and Rhode Island adopting no changes at all aside from renouncing allegiance to the Crown. Connecticut after independence still sought to keep its "King Charles Charter." In the constitutional debates of the 1770s and 1780s, complained Paine, Price, Priestley, Mazzei, Filangieri, Turgot, and Condorcet, tradition and precedent by and large eclipsed "reason." Such obstinate "imitation," Turgot assured Price in 1778 (much to John Adams's indignation), had deplorable consequences. Instead of concentrating legislative and executive power in their assemblies, forging an orderly hierarchy of power, Americans, following Montesquieu, opted instead for separation of powers, dividing authority between governors, upper chambers, and lower chambers, emulating Britain where power and authority were divided between the monarch, an upper chamber (the Lords) dominated by the peers and bishops, and a lower chamber (the House of Commons) controlled by the gentry.[1]

From 1776 onward, the dichotomy of opposing principles within the American Revolution, "aristocratic" and "democratic," persisted both as an intellectual quarrel and active political struggle. If many among the elite abhorred the broad-based electorate and wide representation adopted in 1776 in Pennsylvania and Vermont, others judged most of the state constitutions far too oligarchic. According to Ethan Allen, a Connecticut-born frontier pioneer, farmer, and land investor who was also a homespun philosopher and deist, there existed, as he put it in 1778, "less dissatisfaction in the state of Vermont, as to matters of government, [than] in any of the eastern states, Connecticut excepted."[2] Although independence was secure, argued an editorial in the *Gazette of South Carolina* on 7 September 1786, "the American Revolution is just begun [since] the whole government must be made to conform to democratic principles."[3] That two fundamentally different, competing interpretations of the American Revolution and its true character existed—one more radical and republican (with Jefferson as its chief hero), the other more "aristocratic," proto-nationalist, allied to the churches, and less individualistic (with Hamilton as the driving force and Jefferson as chief culprit)—has often been remarked on by modern historians.[4] The "moderate," "aristocratic" revolutionary outcome sought by Adams, Hamilton, Jay, Livingston, and Morris, conserving the pre-1776 American gentry elite's ascendancy intact, had become locked by revolutionary circumstances in an unresolvable tension with the democratic and egalitarian challenge. The American Revolution, by 1783 in one sense an accomplished fact, in other respects remained an unresolved clash of principles dividing society, education, and a political arena that was fast also becoming a polarizing transatlantic divide.

After the American War, European "moderate" enlighteners like Burke who had in any way justified or condoned the American Revolution found they needed categorically to retrench and qualify their endorsement to curtail the more grandiose constructions being built on it, if only by discussing it as little as possible. They felt compelled to check its potentially radical democratic and egalitarian implications and consequences. For decades after 1783, conservative commentators defended the tendency for American legislatures to distance themselves from their earlier willingness, in 1776, to proclaim a generalized conception of the "Rights of Man" elevating the innate status and dignity possessed by all humans to the first principle of government and worthy legislation.[5] Far from agreeing that the American example promised vast political and social benefits for all, and an end to oppressive government globally, obstinate resistance arose, in both America and Europe, to espousing American revolutionary principles in their equalizing, democratizing mode. For supporters of the American proto-democratic, secularizing, and egalitarian tendency, those to whom "the rights of humanity are dear" and who "groan to see them usurped everywhere," as one Dutch pamphleteer put it,[6] increasingly confronted detractors—on both sides of the Atlantic the majority—defending the social status quo allied to religion and tradition.

"Mixed government" was denigrated by radicals for dividing sovereignty and entrenching privilege and social status. In Europe, it enabled aristocracy to preside while formally deferring to a monarch for aristocratic titles, honors, military commands, colonial governorships, and high offices of state, and as a shield against any popular challenge. In America, Montesquieu's "mixed government" recipe buttressed oligarchic elites and entrenched the preference, more redolent of monarchical than republican practice, for powerful state "governors," a trend pronounced in states such as Maryland and New Jersey. If king and ministers habitually fostered corruption and manipulated members of Parliament, state governors were equally well placed to bribe and twist legislatures and judiciaries. Hence, in Europe and America, the "mixed government" construct ultimately represented a blend of surrogate monarchy and "aristocracy," sanctioned by the pulpit, that bolstered a select few at the expense of everyone else.[7] It was hardly likely that the practical repercussions of such a clash of principle and ambition would not rapidly become universal. "The gulf between Burke's oligarchic and Paine's democratic perspectives," as one scholar expressed it, "could hardly be wider, while the hopes raised by the French Revolution lent this contrast dramatic practical relevance."[8] This applied throughout the Western world.

The success of the Pennsylvania (and Vermont) radicals, in 1776, consequently triggered a war of constitutions that spread throughout the Thirteen Colonies with lasting and increasing transatlantic significance. In some cases, the ensuing struggle was relatively subdued. In uncompromisingly aristocratic South Carolina, among the richest states but one controlled by a particularly narrow slave-owning landed oligarchy with property qualifications for the suffrage set so high that only a small minority of adult white males possessed the vote for both houses, the legislature tightly controlled local affairs and appointments to state offices and was only marginally and sporadically challenged by the white majority excluded from full representation.[9] Maryland, by contrast, featured one of the fiercest constitutional tussles. During the autumn of 1776, this state's landed "aristocrats," fearful lest their "poor deluded countrymen," misled by the "detestable villainy of designing men" imitating the likes of Young and Allen, should follow Pennsylvania on the "ruinous" path to democracy, had to repel a more determined radical challenge before clinching their heavily restricted suffrage and bicameral legislature presided over by a solidly oligarchic senate. The result left Maryland's senate elected by just a fringe of the wealthiest, those possessing personal estates valued at over five hundred pounds. To reinforce aristocratic control of the state legislature, Maryland's governor received exceptionally broad powers including sole authority to appoint the state's militia commanders.[10]

In Massachusetts, the aristocratic component was balanced by a stronger representative element. Property qualifications for those voting for the state upper house, the senate, and the governorship were set five times higher than for the much broader mass of citizens able to vote for the lower house.[11] Another characteristic oligarchic device was long legislative sittings between elections. In Britain, allowing no more than three years to transpire without a general election under the 1694 Triennial Act had been canceled by the Septennial Act of 1716, stipulating elections must be held every seven years to limit electoral influence on government. After 1716, the House of Commons was reelected infrequently, only every seven years, purposely releasing the legislature from review by the electorate between elections to restrict its influence over the proceedings, and the rebel colonies, radical critics complained, often adopted this same "pernicious" mode of infrequent elections rendering it easy for representatives to betray their constituents and "sell their liberty."[12] Paine attributed the failings of American revolutionary constitutionalism at both state and federal levels largely to the lingering appeal of Britain's "corrupt" constitution. "As the Federal Constitution," he wrote in 1796, is "a copy, though not quite so base as the original, of the form of the British Government, an imitation of its vices was naturally to be expected. So intimate is the connection between form and practice, that to adopt the one is to invite the other."[13]

"Mixed government" and separation of powers, sanctioned by Montesquieu, persuaded most post-revolutionary politically engaged, pamphlet and newspaper-reading Americans that their political and legal institutions approached perfection. With the Federal Constitution secured by late 1787, little more, many believed, was required. Hence, anti-democratic discourse in the press and legislatures remained broadly prevalent in the United States until well after 1800. Between 1775 and 1820, those dissatisfied had to combat a deeply ingrained bias that America's political order possessed a degree of perfection that only a fringe were prepared publicly to claim it had not achieved. "It is not to be presumed," Elihu Palmer assured his New York audience in 1797, that in "any country man has arrived at perfection in political science." American state constitutions and that of the federal union were "undoubtedly more perfect than any others that ever were formed," he was willing to grant, and had many welcome practical "effects." "But will anyone dare to say that there is no room for improvement?" New Yorkers should remember "what blind attachment was bestowed for many ages upon the British government." Few had protested until a late stage despite their being thoroughly defective, unrepresentative, monarchical, and aristocratic in reality. "And shall Americans at this time exhibit similar imbecility and prejudice, by proclaiming the impossibility of improvement in the primary arrangements of our political institutions?"[14]

The basic clash of principle and of systems was a fight for opinion and perceptions as much as a clash of ambition and economic interest. Part of the lingering power of the "mixed government" doctrine was its formidable capacity to unite the landed and mercantile interests. Britain could never be the model of nations, "le foyer de la liberté" (the foyer of liberty), eighteenth-century observers customarily maintained it was, the Baron d'Holbach (1723–89), among the prime radical theorists of equal rights and among the foremost political theorists of the age, had pointed out in his *Système sociale* (1773), until she awoke from her proud complacency, eradicated aristocratic control, and broadened her restricted suffrage.[15] In addition, Britain would also need to become less preoccupied with building commercial hegemony at the expense of other peoples and halt the senseless mercantilist wars on which her eighteenth-century governing elite continually embarked with a view to imposing ever greater maritime and imperial sway on others to the exclusive benefit of her aristocrats and merchants.[16]

Legal culture survived still more untouched after the Revolution, something manifestly inconsistent with the dignity of a true republic, warned Mirabeau and Démeunier, and a further inducement to ordinary men's "superstitious" veneration for precedent and origins. "There are still preserved here," complained Jean-Pierre Brissot (1754–93), the later leader of the French revolutionary faction known as the Girondins, writing of Boston in his *Nouveau Voyage dans les États-Unis de l'Amérique septentrionale* (3 vols., 1791), narrating his 1788 American tour, the "costly forms of English legal procedure, forms common sense and a taste for orderly methods will undoubtedly eliminate," but which, for now, rendered excessive numbers of lawyers unavoidable. Radicals followed the *Histoire philosophique* in deploring American "blindness" to the political and social harm stemming from the overall shapelessness and lack of principle of a customary legal system scorned by *philosophes* (but not Hume) as a "chaos exceedingly difficult to unscramble."[17] American lawyers not only maintained the pre-1776 tradition of inflated fees but exploited the law's vast intricacy to exact undue influence in state legislatures, enabling them to "worm their way into the houses of the legislature and the administration," noted Brissot of Massachusetts, "which they infiltrate with their vexing disputatiousness."[18]

Brissot was amazed by the curiously high status Americans all too willingly accorded to lawyers.[19] With respect to antiquated, unreformed legal usage, America seemed to have joined instead of detached itself from ancien régime archaism and outmoded usage. Adherence to archaic forms specially devised to "increase the expense and to mysticize the entire procedure of law" struck many as yet another device for advancing the interests of the landed and financial elite over the disadvantaged.[20] If English and American law's vast web of intricacy looked suspect, producing opaqueness that greatly encouraged the growth of a rapacious lawyer class amassing personal fortunes by exploiting the less affluent with a mass of clever expedients, preserving intact an antiquated legal tradition based on case law, and perpetuating a legal system devoid of clear principles, proved the perfect means to circumvent equality and universal human rights. State officers and officials in the South were mostly appointed by the legislatures and were usually landed proprietors; in the North they were more frequently locally elected and often lawyers.[21]

Despite such strictures, Brissot figured among those depicting America's transition toward republican equality and emancipation in a highly optimistic fashion, presenting the country as a bastion of innocence, simplicity, individualism, and liberty. His worry, and that of many others, was that equality is a delicate plant. In a passage of the *Histoire philosophique* composed shortly after 1776, closing the ninth volume of the 1780 edition, Diderot had expressed confidence the Americans would win their war against the colonial oppressor but urged them to remember, in building their new society, not to allow inequality of wealth to grow excessive.[22] "Fear too unequal a division of wealth resulting in a small number of opulent citizens and a multitude of citizens living in misery from which arises the arrogance of the former and abasement of the latter." For this would "undermine the equality comprising the fundamental principle of the democratic republic."[23] Price, an author much read in America and Europe, likewise greatly prized the de facto equality prevailing in early America. Most inhabitants of Connecticut, he had learned, consisted of a "hardy" middling sort in which the "rich and the poor, the haughty grandee and the creeping sycophant," were "equally unknown." "This is the equality to be found in all the productions of nature, the equality and the only equality necessary to the happiness of man."[24] At the same time he summoned Americans never to forget the dangers of "too great an inequality in the distribution of property."[25]

It particularly disturbed European and American radical enlighteners— and behind the scenes and less articulately a great many others, albeit a minority—that the new United States constitutions and laws nowhere made any explicit commitment to equality or democracy as social and political principles. In their new constitutions, states like Rhode Island, Connecticut, and the Carolinas signally failed to embrace any clear, meaningful principle of broad representation.[26] The states evinced no "véritable amour de la démocratie" (true love of democracy), objected the *philosophe* and eager *Américaniste* François-Jean, marquis de Chastellux (1734–88), a veteran of the American War, writing to Madison in 1784. In 1776, when the *Declaration of Independence* proclaimed men equal, Americans, he thought, had been more or less equal in practice. But a temporary state of rough equality provides no lasting basis for a democratic republic. There might be little danger at first, but in time, with shifting circumstances and growth of commerce, crafts, and population, a large and impoverished laboring class resembling that of France and Britain could emerge. The resulting inequality, admonished Chastellux, would assuredly threaten the Republic's foundations. A republican society must take positive, formal steps to curb overweening wealth inequality and limit the resulting social subordination that vitiates society as a whole.[27]

The specter of a resurgent "American aristocracy" deeply alarmed *philosophes* such as Diderot, Condorcet, Chastellux, Brissot, Mirabeau, Mazzei, Miranda, Priestley, and Price. "There are three enemies to equality against which America must guard," warned Price.[28] First, granting hereditary honors and titles of nobility; second, right of primogeniture, a legal device designed to "raise a name, by accumulating property in one branch of a family," disparaged by him as "a vanity no less unjust and cruel, than dangerous to the interest of liberty"; third, an unbalanced, exploitative mercantilist foreign trade, like Britain's, designed to benefit a restricted merchant, financial, and aristocratic elite. Of these, formal "aristocracy" seemed to Price the immediate menace. Unfortunately, reports reaching Europe suggested pressure was reviving for a defined nobility, for "granting hereditary honours and titles of nobility" in America. Price considered this a looming disaster. Men distinguished by such titles, "though perhaps meaner than the meanest of their dependents, are apt to consider themselves as belonging to a higher order of beings, and made for power and government." Birth and rank necessarily dispose them to be "hostile to general liberty"; and when they are not and do recognize the "rights of mankind, it is always a triumph of good sense and virtue over the temptations of their situation."[29] Far better for the United States to remain forever "what it is now their glory to be—a confederation of states prosperous and happy, without lords, without bishops—and without kings."[30]

Honoré Gabriel, comte de Mirabeau (1749–91), later among the key early leaders of the French Revolution, in 1784 was another outside observer expressing alarm lest the American Revolution, the "most astonishing of all revolutions" and the only one "philosophy" could endorse, fall victim to "aristocracy." An American Revolutionary War veteran officers' initiative, originating in the summer of 1783, with one of Washington's closest aides, General Henry Knox (1750–1806), among its chief promoters, aspired to create a permanent order of officers that "fought and bled" with Washington. Complete with ranks, medals, and marks of distinction, this Order of Cincinnatus would be hereditary and its members' descendants automatically succeed to their status. Nothing was likelier to undermine the Revolution, protested Mirabeau, or degrade to unprofitable theory instead of man's true destiny the republican legacy of Sidney, Locke, and Rousseau.[31] Just when America's achievement drew all eyes admiringly to the western hemisphere, an officer clique attempts to erect a new *noblesse* in the nascent republic! Worse, in their naïveté, ordinary Americans, complained Mirabeau, seemed little perturbed (though actually there was a considerable outcry, lasting many months). If Paine, Lafayette, and John Adams in Holland did seem complacent about this, Franklin, a great foe of hereditary nobility and primogeniture, was appalled.[32] It was Franklin, then in Paris, who spurred Mirabeau—himself a renegade noble—and Chamfort to intervene against the threat of American "aristocracy" at this juncture, coordinating what became a transatlantic anti-aristocratic campaign drawing in others. Démeunier denounced the society of Cincinnatus for introducing the "funestes suites de l'aristocratie héréditaire" (lamentable consequences of hereditary aristocracy).[33] Francisco de Miranda, first of the great South American "liberators," conferred at length about the controversy while in Charleston, in 1783, with Aedanus Burke (1743–1802), author of the fiercest American tract denouncing the Cincinnati project. This French-educated South Carolina judge of Irish background pronounced the newly established "order" possibly fitting for the "petty princes of Germany" but not for America, a pernicious assault on republican liberty apt to produce fresh "Caesars" and "Cromwells."[34]

The society remained for years an American and transatlantic ideological battlefield.[35] The anti-Cincinnati backlash sufficiently impressed Washington, ever vigilant to safeguard his image and reputation, to prompt his withdrawing his earlier acceptance of the order's invitation to become its first "president."[36] Burke's anti-aristocratic brochure was forwarded by Franklin to Paris, together with a letter on the topic of his own, both texts becoming absorbed into Mirabeau's hard-hitting *Considérations sur l'Ordre de Cincinnatus* (1784), a reworking of Aedanus Burke and Franklin that caused a considerable stir in Europe. Rendered back into English, it reappeared, in 1786, at Philadelphia, now solely under Mirabeau's name—much to Aedanus Burke's irritation.[37] Equality, affirmed Burke, Franklin, and Mirabeau, is the American Revolution's fundamental principle and chief constitutional ingredient. All pretensions to nobility, and whatever encourages the ignorant to defer to noble status, the American public must abjure as "préjugés absurdes et barbares," an immediate threat to America's well-being and Constitution.[38] Nothing more damages society than endorsing military prowess as the foundation of a privileged elite. Reason and virtue make the only genuine "nobility" existing on this earth.[39]

If formalized nobility looked menacing to some, the real threat to the American Revolution in all radical eyes was that of informal "aristocracy." According to Paine, Franklin, Young, Mazzei, Barlow, Mirabeau, Brissot, and Jefferson, as earlier Raynal, Diderot, and d'Holbach, the Revolution was threatened by practices, laws, and political traditions, especially primogeniture and restricted suffrages, inherited from the past and everywhere cherished by conservative revolutionary leaders. The perceived threat in the United States was the continuing ascendancy of large property owners and big merchants over state legislatures bolstered by restricted suffrages controlling access to office, legislatures, and governorships. "Aristocracy," consequently, remained an abiding theme of social criticism throughout the post-revolutionary era down to the mid-nineteenth century in America as in Europe.[40] In discussion with Sam Adams at Boston in 1784, a worried Miranda asked how was it that in the United States, a budding democracy whose basis was republican "virtue," offices and dignities were allocated not according to virtue and accomplishment but, instead, according to social standing and property? Surely this was a thoroughly unenlightened, inherent contradiction disfiguring the Revolution. Adams offered no answer.[41]

Oligarchic hegemony had only been incipiently challenged in most states. Yet when projecting the new American reality to the outside world, enthusiasts inevitably showed little inclination to advertise this too openly. A tendency to overstate the Revolution's democratic credentials when publicizing these in Europe characterized the publicity efforts of Jebb, Price, Mazzei, Mirabeau, Lafayette, and Brissot alike. Connected to radical networks in Britain and America, Brissot retained close ties to exiled "democrats" opposing patrician oligarchy in Switzerland, where he had traveled to observe firsthand the memorable and widely influential but short-lived Genevan democratic revolution of 1782. Eighteenth-century Switzerland was a federation of small cantonal republics of which none was yet democratic but where, in several, resentment was building against the closed hereditary patrician oligarchies, closely allied to the clergy, controlling their politics and institutions and where, by 1780, democratic discourse was more rife than elsewhere in

Europe and perhaps more so than in the United States. As Brissot realized, the Swiss cantons were decidedly more ripe to embrace and benefit from "American" principles than from the American reality, and the same applied to all of Europe.[42] Brissot aspired to assist his Swiss, British, and French friends in democratizing their respective countries not least by promoting the image of a free and near-democratic America.

Federal Government

The great majority of those who participated in the framing of the United States Constitution of 1787 had no wish to extend the reach of popular participation in political life; their main goal was to retain control within the hands of the existing political elites.[43] In the United States, pressure for a closer union and stronger central government, especially to create a federal infrastructure of trade regulation, customs, and banking and to allow more effective negotiation with foreign powers, had by 1787 become intense. A new federal constitution was necessary, many delegates to the state legislatures agreed, for a range of reasons, not least because the war's successful conclusion did not mean an end to international disputes. Differences with Britain, Spain, and France persisted over the Newfoundland Fisheries, customs duties, maritime rights, and Great Lakes navigation and Mississippi traffic. "Spain thinks it convenient to shut the Mississippi against us on the one side," noted John Jay, "and Britain excludes us from the St. Laurence on the other; nor will either of them permit the other waters, which are between them and us to become the means of mutual intercourse and traffic."[44] To defend the common rights of the Union in these and other areas, a stronger mechanism of central government was essential.

Jay published his views on the inadequacy of the existing Articles of Confederation in *The Federalist*, a soon famous set of tracts appealing to the public, during the ensuing public debate, to support the originally confidentially proposed, sketched-out, and debated closer federal union. Alexander Hamilton (1755–1804), Washington's chief of staff and among his closest political allies, joining in the public debate, added the consideration, in November 1787, that even accepting the republican plea that "commercial republics, like ours, will never be disposed to waste themselves in ruinous contentions with each other" and "will cultivate a spirit of mutual amity and concord," history suggested it would be foolhardy to rely on any such assumption. "General or remote considerations of policy, utility or justice" often yield to "aversions, predilections, rivalships and desires of unjust acquisition that affect nations as well as kings." Ancient Athens and Carthage were commercial republics but both were warlike. "There have been, if I may so express it almost as many popular as royal wars."[45] The United States simply could not dispense with a regular standing navy and army maintained by all the states in common.

In another article for *The Federalist*, Hamilton cited the disputes over Vermont as further evidence of the need for stronger central government. The territory of Vermont had been French until 1763, though mainly peopled by Iroquois and other Indians. After 1763, when the area began to be settled by Anglo-Americans, it was originally called the "New Hampshire Grants." However, incompatible and overlapping land grants were issued by the legislatures of New Hampshire, New York, and Massachusetts, which all claimed the territory. The local militia, the Green Mountain Boys, had played a key role in capturing Fort Ticonderoga and occupying Montreal under their leader, Ethan Allen.[46] Outlawed in 1771 for resisting royal authority, during the 1775 retreat from Canada, Allen was captured and then spent three years as a prisoner. Claiming the "hatred subsisting between us [and the State of New York] is equivalent to that which subsists between the Independent States of America and Great Britain,"[47] he willingly negotiated with Loyalists and the British while a prisoner, always angling for what he and his supporters really wanted: autonomy for Vermont. Vermonters effectively renounced the Crown *and* the United States, proclaiming their own sovereign republic with the radically republican constitution finalized on 8 July 1777, a text firmly based on the democratic Pennsylvania model but crucially going beyond it in being the first North American constitution to ban slavery.[48]

Revolutionary Vermont surpassed even Pennsylvania in detaching liberty from privilege, property, slavery, and Locke,[49] becoming a temporarily independent entity suspended between Canada and the United States that endured as such, remarkably, for fourteen years. Vermont became the first of only four former independent sovereign states in American history (the others being Texas, California, and Hawaii) that eventually opted to surrender acknowledged sovereignty to join the United States. Vermont was officially incorporated into the Union, as the fourteenth state, only on 4 March 1791. According to Hamilton, in 1787, the Vermont business perfectly illustrated the risks of internal disunion. Plans to incorporate the territory into the Union as a separate state were blocked by New York, while New York's efforts to absorb it were obstructed by New Hampshire, Massachusetts, Connecticut, New Jersey, and Rhode Island, all of which acted chiefly through fear and envy of New York, being "more solicitous to dismember this state," according to Hamilton, "than to establish their own pretensions." Maryland too evinced "warm zeal for the independence of Vermont."[50] Such squabbles threatened the Union, as did the huge public debt. How the public debt issuing from the war should be apportioned and liquidated was bound to be "productive of ill humour and animosity" given the widely differing views about how to discharge it. "A firm Union," affirmed Hamilton, "will be of the utmost moment to the peace and liberty of the states as a barrier against domestic faction and insurrection."[51]

Under the surface there were tensions between the three Founders who composed *The Federalist* over basic principles; but these they agreed to paper over for the moment for the sake of mobilizing a broad spread of opinion behind the proposed federal constitution. Hamilton acknowledged the "aversion of the people to monarchy,"[52] but, unlike Madison and Jefferson a true Lockean, believed that government originates and should be conceived as a compact between people and their sovereign rulers, and that ideally not only the justices of the supreme court but the executive officer and perhaps even the Senate members should be chosen for life in order to minimize the democratic tendency.[53] Inevitably, the form and character of the proposed United States Federal Constitution became a matter of intense scrutiny and public debate during the long and fiercely contested ratification process. Formidable "anti-Federalist" opposition to the new proposed constitution arose from various quarters including in some state legislatures and in the press, opposition that focused even more on the "aristocratic" character of the proposed federal senate than on the powerful new presidency: until the end of the nineteenth century the Senate consisted not of popularly elected members but delegates chosen by the state legislatures, hence specifically on the basis of wealth and property.[54] Among other strategies, opponents of the proposed new union circulated with great assiduity, noted Hamilton, the "observations of Montesquieu on the necessity of a contracted territory for a republican government." New York, Pennsylvania, and Virginia, however, were already much larger than the kind of republic Montesquieu had in mind, Hamilton pointed out, as were Massachusetts, Georgia, and North Carolina; and so far was "that great man" from "standing in opposition to a general union of the states, that he explicitly treats of a confederate republic as the expedient for extending the sphere of popular government and reconciling the advantages of monarchy with those of republicanism."[55]

Each side had their favored political theorists. "Mixed government" combining elements of monarchy, aristocracy, and democracy was in the eyes of Adams, Hamilton, and other "moderates" the way to counter democracy's inherent instability and vulnerability to popular passion and tumult. Should unrest destabilize "one of the confederate states," Hamilton quoted Montesquieu as affirming, "the others are able to quell it."[56] Such a state could viably withstand both despotic leanings and internal dissension. The most renowned

French political thinker of the day after Montesquieu and Rousseau, Mably, did consider the vastness of even such individual states as New York, Pennsylvania, and Virginia, let alone the whole confederation, problematic from a republican standpoint. Unlike Montesquieu, he was sufficiently radical to prefer unqualified universal male (white) suffrage in principle, but worried lest the representative democracy embodied in the 1776 Pennsylvania and 1777 Vermont constitutions would prove seriously unstable. The daunting size of the bigger states, he apprehended, direly threatened their republican character, leaving them vulnerable to some "new House of Medici."[57] Consequently, it was better for the time being that the remaining American state constitutions under revision should avoid Pennsylvania's universal suffrage principle. Under existing conditions, stiff property qualifications excluding the less affluent from voting, representation and power should be retained.[58]

"Despite the revisions to the state constitutions during the Independence war," argued one of the young republic's most avid political theorists, James Madison (1751–1836), a leading Virginia delegate, also in *The Federalist*, complaints had flowed in from well-meaning, virtuous citizens that "our governments are too unstable; that the public good is disregarded in the conflicts of rival parties; and that measures are too often decided, not according to the rules of justice, and the rights of the minor party; but by the superior force of an interested and over-bearing majority."[59] A factious spirit, motivated by popular impulses and passions, "tainted our public administrations." Only via a stabilizing union could "we behold a republican remedy for the diseases most incident to republican government. And according to the degree of pleasure and pride, we feel in being republicans, ought to be our zeal in cherishing the spirit, and supporting the character of Federalists."[60] Federalism gained ground.

Since the United Provinces (Dutch Republic) and Helvetic Confederation (Switzerland) were then the only existing, longstanding, modern examples of republican confederacies, it was natural that while forging and finalizing the United States Constitution in late 1787 and early 1788, the Founding Fathers should examine their constitutions much more closely than those of ancient Rome and Greece, or any others. The Dutch example appeared especially relevant since the United Provinces had participated in the American War and was now plunged in severe crisis. The modern world's first avowedly democratic revolution had developed there since 1780 expressly invoking the example of the United States, but in September 1787, following Prussian and British intervention, it dramatically collapsed just when deliberations surrounding the United States Federal Constitution were at their height. "This unhappy [Dutch] people," noted Hamilton and Madison, were "now suffering from popular convulsions, from dissensions among the States, and from the actual invasion of foreign arms, the crisis of their destiny. All nations have their eyes fixed on the awful spectacle."[61] The Dutch union revealed so many vulnerabilities, contended Madison and Hamilton, as to produce "imbecility in the government, discord among the provinces, foreign influence and indignities; a precarious existence in peace, and peculiar calamities from war," the last point alluding to the Dutch suffering more from the American War (owing to Britain's pillaging their colonies to compensate for her American losses) than any other combatants, even than most American states.[62]

The Dutch crisis of 1787–88 was only one of many considerations guiding the Founding Fathers but among the most obviously relevant and urgent. The Dutch Republic's two great weaknesses were the States General's inability, just like the pre-1787 American union, to raise taxes directly within the confederacy (except in a few dependent territories and on overseas trade) and its incomplete control, as with the American Congress before 1787, over war and peace, the armed forces, and foreign affairs. The "first wish prompted by humanity," commented Hamilton and Madison, was that "this severe trial may issue in such a revolution of their government, as will establish their Union, and render it the parent of tranquility, freedom and happiness." Should the Dutch fail to extricate themselves from their disastrous predicament, then the "asylum under which, we trust, the enjoyment of these blessings, will speedily be secured in this country, may receive and console them for the catastrophe of their own." Under the outgoing American Articles of Confederation, the "efficacy of the federal depends," as in the Dutch United Provinces, "on the subsequent and voluntary resolutions of the states composing the union." Inefficient in peacetime, such a format could be calamitous in war. By assigning to the new federal government authority to take decisions without this requiring the individual states' approval, the new United States Constitution substantially diverged from both the Independence War American confederation *and* the Dutch union. Under the new constitution, whenever majorities were secured in both houses of the legislature, Senate and House of Representatives, federal acts became effective without requiring the concurrence of individual states, a crucial departure from previous transatlantic federal culture and practice whether Dutch, Swiss, or American.[63]

Another striking innovation was the new American Constitution's adeptly combining representation of the citizenry with the trappings of sovereign equality between the states. The lower house reflected differences in population between states; the upper house (Senate) equalized the states' standing by allocating an equal number of senators (two) to each. "The House of Representatives will derive its powers from the people of America," explained Madison, "and the people will be represented in the same proportion, and on the same principle, as they are in the legislature of a particular state. So far the government is national not federal." The Senate on the other hand derived its powers from the states as equal sovereign entities enjoying equality in the upper house. "So far the government is federal not national." The executive power was meant to be an ingenious mix of the two principles: election of the president by a college of electors representing the states but with the electors allocated to each state proportional to the population of these supposedly co-equal societies. "The proposed Constitution therefore is in strictness neither a national nor a federal constitution, but a composition of both."[64]

The American Constitution represented a distinct advance on the inefficient and now obsolete Dutch and Swiss federal constitutions of the early modern era, and this was as obvious in Europe as America. It transcended the closed ruling oligarchies of the past in being more workable and efficient, and in compromising more, symbolically at least, with popular sovereignty and democracy. In this respect it was truly a modern landmark. In making the new constitution, the Thirteen States, Federalists claimed, were not really innovating. Careful scrutiny would convince the interested inquirer that the change "consists much less in the addition of new powers to the Union," held Madison, than "invigoration of its original powers."[65] This was greatly to underestimate its innovative character. Madison in any case was no radical during this period in which he collaborated with Hamilton and Jay, steadfastly maintaining, against Jefferson's view, that a federal Bill of Rights was an unnecessary addition to the Constitution.[66] But innovative or not, the Constitution did little to resolve the fundamental divide within the Revolution between the democratizing tendency and traditional oligarchic control. As with slavery, restricted suffrages, property qualifications for voting, and the exclusive character of the Federal Senate, the 1787 new United States Constitution simply shelved the Revolution's deepest inner contradictions.

Church and State Separated?

As delegates convened to draw up the United States Federal Constitution in 1787, there was no way they could agree to establish a single state or public church. This was because in the past divergent ecclesiastical traditions had prevailed in different parts of the Thirteen Colonies. In the South and Pennsylvania, the formerly dominant Anglican Church had been much weakened during the Revolution and lost its privileged position but reemerged renewed after 1783 as the Episcopal Church, regaining a patchy primacy in some regions. By contrast, in New England and New York the three main Calvinist churches, the Presbyterians, Congregationalists, and Dutch Reformed, had been and remained largely preponderant. However, in many areas, dissenters—Baptist and Methodists especially—increasingly outstripped both main older blocs, Anglicans and Calvinists. Of all the churches during the revolutionary era, the Baptists expanded the most dramatically, rising from 94 congregations in 1760 to no less than 858 in 1790, becoming the largest denomination in the republic.[67] But if there was no possibility whatever of a single federally protected and promoted public church, the Thirteen Colonies could have agreed to an overarching comprehensive formula of public religion declaring civil power and sovereignty to descend from God, covering main points of doctrine especially belief in the Trinity, and instituting state support and regulation. Furthermore, there was sustained, considerable pressure, in the form of petitions and memorials, for Congress to adopt such a scheme.[68]

For freethinkers, Unitarians, Catholics, and Jews, it was among the Revolution's principal gains that this formidable combined Protestant theological pressure was successfully resisted, though it was by no means freethinking or radical ideas that achieved this result. From a secularizing standpoint it was largely fortuitous that the apprehension felt by dissenters, especially the Baptists, regarding state intrusion into religion worked strongly in their favor. Dissenters worried that state protection of religion could encourage elite oversight of ecclesiastical affairs and doctrine to their detriment. This enabled the Founding Fathers who were deists, freethinkers, and atheists to secure one of the most resounding triumphs of the late eighteenth-century radical tendency: the United States Constitution was finalized, in unprecedented fashion, without any declaration in its articles that civil power descends from God or is responsible for the promotion or protection of religion.[69] Separating church and state, disempowering state-backed religious authority, and disestablishing state churches, the absence of any religious test or oath for holding office in the government of the United States, together undoubtedly figured among the most internationally influential dimensions of the American Revolution.[70] Condorcet identified this absence of formal connection between state and religion as among the American federal constitution's historically and philosophically most decisive and significant innovations.

All seven states where the Anglican Church had been the officially established public church prior to 1776 had, by 1783, disestablished that church (South Carolina in March 1778), officially removing ecclesiastical authority from involvement in public ethics and governance;[71] and if radical success in these seven state legislatures in achieving this outcome stemmed less from

Enlightenment ideas than from proliferation throughout revolutionary and post-revolutionary America of the new dissenting churches, convergence of interest here held for a time. Evangelicals and radicals both sought disestablishment, a broad toleration, and termination of state supervision of church affairs. Both aspired to end church dependence on state-exacted taxation. But their concurrence ended there. When it came to resisting the post-1790 influence of the "Second Awakening" dissenting preachers, the dissenters ceased to be allies and took to targeting the radicals' ideological and educational projects. After 1790, Baptists and Methodists were generally ranged on the side of political and social conservatism against the radicals.

Americans often remained (and remain) unaware that their Founding Fathers were predominantly irreligious deists and atheists privately repudiating religion. Freeing the individual as far as possible from clerical tutelage and widening toleration, as well as disestablishing churches, and separating church and state, represented an indispensable goal for the American Revolution's leading figures since most were Unitarians, deists, or nonbelievers. Admittedly, Unitarians and atheistic freethinkers disagreed about the question of God. On this ground, Priestley rebuked Franklin and publicly berated Volney. "It is much to be lamented," he remarked, "that a man of Dr. Franklin's general good character, and great influence, should have been an unbeliever in Christianity, and also have done so much as he did to make others unbelievers."[72] Yet the Unitarian Priestley, deriving his determinism from Anthony Collins, was also a philosophical necessitarian and materialist. Priestleyan Unitarians were as antagonistic to politicized religious authority, ecclesiastical hierarchy, and intolerance as Paineite deists and atheists, and as committed to a culture of science wholly stripped of *supernaturalia*. Radical Unitarians too deemed general emancipation from ecclesiastics essential for free expression, equality, and democracy. Every radical enlightener embraced what Price termed "liberty of conduct in all civil matters" and "liberty of discussion in all speculative matters."[73]

Jefferson's explicit goal with respect to religious authority and church government was to secure freedom *from*, as much as freedom of, religion,[74] and this regarding society as a whole as much as the individual. American radicalism fought religious direction of education, and efforts to introduce theology into politics and impose religious conformity on society, as unwaveringly as Condorcet, Mirabeau, Volney, or Brissot in France and Priestley, Price, Cooper, or Bentham in Britain. "The moral condition of man," held Palmer, will be "as essentially renovated by the American Revolution as his civil condition." Awakened by the "energy of thought, inspired by the American Revolution," he expected, "man will find it consistent with his inclination and his interest to examine all the moral relations of his nature," develop his intellectual capacities, and "relinquish with elevated satisfaction, those supernatural schemes of superstition which have circumscribed the sphere of beneficial activity, for which Nature designed him." Together the Enlightenment and the American Revolution would transform humanity decisively for the better. Educational progress in particular would "overthrow those systems of error and imposition which have so long corrupted the morality of the human heart"; to remove them "it is only necessary that man should take cognizance of their absurdity."[75]

While the Revolution secured far-reaching modifications to pre-1775 colonial regulation of church affairs, and what Madison called "the rights of conscience in the fullest latitude," even in Pennsylvania it failed to eradicate religious "tests" and theological criteria, and in most states, as Price was dismayed to discover, these long remained a lingering bone of contention. The American Revolution can in no way be claimed to have been purely secular in character or to have established a secular state.[76] The new Massachusetts constitution, unfavorably commented on by Miranda during his tour of the fledgling United States in the early 1780s, required "all who take seats in the House of Representatives or Senate" to declare their "firm persuasion of the Christian religion." This oath of office, designed to exclude atheists, deists, agnostics, Jews, and other non-Christians, remained in force until 1820. When he challenged Sam Adams in 1784 about the prevalence of "aristocracy" in America, Miranda added a second incisive question: How was the Revolution's promise to favor no sect or creed reconciled with the state legislatures' test acts debarring those refusing allegiance to Christianity from executive, legislative, representative, and judicial office and functions?[77]

Religious authority continued to intrude and debar in other ways. New Jersey, whose constitution Démeunier ranked among the worst, required state officeholders to be "Protestants" and, like New Hampshire and North and South Carolina, to acknowledge the divine inspiration of the Old and New Testaments; Article XIX of the state's revised constitution, approved in July 1776, explicitly restricted full civil rights to "Protestants."[78] Worse, the 1780 Massachusetts constitution obliged every householder to subscribe to one church or another, requiring all citizens to pay church taxes, each Christian denomination being empowered by the state legislature separately to tax its congregants. Since in Massachusetts the majority attended the Congregationalist Church, this Calvinist confession became virtually "established" de facto and in effect state supported, exercising a rigid ascendancy over whole communities until 1833.[79] Maryland's consummately "aristocratic" constitution, finalized in November 1776, failed explicitly to establish religious toleration as such, granting only a vague, truncated religious freedom to "persons professing the Christian religion" while again authorizing the state legislature to "lay a general and equal tax for the support of the Christian religion" supposedly on a non-confessional basis. Admission to office, under Article XXXV, required a declaration of "belief in the Christian religion" and the same, objected a scandalized Price, was required as a "condition of being admitted into any places of profit or trust."[80]

New Hampshire's constitution in practice maintained the Congregationalist Church with public funds and, despite efforts to change this, expressly debarred non-Protestant officeholders until 1877.[81] Suspending "government under the crown" in June 1776, Delaware instituted a particularly intrusive test for officeholders; the state's revised constitution, approved in September, required all appointed to office to declare their "faith in God the Father and in Jesus Christ His only Son, and in the Holy Ghost, one God, blessed for evermore, and I do acknowledge the holy scriptures of the Old and New Testament to be given by divine inspiration." This requirement to avow the Trinity confined freedom of conscience and equal rights to citizens "professing the Christian religion"—minus the Unitarians—the constitution explicitly excluding anti-Trinitarians from the state legislature and from office.[82] Unitarians, Jews, and radical freethinkers indignantly objected. "Montesquieu," protested Price, "was not a Christian. Newton and Locke were not Trinitarians; and therefore were not Christians according to the commonly received ideas of Christianity (any more than Price, Cooper or Priestley). Would the United States, for this reason, deny such men, were they living, all places of trust and power among them?"[83]

Since all citizens should possess equal rights and are equally concerned in upholding political liberty, every distinction of creed, as well as rank and privilege, should be erased from the state legislatures as well as from state law, federal law, and Congress. Paine, Barlow, Freneau, Palmer, and other radicals repudiated the principle of religious tests in toto, insisting no criterion of belief, and no Church authority, should figure in any legitimate constitution. Beside religious tests and state-authorized taxes to support churches, there was the actual or threatened additional factor in some states of legalized anti-Catholic discrimination. In 1777 John Jay, a leading patrician and landowner, and later First Chief Justice of the United States (1789–95), among the country's foremost adversaries of radical and democratic ideas, only narrowly failed, during revision of the New York state constitution, to secure formal curtailment of the political rights of Catholics refusing to take special oaths renouncing papal supremacy and authority.[84]

Another intrusion into personal liberty under the pretext of religious obligation was enforced Sunday observance. In his account of the United States, Miranda repeatedly complained of the invasive intolerance of small-town America. Religious liberty in the new republic seemed to him much narrower and more grudging than foreign onlookers supposed. Required conformity to what radicals deemed the dismal silence gripping American towns on Sundays scandalized Miranda, Chastellux, and Paine, who in his *Age of Reason* (1794) especially derided Connecticut's "stupid Blue Laws" for their strict rules of Sabbath observance.[85] To non-Christians and secularizing detractors Sabbath observance seemed just another way to extend intolerance and bigotry, observance being unbendingly imposed on all whether concurring or not, forbidding all non-religious gatherings, dancing, feasting, and drinking on the Lord's Day—and Miranda from practicing on his flute. One would suppose, complained Chastellux, a violent epidemic or a plague had compelled everyone to stay within doors.[86]

Religious censorship and obligation were extended further via state "blasphemy laws." Until the early nineteenth century, Pennsylvania, Massachusetts, and New York all continued hearing cases of indictment for "blasphemy" including denial of divine providence and ridiculing passages of Scripture. Young, Price, Paine, Barlow, Jefferson, Brissot, Miranda, Freneau, Palmer, and other radicals were all anxious to counter such intrusion into individual conduct and freedom of thought. Combating intolerance and conventional religiosity seemed to them an essential ingredient in the wider project of democratizing and deconfessionalizing American society. Uncoupling law and morality comprehensively from faith and theology, and curbing the pastors' hold over opinion, to radicals seemed a goal so far only very partially and insecurely achieved. As it stood, American liberty of conscience, they charged, was really a consensus of basic religious agreement imposed on everyone regardless of individual assent or dissent, rather than a framework freely permitting freedom of thought and dissent from majority consensus.[87]

CHAPTER 4

Schooling Republicans

Schools for a Nation

With Independence won, some revolutionaries were tempted to exult in the palpable shift in attitudes already accomplished: "our stile and manner of thinking have undergone a revolution, more extraordinary" than the political revolution, asserted Paine in his *Letter Addressed to the Abbé Raynal* (1782). "We see with other eyes, we hear with other ears; and think with other thoughts, than those we formerly used. We can look back on our own prejudices, as if they had been the prejudices of other people."[1] Confident that further rapid advances would follow, by the time the French Revolution erupted in 1788–89, Paineites either side of the Atlantic believed their style of Enlightenment had won much ground among many new and less educated readers. Events soon suggested, though, that they had exaggerated the advance of their "revolution of the mind" and the diffusion of their ideas through pamphlets, newspapers, and extracts.[2]

The American Revolution created a new form of republic explicitly built on the principle of "liberty." Yet the United States that emerged in 1787 was predominantly undemocratic and by and large not geared to promoting the welfare of society as a whole. The Revolution contained two divergent tendencies within it, rooted respectively in moderate and radical Enlightenment, and this inevitably generated a conflict of attitudes, values, and institutions that could not easily be resolved. On the one hand there was the powerful Lockean legacy. But Locke had justified a revolution, the Glorious Revolution of 1688, led by an aristocracy on the basis of everyone's right to the pursuit of "life, liberty and property," assigning property a decisive role in the possession and organization of power and authority. For Locke, the prime reason men enter into commonwealths placing themselves under government is for the "preservation of their property." Substituting the "pursuit of happiness" for "property" in the

Declaration of Independence consequently had far-reaching implications regarding the purposes of the state and the scope of its responsibilities. Where in Locke property is the basis of social division into classes, Jefferson's formulation marginalized the principle of social class. The landless could no longer be regarded as either so marginal or so subordinate as in Locke. Where Locke nurtured a negative conception of liberty, centered on protection of property, for Jeffersonians liberty was a positive, developmental concept to be upheld and advanced by the state and its agencies.[3] Where in Locke, education is essentially a private matter geared to issues of property without any public role, in radical Enlightenment education is a public matter and something to which everyone has a right.[4] Whereas in Locke, popular sovereignty extends only so far as the "compact" between people and the executive power, in the political philosophy of Franklin, Jefferson, Paine, and Price, the people share continuously in the exercise of government through elections, representation, and the right to free expression of opinion. In the constitution for the colony of Carolina that Locke drew up for the Lords proprietors of Carolina in 1669, and helped revise in 1682, for example, he took care to avoid erecting a "numerous democracy," slavery was retained, the Indians had few rights, and most colonists were left firmly subordinate to the great landowners, or "landgraves" as Locke termed them.[5] Finally, Locke's toleration ruled out secularism, excluding atheists from toleration by the state and placing Catholics and Jews in a subordinate position in relation to the theologically tinted responsibilities of the sovereign.

Locke's philosophy, in other words, constituted an absolute obstacle to the forming of a democratic society. Under the Constitution of 1787, the states relegated to the federal government those powers appropriate to the collective authority of the Union—those of war and peace, maintaining armies and the navy, and regulating commerce. But because everything not expressly assigned to the Union, including education, local government, policing, state electoral issues, and other powers relevant to quality of life, individual security, and the degree of liberty enjoyed by the citizen, was reserved to the state legislatures, the quality and character of the public sphere came to depend in large measure on the state governments, a division of powers reinforced by the Tenth Amendment in 1791. The dual arrangement sufficed to guarantee the United States' republican character but could not, of itself, advance democracy or guarantee political liberty for everyone. As Fenimore Cooper observed later, "A republican form of government is not necessarily a free government. Aristocracies are oftener republics than anything else, and they have been among the most oppressive governments the world has ever known."[6] Eighteenth-century Switzerland, Holland, Venice, Geneva, and Poland amply bore this out.

Those enlighteners wanting the American Revolution to progress beyond what had been achieved by 1783 viewed the Revolution as the outcome of an intellectual shift driving a thus far insufficient political, social, and educational transformation. "The American war is over," averred Rush in 1787, "but this is far from the case with the American Revolution. On the contrary, nothing but the first act of the great drama is closed."[7] A similar remark was made in 1789 by Noel Webster: "a fundamental mistake of the Americans has been that they considered the revolution as completed when it was just begun."[8] Even though Rush and Webster had by then both partly broken with their earlier comprehensive radicalism, they remained leading advocates, on a more fragmented basis, of strands of democratic and radical educational, legal, and medical reform. One of Rush's chief objectives, set out in a plan drawn up in 1786, was for "one general and uniform system of education," publicly supported schools in Pennsylvania "grounded in religion" but under unified direction and with state-trained teachers, the whole organized to turn out morally upright republican-minded citizens, a system that would avoid pushing up the tax burden in the state by raising levels of conduct sufficiently, as he hoped, to significantly cut the cost of fighting crime, constructing jails, and punishing criminals, forging a society that would enable the ordinary citizen "to sleep with fewer bolts and locks on his doors."[9]

One could be selectively engaged in schemes of far-reaching improvement in a wide variety of fields, Rush and Webster proved, without necessarily adhering to a comprehensively radical, that is generalized democratic republican, perspective and without rejecting religious authority. A more limited, itemized reform agenda could achieve much. Rush's campaign to change Pennsylvania's penal code, for instance, eventually scored some success. Brissot, who had opposed capital punishment since the 1770s,[10] and in 1793 opposed the execution of Louis XVI, had long expected Pennsylvania and other states to "free themselves of their superstitious respect for English law and have the courage to give to Europe a great example of justice, humanity and political wisdom."[11] Over stiff opposition, working with the state attorney general and using arguments drawn from Beccaria, Rush secured his pathbreaking capital punishment reform law in 1794. Dividing murder cases into two distinct categories, depending on the extent of intent and malice, this measure introduced for the first time a means to restrict and diminish use of the death penalty, thereby marking the beginning of the degree system in American law. Pennsylvania abolished the death penalty except for premeditated murder.[12]

Yet a wider reformism consonant with the goals of secularism and democratic republicanism (which Rush and Webster repudiated) necessitated a more integrated vision explaining how social problems and injustices were interrelated and collectively arose from the defects of oligarchic rule and religious authority. "Some few fundamental truths," introduced by "strong and benevolent minds," urged Elihu Palmer, should be the "basis on which must be erected the future dignity, improvement and happiness of the species."[13] It was here that radical enlighteners were uniquely equipped to provide a comprehensive and persuasive rationale. Only their texts and categories, they believed, provided critical tools of adequate reach and incisiveness. Only they could hope to mobilize a broad spectrum of opposition to the status quo since their reformism offered systemic solutions for all manner of specific grievances—felt by blacks free and enslaved, religious minorities, women, Jews, homosexuals, the illegitimate—offering a common path to widening, equalizing, and secularizing citizenship and the common good. Despite appearances, the "despotism of kings and priests," urged the radicals, was being conserved in America. To produce free and responsible citizens, society had to comprehensively eradicate the principles of monarchy and aristocracy from attitudes as well as from local and state politics and administration. Among the chief strands of their project was their ambition to reorganize education and free it from the shackles of the past. To ground the new state securely, averred Price, and ensure the "greatest effect on the improvement of the world, nothing is more necessary than the establishment of a wise and liberal plan of education."[14]

Only an unrepresentative fringe agreed, though, with reformers like Franklin, Paine, Barlow, Freneau, Coram, Palmer, Cooper, and Jefferson—and their French counterparts Condorcet, Brissot, and Volney—that education needed to be secularized, equalized in terms of opportunity, and made universal even if it included, as with Jefferson, a strong elitist tendency. Late eighteenth-century American society more generally by no means judged a far-reaching transformation in society's and the individual's moral attitudes, thinking, and ideas requisite to promote citizenship and the common welfare. The schemes for public education were all rejected.

Nor was there any broad perception of a need for a wider emancipation of society's disadvantaged segments. Moderate Enlightenment "mixed government" and aristocratic republicanism was hegemonic throughout the British empire and the United States during the late eighteenth and early nineteenth centuries, underpinning a system in some respects working against the business class as well as the lower orders. Capitalists and businessmen are too attached to their own interests, warned Adam Smith in his *Wealth of Nations* (1776), to make suitable leaders of society; society should keep capitalists out of politics and legislation. Society's natural heads, to his mind, whether in England, his native Scotland, or America, were the "aristocracy."

This raised the question whether American "aristocracy" was sufficiently robust to guide state and society in a responsible, stable fashion. There was a danger, Smith suggested, that democratic thinking and practice of the kind germinating in the United States might destabilize the entire edifice.[15] Adam Ferguson (1723–1816), another pillar of Scottish moderate Enlightenment, likewise rejected Price's arguments for equality and democracy. Civil liberty, he argued, is by no means "popular power"; indeed, popular government is dangerous to liberty: "liberty does not consist in the prevalence of democratic power," and there is "no species of tyranny under which individuals are less safe than under that of a majority or prevailing faction of the people." Wherever the uneducated and unenlightened are masters, despotic leaders quickly emerge to exploit men's passions and prejudices, so that liberty withers.[16]

In America, "moderates" like John Adams, facing broader electorates than in Europe, were undoubtedly more amenable than Ferguson, Adam Smith, or Voltaire to the idea that republics require a larger base of literacy and education than monarchies, so as to enable prospective voters to appraise arguments, express their views, and identify the candidates with most merit. This entailed greater willingness to acknowledge the need for education reform. Adams ensured that it was written into the Massachusetts constitution that support of public schools at elementary and secondary levels was a state obligation.[17] Many Americans, approaching the issue from a similar standpoint, criticized the widespread lack of state support for education outside New England and New York. But since Adams and other moderates rejected democracy and universal suffrage, their plans still remained substantially different and far narrower in scope than those of the radical minded. Where Adams wanted a more exclusive education for boys from affluent families, placing a higher value on learning Latin and Greek, radicals sought to widen political participation and access to office by broadening educational opportunity. Where moderates in New England and the middle states preferred to expand public schooling while preserving some distance between the lower orders and "aristocracy," providing basic schooling for those lower down in society without designating paths to, or public support for, intermediate and higher education,[18] Jefferson preferred a layered system rising from elementary to intermediate and then higher education, providing a publicly subsidized route for the most able and meritorious to rise into the professions and political elite whatever their social background.

Lack of explicit republican principles in popular consciousness, education, and numerous state constitutions, including those of Massachusetts, New York, Maryland, the Carolinas, Rhode Island, and Delaware, struck Paineites, Jeffersonians, and foreign *Américanistes* like Brissot and Miranda as dangerous neg-

ligence requiring urgent attention and correction.[19] "Democracy" in America
Miranda scathingly dismissed as a republicanism locating legislative power
in the hands of "ignorance."[20] One of the features of the new republic that
struck him as decidedly odd "considering the many illustrious persons in
America who through their vigor and talents have accomplished the great and
complicated work of independence" was that "none have either a general approbation or the popularity" of Washington; in fact, he added, "nobody" had
any standing as popular hero of the Revolution "except him." This excessive
concentration of "all the glory" on Washington seemed to him inadvisable in
a republican society, a "usurpation as capricious as it is unjust."[21] On a later
occasion, Miranda referred to Washington disparagingly as "the idol."[22] Designing "American republics where government is in the hands of the people"
without building a society that acknowledges the "natural equality of men"
and consolidates equality and democracy through education and public civics
was to invite grave peril.

Certainly, it was a resounding turning point in the history of the world that
merchants, financiers, professionals, retailers, and manufacturers sat in the
state legislatures, but Miranda's impression, after witnessing debates in the
Massachusetts state assembly "on various occasions," was that the "defects
and inconveniences" arising from "all the influence being given by the [state]
constitution to property" were considerable. Instead of the senators and as-
semblymen being "the wisest," the Massachusetts constitution ensured they
were the wealthiest, which in America meant generally "people destitute of
principles and education."[23] To counter this defect, the United States needed
to ensure knowledge was "universally diffused by means of public schools,"
which must be free, be compulsory, and eschew "modes of faith."[24] Ending ecclesiastical supervision of education was indispensable not least for instilling
into their universal enlightened society the "principle of universal toleration,"
all sharing liberty equally without any distinction on the basis of belief, ethnic-
ity, or lineage.[25]

Democratic critics, unlike the "moderates," felt that if democratizing education was not vigorously pushed forward, all the Revolution's achievements
thus far would inevitably unravel. "A universal attention to the education of
youth, and a republican direction given to the elementary articles of public
instruction," asserted Barlow in 1801, "are among the most essential means
of preserving liberty in any country where it is once enjoyed; especially in the
United States. The representative system must necessarily degenerate, and
become an instrument of tyranny, rather than of liberty, where there is an
extraordinary disparity of information between the generality of the citizens
and those who aspire to be their chiefs."[26] Ignorance was everywhere such

an infallible tool of despotism, held those embracing radical views, that there could be no hope of "continuing even our present forms of government, either federal or state, much less that spirit of equal liberty and justice on which they were founded, but by diffusing universally among the people that portion of instruction which is sufficient to teach them their duties and their rights."[27] "Unequal governments are necessarily founded in ignorance," held Barlow, and "must be supported by ignorance; to deviate from their principle, would be voluntary suicide. The first great object of their policy is to perpetuate that undisturbed ignorance of the people which is the companion of poverty, the parent of crimes, and the pillar of the state."[28]

Unlike the socialists later, radical enlighteners recognized that a wide range of social reforms to alter society's character must include economic adjustments, mitigation of poverty, removing all vestiges of "feudalism," and a drive for greater economic equality, but they refused to center their analysis around the economic issue. In the economic sphere, they never overstepped certain limited goals or questioned the right to private property as such, a "right" the first socialists began identifying as a theoretical weakness in the thought of Paine, Jefferson, and the radical tradition as early as the 1820s.[29] In his *The Rights of Man to Property!* (1829), a fierce attack on economic inequality, simultaneously a eulogy and critique of Paineite radicalism, the New York early socialist Thomas Skidmore (1790–1832), dismissing Jefferson's account of universal and equal rights as "very defective and equivocal," refused to acknowledge property as a personal, individual right.[30] Gross inequality needed combating, agreed Jeffersonians; in the democratic republic "men should by every fair means be legally prevented from becoming exorbitantly rich" because, as the New York radical poet and pro-Jefferson journalist of Huguenot descent Philip Freneau (1752–1832) expressed it in 1797, "in an assemblage of rich men there is a natural aristocracy which evermore has, or makes a separate interest from that of the people."[31] But while much hinged on curbing excessive economic inequality via fiscal means and inheritance laws, radicals never sought to curtail individual economic freedom or acquisition of property as such and regarded socialist efforts to do so as contrary to liberty. Exploitative luxury and poverty, they maintained, could be constrained and would in fact diminish with more equitable tax systems and inheritance laws.[32] Modifying the economic order was no insignificant dimension of their thinking, but it always remained secondary compared with their broader concern with republican liberty, secularism, political equality, and equality of educational opportunity.

The conviction that "progress of letters and philosophy alone could enlighten men about their true interests," as Chastellux put it in 1772, and adequately transform Man's political and social world,[33] originated in *ency-*

clopédiste circles prior to the American Revolution and was carried furthest by Helvétius. But the Revolution lent major new impetus to the idea. Reflecting on the American Revolution contributed to making Brissot among the most insistent of all enlighteners on the need for mass education: it was education's task to rescue mankind from "the degradation" to which monarchy, aristocracy, and the clergy had subjected it, the government's responsibility to educate its citizens, and philosophy's task to equalize, secularize, and rationalize education.[34] Schooling was essential for every individual's personal development *and* for the viability and well-being of the democratic republic itself. It was also manifestly the best way to integrate free blacks into society, one of Brissot's main concerns. Failure to educate the masses for citizenship in the democratic republic must spell its decay and downfall, and in the process vindicate the prognostications of "moderates" warning that mass passions would decimate liberty. Insufficient educational reform could only reinforce the moderates' insistence that liberty, stability, and social well-being are best secured by the aristocratic republic.

To this Freneau added that defeating "ignorance" mattered greatly also for maintaining freedom of the press. The vitriolic American press polemics of the 1790s plainly demonstrated that where ignorance prevails the papers are easily captured and mobilized against, rather than for, democratic and secular ideas. "It appears that the press, if kept free, and in the hands of uncorrupted men, will of itself support the flame of republicanism that is now happily raised in the world: but it lies with the people themselves to encourage this great engine of liberty, and to prevent it from becoming an instrument of slavery."[35] The people could do this, but only if and when schooled as republicans. The Revolution must entail a general metamorphosis of education in schools and colleges, and in adult education and pastimes, to create a more aware public. However, this was not the general view of the public or the legislators. In New England, state education policies accepted that local town meetings would raise taxes only for church schools. Only six out of the sixteen post-Revolution American state constitutions drawn up by 1800 expressly stipulated the need for public support for education; aside from New York hardly any set up boards of regents to supervise a coordinated statewide educational policy.[36] Yet, even in New York City, as late as 1805, by which time the city's population exceeded 60,000, the only schools available were church schools or private schools for profit.[37]

Conquering "ignorance" for radical enlighteners meant propagating critical independence of thought and the ability to weigh evidence and criteria, in scientific fashion, to form sound rational judgments. "The end of education," contended Price, quite remarkably for a preacher, is to "direct the powers of the mind in unfolding themselves; and to assist them in gaining their just bent and force." Education should be an initiation in honesty and how to employ reason "rather than into any systems of faith." It "should form a habit of cool and patient investigation, rather than an attachment to any opinions." Price urged Americans to establish a "wise and liberal plan of education," especially to teach young people to think independently and critically rather than religiously, education displacing traditional schooling of the kind that instills dogma, zeal, and submissiveness to authority. Traditional and still prevailing education he dismissed as a "contradiction, not an enlargement of the intellectual faculties; an injection of false principles hardening them into error, not a discipline enlightening and improving them."[38]

Since in the United States the state legislatures, not the federal government, retained sole responsibility for schools and colleges, the outcome varied considerably from state and state. Yet no state instituted compulsory, universal elementary education in the way the French Revolution attempted to do from 1792 to 1793 until Massachusetts proclaimed compulsory education in 1852. As Virginia's second revolutionary governor, in the years 1779–81, Jefferson tried to introduce a system of centrally directed republican public education at all levels, encompassing higher education as well. The way to avert future tyranny, he assured the state legislature, is to "illuminate, as far as practicable, the minds of the people at large." Under his fiercely contested and in the end rejected 1778 education bill "for the more general diffusion of learning" in Virginia, he proposed three years of free schooling for all free boys and girls in which they would learn reading, writing, arithmetic, and Anglo-American history rather than Scripture.[39] Modified subsequently, Jefferson's scheme later divided the Virginia counties into wards, or townships, each of five or six square miles, to "establish in each a free school for reading, writing and common arithmetic, to provide for the annual selection of the best subjects from these schools who might receive at the public expense a higher degree of education at a district school." To oversee the process the legislature would appoint a board of three to be renewed each year. At the secondary level, his projected twenty or so secularized state grammar schools, boys from families in easy circumstances would pay tuition and boarding fees; but sixty or seventy "public foundationers" would be selected every year via rigorous exams for free tuition through six years at secondary school. The best, the surviving half or so of the original "public foundationers," would then proceed to secularized, state-supported university study at William and Mary College: "Worth and genius would thus have been sought out from every condition of life, and completely prepared by education for defeating the competition of wealth and birth for public trusts."[40] What he proposed was an Enlightenment elitism excluding the clergy from both educational and political influence that still left most of the free population unequipped to participate at the higher levels of political life but would ensure that all could participate in elections and safeguarding republican values and ensuring that only the best and most enlightened minds, whatever their social origin, were selected for high office.[41]

Jefferson's other more successful reforms having "put down the aristocracy of the clergy, and restored to the citizen the freedom of the mind, and those of entails and descents nurturing an equality of condition among them," he had hoped that "this on education would have raised the mass of the people to the high ground of moral respectability necessary to their own safety, and to orderly government; and would have completed the great object of qualifying them to select the veritable aristoi, for the trusts of government, to the exclusion of the Pseudalists."[42] State-supported educational equality, enabling society to select public servants according to merit rather than birth and money, would, he hoped, neutralize family connection and privilege, as would his plan to add a dose of direct democracy to the representative system. Besides education, the proposed county wards would be responsible for roads, policing, and poor relief, and make possible a "general call of ward-meetings by their wardens on the same day thro' the state at any time." This would allow a mechanism for determining the "genuine sense of the people on any required point," enabling Virginia "to act in mass" as, during 1765–75, "sections of New England had done with so much effect, by their town meetings," popular intervention that contrasted sharply at that time with Virginia's relative quiescence.[43] His epoch-making initiative was rejected by both the Virginian public and the state legislature.

Jefferson sought to systematize state support for education, equalize educational opportunity, and curtail theology, replacing the latter as the guiding value system with science and republican principles. He helped abolish the divinity school at William and Mary, America's second oldest college, dating from 1693, hoping the college would become a state institution focusing on the sciences and philosophy, with a supervisory role over the entire state education system.[44] Its most vital function, according to his conception, would be to serve as a "seminary" for training in political thought and the study of government, the essential basis, as he conceived, for individuals becoming qualified to enter political life at the higher levels. His whole educational agenda—secular, libertarian, republican, anti-aristocratic, and *philosophique*—aimed to ameliorate humanity by enlightening it en masse, revolutionizing lower and higher education together in accordance with the idea of the "common benefit"—but placing higher education in charge of the whole. This unLockean and unRousseauist style of Enlightenment, asserting the need to educate the people to enable men and women to make informed judgments independently while training an elite to occupy all offices in the state, remained Jefferson's consistent creed until his death.[45] It was a vision he shared with such close allies as Condorcet, Volney, Barlow, and his friend Philip Mazzei (1730–1816), a Tuscan physician and one of the most ardent propagators of republican *Américanisme* in Europe. Paine and later Barlow shared this vision.[46] After seeing his educational schemes rebuffed several times by the oligarchic governing elite in Virginia, finally in 1796 Jefferson scored a semi-success when the state legislature approved a state-endorsed elementary schools system; however, apprehensive of the expense, the legislators still left it to each county administration to implement the principle on its own initiative, which to Jefferson was tantamount to allowing counties to emasculate what the legislature stipulated.[47]

A prominent Paineite much preoccupied with educational issues in Delaware was Robert Coram (1761–96). Coram, steeped in the French *encyclopédistes*, Catherine Macaulay, and especially Beccaria and Godwin, and a habitué of Delaware's main library, the Wilmington Library Company, critically scrutinized every aspect of American society "with a philosophic eye." Ardent for democracy, one-chamber legislatures, reducing economic inequality, and more justice for the poor, he fiercely deplored the sway of preachers and the practice of basing political rights on property qualifications. Although like Paine of English origin, in his *Political Inquiries* (1791), Coram lambasted American veneration of England in constitutional matters and desire to "imitate them in the establishment of a nobility also." Indignant that Americans mostly went along willingly with black slavery, it angered him too that they were so "much prejudiced against the Indians." Above all, he sought to show how all these issues were linked socially and politically, and that their close interaction needed to be grasped philosophically. To his mind, they could be resolved only by far-reaching education reform.[48]

A veteran who had fought for the Revolution at sea, in the republic's fledgling navy, Coram demanded schools that were free, public, secular, and uniform, foregrounding Montesquieu's principle that a country's education system should "correspond to the principles of government."[49] He derided the "absurdity of our copying the manners and adopting the institutions of monarchies" with regard to social privilege and education. Since the Revolution several states had introduced laws "establishing provisions for colleges and academies where people of property may educate their sons; but no provision is made for instructing the poorer rank of people, even in reading and writing. Yet in these same states, every citizen who is worth a few shillings annually, is entitled to vote for legislators. This appears to me a most glaring solecism in government. The constitutions are republican, and the laws of education are monarchical."[50] Coram tried to promote his program as a delegate to the Delaware constitutional convention of 1791, but he and his allies were repulsed by Delaware's affluent gentry elite preferring two chambers, a strong governor, and especially a restricted suffrage with stiff property qualifications for the upper chamber. A journalist as well as a librarian and teacher, Coram fought back through the press.[51] To him, "tyranny" and social oppression accentuating economic inequalities remained a plague as real in America as Europe, Africa, or wherever: "too much reason had Raynal [in fact, Diderot] to say," he exclaimed, that "everywhere you meet with masters, and always with oppression. How often, says this venerable philosopher, have we heard the poor man expostulating with heaven, and asking what he had done that he should deserve to be born in an indigent and dependent station."[52]

Men should not seek a doctrinaire "mathematical equality," concurred Coram, but genuine democracy does necessitate a formal equality in which the "generality of men educated under equal circumstances, possess equal powers." Raynal and the *Histoire philosophique* "whose philanthropy I revere, and of whose works I am far from being a willing critic," he rebuked for expounding ideas of equality equalizing every individual's right to "happiness" but falling short, in his view, with respect to education.[53] A more complete concept of equality, including equality of educational opportunity, was indispensable to the "happiness of man."[54] All enlighteners sharing Coram's zeal for universal rights rued the lamentable effects of mass ignorance, but few so loudly decried absence of publicly supported secular schools as a deliberate stratagem of ancien régime despotism and oppression, remnants of which, in his view, were seriously obstructing liberty's progress in America. The "security" and effectiveness of all government, he held, "must in a great measure depend upon the people." "Humanity is wounded by the outrages of the mob in France; but what better can be expected from ignorance, the natural parent of all enormity?"[55] "In our American republics, where government is in the hands of the people, knowledge should be universally diffused by means of public schools."[56] The indispensability of universal secular education exhorted by Jefferson, Barlow, Freneau, Palmer, and Coram perhaps typified American philosophical radicalism even more than European.

Correcting what Thomas Cooper (1759–1839) called the "present imperfect state of society and of knowledge" depended above all, according to all these revolutionary critics, on extending and changing the character of common schooling. Cooper, a Unitarian, materialist, and founding member of the Manchester Constitutional Society in 1790, emigrated from England to

America at a time when radicals were being systematically hounded in Britain. Religion, it has been rightly said, "probably meant very little to Thomas Cooper": the "God he worshipped was Truth and his creed was Freedom."[57] Together with his friend Priestley, he settled in Northumberland, Pennsylvania, in 1794. In America, he exemplified the characteristic radical Enlightenment cult of better, more secular, and more widely available education as the solution to all problems, even economic deprivation and drudgery. "I hope to see a time," he averred, "when not only the childhood, but the youth of the poorest inhabitant in this country, female as well as male, shall be employed in the improvement of their understanding, under some system of national education." For many, in existing circumstances a life of "drudgery and unrelenting labour" might be unavoidable, yet he did not doubt that "the universal annihilation of absolute ignorance among us will tend in time to material improvement in the means of promoting human happiness."[58] Some progress was being made. Thanks largely to church schools, literacy rates stood higher than in Britain or any part of Europe. In contrast to France, where by 1829 seventeen out of thirty million remained unable to read, according to Skidmore's calculations, "in the state of New York, as well as most of our sister States, scarcely one twentieth" were "incapable of reading, with a full understanding of what they read."[59]

Reforming the Colleges

During the 1790s, many leading reformers, Rush, Coram, and Webster among them, put forward schemes for a national school system; but all such comprehensive schemes were set aside by Congress and the individual states.[60] Scorning most states' governance of schooling, critics deplored even more what they regarded as the stagnant, tradition-bound state of the university colleges. America's stock of colleges expanded impressively in number from 1775 to 1800, from nine to twenty-five or, depending on one's definition, slightly more but were strikingly uneven in quality and invariably narrow in scope.[61] Moreover, they remained private institutions largely free of supervision by the states, with severely limited, traditional curricula principally intended for training the clergy and, beyond that, finishing "gentlemen" in the classics.

Franklin had founded the Academy of Philadelphia in 1751 (from 1755, a chartered college, today the University of Pennsylvania) and organized its library and "philosophical apparatus [i.e., equipment for physics demonstrations]" with the conscious aim of fashioning accomplished men of the world and of business, rather than gentry, and of promoting scientific, useful, and commercial skills rather than traditional subjects. He was keen to include instruction in mathematics, "natural history," and public speaking.[62] While it is often noted that Franklin sought to revolutionize higher education in America, and heavily stressed the need to institutionalize "useful" knowledge, to favor teaching that can contribute to the self-advancement of individuals, it is rarely pointed out that he by no means meant by this just vocational training and what he termed "mechaniks." In fact, most "useful" of all to society, and ultimately to individuals, in his estimation, is the teaching of "universal history"; for it is by teaching this subject that "the first Principles of sound Politicks [may] be fix'd in the Minds of Youth."[63]

Although the college at Philadelphia did teach agriculture and its mathematical school was "pretty well furnished with instruments," much of Franklin's approach and proposed curriculum was later discarded. In approving William Smith as the academy's first provost in 1754, counting on his "great abilities and indefatigable application," hoping "that noble institution will go on prosperously,"[64] Franklin unwittingly installed a tenacious Anglican theological tendency that at first discreetly but later more forthrightly promoted old-style Tory and Loyalist attitudes. Once established, Smith proceeded to purge Quaker and Presbyterian influences and later managed to ease Franklin from his governing role. By the early 1760s, Franklin and Smith were already bitter enemies.[65] Smith's college set reading lists prioritized Locke, Hutcheson, and Newtonian physico-theologians like Ray.[66] Tolerant theologically, Smith, like many in the colonies, was at the same time an Anglophile cultural chauvinist, continually trumpeting "British liberty" and "mixed government" in speeches and advocating schools to teach Pennsylvania Germans (upon whom both Franklin and Smith looked down) the "superior advantages" of the English language, law, and institutions. Deposed as rector in 1779 because of his Tory sympathies, Smith later recovered his post; by the time the college was reconstituted in 1791, the old oligarchy had returned to power in Pennsylvania and Franklin's design was never fully adopted.

Jefferson's alma mater, Virginia's William and Mary, he despised as a bastion of Anglican traditionalism long notorious for combating Enlightenment "deism,"[67] which persisted in the "miserable existence to which a miserable constitution has doomed it." To replace the old William and Mary, Jefferson wanted a "university on a plan so broad and liberal and modern, as to be worth patronizing with the public support," a university discriminating in choice of sciences taught and endowed with professorships capable of drawing the "youth of other states to come and drink of the cup of knowledge and fraternize with us."[68] Like Condorcet, he especially recommended studies pertinent to an enlightened society—botany, chemistry, zoology, medicine, agriculture, mathematics, geology, and geography—together with the social and political humanities, namely politics, history, ethics, law, and the fine arts. Yet, defying torrents of scorn from its detractors, post-1783 American higher education policy, directed by champions of theology and Scots moderate Enlightenment, sought to modify the curricula in a limited fashion, not least to stiffen resistance to more fundamental change.

Much later, Jefferson enjoyed some success when founding the new University of Virginia (1819) at Charlottesville, which he conceived as an early form of campus college complete with a classical style rotunda recalling the ancient Roman Pantheon—a university supported by the state on a strictly nonsectarian basis and offering a wide range of scientific and other subjects. He and Madison devoted much time and energy to the institution over the years and both were extremely proud of it.[69] They judged it essential the professors should broadly share their republican political perspectives and that the students learn republican political theory from a range of texts. Neither Sidney nor Locke, Madison stipulated, was sufficiently anti-monarchical or oriented to guard against slippage from genuine republican values.[70] One scholar of whom Jefferson approved for a science chair was Thomas Cooper, whose appointment, however, was overturned by the state legislature (prompted by Virginia Presbyterians) owing to his too obviously anti-Trinitarian and anti-clerical views.[71] Jefferson's influence succeeded, though, in getting him appointed, in 1820, to the chemistry chair at South Carolina College (today the University of South Carolina), an institution founded in 1801, at Columbia, with the design of bringing the planter-dominated east and backcountry west of the state closer together. Classes had begun in 1805 with nine students. A superior scholar and excellent teacher, in 1821 Cooper was appointed second college president in succession to the deceased Baptist proponent of the "Second Awakening" hitherto presiding, at which point he embarked on one of the most embattled college presidencies (1821–34) of the era despite becoming a decided enthusiast for the Southern way of life and abandoning his earlier opposition to slavery.

Should a college president perchance pertain to the wrong variety of the Enlightenment—or at least still partly, given his betraying his own pre-1820 ideals to the extent of becoming an apologist for Southern slavery—a fraught outcome was inevitable. From 1822, Cooper's (white) democratic leanings and past doctrine of "justifiable Revolution" were scrutinized by statesmen and churchmen, provoking a public scandal. Investigated for undesirable opinions by the state legislature, he used all his skills to ward off the pressure. His materialism, denial of all supernaturalism, and opposition to "Scottish meta-

Jefferson and Madison's "University of Virginia" in 1826. Photo credit: The New York Public Library / Art Resource, NY.

physics" blended with scorn for preachers and their "intolerance" generated a protracted, famous battle.[72] The ascendancy of his religiously conservative foes he attributed primarily to "ignorance": "the people, not aware of the frauds committed are the gross dupes of missionary societies, Bible societies, and theological seminaries," so that "every head of a family of a religious turn, or in any way connected with that sect, must submit to the power these parsons have acquired,— acquired by making the females of the families which they are permitted to enter the engines of their influence over the male part." He predicted "another night of superstition, not far behind the Inquisition; for so rancorously is every opponent calumniated that the persecution becomes gradually irresistible, and the men who hate these impostors and their frauds are actually compelled to bow down to them."[73] Refusing to retract his slights on the clergy, after an eleven-year struggle with the local establishment and legislature, he was finally ousted from the college presidency in November 1833.[74]

Charlottesville, Virginia, and Columbia, South Carolina, in any case, were definitely not characteristic of the main line of higher education policy. At Yale, the largest and most Calvinist college in New England, Ezra Stiles (1727–95), a Congregationalist minister and proponent of a moderate Calvinist Enlightenment, the college's seventh president (1778–95), and Timothy Dwight (1752–1815), the college president for twenty-two years (1795–1817), scorned deists, Baptists, Quakers, and Universalists as well as Arminians and Anglicans but strove to accommodate and steer between the Enlightenment and New England's growing zeal for revivalist preaching. Stiles has been designated the "best specimen of the special New England compromise between Protestantism and Enlightenment just before this compromise broke down" (in the 1790s). A firm republican, advocate of equality, and friend of Franklin, he encouraged the young Barlow to develop his talent for poetry. Although he dismissed Ethan Allen as a "profane and impious Deist," his own inner thoughts harbored more than a hint of struggle between deism and Christianity.[75] More abrasive and emphatically aligned with Scottish moral philosophy, Dwight strove to combat "infidel philosophy," a designation in his eyes covering deism, atheism, materialism, Universalism, and Humean skepticism, and, very differently from Stiles, reviled democratic ideas.[76] A popular, influential speaker and key educationalist, Dwight stabilized the Yale curriculum and Connecticut's academic culture, severely pruning old-style Trinitarian and other theological dispute while fighting the "infidel" challenge. Seeking broad collaboration among the Calvinistic churches on the basis of a minimum of doctrine, he constructed a new orthodoxy avowedly anti-Unitarian, anti-Baptist, and anti-Catholic but otherwise deemphasizing theology and martialing a plurality of Protestant churches aimed more against philosophic irreligion and deism than wrong religion.

Reductive theologically if "politically Congregationalist," Dwight's education philosophy proved formidable in the years around 1800 as a conservative moral, social, and political force. "Infidel philosophy," having stricken a corrupt and declining Europe, now menaced the "land of freedom, peace and virtue," the United States. Despised by Barlow as a "bigot and Tory," Dwight staunchly supported the anti-democratic stance of the Federalists, dismissing Jeffersonian republican and democratic agitation as the despicable dual tool of Paineite social subversion and "infidelity."[77] Such philosophy, he assured Yale students in his lecture series *The Nature and Danger of Infidel Philosophy*, was as indefensible intellectually as it was insidious morally and politically. Assailing their "vile hypocrisy" in September 1797, he denounced Hobbes, Blount, Shaftesbury, Toland, Tindal, Bolingbroke, Paine, and other authors he assumed his students might read, claiming "infidel philosophy has not hitherto been able to support itself, nor to make any serious impression on the evidence of the Divine Origin of Scriptures."[78] "Rational freedom," the kind of liberty that is useful to society and upholds morality, "cannot be preserved without the aid of Christianity."[79] "Infidel philosophy" was false and dangerous, and encouraged immorality and sexual depravity, "holding out a general license to every passion and appetite."[80]

In his noted satirical poem *The Triumph of Infidelity* (1788), Dwight oscillated between warning readers against the dire "threat" to society and ridiculing Satan for imagining he could "triumph" over Christianity using such feeble means. "Most American men, and practically all women," he was glad to say, remained faithful: fortunately, "atheists are few, most nymphs a Godhead own."[81] But Dwight also knew an underlying clandestine radicalism flourished at Yale and other colleges, indeed felt that the Revolution had heightened the threat of infidelity and sexual license. "Infidels" mostly kept quiet but were more numerous than appeared. One concealed "infidel" enlightener was the dramatist and New York theater manager William Dunlap (1766–1839), among the founders of the nineteenth-century New York theater world, a personage convinced the theater could help reinforce the American Revolution by reeducating the public in republican values but who felt intense frustration that "mercenary" theater managers preferred to stage "such ribaldry or folly, or worse, as is attractive . . . to the uneducated, the idle and profligate."[82] Friendly with Dunlap despite regarding the theater as immoral, Dwight had no idea he was privately a staunch deist, follower of Godwin, and foe of "religionists." One evening Dwight read Dunlap sections from his satire condemning "all Frenchmen, innovators and infidels" to which Dunlap listened, Dwight thought, approvingly, without uttering a word of criticism. But on returning home, Dunlap noted in his private diary that Dwight was a hopeless bigot whose anti-Jacobin tirades were merely an "inveterate farrago of falsehood and abuse."[83]

Still more illiberal during his long college presidency (1768–94) was the Scots academic John Witherspoon (1723–94), a doughty opponent of Hume's skepticism who signed both the *Declaration of Independence* and the Articles of Confederation on New Jersey's behalf. If William and Mary was a bastion of Anglicanism, Witherspoon's Princeton where the young Madison studied in the years 1769 to 1772 championed Presbyterianism while no less powerfully combating "infidelity." Witherspoon heavily entrenched Scottish "moderate" Enlightenment and the "argument from design," especially the austere moral thought of Reid, as Princeton's dominant intellectual creed and the backbone of its social conservatism.[84] With Witherspoon still nominally president, from the late 1780s onward the next Princetonian driving force was Samuel Stanhope Smith (1751–1819), later the college's seventh president (1795–1812), who similarly strove for an enlightened, up-to-date version of Calvinism that blocked the dogmatic Counter-Enlightenment proclivities of the "Second Awakening" but was socially and politically unbendingly conservative. Stanhope Smith's double strategy eventually landed him in difficulties with Calvinist theological hard-liners, forcing his resignation as college president in 1812. By that date, the "stance of the Moderate Enlightenment," concluded Henry May, had become "difficult for any Presbyterian, and for a president of Princeton impossible." At Princeton, during the early nineteenth century, anti-Anglican and anti-Baptist conservatism verging on Counter-Enlightenment triumphed.[85] Calvinist theology's primacy and the Scottish emphasis were further reinforced in 1812 with the founding of the soon renowned Princeton Theological Seminary.

The president of Harvard College, Joseph Willard (president: 1781–1804), was a Congregationalist pastor who knew his Latin and Greek but was characterized by Miranda as "unsociable, austere and of an unbearable circumspection." Miranda praised the college's "philosophical apparatus," that is, its physics and chemistry equipment, but otherwise thought the college "better calculated to form clerics than capable and educated citizens." "It is certainly an extraordinary thing that in this college there is no professorship whatever of the living languages and that theology is the principal professorship."[86] His only other comment concerned the extraordinarily slovenly appearance of Harvard scholars. Harvard boasted hardly any impressive scholars, agreed Brissot, which was unsurprising since "interest in learning is not widespread among Bostonians. Trade occupies all their thoughts, turns their heads and absorbs all their speculations. Consequently there are few writers and few great works."[87] Resisting moves to convert the college into a state institution with public responsibilities within the framework of the 1780 Massachusetts constitution, Harvard, like the other leading colleges, remained a private establishment. Its structure of studies, according to Brissot, resembled Oxford's, being entombed in theology and the past. Like Condorcet, Brissot believed "education is perhaps the only way to draw men from the shameful state of degradation in which they remain sunk,"[88] and in the United States judged it inconceivable the "recent Revolution will not bring about a great reform. Free men," he argued, must participate as citizens, "swiftly cast off their prejudices," and realize that dead languages and "tedious philosophies [i.e., academic scholasticism]" and theology should occupy few hours of their lives. Bostonians needed "studies more suitable to the great family of mankind."[89] Appalled by the craze for gambling, he concluded this was a natural by-product of an America providing leisure and dignity to all for the first time but where "men read few books" and spend little time courting women, and practically no time on learning and the sciences: this "taste for cards is certainly very unfortunate in a republican state; it is a habit that stultifies the mind."[90]

David Tappan (1752–1803), Hollis Professor of Divinity at Harvard, another fervent adherent of Scots moral philosophy and unbending Calvinist adversary of Unitarians, joined forces with Dwight and others to instill among students the myth that the recent rush of "infidel philosophy" in America flowed from a conspiracy in Europe against all government and religion fomented by the German Illuminati. According to this obsessional conspiracy theory, "infidel philosophy" either side of the Atlantic was not just a "plan formed, and to an alarming degree executed, for exterminating Christianity," and "moral obligation" along with chastity and decency, but also "for rooting out of the world civil and domestic government" and big property ownership. There was no hiding the reality that "under the pretense of enlarged philanthropy, and of giving mankind liberty and equality," faithless subversives "carefully concealed the true end, which is no less than to reduce the whole human race under a complete subjugation to these Philosophers."[91] When the "Old Calvinist" Tappan died, strife between Unitarians and Calvinists at Harvard intensified. A battle ensued in 1804–5 over the appointment of his successor to the Hollis Chair, the crypto- and soon openly Unitarian minister Henry Ware (1764–1845).[92] When Ware emerged triumphant, the old-style theologians abandoned the college with its famous new School of Divinity to New England's moderate Socinian creed, rendering Harvard more liberal theologically than it had been, but left it as much the preserve of privilege and theology as before. Harvard remained a fortress of moderate Enlightenment aversion to Jeffersonianism, secularism, and democracy.

On the surface, it was an easy matter for college presidents balancing moderate Enlightenment against Counter-Enlightenment Calvinism to direct the colleges against the dual threat of "infidel philosophy" and democratic ideas. There were pious Calvinists, Catholics, and Lutherans among the avowed republicans and democrats, but such a combination was hardly to be found among the leadership or foremost publicists on either side. As with the Catholic revolutionary democrats of the French Revolution, religiously devout republicans found themselves politically and culturally isolated. Nearly all college presidents were steadfast political conservatives inculcating educational values that struck detractors as belonging to the same theological-ecclesiastical system buttressing worldly and spiritual despotism in the Old World. In their political, historical, and moral philosophy curricula, all the principal colleges prior to 1819 promoted exclusively conservative principles, endorsing "mixed government" and the British model, rejecting democracy and irreligion outright. They were as inclined to couple irreligion and democratic republicanism as their radical foes. Consequently, the colleges became overtly an intellectual and political as well as religious battleground. Leading democratic spokesmen and intellectual voices, especially those known to be irreligious freethinkers, materialists, and atheists like Franklin, Paine, Jefferson, Freneau, Coram, and Palmer, or alternatively extreme radical Unitarian latitudinarians, like Cooper and Priestley, were condemned as inveterate enemies of society, religion, and morals. Quantitative analysis of American library holdings, reading habits, and editions in the 1790s and first decade of the new century reflects a marked escalation of ideological conflict among academics and the student fraternity with radical works by Paine, Raynal, Rousseau, Volney, Beccaria, Condorcet, Godwin, and Wollstonecraft being read widely.[93]

Disputing the moral, social-political, and religious aspects of the Revolution permeated higher education and the public sphere, with the battle of beliefs and ideas figuring prominently in sermons. This turned the colleges simultaneously into moderate Enlightenment foci fomenting public conservatism and, behind the scenes, notorious centers of clandestine radical critique. One example was the conversion of Barlow and his friend Noah Webster (1758–1843) to radical ideas while Yale students.[94] Webster later changed his views but, when young, was a zealous reader of Price, Priestley, and Rousseau. On reading *Common Sense* as a student in 1776, he became an apostle of equality and, like Barlow, a Paine admirer. As a young radical, he abhorred Dwight's *Triumph of Infidelity*, the anonymously published 778-line satirical denunciation of Yale deism, not realizing its author was his future college president and ally, whose poetry he otherwise admired. Breaking with Paine and Barlow in the early 1790s, Webster joined Dwight to become yet another noted public foe of "infidel" philosophy.[95]

American "infidels" derived from very various educational backgrounds. Some, like Franklin, Paine, Young, Allen, and Rittenhouse, were self-emancipated autodidacts; others, like Jefferson, Mason, Madison, Barlow, and Monroe, belonged to the highly educated, privileged elite. All were intensely American but—in a sense emphasized by their foes in the colleges—also allegedly un-American, owing to their sympathy for French radical *philosophes* and supposed solidarity with Jacobins. American "moderation" and conservatism, dominant at home, could not prevent the Revolution's radical dimension from capturing the outside world's perception and interpretation of what the United States represented—at any rate down to the 1850s. Yet, while the radical tendency was inherent in the Revolution, drawing on both its legacy and its failure to fulfill its promises, American radicalism could not deny its vast intellectual debt to European writers. This helped American adversaries project their "infidelity" as a highly extraneous intrusion into the "authentic" American reality. American radicals cited European more than American authors and, like Franklin, Paine, Barlow, and Jefferson, refined their philosophical views as much or more in Europe as America. After leaving Princeton and Witherspoon's spell, Madison became as addicted to French thought, as steeped in Condorcet, Raynal, Chastellux, Mercier, Volney, Mirabeau, Brissot, and Mably, as Jefferson.[96] A homegrown Paine admirer and zealot for "philosophy" and the "empire of reason," already at Yale, Barlow grew into a full-blown materialist and atheist swayed by Boulanger and d'Holbach, unwaveringly opposing monarchy, clergy, and aristocracy, only after settling for business in France, in 1788, and plunging into the French revolutionary ferment.[97]

The insidious myth that the American Revolution differed fundamentally in character from the French, concocted in the mid-1790s, made headway in the late 1790s largely due to Federalist press efforts to tarnish radical thought as irreligious and "un-American." The pro-Federalist *Gazette of the United States* styled Jefferson's leading supporters the "French faction," a clique that "may with truth be pronounced in the wane": the "star of Jacobinism must soon cease to shed its malign influence; for shadows, clouds, and darkness rest upon it."[98] From the 1790s, radicals steadily lost ground in the public sphere even though the very impetus and zeal of the "Second Awakening" generated a degree of unease and intellectual reaction among citizens of all kinds. In restricted circles, the Awakening's emotionalism, populism, and anti-intellectualism, which also disturbed Dwight, intensified the countervailing impulse further encouraging immersion in deistic and materialist irreligious books, with those of Paine, Godwin, and Volney in especially strong demand during the decade 1800–1810.[99]

Another battleground for the soul of the Revolution was public support for the arts and sciences. It was taken for granted by some "moderates," including Washington and Adams, as well as radicals, that any republic worthy of general esteem should actively champion and patronize the Enlightenment publicly, especially by promoting the arts and sciences. Jefferson, who closely studied architecture, and whose design for Virginia's Capitol building became the first neoclassical edifice of its eventually ubiquitous type in America, was convinced that an entirely new public architecture, art, and museum culture was requisite for attiring the new republic and giving expression to its values.[100] Nevertheless, public support for the arts and sciences, such as characterized the French Revolution between 1789 and 1793, was broadly rejected in the wake of the American Revolution by indifferent legislatures and a largely uninterested public, both being as stubbornly reluctant to support the arts and museums as to incorporate schools and colleges into the public sphere under the mantle of republican criteria.[101]

In 1782, Congress turned down proposals to appoint the uniquely qualified Pierre-Eugène du Simitière (1737–84) as "historiographer of the United States," which, given his impoverished circumstances, meant refusing to help the nation's most assiduous researcher into the revolutionary era to complete his research and his projected large-scale history of America's revolutionary struggle and republican institutions. Elected to the American Philosophical Society in 1768, and one of its leading naturalists, Du Simitière, a native of Geneva who had lived in the West Indies, New York, and finally, from 1774, Philadelphia, owned a renowned collection of manuscripts and rare materials, as well as objects, relating to North America's early history and the West

Indies and had zealously collected every pamphlet, broadside, and newspaper article relating to the Revolution he could locate. A fervent public-spirited *Américaniste* among the most stalwart republicans in the colonies, he opened his collection, including his numerous natural curiosities, to the public in May 1782, naming it "The American Museum." It was Philadelphia's first public museum and the second in the United States after the Charleston Museum but cost more to maintain than accrued from ticket receipts. Incredulous that Congress could be indifferent to his great project, as well as his past heavy outlay and present impecunious predicament, Du Simitière reportedly never recovered from the blow.[102] Following his premature death, two years later, the museum had to close and auction off its contents, many of his manuscripts going to the Library Company with which Franklin was associated.[103]

When Miranda began his tour of the United States, at Philadelphia, in November 1783, the only real memorials to revolutionary values and striving were private collections such as Peale's where one could see "one hundred portraits of middling merit done by this artist of the leading citizens and foreigners who contributed to the American Revolution."[104] During following decades artists such as John Trumbull (1756–1843) devoted to commemorating the Revolution and its principles found it difficult to interest the American public in "history" scenes depicting themes and episodes from the Revolution. Commiserating with him in 1817, ex-president John Adams agreed that there then existed in the United States "no disposition to celebrate or remember . . . the characters, actions or events of the Revolution."[105] Even Jefferson as president, during the first decade of the new century, felt helpless to promote Barlow's scheme for systematic state support for the arts, learning, and sciences. While enthusing over the principle, he excused inaction on the ground the American public would simply refuse to support it.[106] In 1805–6, he did back Barlow's plan for a "national university" to lead America in higher learning and end theology's ascendancy; but here too Jefferson, like Madison earlier, was roundly rebuffed by the United States Congress.[107] Paine's confident claim, in 1782, that the Revolution had freed Americans from the "beaten track of vulgar and habitual thinking" and that "both with regard to ourselves, to France and to England, every corner of the mind is swept of its cobwebs, poison, and dust, and made fit for the reception of generous happiness," so that "we are now really another people, and cannot go back to ignorance and prejudice"—his belief that the "mind once enlightened cannot again become dark"—can scarcely have sounded convincing to some surveying the American scene around 1800 and striving to expand and restructure education for the American people.[108]

CHAPTER 5

Benjamin Franklin: "American Icon"?

The Making of an American Revolutionary

Benjamin Franklin came to represent the democratic tendency and embody the highest values of the American Revolution with unparalleled resonance internationally. Shortly after his death in 1790, a French commentator on the Revolution then unfolding in France described him as the republican *philosophe* who, first among the revolutionary era's "heroes of liberty," initiated the rupture with older constitutional forms and contexts classically expounded by Montesquieu, originating the drive to renew political thought on the basis of equal "natural rights" and the "pursuit of happiness."[1] On multiple levels Franklin was iconic for the Enlightenment and American Revolution in ways exemplary yet also, in key respects, more divisive than historians usually acknowledge.

Franklin's extraordinary career reflected perhaps more consistently and memorably than any other apart from Jefferson's the American Revolution's fundamental creativity and innovativeness, the depth and scope of the resulting rift between moderate and radical tendencies, and the paradox and dilemmas of its later legacy. The biographical dimension here provides an indispensable perspective for conveying the full scope and implications of the wider picture. For Franklin's role both within and outside America affords a unique vantage point from which to consider the interlacing of the American Revolution with the Enlightenment's long-term trends, its prolonged but meandering impact on Canada, France, and Holland.

More than most Founding Fathers, Franklin was a self-made man. Born in Boston in January 1706, his father was a humble artisan, an English candle and soap maker from Northamptonshire. Receiving less formal education than other American revolutionary leaders, in science and learning he eventually outstripped all the rest. Apprenticed initially for candle making, his zest for reading led to his switching instead to the printing trade. From age twelve a Boston printer's assistant, he vested his surplus energy in reading and learning to write correctly. "My time for these exercises," he recorded, "was at night, after work or before work began in the morning; or on Sunday when I contrived to be in the printing house alone, evading as much as I could the common attendance on publick worship, which my father used to exact of me when I was under his care: and which indeed I still thought a duty; tho' I could not, as it seemed to me afford the time to practice it."[2]

Early on, Franklin discovered the meaning of political criticism and opposition. In August 1721, his older brother James, for whom he worked, established the *New England Courant*, Boston's fourth newspaper. When, two years later, his brother was jailed by the Massachusetts General Court and House of Representatives for criticizing them and infringing court orders not to publish without submitting to prior censorship, Franklin found himself embroiled in the last serious attempt to impose formal political censorship on the Boston press. During his brother's imprisonment, he edited the paper, and "made bold to give our rulers some rubs in it, which my brother took very kindly, while others began to consider me in an unfavourable light, as a young genius who had a taste for libeling and satire." He was summoned and severely rebuked for lampooning the authorities, an experience which, along with repugnance for Calvinist piety and his brother's "harsh and tyrannical treatment of me," instilled in him that "aversion to arbitrary power that has stuck to me thro' my whole life."[3] Quitting Boston shortly afterward, in October 1723, he migrated to Philadelphia.

Franklin became an outright rebel against conventional religion from an early stage. Privately, he denied Christianity and especially the authority of the pulpit throughout his adult life. Already at fifteen, he doubted the truth of Revelation and, after reading Shaftesbury, Collins, and the Boyle Lectures refuting atheism (in his opinion not very successfully), became a "thorough deist." Arriving in England for the first time at barely eighteen, in December 1724, he worked in a London print shop, assisting with the third edition of Wollaston's *The Religion of Nature Delineated*, a book that stimulated him to produce an incisive tract of his own, *A Dissertation on Liberty and Necessity, Pleasure and Pain* (most copies of which he later destroyed). Extolling reason and science, he followed Collins in expounding a philosophical necessitarianism eliminating free will and predicating an omnipotent God so minimally, it amounted virtually to "atheism" rather than deism.[4]

The conventional-minded considered Franklin's views "abominable."[5] During the mid-1720s, frequenting London coffeehouses and clubs, he encoun-

be impracticable for ten or a dozen English colonies, to whom it is more necessary, and must be more advantageous; and who cannot be supposed to want an equal understanding of their interests."[10]

In philosophy and science, Franklin's chief preoccupation, from 1746, was research into electricity, which he undertook "with great alacrity," his first publications on "Electrical experiments" appearing in the Royal Society's *Philosophical Transactions* in 1748. It was the French translation of his writings on electricity, on the initiative of the renowned naturalist Buffon, in 1752, that transformed him into an international celebrity. Challenging the explanations of the then presiding authority on electricity, the Abbé Jean-Antoine Nollet (1700–1770), from 1734 first professor of experimental physics at the Sorbonne, Franklin became the first American to figure prominently in international scientific controversy. Suddenly famous across the Atlantic, his achievements in the "electric branch of natural philosophy," especially his account of lightning, in turn established his reputation in Britain and America, belatedly securing honorary degrees from Harvard, in July 1753, and Yale soon afterward.[11] In 1767, and again in 1769, Franklin visited France and was presented at court. In 1772, he was elected a corresponding member of the Académie Royale des Sciences, an honor rarely bestowed on foreigners.

Unusually, Franklin became simultaneously an ardent Francophile and Anglophile. Until 1775, his staunch Francophilia by no means prevented his remaining an ardent British patriot and friend of England. Despite his aversion to hereditary aristocracy, he remained loyal to Crown and empire for decades and an indefatigable negotiator eager to defuse the mounting tension between Britain and the colonies. He returned to London, in October 1763, as Pennsylvania's agent, just when the empire emerged from the Seven Years' War as the largest and most powerful the world had yet known. Disregarding the deep resentment at home, Franklin, unlike practically every other American spokesman or publisher, appeared willing even to stomach the Stamp Act. Temporarily, this cost him his American popularity: "all the papers on the Continent, ours excepted," reported Hall from Philadelphia, were "full of spirited attacks on the Stamp Act"; but because they did not "publish those papers likewise," Hall (and Franklin) were "much blamed, got a good deal of ill-will," and "on that account" lost many customers. So did their partner in New York, James Parker, accused of being "no friend of liberty," and their Charleston associate, Peter Timothy, who "from the most popular" became the "most unpopular man" in South Carolina.[12]

Nothing more delighted Franklin and his London friends than the repeal of the Stamp Act. Relations with England, he remained confident, would

tered Bernard Mandeville, whom he found a "most facetious ente companion" and whose ideas about human nature he studied, furtl stering his irreverence, oppositional attitude, and aversion to religior deville became—with the possible exception of Shaftesbury—the si single intellectual influence over Franklin's emerging radical views his early outright rejection of religious notions he may have retreated later, toward a more ambivalent "deism" that did not wholly exclud providence.[7] In any case, in subsequent decades Franklin did not pa religious unorthodoxy publicly, not wishing to affront others or an the church authorities. In his maturity he also increasingly evinced ぇ ful moral sense, a robust awareness of the need for integrity for a hap vidual life and society's well-being.

A paragon of Enlightenment sociability, seeking social amelioration meetings, discussion, and group reading, after returning to his Phili printing business, in late 1726, Franklin formed his own "club for improvement, which we call'd the Junto," gathering every Friday Besides an essay every three months, members had to offer "quer comments on "any point of morals, politics or natural philosophy" d by the group. The stated goal was calm, thoughtful deliberation, ii after truth avoiding all "fondness for dispute," "warmth of expressi "desire for victory," enlightened rules enforced with "small pecuniai ties" for infraction. The Junto assembled a modest library featuring e the works of Locke, initially attended mainly by book-loving artisar it also attracted members from the middle and gentry classes. Contir many years, the club evolved into the "best school of philosophy, mc politics that then existed" in Pennsylvania.[8]

By the late 1740s, Franklin had made sufficient money to retire con and assume the lifestyle and political activity of a "gentleman." He tra management of his printing business to his young partner, David Hal quently devoting himself partly to "philosophical studies" and partly affairs. A member of the Philadelphia city council from 1748, and a from 1751, he soon afterward became a member of the Pennsylvania ℐ despite being a poor public speaker and noticeably reserved, even a in public spaces.[9] Far from dealing only in local affairs, Franklin, alre ing the 1750s, displayed an unusual interest in the collective well- the colonies and repeatedly proposed the need for a permanent unio them. "It would be a very strange thing," he remarked in March 175 Nations of ignorant Savages [i.e., the Iroquois] should be capable of f scheme for such an Union, and be able to execute it in such a manne it has subsisted ages, and appears indissoluble; and yet that a like unio

mend. When, despite the repeal, friction resumed in 1766–67, he urged ministers to grant the Americans representation in Parliament, maintaining that a durable and flourishing union, like that with Scotland, could only consolidate and strengthen the empire. Slowly, though, he began suspecting that British ministers, following their unprecedented global triumph, had simply grown too haughty and imperious to admit America to an "equitable participation in the government of the whole."[13] His undeviating advocacy of reconciliation nevertheless persisted right down to 1774. Franklin "took every method in his power to prevent a rupture between the two countries," recalled his Unitarian friend and fellow scientist Joseph Priestley. "He urged so much the doctrine of forbearance," recorded Priestley, who knew him well at that time and often debated theology and politics with him, that for "some time he was unpopular with the Americans on that account, as too much a friend of Great Britain."[14]

Besides Priestley, Franklin drew close to several other London radical dissenters, including John Jebb and Richard Price, frequenting the "Club of Honest Whigs," a hotbed of opposition to the British establishment and staunch supporters of American resistance to the ministry's coercive stance in the colonies.[15] But he also expanded his contacts in France. In February 1769, he provided the young Benjamin Rush, who had just completed his medical studies at Edinburgh, with letters of introduction to Paris, resulting in a conversation between Rush and Diderot at a time when the latter was laboring on the politically and religiously seditious *Histoire philosophique des Deux Indes* (1770). Rush and Diderot discussed how to oppose British "tyranny," Diderot finding it ironic that England, once associated with the fight *for* liberty, was now the world's foremost oppressor, and that while "we write against despotism" from London stream printed pamphlets "favoring tyranny."[16] As Rush departed, Diderot provided a letter recommending "my young Pennsylvanian" to Hume. During 1772–73, Franklin, now Massachusetts's agent in England, defied the steady escalation of American ill-feeling, striving still to mend the fences by pinning responsibility and blame for the deteriorating situation not on the Crown, or colonial assemblies, but misjudgment and ineptitude of royal subordinates like his former friend Hutchinson, Massachusetts's beleaguered governor.

Briefly, during 1773, Franklin felt America's angry resentment was already "much abated"; but by September when writing his hilarious essay "Rules by Which a Great Empire May be Reduced to a Small One" pillorying the London ministry for its arrogance and crass mishandling of the issues, he was well on the way to a complete rupture. If the settlers in the colonies "happen to be zealous Whigs," he advised, mockingly referring to American veneration for the Glorious Revolution of 1688, if they were "Friends of Liberty, nurtured in Revolution Principles, remember all that to their prejudice, and contrive to punish it: For such principles, after a Revolution is thoroughly established, are of no more use, they are even odious and abominable."[17] This older notion of "Revolution Principles," as inherently linked to 1688 and long deeply venerated, remained ingrained in America.

Franklin's political volte-face was completed in January 1774 when the British ministry vilified him in the press for transmitting back to Boston copies of secret letters to London, from Governor Hutchison, recommending use of force. The British ministry and press henceforth portrayed him as not just "a very factious man," as Hume put it in a letter to Adam Smith, but a cunning, devious intriguer, false to Britain and the king, guilty to an "extreme degree" of inspiring the latest escalation.[18] Condemned also in Parliament, Franklin resigned his official functions but on his own initiative stayed in London for over a year more in the increasingly forlorn hope of somehow averting war. Only after a final round of fruitless negotiations with British ministers, in December 1774 and January 1775, and the Lords' rejection of all compromise proposals did he grow indignant at Parliament's overweening, bullying tone and, "soured and exasperated," according to Burke, who had a long conversation with him just before he left, finally abandon all hope of preventing war, albeit in Burke's understanding he was still committed to a reversion to the pre-1763 status quo rather than a total break with Britain.[19]

Franklin sailed for America in March 1775, fully persuaded of the inevitability and justice of the looming rupture. Back in Philadelphia shortly after the clashes at Lexington Green and Concord, he discovered that he urgently needed to repair his American reputation. In Pennsylvania and Massachusetts, many suspected he still privately adhered to England.[20] He needed to show unambiguously which side he was on, not least because his son, William Franklin (1730–1814), with whom he now openly quarreled (and was never afterward reconciled), was the royal governor of New Jersey (1763–76), remaining in this position until June 1776 when—the last royal governor still in post—he was interned. Released later in the war, William Franklin set up base in British-occupied New York City from where he actively organized Loyalist armed opposition to the Revolution.[21]

Franklin paraded his patriotism, assuring all and sundry that only indomitable resistance could save America from the "most abject slavery and destruction." He encouraged Paine, whom he met for the first time in London in 1774, to write subversively. Attracted by his radical republican and irreligious views, and appreciating that Paine, like himself, had acquired an advanced education purely by his own efforts, Franklin urged him to settle in Philadelphia and join forces with him politically. Armed with Franklin's letters of introduction, and backed by Franklin's son-in-law, the businessman Richard Bache, Paine emerged as a front-line opposition journalist almost from the moment he arrived, in November 1774, several months before Franklin himself. "Your countenancing me," Paine assured Franklin in March 1775, recalling his initial three months in Philadelphia, "has obtained me many friends and much reputation, for which, please to accept my sincere thanks." Paine's backers helped lever him into the editorship of the *Pennsylvania Magazine*, in effect rendering him Franklin's revolutionary voice in print.[22] In a similar way, Franklin later, in 1787, introduced Paine to the innermost radical circles in Paris by providing him with warm letters of introduction to Condorcet, Chastellux, La Rochefoucauld, Jefferson, and others.[23]

Committed republicans spearheaded the Revolution and led opinion in the colonies, but there also remained numerous ardent Loyalists and moderates of the sort Franklin himself was until 1774, urging reconciliation. Franklin needed to display republican as well as revolutionary ardor, that he had changed his views not only about Britain and independence but also about monarchy, aristocracy, and much else. Allied to Rush, Paine, Young, and the other Philadelphia radicals, he began reflecting seriously on republicanism, democracy, equality, and secularism in politics. The most eloquent and vocal of the Pennsylvania "moderates" opposing Franklin and Paine was the prominent Scottish educational reformer William Smith (1727–1803), Franklin's former ally, who, from 1755, on Franklin's recommendation, headed the new Philadelphia academy (later the University of Pennsylvania). An Anglican Latitudinarian, eulogizing England as the throne room of enlightened rational religion, Smith scorned sectarianism, intolerance, and religious polemics while also censuring Quakers and their pacifism. During the Seven Years' War, he had urged vigorous imperial expansion (like Franklin) and continued to do so.

In Philadelphia's intellectual and political life Smith was a force to be reckoned with. In January 1769, he had been instrumental in uniting the American Philosophical Society, founded in 1767 (and backed by a distinguished group of patrons and the colony's governor and assembly), with the earlier Philadelphia-based American Society for Promoting and Propagating useful Knowledge, whose library was warmly praised by the *Histoire philosophique* as North America's best.[24] While Franklin, the new society's president, was in England as Pennsylvania's agent, this combined body had become America's foremost learned society already well before the Revolution. Although Smith loudly denounced the Stamp Act, unlike Franklin, and condoned limited resistance to Parliament, there was a line beyond which he refused to step.

Penning a powerful retort, signed "Cato," to Paine's *Common Sense* in 1776, Smith emerged as the democrats' foremost local ideological adversary, the leading spokesman for "reconciliation." Styling "our connection" with Great Britain "our chief happiness," from 1775 Pennsylvania's leading standard-bearer of "moderation" and anti-republicanism regularly lambasted Franklin's and Paine's arguments for independence, "confident that nine-tenths of the people of Pennsylvania" disagreed with their plans for "demolition of monarchical government," urging fellow citizens not to "acquiesce in such a horrible doctrine."[25]

Paine's *Common Sense*, held Smith, was full of "mischievous tenets and palpable absurdities." "The true interest of America," he proclaimed in "To the People of Pennsylvania" (March–April 1776), published in the *Pennsylvania Gazette*, "lies in reconciliation with Great Britain, upon constitutional principles." In his "furious antipathy to mixt governments" in which he "surpassed all the writers I have met with," sneered Smith, "the author of *Common Sense* stands singular in his rage for condemning the English constitution in the lump," in utter contradiction to Montesquieu, Locke, and the "immortal Sidney."[26] Monarchies, replied Paine in his *Letters* answering "Cato," are by nature ambitious, violent, and warlike; only republics, like the Dutch United Provinces, pursue stability and peace.[27] On the advance of the British under General Howe into Pennsylvania in 1777, Smith was arrested with other Tory sympathizers and removed from his college rectorate for the war's duration.

This clash of ideologies at Philadelphia was part of the wider political and ideological battle waged at the heart of the American Revolution. During the summer of 1776, John Adams, becoming friendly with Rush at this time, persuaded him of the urgent need to minimize internal friction within the republic and of the commanding virtues of "mixed government." By early 1777, Rush was blaming "Cannon, Matlack and Young" for detracting from the "strength of the state by urging the execution of their rascally government in preference to supporting measures for repelling the common enemy" while warning correspondents that in Pennsylvania "our people (intoxicated with the *must* or first flowing of liberty) have formed a government that is absurd in its principles and incapable of execution without the most alarming influence upon liberty."[28] Pennsylvanian democracy under the likes of Paine, Matlack, and Charles Wilson Peale (1741–1823), America's leading artist (and revolutionary spokesman in the arts), he assured Lee, had become a "Mobocracy."[29] Franklin disagreed but by then had departed the scene, leaving Matlack, Paine, Young, Cannon, Peale, and Rittenhouse to lead the fight for democratic values. In December 1778, in another address to "The People of Pennsylvania," Paine defended the manner in which the constitution was formed, the cool deliberation "amidst which it was forged" and the convention's having the "wisest and ablest man in the State, Dr. Franklin, for their president, whose judgment alone was sufficient to form a constitution, and whose benevolence of heart would never concur in a bad one."[30] Franklin had indeed approved of and contributed to the constitution's strong democratizing tendency and its bestowing full religious freedom on every individual.[31]

Asked to transfer to Paris, in September 1776, as part of a three-man commission with Silas Deane and Arthur Lee to seek military and political aid from France, Franklin readily accepted. "The common toasts in Philadelphia," reported Rush, "now are: 'His most Christian Majesty' [i.e., the French king] and a 'speedy alliance between the King of France and the United States.'"[32]

The Revolution Comes to Paris

Arriving in Paris in December 1776, Franklin found himself "the only man from America," as Condorcet put it, "to enjoy a great reputation in Europe."[33] An immediate sensation—the supposed embodiment of American naturalness and plainness of dress (however bogus the supposedly backwoods attire and caps he sometimes affected)—he enjoyed exceptional stature in France as the quintessential American republican and egalitarian before attaining remotely comparable renown in America. The imagery of egalitarianism and simplicity swept Paris's fashionable circles in 1776–83, contrasting starkly with European court culture, with Franklin, much to the satisfaction of innumerable Rousseau admirers, becoming the very emblem of radical critique of ancien régime artificiality and social hierarchy. Reformers, especially followers of Diderot, d'Holbach, and Helvétius of the circle of Mme. Helvétius, doyenne of the radical *philosophique* circle, tended all to be ardent *Américanistes*. Lodging nearby at Passy, Franklin frequented her salon, in the suburb of Auteuil, seeing much of Mirabeau, Cabanis, Chamfort, and Turgot besides the chemist Lavoisier and Condorcet, later a leading radical *philosophe* of the French Revolution—personalities he encountered frequently also at sessions of the Académie des Sciences.[34]

Franklin's arrival spurred the ardent enthusiasm for the American Revolution manifested in French radical intellectual circles since 1774–75, especially personages associated with the *Histoire philosophique* and with Turgot and Condorcet. This point needs emphasizing because, as a rule, both French and American historians have tended greatly to underestimate the strength of crypto-republican tendency in French thought prior to 1789.[35] French radical

philosophes did not admire everything about the American Revolution, especially not its failure to abolish slavery, or the checks and balances retained in
most state legislatures, or the religious tests. Like Diderot, d'Holbach, Rousseau, and others, they preferred to see just one legitimate source of political
authority, the "general will," as Diderot was first to call it, a single chamber
armed with legislative supremacy presiding over both executive and judiciary,
as in the recently recast Pennsylvania constitution, of which they, like Price,
wholeheartedly approved.[36]

Condorcet, typically for radical enlighteners, viewed the Enlightenment as
the chief step in human progress since the rise of sedentary agriculture and
the most essential for freeing the human mind, setting modern science on its
path, and achieving liberty. It was in building on the new principles of the Enlightenment that the United States had preceded Europe, becoming a land
"where the rights of man are respected." Notwithstanding differences of climate, manners, and constitutions, America's impact on the wider world, Condorcet averred in 1781, would prove immense.[37] During the 1780s, before the
French Revolution, Condorcet and other radical publicists produced several
texts predicting what they believed would be the vast impact of the American
Revolution on Europe.[38] The Revolution would soon reach Europe, and the
likeliest place for its first incursion across the Atlantic was France.[39] America
would determine "if the human race is destined by nature for liberty or slavery," agreed another key propagator of radical ideology, the future revolutionary Mirabeau, in 1784.[40]

Their championing the 1776 Pennsylvania model as the ideal and most authentic American constitution was seconded by Condorcet's later ally during
the French Revolution, Brissot. Like most orators and journalists of the democratic Left during the French Revolution, personages such as Condorcet,
Desmoulins, Bonneville, Carra, Gorsas, Pétion, Robert, and Lafayette, Brissot was already before 1789 an ardent republican, anti-monarchist, *Américaniste*, and anti-aristocrat. A keen supporter also of the Genevan democratic
revolution of 1782, Brissot penned the "Plan de conduite," one of the most
influential proposals published prior to the gathering of the 1789 Versailles
Estates-General. Criticizing separation of powers, bicameralism, and one-
person executives, Brissot steadfastly rejected Montesquieu and the "British
model" as altogether contrary to the interests of the majority.[41]

Ties to the Auteuil circle helped Franklin propagandize openly on behalf of America's Revolution in France, ensconced among one of Europe's
most vibrant intellectual circles—*philosophes*, journalists, economists, and reformers ardently supporting the American Revolution for itself but equally
for what it signified for France and mankind. The American people, Turgot

Benjamin Franklin (1706–90), by the court portraitist Joseph Siffred Duplessis (1725–1802), painted in Paris around 1778. Photo credit: National Portrait Gallery, Smithsonian Institution / Art Resource, NY.

assured Price in March 1778, "are the hope of the world."[42] The distinctive image Franklin exuded in France owed much to his personal style, quiet and modest but firm, scrupulously avoiding the attire of court and aristocracy. During 1777–78, without wig and plainly attired, he sat for several artists, including Jean-Baptiste Greuze. However, his shunning aristocratic attire and manners, and Paine's well-publicized "attachment" to him, hardly enhanced his image among the entrenched gentry oligarchy of Pennsylvania, Virginia, or New York.[43] At first, while France made no overt move to support the American Revolution, Franklin proved so taciturn at receptions and dinners that some grew concerned. One dinner guest engaging him in conversation ventured to remark that the American Revolution offered the world a "grand

et superbe spectacle." "Oui, Monsieur," answered Franklin, "but the spectators are not paying."[44]

Thriving intellectually, socially, and politically in France, Franklin got to
know most of the *philosophe* elite, several times encountering the now aged Voltaire, who, in 1778, at the end of his long life, returned to Paris from Ferney.
They met publicly at the Académie des Sciences. John Adams, then also present in Paris and antagonistic to both Franklin and French "modern philosophy," noted how these "two aged actors upon this great theater of philosophy
and frivolity" embraced "by hugging one another in their arms and kissing
each other's cheeks" until the great tumult around them subsided and the
audience were finally satisfied.[45] If Franklin impacted impressively on Paris,
France equally drew him, and in the politically crucial position in which he
found himself, he further absorbed radical ideas and texts, increasingly discarding the strands of moderate outlook shaping his views before 1775. In October 1778, Bentham, at this time deeply affected by Helvétius's utilitarianism,
sent on from London a report originating with Jan Ingenhousz (1730–99), a
Dutch physician and chemist friendly with Franklin in Paris, that "Franklin
has Helvétius constantly on his table."[46]

Franklin's diplomatic role as such arguably mattered less for the Revolution
than the symbolic value of his presence. Even so, during 1776–78, his early Parisian period, he scored a major diplomatic breakthrough, his knack for court
diplomacy helping secure and shape the French alliance. After months of hesitation over whether to assist "rebels" against royal authority, but tempted—like
every rival power—by the opportunity to strike at Britain, Louis XVI eventually signed his military pact with the United States on 18 February 1778. "All
Europe is for us," wrote Franklin jubilantly to Richard Bache, "and England
in consternation."[47] Franklin used his European success not least to counter
those Loyalists in America, including William Smith, who, following the alliance with France, still urged reconciliation with Britain and, as he put it, "are
for returning to the Dependency." "America at present stands in the highest light of esteem and respect thro'out Europe," he assured Sam Adams in
March 1778; "a return to dependence on England would sink her into eternal
contempt."[48] Displaying his love of fine food and wine, Franklin celebrated
the third anniversary of American Independence, on 5 July 1779 (the fourth
was a Sunday), by arranging a banquet in his Passy residence for forty distinguished guests seated at a dining table under a full-length portrait of Washington (which Lafayette had brought back from America), depicting the general
holding the *Declaration of Independence* in one hand and the Franco-American
treaty in the other while trampling under foot proposals for reconciliation with
England.[49]

No sooner was the treaty signed than Franklin utilized the boost to American prestige and the expectations to foster support for America in Holland too, employing as his "Agent for the United States" there a German-born Huguenot translator, Charles Frédéric Dumas (1721–96), familiar with the Amsterdam bankers and with the merchants shipping munitions to the American rebels via the Dutch Caribbean.[50] Dumas's tasks on Franklin's behalf included planting pro-American reports in Leiden's *Gazette de Leyde*, then among the most prestigious papers in western Europe.[51] From 1777, considerable American effort, not least on Franklin's part,[52] was devoted to cultivating the United Provinces, the Netherlands being, after France, the second likely chief source of assistance for the American Revolution—at any rate for finance and munitions as well as Protestant Bibles. (In 1776, with the usual flow of Bibles from England suddenly cut off, and until 1782 none yet being printed in America, Congress made provision to import thousands of Protestant Bibles from Holland—as with tea, pepper, gunpowder, and spices then the only practicable alternative source to Britain.)

Among the initiatives reflecting this cultural, logistical, and diplomatic offensive was a "Memorandum for the Dutch," written in 1777 by Arthur Lee (1740–92) in his capacity as one of the American commissioners in Europe, signed by Franklin and Lee and published in Holland by Dumas, in April 1778.[53] Lee, a Virginia gentleman who had studied in Edinburgh but disliked English attitudes, was a leading adversary of British maritime and imperial aspirations. A cantankerous character who got on badly with Franklin, he was an effective propagandist for America devoted heart and soul to the American cause and a resolute abolitionist. Before Cromwell instituted the British Navigation Laws in the 1650s, "when the commerce of America was free," he reminded the Dutch, "the number of Dutch vessels in the American ports outnumbered those of England." The Navigation Acts had caused the First Anglo-Dutch War of 1652–54, a "usurpation" that greatly damaged Holland but, in the end, also diluted Britain's preponderance: "the wealth and power arising from this very monopoly so intoxicated Great Britain as to make her think there were no bounds to the exercise of the control she had usurped." Since the Dutch lost most through British expansion and mercantilism, "from them therefore America in a most special manner looks for support."[54]

Franklin's diplomatic success was accompanied by one of the century's most effective propaganda coups against monarchy, aristocracy, and empire—a text almost rivaling Paine's *Common Sense* as a foundation for the late eighteenth-century revolutionary consciousness. In 1777, helped by his French friends, Franklin issued *La Science du Bonhomme Richard, ou moyen facile de payer les impôts*, supplemented by the entire text of the 1776 Pennsylvania constitution and an account of his interrogation by the London Parliament over the Stamp Act protests. Back in 1733, Franklin had begun publishing annual installments of his "Poor Richard" almanac replete with homely proverbs, "scattering here and there some instructive hints in matters of morality and religion" for the "public good,"[55] and in 1758 published *The Way to Wealth*, further instructing "Poor Richard." His mythical poor but inquiring and honest laboring man, having been earlier taught how to prosper through one's own efforts, was now being taught how to conquer political liberty. It became the best-known American text of the age in France. The implications of *Bonhomme Richard*, underlined by editorial comments, were so republican and subversive, it would have been impossible in other circumstances to produce multiple editions in pre-1789 France; but, in 1777–78, the French authorities were sufficiently captivated with their pending American alliance, and tied by promises to discreetly allow pro-American publications,[56] to turn a blind eye to the book's manner of elaborating American grievances against the British Crown.[57]

A man of the people, devoted to fighting despotism, Bonhomme Richard openly justifies armed rebellion against tyrannical government wherever entrenched, including India. Later, in 1789, this mythical personage epitomizing the soundly instructed ordinary man reappeared in various French revolutionary pamphlets.[58] A generalized apology for revolution, *Bonhomme Richard* urges citizens to elect their public officeholders and directly participate in framing laws themselves so as to protect their liberty and promote the common good, claiming no government possesses legitimacy unless organized for the "l'advantage commun" rather than that of a hereditary elite or of vested interests.[59]

Bonhomme Richard's impact was heightened by the now established tradition, beginning with Voltaire's *Lettres philosophiques* (1734), of depicting Pennsylvania as a haven of "Quaker" uprightness, simplicity, and toleration. A new layer to Pennsylvania's iconic status had accrued in 1774 with Diderot's passages, in book eighteen of the *Histoire philosophique*, exalting Pennsylvania as the epitome of enlightened good government based on consultation and freedom of thought and expression, being more democratic, more tolerant, and (supposedly) more just to its black and Native American populations than other American colonies. With its libraries and reading societies, Philadelphia became mythologized into the quintessential Enlightenment city, combining "philosophy" with individual initiative, collective responsibility, and social amelioration. Diderot's and Raynal's contribution to the ground-plan for the late eighteenth-century Atlantic democratic revolutions was nowhere clearer than in their extravagant praise of this particular colony.[60]

Franklin took full advantage of this *philosophique* image-building. From 1777, he became internationally closely associated—especially in France but also in America, Germany, Italy, and Britain—with the 1776 democratic Pennsylvania constitution owing to *Bonhomme Richard* and the political mythology it forged.[61] Its international resonance was enhanced further by America's first noteworthy naval commander, John Paul Jones (1747–92), hero of America's sole important maritime battle of the Revolutionary War, fought in the North Sea, off the Yorkshire coast, on 23 September 1779. In Paris, Franklin had deliberated various schemes for naval action around Britain's coasts with Lafayette, who eagerly suggested Franco-American landings at Liverpool, Cork, and elsewhere.[62] Operating out of Nantes and Brest, under Franklin's supervision, Jones's squadron consisted of a flagship (40 guns) tellingly named the *Bonhomme Richard* and *The Alliance* (36 guns), both manned by Americans, and four other warships manned with French crews. Although Jones's squadron was mostly French-built and donated by France, and the crews more French than American in total, the whole flotilla sailed under the stars and stripes around Ireland and Scotland into the North Sea.[63] Overall, the encounter off Flamborough Head, a long and famous battle with the loss of many men, was an American victory but one in which Jones lost his flagship. Shattered by British broadsides, but with the surviving crew and America's first admiral successfully rescued, *Bonhomme Richard* slowly sank.

Back in Paris, Jones was publicly feted, presented to the king, and ecstatically applauded at theaters and everywhere he went, "especially at the Opera."[64] Another major propaganda coup with lasting impact on the French intellectual scene was Franklin's collaboration with Louis-Alexandre de la Rochefoucauld d'Anville (1743–92), a liberal-minded aristocrat and friend of Turgot and Condorcet, much interested in constitutions. In February 1777, La Rochefoucauld (the great-great-grandson of the renowned aphorist) published the 1776 Pennsylvania constitution, translated by him into French in collaboration with Franklin, in the *Affaires de l'Angleterre et de l'Amérique*.[65] He then undertook translating the Virginia and Maryland constitutions and several other newly revised American state constitutions. Along with the *Declaration of Independence*, all thirteen American state constitutions then appeared together at Paris (albeit with "à Philadelphie" on the title page) in 1783, with the (grudging) permission of French ministers, under the title *Constitutions des Treize États-Unis de l'Amérique*. This compilation included the Articles of Confederation and the 1782 Dutch-American Treaty, all laced with notes by Franklin, who made a point of distributing the book widely among influential figures.[66] During the years leading up to the French Revolution, this

key publication served as *the* primary source for American constitutionalism among the French and European intelligentsia and for the revolutionary
French National Assembly.

American revolutionaries, the historiography suggests, did not intend to
"establish a new form of society."[67] Correct for the moderate Enlightenment
American Revolution, this is unquestionably and entirely incorrect for the
democratizing radical American Revolution. As championed by Franklin,
Paine, Young, Cannon, Allen, Peale, and Matlack, and also Jefferson and
Madison, the Revolution certainly *did* mean a "new form" of society and
politics, and was viewed in this light by Europe's key intellects. "Men whom
books of philosophy had secretly inclined to the love of liberty," explained
Condorcet, doubtless thinking of his friends and himself, "became enthusiastic about the freedom of a foreign people, while waiting to be able to turn their
attention to recovering theirs, and joyfully seized the opportunity to acknowledge
sentiments publicly which prudence had forced them to keep silent about."[68]
In his public eulogy following Franklin's death, Condorcet stressed the "noble
aims and profound intentions" of Franklin's political thought, his idea that
individual effort and virtue must combine with good social and political organization based on "reason" to maximize human happiness. *Bonhomme Richard*
would later be recognized as an early joint manifesto of the American and
French revolutions, elevating the 1776 Pennsylvania constitution into the model
of all that is democratic, anti-monarchical, and anti-aristocratic, and against
religious authority's sway over private and public life.[69]

Another notable Franklin propaganda coup was a carefully designed commemorative silver medal issued in 1781–82 to celebrate "la liberté américaine" (see figure 6). Conceived by Franklin and engraved by Augustin Dupré
at the mint for medals at the Paris Louvre, it depicts on one side "Libertas
Americana" vigorous and pure, her hair blowing freely in the wind, holding
a Phrygian liberty cap on her lance point;[70] on the reverse stands the infant
Hercules with each hand strangling a serpent—the British armies defeated
at Saratoga and Yorktown—aided by Minerva with the fleur-de-lis on her
shield (France), nobly fending off the oppressive, raging British Lion. Even
the most formidable infant, implies the medal, needs a powerful backer.

Scorning French *philosophes*, especially of an Epicurean variety, Adams
considered Franklin an intellectual fraud combining affected modesty with
luxuriating in "all the splendor and magnificence of a viceroy," his wine cellar
stocked with "a thousand bottles of the choicest wines." Franklin had a "passion for reputation and fame as strong as you can imagine, and his time and
thoughts are chiefly employed to obtain it, and to set tongues and pens, male
and female, to celebrating him. Painters, statuaries, sculptors, china potters

The two sides of Franklin's propaganda medal "Libertas Americana" by Augustin Dupré (1781). Photo credit: Yale University Art Gallery.

and all are set to work for this end." Although he generously charged Adams no rent for his Paris lodgings and was no intellectual fraud, Adams labeled him a rich-living "charlatan" posing as a philosopher, excessively inclined toward France politically. His style of diplomacy and general demeanor exasperated not only Adams but also other American founding oligarchs disdaining French culture and attitudes in the English manner.[71]

Franklin succeeded admirably in his diplomatic mission despite apparently never realizing his fellow naturalist and friend Edward Bancroft (1744–1821), the American legation's secretary, whom he had recruited as a spy for America in England in 1774, had defected, becoming a spy for Britain passing, inter alia, secret communications about Jones's flotilla to George III's ministers. In September 1778, Congress recalled its other commissioners and appointed Franklin sole minister plenipotentiary at the French court, leaving him alone to pilot America's most crucial foreign relationship and generally America's affairs in Europe. Franklin presided over the Franco-American pact through the next critical four years until the alliance had clinched their resounding, decisive military-naval breakthrough—the trapping of the British army at Yorktown, in October 1781, forcing the surrender of Cornwallis's entire force to Washington, thereby greatly accelerating the war's end.

Before Yorktown, but also after, Franklin's mission in Paris was no simple task. The Revolution jarred against ancien régime sensibilities in numerous ways. A particular irritant was the distaste of foreign envoys in Paris for any sort of dealings with the United States, a new republic born of rebellion against a monarch. In the past, Parisian court protocol assigned aristocratic republics like Venice, Genoa, Berne, and the United Provinces a status in palace ceremonies and etiquette decidedly below even small monarchies and principalities. The United States, still unrecognized by most European states, lacked even the character of being an established aristocratic republic, ensuring lower standing than pertained to any other sovereign power. Envoys of princes and aristocratic republics alike took every opportunity to insinuate America's "inferiority." "I hear Washington ridiculed in Russian," complained Franklin, "and myself in all the jargon of Germany" while enduring the "contempt of the wretched envoys of every paltry principality." These included the Dutch envoy claiming his compatriots rebelled against Spain in 1572 "for religion, not taxes," Venetian diplomats who admitted "Venetians hate anything but a nominal republic" and that there was nothing genuinely republican about their empire, and the papal nuncio cheerfully designating America's minister plenipotentiary a "Quaker."[72]

After Yorktown, Franklin stayed several more years in Paris, hosting the American delegation handling the peace negotiations ending the Revolutionary War with the Treaty of Paris, finalized in the autumn of 1783. Besides friction between Americans and British, the negotiations produced tension between the Americans and French and between the three American commissioners, Jay, Adams, and Franklin, Jay proving even touchier and more suspicious of France than Adams. For months, Adams and his son, John Quincy, figured among Franklin's regular Paris entourage along with Jefferson and Lafayette, back from America "cover'd with laurels." Lafayette's gallantry in Rhode Island and at the New Jersey battle of Brandywine, Washington wrote to Franklin, had "endeared him to America"; his "bravery and good conduct" had "gained the esteem and affection of the whole continent."[73] In Paris too, Franklin was gratified to find, the young hero and his "suite speak very handsomely of the Americans and of the present condition of our affairs."[74] Lafayette's particular friends, Condorcet and Mazzei, like him staunch *Américanistes*, continued to propagandize vigorously for the American Revolution in Europe.

Jefferson got on with Franklin, whom he admired, and with Lafayette, and briefly was a close companion to John Quincy. John Adams, detesting Franklin, Jefferson's Francophilia, and Lafayette (and as anxious as Jay to prevent reversion of Canada to France), sought to minimize the influence of all three on the negotiations and on his son. Although Britain conceded American independence in principle in October 1782, the treaty was finalized only on 3 September 1783. If England did little for expropriated Loyalists or defected black slaves seeking refuge in British-occupied enclaves, and nothing for her Native American allies, the United States, at Jay's and Adams's insistence,

The American Rattlesnake presenting Monsieur his Ally with a Dish of Frogs (refers to the United States negotiating a preliminary peace with Britain, in November 1782, without conferring with France). Courtesy of the John Carter Brown Library at Brown University.

made not the slightest effort to oblige their French allies by seeking concessions to France and refused even to consult seriously with them.[75] The peace was sealed in the Hotel d'York, with Franklin, Adams, and Jay signing for the United States and a solitary British MP for George III.[76]

Not until May 1785 did Franklin receive Congress's instructions to terminate his mission and return home. Outside America, he had become the Revolution's icon to such an unparalleled degree that his was now the only name regularly placed alongside Washington's in accounts, ceremonies, and publicity relating to the American Revolution. "The father of American liberties," as the Irish radical William Duane put it some years later, Franklin "became the general object of respect and love."[77] A French cult figure, his portrait appeared on snuffboxes, medallions, miniatures, Sèvre porcelain, and rings, and as busts in plaster, marble, and bronze.[78] Most Americans, however, remained barely aware of his towering international reputation; and those who knew of it were not necessarily enthusiastic about its implications for the Revolution's transatlantic profile. Eulogized by republican-minded French *philosophes* and radical democrats in Britain, Holland, Germany, and Italy, Franklin was distinctly less esteemed by the privileged political elite of his own country. He represented an Enlightenment philosophy and irreligious democratic tendency distasteful to America's landowning gentry and top merchants, a radical standpoint firmly entrenched only in Pennsylvania where, for the moment, the old oligarchy were unseated and in Vermont, which possessed a constitution sharply contrasting with the "aristocratic" constitutions of New York State and Massachusetts, and resembling Pennsylvania's in its democratic structure in terms of suffrage and election of officials.[79]

The Icon Shelved

Back in Philadelphia, in 1785, Franklin was elected to the Pennsylvania legislature's executive council and subsequently became its "president." He divided his time between politics and reinvigorating the American Philosophical Society of which he had long been president, a body sunk into "a very languishing state" since 1776,[80] presiding over debates and contributing handsomely to the cost of building Philosophical Hall, the society's future headquarters. It was unclear, though, what exactly Franklin did symbolize. In March 1787, the Pennsylvania Assembly elected him to the state's delegation attending the national convention meeting in Philadelphia to revise the republic's Articles of Confederation and decide on the Federal Constitution. Many members of the governing elites wanted to balance the thirteen legislatures (Vermont was not yet included) with greater cohesion and authority at the center. Political theory was the order of the day. Several Founders, Franklin prominent among them, specially applied themselves to studying political ideas in preparation for the revision. He convened a "Society for Political Enquiries," meeting weekly in his large library, including Rush, still a leading figure in Philadelphia's intellectual life if now openly opposed to the 1776 Pennsylvania constitution, and Gouverneur Morris, who had always detested it.[81]

Both the national and state constitutional debates converged on Philadelphia, but Franklin was less involved in debating the new federal arrangements than the local Pennsylvania constitution. With the war over, pressure to exclude former Loyalists from politics lessened while many wartime temporary activists withdrew. By the late 1780s, the battle between opponents and defenders of the 1776 democratic constitution—with the Quakers aligning with the former—tilted increasingly against the "constitutionalists," as the radicals were known.[82] Outside Pennsylvania, antipathy to the Pennsylvania constitution was especially fomented by the Federalist faction urging stronger central government for the Union as a whole. Adams, Jay, Hamilton, and Morris, like

Rush, cited Pennsylvania as illustrative of the disunity and strife allegedly resulting from abandoning the "aristocratic" format of senates and governors uniformly present in the other states, deemed indispensable by Adams and Morris. For his part, Franklin persisted in rejecting bicameralism on principle, deeming it a pernicious vestige of the aristocratic British past. Senates, or upper houses based on social privilege and property qualifications, were admired by conservatives, he perceived, chiefly as a device for entrenching oligarchy and averting capture of American society and politics by the democratic tendency. The drive for an upper house in Pennsylvania Franklin called a "disposition among some of our people to commence an aristocracy, by giving the rich a predominancy in government, a choice peculiar to themselves in one half of the legislature."[83] Like Turgot, Condorcet, and his *philosophe* friends, he disparaged the institution of state governors, indeed single-person executives generally, as an undesirable remnant of the toppled monarchical system.[84] "Who is to watch and control" this one-man executive? he demanded, "and by what means is he to be controuled? Would not those means, however constructed, cause the 'same inconveniences of expence, delay, obstruction of good intentions, etc., which are objected to the present Executive?' "[85]

However powerless to stem the conservative tide, Franklin in his last years firmly adhered to his radical anti-oligarchic stance. In 1789–90, the Pennsylvania elites, Anglicans, and Quakers, renewing their drive to overthrow the 1776 constitution, finally regained control of the assembly. With "anti-constitutionalists" now the majority in their legislature, there was little Franklin and his allies could do to prevent replacement of the 1776 constitution with a revised framework introducing bicameralism, informal aristocracy, and a state governor.[86] In December 1790, fourteen years after the radical coup of 1776, Pennsylvania finally discarded its one-chamber democratic format and aligned with the rest—though compared with the others, Pennsylvania still remained exceptionally liberal as regards voting rights, property and religious qualifications, and access to the state senate.

Franklin died on 17 April 1790. In America, reaction beyond Philadelphia was curiously muted. If Jefferson extolled Franklin's "wisdom" and contribution to the "establishment of our own freedom," celebrating the "memory of our great and dear friend, whom time will be making greater while it is sponging us from its records," and remarking in a letter to William Smith that "philosophy has to deplore one of its principal luminaries extinguished," other American leaders took a decidedly less flattering view.[87] Although, on 22 April, the House of Representatives adopted a motion of tribute proposed by Madison, the federal Senate pointedly declined to follow suit. Adams, now chairman of the Senate, did *not* think it appropriate to honor Franklin with special national recognition and was backed by an array of senators disliking Franklin's libertarian attitudes and (since July 1789) the French Revolution's democratic proclivities. Franklin's name had become inextricably linked to radical ideas, democracy, anti-aristocracy, and black emancipation in France *and* the United States. Since he championed unicameralism and a subordinate, consultative rather than a one-man executive,[88] Adams, Jay, Hamilton, and other Federalist adversaries of democratic revolutionary values rightly associated Franklin's political legacy with the French republican tendency they loathed. As Condorcet, Brissot, and the other French commentators continued criticizing the American state constitutions for compromising popular sovereignty and secularism, and blocking democracy, it was logical to connect Franklin to the growing *philosophique* assault on Montesquieu, gentry republicanism, privilege, religious tests for officeholders, and the British model.

On learning of Franklin's death, the French National Assembly declared three days of public mourning. The only two busts presiding over the National Assembly's deliberations (until the bust of Rousseau by the sculptor Jean-Antoine Houdon [1746–1828] was added shortly after Franklin's death) were those of Washington and Franklin. They had become the visual dual embodiment of America's Revolution in France and all Europe. France, though, since 1789, was effectively the sole other country thus far sharing America's republican constitutional principles in both their "moderate" and radical guises. On 11 January 1790, Belgium's "Congress" of supposedly sovereign "states" issued their declaration of independence from the Austrian Crown, officially establishing what they called, in imitation of the United States, the "United States of Belgium" albeit with a conspicuously weak executive authority whose powers were limited to defending the country and issuing money. The new "United States" (on documents styled the États-Belgiques Unies or, alternatively, Verenigde Nederlandsche Staten) consisted of eight supposedly sovereign "states" (without Liège): Brabant, Flanders, Luxemburg, Namur, Hainault, Mechelen, Guelders, and Limburg. These now came together to form a federal union broadly on the American pattern, indeed became the world's first federal republic explicitly constituted on the American model.[89]

But while the American parallels were striking, the Belgian revolution of 1789–90 reflected only the "moderate" dimension of the American Revolution. Since 1789, Belgian pamphlets and papers, recognizing his success in rousing local sentiment against the Austrians, had taken to styling Hendrik van der Noot (1731–1827), leader of their revolution against Emperor Joseph II, alternatively as the Belgian "George Washington" and "le Franklin des Pays-Bas." The latter epithet seemed especially misleading as Van der Noot was a Brussels lawyer commissioned by the States of Brabant to formulate legal objections to Joseph's enlightened reforms, called for a revolution that was purely aristocratic and "moderate" in character, and was unbendingly Catholic and explicitly opposed to democratic and republican tendencies. The German enlightener Georg Forster (1754–94), who was in Brussels when Van der Noot's adherents had captured the city late in 1789, was among those scandalized by this labeling of a staunchly conservative revolutionary propagandist a second "Franklin." Public celebration of the Belgian "Franklin" certainly played a role in the 1789–90 Belgian upheaval but remained an epithet that, in radical eyes, Van der Noot in no way deserved.[90]

By contrast, in Grimm's *Correspondance Littéraire*, as elsewhere, Franklin was proclaimed a key figure in the advance of the Rights of Man.[91] In June and July 1790, his demise was marked in Paris with a series of commemorative celebrations further highlighting his centrality in the shared legacy of the French and American revolutions, among them a famous banquet at the Café Procope. Various cafés and clubs dedicated hecatombs to Franklin's memory, featuring funerary busts adorned with revolutionary epitaphs. An unprecedented series of public orations eulogizing Franklin impressed on the public his importance for France, Belgium, and the wider world, as well as America. Mirabeau, in his speech in the National Assembly on 11 June, styled Franklin the "genius" who "emancipated America and poured torrents of Enlightenment on Europe," helping inspire mankind's progress in both hemispheres. To Mirabeau, Franklin was the very symbol of the idea that it is "philosophy" and not religion, royalty, or aristocracy that improves the world and enhances the lives of men. For centuries, European governments had publicly mourned stuffed-up aristocrats and courtiers who were not at all great except in florid funerary orations. Instead of the "hypocritical mourning" laid on by royal courts, nations should publicly mourn only their true "benefactors," "les héros de l'humanité," personages like Franklin. Belgians and others might not mourn him as they should, but at least France, "eclairée et libre" (enlightened and free), would demonstrate to the world her sense of loss and show the entire world that she remembers one of the greatest men "qui aient jamais servi la philosophie et la liberté" (who have ever served philosophy and liberty).[92]

Condorcet's oration at a public session of the Académie des Sciences in Paris declared the 1776 Pennsylvania constitution, distinguished "from most of the others by a greater equality, and from all, by entrusting the legislative power to a single chamber of representatives," to be "in part his work": "Mr. Franklin's opinion alone determined this last provision."[93] The Abbé Claude Fauchet (1744–93), among the Revolution's finest orators, delivered his eulogy of Franklin before the Paris city council and prominent National Assembly deputies, among them Mirabeau, Sieyès, and "Dr. Guillotin."[94] He hailed Franklin as a benefactor of the human race "claimed by two worlds," one of those enlighteners who, in recent decades, had transformed mankind for the better. A passionate democrat, Fauchet too derided the "ridiculous etiquette" of monarchical courts that for centuries considered only royal deaths and the demise of high-born aristocratic personages worthy of ceremonies of public mourning.[95] Great public commemorations celebrating the true benefactors of humanity would henceforth characterize the new revolutionary era. In the future, enlightened societies would reserve for major public homage exclusively "les héros de l'humanité," genuine benefactors of the human race "like Franklin."[96]

The publicly projected revolutionary "Franklin" trumpeted in Paris, contrasting with that projected in conservative Brussels, conveyed the message that the democratic republican tendency—destined to pervade the French Revolution until June 1793—was the fruit of "philosophy" and Enlightenment and constituted a powerful transatlantic impulse. Franklin, a freethinker more discreet than Voltaire, had sufficiently avoided antagonizing the devout to remain acceptable to religious proponents of the democratic republican and egalitarian Revolution like Fauchet, while simultaneously endearing himself to Condorcet and the irreligious.[97] Included in the dictionary of famous atheists, published by the materialist *philosophe* Sylvain Maréchal and the unbelieving astronomer Jerôme Lalande in 1800, the editors proclaimed him "Pythagoras of the New World" and (after Washington) second Founder of American liberty.[98]

The speeches exalted Franklin not as a statesman or "genius" but specifically as a "philosophe," whose ideas and insights helped prepare both the American and French revolutions. The eulogy delivered at the "Club of 1789" by La Rochefoucauld, now a leading National Assembly deputy (and supporter of the Revolution until August 1792), emphasized Franklin's opposition to Montesquieu, to separation of powers and "mixed government"—a construct, in his view, unfortunately emulated by all the American states except Pennsylvania. It was Franklin's insistence on a single-chamber legislature controlling judiciary and executive, removing checks and balances, that had established a new, more coherent constitutional framework that the French National Assembly had then accepted and "had now become the basis of the French [1791] Constitution." Franklin he pronounced the "first to dare to put this idea into practice; the respect Pennsylvanians have for him made them accept it." Franklin had demonstrated great courage in this regard as practically all political writers of the age—excepting only Turgot, Condorcet, and La Rochefoucauld, in France, and Price in England—wholly disagreed with him about this.[99] The Society of 1789 marked Franklin's demise by installing a famous bust of him in their meeting hall.

Through late 1790 and early 1791, the United States Congress received several representations from the French National Assembly and other bodies honoring the "great Benjamin Franklin," styling him the chief link between the French and American revolutions. Congress was understandably disconcerted by this and decided not to respond. The Franklin cult, like the wider *philosophique* message pervading the Société de 1789, the Cercle social, and the Cordeliers Club leadership, inevitably displeased everyone opposing democratic, egalitarian, and emancipatory principles, hence most of the American political elite.[100] The testy pro-democrat and pro-Franklin Pennsylvania senator William Maclay (1737–1804)—who uniquely kept a diary of the Senate's proceedings—noted that the American Senate reacted with undisguised "coolness and apathy," a "coldness that was truly amazing." He wondered what the effect in France would be. "I cannot help painting to myself the disappointment that awaits the French Patriots, while their warm fancies are figuring the raptures that we will be thrown into on the receipt of their letter, and the information of the honours which they have bestowed on our countryman, and anticipating the complimentary echoes of our answers, when we, cold as clay, care not a fig about them [the French National Assembly], Franklin or freedom. Well we deserve—what do we deserve? To be d——d!"[101] The effect was to drive a wedge not between the French and American revolutions as such but rather between the two sets of opposed radical and moderate Enlightenment ideological blocs either side of the Atlantic.

Unlike the United States Senate, the American Philosophical Society could hardly avoid putting on a public commemoration honoring its founder. However, like Congress, its members found themselves divided into pro- and anti-democratic (and pro-and anti-Franklin) factions, generating a clash of principles and ensuing deadlock over who should deliver the society's eulogium. It eventually became a choice between Rittenhouse, designated Franklin's successor as president who esteemed his legacy highly, and the Anglican oligarchy's spokesman, William Smith, now restored to prominence. Smith could be relied on to minimize Franklin's democratic significance and help manipulate his memory into a tool of conservative attitudes. The imbroglio lasted practically a year until the democrats were overruled and Philadelphia's "Belgians" secured Smith to pronounce. In his subsequently much-discussed oration, he scrupulously avoided praising or even mentioning Franklin's political propensities or irreligion. "People say much of it," reported Senator Maclay, who was present: "I thought little of it. It was trite and trifling." Smith even contrived to pronounce Franklin a "friend of Revelation" while not believing, according to his own daughter, one-tenth of his eulogy of "Old Ben Lightning Rod." Smith, jotted Maclay in his Senate diary, "certainly is a vile character."[102]

Restrained acclaiming of Franklin's achievements in America (and Belgium) clashed with the French revolutionaries' "Franklin cult," reflecting oligarchic America's antipathy to the democratic upsurge of the American Revolution's early years (1774–76). Franklin's legacy as a beacon of Enlightenment and propagator of the radical tendency ever eager to keep religion out of public life contrasts also with his curious image in American culture today. "What we most remember about Franklin," comments one historian, and the image that "will continue to dominate American culture" in the future, "for as long as it is seen as a land of opportunity," is the "symbolic Franklin of the bumptious capitalism of the early republic—the man who personifies the American dream," an "inspiration to countless young men eager to make it in the world of business."[103] Ironically, honoring Franklin "for his success" in business, and supposedly voicing the typical values of his countrymen, eventually did dominate his legacy.[104]

In reality, what is far more to the point is that Franklin, though not usually classed as a radical,[105] had by 1775 become a leading light of the "Radical Enlightenment." His hopes for black emancipation, which became well-known in Britain and France as well as America, and for the French revolution, expressed toward the end of his long life in a letter to David Hartley dated Philadelphia, 4 December 1789, exactly captures the perspective of radical thought: "the Convulsions in France," he granted, "are attended with some disagreeable circumstances; but if by the struggle she obtains and secures for the nation its future liberty, and a good constitution, a few years' enjoyment of those blessings will amply repair all the damages their acquisition may have occasioned. God grant, that not only the love of liberty, but a thorough knowledge of the Rights of Man, may pervade all the nations of the earth, so that a philosopher may set his foot anywhere on its surface, and say, 'This is my country.'"[106]

Franklin and Jefferson, it has been justly noted, were "by far the best writers" of the Revolution: this was partly a question of style but also of message,[107] and Franklin's authentic admirers kept alive the conception of the American Revolution as a post-1783 continuing commitment. Among them was Emerson, who "loved and celebrated America to the extent that he saw it carrying out" its special role "in the ever unfolding world-historical realization of the values of human freedom and rationality." "If there is any period one would desire to be born in," exclaims Emerson in "The American Scholar," originally delivered as a speech in Cambridge, Massachusetts, in August 1837, "is it not the age of Revolution; when the old and new stand side by side, and admit of being compared; when the energies of all men are searched by fear and by hope; when the historic glories of the old, can be compensated by the rich possibilities of the new era? This time, like all times, is a very good one, if we but knew what to do with it. "[108]

Emerson was then (in contrast to his post-1848 view) reasonably optimistic that America would perform the role in the world that he envisaged for it: "I read with joy some of the auspicious signs of the coming days, as they glimmer already through poetry and art, through philosophy and science, through church and state." He gazed back on Franklin and his allies as the makers of a revolution so grand that "it bears the palm away from Greek and Roman achievement." For those conceiving the American Revolution as a world event of surpassing significance, Franklin stood at the head of the group that had most powerfully articulated and promoted the Revolution's core meaning.[109]

CHAPTER 6

Black Emancipation: Confronting Slavery in the New Republic

The Revolution and the Blacks

If Americans were fighting for "freedom," sneered one pro-British Dutch pamphleteer, why do they not set free their black slaves? Why do they participate themselves in that accursed trade in human beings? Or do Africa's ill-fated inhabitants transported against their will to American shores possess no natural rights as white men do? Does not their reluctance to liberate them prove, in the plainest fashion, the "vile hypocrisy and most crafty duplicity of the Americans"?[1] Black slavery was universally recognized as the prime contradiction of the American Revolution and defect of the new republic. Far more numerous in the nascent republic than Native Americans, who numbered at most 150,000, the nearly half a million slaves in the thirteen United States of 1775, virtually 20 percent of the republic's population, rose to around 700,000 by the 1790s.[2] The blatant contradiction involved in retaining slavery while declaring as "self-evident" that "all men are created equal, that they are endowed by their Creator with certain unalienable Rights, that among these are Life, Liberty, and the pursuit of Happiness," impressed itself forcefully on friend and foe alike, a bitter irony in no way lost on the roughly 430,000 blacks in the South (the vast majority slaves), forming nearly 40 percent of the population there, and roughly 50,000 more, slaves and freemen, in the North.[3] In the Middle Colonies, blacks, free and enslaved, constituted around 6 percent of the population.

Yet if this "vile hypocrisy" was widely sneered at by the Revolution's opponents in Europe, it would be wrong to suppose Europeans generally believed in black equality or favored black emancipation. Neither should we assume "moderate enlighteners" in general did. How strange and indefensible, protested John Millar (1735–1801), that those declaiming loudest about "liberty" as the birthright of everyone in America, as an "inalienable" human property, should not scruple to enslave "a great mass" of their fellow humans as property devoid of practically all rights.[4] Millar, though Scottish, opposed the conservative political stance of Hume, Smith, and Ferguson, indeed unlike the rest of the Scottish Enlightenment was a radical enlightener against whose politically subversive views, Hume, in December 1775, warned a nephew.[5] An ardent enthusiast for universal and equal human rights, he fully embraced the democratic side of the American revolutionary coin—but only because of his own prior radical posture. His criticism of the Founding Fathers for failing to abolish slavery was an integral part of a much wider critique of political and social conditions at the time. Loudly condemning the "corrupt" features of Britain's monarchy and Constitution, Millar in addition supported Irish rebellion against that country's aristocratic "Ascendancy" and also advocated women's rights. It was by the same radical standards of universal human rights, not on any traditional notion, that he championed the American Revolution and yet simultaneously denounced the United States for retaining slavery.

Nothing more forcefully underlined the inner contradiction permeating the American Revolution than the congressional proceedings in July 1776 when Jefferson's draft clause denouncing the British Crown for introducing black slavery into America as "a cruel war against human nature itself" was deleted from the final version of the *Declaration of Independence*.[6] A gaping blemish in principle, it was an obstacle to building the republic on sound principles of which Jefferson and Madison were painfully aware. Jefferson long vacillated over this matter, while Madison, in his contributions to *The Federalist*, tentatively defended the unavoidable need for the uncomfortable compromises the United States Constitution, of which he was one of the prime framers, conceded to the Southern slave states.[7]

Inevitably, the American Revolution's core values, given their content and scope, were to some extent bound to encourage, reinforce, and broaden the movement to weaken and abolish slavery in the Americas and the rest of the European colonial world; and while the resulting slow-moving process remained marginal in terms of its overall effect, this was soon widely perceptible on both the intellectual and social levels. The arduous incipient shift toward emancipation included a precarious trend, hampered on every side, toward revolutionary self-emancipation by insurgent blacks, rendering black rebellion an inherent component of the revolutionary process itself.[8] Prior to 1775, only a small fraction, under 5 percent of the black population in the Thirteen Colonies, consisted of free blacks; during the revolutionary upheaval, which offered several paths whereby blacks could aspire to win their freedom, this initially low percentage rose somewhat to over 8 percent of the black total.[9]

Even before the Revolution began, those chiefly resisting British demands in the colonies in the name of liberty and rights were conspicuously silent on the subject of slavery. At the war's outset, Congress issued a regulation, dated 12 November 1775, that all blacks, freemen or slaves, were ineligible to serve in the revolutionary army—categorical exclusion of black men from the fight for freedom. But as the war widened, Congress could hardly afford to see black units recruited on the British side alone, with no blacks in the Patriot army. Although in early 1776 both Washington and Congress reaffirmed their preference for not enlisting black soldiers, by late 1776 the position had changed. Dunmore's "diabolical schemes" offering freedom to slaves joining the British troops in Virginia had scared Washington and congressional leaders sufficiently for them to cancel their initial general prohibition, prompting the northern and Middle Colonies especially to reconsider the issue of black enlistment.[10] Blacks began serving attached to black units in the revolutionary forces, albeit mainly in New England regiments and those of Pennsylvania.[11]

In 1778, the Massachusetts and Rhode Island legislatures, chronically short of soldiers, began more publicly and systematically authorizing black recruitment. Offering immediate freedom to slaves enrolling, they set up standing committees to supervise and effect payment of compensation to slave owners. Black troops—along with some Native Americans—subsequently played a prominent part, fighting both British and Hessians, in the battle ending the fight for Rhode Island and siege of Newport on 29 August 1778. When the Rhode Island black regiments were disbanded at the end of the war in 1783, the blacks, like many of the white soldiers, never obtained most of the pay due to them and were cheated of the promise of land. But at least all were freed. Only in the 1820s did Rhode Island make some attempt to provide land and pensions for surviving veterans of its black units. Connecticut, by contrast, did not even emancipate all the blacks enlisted into its regiments.[12]

From 1779, the brunt of the Revolutionary War shifted to the South, where chronic shortage of poor whites for the militias was aggravated by a widely commented on, generalized fear among whites of leaving home amid the heightened risk of black insurgency. While Washington and other Virginian leaders vacillated, Congress, after much debate, issued directives for the raising of Southern black units, partly to assist in fighting the British but also to "lessen the danger from revolts and desertions, by detaching the most vigorous and enterprising from among the Negroes." Owners of able-bodied slaves enlisting were to receive a fixed rate of compensation determined by Congress, in United States dollars. For Congress, this was a cheap way to raise troops as there was no immediate proposal to pay enlisted black soldiers on a regular basis. At the war's end, they obtained only confirmation of their freedom plus fifty dollars each. In North Carolina, Georgia, and Virginia, manumission was intended for strictly limited numbers, chiefly as a means of forestalling a wider black movement toward resistance and emancipation, while in South Carolina the legislature refused to comply altogether.[13]

Fear of mass slave revolt in the South where, by 1790, blacks formed well over a third as compared to slightly under 20 percent of the Thirteen Colonies' population as a whole[14] prompted the Southern gentry to employ every conceivable argument to get Congress to prioritize military operations in New England and the Middle Colonies rather than the South so as to deflect the conflict as far as possible away from their own racially fraught region. Unsurprisingly, despite Dunmore's offer of freedom in Virginia—and later in the Carolinas and Georgia—being restricted to slaves of known Patriots, substantial numbers of blacks, especially but not only in the South, (eventually) sided with Britain rather than the United States. The British endeavored to avoid alienating white Loyalists.[15] But many blacks, whatever their owners' sympathies, simply took advantage of the general turmoil to escape their shackles. While New York City was in British hands, from 1776, numerous escaped slaves sought refuge there, rendering New York for the first time a substantial center of free black settlement. When Charleston fell to the British in May 1780 after a six-week siege, thousands of blacks flocked to the city. Where only a few hundred black slave runaways joined Dunmore in 1775–76, when Cornwallis invaded Virginia during the spring of 1781 over 4,500 black insurgents came over to the British troops and Hessians, including no less than twenty-three from Jefferson's estates alone and a number of Washington's slaves.[16] During the long and arduous siege of Yorktown, in the summer and autumn of 1781, numerous blacks, wounded, diseased, or hungry, expired in miserable conditions.[17]

None of this, though, inhibited the British Crown, during the preliminary negotiations preceding the final peace with the United States, provisionally signed at Fontainebleau in November 1782, from consenting to deliver up to their "masters" those black men and women who had joined them during the conflict, promising to depart without "carrying away any negroes or other property of the American inhabitants." On evacuating the South in 1783, British commanders were instructed to take with them only such blacks who had received explicit promises of freedom, leaving behind the majority of the ten thousand or so fugitives from Patriot plantations or who had been sequestered by the British. Such was the outrage this betrayal provoked among the refugee black population that the departing army found themselves obliged to take with them a considerable portion of the runaways and sequestered slaves. On evacuating Savannah, Georgia, in July 1783, the British took around three thousand black men, women, and children with them, slaves of Loyalists mostly but also runaways and rebels. On evacuating Charleston in December 1783, the British departed with around five thousand former black slaves, many transferring to Nova Scotia.[18]

From around 1780, for the first time, and directly linked to the Revolution, the antislavery movement in the nascent United States gained momentum as a powerful social impulse and organized emancipatory political force. It was at this point that a planned, sustained antislavery strategy, commencing in Pennsylvania, began to accost the state legislatures. The first enactment for the abolition of slavery, that of Pennsylvania passed on 1 March 1780, proved considerably more gradual, due to opposition, than its principal authors—Matlack, Bryan, Paine, and Benezet—desired.[19] A key abolitionist among Philadelphia's French community, Franklin's Quaker friend Anthony Benezet (1713–84) was the originator both of abolitionism as an organized movement in Pennsylvania and of supported schools for the children of freed blacks. Ardent for black emancipation and integration into society, in 1772 Benezet was among the relatively few in America who immediately seized on the second paragraph of the *Declaration of Independence* (and the first article of the Virginia *Declaration of Rights*) to underline in print the radical understanding of basic rights and the enormity of the contradiction in thus professing basic human rights and yet retaining slavery.[20] Franklin, only recently questioning the legitimacy of black slavery himself, agreed with him and was soon to set up the first American antislavery society (of which Paine, too, was a founding member). Franklin urged Benezet to join them in linking the abolition campaign to the Revolution;[21] Benezet, though, as a Quaker, discerned no intrinsic link between black emancipation and renouncing monarchical and aristocratic government. He preferred to remain neutral.

In March 1780, for the first time in history, a black slavery abolition decree issued from a Western legislature—powered by a broad cultural and intellectual movement generated by pamphlets and sections of the Northern press fiercely stigmatizing slavery and enslavement, and actively propagating the idea of universal human rights. Yet one should not to overstate its significance. A majority of Patriots still preferred to prolong rather than resolve the Revolution's great contradiction. Even Paine was noticeably more reticent in public (and private) on the subject of abolition throughout the revolutionary era than one might guess from his general stance. If the American antislavery movement of the 1820s and 1830s "did not cite Paine as one of its forebears," this was not just, as has been noted, because religious abolitionists abominated Paine's irreligion but also because he had remarkably little to say on the subject.[22] The fact is that abolitionism, as Rush noted three decades later, was generally unpopular with white Americans during the Revolution.[23] Abolitionism was confined to a small, highly motivated fringe—an alliance of a few radicals, like Matlack, with a few religious dissenters. Meanwhile, if the personal and general goal of the black rebels was to fight for emancipation and their freedom, their general understanding of the slavery issue, except for a small minority, remained stunted by lack of education, inability to read, and most blacks' dogged adherence to monarchism and piety.

During the 1780s and 1790s, self-emancipation and the Revolution together freed only a modest fraction. Yet, despite the obstacles, solid progress was eventually achieved. A few whites underwent a change of heart. The radicals were joined by a few Northern "aristocrats"—notably Gouverneur Morris[24]—and by more Christian dissenters. In the 1780s, a substantial fringe of Baptists, Methodists, and other Protestants vigorously embraced the cause of abolition, whereas for the most part they had done nothing comparable previously.[25] Even if most American whites remained unsympathetic, humanity's "great project" of freeing the blacks from slavery was now at last underway, affirmed the German journalist and Diderot disciple Wilhelm Ludwig Wekhrlin (1739–92) at Nuremberg, in 1784, thanks to the American Revolution.[26] While pro-British pamphleteers continued emphasizing American "hypocrisy," Methodist, Quaker, and other American religious leaders began pressing hard for abolition on Christian grounds.

It would, however, be misleading to consider the "Christian" and radical Enlightenment abolitionist movements as broadly parallel or equivalent in their aims. If just one of several impulses generating the transatlantic abolitionist movement on both sides of the Atlantic more broadly, the *philosophique* summons for black emancipation of the 1780s diverged from, and went beyond, the dissenting initiative in several ways besides in being secular and lacking a theological basis. Condorcet, whose views on black emancipation evolved during the early stages of the American Revolution, certainly no later than 1777,[27] wrote his most far-reaching assault on slavery and oppression of the blacks in 1781 (reprinted in 1788), encasing his analysis within a much wider critique of contemporary values, moral standards, and social practice, and harsh condemnation of colonial planter society, than did Christian abolitionists. Slavery to him was part of a generally corrupt social and moral system which, along with its other oppressive practices, laws, and institutions, deliberately incited strife and instigated local wars in Africa to promote European mercantile interests. "Politically regulated society can have no other goal than maintenance of the rights of those who make up society. Hence every law contrary to the right of a citizen or outsider is unjust, a veritable crime, authorizing violent resistance."[28] According to the *philosophique* cult forged by Diderot, d'Holbach, Helvétius, and the *Histoire philosophique*, universal human rights override every commercial consideration and every other value system.

Distinct from the dissenting movement for black emancipation,[29] the radical strategy pivoted on the idea that "natural morality" and universal natural right apply everywhere and to all men, that the "right of men" is inviolable and universal, rooted in the inherent equality of all, so that even wholly voluntary slavery is unjustifiable.[30] Accordingly, the idea that black men are "our equals" in a moral, social, intellectual, and political sense was a principle embraced during the mid-1780s only by "Radical Enlightenment" writers like Condorcet, Raynal, Diderot, Helvétius, Pechméja, and Brissot.[31] "You want to know why there are no black authors," wrote Brissot in 1786, "or even any enlightened black men? What made you what you are?" Education, circumstances; have either the one or the other ever favored the blacks? Rendered miserable by African despotism, enslaved in the Americas, "in Europe, they are condemned by public opinion, everywhere proscribed, like the Jews; in a word, they are everywhere in an abject state."[32] A black, Jew, Turk, or Indian, held Brissot, can be raised up and converted into a "républicain éclairé" (enlightened republican) with no more or less difficulty by wise government and education than can a thoroughly ignorant, credulous, and prejudiced white.[33] This was the authentic radical stance. From this perspective, widely promoted by the huge transatlantic impact of the *Histoire philosophique*, eradicating black slavery must and could only be achieved by society itself, by the legislative power of the state, in a comprehensive, revolutionary fashion.

According to the radicals, slavery needed to be eradicated fully and compulsorily without compensating slave owners, and in the most comprehensive fashion, using public resources and funds to assist, educate, and support the freed blacks.[34] At a key strategic meeting at the house of the duke de La Rochefoucauld in Paris in June 1789, shortly before the fall of the Bastille, Condorcet, Mirabeau, Lafayette, and the Abbé Grégoire unanimously concurred that abolition should be brought about in carefully prepared and publicized stages. Emancipation was understood as a political and educational as much as a legal transformation. The free blacks and mulattoes of the French Caribbean and, eventually, all blacks under the French flag "should be assimilated with the whites as regards political and civil rights," the program actually implemented by the Brissotins three years later.[35]

The radical critique also diverged from other abolitionist movements, first tentatively and after 1780 more insistently, in affirming the potential equality of black men in intelligence, capacities, and moral standards. During the 1770s there was still some lingering uncertainty and hesitation in advanced circles about the reality of black equality in terms of intelligence and abilities. "The Negroes who are free," explained Franklin, answering a query from Condorcet in March 1774, "live among the white people, but are generally improvident and poor. I think that they are not deficient in natural understanding, but they have not the advantage of education. They make good musicians."[36] Jefferson and some other radicals continued to harbor doubts, especially privately, as to whether black capacities were really equivalent to those of whites. But publicly, in a striking parallel to Dohm's dismissal of commonly alleged Jewish "defects" and "vices" in Europe as essentially the outcome of "Christian" oppression in his 1781 text on Jewish emancipation in Germany, Enlightenment philosophical republicans viewed the ignorance, indolence, monarchism, and other widely deplored "deficiencies" of blacks essentially as culturally, socially, and institutionally induced. Their "vices" were fomented, like the faults of their oppressors, the white planters' moral and social failings, by the wider structural flaws of society, monarchy, and religion.[37] In aptitude, argued Brissot, Condorcet, and other radicals, whether for education, the arts, or business, blacks were actually no different from whites. On this basis, Brissot redoubled his endeavors not just to promote abolition of slavery but to more comprehensively emancipate the blacks through education and helping find appropriate work.[38]

"We perceive already the good effects of the abolition of Negro slavery in Pennsylvania," Rush assured Price in October 1785: the "slaves who have been emancipated among us are in general more industrious and orderly than the lowest class of white people. A school has been set on foot for their children by the Quakers in this city; and we have the pleasure of seeing them improve in religion and morals under their instructions, as well as in English literature."[39] After Benezet had founded the first school for blacks in Philadelphia in 1770, several more appeared both there and in New York. What he witnessed in Philadelphia schools and shops permanently persuaded Brissot that the "mental capacity of Negroes is equal to any task, and that all they need is education and freedom."[40] "If then, Negroes here [in Philadelphia] are limited to the small retail trade, let us not attribute it to lack of ability but rather to the prejudice of the whites, who put obstacles in their way."

"This discrimination," observed Brissot, "is apparent everywhere. For instance, Negro children are admitted to the public schools, but cannot cross the threshold of a college."[41]

Abolition in the North (1780–1848)

At the close of his long and fruitful life, Franklin's final political intervention helped elevate his legacy and the Revolution's international significance—as well as his standing as its foremost transatlantic spokesman. Propagating ideas of emancipation, equality, secularism, free thought, and democracy, and rejecting "mixed government" doctrine, Franklin continued projecting the Revolution as a program of social and moral amelioration.[42] Until the 1770s, he had given relatively little time and thought to the slavery question. It was his enlightened Quaker friend Anthony Benezet's influence, and discussion with Condorcet and the Paris radical *philosophes*, that prodded him further. In 1787, he became president of the Pennsylvania-based "Society for Promoting the Abolition of Slavery and the Relief of Negroes Unlawfully held in Bondage," which denounced black slavery as "an atrocious debasement of human nature" and publicly proclaimed the need for a more concerted political effort to achieve the equality of rights spelled out in the *Declaration of Independence*.[43] In November 1789, the society issued "An Address to the Public" from Philadelphia under Franklin's signature, setting out its scheme for advancing abolition and accelerating the integration of freed blacks into society, a plan subsequently published by Brissot and the Amis des Noirs in the pro-Revolution newspapers in Paris. Franklin, Paine, Rush, Rittenhouse, and other radical enlighteners of the society agreed that former slaves needed continued assistance to integrate into society as free men.

Continued imposed post-Independence social subordination of blacks in the North resulted not just from excessively staged abolition but other factors too. Of itself, legal emancipation proved no solution to the social and economic problems slavery had created. "The galling chains that bind his body, do also fetter [the slave's] intellectual faculties, and impair the social affections of his heart," the 1789 address asserted, so that successful social integration required education and training to "qualify those who have been restored to freedom, for the exercise and enjoyment of civil liberty, to promote in them the habits of industry, to furnish them with employments suited to their age, sex, talents and other circumstances, and to procure their children an education calculated for their future station in life." This "we conceive will essentially promote the public good, and the happiness of these our hitherto too much neglected fellow creatures."[44] The last public document Franklin signed, in February 1790, two months before his death, was the Pennsylvania Abolition Society's renewed petition to Congress for the prompt outright abolition of slavery in America.[45] A fitting conclusion to an extraordinary career, it achieved little beyond being read out in the Senate, by Adams with "rather a sneer." Backed by a few republican senators like the Pennsylvania Scots democrat Maclay, it provoked angry reactions from most Southern congressmen and several personal attacks by senators on Franklin, confirming the deep divisions over Franklin as well as slavery.[46]

Hence, if Quakers and dissenters spearheaded American and British abolitionism, the campaign to emancipate the world's blacks in a more comprehensive sense, in America, Britain, and France alike, claimed Condorcet in 1781, was led by (radical) *philosophes*.[47] It was not religion but rather "philosophy" that played the primary role and afforded the real impetus.[48] This was the view also of Diderot's German disciple Wekhrlin, who in 1788 rejoiced that the "eyes of the Quakers" had been opened to reveal that slavery could not be reconciled with "the principles of equality, gentleness and humanity which they profess," and joined Condorcet and Brissot in lauding the Quakers for initiating a process philosophical radicals aspired to help extend throughout the world, but at the same time reminded readers that in this immense struggle to emancipate the black peoples, all the churches—except the Quakers and a few other dissenters—had hitherto persisted in the reprehensible and obnoxious policy of acquiescence in slavery, the slave trade, and worldwide oppression of the blacks. "Christianity" had generally accepted and endorsed slavery for millennia and mostly still did. Churches, Protestant and Catholic alike, instead of furthering emancipation, in the main actively hampered the process, preaching acceptance and submission on the basis that it is Christian souls, not bodies, that are equal.[49] American Anglicans, like those of Jamaica, were among the most obstructive. Yet even the Methodists, generally keener than Anglicans and Catholics to instruct slaves in Scripture, publicly urged abolition becoming the second dissenting church to do so, only late in the Revolution, well after the Quakers. Prodded by Francis Asbury (1745–1816), a recent English immigrant figuring among the principal founders of Methodism in America and the "Second Great Awakening," the Methodists first categorically declared slavery "contrary to the laws of God" at their Baltimore conference in 1780.[50]

The lamentably slow progress of black emancipation in America presented European radicals with a serious dilemma. Brissot, Condorcet, Chastellux, La Rochefoucauld, Lafayette, Price, Paine, Wekhrlin, and Kościuszko genuinely sought to advance the antislavery movement and improve the lot of former slaves. But they also needed to shield the American Revolution's reputation and credentials against British and European disparagement aimed at discrediting it by publicizing its abject failure to fulfill its promises. With Independence won, the stain of black slavery, radical enthusiasts for the Revolution on both sides of the Atlantic expected, would not long sully the "purity of American laws" or the Revolution's transatlantic image.[51] Price urged all possible haste on this vital question while acknowledging the need for some delay.[52] Chastellux accepted the inevitability of a gradual emancipation process while demanding concrete initial steps to materialize rapidly.[53] Such concessions to gradualism were sharply criticized by Brissot, who, like his ally Condorcet, stressed the urgency of a prompt, systematic emancipation together with the principle of full equality of rights and social integration for freed blacks and other non-whites along the lines Franklin, Paine, and the democrats were advocating.[54] On establishing the Amis des Noirs in Paris in 1788, Condorcet and Brissot assured their supporters that most American states had now suspended the slave trade and that "Georgia and North Carolina are currently the only States where the importation of negroes is permitted."[55] If there was no denying the extent of suppression of black rights in the South, attitudes in the North were supposedly very different. In the 1770s and 1780s, European radicals had little alternative but to loudly acclaim the antislavery movement in the Northern states while simultaneously denouncing the inhumanity and stubbornness of the slave-owning Southern "aristocracy" as a detestable aberration from the American norm. Démeunier, in 1776, depicted South Carolina's slave-ridden society in the harshest terms proclaiming that colony incapable of truly supporting America's fight for freedom.[56]

"Slavery, my friend," Brissot assured an ally in Paris, from Philadelphia, "has not defiled all of the United States as is generally believed."[57] Northern blacks, slaves and non-slaves, it was often claimed, were treated more humanely and lived better than those in the Southern states.[58] But the battle over slavery, and the future of the blacks, was actually far from concluded even in Pennsylvania, let alone the rest of the North. The 1780 edition of the *Histoire philosophique* proclaimed Pennsylvania socially and "philosophically" the most advanced of the Thirteen Colonies, and no doubt this is why Brissot, when contemplating settling in America early in 1789, prior to the Revolution in France, chose that state for his future domicile.[59] Yet, despite the much-applauded Quaker initiative in emancipating their slaves, most of the black population still remained slaves even in Pennsylvania. Pennsylvania's pathbreaking first emancipation decree, voted by the state legislature in 1780, required slave owners to register existing slaves, acknowledged the rights of young slaves to be protected from despotic masters, and "declared the children of slaves [but not the slaves themselves] free at the age of twenty-eight."[60] The number of black slaves in Pennsylvania declined from 3,737 in 1790 to 1,706 in 1800, and to 795 by 1810. This might seem slow, but it was far more precipitate than in New York State where slave numbers fell from 21,324, in 1790, to 20,343, in 1800, and where still 15,017 slaves remained in 1810, and 10,088 in 1820.[61]

Pennsylvania's decree was a modest but significant first step, the result of unavoidable compromises needed to get the bill through. Inevitably, this outcome gravely disappointed committed abolitionists and integrationists. Paine, Rush, and others had hoped for emancipation at least from the age of twenty-one and for setting a time frame (which was not conceded) for final, comprehensive abolition. "Why did this respectable assembly not go further? Why, for example, did it not grant freedom, or at least the hope of freedom, to Negroes who were slaves at the time of the enactment?" It seemed highly unjust and unsatisfactory that the child of a "Negro slave in Pennsylvania," complained Brissot, "can hope to enjoy liberty some day and his master cannot withhold it from him when he has worked for him till the age of twenty-eight, yet the unhappy father of this child is forever deprived of his freedom." To add insult to injury, the 1780 law stipulated that a "slave may not bear witness against a free man." What possible justification could there be for that in terms of equality, moral equity, or any philosophical principle?[62]

Yet Pennsylvania's was the first American decree to proclaim an eventual permanent abolition of slavery in principle, and for publicity purposes radicals needed to extol, not blacken, Pennsylvania's initiative. Much praise was due, averred Brissot, to the "spirit of equity and liberty that inspired the Pennsylvania Assembly with the humanitarian principles expressed during the debates preceding the enactment" of the 1780 law. In New Jersey and New York, meanwhile, nothing comparable transpired; indeed slave numbers in these states actually increased down to the 1790s, practically doubling in New Jersey between 1760 to 1790 from 6,567 to 11,423, and by 1800 to 12,422,[63] most of these enslaved living in the extreme northeastern part of the state, at a time when slave numbers in Delaware fell somewhat, to 6,153, and in New York grew more marginally.[64] New Jersey finally passed a Gradual Abolition Act in 1804, freeing children born to slaves after 4 July 1804—a day marked by no public festivities relating to this—on having served the mother's master until the age of twenty-one, for females, that is until 1825, and, twenty-five for males, at the earliest in 1829![65] Thanks to Jay and Livingston, slaves in New York State likewise had considerably less prospect of being freed within a foreseeable time frame than children of slaves in Pennsylvania. New York's and New Jersey's less enlightened attitude when set beside that of Pennsylvania Brissot attributed to the fact that the "base of the population is made up of the Dutch, that is, of a people less willing than others to part with property." In New Jersey, the original Dutch demographic base was indeed mainly in the state's northeastern stretches, Bergen, Passaic, and Hudson counties, so that while the west "inclined toward emancipation, those in the eastern part are opposed."[66]

Radicals abominated slavery but had to deal with intractable resistance in the Southern legislatures combined with the widespread inertia of most of the Northern elite and public. The "aristocratic" revised New York State constitution, finalized in April 1777 at Kingston, thirty miles south of Albany, was drafted by a committee dominated by unyielding conservatives, Jay, Morris, and Livingston, collaborating to thwart democracy and ensure nothing resembling the overthrow of the Pennsylvania gentry occurred in New York, assigning the governor of their state overweening powers, including that of vetoing the legislature's own enactments. Livingston and Morris themselves belonged to slave-owning families. Gouverneur Morris blocked Jay's efforts to add institutionalized anti-Catholic discrimination to their conservative proposals but received scant backing from the others for his singular efforts to prohibit slavery under the state's new constitution. Over 20,000 blacks lived in bondage in New York State when Morris proposed enacting that "every being who breathes the air of this state, shall enjoy the privileges of a freeman." The rest of the committee gave token verbal support to the principle but refused to act on it, deferring further consideration of the slavery question to the state legislature.[67]

The New York State legislature took a tentative first step toward black emancipation in 1781 when it freed slaves resident in the state who had served in the revolutionary army. But where, in 1783, Massachusetts became the second state (after Vermont) to abolish slavery fully and absolutely, it was only considerably later, despite growing support for abolition in the press,[68] that the New York State legislature passed a general measure for staged abolition— not until 1799. Massachusetts had been hesitantly followed by Connecticut and Rhode Island in 1784, albeit these states adopted much more gradual procedures, so gradual that it was not until 1848 that final abolition was decreed in Connecticut and the last remaining slaves freed.[69] The New England states, meanwhile, though slowly abolishing slavery, did practically nothing to help integrate freed blacks, provide them with land, educate them or break down the organized discrimination denying them equality of status and political rights, and underpinning the long widely accepted and imposed ban on mixed marriages.

Overall, observed Kościuszko, on returning to America from Poland in the summer of 1797, resistance to ending slavery and integrating free blacks persisted tenaciously in the middle and northern states, as well as the South. Revisiting New Jersey, he was appalled to find slaves still numbered "around 9,000" (actually over 12,000), and that all efforts in the state legislature to abolish slavery had thus far been thwarted by conservatives (with Witherspoon's backing). New Jersey abolished slavery in principle only in 1804, and even then black slave children born in the state had to serve until the age of twenty-five (for males) and twenty-one (for females).[70] Ungenerously, slaves born before 4 July 1799 in New York State were reclassified as "indentured servants" but in essence remained slaves for life. Slave children born after that date remained slaves until the age of twenty-eight and were only then declared free. As late as 1810, with still over 15,000 slaves in the state, no less than 40 percent of New York City households included slaves. Complete abolition of slavery in New York State was only finally achieved and publicly celebrated in July 1827, over half a century after commencement of the Revolution![71]

"Every master of slaves is born a petty tyrant"

If unedifying in the North, the situation was far worse and more depressing in the South, as well as in parts of the newly opened up West. "When you tour Maryland and Virginia [the furthest south he traveled]," commented Brissot, "you suppose you are in a different world, and think so again when speaking with the people of these states. There, differently from in the North, there is no talk of freeing the Negroes, and no praise of the anti-slavery societies in London, Paris and America." Nor would this obstinate mind-set be easily changed.[72] "The strongest obstacle to abolition," Brissot continued, "lies in the character, inclinations, and habits of the Virginians. They like to live off the sweat of their slaves, to hunt, and display their wealth without having to do any work."[73] Majority-white attitudes toward black emancipation were even less liberal in Maryland, according to some, than in Virginia.

Virginia had supplied some of the Revolution's foremost leaders but scarcely seemed to be playing an active role in the process of black emancipation. Lafayette, whose abolitionist zeal was warmly praised by Franklin's Pennsylvania Society, tried to spur Washington to accelerate the incipient emancipation process in Virginia. Like Brissot a few years later (who visited Mount Vernon bearing a letter of introduction from Lafayette),[74] he tried to mobilize Washington for concerted action on behalf of the abolition movement, in 1783 proposing an emancipation scheme that he afterward proceeded with alone, purchasing a plantation in Cayenne where he planned to liberate "my Negroes in order to make that experiment which you know is my special concern."[75] By agreement with the intendant of Cayenne, Lafayette retained this South American estate for some years, complete with school and other facilities where he endeavored to prepare blacks for emancipation and a better subsequent life as free men. Washington commended this "generous and noble proof of your humanity. Would to God, a like spirit would diffuse itself generally into the minds of the people of this country, but I despair of seeing it—some petitions were presented to the [Virginia] Assembly at its last session, for the abolition of slavery, but they could scarcely obtain a reading." Washington qualified his apparent concurrence, though, adding: to set the blacks "afloat at once would, I really believe, be productive of much inconvenience and mischief; but by degrees it certainly might and assuredly ought to be effected, and that too by legislative authority."[76]

This was not unreasonable. But there is no indication Washington took any steps to support Lafayette's scheme (which was eventually aborted in 1792 when the latter fled France, and his property was confiscated by the revolutionary Republic both in France itself and French Guyana) or to sponsor his campaign on behalf of the blacks in any way. When in November 1785 the Virginia legislature considered a petition submitted by the Methodist leaders Thomas Coke and Francis Asbury for the gradual emancipation of the slaves in their state, and promptly rejected it, the future first president made no effort to support the Methodist motion—not even by letter as he had promised Asbury he would.[77] Worse, so intense was the opposition to this Methodist initiative in Maryland, Virginia, and the Carolinas that, at their next conference, the Methodists reluctantly agreed to suspend the whole business of abolition for the time being.

Unfairly or not, by the 1790s, if not earlier, some radical observers concluded that George Washington was, as Paine called him, "a hypocrite in public life." "The world will be puzzled to decide whether you are an apostate or an impostor, whether you have abandoned good principles, or whether you ever had any," declared Paine scornfully in his open letter to the president, dated July 1796 and published three months later in the Philadelphia *Aurora* by Franklin's grandson, Benjamin Franklin Bache. In this, the most virulent and derogatory attack on Washington ever published, Paine accused him of being "cold" and "treacherous," and of concentrating chiefly on enhancing his presidency in the eyes of the nation and seeking flattery, "encouraging and swallowing the grossest adulation," and traveling "America from one end to the other to put yourself in the way of receiving it. You have as many addresses in your chest," he added with calculated insult, "as James II."[78]

Nevertheless, also in Virginia, where there were 293,427 registered slaves in 1790 rising to 345,796 by 1800,[79] representing 40 percent of the population, it was during the Revolution that the radical fringe in the state legislature, Jefferson, Madison, and Mason, first initiated political moves to tackle slavery, sharing an unpublicized pledge to work behind the scenes for the gradual emancipation of the slaves in their state. In 1784 Jefferson, as chairman of the congressional committee appointed to devise a plan for regulating the boost in westward migration following the war's end, proposed abolishing slavery in all the lands west of the Alleghenies from 1800.[80] The full scheme, opposed by almost all his Virginian colleagues, narrowly failed to pass. Thus Congress failed to prevent the legal extension of slavery into Kentucky and Tennessee. However, a more limited enactment, the so-called Northwest Ordinance, issued by Congress in 1787, proved of appreciable significance in limiting slavery's westward expansion north of the Ohio River. Intended to establish a framework within which the new territories could evolve into fully-fledged states of the Union while preventing the emergence of any future independent "Vermonts," the measure went beyond Jefferson's original recommendation (no slavery after 1800) by abolishing slavery outright immediately throughout "the Northwest," the whole territory west of Pennsylvania and north of the Ohio River as far as the Mississippi.[81] The decree guaranteed white settlers that "the Northwest" would eventually constitute between three and five states and enjoy equal civil and political rights with the Union's existing states. However, this key ordinance made little significant provision to protect Indian rights and none at all to secure those of free black immigrants and freed slaves.[82] An integral feature of the Northwest Ordinance, as of the Constitution itself, was the obligation to return fugitive slaves to those states whence they had fled; worse still, the "no slavery" rule applied to the Northwest was part of a complex package of compromise between the states, carrying the firm implication that slavery *would* be institutionalized by the Union in the Southwest.[83] Furthermore, in the southern part of the Northwest, the territory designated "Indiana" (modern Indiana and Illinois), which acquired its own legislature in 1804, pro-slavery elements subsequently sufficiently gained ground to circumvent the prohibition on slavery by introducing a form of indentured labor for blacks similar to that in New York, a scheme that by 1810 officially held 630 blacks in quasi-slave servitude.[84]

In August 1787, during the United States Constitutional Convention, the most formative episode in the young nation's history after the Revolution, some of the fifty-five delegates from the Thirteen States concurred that slavery was entirely "inconsistent," as Maryland representative Luther Martin expressed it, "with the principles of the Revolution."[85] Gouverneur Morris denounced slavery vehemently. George Mason (1725–92) deplored the slave trade as "an infernal traffic," roundly condemning the effects of slavery on American society, but, as often earlier, sounded (like Jefferson) distinctly more worried about slavery's negative influence on the white population and their attitudes and work habits than the injustice done to the blacks: "slavery discourages arts and manufactures"; poor whites "despise labor when performed by slaves"; "every master of slaves is born a petty tyrant."[86] A number of delegates opposed permitting South Carolina and Georgia, the two states wanting to continue the slave trade, to do so. Yet there was no realistic means of bringing the Southern states into a firmer union if slavery as such was abolished or seriously curtailed. Delegate Charles C. Pinckney made doubly clear that South Carolina and Georgia "cannot do without slaves" and under no circumstances would agree to suppress the slave trade, let alone slavery itself.[87] "Great as the evil is," commented Madison, "dismemberment of the Union would be worse."[88]

Accordingly, no motion in favor of abolition was ever tabled at the Constitutional Convention that drew up the United States Constitution. In the end, Northern as well as Southern delegates colluded in burying the whole issue and excluding direct reference to "slavery" in the Constitution's final wording so as to avoid offending the sensibilities of those unwilling to include the word "slavery" in the nation's foundation text. The result was that the United States Federal Constitution, utilizing respectable circumlocutions, condoned slavery indefinitely, precluded Congress from prohibiting the slave trade for two decades (whereas the Continental Congress had suppressed it in 1774), and required all states, under strict rules, to return fugitive slaves to bondage and their owners.[89] While most American and European opinion was not especially critical of these compromises at the expense of the black population, the outcome placated Southern white opinion and positively appealed to restless elements among the planters of the Caribbean, Brazil, and Spanish America. The lesson of the American Revolution appeared to be that there were ways to gain political independence and reject monarchy while yet keeping the power and privileges of the landowning elite intact—and without running the risk of freeing the slaves.[90]

Equally deplorable in radical eyes, under a crucial compromise with the Southern states reached in July 1787, the Constitution supplemented the representation of the slave states in the future national House of Representatives by stipulating that in determining the number of representatives for each state, black slaves should be represented in a ratio of three to five in relation to citizens. As Madison noted in *The Federalist*, this was a principle that sharply contradicted all the state constitutions since no such principle had been admitted before: in the state legislatures slaves were "not included in the estimate of representatives in any of the states possessing them." But the new arrangement did accord with the undemocratic suffrage restrictions and more general anti-democratic tendency everywhere applying outside Pennsylvania and Vermont affecting poor disadvantaged whites too: "the qualifications on which the right of suffrage depend [*sic*]," granted Madison, "are not perhaps the same in any two states."[91] A cruel supplement to the wider contradiction, this article of the United States Constitution signified that the nearly 20 percent of America's population that remained enslaved were henceforth represented in the national legislature by additional Southern white delegates expressly committed to perpetuate the institution of slavery.[92]

CHAPTER 7

Expropriating the Native Americans

Tory Loyalists, disaffected slaves, and landless whites were not the only ele-ments either reluctant to join the Revolution or stoutly resisting it. The Iro-quois, Cherokee, Shawnee, Delaware (Lenape), Creek, and other native peoples were deeply divided over whether to side with the American Revolution, the British, or stay neutral. Under the 1774 Quebec Act, some of the strategically most crucial predominantly Native American areas were now theoretically in—or else bordering—Canada and hence more directly under British control or influence than previously.

In the radical critique of the American Revolution, after 1775, the Indian question never loomed anything like as large as slavery and black emancipa-tion, or the travails of landless whites. A long tradition of Radical Enlighten-ment sympathy for the Indians reached back to the Dutch ex-Jesuit opponent of Louis XIV's absolutism Franciscus Van den Enden (1602–74), the first of the radical enlighteners (preceding Spinoza) to clearly couple rejection of religious authority with proposing sweeping reform of the social and political system. Van den Enden had praised the Indians of New Netherland for their social system based on equality when formulating proposals for a new kind of colonization in the then Dutch colony in the early 1660s.[1] This approach was renewed by Louis-Armand, baron de Lahontan (1666–1715), who spent eleven years in Canada between 1683 and 1694 and whose memorable account of the Iroquois, published in 1703, further fixed the Indians' reputation for a naturalistic morality and powerful egalitarian sense recognizing no social ranks.[2] But if the young Jefferson had been "very familiar" with the Cherokee, as in later life he assured Adams he had been, and "acquired impressions of attachment and commiseration for them which have never been obliterated,"[3] in general radical awareness, criticism and debate focused less on Native Ameri-can issues than any other major question.[4] Paine, Coram, Freneau, and others, especially Ponceau and Volney, followed in the tradition established by Van den Enden and Lahontan. But even Volney qualified his considerable sympathy while in America, viewing the Native Americans he investigated as somewhat less praiseworthy than the Bedouin of the Arabic world whom he had studied many years before. Where the latter were compelled to remain nomads by the harsh inhospitality of the desert, the Indians inhabiting the fertile lands between the Mississippi and the Appalachians actually preferred their "primitive" state as hunters and gatherers, continuing without making much effort to adjust to sedentary agriculture and society.[5]

Paine and his fellow radicals only rarely came into direct encounter with Indian issues during the revolutionary era, though Paine did serve as secretary to one of the main conferences between Patriot leaders and Iroquois chieftains, convened two years into the Revolutionary War, in January 1777, at the church at Easton on the Delaware River fifty miles north of Philadelphia. A commission of four Pennsylvania delegates, and two from Congress, persuaded the chiefs to sign a treaty committing the Iroquois Six Nations (Mohawk, Onondaga, Oneida, Tuscarora, Cayuga, and Seneca), a confederacy dating back to the mid-fifteenth century, to a pact with the United States directed against Britain; but Congress itself afterward rescinded the agreement on hearing the Iroquois tribes were in internal disagreement and that many Iroquois disregarded its terms. Paine, like Brissot, was impressed by the Indians' egalitarian tendencies, love of liberty, and general demeanor, and staunchly defended their right to an independent existence; nevertheless, he too only occasionally broached the topic of the Indians' bitter struggle to defend their land and resist encroachment and imposed land sales.[6] Radical views of the Indian predicament, despite being inherent in the *Histoire philosophique*'s uncompromising anticolonialism and defense of colonized non-white peoples, and constituting a more than a century-old tradition of eulogizing Native American customs, moral thought, and society, counted for little during the drama of 1775–83. Radicals claiming Indians make trustworthy allies and "good friends," as Brissot put it, praising their egalitarianism and social harmony, and sympathizing with their difficulties and plight, simply had scant impact on the wider scene. Sentiment in the colonies was mostly highly unsympathetic and not infrequently explicitly hostile to the native peoples.

In 1775, Native Americans within the borders of the Thirteen Colonies found themselves trapped in a quickly deteriorating situation. Even in the case of the Iroquois, who possessed the longest and most impressive tradition of fostering a confederacy of peoples with a firm identity, the long familiar political problem hampering their response to white encroachment—how to sustain and consolidate their unity, overcoming local disputes and animosities, in the midst of the Revolutionary War—arose on a scale and with an urgency they had never previously experienced. For Native Americans, the Revolution became a great internal political crisis verging on civil war, as well as a vast intensification of their struggle with the white settlers and their political representatives. The most renowned Indian war chieftains of the revolutionary era emerged as a new kind of Native American leader with concerns that were profoundly political and cultural as well as strategic.[7]

Where Indian tribes were surrounded or boxed in by white settlement, they had little alternative but to align with the stronger side or, where in doubt, endeavor to stay neutral. The Iroquois inhabiting the northern stretches of New York State, long resentful and aggrieved over settler intrusion and loss of their lands, carefully pondered their situation. Especially Ethan Allen's capture of Fort Ticonderoga (May 1775), a key stronghold in the Northwest, gave the Iroquois Six Nations reason to hesitate. A Grand Iroquois conference attended by 1,600 Native Americans held in Montreal in July 1775 weighed Governor Guy Carleton's bid for their alliance and promise that Britain would return stolen land to them once the American rebels were beaten and compelled to submit to the Crown. Carleton, though, remained distinctly hesitant about seeking Native American allies against the Americans; he wanted to recruit them for defensive purposes but not for attacking American settlements. Most Mohawk and other Iroquois, in any case, continued to waver, doing little to hinder the American capture of Montreal a few months later, in November. Their preferred policy was one of vigilant and flexible neutrality.[8] Carleton's successor as governor of Canada, General Frederick Haldimand (1718–91), a French-speaking Swiss and veteran of the Seven Years' War, was decidedly more fervent in seeking an offensive British-Iroquois pact against the Revolution as well as for bringing Vermont back under the British Crown.[9]

During 1775–77, Congress strove to keep the still wavering Six Nations neutral while the British Crown's agents urged them to fight for their land against the "rebels." Unlike most other Iroquois chiefs, Joseph Brant (Thayendanegea) (1743–1807), a Mohawk leader, did formally ally with the British Crown, celebrating the alliance with a feast including the ceremonial devouring and drinking the blood of a roasted ox deemed a symbolic "Bostonian." In November 1775, Brant accompanied Guy Johnson (c. 1740–88), nephew and successor of Sir William Johnson (1715–74), British "Superintendent of the Northern Indians," on an embassy to London to plead the Iroquois's grievances against the settlers. William Johnson had long complained of the American settlers intruding on Indian lands, their tendency to "ill treat, rob and frequently murder the Indians" as well as their general unruliness and "fondness for independency" rooted in their "ignorance, prejudice, democratical principles, and their remote situation."[10] William Johnson's influential and widely renowned common-law wife, Molly Brant, was Joseph's older sister. In exchange for his people's alliance, Brant demanded a written undertaking that they would receive back lands previously wrested from them when the "rebels" were defeated. Brant stayed several months in London negotiating with George III's ministers, being treated as a celebrity and sitting for his portrait wearing his chieftain's headdress. James Boswell interviewed him for the *London Magazine* (July 1776). Trusting the assurances he received about land restitution, he returned to Canada eager to rally the Six Nations behind Britain.[11]

From the summer of 1776, substantial numbers of Mohawk and Oneida warriors, roused by the American defeat in Canada and by Haldimand's efforts, as well as Brant, finally did take the field against the "rebels" together with white Loyalist and British frontiersmen mingling with the Iroquois. Simultaneously, British agents based in East Florida began inciting the Creeks, Cherokee, and Seminoles living along the southern frontier to attack settlements in Georgia and South Carolina. These southern attacks commenced in July 1776.[12] Brant vigorously canvassed among his people, urging them to take up arms for their rights with British help, precipitating an open rift among the still mostly undecided Six Nations. Concerting with Governor Haldimand, he began attacking farmsteads in northern New York while other Iroquois chiefs refused or hesitated to become actively embroiled—despite the fact that they all hoped for a British victory knowing that in the past the British Crown and its officials had made some effort to check the colonists' land-grabbing whereas the state legislatures generally had not. Most Iroquois steadfastly remained neutral.[13] Brant's harassment of outlying farmsteads briefly enhanced his stature and alarmed American sentiment across a wide inland area but also further deepened the festering split among the Iroquois chiefs especially when they perceived the first signs of the retaliation to come. This fraught, shifting mix of engagement and non-involvement in the war soon proved disastrous for all the Iroquois in every respect.[14]

Hundreds of Brant's braves, mostly Seneca, Cayuga, and Mohawk warriors, were cut down during General Burgoyne's failed offensive, at the battle for Fort Stanwix, and nearby at the bloody battle of Oriskany (6 August 1777), east of Lake Ontario, in northwest New York. The heavy losses disrupted the Iroquois confederacy further by turning disagreement among the Iroquois tribes into internecine strife with Mohawks fighting Oneidas.[15] Retaliating, a combined contingent of Loyalists and Seneca Iroquois, one of whose commanders was the renowned Seneca chieftain Cornplanter (c. 1740–1836), on 3 July 1778 decimated an American force, killing over three hundred Patriots near Forty Fort, in the Wyoming valley in Pennsylvania, then captured and burned the fort. But there were few other victories to celebrate, and vastly exaggerated reports of Iroquois cruelty in Pennsylvania and in the so-called Cherry Valley massacre in eastern New York, in November 1778, and elsewhere circulated in the Patriot press, materially adding to the growing aggressiveness with which most Americans viewed the Iroquois confederacy at this time and for decades after. If the scaremongering generated psychological pressure that temporarily aided Britain and monarchy, the Iroquois paid an exorbitant price. For the remainder of the Independence War the Six Nations remained hopelessly divided with the Mohawks and Senecas allied to the British and Oneidas and Tuscaroras to the "rebels." In 1779, a large American force dispatched to retaliate, commanded by General John Sullivan, carried personal orders from Washington to effect the "total destruction and devastation of their settlements" and "ruin their crops now in the ground and prevent their planting more"; Sullivan did as he was told, thoroughly decimating the Iroquois lands in western New York State and western Pennsylvania, burning around forty villages, killing and scattering large numbers, and destroying their food stocks.[16]

Along the northeast frontier, separating what is now Maine (then ruled by the Massachusetts legislature) from British Nova Scotia, a similarly fraught and confused situation reigned. Substantial numbers of Tories had migrated from further south, but white opinion in the border area remained predominantly hesitant or neutral,[17] while a few Nova Scotians, like the Scots colonel John Allan (1746–1805), moved southward and joined the "rebels." Edinburgh-born Allan, earlier a key figure in the Nova Scotia House of Assembly in Halifax, figured prominently in relations with the Native Americans of the Northeast during the Revolutionary War. In 1776, he negotiated the neutrality of the Wabanaki or Dawnland Indians, a confederacy of five Christianized Algonquian-speaking peoples (Abenaki, Penobscot, Maliseets, Passamaquoddy, and Micmac) inhabiting much of Maine, New Brunswick, Nova Scotia, and the islands straggling the Canadian east coast—a considerable setback strategically and in terms of prestige for the British who had hoped for their allegiance. Taking up residence on the American side (leaving his wife and five children in Halifax), Allan was appointed commanding officer at Machias, a frontier settlement and refuge for Nova Scotians defecting from the British, lying some two hundred miles northeast of what is today Portland. In 1777, Allan was appointed "Continental Superintendent for the Eastern Indians" by Congress, holding the rank of colonel.

Of the Wabanaki Confederacy, the Penobscots inhabiting the Penobscot River Valley between Portland and Machias, who still today possess a small remnant of sovereign territory close to Bangor, in southern-central Maine, were the most embedded in American territory. They were also the most staunchly neutral, encouraged in their neutrality by a Congress ruling prohibiting white intrusion into their then extensive territory. But the remaining four Wabanaki tribes who through the early and mid-eighteenth century had supported the French in their struggle with Britain and her American colonists were less easily kept neutral. The Passamaquoddy inhabiting the area to the north and the Maliseets, their neighbors further to the north, became a particular focus of the diplomatic tussle for Indian allegiance between the British and rebels, owing to the obvious strategic importance of their territory.

All the Wabanaki strove to keep their options open while preserving their independence and loyally adhering, as they had for many decades, to the French Catholic Church. Even the furthest north, the Micmac of the Nova Scotia islands, who had no realistic prospect of detaching themselves from Britain, nevertheless closely followed the ebb and flow of the struggle, negotiated with the Nova Scotia rebels, and sent emissaries to Allan declaring their intention to befriend both sides.[18] In 1777, the British constructed a new fort, Fort Howe, on the border, at St. John, to consolidate their grip on the area, causing the local Wabanaki, the Maliseets, to divide. One faction, remaining where they were, sided with the British, retaining control of their territory, while the other faction, mindful of more than a century and a half of fighting Britain in alliance with the French, manning twenty-seven canoes commanded by Chief Ambrose Saint Aubin and leaving their ancestral lands by a highly tortuous route, transferred to rebel territory, joining forces with Allan at Machias.

In August 1777, small groups of Passamaquoddies, Maliseets, and Penobscots, together with white rebel militia, repelled an attack launched from four British vessels at the river mouth at Machias. Yet even the Penobscots, while assuring Congress of their loyalty and promising to guard the northern approaches to their territory, proved only lukewarm allies and refused to raise the contingent requested from them to join the Continental militia. When, in 1778, the British called a conference at Fort Howe, not only Maliseets and Passamaquoddies but also some Penobscots turned up to hear what the British had to offer. Their loyalty was for sale if the price was right. To prove their nondependence on Congress, Indian delegates even handed in to the British commander their letters, medals, and other gifts received from George Washington. Once the alliance between France and Congress was proclaimed, Allan, knowing the French connection would appeal strongly to all the Wabanaki and strengthen his hand, at once dispatched messengers carrying the news to all five tribes. Several groups of Wabanaki traveled to Boston and Rhode

Island in late 1778 to witness the arrival of French troops and supplies for themselves. The French agent in Rhode Island assisted them in finding a French priest who then dwelled among the Penobscots from 1780 to 1784.[19]

Native American resistance to the American Revolution gained two notable recruits in March 1778 when Alexander McKee, a former official of the British Department of Indian Affairs, married to a Shawnee woman, deserted to the British along with the legendary "white savage" Colonel Simon Girty (1741–1818). Their defecting group joined the Delaware Indians in Ohio. Girty had been a child captive of the Seneca in Pennsylvania and later built his career as an interpreter and mediator with the Iroquois. An incident a few weeks before their flight when a revolutionary commander launched an unprovoked attack on a neutral Delaware Indian village had convinced Girty the Americans, once their independence was secured, would simply discard all promises and ignore the Ohio River as the agreed demarcation line, driving the western and the northern tribes wholesale from their ancestral lands, as indeed they did. To the whites, Girty, who spoke no less than eleven native languages, became "frontier America's most infamous traitor-renegade," to the Indians a hero fighting to defend them and their hunting grounds.[20] Over the next years down to the end of the Revolutionary War, he and his younger brother, living with the Indians while also making frequent visits to British officers at Fort Detroit, the British headquarters in the west, incited the Delaware and Shawnee, and encouraged Brant in fomenting Iroquois, to resist the "rebels" all along the northwestern frontier, keeping a large zone in constant turmoil.

The raiding added to the concerted pressure on the Americans at a crucial stage: "while we are threatened with a formidable [Indian] attack from the northward on our Ohio settlements," remarked Jefferson in 1780, and from the "southern Indians on our frontiers convenient to them, our eastern country is exposed to invasion from the British army in Carolina."[21] But the only result was that at the war's close, the Native American confederacies figured among the heaviest losers of people, lands, and influence in the Revolution.[22] The so-called second treaty of Fort Stanwix (1784) supposedly secured what remained of the Six Nations' lands, but Congress in its post-1783 enfeebled state showed little capacity or willingness to defend their rights and interests. Neither did the new Federal government from 1788. The Seneca chieftain Red Jacket (c. 1750–1830) also called Sagoyewatha (Keeper Awake) due to his fine oratory, delivered an eloquent speech of protest before Washington himself in Philadelphia, in 1792, recalling the horrific 1779 campaign when revolutionary troops under Washington's orders had ruthlessly ravaged Iroquois villages and lands. He urged Washington to evince greater vigor in protecting them and what was left of their territory and really be a "Father of his country."[23] Exceptionally, Brant, Molly Brant, and the Mohawks did receive significant compensation from the British government in 1786, and from that date built a new center for their largely exiled and expelled people at Brant's Town, a Mohawk village that also welcomed refugees from other peoples, on the Grand River in southwestern Ontario.[24] Brant's well-appointed home long remained a focus of Native American British Loyalism.

Discussion of and special provision for the Native American peoples in the American Constitution of 1787 was in fact astoundingly cursory.[25] The status and rights of the Indian communities coexisting beside the whites in the Thirteen States and around their northern, western, and southern edges had already been extremely obscure in 1775 and remained so throughout the revolutionary and post-revolutionary era. To what extent and in what ways Indian peoples retained their autonomy and separate laws were pointedly described by Madison as among the most incoherent and confusing aspects of the nascent republic's laws and those of all the states. "What description of Indians are to be deemed members of a State," he noted in *The Federalist*, in 1788, "is not yet settled; and has been a question of frequent perplexity and contention in the Federal Councils. And how the trade with Indians, though not members of a State, yet residing within its legislative jurisdiction, can be regulated by an external authority [the United States government], without so far intruding on the internal rights of legislation, is absolutely incomprehensible."[26] The situation scarcely improved subsequently. In 1795, President Washington appointed a congressional commission to study the perplexing legal anomaly that the southern Creek confederacy in Georgia and Alabama had signed one treaty in 1785 placing themselves apparently under the jurisdiction of Georgia and another, in 1790, with the federal government in which they placed "themselves under the protection of the United States alone and bound themselves not to enter into any treaty with any other individual, state or power."[27]

The so-called Western Indian Confederacy of Indian peoples, headed by the Shawnee, Miami, and Delaware (Lenape), escaped the 1779 retribution visited on the Iroquois; but later they too lost massively despite (and due to) their vigorous efforts to resist. The so-called Northwest Indian War (1785– 95), or Little Turtle's War as it later became known, erupted because Britain had done nothing to secure the lands of (most of) her Indian allies in the 1783 peace treaty concluding the War of Independence and the United States refused to recognize the lands reserved for the tribes by Britain prior to 1783.[28] This vagueness affected a large area still residually under the influence of the British at Fort Detroit but over which the United States was anxious fully to assert its sovereignty. In the autumn of 1790, the chieftain Little Turtle (1747–1812), who had participated in the fight against the Americans and French during the Revolutionary War and was soon to become the most renowned of all the Indian war heroes, trapped and defeated an American force that had invaded their lands, attempting to control the junction of rivers, the key to their territory, and had burned the principal Miami village, Kekionga (today Fort Wayne). In October 1791, starting from Fort Washington (Cincinnati), a punitive American force of 1,486 regulars and militia, led by the governor of the Northwest Territory, General Arthur St. Clair, advanced northward from the Ohio River under President Washington's direct instructions forcibly to reduce these tribes to submission. Surprised on 4 November, at the Wabash River, St. Clair's army was defeated with heavy loss by a combined army of Miami, Shawnee, and Delaware under Little Turtle (with Girty among their commanders). Most of the American force was killed or wounded (628 men killed and 258 wounded) in arguably the heaviest reverse the United States Army ever suffered combating Native Americans.

Despite this sensational victory causing quite a shock to Washington and the members of his administration in Philadelphia, a setback costly to the United States financially as well as in men, negotiations with the western tribes, held in 1792, with Girty (dressed as an Indian) as interpreter, quickly collapsed. The Indians demanded the Ohio line as the eastern border of their territory; the government refused.[29] Washington felt the humiliation of the 1790–91 military defeats keenly and, like his grasping, famously obese secretary of war, General Henry Knox (1750–1806), preferred to strengthen the Federal government's authority than compromise. Washington and Knox would countenance neither defeat nor the Ohio line, instead increasing military spending with the aim of overcoming Indian resistance by force. "No other remedy remains," Knox assured the commander at Fort Washington, "but to extirpate, utterly if possible" those resisting American authority.[30] A larger force was gradually prepared from mid-1792 and organized as a standing army maintained in forts, an army that finally crushed the resistance at the Battle of Fallen Timbers (20 August 1794) fought near what is today Toledo, Ohio.

With this, organized resistance collapsed for the time being and Indian possession of the territory between the Great Lakes to the north and the Ohio in the south (bounded by the Mississippi to the west), originally established by the British under the first treaty of Fort Stanwix, in 1768, largely disintegrated.[31] Pivoting on Fort Wayne, named after the victorious commander at Fallen Timbers, Anthony Wayne (1745–96), a line of forts was constructed during 1794–96 to house the standing force intended to overawe the Great

Lakes tribes permanently. Under the peace signed at Fort Greenville (Ohio), finalized on 3 August 1795, the Shawnees, Delawares, Miamis, and other Great Lakes peoples, after twenty years of warfare, ceded Ohio and much of Indiana to the United States.[32] The Greenville Treaty Line that was now established supposedly reserved the rest of Indiana for these people, but the new line was hardly respected either, resulting overall in a vast setback for the Great Lakes peoples followed by British abandonment of Fort Detroit in 1796. Driven off vast tracts, many Shawnee, Miami, Delaware, and Seneca, and among them Girty and his family, migrated northward into Ontario where, since the end of the Independence War in 1783, the Native American population had substantially increased.[33]

This was not quite the end of the story, however. In the response to their defeat and capitulation and the demoralizing losses of land and transfers of population that followed, the Shawnee "prophet" Tenskwatawa admonished his own people and soon neighboring tribes over a vast area to renew their communities further west, eschew white "customs," and collaborate together to revive and cherish their own traditions. From 1805, based on his "visions" and organized by his warrior brother Tecumseh (1768–1813), a powerful utopian, militant movement, involving repentance and renouncing whiskey, developed that from 1808 established its headquarters in Prophetstown, located in western Indiana Territory close to where the township of Lafayette would be founded in 1825. Having rebuilt a northwestern (mainly Shawnee confederacy) to resume the fight against the Americans during the first decade of the new century, Tenskwatawa and Tecumseh injected fresh hope into the minds of Native Americans across an immense area, on the southern side of the Great Lakes.[34] To spread their message, Tecumseh personally visited and sent agents over a vast expanse designing to bring as many tribes and factions as possible, to the north and south, into his combined spiritual and resistance movement.

The brothers boosted morale for a time, reinstilling the will to oppose white settlement and domination and by reaffirming Native American traditional cultures and beliefs to resist the plague of alcohol, passivity, and demoralization decimating the tribes.[35] The Prophet's exuberant followers were crushed at the battle of Tippecanoe (7 November 1811) by the politically ambitious governor of Indiana, William Henry Harrison (1773–1841), who, alarmed by the reports of Tecumseh's wide-ranging diplomacy and directly contrary to President Madison's orders, had invaded their territory commanding over a thousand men. Next Harrison, who, like Tecumseh, had fought at Fallen Timbers, burned down Prophetstown. But this only further stiffened the resistance, and during the early stages of the Anglo-American War of 1812–15 Tecumseh's warriors played a conspicuous role as allies of the British (whom the United States government blamed for stirring them to armed resistance in the first place).[36] In August 1812 Tecumseh's men played a key part in forcing the surrender of the two-thousand-man U.S. garrison of Fort Detroit to a combined Native American–British army. It was Tecumseh's greatest feat. He died in battle in October 1813, in Ontario, defeated together with a British force, by Harrison, at the Battle of the Thames (5 October 1813), one of the few American victories of the war in Canada, but only after establishing a lasting legend. A Virginia aristocrat who became a popular hero, Harrison went on to become the ninth president of the United States and the last born before Independence—but only for a month, dying of pneumonia in April 1841.

The position of Native Americans throughout the rest of the nascent republic likewise generally deteriorated rapidly during the Revolutionary War and even more rapidly after 1783. The Maine Wabanaki, having initially profited from their role as judiciously wavering neutrals benefiting from gifts, rum, and provisions from both sides, lost such leverage as they still possessed after hostilities ended in 1783. Peace deprived them of their former military and political usefulness. Congress made no further effort to shield them from land-grabbers and dishonest traders selling shoddy goods at exorbitant prices and bad whiskey and rum, which, in Maine as among the northwestern confederacy, the Indians found irresistible. In 1784 Allan, who, like Girty, had time and again evinced profound respect for the tribes, was dismissed as superintendent and told his role in American-Indian relations was over. The Massachusetts state legislature, by stages opening up their lands to white settlement, in effect canceled the prohibition of white intrusion into Penobscot territory. Congress, the Penobscot angrily protested, had recognized their possession of all land six miles either side of the river along its length. The state commissioners replied that Massachusetts had only provisionally recognized their claim, not passed a definitive measure. Friction and acrimony dragged on until an imposed highly disadvantageous treaty ended all negotiation in 1796. Under its terms, in exchange for consignments of clothing, ammunition, food, and alcohol, the Penobscots were obliged to surrender 190,000 acres of territory.[37]

Equally catastrophic was the plight of the Cherokee, bordering on Georgia and the Carolinas, in the South. In Tennessee and Kentucky, the Cherokee peoples found themselves as deeply divided by the Revolutionary War as the Native American peoples further north. During the summer of 1776, the Virginia and Carolina legislatures received reports that the Cherokees and Creeks were responding to British overtures, from Florida, and harassing frontier areas; a prompt preemptive drive commanded by Charles Lee soon defeated the Cherokee tribes, and burning Cherokee villages, destroying their crops, and slaughtering their livestock forced them into humiliating terms signed in May 1777. Under this "agreement" the Cherokee had to evacuate a major part of their ancestral lands.[38] From that point on, most Cherokee elders felt armed struggle to defend their ancestral lands from white encroachment had become hopeless.[39] They opted for reluctant acquiescence in the 1777 "peace treaties," which, in practice, meant wholesale loss, subordination, and marginalization.

By 1783, the Cherokee had lost three-quarters of the land they held before the Revolution, despite which their villages were often devastated in retaliation for sporadic continuing attacks on white settlements by other, recalcitrant Cherokee and Creeks.[40] Jefferson sought to prod the Virginia and Carolina legislatures into offering some protection from grasping frontiersmen and providing peaceful Cherokees, Creeks, and Shawnees with food, supplies, and gifts but without success.[41] At that time his attitude remained one of explicit respect for Indian abilities and rights. Most Cherokee continued to coexist peacefully, submitting to the disadvantageous treaties forced on them in 1777. Accelerating attrition of their lands, though, and the elders' seeming encouragement to humiliating surrender eventually provoked a substantial "secession" of younger warriors resolved to renew the fight and stay independent whatever the cost. Under chieftain Dragging Canoe (c. 1732–92), this recalcitrant faction trekked westward, setting up a fresh confederacy in Tennessee, to the north of what is now Chattanooga.[42] Supplied with ammunition by the British, the Chickamauga—the Cherokee militants gathered at Chickamauga Creek—from 1780 waged a defiant war of harassment along the southern frontier, refusing to surrender even after 1783, for over a decade after the Revolutionary War.[43] During the early 1790s, still led by Dragging Canoe, they were joined by some Creeks and also a Shawnee contingent from Ohio led by another brother of the renowned Shawnee chief Tecumseh.[44] Simultaneously with the Indians of the Northwest, they were defeated by overwhelming force only in 1793–94.

In Georgia and Alabama, the Creek confederacy fared better for a time. Having formerly allied with the British in the Floridas, they now allied with Spain and in the later 1780s succeeded in driving back white encroachments from coastal Georgia. The treaty of Colerain (29 June 1796), drawn up during Washington's presidency, expressly guaranteed the Creek confederacy's territory.[45] The Creeks became the special care of a North Carolina congressman, Benjamin Hawkins (1754–1816), an expert on the Cherokee and Choctaw as well as the Creek, deeply involved in Indian affairs since 1785, who served as Congress's general superintendent of all the Indian tribes south of the Ohio River from 1796 to 1814. Married to an Indian woman and deaf to missionizing calls to spread Christianity, he strove to preserve the cohesion of Creek society by teaching them to adjust to sedentary agriculture. From the 1780s, some of the Creeks and other southern Indians did, as Jefferson put it, become "far advanced in civilization," enclosing fields, acquiring herds of cattle and hogs, spinning and weaving their clothes, and building "good cabins."[46] Some became prosperous individuals; rather more lapsed into poverty and deprivation.

Still more unfortunately for the Creeks (and Hawkins), Jefferson's prediction at the start of the Anglo-American War of 1812–15 that "on those that have made any progress, English seductions will have no effect" but that the "backward will yield, and be thrown further back" and "lose numbers by war and want" proved all too accurate.[47] British agents persuaded many of the Upper Creeks to again take up arms allied to Britain against the United States, plunging Alabama and the western fringes of Georgia into a bitter local conflict—with Creeks taking both sides. The pro-British Creek Red Sticks were traditionalists resenting the encroachments of sedentary ways and agriculture and the loss of much of their ancient culture and prowess. Inspired by the famed Shawnee leader Tecumseh and joined by some runaway blacks, the Red Sticks became allies of Tecumseh and the Prophet, fighting to defend their traditional way of life as hunters on their communal lands. They were soon crushed by a mixed force of whites and pro-American Creeks under Andrew Jackson. Hawkins hoped for a new start. Although during the war many Creeks and some Cherokee "took part with Great Britain against the United States, and did us much injury," Hawkins hoped that the resulting "retaliation on our part is to forgive them, because they were a poor deluded people," and "enlighten their understandings" and "better their condition by assisting them with tools and implements of husbandry, and teaching them the use of them."[48] In fact, the ensuing treaty of Fort Jackson (August 1814), imposed by General Jackson, peremptorily confiscated two-thirds of Creek lands, over twenty million acres comprising half of Alabama and much of Georgia's interior, regardless of whether localities had sided for or against the United States and over the protests of the chiefs rejecting the Red Sticks. Hawkins was so disheartened by this disaster for the Creeks that he soon afterward resigned his superintendency in disgust.

Irrespective of whether they supported the Revolution or Britain, or stayed neutral, all the Indian confederacies and tribes, from the Nova Scotia borderlands and Vermont to the southernmost limits of the United States, eventually including the Creeks, lost ground disastrously during and, still more disastrously, after the Revolutionary War.[49] If Washington and Knox initiated the military sweeps driving the Indians from extensive lands, Jefferson, before becoming president, favored guaranteeing Indians possession of their land combined with a policy of sympathetic negotiation, assimilation, and integration. He endorsed Hawkins's approach, his promoting the federal "plan for civilization" from his base on the Creek lands in Georgia. This was designed to accelerate the shift from a nomadic existence over vast expanses to utilizing land under a sedentary way of life in far smaller enclaves based on crop growing, cattle rearing, and cloth weaving.[50] Native Americans had no choice, Hawkins and Jefferson were agreed, but to abandon their traditional lifestyle as hunters and gatherers since the "business of hunting has already become insufficient to furnish clothing and subsistence to the Indians. The promotion of agriculture, therefore, and household manufacture, are essential to their preservation."[51]

On becoming president in 1801, Jefferson initially continued to uphold his theory, that being helped to adjust to sedentary agriculture and acquire a "sense of the superior value of a little land well cultivated, over a great deal unimproved," would enable the Indians to survive where they were and that "while they are learning to do better on less land, our increasing numbers will be calling for more land, and thus a coincidence of interests will be produced between those who have lands to spare, and want other necessaries, and those who have such necessaries to spare, and want lands. This commerce, then, will be for the good of both, and those who are friends to both ought to encourage it."[52] On no other question did Jefferson's republican radicalism so clearly reveal its underlying ambiguity and destructive potential. Though his stance, down to the last years of his presidency, was basically an integrationist one, guaranteeing to the Indians vestiges of their land, he was convinced the Indians must vacate much of their ancestral lands to the whites. The Louisiana Purchase (1803) renewed the debate about the indigenous population, with Jefferson still professing sympathy for their plight. "The aboriginal inhabitants of these countries," he stressed in his Second Inaugural Address (March 1805), "I have regarded with the commiseration their history inspires. Endowed with the faculties and the rights of men, breathing an ardent love of liberty and independence, and occupying a country which left them no desire but to be undisturbed," the spread of the United States and the stream of immigration from Europe had tragically "overwhelmed" them.[53]

The president repeated his view that now the Indians were "reduced within limits too narrow for the hunter's state, humanity enjoins us to teach them agriculture and the domestic arts; to encourage them to that industry which alone can enable them to maintain their place in existence, and to prepare them in time for that state of society, which to bodily comforts adds the improvement of the mind and morals."[54] Yet he now also declared that "endeavours to enlighten them on the fate that awaits their present course of life" confronted powerful obstacles, in particular their stubborn adherence to their obsolete style of life, blaming the "prejudice of their minds, ignorance, pride, and the influence of interested and crafty individuals among them." On this pretext, he justified what became an all-out assault on Indian tradition, culture, and manner of life, denouncing—alluding to Tenskwatawa and Tecumseh—those propagating among them a "sanctimonious reverence for the customs of their ancestors whatsoever they did," for teaching them that "reason is a false guide, and to advance under its counsel, in their physical, moral or political condition, is perilous innovation; that their duty is to remain as their Creator made them, ignorance being safety, and knowledge full of danger." Native Americans too, it transpired, had "their anti-philosophers, who find an interest in keeping things in their present state, who dread reformation, and exert all their faculties to maintain the ascendancy of habit over the duty of improving our reason, and obeying its mandates."[55] Indian society, insisted Jefferson, urgently needed to reject their "Prophet."

Before 1803 Jefferson favored gradually integrating Native Americans into American society, as he repeatedly assured Hawkins. He, too, believed the "ultimate point of rest and happiness for them is to let our settlements and theirs meet and blend together and to intermix and become one people."[56] But after the acquisition of the Louisiana Territory, and Tecumseh's revolt, Jefferson drastically changed his stance, rejecting assimilationism and adopting instead the idea that the Indian population east of the Mississippi should be resettled on the western side, in the newly acquired territory, thereby eliminating the problems posed by their presence in already settled areas. Abandoning his enlightened policy of gradual integration with help, Jefferson shifted to the opposite strategy: "instead of inviting Indians to come within our limits, our object is to tempt them to evacuate them." In practice, this meant driving them out. He gradually abandoned integrationism, moving to a policy of organized pressure and large-scale "purchases" of Indian lands west of Appalachians, initiating the process of Indian removal and transfer great distances further to the west that Andrew Jackson (1767–1845), as seventh president of the United States (1829–37), subsequently resumed with still more unrelenting sweep and vigor.[57]

Catastrophic losses during and immediately after the Revolutionary War, in terms of territory, jurisdiction, standing, and self-esteem, exerted a hugely traumatic and demoralizing effect on Indian society and on Girty, Allan, Hawkins, and all who devoted their lives to assisting the tribes. A few idealistic and committed enlighteners such as Du Ponceau and Gallatin persisted in taking a keen interest in Native American cultures, languages, and traditions and efforts to conserve them, but American political, educational, and church leaders mostly sought to justify, usually theologically, the tendency to drive the Indians back and exclude them from society and legal and political rights (except in a marginal fashion), often expressing intense scorn for their moral condition and "decay." Contempt for Indian alcoholism, indolence, vagrancy, and willingness to engage in seemingly casual interracial sex helped underpin the abysmally low esteem in which Indian society was predominantly held, in direct opposition to the elevated view of the Indians propagated by radical thought reaffirmed by Volney during his travels in America during 1795–97.

In the case of Timothy Dwight, president of Yale College and leader of the intellectual campaign against deism, radicalism, and freethinking in New England, contempt for Native American morals merged explicitly with antagonism to radical thought. Visiting Stonington, Connecticut, on the edge of the Pequot Indian reserve in 1807, he remarked that the tribe's former renowned energy and prowess had now vanished entirely, and that these Indians had sunk into an utterly passive torpor in his opinion owing to vice and sinful living. "Godwin's great and favorite step toward perfection," he observed with satisfaction, referring to Godwin's subversive ethics of personal freedom, "they practice in the most unlimited manner." Despite their attending Baptist services, they were a people living in his view "without the restraint of law, morals or religion," perfectly illustrating the horrifying danger of humans living "free in the fullest sense," of degenerating into unbounded promiscuity governed only by their passions and appetites, and the ideas of Godwin.[58]

Understanding of the real nature of the Native Americans' tragic plight and sympathy for their fate in the American Enlightenment was to be found only in a few restricted circles—often specialists with intimate knowledge of their culture and customs.

CHAPTER 8

Whites Dispossessed

Poor Whites

Among the many striking parallels between the American and French revolutions were the widespread disruptive and radicalizing political repercussions of growing economic distress among poor whites—a feature that in the American case has been often downplayed or ignored. In fact, the vast scale of economic dislocation and deprivation caused by the inexorable pressures of the Revolution—the disruptive impact of heavy taxes to finance the war, high prices for necessities, systematic price manipulation, flour and bread shortages, currency instability, and burdensome troop quartering and movements, along with chronic difficulties in paying the troops—became a powerfully destabilizing social and political mechanism in town and country in both cases.

Philadelphia, chief seedbed of political radicalism during the American Revolution, was also a key focus of economic friction. But the relation between economic stress and political and intellectual radicalism was no simple one. Rather, economic discontent was as likely to destabilize and disrupt as reinforce the radical tendency in attitudes and politics. Among incidents illustrating the complexity of the relationship between socioeconomic friction and political and intellectual radicalism was the so-called Fort Wilson Riot of October 1779. When the British evacuated Philadelphia in June 1778, they left behind a morass of tension, resentments, and feuds besides various sicknesses. At the same time, Philadelphia's storekeepers, anticipating the British descent on Virginia and the South, raised prices of supplies almost across the board even before coastal routes to the South were disrupted. During 1778–79, contemporary letters, newssheets, and pamphlets confirm, increasing currency instability and the profiteering of "combinations" of "monopolizers"— cliques of local merchants combining to drive up prices by exploiting flour and bread shortages and manipulating other supplies—exacted a heavy toll on Philadelphia's artisans and poor.

Apart from rum, which remained stable, food and dry goods articles rose spectacularly in price during 1778–79. Paine later recalled his shock at having had to pay "three hundred paper dollars" for a few worsted stockings.[1] An all-too-familiar method of "monopolizing" was to hold back newly arrived flour supplies and other necessities for weeks on ships anchored in the harbor or in warehouses, a practice known as "forestalling." Of the leading "forestallers," Robert Morris (1734–1806), "our celebrated financier" as Rush called him, a politically influential elite merchant who as Congress's Superintendent of Finance from 1781 to 1784 was soon a powerful figure in the fledgling United States government and stalwart of the Pennsylvania anti-democratic "republican party" aiming to overthrow the 1776 democratic constitution, was reputed among the worst.[2] Popular pressure for price controls and regulation, expressed in rowdy informal gatherings and town meetings, intensified.

Raucous gatherings in State House Yard produced two committees charged with drawing up a price regulation strategy for the city with Paine figuring on both. Neither committee nor the Pennsylvania General Assembly's Supreme Executive Council, which also tried to impose regulations to restrain prices, could devise a coherent strategy rendering price regulation effective, however, or overcome the merchants' tenacious resistance, any more than proved possible in France in 1793–94. Later, in the midst of the French Revolution, Paine recalled this earlier episode, pronouncing all such attempts to impose price controls unworkable and counterproductive, resulting only in further price increases.[3] Beside the inherent difficulty of implementing such a policy, the reviving strength in the unicameral legislature of conservatives like Robert Morris and John Dickinson, now recovering somewhat from their nadir during 1775–76, presented a growing obstacle. The democratic trend lost ground, after 1776, due to low voter turnout in the 1776 Philadelphia autumn elections and the relative indifference of the needy to the intricacies of the state constitutional debates and politics. This was one of the main factors causing economic deprivation to cut across and sap the radical tendency.[4] In addition, there were quarrels and defections. Rush, earlier an ally but opposed to food price regulation, broke with the radical leadership during 1778–79, estrangement that eventually produced total disillusionment with the Revolution.[5] He swung to Adams, who more than any other commentator, insisted that "perfection of government" resides in "providing restraints against the tyranny of rulers on the one hand and the licentiousness of the people on the other."[6]

The inability to stem the relentless rise in prices of necessities aggravated economic distress in Philadelphia, as was attested by many contemporaries. Growing economic distress heightened the pressure within the city militia companies for action generating more pressure to apply coercive methods.[7] In the autumn of 1779, gangs of militiamen with clubs toured Philadelphia stores "obliging" retailers to lower their prices. On 4 October 1779, a crowd of two hundred or so militiamen seized four notorious "monopolizers" and paraded them through the streets in humiliating garb, shouting populist slogans. This "beating the rogues' march" was followed the next day by an "insurrection," as some called it, caused by militiamen demonstrating in the city center against merchants resisting price regulation. "The objects of the mob were unknown or confusedly understood," Rush wrote to John Adams, "they were enraged chiefly by liquor." Passing a large residence on Walnut Street belonging to James Wilson, a leading conservative lawyer, defender of Tories and opponent of price controls, the crowd were fired on. Wilson and Morris had barricaded themselves inside with armed friends, thirty or forty "gentlemen." "A battle ensued" with fusillades of firing both ways but mainly into the crowd from those inside, leaving six or seven dead and around nineteen wounded. "Our streets were for the first time stained with fraternal blood." To halt the violence, other militia companies were summoned. The demonstrators were dispersed, some briefly imprisoned. The Supreme Executive Council, whose secretary at the time was the radical Timothy Matlack, sought to smooth things over as swiftly as possible. Everyone detained was soon released; no further punitive action was taken. "Since this melancholy affair," added Rush, "we have had a calm in our city. But every face wears the marks of fear and dejection."[8]

The revolutionary leadership had failed to back up the crowds. Philadelphia's radical elite—now lacking Young (who died two years earlier)—directed the movement for price controls and the campaign against "monopolizers" but refused to align with their lower-class supporters when it came to violence and unruly methods. Aspiring to remain political mentors of the people, Matlack, Paine, James Hutchinson, the artist-revolutionary Charles Willson Peale (1741–1827), who produced portraits of many revolutionary leaders (including over a dozen of Washington), and the merchant and militia officer General Daniel Roberdeau (1727–95) all firmly disassociated themselves from uncontrolled mob behavior.[9] Roberdeau held that if "combinations" of merchants could manipulate prices, the people must be allowed to defend themselves by forming "combinations" to enforce price regulation but refused to tolerate spontaneous crowd action and rioting. The Philadelphia violence might easily have escalated and grown seriously disruptive in the midst of the Revolution.

The nervousness it caused was widespread. "We are at this moment on a prec-ipice," reported one prominent congressman to Adams the day after the inci-dent, "and what I have long dreaded and often intimated to my friends, seems to be breaking forth—a convulsion among the people."[10]

In conflict with the radicals, Philadelphia's top merchants and "monopoliz-ers" mostly sympathized with the Philadelphia Republican Society, founded in March 1779 and dedicated to overthrowing the Pennsylvania democratic constitution of 1776, wanting a more restricted, "aristocratic" voting and leg-islative system. Radicals resisted but, on both sides, the degree of convergence between economic and social forces and pressures, and ideological stance, was limited. None of the four "rogues" paraded on 4 October, for instance, belonged to the society.[11] Equally, the Constitutional Society founded shortly afterward to counter the Republican Society by organizing radical sentiment in defense of the 1776 constitution, an organization explicitly democratic and in favor of price control, did not automatically endorse the aims and activities of the discontented militia and crowds. Radical revolutionary lead-ers pursued a broad program of democratic republican political, social, cul-tural, and economic objectives justified by enlightened concepts; the rioters, while resenting the ability of the rich to evade military service exacerbated by the army's maintaining an obvious gap between "gentlemen" supplying the officer class and the ordinary soldiers, chiefly wanted cheaper flour and bread, compulsory price regulation, and punishment of Tories (with whom they routinely associated the "monopolizers"). If the two levels of friction, the socioeconomic on the one hand and between democrats and "aristocrats" fighting the political battle on the other, closely intersected, they remained significantly distinct. The two levels continued to closely interact, though, during the later war years and after, against a grim background of price insta-bility and fiscal pressure.[12]

While hoarding and food price manipulation eased during the Revolu-tionary War's immediate aftermath, other economic and financial difficul-ties grew more acute. Renewed social unrest after 1783 stemmed principally from the mounting fiscal pressure together with the resumed demands of large rentier landowners. Earlier, between the Revolution's commencing and around 1780, paper money and ensuing steep inflation helped ease indebted-ness and clear tax arrears. In addition, with New York City occupied, protest-ing small tenant farmers in the surrounding area, the "anti-renters," saw the New York landowners' ascendancy and revenues curtailed to some degree after the New York State legislature banished nearly sixty Tory property own-ers in 1779 and authorized confiscation of their estates.[13] In the most no-table setback for the gentry, Loyalist landlords in Westchester and Duchess counties had around 66,000 acres of their estates expropriated and sold off to rebellious farmers.[14] But after this relatively benign early phase, during and after the second half of the war the trends rebounded on tenants and small independent farmers.[15] The "Great Proprietors" tightened their grip after 1780 throughout the Hudson Valley running the length of New York State, as in Virginia, Maryland, Maine, and other areas where large numbers of small-holders rented farms from big landowners often on disadvantageous terms, producing a growing problem of rural indebtedness and inability to pay taxes.

Leading gentry dynasties like the Livingstons, Philip Schuyler, Timothy Pickering, and Henry Knox—some longstanding, others recently emerging big speculators—wanted an American Revolution placing government, power, and privilege squarely in their own hands and safeguarding their property rights.[16] As the fighting receded from New England and the Middle Colonies, the Livingstons, Van Rensselaers, Schuylers, and other "aristocrats" resumed their efforts to build up their holdings, contracting with new waves of settlers and offering long-term tenancies for substantially raised rents. In the domain of Rensselaerswyck, once a Dutch patroonship allocated by the Dutch West India Company in 1630 to Kiliaen van Rensselaer, an estate to the north of the Livingston domain (160,000 acres) that had grown far beyond the 250,000 acres estimated at an earlier stage, encompassing huge tracts around Albany on either side of the Hudson River, the number of tenant households increased by three times between 1779 and 1800, from 1,000 to 3,000 farms. Stephen van Rensselaer (1764–1839) inherited the estate on his twenty-first birthday in 1785 and as its young proprietor assigned more and more farms under tenancy agreements, enabling him to accumulate an unprecedented rent mountain. Although he was reputedly more lenient in fixing and exacting rents than some other Great Proprietors, as a group the landlords vigorously expanded their rent "mountains" and financial status, exacting social deference and, where applicable, votes, exerting a range of pressures to force compliance. Albany County was almost completely dominated politically, as well as economically and legally, by Van Rensselaer and his father-in-law, the Revolutionary War commander Philip Schuyler. At the same time, Van Rensselaer established dozens of churches, moral reform societies, and other ecclesiastical charitable establishments and financed the Rensselaer School, later to become the Rensselaer Polytechnic Institute.[17]

While settled areas dominated by large domains became more densely farmed, fresh zones in western New York, Virginia, Pennsylvania, and Maine were opened up by or for Great Proprietors. For roughly two decades (1780–1800), conflict between big landowners and anti-renters, and local "liberty-men," both grew in intensity and expanded geographically, spreading westward through the backcountry. In Virginia, tension between the pro-Revolution gentry and poor white tenant farmers manifested itself throughout the war, especially in the notorious reluctance of the latter to serve in the revolutionary militia. Although Virginia boasted the second-largest white population of any state, at around 280,000, mobilizing poor whites behind the Revolution failed more dismally there than virtually anywhere (aside from the Carolinas).[18] In 1775–76 early disruption of Virginia's prewar rural economy and tobacco sales, making it harder for poor white tenants to pay their rents, stoked rural unrest, rent strikes, forcible closure of courts, and other armed demonstrations albeit stopping short of violence.[19] These tensions associated with fraught tenancy and poor white landlessness evolved into a major destabilizing factor within the Revolution after 1783; this was especially due to the fact that the state legislatures (except Pennsylvania and Vermont) generally denied the vote and political rights to the propertyless under the newly revised state constitutions. The overall situation worsened for a time, from 1783, with Congress's decision not to directly assign vacant lands in the western reaches of New York and Pennsylvania (from where the Iroquois were expelled), the Northwest, and other areas along the frontiers that had been promised to the Independence War common soldier as belated remuneration in lieu of pay or compensation for hardship.

The problem of the released soldiery, from 1783, weighed especially heavily. In the mid- and late 1780s, a profound bitterness and anger gripped many war veterans. "When the country had drained the last drop of service it could screw out of the poor soldiers," recalled Sergeant Joseph Plumb Martin, from Connecticut, "they were turned adrift like worn-out horses, and nothing said about land to pasture them on." Congress, which in 1776 had promised each man enlisting one hundred acres in unspecified locations when the war ended, did in fact appropriate tracts in Ohio and elsewhere in the West under the category "Soldier's Lands," Martin explained, but "no agents were appointed to see that the poor fellows ever got possession of their lands; no one ever took the least care about it, except a pack of speculators" who did their utmost "to pluck the last feather from the soldiers."[20] Among those attesting to this, and Washington's own hand in the outcome, was Tom Paine, who in his published attack on the president in 1796 claimed the "lands obtained by the Revolution were lavished on partisans; the interest of the disbanded soldier was sold to the speculator; injustice was acted under pretense of faith; and the chief of the army became the patron of fraud."[21] The disarray and confusion surrounding land plots designated for veterans was aggravated by these often being ill-defined and hard to extricate from legal tangles surrounding disputed titles to larger areas encompassing whole batches of farms, forcing most soldiers to relinquish instead of settle on their assigned lands, often selling to speculators much too cheaply. Seething with resentment, disbanded ex-soldiers settled where they could.

One group, including Martin, established farms on Maine's Cape Jellison, a tongue of land forming part of the huge 576,000-acre Waldo Patent, a large slice of mid-Maine between the Kennebec and Penobscot rivers, including Camden, forming the estates of a departed Tory dynasty. The veterans soon became locked in a land war with Washington's grasping former artillery general, Henry Knox, beginning in 1785–86, when Knox, who had inherited his claim through marriage, obtained legal title to estates occupying most of mid-Maine.[22] To drive the small independent farmers into submission or away, Knox launched an epic campaign of lawyers' actions, court cases, and extra-legal harassment verging on outright violence that lasted thirty years. Several of Knox's survey teams sent into the backcountry to subdivide his territory into plots for renting out were ambushed or shot at by desperate resisters. On one occasion, in July 1800, a group of "liberty-men," "blacked and disguised like Indians"—a recurring feature in the Maine unrest—ambushed seven of Knox's surveyors, wounding three and forcing them to evacuate the area. Martin himself was among the recalcitrant refusing rents and eventually reduced to landless poverty by Knox's offensive.[23]

New York State's main artery, the Hudson River Valley, remained a particular focus of such friction.[24] Earlier disturbances in the 1750s and mid-1760s, the milieu in which the radical Thomas Young grew up, had been stamped out by the colony's officials, at the behest of the Livingston, Schuyler, and Van Rensselaer dynasties, using a variety of methods including intimidation and violence. The 1766 repression left many small tenant habitations in a sorry state, noted an eyewitness, "some demolished, some robbed and pillag'd, and others of them invelop'd in flames of fire."[25] During the Revolution, while New York's mercantile leaders and big landowners concerted resistance to the Crown, Hudson Valley tenant farmers often resented the "great state and magnificence" of those Ethan Allen dubbed New York's "junto of land thieves"[26] more than they did the British. Much as Vermont's Green Mountain Boys threatened to defect and join Canada rather than succumb to the New York landowners' efforts to absorb Vermont into their patrimony, Hudson Valley anti-renter tenant farmers remained distinctly ambivalent toward the main revolutionary conflict while tenaciously resisting exploitative short-term leases and landlord harassment. On the 160,000-acre estate belonging to Robert R. Livingston (1746–1813), a leading pillar of the New York State aristocracy's efforts to avoid being ejected from the state legislature like their Pennsylvanian colleagues, many tenants aligned with Toryism and the king as a way of opposing Livingston in the hope of ultimately wresting their "lands" from him.[27] Unrest, punctuated by local risings of disgruntled rural tenants, continued throughout the period between 1783 and 1811.

Rents likewise provided the main income of many big Virginia landowners, including Washington, now among the richest men in America. In December 1793, Washington noted that "all my landed property east of the Appalachian Mountains is under rent, except the estate called Mount Vernon"; but this too he now considered renting out.[28] Mount Vernon actually amounted to only 7,000 acres, a modest component of his domain compared with the approximately 45,000 acres he owned elsewhere, in Virginia, New York, Pennsylvania, and Ohio. Small by comparison, Jefferson's estate by 1794 totaled 10,647 acres, divided between three different Virginia counties. Possessing 150 slaves, he worked much of his land directly, as large plantations.[29] Since land was the key to political power and landowner control in the state legislatures, rural tension in Virginia, the Carolinas, and Maryland, as in New York, Massachusetts, Maine, and Vermont, tended to be simultaneously economic, social, and political.[30]

Of course, many unresisting tenants did not oppose landlord sway since rebellion held out little prospect of success while loyalty and deference to the estate system was "rewarded." Post-revolutionary stability, rising rents, and the subsiding of insurgency assisted what has been termed the "revival of the gentry," enabling landlords to stabilize their control, expand their aristocratic lifestyle, develop a genteel code and culture, and become local patrons on an unprecedented scale. Gouverneur Morris was among the most prominent and politically active of the New York "aristocracy." Morrisania, the family estate near New York City, though thoroughly ravaged by British troops during the war, recovered afterward along with another estate acquired in New Jersey and, during the 1780s, prospered under his direction, elevating his social status and aristocratic demeanor.[31]

Until the early 1790s, tenants and landlords, the two opposing sides in rural New York land and legal battles, by no means always corresponded to the two rival factions embroiled in the increasingly fierce ideological conflict between "democrats" and "aristocrats" in the political arena. New York City artisans, at times, looked to the Federalists as much as the Jeffersonians. By the late 1790s, though, the continuing social and legal tension over rents had produced a situation where most New York large landowners identified with the Federalist party while tenant disgruntlement and opposition led anti-renters to gravitate to Jefferson's republicans, though the latter retained the support of some major landowners.[32]

Shays' Rebellion (1786–87)

Rents, oppressive landlords, and the frustrated quest for independent propri-
etorship were the socially most divisive factors in rural New York, Virginia,
Maine, and other parts. This was not at all the case, though, in Massachusetts,
where Shays' Rebellion, the most significant post-Revolution insurgency, occurred. This rebellion commenced in June 1786. Crowds of protestors closed
courthouses and stopped debt hearings and other cases over a large area to
prevent creditors and their lawyers from jailing them or foreclosing on farms.[33]
Mobs, often carrying arms and given to intimidation, forcibly released debtors from prison and besieged judges and federal officials while the Worcester and other town militias refused to act against the demonstrators.[34] The
heavy-handed methods used to suppress the disorder and prevent "stopping
of the courts" by "bodies of armed men" resulted in scattered violence and
several miniscule "battles" with hardly any fatalities that ended only in late
February 1787, followed by continuing small-gang harassment of particularly
unpopular merchants, lawyers, and officials until June.

   The rising was widespread in the western half of Massachusetts, especially
Worcester, Hampshire, and Berkshire counties, areas with many independent
small farmers and few rural "aristocrats," but was scattered, the movement
being curiously uneven. Some widely dispersed places such as Springfield, Colrain, Concord, and Pelham became heavily implicated while others in the same
areas remained quiescent. The rebels' nominal leader, Daniel Shays (c. 1747–
1825), was an indebted small farmer from Pelham, a Scots-Irish community
some seventy miles west of Boston, notorious for harassing Tories at the start
of the Revolution.[35] A veteran army captain who had served at Bunker Hill,
Ticonderoga, and Saratoga, Shays's financial plight forced him, among other
measures, to sell a sword with a golden handle Lafayette had presented him
with, a transaction detractors later widely publicized to "prove" his supposedly
despicable character. But he possessed charisma. "If Shays had not been a
desperate debtor," remarked Hamilton dismissively in *The Federalist*, in November 1786, "it is much to be doubted whether Massachusetts would have
been plunged into a civil war"; Hamilton would have preferred to see the Federal government take over the state's debts and redistribute the burden more
equitably.[36] The upheaval Shays's name was attached to was unquestionably
serious even if he afterward disavowed any intention to provoke large-scale
violence and when commanding "at the head of about 1,200 men" in the biggest encounter, at Springfield on 25 January 1787, his "army," once intimidation failed, was quickly scattered by a Federal force of 900 with a burst of cannon fire, leaving four dead and twenty wounded.[37]

Many smallholders implicated in the western Massachusetts insurgency were Revolutionary War veterans who had exchanged state promissory notes they were unable to use for purchases, paying taxes, or settling debts, for a miniscule fraction of face value in cash, and become increasingly indebted. "Much the greater part of these securities," noted one observer at the time, "are now in the hands of people who either from principles of Toryism or avarice have either wholly oppos'd the exertions" of the people against Britain or contributed only a minimum.[38] Farmers' indebtedness was undoubtedly a major factor in the insurgency. However, veteran and small farm indebtedness was a general phenomenon equally prevalent in the rest of the United States, in Virginia, New York, Pennsylvania, Maryland, Connecticut, or Vermont no less than Massachusetts. Hence other factors must be brought into the equation to explain the unparalleled proportions, the scale of the unrest fomented by Shays' Rebellion.

Several specifically local factors, political, fiscal and financial, aggravated the situation. Though rivaled in some respects by New York or Maryland, no state since 1780 boasted a more "aristocratic" constitution with a more restricted suffrage than Massachusetts, and while backcountry farmers were often not especially interested in constitutional affairs, a direct consequence, experience soon proved, was a power shift toward the wealthy mercantile elite living in Boston and the eastern counties. This, in turn, translated into a regressive tax policy, placing the burden on farms rather than consumption, trade, or fortunes, disproportionately affecting the west and transferring wealth from west to east—a much-resented setback for small farmers.[39] In particular a poll tax levied without regard to income weighed heavily on the less prosperous. In locations like Colrain, near the Vermont border, a small town with one of the highest proportions of citizens involved in the rising of any of the western Massachusetts townships, another place where many Scots-Irish had settled, the democratic Pennsylvania model adopted by Ethan Allen and the Green Mountain Boys for Vermont in 1777 now looked decidedly preferable to that of Massachusetts.[40] Many feeling cheated by the state legislature reportedly wanted to discard John Adams's constitution, eliminate the senate, and acquire a single-chamber legislature that would remove wealth qualifications for officeholders in Massachusetts and choose officials annually.[41] The same conclusion was reached by some in the Maine backcountry, where (as in Connecticut) there were rumblings of sympathy with the neighboring insurgency, helping foment an incipient movement for separate statehood. Though thwarted for the moment (Maine became a separate state only in 1820), moves for separate statehood became a factor in local politics beginning in 1786–87, especially among backcountry farmers abhorring the Boston "aristocracy."[42] Their detractors in Portland (formerly Falmouth) and coastal areas allied to the Boston elite, and opposing separate statehood for Maine, responded by denouncing the Maine separatists as seditious "Shaysites."[43]

Still more unique to Massachusetts was the unbendingly "aristocratic" financial strategy of the state legislature. Elsewhere, state legislatures decreed that much of the face value of the promissory notes and "securities" issued to creditors and soldiers during the war had eroded for good. Various schemes to consolidate and pay off wartime state debts were devised, some more generous to the financiers and merchant investors than others but all, except that of Massachusetts, laying some of the loss on the creditors while seeking to hold the tax burden in check. Protesting indignantly in Rhode Island, John Brown and other wealthy Providence and Newport speculators in the end pocketed only one-eighth of the face value of their acquired notes.[44] This was not unjust, answered the state legislature, since this still exceeded what they had paid out to the soldiers for them. Massachusetts alone ignored the notes' sunken current market value, undertaking to pay what they were nominally worth when issued.[45] The result was an unparalleled bonanza for the Boston financiers and merchant elite and a heavier tax burden for everyone else than applied elsewhere, given that liquidating the nominal debt at face value proved exceedingly costly. "The Massachusetts Assembly had, in its zeal to get the better of their debt," Adams admitted to Jefferson, "laid on a tax rather heavier than the people could bear."[46] Furthermore, where other states eased somewhat their laws and procedures concerning debt during the Independence War's difficult aftermath, Massachusetts did not, rendering the burden still harder to shoulder.

It was a social tragedy. Anger at the way the state debts were settled to the advantage of the financial elite and disadvantage of ordinary folk was by no means confined to Massachusetts. But the resentment there reached an intensity seen nowhere else. By the mid-1780s, no less than four-fifths of the Massachusetts state public debt in promissory notes and "securities" had been transferred from soldiers and ordinary householders to the financial elite, 40 percent of it to just thirty-five wealthy Boston investors. These persons were enormously enriched at the expense of the rest. Particularly furious were the rural war veterans who now found themselves crushingly taxed by their state legislature to redeem notes they themselves, driven by hardship, had relinquished to investors at a fraction of face value.[47] "How shocking to humanity," wrote William Whiting (1730–92), an erudite Berkshire County chief justice strongly sympathizing with the rebels, "must be the idea that the poor soldier who has for many years through dangers, hardships and nakedness wrought out the salvation of his country, must now be compelled to pay his proportion of the interest and principal of twenty shillings for every two shillings and sixpence [i.e., 12.5 percent of face value] he has received as wages for his arduous and important services. It would certainly have been much better for him to have received no wages at all."[48] In effect, it was a massive state swindle in favor of the financiers.

The disaffected did not rise "into mobs and tumults upon small oppressions," recorded Whiting: besides crushing taxation and heavy indebtedness, they faced immediate confiscation of indebted lands and properties that were then auctioned off at wretched prices. Besides this, under Massachusetts laws they had to pay exorbitant lawyers' fees every time creditors cited householders for debt in court or threatened confiscations, even when debtors just delayed rather than refused payment.[49] The insurgents did not consider themselves "rebels," instead calling themselves "regulators" or the "New England Regulation" and erecting "liberty trees" as revolutionary emblems. They resorted to arms, replicating revolutionary rhetoric and invoking popular sovereignty and "natural rights," to suppress the "tyrannical government in Massachusetts" plundering the people under a state constitution they denounced as "iniquitous and cruel." Concurrent rumblings resounded in adjoining parts of New Hampshire and Vermont as well as Connecticut and Maine. A few prominent figures besides Whiting clearly sympathized with the rebellion, including Jefferson in Paris and several preachers among the many throughout Massachusetts and nearby who nevertheless preached against insubordination and resort to violence and did much to dampen the movement in most west Massachusetts towns.[50] Ethan Allen, in neighboring Vermont, expected to sympathize, was offered command of the insurgents but declined, professing contempt for both sides. Tired of war and keen to pursue "his philosophic studies," Allen readily agreed the Massachusetts oligarchy were a "pack of damned rascals and that there was no virtue in them" but viewed Shays's adherents too as a "damned bunch of rascals."[51]

Whiting published an open letter under the name "Gracchus," justifying the rebellion in principle, albeit remaining ambivalent about their resort to violence. He pronounced the eastern elite an "odious and detestable" aristocracy, "overgrown plunderers tyrannizing over the rest of the people, whom they have impoverish'd and rendered incapable of resistance."[52] At the same time, he identified as the episode's key feature—and that of greatest relevance to the wider American situation and future—the "aristocracy's" remarkable success in swinging most opinion, and all twelve other States, firmly behind the repression. In this the financial oligarchy were aided by the lawyers, sheriffs, editors, and military men, the "contemptible tools, vassals and dependents" of those

186 / *Chapter 8*

seeking to "enrich themselves by the plunder of their fellow-citizens." With disturbing ease, the Boston elite and their "tools" swayed not just Congress but the general public to condemn the insurgents as "mobbers, rioters, and disturbers of the peace" and approve every repressive measure taken against them by deliberately misrepresenting the insurrection's real character. Eager to persuade Washington to come in person, Knox grossly exaggerated the scale of the rebel "army" while simultaneously claiming only a "few wretched officers" had joined the "rebellion." In reality, the total of armed insurgents was considerably less than he reported but rather more, at least forty, veteran officers *were* implicated.[53]

Whiting viewed the "rebellion" as clear evidence that the true principles of "natural rights" and democratic republicanism, the veritable basis of the Revolution, were being subverted in the new United States by "designing men." "The design of all government is or ought to be the equal protection, prosperity, and happiness of all its subjects: and whenever it happens in any republican government or commonwealth that some part of the citizens have it in their power by compulsion to enrich themselves by the same means that impoverishes and depresses some other orders of people, that government is either defective in its original constitution, or else the laws are unjustly and unequally administered." Any fair-minded observer should be horrified to "what a pitch of affluence and opulence a certain set of men have arisen in the course of a few years, and that principally drawn from the very vitals of the people." They had achieved spectacular European-style inequality within a short time, even if using methods different from those customary in Europe. America's situation doubtless diverged from that of those parts of the world where the common people had no choice but to "bow down to that double-headed monster of ecclesiastical and civil tyranny," namely absolutist monarchy and the Church, but in the final reckoning the American outcome did not appear very different from the European.[54]

Whiting stemmed from an elite family and had been a conservative until 1783, veering to a radical standpoint only in the mid-1780s, immediately preceding the rebellion. He was moved by the "extreme poverty and distress great numbers of the poorer sort of people are reduced to."[55] But while he sympathized, he also blamed the dissolution of republican principles in America on the protesters, on Massachusetts citizens and the American people generally, no less than "the aristocracy." The disaster was as much due to their "inattention to public affairs for several years past" and failure to grasp and promote republican values as anything else. Those eligible to vote were by no means fulfilling their duty to "watch and guard their liberties" and ensure the election of worthy representatives. Americans had risked their lives and fortunes to "free themselves from the tyrannical claims of Great Britain: Take heed how you are duped in to be the wretched instruments of inslaving your brethren in the other states"; for liberty is easily lost and "once this game is played in any one of the States, of subjecting the major part to the minor," he admonished, "it will soon run through every other state, and your liberties, dear bought as they are, will be gone forever."[56]

"Inattention," ignorance, and failure to involve themselves in politics lay at the root of the malaise. Those orchestrating the Massachusetts repression enjoyed the backing of powerful elements in central government but also of large segments of the public swayed by the insidious clique through their remarkable leverage over the press. Why did they fill the public papers, protested Whiting, "with lampoon, satire and ridicule pointed at all those who are opposing them in their ambitions and lucrative pursuits, branding them with all the opprobrious and odious epithets their fruitful imaginations can suggest" while deterring the "printers from publishing any defense of the conduct of those they call insurgents"? They designed to "raise the indignation of the people in the other States to that degree as to induce them to assist in entirely destroying all those that oppose them in this State and thereby enable them to introduce and establish their favourite aristocracy." Equally, oligarchs and editors deliberately obscured the war veterans' participation in the unrest. If things continued as they were, the "principle of republicanism will be totally destroyed, and an aristocracy succeed of course."[57]

Sporadic, inarticulate, and widely misrepresented, Shays' Rebellion had a considerable impact psychologically and politically. "It has given more alarm," commented Jefferson, "than I think it should have done."[58] In Massachusetts and the Thirteen States generally, the insurrection caused a considerable shock; many Federalist leaders grew agitated, not least Washington, who feared that "combustibles" elsewhere "may set fire," meaning that the unrest might spread.[59] But the key feature was the strikingly negative reaction of the press, clergy, and most onlookers. The rebellion deepened the basic rift in American politics and society, consolidating the anti-democratic tendency and hostility toward the Pennsylvania-Vermont model. Successfully vilifying Shaysites as treacherous fomenters of sedition, prominent political figures such as the state governor James Bowdoin, Knox, and Sam Adams (who denounced them with particular vehemence) called for suspension of normal justice rules and the death penalty for rebel leaders. Officials, press, clergy, and people strengthened the hand of those, like Knox and Washington, urging a stronger central administration and larger Federal army, thereby aiding the "Federalists" at a crucial moment in deliberations over the United States Constitution.[60] "Who can determine what might have been the issue of the late convulsions," demanded Hamilton rhetorically in December 1787, given the "tempestuous situation from which Massachusetts has scarcely emerged," had the "malcontents been headed by a Caesar or by a Cromwell?"[61]

As the insurrection petered out in the face of the over four thousand militiamen sent by the governor from Boston to crush the rising, there was a general feeling that a dangerous crisis had been surmounted and that its aftermath required delicate handling. Bowdoin's faction in the Massachusetts state legislature were punished by the electors, however, the following spring, with the governor and his friends ousted from office, followed by the state legislature adjusting its course somewhat in fiscal policy, lessening the tax burden on farms and raising taxes on consumption and trade so as to head off further trouble. Massachusetts thus blended initial judicial rigor with subsequent flexibility.[62] Thousands of vanquished "rebels" were brought to court and stripped of citizenship rights (later restored), with hundreds indicted in Worcester, Springfield, and neighboring towns for "treason," "insurrection," and "sedition," the process dragging on for months with conflicting voices alternately urging harsh and lenient punishment. Four thousand insurgents signed confessions admitting complicity in return for amnesty. Finally, the elections and fear of aggravating tensions inclined the legislature to leniency. Eighteen of the "rebels" indicted were sentenced to death but only two were actually hanged, the rest, with Shays himself among those remitted, incurring fines and terms of imprisonment. Justifying rebellion in print was deemed more pernicious than rebellion itself. Arrested in February, Whiting was tried in April for endorsing insurrection and sentenced to seven years' imprisonment and a hefty fine.[63]

The repression, energetically urged by the popular press and clergy, aided the Federalists in persuading the American public that their country was "in crisis" and that a more powerful and centralized authority was requisite.[64] "The horror excited in our minds by the late spirit of insurrection," commented one Congregationalist minister, "flies away before the New Congress, like the darkness of the night before the rising sun."[65] Shays' Rebellion was likewise seized on by the British ministry and German princes as palpable evidence of the "anarchy" American subversion encouraged and of the inferiority and undesirability of republics compared to "monarchy." Ministers in London were anxious to counter the eulogies and hyperbole celebrating the American Revolution as the birth of a new and better kind of society and to foment the intellectual anti-Americanism fashionable in Britain in 1780s and 1790s, which if mainly designed to discourage republican sentiment at home was partly aimed at dimming America's appeal and discouraging large-scale emigration from Britain and Ireland to America.[66] Not just British opinion but also most European newspapers and pamphlets during the later 1780s brimmed with derogatory misrepresentations of America. "After informing Europe for several consecutive years about imaginary uprisings that allegedly took place," supposedly casting the nascent United States into constant anarchy and turmoil, in 1786–87, remarked Condorcet, the derogatory reports in British gazettes identified a real tumult—Shays' Rebellion, which threw all Massachusetts into confusion and spread alarm in all the states—as material ideal for denigrating the Revolution.[67]

In Europe, commented Condorcet further two years later, advocates of "mixed government" and monarchy began regularly citing Shays' Rebellion to illustrate the undesirability and instability of "popular governments."[68] This was absurd: the disruption and harm caused were wholly insignificant compared to what took place in Britain itself, for example, during popular risings like the anti-Catholic Lord Gordon Riots of 1780 when much property was damaged, the Irish immigrant district of Moorfields in London was sacked, and hundreds were killed and wounded. "Those who rioted in Massachusetts did not use violence against any individual, his person or his property, and paid everywhere the fair price for what was needed."[69] There were just a handful of deaths. But the absurdity of the charge did nothing to detract from the effectiveness of claiming republics were undesirable and disruptive. "The British ministry have so long hired their gazetteers to repeat and model into every form lies about our being in anarchy," wrote Jefferson to William Smith from Paris in November 1787, "that the world has at length believed them, the English nation has believed them, the ministers themselves have come to believe them and what is more wonderful, we have believed them ourselves. Yet where does this anarchy exist? Where did it ever exist except in the single instance of Massachusetts? And can history produce an instance of a rebellion so honourably conducted?" Congress and the nation had been "too much impressed by the insurrection of Massachusetts." It was in this connection that Jefferson made his notorious remark about the "tree of liberty" needing to be "refreshed from time to time with the blood of patriots and tyrants. It is its natural manure."[70]

The seething, sporadic backcountry unrest characterizing America in the aftermath of the Revolution subsided from the end of the 1780s and especially after Jefferson's unexpected electoral victory of 1800. The pressure eased partly as a result of changing circumstances, in particular the spread of both great estates and small independent farms onto forcibly vacated Indian lands, and partly party policy.[71] Once in power, Jefferson's Republicans took steps to limit the Great Proprietors' legal and political clout, including the Compromise Act in Pennsylvania, under which state commissioners, chaired by the radical Thomas Cooper, obliged the big proprietors to allow Susquehanna Valley settlers who had arrived before 1783 to purchase small farms of up to three hundred acres at fixed low prices, drawing on state funds to compensate the affected landowners. Improved economic conditions owing to the accelerating westward expansion softened the accumulated resentment. But the essential clash of principle—the view of the American Revolution promoted by the radical tendency versus the "aristocracy's" and clergy's interpretation of it—continued to loom. Essentially, the underlying political, social, and intellectual problem of "aristocratic" versus "democratic" legislatures and forms of government reflected in Shays' Rebellion (and other subsequent disturbances) remained entirely unresolved in practice and principle.

CHAPTER 9

Canada: An Ideological Conflict

The Americans Invade Canada (1775–76)

Radicals predicted a rapid spread of the American Revolution's internationally proclaimed principles to Canada, the Caribbean, Ibero-America, Ireland, India, and Europe. The entire western hemisphere, suggested the *Histoire philosophique* in its 1780 version, "must eventually detach itself from the old world," abandoning monarchy and aristocracy as well as colonial subordination, ecclesiastical tyranny, and intolerance. A vast program of emancipation— social, religious, and ideological—seemed bound to follow what the *Histoire philosophique* described as the "fermentation and shock to our opinions" precipitated by the American Revolution.[1]

With American Independence declared, in 1776, all that bound the Thirteen Colonies together was a loose treaty of confederation that did not exclude the possibility of adjoining British dependencies—East and West Florida and Canada—breaking free from their colonial masters and joining the Union.[2] Extending the rebellion to the French-speaking territory conquered from France and annexed in 1763 and to "the maritime provinces" (Nova Scotia, New Brunswick, and Prince Edward Island, acquired by Britain earlier) was a possibility that the American insurgents were keen to explore. Canada's defenses, already dangerously overstretched and denuded, were weakened further in 1774–75 by Ethan Allen's capture of Fort Ticonderoga and the strategic decision to concentrate Britain's inadequate troop strength at Boston, leaving Guy Carleton, the British governor-general at Quebec, with under a thousand British regulars to defend all of then Canada.[3]

Exploiting this gap and vast open terrain was an obvious strategy for the rebel leadership to adopt. By invading Canada, Congress could hope to deny Britain use of the Saint Lawrence River Valley, thereby blocking access to the interior and to the West and hindering Britain's ability to communicate with, and supply weapons to, the mostly pro-British Indian tribes straddling New York, Pennsylvania, and other northern colonies. If the rebel campaign succeeded, not only would Britain's strategic position in North America be vastly weakened but Congress would gain splendid bargaining counters should prospects arise for a favorable negotiated settlement.

But Canada was not just a question of strategy and military operations; there were also important political and ideological factors involved. Canada's total population in 1770 (without counting the Maritime Provinces) was still reckoned at below 100,000, including between 80,000 and 90,000 French speakers and 3,000 English speakers. It was rising rapidly, though, and due to reach around 200,000 by 1790.[4] The nascent United States, from 1776 the world's largest republic in population as well as territory, boasted two and half million, just surpassing the Old World's most populous and prosperous republic, the United Provinces. Even counting Nova Scotia, from where most of the French speakers had been expelled by the British in 1760s and replaced with Scots, and around 8,000 settlers from New England—making New Englanders now the province's majority[5]—four-fifths of Canadians were French speaking and traditionally hostile toward England. On the other hand, the French Catholic clergy and seigneurs dominating most of Canada saw little to be gained by joining Protestant republican rebels. The 1774 Quebec Act, guaranteeing the status of the Catholic Church and French law, contributed to keeping the populace neutral, albeit at the cost of bitter American Protestant recrimination and some resentment also among Anglo-Canadians in Montreal and Nova Scotia.[6] Canada was too eager to preserve the benefits Britain had so generously bestowed on her ever to wish to secede, a leading pro-British pamphleteer, Isaac de Pinto, in Holland, assured European readers.[7] It was supposedly only to satisfy the Thirteen Colonies that Britain acquired Canada during the 1763 peace negotiations, ending the Seven Years' War, disregarding potentially more lucrative gains in the Caribbean and sacrificing her own interest for her ungrateful American subjects: "everything proves the unnatural ingratitude of the rebel colonists."[8]

From 1775, Loyalism in Canada gained fresh vitality from the growing influx of Tories expelled from, or choosing to leave, the Thirteen Colonies, though much of this immigration arrived only at the end of the Revolutionary War. Of approximately 70,000 Loyalists forced into exile from the United States, over 40,000 settled on Canadian territory. At first, most gravitated to Nova Scotia, where more than 20,000 found refuge, and New Brunswick. Prior to 1783, only a few migrated to the Niagara frontier; the real influx to "Upper Canada" (Ontario) occurred in the 1790s when many American Loyalists and other English speakers settled there. In relation to Canada's modest pre-1775 population, the American émigré immigration arriving between 1775 and the mid-1780s represented a massive addition of people and wealth. Indeed, the number of exiles *from* rebel territory in Canada was actually considerably greater in proportion to the total population of the Thirteen Colonies than the approximately 145,000 émigrés from revolutionary France (a country with a population over ten times as large) going into exile in the years 1789–94. The relative size and value of the American Tory land and property seized and expropriated by the revolutionary authorities was likewise much greater than in France.[9]

Yet despite this massive Loyalist infusion reinforcing Britain's grip, the American effort to detach Canada began on an optimistic note. The expectation was that American Loyalist and French Canadian opposition could be effectively countered by rekindling Canadian resentment against the British Crown and persuading the French, Scots, and non-Loyalist New Englanders of Nova Scotia of the advantages of participating in the colonies' rebellion. The obvious reluctance of Canadians to respond to Governor Carleton's summons to rally to the local militias seemed a distinctly promising sign. Initially, allocating high priority to the Canadian venture, some elements in Congress were eager to adopt an expansive policy.[10] Canada was the first country outside the Thirteen Colonies in which the American Revolution's republican ideology was deliberately and systematically diffused. Washington personally joined in this ideological effort by forbidding expressions of anti-Catholic zeal among his troops at a time when he and his colleagues were seeking the "alliance of the people of Canada, whom we ought to consider as brethren embarked on the same cause; the defense of the general liberty of America."[11] Ideologically, Canada in fact played an especially significant role in American denunciation of British "tyranny" in 1774–76 because, unlike the Thirteen Colonies, Canada (apart from Nova Scotia) lacked a representative assembly. An official letter from the Boston Committee of Correspondence "to the inhabitants of the province of Quebec," written by Sam Adams (one of the revolutionary leaders most involved in the Canadian sedition) and dated 21 February 1775, cited the Quebec Act as irrefutable evidence of British ministers' intention to deprive Canadians of the rights and "protections" guaranteed by the British constitution.[12] Canada was the "only part of the British empire," as Rush expressed the point in February 1776, "in which arbitrary power is established by law."[13] Some Canadians, English and French speakers, proved receptive to this notion even though most, especially the illiterate and partly literate who constituted a relatively larger segment in Catholic French-speaking society than in Protestant English-speaking America, proved impervious to Congress's propaganda.[14]

The rebel propaganda campaign in Canada commenced as early as October 1774. A first subversive pamphlet titled *Lettre adressé aux habitants de la Province de Québec, ci-devant le Canada* (Letter Addressed to the Inhabitants of the Province of Quebec, formerly Canada), championing the revolutionary cause there, printed in two thousand copies, appeared that month at Philadelphia, produced by an experienced Lyon printer, Fleury Mesplet (1734–94), who had settled in America shortly before the Revolution. An able journalist as well as printer, and radical disciple of the French *philosophes* eager to sever Canada from Britain, end black slavery (there were only around three hundred black slaves in Canada), and secure better terms for Native Americans, Mesplet was an obvious recruit for Franklin's program. On Franklin's recommendation, Mesplet became Congress's official printer of American French-language propaganda directed toward Canada.[15] Late in 1774, Mesplet made a first brief reconnoitering visit to Montreal, bringing a stock of revolutionary pamphlets with him. In February 1775, Congress sent additional agents incognito to distribute printed literature, organize meetings, and rally English-speaking business leaders behind the conspiracy.

Despite Governor Carleton's efforts to suppress it, this first printed *Lettre adressé*, of October 1774, circulating from December 1774 in Montreal but preceded by some manuscript copies, diffused widely in Canada.[16] Composed by a congressional committee, the translation into French was by Franklin's Genevan republican friend, Du Simitière. British power in Canada, contended the *Lettre adressé*, was chiefly supported by rapacious landowners and clergy. Canadians should not be dupes of haughty seigneurs and priests, abandoning the "liberty and happiness of all" for the sake of the privileged few. Reminding the Quebecois of their "courageous and glorious" resistance to the British in 1759, the pamphlet urged them to cast off the yoke of oppression and send delegates to Philadelphia to join the "United Colonies" and form this "highly desirable union." Repeatedly citing Montesquieu and Beccaria, and uncompromisingly republican, the *Lettre adressé* exhorted Canadians to think in political terms and ignore religious differences, pointedly eulogizing the Swiss union, the Helvetic Confederation, as a shining exemplum of a united federal republic accommodating both Catholic and Protestant states (cantons).[17] The London ministry, Canadians were reminded, were as "absolute throughout the entire extent of their province" as the "despots of Africa and Asia" in those parts. The great "compatriot" of the French Canadians, Montesquieu, an authority revered by all Europe, had proved that governments in which the people do not participate and where there is no curb on royal authority decimate liberty, while the "celebrated Beccaria" showed that "in every human society there is a force that continuously tends to confer control and happiness on one party and reduce the rest to misery and complete lack of power." Good institutions must oppose this tendency and extend the influence of the laws "également et universellement."[18]

The first and foremost "right" of the people is to participate in government through its representatives and be governed only by laws of which it has approved. Press freedom and full freedom of religion were further overriding priorities. Only a free press could impose broader, more responsible, and generous sentiments on those who govern and, by informing and criticizing, prod them into comporting themselves honorably and equitably in administering the people's affairs.[19] In May 1775, at Philadelphia, a second formal letter addressed to Canada's French-speaking populace in the name of Congress appeared in print, composed by Jay, Sam Adams, and Silas Deane and translated by Du Simitière. Again Canadians were exhorted to cast off the yoke of arbitrary power and the straightjacket of two established churches—Anglican and Catholic—being assured the Americans were their friends, not their enemies, and that the future of the Catholic and Protestant colonies would be closely conjoined.[20]

Predominantly, French Canadians were a community little touched by Enlightenment ideas and unswervingly deferential to their priests. Since the British conquest in 1759, the French Canadian priesthood had diminished from 181 (including around 70 parish priests) to 138, in 1772, but were still numerous enough to keep a firm rein on their flock.[21] Seeing the clergy and seigneurs solid for Britain, and the pious firmly behind their priests, Governor Carleton was initially confident that few would heed the stream of American printed political propaganda. Nevertheless, warned the bishop of Quebec, Monseigneur Jean-Olivier Briand (1715–94), a minority did know about "philosophy," were discussing the new ideas, and resented Britain. Briand had no notion why the divine will had delivered the land of Canada to the English but, whatever the reason, as head of the Canadian Catholic Church, he was determined to support royal authority and exhort his flock to lend no succor to revolutionaries.

As the crisis in the Thirteen Colonies escalated, Briand issued a general *mandement* (22 May 1775) admonishing French Canadians not to stir from their allegiance to George III, "your king," and enjoining them to promote the British Crown's interests, show gratitude, and shun the "pernicious design" of "the enemy."[22] He was not preaching war against the Thirteen Colonies, he claimed in subsequent *mandements*, simply following the dictates of the Church in demanding unquestioning submission to authority. Yet it was not only disgruntled English speakers who attended town meetings to discuss American events and who responded to the summons to join the Revolution, and although the French-speaking peasantry did mostly defer to their clergy, some tenant farmers of the rural parishes around Trois-Rivières between Quebec and Montreal vacillated. According to several reports, including one from René-Ovide Hertel de Rouville (1720–92), leader of the Montreal Loyalists and one of the first two French-speaking judges appointed under the Quebec Act in Canada, some French as well as Scots, Irish, and some other English speakers in Montreal and outlying areas supported the revolutionary cause. English-speaking merchants formed a pro-Patriot Montreal "committee of correspondence," headed by Thomas Walker, James Price, and John Blake— all migrants from the Thirteen Colonies since 1763—that assumed the lead in distributing Congress's (and Boston's) revolutionary pamphlets.[23]

On 1 May 1775, the bust of George III, standing in the main square of upper Montreal, was attacked during the night, smeared with muck, crowned with a papal miter, and defaced with insurrectionary graffiti, proclaiming King George III "the Pope of Canada." The early troubles in Boston had featured disfigurement of royal statues, and Carleton reacted energetically, repeatedly publishing a proclamation in the *Gazette de Quebec* condemning the offense and offering a monetary reward for information resulting in the arrest of the miscreants who had dared soil the monarch's statue and attached a *libelle diffamatoire*. The informer was promised a royal pardon should he be among the culprits. On 22 May, spurred by the governor, Briand issued a further *mandement* read in all the Catholic parishes of Canada, commanding the faithful to shut their ears to the *séditieux* undermining religion and submission to legitimate authority.[24] While most French Canadians did refrain from assisting the American invasion during 1775–76, Briand knew perfectly well that most wanted it to succeed and that very few were willing to serve the Crown against it.[25] Reporting to Lord Dartmouth in London on 7 June 1775, Governor Carleton now confessed to being seriously disturbed by the effect of American propaganda in Canada and growing signs that dissidents were defying their priests and seigneurs.[26]

A sure sign that American propaganda was swaying some was an article that appeared three times in the *Gazette de Quebec* during July, insisting the rebels were not "the friends" of Canadians and their religion they claimed to be in the "papers" they were distributing in Canada.[27] By July, American preparations were underway for a full-scale invasion. On instructions from Congress, from late June 1775, a sizable army of up-country New Yorkers and Vermonters assembled on Lake Champlain, at Fort Ticonderoga, advancing in late August and setting siege to Fort Saint John (Saint Jean) commanding the Richelieu River and the southern approaches to Montreal. The siege of Fort Saint John—the key to Canada—dragged on for ten weeks. Despite Carleton's efforts to concentrate a significant force and encourage the Iroquois to assist, local Canadians failed to help and the British garrison surrendered on 2 November 1775 to the American invasion force of around 1,700 men under General

Richard Montgomery (1738–75), an Irishman who had served sixteen years in the British army until 1772. Montgomery and his men occupied Montreal soon afterward. In and around Montreal, a Canadian regiment, which included some French Canadians, was formed to serve as an integral part of the "Continental Army." In all, around 500 Canadians joined the rebel army.[28]

A second American invasion force, under one of the rebels' most renowned commanders, Benedict Arnold (1741–1801), moving over exceptionally rough terrain and only slowly surmounting the difficulties, meanwhile edged northward from upper Maine toward the headwaters of the River Chaudière that from there flowed down to the Saint Lawrence, at Quebec. Weakened by exhaustion and sickness, this force arrived unopposed by the local inhabitants, opposite Quebec in early November. In early December 1775, the Americans (who had not yet declared their independence) commenced a determined siege of Quebec, culminating in an unsuccessful general assault, on the last day of 1775, that was repulsed with heavy loss (Montgomery being among those killed). When news of this first major debacle for the Americans—one of the most disastrous reverses of the Revolutionary War—reached Philadelphia, some members of Congress urged evacuation. But most followed Sam Adams and others in wanting to continue the siege and in ordering fresh units to be raised and sent to Canada, despite the risk that this would dangerously weaken Washington's army in and around New York.[29] There seemed a good chance Quebec and all Canada could be secured before the iced-over river thawed sufficiently to enable British reinforcements to arrive in the spring. In January 1776, rumors that Quebec had actually fallen circulated in Nova Scotia, stiffening the "encouragers of Rebellion" there.[30]

The siege of Quebec continued through the opening months of 1776, despite severe difficulties in obtaining adequate supplies. In January 1776, Congress dispatched a third official letter to the Canadians announcing that the Thirteen Colonies, despite the heavy repulse from Quebec, would never abandon their Canadian brethren and that more forces were being sent.[31] In March 1776, Congress appointed Benjamin Franklin head of a commission to direct the American effort in Canada, a delegation including another congressman and a Catholic priest from Maryland.[32] Franklin and Congress's commissioners arrived in Montreal in April 1776 with instructions to establish good relations with the Indians and "assure the inhabitants of Canada, their commerce with foreign nations shall in all respects be put on an equall footing with, and encouraged and protected in the same manner as, the trade of the United Colonies." The Catholic Church too would be respected; pro-American mass began to be celebrated in Montreal under Jesuit auspices (the Jesuits were at odds with Bishop Briand). The commissioners also had instructions to "establish a free press and to give directions for the frequent publication of such pieces as may be of service to the cause of the United Colonies."[33]

The commissioners arrived with Mesplet in tow bringing printing equipment, books, stores of pamphlets and paper and print, several servants and artisans, and another French radical, Alexandre Pochard, among whose tasks was to prepare a French translation of Paine's *Common Sense*.[34] Mesplet began printing in Montreal in May 1776. The Americans were invading militarily, politically, and intellectually. Bishop Briand instructed his clergy not to administer the holy sacraments to, or marry, anyone in the parishes reputed to be helping the Americans. The Loyalist cause in Montreal under American occupation, directed by the higher clergy, continued to be vigorously promoted by anti-Jesuit Augustinian Récollets and their students. For disobeying their priests, rebels were to be pronounced "heretics" in rebellion against the Church.[35]

To sway Montreal's inhabitants, Franklin and his colleagues stepped up their publicity drive while simultaneously appealing to the Iroquois Six Nations adjoining the Great Lakes. Franklin had been recommending greater effort to convert the Iroquois into allies ever since the 1750s.[36] To counter British appeals to the tribes, or what Franklin called their exciting the "savages to assassinate our innocent farmers with their wives and children," Mesplet later, in 1777, issued a remarkably subversive tract, the *Apocalypse de Chiokoyhikoy*, exhorting the Six Nations and all the Indians of the Great Lakes to rise against royal tyranny and fight alongside the Americans. This text, probably issued at Montreal (not "Philadelphia" as stated on the title page), dramatically called on all the Indians of both North America and Spanish America to rise against monarchy and colonial oppression. Some copies apparently eventually reached Peru, for the *Apocalypse* was later condemned in Spain and repeatedly banned in Peru and Chile after the Inca Tupac Amaru rising of 1780.[37]

The escalating propaganda war in Canada had multiple dimensions, tying in every strand of eighteenth-century political theory and connecting all the Americas. Oddly enough, among the most formidable of Franklin's, Du Simitière's, and Mesplet's opponents in the propaganda battle over Canada were two different William Smiths—Franklin's Scottish adversary in Philadelphia, the Anglican William Smith (1727–1803), who in the *Pennsylvania Gazette* in March 1776 insisted it was vile treason for Americans to seek military help abroad, particularly France, and American-born Presbyterian William Smith (1728–93) in New York, later chief justice of Canada. The first adopted the "illustrious Montesquieu" for his "chief guide" in political thought. Lacking an adequate fleet "has been the great bar to [France's] numerous projects for universal empire," argued Smith of Philadelphia: "can any Protestant, can you my countrymen, ever wish to see [France] possessed of such a fleet, assist her in attaining it, or willingly give her footing in America? Would she then be content to be the humble ally of these colonies; or would she not, in her own right, resume Canada, which, according to the limits she formerly claimed, is larger than all our provinces together?" The French would colonize northern and western North America, confining the British colonies to the eastern seaboard. Only the British monarchy could protect Americans from being thus penned in by a revived French Catholic empire while, at the same time, responsibly maintaining "separation of powers" and "moderation," the supreme principle guaranteeing liberty.[38]

Over the next months, Canada was a scene of deadlock. Montreal remained in American and Quebec City in British hands. But the American occupation force was deteriorating rapidly. "We understand that the troops now before Quebec have not ten days provision," reported the commission to Congress on 1 May 1776, after receiving word from Arnold, "but hope, as the lakes are now open, supplies will soon reach them."[39] A week later, conditions in the besieging camp at Quebec, the militia commander appointed by Congress to replace Montgomery, John Thomas (1724–76), informed Franklin, were so bad that of a nominal force of 1,900, only a thousand, including officers, were "fit for duty," the rest being invalids, wounded, or stricken with smallpox. Three hundred effectives were "soldiers whose enlistments expired the 15th ultimo, many of whom refused duty, and all were very importunate to return home."[40] Soon his force would be wholly inadequate to continue the siege. The men, Franklin reported from Montreal on 12 May 1776, "must starve, plunder, or surrender."[41] The invading "rebels" had little alternative but live off the land, which rapidly alienated most French Canadians who were understandably "provoked by the violences of our military in exacting provisions and services from them, without pay; a conduct towards a people, who suffered us to enter their country as friends, that the most urgent necessity can scarce excuse." The invading army's growing plight "contributed much to the changing their good dispositions towards us into enmity," explained Franklin, "makes them wish our departure; and, accordingly, we have daily intimations of plots hatching and insurrections intended for expelling us, on the first news of the arrival of a British army."[42]

Even so, the commissioners still hoped to "regain the affections of this people, to attach them firmly to our cause, and induce them to accept a free government."[43] Until June 1776, Franklin and Mesplet plied their propaganda campaign in Canada against the landowners, clergy, and Canadian Loyalism while simultaneously appealing to the Quebecois and Iroquois, but now with rapidly waning success. On 7 June 1776, following the arrival of British reinforcements, the Americans were decisively beaten at Trois-Rivières and forced, riddled with smallpox, which added many fatalities (among them their commander, Thomas), to evacuate Canada completely, greatly heartening the British and casting considerable gloom in the Thirteen Colonies. Keeping Canada "was of the utmost consequence," Adam Smith assured a correspondent, "as had it been lost, our affairs in America would have been nearly desperate."[44] The fleeing army took the commissioners with them, though Mesplet and Pochard stayed behind as Franklin's agents and, after a brief imprisonment, resumed printing, publishing the *Gazette de Montréal*. During their incarceration, their French rendering of Paine's *Common Sense* remained well concealed. What happened to the unpublished manuscript subsequently remains unknown.[45]

The *Declaration of Independence* on 4 July 1776 and its eager reception across the rebel colonies a month later, Rush assured Lee, helped revive morale just when the "loss of Canada had sunk the spirits of many people who now begin to think our cause is not desperate and that we shall yet triumph over our enemies."[46] In Canada, the mood was submissive: "everyone, the priests, and some gentry at their head," reported Pochard to Franklin in October 1776, "basely prostrate themselves before the idol of tyranny. The few honest types who sigh for the return of your troops are persecuted."[47] Beaten in Quebec, Americans were hardly eager, most histories of the Revolution relate, to renew the invasion attempt. But there were still real opportunities for subverting British Canada. In November 1776, a veteran militia colonel, Captain Jonathan Eddy (1726–1804), a former member of the Nova Scotia General Assembly but born in Massachusetts and an ardent revolutionary, in contact with Sam Adams and accompanied by several hundred volunteers, many local, with some Acadians and Maliseet Indians,[48] stirred rebellion in the Maritime Provinces. Eddy's force besieged strategic Fort Cumberland (the former French Fort Beauséjour), controlling the isthmus between Nova Scotia and New Brunswick for three weeks. When British regulars relieved the fort, scattering Eddy's force, they torched the farms of the New Englanders and Acadians in the area around in retaliation.[49]

Empire versus Republicanism (1777–1812)

In particular, the decisive American victory at Saratoga in October 1777 dramatically reopened the question of Canada's future. "I make no doubt," Thomas Walker assured Franklin, "the Canadians must be struck with astonishment at this unlook'd for event; and that they will heartily join us in any future attempts upon that colony, which I ardently wish to see added to the

United States."[50] Walker was among the Americans who had settled in Canada in the 1760s, supported the Revolution, and fled to the United States after the repulse of the 1775–76 invasion. Given the changed military position, British opinion too now had to reckon with the possibility that "Canada, Nova Scotia, and the Floridas" could be "all conquered by them." Adam Smith, whose view of Britain's North American prospects had become increasingly gloomy, believed that the "complete submission of America" would be impossible without conceding the "most perfect equality" between mother country and colonies, "both parts of the empire enjoying the same freedom of trade and sharing in their proper proportion both in the burden of taxation and in the benefit of representation." If the government remained unwilling to concede this much, Britain must now contemplate the "complete emancipation of America from all dependency upon Great Britain." Smith's views, though, were highly unrepresentative of British perspectives in one respect. Should America refuse "such a union with Great Britain as Scotland made with England in 1707," it might be judicious, he advised ministers in London, to return "the two Floridas to Spain" and Canada to France. By so doing Britain would "render our colonies the natural enemies of those two monarchies and consequently the natural allies of Great Britain. Those splendid, but unprofitable acquisitions of the late war, left our colonies no other enemies to quarrel with but their mother country."[51] A restored French Canada would render a "federal union with America," and restoration of British primacy, again possible.

Over the winter of 1777–78, prior to and especially after the signing of the Franco-American alliance (February 1778), a new U.S. invasion of Canada, possibly in conjunction with the French, was planned with the support of many Congress members but against the advice of Washington. Those supporting the project pointed out that the French alliance offered a real opportunity to break Britain's hold on Canada, a breakthrough certain to wreck Britain's entire strategic position in North America. But the possibility the French would retain Canada, once they had a force there, a prospect appealing to Lafayette and Adam Smith for diametrically opposite reasons, tipped Washington against such proposals. The planned invasion was called off in March 1778; nevertheless, rumors of fresh American or Franco-American invasion attempts persisted through 1778 and early 1779.[52]

It was hardly possible to doubt, remarked Condorcet in a pamphlet published anonymously, supposedly in "Londres," in 1778, that Canada would "follow the example of the neighboring provinces," and when it did that French Protestants would at last be free to settle there and combine political liberty with freedom of religion, enjoying all the advantages of the language and usages of their *patrie*.[53] A leading pro-American publicist in Holland,

Antoine-Marie Cerisier, forthrightly championed what he called "Canadian liberty." In a pamphlet attacking the prominent pro-Orangist and pro-British propagandist Isaac de Pinto in 1779, Cerisier summoned Canada to secede and join the United States, embracing the "spectacle de la liberté" transfixing all the New World colonial empires.[54] Like Condorcet and Lafayette, he hoped to see Canada emerge "in freedom" as the fourteenth state (Vermont still lacked that status). Should the United States and France fail to liberate Canada, the consequence would be further consolidation of the Quebec *noblesse* and clergy subjecting all Canadians to their tyranny.[55]

During early 1779, Congress deliberated a renewed incursion, responding in part to pleas from Vermont where there was considerable appetite to resume operations in Canada, while Lafayette and a small band of Canadians with him eagerly awaited a fresh incursion into "La Nouvelle-France," as they still called the country. In secret talks held in Paris in 1779, collaborating with Lafayette (when temporarily back in France), Franklin proposed a joint Franco-American effort to annex Canada, a project Lafayette promoted vigorously.[56] Franklin and Lafayette urged the French to invade by land and sea, starting by clearing the Canadian east coast north of Maine and sacking the British base at Halifax. In addition to some Indians, French Canadians, and settlers in border areas, the "inhabitants of Nova Scotia too, except those in the town of Halifax are known to be generally well affected to the American cause," Franklin assured Louis XVI's foreign minister, Vergennes, in February 1779, "being mostly settlers who formerly emigrated from New England."[57] The British, informed of these Franco-American deliberations, organized a further crackdown on pro-American dissidents; Mesplet was locked up for a second time along with Valentin Jautard (1736–87), another subversive French-born journalist who had supported the American invasion in 1775–76.[58]

Congress eventually countermanded the 1779 invasion plan too, again chiefly owing to Washington's unwillingness to detach significant forces from his main army and deep distrust of French ambition and designs. Subsequently, further successive invasion scares swept Canada. At the point the Revolutionary War ended with the peace preliminaries signed in January 1783, France and Spain were preparing a dual land and sea offensive in the Caribbean and Canada, causing Lafayette's hopes to surge once more. He was assigned to lead a repeat American invasion of the Saint Lawrence Valley. The end of hostilities hence greatly dismayed Lafayette, who pointedly reminded Washington of his keen desire "to add Canada to the United States" and longing to "embrace" General Washington in Montreal.[59]

The Revolutionary War had ended. But this did not dispel expectations that Canada would eventually secede. Not only did many contemporaries ex-

nsurgents.[71] Tecumseh was an exceptional leader who
ing Indian morale throughout the Great Lakes region.
within Canada was the increasingly repressive, reac-
tish authorities during the Napoleonic era, memories
1798 Irish revolution also played a part in feeding anti-
of the rebels imprisoned in Ireland having later found
men in New York and Pennsylvania, and many fellow
he war of 1812 would develop into a wider republican
iently breach the walls of the British empire to release
on.[72] In connection with the ideological struggle in the
sonian bloc at odds with the anti-democratic, Feder-
mained strong in New England) was not averse to
ity toward British institutions, "mixed government,"
on both sides of the border.
sm to king and Church, most Englishmen and some
iples of the democratic wings of the American and
ditional and nationalist grounds, evincing little sym-
laints. But in the United States, even some moderates
al features of the British mixed-government model
ritish empire and its defenses in Canada. Adams was
ice is humbled," Adams assured Jefferson in 1814,
Bona is banished a greater tyrant and wider usurper
ll is quite as unfeeling, as unprincipled, more pow-
od, than Bona. John by his money, his intrigues and
n after coalition against him made [Napoleon] what
ie is. How shall the tyrant of tyrants be brought low?
But where Jeffersonian democrats deplored both the
evolutionary reactionary flavor of post-1790 British
n the Adams vein, while loathing the imperial pre-
e basic form of the British domestic political system.

Suppression of Canadian

Canada developed into an inconclusive, bitter, three-
forces, in which recent Irish immigrants were dis-
ed, attempted repeatedly to break into Upper Can-
n, initially invading with an air of great confidence
fact that many American, Irish, and Scots English-

pect Francophone Canada to break away from the British Crown, a strong anticipation lingered that the British settlements in Canada too "will become part of the United States of America," and that this would happen, Paine suggested, not only "against all [Britain's] contrivances to prevent it" but even "without any endeavours of ours to promote it."[60] In the minds of many, the projected Canadian revolution was thus postponed rather than aborted.

In 1791–92, the British government took wide-ranging measures to counter the worrying circumstance that the French Revolution was reviving anti-British republican sympathies among the rapidly increasing Francophone population, now numbering around 140,000, and also among non-Loyalist Anglo-Americans in Canada. Parliament passed the Canada Act (1791), as an antidote against the now combined threat of the French and American revolutions.[61] If by this time there seemed little likelihood that Canada would ever rejoin France, many observers thought Canada would eventually be absorbed into the United States or else become an associated separate republic like Vermont. "If, as is almost impossible to doubt," reiterated Condorcet in 1791, "Canada should follow the example of the neighboring colonies [in throwing off allegiance to Britain], there will be a region in North America where prospective French settlers would enjoy, besides many other advantages, both the language and usages of their homeland."[62] Ministers in London grew distinctly worried.

The lesson of the American Revolution, it seemed to them, was that any resurgence of disaffection should be handled less heavy-handedly than in 1774–75. At the same time, though, there was a growing sentiment in England, and among Loyalist English speakers in Canada, that the English-speaking social elite should in future be more firmly dominant over the French. Both considerations, and the desire to attract more American settlement into Ontario, contributed to the elaboration of new arrangements for royal authority. Mainly drafted in London, the 1791 Canada Act, effectively Canada's first constitution, became a cornerstone of a new, more sophisticated imperial system. Its guiding principle was that Franco-American democratic republicanism could be permanently thwarted by a vigorous injection of institutionalized "mixed government" dominated by "aristocracy."[63] If colonial Canada possessed no real nobility in the European sense, the gap could be filled with selected nominees chosen for their wealth and loyalty by the governor-general. On this basis, representative bodies, two-chamber assemblies, were established in Canada proper for the first time (New Brunswick had acquired a legislature in 1784).

The Canada Act aimed to check revolutionary tendencies by bolstering Crown and landowners along with the Anglican and Catholic churches by making limited concessions to the principle of representation and instituting restricted voting rights. Both Upper and Lower Canada acquired an elected lower house, which however was deemed subordinate to the "Legislative Council," the appointed upper house formed from the governor's nominees into what now became a self-perpetuating oligarchy. In Lower Canada, this Legislative Council comprised a mix of British and French nominees and wealthy landowners. Crown-appointed nominees rather than elected representatives, functioning on the model of the London House of Lords, in this way came to wield effective power. At the same time, the Act enlarged Upper Canada by slicing off the western part of Quebec and instituting English law in Upper while retaining French law in Lower Canada. Further, the Anglican Church became the principal established church with a full seventh of land in all new townships in both Canadas allocated to endow its vicars' livings.

To match the political change, vestiges of French absolutism and divine right theory still being taught in French Canadian seminaries and colleges were now replaced by formal "mixed government" doctrine integrating Crown, aristocracy, and a mixed Protestant-Catholic ecclesiastical establishment in a joint system of authority. Despite Britain's military garrison in Canada, and Upper Canada's executive and judiciary, being mainly paid for by the home country, which had the advantage of keeping taxes much lower, a mere fraction of those payable in neighboring American states struggling to pay off their war debts,[64] a measure of French and Scots-Irish disaffection persisted and remained focused on American and French revolutionary principles as was hardly surprising given that the Canadian legislatures, as formed in 1791, were considerably less democratic than either the neighboring New York State legislature or that of revolutionary France.

With the Revolution in France now in full swing, the British authorities in Canada stepped up surveillance and took added precautions much as occurred at this time also in Scotland, Ireland, and England itself.[65] The memory of the 1774–79 Franklin-Mesplet-Jautard conspiracy still suffused French-speaking Canada, and no disciple more ardently celebrated its legacy than Henri-Antoine Mézière (1771–1819), a young Montréalais who had received his secondary education at the College of Saint-Raphael in Montreal (which he afterward reviled as an intellectual "tomb" run by ignorant ecclesiastics) and whom Mesplet had introduced to "Rousseau, Mably, Montesquieu and other philosophes" and encouraged to dream of Canada's reacquisition by France. Expelled by the British authorities in May 1793, Mézière transferred to Philadelphia to assist the French revolutionary emissary to the United States, Edmond-Charles Genet (1763–1834), in promoting the democratic principles of the Brissotin republican regime in France (1792–93)—and in inciting insurrection in Canada. Although most French and British Canadians, together with the many American Loyalists in Canada, stoutly resisted their calls, the French

being a "people ⋯
ows of ignorance ⋯
pathizers with Ar ⋯
noticeably resurge ⋯

During 1792–9 ⋯
garrisoned by sor ⋯
and Quebec inten ⋯
lican clandestine ⋯
phlet titled *Les Fr* ⋯
fused in 1793–94 ⋯
the ideas of Fran ⋯
ans to follow the ⋯
the Club des Patr ⋯
some two hundr ⋯
group, they aime ⋯
the United States ⋯
all British-maint ⋯
leges, as well as t ⋯
encouragement ⋯
forts, noted Méz ⋯
culated in Canad ⋯
of Man. He stres ⋯
dians had suppo ⋯
invading Americ ⋯
aversion to Mor ⋯
him in prison. H ⋯

Pro-American ⋯
not just among ⋯
rived English sp ⋯
their way to Up ⋯
five times since ⋯
proaching 60,00 ⋯
Anglo-American ⋯
rels over maritir ⋯
British ships pr ⋯
not yet settled ⋯
stretching westv ⋯
the American N ⋯
the massive revi ⋯
(1768–1813), co ⋯

of the Native American ⋯
succeeded in briefly rev ⋯

If the principal facto ⋯
tionary stance of the Br ⋯
of the suppression of the ⋯
British sentiment, some ⋯
their way to Canada. Iri ⋯
Irish in Canada, hoped ⋯
crusade that would suffi ⋯
Ireland too from subject ⋯
United States, the Jeffe ⋯
alist tendency (which r ⋯
gently encouraging host ⋯
and imperial pretensions ⋯

United in their loyal ⋯
Scots scorned the prin ⋯
French revolutions on ti ⋯
pathy for Canadian com ⋯
attracted to the theoreti ⋯
remained hostile to the ⋯
one such. "Though Fra ⋯
"Britain is not. Though ⋯
still domineers. John B ⋯
erful, has shed more blc ⋯
arms, by exciting coaliti ⋯
he was, and at last, what ⋯
Aye! There's the rub."[73] ⋯
system and the counter ⋯
government, moderates ⋯
tensions, still adulated t ⋯

The War of 1812 and
Radicalism (1812–38

The War of 1812–15 in ⋯
year struggle. American ⋯
proportionately represer ⋯
ada via the Niagara regi ⋯
based on the indubitable ⋯

speaking newcomers settling there since the 1790s nurtured greater sympathy for America than for Britain.[74] Ministers in London could still count on the ardent loyalism of descendants of American Tory immigrants of the Revolution era, but that hardly extended to the rest of the population, and especially not recent Irish immigrants, the largest slice of immigration into Canada from the British Isles since 1783.[75]

But the American war effort too was sapped by internal disaffection: a number of American officers with Federalist sympathies, including their commander at Niagara, New York State's richest aristocrat, General Stephen van Rensselaer (1764–1839), and his cousin, another commander at Niagara, Solomon van Rensselaer (1774–1852), both appear to have desired Britain to win in the expectation of thereby weakening American republicanism, checking Jefferson and strengthening "aristocracy" on both sides of the Canadian border.[76] The British renewed their interference in the region around Fort Detroit and again incited the anti-American Shawnee-led confederacy in the Northwest, headed by Tecumseh, who joined them in fighting the Americans, hoping to push them back beyond the Ohio River. With the British occupying Detroit, the struggle came to focus especially around Niagara.

The later, post-1850 Canadian national myth that the Ontario militia loyally bore the brunt of the American assaults and heroically fended them off, historians have shown, was almost entirely a later self-serving fiction. General Sir Isaac Brock (1769–1812), who commanded the successful foray that captured Detroit (August 1812) with Tecumseh's help and who afterward repulsed the initial American invasion of Ontario, at the battle of Queenston Heights (13 August 1812) in which he died, was undoubtedly the principal hero of Canada's stalwart defense but one who entertained little sympathy for, or confidence in, Canadians and was never on good terms with the Upper Canada legislature.[77] The defenses and forts of Ontario did indeed hold firm; every American thrust was repelled. But it was almost exclusively the British regulars without the Canadians who fought off the incursions.[78]

Canada stabilized with the Anglo-American peace of 1815 and 1818 Anglo-American convention ending the border disputes (fixing the border at the Forty-Ninth Parallel as far as the Rockies—with joint control of the Oregon Territory for ten years), except for the border on the Pacific coast. Yet the threat to British Canada posed by Franco-American democratic republicanism was still not wholly expunged. Another notable resurgence of republican sentiment occurred after 1822 when Governor Dalhousie, directed from London and under pressure from the Anglophone Canadian elite, introduced proposals for reuniting Lower (Francophone) with Upper (Anglophone) Canada on a new basis. Opposition to the plans to subordinate French-speaking

Canada to Ontario by integrating the two Canadas under the primacy of the English-speaking "aristocracy" grew intense. The campaign against Dalhousie's plans was led by Louis-Joseph Papineau (1786–1871), a member of the Lower Canada legislature, dubbed the "Mirabeau of North America" for his fiery oppositional oratory, who was to become one of the foremost figures of pre-1848 Canadian political history. Son of a Montreal lawyer and representative in the Lower Canada legislature, the younger Papineau began as an admirer of British "mixed government" and firm disciple of Montesquieu, Voltaire, and Adam Smith, hence a classic "moderate enlightener."[79]

Offended by the 1822 proposals "for union" and the domineering attitude of the "English party," Papineau eventually came to reject, notably during a subsequent visit to England, the aristocratic system he found prevailing there and the extreme economic inequality that buttressed it. From 1826, Papineau emerged publicly as a "democrat" and, from 1830, as a declared republican opposed to the British connection.[80] He tightened his links with the "Philosophical radicals" in London whose leader, Bentham, too had recently become increasingly convinced of the advantages of American democracy and who, in 1827, wrote a paper on Canadian grievances and need for emancipation from oppressive, unrepresentative rule. In effect, Bentham now recommended that Canada *should* join the United States.[81] Papineau pushed his campaign to secure lower house control over the executive to the point of fomenting complete deadlock between the Quebec regional assembly and Lower Canada's pro-British Legislative Council.[82] By this time a convinced disciple in political thought of Franklin, Jefferson, the economist Jean-Baptiste Say (1767–1832), and the French republicans of 1830 as well as Bentham, he had also emerged as a militant anticlerical. In 1831, spurning Catholic and Protestant opinion alike, Papineau successfully sponsored a law in the Canadian legislature granting full equivalent political rights of citizenship to Canada's small community of just a few dozen Jews, more than a quarter of a century before any other part of the British empire legislated for Jewish equality.

The speeches and writings of Papineau and another prominent opposition leader, Ludger Duvernay (1799–1852), prove their republican goals to have been far-reaching. In Canada, the 1830 European revolutions reawakened vivid memories of the 1775–76 American invasion, as well as of the crisis of 1793–94 during the French Revolution and the struggle of 1812–15. Beside French republican sentiment and Irish immigrant rancor, loathing of the obligation to pay one-tenth of all farm produce to the Anglican Church in tithes played a not insignificant role. Although by 1830 there were still only around 270,000 English speakers as against 460,000 Francophones in the country, the Canadian press remained heavily dominated by Anglophone newspapers, which, in concert with the bishops of Montreal and Quebec, unceasingly condemned the French 1830 July Revolution, along with republican and democratic ideas, and Canadian interest in philosophist revolutionary democratic principles. However, two Canadian papers, the *Irish Vindicator*, edited by a physician, Daniel Tracey (who died in the 1832 Montreal cholera epidemic), and the French-language *Minerve*, edited by Duvernay, once again proclaiming Lafayette the "veteran of liberty," made a point of reaffirming the universality of the joint American and French republican revolutionary tradition.[83]

"The cause of Canada and Ireland are the same," insisted one of Bentham's radical allies, John Roebuck, in Parliament in London, criticizing the ministry in March 1837, "it is the cause of self-government and religious liberty—it is the cause of the suffering many" who resist the overbearing insolence of a "miserable monopolizing minority." The majority were Catholic in both countries, "and in both countries a small minority who call themselves English, have hitherto domineered over, and insulted the people at large, whom they always stigmatise as foreigners and aliens. By the power of England, this monopolizing minority has been supported in both countries."[84]

Eventually the mounting turmoil produced armed risings in both Upper and Lower Canada known as the Patriots' War of 1837–38. At this point, the rebels retained the sympathy of Roebuck, John Stuart Mill, Molesworth, and other "philosophic radicals" in England, much as earlier they had that of Bentham, for their grievances and ideas if not for their resort to violence.[85] Papineau, Duvernay, and some other republican leaders who, since 1822, had endorsed Mézière's and Lafayette's view that Canada under Britain was an oppressed land at this point also embraced Bentham's and Mill's reservations about violence. Idealizing Jefferson and the American Revolution together with the democratic French revolutionary tradition, they insisted they were "respectable revolutionaries," "revolutionaries of a philosophical age," publicly rejecting resort to arms as a result of which they hesitated to issue an open call for Canadian independence. Although Papineau (rather hesitantly and evasively) condoned the 1837–38 rebellion, he soon found himself clashing with the uncompromising militant *patriotes* promoting violent action. Accusing his supporters of lacking resolve, the militants labeled his faction the "moutons" (sheep). Papineau could be Canada's "Franklin," retorted his adherents, without needing to be her "Washington."[86] Even so, Papineau's conduct, including his inciting French parishioners to defy the clergy's celebrating and blessing Queen Victoria's succession to the British throne, proved sufficiently incendiary for the governor, in November 1837, to order his arrest along with Duvernay and twenty-five other Patriot leaders implicated in anti-British conspiracy. Both leaders fled in time, Duvernay seeking refuge in Vermont, Papineau in New York. In exile in the United States, they continued championing the ideals of the American and French revolutions as a single combined republican revolutionary program and legacy.

The history of French-speaking and Scots-Irish republican resistance in Canada culminated in the 1837–38 uprising, which began among the French in Lower Canada and ended with pitched battles in the countryside of Upper Canada in which the insurgents, initially successful, were finally crushed by British regulars. For the Canadian Patriots of 1837–38, the American Revolution was undoubtedly still the prime revolutionary model. If in Lower Canada the strife assumed the character of a Francophone revolt against British rule, in Upper Canada, with its large admixture of Irish Protestants and Scots, as well as ex-Americans, it turned into a brief civil war with many echoes of the American Revolution.[87] At Toronto, Scots rebels and pro-American reformers reprinted the American *Declaration of Independence*, as means of further inciting opinion against the British Crown.[88]

Like their predecessors in 1774–83, the bishops of Quebec and Montreal called on Catholics to show submission, exalt the Crown, and wholeheartedly repudiate Papineau's and Duvernay's republicanism, universalism, democratism, philosophism, and secularism. In exile in the United States, Papineau became more than ever convinced Canada's future lay in joining the Union and, briefly, rallied both Canadian exiles and sympathetic Americans to this view. At odds with Canadian Independence militants, though, he left New York in February 1839, migrating to France where he withdrew from active politics, spending his time immersed in libraries and archives until allowed to return to Canada, finally, in 1845. In France, too, he remained less a Quebecois nationalist than stalwart advocate of radical thought, of the great French Revolution (before Robespierre), legislative supremacy, secularism, and universal human rights.

In a significant sense, 1837–38 marks the definitive defeat of Canadian democratic republicanism and Radical Enlightenment in Canada, a belated conclusion to the revolutionary process initiated in 1774–76.[89] However, both the process and its repressive ending were routinely played down and minimized from the mid-nineteenth century onward and eventually almost forgotten. After Canada became officially (virtually) independent of Britain as the "Dominion of Canada" in 1867, Anglophone Canadian nationalism colored by anti-Americanism and assumptions about the superiority of the British race and civilization encouraged a new zeal for the British connection that had little use for the pre-1838 revolutionary republican legacy. As it receded into distant memory, the democratic movement of the 1820s and 1830s came to be generally misrepresented and projected, much as British conservatives saw it at the time, as merely a localized French Canadian revolt.[90]

CHAPTER 10

John Adams's "American Revolution"

America's Need for Foreign Arms, Munitions, and Loans

John Adams, among the foremost of the Founding Fathers, played a key role in the American Revolution, both in Massachusetts local politics and on the national stage. But he was also among the Revolution's most important early envoys abroad and, during the late 1770s and 1780s, intimately connected with the political maneuvering and intricate intellectual debate over propagating the Revolution's core principles in Europe. In particular, Adams acted as a brake on European democratizing interpretations of the Revolution's significance. Here again, as with Franklin, a biographical perspective helps uncover the intricacies of the Revolution's complex interaction with the outside world.

In March 1778, Adams arrived in France as Congress's deputy minister in continental Europe to work with Franklin. His task was to help seal the French alliance at which Franklin, whom Adams considered lacking in concentration and too easygoing in accommodating French demands, had labored since December 1776. Professing to have shaken off the "narrow and illiberal prejudices peculiar to John Bull [i.e., the English]," typical of his youth, Adams battled to transcend his distaste for the French and for Catholicism,[1] while remaining unsympathetic to both, and especially the political and philosophical radicalism of Mirabeau, Brissot, Condorcet, and (until 1791) Lafayette.[2] Blunt, undiplomatic, disliking ceremony, and normally at a loss for small talk, Adams found numerous aspects of French culture grating, not least the boundless enthusiasm for Franklin—among the few French pre-1789 fads to survive intact through the Revolution.[3]

With Dutch enthusiasm for the American cause mounting and friction between the Dutch and British at sea intensifying, France gave the United Provinces formal notice of the Franco-American alliance on 12 March 1778. France's

pact with the United States was not yet a declaration of war or even an unqualified military alliance. Neither French nor British wished to be seen as initiating hostilities. Should France attack first, the Dutch would be bound under
longstanding treaties, reaching back to 1688, to enter the war on Britain's side.
Should Anglo-Dutch relations worsen to the point that Britain blockaded the
Dutch coast, this too would encumber France since Holland remained the chief
entrepôt for Baltic masts, pitch, and other naval stores needed for the French
fleet preparing for war in the Atlantic. Anglo-Dutch hostilities would disrupt
the hard to dispense with flow of naval munitions to France *and* America.[4]

Adams briefly returned to Massachusetts in the summer of 1779 to serve
as a delegate to the 1779–80 winter convention charged with drawing up Massachusetts's revised constitution following rejection by voters of an earlier
version, in February 1778. Early in 1780 the state convention's drafting committee of thirty entrusted the task to a subcommittee of three who, in turn,
devolved it to Massachusetts's foremost constitutional expert—Adams. The
five-year constitutional imbroglio was resolved by the simple expedient of let-
ting Adams write the new constitution himself. Inspired by Locke and especially Sidney, the authorities chiefly shaping his "moderate" outlook whom
he cites at length justifying armed rebellion against the Crown in *Novanglus*,[5]
Adams agreed with Jefferson that "that form of government which communi-
cates ease, comfort, security or in one word happiness to the greatest number,
and in the highest degree, is the best" and that no good government exists that
is not "republican." But he rejected broad suffrages, equality, and unicameralism, and especially Paine's and Condorcet's democratic republicanism.[6] To
Adams, Paine was a half-educated, colossal nuisance, a "mongrel between pig
and puppy" debasing the American Revolution's veritable legacy.[7] He adhered
to his faith in "mixed government" and natural "aristocracy" for decades into
his old age, and was still staunchly defending these principles at the Massachusetts convention called to reform the state constitution in 1820, in alliance with
the young conservative Daniel Webster.[8]

Like Locke, Adams believed armed resistance to authority justified only
when led by the "greater and more judicious part of the subjects of all ranks"
rather than the "vile populace or rabble of the country." In the new Massachusetts constitution, repudiating democracy, Adams incorporated the "mixed,"
British-style "aristocratic" design, checks and balances, bicameral structure,
and anti-democratic safeguards he judged essential for the American body
politic generally, especially stiff property qualifications excluding most potential white voters from the suffrage, thereby adding many newly disqualified
voters to those already lacking the vote (much to the discontent of the Massachusetts and Maine backcountry districts). Even more stringent property

John Adams (1735–1826), c. 1793, by Revolutionary War artist John Trumbull (1735–1826). Photo credit: National Portrait Gallery, Smithsonian Institution / Art Resource, NY.

qualifications applied to those electing the state senate and to those running for election to state offices. Adams deemed it imperative to preserve and institutionalize a republic's hereditary "aristocracy," formal or informal, to balance executive power, on the one hand, and the people on the other.[9] The new state senate was to be elected only by persons belonging to this "informal aristocracy" based on substantial property.

In this manner, though a sincere republican and enlightener, Adams concentrated political power in the hands of the Boston mercantile elite and big landowners beyond anything seen before 1775.[10] Typical of him too was the strong executive, or presiding "representative," empowered to constrain both legislative chambers, a feature particularly unpalatable to radical republicans like Jefferson.[11] In Adams's original scheme, this projected "governor" even chose the state militia commanders, though this power was afterward deleted by the drafting committee as departing too far from popular sovereignty.[12]

Massachusetts's finalized new constitution duly appeared as a fifty-page pamphlet establishing a model that was widely discussed and helped set the pattern for future American constitutional development but also exacerbated rather than eased the tension between "classical republican" gentry rule and the democratic tendency, pitting "mixed government" against the more egalitarian strain in post-1774 American and European republicanism.[13]

Institutionalized support for religion Adams judged an indispensable further prop to a viable constitution, though it was not he who added the crucial article guaranteeing compulsory public financial support for the Congregationalist Church that so antagonized the radicals. It was on Sam Adams's initiative that an amendment was included ensuring freedom of worship but making it incumbent on all to "worship the Supreme Being, the great creator and preserver of the universe," pay for the clergy, and respect the Lord's Day, requiring delegates of both Senate and House to undergo tests declaring their "Christian" belief. Although unbending "incumbency of worship" was partially diluted by the drafting committee afterward, officeholders had to explicitly affirm the truth of the Christian Gospel, which meant that Adams's brainchild formally excluded deists, atheists, agnostics, Jews, and others (Buddhists, Muslims, Confucianists, etc.) from political life. Adams's constitution thus emerged far removed from secularism, equality, and full freedom of expression.

After a brief second stint in Paris, Adams transferred, in July 1780, to the United Provinces—a republic now much less powerful and dynamic than during its seventeenth-century Golden Age when besides "New Netherland" (afterward New York and New Jersey), it colonized South Africa, the Guyanas, Curaçao and five other Caribbean Islands, Ceylon, several enclaves in southern India, and much of what today is Indonesia. But in 1780 the Netherlands remained a key diplomatic forum and publishing center as well as a focus of international finance and trade depot. Although, for the moment, Adams was merely the United States' informal representative (Congress as yet having no official standing in the Netherlands), he aimed to "render my country somewhat less dependent on France, both for political consideration, for loans of money and supplies for our army." Until April 1781, he resided in Amsterdam, then The Hague, and afterward Leiden before eventually returning as "ambassador" to The Hague.[14] Leiden, where he stayed several times and his elder son, the future sixth president, John Quincy Adams, attended the university for periods, was for him hallowed ground, as it was where the Pilgrim Fathers sought refuge before migrating to New England in 1620.[15]

Adams cultivated closer relations with the only power able and likely to lend large sums to the financially struggling United States, the French court being now practically bankrupt and Spain refusing to deal directly with the United

States. The Dutch, though, were a profoundly divided society. The Prince of Orange, Willem V (1748–1806), stadholder since 1751, and his court nobility, found themselves increasingly at odds with the locally dominant urban oligarchies of Holland and Zeeland who were anxious to defend their still extensive maritime and commercial interests against the overweening encroachments of British power. A longstanding alignment between England and the House of Orange dating back to 1688 guaranteed British backing for the dysfunctional Dutch ancien régime, especially Orangist power and dynastic concerns, but strictly in exchange for near complete subservience to British interests, and maritime and colonial supremacy, dependence greatly resented by the town oligarchies.

The pact between the courts of St. James and The Hague had recently come under increasing strain. Since the onset of the American War, powder, shot, and weaponry used to fight the British flowed in conspicuous abundance via the several Dutch Caribbean outposts, especially St. Eustatius, a notoriously "convenient channel of supply to the Americans."[16] Britain banned shipment of weapons and powder from Europe to the colonies in October 1774, but subsequent reports confirmed that foreign, usually Dutch, artillery and powder continued to reach the "rebels" in spectacular quantity. Franklin's dispatches from Paris frequently passed by the same route and, on 16 November 1776, when one of Congress's warships entered the harbor, St. Eustatius's governor became the first official foreign representative ever to salute the stars and stripes in ceremonial fashion with artillery.[17] During a thirteen-month period in 1778–79, with the munitions trade to America burgeoning spectacularly, the number of vessels entering St. Eustatius's harbor attained the astounding total of 3,182![18] Such escalation of a longstanding subversive contraband flow preeminently linked Holland to America's growing rebellion against the British imperial mercantile system, rendering St. Eustatius pivotal to the collision between British mercantilism and both the Americans and Dutch.

Bristling with indignation, London demanded the stadholder halt the massive exchange of arms, munitions, and naval stores for Virginia tobacco, indigo, and cash transacted on St. Eustatius. Outwardly, the States General deferred to the stadholder's wishes, in March 1775, forbidding munitions exports from Holland to North America; but the Amsterdam and Rotterdam city governments refused to comply, citing the 1674 Anglo–Dutch peace treaty (contracted when England had been in a weak position internationally and obliged to settle on unfavorable terms) authorizing Dutch vessels to transport goods of any kind to third parties with whom England was at war. Resentment against British sway over world commerce also boosted objections to the stadholder's permitting "freely to pass through our land the German slaves [i.e., Hessian mercenaries] Britain hired to fight the Americans."[19] If sympathy for the American Revolution stoked friction between Amsterdam and the Orangist court, it also stirred memories, at several levels, of the Dutch Revolt against Spain, led by the first William of Orange, in 1572. Finally, it heightened disaffection among white settlers in South Africa where sentiment decrying the stadholder, "aristocracy," subservience to foreign powers, monopolistic colonial trade, and intolerant Calvinist ecclesiastical authority surged up, becoming seriously divisive just when Adams arrived.[20]

Applause for American defiance of Britain and enthusiasm for American political and, even more, American economic independence substantially worsened an already complex, increasingly tense Dutch domestic political confrontation. A missive from the American commissioners in Paris—Franklin, Adams (Deane having been recalled to Philadelphia), and Arthur Lee— requesting the United Provinces to join France and sign a treaty of amity with America had been circulating among the town governments since April 1778, infuriating Orangists and the British ambassador. Stadholder and ambassador also suspected Amsterdam of secret collusion in Franklin's plot to bring Jones's squadron into Dutch waters with a view to further disrupting the Anglo-Dutch ties.[21] It was the American naval victory at Flamborough Head, off the Yorkshire coast, in September 1779 that brought the simmering quarrel between England and the United Provinces to boiling point. "Our Commodore's ship," reported Franklin, the *Bonhomme Richard*, was "so shattered that she could not be kept afloat, and the people being all taken out of her, she sank the second day after the engagement."[22] But the badly mauled remainder of the Franco-American flotilla crossed the North Sea, reaching the Texel roadstead a week later, with several captured English vessels in tow and nearly four hundred British prisoners. Claiming unintentionally to have been driven by winds rather than be purposely seeking refuge under the Dutch flag, Jones in fact had secret orders, concocted between Franklin and the French, to request asylum in Dutch waters so as to goad Holland into virtual recognition and further provoke England.

The British government demanded immediate release of the captured vessels and prisoners. Neutrality, replied the States General, obliged them to defer any decision regarding the lawfulness of Jones's prizes; they agreed, though, to refuse munitions and bid Jones depart as soon as his ships were seaworthy. America's seamen, meanwhile, were rapturously received wherever they went. "We have been almost smothered at the [Amsterdam] Exchange," reported one sailor, "and in the streets by an innumerable multitude overjoy'd and mad to see the vanquisher of the English."[23] To the stadholder's annoyance, Louis XVI intervened, insisting Jones's ships were a joint American-French force and that he was placing them all under the French flag (Franklin had agreed to using both flags). This scotched hopes of procuring recognition, infuriating Jones, who refused to run up the French royal colors on his vessel. Hauling down the American flag on the rest sufficed, though, to get the squadron safely back to France, in late December, with Jones more than satisfied at having strained "relations between Holland and England to a point past mending. Nothing now keeps Holland neutral except the influence of the ship owners, who are doing almost the entire commerce of Europe at enormous rates. . . . But the Dutch people are for us and the war."[24]

In April 1780, shortly before Adams's arrival, Parliament, seething with anger, formally repudiated the Anglo-Dutch alliance. Britain and the United Provinces were on a collision course. But it was not chiefly economic interest, Jones rightly observed, that caused the Fourth Anglo-Dutch War (1780–84). Economic factors certainly contributed, but commercial interests supporting the American cause were more than neutralized by the many Dutch shipowners and investors in colonial trade dreading the inevitable losses and disruption of conflict with Britain. Rather, the amazing popular fervor for the American cause reflected a widely diffused exasperation felt among ordinary Dutch burghers at their country's demeaning subservience and reduced status, a collective impulse to renew the defiance and stirring resistance of the American Revolution in the Anglo-Dutch context. For the pro-American Dutch opposition, the ensuing struggle was a high-risk strategy affording an opportunity finally to discredit Willem V and disentangle the Republic from the tentacles of European dynastic court intrigue and ambition in the unrealistic hope that the war, and especially emulating the revolutionary spirit and vigor of the Americans, would powerfully revive Dutch patriotism, national stature, shipping, and commerce. For Britain, war with the Dutch, though no minor distraction from the main conflict, presented a convenient opportunity to recoup losses and prestige by seizing Dutch colonies and merchant fleets, a chance cheaply to compensate for setbacks in America at the expense of a prosperous but browbeaten, militarily and diplomatically vastly inferior rival goaded by an angry home populace lacking any realistic notion of how overwhelming Britain's maritime supremacy was.

Colonial Crisis, South Africa, and the "Expanding Blaze" (1780–84)

The Dutch Republic, it soon became evident, had stumbled onto a reckless course leading to unmitigated catastrophe for its trade and empire.[25] The setbacks the war brought only deepened the internal Dutch political crisis by mobilizing the Orangist faction calling for the Republic to support George III against the American "rebels," and against France, to placate Britain and engineer a swift changing of sides. "The English party," Adams reported to Philadelphia in February 1782, seek "to engage the Republick to join the English in the war against France, Spain, and America. The Prince is supposed to wish that this were practicable but to despair of it. Some of the great proprietors of English stocks, several great mercantile houses in the service of the British ministry, are thought to wish it too."[26]

An extraordinary, internationally conspicuous split had developed in Holland and in the Dutch colonies: "one half of the Republic nearly," explained Adams, "declares every day very indecently against France—the other half against England: but neither the one nor the other declares against America, which is more beloved and esteemed than any other nation of the world." The anti-Orangists supporting the United States comprised a large bloc of "moderates," noted Adams, and an (initially) much smaller group of democrats desiring "demolition of the Stadholdership," a lessening of the grip of the colonial companies, and "the people" to possess the "right of choosing the regencies," the town governments. Adams instinctively disliked this democratic fringe without at first considering them a serious threat: "I think these are very few in number, and very inconsiderable in power, though some of them may have wit and genius." Yet Adams faced a thorny difficulty since those "very few" with wit and genius, of whom he remained suspicious, were the only element reliably wedded politically to the American cause and revolutionary principles.[27]

The Prince of Orange's supporters, fighting for dynasty and narrow oligarchical and colonial interests, were staunchly backed by the Calvinist Dutch Reformed Church and by the least educated, poorest strata of the population among whom adulation of the princely house and public Church remained deeply ingrained. The anti-Orangist opposition, by contrast, was backed by numerous Protestant dissenters and Catholics resenting the established Church and led by a fringe of political newcomers, intellectuals, and renegade churchmen, in varying degrees embracing Enlightenment ideals and the American example. Given Adams's official functions, his strategy necessarily needed to be tied to the anti-Orangist camp despite their eulogizing and emulating the American Revolution in a fashion that was not his, with some of them espousing political theories too radical for his liking.

One of those to whom Adams was referring and who became one of his principal allies in the Netherlands was Antoine-Marie Cerisier (1749–1828), a Frenchman resident in Holland since 1774, steeped in Rousseau, Mably, and Raynal and the author of the *Tableau de l'histoire générale des Provinces-Unies*

(10 vols., Utrecht, 1777–84), a general history of the Republic (and critique of French institutions) that Adams studied on arriving to orient himself in the complexities of the Dutch political system. A key publicist "possessed of the most genuine principles and sentiments of liberty, and exceedingly devoted by principles and affection to the American cause," as Adams put it, he was among the foremost propagandists denouncing British pretensions, tyranny, and colonial sway.[28] Cerisier, who had turned his Amsterdam journal, *Le Politique Hollandois*, into a major vehicle of democratic and pro-American ideas,[29] proclaimed the American Revolution the happiest possible development for mankind. The thirteen new "states," a land whose population already exceeded the Dutch Republic's two million by about one-fifth, heralded a new world order and would, to the benefit of all, he declared earlier in a pamphlet published in December 1778, weaken that "arrogant power" (Britain) whose efforts were all directed toward building a "universal monarchy over commerce and the seas."[30] Every nation possesses a right to liberty because liberty is necessary to its conservation and prosperity; to be free means to obey only laws promoting the "happiness of, and approved by, society."[31]

Since European states had failed to correct the abuses, mercantilist trade policies, and arbitrary government plaguing their overseas dependencies, Cerisier expected all colonies everywhere to rise against the "despotisme affreux" to which their imperial masters subjected them. Already the colonists were restless, he insisted, in Dutch Guyana (Surinam) and South Africa.[32] In South Africa, the initial stirrings of local white protest against the rigid colonial framework imposed by the VOC (Dutch East India Company) had indeed gained momentum in direct response to the American Revolution. Friction between small independent farmers, the *vrijburgers*, and the VOC reached back at least to the late seventeenth century but had posed no real threat to the Company's sway until after the outbreak of the American Revolution. The foremost spokesman of the anticolonial movement at the Cape of Good Hope, a schoolmaster, Johannes Hendrik Redelinghuys (1756–1802), was later to become an active democratic leader, critic of the "moderates," and publicist in Holland.[33]

The Dutch colony at the southern tip of Africa, the Cape colony, or "Tavern of the Two Seas," had been established in 1652, at the outset of the First Anglo-Dutch War (1652–54), to secure what the VOC considered a crucial way station on the route between the United Provinces and the East Indies. South Africa's function in the Dutch seaborne empire had always been primarily strategic and logistical, supplying outward-bound and returning VOC fleets with water and provisions. Since there had been no local pool of black labor suitable for the Company's purposes, white farmers often from the most landlocked and least prosperous parts of the northern Netherlands had been encouraged to settle and provided with land cheaply, rendering the Cape the only Dutch colony since the days when New York and New Jersey had been called New Netherland where white colonists worked the land with their own hands, at least to begin with. Slowly the colony expanded, as South Africa's farms, orchards, and vineyards spread beyond the Cape peninsula itself. Huguenots and German Lutherans arrived to supplement the Dutch settlers. By American standards the stream of immigration from Europe down to the 1780s remained small. But demand for provisions expanded vigorously as dozens of ships docked at Cape Town each year, outward bound for, or returning from, southern Asia. Over time, slave labor, mostly imported from West Africa, took on many or most tasks on the larger farms and became an integral feature of South African society.

The underlying economic and social causes of the unrest gripping white South Africa in the late eighteenth century were undoubtedly specific to the region. Although there was a good deal of interest in the American Revolution among the intellectual and professional elite also in Surinam and on the six Dutch Caribbean islands only in South Africa were there small independent white farmers and grievances enough for American protest, boycotting, and armed resistance to become a major stimulus to action. Resentment grew against a rigid mercantilist system imposed by the VOC and its officials, especially the Company's monopoly over importing and exporting and setting the rules, tariffs, prices, and procedures for the sale of agricultural provisions to the Company. That there was room only for a minimum of participation on the part of the white settlers in the colony's affairs had caused discontent much earlier. The Company's desire to keep prices for imported goods in South Africa high and prices for local agricultural products low created a permanent pool of resentment against the system.[34] But in the late 1770s this situation came to seem more obviously unacceptable, more of an affront to the citizenry's rights, than earlier. Especially, continuing exclusion of local men from the governing political council of the Cape rendered the colony fertile ground for the slogans and ideas of the American Revolution. The timing and character of more organized opposition to the VOC regime at the Cape under its Orangist governor, Baron Joachim van Plettenberg (1771–85), were closely tied to the example and stimulus of the American Revolution.[35]

Since 1747, South Africa's colonial governors had been chosen by the stadholder and were invariably firm Orangists and anti-democrats, a circumstance that to an extent strengthened local attachment to the Dutch Patriot and American cause during the war with Britain and opposition to Orangism. The governor ruled the colony through a "Great Council" of Nine, all of whom were

Company agents and officials, allowing the colonists no representation whatever. Secret meetings to mobilize resistance to Plettenberg and the VOC occurred regularly from 1778 onward in Cape Town and Stellenbosch, the second oldest and then the second most flourishing and substantial Dutch town in South Africa presiding over the region where in the late seventeenth century Huguenots had established South Africa's wine industry. In 1779 delegates were sent, under cover of private business, to present a formal petition of protest to the VOC directors in the Republic. When this proved fruitless, South Africa's opponents of the VOC widened their campaign for greater political and economic "freedom" and began petitioning the States General in The Hague.

In 1783, a sensational 322-page book with which Redelinghuys was closely connected appeared anonymously in Holland in French (and soon Dutch) under the title *L'Afrique hollandoise, tableau historique et politique de l'état originaire de la colonie du Cap de Bonne Espérance*, reminding the public and town oligarchies that the "Anglo-Americans can be imitated by the colonists of the two Indies [East and West]": especially in the colony of South Africa where conditions were ripe for rebellion against tyranny: the American revolutionary "example could become contagious."[36] The author, supposedly a certain François Bernard, well versed in Raynal and the *Histoire philosophique*, provides a detailed account of the political, fiscal, and economic situation of South Africa couched in an unmistakably Radical Enlightenment rhetoric assuring readers that "philosophy," that is to say *la raison eclairée* (enlightened reason), had now made Europeans so aware of basic universal rights and the iniquity of despotism that practically all European monarchies had moderated their former absolutism and attitudes leaving only the colonial world of the Americas, Africa, and Asia under older forms of mercantilist despotism. But even in the Americas, Africa, and Asia, European colonists, being freer of "superstition" than the native populations, would no longer submit to the "awful despotism" imposed hitherto. The Americans had set the example of how to break the yoke of oppression and unjust government and it was an example that would be followed. In South Africa where the Company's agents and officials were imposing intolerable oppression, if the VOC "continues to authorize their unjust exactions, the colonists will revolt and will seize justice for themselves; in that case, the colony is lost to the Company and its loss must necessarily entail also the ruin of all the [Dutch] commerce of the East Indies."[37]

Redelinghuys was one of the delegation of representatives sent to Holland to press the demands of the "Kaapse Malcontenten," or South African dissidents, who presented their formal address to the States General in May 1785. According to this radical democrat, as he proved to be, South Africa was a direly oppressed land. But it soon transpired that the white settlers at the Cape were deeply split and that in reality neither the Orangists nor the Reformed Church lacked for vigorous support.

Misery was the lot of most of the world's population, contended both Cerisier and *L'Afrique hollandoise*, echoing the *Histoire philosophique*, primarily because excessive power and wealth were concentrated in monarchical, oligarchic, and aristocratic hands, with commerce outside Europe everywhere encumbered by exclusive monopolies and privileges serving narrow, vested interests. The American Revolution, however, would forge a long-term coalition of the Netherlands and its dependencies with America and France that would finally break the imperial mercantilist stranglehold and transform the entire New World and Old World for the better. America's example would everywhere impact among peoples possessing the same grounds as the Americans for overthrowing exploitative systems that did nothing for the people except exact oppressive taxes and curb personal liberty; ultimately, America's example would everywhere lead to the replacing of the totally unsatisfactory and oppressive existing order with free republics and open trade. Ibero-America would assuredly be happier and freer once rid of the Spanish and Portuguese monarchies, aristocracies, ecclesiastical establishments, and Inquisition, and as part of the chain reaction, it was to be expected, so would the rest of the former French, English, Portuguese, and Dutch colonies.[38] Pleasingly for all equitable souls, the crimes of those who had devastated the New World (the Spaniards) would surely be compensated by North American population growth physically replacing the "numerous peoples of South America that European oppression and cruelty has caused to disappear."[39]

Like the *Histoire philosophique*, Cerisier ventured to assume that the United States would give the world's nations free access to her ports and expect the same from the rest, driving all countries to open their ports to free commerce, thereby permanently shattering the mercantilist systems monarchies like Britain, France, and Spain had imposed, and which the Dutch had rigidly imposed on their own colonies while stoutly resisting those same systems elsewhere. At present, the Cape provided few benefits for South Africa's colonists, over whom the Company, according to the *Histoire philosophique*, tyrannized abominably. In the future, advised the radical *philosophes*, the Cape should become a model of toleration and hospitality to all. The true consequence of the VOC's "vile treatment" of its employees and *vrijburgers* was a "contagion" of corruption that betrayed the Company's affairs at every step and ensured rapid deterioration of its colonies, garrisons, and ships' crews. An altogether freer and more benign social and economic regime was the only conceivable way in the long run for the Dutch to defend and retain the Cape of Good Hope and the

Company's strongholds in Ceylon and elsewhere.[40] If the ships of all nations were freely admitted and South Africa's colonists permitted to trade also with North America, the colony at the Cape would flourish and successfully attract fresh colonists from all parts.

The *Histoire philosophique* offered its far-reaching recommendations, its authors claimed, disinterestedly, philosophically, purely out of what they termed devotion to "le bien général des nations."[41] Since the principal cause of international jealousy, rivalry, and wars in the eighteenth century was disputes over colonies and commerce, the American Revolution by demolishing Britain's Atlantic mercantilist system, Cerisier and *L'Afrique hollandoise* wholeheartedly agreed, was indeed preparing a new world order. Eventually, through America's example, all the colonial empires would become "la source d'une paix universelle et du bonheur des nations" (the source of a universal peace and the happiness of nations).[42] Once independent, the United States would drive a general process of maritime and commercial amelioration and expansion that, together with the anticipated political changes, would render the entire world happier, more prosperous, and more peaceful.[43]

Like Raynal, Diderot, and Paine, Cerisier also linked American rebellion to the recent dramatic expansion of British power in India, accusing Britain of extending her rapacious tentacles throughout the East, everywhere provoking wars and imposing her vastly oppressive colonial system. In Bengal, England had forged *un despotisme* "so revolting" it produced atrocities even worse than those Spain had perpetrated in the New World.[44] It was not the British people, however, who deserved the blame. Again echoing the *Histoire philosophique* and Diderot, Cerisier blamed rather "corrupt" laws and the mercantilist imperial system. England abounded in "reasonable men" like Price and Priestley who knew Britain could not maintain vast dominions around the world without increasing the "repressive force of government," or cow her rebellious American colonists without building a militarized tyranny so repressive it would eventually extend despotism to British society itself.[45] Overpowering the colonies and maintaining its tyranny in India, predicted Cerisier, would render Britain first an "aristocratie tyrannique" and, finally, an absolute monarchy.[46]

Cerisier's stance, and that of the *Histoire philosophique* and *L'Afrique hollandoise*, was diametrically opposite to that of the best-known defender of the British connection with Holland and the Dutch colonial system, the wealthy Amsterdam patrician and pro-Orangist enlightener and economist Isaac de Pinto (1717–87).[47] American Independence, de Pinto had stoutly maintained since 1776, would inflict colossal harm on the Dutch, politically and economically. What he considered the mistaken principle of popular sovereignty mainly pleased those Dutchmen who seemed to have forgotten the centrality of imperial trade and colonies to their own republic and prosperity. It was assuredly in the Dutch interest to back England, whose political constitution, a mix of monarchy, aristocracy, and democracy, was "admirable et même divin," as Montesquieu asserted, the best ever devised.[48] Should the American "rebels" triumph, they would extend their seditious sway over the entire New World: Curaçao, Surinam, the islands of Jamaica, Martinique, St. Domingo, and Guadeloupe, "all the European possessions in the West Indies would pass under their dominion," ruining Holland's commerce—"no more would that republic boast her riches and greatness!" American insurgency threatened all European political systems and colonial empires together with Holland's seaborne trade. "Spain, Portugal, and all Europe should therefore join with England" to "prevent or at least retard that independency."[49]

The Fourth Anglo-Dutch War assisted the United States by diverting British resources away from North America and adding an additional ally. However, the losses the war inflicted on the Dutch trading system and the two great colonial companies, the VOC and the West India Company (WIC), were so massive that these never subsequently recovered, the VOC spiraling downward from this point on until its final liquidation in 1796. In the Dutch colonies the American War had the effect of simultaneously destroying the fabric of ancien régime and Company rule while also, in South Africa especially, instilling hope for renewal on the basis of American revolutionary principles.

"A war with Holland being resolved upon," records the contemporary historian Ramsay, "the storm of British vengeance first burst on the Dutch Island of St Eustatius."[50] When a British fleet under Admiral Rodney appeared off the "grand free port of the West Indies and America" in February 1781, aiming to sever the chief artery for munitions supplies, the island's diminutive garrison of 60 men had not yet even heard that hostilities had broken out. Resistance was in any case useless against Rodney's powerful assault force of 3,000 troops. All the merchant shipping in St. Eustatius's harbor—130 sail, including 60 flying the stars and stripes, many loaded with tobacco—were taken, together with dozens more subsequently lured into the bay by the simple device of leaving the Dutch flag flying for another month. Rodney also permitted his men to sack St. Eustatius port, "that nest of vipers that preyed on the vitals of Great Britain" that had "done England more harm than all the arms of her most potent enemies, and alone supported the infamous American rebellion."[51] Immense quantities of munitions were seized, including thousands of tons of cordage. With over 2,000 American sailors and tradesmen in detention below deck, Rodney captured another 40 vessels in and around Saba and St. Martin, the two other northern Dutch Antilles that were likewise swiftly overrun. Altogether Rodney seized (and pillaged) around 250 French, Dutch, and American sail in the Caribbean, delighted, as he informed the governor of Barbados, that "France, Holland, and America will most severely feel this blow that has been given to them."[52]

The wholesale pillage of St. Eustatius, with the Jews being "designated as objects of particular resentment," was afterward condemned as "inhuman severity" and "tyranny" by Burke, in Parliament, in his famous "Statius" speech of 14 May 1781. Rodney's sentence of expulsion allowed the 101 menfolk of the island's Sephardic community, accused of collusion with American rebellion, just a day's notice prior to deportation: "they were ordered to give up the keys of their stores, to leave their wealth and merchandize behind them, and to depart the island without knowing the place of their destination."[53] Total plunder from the Americans, French, Dutch, and Jews was estimated at between three and four million pounds sterling.[54] Equally gratifying to the king's ministers, Rodney dispatched part of his force to the western Guyanas, capturing the Dutch colonies of Essequibo, Demerara, and Berbice.[55] He was duly raised to the peerage, receiving a magnificent pension of two thousand pounds per annum, albeit some shine rubbed off his glory when it emerged afterward that his prolonged stay at Eustatius had facilitated the junction of French naval squadrons that secured Chesapeake Bay, in Virginia, enabling the combined American and French forces to trap the British at Yorktown.

But if British diversion contributed to the Franco-American triumph, it did nothing to mitigate Dutch humiliation. In November 1781, the main Dutch base at India's southern tip, the fortress town of Negapatnam, and other nearby Dutch forts were captured and dynamited, leaving only rubble. The former Dutch enclaves in southern India were annexed to Britain's Madras presidency. Of course, the British planned to overrun South Africa too, but the fleet sent for this purpose, under Commodore George Johnstone, was intercepted in the Cape Verde Islands by a French fleet, also heading for South Africa. The ensuing battle at Porto Praya was a draw, but the French fleet subsequently reached the Cape of Good Hope first and sufficiently reinforced the Dutch garrison to prevent its fall—on this occasion.[56] But the precariousness of Dutch South Africa, external and internal, had been amply demonstrated. When the British resumed their efforts to overrun the colony in 1795, after the Batavian Revolution had swept away the old United Provinces and sent the stadholder into exile in England, the efforts of the new regime to get a French fleet in place before the English arrived on the scene failed and this time the colony fell. Strikingly, there were not a few Orangists and strict Calvinists at the Cape who supported the British takeover as a way of defending the Prince of Orange and traditional oligarchy and defeating the democrats, Americanists, and pro-Patriot elements.[57]

"Moderation" versus the Democrats

The Dutch domestic democratic revolution evolved in stages from 1780 onward and, by 1785, had partially broken the stadholder's power, reformed the town militias, and ejected the old oligarchies.[58] This escalating Dutch drama was carefully analyzed by moderates, reactionaries, and radicals alike in neighboring countries since both Britain and Prussia had much to lose should the Dutch ancien régime disintegrate and the Orangist court at The Hague be emasculated. Adams's efforts to promote the American cause in the Netherlands further complicated the internal political crisis, weaving the American Revolution into the very fabric of one of the most important philosophical and ideological clashes of late eighteenth-century Europe: Europe's first major democratic revolution. The American Revolution in this way became embedded in what was virtually a second "Dutch Revolt" of far-reaching ramifications for the entire Western transatlantic world, with Britain and the Prince of Orange standing in, in the minds of some, for Spain and the duke of Alva.

To fight America's propaganda war, Adams recruited an impressive team, among them Cerisier and the Huguenot editor and academic Jean (Johan) Luzac (1746–1807), owner of the *Gazette de Leyde*, internationally the most influential of the Dutch papers and among the few in Europe openly championing the American cause. The first European journal to publish the American *Declaration of Independence* (on 30 August 1776), this twice-weekly paper with a circulation of over seven thousand and readership distributed across Europe was a key vehicle of opinion that evinced a close interest in the new republic's constitutional debates.[59] On 3 October 1780, the paper carried a French translation of Adams's Massachusetts constitution written the year before, rendering it a continuing talking point in Patriot circles and among Belgian radicals (and conservatives) offended by Joseph II's autocratic reforms.[60] Luzac, who also befriended Adams's then thirteen-year-old son, John Quincy, like Adams, favored Montesquieu's political doctrines and advocated informal aristocracy and division of powers in both the American and Dutch contexts. In the *Gazette de Leyde* Adams regularly planted pro-American reports and articles, through Dumas, whom Franklin had recruited as American agent in Holland in 1775.

America's agent organizing munitions shipments and acting as go-between with the Amsterdam bankers, Dumas was also chargé d'affaires in Adams's absences, reporting directly to Philadelphia.[61] Despite his loathing for the "old conjuror" (Franklin) and for Jones (whom he considered simply Franklin's naval stooge),[62] Adams appreciated Dumas as a "man of letters and of good character." Altogether, Luzac's *Gazette* proved an invaluable tool for countering the torrent of adverse publicity pouring from the British and German press, decrying the American Revolution and the Dutch democratic movement. Even so, Adams and Luzac occasionally disagreed, particularly when the latter served his paper's interests rather than those of the United States or ventilated his notion that America might not secure full independence. At a low point in American fortunes, in late 1780, Luzac reported that Congress's financial position was fast deteriorating against a background of military defeat in the South and Native American offensives on the frontiers. The United States might need to make concessions, he predicted (like many prior to Yorktown), leaving only some states independent, much as the seven northern provinces of the Low Countries had won independence from Spain in 1609 while the southern Netherlands (Belgium) remained under Spain. Adams was furious. He did not want the *Gazette* plying discouraging news at a time when he was seeking Dutch loans.[63]

Another close collaborator was François Adriaan Van der Kemp (1752–1829), an anti-Calvinist preacher and leading publicist of the anti-Orangist Patriot party who figured among Franklin's and Adams's regular publicists promoting the American Revolution in Holland. Van der Kemp's *Verzameling van stukken tot de dertien Vereenigde Staaten van Noord-Amerika betrekkelijk* (Collection of Tracts relating to the Thirteen United States of North America) (Leiden 1781) diffused knowledge about the American Revolution and was comprehensively anti-Orangist and pro-democrat.[64] America Van der Kemp proclaimed the great example to the world, filling "every bosom with a craving of freedom." Allied to the Americans against Orangist and British oppression, he preached from the pulpit, the Dutch would counteract "degeneration of the national character, check corruption of morals, suppress the seeds of tyranny," and restore Holland's "moribund liberty to health." Allying with America would revive Dutch trade and "restore Leiden to its former luster." "America is ordained," he proclaimed in a sermon, published in 1782, to "heal the flaws of the Dutch people provided they follow in [America's] footsteps and are ready to be converted and to live."[65]

"Having read some of his writings and heard much of his fame," Adams had sought Cerisier out, soon after arriving in Holland, and "furnished him with intelligence and information on American affairs," introducing "him to the acquaintance of all the Americans who have come to this country, from whom he has picked up a great deal of true information about our affairs and perhaps some mistakes. His pen has erected a monument to the American cause," Adams added in May 1782, "more glorious and more durable than brass or marble. His writings have been read like oracles and his sentiments

weekly echoed in gazettes and pamphlets both in French and Dutch for fifteen months."[66] In February 1782, Adams had recommended Cerisier to the
Massachusetts Academy of Arts and Sciences as "one of the greatest wits and
historians of Europe, and the best grounded in the American Principles of
any I have found."[67] "It especially pleased Adams, he assured Cerisier in February 1784, to find the "pens of a Mably, a Raynal, a Cerisier, a Price, turned
to the subject of government. I wish the thoughts of all academies in Europe
engaged on the same theme, because I really think that the science of society
is much behind other arts and science."[68]

Diametrically at odds with Cerisier and the South African agitators as well
as Adams, de Pinto published a whole series of widely read pamphlets denouncing the American Revolution. No less a champion of the Enlightenment
than they, to de Pinto too the Enlightenment was the glory of the age, "nos
philosophes modernes" having forged a general spirit of humanity, toleration,
and moderation. The common people could indeed no longer be treated as if
of no account, dragooned and sacrificed to the undisguised interests of small
elites. Personally, he felt immensely grateful to the *philosophes* for enabling
him, as a Jew in Christian society, openly to participate in public debate. Royal
ministers, whatever their intentions, nowadays had to abandon the monarchical absolutism of the past. In educated society a tyrant like Louis XIV, proclaiming divine right and nurturing aggression and intolerance, no longer
possessed admirers or apologists. The Enlightenment was undoubtedly an
intellectual revolution: "maxims flatly contrary to the arbitrary and tyrannical principles of the past" had conquered generally.[69] It was a marvel that all
governments now professed to serve the best interests of their subjects instead
of being solely concerned with royal glory and that of a church. But sympathizers with the "rebels" were abusing legitimate "enlightened" maxims and
adopting invalid interpretations of the Enlightenment for seditious purposes.
Supporting American "rebellion" meant supporting false and dangerous principles stretching Enlightenment beyond any reasonable point, threatening the
stability of the world political and economic order.[70]

A "great champion of the English system," de Pinto trumpeted a conservative Anglo-Dutch enlightened ideology that—like the political thought
of Adams—built on Montesquieu's idea that "by extending participation in
power," moving toward democracy, political liberty undermines itself. Montesquieu and Voltaire, *philosophes* who, like himself, always lauded England,
were being basely maligned by the likes of Cerisier.[71] Among the opponents
de Pinto had in mind was d'Holbach, who in his *Système social* (1773) had
questioned whether a "people unjust toward others," driven by greed for
wealth, a "peuple conquérant," opposing the liberty of others whenever and

wherever there was economic advantage for themselves, could possess "sound ideas concerning liberty," true liberty meaning love of equity, humanity, and "profound awareness of the rights of the human race."[72] Such "declamations" alleging the "tyranny of the English" de Pinto deemed contemptible—on a level with Raynal, Diderot, and Price pouring forth "abominable praise" of the American "rebels."[73] These writers were twisting Enlightenment maxims of humanity, toleration, and moderation into a pernicious, false creed, a theory of man and government utterly contradicting Locke and useful only for spreading sedition and anarchy.[74] De Pinto vehemently rebutted popular sovereignty deploying his chief heroes—Locke ("contract" should not be confused with popular sovereignty) and Montesquieu ("pouvoir du peuple" [power of the people] should not be conflated with "liberté du peuple" [liberty of the people])—to combat democratic ideas.[75]

Defying experience and precedent, the American Revolution, according to de Pinto, stretched the principles of equality, freedom, and representative government much too far. Americans extolled Locke. But their Revolution was in no way Lockean, promoting as it did popular sovereignty rather than "contract" between monarch and people, the central pillar of Locke's political theory. Hypocritically invoking Locke while really being, like Price, anti-Lockean, the American Revolution was a thoroughgoing imposture, the tool of ambitious conspirators vilely spreading subversion in both the Old World and the New.[76] If the inhabitants of Surinam, St. Eustatius, South Africa, and the Dutch East Indies emulated the "rebels," demanding political representation, would not the Dutch reject such pleas, just as Parliament did?[77] If political liberty is a "right of nature," retorted de Pinto's opponents, how did he justify calling the Americans faithless "rebels" and cruel "brigands"? Parliament, they argued, had flagrantly violated the principles of 1688. If the "principles of the [Glorious] Revolution" justified the Hanoverian dynasty and English constitution, it was inexplicable how de Pinto and his British patrons could claim "Americans have revolted against their legitimate sovereign." Was James II in 1688 any less the legitimate sovereign than George III in 1776?[78]

Orangist propagandists reacted with special indignation to American and anti-Orangist fondness for presenting the American struggle against Britain as a follow-up to the 1572 Dutch Revolt against Spain. Bracketing the Dutch Revolt of 1566–1609 and the American Revolution appealed to many Protestant Dutch, German, and Swiss supporters, and some American Protestants, and was deliberately utilized as a publicity ploy by supportive pastors, German commentators, and the American commissioners in Europe, as well as by Dutch radicals. De Pinto denounced this "odious" comparison perpetrated by enlighteners like Dohm, Goethe, and Schiller together with the

Dutch "Patriots" as a way of falsely legitimating and heroicizing American revolutionary sedition in ordinary people's minds. British rule in America, tempered by wise laws and Protestantism, and authorized by Parliament, could in no way reasonably be likened to the cruel and abominable tyranny of Philip II, Alva, and the Inquisition. Unlike the American "rebellion," agreed another Orangist publicist, the Dutch Revolt was led by a pious prince (William of Orange) and by a Reformed faith pursuing irreproachably religious ends, not subversion against Crown and public Church.[79]

The American Revolution, retorted Cerisier, *was* the Dutch Revolt's direct successor and also the inspiration of the democratic Dutch *Patriottenbeweging* (Patriot movement), "cette hereuse revolution" of which he himself was now a prominent leader. There was no more favorable moment to publish an account of the first Dutch struggle (1566–1609) against despotism, oppression, and intolerance, he claimed, introducing the third volume of his general history of the United Provinces, in 1778, than now when the Americans were renewing the Revolt of 1572 with the "same impact but a more rapid and complete success."[80] In a "memorial" to the States General of April 1781, Adams too exploited this aspect of Dutch zeal for America. "If there was ever among nations a natural alliance, one may be formed among two republics." Many of the colonies' early settlers, he recalled, invoking the Puritan exiles, first "found in this country an asylum from persecution" and had ever since "transmitted to posterity a grateful remembrance of that protection and hospitality and specially of that religious liberty they found there, having sought them in vain in England." The "origins of the two republics are so much alike" that the history of the "one seems but a transcript of the other; so that every Dutchman instructed in the subject must pronounce the American Revolution just and necessary or censure the greatest actions of his immortal ancestors." "There has seldom been a more distinct designation of Providence" to any "two distant nations to unite themselves together."[81]

According to Dohm, it was unlikely the Americans would match the extraordinary heroism and resolve of the Dutch during their Revolt against Spain. Reports reaching Germany from America suggested the Americans, though inspired by the *Declaration of Independence* and the "excellently written" pamphlet *Common Sense* (of Paine), were retreating before Britain's vast global military might backed by hired German regiments. Should the Americans falter, these colonial "sons of freedom" would enjoy some sympathy in Germany; and the outcome would affect Germany, for "we Germans," he added with studied ambiguity, remain "true champions of freedom."[82] Censorship obliged Dohm to mince his words: "I am very far from defending the rights of the colonies against the British ministry," he had affirmed in his

Briefe nordamerikanischen Inhalts of January 1777, a text that leaves little doubt this *was* his intention. In a discreet fashion, Dohm, Wekhrlin, Forster, Wedekind, and other radical-minded German enligheners took up ideological cudgels against conservative writers supporting princes and courts, and hence also the British Crown, although the increasingly strict censorship imposed throughout the German principalities powerfully muted the controversy there on the surface.

The American Revolution's international political and philosophical ramifications could at the time be freely and openly debated only in the Netherlands. Everywhere else, the debate was to a greater or lesser extent muffled by state censorship, and in England by force of popular loyalism. Beside the relative press freedom prevailing there, another reason for the wholly exceptional scale and intensity of the Dutch debate was the domestic political divide firing up both sides to the controversy and further polarizing the rival moderate and radical ideological blocs. Twenty percent of Dutch pamphlets, around ninety-seven tracts, published during the years of the Revolution dealt with the American conflict.[83] But always they divided sharply into two opposed streams. If the *Gazette de Leyde*, the most renowned Dutch journal internationally, backed the Revolution, the *Courrier du Bas-Rhin*, published in adjoining Cleves, also widely read across Europe, was fiercely pro-Orangist. Defenders of British imperial hegemony habitually deployed Locke and Montesquieu in defense of "mixed government" and aristocracy, so that the clash of rival Enlightenment worldviews came to be clearly defined in the terms of rival systems of political thought as well as the Dutch (and Swiss) political struggles of the 1780s, pitting democrats against patricians in an ever more embittered political contest while further polarizing the Enlightenment's competing radical and moderate wings.

The Anglo-Dutch war palpably intensified the domestic Dutch political crisis. Another prominent Patriot leader with whom Adams collaborated was Joan Dirk van der Capellen tot den Pol (1741–84), an idealistic Overijssel baron who had translated Price into Dutch and long opposed the stadholder and the *anglomanes* (pro-British faction). Secretly in contact with Franklin since 1779, he was among the States delegates who had striven hardest, since 1775, to prevent the stadholder sending the Republic's famed "Scottish Brigade" to fight in America at Britain's request.[84] Van der Capellen had triggered the Dutch *Patriottenbeweging* proper with his brochure *Aan het Volk van Nederland* (To the People of the Netherlands), distributed in various towns during the night of 25 September 1781. Banned immediately by the stadholder and States, this key opposition pamphlet was repeatedly reprinted and swiftly gained renown. Van der Capellen wrote the tract, Van der Kemp later recalled, conferring "with me while I visited him at his country seat"; he "entrusted me with its publication and distribution" from Leiden.[85] It was a text that mattered less for its originality than its electrifying rhetoric, its lambasting the Princes of Orange as oppressors of "Batavian freedom" while exalting the common people as the chief source of legitimacy in politics. The point of society (and everyone's duty) is to render the people "happy," society's members being from "nature all equal and equal in relation to each other, with no-one subjected to another."[86]

Citing the "Thirteen United States of North America," and equally lauding American Patriots and seventeenth-century Dutch republicanism, especially Oldenbarnevelt, Johan de Witt, and Dutch Golden Age liberty and freedom of the press, Van der Capellen stressed the need for peoples to elect their own representatives on a broad suffrage in an orderly, responsible manner. America was certainly his primary model, though he also admired "some of the re-publics of Switzerland."[87] His brochure denounced the Prince of Orange's tyranny, spy network, and Anglomania: "how have you conducted yourself to-ward our merchants, our seamen, toward our entire Fatherland and its most precious interests, since the outbreak of the American war?"[88] "There is at present a fermentation in this nation," Adams informed Congress, an "excep-tional excitement surrounding political pamphlets" and "especially one large pamphlet," he added, meaning *Aan het Volk van Nederland*, a tract distributed everywhere, read and discussed by everyone, that appeared also in English.[89]

Since the political agitation Van der Capellen and Van der Kemp instigated aided America Adams supported it, at any rate to begin with. He and Luzac applauded the new citizen militia units or *vrijcorps* (free militia) springing up in the major Dutch cities in the early 1780s that rapidly became the driving force propagating and pursuing Patriot views and goals. These militia units, electing their officers and exuding a whole new democratic revolutionary al-lure, were based chiefly on the American but also on the Irish model. In Lei-den, the *vrijcorps* and their exercise rota, instituted by Van der Kemp and his ally Pieter Vreede (1750–1837), a cloth manufacturer and leading Patriot pam-phleteer, formed in the spring of 1783. It was the American Revolution that awoke the Dutch from their lethargy, Van der Capellen, Van der Kemp, Luzac, Cerisier, Vreede, and Dumas all proclaimed, precipitating the political crisis and mobilizing opinion. Adams soon concluded, though, that a serious prob-lem existed with respect to how the American Revolution was being conceived and projected by the Dutch and in Europe generally.

Troubled that a numerous faction of "proselytes to democratic principles" had suddenly arisen, Adams hoped these men would eschew urging "simple democracies, for these are impracticable." If the "people should have a voice, a share, and be made an integral part," they should defer to "mixed government," rank, wealth, and property. Good government is always an *imperium mixtum*, combining monarchy, oligarchy, and democracy, the one, the few, and the many, in a balanced fashion as in the 1780 Massachusetts constitution. This was Adams's overriding constitutional principle, but not Franklin's, Paine's, or Jefferson's,[90] and while his aristocratic bias was welcome enough to Van der Capellen, Luzac, and other "moderates" within the Dutch Patriot movement, it clashed with the democratic outlook of younger leaders like Cerisier, Petrus Paulus, Pieter Vreede, Johan Valckenaer, Gerrit Paape, Wacker van Zon, the Amsterdam dissident Irhoven van Dam, and Luzac's brother-in-law, the Delft journalist and agitator Wybo Fijnje (1750–1809).

The Dutch Revolution, no less than the American, nurtured competing moderate and radical wings, with the latter, under their new criteria of popular sovereignty and equality, condemning "aristocracy" and practically all existing pre-revolutionary political institutions as oppressive and illegitimate.[91] Intellectually, this democratic wing drew its inspiration from much the same sources as the American radical tendency. The lawyer and journalist Willem Irhoven van Dam (1760–1802), later, in 1795, an ardent ally of the French Revolution, regularly cited Raynal, Diderot, d'Holbach, and Mably alongside Paine, Priestley, and Price as all promoting radical democratic ideas. By 1783, he already employed the term *onwijsgerig* (unphilosophical) to mean anything undemocratic, intolerant, monarchical, and tied to aristocracy. This faction, eyed with growing suspicion by Adams, were convinced "philosophy" alone generates "love of man and the people's liberty." Given the deadlock in Dutch politics, these intellectuals were well placed to capture and mobilize the discontent and frustration gripping their republic and steer the reform movement.[92]

From Adams's perspective, these divergent Patriot blocs somehow had to bridge their differences and collaborate, placing him in a peculiar quandary. Obviously there was no possibility of his aligning with Orangism or the "English party"; quite apart from their pro-British stance all conservative friends of the stadholder, noted Van der Capellen, shunned Adams like "the plague."[93] The irony was that, unbeknownst to them, Adams was a warm friend to precisely the "mixed government" principles and bias toward aristocracy they championed and that were anathema to his more zealous allies while he was saddled with democratic allies proclaiming principles he inwardly repudiated and abhorred. No less emphatic than Orangist theorists in abjuring popular sovereignty and democracy, Adams felt personally most at ease with Luzac, who continued promoting the American cause in the *Gazette de Leyde* from the late 1770s through to 1782 while similarly growing increasingly worried about how the American Revolution was being projected. But if Adams and Luzac understood each other, Luzac's increasingly anti-democratic leanings created mounting difficulties for his paper and his pro-American stance. By 1782, the *Gazette* projected a firmly rejectionist attitude toward the several pro-American democratic movements now stirring Switzerland and Ireland as well as the Netherlands because they were loudly anti-patrician.

Like Adams, Luzac flatly rejected their idea that the new democratic republican movements stemmed from the veritable principles of the American Revolution; but precisely this conviction rapidly reduced his usefulness to the American cause in Europe.[94] Strife between *aristocrates* and *démocrates* at Geneva, in 1781–82, brought Luzac's previously latent antipathy to democracy and preference for Dutch-Swiss oligarchic republicanism obtrusively to the fore. His championing Adams and his conception of the American Revolution, Luzac's coverage of the Swiss and post-1781 Dutch revolutions revealed, was not support for republicanism, democracy, or equality as proclaimed by the radical Dutch Patriots, French radical *philosophes*, Genevan democrats, Irish republican leaders, or the American Revolution's democratic wing but rather endorsement of the "classical" gentry republicanism Adams extolled. The great difficulty they now both faced, Adams noted in his diary, was that Luzac's oligarchic inclinations were increasingly earning him Patriotic "contempt," hence rendering him an impediment to American diplomacy.[95] A decisive turning point was reached when the *Gazette*, to the disgust of the democrats, approved the French Crown's military intervention in 1782 to crush the Genevan democratic revolution by force. In 1783, the *Gazette* similarly condemned the Irish Revolution.[96] It was now obvious that in the Genevan, Irish, Dutch, and American dramas alike, Luzac was simply too tied to "moderation," Montesquieu, and "aristocracy" to be any longer an effective mouthpiece for American interests.

Until 1782, the United Provinces was only unofficially a friend to America. Following Yorktown, popular petitions demanding formal recognition of the United States bombarded the provincial assemblies.[97] By April 1782, the stadholder's authority had receded sufficiently for the Dutch Republic to become the second European power after France to formally recognize American independence (Spain, showing considerable and understandable hesitation and reluctance, had still not yet done so).[98] Adams, who had labored incessantly to reach this point, hence became the first United States "ambassador" to a European country officially accredited as such. A flurry of ceremonies, banquets, receptions, and fireworks displays followed, all rousingly acclaimed by the Patriot press. Celebratory poems and engravings were published. Transferring to The Hague, Adams purchased a fitting residence, renaming it the Hôtel de l'Amérique. Addressing public meetings, he met with many flattering responses styling him the American Revolution's rhetorical embodiment; in Paris he was reportedly being lauded as "le Washington de la Négotiation."[99] "A few of these compliments," he observed complacently, "would kill Franklin should they come to his ears."[100]

Shortage of funds to finance America's independence struggle, meanwhile, had become chronic. On the financial front, there had indeed been a string of mishaps. In 1776, Franklin had failed to negotiate a major loan in Amsterdam despite guarantees offered by the (heavily indebted) French court. Between 1776 and 1780, several American states, endowed with the power to tax that Congress lacked, sought loans on their own account, in Amsterdam, but without success. The loans Adams eventually obtained in 1782, and again in 1784, were indispensable to bolstering the fledgling republic and its financial creditworthiness, though it was less diplomatic skills that secured the breakthrough than the recovery of American standing following the decisive victory in Virginia. Yorktown, Dutch recognition, and receding Orangist fortunes rendered investing in the American Revolution relatively safe, lucrative, and soon fashionable. Dutch Patriot political success also removed the risk of political developments in the United Provinces endangering the position of pro-American Amsterdam bankers. The first large loan was unnecessarily delayed only because Adams could not see why the United States, even if still unrecognized by most states, should pay higher interest, at 4 percent, than some other powers (the heavily indebted French Crown could borrow only at 6 percent). With the peace accord of 1783, major financial risk for the Amsterdam bankers wholly subsided (until 1787).

Peace negotiations to end the American War ensued in Paris from the autumn of 1782. Adams joined Franklin and Jay as one of the three principal American negotiators. Jay and Adams hit it off well—both worried Congress was being too deferential toward France, risking French intrusion in Canada and expansion in the Caribbean while detesting Franklin's Francophilia or what Adams construed as his countenancing French resolve to "keep us weak. Make us feel our obligations. Impress our minds with a sense of gratitude."[101] Adams had already earlier displayed an obsessive hatred for Franklin but over the winter of 1782–83, infuriated by almost everything Franklin said and did, continually complained of his love of French habits and wine, womanizing, and proximity to French ministers. "I hope the ravings of a certain mischievous madman here against France and its ministers," reported Franklin, "which I hear of every day, will not be regarded in America, so as to diminish in the least the happy union that has hitherto subsisted" between France and the United States.[102]

The Orangist Coup d'état of 1787

Dutch financial assistance remained indispensable even after the peace for several more years. Not unnaturally, the Dutch hoped to benefit from the United States' need for loans and new open-door trade policy, though only in June 1783, with the peace almost finalized, did the United Provinces send their first ambassador to America escorted by a large naval squadron (Anglo-Dutch hostilities had not yet ceased). The ambassador, Pieter Johan van Berckel (1725–1800), was an insignificant figure but a brother of the powerful Amsterdam city secretary, Van Berckel, and came with a large entourage including Gijsbert Karel Van Hogendorp (1762–1834), among the acutest European political observers and defenders of monarchy and aristocracy of the revolutionary era. Van Berckel and his entourage were received with unprecedented pomp by Congress in Princeton, New Jersey, the United States' temporary capital (July to October 1783). Van Hogendorp was not impressed by the America he toured in 1783–84, and least of all by Princeton. He at once grasped the basic rift in American society: there was a general division between "gentlemen" and "persons in lower life"—a distinction based on wealth. The only real difference from the European situation was that society's ranks were not legally or politically defined. To begin with Hogendorp was almost disdainful of the United States Constitution, but in later years, after returning to Holland, he came to discern potential advantages in the Constitution from an aristocratic, anti-democratic standpoint.[103]

From the autumn of 1782 until May 1785, Adams resided mainly in Paris, making short trips to Holland for financial negotiations. From May 1785 to March 1788, he served as the United States ambassador in London, where he predictably encountered great coolness. Most people found it very difficult to reconcile themselves to what had happened, and the London press was even prone to suggest that most Americans had come to regret their independence.[104] Efforts to negotiate a commercial treaty in London foundered as a result of this iciness, and aside from negotiating a third and fourth Dutch state loan, Adams achieved little during his English stay. This left him ample free time for conversation and writing *A Defense of Constitutions*, his theoretical polemic against Paine and democratic ideas. His problem was that in England too no one would talk to him except the democrats. During his period in London, he later informed Jefferson, "I was intimate with Dr. Price. I had much conversation with him at his own house, at my houses, and at the houses and tables of my friends."[105] Adams and his wife also saw much of John Jebb (1736–86) and a "few others like them." These were men distinguished in learning and international politics but thoroughgoing democrats, staunch critics of "mixed government" and the British constitution. No other Britons "professed friendship for America." Where Franklin assured Price that his political contribution was "a valuable one," his writings making "serious impressions on those who at first rejected the counsels you gave" but acquiring "new weight" every day and likely to remain "in high esteem when the cavils against them are dead and forgotten,"[106] Adams and Price disagreed so profoundly that they could not discuss politics at all. The paradox of Adams's position in England, like his quandary in Holland, was that the only prominent persons willing to associate with him interpreted the American Revolution quite differently than he did. For this reason, bizarrely, "unitarianism and Bible Criticism," Adams recalled later, were their sole topics of conversation.[107]

During return visits to The Hague and Amsterdam, between 1785 and 1788, Adams increasingly distanced himself from the democratic movement that so staunchly supported the American cause during the independence struggle. Luzac, too, grew wholly disillusioned with the Patriot movement. By 1785, the "moderates" dominating the early phase of the movement, diverging increasingly from the views of Cerisier, Van der Kemp, and Fijnje, had been largely marginalized. The initiative now lay with radical Patriots with explicitly democratic aims, pressing for abolition of the stadholderate (which Van de Capellen had sought to emasculate but not erase) and nullification of all privilege, ecclesiastical influence, and oligarchy.[108] By 1785, the Dutch Republic was a deeply divided land politically and ideologically, and the main cities, including Leiden and Utrecht, were plunged in continual crisis and intermittent riots. In April 1785, with Patriots gaining in Leiden, as well as Utrecht, Rotterdam, Delft, and other cities, Luzac had to transfer his paper's editorship to Cerisier, who promptly realigned the *Gazette de Leyde* behind the radical Patriot leadership. From April 1785, the paper changed tack and backed calls for extensive reform of the Dutch ancien régime constitution still consisting of seven provincial assemblies alongside the Republic's general assembly exclusively comprising delegates co-opted from the closed oligarchies running the towns and provinces.

The *Gazette* took to echoing the Patriot charge that the United Provinces were no true republic but just the mask of one manipulated by a stadholderate exploiting the ignorance of a too easily misled people, precluding any true equality of status among the citizenry. Not only did the stadholder's court and regent oligarchy enjoy exclusive access to officeholding, but Dutch Reformed Church members, despite possessing no explicit electoral or representative privileges under the constitution, enjoyed "rights" and advantages most obviously (until the early 1780s) in central government, town government, and the local militias from which, in the past, Catholics, dissenters, and Jews were generally excluded. There was no talk yet of Jewish (or black) emancipation in Holland, South Africa, or other Dutch colonies. But Cerisier did advance proposals for equalizing the status of Catholics and Dissenters with that of the Reformed. The Republic's political apparatus had to be adjusted to a people equalized and defined without confessional bias.[109]

Adams carefully observed the evolving Dutch political crisis, participating during his visits in numerous discussions in Leiden restaurants. Designating the Orangists the party of the upper and lower classes, and Patriots that of the middle class, in a long letter of the summer of 1785, he acknowledged that it was the American Revolution that pervaded the rhetoric, ideas, and symbolism of the Patriot movement, as well as their militias and parades. The American Revolution had inspired the local coups in towns like Delft and Leiden now bringing them to a precarious ascendancy: "This party views America with a venerating partiality, and so much attached are they to our opposition [to tyranny], that they seem fond of imitating us wherever they can, and of drawing parallels between the similar circumstances in the two countries."[110] Yet Adams and Luzac stubbornly maintained the Dutch democrats were on the wrong path. In late 1785, Luzac broke openly with the Patriot movement and found himself publicly pilloried in papers and pamphlets as an "out-and-out aristocrat."[111]

A culminating episode of the Dutch Revolution was the gathering of Patriot leaders in Leiden on 4 October 1785, headed by Pieter Vreede, Wybo Fijnje, Cerisier, and Van der Kemp, to draft the movement's general manifesto, the so-called *Leids Ontwerp*.[112] This "project" affirmed popular sovereignty (which Orangists denied), its first article stating that "freedom is the inalienable right of all the federation's citizens" and openly calling for "eene waare representative Demokratie" (a true representative democracy).[113] The people's foes were designated "domineering aristocrats" and the stadholder and his court an "illegal aristocratic cabal." Although its democratic tendency should not be exaggerated (the document also had backward-looking features), it was broadly a radical program.[114] In Utrecht, Leiden, Delft, and other cities where the Patriots gained a firm grip, the reforms ended the stadholder's local influence and the reign of the old regent oligarchies, instituting elections for the city governments and main municipal offices. But while by the summer of 1786 the democrats were preponderant in most parts of the provinces of Holland, Utrecht, and Overijssel, Orangists retained the upper hand in Zeeland, Friesland, and parts of Gelderland, and there were repeated outbreaks of populist rioting against the Patriots in Rotterdam, The Hague, and other main cities.[115]

Democratic discourse invoking America resounded continually during the mid-1780s in Holland, as among the British radical intelligentsia and the French radical pro-American intellectual elite, more and more unsettling Adams (as well as Luzac and de Pinto). Adams found himself embroiled in a European contest that was at once political and intellectual while believing his adversaries had little true grasp of political theory. Years later, he recalled how, in 1785, when "Lafayette harangued you [Jefferson] and me, and John Quincy Adams, through a whole evening in your hotel in the Cul de Sac, at Paris, and developed the plans then in operation to reform France," he felt "astonished at the grossness of his ignorance of government and history, as I had been for years before at that of Turgot, Rochefoucauld, Condorcet and Franklin. This gross Ideology of them all, first suggested to me the thought and the inclination which I afterwards hinted to you in London of writing something upon aristocracy." Yet, at the same time, Adams dreaded making "enemies of all the French Patriots, the Dutch Patriots, the English republicans, Dissenters, Reformers, call them what you will; and what came nearer home to my bosom than all the rest, I knew, I should give offence to many, if not all of my best Friends in America, and very probably destroy all the little popularity I ever had." His 1786 *Defense of the Constitutions*, Adams later believed, "laid the foundation of that immense unpopularity, which fell like the Tower of Siloam upon me."[116]

By contrast, in America, Jefferson's "steady defense of democratical principles, and your invariable favourable opinion of the French Revolution laid the foundation of your unbounded popularity." Yet, while rejecting Lafayette's, Turgot's, and Condorcet's "general will" and unicameralist, democratizing principles, Adams nevertheless believed there was much amiss with America's state constitutions. He discerned evident risks to his republicanism, that of Sidney and Locke as he believed, from below and from above: "If a warrior should arise to attack our constitutions where they are not defensible, I'll not undertake to defend them. Two Thirds of our states have made constitutions, in no respect better than those of the Italian republicks, and as sure as there is a Heaven and an Earth, if they are not altered they will produce disorders and confusion."[117]

During the Philadelphia Constitutional Convention debates, in 1787, the Founding Fathers, not for the first time, stressed the parallels between the 1578 Dutch confederation and their own.[118] In late 1787, the comparison even briefly became a central theme of American deliberation. This was highly ironic, given that Americans were fixing their attention on the United Provinces just as the Dutch Patriots were organizing to demolish it.[119] The Dutch Republic illustrated the dangers of creating too weak a federation, and the Philadelphia delegates were keenly aware of the need to institute a federal structure with authority to tax and—unlike the Dutch Republic—possess direct control over the armed forces and diplomacy. But there were also features of the pre-1780 Dutch constitution that both sides in the American constitutional arena could invoke with advantage. Bitter strife over the Dutch stadholderate's powers gave force to what many perceived as a disquieting concentration of power in the presidency in the American draft Constitution. Franklin and Jefferson were profoundly troubled by the broad dimensions of the proposed presidency. The stadholder's actions "would have sufficed to set me against a chief magistrate eligible for a long duration," remarked Jefferson, "if I had ever been disposed towards one."[120] In one respect the American president and state governors (also regularly compared to the Dutch stadholder) stood to acquire powers exceeding those of any Prince of Orange: their veto over legislation in the state legislatures. The president's proposed powers included the power to veto acts passed by both houses of Congress, authority unparalleled by any prerogative of the stadholder.[121] When he next met Adams, Willem V himself underlined this imposing fact: "you are going to have a king under the title of 'president.' "[122]

Disdaining the Dutch democratic movement and its envisaging the American Revolution as democratic, it nevertheless came as a profound shock to Adams, as likewise to Jefferson, Mirabeau, Godwin, and Price, when the Dutch republicans were suddenly overwhelmed by an international coalition of powers organized to suppress them. This disastrous denouement occurred in September 1787 when the new Prussian king, with British backing, intervened on the flimsy pretext of an insult to his sister, the stadholder's wife. On 13 September 1787, four days before the signing of the United States Constitution in Philadelphia, Friedrich Wilhelm sent a twenty-thousand-man-strong Prussian army under the duke of Brunswick to occupy the United Provinces temporarily and assist the Orangists to retrieve power and purge Patriots from the militias and town governments. Avid for word from America, Adams and Jefferson heard of the fall of Utrecht and then Amsterdam, and complete crushing of the Dutch democratic movement, before hearing the American Constitution was finalized.

The Prussian invasion outraged Lafayette, who aspired to place himself at the head of the Dutch Patriots and was already on his way when he learned that all resistance had petered out before he could intervene.[123] Orangist triumph entailed extensive purges and imprisonment of anti-Orangist leaders,[124] prompting a massive exodus of thousands of officials, journalists, lawyers, manufacturers, and professors. All projects and schemes for reform were ditched, including the schemes for reform in South Africa. Though directed by the Orangist court and Prussian troops, the repression's wide scope and intensity flowed from the furious loyalism of the less informed and literate. Devotion to the House of Orange and established Church drove an anti-intellectualist upsurge and banning of Patriot papers and other publications, utterly demoralizing for the fleeing and uprooted radicals and dismaying for their allies abroad.[125] "Are we to suppose the game already up," exclaimed Jefferson, writing to Adams from Paris on 28 September 1787, "and that the Stadtholder is to be reestablished, perhaps erected into a monarch, without this country [France] lifting a finger in opposition to it? If so, it is a lesson the more for us. In fact what a crowd of lessons do the present miseries of Holland teach us? Never to have an hereditary officer of any sort: never to let a citizen ally himself with kings: never to call in foreign nations to settle domestic differences: never to suppose that any nation will expose itself to war for us etc." Jefferson, though, had not yet wholly abandoned hope that France would intervene, if not for the Patriots' sake then to check British and Prussian arrogance: "still I am not without hopes that a good rod is in soak for Prussia and that England will feel the end of it."[126]

"I tremble and agonize for the suffering Patriots in Holland," agreed Adams, from London, on 28 October.[127] Orangist vengefulness surpassed all precedent, affecting many individuals and families. Years of demonstrations, parades, slogans, and ideological warfare, in addition to political intervention from the pulpit, had set the scene for a full-scale populist reactionary repression closely akin to the English "Church and king" loyalism that afterward vilified and purged radicalism in Britain. At Delft, the plebs showed what they thought of democratic ideas by smashing up an entire hall full of revolutionary Delftware adorned with liberty symbols and hurling the shattered porcelain into the canals. Great numbers of officials and officeholders were targeted and dismissed, some beaten up in the streets or in their pillaged homes by angry mobs. Every Patriot officeholder was relentlessly purged, even in distant Philadelphia the inept Van Berckel (who stayed in America, on a farm near New York). Among thousands of refugees driven from their homeland were Cerisier and Luzac's sister, Emilie Luzac, with her husband, Wybo Fijnje. Fijnje and his wife fled to Brussels, Cerisier to France. Van der Kemp, released after six months' imprisonment with bail money put up by Luzac, fled with his family via Antwerp in May 1788, abandoning house, library, and his famous collection of busts and medals, to America, settling in the Dutch village of Barneveld, near Utica, in New York State. Redelinghuys, by contrast, was prevented from leaving, the new Orangist regime being anxious to pre-clude his returning to South Africa and helping prolong opposition at the Cape.[128]

As a friend of the "Patriotic Party against the Statholder," the American legation's secretary, Dumas, likewise incurred "censure and displeasure." Adams received a formal communication from the purged States General requiring "me to employ him no longer but to appoint some other person in my absence."[129] Since Dumas as "Agent for the United States" officially held his post from Congress, not the ambassador, Adams simply forwarded their demand to Congress. Not the least disquieting aspect for both Jefferson and Adams was the possibility Orangist vengeance might descend also on the banking house of Jakob and Nicholas Van Staphorst, which, with Dumas as go-between, handled the United States' loans. In the event, the pro-French firm was left unmolested.[130] A posthumous victim of the repression was Van der Capellen. In March 1785, Patriot leaders had commissioned a statue of him to be wrought in Carrara marble by the Italian radical-minded sculptor Giuseppe Ceracchi (1751–1801). Finished in August 1789, the work could neither be transported to the Netherlands nor paid for, those who commis-sioned it having fled abroad.[131] For decades, the grandest Patriot monument to the people's democratic striving thus stayed bizarrely stranded in Rome.

"My worthy old Friends the Patriots in Holland are extreamly to be pit-ied," affirmed Adams in November 1787, "and so are their deluded persecu-tors. That country I fear is to be ruined, past all remedy. I wish that all the good men had sense and spirit enough to go to America."[132] A few did; but if Adams sympathized with their plight, he felt none for their cause. From September 1787, the *Gazette de Leyde*, for the second time since Adams's arrival, lurched rightward. Like the Orangist repression more generally, this shift corresponded to Adams's views well enough, despite his dismay at the purges. Genuinely appalled by "what lengths the spite extends," he nonethe-less approved Orangist political theory, rejection of popular sovereignty, and its blending monarchy with oligarchy. In this he resembled Edmund Burke, who at this point, delighted by this "opportunity of restoring that party to power, which was most likely to prove a valuable friend of Great Britain," slackened his efforts for domestic reform, retreating into the uncompromis-ing conservatism and insistence on the primacy of British interests for which he is remembered. Remarkably for a former champion of "liberty," Burke judged the "entire destruction" of the Patriot movement, and the "French interest" in Holland, "a good event to this country [i.e., Britain]."[133]

Adams longed to return to America and was planning his departure. This worried Jefferson owing to the uncertainties still surrounding the state loans.

With America's Revolutionary War debt to France not yet repaid, interest repayments falling into arrears, and Congress encountering mounting difficulty in servicing its schedule of repayments, fresh loans were essential to the functioning of the United States government especially overseas. Jefferson implored Adams's wife, Abigail, to help persuade her husband to defer their departure.[134] Congress's precarious finances in the event kept Adams in Holland for several more months, deferring his departure until May 1788. In March, Jefferson, traveling from Paris, joined him for his last weeks in The Hague, the two Founding Fathers together negotiating with the Amsterdam banks to finalize the new arrangements.[135]

During Adams's last sojourn in Amsterdam, in early 1788, his hostility to the democratic movement—and its idolizing the American Revolution as a democratizing world event—became still more marked: "the Patriots in this country were little read in history, less in government; knew little of the human heart and still less of the world. They have therefore been the dupes of foreign politics and their own undigested systems."[136] To him they were deluded ideologues, victims of defective "philosophy." By contrast, for Jefferson and the French radicals the 1780–87 Dutch Revolution was the first sister revolution manifestly the offspring of the American upheaval and its Paineite republican reforming principles, a bid for enlightened republican equality and democracy. This disagreement over the Dutch crisis of 1787 reflected the deep contradiction within the American Revolution and political system itself. The clash between the American Revolution as a pillar of "moderation," as an ideological construct of Adams, Jay, and Hamilton, and the American Revolution as the democratic future of mankind inspiring the Dutch democrats by no means ended in 1787. Among the thousands of exiles, many were soon building networks abroad, creating a kind of liberation movement in exile, aspiring one day to reverse the outcome of 1787 and drive out the Orangists in their turn. Inside and outside the Netherlands, an ideologically hardened rejection of the Dutch ancien régime consolidated.

The new American ambassador to the Netherlands, Jay, was a conservative chosen by Washington as someone who needed no reminding that the United States should avoid showing partiality for the exiled radicals and their democratic cause. However awkward in terms of publicity, Orangist repression suited the political instincts of Washington, Jay, Hamilton, and Adams, and fitted their vision for America's future. Informal aristocracy and the old system, not democracy, was their goal. After Jay, John Quincy Adams (1767–1848), later sixth president of the United States (1826–29), returned to Holland, in October 1794, as the United States' envoy, six years after his father's departure, acutely aware of the continuing stresses. He too wrestled with the irony that the Dutch faction devoted to "mixed government" and Montesquieu considered themselves totally at odds with American principles. "The Court party" and "all the Orangist faction in the Netherlands," he informed his mother, "never look upon the United States but with eyes of terror and aversion, sometimes shaded with a veil of affected indifference and sometimes attempted to be disguised under a mask of respect and veneration." The stadholder and old oligarchy, like Europe's patrician elites generally and Europe's monarchies, feared and detested the United States' democratically tinted republicanism and rejection of the hereditary principle. The Dutch ancien régime retreated more than ever into the arms of Britain. Since 1787 "the British government," John Quincy informed Congress, "has been much more absolute in The Hague than in London."[137]

John Quincy liked neither Orangism nor Britain's ascendancy over the Dutch Republic. But the same basic contradiction within the American Revolution that so disturbed his father in the Dutch context dismayed him too. He was not at all disposed to renew his father's pre-1783 outwardly amicable ties with the democrats, proving even more unsympathetic to the radicals venerating America than his father. As a youth in Paris, John Quincy had often heard Franklin, Jefferson, and Lafayette debating democratic republican principles but now followed his father (and Luzac) in despising such ideas. As with the earlier appointments of Gouverneur Morris as minister plenipotentiary to France, and Jay in Holland, this was doubtless why he was chosen for The Hague. The Federalist administration wanted to be sure of having ambassadors who, unlike Jefferson and Monroe, would not assist democratizing, revolutionary movements. Invited to join one of the Dutch democratic clubs, John Quincy flatly refused, having been directed to avoid "every act that could be charged with partiality to the Patriots."[138]

John Quincy's aloofness could not have contrasted more with Jefferson's active support for the democratic republicans in France. Fundamental divergence over America's role in the world and the Revolution's legacy reflected America's divided self-awareness at home. But the bitterness of the Dutch ideological polarization also served, John Quincy pointed out, as a warning of the dangers of such strife. With the French conquest of the Low Countries in 1794–95, a new regime assumed power in Holland that turned the tables on the Orangists and renewed the ferocity of the ideological conflict. Before 1787, in "most of the cities and villages throughout the provinces," explained John Quincy, "certain clubs or popular societies had formed themselves, similar in their nature to those which have since been so notorious in France, and to those which upon their model have recently arisen in the United States." After September 1787, these political clubs, having drawn considerable bodies of adherents, were "prohibited from assembling, and others, consisting only of partisans of the House of Orange, were substituted in their stead." With the French invasion and the "revolution consequent upon that event, the Orange societies have been prohibited in their turn and the patriotic clubs have been revived." The result was a deepening of the ideological split, the Netherlands becoming, like France, a land of entrenched warring political clubs and local factions. If care was not taken, the same paralyzing deadlock would permeate and polarize the United States too.[139]

CHAPTER 11

Jefferson's French Revolution

Jefferson's Radicalism

In his own accurate estimation, Jefferson was the most consistent, unambiguous, democratizing republican among the Founding Fathers. A classic "radical enlightener," the common people, he always insisted, whether American, French, British, or South American, with no nation or group being potentially more suited to it than any other, can be trusted to make, and sustain, a free, liberty-loving, and viable representative democratic republic provided only that they are sufficiently "enlightened" to detach themselves from religious authority—history furnishing "no example of a priest-ridden people maintaining a free civil government." The "people are the only safe depositaries of their own liberty," undoubtedly, but all liberty, American, French, or otherwise, is but a "short-lived possession unless the mass of the people" become "informed to a certain degree."[1] Democracy works but only when ignorance is checked and religious authority shut out of public life. With Jefferson, "Radical Enlightenment" was the whole essence: without discussing his "Radical Enlightenment" one understands nothing about Jefferson or his role in the American Revolution.

Throughout the revolutionary years, and his post-Independence political career, Jefferson strove to broaden the Revolution's scope and significance, which to him meant considerably more than just achieving independence from Britain. Steady in his views for decades, he strove to strengthen and build on the Revolution's core values as he understood them and render the United States the world's prime exemplum of modern democratic republican political and social principles and keep it on that path. He came to represent, and speak for, the abiding ties between the American and French revolutions more eloquently and incisively, and in a more far-reaching (and more typically "Radical Enlightenment") manner, than any other major figure of the American Revolution, seeing the two as interacting closely on many levels and in many places. In 1793, for example, he sympathized with French revolutionary plans to arouse the French in Canada to revolt against their British "oppressors" (while continuing to hope for Canada's conquest and the "final expulsion of England from the American continent" in 1812).[2]

A voracious reader with an enormous library, much of it philosophical and anticlerical, Jefferson was thoroughly steeped in Enlightenment literature from early on. The quintessential American enlightener in general as well as in "radical" terms, he also had firm preferences, leaving Rousseau strikingly absent from his thinking.[3] Another notable bias was his conspicuous dislike of Hume, Montesquieu, and Blackstone, three principal pillars of moderate Enlightenment and veneration for the British model (which Jefferson regularly disparaged).[4] Hume especially he came to see as a fount of "Tory" principles and dangerous aristocratism.[5] Chief author of the *Declaration of Independence*, written to justify the Revolution and repudiation of the British Crown, Jefferson made no claim to originality for the ideas it contained, and allusions to particular strands of political philosophy in this epoch-making document are too sparse to indicate derivation from any specific intellectual tradition.[6] While "classical republicanism" figured prominently in Jefferson's education and subsequent thinking, by 1775–76 he had developed a conception of human rights as "natural," primary, and transcending any written constitution, thereby from the outset of his political career projecting a distinctly radical philosophical perspective.[7]

Studying at William and Mary College in Virginia, Jefferson was taught by, and had been close to, William Small (1734–75), a Scottish mathematician and scientist whose short career ended (back in Britain) with his premature death at age forty-one from malaria contracted in Virginia.[8] From Small, an associate of Franklin, Priestley, and another prominent English radical, Erasmus Darwin (1731–1802), grandfather of Charles Darwin and one of the founders of the renowned Birmingham Lunar Society, Jefferson acquired his first grounding in radical thought: "I got my first views of the expansion of science and of the system of things in which we are placed," a nominally deistic style of thinking stressing the immutability of nature's laws and their inherent incompatibility with biblical religion, miracles, Revelation, and "priestcraft."[9] Virtually the entire Birmingham Lunar Society, including Darwin, venerated Franklin and, going against the inclinations of their countrymen, warmly supported the American rebellion against the ministry of George III.[10]

Jefferson's "deism" was indebted also, recent research shows, to Henry St. John Bolingbroke (1678–1751), a writer in whom Jefferson took a keen interest while at William and Mary, and from whom he took extensive notes. How far Bolingbroke derives his Bible criticism, rejection of miracles, and theory of "imposture" and priestcraft, and notions of the relationship of politics to religion, directly from Spinoza rather than indirectly, via Toland, Collins, and Thomas Gordon, remains to be investigated, as does Bolingbroke's and Gordon's (appreciable) debt to Bayle. But since specialists now accept that Toland and Collins, both among Bolingbroke's prime sources, were closer to, and more dependent on, Spinoza than scholars once supposed,[11] Jefferson's system can safely be said to blend a Spinozistic critique of providence, ceremonies, miracles, priestcraft, Bible criticism, and religion generally with Bayle's questioning of the justice of the biblical God and Bolingbroke's equally Spinozistic doctrine of the equal moral status of all men and peoples before "Nature's God." For Jefferson, all peoples with their distinctive cultural and physical features and differences are formed by the same set of universal laws.[12] Esteeming Bolingbroke, Toland, Collins, Mazzei, Gordon, and Priestley (and later Condorcet and Volney), Jefferson, like Franklin, also admired Paine. The egalitarianism and democratizing impulse that decisively shaped his views can thus be said to have been a cumulative outcome from the republican, non-providential "deist" proclivities of all these Radical Enlightenment writers.[13]

Virginia was the first state to revise its constitution fundamentally. Despite the conservative temperament of most of the state assembly, it was agreed that the emerging new state constitution required a broad *Declaration of Rights*. Drafted by George Mason, among the richest Virginia planters but unusual for the earnestness of his republican commitment,[14] this declaration, of May 1776, was highly innovative in its terminology, being the first modern declaration of rights to be based on a universal conception of equality. Jefferson was among those most eager to ensure that the text included no direct reference to "Christ" or to Virginia being a "Christian" society.[15] The new state constitution itself followed in June. Jefferson later described Mason as a "man of the first order of wisdom among those who acted on the theater of the revolution, of expansive mind, profound judgment, cogent in argument, learned in the lore of our former constitution, and earnest for the republican change on democratic principles."[16] The Virginia *Declaration*, like that of Pennsylvania a few weeks later,[17] surpassed Congress's subsequent *Declaration of Independence* of July 1776 by emphasizing even more men's natural equality and the inalienability of their natural rights, and in stating the purpose of government to be the "common benefit, protection, and security of the people." The United States' *Declaration* acknowledges the function of governments to be to protect universal basic rights but is notably vaguer with respect to the "common benefit."[18]

From July 1776, fundamental changes followed thick and fast. "At the first session of our legislature after the *Declaration of Independence*," Jefferson recalled thirty-seven years later, "we passed a law abolishing entails. And this was followed by one abolishing primogeniture, and dividing the lands of intestates equally among all their children, or other representatives. These laws, drawn by myself, laid the axe to the root of pseudo-aristocracy." Admittedly, these initiatives failed to introduce anything approaching universal male suffrage in Virginia and left political control with the landowning "aristocracy"; but Jefferson succeeded in having the suffrage qualifications set low with even small plots of land qualifying their owners for the right to vote.[19] Other late 1770s initiatives proposed by Jefferson and his colleagues were similarly pathbreaking in terms of social and constitutional principle but failed to pass because few Virginians, in the townships or the state assembly, were as secular, anticlerical, and republican-minded as Jefferson, Mason, and Madison. Their ardent republican revolutionary creed was not, in fact, particularly widely shared among the Virginia elite—or at the grassroots level. Benjamin Rush, who turned against democracy already in 1776 (but not until much later against the Revolution's republican legacy), remarked in a letter to Jefferson of August 1800 that where the "citizens of Boston in the republican years of 1776 and 1777 rejected the royal names of several streets and substituted in the room of them names that comported with the new and republican state of their town," Virginia did nothing comparable. Rather, Virginia counties retained designations distinctly reminiscent of British royalty and the "disgraceful remains of your former degraded state as men."[20]

For Virginians generally, and indeed most Americans, monarchy, aristocracy, and ecclesiastical authority were not the outright foes and revolutionary targets they became for Franklin and Jefferson. Nowhere else was there such a fierce battle in the legislature and society over disestablishing the public church and its system of belief imposed by statute. In December 1776, religious dissenters, among whom, in Virginia, the Baptists were now the largest group, were finally exempted from obligatory taxes to support the Anglican Church—a major shift, albeit for the time being the Anglican clergy remained state supported and privileged with "heretical" notions still theoretically subject to legal action by them. Strikingly, Jefferson's 1779 draft bill for "religious liberty" with its abjuring the Anglican Church's "spiritual tyranny" initially failed to pass. When Virginia's "law for religious freedom," softening Jefferson's original phraseology, did finally pass in 1786, after a decade-long contest, steered through by Madison in Jefferson's absence, it succeeded only thanks to the Baptist Evangelicals, who had their own reasons for opposing the state's "right" to privilege one particular church and counter "heresy" as its clergy directed. But even then, the legislature deleted his affirmation that the "opinions of men are not the object of civil government, nor under its jurisdiction," tying in mitigating phrases confirming that the state government could still punish individuals for "blasphemy" and, in theory, for irreligious and "heretical" beliefs. But the core was secured, and Jefferson always reckoned this law among his prime achievements.[21]

Having contributed as much as, or more than, any Founding Father except Franklin to broaden the scope and implications of America's independence, Jefferson found himself dispatched to France precisely at the point the ancien régime there disintegrated. Arriving in the late summer of 1784, with Franklin still presiding over the American Revolution's reputation, interests, and legacy in the Old World, he joined with him and with Adams (over from The Hague) in meetings in Paris to fix America's overseas trade policy and prepare commercial treaties with European powers. Such agreements were a means of advancing America's trade, reinforcing the Union, and elevating the federal principle by establishing responsibilities directly under Congress rather than the individual states. When Franklin finally departed for America, having long charmed the Passy neighborhood with his inexhaustible fund of bons mots, "it seemed as if the village had lost its patriarch."[22]

On 17 May 1785, Jefferson was officially received at Versailles in succession to Franklin. Diplomatic duties rendered him a frequent visitor to the palaces, grounds, and gardens but left him with no particular fondness for the royal court.[23] He greatly preferred the literary and philosophical salons of Madame Helvétius, the Comtesse de Tessé, an aunt of Lafayette's wife, and the wife of Louis XVI's chief minister, Madame Necker. By 1789, if not earlier, he evinced a special aversion to the queen, Marie Antoinette. Yet, he concurred with Franklin, France, for which he acquired a lifelong affection, was America's sole dependable friend. Cultivating America's relationship with the French court remained in both their eyes a vital priority. With Lafayette, who returned to Paris from his triumphant postwar tour of the Thirteen States in January 1785, Jefferson remained in close contact, despite reservations regarding his "unmeasured ambition" and thirst for popularity, defects that remained abiding features of Lafayette's personality.[24] Lafayette's house, a key focus of the American colony in Paris, became the channel of Jefferson's discreet interventions in the French revolutionary scene.

If Lafayette—at the time more renowned in America than in France—remained an ardent champion of the American Revolution and (until 1791) of republicanism, Jefferson, like Franklin, found the prevailing view of the new republic among Europe's courts and aristocratic elites to be distinctly hostile. Most countries and diplomats viewed the United States as a threat to monarchy, aristocracy, and ecclesiastical hierarchy. According to anti-American propaganda still emanating from London, The Hague, and the German courts, America nurtured a disorderly and politically, religiously, and morally anarchic society, and, if militarily successful, at a more fundamental level should be pronounced a failure. Jefferson's friends and allies, as with Franklin earlier, were chiefly enthusiastic *Américanistes* drawn from the circles of the radical *philosophes*, notably Mazzei, Chastellux, Démeunier, La Rochefoucauld, Condorcet,[25] and the Baron Grimm, from whom he learned everything he needed to know about Diderot, d'Holbach, Helvétius, and the *Encyclopédie*. Grimm he got to know "most intimately. He was the pleasantest, and most conversible member of the diplomatic corps whilst I was there," he recalled later, a "true expert in conversation, painting, sculpture and literature." Despite quarreling with Diderot over the latter's growing anti-monarchism in the early 1780s,[26] Grimm identified with the "school of Diderot, d'Alembert, d'Holbach, the first of whom committed their system of atheism to writing in *Le Bon Sens*,[27] and the last in his *Système de la nature*," texts Jefferson studied carefully. Years later, on reading Grimm's "compleat review of French literature and fine arts from 1753 to 1790," Adams concurred that he was certainly a brilliant critic.[28] Drawn to French materialism and radical irreligion, Jefferson equally gravitated toward the growing crypto-republican tendency among the followers of Raynal, Diderot, and d'Holbach. The 1782 Genevan Revolution, presented to the world as a struggle between "aristocrates" and "démocrates" and the Dutch democratic movement having adopted similar terminology, by the early and mid-1780s these labels, important to Jefferson, were firmly established as pan-European badges of identity, familiarizing onlookers everywhere with the essential split between "aristocratic" and "democratic" republicanism.[29]

Eager to broaden his European knowledge, Jefferson toured southern France and Piedmont from February to June 1787, sampling the Burgundian vineyards, visiting Roman arches and aqueducts, proceeding to Marseille, Nice, and the Po Valley as far as Milan, and westward to Bordeaux. He admired the culture, history, and art, while attentive also to the poverty of most of the French and northern Italian rural and urban population, becoming keenly aware that the "general fate of humanity here [is] most deplorable."[30] To the small extent he participated in the American debate over the Federal Constitution, hammered out by Congress during the summer of 1787—he was unable to peruse a copy of the proposed document until mid-November—he did so consulting with Lafayette, Mazzei, and Paine, who had arrived in May. Like his French and Anglo–American republican democratic allies, Jefferson harbored substantial reservations, especially disliking (along with Paine, Mazzei, and Franklin) the strong presidency, the reeligible one-person executive, "a bad edition of a Polish king," or Dutch stadholder, as it seemed to them.[31] "A plurality is far better: it combines the mass of a nation better together: and besides this, it is necessary to the manly mind of a republic that it loses the debasing idea of obeying an individual." Like George Mason (who refused to sign the Constitution), Jefferson also sharply criticized the absence of "express declarations ensuring freedom of religion, freedom of the press," and "trial by jury," along with the "long duration of the senate" and relative weakness of the House of Representatives.[32] Yet, while opposing presidential reelection to the last, he was eventually persuaded by Madison to endorse the Constitution with assurances that a Bill of Rights would quickly be appended, following ratification, by way of amendments.

Championing Revolutionary France (1788–93)

During the French Revolution's early phases, Jefferson was more than just an enthusiastic eyewitness. At times, he figured almost as a direct participant. For him, this new revolution was an overwhelming experience that indelibly impressed itself on his outlook and thinking. It decisively shaped his understanding of the meaning and principles of the American Revolution itself, as well as his attitude to his American opponents during the bitter 1790s antagonism between Federalists and Anti-Federalists over the general direction and future path of the United States. He judged the two revolutions so closely bound together, he assured Mason (who similarly fretted that there were factors "sapping the republicanism of the United States"), that he came to view the French Revolution's success and the consolidation of French liberty "as necessary to stay up our own [Revolution and liberty]" and prevent America "falling back to that kind of half-way house, the English constitution."[33]

At first, like his friends Mazzei, La Rochefoucauld, and Lafayette, with whom he conferred regularly in 1788–89, Jefferson did not consider France yet ready for the transition from monarchy to (de facto) republicanism to which his *Américaniste* allies and some other leaders of the new revolution were committed. France could not easily or quickly dispense with her ancient legal and institutional structures. Initially, they agreed, France would follow America's path only partially—and by degrees.[34] During the summer of 1788, though, as the French pamphlet war heated up and political controversy grew more strident, Jefferson became impatient, and before long disgusted, with the French nobility's and privileged elites' conduct. Especially, he despised the regional high courts or *parlements*, realizing these age-old bodies were mobilizing and misleading popular resistance to the Crown purely for their own advantage. Optimistic that at least the younger French nobles would forsake privilege and support the Third Estate leaders, until early 1789 Jefferson, Lafayette, and Mazzei continued urging allies to see the wisdom, in the current context, of a cautious, middle-of-the road approach.[35] This was not because they believed what was good for America differed from what was good for France, or any other nation, but because the distance the French needed to traverse to reach republican ground seemed so immense. They feared a possible aristocratic backlash or that the republican Left would seek too much too soon and, like the Dutch Patriots in September 1787, be overwhelmed by a combination of domestic opposition and foreign intervention.[36] Already months before the Estates-General met, Jefferson knew republican-minded French Patriot leaders would push for "a declaration of rights" and "flatter themselves," he informed Price, that "they shall form a better constitution than the English. I think it will be better in some points—worse in others. It will be better in the article of representation, which will be more equal. It will be worse, as their situation obliges them to keep up the dangerous machine of a standing army."[37]

Condorcet, subsequently the most significant of Jefferson's French associates, was certainly an avowed "republican" by 1786 and probably earlier. During 1788, he published a series of anonymous papers, supposedly in "Philadelphia" (actually Paris) under the pretense of being an "American" republican observing the French scene. By then he had already noted, in his 1786 text "Influence of the American Revolution on Europe," some of the ways he and his friends believed the American Revolution had galvanized educated opinion in France. How could laws supporting religious intolerance possibly remain in force in Europe when governments witnessed that the "most extensive tolerance ever enjoyed by any people, far from inciting unrest, is making peace and fraternity flourish in America?"[38] Religious toleration did indeed rapidly advance in France in the 1780s. Public discussion of key issues in the papers, revolutionary America had also proved, helps dispel prejudices and prepare the way, building support for unfamiliar but necessary changes. Publicizing the Independence struggle had bound the populace to its commitment to create a new polity. Publishing deserters' names in local gazettes achieved more in curbing desertion from the ranks than threatening severe penalties. Whereas liberty of the press in England, held Condorcet, was fatally eroded by strict libel laws, by corrupting journalists, and by the "practice of circumventing, with often ridiculous subtleties," the essence of press freedom, "we have seen in America that information, easily and quickly disseminated throughout an immense country by the printing press, gave the government, in difficult circumstances, a weapon often more powerful than the laws."[39]

When the Americans commenced their Revolution, they had convened their representatives in a Congress, Condorcet pointed out, permitting no distinctions between orders, no ecclesiastical presence, and no hereditary privileges.[40] Furthermore, the effectiveness of Congress during the American Revolutionary War sufficiently proved that numerous heads representing the people could act more forcefully and decisively than a single head, or a small aristocratic group, and that it was a fallacy to suppose either monarchy or aristocracy functions more efficiently than a democratic republic.[41] The distinctions between French society's three orders—clergy, nobility, and Third Estate—he declared, must be erased by the forthcoming meeting of the Estates-General and the privileged orders merged with the Third so as to create a "national assembly." Eventually, Condorcet went on to chair the drafting of Europe's first democratic republican constitution (February 1793). Between 1791 and June 1793, Condorcet was among the principal leaders of the French Revolution, remaining so until declared an outlaw by the ruthlessly repressive populist Montagnard regime and forced into hiding.

As the months passed, Jefferson realized that there was scant genuine convergence on basic "rights" in France and that the conflicting goals and interests of what soon became vehemently warring factions and interests were too incompatible, and the political struggle too embittered, for the Third Estate to accept any outcome short of fully demolishing the privileged status of the nobility and clergy and thoroughly emasculating royal power. This meant there could be no revolutionary settlement of the kind he and his French republican friends (then including Lafayette) desired to witness without a prolonged struggle. By the early summer of 1789, Paris and all France seethed with political excitement and turmoil fomented by high-level deadlock. The Revolution had no choice but to radicalize and follow America's republican path more forcefully and rapidly than Jefferson, Mazzei, Lafayette, Condorcet, Démeunier, and the rest had initially judged realistic—or else simply collapse.[42]

At Versailles, where the Estates-General convened, still for the moment organized on traditional lines in three separate chambers—clergy, nobility, and the Third—Louis XVI's efforts to fix attention on the spiraling state debt and need for additional royal revenue were swiftly laid aside. Attention focused on the quarrel over privilege and the status of the three estates, producing a momentous clash that brought the routine processes of government to a halt. The Patriot leadership contended that practically the entire existing French constitution and tax system was illicit and needed reforming. Regarding the projected new constitution, they also agreed, in principle at least, on the necessity "as preliminary to the whole" of a "general Declaration of the Rights of Man." One proposed draft Jefferson reviewed with particular care was the "Declaration of Rights" that Lafayette drew up in nine articles in January 1789. Besides his Virginian deputy and protégé, William Short (1759–1849), Jefferson discussed it with Lafayette himself and with Jean-Paul Rabaut Saint-Étienne (1743–93), a noted champion of toleration and freedom of the press (later guillotined by the Montagne), the leader of the Protestant group in the Estates-General. Despite being the American ambassador, or rather in his own eyes and those of his friends because he was the American ambassador, Jefferson unhesitatingly participated in the discussion, sending a copy to Madison in America and endorsing Lafayette's revised second draft "Charter of Rights" in ten articles, formulated in June, hopefully to be granted by the king and signed by every member of the Estates.[43] Jefferson defended his "presumption" in intervening in the French discussion of universal rights, his urging revolutionary leaders to back Lafayette's draft "Declaration," by citing his "unmeasurable love for your nation," as he expressed it to Rabaut, and "painful anxiety lest despotism, after an unaccepted offer to bind its own hands, should seize you again with tenfold fury."[44]

Lafayette and Jefferson's circle affirmed that all men are born free and equal, demanding abolition of privilege and the granting of press freedom, annual convening of the Estates-General, transfer to the legislature exclusively of the power to tax, and that "laws shall be made by the Estates General only, with the consent of the king"—in other words an unmistakably republican outcome. The revolutionary new concept of "universal and equal rights" had been in the air in France for some years. Although it is true, as historians claim, that even British-style gentry republicanism, let alone democratic republicanism, at this time had little resonance in French society as such, among the Enlightenment intelligentsia identifying wholeheartedly with the Revolution, men such as Condorcet, Brissot, and many key newspaper editors, like Carra, democratic republicanism was already dominant and this now shaped the radical revolutionary thrust. In fact, the *philosophes*, held Condorcet, had rediscovered the long-lost notion of universal and equal rights well before the American Revolution; however, they faced the great difficulty of how to diffuse this republican concept more widely in society. The

The marquis de Condorcet (1743–1794), portrait engraving by Augustin de Saint-Aubin (1736–1807), from 1777 official engraver at the Paris Bibliothèque Royale (from 1791, the Bibliothèque Nationale). Photo credit: © Roger-Viollet / The Image Works.

"ignorant" need concrete, working examples and here the American Revolution proved decisive for France by providing with its "Declaration of Independence, a simple and sublime exposition of these rights, so sacred and so long forgotten."[45] Among the most fundamental universal rights, held Condorcet in 1786, were the right to "contribute, either directly or through representatives, to the making of the laws and all actions taken in the name of society at large."[46]

Most nobles and higher clergy in the Estates-General resisted the Third and its eloquent leaders, Sieyès and Mirabeau, but, receiving no guidance from the court and intimidated by popular agitation, for the moment offered mostly just sullen recalcitrance. For weeks, Louis evaded aligning with the nobility or the Third. Jefferson remained hopeful that France's affable, peace-loving but pliable king would finally back the Third, and subsequently believed Louis would have done so but for his insidious queen, Marie Antoinette, and the court hard-liners around her.[47] The standoff left all further revolutionary progress blocked until some clergy and a few nobles joined the fifty-eight "nobles" already elected deputies of the Third (including the *philosophes* Mirabeau and Volney) in opposing voting and deliberation by orders. On 17 June 1789, the resulting inflated Third Estate, contrary to all precedent, and defying both Crown and nobility, proclaimed itself the "National Assembly" of the French people—"by 400 and odd against 80 odd," reported Jefferson. More clergy and aristocrats defected from the privileged orders.[48]

The Revolution had reached its first major crisis point. "We shall know I think within a day or two," Jefferson informed Madison excitedly, "whether the government will risk a bankruptcy and civil war rather than see all distinction of orders done away with which is what the Commons will push for."[49] The declaration of 17 June 1789 surprised onlookers and constituted a stunning revolutionary act in itself, signifying rejection of not just noble and ecclesiastical privilege but France's entire existing political, legal, and institutional structure and tradition. Abandoning his earlier tentativeness, Jefferson waxed increasingly enthusiastic. "The debates of the States General [have] been so interesting lately," he noted on 18 June, "as to carry me almost every day to Versailles."[50]

Compelled to act, Louis XVI finally intervened on 20 June: royal troops appeared and the Assembly deputies arriving at the meeting hall "found the doors shut and guarded, and a proclamation posted up for holding a *séance royale*, on the 22nd, and a suspension of their meetings until then."[51] Open conflict, it seemed, must follow; but a direct trial of strength between Crown and Assembly was avoided. Convening in the nearby royal tennis court, and urged on by the astronomer Bailly, those deputies resolved to resist (technically not quite a majority of the Estates-General's 1,200 deputies but the vast majority of the Third), 577 deputies (with only one dissenting) collectively enacted the famous Tennis Court Oath of 20 June 1789, immortalized later in a stirring painting by the Revolution's greatest artist, Jacques Louis David (1748–1825). Those present vowed "never to separate" until France's constitution was entirely recast eliminating privilege and separate orders.

At this point a worrying rift opened up between Jefferson and the next most prominent American then in France, Gouverneur Morris, over how precisely to connect the French Revolution with the American. Morris, an avowed "aristocrat" and champion of Locke and property in the American context,[52] had arrived in France in January 1789 with instructions from Congress to find investors to purchase American debt from the insolvent French Crown and handle several other Franco-American financial negotiations. Like

Jefferson, he too became engrossed in the salon debates accompanying the French Revolution's early stages. Both statesmen considered France America's natural ally and professed to "love France." Each drew far-reaching lessons from America's experience. But their conclusions proved diametrically opposite.

Morris, convinced America had vindicated Montesquieu and proven the excellence of "mixed government" and the British model, wanted the French National Assembly to embrace bicameralism and base the French upper house on wealth and property to counterbalance the broader electorate represented in the lower chamber. Jefferson, by this time, swayed by his friends Condorcet and La Rochefoucauld, had discarded all trace of respect for Locke, "mixed government," and "moderation." At a dinner in late June 1789, Morris found himself seated next to Lafayette, who sternly rebuked him, claiming "I injure the cause, for that my sentiments are continually quoted against the good party. I seize this opportunity to tell him that I am opposed to the democracy from regard to Liberty. That I see they are going headlong to destruction and would fain stop them if I could. That their views respecting this nation are totally inconsistent with the materials of which it is composed, and that the worst thing that could happen would be to grant their wishes."[53] Morris proved relentless in advising against the democratic republican Left endorsed by Jefferson. "I preach incessantly," he noted on 3 July, "respect for the prince, attention to the rights of the nobility, and moderation."[54]

On 23 June, the king, surrounded by nobles and ecclesiastics, offered a detailed and in traditional terms reasonable compromise, which he read out in person. Conceding many of the Third's demands outright—abolition of privileged fiscal immunities for nobles, clergy, and some others, ending arbitrary arrest under *lettres de cachet*, and abolishing rural forced labor on roads and bridges under the *corvée*[55]—the king expressed readiness to negotiate also on other key points, inviting "the Estates" to propose how to reconcile "liberty of the press with the respect due to religion, morality and the honor of citizens."[56] But those demands most strongly opposed by the nobility and clergy he rejected outright, refusing to countenance abolition of voting by orders in "the Estates-General" or to suppress honorary privileges. The orders should remain separate entities with distinct rights and in part separate functions, the "particular consent of the clergy" remaining "necessary for all resolutions concerning religion." Likewise, Louis reaffirmed his sole sovereignty and control over police powers and the military.[57]

The royal response, noted Jefferson, threw the people into a "ferment." The Third, aroused by spellbinding oratory of Mirabeau, seconded by Barnave, Pétion, Buzot, and Sieyès, rejected the compromise, repudiated separate orders, and demanded recognition of their unilaterally declared title Assemblée Nationale.[58] More clergy joined them. Yet most of the nobility and a narrow majority of the First Estate, 132 churchmen in all, continued obdurately to resist. Louis answered the Assembly's continued defiance by suspending public attendance at its sessions. "I found the streets of Versailles much embarrassed with souldiers," reported Jefferson to Jay: "there was a body of about 100 horse drawn up in front of the hotel of the States, and all the avenues and doors guarded by souldiers. No body was permitted to enter but the members, and this was by order of the king; for till now the doors of the common rooms have been open and at least 2000 spectators attending their debates constantly."[59] However, the grave confrontation Jefferson describes in his letters to Philadelphia suddenly dispelled on 27 June, albeit with the court—not the Third—backing down.

This was less due to royal spinelessness than to the growing unrest destabilizing Paris, which had now spread to "all the troops except the Swiss soldiers." The French guards "began to quit their barracks, to assemble in squads, to declare that they would defend the life of the king, but would not cut the throats of their fellow citizens," leaving onlookers in "no doubt on which side they would be in case of a rupture."[60] Jefferson could scarcely contain his excitement. Humiliated, Louis found himself with no alternative but to acknowledge the National Assembly. "Inviting" the recalcitrant *noblesse* and rump of rejectionist clergy to rejoin that body, he finally opted to address and cooperate with the "National Assembly." With social orders and privilege eliminated and the eminent astronomer Bailly elected its "president," the National Assembly inaugurated its first official session on 30 June.[61] In theory and practice, sovereignty had now been transferred from Crown to the people, just as occurred in the United States in July 1776. The French Revolution was truly underway.

The agitation building in Paris had meanwhile created a third revolutionary engine beside the National Assembly and continuing popular turmoil around the Palais Royal. This was the Paris electoral assembly meeting in the Paris Town Hall, a council of 407 "electors" established to sift the capital's petitions and cahiers of grievances and instruct the city's representatives in the National Assembly. This body now became the mouthpiece of Paris and focus of feverish debate. Brissot, chosen "elector" by one of the Paris wards or "sections," and one of the Revolution's leading journalists as editor of the *Patriote françois*, quickly made his mark, persuading his district, at a meeting on 21 April, of the need for a correspondence committee enabling the Paris wards to direct their National Assembly deputies. Disliked by lawyers and businessmen owing to their republican social and political views, Brissot and Condorcet had failed to get elected to the Estates-General. But their Parisian committee enabled them to play a prodding role, ensuring their democratic republican program—at this stage even more ambitious and more *Américaniste* than the schemes of Lafayette, La Rochefoucauld, Démeunier, and Jefferson—echoed in the National Assembly. Brissot was especially eager, like Lafayette, to secure a broad *Declaration of Rights* along American lines. Among those chosen by other Paris electoral districts, and now a ward "president" supporting Brissot's strategy, was Nicolas Bonneville (1760–1828), a professional scholar, writer, and translator expert in English and the main documents of the American Revolution. From the autumn of 1789 onward, Bonneville and his (subsequently) close friend Paine were among Condorcet's and Brissot's firmest allies in Paris.

As a legal theorist and social reformer, Brissot was especially indebted to Beccaria, Helvétius, and Rousseau. Having (like Mirabeau) personally witnessed the Geneva revolution of 1782 and, again like Mirabeau, being a longstanding spokesman for Jewish emancipation, Brissot had by this time long been active in the Franco-British-American antislavery movement to which he, along with Condorcet and Lafayette, was passionately committed. In their principles, the emerging revolutionary leadership in 1789 was hardly representative of any of French society's main strata, any more than Mason, Jefferson, and Madison had been in Virginia in 1776. Rather, what was entirely obvious—as some loudly complained—was that the French Revolution's Left-leaning spearhead comprised the leading publicists and pamphleteers of the 1788 public controversies, that is, they were predominantly ardent republican *philosophes* and *Américanistes*.

Already by early July, the general assembly of the capital's "electors" had emerged as a provisional city government, the forerunner of the revolutionary Commune.[62] The group headed by Brissot, Bonneville, Gorsas, and their republican allies (Condorcet joined them only in September)[63] gave crucial backing to Mirabeau, Sieyès, La Rochefoucauld, Lafayette, Volney, Démeunier, and other radical reformers inside the National Assembly, helping them take the lead (at least for much of the time) despite the National Assembly's hostile conservative and "moderate" majority. Even so, the predominantly "moderate" monarchist National Assembly, hopelessly torn between the warring ideological blocs, could only with much difficulty be prodded by the pro-Revolution press (dominated by republican radicals), the popular agitation, and the Paris electoral assembly into adopting the measures the radical republican fringe of *philosophe* intellectuals, led by Mirabeau and Sieyès, demanded.[64]

"The condition of man thro' the civilized world will be finally and greatly ameliorated"

The French democratic republicans pursued their philosophically couched far-reaching goals not by directly controlling the National Assembly but by continually goading it via the strident pro-revolutionary press and by harnessing the restless discontent gripping the capital. By dominating the pro-revolutionary press (and theater), the radicals emerged as the strongest faction in the Paris city government. In this way, a vigorously republican, democratic, and egalitarian tendency, bolstered by the ceaseless ferment in the streets and cafés, achieved remarkable success despite the relatively small number of *philosophe-révolutionnaires* in the National Assembly and the lack of sympathy for their views among a majority of Frenchmen.[65]

Coordination between the streets, Paris electoral assembly, and National Assembly was orchestrated, observers noted, many with marked distaste, by "philosophes," a mix of intellectuals and literary people, with outright republicans like Brissot, Bonneville, Carra, Gorsas, Pétion, Desmoulins, Cérutti, Beaumarchais, Robert, Pétion, and Mandar prominent among them. Personalities enthusiastic about the Belgian and Dutch revolutions as well as American were generating crowd power by trumpeting anti-aristocratic slogans through crowd leaders one witness called "demi-philosophes" because of their ability to mobilize discontented elements around the Palais Royal by loudly amplifying their leaders' rhetoric in watered-down simplified form.[66] With the Paris "electors" assembly pushing the National Assembly, the projected *Declaration of the Rights of Man* to which some Paris primary districts had been committed since April was energetically promoted by Paris as well as in the National Assembly by Sieyès, Volney, Pétion, and their following, beside Lafayette.[67]

The Revolution having now "prostrated the old government," the new "constitution should begin," agreed Jefferson, with a "Declaration of the natural and imprescriptable rights of man."[68] By this point, Jefferson's and Lafayette's (third) draft Declaration had grown to thirteen articles but was still markedly shorter and closer to the American (Mason-Jefferson-Madison) model, especially the 1776 Virginia state *Declaration of Rights*, than the far longer, more complex formulations offered by Mirabeau, Sieyès, and, outside the Assembly, Brissot, who subsequently supported Mirabeau's draft against Lafayette's.[69] Beside these divergent drafts, collaboration among the principal radicals was troubled by lack of trust between Mirabeau and Lafayette, whose relationship gradually deteriorated until by the autumn of 1790 it had reached the point of open hostility. Since Lafayette, now prominent in the National Assembly, increasingly tried, with Jefferson's help, to seize the initiative behind the scenes, Jefferson found himself backing a group publicly at odds with Mirabeau, whom Jefferson too disliked, was suspicious of, and deemed less enthusiastic about the United States and the American revolution than Brissot, Condorcet, or Lafayette.[70]

Demonstrations and street clashes continued in Paris and Rouen. Deferring to the king, the National Assembly remained at Versailles; but opinion differed over whether king and court really embraced the changes introduced so far or were merely playing for time while preparing some grand countercoup. Although in Jefferson's view, Louis probably had no intention of bombarding Paris and trying to crush the Revolution by force, many Parisians assumed the king, or at least those around him, did.[71] As the general expectation of a dramatic confrontation intensified, the National Assembly met in emergency session on 8 July. Despite the grave situation, the instability, uncertainty, and soon widespread peasant disturbances unsettling all of France, the republican faction, stiffened by the Paris electoral assembly, remained adamant. On 9 July, the National Assembly's steering committee adopted a proposal introduced by Lafayette and the Brissot faction that France's traditional constitution was archaic and obsolete, and that the country required an entirely new constitution. The Assembly "are now beginning to build one from the foundation," Jefferson assured Paine, then in London, news the latter shared with Edmund Burke, with whom he was then still friendly, vainly hoping to win him over to support the Revolution.[72]

By this point, a large body of royal troops, mostly Swiss guards and German mercenaries, were positioned with artillery between Versailles and Paris, with more expected shortly. "Great inquietude took place," recorded Jefferson, and the "Assembly voted an address to the king."[73] Composed by Mirabeau, this was delivered to the palace on 10 July by a deputation of six nobles, six clergy, and twelve of the Third. The massing of troops contradicted the king's stated desire to restore order and tranquility, complained the Assembly, and constrained their liberty.[74] The troops, answered Louis, simultaneously rejecting the Assembly's request to transfer their meetings to Paris, were requisite to maintain stability in the capital. Even more dismaying, on 11 July, as the National Assembly deliberated over Lafayette's (and Jefferson's) draft *Declaration of the Rights of Man*, Louis ill-advisedly dismissed his popular Swiss minister, Jacques Necker (1732–1804), a reformer of the liberal monarchist tendency committed to "moderation."

Dismissing Necker, the minister best placed to salvage the king's credit with the people, heightened tension between king and Assembly and simultaneously deepened the growing split within the Assembly between constitutional monarchists and the republican-dominated Left. Necker's removal looked like proof of the royal court's underlying rejectionist attitude and what Jefferson called the "aristocracy's perfidious intentions." Allied to the regional magistrates' high courts, or *parlements*, most nobility desired the "great project" of France's regeneration aborted. Removing Necker provoked an outright confrontation in the capital's streets and squares between foreign troops and demonstrators, gravely aggravating the crisis gripping the country, a development that could easily have been avoided. Particularly disturbing, noted Jefferson, were the additional "great bodies of troops and principally of the foreign corps" approaching the outskirts of Paris from different parts of France. "They arrived in the number of 25, or 30,000 men."[75] Consequently, an already dangerous confrontation further escalated. "The mobs immediately shut up all the play houses"; before long the "foreign troops were advanced into the city. Engagements took place between some of them and the people."[76]

The fringe of ardent crypto-republicans with whom Jefferson associated aimed to render royal ministers fully responsible to the legislature. The considerably larger National Assembly centrist bloc, headed by the anglophile monarchist Jean-Joseph Mounier (1756–1806), preferred to see "philosophy" and American principles roundly rebuffed and the king retain if not full sovereignty then unrestricted choice of ministers in the English manner with the constitutional right to dismiss them at will. Venerating Montesquieu and "mixed government," "moderates" recommended Britain's constitution as the ideal model to follow in preference to the American system but lacked the support in the streets and cafés the Left leadership commanded. By late June and early July 1789 Jefferson was positively jubilant. The democratic republican leaders, he assured Paine, having "shown through every stage of the transactions a coolness, wisdom and resolution to set fire to the four corners of the kingdom and to perish with it themselves rather than to relinquish an iota from their plan of a total change of government, are now in complete and undisputed possession of sovereignty."[77]

However, the real struggle was just beginning. Serious unrest ensued on 11 July and continued for four days. Fear and uncertainty, sharpened by grain shortage, did most to provoke disturbances now spreading well beyond the confines of Paris, resulting at Rouen in spontaneous pillaging of shops and grain stores, leaving several killed or wounded.[78] In Paris, by contrast, the rioting assumed a strikingly disciplined, organized character with virtually no pillaging or local violence. Desmoulins and Mandar, both outstanding orators, delivered rousing speeches in the Palais-Royal cafés, exhorting action and a call to arms while carefully avoiding incitement to violence against individuals or looting of stores.[79] "There was a severity of honesty observed," noted Jefferson with satisfaction, of which "no example has been known." Throughout these months, Jefferson, thrust in the midst of the French Revolution, continued to be greatly irritated by the extremely hostile appraisals of the French situation emanating from England, reports now heavily influencing American opinion: having "observed the mobs with my own eyes in order to be satisfied," he sought to convince his colleagues in America that on the whole the rioters behaved with commendable restraint and dignity.[80]

On the evening of 12 July 1789, having earlier that day attended at Versailles, Desmoulins delivered a highly inflammatory speech at the Palais-Royal Café de Foy, insisting a court plot to forcibly crush the Revolution undoubtedly existed and that the foreign regiments would be used to slaughter everyone defying the royal will.[81] He had already written (though not yet published) his *La France libre*, among the most uncompromisingly democratic republican pamphlets of 1789 (it appeared in August). Surrounded by a cheering crowd, this remarkable journalist famously leaped onto a table exhorting the people to save themselves and the Revolution by resorting to arms. That evening, on the Champs-Elysées where units of Swiss and German dragoons were encamped, armed rioters staged a noisy demonstration to which the troops responded by firing blanks into the air.[82] The mob, led by veterans like Mandar (a former soldier), obtained arms by breaking into the civic arms store. What followed turned into a catastrophe for royal authority and the Crown's capacity to act: the demonstrators were joined by hundreds of the French palace guard.

For days, the city experienced unprecedented turmoil. Following dissolution of the old city council, control was transferred to the assembly of electors' steering committee dominated by Brissot, Bonneville, Carra, Fauchet, and the democratic republican leaders. Accusing the court of conspiring against the National Assembly, these delegates assumed responsibility for restoring order and the capital's grain supplies. Having secured control of Paris, it was this emergency committee, on 11 and 12 July, that established the new civic militia, the "National Guard," under Lafayette, who suddenly now assumed a crucially prominent position in the Revolution. Lafayette, Brissot, and the new Paris city government instructed their freshly formed militia to mount day and night patrols and largely succeeded in preventing pillaging and break-ins, the sort of uncontrolled disorder witnessed in parts of rural France and in Rouen. In Paris, much to Jefferson's satisfaction, there were no attacks on shops, food stores, or the homes of the wealthy. Before long Lafayette's force, expanded to the level of 31,000 men and modeled partly on the

The marquis de Lafayette as commander of the Paris National Guard, 1790. Photo credit: National Portrait Gallery, Smithsonian Institution / Art Resource, NY.

example of the American militias, decked out with new uniforms and tricolor cockades, became the principal pillar of order in the capital.[83]

On 14 July, crowds of artisans, shopkeepers, and journeymen, denouncing the "conspiracy" at court, spent the morning roaming the streets indecisively until some urged a march on the Bastille to seize that "monument of *despotisme.*" A vast throng then marched to the Bastille with Bonneville and Fauchet among the "electors" in the lead.[84] At the Bastille, Bonneville tried to persuade the garrison to surrender peacefully. The governor, the Marquis de Launay, refused. As the crowds pressed forward, the 150 defenders lining the walls under the royal white banner opened fire. The crowds, led by French Guards, answered by using cannon to breach the walls. After five hours of bombardment they stormed the fortress, massacring everyone refusing to surrender, including de Launay. The fighting over, a liberty hat was hoisted to vast applause, the prisoners inside released, and the cannon removed to the Town Hall. The Bastille was handed over to the new city militia, which afterward quickly restored order throughout the capital.

Many now expected a full-scale royal onslaught on Paris from several directions, using the foreign troops deployed around the capital. Uneasy crowds of armed citizens lingered in the city center, especially around the Palais-Royal. Trenches were dug and barriers thrown up around a ring of streets to hinder royal cavalry incursions. But the court remained too stunned to react, paralyzed by army desertions and Louis's personal distaste for bloodshed and disinclination to attack the crowds. Moving within hours from dread to exultation, Paris grew positively euphoric. The Bastille's storming was a decisive event affording the "people" the psychological and political upper hand. Democratic republicans and the Paris assembly of electors' steering group soon became inebriated figuratively and literally. As word of the Bastille's fall spread, one group of intellectuals conversing in a café, including Volney and Jefferson, erupted into excited laughter and shouts of joy with much stamping of feet and jigging around tables. No longer doubting French capacity to embrace American principles, Jefferson ventured: "Messieurs, you are delighted by this triumph. But you must contend with the nobles and priests, and until you have dealt with them you will never have liberty."[85]

Until 14 July 1789, despite differences of emphasis, moderate and radical enlightened opinion in France had stayed broadly united in favor of reform. Liberty, toleration, "horror of despotism and superstition," and desire to see abuses reformed had long been common ground for all enlighteners.[86] Only now, with emotion running high, did opinion polarize with the disciples of Diderot, Helvétius, and d'Holbach pushing one way and moderate enlighteners like Marmontel, Morellet, and Suard declaring against the Revolution. Opposing the Revolution meant breaking with committed *réformateurs* aiming to change society and institutions, abandoning the Helvétius salon and withdrawing into segregated near silence.[87] In this manner, the rift between moderate Enlightenment and the radical tendency in France became more polarized, politicized, and permanent. Instead of remaining neutral between the disputing *philosophe* cliques, as some thought she should, Mme. Helvétius (who had not forgiven court or clergy for persecuting her dead husband) aligned with Volney, Garat, Cabanis, Chamfort, Jefferson, Sieyès, Brissot, Condorcet, and Mirabeau.[88] The Bastille's fall thus exacerbated but also clarified the longstanding rift between the two now openly competing Enlightenment wings—moderate and radical—with respect to democracy, republicanism, and liquidating censorship and religious authority.

Bailly, secretary of the council of electors and Condorcet's rival in the Academy of Sciences, was chosen mayor of Paris by the capital's electors' assembly on 15 July, and Lafayette was confirmed as commander of the National Guard.[89] A longstanding critic of the ancien régime but no republican or democrat, being a staunch constitutional monarchist (even if more liberal than Mounier), in the new Paris city government, Bailly headed the "moderates."[90] But this did not end the simmering ferment, particularly in the so-called Cordeliers district, in the heart of Left Bank Paris, where a debating forum emerged, later to be second in revolutionary renown only to the Jacobins. If the Jacobins later became militant egalitarians, until 1792 they remained predominantly moderate and deeply divided; the Cordeliers Club, by contrast, evolved much earlier as a focus of both radical sentiment and popular unrest. Dominating a mixed, partly working-class district, skilled artisans supplied most of the club's membership, infusing it with vigorous social discontent. However, the leadership until late 1792—Danton, Desmoulins, Fabre d'Églantine, Mandar, Maréchal, Manuel, Prudhomme, and Pierre-François Robert (1762–1826), a prominent revolutionary journalist and author of another notable republican tract of 1789, *Le Républicanisme adapté à la France*—were again, aside from Danton (a brilliant orator but no intellectual), mostly journalists, writers, and editors. What gave the Cordeliers its distinctive stamp, commented Desmoulins, was the intensely literary Café Procope, now, as in past decades, a regular focus of *philosophique*, republican, and *Américaniste* debate.[91]

Psychologically and politically, the Bastille's fall was the most decisive event of the early Revolution. Royal power and prestige never recovered. The seal was put on the National Assembly's conquest of sovereignty. Within days, some were proposing that 14 July should become a national festival.[92] For the next four years, until Robespierre's June 1793 coup d'état, which fundamentally transformed (and perverted) the French Revolution's character, freedom of expression and full press freedom prevailed. While the authoritarian populism of the Montagne—the hard-line faction that by mid-1793 dominated both the National Assembly and the Jacobin Club—was for the moment held at bay, a combination of *philosophique* leadership and artisan support promoted republicanism, press freedom, democracy, human rights, *Américaniste* individual liberty, and general emancipation.

The impact throughout France, Germany, and Britain was overwhelmingly negative in court, church, and most popular circles, as it was too among Adams, Morris, Hamilton, and other leading Federalists in America, but massively positive in radical intellectual circles. Democrats and egalitarians everywhere rejoiced. Price wrote to Jefferson enthusiastically, on 3 August, acclaiming the "progress and completion of one of the most important revolutions that have ever taken place in the world, a Revolution that must astonish Europe; that shakes the foundations of despotic power; and that probably will be the commencement of a general reformation in the governments of the world which hitherto have been little better than usurpations on the rights of mankind, impediments to the progress of human improvement, and contrivances for enabling a few grandees to suppress and enslave the rest of mankind." This crucial global impulse resulted from the conjunction of the American Revolution's radical tendency with the democratic republican leadership of the French Revolution. It was not the product of social forces, crowds, or national character, and least of all of long-term trends in social practice and sociability. Convinced the "General Revolution" was now transforming Europe and the world, Price, airing his Unitarian sympathies, stressed the need to safeguard individual religious conscience "from the interference of civil power."[93]

A religious man, like Priestley and Fauchet, Price was no atheist or Jeffersonian deist. Unlike most American and French radical democrats, he preached an ardent but heterodox Christianity that rejected church hierarchies and dogmatic theology. However, he fully concurred with the Jeffersonians (and disagreed with Adams) in wanting to go beyond Locke, to fully dismantle the edifice of ecclesiastical authority and end religion's intrusion into politics, law, and education. "The United States of America have happily taken this step. It cannot, I suppose, be at present attempted in France without too much danger; but it seems likely to be gained there long before it will be gained in England. Indeed, the [moderate] Patriots in France pay us too great a compliment by speaking of us [the British] as they do, as their model, and considering themselves imitating us. I scarcely believe we are capable of making such an exertion as the French nation is now making with a spiritual unanimity altogether wonderful. We are duped by the forms of liberty."[94] Most Britons, Price believed, failed to understand that their constitution was a sham perpetrated by Crown and aristocracy, stiffened by Anglicanism.

The "moderate" faction seeking to dominate the French National Assembly did indeed exalt England and the British model; but Price was wrong in assuming admiration for the British legacy and constitution extended to the revolutionary leadership more generally. As Adams and others pointed out, the democrats were by no means getting their ideas from Locke, or more generally from England, but from French sources. This did not mean, though, as Adams was perfectly aware, that the French scenario differed radically from the American. On the contrary, held Adams, the French, like "too many Americans, pant for the equality of persons and property."[95] Edmund Burke, for his part, was outraged by all suggestion that British influences were at work. Unpersuaded by Paine, Price, and Jefferson, and indignant that democratic and republican ideas were gaining ground in France and had intruded and now captured a "cabal" in England too, he denied any of this had a "British" origin.

Angry that it was "given out in France" that their course followed England's example, he retorted that practically nothing done in France "originated from the practice or the prevalent opinions of this people [the English], either in the act or in the spirit of the proceeding. Let me add, that we are as unwilling to learn these lessons from France, as we are sure that we never taught them to that nation."[96] Deplorably, among the French, this "cabal, calling itself philosophic, receives the glory of many of the late proceedings" and many people believed "their opinions and systems are the true actuating spirit of the whole of them." But if France had disastrously succumbed to nefarious "atheists and infidels," French counterparts of Collins, Toland, Shaftesbury, Chubb, Morgan, and Bolingbroke, the ideas of such "freethinkers" and republicans, Burke was glad to point out, generally lacked support and influence in the Britain of 1789.[97]

With Adams alarmed, Burke disgusted, Price optimistic, and Paine and Jefferson exhilarated, the French National Assembly found itself trapped in a three-way tussle. After the Bastille's fall, a bitter power struggle developed in the press, clubs, and Paris city government, replicating the same three competing political factions splitting the National Assembly. Irreconcilably divided between an aristocratic Right, constitutional monarchist Montesquieuian center, and a democratic republican Left, the legislature had little immediate prospect of resolving such deep-seated ideological contradictions even without taking account of France's fourth ideological bloc, the ultra-royalist and Catholic rejectionist constituency, powerful throughout provincial France, refusing to have anything to do with the Revolution or the National Assembly.

Once the French upheaval seized the attention of the European, British, and American publics, every commentator, and especially every American political observer, felt impelled to compare the American and French revolutions, even while drawing strikingly diverse conclusions. No other Founding Father, however, was so acutely aware as Jefferson of the deep intertwining of the two revolutions and their fundamental parallelism, or so conscious, as Condorcet put it, of the "benefits humankind as a whole should expect from America's example."[98] "It is impossible to desire better dispositions toward us," Jefferson wrote to Madison, on 27 August 1789, "than prevail in this [National Assembly]." "Our proceedings have been viewed as a model for them on every occasion; and though in the heat of debate men are generally disposed to contradict every [authority] urged by their opponents, ours has been treated like that of the Bible, open to explanation but not to question."[99] Jefferson's observation was accurate, but only regarding the republican and near republican leadership; and, even there, the American federal principle lacked appeal. On the other hand, Jefferson's comment in no way applied to the centrists and constitutional monarchists. America's example weighed decisively, and more pertinently than the British constitution, undoubtedly, but exclusively among republican foes of monarchy, aristocracy, inequality, and ecclesiastical authority, the democratic revolutionaries.

Jefferson, Price, and Paine, like their Polish revolutionary comrade, Kościuszko, now back in Poland, though hopeful, were also acutely aware of the tremendous risks confronting the French Revolution. Especially, they feared the deep divisions not just in French society but even among genuine, sincere "amis de la liberté," in the National Assembly and Paris administration. These occasioned "strong differences of opinion and produced repulsive combinations among the Patriots" much deplored by Lafayette.[100] With every passing week the National Assembly's principal factions—conservative constitutional royalists, centrist constitutional monarchists, and democratic republicans—were more and more at loggerheads. "Philosophy," commentators agreed, won most clashes during the arduous and protracted National Assembly debates over the *Declaration of the Rights of Man and the Citizen* but not all, being defeated specifically on Articles Ten and Eleven concerning freedom of expression and religion, clauses provoking many angry exchanges especially between the clergy and those Brissot termed followers of a "philosophy of gentleness and toleration," with Mirabeau, Mounier, La Rochefoucauld, Pétion, and Démeunier all prominently intervening in the Assembly debates.

Opponents of the radicals, including monarchists and clergy, rallied around the draft "Declaration" presented by one of the Assembly's standing committees, or "bureaus," the Sixth Bureau, chaired by the vehemently anti-Semitic Bishop of Nancy, demanding reference to God's name and the Ten Commandments in the "Declaration," and that freedom of expression be curtailed with the proviso that no one should be permitted to "trouble the established creed," and that freedom of thought and conscience should apply only in a limited way so as not to "trouble" the publicly established religion of the state.[101] These restrictive Sixth Bureau recommendations were backed by the center and less committed, but, with Mirabeau and the radicals fighting them, the Sixth Bureau's conservative strictures were eventually largely (but not wholly) discredited and defeated.[102] Radical success, admittedly, as Mirabeau complained, was incomplete, but in vigorously countering the Sixth Bureau, Mirabeau, Brissot, and their adherents nevertheless gained a crucial victory: they largely secured liberty of the press, freedom of thought, and abolition of state-backed religious coercion.[103] Finalized on 26 August, the *Declaration of the Rights of Man and the Citizen*, shorn of most of the Sixth Bureau's provisos, envisaged society's renewal on a completely fresh basis, not one supposedly inherent in the nation's legal past (a fiction still present in the American *Declaration*).[104] All agreed, though, that it was American Independence that had "opened our eyes about the true destiny of peoples," their "natural rights, and the equality of everyone's rights," affirmed Carra, one of the leading republican journalists, in October. He and his colleagues confidently expected the entire world to be transformed by their victory in curtailing religious authority and securing the principle of human rights based on equality.[105]

Jefferson too was full of optimism at the time and some of this never left him. "The appeal to the rights of man, which had been made in the U.S.," he recorded in his autobiography, thirty-two years later, "was taken up by France, first of the European nations. From her the spirit has spread over the South [of Europe]. The tyrants of the North have allied indeed against it, but it is irresistible. Their opposition will only multiply it's [*sic*] millions of victims, their own satellites will catch it, and the condition of man thro' the civilized world will be finally and greatly ameliorated."[106]

Lafayette, ambitious but not an especially good judge of men or situations, in the end proved to be less republican and democratic than he professed in 1789–90. But he may have been more realistic than Condorcet, Brissot, Pétion, Bonneville, Carra, and Paine in realizing the Revolution could succeed only by reconciling or bridging moderates and radicals. His tactic in both National Assembly and Paris city government, he explained on 25 August, was to weld a lasting compromise between center and Left and unite their leading figures, "eight of us whom I want to coalize, as being the only means to prevent a total dissolution and civil war. The prime obstacle dividing them," he assured Jefferson, "is the king's veto. Some want it absolute, others will have no veto, and the only way to unite them is to find some way for a suspensive [i.e., temporary] veto so strongly and so complicated as to give the king a due influence."[107] Jefferson appreciated the logic of Lafayette's strategy, and the need to bridge the gulf between constitutional royalism and democratic re-publicanism, the gap between Montesquieu and the *Declaration of the Rights of Man*, between "moderates" and radicals. Lafayette's "attachment to both [factions] is equal," noted Jefferson in September, "and he labours inces-santly to keep them together."[108] The only way to avert a ruinous rift, Jeffer-son agreed, was to seek a temporary or "suspensive veto," drastically limiting the king's influence and ensuring the legislature (and the republicans) the permanent upper hand while leaving a fig leaf for the liberal monarchists.

With the constitutional Right demanding balance between king and leg-islature, and some republicans resisting a royal veto, Lafayette—who until 1791 continually assured his friends Condorcet and Brissot that he too was a "republican"—showed more willingness than they to court Mounier and Bailly and endeavor to reconcile Left and center. For a time Jefferson encour-aged him. Negotiations to conclude this "concordat" on the basis of a "sus-pensive veto" and one-chamber legislature, leaving the Crown only minimal power, which (despite Sieyès's firm opposition) patched over the rift tempo-rarily, were held in Jefferson's elegant Paris residence, the Hôtel de Langeac. At a key six-hour secret "conference" at Jefferson's residence over dinner and wine on 26 August, Jefferson listened as Lafayette, "who had no secrets from me," Mounier, Barnave, Alexandre de Lameth, and four others, all "leading Patriots of honest but differing opinions sensible of the necessity of effecting a coalition by mutual sacrifices," strove to forge a viable and united moderate-radical bloc.

Lafayette and Jefferson designed a center-Left coalition to dissolve Mou-nier's hitherto formidable center-Right conservative "moderation," and in this way reduce the "aristocracy to insignificance and impotence," as Jefferson put it, as well as outflank uncompromising hard-liners aiming to shear the king of all power. After the "veto debate" on 15 September, the "suspensive veto" was carried by 673 to 352 votes, a supposedly happy compromise accompanied by rapprochement between Lafayette and Mirabeau.[109] Although revolution-ary France nominally remained a constitutional monarchy until August 1792, those revolutionary leaders repudiating the "mixed government" model in August 1789 rightly conceived and described the new system in France as "basically a democratic republic," as one of its key framers, Roederer, later ex-pressed it, "with a phantom of royalty."[110]

Throughout 1789–91, there was as yet little sign—except in Marat's crassly populist paper, *L'Ami du Peuple* (the Friend of the People)—of the future Counter-Enlightenment populism, authoritarianism, and intolerance that, from mid-1793, undermined the Revolution and altogether discredited it in the eyes of De Gouges, Wollstonecraft, Paine, and enlighteners of every description. With the constitutional Right in the Assembly (a residue of nobles and ecclesiastics) marginalized, the main obstacle to the democratic republicans from late 1789 until late 1791 remained the constitutional monarchist segment—first under Mounier and later under Maury and Malouet. Extolling Locke and Montesquieu, these men vigorously opposed universal male suffrage, republicanism, and egalitarian laws, as well as compulsory universal education. Like Morris, they were principally concerned less to defend the existing social order than promote a new informal aristocracy of inherited wealth and property. Constitutional monarchists in turn divided into center-Right and liberal monarchist factions, making four principal groupings in the Assembly altogether.

It was in fact Jefferson who, in the English language, most expertly and succinctly analyzed the four principal blocs vying for dominance of the National Assembly during the Revolution of 1789. The French National Assembly, he explained, writing to Jay on 19 September, comprised four main factions. First, the "Aristocrats," as he termed the participating constitutional Right, comprising most of the nobility, bishops, and higher clergy, together with the representatives of the *parlements*; these strove to retain as much monarchy, aristocracy, and ecclesiastical authority as possible. Second came the "moderates," royalists desiring "a constitution nearly similar to that of England" and separation of powers according to the ideas of Montesquieu. The third faction was an offshoot from the center, a group promoting the liberal Orléanist branch of the royal house, dismissed by Jefferson as "wicked" and "desperate." Finally, smallest but for the moment the faction with the greatest outside resonance and most popular backing, as well as the most press and international ties, were the "republicans, who are willing to let their first magistracy be hereditary" but (in Lafayette's, Sieyès's, Pétion's, and Mirabeau's formulations) intended to render the French monarchy "very subordinate to the legislature, and to have that legislature consist of a single chamber."[111]

Jefferson had no hesitation about indicating his preference for the last of the four blocs, the "republicans," to his colleagues and the government in Philadelphia. However, this posed a problem. His second, third, and fourth blocs, including the republicans, though severely at loggerheads, all designated themselves "Patriots." Paradoxically, but significantly, despite being furiously at odds, both moderates and radicals in this escalating bitter contest could accurately, as well as sincerely, extol the American Revolution. Each embraced the American example but differently and on sharply divergent principles, here too demonstrating how closely and intricately the twin American and French revolutions paralleled each other and intertwined. The "moderate" center, headed in 1790–91 by Barnave, Bailly, and the De Lameths, admired the American Federalists' achievement in creating a republic with a strong executive, restricted suffrage, and firm commitment to property, wealth, and informal aristocracy—the American Revolution of Adams, Hamilton, Morris, and Jay. Condorcet, Brissot, Bonneville, Pétion, Desmoulins, Carra, and the "republicans," by contrast, admired the democratic, egalitarian Revolution of Franklin, Paine, Madison, Short, Lafayette, and, of course, Jefferson.

Repudiating Robespierre and the Montagne

Briefly, despite the grumblings of Brissot and Sieyès, it seemed Lafayette (and Jefferson) had succeeded in reconciling center and Left. "The result was," in Jefferson's words, that the "King should have a suspensive veto on the laws, that the legislature should be composed of a single chamber only, and that to be chosen by the people. This Concordate decided the fate of the constitution. The Patriots all rallied to the principles thus settled, carried every question agreeably to them, and reduced the Aristocracy to insignificance and impotence."[112] But Jefferson, in October 1789, was far too optimistic. Beyond a certain point—albeit after his departure from France—Lafayette clashed increasingly with his former friends Condorcet, Brissot, and Paine, leading eventually, in 1791, to outright rupture. For a time, Jefferson continued to express confidence in Lafayette, a "powerful band of union between these two parties," and in his ability to overcome what throughout 1789–91 remained the principal rift in revolutionary ranks, that between the republicans and the moderates to whom Lafayette was increasingly drawn. Before long, though, reality entirely undid those hopes.

Subsequent developments soon revealed the limitations of Jefferson's early optimism. Jefferson was delighted with the basically republican outcome of 1789 but deeply disturbed by the continuing divisions among the pro-Revolution factions. At the same time, there existed also another dimension to the Revolution, he perceived, likely to transform the Caribbean and eventually powerfully affect the Americas generally as well. His and Lafayette's friend Condorcet had articulated a plan in the second version of his treatise on black emancipation in 1788 by which, once freed, the blacks of the New World could integrate into society as wage laborers.[113] Lafayette, Kościuszko, Brissot, Condorcet, and Paine, among Jefferson's closest allies, were all passionate for black emancipation and, while residing in France, Jefferson himself could hardly fail to align with them on this issue at least theoretically. "The Emancipation of their islands," he informed Jay on 27 August 1789, referring to Saint-Domingue (Haiti), Martinique, Guadeloupe, Cayenne, and the other French New World possessions, "is an idea prevailing in the minds of several members of the National Assembly, particularly those most enlightened and most liberal in their views," meaning Lafayette, La Rochefoucauld, Sieyès, Volney, Destutt de Tracy, Mirabeau, and those delegates collaborating with Condorcet and Brissot on behalf of black emancipation through the society of the Amis des Noirs. Brissot, Condorcet, Carra, and Gorsas were not yet members of the Assembly but still external allies influencing the Revolution's course through newspapers, organizations, and the Paris city government.

Black emancipation was an aspect of the revolutionary turmoil in France that promised to additionally link the American and French revolutions, with vast implications for the entire New World's future and for black people generally. In the Caribbean, "such a step by this country [France] would lead to other emancipations or revolutions in the same quarter."[114] Jefferson, given his reluctance to accept racial equality, and reservations about blacks in particular, doubtless felt much less zeal for this aspect of the joint American-French revolutionary impulse than his *Américaniste* friends (and Polish comrade Kościuszko) but took care, on the surface, not to diverge from his allies' idealistic fervor. When Brissot requested that he join the Amis des Noirs in 1788, he had replied that he definitely sympathized but could not, as United States ambassador, conduct himself merely according to his own personal convictions. His closest associates and friends, and his predecessor Franklin, all proved more active and passionate for this cause than the future American president.[115]

Another fundamental democratic tendency conspicuous in the French Revolution that Jefferson hardly embraced—and had been wholly absent from the American Revolution[116]—was the cause of women's emancipation first forcefully championed by Olympe de Gouges and Mary Wollstonecraft. A major figure in history whose role has often been understated, no one else stood up for women's rights during the French Revolution with the boldness and insistence of Olympe de Gouges (1748–93), or so unequivocally condemned the age-old systematic subordination of women by men. The fearless De Gouges also later publicly denounced Robespierre as a despot and a monster (she was guillotined during the Terror), not because Robespierre ignored women's rights but because of his dictatorial tendencies and because, from early 1793, he suppressed the Revolution's democratic features. Among male leaders of the Revolution receptive to the notion of women's equal rights including political rights, those who stood out, in the first place Condorcet, were invariably out-and-out opponents of Robespierre, Saint-Just, Marat, and the Montagne. This is yet another reason why it is unfortunate that still today historians label figures such as Condorcet, De Gouges, and Paine "moderates" when it is they who were radical enlighteners, and "radical" in terms of the sweeping new principles they sought to introduce, and Robespierre and his colleagues "radical" when it was they who, like Rousseau, had by far the more traditional views about women and blacks, as well as about restricting individual rights and the need to curb free expression and suppress criticism of the government.[117]

By 5 October 1789, the day of the famous march of the hungry women on Versailles, Jefferson had already departed Paris and was awaiting ship at Le Havre to return to America. Officially, his mission as United States' minister plenipotentiary in Paris still had two years to run, and he expected to return after six months or so to continue his simultaneous role in the American and French revolutions there,[118] having no inkling President Washington preferred to remove him from the scene by promoting him to the higher position of secretary of state. Shortly after returning to America, in March 1790, he visited the aged Franklin lying on his sickbed in Philadelphia (not long before he died) to deliver a detailed account of the changed state of the "country in which he had so many friends, and the perilous convulsions to which they had been exposed" relating "what part they had taken, what had been their course, and what their fate."[119] He sought to reassure the old man who had found many of the reports he had received from Paris detailing violence and chaos "very afflicting" and who worried that the "voice of Philosophy . . . can hardly be heard among those tumults."[120] The long and detailed discussion of so much crucial French material relevant to America and Britain was almost too much for Franklin.

Yet what Jefferson had thus far experienced was only just the beginning. The women's march that shook France on 5 October led directly to the transfer of Louis XVI and his entire court, under Lafayette's escort, from Versailles to the Tuileries Palace, in Paris, rendering the royal family virtual prisoners of the Revolution. At first, this seemed only to confirm the democratic republican Revolution's triumph over its conservative and "moderate" adversaries. Jefferson, while still at Le Havre overseeing the packing of his pictures, sculptures, and cases of wine for shipment across the Atlantic, received word of the latest momentous developments from Short, whom he left as secretary of the Paris embassy. Unlike Jefferson, Short *was* a founding member of the Amis des Noirs. An ardent admirer of Franklin and Lafayette whom Jefferson later called his "adoptive son," Short continued sending Jefferson detailed private reports about affairs in France but he was less of a solid republican, events soon proved, than adherent of the 1791 "mixed" French constitution.

It soon became obvious, moreover, that while Short was "acting minister," it was Morris rather than Short who enjoyed President Washington's (and Hamilton's) confidence and, equally, that tension between Washington and his new secretary of state, Jefferson, over French affairs was growing. Like Morris, Hamilton was convinced that it is experience that counts in politics, not principles, and around the time of Jefferson's departure from Paris, he wrote to Lafayette, in Paris, communicating his view that developments in France were deeply worrying, that the nobility would resist the proposed constitution to the utmost, and that he especially dreaded the "reveries of your philosophic politicians who appear in the moment to have great influence and who being mere speculatists may aim at more refinement than suits either with human nature or the composition of your nation."[121]

By January 1790, Morris was confident enough to write to the president assuring him that his views "on the Revolution effecting here I believe to be perfectly just because they perfectly accord with my own." Leaving aside "the Aristocrats" and high clergy who still "think they ought to form a separate order," Morris continued supporting the moderate middle bloc "which consists of all sorts of people, really friends to a good, free Government" while loudly disparaging the third faction "composed of what are called here the *Enragés*, that is the Madmen. These are the most numerous," though, he explained to the president, and unfortunately "this last party is in close alliance with the populace here, and derives from that circumstance very great authority." Heaping scorn on the democrats, Morris especially despised the aspirations and views on politics of the many intellectuals figuring among both the "moderate" and democratic factions: "Marmontel is the only man I have met with among their Literati [i.e., intellectuals] who seems truly to understand the subject."[122] For Morris, it was always political experience that counted. In November 1790, writing to Washington, he accounted the "Assembly at once a master and a slave, new in power, wild in theory, raw in practice. It engrosses all functions tho incapable of exercising any, and has taken from this fierce, ferocious people every restraint of religion and of respect."[123]

Lafayette, well known to Washington, was judged by Morris altogether inadequate in abilities for his now crucial role. Withdrawing from the Assembly to concentrate on his command of the thirty-thousand-man National Guard, on whom order in the capital, and hence the country, depended, Lafayette remained a pivotal figure in the French Revolution until the elimination of the French court and monarchy with the rising of 10 August 1792 when he was forced to flee the country. Until then he battled vainly to prevent the Revolution's descent into hopeless strife and chaos. Whether it reflected realism or naïveté on his part, Lafayette continued striving to narrow the gap between the two pre-1793 main rival revolutionary blocs, moderate and radical. Brissot and Condorcet likewise strove to maintain their collaboration with Lafayette, and steady him on a "republican" path, persisting in this until the Champs de Mars "massacre" in Paris (17 July 1791) when National Guard troops under Lafayette's orders fired on demonstrators, killing or wounding dozens. At that point, their alliance with Lafayette collapsed—as did Paine's: in the second part of the *Rights of Man*, Paine treats Lafayette very differently than he does in the first.[124] Yet, in early 1792, Brissot still tried to bring Lafayette back to the democratic republican fold, opposing his being publicly vilified (which later figured among the damning pieces of "evidence" Robespierre adduced to brand Brissot and Condorcet too as "enemies" of the Revolution).[125]

In January 1792 Congress finally approved Washington's nomination of Morris as ambassador to France despite a continuing sharp split over this, in both houses, with Monroe leading the opposition, to Morris as a "monarchy man." By insisting on Morris, whom Jefferson disliked and vigorously disagreed with, Washington was indicating to the world, in no uncertain terms, that he rejected Jefferson's appraisal of how things stood in France and repudiated the democratic thrust of the French Revolution.[126] Leading opinion in England was delighted. The London papers began spreading the reports that Morris is "come over," as he himself expressed it, as an "Agent for the Aristocrats."[127] As secretary of state, Jefferson now had to both congratulate and direct Morris.

In doing so, Jefferson took the opportunity both to admonish him to remain as neutral as possible and, yet, if forced to incline to one side, to follow the inclinations of most Americans and support the democratic wing: "I have the pleasure to inform you that the President of the United States has appointed you Minister Plenipotentiary for the United States at the Court of France, which was approved by the Senate on the 12th instant, on which be pleased to accept my congratulations. . . . With respect to their Government, we are under no call to express opinions which might please or offend any party; and therefore it will be best to avoid them on all occasions, public or private. Could any circumstances require unavoidably such expressions, they would naturally be in conformity with the sentiments of the great mass of our countrymen, who having first, in modern times, taken the ground of Government founded on the will of the people, cannot but be delighted on seeing so distinguished and so esteemed a nation arrive on the same ground, and plant their standard by our side."[128] Jefferson here again stressed the parallelism of the American and French revolutions of which Morris was just as aware as he. Of course, Morris had no intention of siding with the democratic faction and continued to intrigue with the court and aristocratic faction for an "aristocratic" outcome.[129]

For many months, striving to check Hamilton's fiery speeches in the Cabinet and Morris's influence exerted from Paris, Jefferson continued trying to bring Washington round to his way of thinking and, as late as December 1792 and early 1793, briefly supposed he had succeeded; but this soon proved to be an illusion.[130] When Jefferson's allies the Brissotins strengthened their position with the elections of September 1791 and dominated the new assembly, Morris complained that "the new Assembly as far as can at present be determined is deeply imbued with republican or rather democratical principles."[131] As the democratic republican tendency in France further consolidated its grip, Morris grew gloomy while showing he was just as aware as Jefferson and Monroe of the strange public transatlantic paradox created by an American ambassador (and president) doing everything possible to oppose the spread of democratic republicanism in Europe. "The mission to France must be a stormy one," he confided to a political ally in Philadelphia in February 1792, "let it fall on whom it may. [France] is split up into parties whose inveteracy of hatred is hardly conceivable and the Royalists and Aristocrats consider America and the Americans as having occasioned their misfortunes. The former charge it upon us as Ingratitude seeing that it was the King [of France] who stepped forward to our relief. Should this party get the better in the struggle there are very few Americans who would (for the present) be well received. On the other hand the Republicans consider everything short of downright democracy as an abandonment of Political principle in an American. I could dwell minutely on both sides of this question but a word to the wise is sufficient. To stand well with all parties is impossible."[132]

The situation in France changed still more dramatically with the rising of 10 August 1792, known to many at the time as the "Second Revolution," when the Tuileries Palace was stormed, the Swiss Guard massacred, and the liberal aristocracy and Feuillant center bloc along with Lafayette eliminated from the scene. In August 1792, the monarchy ended and France became formally the republic it had been in substance since July 1789; but almost at once a new basic rift replaced the earlier split between Left and center— democratic republicans precariously controlling the National Assembly versus Montagnard authoritarian populists invading the Paris city government with a new set of slogans and labels. If Short was shocked at how those who had accepted the 1791 monarchical constitution now overturned it, initially the 1792 upheaval only reinforced the optimism and commitment to the Revolution of a Jefferson lacking his former proximity to French developments but as committed to the success of the democratic republican French Revolution as ever. Even though it aborted Lafayette's role in the Revolution, Jefferson expressly condoned the 10 August uprising in Paris: "it was necessary to use the arm of the people, a machine not quite so blind as balls and bombs, but blind to a certain degree." He regretted the bloodshed attending the overthrow of the French monarchy and aristocracy (that drove his friends La Rochefoucauld and Lafayette into exile), but the "liberty of the whole earth was depending on the issue of the contest," he reminded Short, "and was ever such a prize won with so little innocent blood?" "Rather than that it should have failed, I would have seen half the earth desolated."[133]

Formally proclaiming France a republic in 1792 was deemed by democratic republicans like Condorcet, Brissot, Pétion, Bonneville, Paine, and Jefferson an inevitable consequence of Louis XVI's betrayal of the Revolution and the Constitution. They had warned all along that constitutional monarchy of the kind instituted in France in 1789 was inherently self-contradictory and unworkable (Morris agreed with that). Most Frenchmen had earlier been impervious to a conclusion that by the summer of 1792, owing to force of circumstance, nearly everyone supporting the Revolution had reached. Proclaiming France a "republic" inevitably further worsened relations with Europe's monarchies but, equally, was widely expected on both sides of the Atlantic to bind revolutionary France more closely to America. "Why should not the French nation accomplish with respect to Louis XVI," asked Condorcet, "what the American populace did regarding George III?" Will the European powers refuse to recognize the French Republic, when in 1783 they had been compelled to recognize the American republic? "By their conduct will they admit that principles true in America are untrue in Europe, and that the same maxim stands true or false, crime or virtue, according merely to the requirements of their insidious policies?"[134]

From August 1792, growing economic distress and bread shortage, especially in the cities, generated sufficient exasperation among the working poor and lower-middle strata, the so-called sans-culottes, to enable Marat, Robespierre, Danton, and the other Montagnard leaders to steer the Revolution fitfully, using their slogans, toward the authoritarian, aggressive populism and anti-democratic oppression they preached. Robespierre contemptuously rejected the enlightened ideas and aspirations of Condorcet, Brissot, Mirabeau, and Lafayette, those who, during 1789–93, had sought to emulate and improve on the American Revolution by forging the world's first human rights and freedom-based democracy. While Brissot, Condorcet, and most of their faction rejected constitutional monarchy and sought to discredit Louis personally, in contrast to the Montagne, they did not seek his execution. (Rather

than face the scaffold, Paine hoped that Louis and his family could be transferred, as exiles, to America.) By contrast, Robespierre and the Montagne
insisted on the king's public execution. For his part Jefferson always refused
to say whether he thought the execution of Louis XVI was justified or not:
"I shall neither approve nor condemn."[135] Robespierre in any case detested
Condorcet, Brissot, and the intellectuals leading the democratic republican
Revolution and always made it a point to oppose them on every issue, scorning and denouncing their radical ideology repeatedly in his speeches during 1792, 1793, and 1794. Entirely anti-republican and monarchist in the
years 1789–91, from late 1792 Robespierre relented to the point of becoming
a nominal "republican" but, of course, was never a republican in any authentic sense, and much less a democrat. Robespierre in fact was consistently the
French democratic republicans' principal adversary, rejecting their policies
comprehensively while charging them with "betrayal" and being a new kind
of "aristocracy."

The Montagne, a coalition of three main populist groups, finally seized
power through the organized coup on 2 June 1793 when the democratic republican Revolution was overthrown, freedom of thought, expression, and
the press ended, and the steps that led to the suspension of the democratic
constitution initiated. A very different kind of French Revolution then rapidly evolved during the summer and autumn of 1793 into the unconstitu-
tionality, repression, horror, organized popular coercion, and bloodshed of
the Terror. Ardently Rousseauiste and aggressively Counter-Enlightenment,
Robespierre and the Montagne in no way shared the admiration of the American Revolution and its values divergently shared by both the democratic republicans and the constitutional royalists, having no interest in either competing American ideological tendency. At this point all parallelism ceased.

The French populist authoritarianism generated by Marat and Robespierre
was not in any way an offshoot of the democratic republican Revolution of
1789–93 but an entirely separate and fiercely antagonistic social, cultural, and
political trend. When their bloc, the Montagne, captured power in June 1793,
the effect was not to fulfill but entirely alter and in large part wreck the Revolution and all the freedoms and "rights" of the democrats. Unsurprisingly,
Enlightenment intellectuals both moderate and radical, in France or abroad,
to a man rejected the Montagne and denounced the calls for dictatorship and
systematic election-rigging, intimidation, and elimination of all criticism and
muzzling of the press emanating from Marat, Hébert, and Robespierre.[136] No
enlightener, moderate or radical, could support Montagnard ideology or their
coup, or sympathize with the political repression gripping France from June
1793 to Thermidor (July 1794). Even so, for previously firm supporters of

the Revolution now at a distance, men like Jefferson back in the United States or the Swedish radical Thorild, repudiating the French revolutionary regime and abandoning their zealous commitment to the Revolution proved agonizing, difficult, and protracted. True republicans closer to the scene, like Paine, Brissot, Gorani, Paape, Pétion, and Short, especially if in Paris at the time of the politically instigated "September massacres" of 1792,[137] conspicuously broke with Montagnard populist ferocity markedly earlier.

The time lag needed for the Montagnard group dictatorship's true nature to become universally manifest outside France, including across the Atlantic, briefly interrupted the amicable relations between Jefferson and his hitherto loyal protégé Short. By late 1792, with the Brissotins still dominating the National Assembly but the Montagne daily gaining ground, Short was already sending highly negative evaluations of Robespierre and the Montagne back to Philadelphia. Jefferson, then still striving to prod Washington into a more sympathetic attitude toward the French Revolution, was horrified. "The tone of your letters had for some time given me pain," he admonished Short, in January 1793, "on account of the extreme warmth with which they censured the proceedings of the Jacobins of France."[138] Condorcet was now completing the world's first democratic constitution; but the Paris Commune and now solidly populist clubs under the Montagne were blocking all democratic efforts in the National Assembly. Jefferson then still supposed the Jacobins to be heirs to the ideas and policies of the Left republicans he had supported in 1789–92. As yet, he failed to grasp that since September 1792 Brissot, Pétion, Condorcet, and his republican allies were being politically targeted and boycotted by the Jacobins with Robespierre and Marat launching an all-out onslaught against them.

By early 1793, Short's dispatches thoroughly alarmed Jefferson. For a time, he believed Short was damaging both the French and American revolutions given that there were in the United States "some characters of opposite principles" to theirs, "some of them are high in office, others possessing great wealth, and all of them hostile to France and fondly looking to England as the staff of their hope." If Washington had never evinced any sympathy for the French Revolution, his closest aide, Jefferson's principal foe, Hamilton, was vehemently opposed.[139] Thankfully, for the present, those exploiting the weak points of the American Constitution and Revolution as a stepping-stone to informal aristocracy and monarchy, Jefferson admonished Short, were being held in check by ordinary Americans. If one excepted the few Anglophile aristocrats, "this country [i.e., America]," he asserted, "is entirely republican, friends to the constitution, anxious to preserve it and to have it administered according to its own republican principles." Americans were being bolstered in their republicanism by what he still construed as French democratic success. Jefferson wanted nothing said or done by his subordinate in Paris that could assist the "little party above mentioned" in turning the tables on American republicanism in favor of "aristocracy."[140]

But within months, Jefferson discerned his error and rallied to Short's and Paine's view: from 1795, he repudiated the Montagne, roundly denouncing the "atrocities of Robespierre."[141] Paine had rightly protested to Danton, in May 1793, shortly before the populist authoritarian takeover, complaining of the Montagne's tirades against his democrat republican allies in the National Convention, insisting the Montagne's accusations were just "calumny": "I know there are not better men nor better patriots than what they are."[142] By the spring of 1793 it was obvious in Paris at least that the new revolutionary bloc headed by Robespierre relied on lies and deception, proceeding with no regard for "moral principles." In later years, Jefferson readily accepted that the French Revolution had ultimately failed, but he insisted that Robespierre and the Terror destroyed the Revolution by means of city mobs "debased by ignorance, poverty and vice"; the deception and lies that made the Terror possible followed specifically, he believed, from the people's ignorance.

Jefferson's repudiation of Robespierre, Marat, and the Montagne by no means signified that he had now lost faith in the common people; it merely stiffened further his insistence that democracy works only when the people are sufficiently enlightened and informed. After Thermidor, Jefferson, Paine, and Short again grew hopeful that the neo–Brissotin revolutionary regime that emerged following Robespierre's demise, between July 1794 and February 1795, would succeed in steadying the French Revolution on the democratic republican basis shared with the American Revolution. Jefferson termed himself, writing to Démeunier from Monticello on 29 April 1795, as "a warm zealot for the attainment and enjoyment by all mankind of as much liberty, as each may exercise without injury to the equal liberty of his fellow citizens," while lamenting that "in France the endeavours to obtain this should have been attended with the effusion of so much blood." "I was intimate," he recalled, "with the leading characters of 1789. So I was with those of the Brissotine party who succeeded them: and have always been persuaded that their views were upright." Those who came afterward, the Montagnard leaders, Jefferson did not know personally and he now accepted that the "party which has lately been suppressed [i.e., at Thermidor]" betrayed the Revolution. Fortunately, the "government of those now at the head of affairs appears to hold out many indications of good sense, moderation and virtue."[143]

In April 1796, Jefferson wrote to one of the greatest foes of the Montagne and exponents of radical ideas, the former French National Assemblyman, abolitionist, atheist, orientalist, and revolutionary journalist Constantin-François Chasseboeuf, comte de Volney (1759–1820), who had just arrived in America for a three-year *voyage philosophique*. Like Paine, Volney was a close observer of both the French and the American revolutions. As a *philosophe* supporting the democratic republicans, he had been imprisoned by the Robespierre regime and barely survived. It was no mere empty courtesy that moved Jefferson to write: "I shall have a great deal to learn from you of what passed in France after I left it. Initiated as I was into the mysteries of the Revolution, I have much still to learn which the newspapers never knew."[144] Advised by Short, Paine, Lafayette, and Volney, Jefferson never subsequently doubted that Robespierre was a cruel and utterly corrupt dictator and the Terror an unmitigated disaster for both the French and American revolutions. The French Revolution he supported had been "defeated by Robespierre" he stressed again, years later, writing to John Adams.[145] His brief altercation with Short was soon left far behind them, the two resuming lifelong friendly relations and corresponding amicably not least about the French Revolution and its principal figures. "I am glad the bust of Condorcet has been saved," agreed Jefferson, writing to Short, long afterward, in October 1819, "and so well placed." "His genius should be before us while the lamentable, but singular act of ingratitude which tarnished his latter days [Condorcet's being outlawed, hounded, and driven to suicide by the Montagnard group dictatorship] may be thrown behind us."[146]

Robespierre, Paine assured the French Convention, after Thermidor, was "my inveterate enemy, as he was the enemy of every man of virtue and humanity."[147] Jefferson fully agreed, deeming him every bit as much a betrayer of the Revolution as the post-1800 Napoleon. "Robespierre met the fate," he assured Mme. De Stael in May 1813, "and his memory the execration, he so justly merited."[148]

CHAPTER 12

A Tragic Case:
The Irish Revolution (1775–98)

"Ireland has much the air of Americanising"

Nothing seemed more probable, even prior to the American rebellion becoming an Independence movement proper, in 1776, than that American developments would have a profound impact on Ireland. Owing to the country's chronically disordered social and political condition in the eighteenth century, it was potentially more profoundly divided than almost any other western European land. After Canada, Holland, and France, Ireland was in fact the fourth country on which the American Revolution directly impinged as an inspiration, ideological divider, and guide for action.

Ireland possessed an ancient constitution, legal tradition, and local parliament that had all been overturned by statute and remit, in effect by force, following the Glorious Revolution (1688–91), which subjected the country to the Parliament of England without any pretense of justification. Catharine Macaulay (1731–91), among Edmund Burke's principal ideological adversaries, argued in the last volume of her *History of Great Britain*, in 1783, that the revolutionaries of 1688 had been false friends of liberty intent only on self-promotion and enhancing aristocratic power.[1] Nowhere did this sound more plausible than in Ireland. The 1688 Revolution extended the preponderance of the London Parliament and English aristocracy over Irish and Scottish politics and economic life, and generally the lives of the Irish and Scottish peoples, but in Ireland in a much more direct and brutal fashion than in Scotland.[2] In Ireland, conflict between Williamites and Jacobites (1688–91) bequeathed a legacy of bitterness deeper and more general than any Jacobite disaffection in England or Scotland south of the Catholic Scottish Highlands.

Dethroning James II and ejecting the House of Stuart, contended champions of the Glorious Revolution, had emancipated Ireland from popish oppression and arbitrary power. The Protestant minority generally concurred. But some Irish Protestants found the political outcome unsatisfactory even so and the economic outcome indefensible. The 1688–91 Revolution in Ireland entailed not just a change of dynasty and, in Catholic areas, firmer Protestant dominance but an imperial shift, concentrating power at the center, in London, extending English hegemony to every aspect of Irish life. Burke, himself of Irish birth, despite accepting the political, and only mildly opposing Ireland's economic, subordination, nevertheless, like many others, acknowledged that a revolution which, in England, largely benefited the "great body of the people" occurred in Ireland at the "expense of the civil liberties and properties of the far greater part; and at the expense of the political liberties of the whole. It was, to say the truth, not a revolution, but a conquest, which is not to say a great deal in its favor."[3]

An early protest against Ireland's ruthless subordination was the renowned tract titled *The Case of Ireland* (Dublin, 1698) by the Dubliner William Molyneux (1616–93). Gently protesting the Irish parliament's drastically reduced status and appealing to William III to honor promises made in his *Declaration of the Hague*, of October 1688, to the Irish, Scots, and English alike and "rescue these nations from arbitrary power," Molyneux pronounced liberty "the inherent right of all mankind" and the Williamite settlement in Ireland fundamentally unjust. An Anglican whose family had directly benefited from the forfeitures of land following the 1641 Irish Catholic rebellion, questioning the London Parliament's supremacy and the mercantilist economic system imposed on Ireland, Molyneux saw Anglican Church domination as a natural outgrowth of Irish history. He sought, he assured Locke, to avoid antagonizing the king's ministers by couching his complaint against Parliament's imposed revolutionary settlement with carefully calibrated "caution and submission." He was evidently not deferential enough: his text was condemned and publicly burned by the common hangman in London, on Parliament's orders and, on those of the Anglo-Irish administration, in Dublin.[4]

Molyneux was no radical. He registered his opposition to the revolutionary settlement of 1688–91, relying exclusively on traditional arguments and citing broken promises to buttress his case, providing no path to broader, more comprehensive arguments.[5] Over the next decades little changed. In Ireland, the land was dominated by Anglican landowners possessing estates deriving from the earlier Cromwellian confiscations supplemented by those seized from exiled Jacobite rebels in and after 1691. The 1690s confiscations were resented not only by those directly deprived but also by Catholic tenant farmers, the

Dublin legislature, and some landowners aggrieved at the high-handed manner in which the land was selectively redistributed by ministers in London.[6] From the 1650s down to the mid-eighteenth century, the total amount of land in Ireland remaining in Catholic ownership shrank drastically, by the 1760s totaling no more than around 14 percent. The Catholic majority, over 70 percent of the Irish population, largely illiterate, remained completely excluded from landowning as well as from the country's political and most of its professional life, subject to a range of disabilities and marks of inferior status. Social resentment gave added edge to the longstanding religious and cultural divide separating the Catholic rural and urban masses from two rival and mutually antagonistic Protestant minorities: the landed aristocracy and Dublin Anglican elite beside the less affluent and less dominant but more numerous Scots-orientated Ulster Presbyterians. Even the principal privileged groups, Anglo-Irish noble landowners and the Anglican clergy, whose livings and churches were financed from rents raised from confiscated lands and tithes imposed on the largely non-Anglican peasantry, while approving most of the prevailing social, economic, and religious hierarchical post-1688 Irish order, followed Molyneux in resenting their dependent status under the Crown.

Psychologically and socially, eighteenth-century Ireland was undoubtedly a potential powder keg but, prior to the American Revolution, predominantly quiet and submissive. There was no non-religious critique of the country's wretched condition, only a striking lack of tools for analyzing and comprehending its situation and for political debate other than longstanding theological dispute that entirely obscured the basic social and historical divisions. Fear and suspicion permeated Irish society and profoundly divided Catholics from Protestants, and Presbyterian from Anglican, but contributed little to resolving the country's chronic difficulties. Socially, "Dissenters," Ireland's non-Anglican Protestants, occupied an intermediate space between conquerors and conquered but one so tightly hemmed in as to permit little scope for any form of mobility upward or downward. Ulster Presbyterians, with their Calvinist traditions and Scottish origins, resented Anglicans and disdained the Catholics, while Catholics detested "the Ascendancy" and the Presbyterians, heartily loathing the internal political and economic sway of the dominant Anglican landed class while expressing their opposition and resentment still primarily in religious terms.

Organized discrimination shaped life and culture at every level. Especially oppressive were the stringent economic restrictions maintained by the London Parliament, preventing Ireland's woolen and other textile industries from competing either in the domestic British market or in the American colonies. Statutes subordinating Ireland's economy rigorously to England's, including those restricting Irish shipping and shipbuilding, had long been in force. But during the eighteenth century, additional mercantilist legislation was brought in to exclude Irish shipping from trade with the American colonies, Africa, and Asia more systematically and effectively than before. The Dublin executive, viceroy and council, imposed from London without consultation, applied the new restrictions even where most obviously detrimental to Ireland's interests. It was not Ireland's place to share the advantages of an imperial system reserved for England and Scotland. Locked into a system of preference and exclusion, Ireland struck Diderot's friend Chastellux as the most vulnerable link in the empire's structure.[7]

Grievances, though, no matter how great, cannot in themselves supply a rationale for rejecting and replacing an entire system of political, social, religious, and economic dependency and repression where there was no intellectual basis for overturning it and where religious authority, martialed in competing sectors, infuses the entire culture. Before the mid-1770s, there is no room for a conceptual framework capable of yielding programs for comprehensive reform. One representative of the Irish mainstream Enlightenment, James Gordon (1750–1819), an Anglican schoolmaster and eventual rector of Cannaway in Cork diocese who later composed a perceptive history of the Irish Revolution (1801), noted the hopeless plight of those, the great majority, locked in the dogmatic straightjacket of age-old confessional thinking. Although personally espousing the benign and tolerant aspects of Ireland's incipient "religious Enlightenment," he also sensed its limitations. Since the clergy exercised massive sway in Ireland, cross-denominational negotiation among liberal-minded churchmen might have promoted toleration and ameliorated matters, but in practice interfaith discussion seldom occurred and, to Gordon, seemed unlikely ever to on any scale. All three main denominational blocs were debarred by confessional pressure from pursuing Ireland's true interest while the fringe churches and small immigrant communities seemed little better. Despite centuries of persecution and banishment from France, and the "kindness" and advantages they encountered in Ireland, even the country's Huguenot pastors remained so unbending in confessional dispute and resistant to Enlightenment thinking that Ireland's desperate plight "never mitigated their bigotry, nor drew from them one sentiment in favour of toleration." Those recommending comprehensive toleration found themselves trapped between "counterfeit loyalists" (Protestant zealots) and "monk-ridden Catholics" projecting the "old religious hatred of the Romanists." Though "mutually eager to cut each other's throats," commented Gordon ruefully, these rivals would with the greatest ease join together "cordially" to annihilate the few like himself demanding a more enlightened solution.[8]

Given the prevalence of confessional loyalties in Ireland, freethinkers, deists, and atheists were popularly loathed and abjured to a degree beyond what was usual abroad. In 1765, Ireland's new lord lieutenant, Lord Hertford, who as Hume's superior in Paris had admired his good sense, having planned to bring him to Ireland and install him as his secretary in Dublin Castle, abandoned the idea on discovering that Hume's "character as a philosopher is an object of universal disgust not to say detestation in this country; and his historical character [i.e., historical interpretations] where Ireland and the Stuarts are concerned, is excessively disliked." It was "impossible for Hume to take up such a function in Dublin" and intermediaries had to be found to impress on him the exceptionally bigoted character of the country so as to extricate Hertford from the "disagreeable necessity," in "contradiction to all his feelings for Mr. Hume," of laying an "absolute embargo upon him and his philosophy."[9]

It was by no means, therefore, social and economic pressures as such that generated the late eighteenth-century Irish Revolution. Until the century's third quarter, practically no one thought or talked in terms of popular sovereignty, equality of status and inherent universal and equal rights, freedom of expression and thought, or parliamentary representation of the whole of society. Rather a revolutionary situation led by figures intending to transform the entire picture fundamentally ensued, and could only have ensued, from a preceding "revolution of the mind." Already in the late 1760s the growing American crisis made a deep impression on enlighteners averse to the bigotry and intolerance of Ireland's past, encouraging enlightened circles in Ireland and in England where open to reconsidering Britain's overweening relationship with Ireland. Confronting an unyielding aristocratic-ecclesiastical establishment in both Britain and Ireland, during subsequent years English critics like Price, Priestley, John Jebb, and Robert Bage projected their new zeal for revolutionary change, aroused by the American Revolution, with particular emphasis onto the Irish context[10]—and to an extent likewise on India.[11] The ex-Quaker Derbyshire manufacturer and novelist Robert Bage (1730–1801), a friend of Erasmus Darwin and enthusiast for both the American and French revolutions, projected his philosophical radicalism through fictional projections set in both America and India. The American Revolution, itself a warring duality of radical (democratic) and moderate (aristocratic) tendencies, thus helped drive an identical polarization process characterizing British and Irish political thought and general culture during the last third of the century, as it turned out with a sharpening of unease with regard to India and explosive consequences for Ireland.

After the Americans secured their Independence, Jebb congratulated Franklin on America's success and "glorious institutions" that ensured an asylum of liberty for all mankind. Its fortunate citizens now possessed a "larger proportion of civil and religious liberty, than hath been indulged in any age or clime."[12] But while transforming America, the Revolution had also transformed onlookers across the seas including himself—even though he had never visited the New World. America's example had brought about his personal conversion to political and intellectual radicalism, his post-1774 "enlightenment" turning him into an avowed fighter for annual parliaments and universal suffrage in England and profoundly transforming his view of Britain's relationship to Ireland. Prior to 1774–76, Jebb had "gloried in the name of Englishman," like his compatriots associating the term with everything "generous, manly and humane. I thought it virtue to believe, that my country was the peculiar care of heaven." But the American Revolution had taught him with "pain inexpressible" that the British constitution and Parliament were not what his countrymen imagined. Trusting in the British constitution's much trumpeted superiority over all other political regimes, he had earlier shared a national delusion that was actually a crass prejudice permeating all levels of society. The "birth-place of Milton, and Hampden, and a Sidney" had succumbed to wishful thinking, domineering arrogance, chauvinistic pride, and a rapacious thirst to dominate global commerce, rendering the people positively "eager, at the call of despotism, to destroy the liberties of its more virtuous brethren [i.e., in America]."[13]

Narrow chauvinism, sanctioned by Anglicanism, had fomented erroneous, oppressive ideas justifying "deeds of foul injustice" in America and still worse oppression in Ireland, a land abominably tyrannized over; the Dublin parliament, held Jebb, far from representing the Irish people, was but the "voice of the aristocracy and the inclinations of the crown."[14] Radicals like Jebb repudiated the Williamite Glorious Revolution of 1688–91 in every particular and every constitutional and legal system resting on precedent and "experience" inherited from the past. All systematic opponents of "the Ascendancy" in Ireland naturally turned to the American Revolution to ground their intellectual, moral, and political challenge to what, by the 1770s, they were beginning to see as the insupportably oppressive status quo. But equally "moderate" Enlightenment impinged powerfully on Ireland, vigorously justifying "the Ascendancy" if in revised terms recommending more toleration and some easing of the discrimination. The result was a new-framed clash of basic values reaching into every corner of enlightened thought and endeavor.

Publicists in Ireland during the 1770s and 1780s began routinely to distinguish between what most deemed "True Enlightenment," exalting Newtonianism, Locke, and Montesquieu together with the Anglo-Irish "Ascendancy" (the gentry establishment) buttressed intellectually by Oxford, Cambridge, and Trinity College, Dublin, versus "pernicious" Enlightenment insidiously promoting American democratic revolutionary values, French *philosophie moderne*, and the ideas of the *Histoire philosophique* and of Franklin, Jefferson, Paine, Jebb, Price, Priestley, and Macaulay. Deemed "dangerous" and subversive, the radical challenge was uniformly disparaged and vilified by "moderate" reformers and conservatives as "democratical" and "atheistic."[15] Paradoxically, the very term "Enlightenment" had, by 1775, become structurally integral both to prevailing Ascendancy's political rhetoric reaffirming the political inheritance of 1688–89 and to an opposition discourse rejecting that legacy.[16] The basic rift between Moderate and Radical Enlightenment characterizing eighteenth-century thought and culture everywhere, in Ireland soon grew bitter and pervasive, generating an intellectual dichotomy that fundamentally reshaped politics.

The American Revolution's impact on Irish society—traditional, theologically fraught, and ethnically fragmented—was hence far-reaching and deeply unsettling. If Irish Anglicans were "the Ascendancy's" backbone, and Catholics mostly indifferent to the Enlightenment and American developments, the Presbyterian minority, sometimes encouraged by their clergy, and other non-Anglicans frequently evinced sympathy for the American "rebellion," further aggravating relations with Anglicans.[17] By 1791, this development had proceeded so far that a pamphlet like the *Argument on behalf of the Catholics of Ireland*, published that year by the ex-Anglican Theobald Wolfe Tone (1763–98), later to emerge as a leading Irish revolutionary, stressing the "rights of man" and their equal applicability to all denominations of men, his appeal to "substitute the common name of Irishman in place of the denominations Protestant, Catholic and Dissenter," could appeal fairly widely even if chiefly in Presbyterian society. Some ten thousand copies of Tone's pamphlet were disseminated from Belfast, strengthening a strand of thinking that imparted real impetus to the non-confessional but inherently anti-theological (and anti-Catholic) radicalism that forged the United Irishmen movement.[18] With "religious Enlightenment" hemmed in, radical forms of Enlightenment made rapid strides in certain circles.

The great weakness of Moderate Enlightenment in Ireland was that marginal amelioration of rampant injustices left the basic structure of political, economic, and religious repression and imperial ascendancy intact. Critics of the status quo mostly still aimed at mitigating just the worst abuses, refining what they judged the near perfect British "constitution" of 1688–89 and its Lockean principles. Viewing Ireland as part of an imperial complex permanently under Britain's Crown and Parliament received eloquent support from Burke, whose mother was of Catholic background and father Protestant. If the "several bodies which make up this complicated mass are to be preserved as one Empire," he assured a friend in 1773, "an authority sufficient to preserve that unity and by its equal weight and pressure to consolidate the various parts that compose it, must reside somewhere: that somewhere can only be England." One should deem the "supreme power to be settled there, not by force or tyranny or even mere long usage, but by the very nature of things and the joint consent of the whole body." England "must have the sole right to the Imperial Legislation: by which I mean that law which regulates the polity and the economy of the several parts as they relate to one another and to the whole."[19]

Burke was conscious of the "cruel, oppressive and unnatural" chains imperial mercantilism imposed on Ireland, and disquieted by the unjust discrimination against Catholics, but offered no means of escaping this somber plight.[20] Burke sought mitigation of abuses while broadly justifying the prevailing system, especially the aristocracy's ascendancy in line with Adam Smith's, Ferguson's, and Hume's general approach. Such views long remained dominant. Smith and Ferguson proposed Scottish-style union with Britain as the remedy for Ireland's ills: a union like Scotland's would make Britain more secure while giving Ireland equal economic privileges and softening the Anglo–Irish landed elite's internal sway. "By an union with Great Britain," held Smith, "the greater part of the people of all ranks in Ireland would gain an equally complete deliverance" (as Scotland) from an "oppressive aristocracy." British constitutional procedures would curb the internal sway of the Anglo–Irish landed elite, "an aristocracy not founded like that of Scotland, in the natural and respectable distinctions of birth and fortune, but in the most odious of all distinctions, those of religious and political prejudices—distinctions which, more than any other, animate both the insolence of the oppressors and hatred and indignation of the oppressed, and which commonly render the inhabitants of the same country more hostile to one another than those of different countries ever are."[21] Union with Britain would mean higher taxes, admittedly, but would also compensate Ireland economically for entrusting control over defense, foreign policy, and taxation to England. Via such a union, the Irish would perhaps become less deeply divided; but no more than in Scotland could this solution counteract loss of autonomy, unequal status of the churches, or indeed an adjusted aristocratic dominance. Smith's and Ferguson's "natural and respectable distinctions of birth and fortune" would continue to rule Irish society.[22]

Arguably, given the vast repressive resources at Britain's disposal, acquiescence was sound advice. Either one accepted what Burke called Ireland's virtually but "not wholly aristocratical" Ascendancy under the Crown or subversively opposed the structures of oppression, aligning with Paine, Jebb, and

Price. Burke and Smith possessed a closer interest in, and deeper grasp of, Ireland's predicament than most contemporary commentators. But neither was willing to apply equality or anything approaching radical democratic criteria to the Irish (or any other) context. This applied both before and after Burke's lurch to the right during the 1787 Dutch crisis, a change of stance that baffled many. Burke's earlier apparent "liberalism" was indeed widely misinterpreted. For while Burke had sometimes questioned the wisdom of English economic legislation concerning Ireland (and still more the East India Company's sway in India), he never doubted England's right to impose one-sided mercantilist statutes in principle. Better harmonizing Ireland's interests with those of Britain frequently engaged his attention; but his unwavering aim was to strengthen the overarching imperial supremacy of Crown, Church, gentry, commercial elite, and Parliament more securely.[23]

The American crisis weighed on Ireland from the outset. In the years immediately preceding the American Revolution, advocates of the American cause sometimes drew parallels between Ireland's plight, or what Franklin called the British Parliament's "usurped" dominion,[24] and the growing disaffection of the colonies. In 1771, Franklin visited Dublin, "being desirous of seeing the principal Patriots there," and appeared before the Dublin parliament where he found opinion sharply divided between the "courtiers" and the "Patriots" angered by Ireland's general situation and now by Britain's extracting extra Irish resources with which to coerce the Americans. The Patriots were "disposed to be friends of America, in which I endeavored to confirm them with the expectation that our growing weight might in time be thrown into their scale, and by joining our interests with theirs, a more equitable treatment from [Britain] might be obtained for themselves as well as for us."[25] In reality, Ireland had long been treated far more oppressively than had the American dependencies.

A British Act of Parliament of 1698 had established an Irish standing army of 12,000 men recruited exclusively among Protestants and, in terms of command structure, fully integrated into the British army. The only standing armed force in the country, it was paid for by, and kept order over, Irish society as a whole. Irish troops and money had played a not insignificant part in British success during the Seven Years' War, marking the high point of British imperial expansion. As friction escalated in North America during the 1760s, the British government responded with an array of precautionary measures. Among these was the 1769 Augmentation Act, imposed by George III's viceroy in Ireland, Lord Townshend, and the Irish parliament, expanding the standing force to over 15,000 and broadening its responsibilities beyond maintaining order in Ireland so that it could also be "employed towards the necessary defense of his Majesty's garrisons and plantations abroad."[26] The Dublin assembly agreed to support George III's "just rights" in America, transferring 4,000 troops from Ireland's standing army to fight the American "rebels." The Augmentation Act thus significantly extended commitment of Irish resources to defending colonies with which the Irish themselves remained prohibited from trading, underlining further the glaring injustice of Ireland's subordination and embroilment in the American drama.

Ireland's "Radical Enlightenment"

Before 1774–75, most Protestants in Ireland, as in Britain, belonged to what E. P. Thompson called the "peer-respecting, flag-saluting, foreigner-hating" mass passionately infused with loyalist, traditional, and xenophobic sentiments. Criticism and protest redounded in isolated texts, and two or three private clubs and societies, but nowhere near amounted to a national movement. Although measures were introduced to restore some influence to the Irish parliament earlier, only with the outbreak of the American Revolution was there a significant change of mood in Ireland. During the late 1770s, a vigorous and fairly broad-based (even if predominantly Protestant) movement emerged committed to pursuing a wider-ranging reform agenda. Its principal goal was "a more equal representation of the people in parliament" and less direct subordination of Ireland to British interests; but almost from the first this growing reform impulse, like the Irish Enlightenment that gave birth to it and supplied its rationale and terminology, revealed an irreconcilably divided, dual character.[27] Ireland's unenviable subjection inexorably deepened the rift between the two rival "enlightenments."

Untypical in many ways, Ireland was characteristic of eighteenth-century ancien régime Europe in its dual reception of Enlightenment ideas. From the 1770s, old social pressures together with new intellectual impulses drove intellectual polarization, rendering conciliatory, harmonizing, middle-of-the-road positions increasingly inapplicable. Yet more comprehensive opposition or criticism had scant prospects in the Dublin parliament where by 1776, as Franklin saw, the Irish "Patriots" represented a lively critical voice while remaining an impotent, uncomfortably small minority. Real opposition could surge only from below. But this was impossible until grievances found their vehicle in the further spread of those enlightened ideas that could explain and justify a broad, generalized opposition to "aristocracy," bigotry, ecclesiastical power, political dependency, empire, and monarchy. In general, collision between moderate and radical enlightened impulses with "moderation" keeping the upper hand in the public sphere and higher education complicated and hampered the quest for comprehensive solutions to an oppressed land's chronic problems. For those wanting more meaningful change, there was no alternative but to reject the "moderate" legacy of 1688, Locke, Montesquieu, Hume, Smith, and Burke and opt for stronger fare. Some began to brew "projects of a deeper kind," as Gordon put it, "projects of revolution, the total subversion of the existing government, and the erection of a democratically constituted commonwealth in its place."[28]

The radical tendency, then, exclusively provided a rationale for transforming Irish laws, institutions, and practices fundamentally, offering explanations accessible to the people. "The lower classes," recounts Gordon, "were informed that by a revolution which, in the establishment of a democratic system of government, would give universal suffrage and equal rights, their condition would be exalted and rendered far more comfortable."[29] Although not a few Ulster Presbyterians volunteered for service in the Irish regiments sent to fight the American "rebels," there arose also a good deal of sympathy for the rebellion among this segment of the population, not least because emigration from Ulster had been rising sharply in recent years, with over twenty thousand Ulstermen migrating across the Atlantic to the American colonies just in the years 1769–74, newcomers who frequently became participants in the American insurgency.[30] According to one "New Light" Presbyterian minister, Dr. William Campbell of Armagh, the "Presbyterians of Ulster condemned this war [by England on the American rebels] as unjust, cruel, and detestable. They beheld it with anguish and with horror, as the most wanton, unprovoked despotism. Their friends and relations abounded in the different provinces of America, and they heard with pride that they composed the flower of Washington's army, being carried on by a native love of liberty, to encounter every danger, for the safety of their adopted country."[31]

The Presbyterian connection between Ulster and New England, and obvious risk of opinion below the level of the landed class represented in the Dublin parliament aligning behind the American rebels, together with the alleged similarity of Irish and American interests in the face of British imperial power, undoubtedly disquieted ministers in London. The same manifestations excited Lafayette when back at Paris in 1779; he had contacts among the Irish dissidents and endeavored to persuade Vergennes, the French foreign minister, to support anti-British subversion in Ireland as well as Canada.[32] Meanwhile, just as in Canada, British ministers tried to deflect the danger by placating Catholic opinion. Like French Canadians, Irish Catholics were mostly indifferent to the American cause. Hence, from 1778, Catholics were more often admitted to the Irish army, and measures to lessen discrimination and Catholic disabilities were considered, debated, and partially adopted. A calculated reaction to the mounting crisis in the American colonies and in Canada was the Irish Land Act of 1778 permitting Catholics to own land on the same basis as Protestants. This shift of official policy toward a more accommodating view of Irish Catholicism only provoked disgruntled Ulster Presbyterian ministers—for the first time—to enter the world of public sphere politics, which they commenced doing precisely in the mid-1770s. In particular, they enthusiastically endorsed the Volunteer movement that now began, serving as chaplains and producing Volunteer sermons, and subscribed to the movement for parliamentary reform that soon also took root in Ulster.[33]

As the American crisis escalated, an increasingly concerned London government proposed further parliamentary bills to appease Irish opinion. There was talk of alleviating the condition of Ireland's industries and trade and permitting direct trade between Ireland and the American colonies. When France entered the American War in 1778, at a time when Britain was unable to reinforce the diminished garrison in Ireland, the London and Dublin authorities, worried about the inadequacy of the armed force available in the event of a French invasion, agreed to the forming of an Irish Volunteer militia force under the control of the gentry of "the Ascendancy." This avowedly loyalist force eagerly organized, raised its own funds, and purchased its own arms and uniforms, albeit almost entirely among the more affluent sections of the Protestant population.[34] The numbers joining these volunteer associations, much to Burke's alarm, were imposing, rising from 15,000 in 1779 to over 40,000 during 1780; and they were electing their own officers.[35] Here was an opportunity for Irish Protestants to simultaneously display "loyalty," despite the loathing of many for the war, *and* apply pressure. Ireland's reformers and enlighteners certainly had logic and justice on their side, and the beleaguered British government made profuse verbal and some limited but concrete concessions.

Against these concessions, however, a fierce outcry was whipped up at public meetings in Manchester, Liverpool, Glasgow, and other manufacturing and commercial cities in Britain. Petitions were organized. English public opinion, in a frenzy of loyalism and chauvinism, thoroughly aroused by the press against the American "rebels" and Irish dissidents, was in no mood to permit Irish participation jointly with England in trade with America or access to the British market for Irish manufactures, even on a restricted basis. Although, in Adam Smith's opinion, "all these unjust and oppressive restraints" were of no real economic value and seemed "rather to have gratified the impertinence than to have promoted any solid interest of our merchants and manufacturers,"[36] reluctantly government ministers found themselves forced to bow to public sentiment. Burke's own constituency, Bristol, he regretted to see, more than distinguished "itself by its zeal for that fatal cause," gripped by that "spirit of domination which our unparalleled prosperity had but too long nurtured."[37] But the rebuff to Irish demands in the London Parliament did not go unanswered. English obstreperousness provoked fierce indignation in the Northern Irish Presbyterian community and heightened sympathy for the American "rebels." What has been called the "first active step" in the Irish Revolution, and perhaps its most successful, began in 1779. In April that year, in undisguised emulation of the Americans, Dublin public gatherings adopted several confrontational resolutions including a non-importation agreement to promote among the people a movement to boycott such "British goods as could be made in Ireland."[38] The militia associations enthusiastically adopted these resolutions even while trumpeting their British loyalties. The Volunteer organizations had become a formidable opposition force. As Burke expressed it in 1780 with evident alarm, the "people of Ireland demand a freedom of trade with arms in their hands. They interdict all commerce between the two nations. They deny all new supply in the House of Commons, although in a time of war."[39]

The Irish Revolution had incipiently begun. "It is now too publicly known to be disguised any longer," confessed Horace Walpole in May 1779: "Ireland has much the air of Americanising."[40] As realization spread, in republican-minded circles spirits rose. Lafayette wrote assuring Franklin in Paris, in November, that the Irish "begin to speak a bold language and mention the blessed words of independency and the Rights of Mankind."[41] The effects of Irish action "when England was embarrassed by her frantic crusade against America," as Wolfe Tone later observed, were spectacular. A massive gain was achieved by a show, albeit not the use, of force, a technique learned from the American Revolution soon put to further use. "The British Parliament, in a former session frightened into a limited concession by the menaces of Ireland," in Burke's words, but subsequently "frightened out of it by the menaces of England, were now frightened back again, and made a universal surrender of all that had been thought the peculiar, reserved, uncommunicable rights of England—the exclusive commerce of America, Africa, of the West Indies— all the enumerations of the Act of Navigation—all the manufactures, iron, glass . . . all went together"; the ensuing Irish "Free Trade Act" was greeted throughout Ireland "with rapture." The Anglo-Irish leadership, "taught wisdom by humiliation," had been forced into a thoroughly humiliating climb-down.[42] But this was insufficient for those convinced by the logic of radical ideas: "we extorted from Britain's necessities," later remarked Wolfe Tone, the upwardly mobile son of an Anglican Dublin coach maker, "the extension of our trade; this is a great improvement; but is it the connection with England we are to thank for that?"[43]

Irish sentiment, royal ministers knew, had to be placated while the American conflict dragged on. Most formal disabilities and penalties affecting the Catholic population were lifted under the 1778 Catholic Relief Act, which unmistakably hinted that the repression of Catholicism in Ireland was being alleviated by His Majesty's government in recognition of the Irish Catholics' "peaceable behaviour" (in contrast to American rebelliousness) and to strengthen the monarchy in its present conjuncture.[44] Parliament in London, which had thus far denied the Protestant majority equality of civic status with Anglicans, soon had to accept abolition of sacramental tests for Dissenters too. In April 1780, the Irish legislature's reforming Whig leader, Henry Grattan (1746–1820), a liberal member of the Anglo-Irish elite combining pressure for autonomy in domestic affairs with acceptance of imperial direction in international and strategic matters, demanded that the Irish parliament "deny the claim of the British Parliament to make law for Ireland." The Irish parliament, dominated by landed gentry whose careers and interests were closely tied to Britain's dominance, defeated the motion but only somewhat narrowly, by 133 votes to 99; the cry for an autonomous legislature was then vigorously taken up, outside the legislature, by the militia associations.

Again the Volunteers demonstrated their feelings in no uncertain terms. With the American struggle absorbing Britain's attention, "we broke another, and a weighty link of the chain, which bound us to England," recalled Tone later, "by establishing an exclusive right of legislature for ourselves."[45] Ireland's parliament gained in stature in 1782, though perhaps more impressively on paper than in practice and with little real impact on society below the top strata given "the Ascendancy's" continuing grip over Irish life.[46] But such symbolic successes whetted the appetite for more far-reaching reform and for widening the suffrage. "From the year 1782 when by the spirited exertions of the volunteer associations of Ireland," recorded Gordon, the "legislature of this kingdom was rendered legally independent of that of Britain, and the odious restrictions, which had been most unwisely imposed on its trade and manufactures by the British government, were in a considerable degree removed, many of the Irish extended their views to a wider sphere of political freedom."[47] Even some Catholics were now invoking "brave, daring Washington" as radical enlighteners increasingly embraced cross-denominational integration as the means to advance their cause.[48]

Ireland's parliament remained unrepresentative and dominated by the aristocracy; but growing Irish disaffection was now exerting a destabilizing effect on not just Ireland but to an extent the entire empire. Burke acknowledged the justice of the Volunteers' demands but greatly feared the effect of American Independence on Ireland. He shrank from all talk of Irish independence and kept a low profile even in relation to calls for more autonomy, desperately hoping that 1782 would be the "last revolution in Ireland."[49] With the protest movement gathering momentum, a provincial assembly of militia delegations gathered several times, first in February 1782, at Dungannon, in Ulster, where most of the Volunteer associations were located. Representing 143 Volunteer contingents, it met "with design, among other objects, to plea and petition for a parliamentary reform, or a more equal representation of the commons in parliament."[50] In 1783, the reformers convened a national assembly of delegates from the counties, at Dublin, meeting under the "invidious title of Congress, invidious undoubtedly," averred Gordon, "since under the conduct of an assembly so denominated, the British colonies of North America had recently, by a successful war against the power of Britain, established an independent republic in the western hemisphere."[51] But even if inspired by American example and orchestrated by a group of highly educated leaders backed by Volunteer associations, this fresh challenge avoided pressing for Catholic political equality and emancipation. In any case, it failed to secure any further concession. With the American Revolution winding down, the Ascendancy's and British amenability ceased and "in November, the same year, . . . the petition of the Irish 'Congress' was contemptuously rejected by Parliament."[52]

With the end of the American War, Irish efforts to exert pressure by emulating America, unlike the democratic movement then gaining momentum in Holland, slackened, losing its impetus. From 1783, there were several attempts to revive the open, effective, and legal opposition of the 1778–82 period, but these were unsuccessful. In April 1784, students of Trinity College, Dublin, led by a committee including the young Wolfe Tone, urged the Irish again to boycott British goods and purchase only Irish manufactures. But such endeavors had lost their edge and capacity to intimidate. After 1783, the Volunteer associations dwindled in numbers and became increasingly divided over how far to admit Catholics and remove discriminatory measures against them.[53] Both "the Ascendancy" and the main Presbyterian bloc opposed relaxing the barriers further. Unlike John Jebb and the small band of English cosmopolitan radicals supporting the Irish protest movement, the Volunteers remained deeply divided over this question and relatively few Irish Protestants proved willing to accord full citizenship rights to Catholics.[54] Scope for exerting pressure without violence hence largely vanished. From 1783 onward, the choice was either acquiescence or underground revolutionary conspiracy, stark alternatives that could only further polarize Irish politics and divide Ireland's

Enlightenment between its moderate and radical streams. The middle ground began to crumble.[55]

The American Revolution had shown the way in terms of principle and technique, and helped stoke the general revolutionary ferment of 1785–98 in Holland, Switzerland, France, Italy, Poland, and Germany, by infusing Europe's radical philosophical criticism of the old order with a vigorous practical political dimension. American equality and social harmony European radicals often overstated less from naïveté than deliberate subversive intent. Jebb's radicalism was keenly esteemed in Ireland during the 1780s. Brissot's 1788 account of America was among those most loudly acclaiming the United States for teaching the contemporary Swiss, Dutch, French, British, Belgians, and Irish how to conquer liberty and conserve it.[56] During the 1780s, while activism in Ireland waned, there was a further expansion of all kinds in numbers of bookshops, reading rooms, coffeehouses, and literary societies in both Dublin and provincial towns, and the founding of the Royal Irish Academy (1784), and taste for reading and discussing Enlightenment historical, philosophical, political, and religious works widened. It was at this stage that the Dublin publishing industry began regularly to reproduce radical literature. Key texts like Paine's *Common Sense* and Raynal's *Histoire philosophique*, which appeared in several English-language editions at Dublin, stimulated diffusion of radical thought alongside the wider Enlightenment.

Leading figures in the radicalization of Irish opposition in the late 1780s and 1790s, inevitably, were university-educated cosmopolitans immersed in enlightened literature. Belfast-born William Drennan (1754–1820), founder of the underground organization United Irishmen, was a Glasgow University physician, poet, and educationalist as well as zealot for the American Revolution. Tone's close friend Thomas Russell (1767–1803) was an ex-Anglican British army officer who had served in India; he was to be hanged in 1803 for revolutionary conspiracy. Lord Edward Fitzgerald (1763–98), fifth son of the first duke of Leinster, was a dashing Irish nobleman who was to sit as an MP for County Kildare in the Irish parliament of 1796–97. Other figures to the fore in demanding full adult male suffrage and annual elections, and from 1789, collaboration with the French and Dutch revolutions, were Thomas and Robert Emmet, sons of the state physician for Ireland. William James MacNeven (1763–1841), one of only two Catholics among the twelve founding members of the United Irishmen's Dublin branch, another enthusiast for the French Revolution who read and spoke German, Italian, and French (besides Gaelic), having been educated in Prague and Vienna by an uncle, a physician at the court of Maria Theresa. Like Tone, these all became revolutionary leaders through university study, student clubs, reading, debate, and international connections.

The ardent conviction that the rights of all Irishmen were violated by the existing system of dependency undeniably derived from immersion in Enlightenment debate and concepts.[57]Anti-monarchical and democratic from the outset, Ireland's radical tendency was especially emphatic in its internationalism and denouncing religious intolerance and calling for Irish unity and Protestant-Catholic harmony. Until August 1792, the French Revolution was officially constitutional monarchist, which meant that the British establishment did not yet evince that blanket hostility toward it that developed later in 1792. Nevertheless, the outbreak of the French Revolution further sharpened the clash between moderate and radical Enlightenment in Ireland even more than in Britain, causing the mounting pro-revolutionary enthusiasm welling up in Dublin and Belfast during 1788–91 to be publicly displayed in undisguised ardor for the French Revolution. The growing practice, borrowed from revolutionary France and Holland, of flaunting green cockades helped foment Irish patriotism and incipient republicanism. All this proved profoundly disquieting to ministers in London.[58]

Having established the United Irishmen, soon Ireland's foremost secret organization, early in 1791, Drennan built what he called "a benevolent conspiracy—a plot for the people," organized, he explained, writing to a friend, to secure "the Rights of Man and the Greatest happiness of the Greatest Number." Although, like Tone, fiercely anti-Catholic theologically, political reconciliation of Catholics and Protestants erasing all theological distinction always featured among Drennan's principal goals.[59] In October 1791, Tone and Russell established the organization's first functioning branch at Belfast. A Trinity College graduate, tutor, and now barrister possessing firm leadership qualities and a "ready and excellent pen," according to Drennan, Tone presided at the first Belfast meeting and drew up the society's early resolutions.[60] A second "Society of United Irishmen" lodge founded soon after, in Dublin, emulated the Belfast format in meeting weekly and keeping formal "resolutions." The United Irishmen set out, noted Gordon, "to tincture the minds of their countrymen with republican ideas, by the dissemination of Paine's *Rights of Man*, and other democratic publications," aims closely tied to discrediting all conventional notions and weakening confessional faith.[61] By late 1792, the movement had already won considerable backing, and its illegal propaganda sheets were being perused by many who found its arguments persuasive, much to the consternation of Burke, who, despite acknowledging its arguments were "rational, manly and proper," detested and deeply feared Irish republicanism's widening reach.[62]

The second anniversary of the Bastille's fall was celebrated in 1791 with lively marching parades in Dublin and Belfast where "Franklin" and "Mirabeau" were the two principal "heroes" proclaimed on the parade banners and in effigy.[63] The third anniversary of the Bastille's fall, on 14 July 1792, was again triumphantly celebrated in Protestant towns with parades featuring increasingly subversive devices. One publicly flaunted slogan read: "Our Gallic brethren were born July 14, 1789:—alas! We are still in embryo"; its reverse side read: "Superstitious jealousy, the cause of the Irish Bastille: let us unite and destroy it!" A Belfast banquet for a mix of Catholic and Protestant local notables held shortly afterward featured four "national" flags—those of America, revolutionary France, revolutionary Poland, and Ireland.[64] Among toasts raised at the 14 July 1792 banquet at Newry were: "may Great Britain, France and Ireland vie with each other in restoring the spirit of free government over the face of the earth; to Thomas Paine, the celebrated vindicator of the human race"; to President "Washington, an ornament of the human race!"; to "short Parliaments and an equal representation to the people of Ireland and Great Britain"; to "the memory of Dr. Price" and "to Dr. Priestley"; "may the demolition of the Bastille be followed by that of the Inquisition"; and, finally, health to "All those who sincerely rejoice in the French Revolution, and disappointment to its enemies."[65]

The years 1790–92, during which the Irish Enlightenment's political face was increasingly riven between "aristocrats" and "democrats," witnessed a marked intensification of popular agitation in Ireland together with fierce escalation in the "civil war" within the Enlightenment sometimes called a split between "empiricists" and "rationalists."[66] The polarity was becoming stark though there was still confusion in the minds of Paine, Price, Cloots, and Priestley concerning Burke's abruptly changed stance. "That an avowed friend of the American Revolution should be an enemy to that of the French, which arose from the same general principles, and in a great measure sprung from it," admitted Priestley in 1791, "is to me unaccountable."[67] Burke's lurch to the right actually dated from 1787 but still met with scant comprehension among radicals and Ulster Presbyterians.[68] Irish opponents of the status quo had expected him to support the Dutch, French, and Irish revolutions since he had been (mistakenly) judged a friend of the American Revolution—though Catharine Macaulay at least had long clearly identified a marked "aristocratic" subtext to Burke's generally presumed progressivism that she thought needed exposing.[69] Paine, too, attributed his former friend's seeming defection to his aristocratic connections, his "praising the aristocratic hand that hath purloined him from himself."[70] Burke still pressed for constitutional adjustments in Ireland but not many, prompting Priestley's complaint that under Burke's newly revised principles "mankind are always to be governed as they have been governed, without any enquiry into the nature, or origin, of their governments. The choice of the people is not to be considered, and though their happiness is awkwardly enough made by him the end of government; yet, having no choice, they are not to be the judges of what is for their good."[71] Despite the growing focus on the drama in France, until September 1792 America remained the "only real republic in character and in practice, that now exists," as Paine expressed it. America's "government has no other object than the public business of the nation, and therefore it is properly a republic and the Americans have taken care that this, and no other, shall always be the object of their government, by their rejecting everything hereditary, and establishing government on the system of representation only." This stood in blatant contrast, noted Paine, to post-1787 Holland, which despite still calling itself a republic "is chiefly aristocratical, with an hereditary stadholdership."[72] Irish radical republicanism drew additional impetus from the openly republican turn taken by the French Revolution with the 10 August 1792 rising in Paris.[73] (In Scotland a similar wave of republican sentiment swept certain taverns, associations, and clubs.)[74] On hearing that the "king of France is dethroned," certain Irishmen, Tone conspicuous among them, loudly rejoiced alongside English, Scottish, and American radicals. France would shortly stand beside the world's first supposedly non-aristocratic republic across the Atlantic. At the same time, republicanism and the assault on ecclesiastical authority provoked a growing torrent of reactionary "King and Church" outrage, chauvinism, bigotry, and parochialism in Ireland as in Britain that moderate enlighteners, like Burke, now had little choice but to publicly embrace. In Parliament and the press, Burke bitterly denounced the radicals as dangerous "foreign" elements blending American, French, and Irish subversion under the banner of "French doctrines" to the ruination of all proper and respectable thinking.

Not only the Anglican Church but the Presbyterian and Catholic churches too were all "menaced alike," he assured his son, Richard, a Protestant spokesman for Catholic rights (but of more moderate stamp than Tone), in 1792, by the advance of French revolutionary republicanism. Through the influence of the "modern philosophers," deism and atheism would spread in Ireland and have "pernicious" effects.[75] If there were fanatics enough already, there were not yet persecutors cruel and hard-hearted "such as those beings of iron, the Atheists."[76] Should government and constitution be overwhelmed by revolutionary principles, "it is the new fanatical religion, now in the heat of its first ferment, of the Rights of Man, which rejects all Establishments, all discipline, all Ecclesiastical, and in truth all Civil order, which will triumph." Such a revolution would "destroy your distinctions," "lay prostrate your Church," and "put all your properties to auction, and disperse you over the Earth," bringing about the end of empire and aristocracy. "If the present Establishment should fall, it is this religion, which will triumph in Ireland and in England, as it has triumphed in France."[77]

In September 1792 Paine fled to Paris but continued, together with Barlow, at the helm of the international English-language propaganda campaign incisively answering Burke's hardening conservatism. Barlow's satirical poem, *The Conspiracy of Kings* (1792), poured derision on Burke's royalist "mad foam," deriding "Rank, Distinction, all the hell that springs from those prolific monsters, Courts and Kings."[78] Reminding readers that he was neither French, British, nor Irish but "American," a product of the land "where justice reigns, and tyrants tread no more," Barlow poetically inquired of Burke whether, by "thy infuriate quill," he aimed to "rouse mankind the blood of realms to spill? Then to restore, on death devoted plains, Their scourge to tyrants, and to man his chains?"[79] The audience for such sallies in Ireland only grew. On 27 October 1792, at yet another republican banquet at Newry, the main town on the highway between Dublin and Belfast, there were repeated toasts to the "Republic of France" and her victorious "citizen-soldiers," to the confusion of despots everywhere and "annihilation" of "despotism," and health to "President Washington and the United States of America" and the Irish people.[80] To counter "this new, this growing, this exterminatory system," Burke urged Anglicans, Presbyterians, and Catholics to unite, forgetting their previous disputes.

On 18 November 1792, over a hundred prominent British, American, and Irish visitors gathered at White's Hotel in Paris, also known as the "British Club," to celebrate the French Revolution and its achievements and denounce Burke. While the British people had now mostly turned against the French Revolution, egged on by the London government and most clergy, much of the intellectual and literary fraternity of Britain, the United States, and Ireland remained enthusiastic. Although Mary Wollstonecraft only arrived at White's shortly afterward, and Coleridge, during the 1790s likewise a fervent revolutionary ideologue, was absent, those attending formed an impressive coterie. Paine, Barlow, and several other poets including Helen Maria Williams, Robert Merry, and possibly Wordsworth were present,[81] as were David Williams (1738–1816), author of the *Letters on Political Liberty* (1782), Sir Robert Smyth (1744–1802), a former MP for Colchester, Lord Fitzgerald, and Colonel Eleazar Oswald (1755–95), a renowned American Independence war veteran who had participated in the 1775–76 invasion of Canada and later became editor of the Philadelphia *Independent Gazette*. Oswald had now joined the French revolutionary army and was the most prominent American participating in the revolution gripping Belgium. All this was a reminder that, aside from Gibbon and Burke, politically aware British, American, and Irish intellectuals, poets, journalists, and authors, like their Continental counterparts, mostly applauded the French Revolution as a worthy offshoot of the American and true parent to the Canadian, Belgian, Dutch, Swiss, and Irish revolutions. Arm in arm with their American and Irish counterparts, British radicals fervently celebrated the French Revolution.

The high point of the 18 November 1792 daylong banquet at the Paris "British Club," attended also by delegations from other nations, was a series of sixteen toasts. The fourth was to the coming constitutional "Convention of Britain and Ireland," proclaiming Ireland a land unjustly "enslaved" by England and stipulating that Britain, too, needed a democratic revolution. The fifth was to the "perpetual union" of the peoples of Britain, France, America, and the Netherlands: "may these soon bring other emancipated nations into their democratic alliance"; the sixth was to prompt abolition of "all hereditary titles and feudal distinctions" in Britain, a toast jointly proposed by Smyth and Fitzgerald, who threw their aristocratic titles on the fire—gestures greeted with outrage when afterward reported in the London papers, leading to Fitzgerald, who ranked as a major, being promptly cashiered from the British army.[82] Years earlier, in September 1781, he had been wounded fighting "rebels" in South Carolina, at the battle of Eutaw Springs. Later, in 1787, he was a British officer in Canada. In 1789, he undertook a remarkable journey overland from New Brunswick to Quebec and then Ontario, accompanying the renowned Independence war chieftain Joseph Brant to Detroit where he fraternized with the pro-British tribes and was formally adopted as one of their "chiefs." Afterward, he descended the Mississippi to New Orleans. Fitzgerald's gradual conversion to radical republican ideas was completed in Paris, in the autumn of 1792 while lodging, he informed his mother, "with my friend Paine—we breakfast, dine and sup together. The more I see of his interior, the more I like and respect him."[83] This was in contrast to Tone, who was not especially impressed with Paine personally and dismissed the second part of *The Age of Reason* as "damned trash."[84] A warm admirer also of Rousseau, from early 1796, Fitzgerald emerged alongside Tone as a principal organizer of the United Irishmen movement.

The most effective text propagating radical ideas and stoking discontent in Ireland—as in Scotland—was undoubtedly Paine's *Rights of Man* published in February 1791. Received in Ireland with distinctly more acclaim than Burke's *Reflections on the Revolution in France* (1790), it sold faster in Ireland and Scotland than in England, achieving what by Irish and Scottish standards was an enormous diffusion, the seven Irish editions amounting, reportedly, to forty thousand copies sold by November 1791.[85] Before long, according to one Belfast bookseller, *The Rights of Man* had been "read perhaps more universally than any pamphlet during the previous century."[86] Given the greater literacy of the Protestant population, it must have been mainly Protestants who read it; in Dublin Paine was advertised as "the Luther of political reformation." The radical republican group at Cork, led by Denis Driscol (1762–1810), were all Paineites. This was all much to Paine's own gratification, and for the first time he began to take a lively interest in the Irish situation.[87] Among other organs spreading subversive ideas, from its launch in January 1792, was the Belfast *Northern Star*, a workingmen's newspaper dedicated to the "reform of parliament" through the "union of Irishmen." Although it represented only a minority trend among Ulster Protestants, and its editor, another of the founders of the Belfast lodge of the United Irishmen, Samuel Neilson (1761–1803), was the son of a Presbyterian minister, his paper solidly supported the French Revolution and propagated the views of Paine, Jebb, Macaulay, Price, Godwin, Raynal, and Priestley during the five and a half years down to May 1797 when its office was ransacked and printing apparatus wrecked by outraged Loyalist militia.[88] Another paper propagating radical republican ideas, from late 1792, was the *Cork Gazette*, edited by Driscol, an ex-Catholic priest who had converted to Anglicanism some years before and become an Anglican curate in Cork but who, from 1792, embraced revolutionary Jacobinism and urged universal male suffrage, annual parliaments, and abolition of property qualifications for parliamentary candidates.[89]

Most Irishmen were far from being republican, but the likes of Tone, Fitzgerald, Russell, Neilson, and Driscol, the radical intellectual vanguard, unhesitatingly adopted a pro-French republican stance. A local movement of ideological subversion aligned with "leading men [in radical thought and conspiracy] in France, England and America," these Irish radicals sought to infuse the United Irishmen with the universal objectives of the international radical tendency. Working in secret within Ireland, they conceived their movement as part of an international Enlightenment brotherhood and project closely linked to France, Dutch anti-Orangism, and the United States,[90] systematically applying the principles of the American and French revolutions in the Irish context. Like Adam Weishaupt (1748–1830), founder of the German Illuminati in the 1770s, Drennan wanted his organization to adopt "much of the secrecy and somewhat of the ceremonial of Freemasonry" as a way of promoting their cause, transforming the present "sand of republicanism into a body" and propagating a strong republican awareness around the country. Not least, he and his group aspired to raise the consciousness of the Catholic population and secure an effective cooperation between Catholics and Protestants opposed to British rule.

Nevertheless, the United Irishmen were divided from the outset. Drennan aspired to foment civil action against the Irish executive, parliament, and gentry, as the Irish had during the American War using publicity and purely legal means, organizing an open campaign rather than secretly organize a violent uprising in alliance with revolutionary France. "Why should we not refuse to pay taxes," urged Drennan in a letter of November 1791, "as well as America? Are we better represented than they were? Or are we more lightly burthened?"[91] However, the view that conspiracy and armed rebellion were unavoidable, later promoted energetically by Tone, Fitzgerald, Neilson, and Driscol, increasingly swayed a segment of United Irishmen, records Gordon, as early as 1792.[92] Money began to be "raised by subscription to arm and embody a number of men in the metropolis"; there was talk of naming them the "national guards" and giving them a "uniform distinguished with green, which was adopted as the national colour."[93] The leaders of the underground were generally ex-Protestants, deists, and atheists and hardly ever Catholics. Burke at this point was perfectly aware that it was not the Catholic population who were driving the subversive tendency destabilizing the country. The main subversion derived from the "strong republican Protestant faction in Ireland" that once persecuted the Catholic majority—Protestant "conspirators and traitors who were acting in direct connection with the enemies of all government and religion" now strove also to seduce Catholics from their proper allegiance.[94]

In January 1793, with the outbreak of war between France and Britain looming, Grattan and the moderate reformers in Ireland's parliament reaffirmed their loyalty to the Crown, and willingness to support Britain against France, further widening the split within Irish reformism between moderates and radicals. The campaign of vilification of Paine unleashed in England over the winter of 1792–93 with mass burnings of effigy and books was followed by a crackdown on printers and booksellers that soon extended also to Ireland. Indictments were issued against publishers issuing Paine's works and other radical literature. When Britain entered the European conflict, in March 1793, the Dublin authorities moved swiftly to suppress the United Irishmen and those, like Fitzgerald, denouncing the war against France as "unjust" and calling for Irish independence. Under suspicion, several students were expelled from Trinity College, Dublin. Driscol was tried for "seditious libel" at Cork assizes in April 1794, fined, and imprisoned. The intensified crackdown compelled radicals unambiguously to become armed conspirators and revolutionaries, marking the beginning of the originally non-confessional Irish underground "republican" resistance.[95] Below the level of the dominant

Anglican gentry class and college curricula, radical ideas in this way emerged as the predominant Enlightenment form in Ireland—the Enlightenment of the underground republican opposition. Paine, now residing in Paris, at this point developed close links, often at the "Irish Coffee House," with several leading Irish subversives particularly, as we have seen, with Fitzgerald.[96] Fitzgerald, Drennan, Tone, and the Emmets interpreted Britain's war against France as a counterrevolution aimed at restoring the French monarchy and aristocracy and helping Prussia, Russia, and Austria "stop the progress of liberty throughout Europe." Their rival strategy, Irish radicals realized, meant seeking French (and Dutch Patriot) revolutionary assistance against England.

Paradoxically, therefore, Catholicism and the Catholic Church had virtually nothing to do with the early rise and ideological origins of the Irish republican movement that in later times was to become solidly "Catholic" socially. At the time, the episcopate and leading Catholic voices in the Irish political arena steadfastly denounced the principles of the American, Dutch, French, and Irish revolutions together, adhering to rigidly conservative positions. "The exclusion of the Catholics from the privileges of the Constitution," declared Theobald McKenna (d. 1808), the foremost Irish Catholic political writer of the 1790s, in his *An essay on Parliamentary Reform* (1793), was a "great grievance" and the source of many other grievances; and "until this be addressed, it is vain to seek for improvement of any kind in Ireland; the emigration to foreign service; the cast of dissipation; the idleness, the inclination to petty insurrections, which a quibbling pedant imputed to our national character, are all occasioned by either the past or present oppressions of this system."[97] Yet, while vividly conscious of Ireland's plight, McKenna, in sharp contrast to Tone, Fitzgerald, and the Emmets, was equally forthright in assailing Paine and Barlow together with their adherents in the United Irishmen movement for their Franco-American republicanism and zeal to demonstrate the "uselessness of sovereigns." He fiercely denounced all lack of submission to religion, monarchy, and the peerage.[98]

The equality and democracy fomented by the American Revolution, held McKenna, were simply not natural or justifiable principles. Men are made by God to live under monarchy and aristocracy. Even "Holland, which was much more adapted for its size, than Ireland for a republic, has subsided [i.e., since 1787] into an aristocracy, or rather a limited monarchy." The Dutch and French examples both amply demonstrated the superiority of British "mixed government," he suggested, unshakably convinced the "oppressions of absolute monarchy, the convulsions of democracy, constitute alike the panegyric of the English constitution." Fellow Irish Catholics he admonished against what he saw as the ruinous social and moral peril embedded in republicanism.

"The truth is," he declared, that the upheaval and "civil war in America" and consequent dissolution of the "connection with Britain, proceeded from the prevalence in the colonies, of that republican spirit, and republican constitution, which many desire, at this day, to introduce in Ireland."[99]

Preparing the Revolution

Irish Catholics were directed by all their bishops and clergy to spurn republicanism, democracy, and the American, Dutch, and French examples. To escape "slavery," countered Tone and the international radical fraternity, Irishmen must fight for their independence. After fleeing via Ireland and reaching Philadelphia, James Thomson Callender (1758–1803), a Scots pamphleteer expelled from Scotland in 1793, published a new edition of his subversive *The Political Progress of Britain* (1792), comprehensively denouncing imperial sway and warmongering, emphasizing that the overly vaunted Glorious Revolution of 1688 had failed to offer "much relief to Ireland. The Irish people continued to groan under the most oppressive and absurd despotism." During the American War, their resistance convinced the English of the "hazard of contending with a brave, an injured and an indignant nation," but, unfortunately, the Irish failed to maintain the pressure. Reviling both the Scottish Union and England's sway over Ireland, Callender predicted an imminent great Irish uprising: "it is to be hoped that a short time will extinguish every vestige of a supremacy, dishonourable and pernicious to both nations."[100] He also predicted a "revolution will take place in Scotland before the lapse of ten years at farthest, and most likely much sooner."[101]

Both the tension and the repression intensified in Ireland during the mid-1790s. With Belfast and Dublin the revolutionary movement's twin headquarters, the United Irishmen succeeded in extending their cells across the country. At the same time, though, the internal split within the United Irishmen movement between Tone, Fitzgerald, Neilson, Driscol, and the more radical faction, on one side, and, on the other, Drennan, Thomas Emmet, and the Catholics preferring a more cautious, limited strategy grew deeper from 1794. Threatened too with arrest for sedition, Tone emigrated with his wife and two children to America in June 1795, gravitating briefly to Princeton.[102] But not unlike other dissidents driven across the Atlantic during the harsh repression of the 1790s in Britain and Ireland, he abhorred the "aristocratic" tone of Washington's administration and the rampant commercialism now suffusing America. The United States struck him as having abandoned the true ideals of their own Revolution. Early in 1796, he changed his mind about settling in New Jersey and recrossed the Atlantic to resume a life of conspiracy in Europe, in Paris.

Indeed, Tone's reaction against the dominant trends in American politics and society in the mid-1790s was so violent that it profoundly shaped the character of his political thought from this point on, his ideas developing into a fully-fledged republicanism, bent on seeking Irish independence from Britain, only after he arrived in France.[103] It was not national independence as such, though, that Tone, Fitzgerald, and the United Irishmen leadership now began to advocate and seek for Ireland but an independence conforming to Paine's "General Revolution" emancipating all mankind. The impoverished Irish peasantry needed to advance materially and in their ideas both together, so that superstition, religious bigotry, and fanaticism would be overcome and the door opened to a better life for them—and a new brotherhood of man. It would be the future "interest as well as the duty of national government," affirmed Tone, "to redress their grievances and enlighten their minds."[104] In Paris, Tone associated with James Monroe, an American envoy who was far from sharing the Washington administration's antipathy to French revolutionaries. Most Americans, Monroe reassured European republicans, had not forgotten their own revolutionary ideals. Besides extricating Paine from prison, and assisting Barlow, Monroe had in January 1795 secured the release of Lafayette's wife, Adrienne; he opposed what he deemed the pernicious influence of Jay's commercial treaty with Britain. Monroe's promoting American revolutionary principles as he understood them, however, sufficiently displeased Washington and Hamilton to get him soon recalled to America.[105]

Well-read, eloquent, and competent in French, an avowed intellectual despising merchants (whom he thought made extremely poor revolutionaries), Tone produced several "democratic publications" preparing the Irish for the pending irruption of the revolutionary fervor from Europe, explaining that the French were coming to "emancipate, not to conquer your country."[106] Among these was *An Address to the People of Ireland*, clandestinely printed at Belfast in 1796. "Six hundred years of oppression and slavery have passed in melancholy succession over our fathers' heads and our own," lamented Tone, during which "we have been visited by every evil, which tyranny could devise and cruelty execute. . . . Nothing but the pressure of an incumbent force has prevented the indignant spirit of Ireland, from bursting forth long since, and leveling with the dust the edifice of her oppression."[107] Yet no significant resistance had occurred prior to 1776. It was the American Revolution that first awakened the Irish to the dismal plight in which they languished. Only a comparable "revolution" could secure for Ireland genuine legislative independence,[108] improve life for the peasant tenant farmers, dissolve the "unnatural union between church and state, which has degraded religion into an engine of policy," and abolish "tithes, the pest of agriculture" (and mainstay of the Anglican Church of Ireland). Ireland's parliament and the "prostitutes who compose it know this and tremble." To extirpate bigotry and intolerance Ireland had to create conditions in which "no sect shall have a right to govern their fellow-citizens" and "each sect will maintain their own clergy, and no citizen shall be disenfranchised for worshipping God according to his conscience."[109]

"The new doctrine" of liberty and equality would surely displace the old ways of thinking and believing. Since the outbreak of the French Revolution, the term "Enlightenment," already central in Irish political and general debate, had grown more and more divisive.[110] That a new order of things was "commencing in Europe," Tone, like Paine, Jebb, Macaulay, Price, and Fitzgerald, trusted with a fervor bordering on millenarian expectation. "As the Mosaic law subverted idolatry, as Christianity subverted the Jewish dispensation, as the Reformation subverted Popery, so, I am firmly convinced, the doctrine of republicanism will finally subvert that of monarchy, and establish a system of just and rational liberty, on the ruins of the thrones of the despots of Europe."[111] "Look, I beseech you," he urged the Irish, "to America!" "See the improvement in her condition since she so nobly asserted her independence, on a provocation, which set beside your grievances, is not even worthy to be named."[112] Plotting with the French Directoire in Paris, Tone disclosed little about his subversive strategy to secure Ireland's independence with French and Dutch assistance. Publicly, he expressed the hope that major violence would be averted and Irish resolve and readiness to use force suffice to extract the major concessions needed. If England sees "all ranks and descriptions of Irishmen united and determined, she will balance, after the experience of America and France, before she will engage in a third crusade against the liberties of an entire nation."[113] But this proved wishful thinking.

In December 1796, Tone sailed as the Irish leader on the ill-fated French fleet, crowded with troops, that sailed for Ireland from Brest under the able and irascible but unfortunate General Lazare Hoche (1768–97), a close friend of Tone's and ardent convert to the cause of Irish republicanism.[114] Franco-Dutch intervention in Ireland, as urged by Tone and Fitzgerald, was indeed a favorite project of Hoche's; but his attempt to land at Bantry Bay and invade Ireland was disrupted by storms.[115] Following this setback, Tone returned to Paris, then migrated, spending most of 1797 in Holland and Germany. He was delighted with Amsterdam: "it is the first city in the world to walk in, and in that respect I prefer it infinitely to either London or Paris." "In point of cleanliness, to speak the truth, we [i.e., the Irish] are most terribly behind the Dutch." Tone admired what the democratic revolutionary movement had achieved there since 1780 and especially since recovering control with French help in 1795. If the renewed Dutch democratic movement's momentum since 1794–95 was owing to the French, it was the American Revolution that had originally roused the people and inspired the ferment that produced the initial Dutch democratic agitation of 1780–87. He delighted in the Dutch democrats' opposition to any "church establishment" and plans to oblige churchgoers to pay the clergy themselves, and in the fierce antipathy to lawyers of his friend Pieter Leonard van de Kasteele (1748–1810), the town secretary of Haarlem.[116] Among the Batavian Revolution's ablest leaders, Van de Kasteele urged the post-1795 Dutch National Convention to exclude all clergy and lawyers from the assembly, rightly deeming these responsible for the fiasco of the failed Dutch 1796 constitution. He viewed the clergy as enemies and the lawyers as "intriguers and caballers, and, from being more in the habit of public speaking and of confounding right and wrong," being "often able to confute and silence abler and honester men than themselves. I could not help laughing internally at this sketch," commented Tone: "I find a lawyer a lawyer all over the world. The most scandalously corrupt and unprincipled body, politically speaking, that I ever knew, is the Irish bar. I was a black sheep in their body, and I bless God that I am well rid of them. Rot them!"[117]

No nationalist, but a typical radical enlightener, Tone hugely despised businessmen, clergy, aristocracy, and lawyers. But neither did he hold the Irish people in general, especially the less literate, in particularly high esteem, despite intense sympathy for their predicament. What chiefly disquieted him while lounging, jotting notes from the *Gazette de Leyde* in Amsterdam coffeehouses, were the indications that despite all the repression and resentment, and appeals to emulate America, his countrymen mostly still ventilated discontent in a conventional, purely local manner, confined to petty, narrow schemes like demolishing enclosure fences and harassing tithe collectors and eviction agents. Ordinary Irishmen seemed insufficiently capable of taking a wider view, transcending centuries-old petty religious feuding, or thinking in terms of a full-scale democratic and secular revolution. What depressed Wolfe Tone was that Irishmen had broadly failed to become "enlightened." "I do not at all believe that the [Irish] people are prepared for a serious and general insurrection," Tone gloomily remarked privately in June 1797, "and in short (why should I conceal the fact?) I do not believe they have the courage. It is not fear of the Army, but fear of the law and long habits of slavery that keep them down." He viewed his countrymen as "a people easily roused and easily appeased." In general, he was much more emphatic about overthrowing Anglo-Irish aristocratic dominance of Ireland than raising the peasantry from their poverty and degradation.[118] His hopes he placed increasingly in Franco-Dutch collaboration. "If either the Dutch or the French can effectuate a landing," he noted in August, "I do not believe the present submission of the [Irish] people will prevent their doing what is right, and if no landing can be effectuated, no party remains for the people to adopt but submission or flight."[119] Tone was far from optimistic about the Irish revolutionary underground's capabilities (whatever he assured the Directoire and the Dutch leadership).

During the spring and summer of 1797, the French prepared another fleet at Brest, hoping to draw part of the British fleet westward, opening the way for a double invasion attempt. The Dutch revolutionaries meanwhile assembled a formidable fleet of twenty-five warships, twenty-seven transports, and fourteen thousand troops, intended for a landing in Ireland in conjunction with the French and Irish. The French and Dutch regimes proceeded together in the name of revolutionary solidarity and to help the Irish but, more especially, to weaken British maritime and colonial power in their own interest. The Dutch assembly's secret committee planning their Irish expedition concerted with Tone, other Irish leaders, and Hoche. When a member of The Hague committee remarked that "no country in Europe had so crying a necessity for a revolution" as Ireland, to judge from the "extreme misery" of the people, Tone was gratified: the Batavian revolutionaries' belief in the "wretched state of our peasantry and determination, if possible, to amend it" gave the Irish revolutionary leadership a unique opportunity to collude against oppression with Holland and France together.[120] Tone would remain with the Dutch commanders on their flagship, the seventy-four-gun *Vrijheid*, invading from the east.

What Burke termed the "Jacobinization" of Ireland under the auspices of the French and Dutch gained momentum, advancing, he believed, owing to a peculiarly noxious blend of French ambition, British mismanagement, and Irish bigotry with the result that by the late 1790s a major explosion was not just a possibility but a virtual certainty; and in this conviction he was far from alone.[121] The British strove to counter the rising tide of subversion with a campaign of intensified armed repression in Dublin and especially northern Ireland known as "the dragooning of Ulster." The crackdown, which even Burke found obnoxious, undoubtedly weakened and disoriented the clandestine revolutionary leadership inside the country. Neilson's paper and Driscol's *Cork Gazette* were forced to shut down. According to two Irish rebel leaders, Alexander Lowry and John Tenet, who joined Tone on the Dutch flagship in August 1797, valuable opportunities were lost and "there seems to have been a great want of spirit in the leaders in Dublin."[122] The protracted stand-off in the North Sea and Atlantic continued for months. Unfortunately for Tone's plans, on 11 October 1797, the British cornered the Dutch fleet (when Tone was on land) off Camperdown (Kamperduin) and, after a great deal of firing with heavy loss on both sides, captured the *Vrijheid* and ten other vessels, a disaster for the Dutch and boost for Britain that effectively ended prospects for a joint invasion.[123]

The invasion scheme of 1797 was in fact the last time the Dutch ever attempted to use naval and military power to defend their trade and empire against their overweening neighbor. Despite this reverse, the dual threat of invasion and revolution in Ireland lingered and the situation continued exerting an unsettling effect in Britain. In northwest England fears were frequently voiced among Loyalists that the United Irishmen might seduce or delude elements of the working population also in Lancashire into embracing radicalism and democratic ideas.[124] During the spring of 1798, under instructions from the Directoire, fleets intended to weaken Britain by liberating Ireland were again prepared in the French Channel ports, this time supervised by then still firmly republican General Bonaparte. In America, the press divided with Federalist organs backing Britain "railing against the Irish for accepting aid from the French," and democratic papers supporting Irish sedition denouncing—as the Jeffersonian Philadelphia *Aurora* put it—America's "panders of corruption and monarchy."[125]

Irish Catastrophe (1798–1803)

By early 1798, the Irish crisis was more acute than ever. Britain responded by proclaiming martial law. Backed by armies of spies, the Dublin government strove to nip the unrest in the bud with vigorous military sweeps to disarm rural opposition and further arrests among the underground leadership and another crackdown on "French principles" at Trinity College. On 12 March the authorities succeeded in arresting most of the conspiracy's leadership in Ireland, including Thomas Emmet and William James MacNeven, incarcerating them in the new, specially designed Kilmainham prison and other Dublin jails.[126] When the insurgency finally broke out on 30 March 1798, it was almost leaderless. Through late March, April, and May armed rebellion spread fitfully over parts of the country. Informed of his whereabouts, British officers, on 19 May, surprised Fitzgerald—the last remaining chief planner and de facto head of operations south of Ulster,[127] recovering from fever in a central Dublin hiding place. Wounded in the ensuing affray, he was incarcerated in Dublin castle where, his wound left untreated, he died delirious from blood poisoning in June.

By June 1798 scattered resistance had developed into a more general rising in villages west and south of Dublin, insurrection spreading within days to most of southeast Ireland. Columns of peasants appeared, rampaging and pillaging in and around Wexford, Kildare, and Wicklow, proclaiming "the Irish Republic." Wexford became the center of this short-lived "republic," which had a "senate," an army, a printer to the "Wexford Republic," and a people's government whose leaders addressed each other as "citizen."[128] It also had a miniscule navy commanded by John Howlin, former captain of a privateer in the American War of Independence. Despite the Wexford "republic's" ragged army being repulsed with heavy loss on 5 June, when assaulting New Ross, a setback barring the rebels from Waterford County, the insurrection subsequently also spread to Ulster. Counties Antrim and Down and the whole eastern side of Ulster flared into open revolt. As sedition and repression spread, the rebel bands became increasingly disorganized, vicious, and blatantly sectarian. Green cockades and slogans proclaiming "liberty and equality" were everywhere in evidence. Despite their common hatred of French republicanism, some Catholic and Presbyterian clergy participated. But amid the turmoil, republican ideals and ideology were quickly forgotten and bigotry took over. Catholics and Protestants began slaughtering each other indiscriminately and with this the veritable Irish Enlightenment as a joint Protestant-Catholic project collapsed.[129] The commander of the short-lived "republic of Ulster," Henry Joy McCracken (1767–98), vainly strove to establish some semblance of order. Leader of the Belfast United Irishmen's lodge, son of a Belfast shipowner of Presbyterian background, McCracken, like Tone, was a revolutionary idealist urging toleration, Protestant-Catholic union, liberty, equality, and Enlightenment values.[130] Horrified, as were many United Irishmen by the savagery of the sectarian killing disfiguring the rebellion,[131] he grew demoralized. His army of 4,000 was defeated with heavy loss, on 7 June, in the battle for Antrim town.

By late June the rebellion was crushed north and south. Suspected ringleaders were hanged, thousands of cottages were torched, innumerable families left homeless and penniless, and at least thirty Catholic chapels decimated. Wexford was pacified and the last vestiges of the fleeting green cockade republic extinguished. The "deep-laid conspiracy to revolutionize Ireland on French principles" had failed, commented Britain's new military commander in Ireland since the previous June, Lord Charles Cornwallis (1738–1805). The presence of this Eton and Cambridge nobleman who had humiliatingly surrendered Britain's army in Virginia in 1781 and was now lord lieutenant and commander-in-chief in Ireland inevitably provoked mocking resonance

The Irish rebellion: the British caricaturist James Gillray (1756–1815) represents the
Irish Revolution of 1798 as inspired by French revolutionary influence. Photo credit:
Eileen Tweedy / The Art Archive at Art Resource, NY.

in America. "If Washington, Rochambeau and Lafayette took Cornwallis at
Yorktown," commented Bache's *Aurora*, "why may not an Irish general and
one or two French generals take Cornwallis in Dublin?" Were the Irish more
blameworthy for desiring representative government, demanded the democratic press, "than we were"—or the French more blameworthy for assisting
Irish than helping American revolutionaries?[132]

The uprising, seemingly, had ended in total defeat. On 23 August, though,
at Killala, in County Sligo, a remote outpost in northwestern Ireland, a diminutive French army of 1,099 men from La Rochelle landed, commanded by an
able subordinate of Hoche's, General Jean Joseph Humbert (1767–1823), a
hard-core republican later (in 1803) dismissed from the French army for opposing Napoleon's dictatorship. Accompanied by Tone's brother, Matthew
(dressed in French uniform), and bringing additional weapons, powder, and
stocks of revolutionary pamphlets proclaiming liberty, union, and the "Irish
Republic," Humbert's force was meant to be followed by another 4,000 men
from Brest, including Tone himself. The French unfurled green banners in-
scribed (following Tone's advice to the Directoire) "Erin Go Bragh," Gaelic

for "Ireland forever." Humbert was shocked and dismayed by the ignorance and sectarianism of the local population. Hardly anyone, he discovered, had the slightest idea what republicanism was; nearly all seethed with religious bigotry.[133] To the local Anglican clergy's surprise, the French "abstained from the plunder of houses and preserved a very laudable discipline."[134] What shocked and dismayed Ireland's Anglican, Presbyterian, and Catholic clergy were Humbert's democratic republican revolutionary principles and undisguised irreligion.

Nevertheless, when Humbert's small French column succeeded on 27 August in driving the British from Castlebar, capital of County Mayo and a key strategic point in the northwest, and he proclaimed the "Republic of Connacht" with its capital in Castlebar around 4,000 Irish volunteers flocked to his banner from all across the west and the central Ireland "midlands."[135] Although his landing came too late and on too small a scale to change the course of the main revolt, Humbert's feats bore out Tone's assurances that with revolutionary help the Irish people would rise en masse. With more coordination, troops, and earlier and larger landings, the uprising of 1798 might conceivably have had a much vaster impact, though short of the Franco-Dutch parity with the British at sea, of which there was scant prospect, it was hard to see how Ireland's subjection could have been more than temporarily cast off. Still, Humbert's small invasion force, humiliatingly for Cornwallis, was not finally trapped and beaten until the battle of Ballinamuck on 8 September. The French were made prisoners of war; the local Catholic Irish were treated with considerable brutality. Four hundred Irish volunteers were officially hanged for "treason," among them Tone's brother and Humbert's aide-de-camp, Bartholomew Teeling (1774–98), a Catholic member of the United Irishmen and former deputy of Fitzgerald, son of a Lisburn linen merchant.[136] The wider Mayo peasant insurgency ended in late September, with the rebel defeat at Killala.

The culminating setback for the 1798 Irish Revolution occurred on 12 October when a British fleet intercepted the main Brest naval force and, after a ten-hour running battle, captured most of it, including 2,500 French troops and the Irish commander, General "Smith," alias Wolfe Tone. Brought to Dublin Castle in irons to face trial, he was certain to meet the same fate as his brother. He had planned the rising from "principle and the fullest conviction of its rectitude," he declared, speaking from the dock, "splendidly dressed in French uniform," reported the Philadelphia *Aurora* the following January.[137] His purpose was to raise the Irish to the "rank of citizens" and secure Ireland's independence. He had striven for the people's happiness following the "path chalked out by Washington in America." His request to die by firing squad denied, he cheated his executioners, according to the accounts reaching Philadelphia, by "cutting his own throat" in his cell.[138]

Its leaders dead or in irons, the insurgency withered, though sporadic unrest continued until well into 1799, as did its provoking fierce chauvinistic and xenophobic "Church and King loyalism" in England.[139] Yet, despite the defeats and intensified repression, there was a sense in which the Irish Revolution lived on, its ties to the American revolutionary legacy strengthened and perpetuated. In July 1798, MacNeven, Thomas Emmet, and Arthur O'Connor, representing the "state prisoners" in the Dublin jails, signed an agreement in Dublin Castle whereby they and the remaining prisoners acknowledged their "treason" and supplied information to ministers in return for their lives on the basis of permanent exile. The government's goal was to display these men as "penitent traitors," as Prime Minister Pitt called them, using signed admissions of guilt to tar French "principles" as unmitigated deceit and betrayal, liquidating high-level Irish political subversion with a propaganda victory vindicating the regime in the eyes of its many domestic critics and affording an opportunity to permanently remove a large batch of veteran Irish conspirators from the scene.

British ministers wanted to ship the prisoners to America. A wave of exiled Irish radicals did cross the Atlantic in 1798–99, including Driscol and John Daly Burk (c. 1776–1808), one of the students expelled from Trinity College in 1793–94, who became editor of the Boston *Polar Star*, a paper in which the "British were well peppered."[140] But the Dublin state prisoners as such did not, as yet, owing to the "remonstrance of the American minister" in London, following what the Philadelphia *Aurora* called a "first direct exercise of the powers given to the President by the unconstitutional, inhuman Turkish law respecting aliens [i.e., under the 1798 Aliens' Act]."[141] The Irish "state prisoners" were told America's president would not allow them to "go to any part of the United States as had been proposed." Twenty Irish revolutionary leaders, including Emmet and MacNeven, were confined instead at Fort George in Scotland. Following the Peace of Amiens (1802), though, after the dismantling of the Aliens' Act under Jefferson's auspices, Emmet, MacNeven, and several other prominent subversives were deported from Scotland to Hamburg, from where they finally crossed the Atlantic with their families, joining the Irish and Scottish émigré radicals in New York, Boston, Philadelphia, and Canada. Commencing new careers, in several cases as journalists, teachers, or agitators, they nurtured the Irish Revolution's democratic and republican ideals in their new milieu. Irish revolutionary rumblings also reached Australia where, on 29 December 1801, a bloody mutiny occurred among Irish prisoners on a convict ship, the *Hercules*, entering Botany Bay. Eighteen United Irishmen died from wounds received in the ensuing bitter affray.

The ideological legacy of the "Irish Revolution" lingered in the United States and Australia, and helped perpetuate memories of the Revolution within Ireland itself. So did the demise of one of the most impassioned of the group, Robert Emmet (1778–1803), converted to the revolutionary cause by his older brother and by Tone at only fifteen.[142] A member of a revolutionary cell at Trinity College, Dublin expelled when the cell was suppressed in April 1798, a month after his brother's arrest,[143] Emmet subsequently devoted himself to rebuilding the United Irishmen's shattered secret organization by creating a new underground centralized "Directory" that was already functioning in 1799. In 1801, he visited France in a fresh effort to persuade Napoleon to organize landings in Ireland. The British government, meanwhile, kept up the repression in Ireland but also sought a more stable political solution. The Act of Union, proclaiming the "United Kingdom of Great Britain and Ireland," introducing elements of concession as well as institutionalized repression, was brought in by the London Parliament to more tightly embed Ireland in the empire in January 1801.[144]

With Thomas Russell and another Ulster Presbyterian prominent in the organization, James Hope (1764–1847), Emmet established secret arms depots for their planned Dublin insurrection. Manifestos were prepared promising confiscation and redistribution of the lands of the Anglican Church, English aristocrats, and counterrevolutionaries to the people.[145] The "Emmet rising," intending to seize strategic points and occupy Dublin Castle in the hope of triggering a wider rebellion, erupted amid diffusion of thousands of copies of its revolutionary proclamation, after five years of conspiracy, on 23 July 1803, but lasted only a few hours. The rebellion was swiftly crushed with the loss of twenty soldiers and fifty rebels killed; most of the insurrection's stock of its manifesto was seized and destroyed. The leaders escaped but in Emmet's and Russell's cases not for long.[146] Over the next months, several thousand more United Irishmen were rounded up and imprisoned, and around forty, including Russell, executed.

Emmet was brought to Kilmainham prison. Condemned as a "traitor" and "emissary of France" at the end of his trial, on 19 September, he delivered a famous reply. Explaining the motives that led him to seek French help, in the hope of "delivering my country from the yoke of a foreign and unrelenting tyranny," his speech posthumously rendered him one of the most famous of all United Irishmen. "I wished to procure for my country the guarantee which Washington procured for America.—To procure an aid [from France] which, for its example would be as important as its valour; disciplined, gallant, pregnant with science and experience, that of allies who would perceive the good, and polish the rough points of our character."[147] The day after his trial for treason, he was publicly hanged in Thomas Street, Dublin, where in July 1803 the insurrectionary violence had begun. After the hanging, his head was publicly cut from his corpse as a "traitor."

The worst of the Irish tragedy, Gordon understood, was that by the 1790s, during the lead-up to the massive uprising of 1798, the United Irishmen's aspiration to establish an independent Irish republic on democratic principles in emulation of the United States, France, and post-1795 Holland was simply not embraced or even understood by the rebel masses. Irish ideologues and propagandists used the democratic and egalitarian Enlightenment concepts that everywhere resounded to mobilize the illiterate and barely literate against those upholding the harsh existing order but could not mobilize Enlightenment ideas extensively and powerfully enough to steer the agitation effectively or mitigate the vast disruption, violence, fanaticism, and bloodshed that ensued.

CHAPTER 13

America's "Conservative Turn": The Emerging "Party System" in the 1790s

Two Opposed Revolutionary Traditions

Ideological strife in the United States reached a peak of ferocity and apparent deadlock in the 1790s. Historians have often remarked that the 1790s was a crucially formative decade in American politics in terms of widening participation and press involvement, and consequent growing polarization into warring proto-parties: "Federalists" supporting Washington, Adams, Hamilton, and Morris, and the "anti-Federalists," or "republicans," headed by Jefferson, Madison, and Monroe. During the early 1790s, supporters of Jefferson in American politics began styling themselves "true republicans" and their Federalist opponents adhering to the factions of Adams and Hamilton "anti-republicans." Even more resonant of the depth of the rift between America's proto-parties, and the significance of the intensifying campaigns to mobilize supporters in state elections, was the growing use of the labels "democrat" and "democracy" as positive terms by one side in the mounting political conflict, from late 1792 onward, and denunciation of "democracy" and "democrats" and as insidious French Jacobin infiltration by their opponents.[1]

Behind such labels hovered a hint of social division. Federalists, suggested Jefferson, were the party of the established old gentry and office-seekers, merchants, and Tories, "true republicans" that of the people—farmers, laborers, and artisans.[2] Sometimes geography was a factor: in Vermont the hilly western part of the state cherished the libertarian traditions of Allen and the Green Mountain Boys; eastern Vermont preferred religion and New Hampshire–style conservatism. But the socioeconomic and geographical divides were always extremely fluid and shifting. No doubt personal self-interest regularly pervaded the choices politicians made as well as the growing bifurcation of the electorate more broadly. But neither social origin and background nor current interests decisively shaped the characteristic rhetoric and terminology used by the vying sets of rival leaders, and while "interest" often figured in the vehement reproaches and accusations each side made about the other, thirst for money and power, however ubiquitous, always needed to be dressed in political programs and justifications and always had to compromise with those striving for higher ideals. All kinds of factors helped determine how any given individual responded intellectually and emotionally to the transatlantic revolutionary drama. Jefferson and Madison were Virginia "aristocrats" seeking to widen the American Revolution's republican and democratizing tendencies who publicly celebrated visiting spokesmen for the radical tendency from Europe and Ibero-America. Alexander Hamilton, secretary of the treasury (1789–95), himself of humble origins, shunned foreign revolutionaries like Volney and Démeunier visiting America, preferring the company of Talleyrand, the corrupt "bishop," aristocrat, and, later, betrayer of both Napoleon and Louis XVIII during his two years in America (1794–96), engrossed in land speculation as doyen of the exiled and fast-growing Philadelphia French aristocratic (and Caribbean landowner) clique.

For some, the theoretical issues involved were of deep, abiding, personal significance. During 1790 and early 1791, James Madison, among the most resolute of Founding Fathers in assailing "antiquated bigotry," ecclesiastical authority, and church intrusion into politics, shifted to an unambiguously anti-Federalist stance following his personal rupture with two leading conservatives in Washington's cabinet, Hamilton and John Jay, the United States Chief Justice (1789–95).[3] Setting aside Locke and Montesquieu, and veering away from Hamilton and closer to Jefferson while deepening his theory of republicanism,[4] he composed his "Notes on Government" rejecting Federalist plans to steer the American Revolution toward the British system and, as he saw it, subvert the authentic republican framework he and his ally, Jefferson, aimed to build. He especially disliked Hamilton's plans to consolidate the states' debts into a national debt by issuing new securities that could be readily bought and sold, further rewarding wealthy investors and speculators who had bought up state certificates, thereby compounding, by raising more taxation to fund the new national obligation, losses suffered earlier by farmers and widows who had parted with their bonds at a fraction of face value.[5] But, for Madison, such bread-and-butter specifics needed to be viewed within the broad ideological framework of democratizing republicanism versus aristocratic "mixed government." Firmly repudiating classical republicanism and Locke's theory of contract between people and sovereign, Madison recommended a representative democratic republicanism in which the key component was broad representation and the "sovereignty" of public opinion. The need for "balance" and division of powers in constitutions stipulated by Adams struck him as profoundly erroneous theoretically but typical of Adams's, Hamilton's, and Morris's "aristocratic" bias—and efforts to subvert equality and republicanism. Embracing the "perfect equality of mankind" and aspiring to treat the interests of all equally, he viewed his Federalist opponents' plans and proceedings, and their Lockean (and Montesquieuian) leanings, as directly contradicting the American Revolution's authentic spirit and principles. The American Republic, he believed, needed to eradicate every lingering vestige of monarchy, aristocracy, and unequal representation.[6] During 1790–91, as he broke with Hamilton, Adams, and Jay, he aligned and conferred more and more with Jefferson.

Given the depth of the ideological split, it is hardly surprising that high points in the escalating political struggle often revolved around particularly sensitive texts and intellectual controversies. Tom Paine's *Rights of Man*, having provoked uproar in Britain and Ireland in the summer of 1791, appeared in a Boston edition reinforced with a preface by Jefferson, now secretary of state, noting the "political heresies that have sprung up" in America while he had been away as ambassador in France. An obvious public rebuke to Vice President Adams and his allies, this sally was "read with general applause," according to Jefferson. Inevitably, Jefferson's robustly pro-Paine stance provoked an angry response from opponents such as Hamilton and Adams. John Quincy Adams felt especially stung; but the clash also confirmed that during the early 1790s most newspaper-reading Americans felt scant sympathy for core Federalist ideas and remained sympathetic to Paine, the French Revolution, and democratic values. Adams's polemics against Paine, Madison reported from New York, only increased the vice president's mounting unpopularity, drawing "attention to his obnoxious principles, more than everything he has published."[7] In the ensuing lively newspaper exchange, Jefferson was gratified to see, most of the public and press unequivocally sided with him. "There are high names here in favor of this [aristocratic] doctrine," but these publications, he assured Short, in Paris, "have drawn forth pretty general expressions of the public sentiment on this subject, and I thank God to find they are, to a man, firm as a rock in their republicanism."[8]

To counter the *Gazette of the United States* edited by John Fenno (1751–98), a paper supporting almost everything Hamilton proposed, Madison and

Jefferson, early in 1791, engaged a committed republican and foe of bankers, the New Yorker Philip Freneau (1752–1832), to edit the first explicitly anti-Federalist paper, the *National Gazette*. A counterweight to Hamilton and Morris, Freneau's paper also became a vehicle for disseminating reports from the *Leiden Gazette* likely to provide "a juster view of the affairs of Europe," and especially the French Revolution, than stemmed from the usual source— the virulently anti-French British press.[9] Son of a Huguenot wine merchant, an accomplished poet, veteran of the Revolutionary War, zealot for the Revolution, and foe of both landed and business "aristocracy," Freneau liked to publish extracts from Paine, Condorcet, and Barlow. Reviling the rising power of the pulpit, he later defended Paine's irreligious *The Age of Reason* (1794–95), which, in contrast to the *Rights of Man* three years earlier, was deluged in hostile criticism;[10] likewise, he assisted Elihu Palmer in finding rooms to deliver his freethinking talks in New York. In an article of May 1797 explaining the "leading principles of government, on the reformed system of Democracy," Freneau specified the core of the for now common American and French republican ideology as press freedom, "frequent and uncorrupted elections," absence of "hereditary dignities," full freedom of conscience without state "establishment of any religious sect or sects," "rotation of men in office at stated periods (and those as short as conveniently may be)," and, finally, vigilance to avert liberty's overthrow via the emergence of an Oliver Cromwell (or Robespierre) figure.[11]

During the fraught 1790s, the French Revolution was the only foreign issue regularly embedded in American domestic politics and featuring in American newspapers that the public generally could be said to take a lively interest in, even in the backcountry on the farms of Kentucky and Tennessee. No other single controversy injected as much enthusiasm or rancor, or reflected the range of ideological divergence infusing American politics at this formative stage, so clearly. During the early 1790s, it remained usual among Americans generally, and not just avowed democrats, to recognize a much wider gulf between the British and American models and constitutions than between the American and French republics. The growing rift between the rival competing political coteries in America at first reinforced the tendency of American opinion generally to be pro-French and pro-Revolution with just a small privileged fringe antithetical and antagonistic to the Revolution.

America's disciples of Burke and Adam Smith, however, though an unrepresentative fringe during 1789–93, were both powerful and persistent. To Morris, a "high-flying Monarchy-man" and "aristocrat to his finger-tips," according to Jefferson, supremacy of the "aristocracy" generally, particularly his own clique, counted for more than any constitution and any suggestion the American Revolution should be a universal role model. Morris held (following Montesquieu) that every country requires a constitution adjusted to its own specific circumstances. No aspect of the American Constitution could in principle be said to possess a broad validity for other nations or for all mankind. From the moment Morris replaced Short as American envoy in Paris, early in 1792, he displayed a marked antipathy to the Revolution and especially Parisian street demonstrations, claiming it was "impossible for such a mob to govern this country." Reversing Jefferson's earlier role, Morris labored indefatigably, on both sides of the Atlantic, to defeat the Jefferson-Madison principle that the large "representative republic" built on popular sovereignty and equality is universally, for all peoples, the best form of government. In Paris, allied to Malouet and the monarchist moderates, he pressured Lafayette (whom he considered wavering and incompetent) and the emasculated French court while it survived (until August 1792), trying to prod the Revolution into a more conservative "British" course. Lafayette desired two French chambers on the American model but with no division into orders and no social distinctions. An "American Constitution will not do in this country," retorted Morris; two such chambers "would not answer where there is an hereditary executive." Stressing the "necessity of restoring the nobility" to primacy in the theory and practice of the new French constitution, Morris judged England's constitution based on "moderation, balance and experience," and on its own particular aristocracy not "philosophy," the right solution for France, as ultimately for America.[12]

That some in government circles had a "design of breaking our connection with France" became obvious to close observers of the American political scene as early as January 1791. "Should we differ with France," noted the avowedly republican Pennsylvania senator William Maclay,[13] "we are thrown inevitably into the hands of Britain, and should France give any occasion, we have thousands and tens of thousands of anti-Revolutionists ready to blow the coals of contention."[14] From April 1791 onward, Jefferson and Hamilton, though still serving under Washington in the same administration but now outright ideological as well as political adversaries, clashed continually. Hamilton had always venerated Locke and "moderate" Enlightenment, and insisted on the primacy of "experience," scorning "mere speculatists" and making no secret of his disdain for the "reveries of your [French] philosophic politicians," as he admonished Lafayette in October 1789.[15] With fellow "anti-Revolutionists" Morris, Jay, and Adams, Hamilton deliberately fomented antipathy to French revolutionary values among Washington's governing inner circle, creating a situation that, by early 1791, occasioned some decidedly odd international dissonances.

Jefferson was astounded by Washington's reluctance to congratulate Louis XVI on the finalization of the 1791 French constitution by which he and Lafayette set great store. Jefferson was convinced this constitution would assist the progress of liberty in Europe *and* the Americas, by entrenching republican and egalitarian values at the heart of government and thwarting the French center-conservative Malouet-Maury bloc favored by Morris. The great failing of the 1791 constitution for "moderates" and centrists was that it was obviously only cosmetically monarchist, being in reality anti-aristocratic, virtually republican, and thoroughly opposed to Locke, Montesquieu, and "mixed government." It was a construct Morris did everything possible to sway both Washington *and* Louis's advisors against—precisely because he and Hamilton judged it likely to bolster the democratizing tendency in America as well as France.[16] The president delayed until March 1792 before belatedly dispatching perfunctory "congratulations."

In March 1792, an alarmed Lafayette wrote warning Washington against Morris's "aristocratic and indeed counter-revolutionary principles." Morris's views were highly unwelcome to all anti-monarchical and anti-privilege French revolutionaries, that is, everyone in the French Revolution venerating the American example and Constitution: "I cannot help wishing that American and French principles were lodged in the heart, and on the lips, of the American ambassador in France," as when Jefferson was America's representative.[17] But Lafayette could no more check Morris's influence as America's "minister plenipotentiary" in France than resist Hamilton's growing hold over the president, which, from 1792, meant abandoning the close relationship with France kept up since 1776 under Franklin's, Jefferson's, and Short's management.[18] "While you are exterminating the monster aristocracy, and pulling out the teeth and fangs of its associate monarchy" in France, Jefferson advised Lafayette on 16 June 1792, a "sect has shown itself among us, who declare they espoused our new constitution, not as a good and sufficient thing itself, but only as a step to an English constitution, the only thing good and sufficient in itself, in their eye. It is happy for us that these are preachers without followers, and that our people are firm and constant in their republican purity. You will wonder to be told that it is from the Eastward chiefly that these champions for a king, lords and commons come. They get some important associates from New York, and are puffed off by a tribe of Agioteurs [stocks and share dealers] which have been hatched in a bed of corruption made up after the model of their beloved England." These "stock jobbers" and "king-jobbers," suspected Jefferson, were actively propagating anti-revolutionary views in the Federal legislature and trying to sway the public.[19]

By the time Jefferson penned these lines, Lafayette, as it happened, had broken with Brissot and Condorcet and aligned with a newly dominant centrist constitutional monarchist faction headed by Barnave and the brothers De Lameth, who precariously directed the revolutionary regime during 1791 and early 1792. Increasingly, this faction's ideal was in fact constitutional monarchy and "mixed government" with a limited suffrage, albeit less on the British model (where the suffrage was narrower, the monarchical element stronger, and the principle of aristocracy more dominant) than a modified, liberalized "mixed government" model like that favored by Jefferson's archrival, John Adams, whose ideas appealed to their moderate Jacobin breakaway bloc known as the Feuillants. With the French democratic republicans temporarily marginalized, during late 1791 and early 1792, Feuillant revolutionary France aligned with the American Republic as conceived by Adams and the Federalists rather than either British parliamentary monarchy or Jefferson-Madison republicanism.

Feuillant "aristocratism" steadfastly opposed the democratic tendency simultaneously in the French *and* American revolutions. In addition, undisguised Feuillant collusion with the French Caribbean slave owners defending black slavery prompted Brissot and Condorcet to accuse them of conspiring with the white planters *and* America's Federalists to smuggle the English model of government into both France *and* the United States as a way of preserving the primacy of property and slavery. Feuillants and Federalists, it seemed to the French democratic republicans, shared a common transatlantic strategy to block democracy, salvage "aristocracy," patronize the white French colonial local assemblies, and prolong black servitude.[20] From August 1792 until June 1793, Brissot headed not the "center" and moderates, as has mistakenly been claimed,[21] but the radical democratic republican bloc during their brief ascendancy within the French Revolution. News of the French monarchy's formal abolition following the mass uprising of 10 August 1792 reached America in December that year and, predictably, was joyously applauded by most, indeed, noted Jefferson, by the vast majority of Americans who welcomed their sister republic with open arms.[22]

Until the later 1790s, it was almost exclusively the Federalist governing elite that articulated a deep-seated blanket antipathy to the French Revolution, its republican, democratic principles, and what Hamilton called its "disorganizing" tendency.[23] Most Americans—even for a time after Robespierre's downfall (Thermidor) in July 1794—viewed the late eighteenth-century Atlantic world's two premier revolutions as essentially a joint enterprise with broadly identical aims: to liberate and ameliorate humanity on a democratizing basis.

Accordingly, until 1796–97, most Americans expressed keen sympathy for their fellow revolutionaries across the Atlantic and regarded "events in France as confirming and validating their own revolution."[24] The bloody repression of the 1793–94 Terror and violent 1793–94 de-Christianization campaign were certainly widely publicized in the United States but, initially, in a subdued fashion and for a time being (rightly) dismissed as aberrations wholly at odds with the stated democratic revolutionary values of the French *and* American revolutions. It is a basic and thoroughly misleading historiographical error, though a stubbornly tenacious one, to suggest most Americans viewed the 1792–94 phases of the French Revolution "with horror."[25]

That Americans predominantly endorsed the French Revolution until 1796–97 requires emphasis because American opinion diverged dramatically from general sentiment at the time not only in Britain and the British press (which remained undeviatingly hostile to the French Revolution throughout) but in most of Europe and the colonial world, a fact of great historical significance. This sense of sisterhood and basic affinity between the American and French revolutions proved pivotal in immediate post-Revolution American history and the emergence of America's long-term internal ideological stresses. It was entirely logical for Paine, both before and after his release from prison in France, to claim that the American and French declarations of rights were the "same thing in principles" and that his active participation in the French Revolution in 1792–93, and again in 1795–96, neither compromised nor qualified the American character of his principles, or right to American citizenship. "On the contrary," he insisted in 1796, "it ought to be considered as strengthened, for it was the American principle of government that I was endeavoring to spread in Europe."[26]

The irresolvable dispute about the French Revolution's significance in American politics was thus an extension of the clash of theories and interests inherent in the American Revolution itself, and ultimately a collision over the future of America's own constitutional principles. The Franco-American alliance of 1778, Hamilton held, after Louis XVI's execution in January 1793, the only alliance revolutionary France then possessed, should now be considered aborted as having been contracted with the French king, not the National Assembly. Jeffersonians furiously disagreed. Washington initially hesitated; but, by 1793, swayed by Morris's reports, sided increasingly with Hamilton in choosing an anti-revolutionary, pro-British posture. Condemning Washington's and Hamilton's refusal to "satisfy the French and our own citizens of the light in which we viewed their cause, and of our fellow feeling for the general cause of liberty,"[27] and as yet unaware of how far Robespierre and Montagne had debased and betrayed the democratic republican core of the

Revolution as represented by his friends Condorcet and the Brissotins, Jefferson pointedly resigned from the administration in December 1793.

The "Democratic Societies"

If the United States and France, the Atlantic world's only two large republics based on enlightened criteria, according to most observers shared a common legacy, symbolized by the presence of the busts of Washington and Franklin in the hall of the French National Assembly, it was dangerous and undesirable, contended Hamilton, Morris, Jay, and Adams, for the United States to align with republican France. Their hand was strengthened by the disturbing, intrusive activities of Edmond-Charles Genet (1763–1834), the handsome young "minister plenipotentiary" sent by the Brissotin republican regime to Philadelphia. Genet's distinctly undiplomatic revolutionary fervor, including demanding publicly whether Americans had forgotten their own revolutionary ideals, quickly caused serious offense.[28] Jefferson and Madison initially encouraged his republican endeavors and would have continued to do so had he been less tactless and disrespectful. Jefferson quickly concluded he was hotheaded and lacked judgment.[29] From April 1793, Genet tried to mobilize support for the newly proclaimed French Republic via all manner of inappropriate publicity forays (not without some success), interfering in American domestic affairs even so far as to hire and help fit out privateers in Charleston and Philadelphia to raid British shipping, thereby directly threatening America's neutral status. Nevertheless, contrary to what is often suggested, Genet's activity by no means reversed Americans' broad sympathy for the French Revolution or dented the homegrown democratic tendency.

Genet's influence, in any case, rapidly dissolved from January 1794 when the Robespierre regime ordered his arrest. The months of his stay were not in fact a time when the Federalists gained much ground except via the influx of the many white refugees from Haiti, fleeing Caribbean French whites mostly being royalists and foes of republicanism and racial equality.[30] During the early 1790s, the Federalists who, in 1789–90, had enjoyed some backing among artisans in New York and other big cities, actually lost support among ordinary Americans owing to their increasingly elitist financial and fiscal policies. It looked obvious, moreover, that the Federalists were deliberately exaggerating and exploiting Genet's indiscretion. The "great bustle" Washington, Hamilton, and Adams fomented over Genet's conduct, objected Paine, was blatantly biased. If Genet offended, Washington's envoy in Paris, Morris, was "infinitely more reproachable." If Genet was "imprudent" and "rash," he was not "treacherous" whereas Morris "was all three." Morris abhorred the French Revolution "in every stage of it," purposely interfering there as an "enemy of the principles of the American Revolution too."[31] What did intensify during 1792–93 was the ferocity of domestic division and Federalist nervousness due to the reenergizing and mobilization of those convinced the American Revolution had stopped too early and failed to secure essential goals. Anti-revolutionary sentiment, heightened among Southern planters by the Haitian Revolution, gained ground in certain circles, reinforced by the French Revolution's entering its openly democratic republican phase from August 1792 down to the Montagnard coup d'état in June 1793. Washington's antipathy to the French Revolution and radical *philosophique* principles became more public as part of what Paine construed as a plan to strengthen the oligarchic character of the United States Constitution and government. If more discreetly expressed, the view of Madison and Jefferson scarcely differed. After Thermidor, but prior to being released from prison, Paine privately protested in writing to Washington. He followed this up later with his public letter of 1796 claiming Robespierre imprisoned him for the "interests of America as well as France," which he would never have contemplated had he not construed the "silence of the American Government" as "connivance and consent." "For whether your desertion of me was intended to gratify the English Government, or to let me fall into destruction in France that you might exclaim the louder against the French Revolution, or whether you hoped by my extinction to meet with less opposition in mounting up the American Government—either of these will involve you in reproach you will not easily shake off."[32]

Ideologically driven partiality for Britain culminated in June 1795 with ratification of "Jay's treaty," an Anglo-American treaty of "Amity, Commerce and Navigation" negotiated in London by Jay, Thomas Pinckney, and Adams's son John Quincy. According to its numerous critics, this accord, signed on 19 November 1794, smacked of deference and was disadvantageous to the United States.[33] The negotiations had been intended to remove practical difficulties complicating the Anglo-American relationship, especially Britain's embargo on neutral vessels sailing to French colonies. But Britain refused to lift the prohibition that had resulted in dozens of American vessels being seized on the high seas by the British navy. Refused likewise was redress for forced impressment of American seamen into the British navy and any easing of Britain's constricting Navigation Laws. Hamilton's request for the return of two thousand slaves freed during the Revolutionary War by the British, now in the Caribbean and Nova Scotia, was refused too (guaranteeing Southern slave owners' hostility to the treaty).[34] Yet denouncing the treaty as "servile" was unjust as it did secure withdrawal of British troops from the Northwest Territory to behind the Canadian border, a key American objective and a better basis for Anglo-American trade. Needing a two-thirds majority, the accord just scraped through the Senate without a vote to spare by 20 votes to 10. But its reception by the public was vehemently negative, particularly in the main ports. Jay and Hamilton were heaped with acrimony and Jay's effigy burned in many places.[35]

Anti-Federalist agitation in favor of democratic principles, especially in Philadelphia and New York, swelled rather than receded from 1792–93, as democratic republicanism replaced what had officially been a constitutional monarchy in France. The words "democrat" and "democracy" began to be used far more frequently in the American as well as the French press than before.[36] The call to live up to the ideals of '76 and trumpet the cause of "liberty" intensified. America's political elites found themselves challenged in a way they had not been hitherto. Much as the Brissotins mobilized public support among foreign democratic republican ideologues like Paine, Priestley, Gorani, and Forster in Europe, they helped inspire the democratic-republican societies, heirs of the Sons of Liberty and committees of correspondence of 1774–83, mushrooming in the United States. Totaling around thirty-five during 1793–94, these clubs owed their popularity and impetus less to French example, though, than to resentment at Federalist policies and the feeling that America's Revolution had not completed its task.[37] "It is a truth too evident to be disguised," affirmed Tunis Wortman (1773–1822), secretary of the New York Democratic Society, the man who wrote its constitution and a close ally of New York's most dissident printer, Thomas Greenleaf, that "since the completion and final establishment of our revolution, the flame of liberty has burned less bright and become less universal in its operation."[38] Ardor for liberty, protested these societies, was dissolving in love of wealth, ease, and aristocracy.

The democratic societies' enlightened radicalism drew inspiration from the American and French revolutions jointly. Philadelphia also witnessed an influx of German radicalism. The earliest of the new associations circulating Paine's *Rights of Man*, challenging the United States government's bias and contesting the state of the country, was actually the German Republican Society of Philadelphia, established by Peter Muhlenberg, Henry Kammerer, and the remarkable physician, Paineite, and admirer of Godwin, Dr. Michael Leib (1760–1822), set up six weeks before Genet's arrival. Its organizers were energized chiefly by the Mainz democratic revolution of November 1792 and subsequent short-lived Rhineland Republic headed by the German democratic republicans Forster, Wedekind, and Dorsch.[39] "In a republican government," declared its initial circular in German, diffused in the *Philadelphische Correspondenz* and signed by its vice president, Kammerer, a member of the Pennsylvania Assembly, "it is the duty incumbent on every citizen to afford his assistance, either by taking part in [the republic's] immediate administration, or by his advice and watchfulness, that its principles may remain uncorrupt; for the spirit of liberty, like every virtue of the mind, is to be kept alive only by constant action." This first American democratic society urged fellow Americans to "guard against every encroachment on the equality of freemen" and impress the "advantages of education upon the minds of their brethren throughout the state."[40]

Organized to channel popular sentiment, the societies summoned the public to play a more active role in politics and clap a wary eye on the authorities. The largest, the Democratic Society of Pennsylvania, urging the formation of like associations throughout the country, was formed in May 1793, again in Philadelphia. Among its leading members were Rush and Benjamin Bache, Franklin's grandson (later a journalistic scourge of the Federalists known as "Lightning Rod Junior"), an American undoubtedly but one who had spent much of his youth alongside his grandfather in France (and Geneva) and whose democratic radicalism was as much Franco-Genevan as American.[41] Its constitution, circulated in the American press, condemned the monarchies "unparalleled in iniquity" waging war on the French Republic as a "coalition of tyrannies that, menaces the very existence of freedom," having already engineered the "tyrannical destruction of Poland," a reference to Russian suppression of the Polish constitution of 1791. Should France succumb, it was likely the United States too, the "only remaining depository of liberty, will not long be permitted to enjoy peace, the honors of an independent, and the happiness of a republican government." Diffusing Paine's *Rights of Man*, the Philadelphia society resolved to fight trends whereby the "spirit of freedom and equality" in America was threatened with eclipse "by the pride of wealth and the arrogance of power."[42]

The fight back against the Federalist "aristocracy" and bankers had begun. Daughter clubs sprouted from Maine to Georgia, among them the New York Democratic Society, New York's Tammany Society, and New Jersey's Newark "republican society," along with the Democratic Society of Kentucky at Lexington, the Republican Society of South Carolina at Charleston, the Bourbon County Democratic Society (Kentucky), and Connecticut's New Haven "republican society." Where the Philadelphia society attained a membership of 315, mostly craftsmen and artisans, and the New York society between a hundred and two hundred, the rest were mostly far smaller, though Charleston's boasted 114 members.[43] These societies utilized the free press to exert an

Triumph of Liberty, dedicated to its Defenders in America (c. 1793). An Allegory of Liberty flourishing alongside monarchy and tyranny wilting away. The image of Plenty holds a torch to a pile of titles of nobility, crowns, scepters, and other attributes of monarchy. Two urns on the monument are labeled B. Franklin and Montgomery. Below the column (center-right) is an open book labeled "The Rights of Man." The Genius of Liberty points to the *Declaration of Independence* and the American Constitution. Photo credit: © Mary Evans Picture Library / The Image Works.

impact, flourishing mainly where there were sympathetic newspaper editors, like Greenleaf eager to publicize their speeches and activities.[44] By late 1793 the agitation greatly disturbed Washington, Hamilton, and Adams. Twenty years later, in 1813, Adams recalled "when ten thousand people in the streets of Philadelphia day after day threatened to drag Washington out of his house and effect a revolution in the government or compel it to declare war in favor of the French Revolution against England." Only thanks to Philadelphia's devastating 1793 "Yellow Fever, which removed Dr. Hutchinson and Jonathan Dickenson [*sic*] Sergeant from this World," suggested Adams, were the United States "saved from a fatal revolution of government."[45]

Jonathan Dickinson Sergeant (1746–93), son of the first president of Princeton College, a Philadelphia lawyer linked to Eleazar Oswald, the most prominent American fighting in the French revolutionary war, figured among Genet's chief backers. Dr. James Hutchinson (1752–93), surgeon-general of Pennsylvania in 1778–84, was a leading advocate of the radical 1776 Pennsylvania constitution prominent in both the Democratic Society of Pennsylvania

334 / Chapter 13

and Society for Promoting the Abolition of Slavery. Close to Rittenhouse, like many leading the 1793–94 agitation, Hutchinson venerated Franklin's political legacy and was thrilled by the zeal for emancipation and democracy evinced by crowds of less educated supporters.[46] Another Philadelphia activist was Dr. George Logan (1753–1821), an Edinburgh University medical graduate and protégé of Franklin who, in 1779–80, had served the Revolution in Europe as a courier for Franklin and Adams. Ostracized by the Quakers for his republican allegiance, Logan was prominent too in the Philadelphia-based Société française des Amis de la Liberté et de l'Égalité and the Pennsylvania Society for Promoting the Abolition of Slavery.

Philadelphia radicalism was paralleled in New York by Wortman, Mitchill, Nicholson, and Freneau, all belonging to the local Democratic Society and abolition society, and in Delaware by Robert Coram and his circle. Samuel L. Mitchill (1764–1831), later a senator, was considered a "living encyclopedia": he pedantically suggested combining the English "freedom" with a Latinate suffix to rename the United States "Fredonia." A renowned defender of press freedom, Wortman was a publicist and orator sworn to propagate democratic principles among New York's artisans. Well-read, eloquent, and energetic, like Dickinson Sergeant, Hutchinson, Leib, and Logan, he too represented an enlightened cosmopolitanism seeking to convert Americans into democrats and citizens of the world aiding the cause of liberty and emancipation everywhere.[47] Coram figured among the most fervent, urging more economic equality in Britain and America and lampooning the "policy of the English government" for seeking to "make the mass of the people poor, and then to persecute them for their poverty" via the Vagrancy Acts. As editor of the *Delaware Gazette* from 1795, he promoted radical ideas by printing extracts from Godwin's *Enquiry concerning Political Justice* (London, 1793) twice a week for three months. Coram demanded public schools "upon proper principles" to ensure the future in America of true republicanism as proposed by all the societies.[48]

The Whiskey Rebellion

America's democratic societies practically all arose in 1793–94, with hardly any emerging from 1795 onward. They gained widespread support briefly, but their emphasizing the affinities and joint democratic commitment of the American and French revolutions quickly also provoked a considerable backlash. They were already being marginalized by late 1794, following a concerted Federalist campaign to discredit them combined with the onset of the Terror in France.

The societies had arisen, insisted Hamilton, Adams, and Morris, with the connivance of local dissidents on French (or at least not American) principles and were implicated in stirring and aggravating the western Pennsylvania disturbances Hamilton derisively called the "Whiskey Rebellion" of 1793–94.[49]

President Washington personally widened the campaign, denouncing the societies in a key speech before Congress in November 1794 that unleashed a virtual hue and cry in the state legislatures and press, thoroughly alarming Madison and Jefferson.[50] It was true that several local societies in western Pennsylvania had had a hand in stoking local unrest and that the principal leader and chief orator of western Pennsylvania's insurgency, David Bradford (1762–1808), a local lawyer of Irish origin and embittered adversary of the Funding Act, was vice president of the Democratic Society of Washington County, but, for the most part, the societies were not advocating violence as a means to press their complaints. To a degree the whole thing was deliberately blown up and manipulated to fan paranoia and mobilize opinion against the democrats.[51] The outcome was that the broad-based rural protest movement in western Pennsylvania verging on violent revolt, disdainfully called the "Whiskey Rebellion," ended up by fatally weakening the "democratic societies" and American radicalism generally.

The "Western insurrection," or "Whiskey Rebellion," briefly convulsed the Alleghenies, especially Pennsylvania's four southwestern counties, in protest against a new tax on grain surpluses used for whiskey distilling that backcountry farmers greatly resented and rightly suspected as serving the interests of a few large distillers.[52] The measure was among the new taxes introduced to raise revenue and accelerate wealth transfer from the wider public to the East Coast elite in the aftermath of the 1790 Funding Act, Hamilton's scheme to pay off war debt speculators at the face value of their bonds, at the taxpayers' expense. Across a sizable region, angry, poor, and landless protesters joined with more substantial farmers in large, mostly peaceful groups in expressing indignation over what many deemed blatant misuse of government for the benefit of the East Coast elite. In an effort to "regulate" corrupt government, a campaign of intimidation directed at Federal tax collectors and officials and of organized obstruction of property foreclosures culminated in a brief armed insurrection sparked by the so-called Battle of Bower Hall (17 July 1794), an encounter in which some six hundred armed rebels led by a Revolutionary War veteran, Major James McFarlane, exchanged shots with Federal officials and soldiers near Pittsburgh.

The unrest possessed little social or economic cohesion but did gain coherence from declaiming revolutionary slogans and principles and displaying emblems that were as American as French. At the gathering of some six thousand small and larger farmers, and a few professionals and local "gentry" as well as laborers, at Braddock's Field on 1 August, the demonstrators denounced Hamilton's tax measures, accused the federal government of betraying the ideals of the American Revolution, and spontaneously erected Liberty poles covered with revolutionary slogans and symbols,[53] while their leader, Bradford, proposed marching on Pittsburgh, got them to chant in praise of the French Revolution, and even suggested a need for "the guillotine" in America. Bradford and some of his supporters felt so aroused and alienated by the predominance of "aristocracy" in America, and the use of the tax system and land sales procedures to favor the nation's "moneyed men" against the rest, that he and they even pondered the suggestion that the interior West should secede from what they viewed as an irretrievably corrupt federal union, deeming this the only way to make government and society more "democratical."[54] Bradford (whose legal practice, ironically, was based in the town of Washington) was prepared to lead a full-scale armed revolt.

The demonstrations against the East Coast "aristocracy" across five counties so provoked President Washington that, encouraged by Hamilton, he resolved to make an example of the protesters. To stamp out the "rebellion" a force of 12,950 militia assembled by the governors of Pennsylvania, New Jersey, Virginia, and Maryland shouldered arms under the president's personal command, the sole occasion in American history when a sitting president personally led an army in the field. As his army advanced deep into Pennsylvania to crush the farmers' defiance, "rebel" resistance dissipated without further resistance. Hundreds of activists fled to Kentucky and Ohio, Bradford to Spanish Louisiana (where he bought a cotton plantation and became a slaveholder). One hundred and fifty "Whiskey rebels" were arrested, brought to Philadelphia, and tried for treason, two sentenced to death but then pardoned by the president. While American opinion mostly backed the government, in backcountry areas the disproportionate use of force was fiercely resented.[55]

Was the "Whiskey Rebellion" grave sedition or just a trumped-up show? As it petered out, it was hard to know how seriously destabilizing it potentially was. But in terms of rhetoric and emotion, the "Western rising" certainly exerted a substantial divisive effect, if one mitigated by Albert Gallatin (1761–1849), a radical enlightener of Genevan patrician background whose speeches exhorting the "Whiskey rebels" to eschew armed resistance and seek peaceful compromise helped defuse the violence.[56] Vilification of the demonstrators in speeches, sermons, and the press was widespread even by orators like the Boston preacher Jedidiah Morse (1761–1826), father of the future telegraph pioneer Samuel Morse, then still esteeming the French Revolution highly.

If mass protest was legitimate in France that was no justification for insurgency in post-Revolution America, held the many extravagantly praising the "wise, decisive and seasonable measures" of Washington and the "Supreme Executive" in quelling the "poisonous seeds of a party, disorganizing spirit" in America. The ideas of the "Whiskey rebels," claimed Federalists, were foreign intrusion. But the Liberty Pole was a common symbol cherished by republicans everywhere with its origin in America, not France. The element of contradiction in Morse's combining continued support for the French Revolution with harsh words for the Pennsylvanian "rebels" was shortly to be resolved, in 1796, by his sudden, dramatic turn against the French Revolution.

The Federalists exploited the furor generated by the "Whiskey Rebellion" to discredit the "societies" in which they were aided by the fact that local "Democratic societies" had in fact played some part.[57] The idea that the societies were a foreign intrusion was seized on despite the numerous links between them and the Sons of Liberty of 1776. Dickinson Sergeant had been a prominent revolutionary in New Jersey and had his house in Princeton burned down by Hessian soldiery. Henry Rutgers (1745–1830), vice president of New York's Democratic Society, and Udney Hay, another activist well to the fore in 1793–94, were likewise prominent former 1776 Sons of Liberty.[58] Paine's *Rights of Man*, the rebels' favorite text, was as Anglo-American as French. But none of this prevented what Madison called the "unfortunate scene in the western parts of Pennsylvania" becoming in "several respects a critical one for the cause of liberty." He assured Monroe, then in France, that "the real authors of it if not in the service, were in the most effectual manner, doing the business of despotism. You well know the general tendency of insurrections to increase the momentum of power."[59] The riots, agreed Franklin's grandson, Benjamin Franklin Bache, "show how dexterously the [Federalist] faction can make the most untoward circumstances turn to the advancement of their dark designs."[60]

The "Whiskey Rebellion" compromised democratic republicanism in America and further damaged it in Europe where the turmoil was seized on as proof of the lawlessness and unviability of representative democracy whether American, Dutch, Swiss, Irish, or French. "An American cannot know," commented John Quincy Adams, then ambassador at The Hague, in September 1795, "without seeing Europe to witness the fact, what pleasures and exultations all the partisans of monarchy receive" from the accounts of "popular commotions in America." The "Whiskey Rebellion" was a "delicious feast for them." European conservatives, including Dutch Orangists, reported John Quincy, were "all inimical to the government of the United States, because it furnishes a constant example to those who maintain the superior excellence of a republican system. They wish to see some proof of extravagance or folly in America, which they can have the pleasure of attributing to the prevalence of republicanism, as they have done very successfully with respect to the frenzies of France."[61]

In his November 1794 annual address to Congress, Washington purposely blended the "Whiskey Rebellion" with a fierce, outright attack on the democratic societies. The radical societies were seriously weakened by this and generally by the fallout from the "Whiskey Rebellion." Jefferson was deeply disturbed that the "President should permit himself to be the organ of such an attack on the freedom of the discussion," freedom to gather, "freedom of writing, printing and publishing" and at how the alleged insurgency was manipulated to stoke up "denunciation of the democratic societies" despite their "avowed object" being the "nourishment of the republican principles of our Constitution." It came as a still greater shock that popular support could so readily be martialed behind such condemnation. In sum, Americans were unduly impressed, complained Jefferson in December 1794, by the "extraordinary acts of boldness of which we have seen so many from the fraction of monocrats."[62]

The notion that America's republican democratic upsurge of 1793–94, an essentially American development, was seditious, destabilizing, and a foreign intrusion gained plausibility from the influx of Scottish, English, and Irish radicals escaping the "Church-and-King" repression in Britain during 1792–94, as well as, from June 1793, French democratic republicans fleeing the Terror.[63] If some of these political refugees, like some members of the "democratic societies," were barely literate artisans, most were Paineite journalists, teachers, tutors, lecturers, and professionals who further enriched America's, and especially Philadelphia's and New York's, burgeoning intellectual life.[64] With the Federalists pro-British, and the Irish community solidly anti-British, Irish immigrants mostly gravitated to the anti-Federalist camp.[65] Irish refugees played a conspicuous role in both stoking American radicalism and aggravating the growing suspicion of democratic republicanism. From 1784, the brothers Matthew and James Carey, southern Irish Catholics who had earlier assisted Franklin in Paris and, now, helped financially by Lafayette, issued a series of publications in Philadelphia deploring the "despotism of England" and England's "rapid strides towards the utter extinction of the liberty of the press" beside the "chains of tyranny" in Ireland.[66] Matthew reissued Paine's *Rights of Man* in 1796 and James Carey a two-volume edition of Paine's *The Age of Reason* in 1797.[67] The brothers lambasted Hume for distorting Irish history in his *History of England* (1754–61),[68] and in 1799, in a mocking style reminiscent of Franklin, satirized the British constitution under which: "government is continued and supported 1) to secure to a few the enjoyment of the jurisdiction over the territory of England and its dependencies; 2) to prevent foreigners from interfering in their affairs, and 3) to secure to the rich the enjoyment of the rents, tithes and taxes issuing from the labour of the industrious poor." Carey's third article reads: "As men are not equal by nature, neither are they considered equal by the law." The fourth reads: "Birth and Situation have privileges and protection; to which subjects not possessed of these qualifications are not entitled."[69]

Britain's persecution of radicals during the early and mid-1790s was doubtless fiercer in Scotland and Ireland than in England.[70] James Tytler (1745–1804), editor of the *Encyclopedia Brittanica*'s early editions, outlawed by the Scottish High Court for sedition in January 1793, fled to Massachusetts where he edited the *Salem Register*. Indicted for his *Political Progress of Britain* (1792), Callender escaped in January 1793 to Philadelphia where, by 1794, he counted among America's most trenchant commentators.[71] But the repression proved relentless in England too. While Burke rejoiced at finding himself now prime spokesman of British "sentiments,"[72] and seeing Paine generally discredited, in December 1792, a "Church-and-King" mob attacked the print shop of the *Manchester Herald*; its publishers, Matthew Falkner and William Young Birch, abandoning their paper, fled to America. The radical group in Manchester, headed by Thomas Cooper (1759–1839), an ardent democrat, economist, and scientist and advocate of the *Rights of Man*, was broken up. Cooper had built up a calico printing business near Bolton but had become "so offensive" to the "present spirit of the British government, that he can no longer in safety reside in this country" and "therefore goes to seek asylum in the United States," Jefferson was informed, in August 1793, by an English disciple of Paine, Joseph Barnes, for whom Jefferson was "our great patron of republicanism, and of virtue."[73] James Cheetham (1772–1820), later Paine's first biographer, a Manchester hatter, one of Manchester's "Three Jacobin Infidels" with his two brothers, after being imprisoned, likewise migrated to America.

Joseph Priestley's Birmingham home and laboratory were wrecked by a raging "Church-and-King" mob propelling Priestley too across the Atlantic with his family in June 1794. On arriving in Manhattan, Priestley was greeted by a delegation from the Democratic Society of New York, which read out an address by its president, James Nicholson (1763–1804), a retired naval captain converted from Federalism to republican views. "The governments of the old world present to us one huge mass of intrigue, corruption and despotism," he declaimed, "most of them are now basely combined, to prevent the establishment of liberty in France, and to effect the total destruction of the Rights of Man."[74] Together with Cooper, Priestley settled in the village of Northumberland, Pennsylvania, where they aspired to establish an entire community of English radicals which, however, never materialized. Their move to that remote spot was ill-advised, in Jefferson's opinion, preventing their making as much impact in America as true republicans would have wished.[75]

Cooper utilized the months prior to Priestley's arrival compiling a survey of American life and conditions intended to encourage more persecuted democrats to leave Britain. Philadelphia he declared America's largest city with 42,520 inhabitants, New York second with 33,131, and Boston third with 18,038.[76] "In Boston, New York, Philadelphia and Baltimore, the state of society is much the same as in the large towns of Great Britain, such as Birmingham, Bristol, Liverpool, and Manchester. . . . Nor are the people ignorant; newspapers are as plentiful in America as they are now in France: book societies are everywhere to be found, and though learning, in the European acceptation of the word, is uncommon, good sense, and some reading are universal."[77] Despite slavery, he was delighted by America—at any rate initially—although, unlike Miranda, who ten years earlier had pronounced New Jersey "so delightful that it is commonly called the Garden of America," Cooper advised prospective immigrants to avoid that state's "unpleasant" climate, swamps, and mosquitoes. Chiefly, he worried about economic change. "I detest the manufacturing system" because of the "fallacious prosperity it induces, its instability, and its evil effect on the happiness and the morals of the bulk of the people. You must on this system have a large portion of the people converted into mere machines, ignorant, debauched, and brutal, that the surplus value of their labour of 12 or 14 hours a day, may go into the pockets and supply the luxuries of rich, commercial, and industrial capitalists." He "grieved to see that so sensible a man as Mr. Hamilton can urge, their furnishing employment to children, as an argument for [manufacturing] being established in America."[78]

Until 1795–97, mainstream American opinion stuck to the emancipating rhetoric of the Revolution and a sense of sharing in a common enterprise with France. America and France, Jedidiah Morse proclaimed in 1795, together sought to transform not just their own societies but the entire globe: "While we felicitate ourselves in a freedom from the various calamities which afflict this magnanimous nation [i.e., France], we cannot but feel deeply interested in their happiness, and wish for their success, in all virtuous measures, to advance a cause dear to mankind, and in defense of which we formerly experienced their generous aid." Americans Morse still exhorted "not to confine our benevolent regards to the narrow circle" of their own country but help "impart all the blessings we possess, or ask for ourselves to the whole family of mankind."[79] Wherever establishing men's rights was required, urged Morse, the conjoined principles of the American Revolution and the French led the way. In India, the "condition of the lower classes of people is wretched and horrible in every respect," he assured Bostonians, influenced like so many educated readers at the time by the *Histoire philosophique*, repeatedly citing the English version of "Raynal" (unaware Diderot wrote much of it). If "with respect to morals" America was often "deplorable" and had little to teach India, the "most enlightened, the best governed, and the happiest among the numerous nations" of Asia fell "far below these United States" in constitutional matters and "religious and political organization, in their laws—in science—in their knowledge of useful arts."[80]

An orthodox Calvinist (and noted geographer), Morse championed the French Revolution throughout the Terror, switching to becoming one of its foremost American detractors only from 1796. "We cannot but rejoice most sincerely," he repeated in 1795, echoing a post-Thermidor sermon of 20 November 1794, "in the success of any part of mankind living under oppression whether in Asia, Africa, Europe or the New World" that rises up in arms to fight for that "genuine liberty, which is the right of every man."[81] On 19 February 1795, a day of public thanksgiving seven months after Thermidor, Morse again powerfully sermonized in celebration of America's sister revolution, as he had frequently in the past. France had "arisen from the darkness of slavery to the light of freedom" and "espoused the cause of liberty, which is the birth-right of mankind," bursting the "chains of civil and ecclesiastical tyranny." Repelling external enemies, France would regain internal stability: the "dangerous combination of sanguinary men" led by the "Dictator" Robespierre was now "checked, if not wholly suppressed, which has happily paved the way for the adoption of moderate and rational measures."[82]

"Long may America enjoy the blessings of such aristocracy!"

Until 1796, orthodox Protestant clergy in America made allowances for the irreligious campaign in France, relegating it to secondary significance. If they demanded an end to the de-Christianization, "vandalism," and destruction of Christian monuments and images sweeping France over the winter of 1793–94, revolutionary assault on the Catholic Church as such did not overly disturb them. It *was* shocking that Christianity's "sacred institutions, are spurned at, and rejected," granted Morse in February 1795, but "rejection of the Christian religion in France is less to be wondered at when we consider, in how unamiable and disgusting a point of view it has been exhibited, under the hierarchy of Rome." Once freedom was secure and the "people have liberty and leisure to examine for themselves, we anticipate, by means of the effusions of the Holy Spirit, a glorious revival and prevalence of pure, unadulterated Christianity:—May the happy time speedily come!"[83]

If there was already a deep rift between Federalists and Anti-Federalists long before 1796, there was no basic split among the wider public regarding either the republican character of the American Revolution or its consanguinity with the French Revolution. During 1794, the sway of the French and democratic cause in New York's streets was still so strong that it was unsafe for English sailors to evince unabashedly anti-French opinions ashore when their vessels docked.[84] Yet while there was no decisive shift in popular sentiment until 1796–97, the components of a new American political mythology already existed. Working men were generally drawn to the democratic republican opposition but drew a red line at deism and irreligion. Despite the presence of Palmer and some support for his views among the Democratic Society in New York, at the popular level the irreligious dimension of Paine's legacy was reacted to with overwhelming hostility. Artisans continued to celebrate Paine's *Rights of Man* but even more zealously denounced his *Age of Reason*.[85]

Among notable figures half turning earlier was Noah Webster (1758–1843), educationalist and lexicographer, among the most renowned American journalists and scholars of the age, whose *American Spelling Book* (1783) sold more copies in the early decades after 1776 than any work bar the Bible. Passionate devotee of the American Revolution and former radical ally of Barlow, the Webster of 1794 still desired to witness "republican governments established over the earth, upon the ruins of despotism," convinced the "cause of the French nation is the noblest ever undertaken by men."[86] America's gentry oligarchy, moreover, had often been blameworthy. It was appalling how America's revolutionary veterans had been short-changed by the state legislatures and by Hamilton. "To pay the debt to the men who now hold evidences of it," that is, to the financiers and speculators who had bought up the notes issued to the soldiers during the war at a small fraction of their face value and who, in Massachusetts, received both interest and the full face value at the taxpayers' expense, was indeed highly iniquitous—"a violation of [the states'] own engagements as well as of the compact by which society exists."[87] Nevertheless, Webster, nurtured growing reservations regarding the French Revolution's irreligion, universalism, and cosmopolitanism and its onslaught on "aristocracy."[88]

An erudite Yale graduate descending from a long-established Connecticut gentry family, Webster, like Hamilton and Adams, especially abjured the "modern philosophy that rejects all ancient institutions, civil, social, and religious, as the impositions of fraud, the tyranny of cunning over ignorance, and of power over weakness." Dismissed by Jefferson as a "mere pedagogue of very limited understanding,"[89] he did not "believe with the French atheist, that the universe is composed solely of matter and motion, without a Supreme Intelligence; nor that man is solely the creature of education." Rather, "God, and not education, gives man his passions"; the "business of education" is not to refashion human individuals and society on a new basis but to "restrain and direct the passions to the purposes of social happiness." "Helvétius and other profound philosophers may write as much as they please," exclaimed Webster, "to prove man to be wholly the creature of his own making, the work of education; but facts occur every hour to common observation, to prove the theory false. The difference of intellectual faculties in man is visible almost as soon as he is born, and is more early and more distinctly marked than the difference of his features."[90] Appalled by the "Festival of Reason" and Jacobin repudiation of organized religion, Webster during the mid-1790s discarded his former ardent support for the French Revolution pronouncing the new American "Democratic republican societies" "dangerous to good government."

Allying with Hamilton, albeit still stressing the United States' republican character, he had earlier moved to New York, in December 1793, to establish the city's first daily, the *American Minerva*.[91] Focusing attention on atheistic "modern philosophy," grasped Webster, could ultimately detach the American public from its still prevailing sympathy for the French Revolution even if, during 1794–95, there was as yet little sign of this.[92] Championing Jay's treaty, he blasted Jeffersonians in pamphlets aimed at widening Federalist appeal and tying their cause to what he considered the American Revolution's veritable values. Pronouncing Rousseau "too democratic" and given to ideas unwarranted by "experience," he proclaimed Adams a "firm, intelligent republican" restraining the undesirable "spirit of aristocracy in America."[93] Adams championed "aristocracy" not in its European sense with "exclusive privileges" but rather the "nature and tendency of this principle in men," adopting "cautions and expedients for guarding against its pernicious effects in government." "Aristocracy" in Adams's supposedly benevolent sense was innate in human society. Natural distinctions bolster "personal influence" constituting a "natural aristocracy of men, in all countries and in all governments," an "insensible aristocracy of opinion and respect, that now forms the firmest band of union between the States."[94] "If my ideas of natural aristocracy are just the President of the United States is a most influential, and most useful aristocrat; and long may America enjoy the blessings of such aristocracy!"[95]

The Providential Detection: divine providence keeps a protective eye on America and prevents Jefferson, aided by the Devil, from throwing the United States Constitution into a fire on the "Altar of Gallic Despotism" fed by the radical writings of Paine, Godwin, and others. Photo credit: American Antiquarian Society, Worcester, Massachusetts, USA/Bridgeman Images.

Among America's foremost publicists, in the mid-1790s Webster began systematically linking the French Revolution (and its American supporters) to "atheism," de-Christianization, and irreligion, in this way helping develop what soon proved a winning strategy. Unapologetic elitism, Hamilton, Jay, and their allies knew, could not widen their appeal. Pulling the people round to a comprehensively conservative, pro-Federalist stance required a socially broader lever and that could only be religion. In November 1798, in the *New York Spectator*, he declared Barlow "wrong in all the principles which regard the French Revolution and the connection of the United States with France."[96]

Yet, while lambasting France as the engine of "atheism" and immorality, and his American opponents for "infidelity,"[97] Webster grew worried at the escalation of factional strife. He believed that nothing was more detrimental to the "cause of truth and liberty than a party spirit." Political passion all too readily becomes bigotry and illiberality.[98] As rival parties form, they nurture contrasting modes of rhetoric, become more dogmatic, and adopt "some badge of distinction, a button or cockade," all of which serves to widen the "breach, and create disaffection, suspicion, and hostile passions. Such trends were very visible in America," he admonished in 1794: "should the present controversy in Europe continue two or three years longer, I should not be surprised to see party spirit in America, which grew out of a mere speculative question, proceed to open hostility and bloodshed."[99]

Webster's remaining a firm republican unable wholly to repudiate the French Revolution before long got him into difficulties with his Federalist allies. He rejected the Burkeite creed dominating Britain since 1792 and America from 1796, possessing too clear a vision of the American Revolution's role in the transatlantic progress of democratic values ever to forget that American and French revolutionary principles were intimately entwined in their origins. Estranged from the vehement British-style attack on French revolutionary values stirring conservative America during the 1797–98 "quasi-war with France," he eventually broke with the anti-democrats. He was then in turn exposed to merciless pillorying by less punctilious adversaries of democracy like the later famous journalist, renowned for stinging epithets, William Cobbett (1763–1835), then in Philadelphia writing under the pseudonym Peter Porcupine. (After returning to Britain, Cobbett abandoned pugnacious conservatism to become a leading British reformer.) In 1797–98 Cobbett, fresh from lacerating Priestley in his *Porcupine's Gazette*, styled Webster a "traitor to the cause of Federalism," "prostitute wretch," "viper," purveyor of "silly, idle projects," and "toad in the service of sans-cullotism."[100]

From the late 1790s, religious authority mobilized massively against Jefferson and Madison, playing the chief role in detaching the American Revolution from the French. Generating a more pulpit-orientated, particularist, and nationalistic conception of American identity, repudiation of the cosmopolitan, universal dimension of the "spirit of '76" now proceeded apace aided by the Protestant clergy. During the late 1790s, the Federalist press and pulpit together first forged the modern myth, the first seed of American "exceptionalism," that the American Revolution differed fundamentally from the French, greatly assisted by the widespread revulsion against the religiously subversive texts of Paine, Condorcet, Volney, Priestley, Godwin, and Palmer. The dramatic reversal of values during 1796–99 drew impetus especially from the "Second Great Awakening" and its successful rallying of populist anti-intellectualism and Counter-Enlightenment behind the Burkeite, anti-radical journalism replicating in America the vehement biases of the British papers. Together the "Awakening" and pro-Federalist journalism shifted American political sentiment sufficiently to fundamentally divide the country. After the Terror in France, the "Whiskey Rebellion," and the preachers' volte-face, the foes of democratic republican thought in the United States, headed by Adams, Morris, Jay, and Hamilton, were no longer an unrepresentative, isolated elite. A broad, growing impulse within American society and culture in the late 1790s toward anti-*philosophisme*, anti-republicanism, and anti-cosmopolitanism blended with resurgent organized religion to verge on becoming the new American mainstream.

Mainstream clergy whose views appeared extensively in print broadly continued affirming the French Revolution's basic legitimacy, positive character, and proximity to the American model until the mid-1790s.[101] For a time, many Americans holding conventional religious views conceived the French Revolution as part of the divine design, an intervention of providence that confirmed the providential nature of the American Revolution that preceded it. But they did so guided by their clergy. Time and again the pastors had demonstrated their political and social clout not least by deflecting disgruntled farmers from supporting Shays's insurrection against the Massachusetts "aristocracy," a rebellion energetically supported only where there was a temporary absence of ministers discouraging armed insurrection with the result that only certain widely scattered rural districts and small towns participated.[102] Already earlier loudly deploring American post-revolutionary sedition, from the late 1790s, leading Protestant preachers, especially of the Presbyterian and Congregationalist denominations, took to condemning the French Revolution outright, denouncing not just its unruliness and violence but the Revolution as such, as an unmitigated evil fomented by "infidel philosophy."[103]

The shift in American culture and politics, from 1796, was palpable, reflected at many levels including in the theaters and music halls. Until the mid-1790s, popular taste in New York's and Philadelphia's streets and theaters leaned so strongly in the French Revolution's favor that revolutionary songs like "Ça ira" and "La Marseillaise" enjoyed the status of de rigueur fixtures of the American stage. During a performance sponsored by the Tammany

Society at New York's John Street Theatre on 4 March 1794, the audience became so infuriated by the band leader's refusal to play these much-loved revolutionary songs that the audience attacked the orchestra.[104] The streets of Philadelphia, complained an embittered Cobbett, in late 1794, resounded with revolutionary songs and the delirium of "French bombast," an "outlandish howling" of sailors, women in "masculine style," and even children. By contrast, from 1796, New York and Philadelphia switched to musical events with an emphatic anti-French, pro-Federalist message.[105] Radical supporters of the French Revolution and its universal values still mounted the occasional public celebration of French republicanism's victories, but these were becoming much rarer. In August 1797 the Paris press featured letters from Philadelphia reporting that nearly three hundred citizens had gathered for a banquet to celebrate Bonaparte's conquest of northern Italy. After toasting the French Republic's triumphs, the banqueters raised their glasses "To the American republic! May the radiance of her Revolution never be dimmed by ingratitude or by her allying with enemies of Liberty!" This was followed by: "To the memory of Franklin and Rittenhouse! May their virtues become the heritage of every American!"[106]

Jefferson and Madison, steeped in Enlightenment literature and political and moral theory, could hardly dissociate themselves from the legacy of French revolutionaries or "infidel philosophy" and made no attempt to do so. The day before his inauguration as vice president, in March 1797, after losing the presidential contest to Adams, Jefferson was sworn in as the American Philosophical Society's president, in succession to Rittenhouse. Taking the chair for the first time, on 10 March, he was flanked by Priestley seated to his left and Volney to his right. But with the new populist anti-intellectualism gaining ground, "philosophy" was now undoubtedly a target and a political liability. What awaited the nation, asked the vitriolic Cobbett, from this "triumvirate of atheism, deism and nothingness"?[107] His detractors rightly connected Jefferson to irreligion, "philosophy," and foreign intellectuals extolling universal emancipation.

The Alien and Sedition Acts

The shifting mood in the late 1790s and first decade of the nineteenth century steadily strengthened the Lockean current in the American Revolution, making it possible to reassure the public that religion was indeed the only "sure basis for free government," as one Massachusetts preacher put it in 1804, that separation of church and state did not mean freedom "from religion" or any uncoupling of revolutionary politics from divine providence. Only a small fraction of the Founding Fathers agreed with Sam Adams, Benjamin Rush, and John Quincy Adams that the Revolution's essence was the blending of liberty with Bible-based Christianity but most of the American public unquestionably did, and there were enough Founding Fathers in Sam Adams and Rush's camp to lend a semblance of veracity to the new religious mythology of the Revolution, insisting that the "founding" of America—the framing of the Constitution, the Bill of Rights, and forging of thirteen states into a unified federal republic—was a religious, Bible-based enterprise rooted in the people's piety.[108]

Reviving anti-French prejudice accompanied the fierce quarrel between France and the United States that broke out during 1797–1800 over neutral shipping and cargoes on the high seas (French privateers seizing British-bound cargoes from American ships), which, in turn, further contributed to the fundamental new ideological divide in American society. The sharp deterioration in Franco-American relations helped garner popular backing for the Federalists' particularist concept of Americanism, anti-French indignation being fed by an increasingly Anglophile press acclaiming every French reverse. In 1796, Washington replaced Monroe as ambassador in Paris with the fiercely Anglophile Charles Cotesworth Pinckney (1746–1825), offspring of an aristocratic South Carolina planter family, one of his former colonels, later president-general of the Society of Cincinnati from 1805 to his death, and the man who at the 1787 Constitutional Convention had originated the proposal to institutionalize slave representation at three-fifths the equivalence of citizens. It was impossible to select a more adamant foe of equality and democracy, or advocate of nobility and slavery, to represent the United States in France. The revolutionary Directoire not unreasonably construed his appointment as an outrage.[109] When Pinckney presented his credentials, in November 1796, these were refused, provoking officially fanned public fury in America. A commission of three, including Pinckney, was sent by President Adams to settle the dispute but was predictably snubbed by Talleyrand, provoking a fresh wave of populist indignation that Adams and Hamilton—and the British government—adeptly exploited. Religion, maritime disputes, and the "Pinckney affair" brought the United States and France to the verge of war.

Conservative insistence that America's Revolution differed fundamentally from the French pivoted on the claim that the first was "Christian" in character while the second was "philosophic" and irreligious. From the late 1790s, such pretensions were actively propagated and molded into a mythology permeating the American public realm. Anti-secularists backing the Federalist cause, like Webster, Morse, Tappan, and Timothy Dwight, president

Cinque-Têtes, or the Paris Monster, depicting Franco-American diplomatic tension in 1797: the worthy envoys sent by President Adams recoil with horror at the corruption they encounter in France under the Directoire. Photo credit: Archives du Ministère des Affaires Étrangères, Paris, FranceArchives Charmet/Bridgeman Images.

of Yale who delivered over two hundred sermons warning against the danger of "infidelity," atheism, and deism, turned this mythology into a formidable propaganda onslaught.[110] Informal "aristocracy" was successfully hitched to anti-*philosophisme* and Counter-Enlightenment anti-intellectualism. Spearheading the new ideology was a vehement polemic against *philosophists*—depicted as a menacing contagion vitiating the vitals of America spread via clandestine channels by the same malignant conspirators responsible for the French Revolution's irreligion.[111] This Counter-Enlightenment aspect of the reaction prompted Madison to remark to Jefferson that the Federalists, now just as given to exploiting popular credulity and maliciously maligning opponents as Robespierre, could thankfully never quite "adopt the spirit of Robespierre without recollecting the shortness of his triumphs and the perpetuity of his infamy."[112]

In his last years, an Edinburgh professor and scientist, John Robison (1739–1805) had diffused in English through his *Proofs of Conspiracy Against all the*

Religions and Governments of Europe (1798) the strange obsession of the Abbé Augustin Barruel (1741–1820) that the French Revolution was concocted by a secret "atheist" conspiracy originating in the 1770s among Bavarian Illuminati. To further their anti-philosophist agenda, Dwight at Yale and Tappan at Harvard together with "illuminate Morse," as Jefferson derided him, did not scruple to foment a general "hue and cry" deploying Robison's vehemently Counter-Enlightenment "Illuminist" pseudo-history, a conspiracy theory Jefferson called the "ravings of a Bedlamite." Morse publicly endorsed Robison's, in effect Barruel's, theories in a sermon in Boston's North Church in May 1798 and, in concert with Dwight and Tappan, began publicly shepherding the less well-informed among the New England Calvinist congregations against "philosophy" and democratic republicanism. Malevolent Illuminist conspiracy, held these publicists, had now attained fresh levels of perfidy by employing Jefferson's adherents to undermine religion, morality, and government in America.[113] As propagated by Morse, Dwight, and Tappan,[114] this peculiarly paranoid strand of Federalist anti-democratic, anti-Jacobin fervor further fortified the myth that "infidelity" and Jeffersonianism represented a truly insidious, un-American foreign menace, which among other calamitous effects had helped engineer the Haitian Revolution.[115]

The charge that America was being "contaminated" by intellectual subversion introduced by "aliens" infiltrating through the clubs, societies, and press spearheaded the late 1790s American conservative reaction pervading American political culture. A change engineered by preachers and populists, it precipitated a sharply escalating press war. "The press is the great political machine of nations; the instrument in the hand of man to chase tyranny from the earth," declared Palmer in an oration at New York in 1797, the "severest scourge of despots, the bitter enemy of error and superstition, the lever by which to elevate the moral world above the horizon of ignorance, and to present a luminous day, cheering to the hopes of every rational being."[116] Perhaps, but it now proved equally adapted to Federalists aborting America's alliance with France and propagating fear of clandestine subversion by insidious Irish journalists and French "philosophists." Having helped silence the Shays and Whiskey risings, the newly emboldened right-wing press applauded the Federalist-dominated Congress for passing the Alien and Sedition Acts, marking the advent in America for the first time of institutionalized, systematic repression of radical views. These four edicts, proposed by an anti-Jeffersonian caucus, passed Congress aided by the slave-owning interest and the "three-fifths rule" concerning slave representation.[117] The Sedition Act (July 1798), which Adams did not initiate but willingly signed and Hamilton, despite initial reservations, soon rebuked Adams for not enforcing firmly enough, authorized the federal government, to thwart French revolutionary influence in America, to restrict entry of foreign radicals and deport suspect "aliens."[118] Where Jefferson, Madison, and democratic republican editors like Greenleaf deemed the Act scandalous assault on liberty, the culminating offensive to entrench religious bigotry, aristocracy, and expand the presidency's powers, hence also "informal monarchy," Hamilton judged it necessary to curb "immoderate criticism" of government and "approbation" of France and took the view that the "mass [of aliens] ought to be obliged to leave the country."[119]

If anti-French ire opened the door to the Alien and Sedition Acts, support for them was boosted by wider prejudice against recent immigrants. Hamilton, though exceptionally free from the prejudice against Jews usual at the time, during these years made a point of targeting aliens and recent immigrants as a particular threat to America and source of sedition.[120] Timothy Pickering (1745–1829), the secretary of state, who was in charge of implementing the Acts, was a Massachusetts church deacon's son, an ardent disciple and ally of Hamilton, and a notoriously self-righteous, paranoid xenophobe who regarded Irish immigrants as especially seditious and even toyed with additional measures to restrict Irish immigration. Among Jefferson's chief ideological foes, and an ally of Cobbett, Pickering was second only to Pinckney as a foe of democracy and revolutionary France.[121] Collectively, the eventually four Alien and Sedition Acts exerted a considerable impact, indeed marked a sea change in early United States history, by deepening the ideological rift in the nation and imposing severe restrictions on the right to criticize and on collaboration with foreigners, in addition to prolonging the interval immigrants had to wait to become citizens. The greatest infringement of the Constitution and freedom of expression thus far, according to Jefferson and Madison, every single Supreme Court justice (with no democratic republican sympathizer on the bench) endorsed the Acts' constitutionality. Nevertheless, the four Acts deeply divided American public opinion and the state legislatures and revealed just how embedded ideological strife was in the America of 1798. Jefferson and Madison strove to mobilize congressional resistance and although only Virginia and Kentucky followed them in forthrightly declaring the Acts unconstitutional, Tennessee pronounced the Acts "impolitic, oppressive and unnecessary," Georgia backed the calls to get them rescinded, and there was sustained opposition in Pennsylvania, where Gallatin organized a series of popular petitions demanding repeal of the Acts and in New Jersey. Even in New York, only the senate declared the

Acts "constitutional," while only Rhode Island, Massachusetts, Connecticut, and New Hampshire wholeheartedly backed the Federalist administration.[122]

Altogether twenty-five New York, Philadelphia, Boston, and other journalists were arrested during 1798–99 under the Sedition Act, eleven being tried and ten convicted.[123] Some were native born; others had resided in the United States for decades. Dublin-born Matthew Lyon (1749–1822), the first tried under this Act, had earlier, in January 1798, been the first person to start a brawl in Congress (by spitting on a Federalist congressman who allegedly had insulted him). A caustic foe of lawyers and "aristocrats," in America since 1764, he had joined the Vermont Green Mountain Boys in the 1775 invasion of Canada. An ardent supporter of the democratic societies, elected to Congress for Vermont in 1797, this "singular animal" from the "bog of Hibernia," as Cobbett styled him, practically the only avowed Jeffersonian congressman in New England, caused uproar in Washington by openly ridiculing Congress's stilted etiquette of address and reply.[124] Indicted for deriding the administration's "aristocratic" proclivities and Washington's fondness for "pomp, idle parade, and selfish avarice" in the *Vermont Journal*, "spitting Lyon" was jailed for four months and fined $1,000. The only book accompanying him to prison, he announced defiantly, was Volney's (atheistic) *The Ruins*. His incarceration was by no means as unpopular as the Philadelphia *Aurora* implied when praising his "preventing, by his entreaties and arguments, the violence which the people were about to commit upon his confinement." Returning to Vermont after his release, he was besieged in Trenton and New Brunswick by hostile mobs: "the hisses and hooting of the crowd were loud and universal."[125]

Another indictment for "libeling" the president "in a manner tending to excite sedition" was that of Franklin's grandson, Benjamin Franklin Bache. Jailed in June 1798, he died soon afterward during a fresh Philadelphia yellow fever outbreak at the age of only twenty-nine, prematurely ending what Adams termed his "detestable career."[126] New York's prime dissident editor, Thomas Greenleaf, died from the same outbreak before his trial, which did not prevent Hamilton together with "the Scourge of Jacobinism," Pickering, indicting his widow, Ann, who (continuing to publish Greenleaf's paper, the *Argus*) became the only woman brought to trial under the Acts, indicted for denouncing Adams administration as "corrupt" and conducting herself as a "malicious person seeking to stir up sedition."[127] Another obvious target, the Scotsman Callender, fled to Virginia but was indicted there for styling Adams in his *The Prospect Before Us* (1799), a book approved by Vice President Jefferson, a "repulsive pedant, a gross hypocrite and an unprincipled oppressor," a "strange compound of ignorance and ferocity, of deceit and weakness"; he received nine months' imprisonment and a $200 fine.[128] More unedifying still was the trial of Thomas Cooper, abolitionist, Unitarian, and materialist, comrade of Paine, Priestley, and Jefferson, veteran foe of Burke. Accused of sedition in England in November 1792 for visiting Paris on behalf of the Manchester Constitution Society and conferring with Condorcet about the world's first democratic constitution, in Pennsylvania Cooper had become a journalistic scourge of the Federalists. In retaliation they stigmatized him as a "fugitive Englishman," disciple of Priestley, and "journeyman of discontent and sedition."[129] In November 1799, Cooper published a piece, approved by Priestley, accusing Adams of incompetence and meddling with the judiciary—comparatively mild criticism pronounced "scandalous and malicious libel" by the judge who convicted him for "defaming" the president, fining him $400 and sentencing him to six months' imprisonment. Scorning offers from friends to petition the president for early release, he served his sentence in full, until October 1800.[130]

The Alien Act additionally empowered the president to register, place under surveillance, and deport non-naturalized foreign nationals judged "dangerous to the peace and safety of the United States." Writing to Jefferson on 20 May 1798, Madison styled the bill a "monster that must forever disgrace its parents." Adams's justifications he designated "abominable and degrading" albeit throwing "light on his meaning when he remarked to me, that there was not a single principle the same in the American and French Revolutions." Abolishing royalty, seemingly, was "not one of his revolutionary principles."[131] Among internationally renowned foreign revolutionary freedom-fighters threatened or actually hounded from America under the Alien Act—none were actually prosecuted—were Priestley, the Genevan radical Gallatin, Volney, among the Act's principal targets, and Morse's former Polish hero, Kościuszko, whose hasty departure, to evade deportation, his friend Jefferson helped arrange.[132]

A leading radical *philosophe* and Brissotin republican, Volney had embarked on what he called a *voyage philosophique* in the United States, albeit spending much of his three years there in Philadelphia collaborating with Jefferson and quarreling with conservatives (and also Priestley, who in 1797 publicly rebuked him for his "atheism"). Volney plunged into the mounting "quarrel of English against French principles," the struggle between American democratic republicanism and Americans striving for "aristocracy," the reign of finance and an empowered clergy. To Americans, their republic was a "new" and pristine country, but by any objective appraisal, concluded Volney, after touring the country, one sees that Americans exhibit neither greater good faith in politics, nor greater probity or thrift in financial affairs, nor greater decency in public morality, let alone less bias and party spirit than Europeans. Nor was there greater emphasis in the United States than in Europe on education and public instruction. He thought America had noticeably regressed since 1783.[133] Denounced as an agent of the Directoire plotting a French takeover of the (still Spanish-held) Louisiana Territory, which elements in the French government were indeed angling for, Volney had hurriedly to depart American shores.[134]

Before leaving, he received the manuscript of Jefferson's improved translation of part of his *Les Ruines* (1791). An unsatisfactory first English-language edition translated by the Welsh antislavery activist Morgan John Rhys (1760–1804), a radical Baptist minister who had migrated to Philadelphia, had appeared in America in 1796 after being published earlier by the London Corresponding Society, in 1792. Exceptionally successful in Britain, according to the radical publisher Richard Carlile (1790–1843), this book had "made more Deists and Atheists than all the other anti-Christian writings that have been circulated in this country."[135] Jefferson retranslated the sections concerning politics, oppression, and economic inequality. Back in France, in July 1798, Volney asked Barlow to complete Jefferson's version, by translating also the last section, "The Origin and Filiation of Religious Ideas," where Volney claims men created God rather than the reverse, to answer baffling cosmological questions.[136] This Barlow undertook "under the inspection of the author." *Les Ruines* was a philosophical classic, affirmed Barlow, that "takes the most liberal and comprehensive view of the social state of man, develops the sources of his errors in the most perspicacious and convincing manner, overturns his prejudices with the greatest delicacy and moderation, sets the wrongs he has suffered, and the rights he ought to cherish, in the clearest point of view, and lays before him the true foundation of morals—his only means of happiness."[137] The Jefferson-Barlow version appeared at Paris in 1802 but without either Jefferson's or Barlow's name on the title page as neither could afford, with the fervor of the "Second Great Awakening" mounting by the day, to be publicly associated with Volney.[138]

The deterioration in the Franco-American relationship aggravated by "this war-whoop of the pulpit," as Paine called the political rallying of the preachers, drove a deep psychological and ideological wedge between the two republics—and between American mainstream society and the radicals. Many clergymen responded to the Federalist appeal, eager to denounce the French Revolution and its "philosophist" admirers while trumpeting what they styled the "Christian" loyalty of Adams and Washington.[139] Indeed, the pulpit took the lead in constructing a whole new interpretation of the Revolution, which the Federalist press took up with alacrity. On 14 August 1798, the *Gazette of the*

United States, the semiofficial paper of the Federalist regime edited in Philadelphia by John Fenno, announced that America's civil privileges were threatened by the "deathly embraces" of the "French fraternity" and that the "philosophical fanatics" attempting to raise a "cry of religious hatred and persecution" were at war with the "religious principles of the intrepid founders of our independence."[140]

That the American and French revolutions had nothing in common suddenly became an ineradicable dogma, an immensely popular conventional wisdom, swathed in the Founding Fathers' supposed "religious principles." In 1800, John Quincy Adams, soon to become a Federalist senator for Massachusetts (1803–8), warmly praised a new book emphasizing the alleged vast differences between the two revolutions, the English rendering of a notable product of (moderate) enlightened anti-republicanism, *The Origins and Principles of the American Revolution*, by the Prussian official Friedrich von Gentz (1764–1832). Americans were indebted to Gentz, averred John Quincy, for rescuing the American Revolution "from the disgraceful imputation of having proceeded from the same principles as that of France."[141] Once an enthusiast for both revolutions, from late 1792 Gentz figured among Germany's "most eloquent and passionate opponents" of the French Revolution. A constitutional monarchist, Gentz venerated Locke, pronouncing revolt on the basis of a contract broken between ruler and people (as in Britain's 1688 Glorious Revolution and as in 1776) justified but popular sovereignty, democracy, the *Rights of Man*, and the French 1789 Revolution illicit and abominable.[142] Declaring monarchy and aristocracy indispensable, Gentz helped entrench Adams's and his son's highly dubious thesis that where the American Revolution's principles, idealism, and republicanism were rooted in Locke, the French Revolution was profoundly un-Lockean, helping render this dogma integral to America's political landscape.

Festering social and economic grievances and divisions aggravated the ideological rift at every stage. A relatively minor disturbance—the eastern Pennsylvania "Home Tax Rebellion," or "Johan Fries's rebellion"—flared in March 1799, illustrating how readily disparate social and economic tensions could be sucked into the ideological warfare. By physically resisting recent additional taxation imposed by Hamilton on houses (and stamped documents), in July 1798, to fund the "quasi-war" with France and expand the army and navy, farmers in German-speaking districts of eastern Pennsylvania created a ferment in "Pennsylvania Dutch," called the "Heesses-Wasser Uffschtand," that eventually unsettled six counties, especially Bucks, Berks, Northampton, and Montgomery counties.[143] Demonstrators once again employed revolutionary slogans and symbols to energize the agitation. With armed gangs led by Johan Fries forcibly releasing tax resisters arrested by the authorities, Adams ordered troops to the scene and issued a presidential proclamation denouncing the "rebels" for acting in a "manner subversive of the just authority of the government by misrepresentations to render the law odious, by deterring the public officers of the United States to forebear the execution of their functions, and by openly threatening their lives." But Adams left most of the work of suppressing the revolt to Hamilton. The Federalists, spurred by Hamilton, orchestrated another disproportionately large and intimidating militia sweep on the model of the "Whiskey insurrection" suppression of 1794.[144]

"Whence this precipitation on the part of the government of the United States," demanded the Philadelphia *Aurora*, to "march troops against the people of Northampton and Bucks?"[145] Around sixty "No-Tax insurgents" were arrested, of whom three, including the "rebel" leader, Fries, an Independence War hero furious over the Alien and Sedition Acts and habit of blaming Pennsylvania farmers' protests on "the French," were convicted of "treason." Sentenced to hang, Fries was afterward pardoned by the president. The political fallout was mixed: widespread prejudice against "the Germans" helped depict the insurgents as a "numerous and desperate faction, resolved on the overthrow of the Federal government," generating a vigorous backlash against them among the less informed.[146] But a wide section of Pennsylvania opinion was angered by the—on this occasion—all too obviously trumped-up furor. A notably stern critic of the government's handling of the "Home Tax Rebellion" was Jefferson's aide Freneau, who followed Young, Paine, Palmer, Volney, and Barlow in propagating democratic, egalitarian ideas in an integrated fashion, stressing the American Revolution's significance for the entire world. Freneau propagated a Paineite and politically revolutionary "philosophy" that was simultaneously American and French. Recommending "that mild and peaceful philosophy, whose object is the discovery of truth, and whose first wish is to emancipate the world from the double despotism of church and state," he especially deprecated and decried Federalists for their duplicitous ways of mobilizing the uninformed.[147]

American reaction against irreligion, and revolutionary principles in the years 1797–1800, stirred by the Federalist press, the pulpit, and the Alien and Sedition Acts briefly plunged the democratic papers into discredit and circulation loss. What Madison called the "Anglican Party" briefly partly succeeded in representing the attitudes of the commercial and landowning elite as public opinion itself, significantly depleting what opponents called the "real sentiment of the people," the pro-Revolution sentiments of independent farmers and artisans.[148] For several years, intimidation and loss of readership noticeably weakened the republican press. The virulently anti-British *Polar Star* of Boston edited by John Daly Burk (c. 1776–1808), among the recently arrived Irish émigrés now prosecuted for criminal sedition after strident attacks on President Adams, shut down in 1797.[149] (Burk was afterward killed fighting a duel in Virginia.) Bache's *Philadelphia Aurora*, labeling Adams the "friend of monarchic and aristocratic government" wanting a "titled nobility to form an upper house and to keep down the swinish multitude," briefly ceased publication, like the Carey brothers' *United States Recorder*.[150] Yet, while the chorus denigrating the French Revolution, irreligion, and Jacobinism as such proved permanent, with lasting consequences for the American domestic political arena, by 1799 domestic circumstances swung round to revive the anti-Federalist press and the Acts became decidedly unpopular— for which Adams blamed Hamilton. The Alien and Sedition Acts designed to entrench Federalist control soon backfired.[151]

From early 1799, the Federalists lost momentum due to opposition to the Acts and especially an unseemly quarrel that erupted between Adams and Hamilton sparked by Adams's decision to refuse further expansion of the armed forces. An ugly feud ensued, rooted in their clashing personalities and colliding principles. Although both leaders were proud and impetuous and both advocated "aristocracy" and abominated the French Revolution, Adams, whom Hamilton judged far less "able in the practice, than in the theory, of politics," frowned on standing armies and navies and on land speculation and the financial interest. He was also less pro-British and anti-republican than Hamilton, who struck many observers as "on principle," as Morris put it, "opposed to republican and attached to monarchical government." Ruinously for the Federalists, their leaders' personalities proved totally incompatible. Hamilton scorned Adams as arrogant, petty, and mentally unbalanced, given to "unfortunate foibles of a vanity without bounds" in refusing to prepare the nation's defenses; Hamilton Adams deemed the most "artful, indefatigable and unprincipled intriguer in the United States if not the entire world."[152]

Among other stratagems, Adams greatly resented the Hamiltonians' elaborate stage-management of Washington's state funeral in Philadelphia on 26 December 1799. The obsequies for Washington (who died on 14 December 1799) "presented a scene of public mourning, of solemnity and respect," reported the *Aurora*, "which this city has never before on any occasion witnessed in an equal degree."[153] Imposing funerary ceremonies were organized throughout the land, with public eulogies delivered by the hundred in churches across America. But the obsequies were slanted so as to project the heroic, conquering hero, playing down revolutionary, republican, and democratic values as the Revolution's legacy while stressing the supposed ties between religion and the Revolution and Washington's alleged status as the "instrument of providence." Among wide sections of the population there existed an abiding thirst to connect Washington to biblical faith rather than republicanism, democracy, or Enlightenment.[154] "The death of Washington," recalled Adams in 1816, "diffused a general grief. The Old Tories, the Hyperfederalists, the speculators, sett up a general howl. Orations, prayers, sermons, mock funerals were all employed, not that they loved Washington, but to keep in countenance the Funding and Banking systems; and to cast into the background and the shade all others who had been concerned in the service of their country in the Revolution."[155] Adams, like Jefferson and Madison, genuinely resented the overly close association of American values with the commercial and banking interest and the Washington personality cult.

Memorial sermons extolling Washington continued uninterruptedly through early 1800. Though not all denounced Jeffersonianism, the predominant drift was to elevate Washington infinitely above every other revolutionary figure into "a new Moses," the instrument of God, the very tool of divine providence. The United States, Americans learned, was a land under God's special protection, a "new Israel," unlike any other society. Washington supposedly identified wholeheartedly with Christianity—though this was decidedly stretching a point. The obsequies thus became themselves part of the drive against "deists, atheists and infidels of every description" and the growing use of congressionally sanctioned public days of prayer, commemoration, and thanksgiving in a partisan spirit against the republicans. Preachers took to routinely interfering in the political process, influencing its course in ways not witnessed prior to the mid-1790s. Concealing the truth that if the *Declaration of Independence* contains a "founding religion," it is more "a religion of reason than of revelation," a philosophical religion, an essentially secular project, devoid of theological content,[156] theologians taught that the true spirit of Washington's providential leadership, aligned with Bible religion, had devolved specifically on the Federalist party.[157] Excoriating this new "Washington" cult, the Jeffersonian press reminded "sincere republicans" that when Franklin died and was eulogized in the French National Assembly, Mirabeau led the deputies in observing a profound silence and paying homage in the "sight of the universe, to the Rights of Man and the philosopher who most contributed to extend the conquests of liberty over the face of the whole earth."[158]

From 1799, the republican papers, boosted by the Adams-Hamilton feuding and resentment against Hamilton's taxes, recouped lost ground. The stock of republican papers assailing Federalism rebounded and regained if not all their former ideological baggage then certainly their verbal audacity. Callender, a great foe of big investors and landowners, turned the *Richmond Ex-*

aminer into a major vehicle of anti-Federalist reporting.[159] The *Aurora* was relaunched and recovered circulation under the editorship of William Duane (1780–1865), a Paineite deist who fled Britain for America in 1796, became Bache's chief printer, married his widow, Margaret, and now emerged among the leading anti-Federalist editors. Duane had lived in both Ireland and India and nurtured a generalized, global view of British imperial oppression that he blended with loathing for Federalists. A Federalist senator was heard to remark, boasted Duane's paper on 10 March 1800, that "if the *Aurora* is not blown up soon, Jefferson will be elected in defiance of everything!" "But while the people are returning so rapidly in all parts of the Union to . . . the principles of 1776, in opposition to the monarchical innovations and doctrines which have been imposed on this nation," admonished Duane, the "innovators redouble their activity for mischief."[160]

Chiding the Federalists in a new vein, Duane celebrated St. Patrick's Day, 17 March 1800, by expressing pride in the "Irish blood that flows in his veins and the Irish virtues which he imbibed in that happy but politically oppressed nation," announcing his hope that his American compatriots would share the spirit of the Fraternity of United Irishmen, the Rights of Man, and the "Liberty of the Press; may it flourish in spite of Sedition Laws and surmount the attacks of Committees of Privilege"; he wrote referring to his summons to appear before the Senate for publishing statements Federalist opponents termed "false, defamatory, scandalous and malicious." Despite Adams's deeming the "matchless effrontery of this Duane" fitting material for "the alien law," the proceedings dragged on inconclusively and were then wholly thwarted by Duane's going underground and disappearing.[161]

The presidential election of 1800 proved a decisive watershed, wrecking Hamilton's system and ending Federalist hegemony in Congress. Official emulation of British hounding of radicals ceased, the apparatus for countering alien "sedition" was dismantled, and government repression of democratic republican ideas lapsed, making America safe for political émigrés fleeing Britain, Ireland, and France. America's image as a safe refuge for the persecuted abandoning Europe revived.[162] Yet it was far from clear that by electing him president the American people thereby proved, as Jefferson claimed, that they remained "substantially republican." Their good political instincts had "been played on by some fact with more fiction; they have been the dupes of artful manoeuvers, and made for the moment to be willing instruments in forging chains for themselves." But time and truth "have dissipated the delusion," he concluded optimistically, "and opened their eyes."[163] "What an effort, my dear Sir," he assured Priestley, "of bigotry in politics and religion have we gone through! The barbarians really flattered themselves they should be able to bring back the times of vandalism, when ignorance put everything into the hands of power and priestcraft."[164]

But few others interpreted the 1800 contest as no less "a real revolution in the principles of our government as that of 1776 was in its form," as truly a democratic triumph over ignorance and "kingly government." Rather, incidental factors had intervened to preserve appearances. An unmistakable factor in Jefferson's electoral victory was a growing willingness of many backers to appeal to the middle ground by watering down democratic and revolutionary discourse, repudiating Jacobin excesses, playing to the rapidly growing Baptist and Methodist constituency and acknowledging the nexus between Bible religion and politics.[165] Those comprehensively in accord with Jefferson's views, like Gallatin and Paine, remained very few in number.

If the "democratization of the American mind" during the 1790s proceeded, as is often claimed, from below—the farms and countryside—the bifurcation of American society into democratizers and conservatives was driven less by social or economic factors than by the pulpit, the "Second Great Awakening," and the populist press. Having strengthened their position in the years 1796–98, in the end the Federalists simply divided American society more deeply rather than gained the upper hand.[166] The lasting consequence was that the public domain languished in deadlocked contention in a way that left the Revolution's legacy more ambiguous than ever. Up to a point, Jefferson's electoral victory confirmed that the "spirit of 1776 is not dead. It has only been slumbering." But the slumber was set fitfully to return and profoundly affect his presidency and what came after. Philosophical radicals, like Palmer, discerned in the "progressive movement of intellectual power, the certain ruin, the inevitable destruction of those pernicious systems of error and superstition, of civil and religious despotism which have so long desolated the world and degraded the character of man."[167] But this seems to have been wishful thinking distorting what was just a momentarily victorious blend of revived newspaper protest, aversion to Hamilton's taxes and financial system, and revulsion at the Adams-Hamilton feuding.

CHAPTER 14

America and the Haitian Revolution

Long regarded by white America as the most horrific and threatening of the revolutionary upheavals, the Haitian Revolution of 1791–1804 threw the entire Caribbean into turmoil and affected relations between whites and blacks throughout the New World for decades. This great eruption was not directly inspired or driven by the American Revolution but rather by the French; it powerfully interacted with developments in the United States, though, and impacted on the American Revolution's legacy in a way that had enduring consequences for both the United States and Haiti, as well as profoundly changed the relationship between the United States and France.

The *Declaration of the Rights of Man and the Citizen*, of August 1789, marked a new stage in the unfolding of the French Revolution and quickly injected a degree of social and political tension throughout the Caribbean, even though the white planters' local assemblies in the French colonies for the moment remained sufficiently dominant to resist concrete changes in the islands' institutions, laws, and caste system. During 1789–92, the ancien régime continued in the French Caribbean with only whites owning at least twenty-five black slaves being admitted to the island assemblies. Complete exclusion of free blacks from what some now considered to be their political rights, and their debarment from expressing their views, and from every public office and opportunity for upward mobility persisted without being directly challenged until the highly divisive five-month debate in the French National Assembly about the colonies and slavery that took place between May and September 1791. An especially pressing question was whether the French legislature's colonial committee should be permitted, as moderate royalists urged, to relegate everything concerning the status and conditions of free blacks in the colonies to the white-dominated colonial assemblies.

Brissot and the Society of the Amis des Noirs, especially Grégoire, Pétion, and Destutt de Tracy, who led the *philosophique* denunciation of the "moderate" wing in the National Assembly, accused the French Caribbean's white planters of unjustly denying the free blacks (estimated at over well over twenty thousand) their citizens' rights and treating both free blacks and slaves despotically. Free blacks, contended Brissot, Condorcet, and their supporters, were as numerous as whites on the French Caribbean islands and denying them positions of responsibility and dignity was both unconstitutional and a violation of reason itself since they were often cleverer, braver, and more useful to the *patrie* than the mostly more indolent whites. The torrent of hostile publicity conservative elements within the Revolution poured on Les Amis des Noirs they denounced as a "vile pillar" of the most "horrible aristocratie."[1]

Due to the vigorous efforts of the Société, the Brissotins, and the mulatto circle around the black leader, Julien Raimond (1744–1801), a slave-owning indigo planter from Saint-Domingue, son of a white planter and a mulatto woman (the daughter of a planter) resident in Paris since 1785 where he had been endeavoring, working with various bodies, to raise the legal status of free blacks and mulattoes in the French Caribbean, the colonial planters' assemblies slowly lost ground. In May 1791, the National Assembly ruled that, despite the unremitting opposition of the colonial assemblies, free blacks must now receive full voting rights wherever they met the requisite property qualifications. While the Caribbean assemblies still flatly refused to accept the National Assembly's edict,[2] the French democratic republicans stepped up the pressure. The free blacks of Saint-Domingue, declared Destutt de Tracy in a major speech on 23 September 1791, if liberated "by us from oppression, will be our natural allies; it is neither just nor *politique* to abandon them."[3]

To justify the hegemony of landed oligarchy and slavery in the colonies, and bolster their monarchist preferences, the white planters' spokesmen in the French National Assembly opposing Raimond regularly employed Montesquieu's relativism of climate and conditions. This offered a counterrationale to radical claims that slavery was morally unjustifiable. Montesquieu, the single most cited political philosopher of the American Revolution, was no defender of slavery as such but did defend the necessity of black slavery in certain circumstances. Montesquieu was not an abolitionist because he believed considerable practicalities stood in the way of ending slavery. Especially the passage in book 7 of part 3 of the *L'Esprit des Lois* affirming "there are countries where the heat debilitates the body, and so weakens resolve, that men are not brought to arduous labour except through fear of punishment: there black slavery seems less shocking to our reason" was utilized by colonial apologists such as Médéric-Louis Moreau de Saint-Méry (1750–1819), lawyer and author of several books on the Caribbean, to assert the unavoidable necessity of retaining black slavery. A deputy for Martinique in the National Assembly frequently citing Montesquieu, Saint-Méry later fled into exile at Philadelphia, where he opened a book shop that became a major focus for ousted French white royalist émigrés congregating in the United States.[4]

Montesquieu's moral, social, and political relativism was regularly used to buttress Caribbean "aristocracy" by the colonial lobby. This added to the reasons why Montesquieu's thought, a great pillar of moderate Enlightenment in the United States and France alike, came under growing assault from 1789 among the radical *philosophique* fraternity. The relativism inherent in Montesquieu's enlightened perspective had begun to be fiercely criticized on political grounds during the 1780s especially by Condorcet, who also disliked Montesquieu's benign attitude to monarchy and general conservatism, Volney, and the Swedish Spinozist and poet Thomas Thorild (1759–1808), who vigorously rejected Montesquieu's political ideas, claiming these obscured and obstructed mankind's need for a single equalizing and universal democratic republican model. Only one universal set of laws and political values can buttress equal rights and the best interests of the majority internationally and throughout the globe, which means that Montesquieu was an antiquated obstruction to human progress.[5]

The anticolonialism stemming from the *Histoire philosophique* and other radical Enlightenment texts of the 1770s and 1780s hinged intellectually on the idea of the basic unity of mankind, equality of the races, and the concept of "universal human rights." "Universal and equal rights" dramatically called into question all existing theological and intellectual justifications for the then still prevailing notion that white peoples, Europe as a continent, and the Christian churches possessed some special responsibility, authority or superiority, mission or civilizing role, based on a God-given "right," to rule those parts of the world deemed inherently deficient and inferior. Mainstream Enlightenment writers, ranging from Locke and Montesquieu to Hume and Robertson, offered widely diffused and adopted theories and doctrines useful for wresting land from Amerindians and classifying allegedly backward regions far from Europe as innately primitive besides defending black slavery. Such writers provided intellectual muscle for propping up exploitative colonial structures, but all were potentially undermined by the Radical Enlightenment's principle of "universal and equal rights of mankind." This revolutionary new concept clearly had very little to do with earlier notions of "rights" and had emerged rather suddenly in the 1770s. Thus, far from the "invention of human rights" being due to slow cultural changes in sensibility, or processes like reading novels—one of the great errors of contemporary

historiography—it was unquestionably sudden and highly divisive, and derived predominantly from furious intellectual feuding between moderate and
radical enlighteners.[6]

Only the Radical Enlightenment operated comprehensively and systematically against ancien régime social and legal structures *en bloc*, condemning
not just slavery—even Burke was capable of that—but black social and political subordination to whites generally. Haitian insurgency against unremitting
social oppression began with a free black *and* slave revolt in the northern interior of the island in August 1791, a rising that over the next year liberated
around 15,000 slaves, devastated hundreds of coffee and sugar plantations, and
killed around 1,000 whites; and it was in the northern hills that Pierre Domi-
nique Toussaint Louverture (1743–1803), a former slave taught to read, first
emerged as a prominent insurgent leader. Paine wrote to Short, in November
1791, noting the "distressing accounts" received from Haiti and remarking
that the violence of the blacks was a "natural consequence of slavery and must
be expected everywhere."[7] The insurrection in the northern interior of Saint-
Domingue reached a crucial turning point growing into a full-scale revolution as a consequence of the Paris Assembly's edict of 4 April 1792 officially
abolishing the white colonists' hitherto extensive autonomy. This was the culmination of a mounting revolutionary campaign in France aimed at defeating
Caribbean French white conservatism, aristocratism, and monarchism.

Partly a response to the initial Haitian revolt, and partly a consequence
of the Brissot circle's ideological drive in France,[8] the initiative for this edict
in the National Assembly was taken by Brissot amid an intensified flurry of
antislavery rhetoric. The measure formed part of the *partie de philosophie*'s
deliberate strategy of expanding what they conceived as a war of liberation of
peoples in Europe. Charging the colonists with violating basic human rights,
the decree dissolved the old colonial assemblies and declared full equality of
persons among the free population, white and black. The Brissotin strategy
was to tighten France's grip over her colonies and commence the demolition of the ancien régime racial hierarchy by comprehensively emancipating
the free blacks while postponing the ending of slavery itself, temporarily, until this could be tackled in an orderly fashion without devastating the colonies. The democratic republicans sought first to win over France's Caribbean
free blacks, converting them into supporters of the Revolution and once the
power of royalism and aristocratism in the French Caribbean was broken proceed to end slavery.[9] This first partial black emancipation decree reached the
outraged French Caribbean colonial assemblies of Martinique, Guadeloupe,
and Saint-Domingue during May and June 1792.

The democratic republicans had opted for a high-risk strategy and become the principal agents of the Haitian and wider Caribbean revolution. Following the downfall of monarchy and of the Feuillant ascendancy in France in August 1792—and closure of the principal colonial lobby in Paris, the Club Massiac, and seizure of its papers—an army of 6,000 troops (bringing 30,000 rifles) was dispatched to Saint-Domingue to assert the now emphatically republican French Assembly's authority. With the revolutionary troops arrived a civil commission chosen by the new republican regime headed by Léger-Felicité Sonthonax (1763–1813) and Étienne Polvérel (d. 1796), the historian of the Navarrese constitution. A youthful republican ideologue, advocate of universal education, and vehement foe of the Church (and all churchmen) of only twenty-nine, Sonthonax had predicted, writing in the *Révolutions de Paris* in September 1790, that Europe's monarchies would not long be able to resist the "cries of philosophy and principles of universal liberty" spreading among the nations.[10] He headed the commission mandated to transform France's entire posture in the Caribbean (where he had never set foot before). During his first months on Saint-Domingue, Sonthonax vigorously implemented his instructions regarding "free blacks," especially the April law reconstituting the colony's assembly on a democratic basis so as to equitably represent free blacks, free mulattoes, and poor whites.[11] The planters resisted in every way they could, some conspiring with the exiled monarchist leader Malouet (now in London, whose family fortune was vested in land and slaves on the island) to wholly subvert the revolution in the Caribbean and bring Saint-Domingue under British control.[12]

Sonthonax precariously established a functioning revolutionary government, enlisting some of the (mostly traditional-minded) "free blacks" to the republican cause, no mean feat given the increasingly tense and chaotic situation in which he operated. Dissolving the Saint-Domingue colonial assembly in October 1792, Sonthonax replaced it initially with a provisional commission of twelve, comprising six whites and six blacks co-opted by the commission. The *commissaires* also introduced a mixed-race political club at Cap Français affiliated to the (pre-1793 Brissotin) Jacobins. Royalist and other protesting white officers were purged. The island's blacks remained mostly puzzled or alienated by republican discourse, however, and detested the democrats' overt irreligion. Their difficulties in grasping the abstract principles of republican equality, Sonthonax reported to Paris, remained a major problem for the Revolution since blacks liked to think it was "their king" who had sought to free them and that his royal will was being thwarted by evil councillors and slave owners.[13] Slaves seemed even more fervent for monarchy and religion than free blacks. Priests remained influential in the insurgent districts. This only confirmed, for Sonthonax, that humans lacking *la philosophie* are entirely blind to their own real interests. The commissioners failed to resolve the slave revolt in the hills, but in a way this helped their cause since Saint-Domingue's whites remained too frightened by the continuing black insurgency to go all out in opposing the revolution emanating from Paris.

For a time, the *commissaires* kept France's wealthiest colony largely under French control. On 2 December 1792, Sonthonax summoned a force of several hundred mulatto and free black National Guard to face down a white militia unit encamped on the Champ-de-Mars outside the town, refusing officers of mixed race. An armed clash occurred resulting in the deaths of thirty whites and six free blacks that only narrowly avoided becoming a pitched battle.[14] Before long, though, these Brissotin *commissaires*, open foes of the planters and constitutional monarchists, came under fire also from the Montagne in France. Montagnard authoritarian populism (like Rousseau himself) showed considerably less concern for universal human rights, ending slavery, and black emancipation (and noticeably more sympathy for the white planters) than the Left republicans proclaiming the Revolution's democratic principles.

If Sonthonax aimed to emancipate the free blacks and had sympathy for slaves, he had none whatever for the continuing insurgency, defying the revolutionary regime in the hills that to him was madness fed by religion and royalism. The white oligarchy of the colony's other main town, Port-au-Prince, meanwhile, also defied the revolutionary regime and, in April 1793, had to be blockaded with the aid of local free black supporters and bombarded into submission. As the town fell, hundreds of royalist, counterrevolutionary whites fled into the interior; others were caught and imprisoned. Jacmel was similarly reduced with black help. But with the commissioners and their troops operating in the northern interior and then the south, the situation in Cap Français too deteriorated. As at Port-au-Prince and Jacmel, the chief agents of unrest at this point were neither free blacks nor slaves but recalcitrant whites defending the colonists' supremacy and the old colonial assembly. Sonthonax's Cap Français opponents, often white refugees from the black insurgency in the interior, or monarchist seamen and merchants whose trade was now heavily disrupted by the maritime war with Britain, became increasingly turbulent.

A deteriorating situation exploded into a full-scale crisis in June 1793. The Cap Français sailors mutinied and set siege to the commission's headquarters, the governor's house. Units of free black militia rallied to the commission's defense. Fighting erupted and spread. At the height of the Cap Français violence, and on their own initiative, initially just as a local emergency measure, Sonthonax and Polvérel offered local slaves their freedom if they would fight for the Revolution. Sonthonax's famous printed edict of 21 June 1793 released Cap Français's slaves from bondage in exchange for their help in saving the embattled Brissotin regime. Many responded with alacrity, rushing into the streets armed with knives and other implements. With Sonthonax still besieged, the shooting and killing spread. Fires started. Numerous houses were pillaged. Finally, like Port-au-Prince earlier, the entire town was burned to ashes. Mulattoes and blacks often assisted fleeing or wounded whites. But others cut their throats so that besides several thousand blacks, well over a thousand whites were butchered in this horrific episode that came to be luridly publicized in the United States (as well as Europe); it exerted a deep psychological effect on the planter elite of the American South, and not least Jefferson.

Whites who escaped did so mostly by reaching vessels in the harbor, often bringing (usually) female slaves with them. These were then evacuated in large numbers to New York, Philadelphia, and other American ports. As more and more shiploads of traumatized evacuees reached American shores, the most dramatic and exaggerated images began resonating in white American minds. Between 1791 and 1804 the American press carried regular reports on Haitian developments, making a specialty of reporting atrocities and black massacre of whites, thereby generating a widespread sense of alarm, especially in southern states. Despite the slaves of the white immigrants from Saint-Domingue proving to be highly ostentatious in their Catholic piety, crowding the Catholic churches of Philadelphia, Charleston, and Baltimore, their conspicuous presence exacerbated fears that the more than ten thousand Haitian slaves brought by their fleeing masters to the United States might be spreading the contagion of insurrection and impiety among America's native-born blacks.[15] "I become daily more and more convinced," Jefferson wrote to Monroe in July 1793, "that all the West India islands will remain in the hands of the people of colour, and a total expulsion of the whites sooner or later take place. It is high time we should foresee the bloody scenes which our children certainly, and possibly ourselves (South of Patowmac [i.e., Potomac]) have to wade through, and try to avert them."[16] Jefferson's remarks may not have been very prescient, but they reflected the anxiety the Haitian Revolution excited in American minds and the trauma conveyed in America during the 1790s by the thousands of white émigrés.[17]

Mobilized by newspaper reports of the Saint-Domingue upheaval, a powerful wave of emotional sympathy traversed America—but mainly for the white exiles. Relief committees sprang up in Philadelphia, New York, Charleston, Baltimore, and other cities to assist the less well-off among the refugees, especially women and children whose husbands and fathers had been slaughtered, or were missing, or had fled elsewhere. These collected clothes and food as well as money for the often traumatized new arrivals. Fare money was allocated, enabling some of the destitute to return to France. In the autumn of 1793, South Carolina, Maryland, and several other states and, from early 1794, Congress also assigned taxpayers' money to fund relief for Saint-Domingue émigrés.[18] On America's eastern and southern coastal cities, the influx undoubtedly exerted a profound effect socially and culturally. Whether or not there was any substance to suspicions that Haitian slaves carried with them highly pernicious baggage in terms of seditious attitudes and conspiracy, probably the great yellow fever epidemic of late 1793 that decimated Philadelphia originated among this large mixed influx, even though, as Rush noted, the refugees themselves tended to escape its effects.[19] Among the Cap Français exiles in Philadelphia was a military surgeon, Jean Devèze (1753–1829), who stood out among the heroes of the fight against yellow fever, making medical history by applying techniques very different from those employed by Rush and his colleagues. In 1794, Devèze published his *Recherches et Observations* on the great Philadelphia epidemic insisting the fever (spread by mosquito bites) was not contagious from person to person.[20]

Sonthonax's Cap Français emancipation decree, even if the outcome of a sudden emergency, turned into a great landmark in history. Over the next four months, black emancipation in Haiti dramatically broadened under pressure especially from the insurgents in the northern province, which received its own separate local decree, citing the French *Declaration of the Rights of Man*, on 29 August.[21] By October 1793, all former slaves in Saint-Domingue were officially free. Legally, the colony had become a different world from that which it had been in 1789. Initially, this failed, though, to rally the continuing black insurgency in the interior to the Revolution. Rather than allying with the republicans, Toussaint Louverture at first understood "liberty" to mean independence from French control and playing the Spaniards possessing the larger eastern part of the island (today the Dominican Republic) off against the French.[22] In exchange for protection and "liberty for those who fought for the cause of the kings," and allowing black rebel commanders to operate on their own, Toussaint aligned with the Spanish authorities fighting for religion and monarchy against the representatives of the French Revolution.[23] At this stage, Toussaint's propaganda condemned France's republicans for their religious impiety, for killing Louis XVI, and as bloodthirsty tyrants.[24] Failing to persuade most blacks, the Brissotin commission had simultaneously to fight Spain, Britain, and a French white planter force allied to Spain and Britain, both monarchist empires being anxious to quash the Caribbean revolution. Spanish and British troops invaded different parts of Saint-Domingue and other French colonies. Recruiting hundreds of white émigrés from France, as well as Saint-Domingue, for counterrevolutionary action in the Caribbean, the British occupied Tobago in 1793; in early 1794, they extended their enclaves in Saint-Domingue, taking over Port-au-Prince.[25]

To complicate matters further, from June 1793 rumors circulated in the Caribbean (and the United States) that the new masters in Paris, the Montagne, totally repudiated Sonthonax and Polvérel, their actions, policies, and authority. (They were recalled to France in June 1794 to face trial but arrived after Thermidor and were later released.) The victorious Jacobins, after overthrowing their opponents within the Revolution, did not hesitate to cancel the Brissotin commissioners' edicts and counteract their policies. Under "natural law," argued some Montagnards, abolition of black slavery was not really a "patriotic" goal.[26] "Le pacte social," Rousseau showed, is with the nation, not with humanity in general. Leading authoritarian populists close to Robespierre, most notably Jean-Pierre André Amar (1755–1816), the official compiling the National Convention's indictment against Brissot during the summer of 1793, sympathized with the white colonist lobby rather than the emancipationists while—very much in line with Rousseau[27]—none of Robespierre's circle took much interest in black emancipation as such. To "prove" its argument that nation and patriotism matter more than universal human rights, anti-abolitionist Montagnards insistently appealed to "nature" and Rousseau. True *patriotism* and love of one's nation, they held, cannot flourish "except by abandoning a part of the affection that attaches us to the entire human race."[28] Besides diluting Brissotin universalism, it suited Montagnard aims to affix responsibility for the chaos in Saint-Domingue and Martinique on Brissot and his allies. In a major speech at the Paris National Convention on 18 November, Robespierre himself, plying one of his most blatant untruths, charged the Brissotins with being in league with Britain and deliberately arming Saint-Domingue's slaves in order to ruin France's colonies.[29]

Toussaint Louverture, however, in early 1794, making good his chronic shortage of munitions by obtaining new supplies of powder and weapons from American sources, changed his mind about allying with Spain. By May, having grasped the real character of his former "perfidious protectors," as he explained his volte-face, he announced his military alliance with the French republicans. In contact with French revolutionary agents in Philadelphia and New York as well as coastal Saint-Domingue and teaching his men the difference between royalist émigrés allied to Britain and Spain and French "bons républicains," he now fought for the Republic.[30] By June 1794, he was warmly welcoming the general abolition of slavery in the French colonies by the National Convention in Paris and preparing for the advent of peace and the

Toussaint Louverture as depicted in an 1802 French engraving. Photo credit: © RMN–Grand Palais / Art Resource, NY.

chance to restore the colony to order and render it "as flourishing as ever."[31] The plantations lay in ruins and numerous blacks and whites continued to be displaced by constant incursions of Spaniards and British and their émigré allies.[32] When writing to French officials and commanders, Toussaint termed the British and Spanish troops, white and black, attempting to dislodge him from his strongholds as "enemies of the Republic." During 1794, Toussaint officially adopted the French revolutionary calendar in Haiti, renamed the few vessels he disposed of along the coast with names such as "La Liberté," and under the tricolor flag taught his officers the slogans and procedures of the new French revolutionary military code. When in combat with royalist whites and blacks, or Spaniards and English, Toussaint's units were instructed to cry: "Vive la République!"[33]

Briefly something like a general Caribbean slave emancipation movement under French revolutionary auspices seemed to be in motion. During the mid-1790s, the revolutionary contest on Saint-Domingue widened into a pan-Caribbean conflict. The 1795 revolution in the Dutch Republic, and overthrow of the Orangist regime there, deepened an already bitter rift between Orangists and democrats convulsing all six Dutch Caribbean islands as well as in the Guyanas (most of which was then in Dutch possession). Curaçao became the focus of furious strife and while neither side, Orangists or republican Patriots, favored emancipating the slaves, the latter, as French allies, could not prevent revolutionary papers and propaganda—or Guadeloupe mixed-race privateer crews—assuming a new prominence on their island. Major slave and free black revolts erupted on Curaçao and at Coro later in 1795 that were among the biggest in the Caribbean during the revolutionary era and that, contemporary reports suggest, were plainly inspired by the dramatic developments in the French colonies.[34]

On Saint-Domingue itself a few whites who had abandoned their property were allowed back after swearing allegiance to the Republic, some former planters returning from the United States in the hope of evading sequestration of their lands under the Revolution's punitive laws against recalcitrant émigrés. By allowing white émigrés from the United States to return, Toussaint affirmed his commitment to an orderly coexistence of whites and blacks.[35] This welcoming attitude to returning whites and embracing of religious toleration were later eulogized by American abolitionists eager to present Toussaint as a great and tolerant statesman and the former slaves as capable of political responsibility and constructive self-governance.[36] His open-door policy toward exiles returning from the United States also figured, however, among the points of disagreement that subsequently provoked his bitter quarrel with Sonthonax.[37]

The revolutionary gains of the French and Dutch Patriots in the Caribbean in 1795, and especially black emancipation and apparent revolutionary success on Saint-Domingue, gave rise to extraordinary apprehension in London and Madrid. So menacing did the combination of black slave emancipation and resurgent French and Dutch democratic-revolutionary arms, privateering, and rhetoric in the Caribbean appear to be that it prompted one of the largest British military expeditions ever sent across the Atlantic, comprising nearly 100 ships and 30,000 troops. These joined the appreciable British force already in the Caribbean, striving to reverse the Revolution in the islands, turn back the tide on Saint-Domingue, and halt black emancipation. Yet despite committing massive resources and Britain's increased overall naval and military superiority, this counteroffensive, apart from recovering Grenada and Saint Vincent and eventually occupying Curaçao (in 1800), proved broadly a failure. The French dispatched far smaller expeditions, but these sufficed to hold the line in Guadeloupe and, more tentatively, in Saint-Domingue. Yellow fever and malaria exacted an appalling toll on the British forces. Some 40,000 British troops and sailors, it is estimated, died or disappeared fighting the French Revolution in the lesser Antilles and Saint-Domingue between 1796 and 1800, through fighting, disease, and desertion, many sick and wounded expiring in makeshift hospitals in Jamaica. Britain's failure to recover Guadeloupe, the main focus of the French privateers and naval power in the Caribbean, indirectly helped the black movement in Haiti by diverting significant British troop strength away from the struggle there, thereby helping the black insurgents on Haiti consolidate their grip.

Following the Franco-Spanish peace (1795), which ceded Spanish Santo Domingo (where slave numbers were relatively small compared to the western part of the island) to France and in theory extended black emancipation to all of Saint-Domingue, counterrevolutionary pressure on Haiti waned during 1796–98, and the work of restoring order and agriculture proceeded, despite continuing disturbances and conspiracies often instigated by the British and Spaniards (toward whom Toussaint remained highly antagonistic). Maintaining discipline among his men and issuing proclamations in the name of the Republic, Toussaint strove to curb the pillage and disorder instigated by "enemies of liberty and equality."[38] That his allegiance to the French Republic and its revolutionary culture was more than just superficial is suggested by the frequency with which he assured the French governor, Laveaux, that "it is absolutely necessary," as he put it in February 1796, "that the citizens of these quarters conform to the laws of the Republic and keep themselves in good order, that they have a good citizen to command them, wise and very firm in good principles."[39] For continually reiterating his allegiance to the Republic, he was rewarded by being officially appointed lieutenant governor of the island in May 1796 despite persistent hostile rumors being deliberately spread insinuating that Toussaint aimed to betray the country to the British and again "put [the blacks] back into slavery."[40]

De facto control of Saint-Domingue was nevertheless gradually slipping from the grip of the Paris Directoire. The turning point came during 1797 after Toussaint suddenly broke with Sonthonax (who had returned to head the administration of Saint-Domingue in the spring of 1796), sending him and other French *commissaires* and officials back to France. The exact nature of their rupture and brief power struggle has never been fully explained. Assuming effective control of the island's governance and administration, Toussaint in effect rejected the Directoire's authority albeit without saying so. The last remaining *commissaire*, Julien Raimond, threw in his lot with Toussaint, colluding in the deportation of Sonthonax.[41] Raimond's collaboration helped keep up the appearance that Toussaint governed Saint-Domingue on behalf of France under French revolutionary auspices. To all appearances, the black leadership of Saint-Domingue rejected independence and, most important, rebuffed calls to eliminate the island's remaining whites.[42] Toussaint insisted he had no wish for independence, or to turn on the whites, claiming to be firmer in his loyalty to France than Sonthonax. He professed to be insulted that anyone should suppose Sonthonax more upright and republican than he, or "more of a friend to the liberty of the blacks."[43] If Sonthonax seemed to speak in favor of liberty, he was actually a "monster" undermining the "republicans" and disrupting the coexistence policy, a perfidious scoundrel reminiscent of Robespierre in his hypocrisy and in presenting himself as upright. "Robespierre too spoke of *la liberté* but what would have happened to the Republic without 9 Thermidor?" Besides, why would any leader "seeking the merit of working for abolition of slavery on Saint-Domingue want the burden of responsibility of adding to that a declaration of independence"?[44]

Loving liberty and wanting freedom for the blacks, Toussaint still claimed, in June 1798, meant staying loyal to the French Republic and the Revolution.[45] Although black and mulatto representatives remained in the French National Assembly in Paris, from 1794 to 1799, real power on Saint-Domingue had, by 1798, devolved into the hands of local black leaders, especially Toussaint controlling the center and north, and André Rigaud (1761–1811) commanding in the south. Neither repudiated French sovereignty in either practice or theory, until the summer of 1798, while rivalry and soon civil war disrupted relations between them. Rigaud, mulatto son of a wealthy planter and a slave woman,

374 / Chapter 14

nurtured a more racially hierarchical conception of Caribbean society than Toussaint, whose army was principally composed of former slaves. From 1797, Rigaud kept up more active ties with the French and Curaçao than Toussaint; but it was Rigaud, though not finally defeated until August 1800, who lost the internal struggle.

Toussaint's policy of cultivating good relations with the United States and re-admitting refugee Frenchmen with property in Saint-Domingue returning from exile there, or elsewhere, continued through the late 1790s, the years of Adams's presidency. His vision of the coexistence of blacks and whites on the basis of equality—corresponding to the ideas of Brissot and Condorcet—was wholly exceptional for its time.[46] But at this juncture, the sharp deterioration in Franco-American relations of the late 1790s led to a marked increase in French privateering activity in the Caribbean, which, in turn, resulted in so many American ships sailing to and from Haiti being seized that Congress temporarily prohibited the traffic, an interruption unwelcome to American merchants and inconvenient for Toussaint, who relied on American shipping for a range of supplies and munitions. He appealed to Adams to reopen trade relations. Negotiations followed and a formal agreement between Toussaint and the United States was signed that involved more than just commerce. Adams's secretary of state (1795–1800), Timothy Pickering (1745–1829), a leader of the Massachusetts gentry and earlier handpicked by Washington for his anti-revolutionary, anti-democratic, and vehemently conservative Anglophile leanings (he was later to lead a conspiracy aspiring to get New England to secede from the Union and renew the old links with Britain and her empire),[47] viewed closer relations with Haiti as a way of promoting American interests in the Caribbean. Eager for war with revolutionary France, Pickering designed to extend American protection over Haiti by cutting its links with France while at the same time, as some in the United States hoped, lessening the risk of the "contagion" of black insurgency spreading to disaffected slaves in America.

Pickering was indeed much keener than Adams on the prospect of Haitian independence. American primacy would prevent Haiti serving as a base from which French privateers could operate.[48] More dubiously, he and his allies in Washington viewed Haitian independence as a way of containing the threat of black insurgency and permanently reducing French influence in the New World, as well as reducing any future risk of French revolutionary subversion spreading to North America. It was a stance entirely opposite to that of Jefferson, who positively dreaded Haitian independence and considered Toussaint a definite threat to the United States.[49] Toussaint for the first time openly defied France in August 1798 by signing a separate peace with the British (who remained at war with France)—an accord whereby the British withdrew from Port-au-Prince and other occupied enclaves and reopened Haiti's sea-lanes to British and American shipping.[50] Toussaint now took to playing off America against the British. When his American treaty went into effect on 1 August 1799—in further open defiance of revolutionary France—a mass of American ships headed for Haiti's ports.

In France, meanwhile, years of instability followed Thermidor and the crumbling of the group dictatorship of 1793–94. While the 1795 French constitution and two-chamber legislature and committee executive, or Directoire, it instituted was not a total failure, this body, facing great difficulties and mounting royalist opposition internally, was unable to restore confidence or stability. It looked divided and weak. Apprehension lest the Revolution's republican achievements would dissolve under the Directoire's vacillations produced several coups designed to prod the Revolution onto a firmer, more orderly course, culminating in the late 1799 coup of Brumaire. This marked a crucial turning point. Differently from earlier episodes, this coup d'état was inspired neither by the legislature nor the Directoire but by a substantial, high-level group of disaffected political, legal, and constitutional reformers, the Brumairians, a clique orchestrated by Sieyès that comprised the foremost republican theorists and journalists in the legislature and the Paris Institute: Volney, Cabanis, Daunou, Marie-Joseph Chénier, Destutt de Tracy, Garat, and Say. If the Republic persisted on its current indecisive trajectory, they believed, it would inevitably face humiliation, disaster, and collapse.[51] They aimed to realize their political-philosophical vision by securing their new order of liberty, human rights, freedom of expression, secularism, and representative constitutionalism, defeating royalism, Catholicism, and Jacobin repression permanently through authoritarian and extralegal means.[52]

Lafayette shared their perspective and supported the coup.[53] To put their plans into effect Sieyès needed a general to provide troops. Napoleon Bonaparte was at hand, and it was at this point that the Brumaire conspirators made their decisive error of enlisting his help in overthrowing the legislature and constitution. On 18 and 19 Brumaire of the Year Eight (9 and 10 November 1799), power was transferred at bayonet point from the legislature to a provisional consulate of three—Sieyès, Ducos, and Bonaparte—though only after hours of indignant resistance from the legislators defiant enough to cause the troops to hesitate and Bonaparte briefly to lose his nerve.[54] During the hammering out of the Constitution of the Year Eight, promulgated toward the close of 1799, Bonaparte easily outmaneuvered Sieyès, Ducos, and the constitutional commission supposedly drawing it up: the Consulate was formalized with Napoleon as its unchallenged head. Sieyès withdrew humiliated into permanent retirement.[55]

The coup of Brumaire and new constitution of 13 December 1799 effectively ended the French Revolution. There were now three chambers with the most senior and powerful charged with overseeing the legality and constitutionality of the legislature's actions comprising eighty non-elected, non-removable members co-opted by the senators themselves from a short list presented by the First Consul (Napoleon). The new constitution suspended the Rights of Man, press freedom, and individual liberty, as well as democracy and the primacy of the legislature, wholly transferring power to initiate legislation from legislature to executive, that is to say the consulate, rendering Bonaparte the all-powerful figure of the regime. Distressingly for the original Brumairian conspirators, the *Declaration of the Rights of Man* was removed from its preface. In response to Brumaire, Toussaint began formalizing the autonomy from France Haiti now possessed de facto albeit still without directly proclaiming independence.

In 1800, Toussaint, entirely contradicting Napoleon's policy toward Spain, advanced troops into the former Spanish eastern two-thirds of Santo Domingo (ceded to France in 1795) and confirmed the abolition of slavery (and establishment of French revolutionary values) there too. Napoleon was planning to return the territory to Spain with its former institutions intact, to cement his new Spanish alliance. Despite growing encouragement during Adams's presidency to seek full independence, a policy consistently promoted by Pickering, until 1801 Toussaint still formally presided in Haiti and Santo Domingo as a French general preserving the status quo in the name of revolutionary France. Endeavoring to convert Toussaint into a tool of American expansionism against France, Pickering discovered, was no simple matter. He sent a United States consul to Cap Français to encourage Toussaint formally to secede and place the island under United States protection. But, wary of Britain and America no less than of Napoleon, the adroit Toussaint still resisted proclaiming outright independence.[56]

Meanwhile, Toussaint strove to persuade freed slaves that had abandoned plantations and devastated interior areas to return to the land and resume agricultural work.[57] Former slaves having captured the land, the apparent capacity of Haiti's economy to sustain its population and its tenacity and stability under pressure, eventually prompted Jefferson's notion that Haiti might serve as a safety valve for racial tensions in the United States. Haunted by the sheer scale of the slavery problem in America and the nightmarish prospect of the kind of interracial violence and killing seen on Saint-Domingue in 1793 erupting eventually on a larger scale in the United States, Jefferson began to ponder, as he mentions in several letters of the time, systematically resettling a portion of America's blacks in some reserved quarter of North America or the Caribbean—or Africa. "The most promising portion of [the West Indies]," he wrote to Monroe, during the first year of his presidency, in November 1801, "is the island of St. Domingo, where the blacks are established into a sovereignty *de facto*, and have organized themselves under regular laws and government." The idea both attracted and troubled the president: "the possibility that these exiles might stimulate and conduct vindictive or predatory descents on our coasts, and facilitate concert with their brethren remaining here, looks to a state of things between that island and us not probable on a contemplation of our relative strength, and of the disproportion daily growing; and it is overweighed by the humanity of the measures proposed, and the advantages of disembarrassing ourselves of such dangerous characters."[58] Racial fear had become a powerful factor in the American president's thinking.

Napoleon wrote to Toussaint early in 1801, making no mention of any plans to reassert direct French control over Saint-Domingue, merely recommending that Toussaint continue his efforts to restore order and revive the island's agriculture. Nevertheless, it was in response to Napoleon's consolidation of power that Toussaint widened his control during 1800 and, in the summer of 1801, convened a constitutional convention in Haiti. At the zenith of his power at this time, having defeated Rigaud (August 1800) and overrun the Spanish part of the island, abolishing slavery there and uniting the entire island for the first and only time (in defiance of Napoleon),[59] he proclaimed the island's first constitution on 8 July 1801, abolishing slavery on the island forever and making himself governor for life. While formalizing self-rule, his constitution nevertheless still acknowledged French sovereignty nominally.[60]

With Napoleon master of France, the French Revolution at an end, and the Batavian Revolution emasculated, there was distinctly more scope for pessimism regarding human progress than optimism. Yet it was hard to believe the Enlightenment's achievements would be altogether nullified and the French Revolution's promise wholly blighted. "While the Rights of Man have gone wholly out of fashion in the Old World," confided Lafayette to Jefferson in June 1801, "I draw some consolation from the hope that with the coming of peace, the French will consider the favorable situation of my young adoptive *patrie* [i.e., the United States] and that the perfect harmony of liberty and philanthropy, of energy and good order there, will once again summon back the older people to a realization of their rights."[61] This lingering, residual optimism remained characteristic of Lafayette, Volney, Paine, Barlow, and other republican radicals residing in France during the early part of Napoleon's dictatorship, especially before he declared himself "Emperor of the French" in 1804. While some of the international republican revolutionary fraternity, like Kościuszko, angrily condemned Napoleon's quest for power from the outset,[62] many of the original conspirators and their sympathizers, including Benjamin Constant, while entertaining troubling doubts, still hoped the core of the republican achievement and human rights could be salvaged.

Only gradually did all but the most pliant republicans withdraw from active support for, and participation in, the new regime. Despite quarrels, notably over the Concordat with the papacy, which he opposed, Volney remained a close advisor of the First Consul during the dictatorship's early years, breaking with Bonaparte only in 1804.[63] This qualified acquiescence stemming from earlier perceptions of Napoleon as a genuine torchbearer of republican revolutionary values, a leader forceful enough to save the Revolution from the coalition of monarchical powers ranged against it, was neither as naïve or surprising as it later appeared in retrospect. During 1796–1802, Napoleon and his army had transformed Italy and Switzerland more fundamentally than anything else had for centuries, demolishing all the laws and institutions of the past and setting up a string of sister democratic republics alongside the French Republic and the United States. Under Napoleon, the French had dismantled the entire apparatus of Italian "feudalism," noble dominance, and ecclesiastical ascendancy, unfettering the press and emancipating the Jews and all religious minorities, proclaiming equality and human rights, and installing popularly elected legislatures, together with national guards and tricolor flags.

Napoleon had earlier also secured republicanism's first foothold in Greece, setting up the embryonic revolutionary regime in the Ionian Islands (1797–99) and in 1798–99 conducting himself as a fully-fledged republican likewise in Malta, Egypt, and Palestine. Moreover, despite the fact that he did not share the principled stance of the Amis des Noirs, Napoleon's recorded statements about slavery and the Caribbean during 1799–1800 betray no hint of any intention to try to reintroduce slavery into the French Caribbean colonies—quite the contrary.[64] He was perfectly aware that without acknowledging abolition of slavery for good, there was no prospect of collaboration with Toussaint or the black population of Saint-Domingue. It was the news that Toussaint had overrun Spanish Santo Domingo that prompted Napoleon to cancel his initial confirmation of Toussaint's title as lieutenant governor.

Napoleon's dictatorship, consolidated in the years 1800–1802, had a profound effect on France, Italy, Germany, Poland, Spain, and the Low Countries; it also transformed the Caribbean where during the months he negotiated the temporary Peace of Amiens with Britain in late 1801, he made extensive preparations to restore French power, planning (secretly) to reintroduce slavery in the French colonies. Jefferson's narrow victory in the 1800 autumn presidential election ended any immediate threat of war between the United States and France and removed Pickering's agent from Cap Français. In contrast to the situation prevailing in 1799–1800, Napoleon could now be confident the United States would not oppose reassertion of French control over Haiti and the rest of the French Caribbean. Ignoring Volney, who tried to dissuade him from attempting forcibly to resubjugate the former colony, pointing out that the blacks would fight desperately for their freedom and that any European army sent there would suffer catastrophic depletion from yellow fever and other sicknesses, and that his scheme would risk France's newly improved relations with the United States, Napoleon plowed ahead, seemingly oblivious also of the additional drawback that Britain would prefer to resume the just suspended war rather than permit France to regain her power and possessions across the Atlantic.[65]

Unlike Britain, the United States under Jefferson's guidance was willing to countenance reversion to France's earlier status in the Caribbean but not the kind of grandiose scheme Napoleon actually had in mind. In May 1801, the astounding news reached the United States of the secret treaty of San Ildefonso (1 October 1800) whereby in exchange for dynastic concessions to the Spanish royal house in Tuscany, Spain transferred the entire Louisiana Territory to France. Suddenly, a colossal French empire in the Americas seemed about to emerge based on military force. Willing to endorse a limited resumption of French power in the Caribbean to counterbalance the weight of Britain, Jefferson could not accept a revived French New World empire on this massive scale. Realizing the vast scope of Napoleon's New World ambitions, he understood that the troops sent to Saint-Domingue "were to proceed to Louisiana," as he expressed it in April 1802, "after finishing their work in that island." Where, in Jefferson's view, "Spain might have retained it quietly for years," Americans could not accept the French regaining Louisiana with its control of New Orleans and the Mississippi estuary.[66] Such a development would sink Franco-American relations permanently. "From that moment," concluded Jefferson, "we must marry ourselves to the British fleet and nation,"[67] a prospect that distressed him since "of all nations of any consideration France is the one which hitherto has offered the fewest points on which we could have any conflict of right, and the most points of a communion of interests. From these causes we have ever looked to her as our natural friend, as one with which we never could have an occasion of difference. Her growth therefore we viewed as our own, her misfortunes ours."[68] But all that, it appeared, tragically for revolutionary values, had vanished. Jefferson and Madison made known that if France followed through with reacquiring Louisiana, a considerable change for the worse in Franco-American relations must inevitably follow.

If Jefferson and his administration showed scant inclination, despite the libertarian and republican values they routinely proclaimed, to encourage Haitian independence or champion universal black emancipation, or the international movement to suppress slavery, Bonaparte, still more cynically (but as yet only secretly),[69] repudiated the right of Haiti's blacks to freedom and self-determination altogether. Late in 1801, France's First Consul dispatched two powerful fleets to the Caribbean—a smaller fleet to Guadeloupe, Tobago, and Saint-Lucie (all of which were recovered, though the latter two only briefly, being retaken by the British in June 1803), and a larger fleet, prepared in Brest, sent to Haiti under the command of General Charles Victor Emmanuel Leclerc (1772–1802), husband of Napoleon's favorite sister, Pauline. Leclerc had figured among Humbert's officers during the 1798 Irish expedition and had also participated in the coup of Brumaire. The First Consul furnished him with exceptionally detailed instructions as to how to proceed in Haiti.

The Napoleonic armada arrived off Cap Français in February 1802 and landed the largest French force thus far ever dispatched to the Caribbean. Its 22,000 troops were subsequently considerably reinforced, bringing total troop strength dispatched to Haiti by Napoleon to the staggering figure of over 40,000.[70] A massive investment of French power, cash, and resources in the Americas, the aim was to carve out a New World empire that would pivot on Haiti, New Orleans, and Louisiana. On arriving, Leclerc proclaimed that all the people of Saint-Domingue, "whatever may be your origin and your color, are all Frenchmen; you are all free, and equal before God and the Republic."[71] This was part of Napoleon's secret three-stage scheme for Haiti: first promise the blacks their freedom while occupying the island's key strategic points; second, arrest and deport potential opponents; third, proceed with the reintroduction of slavery.[72] Fighting soon erupted, nevertheless, between the troops and former slaves now further supplied with weapons and powder by American merchants using remote ports where Leclerc's blockade proved ineffective. Where British vessels in the Caribbean were under orders to keep away, Jefferson made no effort to prevent Americans supplying the black insurgents. By late March, a serious quarrel broke out between France and the United States over the French embargo and Leclerc's sequestration of American cargoes and heavy-handed treatment of captured American skippers and crews. The French insisted on enforcing their prohibition on American and other merchant ships attempting to reach Saint-Domingue ports not controlled by the French when intercepted at sea, a ban the United States flatly rejected. Before long, Leclerc was finding the United States administration and American merchants much less cooperative and forthcoming than had been expected not just with regard to blockading Toussaint but also with respect to supplies for the French army, in helping ease his financial difficulties, and in cooperating with French agents, suppliers, and commissaries.[73]

After three months of fighting, Leclerc defeated Toussaint and exacted his surrender under agreed terms. These did not, however, specify restoration of slavery.[74] Meanwhile, in March 1802, under the Anglo-French Peace of Amiens, Britain returned Martinique to France after a decade of occupation. When the French, contrary to expectation, then made no move to abolish slavery there (which the British had kept in place) but instead, on 20 May 1802, proclaimed the reestablishment of slavery and the slave trade on recently regained Guadeloupe, and in Cayenne, the news provoked general outrage among the black communities of the French Caribbean and especially on Saint-Domingue, and among radical enlighteners everywhere including in the United States. The hollowness of Napoleon's promises and cynical character of his ambitions were suddenly plain for all to see. France had definitively abandoned her role as herald of black emancipation in the transatlantic world operative since 1792. Black insurgency in Haiti, having only just subsided, immediately flared again as everyone realized Napoleon aimed to reintroduce slavery there too.[75] Toussaint Louverture, seized by Leclerc, was deported to France where, incarcerated in the Jura in July 1802, he died in April 1803.

Napoleonic reversal of the Revolution's legislation on behalf of black equality went so far that a decree of 13 Messidor of the Year X (2 July 1802) even forbade the free entry of free blacks and half-castes into France permitted since 1791.[76] In the end, though, Napoleon's monumental betrayal of revolutionary principles, the Rights of Man, and the Caribbean blacks profited him nothing. In the resumed fighting in Haiti, the French slaughtered great numbers of blacks, conducting themselves with a ruthlessness in no way alleviated by their own heavy and growing losses from yellow fever, which exacted an appalling toll on their army. By November 1802, when Leclerc himself died from the fever, the French army on Haiti was so severely depleted it was but a miserable vestige of what it had been nine months before, and the entire island was in revolt against France.[77] The news that the Louisiana Territory was reverting to France was everywhere in the air. In October 1802, formal title to Louisiana was transferred from Spain to France, and the growing confrontation between the United States and France intensified, especially when in November 1802 the acting Spanish governor of New Orleans, on Napoleon's orders, declared a ban on American Mississippi river traffic passing to New

Orleans as part of the wider scheme to restore French imperial control, causing outrage among the settlers of Tennessee, Kentucky, and Ohio.

The dreadful losses from yellow fever on Saint-Domingue were undoubtedly the crucial factor in wrecking Napoleon's scheme for a major new North American empire, especially after his debilitated forces in Haiti were defeated by the black insurgents at the battle of Vertières (18 November 1803). By this time the formidable army sent from France two years before had lost approximately two-thirds of its men. Napoleon was horrified and pronounced himself thoroughly sick of the New World. "There was considerable dislike in Paris against the expedition to Domingo," Paine recounted to Jefferson over a year later, "and the events that have since taken place were then often predicted. The opinion that generally prevailed at that time was that the commerce of the Island was better than the conquest of it,—that the conquest could not be accomplished without destroying the Negroes, and in that case the Island would be of no value."[78] This culminating setback, together with the resumption of the war with Britain (from March 1803), ended all realistic prospect of France regaining Haiti as the pivot for her New World operations, thereby knocking the bottom out of Napoleon's schemes for a vast French Louisiana.[79] Jefferson encouraged Haitian resistance and continued inconveniencing the French by refusing to join in their naval blockade of Haiti while American skippers increasingly subverted it. Helped by the French losses to fever and American dread of a rival North American empire, the former black slaves of Haiti defeated Napoleon and secured their hard-won freedom. The independence of the world's first black republic was officially proclaimed on 1 January 1804, a landmark event in the history of the Caribbean and the end of Napoleon's New World French imperial project.

Napoleon toward the end of his life admitted that his Saint-Domingue venture "was the greatest error that in all my government I ever committed."[80] Following the decisive defeat of November 1803, the decimated remnant of the army he had sent across the Atlantic was partially withdrawn to Spanish Santo Domingo and partly back to France, opening the way to a potentially closer relationship between the United States and Haiti. But having taken advantage of the Haitian black uprising, Jefferson and his faction in Congress now proved unwilling to recognize Haiti's independence—resorting to this ungenerous stance essentially out of deference to adamant Southern opinion in the United States. Far from acclaiming black liberty, the president proceeded to treat Haiti's independence as a threat, seeking to isolate the island and asking Congress not to permit American merchants to fit out Haitian vessels for war so as to prevent the blacks becoming a force at sea.[81] Despite contributing to America's territorial expansion and emergence as a world power by rendering the impending Louisiana purchase conceivable and soon eminently possible, Haiti, now independent and free, gained nothing at all thereby, earning no esteem, gratitude, or reward from Congress, Jefferson, or from Americans more generally.[82]

If Jefferson, like Lafayette, Paine, and Toussaint, condemned Napoleon no less than Robespierre as an outright foe of human rights and republican liberty, from 1804 his administration nevertheless to an extent colluded with Napoleonic France in isolating and seeking to stifle Haiti's Revolution, toward which Jefferson evinced a growing hostility based on fear.[83] On the eve of Haiti's formal independence, the black insurgents' new leader, General Jean-Jacques Dessalines (1758–1806), Toussaint's former lieutenant and the victor of Vertières, wrote to President Jefferson expressing Haiti's friendship for the United States and desire to strengthen commercial ties. Jefferson balked. After the declaration, Jefferson fretted obsessively about the likely disturbing and disruptive effect of Haiti's independence on America society, especially after Dessalines perpetrated a series of horrific massacres—occurring between February and April 1804—of the remaining 3,000 to 5,000 or so whites still living in Haiti. According to Dessalines, this slaughter was justified vengeance on his people's oppressors. The gruesome details were widely publicized in the United States, causing deep shock waves throughout the South.[84] Besides shock at the massacres of whites, Jefferson worried about the influence of Haitian free black seamen and crews on shipping and attitudes in the Caribbean and Gulf of Mexico.[85]

Having failed to collaborate with Napoleon's efforts to embargo the island down to the French evacuation of Haiti and the withdrawal of the remnant of their army, in November 1803, into Santo Domingo, President Jefferson subsequently opted for a policy of strict embargo against the world's first black republic, even boycotting the name "Haiti," designating the island still as "Saint-Domingue." Relations between the world's sole black republic and the United States worsened further when in October 1804 Dessalines, emulating Napoleon, had himself crowned Jacques I, emperor of Haiti. Britain, meanwhile, deftly exploited the Franco-American boycott to become (albeit only while the war against France lasted) the black republic's principal great power sponsor, helping Haitians weather the blockade and wear down the French military remnant ensconced in Santo Domingo. By February 1806, Jefferson and his bloc in Congress had formalized, partly to mollify Napoleon, and Southern opinion, and partly to isolate Haiti, what became a permanent embargo on American navigation to and trade with Haiti.[86] Even though the new Haitian ruler's autocratic style led to his assassination by opponents at the age of forty-eight in October 1806, the boycott remained in place.[87] This marked the point where Jefferson parted company with the radical *philosophique* tradition and the radicalism of his own youth, a reality that his old comrades Lafayette, Kościuszko, and Paine found hard to digest.

Neither Lafayette, nor Kościuszko, nor Paine can have been much impressed with Jefferson's record as president with respect to black emancipation and the future of Haiti. Refusing to believe the American Revolution's international legacy had simply vanished beyond recall, Lafayette regularly reminded Jefferson, writing from his chateau La Grange, near Paris, of his hopes for the eventual retrieval of the true *principes républicaines* that had inspired and conjoined the American and French revolutions. In late 1806, he attended a banquet in honor of Kościuszko and spoke warmly of Polish freedom and Kościuszko's unbending love of liberty. Congratulating Jefferson on the *Declaration of Independence*'s thirty-sixth anniversary, on 4 July 1812, he reminded him how, years before, that same July date had filled them both with vast, intoxicating hopes for America and France, adding that even now, despite the "violation," "corruption," and outright suppression of republican values and principles by Napoleon, he still believed these principles survived in France to a greater extent than was commonly supposed and would one day again "animate the Old as well as the New World."[88]

Paine's last political initiative, early in 1805, was a vain attempt to persuade Jefferson that the United States should endorse the revolution in Haiti, establish warm relations, and seek to mediate on behalf of Haiti to end the conflict between Napoleon and the island's triumphant blacks, thereby helping to draw them out of their isolation.[89] The United States should, he urged, seek to persuade France to withdraw its remaining forces from the eastern part of the island, using the opportunity to win the friendship of the blacks of all Santo Domingo. He was rebuffed. Kościuszko, in his last letter to Jefferson, before his death, dated September 1817, pointedly reminded him of the solemn oath they had sworn, in 1798, to promote and assist the black cause along with that of the rest of humanity.[90]

Astoundingly, for a self-professed democratic republic, the United States maintained its policy of non-recognition of Haiti until 1862!

CHAPTER 15

Louisiana and the Principles of '76

"A Warm Friend to the Liberty and Lasting Welfare of the Human Race"

The acquisition of the vast Louisiana Territory from France in 1803 was certainly the greatest feat of Jefferson's presidency and among the foremost of any presidency. But in terms of consolidating the American Union on the basis of the revolutionary principles of 1776 it was also in several respects problematic. Doubling the United States' size at a stroke while creating a new vast border with the northern segment of Spanish America still called New Spain (until 1821; then Mexico), it also redoubled the social and political difficulties arising from the unresolved controversies surrounding the Revolution's legacy and the "rights of mankind." It re-created in new forms the ideological clash between the Federalist and Jeffersonian factions over the nature of "true republican values." Growing apace geographically, the "empire of liberty" at this point failed to establish a clear profile of this new entity in terms of basic human freedoms.

In the age of the American Revolution, no one else promoted the "Rights of Man" as trenchantly and accessibly as Thomas Paine. "No writer has exceeded Paine in ease and familiarity of style," noted Jefferson, writing to Washington in May 1791, "in perspicuity of expression, happiness of elucidation, and in simple and unassuming language. In this he may be compared to Dr. Franklin; and indeed his *Common Sense* was, for a while, believed to have been written by Dr. Franklin, and published under the borrowed name of Paine, who had come over with him from England."[1] Jefferson considered Paine among the most important of those who made the American Revolution—and then carried "the spirit of '76" to France and then the rest of Europe.[2] In America, as in Britain, Ireland, and France, Paine's *Rights of Man* (1791–93) caused a public furor. The papers were full of it, dividing American opinion sharply between Burkeites and Paineites. Though for the moment the latter seemed the dominant stream generally, this was obviously not the case among America's governing elite. Jefferson too, like Paine, berated Adams for abandoning his earlier "republicanism" and genuine American principles, succumbing to "apostasy to hereditary monarchy and nobility."[3] There were "high and important characters" in American government abjuring Paine's "lessons in republicanism," averred Jefferson writing to Paine (then in France), in June 1792, a "sect preaching up and pouting after an English constitution of king, lords and commons, and whose heads are itching for crowns, coronets, and mitres. But our people, my good friend, are firm and unanimous in their principles of republicanism and there is no better proof of it than that they love what you write and read it with delight. The printers season every newspaper with extracts from your last as they did before from your first part of the *Rights of Man*," he averred, embracing Paine's now explicit appeal for worldwide general democratic revolution. Burke pronounced Paine's text an "infamous libel" on the British system; Jefferson declared himself Paine's "sincere votary" and "ardent well-wisher."[4]

Until 1796, Paine stayed as salient in America's gallery of national heroes as any Founding Father aside from Washington. "Paine and the Rights of Man!" were "regularly employed," one historian observes, "in ritual affirmations of commitment to the revolutionary ideals on which the American republic had been founded, and in negative judgment of American leaders found wanting."[5] During the early 1790s, Paine not only embodied the combined legacies of the American Revolution's radical wing and the French in the eyes of American and French democratic republicans but, like Jefferson and Madison, invoked the parallelism of their shared principles striving to pull the two revolutions closer together. During the critical debate over Louis XVI's fate in the French Convention during December 1792 and January 1793, Paine tried to dissuade the Convention from carrying out the death sentence by enlarging on the likely negative effect of the monarch's execution in America in a speech delivered in French translation by another deputy, Bancal. The United States of America, argued Paine, were at the time revolutionary France's sole ally and, during circumstances of war with Britain, this ally was the only power that could supply the naval stores and munitions that France would be prevented from obtaining in Holland and the Baltic (by British sea power). Louis was regarded by Americans as the personage "who had procured for them their liberty." His execution would have a universally damaging effect even in remote frontier areas (Louisville, Kentucky, founded in the year of the Franco-American Alliance, 1778, was named after the French monarch).

A new French ambassador, noted Paine, was shortly to sail to America (Genet actually arrived on 8 April 1793). Aligned with Brissot and Condorcet, Paine conferred with Genet several times before his departure and knew of Genet's instructions to assist the republican revolution in Haiti and very likely of his schemes also to subvert Canada and organize a coup to seize Spanish New Orleans for the French Republic, the plot to organize a "little spontaneous irruption of the inhabitants of Kentucky into New Orleans" that Genet afterward discussed privately with Jefferson, in Philadelphia, on 5 July 1793.[6] Nothing would be more pleasing to American ears, declared Paine, before the French National Convention, than if this envoy could declare, on arriving, that "in consideration of the part Louis Capet had had in the American Revolution," and given the "affliction that the Americans would feel in response to his execution," the death penalty was being rescinded. Paine's Parisian speech culminated with an emotional appeal: "Oh Citizens! Do not give to the despot of England [i.e., King George III] the pleasure of seeing the man who had aided my cherished American brothers in removing their chains mount the scaffold." Paine's intervention, commented Robespierre's paper, provoked much hostile Montagnard comment.[7]

During the years 1793–95, at banquets and gatherings of the briefly flourishing democratic societies, Paine and "The Rights of Man!" were fervently toasted at 4 July gatherings celebrating Independence Day and the fraternal union of the French and American republics, a vigorous reminder of the lingering power of the radicalism of '76 and its renewal in the French revolutionary democratic tendency.[8] At a joint meeting of the two Philadelphia societies, on 1 May 1794, eight hundred people assembled and enthusiastically hailed the shared principles of the twin revolutions, asserting their democratic ideology's internationalism in a salute thoroughly echoing the spirit of Paine: "The Democratic and Republican Societies of the United States—may they preserve and disseminate their principles, undaunted by the frowns of power, uncontaminated by the luxury of aristocracy, until the Rights of Man shall become the supreme law of every land, and their separate fraternities be absorbed in one great democratic society comprehending the human race."[9]

Briefly, *The Rights of Man* and Paine himself remained iconic in America, deemed to represent the American Revolution's fundamental values and the deep kinship of the American and French revolutions, revolutions firmly wedded to each other as they still were for most Americans—and always remained in Paine's mind. Before learning of the downfall of the French democratic republican faction, Jefferson could pronounce revolutionary affection for the "French people and its cause" in America to be, as he put it writing

388 / Chapter 15

to Madison in June 1793, "universal."[10] Taking up his post in Paris, in September 1794, Jefferson's protégé, James Monroe (1758–1831), who unlike his predecessor Morris (or mentor Jefferson) was not from a privileged, landowning family, and hence no "aristocrat," reminded the post-Thermidor Montagnard authorities that it was not just Jefferson-Madison republicans who enthusiastically endorsed France's Revolution but in fact most of the American public.[11] Unlike Morris (his and Paine's enemy), Monroe demanded Paine's immediate release from the prison for Brissotin victims, the Luxembourg, where the regime had locked him up. To Paine, Monroe wrote declaring it unnecessary for "me to tell you how much all your countrymen, I speak of the great mass of the people, are interested in your welfare." Few had contributed as much to their Revolution; Americans felt in "their bosoms a due sensibility of the merits of those who served them in that great and arduous conflict." They were not ungrateful. "You are considered by them as not only having rendered important services in our own Revolution, but as being, on a more extensive scale, the friend of human rights, and a distinguished and able advocate in favor of public liberty. To the welfare of Thomas Paine, the Americans are not, nor can they be, indifferent."[12]

"I am not an ambitious man," Paine responded to Monroe, "but perhaps I have been an ambitious American. I have wished to see America the *Mother Church* of government, and I have done my utmost to exalt her character and her condition."[13] Since Paine was "destitute of every necessity, without resource and in bad health," Monroe put him up in his handsome residence on the edge of Paris and, as he expressed it, "supplied his wants and furnished him afterwards with additional aid to some amount" although America's envoy, for a time benefiting from his great knowledge of the French Revolution, eventually tired of Paine's tendency to overstay his welcome and depend on others. Paine's vicious spoken outbursts against Washington and hard to restrain eagerness to publish something in the same vein were also a problem. Anti-Washington sentiment among American expatriates in Paris was indeed soon among Monroe's principal difficulties. At the 4 July 1795 dinner at his residence, matters got out of hand when anti-Federalists present refused to allow a toast to George Washington. Monroe devised a diplomatic compromise, getting the company to toast instead the United States' "executive." Even so, word got out and damaged Monroe in Philadelphia where Monroe's enemies, the Federalists around Washington, before long succeeded in getting him recalled.[14]

Paine's prestige in America markedly receded in the months and years during and after his prolonged stay with the Monroes. During the late 1794 "Whiskey Rebellion," Federalists, with some effect, denounced the "rebels" as

"Jacobins" and "anarchists" endeavoring to impose Paine's *Rights of Man* on America unconstitutionally, by force.[15] By 1796, Federalists had partly succeeded in diverting mainstream opinion from its earlier course: sentiment veered against the French Revolution. Publication of Paine's *Letter to George Washington*, of July 1796, sent from France, assailing the 1787 American Constitution as well as the president, materially contributed to this decisive shift. Many were scandalized by Paine's direct, open attack on Washington (beside Adams and Morris), which was generally considered an unjustified and venomous diatribe. "There was a time," averred Paine, "when the fame of America, moral and political stood fair and high in the world. The luster of her Revolution extended itself to every individual; and to be a citizen of America gave a title to respect in Europe." This glow, he alleged, had now waned owing to the "corruption and perfidy" of Washington's administration.[16]

If Paine viewed Washington and his entourage as "apostates from the principles of the Revolution," Washington towered unchallenged in the public eye as the very symbol of the American Revolution and fight for republican liberty. Successfully building a strong executive for the nation, without using Napoleon's despotic methods, he steered the United States away from France and robustly upheld informal "aristocracy" in the new American context. Until the mid-nineteenth century America's first president was not only often viewed (admiringly or critically) as a champion of social hierarchy and the gentry elite but widely seen as a hero whose values were rooted in Bible faith. Washington always preferred "gentlemen" to ordinary folk for military command and high office, later stressed the French minister and historian Guizot in his own critique of democracy written in 1849. In his opinion, "Washington" was a great hero precisely because this Virginia landowner sought to prevent the United States becoming democratic and egalitarian.[17]

Paine stood almost alone in publicly challenging Washington's unparalleled reputation but headed a sizable phalanx deeply critical of the country's general direction, even if most sympathizers reserved their adverse judgments for Hamilton, Adams, Morris, and Jay among those of "this apostate description," and only faintly insinuating America's first president too was an "apostate" from "true principles."[18] To radicals it was an outrage that the Federalist faction in American political life should have now become the undeclared but willing allies of the despots of the Old World and shackled free expression and criticism with the Alien and Sedition Acts. "Whence this political apostasy," exclaimed Paine's ally, the blind Palmer, an ex-preacher well-schooled in Scripture as eager to dispute with clergy as laymen, "this dereliction of good principles in our own country?"[19] For Palmer, the "primary and fundamental objects of all civil and political institutions are the preservation of personal and individual existence—the establishment of liberty on its true basis, the principles of equality, and the security of the fruits of man's industry, and of his pursuit of happiness in every possible way, not inconsistent with the welfare of any member of the community." These he identified as the essential goals of every well-grounded society: "the more perfectly a civil constitution secures and establishes them, the nearer it approaches the true point of political truth and perfection."[20] The republic must seek to maximize the happiness and liberty of all equally.

Although America had begun triumphantly on its separate path, the United States were beginning to resemble the Old World. In engineering this shift religion could be and by some was construed as the decisive factor. It was especially under the guise of religion, using the "war-whoop of the pulpit," protested Paine, answering Sam Adams, in January 1803, that Federalist leaders sought to "overturn the Federal Constitution established on the representative system, and place government in the New World on the corrupt system of the Old."[21] Washington, Adams, Hamilton, and their allies, radicals were convinced, had succeeded in dominating the American scene and marginalizing critics by deceiving the public aided by the pulpit. "But that so large a mass of the people should become the dupes of those who were loading them with taxes in order to load them with chains," argued Paine, "and deprive them of the right of election, can be ascribed only to that species of wildfire rage, lighted up by falsehood that not only acts without reflection, but is too impetuous to make any." Religious authority and pastors had crucially misdirected the public, supplementing religion with collective emotion and political "falsehood believed to be truth," a furious, immoral "clamor" deliberately whipped up by false claims wreaking vast havoc.[22]

Paine's diatribe against Washington together with his openly irreligious and deistic *Age of Reason* (1794–95), the text that blighted Paine's reputation among the public in Holland, Germany, and Scandinavia as well as Britain and the United States,[23] effectively wrecked his previously high standing. In their published sermons leading American Protestant clergy rounded on the *Age of Reason* as a highly offensive spur to "infidelity," exhorting their congregations against Paine and his books and insisting on the "Christian" character of the American Revolution.[24] Buoyed by the "Second Great Awakening" and the spectacularly rapid growth of the Methodist and Baptist churches, American religion received a powerful boost at the grassroots level, arousing great numbers of individuals who had earlier shown less commitment religious and political. By 1800, the popular religiosity of the "Awakening" had emerged as the most powerful moral, social, and educational force in the country. By expanding personal religious engagement on a scale never witnessed before, a prodigious political impulse was mobilized from the late 1790s onward against all forms of Enlightenment, moderate and radical. While hard-core radicals continued exalting his name, most anti-Federalists consequently ceased invoking Paine and began discarding his legacy as a liability. Americans turned their backs on Paine; and only after Jefferson succeeded Adams, in March 1801, did a United States president officially invite the author of *Common Sense* to return to America from what, since his release in 1794, resembled self-imposed exile.[25] By then, Jacobinism had been so thoroughly vilified by preachers that the transatlantic ideology of the "Rights of Man" was widely considered a dark, pervasive subversive force menacing every pillar of society, morality, and order (not unlike the overblown threat of "communism" of the McCarthy era).

Palmer set up his Deistical Society of the State of New York in 1796–97, with offshoot branches in Philadelphia and Baltimore, to fight the new political power of the pulpit, proclaiming "science and truth, virtue and happiness" the sole "great objects to which the activity and energy of the human faculties ought to be directed." Among his chief allies prior to Paine's return was the Irish ex-priest who had turned violently against Christianity, Denis Driscol. Palmer and his group called themselves the "Theophilanthropists"; their Federalist adversaries, underlining the fact that their radicalism allegedly derived from abroad, styled them the "Columbian Illuminati." The Christian faith, contended Palmer and his clique, had become false to itself and, by entering the political sphere in its newly resumed barnstorming manner with the "Second Great Awakening," especially in its Baptist and Methodist guise, was systematically misleading vast segments of the populace by unleashing powerful but negative emotions promoting terror at sinfulness certainly but also paranoid fear of subversion, infiltration, and "infidelity." Palmer had a rival corpus of "Scripture" to offer. Those most "entitled to the universal gratitude and applause of the human race," he averred in 1801, were Condorcet, Godwin, and Barlow, and among "all the books that ever were published, Volney's *Ruins* is pre-eminently entitled to the appellation of 'Holy Writ' and ought to be read in the churches." No less canonical were Paine's writings, expounding "truth with much simplicity, but with irresistible force."[26]

For Paine, Palmer, Barlow, Coram, Freneau, and their adherents, rejecting conventional religion and religious authority was intimately entwined with their sweeping political and social reformism. Asserting universal and equal rights was inseparably linked to their offensive against organized religion, especially the "Second Awakening" and the Baptist surge. The two impulses remained inseparably linked in their thought and writing. In this respect, this American fringe supplemented by recently arrived dissidents from Britain and Ireland were classic products of Radical Enlightenment. According to Palmer,

Driscol, Cheetham, and another ally, the New York bookseller (and later manager of the New York City waterworks) Colonel John Fellows (1759–1844), a Yale graduate and Revolutionary War veteran who had fought at Bunker Hill and a "personal friend" of Paine, the "Awakening" was a sham. An eager enlightener, Fellows published American editions of *The Age of Reason*, Barlow's collected political essays (1796), and other texts of Paine and Barlow besides d'Holbach in translation;[27] he also sold sets of Diderot's *Encyclopédie* (sent by Barlow from France). To Fellows "religion, which means nothing but belief in idle, fantastic stories, owes its origin to ignorance and fears of mankind in remote and barbarous ages"; worse, organized religion had been "found admirably adapted to the support of despotism" and was hence "sedulously cultivated and rigidly enforced among nations, the enlightened part of which have long since ceased to be the dupes of its extravagant vagaries. . . . In short, it has been made a cheating, money-making business, and kings and priests, both equally useless, have divided the spoil. Kings could not exist without priests. Their trades exactly fit each other."[28]

Those concurring, though, like Jefferson and Madison, by this time often felt constrained to do so tacitly.[29] Won over by the "Second Awakening," the public had grown deaf to all suggestion that anything in post-revolutionary America might have gone seriously wrong. Late in life, after Paine's death, Jefferson still judged Paine and his early inspiration, Bolingbroke, "honest men; both advocates for human liberty" but had absolutely no wish for his private views to be flaunted publicly.[30] By 1800, the hard-core radicals' militant, obdurate stance inevitably threatened to marginalize the entire radical tendency. Desire for further democratization and reform, and a sense of sharing in this with the French, undoubtedly persisted in many quarters.[31] As late as 1800, French revolutionary and republican successes in Italy were being celebrated by farmers in Lafayette County, Kentucky.[32] But only a handful of anti-Federalists aligned with Paine, Palmer, Driscol, Cheetham, and Fellows: most Americans, including most writers and newspaper editors, by this time firmly sided with the pastors. "Pure religion is perfectly republican," insisted the former radical Noah Webster. "Religion has been perverted," he could not deny, "and in many countries made the basis of a system of ecclesiastical domination which has enslaved the minds of men, as political power had before enslaved their bodies." But in the Protestant America of 1800 dominated by Baptists, Methodists, and Congregationalists the situation differed profoundly, leaving no room for that "set of fanatical reformers, called philosophers, charging that oppression to the religion itself, which sprang only from its abuses." And if the tirades of "philosophists" against pastors were wrongheaded, no less so was their exalting democracy, assaulting "aristocracy," and

Federalists, their assailing the existing social and moral order. Their plea for democracy was misconceived, contended Webster in a well-publicized oration at New Haven, Connecticut, in 1802. The doctrine that "universal enjoyment of the right of suffrage is the best security for free elections and a pure administration" was "absurd," democracy's defects being proven by "experience" since a "liberal extension of the right of suffrage accelerates the growth of corruption, by multiplying the number of corruptible electors, and reducing the price of venal suffrages."[33]

Webster called on the American public to repudiate and denounce democracy and the French Revolution together with the "philosophists" who exalted both and "boldly denied the sacred origin of Christianity, and attempted to extirpate its doctrines and institutions."[34] Henceforth, there was no way to defend the French Revolution's reputation and standing, and even most radicals felt constrained to cease doing so, moved by the shift in American opinion and events in France. For Driscol, Napoleon's invasion of Saint-Domingue and reintroduction of black slavery in 1802 was the last straw: it was no longer possible to view Napoleon as continuing the fight for the French Revolution's basic goals.[35] If Federalists and radicals alike continued claiming to represent the American Revolution's veritable spirit and tradition, in the American ideological arena of 1800, the forces repudiating Paineism, Jacobinism, and Jefferson's "infidelity" had dramatically gained ground while those embracing French Revolution principles and the Rights of Man were becoming isolated from mainstream society.[36] Jefferson won the November 1800 presidential election owing to discontents and strong Southern support in no way motivated by democratic principles. The loudly decried republican hard core that persisted in fighting for what they considered the American Revolution's "true principles" after 1800 persevered only as a marginalized and deeply alienated fringe.[37]

Admittedly, during 1799–1800, the republican newspapers recovered lost ground. But they achieved this mainly by switching attention from basic issues to personalities, aided by the internal Federalist split, pitting Adams against Hamilton. This vitriolic quarrel buoyed the gathering counterattack on the Alien and Sedition Acts, which Adams himself now repudiated and blamed chiefly on Hamilton (who was more willing publicly to insist on their implementation).[38] The resumed newspaper offensive against the Federalists and increasingly bad odor surrounding the Sedition Decrees made possible Jefferson's until then unexpected and in the event narrowly won electoral victory. "The newspapers are an overmatch for any Government," complained one Federalist: "they first overawe and then usurp it. This has been done and the Jacobins owe their triumph to the unceasing use of this engine."[39] The reputations of both Adams and Hamilton were wrecked. John Adams's political career, commented Paine with satisfaction, was fated to "begin with hypocrisy, proceed with arrogance, and finish in contempt. May such be the fate of all such characters."[40] Briefly, hard-core republicans had cause to celebrate.

Anxious to purge every vestige of court ceremony and monarchical splendor from the presidency, the first president inaugurated in Washington, Jefferson, distanced himself from the first president by dispensing with all forms of grandeur and display.[41] At the same time, he and his following felt tightly boxed in. His presidential inauguration proved a decidedly more conciliatory, tepid, and less confident affair than radical supporters had eagerly anticipated.[42] His inaugural plea for reconciliation—now "we are all republicans, we are all Federalists"—uttered in a trembling voice, revealed all too plainly his new post-1800 concern with papering over the cracks and dread of ever again becoming embroiled in what Paine, in November 1802, writing in the *National Intelligencer*, termed the "Reign of Terror that raged in America during the latter end of the Washington administration, and the whole of that of Adams." "So far as respects myself," recalled Paine, "I have reason to believe and a right to say that the leaders of the Reign of Terror in America [i.e., the authors of the Alien and Sedition Acts] and the leaders of the Reign of Terror in France, during the time of Robespierre, were in character the same sort of men; or how is it to be accounted for, that I was persecuted by both at the same time?"[43] Here Paine was decidedly stretching a point since the Montagne did not espouse "aristocracy" and were infinitely more authoritarian, populist, and antagonistic to the essential values of '76 and '89 than the Federalists. But when it came to bellowing about "infidelity," suppressing democratic voices, and betraying the public, it appeared "there must have been a coalition in sentiment, if not in fact, between the Terrorists of America and the Terrorists of France, and Robespierre must have known it, or he could not have had the idea of putting America into the bill of accusation against me."[44]

Once ensconced in the newly finished White House, from 1801, Jefferson and Madison, his secretary of state (1801–9), found themselves hemmed in by the fragility of their electoral support. Jefferson unmistakably owed his precarious victory to solid Southern backing. He gained over three-quarters of all the electoral votes in the South (82 percent) compared with barely more than a quarter in the North (27 percent).[45] Almost immediately fierce wrangling set in among his political following over slavery, Indian policy, education, religious tests for officeholding, blasphemy laws, and Sunday observance. Emotionally and rhetorically, many former anti-Federalists had by this point rallied to the originally exclusively Federalist attack on Jacobinism and "infidelity."[46] Certainly, a tentatively republican course was adopted. By 1802, the U.S. army had been cut back, military spending slashed, many Federalist senior army and naval officers purged, and the number of officer cadets being trained at West Point reduced.[47] The Alien and Sedition Acts immediately lapsed and American freedom of expression and to criticize were triumphantly reaffirmed. In November 1800, Palmer and Driscol could establish *The Temple of Reason*, a deist paper published first in New York and then Philadelphia that lasted for three years and, in unprecedented fashion, openly attacked "Christianity" as such.[48] Hamilton's whiskey tax was repealed. But the democratic republican recovery of 1799–1801 in the United States was truncated and partial—a limited victory that largely dispensed with promoting equal rights and democracy, or invoking Paine and the French Revolution.

Ideologically, Jefferson's electoral victory was overshadowed by the continuing anti-Jacobin frenzy, burgeoning Washington cult, and all-embracing "Second Great Awakening." In consequence, his supporters were increasingly divided into two distinct and even opposed categories that Rush differentiated as "moderate republicans" and "violent democrats."[49] The dividing lines between them were doubtless far from always clear. But broadly, those campaigning to end black slavery and integrate the blacks into society separated from those resisting abolition on grounds of "state rights," those opposing religious tests from those backing the pulpit, those demanding secular and universal education, more justice for the Indians, and subordination of the judiciary to the legislature from those opposed, those hostile to strong state senates and governors from those more amenable to lawyers and the status quo. Only the "violent democrats," headed by William Duane, editor of the Philadelphia *Aurora*, the Paine-Palmer clique, and the Philadelphia doctor and activist Michael Leib (1760–1822), a congressman in 1799–1806 and senator from 1809 to 1814, held out as genuine heirs of Paineism, the pre-1800 Jefferson and the republican democratizers of 1776.[50] Continuing the style of public mobilization practiced by the mid-1790s democratic societies, they campaigned against Federalists, big money, and the arcane grip of the lawyers over the judicial process, seeking to expand the influence of Pennsylvania's lower legislative house and lessen that of the governor and state senate.

Jefferson's post-1801 quest to distance himself from recent ferocious battles of principle, however, and the sheer fragility of his supporters' position increasingly constrained him—driving him into an ideological and political retreat and minimalism with profound implications for the future.[51] He may have been the "greatest democrat who has yet emerged from the bosom of

American democracy,"[52] as Alexis de Tocqueville (1805–59) later expressed it, but as president, he was bound to disillusion and, at times, antagonize hard-core radicals since from the outset he chose to narrow and paper over the rift between his side and the Federalists even though such tactics could do little to resolve the underlying clash of principles dividing the Revolution's legacy. If, in the 1830s, De Tocqueville, the greatest nineteenth-century European commentator on America, dreaded most the "tyranny of the majority," the real menace, held Paine, Palmer, and their allies, was how ready the majority were when directed by preachers, finance, and government to support "tyranny" against their own interest.

The new president deliberately passed over his more strident journalist backers, like Duane and Callender, for federal printing contracts, in favor of gentler voices.[53] Among Jefferson's first acts as president, in March 1801, was his official pardon of everyone convicted under the Sedition Act, those exonerated including Callender, who had been fined and incarcerated for affirming in print the "wretched timidity of Mr. Washington," "his abject tameness to England, and his gross duplicity to France."[54] But Jefferson and Madison declined to reward their former ally with the public post, as postmaster of Richmond, he angled for. Anxious to calm the ideological fury of the 1790s, neither were they keen to retain his services as a publicist, preferring the Genevan Albert Gallatin (1761–1849), who, like Volney, had been a target of the Alien Act but was less abrasive.[55] Being dispensed with so affronted the doughty Scot that Callender was never subsequently reconciled. Breaking with his old paper, the *Richmond Examiner*, he became Richmond's prime anti-Republican journalist instead and in September 1802 exacted vengeance by publishing a scathing attack on Jefferson in the *Richmond Recorder*, pronouncing the latter's relationship with his black concubine, Sally Hemings, a fine example to the nation by the "favourite, the first born of republicanism! The pinnacle of all that is good and great."[56] The "Republican" papers turned on Callender. Jefferson too retaliated, styling him a "lying renegade from Republicanism" and claiming he had never employed Callender, an untruth Callender exposed by publishing copies of letters from Jefferson thanking him for assisting against Federalist opponents.[57]

Earlier, Jefferson and his ideological allies had desired Paine (who had left America for Europe in 1787) to return to assist them in the political battle; for a few years after 1794 they keenly awaited his return.[58] No one else contended so publicly that America had lamentably lapsed from its true path and the Revolution's authentic values.[59] Paine, though, understandably preferred Paris under the Directoire to placing himself within reach of the Federalist "Terror." In the United States, he faced a fast deteriorating situation, aggravated by the Alien and Sedition Acts, and he knew it: "The government of England honoured me with a thousand martyrdoms, by burning me in effigy in every town in that country, and their hirelings in America may do the same."[60] Only with the lapsing of the Alien and Sedition Acts did Paine become willing to resume his efforts to influence America's course and help revive Revolution principles by returning. After an absence of fifteen years, shortly after Toussaint Louverture's arrival in France, as Napoleon's prisoner, Paine disembarked at Baltimore, on 30 October 1802, to encounter a small "curious" crowd and generally cool reception.

From the moment he stepped ashore Paine came under torrents of Federalist abuse. The author of *Common Sense* had become the wicked "Jacobin" maligner of Washington, the "living opprobrium of humanity, the infamous scavenger of all the filth which could be raked from the dirty paths which have been hitherto trodden by all the revilers of Christianity."[61] America's newly elected president had offered Paine an American naval vessel to escort him back from France, to preclude interception by the British, ensuring that some of this vituperation rubbed off also on him. In the Federalist press, Paine, the "libeler of Washington," was accounted the "particular friend and correspondent of Mr. Jefferson, patron of all that is base." "Our pious President," deplored the *Baltimore Republican, or, The Anti-Democrat*, "thought it expedient to dispatch a frigate for the accommodation of this loathsome reptile."[62] The Philadelphia *Aurora* and the few other republican papers championing Paine and his cause were swamped. Paine's bitter attacks on Washington and Adams in any case accorded ill with the new post-1800 trend toward reconciliation that Jefferson himself, once the Alien and Sedition Acts were dismantled and the army purged, now favored.[63]

Although the president welcomed him and they conferred, Paine making several visits to the White House (much to the irritation of Federalist critics), in terms of the presidential image in the country, Paine's growing notoriety and soon shabby image, aggravated by his unruly lifestyle and alcoholism, seemed more of a drawback than an asset. Politically and socially he grew gradually more and more isolated. While he lived, Jefferson later confided to Bonneville, "I thought it my duty, as well as a test of my own political principles to support him against the persecution of the unprincipled faction"; but, from 1802, unsurprisingly, the president found this "duty" an increasing strain.[64] If the radical artist Charles Wilson Peale, who had painted Paine's portrait for Jefferson back in 1788 and included both Paine and Jefferson in his renowned collection of busts and portraits of the Revolution's leading figures,[65] like the radical congressman Leib warmly welcomed him back to Philadelphia, and if Palmer proclaimed him "one of the first and best of writers and probably the most useful man that ever existed upon the face of the earth,"[66] after 1802 most former political allies and friends publicly or privately repudiated the returned hero. In the city where he had first won fame several surviving former comrades turned the proverbial cold shoulder. "His principles avowed in his *Age of Reason* were so offensive to me," recalled Rush in 1809, "that I did not wish to renew my intercourse with him."[67]

The now elderly Sam Adams wrote from Boston, in November 1802, acknowledging that *Common Sense* and other writings "unquestionably awakened the public mind, and led the people to call for a Declaration of our national Independence. I therefore esteemed you as a warm friend to the liberty and lasting welfare of the human race." But more recently Paine had aggravated the "spirit of angry controversy." His "defense of infidelity" had "much astonished" and grieved Sam Adams: "our friend, the President of the United States [Jefferson], has been calumniated for his liberal sentiments, by men who have attributed that liberality to a latent design to promote the cause of infidelity." In fact, Paine's ill-advised proceedings had weakened Jefferson's hand, exposing him to the debilitating "noise and violence of faction."[68] Paine's reply reiterated his objections to religious authority and bigotry, inveighing against the mounting intolerance and persecution to which he and his friends were being subjected: "even error has a claim to indulgence, if not respect, when it is believed to be the truth."[69]

Barlow, like Palmer, continued championing Paine's democratic and antiecclesiastical views, but on returning from France, in 1805, he too avoided resuming his former close collaboration with his old mentor. From a letter of 1809 to James Cheetham, editor of the influential New York anti-Federalist paper the *American Citizen* (1800–1810) and the radical expelled from Britain who initially was a close comrade of Paine's in America but afterward quarreled bitterly with him and, after his death, wrote a viciously hostile biography, it seems Barlow still counted Paine "among the brightest and most undeviating luminaries of the age"; but he had become distinctly warier of his failings, his seeking "consolation in the sordid, solitary bottle" and refuge "in low company."[70] He may also have resented Paine's elopement with—or seduction of, as some called it—Bonneville's wife, bringing her to America and then treating her shabbily. Barlow certainly regretted the harm done to the radical cause and to Jefferson by the scandal over the *Age of Reason*; but possibly he kept his distance chiefly because closer association could only compromise his own efforts to enlist Jefferson and Congress for ambitious schemes in educational reform.[71]

Yet few had wholly forgotten *Common Sense*'s decisive impact, and Paine set out to rebuild his once formidable, if always fiercely contested, American reputation with a series of open letters "To the Citizens of the United States," the first appearing in November 1802, aimed at rekindling "sparks from the altar of Seventy-Six." America had fallen prey to a faction of grasping and dangerous men who had abandoned the American Revolution's authentic principles and begun to "contemplate government as a profitable monopoly, and the people as hereditary property. It is, therefore, no wonder that the *Rights of Man* was attacked by that faction, and its author continuously abused." It had distressed him to see America during the 1790s "turning her back on her own glory," and he warned of the dangers of allowing Federalist attitudes to advance: "in the midst of the freedom we enjoy, the licentiousness of the papers called Federal (and I know not why they are called so, for they are in their principles anti-federal and despotic) is a dishonor to the character of the country, and an injury to its reputation and importance abroad."[72] The American and French revolutions afforded the opportunity to refashion all humanity fundamentally by creating a new kind of republican democratic political system in which the "rights of all men would be preserved" and America would serve as the inspiration of the world. But the "Rights of Man" had not been upheld in either America or France, contended Paine, now eager to promote in America his mature political thought and—since 1791 and the second part of the *Rights of Man*—unqualified commitment to universal suffrage and democratic republicanism.[73]

Retreat from the principles of '76 meant erosion of America's example to the world. Insidious efforts were being made to claw back freedom of expression, block democracy, and extend executive power as well as introduce bicameralism and reinforce ecclesiastical authority. The 1790 liquidation of Pennsylvania's 1776 democratic constitution that had earlier encouraged radicals in Vermont and to a degree everywhere was deplorable. Pennsylvania's single chamber had been replaced by a two-chamber legislature with an upper house reserved for the new informal aristocracy of privilege and money. Pennsylvania's legislators had conferred on their governor—together with a "great quantity of patronage" plainly "copied from England"—comprehensive veto powers enabling this public officeholder to block any legislation passed by the legislature he took a dislike to.[74] These, Paine concurred with the German Fries "rebels," were just a few of innumerable damaging reverses.[75]

From the so-called revolution of 1800 onward, with Jefferson in power, the radicals signally failed to make headway against the mounting press campaign directed against them, quite the contrary. No one had fought harder for a fully free press, the resource in which all radical enlighteners vested their hopes, than Paine, Palmer, Fellows, Freneau, Duane, Driscol, Callender, Cheetham, and their allies. Some Federalists too exalted freedom of the press. "In republican governments," declared Webster, in his *American Minerva*, in December 1793, in contrast to monarchies and aristocratic regimes, free newspapers are essential: "like schools, it should be a main point to encourage them; like schools, they should be considered as auxiliaries of government and placed on a respectable footing; they should be the heralds of truth, the protectors of peace and good order."[76] Yet during Paine's long absence American opinion had been largely captured by an uneducated or barely schooled majority guided mainly by revived religion, commercial pressures, and the ambition of lead editors like John Fenno and his son, Jack Fenno, who seemingly specialized in pandering to the lowest common denominator—majority chauvinism, assumptions, and prejudice rather than the ideal of steering readers toward insight, justice, and truth.

Consequently, during the very years the United States expanded geographically most dramatically and began edging onto New Spain's borders, the United States, infused with a new religiosity, was ideologically at war with the tenaciously resisting intellectual residue still vociferously committed to their particular version of the principles of '76.

Louisiana and the Counterrevolution

From 1801, when the news that Louisiana was to be transferred from Spain to France became known in America, Jefferson's opponents, Hamilton, Morris, and Aaron Burr, exploited the new president's Caribbean difficulties to whip up dissatisfaction, urging immediate war with Spain to seize New Orleans by force before retrocession took effect.[77] Louisiana became a pressing issue and Jefferson needed a solution. Paine was among those best placed to inform the president about current conditions in France, Napoleon's chronic cash shortage (not yet known about in the United States), and his strategic predicament with Anglo-French friction intensifying, Austria and Prussia irreconcilable, and Haiti plunged in massive separatist upheaval.[78] From August 1802, during his last weeks in France, Paine sent Jefferson several letters proposing ways, short of war, to acquire Louisiana and outlining precisely how, should negotiations succeed, he thought the Territory should be incorporated into the Union to safeguard revolutionary and republican values. Besides gaining Jefferson's ear, this was a means of countering Bonaparte's harassment of him for his democratic republicanism. Paine could assist Jefferson, elbow Napoleon, bolster Haiti's revolution, and further the Louisiana project and all in one. Back in America, he discussed Louisiana with Leib, who encouraged his renewing his approach to Jefferson.[79]

Thomas Jefferson (1743–1826), 1805, by the Pennsylvanian artist Rembrandt Peele (1778–1860). Photo credit: HIP / Art Resource, NY.

French Saint-Domingue's collapse in 1803 opened the door to an amicable solution to the Franco-American differences over Louisiana. Although Jefferson probably preferred to see Louisiana stay French than go to war with France, the rise of a French empire in North America controlling Mississippi navigation and directly blocking America's westward expansion, he recognized, was wholly unacceptable to his supporters as well as Congress. He was greatly relieved by the rapid erosion of Napoleon's Caribbean army during 1802–3 and eager to exploit France's overall predicament. Congress authorized the funds with which he proposed to take advantage of Napoleon's difficulties. The negotiations commenced in April 1803 with the avowedly Francophile Monroe acting as agent. The talks, following Napoleon's change of heart, went smoothly with Volney strenuously urging the First Consul and his foreign minister, Talleyrand, to agree. These secret negotiations transpired without Napoleon so much as consulting his scorned ally, Spain, despite the projected transfer being apt to greatly weaken Spain's strategic stance in North America and the Caribbean, leaving the entire Spanish American empire more vulnerable to smuggling, conspiracy, and settler infiltration.

Signed in Paris, on 10 May 1803, history's most astounding sale agreement doubled the area of the United States at a stroke, transferring from France to the United States in perpetuity the entire Louisiana Territory, encompassing an area corresponding to the present-day states of Louisiana, Arkansas, Missouri, Kansas, Oklahoma, Nebraska, and the Dakotas, in exchange for fifty million francs. The purchase embraced New Orleans, and control of the Mississippi estuary and navigation, along with no less than 828,000 square miles of land stretching to New Spain and the Canadian border. But this was not all. For the transfer inevitably further aggravated the question of the Floridas, the last remaining segment of southeastern North America outside the United States' bounds, another large territory converging with Louisiana at the Mississippi estuary in a manner inconvenient for settlers along the lower Mississippi Valley. During the Independence war, in 1779, Spanish forces from Louisiana and Cuba had captured first Mobile (today in Alabama), port and chief town of West Florida, founded by the French as part of Louisiana in 1702, and then Pensacola, Britain's base in eastern Florida. Under the Versailles treaty (1783) acknowledging American Independence, "the Floridas" formally reverted to Spain.

Both Floridas, since 1783, formed a single Spanish captaincy-general together with Cuba, administered from Havana. Combined with "Louisiana" the Floridas had constituted a vast Spanish military and naval buffer now plainly conceived as a barrier against American rather than British and French influence in the Caribbean and Gulf of Mexico. Spain, though, lacked the resources effectively to control the extensive slices of North America she regained. "Philosophical" observers hardly expected the hugely expanded but flimsy Spanish North American holdings to seriously impede the American Revolution's further spread. For one thing, the new border with Spanish North America (Texas, California, Arizona, New Mexico, Louisiana, and West and East Florida), fixed in 1783, was ill-defined and porous. Only "liberty," urged Brissot, could develop the vast Louisiana Territory, a land he expected to attract more and more immigrants. New Orleans would be the "first step toward the conquest of Louisiana and peaceful infiltration and civilizing of Mexico and Peru. . . . May this come about soon for the good of the human race! Consider how necessary it is, how possible it is, and what tremendous advantages will result for the whole world."[80] In the early 1790s, New Orleans did in fact become a hotbed of pro-Jacobin, democratic republican sentiment especially among the city's many free blacks and mulattoes.[81]

From 1804, the American government took to openly pressuring a debilitated and divided Spain to surrender the gains made at British expense during the 1779–81 campaigns in North America. These additional territories, present-day Alabama and Mississippi beside Florida, were not yet acquired by the United States in 1803, but with tensions in West Florida rising, Jefferson, negotiating through his envoys, Monroe and Pinckney, at the royal palace at Aranjuez, near Madrid, strove to exploit Spain's weakness and international difficulties trying to lever both Floridas—or at least West Florida—peaceably into American hands. In February 1804, Congress passed the "Mobile Act," a major encroachment on Spanish North American territory and rights, disputing customs rights, demanding concessions relating to Mississippi River navigation to and from the Gulf of Mexico, and requiring compensation for spoliation of American vessels by Spanish and French privateers acting under Spanish authorizations since 1796. Spain should cede West and East Florida, urged the United States, as France had ceded Louisiana, for cash and cancellation of the alleged reparations debt.[82] Some American officials, adopting a considerably tougher stance than Jefferson, proposed seizing Texas, the part of New Spain most closely abutting on Louisiana, as a hostage and threatening outright war to clinch the Floridas too.

In 1803–4, the American republic was immensely enlarged, and verging on being still further expanded, in a manner no previous empire or republic ever had. This certainly presented a unique opportunity for one of Jefferson's favorite democratizing policies: distributing large amounts of public land to landless whites (but not blacks) at low prices.[83] But America was also being transformed into a new kind of continental entity, raising fundamental and troubling questions about its trajectory and general character. When news spread that Napoleon had ceded Louisiana to the United States, New Orleans's French-speaking and Spanish-speaking whites began organizing for the new order. They petitioned Congress for the right to enter the Union as a fully-fledged state with their own existing white majority, traditions, and "rights," including the right to import slaves.[84]

New Orleans's populace, Paine and others had already pointed out, having always been governed by French and Spanish royal and ecclesiastical authority, lacked experience of representative government and possessed no inkling of republican or democratic ideas. For American values to prevail it was imperative, Paine argued, that during the interim before Louisiana gained statehood the democratic and non-slave status of the new territory's group of projected future states should be firmly established and energetic measures taken to secure American liberty in full. Louisiana should remain provisionally, for some years, under a *gouvernement provisoire* so that its inhabitants "may be initiated into the practice [of representative government] by electing their municipal government, and after some experience they will be in train to elect their state government."[85] The boundaries of the projected "states" of the Louisiana Territory should be immediately fixed but with Congress imposing a transitional administration to last until the new "states" were ready to elect their own representatives. It was essential to prevent local Catholic oligarchs and church authorities conserving Louisiana's existing institutions intact, in the way the laws and administration of French royal Canada had been conserved by the British under the Quebec Act, for this would entrench a separate legal, moral, and social identity with the old elites retaining control.

Jefferson evaded the danger of local French planters, royalists, and clergy gaining control of New Orleans and the surrounding area by flatly rejecting his own earlier principle, laid out in the Northwest Ordinance, of provisional government by a local legislative council. He opted instead for provisional government without representation by a federally appointed governor. Since this solution blatantly contradicted his own oft-stated democratic principles, the scheme was laid before Congress in a concealed fashion in a bill presented by the relevant Senate committee's chairman, John Breckinridge (1760–1806), the Kentucky planter and congressman who had acted as Jefferson's right-hand man in mobilizing against the Alien and Sedition Acts.[86] Jefferson's plan to impose a non-elected acting governor and council on the new territory, and hence tax Louisiana without their consent, was inevitably opposed by the town's householders, under their leader, a planter recently chosen mayor of New Orleans, Étienne de Boré (1740–1820). Educated in Paris and among the most enterprising of the Mississippi Delta planters, Boré had revolutionized the technology of sugar extraction from sugarcane and had a large impact on the region's cash crop agriculture. Rather than Breckinridge's scheme, Boré demanded local autonomy prior to statehood on the Northwest Ordinance model of which Jefferson himself had been prime author.[87] Jefferson's "absolute and uncontrolled dominion of Louisiana," as one Federalist critic put it, was opposed as assuming "a power unwarranted by the Constitution and dangerous to the liberties of the United States" by New Orleans, some "republicans," and many Federalists, including John Quincy Adams.[88]

The vast Louisiana Territory entered the "empire of liberty" without having any representative organ of any kind during the era of Jefferson's presidency. Local whites and local free blacks and mulattoes—of whom there were a relatively large number since French and Spanish slavery laws rendered manumission, and the self-emancipation of slaves through money payments, easier to procure than under the Anglo-American system—had no voice in this imposed provisional government. In flagrant dereliction of their own professed ardor for representative government, complained Matthew Lyon, Jefferson and Madison intentionally subjected the entire Louisiana Territory to "probationary slavery."[89] Under the congressional ordinance of October 1803 (which Jefferson had written himself), the president received "sweeping powers, "an assumption of implied power" John Quincy Adams called it, totally at odds with his constitutional role within the United States proper, personally to administer the Louisiana Purchase.[90] The vast new territory was divided by a line today forming the northern boundary of Louisiana, with the expanse to the north, the "District of Louisiana," placed under a separate "governor" and with its capital at St. Louis, a small French town that was the focus of the fur trade for a vast area either side of the Mississippi Valley.[91] To the south, with New Orleans as capital, was the predominantly Franco-Spanish "Territory of Orleans." It was to remain for eight years (1804–12) under an imposed federal administration, directed ultimately from Washington, its officials and garrison headed by Governor William Claiborne (c. 1774–1817). Claiborne, who spoke no French on arriving and almost immediately clashed with local sentiment, was not Jefferson's first choice. The president had wanted Lafayette to "annul the efforts of the foreign agitators [i.e., Saint-Domingue slave-owning royalists] who are arriving in droves"; but Lafayette refused the Louisiana governorship, as did Monroe, Jefferson's second choice, a dependable anti-Federalist fluent in French and chief negotiator of the Louisiana Purchase. Unable to find another prominent ally with French, Claiborne in the end was chosen faute de mieux.[92]

Claiborne's initial steps met with considerable resistance from Boré and local elites. Answerable only to the president, he guaranteed to the French and Spanish inhabitants merely their "rights of conscience and of property"— including slaves—and "to the Indian inhabitants their occupancy and self-government, establishing friendly and commercial relations with them." His most vital task was, as harmoniously as possible, to create a balance between French and English speakers—which soon proved to be no simple matter.[93] The local protest movement opposing the Territorial Government gained momentum at a public meeting in New Orleans on 1 July 1804, with a ringing manifesto demanding immediate autonomy and representative institutions, *The Remonstrance of the People of Louisiana*, approved by some 250 local householders that reappeared in the *Louisiana Gazette* on 24 July 1804. If Congress desired a "free allegiance of citizens attached to your fortunes by choice, bound to you by gratitude," they must accord to Louisiana's inhabitants the rights earlier "territories" had enjoyed.[94] Two weeks later Boré cleverly raised the heat further by reprinting in another New Orleans paper the *Lettre adressé aux habitants de la Province de Québec, ci-devant le Canada*, addressed to Canada by the United States Congress in October 1774, admonishing French Canadians that the first and foremost "right" of the people is to participate in government through its representatives and be governed only by laws of which they themselves have approved.[95]

The charge of hypocrisy and betrayal could hardly have been clearer. In his last major pamphlet, published in September 1804, a tract appearing in both French and English, Paine roundly condemned the Louisiana whites' petition for immediate autonomy and immediate entry into the Union on their own terms (which some in Congress were calling for). Unlike the Americans or inhabitants of France, Paine reminded the Franco-Spanish citizenry, "you are arriving at freedom by the easiest means that any people ever enjoyed it; without contest, without expense, and even without any contrivance of your own. And you already so far mistake principles, that under the name of 'rights' you ask for powers: power to import and enslave Africans; and to govern a territory that we have purchased." There was little justice in this; Louisiana's talk of "rights" was counterfeit. "You see what mischief ensued in France by the possession of power before they understood principles." Despite their protests, it was in the long-term interest of Louisiana's existing French and Spanish inhabitants to undergo a fundamental transformation of their society, to see their people reeducated in a manner that soundly eradicated monarchical, aristocratic, and ecclesiastical influence.[96] To prevent Louisiana following the pattern of French-speaking Canada, foresight and energetic action were requisite. Paine aimed to combine practical improvements to ameliorate conditions of life, trade, and politics with a far-reaching republican idealism.[97]

"The cession of Louisiana is a great acquisition," acknowledged Paine, "but great as it is it would be an incumbrance on the Union were the prayer of the [Louisiana] petitioners to be granted, nor would the lands be worth settling if the settlers are to be under a French jurisdiction." It would "never answer to make French Louisiana the legislators of the new settlers."[98] It would be best, Paine counseled Jefferson, if the "present French inhabitants would soon be a minority and the sooner the better for they give symptoms of being a troublesome set." He would have liked to erase the very name "Louisiana."[99] Especially, he insisted, slavery must be dismantled: "Do you wish to renew in Louisiana the horrors of Domingo?"[100] He advocated creating a society wholly free, republican, and based on representative government, and (unlike the Haiti of Dessalines) on an unrestricted fluid mix of free whites and blacks.[101] The federal government should attract farmers from the eastern seaboard states to settle and also, he added, noting that the "best farmers in

Pennsylvania" were poor Germans, "German peasantry" rather than Scots, Irish—who "in general are generous and dissolute"—or Englishmen. Rather than permitting black slavery in Louisiana, Paine urged congressional encouragement for "our free negroes" to migrate there along with white English and German speakers. It was for Congress "to give [free blacks] their passage to New Orleans" so that they could then "hire themselves out to the planters for one or two years, to learn the business," and then themselves acquire land in Louisiana, paying for it "with a certain quantity of produce."[102]

Jefferson, Madison, Monroe, and the treasury secretary, Gallatin, were, like Paine, keenly aware of the danger to republicanism and equality entailed in absorbing a Franco-Spanish entity accustomed only to authoritarian government by Crown, aristocrats, and ecclesiastics and devoid of regular representation. They understood too the risks in allowing Louisiana's slave population to expand and be extended geographically. Writing to Jefferson, in January 1805, Paine repeated his admonition that "bringing poor Negroes to work the lands [of the Louisiana Territory] in a state of slavery and wretchedness, is, besides the immorality of it, the certain way of preventing population and consequently of preventing revenue."[103] Since the 1791 Saint-Domingue slave revolt, especially during 1793, thousands of free blacks and slaves, as well as French royalist whites, had been relocated to the eastern United States. The white refugees from Saint-Domingue, Genet had warned Jefferson in October 1793, were deeply enmeshed in French and American politics and would tirelessly promote "counterrevolutionary plans" to reverse French Revolution principles and black emancipation especially by arousing the anxieties of Southern whites in America, encouraging the "continual alarms they experience."[104] However, barely a hundred Saint-Domingue white refugees actually settled in Louisiana between 1791 and 1797.[105] Only a further thousand or so arrived down to 1803, not because the Spanish regime sought to block French immigration but because of the distance from Haiti and a bar against importing Saint-Dominguean slaves (deemed by the Spanish authorities corrupted and prone to violent insurrection). Once Louisiana was absorbed by the United States, though, this rule partly lapsed and the influx of French exiles originally from Haiti together with their slaves, often arriving from Jamaica, surged dramatically. Over a thousand entered in the first year and French immigration continued for years afterward to outstrip English-speaking American immigration into Lower Louisiana.[106]

To supporters of the radical ideals of the American and French revolutions it seemed vital to actively counter the social, cultural, and political consequences of this growing hierarchical system. The United States should attract through agents in contact with radicals and dissidents in Britain and Europe, urged Paine in 1803, the right kind of Old World settlers to come to Louisiana to counterbalance, and eventually swamp, the incoming Saint-Domingue planters merging with the original French and Spanish community. Louisiana needed the "thousands and tens of thousands in England and Ireland and also in Scotland who are friends of mine by principle, and who would gladly change their present country and condition."[107] The existing Franco-Spanish inhabitants with their marked Catholic and royalist sympathies should not be permitted automatically to acquire American citizenship but rather be made to wait until circumstances were more conducive to republican principles. Above all, no part of the Territory should be allowed to become a fully-fledged state of the Union until the numbers of newly arriving English-speaking settlers surpassed the Franco-Spanish Catholic-royalist presence. Measures were needed to prevent existing officeholders and landowners dominating the Territory's affairs and regulating immigration and to hasten the substitution of English for French. To Paine, who had always viewed freedom of conscience as a consequence of Protestantism,[108] it seemed requisite also that all special preference and privilege for the Catholic faith be ended and even the practice of organizing public religious processions in the open forbidden. The existing population should be encouraged to learn the art of self-government by electing their local officials and also, following the French revolutionary practice adopted in 1791, electing their own priests—so as to further reduce the papacy's and European episcopate's influence over the region.[109]

Paine's recommendations with respect to religion were ignored, as were his and Barlow's advice that slavery be formally banned and proposal that Congress ship in free black families and sponsor their employment on the plantations, as free men working for pay, recognizing their right to acquire their own tracts to cultivate as independent farmers.[110] His admonitions concerning Louisiana's possible negative effects on the Union were shared to a degree by numerous commentators, including Hamilton, although many, particularly in New England, employed republican arguments merely as a means to channel resentment at the loss of political clout and influence New England experienced in the wake of Jefferson's victory and would suffer further with the advent of fresh states and territories. "I know that the acquisition of Louisiana has been disapproved by some," remarked Jefferson in March 1805, in his Second Inaugural Address, "from a candid apprehension that the enlargement of our territory would endanger its union." But it was impossible to ascertain the "extent to which the federative principle may operate effectively," given that the "larger our association, the less it will be shaken by local passions"; in any case, it was better that both banks of the Mississippi should lie on American soil.[111]

By 1803, Jefferson had long since given up the "expectation of an early provision for the extinguishment of slavery among us."[112] But that he, Madison, and Gallatin made no attempt to hinder slave importing into the Louisiana Territory was by any reasonable reckoning a highly fateful lapse.[113] Their reliance on Southern support and Virginia's and the other southern states' resolve to maintain slavery was doubtless the principal reason; but those seeking to evade constraints on slavery's extension were aided by the fact that Jefferson, who earlier had rhetorically, and for a time actively, supported projects promoting black emancipation,[114] now remained entirely silent on the question. Contributing to his silence were mounting fears during 1803–6 that an independent black Haiti would provoke black unrest and insurrection throughout the American South. Very likely, the president also hoped for a significant westward thinning and dispersal of Virginia's burgeoning slave population, growing slave numbers there raising anxiety as well as depressing prices for slaves to far lower levels than prevailed in Louisiana and West Florida. Privately, Jefferson suggested that slavery's abolition was a task for the next generation, which would "bear it through to its consummation."[115] At times, he liked to imply abolitionism was mainly a tool of Federalist Anglomania aimed at misleading Americans, diluting states' rights, and somehow detracting from genuine "Americanism."[116]

Avoiding responsibility for ending slavery certainly became, if it was not always, Jefferson's prime political and moral deficiency, just as his tendency to resort on occasion to racist appraisals of black capabilities was his chief slippage from the stricter egalitarianism of Paine, Condorcet, Brissot, Kościuszko, and Lafayette.[117] At bottom, he simply felt dismayed and helpless before the whole slavery question. In any case, the president took no steps to impede slavery's rapid extension through Lower and soon Upper Louisiana as Paine and Barlow urged.[118] Nothing was done to hinder the expansion of slavery in the vast new territory aside from a federal law of 1804 supposedly reimposing the ban on importing slaves from outside the United States into Louisiana and on the entry of foreign-born slaves despite it clearly being impossible to prevent a good deal of smuggling along the little-guarded coastline.[119] This stemmed partly from the fears of Jefferson, Breckinridge, and other slave owners regarding the supposedly subversive inclinations of "Santo Domingo" (Haitian) slaves but probably more from expectations that prohibiting importation from outside would boost prices for slaves and thin slave numbers in the southeastern states.

Another reason for the lack of any government curb on slavery's expansion in the new territory, despite a lively debate in Congress, was the outright defeat in the Senate of the amendment proposing to ban slavery in the entirety of the Louisiana Territory introduced by a Connecticut Federalist, James Hillhouse. Hillhouse, like many New Englanders, considered the acquisition of Louisiana highly problematic and staunchly opposed any extension of slavery. In 1803, out of a total population of 60,000, there were already at least 12,000 black slaves in Louisiana, possibly as many as 19,000.[120] A fifth of the total population of the immense territory, they constituted a much higher proportion of those dwelling in and around New Orleans but a relatively small proportion elsewhere. Effective curbs were still possible. Southern senators predictably voted solidly against the Hillhouse amendment; but what effectively killed it was that several Northern Federalist senators did too, including both Timothy Pickering and John Quincy Adams, the two senators for Massachusetts, both stalwart foes of Jefferson and the republican tendency. The result was unmitigated defeat of the congressional effort to prevent slavery's massive extension.[121]

Neither of Paine's main goals in Louisiana, preventing slavery's extension and withholding statehood until the French community were outnumbered by Anglo-Americans, was secured. Slaves already in New Orleans Territory in 1803 remained a relatively small segment compared to the much larger black slave population brought in, mostly from elsewhere in the United States subsequently, especially from 1809 onward. At the point Hillhouse introduced his amendment and Paine composed his pamphlet, and still more during the three years prior to Louisiana gaining statehood in 1812, the state's French and aristocratic character was actually considerably strengthened while, at the same time, the expansion of slavery accelerated. In 1809–10, an unprecedented influx of around 10,000 French refugees, originally from Saint-Domingue, arrived en masse in New Orleans, migrants who between 1791 and 1803 had sought refuge in the Spanish Caribbean Islands, chiefly Cuba, but from where they were now expelled (March 1809) due to the outbreak of war between France and Bourbon (i.e., non-Napoleonic) Spain. At this juncture, a large renewed French influx markedly exacerbated the clash of cultures in the Territory, further intensifying what one historian termed the "chronic tension between English-speakers and French-speakers in New Orleans since the Louisiana Purchase," as well as noticeably increased inequality, poverty, gambling houses, racial miscegenation outside marriage, and prostitution.[122] New Orleans, by 1810 easily the largest American city south of Baltimore, and the one with the largest number of free blacks and mulattoes, was the only major American city unrepresented in any elected legislature. At that point, Anglo-Americans still represented under 5 percent of the white population of the city proper and the parishes immediately surrounding New Orleans.[123]

This renewed French-speaking influx was by no means welcomed by everyone. The "English part of our society (with some exceptions) appear to be prejudiced against these strangers," Governor Claiborne advised Washington, "and express great dissatisfaction that an asylum in this territory was afforded them."[124] Growing Francophone immigration after 1803 energized New Orleans and expanded its free black population but also contributed substantially to expanding Louisiana's plantation system and slavery, and to the unyieldingly conservative tone of Louisiana society, attitudes, politics, and culture.[125] Statehood was granted to Louisiana in 1812 despite the fact that the French community remained a firm majority, mainly because the outbreak of the Anglo-American War of 1812 made it impolitic to withhold statehood any longer. As early as 1810, at 34,660, there were nearly three times as many slaves in Louisiana as in 1803, yielding a now substantial total even if still substantially below the figures for Virginia, the Carolinas, Georgia, or even Kentucky. Louisiana's black element, furthermore, was growing particularly rapidly, being destined to overtake that of both Kentucky and Tennessee during the 1840s.[126] Moreover, if the post-1803 immigration of French- and English-speaking slave owners boosted black slavery in Lower Louisiana, it also established slavery for the first time in Upper Louisiana—in the future states of Arkansas and Missouri.[127] In 1810, there were just 188 slaves out of a total non-Indian population of 1,062 in Arkansas and slavery there had scarcely begun taking root. But from 1803 it did so unhindered by any federal restriction, subsequently spilling over from Arkansas into Missouri and Kansas. Like the new French immigrants in Philadelphia and other northern cities, French refugees from Saint-Domingue migrating to Louisiana, Arkansas, and Missouri vehemently opposed and reviled republicanism, secularism, equality, "rights of mankind," and everything associated with the French Revolution.

Admittedly, this was not the whole story. Following the Holy Alliance's suppression of the Spanish revolution of 1820–23 there was also a considerable influx of Spanish constitutionalist and republican refugees who settled in and near New Orleans, an immigrant group who were the particular audience of Lafayette when he visited New Orleans in triumph in 1824 and delivered a rousing speech exalting the American Revolution together with the defeated and executed Spanish constitutionalist revolutionary leader, General Riego, predicting that *la liberté* would one day return to Spain and redeem Riego and all victims of Spanish "superstition" and "tyranny."[128] Nevertheless, this influx also further bolstered the non-English-speaking element. At New Orleans, as a result, French and Spanish speakers together remained a clear majority until the 1830s when incoming fresh Irish and German immigration finally enabled the combined non-Franco-Spanish population to

James Madison (1751–1836), by George Healy (1808–94). Photo credit: Gianni Dagli Orti / The Art Archive at Art Resource, NY.

outstrip those who closely identified with the Bourbon pre-1803 history of the territory.[129]

Jefferson's successor as president, James Madison, proved just as inert with regard to the slavery issue as his mentor. In October 1810, Madison took no steps to limit the expansion of slavery as he might have done when the short-lived, unrecognized "republic of West Florida," encompassing eastern parts of present-day Louisiana (and wanting Alabama and Mississippi), after rebelling against Spain a few weeks earlier, was finally formally annexed to the United States by presidential proclamation. In Madison's eyes, former Spanish "West Florida" was merely a hitherto unoccupied part of the Louisiana Territory subject to the same rules. This assisted the immediate, uncontested entry into the Union as "slave states" of both Mississippi (which in 1800 counted few slaves but featured over 30,000 by 1819 owing to the rapid extension of cotton production) and Alabama.[130] It was to be many decades and to cost vast strife and loss of life before Louisiana, Arkansas, Missouri, Mississippi, and Alabama finally became even nominally free lands committed to the equality and democratic values introduced by the American, French, and Haitian revolutions.

Both Founding Fathers had long felt politically trapped by the slavery question. Whether or not they sufficiently grasped the force of Paine's arguments against permitting slavery's extension into the Louisiana Territory in 1803–5, in later years America's third and fourth presidents, Jefferson and Madison, certainly understood the enormity of the wrong turn America had taken. By the time Louisiana entered the Union as a fully-fledged state in 1812, expanding local French and Spanish custom and usage were beginning to be balanced politically by a substantial body of Anglo-American newcomers but with slavery expanding more and more rapidly. Governor Claiborne, a Virginian anti-Federalist who had at first been resented by the local population as representing the United States' annexation of their homeland and symbolizing an alien Protestant military occupation, was now elected the new state's governor with wide support and a mandate to sustain the status quo.

Both Jefferson and Madison were clearly horrified by the growing friction between Northern and Southern states over slavery's expansion in the Louisiana Territory that developed during the second decade of the nineteenth century, especially with the "Missouri crisis" erupting in 1819. In Washington, both the Senate and the House of Representatives furiously split over what by then was a raging dispute between all the states now divided into two evenly balanced rival camps. Both ex-presidents were gripped by the nightmare that the Union might fragment under the pressure. "From the battle of Bunker's Hill to the treaty of Paris," Jefferson assured Adams in December 1819, "we never had so ominous a question."[131] The impasse, he told another correspondent, in April 1820, "like a fire bell in the night awakened and filled me with terror. I considered it at once as the knell of the Union."[132] A "scission" of the states would destroy the Union and act as a discouragement to the peoples of Europe, fighting for representation and republicanism against "their oppressive and cannibal governments."[133] The bitter imbroglio pointedly drew attention to the immensity of his greatest failure and to an extent impinged on his reputation, yet Jefferson refused to consider the Missouri imbroglio a reproach to himself or even a "moral" as well as a political crisis calling into question the American Revolution's basic value system.[134]

Alabama with its 40,000 slaves entered the Union as a "slave state" in 1819. The Missouri petition later that year, likewise to enter as a "slave state," not only threatened to expand slavery in the Louisiana territory decisively northward but would render the "slave states" an actual majority of the United States. A proposal put forward in Congress in February 1819 to admit Missouri as a state to the Union but forbid acquisition of fresh slaves, and require the gradual emancipation of the 10,000 or so slaves already there, was hotly debated but eventually defeated. Under the Missouri Compromise hammered out during 1820, slavery would no longer be allowed north of Missouri's southern border or the 36°30′ line of latitude—with the exception only of the new state of Missouri itself—but would remain legally unchallenged south of that line (thereby sanctioning the extension of slavery into Arkansas). To preserve the political balance in Congress between North and South, non-slave and slave states, the outlying northern section of Massachusetts was simultaneously admitted as the "free state" of Maine.[135]

This ominous splitting of the United States into equally calibrated, politically competing, rival halves filled Jefferson and Madison with foreboding and presentiment of catastrophe. The question of how finally to resolve the slavery issue seemed to both former presidents infinitely problematic. Madison, like Jefferson, found it almost impossible to imagine freed slaves and their descendants dwelling, farming, and sharing communities in large numbers alongside whites in the manner proposed by Paine. Like many Virginians unnerved by the rapid growth of the South's slave populations since the Revolution, an expansion much more rapid than that of the whites despite substantial white immigration,[136] both feared an eventual catastrophic black insurrection and slaughter of the whites on the traumatic Haitian pattern of 1793 and 1804. To prevent racial conflict and massacre both believed it essential to disperse America's free blacks widely, removing the bulk of them from Virginia and, if possible, resettling substantial numbers in the Caribbean and Africa.[137]

Paine's "Last Throw" (1800–1809)

From the summer of 1803, Paine divided his time between New York and his farm at New Rochelle in New York State, near the Connecticut border. Shunned by most Americans, he remained an object of suspicion also to the British authorities, and with reason, since he had by no means abandoned hope of toppling Britain's imperial monarchical-aristocratic system. Should Napoleon succeed in invading England—as seemed possible, even likely, during 1803–5—Paine planned, he confided to Jefferson in September 1803, to "make another passage across the Atlantic" so as to "assist in forming a Constitution for England."[138] England's monarchical-aristocratic-ecclesiastical system, he was convinced, had reached "a tottering condition and if Bonaparte succeeds, that government will break up." Among other welcome consequences, the British empire's disintegration would emancipate Ireland and deliver Canada to the United States.[139] His relentless assaults on church authority, Sabbath observance, and Christianity in *The Prospect, or, View of the Moral World*, the journal Palmer founded in 1802 and edited with his wife's help, only further increased his and their isolation.[140] Under the psychological impact of the relentless near universal backlash, from 1802, Paine became depressed and excessively given to brandy.[141] Dying generally despised, only twelve people attended his funeral on his farm in New York State on 10 June 1809.[142]

Returning after an even longer absence in Europe (seventeen years), in July 1805, and settling in Washington thoroughly disillusioned with Napoleon, Barlow received a warm welcome from the president—but was likewise shunned by the public. One Boston Federalist paper styled him a "blood thirsty Jacobin" whose "passion for murder" moved him to hail the "sacrifice of Louis and the Queen, on the scaffold" in "bacchanalian orgies." Former friends and allies cold-shouldered him as they had Paine. Barlow met his old student companion, Noel Webster, after decades apart, in October 1805, only to find the latter had repudiated Paineism and the radical Enlightenment creed they had once shared. Pleased to find Barlow a "little convalescent, chiefly by means of Bonaparte's harsh remedies for new philosophy," Webster was soon disappointed to realize Barlow was only disillusioned with Bonaparte, not with "philosophy" and that "radical cure is impossible."[143] His republican, irreligious outlook remained unshaken. Paine's critique of religion in the *Age of Reason*, generally condemned as "atheism," Barlow still deemed "progress of good sense over the damnable imposture of Christian mummery." The French Republic's downfall left Barlow more than ever persuaded of the "great importance" of proving "to the world, and even to ourselves, that the fabric of this [American] empire is the best organization of liberty hitherto experienced." The Revolution's authentic legacy needed to be projected more effectively throughout the world and strengthened in America itself. Far from respecting Webster's retreat into conventional notions or admiring the America of 1805, Barlow discerned mainly "erroneous habits of thinking" and, like Paine, especially abominated the political and social doctrines of John Adams and the Federalists "which seek the happiness of the few, in the depression of the many."[144]

In January 1806, Barlow finalized plans he had first put forward in 1802 for an American national institute modeled on the Institut de France, a cherished scheme he submitted to Jefferson. America's representative republican system, he argued, was a unique and invaluable innovation in human political development, contrasting fundamentally with Napoleon's blinkered dictatorship. But representative democracy flourishes only on the basis of enlightenment, by expanding secular education and diffusing awareness, knowledge, and science. Welding science conducted in well-appointed laboratories and general research to the American Revolution in a national institute he reckoned an essential step toward conserving and propagating the Revolution's core values at home and abroad. Promoting social and political studies would also enable America to participate more fully in transatlantic debate with European radical republicans and democrats. Europeans "give us credit for what we have done" but also point out, his discussions in Europe taught him, "what we have omitted to do." Interacting with such an institute, they would "perhaps aid us with their lights, in bringing towards perfection a system, which may be destined to ameliorate the condition of the human race."[145]

Congress, "as well as our opulent citizens," presumed Barlow, would gladly join "in making a liberal endowment" for a national institute on the French model. Jefferson, continually pondering educational reform during his later years, proved enthusiastic. "No American had spoken more eloquently or more fully," observes one scholar, "for the radical impulse of the Enlightenment than Jefferson."[146] "I have often wished," he intimated to Barlow in February 1806, "we could have a Philosophical Society or academy so organized" that while the central body should be at the "seat of government, its members dispersed over the states, should constitute filiated academies in each state" so that "all the members wheresoever dispersed might be brought into action, and a useful emulation might arise between the societies."[147] Their joint endeavor resulted in a bill for a "National Academy and University at the city of Washington," combining the characteristics of a university, research institute, adult education center, national museum (incorporating Charles Wilson's Peale's museum), and national academy. Based on Barlow's proposals but drafted at the White House, it was presented to Congress, in March, where, dishearteningly, it progressed at only a "snail-paced gait" before being permanently laid aside.[148]

Unlike Paine, Barlow did cross the Atlantic once more. Back in France, in late 1811, he acted as United States agent in various negotiations with Napoleon's ministers and discussed a scheme, emanating from Joseph Bonaparte, since 1808 "king of Spain," for the transfer of West Florida to the United States that President Madison refused to take seriously since Joseph had no power or authority in Spanish America. Viewing the world from his republican perspective, Barlow equally dreaded the triumph of the despot Napoleon and that of his chief adversary, Britain, which, like Jefferson and Madison, he regarded as also America's principal enemy.[149] Traveling overland to Vilna (Vilnius) in Lithuania, in December 1812, for the purpose of resuming negotiations with Napoleon, Barlow witnessed the last stages of the snow-engulfed chaos of Napoleon's retreat in humiliation and defeat, harassed by Cossack cavalry, from Russia. Traversing Poland as an American diplomatic envoy amid the stragglers and wounded winding their way back from Vilna (which he toured and was impressed by), he found himself surrounded by death, destruction, destroyed projects, and despair. The French Revolution, the resurrected Polish state, and Napoleon's European state system along with the other schemes of late Enlightenment despotism were all disintegrating together. "O God! O God!" he wrote to his wife from Vilna, in one of his last letters: "What did you make mankind for. I want to know.—A creature endowed with so much intellect, foresight, calculation, prudence,—and uses them so little."[150] Reduced to despair, he died in central Poland a few days later.

The entire radical Enlightenment tradition of thought after 1800 found itself under general public condemnation and attack. The striving of "the philosophers" was "denounced by the thundering voice of the church," recorded Palmer, and the "resentful malice of monarchical tyranny."[151] Clergymen and powerful vested interests condemned societies like his in New York because his Paineite critique of religious authority and of the social and political submission, "humility," and deference the churches taught was having an effect. Paineite political and social subversion of the "aristocratic" system the powers of the day aimed to suppress for economic and political as much as religious reasons. "Those who oppose philosophy and bestow upon it harsh and malignant epithets," avowed Palmer, are "interested in keeping up a privileged system of plunder and robbery, which makes nine-tenths of the human race absolute slaves to support the other tenth in indolence, extravagance, pride and luxury."[152] Fortunately, the "cry of vengeance and merciless punishment against the benevolent philosophers of all countries of the present day, has not deterred them from the faithful discharge of their duty, and the most unremitting attention to the best interest of individual and national happiness."[153]

This applied to Paine, Barlow, Freneau, and Jefferson, and to Palmer and his soon to be widowed wife, but also pointed to the growing isolation and ghettoization of the radical fraternity. In the years around 1800, the radical tendency to all appearances noticeably contracted as it came under mounting public pressure. Coram had died young from disease, at only thirty-five, in 1796, in the midst of his journalistic crusade. Two of the most active radical newspaper publishers, Benjamin Franklin Bache and Thomas Greenleaf, both died prematurely in the 1798 Philadelphia yellow fever outbreak. Palmer too, among the most driven of the post-1800 radicals and most capable of organizing a movement, died prematurely in 1806. John Daly Burk died fighting a duel in 1808. From 1798, the "uncrowned poet laureate of the American Revolution," Freneau, entirely ceased his efforts against "aristocracy," "ignorance," and the "worst plague on the human race"—the "dread superstition" pastors foment to "fetter every power of thought; to chain the mind or bend it down." Abandoning his role as leading champion of the French Revolution and scourge of "Cromwells" in America, Freneau ceased publicly contending that the "establishment of true republican principles in the world will work an astonishing change among mankind."[154] Weighed by financial worries, he withdrew to his New Jersey farm where he continued writing poetry but no longer denounced social injustice.[155] Selling most of his land, in old age he was left wandering from house to house seeking odd jobs as a handyman.

Post-1801 gatherings of Jefferson's supporters parried Federalist sallies mostly by distancing themselves from, rather than reaffirming, the intellectual legacies of Paine, Palmer, and Barlow.[156] Yet the urgent tasks identified by the radical critique were by no means yet carried out. Slavery was not yet abolished, free blacks remained second-class citizens, Native Americans were victims of systematic injustice, and "aristocracy" and the pulpit everywhere remained preponderant to a degree that continued to scandalize some.[157] This alone ensured that the onslaught of the "Second Great Awakening" on the radicals could not fully succeed. Those who drew up the Federal Constitution had avoided making the United States formally a Christian state and society, stipulating that the new republic, as the American treaty with the Barbary state of Tripoli stated, stood in no inherent alliance with or opposition to any organized religion.[158] The renewed power of the pulpit in politics inevitably encountered a measure of often silent but still dogged resistance. Paine's *Age of Reason*, having initially run through some fifteen editions in just two years (1794–95), exerted a suffused, veiled impact, being read, often obsessively, by students at Princeton, Yale, and Harvard, suggesting more than a few concurred privately and that, beneath the surface, the Enlightenment's war on conventional and established thinking continued unabated while the correct balance between liberty and religion was not yet found.[159]

The apparent suppression of the "infidels" and Paineite deism on the surface during the early nineteenth century was thus not the whole story.[160] If radical Enlightenment molded the American Revolution's democratic aspirations and spread awareness of the need for more sweeping reform prior to 1800, it also left lasting traces in American religion itself which, after the

Revolution, had little option but to become less dogmatic, less confessionally oriented, and more willing to conform with enlightened ideas and science.[161] The call for greater clarity and simplicity as well as less "establishment" and more direct popular involvement for many meant demanding less theological mystification and a greater focus on Christianity's moral message, moral reform to an extent forging an area of common ground between radicals, Unitarians, and other opponents of "Second Awakening" zealotry.

As part of their project to expand liberty and democracy, late eighteenth-century radical leaders had looked forward to a further rapid "Socinianization" of American religion, considering this a sure path to weakening religious authority and intolerance. Applauding Priestley's ideas and determination to dissolve all traditional structures of theology and church organization, Jefferson confidently predicted Unitarianism to be the American religion of the future.[162] Unitarianism's advance, by bringing deism and Christianity into closer harmony and eliminating the need for theologically trained paid clergy, must inevitably weaken instituted religious authority; and here they were not disappointed. Unitarianism did actually register stunning gains during the late eighteenth and early nineteenth centuries, particularly in New England but also Kentucky where traditionalists had a hard fight on their hands and elsewhere. The battle over the Hollis Chair of theology at Harvard ended in 1805 with a bruising defeat for the orthodox Calvinists headed by Jedidiah Morse. The victor was Henry Ware (1764–1845), before long a declared Unitarian who steered the Harvard Divinity School increasingly toward Unitarianism. Ware made a point of attracting the enlightened, widely read, and "the most elevated," those repelled by what a reformed Harvard conceived as the emotionalism and the crassness of the popular "Second Awakening."[163] Many former New England Presbyterian churches founded by Puritans shifted to strains of rationalist Unitarianism, discarding not just Calvinist severity and theology but numerous inherited dogmas including the Trinity.

Puritan rigidity eroded and dogmatic religion retreated; but this did not mean the old intolerance, preoccupation with theology, and intellectual narrowness gave way.[164] While Priestley's materialism and denial of a non-material immortal soul appealed to some, most obviously Jefferson, it remained broadly unacceptable to most Unitarians.[165] Brissot wildly exaggerated in claiming Protestant "ministers in America will soon be in the position which M. d'Alembert assigned the pastors of Geneva," alluding to d'Alembert's article "Geneva" in the *Encyclopédie* where Diderot's coeditor had notoriously exaggerated the late eighteenth-century Genevan pastors' drift toward crypto-Socinian denial of the Trinity.[166] Rather, the battle between theology and radicalism continued.

New York's freethinkers eventually established a lecture series, newspaper, press association, and debating circles presenting a more coordinated response to the preachers' unceasing assault. Inexpensive reprints of Paine's anti-theological writings, along with Volney's *Ruins of Empires* and the like, reappeared. A prominent celebrity converted to freethinking pantheism by such literature in the 1820s was Abner Kneeland (1771–1884), minister of the New York Prince Street Universalist Church who defected from his congregation, setting up the deistic and rationalist Second Universalist Society.[167] After retreating to Boston, he was prosecuted for "blasphemous" statements in 1833; and while theological assailants eventually got him convicted, in 1838, and sentenced to sixty days' imprisonment for "blasphemy," they succeeded only at some cost to their standing. Kneeland proved to be the very last person imprisoned for religious offenses in the United States.

American separation of church and state undoubtedly afforded a wider toleration than had yet been instituted anywhere else, involving curtailment of ecclesiastical authority and theological dogma to a degree witnessed nowhere else. But this had not been carried through at all systematically into the schools, colleges, and general culture. The menace facing America, contended Palmer, was that "Church and State may unite to form an insurmountable barrier against the extension of thought, the moral progress of nations and the felicity of nature." Yet, belief in the ultimate irreversibility of the (radical, secular, and democratic) Enlightenment, repeatedly reaffirmed by Paine, Barlow, Jefferson, Coram, Cooper, Lafayette, Fellows, and Palmer, was for them an article of faith. With the Revolution's basic principles widely diffused in books and pamphlets, the "guarantee for moral and political emancipation is already deposited in the archives of every school and college, and in the mind of every cultivated and enlightened man of all countries," thus a general reversal, predicted Palmer, in 1801, was inconceivable: "it will henceforth be a vain and fruitless attempt to reduce the earth to that state of slavery of which the history of former ages has furnished such an awful picture."[168]

If the Revolution's most fervent adherents within and outside the United States were typically longstanding adversaries of instituted religious authority and theology, this remained largely masked from the public by the Federalist press and the pulpit. For these entirely succeeded in replacing the historical record with a popular mythology of the Founders' commitment to conventional religious notions. Where opponents of the world's monarchical-aristocratic systems were at the same time leaders of the drive against theological-ecclesiastical primacy and conventional religion, fighting what they considered a joint despotism over body and mind, educators

refused to follow. The universal education of the radicals aimed to secularize and republicanize society, but the presidents of the young republic's colleges were invariably political conservatives imparting a ubiquitous and militant theological dimension to the ceaseless battle of political ideologies and
philosophies.

Paine's reputation in the English-speaking world reached its nadir at the
time of his death but remained in near total eclipse only briefly.[169] During
the 1820s and 1830s, his American and British standing and legacy notably
revived while his renown in Spanish America (where he emerged as one of
the principal guides to the revolutions) grew apace. On 29 January 1825, forty
declared freethinkers, led by Paine's and Palmer's old comrade and publisher
John Fellows—one of the few who had stuck by Paine and helped him financially in his last years—and other noted radicals gathered in Harmony Hall,
New York, the artisan unions' regular meeting place, to deliver eulogies and
drink rousing toasts to mark Paine's birthday and honor the reviled refugee
author who electrified America with *Common Sense* half a century before.[170]
Observed annually from 1825 onward, celebrating Paine's birthday grew in
the 1830s into an elaborate secular ritual with hundreds of hard-core devo-
tees of '76 celebrating political banquets in Paine's honor at Boston, Albany,
and Cincinnati as well as Philadelphia and New York.[171] In mid-nineteenth-
century Cincinnati, the movement to rehabilitate Paine as a great American reformer as well as Enlightenment writer became a particular focus for
numerous recent German immigrant freethinkers and radicals, or "Forty-
Eighters," who gathered there.

Paine and Palmer had fervently embraced the doctrine of Brissot and Condorcet that while the "General Revolution" ranged kings and priests against
the democratic republic, the peoples of the world, the general interest, ultimately supported them, and eventually a whole world of democratic republics would emerge that will not fight each other as monarchies did but
inaugurate instead, for the benefit of the majority, a new and happier era of
"perpetual peace."[172] For a time, this vision revived and diffused from Chile
to Germany. In February 1832, buoyed by the mounting reform agitation
gripping England, British radical groups commemorated Tom Paine's birthday with a series of banquets at which resounded the toast: "To the USA—
may her republican institutions be imitated all over the world!"[173] In this way,
Paine scored a kind of posthumous triumph after all, remaining a lasting inspiration among the "true republican" few, including America's nineteenth-
century literary champions of revolutionary democracy: Fenimore Cooper,
Emerson, and Whitman if not the more cautious Melville. Mankind has a
choice, declared the Paineites: either nothing can stop war and oppression or

the "true republicans" (Radical Enlightenment) will triumph, and with that, as Freneau expressed it in 1797, "conquest will cease—the rights of the weak will be respected, and man will cease to be the oppressor of man."[174]

Hope, toasts, and banquets imparted a timeless, indestructible core to the radical message, rendering Paine's writings and achievement truly universal but also reviving awareness of the American Revolution's abiding significance for the world, the continuing expectation of its "expanding blaze."

CHAPTER 16

A Revolutionary Era: Napoleon, Spain, and the Americas (1808–15)

The Spanish Revolution (1808–14)

Among those Jefferson tried to persuade to accept the governorship of Louisiana, following the Louisiana Purchase, along with a congressional grant of lands, was his old friend Lafayette. Explaining his refusal, in October 1804, Lafayette was by no means unappreciative. It was now fully thirty years since the American Revolution's advent and the commencement of "la liberté américaine," and fifteen since he and Jefferson had together toasted the joint progress of "la liberté française et américaine." Since 1789, American liberty had advanced from strength to strength while in France republican hopes had lapsed to their lowest ebb. For that reason, Lafayette felt honor bound to fight on in Europe, trusting in the "prodigieuse influence" of the veritable French ideas of 1789 and hopeful still that freedom would eventually recover its rightful place in the world; and, in pursuing this goal, he had no choice but to remain in France.[1]

For everyone embracing the ultimate philosophical oneness of the two revolutions, Napoleon's epic career and rise to power were indeed deeply dismaying. If the "cause of humanity is won in America; and nothing can any longer divert it or spoil its progress or arrest it," in France it was now "believed irrevocably lost," Lafayette confided to Jefferson, shortly before Napoleon proclaimed himself emperor of the French, in 1804.[2] Benjamin Constant, preferring exile in Germany to remaining under Napoleon, pronounced Bonaparte a "thousand times worse than the barbarian conquerors of earlier times for violating the tenor of his own age: he chose barbarism, he preferred it; surrounded by Enlightenment, he opted to bring back the night."[3] The reversal of revolutionary values based on the principles of liberty, equality, toleration, and free expression engineered by Napoleon, radical enlighteners typically believed, was comparable to the damage inflicted earlier by Robespierre, leaving the United States, from 1804, the world's sole representative republic. Writing to Lafayette, in 1815, Jefferson expressed their common view by emphatically bracketing together the "unprincipled and bloody tyranny of Robespierre, and the equally unprincipled and maniac tyranny of Bonaparte."[4]

Under John Adams's presidency (1797–1801), rumors that the United States might ally with Britain and declare war on France and Spain, to secure Louisiana and the Floridas, were periodically aired in Paris and Madrid perhaps especially to unnerve Napoleon's floundering ally, Spain, and raise the pressure to cede the desired territories. From 1801, Jefferson pursued the same goals less abrasively, without threatening war. "The present crisis in Europe is favorable for pressing such a settlement," he noted, "and not a moment should be lost in availing ourselves of it." In late 1805, after Trafalgar, the United States resumed negotiations with a humiliated Spain, at Aranjuez, urging transfer of the Floridas in exchange for five million dollars. The new western boundary between the United States and Spanish North America should be fixed provisionally at the Colorado River. But Spain refused to be panicked, for the moment retaining both Floridas and, from 1810, East Florida. In 1812, President Madison had to restrain unruly expansionists eager to invade Florida, from Georgia, and seize the territory by force.[5] Bonaparte too sought to avert an open American-Spanish rupture while simultaneously deflecting American efforts to annex the Floridas. This led him to appear willing to negotiate, as he had over Louisiana, while actually playing for time.

Spanish enlighteners had for decades been expressing deep concern about the American Revolution's implications for Spanish America. Don Francisco Cabarrús (1752–1810), leading advocate of far-reaching economic and financial reform in the Spanish empire, urging liberal economic policies and "free trade" at home, had supported the American rebellion qua rebellion against British power. The former English colonies in North America would cast off royal authority permanently, he hoped, thereby weakening Britain. But he also knew there was no empire for which the Revolution posed a greater potential threat than that of Spain. European polemics over the American Revolution, noted another Spanish enlightener and official, Don Pedro Varela y Ulloa (d. 1797), in 1782, were inevitably in part a debate about the future of the British, French, Spanish, Portuguese, and other European global empires, a controversy that concerned the whole globe and was ultimately a philosophical question. A universal conflict between two antagonistic intellectual-political blocs had begun as to which embodied the Enlightenment's true "espíritu filosófico." Disputing the American Revolution's veritable nature and significance in the last analysis was a quarrel not just about consequences for imperial powers but about the nature of good government, the extra-European world, the proper social and moral order, and the authentic philosophical spirit of the age.[6]

Championing America's fight for independence while officially wholly disassociating itself from American principles, the Spanish Crown proclaimed sovereignty and political power, like the social order, to be ordained by God and sanctioned by the Church, a principle for the moment as binding in the Floridas, Louisiana, and Texas (all still under Spanish rule) as in Central and South America. The Spain of 1776 remained "still the foyer of *despotisme* as Rome is for intolerance," as Chastellux expressed it, an absolute monarchy.[7] Yet, in practice, Spain, like the other powers supporting the United States from 1778 to 1783—France and the United Provinces—had to countenance American principles to a degree, turning a blind eye in the Americas and Europe alike to justifications published by "'rebels' in arms against monarchy proclaiming equality and political liberty," as one Dutch writer put it, "are a right of nature."[8] Insurgents refusing taxation without representation had become Spain's formal military allies. This rendered it impossible categorically and comprehensively to denounce their drive for political liberty and religious freedom as unjustified rebellion against God and religion. Whatever Europe's courts professed, allying with "the rebels" compromised monarchical-aristocratic efforts to suppress an ideology asserting the right of rebellion against tyranny and the universal rights of mankind.

Spain's imperial system was weak and ramshackle, menaced by disaffection among all social strata, especially locally born whites, or Criollos (Creoles). Spain needed to act decisively if she was to forestall mass sedition in emulation of the North American colonies, contended Cabarrús, and avoid risking the loss of her vast New World empire. Hoping to see the United States independent, he wanted Spain's North American territories to form a permanent demarcation segregating Spanish America from such disruptive principles as the right to self-government, toleration, freedom of expression, the invalidity of nobility, and separation of church and state. Grievances that had helped trigger the American Revolution, especially oppressive mercantilist trade restrictions and fiscal policies, should be immediately removed in Spanish America. Far-reaching economic, administrative, and fiscal reform was requisite to broaden participation and prosperity and, via "enlightened" commercial and financial policies, enable the colonies to share equitably in the empire's benefits. It was morally wrong and ruinously unwise to subject Spanish America's population to the oppression, "enslavement," and systematic exploitation that Crown, Church, and colonial bureaucracy had uninterruptedly maintained since the Spanish Conquista of the sixteenth century.

In his 1778 *discurso*, Cabarrús demanded unrestricted, open discussion of everything concerning Spanish America's subordination to Spain. The American Revolution's real significance had not been sufficiently considered, he believed, either in his own or other European colonizing nations to jolt them into reforming promptly and drastically enough to forestall armed rebellion as, for the moment, the most direct route to "humanity and justice."[9] He deplored the dismal failure of the conservative-minded to grasp the urgency of far-reaching reform. In Spain, the American Revolution had perversely developed into the "most powerful argument used by the enemies of liberty" to urge state and Church to persevere in the "system we have hitherto used in our colonies." "The bad results of the contrary system of the English" in their colonies, conservatives opposing Spanish American economic freedom and representation in government calamitously insisted, proved representation and greater liberty would decimate Spain's empire too. Misguided reactionary thinking remained all too prevalent in the Spanish-speaking world.[10]

Deep in difficulties, post–Louisiana Purchase Spain desperately needed to avoid clashing with the United States. She sought a modus vivendi while countering the growing American interference and support for the revolutionary conspiracies now increasingly destabilizing Ibero-America. American diplomacy Madrid viewed as simply a hypocritical extension of the United States' barely disguised post-1803 expansionism and aggression. The Spanish court's fears were heightened by Francisco de Miranda's two attempts, in 1806, to incite rebellion at Caracas. The earlier, involving 180 men sailing in the *Leander*, a vessel actually acquired and fitted out for revolutionary sedition in New York, had a mostly American crew largely recruited and financed by Colonel William Stephens Smith (1755–1816), an Independence War veteran and former adjutant of Lafayette married to one of John Adams's daughters—and hence John Quincy Adams's brother-in-law—who had been Miranda's traveling companion in Germany in 1785.[11]

Miranda regarded the American Revolution as "the infallible preliminary to our own."[12] His attempt to prize Venezuela from Spain, Spanish officials (and many Americans) believed, was planned and prepared in secret collusion with Jefferson and Madison, to whom Smith had been close for decades and afterward publicly claimed had authorized his involvement. The American press was supportive: the "United States of South America," predicted the *Richmond Enquirer*, "like the United States of the North, will represent to admiring Europe another republic independent, confederated, and happy."[13] Both 1806 forays failed without attracting much local support (in the first fiasco Smith's son, William Steuben, who had joined the expedition, was captured and imprisoned). Yet Miranda's conspiracies together with the Haitian Revolution and British and American efforts to subvert the Spanish New World rule were perceptibly heightening tensions in Spanish American society at all levels.[14]

Napoleon, having transformed Italy in 1796–99 and, in 1803, Switzerland, and however ingloriously, the French Caribbean and the American South and West, equally fundamentally reshaped the Iberian Peninsula and, indirectly, Ibero-America. Until 1808, the Spanish king, Carlos IV (reigned: 1788–1808), adhered to his disastrous pact with Europe's overweening despot even after suffering crushing naval defeat, together with the French, at Trafalgar (1805). Part intimidated and part bribed by France (with the prospect of jointly partitioning Britain's dependency Portugal), Spain lingered desultorily at war with Britain, her shipping and trade decimated by England's navy. After Trafalgar, both Spain's and Spanish America's overall situation deteriorated alarmingly under an overwhelming double threat overshadowing her entire empire—British incursion and American patronage of Creole insurgency. On the River Plate, the local militia, in 1806 and 1807, twice repelled British landings aimed at seizing Buenos Aires, feats uplifting local self-confidence that also demonstrated the hopelessly dilapidated state of Spain's defenses and imperial system.

Then, in 1807, Napoleon sent a French army into Spain, ostensibly to join Spanish forces in invading Portugal. This intrusion precipitated an unexpected and dramatic sequence of events. Popular disturbances combined with the paralysis of Carlos IV's power and mounting chaos in the country tempted Napoleon to seize Carlos and his son, Fernando, and impose a French-fashioned "enlightened" constitutional monarchy on the country by transferring the throne to his own brother, Joseph. Madrid was occupied, key strategic points were usurped, and Joseph crowned king of Spain and its empire (although his rule never extended over all Spain or any of Spanish America). This coup Napoleon justified on the basis of the Estatuto de Bayona, the "Bayonne constitution," "that masterpiece of enlightened despotism" one historian called it,[15] that the emperor had drawn up after assembling a convention of largely Spanish notables in Bayonne. This very first written constitution in the Spanish-speaking world Napoleon attempted to foist onto Spain, thereby dividing the Spanish world into two.

As the French military presence became outright military occupation, in early 1808, Spanish and Spanish American reformers faced a profound dilemma. Many, henceforth called *afrancesados* or *josefinos*, including several friends and associates of Goya, opted to back the moderate enlightened reform movement Joseph initiated as a way to end the mounting turmoil and secure much-needed reforms (unaware the Bayonne constitution would never be fully implemented). In their published tracts they sought to convince Spaniards that Joseph's reign and reforms were a continuation of the enlightened project of Kings Carlos III and Carlos IV.[16] From 1808, with Spain divided between warring camps comprising a wide variety of different groups, both sides—that of Joseph and those opposing him and French arms—prominently featured committed enlighteners. If there were staunch Patriots in the regions unoccupied by the French, defending Spain's national sovereignty, "many of the most enlightened and honest Spaniards," recalled one anti-French reformer later, "attached themselves to Joseph Buonaparte," attracted by his far-reaching plans to reduce ecclesiastical authority and Church property and suppress the Inquisition.[17] They included some of the most radical enlighteners in Spain, among them the Brissotin revolutionary, originally from Seville, José Marchena, who became one of Joseph's chief publicists.[18] Until 1810, the French seemed to be slowly gaining the upper hand over the opposition. Between January and March 1810, Joseph overran most of Andalusia, entering Córdoba, Granada, and Seville in triumph. But from 1811 onward, with British help, Fernando's supporters regained lost ground.

The tenacious anti-French opposition whose political headquarters was first Seville (during 1808–9), and then Cádiz, sought to defend but, equally, reform Spain's world empire. These *antibonapartistas* counted numerous champions of the old order along with a "liberal" faction, as it was dubbed, comprising Enlightenment radicals. This latter group eventually became dominant on the regency council and especially in the Cádiz Cortes (parliament), where by 1811–12 the mood tended strongly against conservatism and the interests of the privileged classes. The result was among the most surprising episodes of the revolutionary era, a clear instance of marginal, fringe intellectual groups assuming the lead amid severe upheaval. In this respect, the Spanish Revolution resembled the French. The convergence of uprooted "Patriots" on the isolated, almost besieged, peninsula of Cádiz, successfully defended only with the help of Britain's navy, a focus of resistance and reform from which the aristocracy, great landowners, and churchmen mostly kept away, became the intellectual base of a "political-literary war" that gripped Spain in the years 1810–14, an ideological tussle between rival radical and conservative factions designated by the former *liberales* and *serviles*.[19]

Those seeking to inculcate into the literate middle class and artisans notions of popular sovereignty, national revival, and representation and, through group readings even rouse the peasantry, designing political revolution and organizing a full-scale attack on privilege were mostly estranged secretaries,

"The Spanish Bull Fight, or the Corsican Matador in Danger." James Gillray depicts the popular rising of 1808 against Napoleon's occupation of Spain. Photo credit: Courtesy of the Warden and Scholars of New College, Oxford/Bridgeman Images.

academics, renegade churchmen, and journalists.[20] "No sooner had the liberty of the press been proclaimed," observed one contemporary, "than several eloquent writers, who had travelled throughout the rest of Europe and marked the progress of knowledge, devoted their talents to enlightening the people and showing the advantages of civil freedom."[21] Yet, those most adept at swaying crowds toward uncompromising rejectionism of the French (and their new ideas) were chiefly the clergy and defenders of privilege. Paradoxically, the Cádiz intellectual coterie became leaders of a popular movement superficially radical but actually driven by conservatism, sentiment, and profound emotional loyalism. Deep resentment infused the spontaneous rising of the great mass of the urban and rural Castilian population against the French, with the clergy and magistrates at their head. In 1808, for the first time there consequently developed in the Spanish world a vehemently contested public arena. Printed propaganda directed against the *josefinos* spoke two languages denouncing them as oppressors of the people but even more as purveyors of irreligion corrupted by reading freethinking French literature. Denounced as traitors, *josefinos* were chiefly loathed as "ideológos-filósofos-humanistas."

The intellectuals crowding the cafés of Cádiz and steering the Revolution of 1810–12 can certainly be construed, and were viewed by some at the time, as the spearhead of middle-class strands aspiring to become Spain's new social elite.[22] Few of their leaders, though, came from typical middle-class backgrounds. Rather, the Cádiz reform party was led by essentially unrepresentative intellectuals such as Agustín Argüelles (1776–1844), a former bishop's secretary estranged from the Church who composed the preface to the 1812 Cádiz Constitution, Manuel José Quintana (1772–1857), successful poet, playwright, and enlightened essayist, Bartolomé José Gallardo (1776–1852), a peasant son trained in philosophy at Salamanca, avid for French books and author of the *Diccionario Critico-Burlesco* (1811), the most anticlerical Spanish text of the age,[23] Evaristo Pérez de Castro (1778–1849), an art and theater-loving junior diplomat whose portrait Goya painted sympathetically, Diego Muñoz Terrero, a philosophy professor and rector of Salamanca University, champion of press freedom, and a great orator in the Cortes, and José Maria Queipo de Llano (1786–1843), seventh count of Toreno, whose Enlightenment reading made him radical enough to be disowned by his aristocratic relatives.

Unprecedented pressures to appeal to "public opinion" galvanizing all three main blocs, *josefinos*, *absolutistas*, and *liberales*, imparted a crucial role to tracts, pamphlets, and newspapers, and to proclamations and speeches before large assembled crowds. Intellectuals mixed with renegade nobles, the revolutionary leadership sought to endow the monarchy with a still more libertarian constitution and institutional framework than Joseph offered.[24] In their papers and pamphlets, Quintana, Argüelles, and Muñoz Terrero emphasized the vital importance of press freedom and freedom to criticize for strengthening the "voice of the people,"[25] though what Argüelles meant by the latter was the mostly urban literate segment. The press remained throughout the principal weapon of the radical faction in the soon public ideological war between radicals and conservatives waged from late 1810 and, before long, the Cádiz Cortes's defining feature. Temporarily, radicalism defeated Spanish conservatism, the *absolutistas*, in the ideological war shaping the 1810–13 revolution, but only because newspapers, journals, and pamphlets became, briefly, the main arena and tool of politics: excessive reliance on speeches, manifestos, and slogans afterward rapidly proved the radicals' prime weakness.[26]

Accordingly, while the collapse of the old monarchy and anarchic conditions made the Spanish Revolution possible, it can no more explain the far-reaching character of what ensued, why the pamphlets propounded the Enlightenment culture they did, why the Spanish Revolution declared the sovereignty of the national legislature, curtailed privilege, erased the Inquisition (albeit not permanently), and strove to diminish the Church's power, legislating under the rubric "rights of mankind," than the financial crisis engulfing the French monarchy in 1787–89 can explain the democratic republican tendency that shaped the French Revolution until June 1793. The swift success and then rapid failure of the Spanish Revolution of 1808–14 was rendered possible by the deeply chaotic situation Napoleon's invasion created and ensuing general turmoil. But to explain the Spanish Revolution's ambitious sweep, one must, as with French Revolution of 1789–93, cite rather the deep incursion of Radical Enlightenment ideas among the country's guiding intellectual fringe.

In Spain and Spanish America alike changes came thick and fast; the regency council of officials and ministers leading the resistance to Joseph acted in the name of the Bourbon successor to the throne, Fernando VII (reigned: 1808–33). Fernando himself, meanwhile, remained until 1814 a virtual prisoner of Napoleon in France. In January 1809, the *antibonapartista* leadership announced that all Spain's American dependencies henceforth constituted an integral part of the Spanish monarchy rather than being mere colonies, as in the past. The monarchy would be fundamentally reformed and Spanish America share in the emerging new legal and representative institutions. The city councils of all the realms of Spanish America were summoned to choose representatives for the preliminary constitutional commission to meet in Cádiz; but only a few of these (in the event nine) represented the Spanish New World as against thirty-six commission members for metropolitan Spain. The same gross imbalance applied in the autumn of 1810 when the Cádiz regime called for local elections and proceeded to convene the much larger national Cortes to carry the reform process forward.[27]

Spanish America was thus represented in the 1810–12 Cortes as a relatively minor appendage in blatant defiance of equity and proportionality, a contradiction the philosopher Bentham early on identified as unsustainable.[28] The proportionality principle, invoked as a constitutional issue originally by Franklin and others during the American Revolution, had received more sustained attention during the early French Revolution. The question lingered, subsequently prompting the Spanish American deputies at Cádiz to protest repeatedly at their diminutive representation. But since Spanish America's population was estimated at the time at roughly fifteen million, around 50 percent more than the total for Spain itself (reckoned at ten million), there was no way genuine proportionality could apply without transferring control of the empire across the Atlantic.[29] The proclamations relating to Spanish America issued by the Cádiz Cortes and its leading figures during 1810–13 simultaneously eulogized the Creoles and reproached them for showing insufficient loyalty to their "mother," Spain.[30] The chief split, however, in the regency council at Seville, and then, from 1810, the Cádiz Cortes, as more generally throughout Spain and Ibero-America, was that between the tenacious conservative bloc representing the interests of Fernando's court in captivity (and of the Church and nobility), a mix of Counter-Enlightenment and "moderate" Enlightenment conservatism, confronting the intellectuals, journalists, and ambitious reformers aiming to reorganize the monarchy in a radical, sweeping fashion.

Since outright republicanism was popularly inconceivable in Spain, the radicals sought a constitutional, representative monarchy on the French model of 1791, expressly disavowing all resemblance to British "mixed government" with its hereditary element of aristocratic and ecclesiastical power. Outline proposals presented to the Cortes in August 1811, by the commission of fifteen nominated to determine the new constitution's basic principles, explicitly ruled out both an upper house and assigning the nobility or clergy separate representation, both points marking a fundamental break with the Spanish past and British constitutional practice.[31] All Spaniards would be represented as equals in the single-chamber sovereign legislature. The 1811 *proyecto* included other striking radical elements. Like Louis XVI in 1789, the king stood to lose all control over state finances and would receive only a fixed allocation, or civil list, from the legislature with spending on the royal household remaining entirely separate from and subordinate to public expenditure. Although the Cádiz radicals shared the antagonism to ecclesiastical authority of the French radical enlighteners, and were viewed by opponents as *philosophes* in disguise, they knew they could not afford openly to contradict popular religious sentiment. Rather, they affirmed their Catholic allegiance, accepting that the Catholic religion "will always be the religion of the Spanish nation, with the exclusion of all others" while allying with the austere Jansenist reforming clique within the Church.[32]

Finalized in March 1812 (proclaimed in Mexico in September), the main features of the Cádiz Constitution clearly derived from the French constitution of 1791. Drafted in 141 articles—as against 146 in the "Bayonne constitution"—the Cádiz Constitution vested sovereignty in the people and proclaimed the principle of equality. Although it featured no formal "Declaration of Rights,"[33] it introduced universal and equal rights in various clauses (echoing the French Declaration of 1795), stipulating equality before the law, liberty of the press—a freedom already conceded under a special decree of 10 November 1810[34]—and regular, automatic meetings of the Cortes. All adult male Spaniards could vote to choose representatives for the Cortes except servants, bankrupts, and criminals. Urban government was to be fundamentally reorganized too so that henceforth the empire's cities would be run by democratically elected councils. Cortes deputies would not as in the past represent districts or towns but the nation in general, each delegate notionally representing 70,000 citizens.[35]

The monarch's role was simply to approve laws and head the executive, the armed forces, and the country's diplomacy. Where the British king retained an absolute right of veto over legislation, a severe defect in the eyes of the Cádiz radical leadership to which Argüelles and Pérez de Castro forcefully drew attention, Spain's monarch, like Louis XVI in 1789–92, retained only a temporary veto, enabling him to delay legislation for at most two years.[36] The king permanently lost all right to initiate legislation or impose taxes, subsidies, or financial exactions of any sort, all power of arrest or detention, all authority to introduce exclusive privileges or suspend or prolong the legislature. Like France in 1789, revolutionary Spain had become a republic under the semblance of monarchy. Although Cádiz is sometimes claimed to have followed the American model in instituting a clear division of powers, actually the Cortes rejected the American pattern as well as Lockean theories of contract and "mixed government," following rather the 1791 French precedent in expressly affirming supremacy of the legislature as the voice of national sovereignty while tightly restricting the executive power and subordinating the judiciary. The legislature was pronounced sovereign. Equality of all citizens under the law and fiscal regime was proclaimed. Seigneurial jurisdiction was ended, disentailing a vast category of lands, including the property of the medieval military orders. Use of noble titles, arms, and liveries in municipal and other public affairs was forbidden.

The Cádiz Cortes of 1810–14 thus largely rejected American precedent as well as the reform trajectory of Spanish absolutist enlightened despotism in the style of Carlos III, Carlos IV, Napoleon, and Joseph. No provision was made for the empire to be remodeled on the federal principle, the aspect of the American Revolution that might potentially have been most helpful.[37] No form of regional autonomy was envisaged despite the participation of Spanish American deputies from the empire.[38] Rather, the judicial reforms presupposed a highly centralized system for Spain and its colonies. But American-born Spaniards, the Criollos, whose legal status had been distinct and inferior, now acquired full equality as citizens—a major change sealed by the constitution defining the "Spanish nation as the collectivity of the Spaniards of both hemispheres." Theoretically, Spanish Americans and Hispanic American Indians and mestizos became "Spanish citizens" too. The Cádiz Cortes was highly innovative in granting citizenship in principle to Spanish American indigenous peoples albeit the constitution still sustained a three-tier racial hierarchy by excluding those of African descent. Slavery survived intact in the Cádiz Constitution on much the same evasive basis as in the

1787 American Constitution.[39] Free blacks could secure citizenship through naturalization.

Promulgating the constitution was accompanied by joyful public celebrations throughout those parts of Spain unoccupied by the French. A resounding Cortes decree required that all principal town squares throughout Spain and Spanish America, previously usually called "Plaza de Armas" or given a royal title, must now be designated "Plaza de la Constitución." Marble slabs, bearing the name "Plaza de la Constitución" in gilt letters, were to be affixed "in the main square or market place of every town throughout the monarchy," instructions widely complied with in regional centers throughout the vice-royalties and captaincies-general of Spanish America including East Florida, where the monument in St. Augustine's main square survives to this day.[40]

Emulating decrees promulgated in Josephine Spain, the diocesan clergy were deprived of most privileges and reduced in size. By decrees of 25 January 1811 and 16 June 1812, special taxes were imposed on the Church's remaining property and tithes. Monasteries and convents counting less than twelve inmates were dissolved, in February 1813, and the remaining monasteries had restrictions placed on their recruiting of novices and exacting money from parishioners. The Inquisition was formally abolished in February 1813, albeit only after bitter quarrels: many deputies pointed out that most Spaniards wanted to keep the Inquisition and that a secular body like the Cortes could not abolish a sacred body authorized by papal bulls.[41] The Cortes ordered its decree abolishing the Inquisition to be read out in all the parish churches of the monarchy on three successive Sundays; but the measure met adamant resistance. "Freedom of thought" and expression in any case remained largely theoretical in much of Spain since the Cortes simultaneously issued laws enjoining unqualified respect for the Catholic faith, severely curtailing all personal religious freedom.[42]

According to Jefferson, like most enlighteners at the time, the Cádiz Constitution "had defects enough" but was nevertheless impressive, not least in recognizing that the "rights of citizenship" entailed the necessity of all men being able to read and write. Education was ultimately the key to republican success in Spanish lands as in America: "enlighten the people generally, and tyranny and oppressions of the body and mind will vanish like evil spirits at the dawn of day." Jefferson disagreed with those "enthusiasts" who thought mankind perfectible but did "believe it susceptible of much improvement, and most of all, in matters of government and religion; and that the diffusion of knowledge among the people is to be the instrument by which it is to be effected." For the Spain reborn of 1810–14 Jefferson was filled with hope but also fearful, and with every justification given the powerful countervailing majority tendency rooted in "ignorance and bigotry of the mass."[43]

The Church stood in outright opposition to the Cortes. The bishops indignantly protested that the Cortes was emulating the irreligious French and *josefinos*. Many ecclesiastics openly defied the Cádiz decrees.[44] The Inquisition ceased but only nominally—it was soon to be back. Meanwhile, freedom of expression and the press existed exclusively on paper under the proviso that nothing contrary to the Catholic faith could be expressed. New special diocesan councils were instituted to enforce religious authority and censorship. When the first Cortes popularly elected under the 1812 constitution convened in September 1813, the pro-Enlightenment faction opposing the conservative clergy and nobles found itself already disastrously diminished and weakened.[45]

The Defeat of the Spanish American Republican Revolutions (1808–16)

The Cádiz Cortes of 1810–14 simultaneously impacted on Spain and Spanish America. Since the 1770s, Enlightenment and republicanism, stimulated by the American (and French) example, had become a combined force to be reckoned with in Latin America too. How far matters had progressed by the early 1780s is revealed by the diary of Don Francisco Arias de Saavedra de Sangronis (1746–1819), one of the architects of the Spanish reconquest of the Floridas and a leading reformer of the Spanish administration in Cuba. A royal commissioner touring the Caribbean and Mexico between 1780 and 1783, and afterward *intendante* of Caracas, Saavedra de Sangronis was among the best-informed observers of the day regarding the general condition of the empire. Spain must either lose her empire in a "short time" or else consolidate on a wholly new basis. If the latter, Spanish America's administrative, economic, and cultural institutions and administration must be comprehensively reformed to receive the Enlightenment and deflect the American Revolution's summons.[46] Should Spain proceed "with tyranny and oppression" without changing the attitudes of peninsular Spaniards in positions of responsibility, Spain's empire could not long eschew a "fatal catastrofe."[47]

New World–born Spaniards, the Criollos, insisted Saavedra de Sangronis, "are today in a very different situation from a few years ago, having enlightened themselves a lot in a short time." Crucial, he noted, much like the *Histoire philosophique*, was the transformation in their intellectual orientation. In

Spanish America, the "new philosophy is making much more rapid progress than in Spain itself" while religious devotion, the "most powerful restraint" on new ideas, had receded worryingly. Trade with the United States compounded the threat, introducing more "new ideas about the rights of men and sovereigns." "In our America," thousands of copies of the "works of Voltaire, Rousseau, Robertson, the Abbé Raynal and other modern philosophers which those natives [i.e., the Creoles] read with a special enthusiasm" circulated.[48] Another European radical writer whose ideas pervaded Spanish American elite circles by the 1790s was Filangieri.[49] Forty years later, prominent Spanish American commentators concurred that the 1770s were the decisive decade intellectually and in terms of outlook on the world when elite Spanish Americans underwent "this revolution" in ideas and understanding of toleration and freedom of thought seeding the revolutions.[50] The future great South American revolutionary leaders Francisco de Miranda, whose most formative years were the 1770s, and Simón Bolívar (1783–1830), who spent most of the period 1799–1806 in Europe, especially Spain and France, where he read much *philosophique* literature, exemplified this comprehensive South American "revolution of the mind" ushering in the Revolution proper.[51]

The American Revolution's legacy combined with the influx of French books of which there is "allí immensa copia" (an immense quantity) that "va haciendo una especie de revolución en su modo de pensar" (effects a kind of revolution in their way of thinking), explained Saavedra de Sangronis, representing a fundamental threat to Spain's Crown and empire.[52] Spain desired only to extract everything she can, enlightened Spanish Americans were "now persuaded, from those territories" and hold them permanently in subjection. Only urgent reforms, integration, prudent and responsible officials, and a change of attitude causing the dependencies to be treated like provinces of Spain rather than "colonies" could ward off this encroaching challenge. Reforming Spanish America's colleges too, ending their conservatism, scholasticism, and ecclesiasticism, was essential for tackling the root of the trouble—sons of leading Creole families migrating to France to finish their education.[53]

The revolution in Creole elite education and print culture, bringing Enlightenment ideas into the Spanish New World, not social forces, were undeniably the principal factor driving the transformation and laying the ground for revolution. But inherent in this, stressed the viceroy of New Granada (today Colombia), reporting to Madrid in July 1781 at the height of the insurgency that shook Spain's grip on the northern Andes in the early 1780s, was consciousness of the American Revolution. New Granada's internal strife had worsened "because the form of *independencia* won by the English colonies of the North is now on the lips of everyone [participating] in the rebellion."[54] It was true that the common people understood practically nothing about it; but the social elites of Spanish America grasped the significance of the United States' independence all too well. A fringe, schooled in radical ideas since the 1770s, had gone to war intellectually with a royal and ecclesiastical absolutism seeking the empire's further centralization, militarization, and commercialization and denying popular sovereignty. From 1808, the Creole elite's aversion to the old order gained added impetus from the general disorientation resulting from the Napoleonic invasion of Spain.

Although most of the Spanish American population extravagantly lamented their legitimate monarch's misfortunes, and Spanish America's viceroys, regional judicial high courts (*audiencias*), district governors, and city councils (*ayuntamientos*) loyally adhered to the deposed Bourbon monarch, repudiating Joseph in Madrid, the collapse of effective control emanating from Spain created a chronically destabilizing vacuum. This fomented local power struggles in every regional center throughout Spanish America. Everywhere, rumor, conspiracy, and sedition were in the air, boosting the impact of subversive tendencies already present, aggravated in Venezuela and New Granada by the Anglo-French struggle for Caribbean hegemony and political and social unrest spilling over from the French and Haitian revolutions.[55]

The first major rising of the Spanish American Revolution, at Chuquisaca (Charcas), in Upper Peru, present-day Sucre, began when local *audiencia* and other royal officials divided, in May 1809, with both factions seeking support from leading Creoles in the city council and university. Jaime de Zudañez and Bernardo de Monteagudo, heading the Chuquisaca rising, outwardly professed allegiance to the Crown but voiced a rhetoric of popular sovereignty, republicanism, and the primacy of the interests of the majority. They advocated far-reaching reforms and sought support among the mestizos and Indians; Raynal, Filangieri, Mably, and Rousseau were their chief ideological heroes. Much the same story was soon to recur in New Granada, Venezuela, Argentina, Chile, and Mexico. Signs of unrest proliferated everywhere. In July 1809, the proprietors of Lima's cafés were summoned by royal officials and warned not to permit "subversive conversations" discussing the Chuquisaca insurrection in their establishments on pain of being held responsible and severely punished.[56]

Although the viceroy of Peru acted vigorously and kept Lower Peru a bastion of royalism and anti-Enlightenment for the present, insurgency, preceded by earlier conspiracies in the mid-1790s, soon rocked all Upper Peru (Bolivia) and northern Chile.[57] Revolts erupted shortly afterward in Buenos

Aires and Santiago de Chile besides Quito, where renewed active plotting began in late 1808 following the Bayonne proclamations deposing Fernando. Emergency gatherings of members of the local noble elite established a junta in Quito province (today Ecuador) to represent sovereignty in their region, defend religion, and counter the Napoleonic threat.[58] The royal president of Quito's *audiencia* was deposed on 10 August 1809. Officially, this junta swore allegiance to Fernando, but its actions clearly served the ambitions and interests of the local Creole elite.[59] Royalist troops regained control after three months—but not for long: disturbances erupted again in August 1810 and a second junta seized Quito in September 1810.

In the early stages, Spanish American revolutionaries adopted a continental perspective rather than one specific to traditional borders, proclaiming "la revolución de América" in general. The ubiquity and common characteristics of the revolutionary sedition (as well as of Counter-Enlightenment royalism) in Spanish America in 1808–10 prove clearly enough that the rupture was only *triggered* by Napoleon's invasion of the Iberian Peninsula, not caused by it. Later historians often liked to describe what transpired on both sides of the Atlantic as movements of national sentiment and loyalty, anachronistically imposing a largely posterior political construction. In reality, the Napoleonic invasion stimulated an already powerful enlightened tendency among the literate classes that fragmented both Spain and Spanish America into implacably warring factions. Even in Lima, chief bulwark of royalism, religion, and Counter-Enlightenment during the risings of 1808–14, where the press was more effectively muzzled than elsewhere, a clandestine paper, the *Diario Secreto de Lima*, briefly appeared, in 1811, broadcasting not popular or "national" but Enlightenment views and political subversion.

Edited by a young, Madrid-trained lawyer from Bogotá, Fernando López Aldana (1784–1841), the *Diario Secreto de Lima* preached solidarity among the revolutionary movements, supported the rising in Quito, and broadcast secret reports and copies of the revolutionary *Gazeta de Buenos-Ayres* received from the circle of Manuel Belgrano (1770–1820) and Juan José Castelli (1764–1812), leaders of the May 1810 uprising that overthrew royal control there.[60] Everywhere, insurgent leaders proclaimed the old institutions and ways of thinking obsolete and the need to replace these with the new doctrine of the "rights of mankind." Belgrano had acquired his reforming ideas while in Spain and through studying the French Revolution. Castelli, son of a Venetian doctor, had studied at several universities, including Chuquisaca, and was connected to intellectual networks across Hispanic America. Admiring Rousseau, Voltaire, and Diderot, he was powerfully impressed by the French Revolution but also by the great Andean risings of the 1780s.[61]

The Venezuelan landed elite too, perceived the now highly nervous royal authorities, were steeped in subversive local "conspiracy." Their "secret" meetings were investigated by the regional high court (*audiencia*) and several high-status individuals arrested.[62] In May 1809, the Seville Junta Suprema removed Venezuela's captain-general for vacillation, replacing him with the governor of Cumaná province, Vicente Emparán (1747–1820), who stood out as one of the most distinguished officials in the Spanish New World, a famous enlightener, reformer, and man of culture associated with Alexander von Humboldt (1769–1859), who during the five years he toured Spanish America (1799–1804) had exerted a profound effect on the local intelligentsia.[63] But Emparán sought the applause of the *caraqueño* elite by opening Venezuela's commerce to the outside world against the Seville Junta's explicit orders, bringing him, too, under suspicion. In mid–April 1810, news of the French breakthrough in Andalusia, the fall of Seville, and the blockade of Cádiz brought the tension between Fernando's adherents and Venezuelans suspected of reform-mindedness and in Emperán's case willingness to recognize Joseph to the boil. On 19 April 1810, a mixed group of Creole and peninsular elite figures overthrew the royal regime in Caracas, establishing a Junta Suprema claiming to embody the sovereignty of the "inhabitants of the United Provinces of Venezuela." While reaffirming ultimate loyalty to the Crown, this Caracas junta represented the local landed elite's bid for power. But their coup deeply divided local opinion, being vigorously denounced by Coro and Maracaibo local particularists as well as supporters of the Cádiz regime—and the archbishop, *audiencia*, and the ousted *absolutista* officials.[64]

With Venezuela verging on de facto independence while fast descending into chaos, the Caracas Junta Suprema tried to reorganize the country's administration and fiscal and commercial regime, abolishing some royal taxes, including Indian tribute, ending the slave trade, and formally opening the country's commerce with the United States and Britain, quashing Spain's longstanding, mercantilist trade monopoly. Delegations were dispatched to the United States and Britain to seek backing, supplies, and arms. The latter commission (including Simón Bolívar) conferred with General Miranda, the only prominent Ibero-American veteran of both the American and French revolutions, urging him to return and help guide Venezuela's revolution. The Caracas Junta could not, though, prevent some Venezuelan towns holding elections to choose deputies for the Cádiz Cortes scheduled for March 1811. "Electors" were chosen at parish level by propertied free males over twenty-five and these "electors" then selected the deputies. The quarrel between the Cádiz government and Caracas Junta, revolving around sovereignty, jurisdiction, and commerce, dragged on. To restore sovereignty and imperial trade restrictions, the Cádiz assembly, backed by three Venezuelan provinces—Coro, Maracaibo, and Guyana—sent naval forces from Cuba and Puerto Rico to police Venezuela's coast.

Ostensibly a fight for independence between insurgents and loyalists, Venezuela's internal power struggle was really a four-cornered contest: royalists fought the rebel elite's Junta Suprema while both battled particularists and local foes of the landed elite, with all factions instigating unrest among local *castas*, *pardos*, and *zambos*. Particularist opposition was especially powerfully entrenched at Coro, capital of a region with a large *pardo*, slave, and Indian population.[65] As the chaos worsened, foreign observers grew increasingly gloomy about the prospects and none more so than Joseph Blanco White (1775–1841), a Spanish Anglophile of Irish ancestry residing in London where he edited the foremost independent transatlantic Spanish-language periodical of the day, *El Español* (1810–14), a paper that reached Chile, Mexico, Quito, and Buenos Aires as well as the Caribbean. Blanco White backed opposition enlighteners like López Aldana, Castelli, Roscio, and Irisarri in demanding "liberty" and more toleration but rejected their resort to arms and push for independence. He did not think the revolutions could succeed.[66] Neither Spain nor Spanish America, he declared in 1810, was "prepared to profit by a revolution." Plausible if "led by well-meaning and impartial men, and were it not the interest of many to oppose all their efforts," in the circumstances it seemed probable their revolutionary endeavors would simply implode in slaughter and civil war.[67]

Nearly all Spanish America was by now engulfed in unrest and turmoil. The insurrections had succeeded at Santiago (Chile) and Buenos Aires but even there were obdurately resisted by upcountry regions of what is today Argentina and nearby Montevideo. As yet, no single declaration of independence had materialized. Civil war and division gripped virtually the entire continent while confusion of principle and goals complicated clashes of allegiance between Crown and rebels and within the viceroyalties and captaincies-general between regionalist and centralizing factions. As the Spanish American crisis unfolded, central authority disintegrated everywhere, exacerbating tensions generated by caste, class, ecclesiastical status, and slavery. Amid this vast welter of strife and ideological combat compounded by fears (and hope) of British or American intervention, many perceived an urgent need for more coherent intellectual direction. Given the lack of clear goals and revolutionary focus, a significant development in distant Philadelphia was the translation project of Manuel García de Sena (1780–1816), a Venezuelan based there since 1803, who rendered into Spanish key extracts of Thomas Paine together with the American *Declaration of Independence*, the United States Constitution, and the state constitutions of Massachusetts, Connecticut, New Jersey, Pennsylvania, and Virginia.

García de Sena echoed Paine's idea that the American Revolution represented a giant step forward in man's understanding of government and politics and that it was the American Revolution's essential principles that the French Revolution had carried further.[68] The idea that forging a broader and more coherent Spanish American revolutionary consciousness depended on teaching the American Revolution and its constitutional outcome was reinforced in London by a separate Spanish rendering of Paine's *Common Sense* appearing in 1811, the work of the Peruvian Manuel José de Arrunátegui. García de Sena and Arrunátegui aspired to see the entire New World, North and South America, converge in terms of republican attitudes and practice.[69] Until 1821, the "Tom Paine" propagated by the revolutionary leadership in Spanish America was somewhat fragmentary, consisting only of *Common Sense* plus short extracts from other writings. *The Rights of Man* failed to appear in translation until an abbreviated version was brought out by Matthew Carey, in Philadelphia, in 1821.[70] But what *was* available in Spanish sufficed to help shape Spanish America's incipient radical tendency. Printed in Philadelphia, five thousand copies of the Paine compilation, calling for independence from Spain (and distancing from the British model), presenting the turmoil gripping Spanish America as part of the wider global struggle of "liberty" against "oppression," reached Venezuela with some seeping through to New Granada and New Spain (Mexico) besides Cuba and Puerto Rico.

La Independencia de Costa Firme justificado por Thomas Paine treinta años ha (The Independence of the Mainland justified by Thomas Paine Thirty Years Ago) (Philadelphia, 1811) was followed by García de Sena's rendering of John McCulloch, *A Concise History of the United States until 1807* (Philadelphia, 1812). Both attracted attention in leading reformist Spanish American papers such as the *Gazeta de Caracas* (January 1812),[71] further entrenching Paine's name and ideas in the Ibero-American consciousness, before long rendering him the preeminent publicist evoking American solidarity with the Spanish American revolutions and Europe's "General Revolution." Among those debating Paine's ideas in the *Gazeta* was a leading Caracas republican, the journalist Juan Germán Roscio (1763–1821). In this way, Paine's arguments for republicanism, alongside, and, for some, in preference to, the constitutional monarchism of the 1812 Cádiz Constitution began to penetrate.[72]

Over several months in 1813, the ephemeral Chilean republican paper *Semanario Republicano de Chile* regularly cited Paine's republican views while invoking the need for Spanish American "Washingtones." This paper was edited by the Guatemalan Antonio José Irisarri (1786–1868), a central figure in the Chilean revolution of 1810 and commander of the Santiago National Guard. After completing his education in Europe, Irisarri consistently figured among those Spanish Americans claiming republics pursue the happiness of peoples better than kings and denying monarchy was instituted by God.[73] Reviling royalists, he derided fellow Spanish Americans for lamenting Napoleon's seizure of Spain as an immense calamity when they should welcome it wholeheartedly as an opportunity to be rid of royalty and achieve independence. How contemptible that Spanish Americans continued to "weep over the misfortune of Fernando"![74] "Moderates" of the Spanish reform party, like Blanco White, an influential friend of the Cádiz revolutionary Quintana, Irisarri chided for demanding only modest changes and championing Spain's imperial claims over Spanish America.[75] Irisarri agreed, though, that "lack of enlightenment of the popular masses," exploited by the baseness of ambitious individuals, has "always been the reef on which republics perish."[76] Nothing illustrated this better than the French Revolution. "Thus I believe that the firmest support of republics is Enlightenment and virtue; and I dread with pain in my soul that that people in which these qualities are lacking, cannot be republican," but only become more unhappy and revert to tyranny.[77] Press freedom itself will be "prejudicial instead of beneficial to peoples if it does not offer truth and present it to men cleansed of all error, passion and interest." Enlightenment alone can produce a meaningful and coherent outcome, capable of stabilizing societies, benefiting the whole, and achieving peace under a constitution like that of the United States.[78]

In Spanish America, there was no lack of explicit and outright republicanism expressly extolling the United States as the decisive model—among the intellectual leadership. Conversely to what most Latin American historians have traditionally argued, "national" feeling barely existed; this is hardly surprising since there were no distinct Latin American nations. Miranda's return to Venezuela improved prospects for the radical republican fringe seeking to demolish royal government and ecclesiastical primacy, but only briefly. An avowed, publicly declared foe of monarchy, aristocracy, gender inequality, slavery, and religious authority, and longstanding republican revolutionary steeped in Raynal and French *philosophique* literature (since the 1770s), Miranda possessed an unparalleled transatlantic revolutionary awareness stretching back three decades.[79] Through the press, meetings, and demonstrations, his adherents temporarily gained ground. When thirty delegates representing seven of Venezuela's ten provinces convened as a national Congress in Caracas Cathedral on 2 March 1811, a majority, the "moderates," representing top landowning families, preferred greater autonomy from Spain to full independence. But the radicals mobilized sufficient pressure in the streets, cafés, and through the Caracas press to defeat them. Venezuela's first *Declaration of Independence* was proclaimed, on 14 July 1811, accompanied by a yellow, blue, and red national tricolor flag devised at Miranda's urging in emulation of the French, Dutch, Rhenish, and Italian revolutionary tricolor flags of the 1790s. Celebrations followed, a Bill of Rights was agreed, and freedom of the press promulgated; Bolívar and a few other landowners freed their slaves (something none of the Virginia Founding Fathers had done).

Venezuela's Act of Independence (5 July 1811) and the new republic's constitution, finalized in December 1811, were drawn up by commissions headed by Roscio, editor of the *Gazeta de Caracas* who, like Miranda and Francisco Javier Yanes (1776–1846), another Venezuela founder invoking Paine's *Common Sense*, represented the anti-monarchical and anti-ecclesiastical democratic republican revolutionary vanguard. *Soberanía popular* should always preside in politics: "all should take part in what affects everyone; it is for everyone to approve what concerns everyone."[80] However, Spanish Americans, lamented Roscio, were peculiarly inclined to false notions, and this trapped all Spanish America under the triple yoke of popular ignorance married to ecclesiastical authority, feudal privilege, and monarchy. He defined monarchy as a method of enslaving men with the aid of theologians defending arbitrary power. Citing Paine as chief propagandist of the North American *and* Spanish American revolutions, his later pamphlet, *El Triumfo de la libertad sobre el despotismo* (Philadelphia, 1817), fiercely assailed the Church's teaching that monarchs derive their authority and power from God.[81] In fact, contended Roscio, the Bible does not conflict with sovereignty of the people.

The 1811 Venezuelan constitution abolished hereditary privilege and titles, instituting elections for the legislature and equality before the law (for non-slaves), and suppressed the slave trade (but not slavery), and in the French manner subordinated the executive to the legislature.[82] However, it also followed the 1791 French constitution in electing members of its new legislature indirectly, via "electors," formally distinguishing between "active" and "passive" citizenship, and restricting voting rights to adult males over twenty-five meeting substantial property qualifications (raising the 20 percent of the population that was white into a broad new racial elite). Equally, the constitution's very first article declared the Catholic faith the "one and exclusive religion of the inhabitants of Venezuela," charging Congress with preventing all other "public or private" religions.[83] Eclectically forged by professors, journalists, and professional revolutionaries like Roscio, Yanes, and Miranda, Venezuela's first constitution, like Mexico's several years later, was fiercely criticized by some observers for adopting American-style federalism. Among the rejectionists was Bolívar, who wished to elevate rather than subordinate executive power over both regions and over the legislative authority.

Discarding the designation "Spanish America," the Venezuelan constitution located the country geographically in the "continente Colombiano" (Columbian continent), declaring: "We, the People of the States of Venezuela, using our sovereignty, proclaim the seven provinces here represented Venezuela's "United States."[84] Venezuela followed the American model also in adopting separation of powers, a two-chamber national legislature with the two legislative houses called respectively the "House of Representatives" and "the Senate," and a "federal constitution declaring each state of the States of Venezuela 'sovereign.'" Venezuela's upper house, though, instead of an equal, fixed number of senators per state, as in the United States, emulated Cádiz in providing one senator for every seventy thousand inhabitants. The judiciary was pronounced a separate branch and placed under a Supreme Court in the American manner. However, the 1811 constitution purposely avoided an American-style presidency, adopting instead a three-man executive, or triumvirate (like the 1799 French constitution), one of whom was Roscio. Elected for four-year terms, this executive was kept weak to ensure legislative primacy, a feature trenchantly criticized by Miranda and Bolívar.[85]

The revolutionary wave also swept New Granada (Colombia). In November 1809, the Bogotá city council composed a manifesto comprehensively critical of royal policies, denouncing in particular discrimination against Creoles. Drafted by a leading detractor of the royal administration, Camilo Torres Tenorio (1766–1816), it demanded equal representation for "American Spaniards" in both the Cádiz Cortes and Junta Suprema. True fraternal union between European and American Spaniards could arise only through justice and equality. Had the British Crown considered carefully "perhaps today it would not be regretting the secession of its [American] colonies. Pride and a spirit of superiority ensured the loss of rich colonies unable to comprehend why, being vassals of the same sovereign and integral parts of the same monarchy, they could not (while other provinces could) send representatives to the nation's legislative body, a parliament enacting laws and imposing taxes of which they had not approved."[86] Exhorting "ideas of humanity for all classes of society" and the "progreso de la luces" (progress of enlightenment), Tenorio demanded abolition of "Indian tribute," an end to slavery and the slave trade, and regularization of Indian land tenure rights.[87]

After months of pressure behind the scenes, in July 1810, leading Creole notables, critics, and activists, aided by popular demonstrations in Bogotá's *plaza mayor*, forced the viceroy to set up a local Junta Suprema. Consisting of twenty-seven Creole and peninsular notables, it provisionally assumed the government of New Granada.[88] Before long this junta, abjuring the Cádiz regency council, expelled both viceroy and *audiencia* from the country. Proclaiming an equitable "union" of European and Creole Spaniards while still paying nominal allegiance to Fernando, the Bogotá Junta Suprema found itself defied, however, by several regional forces. In the northeastern provinces of Santa Marta and Río Hacha and the south, its main adversary was a tenacious royalism. In the coastal fortress city of Cartagena, opponents demanded a looser federal confederacy not dominated by Bogotá. New Granada accordingly split like Venezuela into three principal blocs—centralist republicans seeking a unified, independent New Granada, royalists, and those urging federalism tempered by residual ties with the Cádiz regency council.

Here too, García de Sena's Spanish translations of Paine and the American state constitutions helped shape opinion. During the years 1810–13, the Spanish American Revolution's early stages, despite the indispensable military roles of Miranda and Bolívar, it was still the jurists, journalists, professors, and intellectuals, the members of the Enlightenment societies and reading clubs since the 1770s, who headed the New Granadian as they headed the Venezuelan, Argentinian, Chilean, Bolivian, and Ecuadorian revolutions. Among the presiding Creole Enlightenment intellectuals were the veteran enlightener Antonio Nariño (1764–1824), the Popayán-born botanist, academic, and newspaper editor Miguel de Pombo (1779–1816), José Felix Restrepo (1760–1832), a botanist and historian over many years professor at the royal college in Popayán, and the naturalist and journalist Francisco José de Caldas (1768–1816). Nariño, an aristocratic admirer of Franklin and eager zealot for both the American and French revolutions, had, as early as 1794, clandestinely disseminated in his own Spanish translation the 1789 French "Declaration of the Rights of Man and the Citizen" in Peru as well as New Granada.[89] Similarly aroused against royal absolutism, scholasticism, and the clergy before the Revolution, Caldas had collaborated in numerous South American scientific expeditions, like Nariño, Pombo, and Restrepo, with the great geographer and ethnographer Alexander von Humboldt. A founder of the science of mapping and analyzing plant distribution under different geographical conditions, in 1810, Caldas had become coeditor alongside Pombo of the first newspaper printing republican revolutionary rhetoric in New Granada, the thrice-weekly *Diario Político de Santa Fé*.[90]

In its first issue, deploring the confusion of ideas and uncertainty gripping New Granadians, the *Diario Político* stressed the country's need for a genuine, enlightened paper in which "our Francklines and our Washingtones spread light."[91] In October 1810, the paper published a *discurso* on liberty of the press equating political servitude under monarchy with religious *fanatismo* and general ignorance. It was a paper that tied political liberty inextricably to freedom of the press and "Enlightenment," the true salvation of man.[92] Since most of New Granada's populace exalted "superstition and fanaticism" rather than "reason and philosophy," Pombo, Nariño, Restrepo, and Caldas conceived themselves as facing a gargantuan uphill task. A congress of representatives from provinces willing to participate in a "Congreso General" of the viceroyalty convened in December 1810 but proved unable to restore unity. During 1810–11, each New Granadian "state" abandoning royalism adopted its own "Declaration of the Rights of Man and the Citizen," eclectically choosing their own wording and precedents—mostly the French constitutions of 1793 and 1795. Even though most clergy, and all of New Granada's bishops, condemned the revolutionary leadership already, there was no alternative, once again, but to recognize Catholicism as the country's exclusive religion. García de Sena, appreciating the necessity for this in Spanish America, had at the outset carefully deleted Paine's assaults on the Church, clergy, and religious authority from all his editions.

Convening in Bogatá in February 1811, most delegates to the New Granada Congress, "fascinated by the brilliance and prosperity of the United States of North America," were, like the other "Restrepo" prominent in the Revolution, the historian José Manuel Restrepo (1781–1863), secretary of the junta of the province of Antioquía and delegate for that province, guided as much or more by American than French example.[93] In fact, champions of the federal principle and the American model dominated the early constitutional debates.[94] With Pombo, Nariño, and others extolling the merits of the American state constitutions, each of the "states" of New Granada devised its own local constitution on one or another American state constitution. The result was a plethora of divergence: "in one province reigned, with small alterations, the fundamental laws of Pennsylvania," complained José Manuel Restrepo, in another those of Virginia, here those of Massachusetts, and there those of Maryland. Experience soon proved, though, that those "constitutions, although wisely devised for the peoples of North America, were inadequate to maintain order among New Granada's inhabitants" dominated by "superstition," clergy, and the "habit of slavish submission."[95]

In 1811–14, *Republicanos federalistas* successfully promoted a vision of the "United Provinces of New Granada" as a new United States "preserving a wide autonomy" for the individual states, though Nariño and José Manuel Restrepo among others soon regretted this, coming to see the American state constitutions as "too liberal for peoples educated under the harshest despotism." Meanwhile, a distinct, more centralist independence movement coalesced in Bogotá. Like the other provinces the "state of Cundinamarca," as the Bogotá region called itself, adopted its own constitution (March 1811), locating sovereignty, like the 1795 French revolutionary constitution, in the "universality of its citizens" but without relinquishing Bogotá's claims to be the country's effective political center. Meanwhile, yet another confederation arose under the junta at Quito (present-day Ecuador), with Quito's insurgents during the renewed rebellion there (1810–12) aiming less at independence than autonomy from Bogotá and Lima, reserving power for the local Creole elite.[96] Attached to New Granada since 1739, on 15 February 1812 the region under the *audiencia* of Quito was proclaimed a separate union of "provinces forming the state of Quito" by a "congress" of delegates from across Ecuador.

Among the Ecuadorian movement's principal figures was the *guayaquileño* (from Guayaquil) publicist Vicente Rocafuerte (1783–1847), later second president of Ecuador (1834–39). Converted to republicanism in Spain and France as a young man, he became friendly with Bolívar (of whom he later became an incisive critic). Remaining in Spain after 1808, he emerged among the Cádiz *liberales* representing Quito province until 1814. In 1819 he migrated to the United States where he lived until the early 1830s writing many of the numerous texts, filling seventeen published volumes, that made him arguably the Spanish American Revolution's most systematic theorist and publicist. No other leader so emphatically insisted that the Enlightenment was the exclusive seedbed of all democratic republican revolution. Few other Spanish American revolutionaries were as ardent for the American model or as adamantly republican. His political thought Rocafuerte professed to derive from Filangieri in the first place, and secondly Montesquieu and Mably, though he had also studied Rousseau, Adams, Madison, and Hamilton "with some attention."[97] None was more conscious that the accelerating transatlantic flow of information crossing between Europe and the New World and between North and South America, the journals and newspapers, was the lifeblood of the insurgency, the means by which the revolutions of Europe and Latin America connected with the North American fountainhead of the modern world's democratic republican revolutionary impulse.[98]

Residing in Philadelphia between 1819 and the early 1830s, Rocafuerte was keenly aware of living in what had been the heart of the American Revolution's radical tendency and the New World's chief publishing and communication center, its window on all the revolutions of the Old World and Latin America. At Philadelphia, he published his *Necessary Ideas for every Independent American People that Wants to Be Free* (1821), summing up his reflections after twelve years of revolutionary struggle. Like his *Ensayo Político*

(New York, 1823), this text envisaged the Spanish American Revolution as the child of the American and French revolutions together, proclaiming the guiding democratic republican principle that "all men are born equal" and share basic rights, that no other legitimate basis for representative government exists than equality of rights, and that governments exist only to protect these rights. Legitimate government therefore can only be based on popular sovereignty and every government that fails to protect men's rights can legitimately be overthrown. Monarchy must be rejected outright as "superstition" equivalent to belief in "Aristotle's four elements" and the "Holy Office of the Inquisition."[99] The French Revolution began well and should have converted the world to the American Revolution's principles but had unfortunately been wrecked by the "hipocritas Robespierres," "ambiciosos San-Justs," execrable Couthones, and other Montagnard "monsters of humanity" perpetrating the most "atrocious crimes."[100] "All the disorders that have occurred in France during the course of its Revolution," held Rocafuerte, "have had their origin not in the principle of equality of rights, but in violation of this principle."[101]

Rocafuerte extolled the toleration of "England, Holland, Germany, Switzerland, Denmark, Sweden and the United States." The function of "religion" is to bolster the "morality of society" via toleration and "not by maintaining opulent archbishops" like those of Toledo, Lima, and Santiago de Chile expending revenues of thousands of pesos annually.[102] Rocafuerte supplemented his texts with Spanish renderings of the American *Declaration of Independence*, the 1778 American Articles of Confederation, and the American Constitution, and phrases from Paine's *Common Sense* in addition to an entire speech of John Quincy Adams delivered in Washington on 4 July 1821 commemorating the forty-fifth anniversary of American Independence. America's *Declaration of Independence* he declared humanity's "verdadero decálogo politico" (true political Decalogue), which, after many years, would eventually accomplish for the entire world what Moses' Decalogue had taken forty centuries to do in the moral sphere.[103] Thomas Paine "contributed more than anyone else to wresting the despotic scepter from the hands of royalism";[104] especially in his famous work *Common Sense*, although in justifiably dismissing Britain's monarchical constitution as inherently "inferior" to the republican American Constitution, readers should note, Paine merely followed earlier French *Américaniste* writers.[105]

The United States, then, was the most relevant model, its superiority over Britain and Europe gaining further, from the rise of the Holy Alliance since 1814 and the, for many, unappealing contrast the latter offered when compared to the "admirable system of religious toleration and political liberty" prevailing in America.[106] Where courts and kings—even in constitutional monarchies—cost exorbitant sums, the United States' president, following the "immortal example of the great Washington," contents himself with a modest annual salary.[107] The prime model for Hispanic Americans was, and should be, the institutional framework forged by "Franklin, Hancock, Hamilton and that series of great men, whose wisdom the world admires and will admire forever."[108] Praising Washington, Adams, and John Quincy Adams, as well as Franklin and Jefferson, his own chief goal was to help spread "among us the spirit of liberty and tolerance that stems from the wise sentiments of the heroes and great men of North America."[109]

Rocafuerte's insistent political pan-Americanism expressly rejected property qualifications as well as hereditary aristocracy for the right to vote, declaring the principles of universal and equal rights and representative democracy defending these rights the only valid format.[110] For Rocafuerte, like Roscio, Nariño, and Irisarri, the real challenge confronting Spanish America was not Spain's recalcitrance but the ongoing struggle between ignorance and knowledge, "between darkness and light." Without Enlightenment "philosophy" Spanish Americans would justly be scorned by future generations for not attaining the exalted moral and political standards of the "Washingtones, Franklines y Jeffersones," for not cultivating "in our soil the delicate plant of liberty found only in the laurel and cypress shade covering the tomb of the immortal Washington."[111] America's political system should ultimately become that of all the Americas in the broadest sense, a pan-American constitutionalism solidly based on the principles of Washington, Adams, Jefferson, and Madison. The result would be that the entire New World would contrast increasingly with royalist, legitimist Europe, the world of the Holy Alliance, and become the world's chief promoter of human well-being and happiness, "la verdadera patria de la filosofía, de la tolerancia religiosa y de la libertad política" (true patria of philosophy, religious toleration, and political liberty).[112] This elective and representative future common model, jointly forged by Washington and Bolívar, Rocafuerte dubbed the *sistema Colombiano*.

If all revolutionary spokesmen admired American stability, prosperity, and power, zeal for American-style states rights mainly attracted regional particularists resenting the historical dominance of regional capitals like Bogotá, Caracas, Mexico City, and Lima, federalism being certain to weaken central control and strengthen local autonomy. In New Granada, the provisional federal capital was fixed by the federalist revolutionary "states" in Tunja, and later, after efforts by Cundinamarca forces to seize Tunja, in Leyva. Meanwhile, Bolívar and his supporters attributed the political and military divisions debilitating the Revolution precisely to the deleterious effects of the American model. As both the fighting and fragmentation spread, the enlighteners were increasingly marginalized and the leadership came to consist more and more of successful military commanders. Veneration for the American model, so conspicuous in the early stages of the Revolution, steadily receded after 1815 except among a small residue, being spurned by centralists and especially Bolívar, who was eventually to emerge as the unrivaled military leader of nearly all the Spanish revolutions apart from the Argentinian and Mexican. Even though Bolívar spent six months in the United States, in 1807,[113] his authoritarian instincts clashed with the independent legislature and judiciary characterizing America. An increasingly Napoleonic figure as time went on, he demanded a powerful executive embodied in his own person. He approved a separate judiciary, but otherwise, the only feature of the United States' political system he judged worthy of emulation in Spanish America was the "American President's right to choose his own successor," as he styled Washington's succession by Adams, and Jefferson's by Madison.[114]

Unsurprisingly, the New Granadian Revolution quickly disintegrated into a desultory civil war with royalists and Cádiz Patriots controlling the south, Panama, and part of the northeast, centralist republicans holding Bogotá, and *republicanos federalistas* of the "United States of Colombia" the rest. The first Venezuelan republic proved even shorter-lived, enduring only a year and twenty days from July 1811 to July 1812, with regional royalists nominally loyal to the Cádiz Cortes, and often mobilizing *pardos* and slaves against the rich, steadily gaining ground. Eventually, two more Venezuelan "states"—Barcelona and Cumaná—defected to the Cádiz Patriots and royalists (for the moment allied) so that the Venezuelan civil war became a tussle of five provinces against five. What commenced as a political revolution initiated by the Creole elite descended into a chaotic social war characterized by merciless cruelty and slaughter.

Miranda was proclaimed generalissimo of the fledgling Venezuelan republic with greatly expanded powers but was unable to hold the line.[115] The Creole elite seeking independence was simply unable to rally sufficient support. Blanco White's *El Español* accused them of using radical Jacobin principles as a cloak for their own material self-interest, as a means to oppress Venezuela's non-whites.[116] Independent Venezuela's collapse was hastened by the arrival of a royalist force from Puerto Rico that deployed at Coro and overran much of western Venezuela followed by a massive earthquake, on 26 March 1812, which devastated Caracas, killing thousands and wrecking Miranda's barracks and other republican strongholds while leaving royalist areas intact. Jubilant clergy announced that divine providence manifestly endorsed their side— despite the numerous corpses found under collapsed churches and monasteries.[117] In desperation, Miranda ordered the arrest of all peninsular Spaniards and promised freedom to black slaves volunteering to fight for independence.

But the archbishop of Caracas proved better placed to command the lower orders' loyalty. With little grasp of the complexities of republicanism, blacks, *pardos*, and other half-castes mostly declared for royalism and the Crown. On 25 July 1812, Miranda offered to capitulate, submitting to the Cádiz Cortes.[118] Accusing him of treason, Bolívar handed him over to the royalists in exchange for permission to exit westward with his beaten followers.

Miranda, Roscio, and other captured revolutionary leaders were sent for trial to Spain. As Joseph's regime crumbled, the British-backed Spanish Crown, represented by the radical Cádiz regency council, regained considerable ground in Spain in the years 1812–14. Spain's Cádiz-style constitutional revolution gained momentum. In "royalist" areas of Venezuela and New Granada, elections were ordered at parish level on the basis of universal suffrage, including Indian and mixed populations (but excluding the black minority), proceeding with questionable fairness and usually controlled by local Creole elites. For the first time, less affluent whites, mixed bloods, and some Indians found themselves thrown pell-mell into the processes of political participation about which most lacked even the sketchiest notion.[119] Meanwhile, Venezuela ultraroyalists, affronting Creole sensibilities and ignoring Cádiz, tried to capitalize on the republicans' defeat and, in 1813, civil war, more chaotic, brutal, and gruesome than ever, resumed. After crossing into New Granada and joining forces with the *federalistas* there, Bolívar crossed back again, reinvading Venezuela from the west and, by August 1813, had again captured Caracas where the *cabildo* conferred on him the title of "El Libertador." By late 1813 Bolívar was precariously the dictator of Venezuela.

Writing to Lafayette in November 1813, Jefferson looked forward to Spanish America's "emancipation." He did not doubt South America's ability to break free from Spain, eventually, but also anticipated that its populace, plunged in the "most profound ignorance, brutalized by superstition, and in complete subjection to their clergy," would, despite possessing some intelligent and able leaders, prove incapable of breaking out of their local systems of religious and social despotism. To him, these revolutions appeared premature. For men trapped in pre-Enlightenment structures of thought there is no way forward.[120] Representation and democratic republicanism must fail, foreign observers agreed, where the people are not taught what it is and how to sustain it and hold their leaders in check. The civil strife dragged on. Bolívar's second ascendancy in Venezuela likewise proved brief. Royalists managed to mobilize much of the poorer population while retaining the allegiance of some of the upper strata. Defeated, Bolívar withdrew yet again to New Granada, publishing a farewell manifesto attributing the renewed failure to "ignorance" and Venezuelans' natural subservience to tyranny.

In New Granada, as in Venezuela, Ecuador, and Peru, many Indians and blacks flocked to the royalist banner. From mid-1814 the resurgence of popular royalism, opposition to the Revolution fired chiefly by ecclesiastics and religious zeal, only intensified. According to José Manuel Restrepo, the "fanatismo religioso" of the priests and monks successfully aroused the *vulgo ignorante* in part by accusing the revolutionaries of attacking Catholic shrines, images, and crucifixes.[121] New Granada states with American-style constitutions, under increasing pressure, dismantled or suspended their more libertarian clauses, placing themselves under dictatorial rule. Despite promising freedom to hacienda and mine slaves willing to join his army (like Bolívar later) and several victories over the royalists, by May 1814 Nariño too was crushed.[122] Captured for the third time, this staunchest of republican leaders was dispatched to Spain for imprisonment. In October 1814, as royalist victory loomed throughout northern South America, royalist troops, sent southward from Peru, also crushed the Patriots in Chile.

With Napoleon's defeat by the allies in 1813–14, Fernando VII had ample cause for satisfaction. Toppled, Joseph Bonaparte fled, via France, to the United States where he spent the next seventeen years lording it in and near Philadelphia in style on the proceeds of pilfered Spanish Crown jewels brought from Madrid. Restored by Britain and the Holy Alliance, Fernando returned in triumph. After initially endorsing the Cádiz Constitution, he soon performed a dramatic volte-face, adopting an uncompromising Counter-Enlightenment stance, supported by clergy, nobility, and the many reactionary-minded.[123] The *liberales* were swiftly overwhelmed. At Valencia, on 4 May 1814, Fernando formally abolished the Cádiz Constitution, suppressing all constitutional rights and liberties while issuing a peremptory admonition to his rebellious New World subjects to return to their pre-1808 obedience.[124] On 21 July, he issued a further decree restoring the Inquisition tribunals in Spain and, ten days later, in Lima, Mexico City, and Cartagena de Indias with all powers intact.[125] Spain's resplendent monarch did not hesitate to use the royal army to round up the *liberales* who had loyally supported his cause against Napoleon. Many thousands, Argüelles among them, were seized and imprisoned, though Toreno and Rocafuerte fled, in time, to France. Miranda, the Enlightenment hero who began the saga to free Spanish America during the American Revolution in the United States, transferred earlier from Venezuela to Spain for trial, conveniently expired in his cell near Cádiz, ironically on 14 July 1816.

Repression in Spain Fernando followed up, in February 1815, by dispatching a formidable armada from Cádiz across the Atlantic. Comprising forty-seven vessels carrying 10,800 troops, this force extended his triumph first to Venezuela and then South America more generally. The king aimed to restore royal power and authority in the New World viceroyalties with Holy Alliance and British backing and not least secure urgently needed Spanish American silver and other resources to stave off bankruptcy at home. His principal supporters were keen to regain their own lost revenues, posts, ecclesiastical benefices, and New World emoluments but intended few benefits for supporters lower down.[126] (Bentham at this point decided most European Spaniards as well as most Spanish Americans would be better-off materially if Spain lost her American colonies since only the uppermost tip of society profited from her colonies' trade, benefices, and colonial governorships.)

The army sent to the New World was commanded by Don Pablo Morillo y Morillo (1775–1837), conde de Cartagena, a veteran commander wounded at Trafalgar who, from 1808, had been further hardened in the Peninsular War fighting Joseph. Capable but brutal, after pacifying Venezuela, Morillo invaded New Granada where Bolívar, commanding the opposing forces, had recently retaken Bogotá. During the spring of 1815, helped by the fact that the Anglo-American War (1812–15) was still impeding the flow of weapons and munitions from the United States to South America, the royalists won several victories. After an epic, 106-day siege that left the once prosperous commercial metropolis in ruins, in December 1815 the great coastal fortress city of Cartagena, defended by 4,000 Patriots and besieged by 6,000 Spanish troops and 3,000 Venezuela royalists, to the dismay of all *liberales* capitulated.[127] Bogotá was retaken in May 1816.

During 1814–15, the Revolution thus was comprehensively defeated in Spain and most of Spanish America. On the surface, Counter-Enlightenment triumphed over Enlightenment and republicanism everywhere except Argentina. Remaining republican leaders preaching liberty, toleration, and equal rights not yet captured and incarcerated in Spain, including Caldas, Camilo Torres Tenorio, and Miguel de Pombo, were one by one captured and shot, de Pombo at Bogotá in July 1816, Caldas and Torres Tenorio in October. But the very brutality of the repression that continued unremittingly for six months during which Morillo estimated that he executed approximately 7,000 prisoners with thousands more imprisoned or exiled with their families left destitute helped keep resistance and the embers of resistance alive.[128] From the royalist, ecclesiastical, and Inquisition viewpoint, the extremely heavy new financial exactions imposed on the "pacified" areas also ultimately proved counterproductive. On the king's orders, all monuments erected throughout the empire commemorating the Cádiz Constitution and citizen rights were demolished, and Spanish America's civic main squares, lately renamed in honor of the constitution, reverted to royal nomenclature. Jefferson and Lafayette felt highly aggrieved, as did Bentham, but sympathizers with the

Spanish American revolutionary cause in the United States and Europe were distinctly less dismayed by the Spanish court's predictable relentless reactionary rigor than the common people's unwillingness to support the republican journalists and intellectuals battling in their name.[129]

Between 1816 and 1819, Bolívar and his allies retained no real foothold anywhere in northern or central South America, though some insurgents escaped with him to find refuge in the Republic of Haiti, where their leader conferred with the world's sole republican black president. Haiti's "national palace" was found to be appropriately adorned with portraits of Raynal, Grégoire, and Wilberforce. With black help, the revolutionaries regrouped. Should he eventually succeed, Bolívar vowed to abolish slavery in Spanish America, a declaration made in Haiti that further enhanced his stature among radicals even if his promise was made largely out of calculation, to attract more black support.[130] Beyond Haiti, the Spanish American Revolution survived among the many refugees from the mainland in the Caribbean, New Orleans, Philadelphia, and also at sea. Despite longstanding international expectation since 1775 that the United States would wholly subvert European colonial rule in the Americas, this happened to a considerably lesser degree than reformers had anticipated.[131] With U.S. foreign policy geared to avoid foreign entanglements, only a minimum of direct American intervention occurred. Nevertheless, there was some interest and American involvement mattered. If few U.S. citizens joined South American revolutionary armies, great quantities of weapons and munitions were shipped to rebel contingents from 1815 onward and many American sailors participated on privateering vessels commissioned for the South American revolution. Often veterans of the 1812–15 war against Britain, these men included most of the thirty-two captains bearing letters of marque from the sole Spanish American insurgent regime (at Buenos Aires) still boasting an organized army and navy.[132]

In July 1815, President Madison decreed that vessels in rebellion against the Spanish Crown entering American ports would be treated like ships from accredited states. Congress, less sympathetic than Madison, reversed this policy after Fernando's suppression of the nascent republics of Venezuela and Colombia. A congressional act of March 1817 forbade the further outfitting of rebel privateers in the United States; an act of April 1818 rendered it no longer legal for American citizens to enlist on Spanish American insurgent republican vessels, though this seems to have barely interrupted the flow of American sailors (and some soldiers) volunteering to fight in South America.[133] It was obvious, meanwhile, from the papers and from personal reports, that the revolutionary cause in South America was far from dead. "I am anxious for South America," confided Adams to Jefferson in January 1818. "They will be independent of Spain. But can they have free governments? Can the Roman religion and a free government exist together?"[134] "I enter into all doubts as to the event of the revolution of S. America," answered Jefferson. "They will succeed against Spain. But the dangerous enemy is within their own breasts. Ignorance and superstition will chain their minds and bodies under religious and military despotism."[135]

From 1819, in a stunning reversal of fortune, helped by the flow of weapons and munitions from the United States, Bolívar turned the tables on his opponents, reviving the embers of revolution on the South American mainland. Colombia's independence was restored following his victory at Boyacá (August 1819) and that of Venezuela with the fall of Caracas (June 1821). Bolívar still planned to unite as much of Hispanic America as possible under his personal leadership. From 1819 to 1830, he presided over the huge, short-lived republic of Gran Colombia (comprising modern Colombia, Venezuela, Panama, and Ecuador). Nurturing his grandiose vision, he aimed to forge a highly centralized, enduring authoritarian structure, though his Napoleonist tendencies had their benevolent side. Even though only a few blacks, escaped slaves or freemen, ever joined his resumed campaign in Colombia, Venezuela, and Peru, and despite the hostility of most hacendados and landowners, and the severe criticism his policy evoked among Southern congressmen in the United States, he persevered with urging universal and equal rights and sporadically freeing slaves.[136]

The gloomy predictions of Jefferson, Adams, Madison, and Monroe proved all too accurate. Dogged resolve and Bolívar's military skills, together with the victories of the joint Argentine-Chilean forces over the royalist army in Peru, eventually detached Spanish America from Spain but failed to establish free and stable republican institutions. The Inquisition, abolished in Argentina in 1813, was liquidated in Mexico, Peru, and Colombia in 1820–21. But an even greater scourge of humanity, black slavery, continued in Bolivia until 1831, in Colombia and Panama until 1851, in Venezuela until 1854, and in Peru until formal abolition in 1855. Mexico, Colombia, Venezuela, and the other new republics acquired splendid constitutions on paper but exhibited precious little genuine republican liberty or freedom of expression in practice. Gran Colombia, observed President John Quincy Adams in May 1823, had a constitution "almost identical with our own."[137] Nevertheless, it proved a kind of mirage, like the other republics altogether unable to uphold its declared liberties. The most talented and determined of all the South American revolutionaries though he was, Bolívar left no lasting democratic constitutional political legacy of any substance.

CHAPTER 17

Reaction, Radicalism, and *Américanisme* under "the Restoration" (1814–30)

Restoration and the "Holy Alliance"

The Napoleonic Wars plunged all Europe into massive upheaval and, despite Napoleon's failure in the Caribbean, indirectly transformed the New World too by disrupting and fragmenting the entire system of Ibero-American government and administration. Between 1802 and 1814, Napoleonic armies occupied and controlled Italy, Germany, Switzerland, Poland, the Low Countries, and much of Spain, commanded by an authoritarian dictator who dragged all Europe into his grandiose schemes. Napoleon's European state system, at its height from 1805 until his invasion of Russia (1812), transformed Spain, recast the Low Countries, reorganized Switzerland, divided Italy along dramatically new lines, drastically reduced the German confederation in size in particular by emasculating Prussia, and resurrected Poland as an independent state by creating the so-called Grand Duchy of Warsaw. Though small compared to the prepartition Polish commonwealth, the Grand Duchy comprised central Poland and formed a resolute buffer effectively cushioning a drastically weakened Prussia and Austria from Russia and excluding Russia from east-central Europe.

Bonaparte was eventually beaten—in Russia in 1812, in Germany in 1813, and in Spain and France in 1814. By 1815, relentless royalist reaction backed by zealous popular allegiance had also crushed the anti-Napoleonic Spanish Revolution of 1808–14, together with the Venezuelan, New Granadian, Bolivian, Ecuadorian, and Mexican revolutions. By the time of Waterloo, the "General Revolution," as Tom Paine called it, had been effectively crushed everywhere except Argentina and Chile and with it, superficially at least, the late Enlightenment as a reforming creed. After Waterloo (18 June 1815), the "fallen tyrant" who had abandoned his former republican ideals to "dance and revel on the grave of Liberty," as the radical-minded poet Percy Bysshe Shelley (1792–1822) put it,[1] but who, after crowning himself emperor of the French in 1804, toweringly personified the "moderate" late Enlightenment— becoming indeed the single greatest "enlightened despot"—was henceforth permanently eradicated from the scene. By defeating Napoleon the European monarchies, led by Britain and Russia, appeared to have overwhelmed what remained of the revolutionary legacy together with Napoleonic-style enlightened despotism in one fell blow.

The post-revolutionary European reaction known as "the Restoration" sought by every means to bury Napoleonism as well as the republican and democratizing principles of the American and French revolutions. The transition from Napoleon's state system to the Restoration therefore represented a tremendous leap—supposedly to a sacred past—to a global early nineteenth century firmly under British and Holy Alliance hegemony, and more locally Austro-Prussian and Anglo-Austrian domination. Along with other far-reaching changes, this created a new kind of disjunction between the United States and Europe. For the moment there were no "sister republics" to the United States (apart from Argentina and Chile) and, until the 1820s, practically no societies (apart from Norway) officially broadly seeking to align with the ideals of the American Revolution. Although they slowly improved from their conflictual nadir in 1812–15, relations between the United States and a British-led Restoration European world remained after 1815 a tense, cool, suspicious coexistence.

Britain and the United States both stood to gain from the breakup of the Ibero-American empires, but differently and as rivals, and partly for this reason Anglo-American relations remained distinctly frigid down to the mid-1820s. Where the United States condoned and sporadically encouraged the now interrupted drift to democratic republics in Latin America, in principle British and Holy Alliance diplomacy preferred to see independent monarchies, rather than republics, (eventually) displace the manifestly ramshackle and highly unstable Spanish and Portuguese colonial regimes. British ministers wanted an absolute bar on new republics but would gladly countenance fresh Latin American monarchies provided these did not elect the French branch of the Bourbons to reign over them or emerge under post-1814 French royal protection. In theory, this left as a potential source of approved potential candidates acceptable to the Holy Alliance and Britain only the Spanish Bourbon line. However, all princes of this line were debarred from fulfilling such a role by Fernando VII's refusal to permit his relatives to accept thrones in what, to him, were Spain's unalterably God-given New World possessions.[2] Only in the late 1820s did Wellington and his cabinet colleagues finally relinquish their hopes of seeing monarchy, aristocracy, and social hierarchy become entrenched on a pro-British basis in Latin America.

Politically, but also culturally, religiously, and psychologically, the general Restoration following Napoleon's defeat sought to remodel the entire Western world apart from the United States on the basis of monarchy, aristocracy, and ecclesiastical authority, that is, on opposite lines to those sought by democratizing republicans. At the congress of great powers meeting at Vienna (1814–15), Britain, Russia, Prussia, Austria, and Bourbon France strove to stabilize Europe's and the colonial world's new political order, a system of power and ideology subsequently guaranteed by the "Holy Alliance" (September 1815) of Russia, Austria, and Prussia, all aspiring to uphold an uncompromisingly reactionary global order dedicated to the salvation of the world in religious as well as political terms. The great powers jointly proclaimed a new kind of interdenominational Catholic-Protestant-Orthodox conservative orthodoxy exalting throne, altar, and divinely sanctioned authority. This new order was backed by massive international collaboration as well as fierce repression and stringent domestic controls. But though more effective in Europe than Latin America, in substance the Congress powers failed to attain their goals on either side of the Atlantic. The Restoration represented a great world-historical turning point of enduring significance: on the surface, the Enlightenment had ended; reaction and British aristocratic imperial hegemony ruled the globe. For several years, the post-1815 climate was sufficiently overcast to convince both "moderate" Enlightenment reformers like Adams and radical enlighteners like Jefferson that there was no realistic prospect of republican revolutionary success in Europe or Ibero-America in the near future. But the overall outcome, from a conservative standpoint, remained disturbingly incomplete.

Fostering Counter-Enlightenment attitudes was certainly the Congress powers' cultural, intellectual, religious, and political strategy and they promoted reactionary thinking and faith with all possible resolve—but these nevertheless proved relatively puny tools compared to the continuing force of Enlightenment ideas and publications. Under the surface, the post-1815 era remained if not an enlightened age then an age—not of the vague, meaningless "liberalism" historians so often invoke, or "nationalism" but rather of a passionately resurgent democratizing radicalism, and this together with widespread economic and political dissatisfaction virtually guaranteed massive fresh revolutionary agitation and uprisings before long. There was a sense in which reaction was defeated by its own inadequacy. "Ignorance and bigotry," Jefferson assured Lafayette in May 1817, "like other insanities, are incapable of self-government" and have appalling consequences. The Latin American revolutions were simultaneously being blocked but yet were irrepressible. They were almost bound to "fall under military despotism, and become the murderous tools of the ambition of their respective Bonapartes."[3] But yet, feeling himself a "sincere friend and brother" of the Spanish Americans, Jefferson could not help predicting that they would eventually achieve self-government and freedom of expression. As a device to limit the appalling disorder and bloodshed during the interim, they should, he suggested, first settle for a halfway stage—"an accord with Spain, under the guarantee of France, Russia, Holland and the United States, allowing Spain a nominal supremacy, with authority only to keep the peace among them, leaving them otherwise all the powers of self-government until their experience in them, their emancipation from their priests, and advancement in information shall prepare them for complete independence."[4]

Like Paine earlier, Jefferson in 1817 advised leaving Britain out of any such peacekeeping global confederacy. "Her selfish principles," contended Jefferson, "render her incapable of honorable patronage of disinterested cooperation"; this would only change if, as "seems now probable, a revolution should restore to [England] an honest government, one which will permit the world to live in peace."[5] Between 1815 and 1830 there was indeed a good deal of economic and social discontent in Britain as well as Ireland, unrest culminating in the "Peterloo massacre" of 16 August 1819, at a field outside Manchester, when a huge crowd attending the speeches of radical reformers was charged by regular cavalry resulting in hundreds of dead and wounded. Anxiety surged. The British ruling elite were distinctly nervous. That there would be a republican revolution in England, the headquarters of post-1815 global monarchical-aristocratic conservatism, looked at the time no less likely than the eventual resurgence of fresh revolutions in Europe and Latin America. Until such an irruption, nothing could be hoped for, radicals agreed, from a land largely still blanketed in post-1775 reactionary slumber, aglow with pride in her empire and stunted constitution that Lafayette loftily dismissed as "essentiellement aristocratique."[6] Shelley remained a disciple of Paine all his life. For him, in sharp contrast to the moderates, the British establishment and governing class was the essence of the problem confronting the world, not the solution. "Should the English people ever become free," he wrote in 1821, "they will reflect upon the part which those who presume to represent their will have played in the great drama of the revival of liberty with feelings which it would become them to anticipate."[7]

Radicals abhorred the sharp class divisions and narrow suffrage characteristic of early nineteenth-century Britain, the aggressive mercantilist exterior policies as well as the oppression in Ireland, Canada, the West Indies, and

"The Neck or Nothing Man" (1819) by George Cruikshank (1792–1878), depicting the British ruling elite in a panic at the resurgence of democratic reformism. Photo credit: © Collection Gasca / Iberfoto / The Image Works.

other colonies, the economic subjection of Portugal, and Britain's harsh penal code with its exceptionally large number of hangings—allegedly 4,952 in the years from 1811 to 1817 alone.[8] The English gentry's disdain for America and notoriously supercilious superiority complex seemed an additional barrier to the advance of progressive democratic republican attitudes. "The English," grumbled James Fenimore Cooper in 1828, "do not like the Americans. There is a strong disposition in them to exaggerate and circulate anything that has a tendency to throw ridicule and contumely on the national character," prejudice supplemented, he added, noting their zeal for royalty, aristocracy, and their established church, "with the irritation that is a consequence of seeing others indifferent to things for which their own deference is proverbial."[9]

In the Caribbean, a general repression as uncompromising as in Europe, and blanket reaffirmation of slavery, set in from 1815 under British and French royal auspices, leaving the embargoed Haitian Revolution an isolated relic of the revolutionary era. Harsh conditions provoked two major slave rebellions in the British Caribbean—in Barbados (where blacks outnumbered whites by almost five to one), in 1816, and Jamaica, in 1831. Until the early 1830s, British governors of Jamaica, Trinidad, and Barbados relentlessly backed the interests and loyalist pretensions of the white planters, enforcing the slave codes and allowing the white militia to quell all hint of black insubordination, even turning a blind eye when rowdy elements, encouraged by planters, used questionable means to harass and occasionally burn down Baptist and Methodist black churches suspected of preaching against slavery and white supremacy. It was illicit to question divine approval of the white-black caste system. Only when the more benign Earl of Mulgrave replaced the reactionary Lord Belmore as governor of Jamaica, seventeen years after Napoleon's defeat, in July 1832, did Jamaica's colonial government cease collaborating with militia and planter harassment of black gatherings.[10]

Officially, all was convergence and harmony among the victorious monarchies. Briefly, they appeared to have reached collective agreement as to how Europe and the wider world should be carved up and how they were to revert to being, as they had been for centuries before 1789, societies organized around court, aristocracy, church, and colonial empire bolstered by privilege and legally entrenched aristocracy, serfdom, and slavery. However, at Vienna, negotiations to fix terms and boundaries led to much maneuvering and incipient rivalry among the monarchies, especially but not only in eastern and central Europe. Austria, Prussia, and Russia had agreed to dissolve the independent Polish entity created by Napoleon, but not how to divide it up. Despite the efforts of Austria's chancellor, Metternich, to prevent it, Prussia and Austria were permanently stripped of large areas of central Poland seized before 1795, leaving Warsaw, Poznań, and nearly all Napoleon's Grand Duchy as a supposedly autonomous kingdom possessing its own laws entirely under the Russian czar. This brought Russia's borders deep within east-central Europe for the first time, weakening the two major German powers in relation to the expanded Russian empire and (potentially again) France.

Czar Alexander, constantly reminding his allies that Russia had played the largest part in overcoming Napoleon, appeared intent on intruding into east-central Europe in a manner that provoked alarm in Prussia and Austria. Set on reversing Napoleon's scheme to debilitate Prussia permanently by drastically diminishing her German territory, the Congress powers sought to compensate for Prussia's losses in Poland, and to reward her large contribution to Napoleon's defeat, by dramatically enlarging her territory within the reorganized patchwork of German states. This, however, weakened the Austrian Habsburgs in central Europe (despite their being compensated with territory in Italy) while simultaneously lessening the viability and independence of the German middle-sized and small states. In this way, the Vienna Congress while weakening the German confederation neither ended great power rivalries nor produced agreement as to how to reimpose joint Catholic-Protestant-Orthodox conservative principles. It proclaimed an across-the-board blanket rejection of popular sovereignty in every form; but this proved insufficient to preserve a united conservative front.

While the 1814–15 Vienna Congress and the Holy Alliance deliberately negated popular sovereignty by placing Italy under Austrian hegemony, allocating Poland and Finland to Russia, and sanctioning Britain's acquisition of numerous colonial territories seized from her foes, including South Africa, western Guyana, and Ceylon, the consequent vast monarchical-aristocratic-ecclesiastical empires forged in defiance of national identity, colossal though they were, were almost bound to become seedbeds, as the Italian radical Luigi Angeloni (1758–1842) noted, in a text published in Italian, at Paris in 1818, of new centrifugal revolutionary movements.[11] While none of the restored princes failed to support royal-aristocratic reaction to a degree, it was by no means the case that all comprehensively embraced the Counter-Enlightenment as the ideological framework best calculated to underpin such structures. Rather, they embraced the Restoration with varying degrees of resolve and on different ideological platforms, establishing a sharp disjunction and disharmony of political cultures that notably hampered the smooth functioning of both reaction and the Holy Alliance.

The group of out-and-out Restoration monarchies included Austria, Prussia, several other German states, Spain, and in theory at least France. But this absolutist reactionary framework was offset by two other categories of post-1815 monarchy. There remained the "mixed government" model combined with press and religious freedom, exemplified by Britain, Canada, and in practice also France, a system appealing to many moderates. In addition, there existed a group of post-Napoleonic enlightened despotisms, selectively adopting key strands of the Enlightenment and combining these with absolutist forms of monarchical rule. Russia under Czar Alexander I (ruled: 1801–25) initially belonged to this group; more lastingly so did the new united kingdom of Sweden-Norway and, most strikingly, the new monarchy of the United Netherlands (the Netherlands and Belgium), a new medium-sized monarchical-aristocratic entity created by the Congress powers, especially Britain, supposedly to act as a barrier against future French expansionist ambitions.

Having seceded from Denmark and formulated their own constitution in 1814 (after the American Constitution the second-oldest still surviving in the world today), Norway became an eyesore in the new context by successfully retaining her new constitution complete with wide-ranging civil freedoms under the Swedish Crown. Norwegian constitution makers in 1814 had carefully weighed Cádiz against the American *Declaration of Independence* and the United States Constitution of 1787, as well as Adams's Massachusetts state constitution of 1780 and other American state constitutions. The resulting new Norwegian charter, hailed by Bentham and other radicals for abolishing all hint of privilege and nobility, unmistakably resembled its American sources regarding separation of powers, to which it added touches of the 1789 French and the 1812 Cádiz Constitution in ways thoroughly unpalatable to the Holy Alliance.[12] In other respects too, a new Nordic model was beginning to emerge that clashed fundamentally with the ideals of monarchical reaction.

The new United Netherlands was a still bigger problem. To the consternation of the French, British, Prussian, and Austrian courts, exiled French republicans found a ready refuge in nearby Brussels. Exiles from France, including the Revolution's greatest artist, Jacques-Louis David (1748–1825), who spent his last years there, received guarantees of freedom and security from the new joint Dutch-Belgian monarchy, which lasted until 1830. Britain's chief continental pawn, King Willem I (reigned: 1814–43), showed himself to be a ruler who entirely agreed (as he had to) with his fellow monarchs about aristocratic restoration and refusing popular representation but who was unafraid to shock his confreres by firmly rejecting all ecclesiastical authority and privilege. Once a pawn of Napoleon in Germany, King Willem insisted on separation of church and state in the Low Countries precisely in the Napoleonic (and American) manner. He was especially anxious to prevent the Belgian bishops regaining their old social influence and control over education. He also continued Napoleon's emancipation of the Jews. In June 1827, the king imposed a fresh concordat with the papacy based on the model of Napoleon's concordat that recognized the Catholic Church as the majority religion in Belgium but assigned the king veto powers over appointments of senior ecclesiastics and unequivocally placed the state in charge of education. Willem not only refused to return property and privileges to churchmen but, like Napoleon, placed all recognized religions, Calvinism, Protestant dissenters, Catholics, Unitarians, Jews, and secularists on the same basis. A stubborn moderate enlightener, Willem acted entirely against the sentiments of the vast majority of the Belgian people, clashing head-on at every turn with Holy Alliance principles, carrying his refusal to sanction Restoration Counter-Enlightenment so far that, in sharp contrast to Germany, Austria, Italy, and Russia, he even allowed a considerable degree of freedom of the press (especially at the expense of the clergy and aristocracy) provided criticism of his own person and rule remained within bounds.[13]

Czar Alexander's tentative reformism posed a problem only initially. Apart from permitting a measure of Polish internal autonomy until late in his reign, he grew steadily more repressive from around 1820, in response to Polish and Russian anti-autocratic conspiracy. Censorship and repressive methods of rule soon became just as stifling in Russia as in Prussia, Austria, Spain, and

Italy, and eventually more so. "He is now certainly become the watchman of tyranny for Europe," remarked Jefferson in May 1822, tyranny "as dear to its oppressors as detestable to the oppressed."[14] A more enduringly worrying difficulty for Metternich, Prussia, and the British Tories was France, where the newly restored monarch, Louis XVIII (ruled: 1814–24), stood among the victors and closed ranks with the other monarchs but, due to limited domestic support, had little choice but to compromise with the revolutionary and Napoleonic legacy in important respects and was hence unable to embark on a comprehensive reversal of the kind surviving French nobility and clergy had been promised.

The post-1815 French press, to the disgust of devout Catholics, proved far less repressive than in Germany, Austria, Italy, or Spain. Neither the army nor higher education was purged anything like as thoroughly as some desired. If black slavery was confirmed in France's remaining Caribbean colonies, the most important, Saint-Domingue, was now permanently lost.[15] The French Church deprived of all its property in 1790 recovered far less land and revenue than ecclesiastics had expected, having to make do with state financial support and renewed mastery over education. Furthermore, while the most obstinate republicans and everyone tainted with regicide was permanently expelled, Louis XVIII ended up tolerating many former revolutionaries and Napoleonists as well as exiled foreign revolutionaries fleeing from Italy and Spain seeking refuge in France. Among them were Angeloni, Francesco Saverio Salfi (1759–1832), and the key Sevillean publicist, writer, and translator José Marchena (1768–1821), one of the staunchest Spanish supporters of materialism, atheism, and the Brissotin French Revolution who, subsequently, had been a prominent Napoleonist as editor of Joseph Bonaparte's official Madrid *Gaceta*. Marchena did not cease his involvement in clandestine political subversion while in France from 1814; rather, he and his associates maintained contact with underground opposition groups in Spain pouring scorn on the restored Spanish king, Fernando, and continuing to translate and publish Enlightenment texts in Spanish.[16]

Furthermore, many French opponents of the Restoration were soon permitted to return. Benjamin Constant, despite having at the last moment (ill-advisedly) abandoned his longstanding opposition to Napoleon's dictatorship, in 1814, and aligned with the emperor on his return from Elba, trusting Napoleon had really finally converted to constitutionalism, was stripped of his dignities, and post as "archivist of the Empire," and exiled briefly in Brussels and London, but before long could resume his political career in France. A convinced republican and libertarian, and among the stalwarts of the Paris legislature alongside Lafayette and Daunou, Constant reestablished himself in Paris as a professor at the Collège de France and a leading representative of the resurgent republican values of the neo-Brissotin legacy.[17] "France is tranquil," noted Shelley with satisfaction, in 1821, "in the enjoyment of a partial exemption from the abuses which its unnatural and feeble government are vainly attempting to revive."[18]

The inconsistently repressive and intolerant conservative order presided over by the Vienna Congress consequently repelled not only radicals and "moderates" but also right-wing champions of Counter-Enlightenment and orthodoxy. Especially French and Belgian Catholic militants, counterrevolutionary reactionaries, and right-wing Romantics like de Maistre, Félicité de Lamennais, Louis de Bonald, and the young Victor Hugo grew nearly as disgusted with the French Restoration's concessions and pretensions as with the new regime in the Low Countries. Pragmatism, restraint, and moderation looked bogus, utterly ill-advised, virtual sacrilege, to ultraroyalist critics.[19] Wherever reaction failed to secure an uncompromising absolutism steeped in faith and ecclesiastical guidance, a powerful Rightist component henceforth added to the underlying instability, polarization, and general recrimination. Reaction entrapped many an ambitious youth from a plebeian, peasant, or minority religious background in deep personal estrangement from authority and society, subject to the exigencies of the renewed aristocratic-ecclesiastical social system that looked hollow and fragile.

The compromises made by the French, Dutch-Belgian, and Swedish-Norwegian monarchies hugely contributed to weakening Holy Alliance monarchism, censorship, and religious reaction, and in France and Belgium rendered republicans, democrats, and Napoleonists exasperated and disdainful as much as defeated, filled with scorn for the new monarchs and their puny nobility, in France silently fuming and vowing vengeance in the style of the hero of Stendhal's *Scarlet and Black* at seeing young ecclesiastics of noble birth acquiring annual incomes three times larger than those of Napoleon's best major generals.[20] Contempt and alienation pervaded the intelligentsia, the schools, and the teaching profession. Deplorably, complained the journalist Marc-Antoine Jullien (1775–1848) in October 1828, most teachers and most of the French education system were not "directed" by *l'esprit philosophique* or anything sincere but instead by contemptibly pedantic, supposedly traditional religious notions, rendering French education under the restored Bourbon throne incapable of imparting to students a sense of the general direction of things and altogether unpersuasive and uninspiring.[21]

No one expressed the contradictions of estrangement from both establishment and the crowd more vividly than Stendhal in *Scarlet and Black*. His ambitious, worldly young hero from a peasant background, Julien Sorel,

466 / Chapter 17

admires aspects of the Revolution but is far from highly principled; his inner and outer struggle to rise in society operates via the only corridor of upward mobility available (after 1815)—the Church, despite his displaying no vocation or suitability for the priesthood. At crucial moments, his uninspiring career's small reverses drive him to adopt inwardly the rhetoric of radical ideas. Infused with a clandestine revolutionary attitude, revolt motivates him against the system. Like any ideology driven by resentment and ambition, his stance, though opportunistic, channeled personal grievance against society into the fermenting wider collective revolt against royal, church, and aristocratic authority.[22]

Unlike post-1815 Germany, Metternich's Austria, Restoration Italy, or the Spain of Fernando VII where royal absolutism was restored to its full former powers (and indeed expanded powers designed to repress dissident political and religious publications),[23] in France enlightened ideas, moderate and radical, continued to be propagated on all sides. To the distress of the renowned Savoyard writer Joseph de Maistre (1753–1821) and other hard-core anti-*philosophes*, popular sovereignty residually lingered in the "royal charter" with royal ministers partially responsible to the legislature, and liberty of conscience and near equality of cults persisted along with what was undeniably greater freedom of the press than Napoleon permitted. Post-1815 Bourbon France even lacked obligatory payment of tithes and large-scale public religious ceremonies consecrating monarchical power. What was chiefly striking about the post-1815 French regular clergy—the monks and friars—was their limited presence and their remaining permanently stripped of most of their pre-1789 monasteries, social role, and landed property.[24]

French society in the 1820s bore little resemblance to the pre-1789 context and seemed even more vulnerable to harsh criticism. Louis XVIII ruled with a nominal legislature based on a limited suffrage, restricting freedom of the press with respect to political criticism but without seriously repressing radical ideas, philosophy, and denunciation of the Church. Writings of the *philosophes*, though less fashionable in high society than in the 1770s and 1780s, stayed in vigorous demand among other strata and, frequently reprinted, circulated almost as if officially permitted despite being furiously condemned by de Maistre, Chateaubriand, Bonald, and other prophets of reaction as the principal root of the Revolution.[25]

If Louis XVIII's "restoration" remained something of a sham, Spain's restored monarch, Fernando VII, acted in a manner more fully consonant with Holy Alliance ideals. He briefly put up with the Cádiz radicals on returning to Madrid in 1814, confining himself initially to expelling *josefino* supporters of the Napoleonic reforms together with Spanish Americans implicated in the New World unrest (Rocafuerte fled to France).[26] But once assured of popular and noble support, he assailed reform, Enlightenment, irreligion, and constitutionalism comprehensively. With the 1812 constitution suppressed and the *josefinos* purged, he proceeded to expel *liberales* who had supported him against Napoleon, publicly condemning those who had championed his cause on a pro-reform basis as "Jacobins" committed to the 1812 constitution, traitors to the Crown and religion promoting popular sovereignty. Both "moderate" and radical Enlightenment tendencies were before long anathematized in the name of absolutism and Catholic orthodoxy.[27]

Expelling radicals, *josefinos*, and reform-minded loyalists,[28] Fernando massively expanded the burgeoning pan-European exodus of revolutionary émigrés, adding to the droves of defeated radicals, "moderates," and Napoleonists migrating abroad, driven from their homes, posts, and pensions in Italy, Germany, Austria, Poland, Britain, and Ireland and well as France.[29] The total ejected from Spain, in 1814–15, at around 12,000 families, became the largest émigré contingent.[30] Political outcasts scattered across northern and central Europe and North America, their favorite havens being Brussels, Liège, Geneva, Paris, New York, and Philadelphia, where, besides Napoleon's exiled brother Joseph, no less than seven Napoleonic generals and thirteen colonels sought refuge.[31] London too acquired a large community of exiles. The thousands of political fugitives and refugees congregated in semipermanent exile, often remaining committed political activists in their places of refuge. After 1814, both radical and "moderate" Enlightenment ideologies in this way grew into broader, better-connected, and more cosmopolitan networks of political activism with exiled fugitives of all types joining subversive associations, clubs, and secret societies. They became ardent Philadelphes (Filadelfi), Philomaths and Carbonari, Philhellenists, enthusiasts for Polish liberation, and subscribers to the soon revived Spanish, Italian, Polish, and Spanish American revolutions. Despite angry Prussian, Austrian, and French complaints to King Willem, Brussels became the European headquarters of radical subversion well before the 1830 revolution secured Belgian independence from Holland. In Brussels, French and British exiled radicals mixed with fugitive Poles, Italians, Germans, and Spaniards, all provided with a lively cosmopolitan press and eager admixture of local Belgian republicans, among them one of Europe's most notorious foes of the restored papacy and its pretensions, Louis De Potter (1786–1859).[32]

Where exiled moderate enlighteners viewed England as their chief inspiration, radicals extolled the one surviving near-democratic republic, the United

States—and the Cádiz model. Between 1814 and 1830, Italian revolutionaries typically conceived their political ideal as the regime "republicano democratico americano," albeit only a few, like Angeloni, also urged adoption of American federalism, a system the latter believed necessary for stabilizing and perfecting Italian liberty. Angeloni believed federalism had powerfully contributed to the stability of the two republics he admired—the United States and Napoleonic Switzerland—and was the key to combining stability with Italy's regional diversity.[33] More willing to compromise with the moderate tendency, and criticizing Angeloni, Salfi rejected American and Swiss-style federalism as a constitutional solution for a future Italy freed from the shackles of Austria, the papacy, and the Holy Alliance.[34] Italian regionalism needed preserving, he agreed, but the future new independent Italy would prosper best, he thought, under separate constitutional principalities with regional legislatures, and princes retaining a limited executive power, all linked together in a loose confederacy. Europe's mushrooming clandestine networks of exiled republicans and democrats, meanwhile, grew into a veritable radical *internationale*. "Ideologically," claimed Eric Hobsbawm, the "Carbonari and their like were a mixed lot, united only by a common detestation of reaction." But while the Carbonarist brotherhoods encountered numerous difficulties in welding their disparate elements into a viable ideological movement, they moved beyond sharing a pervasive underground culture designed to protect their membership from the police with oaths of silence and rituals of loyalty saturated in ceremony and "mysteries" inherited from eighteenth-century Freemasonry. Rather than inchoate and lacking a sense of direction, as is often suggested, their lodges fomented a strong anti-absolutist opposition culture.[35] In 1819, the radical Carbonarist lodges of southern Italy, a mix of anticlerical constitutionalists and democrats, adopted the comprehensively innovative 1812 Cádiz Constitution as their agreed political program.[36]

Fernando appeared blind to the immanent risks his strategy involved, resisting all suggestion he should divide the Spanish opposition to his rule by splitting the moderates from his radical opponents, by accepting a limited constitution, or "royal charter," on the 1814 French pattern. Among advocates of "moderation" on the Franco-British model was Álvaro Flórez Estrada (1765–1853), formerly a high official of the Cádiz regime who established the influential paper *El Español constitucional* in London, in September 1818, and who aimed to prod Spain's royalty into adopting a conservative constitution based on limited suffrage.[37] By embracing an unbending anti-constitutionalism and absolutism at a time when Spain struggled to check American expansionism, suggested moderates, Fernando was undermining his own authority in Europe *and* the New World. In Flórez Estrada's view, "pernicious" republican principles emanating from the United States represented a much greater threat to the restored Spanish monarchy than any constitutional compromise permitting freedom of expression on an Anglo-French "mixed government" basis. Only via timely, prudent reform could the (American) republican menace to the Spanish-speaking world be countered. Limited suffrage and "mixed government" could best be secured, he insisted, by emulating England, the "wisest, happiest nation, a people headed by the most powerful monarch on earth."[38] Dismayed by Fernando's failure to repel American encroachment in the Floridas and Texas, Spanish exiles abroad routinely contrasted the "España heroica" of their fight against Napoleon down to 1814 with the fragile but bombastic and unbending ultraroyalism of Fernando's post-1814 "España nula."[39]

As in pre-1789 Europe, popular grievances and economic distress were real enough after 1815 but not easily welded into a coherent conceptual framework of opposition. Historians have so often invoked "national" feeling to explain the revolutionary movements that it is essential to remind readers, yet again, that the notion that peoples generated the revolutionary movements is largely a historical myth jointly forged by post-1848 nationalism and Marxism. The people mostly showed little inclination to cease their passive acceptance of "kings and priests" despite onerous economic conditions feeding growing unrest. If the Holy Roman Empire's trappings were swept away by Napoleon, majority sentiment greatly aided the Congress of Vienna in restoring the old Empire's essence and spirit, reinforcing the time-honored passivity of what the "Young Hegelian" social philosopher Arnold Ruge (1802–80) disdainfully dubbed the "old petty-bourgeois consciousness" and Heine called the German "Winterschlaf." Men's outlook, complained Ruge, persisted as if the "old Holy Roman Empire still haunts it."[40] Distressingly for radical-minded democrats who were often novelists, poets, artists, and historians, like Heine, Börne, Stendhal, Büchner, Shelley, Compagnoni, Michelet, Foscolo, and Angeloni, the international Enlightenment had to retreat into a submerged world of the alienated transatlantic intelligentsia and literary coteries, further widening the already yawning gap between Enlightenment and common people as well as between Enlightenment and princely courts.

Romanticism undoubtedly qualified Enlightenment stress on "reason" with a new emphasis on emotion, feeling, and symbolism suffused with melancholia and nostalgia. By while setting the lonely individual starkly against both authority and the crowd, Romanticism remained essentially a cultural filter and intensifier, rather than separate ideological program in its own right. Reinvigorating both Left and Right rather than the middle ground, its effect was to sharpen in some respects but not substantially change the basic triangular split the Enlightenment had introduced into the Western world's consciousness by dividing sweeping reform from "moderation" and setting both against Counter-Enlightenment. Romanticism typically reconfigured this basic divide in literary and artistic terms. If early nineteenth-century Romanticism in political thought, literature, and painting was both conservative and Leftist, and both fed on disillusionment, melancholy, and nostalgia, the frustrations of foreign exile and painful reverses of the great French Revolution and Napoleonic era firmly steered much of this Romanticist longing into resurgent revolutionary ardor and ambition. Backward-looking though it sometimes appeared, Romanticism, Stendhal recognized, with its striving to break bounds, was a decidedly "modern" phenomenon, a highly charged response to the challenges and dilemmas of an age of profound cultural and social alienation.[41]

The people had demonstrated their capacity for political action in and after 1789. In the liberation movements of 1808–9, and 1813–15, in Germany, Spain, and Italy, the masses had become emotionally swept up confronting the French occupation armies with waves of vigorous national sentiment and solidarity. Many townsmen, artisans, and peasants felt deeply involved in driving out the foe from central and eastern Europe as well as Spain, Italy, and Switzerland. But "the people" did so only to find that the 1815 Vienna settlement's rewards and compensations were all for princes, nobles, and clergy, with nothing reserved for ordinary men.[42] "In 1813 and 1815," the Germans, deplored Ruge in his article "A Self-Critique of Liberalism" (1843), "did not think at all, and we still have to pay for our thoughtlessness." In the disappointing outcome, "in our perverse, deeply and unspeakably confused Germanness," the masses simply acquiesced as they subsequently continued to do.[43] It was "their philosophers, their immortal writers" who in 1789 and subsequently had "engendered for the French the new, world-shaking consciousness" enabling them temporarily to break free. When would the German public discard the unthinking deference and conventional piety that accomplishes nothing, the stifling parochialism blocking all striving for a better and freer society? Only total reform of the old political structures could bring liberty and justice: but such a change was impossible without a prior "reform of consciousness" that could arise only from study, literature, and penetrating analysis. Philosophy alone, held Ruge, could elevate the ordinary state of mind and society to a sufficient higher awareness: in a word, "Germans need the dissolution of liberalism into democratism."[44]

Where Stendhal captured the psychology of Restoration alienation, and Heine and Ruge the dispiriting passivity of the conventional, Shelley, a self-proclaimed "democrat, philanthropist and atheist," exemplified the radical Left Romantic poet. For Shelley, the French Revolution was the "master theme of the epoch in which we live."[45] Conceiving nature as a set of immutable laws, and the necessity inherent in nature's laws as the sole path to what is true, he embraced the mechanistic and deterministic concept of "truth" expounded by Spinoza, d'Holbach, and Condorcet to whose texts he repeatedly referred with approval. Of these, to his mind Spinoza's *Tractatus Theologico-Politicus* was the foremost.[46] Philosophers like Spinoza and Condorcet he venerated for forging a comprehensive skepticism about everything society and the common people believed while elevating study, scholarship, and science to the level of politically and socially critical reason.[47] If "philosophy" had identified reality and the path to a better future for mankind, the details of the veritable path had emerged clearly only in the late eighteenth century.

Shelley's principal prose work on political theory, *A Philosophical View of Reform* (1820), adopted a slow, open-ended cumulative perspective on the transatlantic world's renewed revolutionary process, which he conceived as being led by literary and intellectual subversion.[48] "The just and successful Revolt of America," he contended, "corresponded with a state of public opinion in Europe of which it was the first result. The French Revolution was the second." However, France afterward relapsed so that America remained the only extant model for alienated radicals confronting the Restoration, the sole democratizing republic, intending to treat all as equal, and without an established church. America "has no king, that is no officer to whom wealth and from whom corruption flow. It has no hereditary oligarchy, that is it acknowledges no order of men privileged to cheat and insult the rest of the members of the State."[49] This alone sufficed to elevate the American framework above the rest. However, what would eventually abase Europe's sovereigns and privileged was not America, or the people, but Shelley's "new race that has arisen throughout Europe, nursed in the abhorrence of the opinions which are its chains," the international network of revolutionary writers, artists, and critics, and their fraternities, fed on one-substance philosophy and democratic ideas.[50] These thousands of exiles—actual and psychological—found themselves thrown pell-mell into a transatlantic underground conspiracy, dreams and critical endeavor for which the radical *philosophes* of the eighteenth century, the Idéologues of Napoleonic France, and revolutionary publicists like Paine, one of Shelley's principal heroes, remained the prime intellectual sources. Radical Enlightenment was the essence.

Yet Shelley deemed human motivation and inspiration, capacity to grasp reality, elusive and complex so that these always remain in some sense beyond full definition in scholarly or scientific terms. The views of Diderot, d'Holbach, and Condorcet were the primary "cause" of the French Revolution in Shelley's eyes as regards its positive attainments.[51] But there was need to qualify this since the Revolution exerted an additional, exhilarating effect on those caught up in it, inspiration Shelley believed literature could help recapture and intensify. Where Godwin thought men must be reasoned into embracing democratic Revolution step by step with laborious arguments, poetic imagery, Shelley averred, especially after 1815, helps individual intuition leap more directly and incisively to truth. The "oppressed, having been rendered brutal, ignorant, servile and bloody by long slavery," can be marshaled by rousing images and notions poetically expressed to rise against the whole ruling construct and exact a "dreadful revenge." Images can move to revolt and wring concessions by shaming and intimidating the implacable. "This is the age of the war of the oppressed against the oppressors," contended Shelley in a passage deleted by the British censorship, in 1822, from the preface to his poetic drama, *Hellas*, "and every one of those ringleaders of the privileged gangs of murderers and swindlers, called sovereigns, look to each other for aid against the common enemy, and suspend their mutual jealousies in the presence of a mightier fear."[52]

The (Brief) "Lightning of the Nations": The Spanish Revolution of 1820–23

Revolutionary Radical Enlightenment, if curbed and rebuffed, was manifestly *not* dead, even in Spain where the years 1814–20 were rife with conspiracy and a seething revolutionary underground.[53] Following six years of intensely reactionary repression, the Cádiz Constitution was powerfully revived by the Spanish Revolution of 1820, commencing with the mutiny of 14,000 troops Fernando had gathered at Cádiz for his projected attempt to reconquer Argentina and then Chile. At first, the peasantry, especially in Andalusia, evinced only indifference; but as the weeks passed, sufficient support materialized in Galicia and elsewhere in the north to enable the rebels to encircle the capital and finally the royal palace. Cornered, Spain's fuming monarch hurriedly proclaimed the constitution's reinstatement by decree of 10 March 1820, expressing his royal "satisfaction" with a display of hypocrisy that duped no one.

The rebellion's chief feature was its inception as an army coup, or *pronunciamiento*, masterminded by disgruntled young officers, representing a distinctively Spanish style of revolutionary conspiracy soon transferred ubiquitously to Ibero-America,[54] headed by an anti-absolutist general, Rafael del Riego y Nuñez (1784–1823), who for years had plotted restoration of the 1812 constitution. Support was mostly tepid but among restricted groups passionate. Abroad Europe's poets and writers rejoiced. The international enlightened fraternity's enthusiasm was unbounded. National elections for the Cortes followed reinauguration of the 1812 constitution, resulting in the selection, it was optimistically reported abroad, of "men distinguished for talent and virtue, who have been besides proved by persecution and suffering."[55] Onlookers had "no reason to apprehend," averred Edward Blaquiere (1779–1832), a prominent ally of Bentham and radical founding member of the London Greek Committee, that the new Spanish assembly would "not fully justify the expectations of their constituents."[56] Within weeks, the smashed marble plaques designating the former Plazas de la Constitución of 1812 throughout the Spanish world had been "restored and consecrated amidst the rejoicings of the people." Such was the veneration for these symbols of liberty that many "Patriots" had contrived to preserve fragments "which have been restored to light since March last, and are now sought for as valuable relics."[57]

The entire Spanish scenario was abruptly transformed. Political prisoners, Quintana at Pamplona, Argüelles on Majorca, and South American revolutionaries in Spanish jails, like Nariño, were released while radicals, moderates and, despite the reluctance of many supporters of the Cádiz Constitution also some *josefinos* banished from Spain in 1814 streamed back.[58] Among the latter was Marchena, who arrived back in October.[59] The question of returning *josefinos* soon proved highly divisive in Spain, and some returning from France were turned back at the frontier, much to the consternation of French royal police. Those hitherto silenced at home resumed their former writing and gatherings.[60] Mexican and some other Spanish American deputies present, at Cádiz, in 1810–13 returned to Spain hoping to participate in the empire's much-heralded revival on the basis of the 1812 constitution. There was no "liberal ilustrado" (liberal enlightener) in Europe, proclaimed one of the revolution's leading ideologues, the writer, educator, and political activist José Joaquín de Mora (1783–1864), in 1820, in a leaflet introducing the ideas of Jeremy Bentham in Spanish, "who did not look on this event as the 'predecessor y anuncio' of the regeneration of the civilized nations."[61]

For a time, there were extravagant hopes that the Spanish America rebellions could now at last be quieted and resolved through equitable and peaceful compromise. A six-month cease-fire was proclaimed and new constitutional arrangements for the whole empire based on the principles of "Cádiz" and "1812" proposed.[62] The Inquisition was abolished yet again. Patriotic clubs on the French model of 1789 sprang up in Madrid, Seville, and many other cities. Madrid, normally "one of the dullest capitals in Europe," recorded Blaquiere, rose to a "state of the greatest excitement and exultation." For weeks, the city's populace "enjoyed a continual festival." After work, the "Prado, Puerta del Sol, and the numerous streets which branch off from it in every direction, are immediately filled with people of all ranks, ages and sexes: the usual round of serenades and other musical parties, enliven the scene at night, while some popular play or patriotic chief attracts crowded audiences to the theatres. Many hundreds, and these of a respectable class, attend at the societies [i.e., clubs] of the Cruz de Malta and Fontana de Oro, where some of the most eloquent men in Spain emulate each other in impressing the value of rational liberty, and the importance of constitutional government on the minds of their countrymen."[63] Inevitably, however, these clubs also became the scene of bitter ideological splits, with Marchena being expelled by the *moderados* from the Sociedad Patriotica of Seville only a few weeks after returning.[64]

Publishers, printers, and booksellers, intoxicated with the advent of press freedom, and freedom to import books, set to work with energy. In Madrid, Paris, London, and soon Lisbon, translations banned under Fernando's rule poured out in editions intended for a wide diffusion in Spanish. A four-volume translation of Montesquieu's *L'Esprit de Loix* appeared at Madrid, *La religiosa*, the Spanish version of Diderot's *The Nun*, at Paris (1821).[65] Bentham's works became current in Spanish; d'Holbach's *Christianity Unveiled*, first published in English in 1795, appeared under the title *El Cristianismo a descubierto* in London (1821) before reappearing under the more literal title *El Cristianismo Desvelado*.[66] Among its first actions, the reinstated Cortes ordered courses in political science introduced at Salamanca and other Spanish universities. A leading *josefino* resident in France since 1814, Juan Antonio Llorente (1756–1823), former secretary of the Inquisition in the years 1789–91 and recent author of the first full-scale history (and modern assault) on the Inquisition, the *Histoire critique de l'Inquisition espagnole* (Paris, 1817), commented on this Spanish resort to political science in Jullien's *Revue Encyclopédique*.[67] The Revolution required Spain's universities to use the *Cours de Politique constitutionelle* (1818–20) of Benjamin Constant, a work recently published at Paris, in order to modernize and enlighten Spain's political consciousness. Less radical than in the 1790s, and now no revolutionary, the Constant of 1820 still energetically promoted reform, constitutionalism, freedom of the press, and abolition of slavery.

Suddenly Spain became a lightning rod. The shutters went down all over Europe. The 1820 Spanish revolution was widely envisaged as not just a wake-up call for the Spanish-speaking world (where it effectively confirmed the independence of Argentina and Chile)[68] but a blazing beacon for all Europe, instilling fresh hope into the literary and intellectual radical underground scorning kings, nobles, and ecclesiastics. Shelley contributed a stirring "Ode to Liberty" (1820) extolling the revolutionaries, dubbing Spain "the lightning of the nations," a blaze of light in a dark conservative sky.[69] Believing Spain "already free," Shelley rejoiced from self-imposed exile in Pisa as the unrest reached Italy, Portugal, and Greece: "the world waits only the news of a revolution of Germany to see the tyrants who have pinnacled themselves on its supineness precipitated into the ruin from which they shall never arise."[70] The Holy Alliance and all Restoration Europe were profoundly shocked and embittered by the display of revolutionary exhilaration generated among Europe's radical intellectuals, artists, professors, and journalists. Conservative alarm was intensified by the fact that Spain's second "revolution" coincided with the advent of the Greek Revolution and helped precipitate daughter uprisings in Naples (lasting nine months) and Piedmont (lasting under a month), both of which adopted the 1812 Cádiz Constitution as their political program.[71] The Holy Alliance issued a general condemnation and ban on the text of the Cádiz Constitution.[72] This Italian republican upsurge in 1820 expressly linked the American Revolution's legacy with the promise of a new dawn in Italy as well as Spain and Spanish America, the United States being a central theme for idealists championing the new revolutions. Franklin's writings reappeared several times in Italian, and the *History of America* (1821–22) of Giuseppe Compagnoni (1754–1833), a leading legal scholar who had played a distinguished role in the Italian republics of the late 1790s, appeared in Milan.

Multiple Mediterranean outbreaks caused the rest of Europe, including Restoration France and Tory-dominated Britain, to look suddenly insecure. The scene remained promising for radicals into the early months of 1821. But in the spring of 1821, the Italian insurrections were brutally suppressed by the Austrian authorities, brandishing decrees threatening the Carbonari with death. The Church intensified its campaign against republicans and republican ideas. Before long, a renewed stream of defeated and persecuted radicals left Italy, thousands of exiles departing to join the Spanish Revolution and soon also the Greek.[73] The 1820 upheavals also extended revolutionary agitation in Portugal and its empire, commencing with mutiny in the army barracks at Oporto in August, spreading to Rio de Janeiro in February 1821. At Oporto, a junta was formed that convoked the long-moribund national Cortes with its three estates of Clergy, Nobility, and People, and declared the urgent need to draw up a modern national constitution, with the Cádiz Constitution adopted, in November 1820, on an interim basis until a new constitution could be drafted by the Cortes.

As part of its deliberations over the Cádiz Constitution and search for a way out of the moderate-radical clash, the Portuguese Cortes ordered the works of Bentham to be rendered into Portuguese. On both sides of the Portuguese Atlantic, a flood of political pamphlets and new newspapers seized the attention of the educated elite. At the same time, there was much pressure for resumption of programs of enlightened economic regeneration on the model of the Pombal regime and that of Joseph II, aimed at revitalizing Portugal's ailing commerce and society on a Catholic basis. The "disastrous" 1808 and 1810 treaties with Britain were pilloried for ruining Portugal's crafts and industries and turning Portugal into an abject colony. Having burned its last victim to death in Portugal in 1761 and, in 1768, lost control over book censorship, the Inquisition was abolished altogether by the new Portuguese Cortes in 1821. The finalized Portuguese constitution of 1822 was again based largely on the 1812 Cádiz model.

As with the Spanish empire, upheaval in the metropolis meant a mass of complication across the Atlantic. At court in Rio de Janeiro, the king of Portugal and Brazil, Dom João VI (reigned: 1816–25), and his councillors, believing the stability of royal rule equally at risk in Brazil and Portugal unless the agitation was quieted by a conciliatory strategy quickly, made hasty concessions. Ever since arriving in 1808, the Portuguese royal court had adopted a besieged mentality banning printing presses and forbidding the importation of foreign books as well as preventing the establishment of universities to keep out foreign influence and Enlightenment ideas.[74] The Portuguese court had wholeheartedly thrown in its lot with religion and Counter-Enlightenment. But even though, in Brazil at least, royal censorship remained fairly efficient in preventing mass diffusion of republican papers and pamphlets, and the earlier enthusiasm in Brazilian elite circles for the American Revolution and its principles, perceptible in the 1780s, had largely dissipated since the 1790s owing to the Haitian Revolution and fears of slave insurrection,[75] a subversive underground undeniably existed at both elite and lower levels in Brazil, posing an obvious threat to reaction, aristocracy, and royal government.

Earlier, in March 1817, a major mutiny had broken out at a barracks in northeastern Brazil, basically a clash between Portuguese and native Brazilians, following which rebels seized control of Recife (Pernambuco) with the support of the local population and proclaimed the "República de Pernambuco," using rhetoric reviling monarchy, "aristocracy," and dependency, albeit (inconsistently) confirming the institution of slavery.[76] Royal coats of arms were removed, royal officials driven out, and a republican rhetoric and flag adopted, proving that the notion that revolutionary sedition on the part of whites was impossible in Brazil owing to fear of slave insurgency hardly applied wherever resentment at high taxes and European officials prevailed. The sedition spread to the provinces immediately to the north. Portugal, commented Jefferson, writing to Lafayette three months later, "has lost her great northern province of Pernambuco, and I shall not wonder if Brazil should revolt in mass, and send their royal family back to Portugal."[77] Monarchy suddenly looked far more precarious in Portuguese America than had been generally supposed. Within a month, at banquets marking 4 July 1817 in New York, Philadelphia, and Washington, rounds of toasts resounded celebrating the "Pernambucan republic" and the end of "kings and emperors" in Brazil.[78] To lend a hand, a band of veteran Napoleonists set forth for Brazil from Philadelphia, according to some with "King Joseph" among the instigators. In all the "Pernambucan republic" lasted seventy-five days.

Denouncing monarchical tyranny and erasing royalist symbols, the 1817 rising evinced explicit admiration of the United States and republican ideals, eliciting a corresponding wave of sympathy in America despite fears of black and mulatto risings. Even though the short-lived Pernambucan republic collapsed before its envoy sent to the United States had had time to get President Monroe and Congress to consider American recognition, separation from Portugal plainly persisted as a living aspiration among sections of the Brazilian elite and military. The February 1821 revolution in Brazil plunged both the Portuguese royal court in Rio and the landowning and merchant elite into turmoil and division, initiating a period of prolonged confusion as well as exacerbated political debate—barely contained strife between rival absolutist and constitutionalist, and "Portuguese" and "Brazilian" factions. There arose an insistent pressure for the Cádiz Cortes of 1812 to be adopted in Brazil as well as in Portugal (and Spanish America). Even in Rio, which had most to gain from the transplanting of the Portuguese court across the Atlantic, there was a marked resentment among locals at how the best houses, positions, and opportunities had been taken over by newcomers from Lisbon.[79] Originally, the king's aim was to send his son, Dom Pedro, to act as regent in Portugal and remain himself in Brazil. But by April there seemed no alternative, many at court argued, but for Don João himself to return to Europe, while his son, Dom Pedro, stayed in charge of the "provisional government" in Brazil. Don João arrived back in his native Lisbon in July 1821. Shortly afterward, efforts to separate Brazil from Portugal resumed, culminating in Brazil's formal declaration of independence of September 1822. Dom Pedro, reportedly more a devotee of constitutionalist ideas than his father, was crowned first "Emperor of Brazil" in December 1822. War between Portugal and Brazil then erupted (1822–25), years in which the Portuguese court, now based in Lisbon, strove ineffectually to rally the Holy Alliance and Britain in defense of Portuguese monarchy and aristocracy in Brazil.

In March 1824, the United States became the first sovereign power to recognize Brazil as a sovereign state, an intervention for a time pointedly ignored by the Holy Alliance and Britain.[80] American recognition of South America's largest independent state as an empire under the rule of a hereditary emperor looked bizarrely anomalous to Lafayette and many others as was shown by the almost simultaneous outbreak of a second particularist and again explicitly "republican" revolt in Pernambuco province, which was then joined by several other northern regions to form what was called briefly called the "Confederation of the Equator." The new revolt in the Brazilian northeast took Dom Pedro eight months to extinguish.[81] When it was over, an erudite Carmelite friar who had been the revolution's main spokesman in print, Frei Caneca (1779–1825), and several other leaders of the insurrection were shot or hanged at Recife. To curb Brazilian republicanism on a pragmatic basis, Britain and the European monarchies eventually, in November 1825, decided, albeit still with some reluctance, to recognize Brazil as an independent monarchy, after arranging a settlement between what were now the two acknowledged crowns of Portugal and Brazil.

In Spain, meanwhile, the revolution began auspiciously, but, before long, the old rift between moderates and radicals reopened with renewed ferocity, the former seeking to modify the unicameral Cádiz Constitution by introducing a royal veto and second, upper chamber to safeguard Church and nobility as well as royalty.[82] Optimism began to wilt; much time was lost in ineffective debates in the legislature and only excruciatingly slow progress was registered in nearly all legislative areas. Hard-core republicans seeking to curtail ecclesiastical power drastically and dissolve the monasteries had some support but felt frustrated. The Dirección General de Estudios, headed by Quintana, set up to revolutionize Spain's education system, proved largely ineffective in secularizing education, owing to stiff opposition, though it did eventually produce a measure for dissolving monasteries and converting them into schools, in April 1822, which registered some success.[83] Blanco White, Spain's most eminent "moderate" exile, and his ally, the Sevillean poet Félix José Reinoso (1772–1841), charged the 1812 constitution's framers with being doctrinaire, naive admirers of French radical ideas and, worse still, Thomas Paine, who had posthumously emerged since 1810 as Spanish America's principal democratic guide. Resuming contact, from England, with another old ally, Quintana, Blanco White tried to dissuade him and his colleagues from restoring the 1812 constitution with its democratic features unaltered. The Revolution's leaders must urgently dilute the Cádiz Constitution's radicalism, meaning its Franco-American republican tendency: "mixed monarchy" on the British pattern, urged Blanco White and Reinoso, was the correct path.

Proposed by Riego as a deputy for Seville in the Cortes, Reinoso, a former *josefino* who had fled to France in 1814 and returned in 1820, and now a fervent "moderate" and disciple of Burke, eulogized England as ardently as Blanco White. For thus urging a Spanish upper house modeled on the London House of Lords, this Spanish Burkeite "admirer of Monarchical and Aristocratical vetos" was fiercely assailed by Bentham in his 1820 tract addressed to the Spanish Cortes published prior to the suppression of the Italian risings: "Spaniards! Think for yourselves. Think whether, between an assembly of the ruling few thus constituted on the one part, and the interest of the subject many on the other part, there exists not a point-blank opposition, and that opposition an unchangeable one?" Especially pernicious, held Bentham, whether in Britain, Italy, or Spain, was the notion that an upper house, representing a noble class with immense estates and the clergy, should possess the power "in pursuit of its own particular and thence sinister interest, to frustrate all measures proposed by the representatives of the whole for the good of the whole."

Were the opponents of Spain's Burkeites and "moderates," the democratic faction opposing the nobility and clergy, wrong, demanded Bentham, to be inspired "by Yankee-land, whose neck has, for these forty years been free from all such vermin, and who bids the habitable globe observe and declare, whether, in any and what respect, she is the worse for it?"[84] Regarding liberty of the press too, the United States was preferable to the British model because in America—since the rescinding of the Alien and Sedition Acts—the government wholly lacked the pernicious power to persecute contrary opinions in the manner British ministers continued striving to prosecute and suppress those of Paine.[85] The British constitution weighted in the interest of aristocracy and Crown, the increasingly radical Bentham styled the "great Boa Constrictor with a coronet on his head." He summed up sarcastically: "This is legitimacy and social order under the matchless constitution, the envy and admiration of the world." Bentham's radical representations were hotly debated in both the Portuguese and Spanish Cortes as well as the Madrid Club Cruz de Malta, and also, he was delighted to hear, in the universities of Salamanca and Coimbra. Despising Burke, he urged the Portuguese too to cease all hesitation and adopt the Cádiz Constitution: "adopt it as a mass. Take example by your friends in Naples."[86]

Skeptical about the revived Revolution's prospects, Reinoso and Blanco White were soon proved right at least with respect to the insufficiency of popular support: *constitucionales* and enlighteners would soon again be overwhelmed by "superstition" and ignorance allied to European reaction.[87] In parts of Spain, Fernando's adherents soon regained partial control and there civil war erupted. In 1821, in a further volley against "philosophy," the Inquisition, entrenched where royalism still prevailed, renewed its general "ban" on Montesquieu in Spanish.[88] Encouraged by signs of extensive support for ultraroyalism, the reactionary powers convening at the Congress of Verona (October 1822) to discuss Italy, Portugal, and Greece and reverse the Spanish Revolution, authorized Louis XVIII to send the French army across the Pyrenees in the name of monarchical legitimacy, religion, and the Holy Alliance and forcibly suppress Spain's embrace of Enlightenment and constitutionality.[89] Even before the French invaded, the news plunged radical-minded commentators into fresh despondency.

"Are we to surrender the pleasing hopes of seeing improvement in the moral and intellectual condition of man?" exclaimed Jefferson, writing to Adams in September 1821. "The events of Naples and Piedmont cast a gloomy cloud over that hope: and Spain and Portugal are not beyond jeopardy. And what are we to think of this northern triumvirate [the Russian, Prussian, and Austrian imperial rulers], arming their nations to dictate despotisms to the rest of the world?"[90] But Adams had mixed feelings about the new Spanish Revolution. The Cádiz Constitution "appears to me modeled upon that in France in the year 1789, in which the sovereignty in a single assembly was everything and the executive nothing."[91] Cádiz ignored American division of powers and, according to Adams, was hence fundamentally defective. The United States, Adams was inclined to think, should withhold sympathy and support from the revolutions in Spain, Portugal, and Italy. Adams, in Jefferson's view, was missing the point. Spanish defiance of the European reactionary powers gave "confidence that [the Spaniard] will never submit, but finally defeat this atrocious violation of the laws of God and man under which he is suffering; and the wisdom and firmness of the Cortes afford reasonable hope that that nation will settle down in a temperate representative government, with an executive properly subordinated to that. Portugal, Italy, Prussia, Germany, Greece will follow suit. You and I," he assured Adams, "shall look down from another world on these glorious achievements to man, which will add to the joys even of heaven."[92]

Events soon taught the enthusiasts otherwise. In April 1823, 100,000 French troops poured across the Pyrenees. The Spanish army divided while the Church called on the devout not to resist Louis XVIII's "holy" invasion or in any way support Spain's "godless" *constitucionales*. Efforts to mobilize something like the 1808 anti-French fury in reverse, behind the Revolution, Enlightenment, and 1812 constitution, quickly came to naught. There was simply insufficient support. The common people, lamented Quintana, "obedient and submissive" by long habit, showed little ardor for the constitution and none whatever for enlightened values. They preferred the royalist cry: "Absolute King and the Inquisition! Death to the *Liberales!*"[93] With the reactionary powers, and priesthood and nobles behind him, and the United States more concerned to exploit Spain's difficulties in the Americas than aid the constitutionalists, Fernando triumphed yet again, resuming all his old antipathy to popular sovereignty, secularism, Enlightenment, and revolution. The Inquisition was reestablished. General Riego was publicly hanged, in Madrid, on 7 November 1823.

The End of Spain's New World Empire

Louis XVIII's crushing of the Spanish Revolution, in 1823, was warmly endorsed by the European powers, as was its aftermath—a ferocious conservative crackdown on *constitucionales* and all adversaries of royal and church authority. But the unrelenting reaction was loudly denounced either side of the Atlantic by a profoundly shocked and growing international pool of critics and adversaries.[94] In Mexico, Guatemala, and the rest of Central America, as elsewhere in Spanish America, restoration of the 1812 Cádiz Constitution, in 1820, had been warmly welcomed.[95] The Creole elite, hungry for more autonomy, vigorously debated the advantages of remaining within the empire, under the 1812 constitution, against the advantages of outright independence. Both impulses clashed, though, with the formidable royalist reactionary tendency, creating a deadlock skillfully exploited by Mexico's mercurial would-be emperor, Agustín de Iturbide (1783–1824), an overweening veteran officer who had fought the rebels, for Crown and Church, since the onset of the Mexican turmoil in 1810. Denouncing republican and irreligious ideas, Iturbide secured military control of Mexico City in September 1821. Appealing to Creole *absolutistas* and clergy to support his local quasi-independence movement offering religion and aristocracy on the basis of a homegrown Mexican monarchy, he briefly succeeded. Iturbide's Plan of Iguala (February 1821) promised a few token concessions to constitutionality and a minimal relationship with Spain but mainly to uphold ecclesiastical privilege and authority with no concessions to toleration, freedom of thought, republicanism, or radical ideas.[96]

As the 1820–23 Spanish Revolution collapsed, a chaotic, divided New Spain (Mexico) gradually stumbled toward independence without this being a central aim of most participants in the civil conflict or its attendant debates. What mattered to radicals was less independence than whether or not this projected Mexican independence afforded a viable path to emancipation, secularism, equality, and representative government. What conservatives demanded, in or out of the Spanish monarchy, was religion, social hierarchy, and reaction. Mexico's Creole elite at this time were still less drawn to outright independence than a limited constitutional monarchism under the Spanish king or a sovereign of the Spanish royal family. It was mainly the Spanish Cortes's refusal to countenance such a framework that gave Iturbide, that "vile tyrant" as Rocafuerte called him,[97] the opportunity to proclaim himself Mexican "emperor" under the name Augustín I. Subsequently, first Chiapas, in 1821, and then, in January 1822, five other "United Provinces" of Central America—Guatemala, Nicaragua, San Salvador, Honduras, and Costa Rica—drawn to his reactionary program, opted to join his suddenly and almost haphazardly emerging Mexican Empire.

Far from living up to Jefferson's description of him as the Mexican "Bonaparte," Iturbide entirely failed to establish an authoritarian military empire in New Spain. With his initial popularity rapidly turning into general execration, his regime proved spectacularly brief, lasting only from May 1822 to March 1823. Following his downfall, a constituent congress was elected with instructions to draw up what educated Mexicans termed Mexico's "third constitution" (after the Cádiz Constitution of 1812 and the Plan de Iguala). Abolishing both the Bourbon monarchy and Iturbide's "empire," the 1823–24 Mexican constitutional congress forged Mexico's new constitution by judiciously combining ingredients from Paris, Madrid, and Philadelphia. The deputies merged elements of the Cádiz Constitution—several republican clauses of which, fortifying a strong legislature and weak executive, were retained—together with a well-defined federalist framework borrowed from the United States.[98] The new republic, carved from the former viceroyalty of New Spain, comprising nineteen "states" and four territories—Upper and Lower California, New Mexico, and Texas (with Coahuila)—adopted its constitution, in October 1824, under its new name, the Estados Unidos Mexicanos (United Mexican States). This was perhaps the closest of nineteenth-century foreign constitutional constructs to the United States model and among the most enduring—but only in theory. The "United States of Mexico" featured a Supreme Court supposedly independent of the president and legislature, a two-chamber body resembling that of the United States, with a lower house and Senate, the latter featuring two senators for each state. The republic's president and vice president were elected, as in America, for four-year terms. Putting the seal on Mexico's newfound republicanism, federalism, and constitutionalism, liberty of the press was proclaimed. In July 1824, Iturbide, the royalist general turned "emperor" who aspired to rule Mexico with ecclesiastical approval, was executed by firing squad. Yet the 1824 Mexican constitution served merely to underline the general failure of the fledgling Spanish

American republics to escape arbitrary power and establish "free or liberal institutions of government."[99] Mexico descended into unremitting civil strife and violent disorder that with short interruptions continued for decades.

If the Mexican outcome looked grim, the European scene, from 1823, seemed little better. Banished from official culture, princely courts, and higher and lower education, the international radical fringe transmuted further into a movement of exiles and clandestine gatherings from 1824 when Charles X succeeded to the French throne, and the following year when "the hypocritical autocrat," as Jefferson called him, Czar Alexander, was followed by the more openly reactionary Nicholas I (ruled: 1825–55). With Charles X's accession began a more systematic effort to repudiate all vestige of Revolution and Napoleonic reform in France and achieve a purer monarchical-aristocratic and Counter-Enlightenment stance. Destined to become one of the nineteenth century's greatest writers, Victor Hugo (1802–85), just beginning his slow, lifelong political pilgrimage from extreme Right to the Left, was among those invited to the new king's public consecration for which he composed an *Ode au sacre*, commemorating the occasion, roundly condemning thirty years of Revolution and Napoleonic reforms as an age of error, terror, arrogance, and denial of sacred mystery, and exalting Louis XVI as a sacred martyr doubly consecrated "at the altar and the scaffold."[100]

To all appearances the Holy Alliance solidly triumphed after all in 1823–25. Yet Jefferson, Madison, Lafayette, and other democratic visionaries refused to relinquish their hopes. Reaction had won on the surface; yet monarchical legitimacy and aristocratic dominance were hardly popular in France, the Low Countries, Italy, Ireland, Poland, or Germany. In fact, "never was a war more unpopular," affirmed Lafayette in May 1823, "than that of France's counter-revolutionary government on the constitution of Spain."[101] Even in England, radicalism appeared to be growing into a major force. The democratic republicans' faith in mankind's future in any case was a peculiarly tenacious creed. Writing to Jefferson, Adams recounted the story of a visit he received from Dr. Priestley following his arrival in America, subsequent to the "tragedy of Louis XVI when I was vice-President." He found Priestley "very sociable, very learned and eloquent on the subject of the French Revolution" and convinced that it opened a "new era in the world" and presented a "new view of the millennium." Adams disagreed, as he did with Lafayette, Paine, Price, Madison, and Jefferson. "Do you really believe," he retorted, the revolutionaries will "establish a free democratical government in France?" Priestley answered: "I do firmly believe it." Adams was astonished and now, in 1823, put the same question to Jefferson. "Is the devil to be the 'Lord's anointed' over the whole globe? Or do you foresee the fulfillment of the prophecies according to Dr. Priestley's interpretation of them?"[102] The transition from despotism to liberty and democracy, Jefferson granted, choosing his words, is strewn with obstacles: "The generation which commences a revolution can rarely compleat it. Habituated from their infancy to passive submission of body and mind to their kings and priests, they are not qualified, when called on, to think and provide for themselves and their inexperience, their ignorance and bigotry make them instruments often, in the hands of the Bonapartes and Iturbides to defeat their own rights and purposes. This is the present situation of Europe and Spanish America. But it is not desperate."[103]

Successful in Spain, in 1823, by 1825 the royalists had finally lost the vast struggle for Spanish America. Here was one point where American conservatives, like Adams and his son, and the radicals, could narrowly converge with the democrats at the expense of monarchism and the Holy Alliance, though even here, John Quincy Adams was notably more cautious than President Monroe (president: 1817–25). By 1822, both American factions supported the South American and Mexican republicans insofar as they were "contending for independence," freedom, and stability—and, by curbing French and British interference and supplying weapons, were eager to accelerate their success. By the time that France, by capturing Spain for unrestrained reaction, in 1823, simultaneously rendered Spanish America more open to republican advances, to violence and destabilization, and, potentially, to American intrusion and expansionism, American diplomatic intervention had already powerfully entered the scene. In March 1822, in defiance of Spain, France, Britain, and the Holy Alliance, President Monroe had initiated his policy of asking Congress to recognize and support the Spanish American republics: the United States, he urged, "owe it to their station and character in the world, as well as to their essential interests." In June 1822, Congress formally recognized "Columbia" (then including Venezuela, Ecuador, and Panama). During the banquets celebrating 4 July 1822 in the United States there was a vast surge of rousing toasts to the independence of Ibero-America.

Having rejected several requests in earlier years, Congress recognized the independence of the short-lived Mexican monarchy in December 1822, and the first New World republics acknowledged by the United States, those of Chile and Argentina, in January 1823.[104] Meanwhile, following the crushing of the Spanish Revolution, the French court, with the approval of Russia, Prussia, and Austria, began contemplating intervening militarily on behalf of the restored Spanish Crown in Spanish America—even though Britain, fearful of reviving French influence and eager for Latin American trade, now altered her former stance and threatened to use her fleet to prevent this. Rumors of a possible transatlantic intervention swept the Atlantic world. Would the Bourbons regain Spanish America with the czar's and Louis XVIII's help at a time when Brazil was an empire and imperial Russia not only possessed Alaska but (until the Russo-American treaty of April 1824) claimed all the Pacific Northwest, including Oregon? Would the nineteenth-century New World be predominantly monarchical and aristocratic? Jefferson and Madison both encouraged Monroe to support the British Crown in opposing French and Holy Alliance intervention.[105]

Monroe's "Doctrine," or rather announcement, of December 1823 declared the entire western hemisphere closed to further European state intervention and colonization, justifying this by declaring the "political system of the allied powers" to be "essentially different from that of America"; since America's system had "been achieved by the loss of so much blood and treasure," any effort by the allies to "extend their system to any portion of this hemisphere" would be viewed by the United States "as dangerous to our peace and security."[106] This proclamation was made at a moment when reactionary royalist revival in Spanish America and Brazil under Holy Alliance auspices seemed a definite possibility.[107] The effect was to kill all prospect of such a development, rendering the triumph of republicanism in Spanish America inevitable. The Monroe Doctrine blocked the Holy Alliance in Latin America but also reawakened Spanish American fears of their overmighty self-proclaimed northern benefactor.[108] Bolívar did not doubt his precarious South American Federation needed assistance "against Spain, against the Holy Alliance, and against anarchy," but he was equally apprehensive of American motives, viewing the Monroe Doctrine as an obvious intrusion, an attempt to convert the western hemisphere into a United States' sphere of influence.[109]

America: A Global Model?

Following the defeat of the Spanish Revolution of 1820–23 and precarious advent of the Spanish American republics proclaiming American federalism as their constitutional model, there was, once again, nowhere else to look in the world for a relevant, concrete extant example of democratic modernity apart the United States The newborn Spanish American republics uninhibitedly and explicitly based their principles on the American model. If French and British royalists and conservatives deplored the United States for condoning, sanctioning, and even encouraging the insurrections in Latin America, radicals everywhere were enthusiastic about the rash of new republics recognized by the United States during 1822–23 but as yet still boycotted by the European monarchies.[110] Between Napoleon's downfall and the Great Reform Act (1832), more and more former moderates converted to a radical standpoint and hence willingness to disown royalty, aristocracy, and the "mixed government" as exemplified by Britain. The British model simply seemed too strictly class-based, too chauvinist and triumphalist, and, as Angeloni stressed, too fiscally and judicially retrograde and geared for war.[111] The trend, until the 1840s, was for radicals and democrats everywhere to continue styling themselves "friends of America," the American Revolution, and American democracy.

The post-1815 era in Europe and Latin America consequently experienced a conspicuous new wave of cultural *Américanisme* with often suffused but where the censorship was less tight also explicit political undertones. In French journals, superficially nonpolitical articles and reports about American life and conditions, boosted by the enthusiasm surrounding Lafayette's triumphal tour of the United States in 1824, proliferated throughout the 1820s. For those with any discernment, the political dimension was by no means hard to find. Two characteristic features of this once again rather widely diffused fad were the resurgence of the Franklin cult and a craze for Fenimore Cooper's novels. During the 1820s and early 1830s France witnessed a great burst of editions of extracts from, and books about, Franklin. Particularly popular, once again, was *Le Bonhomme Richard*, which reappeared, astoundingly, in over fifty French editions between 1815 and 1852, well over half of these between 1820 and the early 1830s, the text emerging often bound together with other extracts from Franklin or with Mirabeau's eulogy of Franklin of 1791. These reissues appeared mostly in Paris but also in Dijon, Metz, Grenoble, and other provincial centers.[112]

The torrent of Franklin editions between 1820 and 1834 serves as a useful marker to trace the course of resurgent French *Américanisme*, as does the timing of the modish Fenimore Cooper cult set off by the huge success of his novel *The Spy* (1821). This fad proved decidedly more important for its historical significance as a reflection of the French political mood than for its literary impact, though the young Balzac shows some signs of Cooper's influence. During the 1820s and early 1830s Cooper's books about eighteenth-century America especially those featuring Native Americans, above all *The Last of the Mohicans* (1826), first of the "Leatherstocking" novels, poured out in French translation.[113] No less striking, though, the steady receding of French interest in Fenimore Cooper after 1834 reflects the more general waning of European enthusiasm for America from the mid-1830s onward, a phenomenon in the French journals accompanied by a lively debate about why the literary achievement of the nascent United States had thus far been generally so restricted.[114]

Political *Américanisme* briefly surged as a lively trend also among British radicals and Benthamites reacting against conventional English aristocratic and middle-class disdain for America. In 1827, in a blistering attack on Britain's role as chief patron of reaction and royal "legitimacy," Leslie Grove Jones (1779–1839), a former major in the Grenadier Guards, loudly condemned the new world order decreed from Vienna from a specifically British radical perspective. Having visited the United States in 1817, what he saw had led him to revile monarchy and hereditary aristocracy along with Britain's role in international affairs and, in the years preceding the Great Reform Bill, he ceaselessly plied his critique of British Loyalism deliberately infuriating England's gentry establishment with abrasive letters to the London papers. America had taught him to "contrast the free, happy, and flourishing condition of that country with the subjugated and degraded position of France" and all Europe under restored monarchy: "he could not refrain from comparing the principles of freedom and justice" resplendent in America with the principles and practices of "the allies." Neither did Grove Jones spare the Restoration's call for more religion. The churches he denounced along with Europe's kings and aristocrats: everywhere the "pulpit has resounded with the obnoxious doctrines of passive obedience and non-resistance, of the infallibility of ministers and divinity of kings." Assailing the courtly, aristocratic values dominating almost the whole globe apart from America, he contrasted the narrowness of monarchical legitimacy with the values and maxims proclaimed by "Sidney and Locke, by Beccaria and Vattel, by Franklin and Condorcet, by Price and by Bentham."[115]

Earlier a pillar of the British establishment—Wellington's commandant at Brussels prior to Waterloo later posted to Cambrai during the allied military occupation of France (1815–17)—Grove Jones could hardly preach outright rebellion. Familiar with America and also Spain, France, and the Low Countries, he was well placed to draw telling comparisons. Europe needed a different and higher set of goals and the "constitution of the United States of North America both in theory and practice seems to have the claim to the greatest perfection." However, while eulogizing the United States, he argued that in "ameliorating and remodeling the constitutions of the old states of Europe, which becomes necessary from the rapid strides which the human intellect is making, and which all the powers on earth cannot arrest, it should not be recommended to them to imitate entirely the Americans." Europeans should especially eschew armed struggle and seek less violent means than before. In the circumstances of the 1820s, emulating America's example could not altogether "promote the general happiness of the European states" owing to the great strength of the royal courts and bitter legacy of recent wars. Grove Jones feared another vast struggle, renewing the French revolutionary conflict, a useless, bloody resort to methods already tried, exhausted, and discarded. "What is only to be obtained by torrents of blood, should not be sought after, if otherwise attainable."[116] European societies must settle for less initially and then gradually work toward the American model.

Radicals needed a concrete, convincing model and America provided that example. But were the United States truly as admirable and inspiring as 1820s eulogists like Lafayette, Fenimore Cooper, Jullien, Bentham, Rocafuerte, Papineau, Angeloni, and Grove Jones maintained? Was the United States the sole major stable, free republic "where liberty enlivens all institutions," as Jullien expressed it in his *Revue Encyclopédique*, foremost of the journals the new royal French freedom of the press tolerated and which, from its founding in 1819, was among the most active in promoting the new *Américanisme*?[117]

Veteran of the great Revolution, Jullien viewed the United States as the one society that was genuinely democratizing, the "only modern society established from the outset on a rational basis, with no need to compromise with vicious precedents," though he entertained hopes also for Haiti. A striking confirmation of the United States' continuing role, held Jullien, was her carrying through the Enlightenment's (and Napoleon's) grand scheme for the emancipation and integration of the Jews. In the Old World, rigid segregation excluding the Jewish population from mainstream society, anti-Jewish restrictions, and disabilities earlier dismantled by the Revolution and Napoleon were—with the striking exception of the Low Countries—reinstated in 1814–15 not just officially but with eager, widespread popular support most conspicuously in central Europe. Assuredly, Old World bigotry persisted in the United States too; not all barriers to Jewish integration had yet withered there either. In Maryland, Jews still remained legally debarred "as Jews" from holding public office. But in America such lingering tokens of Counter-Enlightenment prejudice and obscurantism lacked basic legal and official status and were already, claimed Jullien, the focus of organized protest. In America, such remnants were merely ridiculous vestiges soon to disappear, not a robust component of an entire refurbished system of reactionary thought, culture, and practice as was the case in Europe.[118] If ignorant and crass, American anti-Semitism was not integral to an entire social and political hierarchical value system powerfully sanctioned by a formidable array of princely and ecclesiastical authorities, sanctioned by the churches and universities in accord with the Holy Alliance and eradicable, if at all, only by massive revolutionary force.

Having consolidated her own Revolution and removed nearly all major social, legal, and cultural barriers that in Europe still blocked progress toward liberty, the United States alone supposedly could now march "directly to a certain level of perfection without having to pass through the dreadful ordeal of [further] revolutions."[119] By 1825, every state of the Union except Rhode Island, Virginia, and Louisiana accepted the principle of universal white male suffrage.[120] America required no new revolutionary upheaval to propel her toward democracy and secularism, whereas post-1815 Europe did. If democracy advanced only gradually and with peculiar inconsistencies and discrepancies also in the United States, it was not systematically opposed like democracy's and equality's severely arrested advance in post-1799 Europe and the European colonial empires in Africa and Asia. Universal male suffrage in America was surely a tremendous landmark in humanity's advance. If the United States still had some way to go to fully realize the American Revolution's radical ideals and become a true democratic republic, America more than ever was *the* supreme model for the radically minded of Europe and the wider world.

"Even should the cloud of barbarism and despotism again obscure the science and liberties of Europe," Jefferson assured Adams in 1821, the United States "remains to preserve and restore light and liberty to them. In short the flames kindled on the 4th of July 1776, have spread over too much of the globe to be extinguished by the feeble engines of despotism. On the contrary they will consume those engines, and all who work them."[121] Here was a stirring prophecy; but were the United States genuinely a beacon of light showing the way for the radical fraternity? The "America" venerated by Europe's and Latin America's radical republicans in the 1820s was not exactly the real America familiar to American citizens. Rather it was an ideological and literary abstraction, a remote ideal nurtured by the vanguard of what the *Revue Encyclopédique* in the 1820s dubbed the advance in the world of *l'esprit philosophique*. By this term, Jullien and his principal contributors, J. B. Say, Sismondi, and the Abbé Gregoire,[122] meant mankind's painfully slow progression to democratic, republican modernity. Their goal was democracy, free expression, and equality with universal secular education, and sharply diminished ecclesiastical authority, mixed with a dash of economic redistribution—in other words, still the ideology of Condorcet and the Brissotins. This late Enlightenment philosophical "Americanism" was laced, as in Paine, Jefferson, and Madison, with decrying Robespierre's "dictatorship" and the Montagne combined with rejecting Napoleon, Britain, and the Restoration.

Here was a potent ideology for the 1820s. Yet a growing number of skeptics harbored doubts. The eminent Genevan patrician, political theorist, economist, and historian Jean-Charles Leonard de Sismondi (1773–1842) in January 1827 published an incisive critique of America in Jullien's *Revue Encyclopédique* that attracted attention in Switzerland and the United States as well as France. A former conservative and foe of the Revolution, since 1815 Sismondi had, much like Bentham, been appalled by the effects of Counter-Enlightenment and "la Restauration"[123] and now become a radical. When he first lost faith in "mixed government," in the 1790s, he had continued to endorse the empirical, experience-based approach of British and American political thinkers, extolling Locke, Hume, Smith, Burke, and Ferguson, defending the old aristocratic order and rejecting the democratic republicanism of Condorcet, Jefferson, and the Brissotins.[124] But when the Vienna Congress powers bullied Switzerland into discarding the Napoleonic federal constitution adopted, in 1803, that had replaced the unitary Helvetic Republic, the first Swiss national state, established by French revolutionary armies in 1798, Sismondi was horrified. Switzerland's reversion, discarding Napoleon's "Act of Mediation" of April 1803, which for the first time entrenched elements of the federal "American model" in Europe, meant relapsing into the pre-1798 Swiss ancien régime system of loosely federated cantons under narrow patrician oligarchies and ecclesiastical privilege. The post-1814 Restoration's uncompromisingly anti-Enlightenment stance quickly propelled Sismondi into an opposite stance. He now loudly abjured all informal aristocracy excluding most of the population from politics, together with British "mixed government."

Converted to the Radical Enlightenment politically and emotionally, Sismondi converted also in terms of economic theory. In his *Nouveaux principes d'économie politique* (1819), he took to criticizing Adam Smith and David Ricardo for overly stressing the idea of a natural equilibrium in economic development. Articulating a new theory of economic cycles, consumption, excess production, and market oscillations, he contended that social and political intervention is always requisite to shield the poor and vulnerable from the unavoidably harsh effects of market downturns. Though never a socialist and later fiercely criticized by Marx, his was among the major voices of the democratic enlightened of the 1820s repudiating classical economics along with American and French veneration of the English model.[125] On one level, American-style federal republicanism was proving a growing inspiration for the world, as recent developments in Spanish America proved; but there were as many worrying as promising signs. With twenty-four American states in the Union and another twenty-four in the newly proclaimed "United States of Mexico," plus seven more loosely confederated "republics" in Central America, American federalism had latterly become the dominant constitutional model for Latin America. Conceivably, Brazil, Peru, and other emerging new nations would eventually all follow the United States by becoming federal republics. But when one delved deeper, admonished Sismondi, the progress these new "republics" represented looked fragile and defective.

History's chief lesson, held Sismondi, in the mid-1820s, is that whatever ideals they announce, governments serve the interests of dominant elites and encourage, or at least fail to curb, the ubiquitous oppression of society's "classes inférieures." The lower classes toil to provide the wealth and services the world's elites appropriate and enjoy, yet, paradoxically and unjustly, exactly these segments were the least protected, favored, and assisted by governments. This was the prime source of injustice in the world, the pattern of all history, and the chief dilemma of philosophy, a conundrum the truly enlightened, like the editors of the *Revue Encyclopédique*, must grapple with. Only by promoting the "happiness" of the poor, by lending support and protection, can the security of the rich and stability of society be ensured. The trend hitherto, not least in Britain, had been to oppress the poor inexorably, strip the destitute of all respect, and brutalize them by keeping them as ignorant as possible.[126]

Was the United States different? The converted Sismondi of the late 1820s saw little reason to think so. In America, the rapidly growing lowest class of society, held in abject slavery, found itself even more wretched and miserable than the oppressed in Britain or France, more downtrodden than the slaves of ancient Greece and Rome or serfs of contemporary Russia and Poland. In the United States, the slaves' misery was intensified by the whites' abiding dread and suspicion of the back race, so that, even after successive generations, aspiring black freemen cannot attain equality with the oppressor. There were a million and a half slaves in United States, according to the latest statistics, recorded Sismondi (accurately),[127] and another 235,557 free blacks,[128] hence nearly two million out of a total of nine million inhabitants of the United States in 1827. Since 1775, blacks had consistently comprised more than 20 percent of American society (in fact between 18 and 19 percent). While the total number of Americans had roughly trebled since 1775, and now surpassed Britain's population, the proportion that was black and shamefully oppressed remained essentially unchanged. "It is necessary to say it, it was for American republicans who have long possessed their liberty and Enlightenment, to set an example of humanity; but they had done the opposite." Racial prejudice Sismondi declared more offensive, degrading, and cruel in the American republic even than in the newly founded Ibero-American republics.

His disparaging remarks provoked a storm of protest. Sismondi, retorted critics, failed to note abolitionism's strength and black emancipation trends in New England and the rest of the North.[129]

More convinced of America's centrality in the progress of democratic republicanism internationally was Lafayette. More so than Sismondi, Fenimore Cooper, and other critics of American oligarchy, Lafayette's confidence in America's credentials as a transatlantic inspiration and model remained intact. For several years he worked closely with Cooper, who wrote a detailed account of Lafayette's visit to New York, in September 1824, projecting him as the "hero" of two worlds whose freedom struggle was a transatlantic enterprise.[130] Cooper also aided Lafayette in maintaining ties with American admirers and helped broadcast his message that "America is the first important country of modern times, in which [distinctions of birth] have been destroyed."[131] Lafayette and Cooper collaborated too in organizing Franco-American support for Greece and for the Polish rising of 1830–31. From 1826 to 1828, and 1830 to 1833, Cooper resided mainly in Paris, punctuated by trips to Germany, Italy, and Switzerland, broadening his original assault on the British and Venetian aristocracies to include the Swiss patriciates and the German nobility.[132] On returning to America in 1833, he declared war on the "narrow and exclusive system" capturing the United States as it had Britain. He stood unrivaled as an American literary foe of the "oligarchical party," the elites ruling society through democracy's outward forms in his native country (to which Lafayette seemed relatively blind). With passionate commitment (until the 1840s) he helped renew the battles of the 1790s on a literary plain, urging Americans to see the distinctiveness of their own political achievement both at home and in international contexts. To Cooper, this meant resisting the Eastern oligarchy's taste for identifying, as they did throughout the nineteenth century, less with America's own republican traditions than their glorified "England" which, though everywhere trumpeted as a liberal "monarchy," was actually, in his view, a "complicated but efficient aristocracy."[133]

Abhorring the gap between appearance and reality, pretense and practice, until the 1840s (when he switched to his late conservative mode), Cooper made it his life's mission to foster what he considered the American Revolution's authentic principles in America and Europe alike. "I own [Jefferson] begins to appear to me," he remarked in 1830, "the greatest man we ever had."[134] His own father, William Cooper, founder of Cooperstown in New York State, had served as a representative in the Lower House during the Washington and Adams presidencies, a politician embracing the "aristocratic" vision of Hamilton, Morris, and Jay presenting himself as an English squire assiduously promoting informal aristocracy and the financial interest. It was a legacy Fenimore Cooper detested until he reached old age when he embraced it himself.[135] American "democratic" political culture and institutions as they functioned around 1830 he viewed as a kind of political mirage, profoundly frustrating for authentic republican democrats like himself. Scorning conventional thinking, he cited popular ignorance as a pervasive threat, a peculiar new species of tyranny that threatened the United States with losing what was most valuable, a blight feeding on deception, myth, and the crassness of opinion manipulated by vested interests.[136]

Certainly, America's past political achievement and present potential were impressive. "Democracies being established for the common interests, and the publick agents being held in constant check by the people, their general tendency is to serve the whole community, and not small portions of it, as is true in the case of narrow governments"; here was a breakthrough not just for America but the entire world.[137] Democracies on the American model, or rather the principles underlying it, represented much the best path forward for all humanity. But within American society, the authentic product was being corrupted and debased by the inability of Americans to grasp the Enlightenment's centrality in their Revolution, democracy, and well-being by uncritical acceptance of commonplace notions. The question why the "truly republican quality" of candor was so little practiced, and so hard to practice in the United States where "political authority is the possession of the body that wields opinion" tormented him: in America there existed "a strong and dangerous disposition to defer to the public, in opposition to truth and justice." Wherever populism, religious authority, and lack of Enlightenment prevail, the "oppression of the public" becomes a suffocating tyranny worse than that of kings.[138] "The people that has overturned the throne of a monarch, and set up a government of opinion in its stead, and which blindly yields its interests to the designs of those who would rule through the instrumentality of newspapers, has only exchanged one form of despotism for another."[139]

By the time Cooper presented his theory of the "new tyranny" of public opinion, in *The American Democrat* (1838), others had reached not dissimilar conclusions, including Emerson and Alexis de Tocqueville (1805–59), who toured the United States in 1831–32 and published the first part of his *Democracy in America* in 1835. The ex–Unitarian minister and essayist Ralph Waldo Emerson (1803–82), who led a philosophical-literary movement, sometimes called Transcendentalism, based in Massachusetts, emerged as another key critic of America's engineered conformism from 1835 onward. In his essay *Politics* (1844) and other writings of the 1840s, Emerson likewise deplored the debasement of "American radicalism" into a shallow, short-sighted, "destructive and aimless" creed to the point that a serious philosopher or reader supporting the democratic cause could no longer endorse it.[140] It was Cooper, though, who most expansively identified American pseudo-democratic cant as a perverse cultural tendency naturally prone to align with conservative rather than radical democratic values.

Since in large democracies the people are less able than in small ones to "scrutinize and understand character with the severity and intelligence that are of so much importance in all representative governments," and are swayed chiefly by preachers, they are "peculiarly exposed to become the dupes of demagogues and political schemers, most of the crimes of democracies arising from the faults and designs of men of this character, rather than from the propensities of the people, who, having little temptation to do wrong, are seldom guilty of crimes except through ignorance."[141] "Misleading of publick opinion," held Cooper, "in one way or another is the parent of the principal disadvantages of a democracy," a malaise wrought chiefly by "prejudice" and unawareness. "Most of its social and moral prejudices" America owed to the "exaggerated religious opinions of the different sects which were so instrumental in establishing the colonies."[142]

Among the worst offenders misleading American public opinion, according to Cooper and Emerson, were the newspapers. While acknowledging the necessity of press freedom for combating tyranny and establishing democracy, Cooper regularly rued the "deleterious influence" of the American press. "As the press of this country now exists, it would seem to be expressly devised by the great agent of mischief, to depress and destroy all that is good, and to elevate and advance all that is evil in the nation. The little truth that is urged, is usually urged coarsely, weakened and rendered vicious by personalities," so that those "who live by falsehoods, fallacies, enmities, partialities and the schemes of the designing, find the press the very instrument that the devils would invent to effect their designs."[143] American democracy's health or sickness, its capacity to survive, for him crucially depended on the common people's ability to discriminate and form sound judgments about what is true or false, a competence, he believed, exceedingly hard to foster and promote because it cannot be acquired except through education, universally available and based on a sound commitment to Enlightenment.

CHAPTER 18

The Greek Revolution (1770–1830)

A New War of Independence

Lamenting the outcome in Spain and Italy, for a time radicals found consolation in—and switched their main international and fund-raising effort to—the Greek national movement.[1] Elements among the now thoroughly agitated Balkan Greek diaspora outside of Greece had for some time been calling for a Greek national revival based on insurrection and liberation. In March 1821, inspired by Greek exiles in Russia, armed insurrection against the Ottomans broke out, simultaneously, in the Danubian provinces (Roumania) and in the Peloponnese. The northern movement was led by Alexandr Ipsilantis (1792–1828), a Greek general in Russian service, fluent in many languages who headed the Philiki Eteria (Society of Friends), a small secret society founded in Odessa in 1814 on the model of the Carbonari. Between 1818 and 1821, the Philiki Eteria underground conspiracy, ardently devoted to the cause of Greek national liberation, had become a network linking Greek "patriots" and the emerging Greek "enlightened" intelligentsia across much of the Balkans, southern Russia, and Anatolia.[2]

Ipsilantis's revolt, disowned by the czar and publicly condemned by the Greek patriarch of Constantinople and twenty-two bishops, faltered after a few months; in June Ipsilantis abandoned his efforts, fleeing into Austrian territory, and was imprisoned in Hungary. The Peloponnese rising, on the other hand, swiftly succeeded, creating a tremendous impression throughout the Western world. This uprising precipitated the process that culminated a decade later in Greek independence. During the autumn of 1821, Shelley, already excited by the restoring of the 1812 Cádiz Constitution (an inspiration also to many Greek enlighteners), composed his stirring poetic drama *Hellas* (1822) celebrating the "glorious contest now waging in Greece," hoping to raise sympathy and money to help drive the revolutionary tide. Above all, Shelley desired Greece's rebirth to be central to what he conceived as the pending and necessary emancipation of all mankind: "We are all Greeks. Our laws, our literature, our religion, our arts have their root in Greece." He presented what he hoped would be the "final triumph of the Greek cause as a portion of the cause of civilization and social improvement." Modern Greek society, he acknowledged, had its defects, "the basest vices"; but through the revolutionary struggle and the new enlightened ideas, the Greeks would no longer be "degraded by moral and political slavery": "The world's great age begins anew, The golden years return."[3]

But by equating the Greek cause and Hellenism with "civilization" and Enlightenment, Shelley helped generate a dangerous illusion that was to prove among the great falsifying myths of the age. The great Greek rebellion as it became arose from a complex social and cultural background that had evolved over centuries and was steeped in tradition and long usage modified, on the one hand, by the recent tradition of revolt against the Ottomans and Islam reaching back to the 1770s and, on the other, by an accelerating post-1750 Greek national Enlightenment. The very failure of the first Greek uprising against the Ottomans, in 1770–74, supported (and partly instigated) by Catherine the Great of Russia, and suppressed by the Turks amid vast loss of life and crushed hopes, had noticeably divided sentiment within the Greek Enlightenment. The aftermath fomented within late eighteenth-century and early nineteenth-century Greek culture a growing tension between the Orthodox Enlightenment symbolized by Eugenios Voulgaris (1716–1806) aligning with Russian autocracy and the Church, and the suffused libertarian republican promise embodied in the American and French revolutions.

For decades, as Catherine's librarian and advisor on Greek affairs, Voulgaris helped inspire and direct a Greek Enlightenment that was conservative theologically, politically, and socially, stretching from Venice to the Aegean Islands, and from Egypt to Odessa, one that ardently eulogized Locke, Newtonian science, and Leibniz, while looking to Russia and conserving religious authority intact. For Voulgaris Locke was the supreme philosopher, the great herald of the Enlightenment, his robust dualism providing the means to reconcile *supernaturalia* with reason. Ignoring his political theory, he emphasized especially Locke's cautious empiricism creating a sharp duality between sense experience and science restricted to a rigorously delimited sphere while simultaneously underpinning Revelation, religion, and what is "above reason" as the higher sphere of theology and church authority.[4]

On the outbreak of the 1770 Greek rebellion, Voulgaris had effectively become the Greek Enlightenment's first political leader, in which capacity he translated into Greek Voltaire's 1767 pamphlet defending Catherine's intervention in Poland on behalf of the Orthodox Church. Despite detesting Voltaire's irreligion and irreverence toward the clergy, and his toleration theory, he willingly espoused his pro-Russian propaganda promoting Catherine and "poor suffering Greece" and championing the Greek dream of liberation from the Ottomans. Above all, he recognized that Voltaire had helped infuse Greece's subsequent cultural self-awareness with the (dubious) notion that modern Greece itself represented global "Enlightenment" and civilization in its struggle with "barbarism" (i.e., the Turks).[5] There was no doubting the intensity of Voltaire's anti-Ottomanism. The treaty of Kutchuk Kainardji (1774) ending the Russo-Turkish War had undermined this approach, though, making obvious Catherine's abandonment of Voltaire's vision for Greece and her former Greek commitments, leaving the Greeks crushed and worse off than before.

The collapse of the 1774 rising just as the American Revolution began set the scene, though, for the eventual emergence of an incipiently radicalized Greek Enlightenment critical of Voulgaris's political and social conservatism, a Greek reaction against autocracy, Russia, orthodoxy, and Locke.[6] Voulgaris's antithesis was Rhigas Velestinlis, or Feraios (1757–98), a true "prophet of revolution" closely associated with the first stirrings of Greek independence.[7] Born in a village in eastern Thessaly, and familiar with peasant life, Rhigas was educated in Constantinople and then the Danubian principality of Wallachia where he became passionately devoted to Enlightenment encyclopedism. During stays in Vienna, in 1790 and subsequently, he published several works contending that Greece's plight could be resolved only by a mix of Enlightenment and republican activism sufficiently vigorous to overcome the country's paralyzing and deeply rooted inertia.

Inspired by Napoleon's instituting republics in much of Italy (1796–1800) and the French republican occupation of the Greek Ionian Islands (1797–99),[8] Rhigas embraced the revolutionary call for a universal transformation in ideas and principles while conceiving the French summons as also entailing a national liberation struggle to overthrow Ottoman rule and liberate the Greek homeland. The Greek Revolution should commence, held Rhigas, with a second great uprising in the Peloponnese. But unlike Voulgaris, Rhigas rejected ecclesiastical authority and appealed for support to Muslims and Jews as well as Christians, drafting a fully-fledged revolutionary program couched in the language of Condorcet, Brissot, and Cloots. He summoned Greeks to establish a Hellenic republic complete with its own legislature, tricolor flag showing affinity to the French Republic, a national anthem modeled on the "Marseillaise," and his draft *Declaration of Human Rights* based on the expanded French Declaration of February 1793. Arrested by the Austrian authorities in Trieste in 1797, he was handed over to the Ottoman governor of Belgrade, who had him and his followers strangled to death in June 1798.

The Enlightenment, all onlookers recognized, was the mother of the Greek liberation movement. But Greek Enlightenment was essentially a diaspora phenomenon, geographically widely dispersed, principally an educational movement beginning in the early eighteenth century and gaining momentum after 1774, especially during Napoleon's mastery of Europe. It was a reflection of the growing commercial preeminence of the Greek merchant elite in southeastern Europe, southern Russia, and the Near East, with its growing need to teach its sons Western languages, science, and the humanities—offering a whole new cultural world to the sons of Greece's merchants and nobles whose financial and moral support, and efforts to foster this "enlightenment," Shelley extolled as "above all praise." It was an educational enlightenment that forged the first modern Greek print culture (based on Vienna and Venice) and during the years of Europe's Restoration (1814–20) witnessed a remarkable further flowering due especially to the vigorous further expansion of Greek diaspora secondary and higher education. By 1820, there was much pride in the newly flourishing academies and colleges established at Chios (which by 1819 boasted some seven hundred students and a French printing press), besides Patmos, Smyrna, Odessa, Jassy, Corfu, and Adrianople, and at Kidhonies (Ayvalik) (also with a French printing press), near ancient Pergamon, in Asia Minor, where a group of Peloponnesian exiles had settled after the first Greek rebellion's defeat.[9] By the outbreak of the 1821 Greek Revolution, the college at Chios boasted eight hundred students, among them several Germans and Americans.[10]

Striking, too, was the growing Greek attendance at western European universities. Whereas in 1815 there had been only seven or eight Greeks studying in Paris, by 1820, estimated Jullien, this figure had reached sixty, with another two hundred Greek students at German universities.[11] The Greeks have "undergone the most important changes," affirmed Shelley, in 1821, the "flower of their youth, returning to their country from the universities of Italy, Germany, and France, have communicated to their fellow citizens the latest results of that social perfection of which their ancestors were the original source."[12] However, it remained largely a diaspora phenomenon, a Greek cultural world concentrated principally outside territorial Greece and the future independent Greek state. Their national revival, Greeks knew, derived principally from an Enlightenment emanating from France, Italy, Britain, Germany, Russia, and the United States, including the ten-year (interrupted) French occupation of the Ionian Islands (1797–99 and 1807–14) which, especially during its first phase, had radically transformed the administration, laws, and institutions of Corfu, abolishing feudal practices and weakening traditional attitudes, firmly on the basis of French republican ideas. All this had a transformative effect; but one could question whether the educated, secular-minded Greek mercantile elite of the 1820s was sufficiently predominant within territorial Greece, as distinct from the wider Greek trading diaspora, to guide the political and general transformation that by late 1821 foreigners already dubbed "the Greek revolution."

In the Peloponnese and Greek islands, the rebels defeated the Turkish forces sent against them, notably at the battle of Dhervenákia where, in July 1822, a Turkish army of 26,000 was overwhelmed and destroyed near Corinth. The insurrection succeeded in the Peloponnese and the islands because local notables and officials collaborated with prosperous shipowning merchants with whose help a considerable fleet was formed, under Admiral Andreas Miaoulis, effective enough to prevent significant Turkish reinforcements by sea. But leadership and power in the "liberated" part of Greece devolved not onto the expanded mercantile elite dominating the Greek Enlightenment and colleges but instead into the hands of local notables and warlords, each tyrannizing over his own locality, with his own armed bands, causing the liberated zone to fragment into armed constituencies based on local authority and family clans. From the outset, the Greek Revolution wrestled with an inner political and philosophical dilemma inherited from Voulgaris, Rhigas, and the 1770s. The secularizing, more tolerant, republican tendency proved incompatible with tradition, autocracy, and theology.

The Russian emperor, fearful of wrecking the Holy Alliance, the reactionary powers' sole guarantee of their collaboration against revolution and radical ideas, refrained from intervening militarily. This avoided the discomforting prospect of a new Russo–Turkish war.[13] But lack of political cooperation between Peloponnese notables and those of central Greece, and the island merchants' placing their commercial interests above everything else, produced an increasingly anarchic situation. The Greek diaspora outside Greece nurtured its own ideas as to how to organize Greece's future but lacked leverage within the country and anyhow was divided in political allegiance. A predominant "moderate" current cultivating "mixed government" and conservative interpretations of the American Constitution clashed with a more radical tendency rejecting "mixed government" stiffened by Bentham's admonition that the Greeks should not stake their future on "division of powers," the Anglo-American model, or Montesquieu, for those influences would only further aggravate their mounting political disarray and fragmentation.[14]

Ordinary Greeks, notables and the common people, were mostly illiterate peasants, lacking any feel for either the glories of ancient Greece or the claims of the "new philosophy" and political ideas. They knew nothing of religious toleration or freedom of thought and deferred chiefly to local magnates and ecclesiastics. Strife and disorder consequently spread throughout liberated Greece. The Jewish community of Tripolis, no longer protected by the Ottomans and suspected of being pro-Turkish, were slaughtered by the insurgents in November 1821, after which sectarian killing rapidly spread. Considered religious foes, traitors, and sympathizers with the sultan, Jews were everywhere dealt with in the most merciless manner. Thousands, recorded the British consul in Constantinople, were tortured and immolated by the insurgents and so-called freedom-fighters in southern and central Greece; hundreds more, reported the British consul in Patras, were massacred in the north.[15] In the Peloponnese, peasants assailed both Muslims and Jews in their midst while the Turks retaliated in kind, ruthlessly butchering thousands of Greeks. Internationally, the ugly side of Greek popular sentiment was deliberately played down, though, to sustain the false parallel, dear to Romantic poets and the press, between modern Greeks and Western culture's highest values. During the 1820s, Western radicals—apart from Sismondi, who was among the first to warn of the viciousness of the underlying reality and extent of Greek oligarchic sway—veiled the truth from the public and themselves.

The Greek Enlightenment Defeated

As the disorder, bigotry, and disruption worsened, many literate Greeks suggested that a constitution and representative institutions must wait until the population became more enlightened and was "purged of its servile habits." Amid so much butchery and chaos, many Greeks grew convinced of the need for a towering leader to restore order, a Greek "Napoleon," "Washington," or "Bolívar," autocratic enough to redeem the country from itself. Against Rhigas's vision of Enlightenment and republican activism arose a strong, conservative Russophile reaction championing authoritarian religion and autocracy, presided over by Ioannis Kapdhístrias (Capodistrias) (1776–1831), who had been among the Greek nobles appointed by the czar to administer the Ionian Islands after the French expulsion in 1799. From 1809, he had served the czar as special envoy including at the 1814–15 Vienna Congress where he vied with Metternich as a champion of unbending absolutism.

Renewing Voulgaris's strategy of alignment with Russian autocracy on grounds of religious affiliation and popular sentiment, Kapdhístrias rebuilt the national movement's alternative identity, its theological and authoritarian Counter-Enlightenment face, with the clear aim of avoiding a constitution and representative institutions. But though soon predominant, this Greek autocratic shift could not prevent the mix of moderate and radical Enlightenment elements generating a widening constitutional debate and the broadly successful international projection, especially by foreign volunteers and Greek newspaper editors and teachers, of the Greek Revolution as "enlightened."[16] During and after protracted debates surrounding a provisional constitution drafted by the First Greek National Assembly, at Epidauros, in December 1821, this underlying ideological struggle continued. On paper, Greece's first constitution provided an up-to-date framework amply providing for religious toleration and freedom of expression. But such a document, spokesmen for Greek republican liberation recognized, could not of itself impart to the new regime an authentically republican character limiting executive power, establishing primacy of the legislature, and instituting toleration, freedom of expression, and political equality.[17]

Foremost among the Greek commentators in these years was the most celebrated Greek enlightener outside Greece and a key publicist of the revolutionary age, Adamántios Koraís (1748–1833). The Smyrna-born son of a Chios merchant, after six years in Amsterdam (1772–78) acquiring French, Dutch, and German and perfecting his Latin, Koraís had transferred to Montpellier where he studied medicine (1782–88). On the eve the great Revolution, he moved to Paris where he spent the remainder of his life. Observing firsthand the storming of the Bastille, Mirabeau's funeral, Voltaire's *panthéonisation*, and other key revolutionary episodes, he took detailed notes at every stage. Though Koraís was once considered just a standard-bearer of Greek national sentiment, today one encounters a wider appreciation of his stature as a general political and Enlightenment thinker, and mediator between the American, French, and Greek revolutions.[18] If historiography once represented "national heroes" like Koraís, Bolívar, Kościuszko, Miranda, Garibaldi, and Mazzini as concerned chiefly with nation-building, with liberating the "nation," in reality such leaders were deeply critical of their societies, and Koraís more than most. Decidedly no admirer of popular attitudes, he saw the "decline" of the Greek language over two millennia as highly deplorable, a calamity due to the prevalent overwhelming "ignorance" undermining Greek society and culture since the end of the classical age. Unawareness, limited horizons, and bigotry, all fostered by the clergy, had filled the void created by lack of self-government and democratic rule under the Romans, Byzantines, and Turks.[19]

Spending his life in the West while remaining in uninterrupted contact via letter with friends, family, and colleagues in the southeastern European Greek diaspora, as well as Greece proper, Koraís developed a general critique of contemporary Greek society and culture. Among its key features were a theory about the degeneration of the Greek language and his dismissing modern Greek culture as essentially the fruit of "ignorance and obscurantism." These views he tied to a political philosophy rooted in his belief that the contemporary Greek reality represented an unending struggle between the values of Enlightenment and Counter-Enlightenment.[20] The Greek people had almost entirely forgotten their ancient classics and, in his eyes, needed an infusion of sound classical ideas from the "healthy ancient" Greece to counter "defective modern" Greece. Koraís's most important project, his Helleniki Bibliothiki (Hellenic Library), was a large collection of translations of ancient texts into his preferred style of modern Greek with extensive notes and comments aimed, he explained in his *Precursor to the Hellenic Library* (1805), at reforming and reeducating his people. Far from targeting only the literate and leisured, he aspired to create a genuinely national culture transmitted ultimately through education, to all of society. Enlightenment philosophy had finally heard Greece's "desperate cries" for help.[21] "Philosophy" wished to return to her birthplace on the vehicle of his Helleniki Bibliothiki. Recovery of ancient Greek philosophy and literature, he was convinced, would help modern Greeks reform themselves, and all humanity to progress, by enabling Greeks critically to reexamine and reevaluate their modern political and religious practices, institutions, and authorities.

Modern Greeks, held Koraís, especially needed to ally with the ancients to combat the main forces of reaction in contemporary Greek society, the Orthodox Church, religious bigotry, and local notables. Most Greeks, though, understood little of this and stood stolidly on the rock of religion and tradition, hurling stones on "philosophy" to prevent her reentry into Greece. Koraís made it his lifelong task to engage with the people and convince them they must abandon their received ideas and embrace "philosophy"—and hence democracy, republicanism, and the *Rights of Man*. Since for Koraís there was nothing automatic about modern Greece's advance toward human rights, he was far from deeming independence and self-government sufficient in themselves to generate social and political improvement. The new post-Independence Greek nation of around 1830, in his opinion, remained highly defective and this was by no means the fault only of the Turks but, equally, of successive Greek generations so imbued with intolerant and authoritarian notions that Koraís termed them "Christian Turks." Modern Greece's reawakening was no national revival in the commonly accepted sense or a "renaissance" reviving the best of classical Greece but, correctly understood, a process of general reeducation and intellectual elevation powered by the reacquisition and reevaluation of the literature, learning, and philosophy of ancient Greece in combination with modern Enlightenment thought, especially American and French democratic-republican ideas.

Central to his political thought was a notion of progress indebted more to Condorcet's sweeping "philosophique" revolutionary reformism than Turgot's more economically and technologically driven conception.[22] Like Condorcet, whom he judged the greatest *philosophe* of the revolutionary age, Koraís was an uncompromising early proponent of compulsory secular universal schooling and educational equality. Social and political progress, for Greece, and men generally, operates by first building a foundation of enlightened thinking and knowledge within society in accordance with Condorcet's maxim that the "history of civilization is the history of enlightenment."[23] A concept optimistic and intensely cosmopolitan on one level, beholding progress as a universal and cumulative tendency, on another it was profoundly pessimistic, seeing vast obstacles to humanity's progress and in his particular nation, barriers of ignorance, theology, chauvinism, vested interests, and despotism. Continued failure would perpetuate the intolerance and political despotism of the past. Precisely here was Greece's tragedy. Post-Independence conservative Greek ideology retaliated against his stern criticism of the Greek Revolution by constructing a self-congratulatory nationalist account that almost wholly erased Koraís's criticism from its reading of modern Greek history.[24]

A committed radical allied to Mirabeau and Brissot, Koraís strongly sympathized with the democratic republican French Revolution. Like all radical enlighteners, he considered Robespierre a "monster" for suspending the French democratic constitution, suppressing freedom of expression and individual liberties, and presiding over the Terror.[25] He entirely approved of France's suppression of noble privilege and titles and the confiscation of the French Church's property.[26] He rejected monarchy and aristocracy, and sought to curb vested interests and ecclesiastical authority. Above all, he advocated the transfer of modern democratic ideas from the West to Greece.

Part of Koraís's significance as a European political thinker stems from his unrivaled ability to compare the French and American revolutions. His radicalism shared much with that of Jefferson, Paine, Forster, Wedekind, Barlow, Gorani, Thorild, Mary Wollstonecraft, and other leading democratic intellectuals identifying with what they saw as the veritable values of the French Revolution. In contact with Bentham and British philosophic radicalism as well as Jefferson, he corresponded also with the Unitarian clergyman Edward Everett (1794–1865), Harvard's young professor of Greek, an outstanding orator, later president of Harvard University, and eventually fifteenth governor of Massachusetts. In 1823, Everett began appealing in his *North American Review* for volunteers to enlist to fight for the Greek cause and formed an American pressure group that included the ambitious young congressman Daniel Webster, who was confronting John Quincy Adams in the House with the cry that it was America's duty, "as the leading republic of the world," to oppose absolutism and support the democratic tendency (despite his also claiming to endorse the Monroe doctrine).[27] Everett's and Webster's circle organized lectures and charity events on behalf of the insurgents and sought to prod the secretary of state into appointing a special American agent, preferably Everett himself, to organize American aid for rebel Greece, pressure John Quincy Adams stalwartly resisted. In October 1823, the *North American Review* published insurgent Greece's provisional constitution. Everett and Webster publicly demanded that America intervene in the conflict and recognize the Greek republic (which no other power had done), denouncing the Ottomans as barbarous and reminding readers that America had been chosen by providence to help remake the world, though Everett at least also endorsed Koraís's concept of progress, his envisaging advancement of knowledge and critical thinking as the primary agent of fundamental improvement.[28]

During 1823–24 America was unquestionably a beacon of hope for the rebels and the scene of a fervent public debate about Greece pregnant with significance for the entire transatlantic world. American moral and financial support for Greece, and moves to build ships for Greece in American ports, gained momentum with successful collections organized in numerous American cities. In his seventh annual message to Congress, on 2 December 1823, President Monroe publicly praised the "heroic struggle of the Greeks" that filled American hearts and minds with the "highest and noblest sentiments."[29] "My old imagination," Adams wrote to Jefferson a few weeks later, "is kindling into a kind of missionary enthusiasm for the cause of the Greeks."[30] Koraís had met Jefferson while the latter resided in Paris as United States ambassador. Drawn to his republican radicalism and Philhellenism, Koraís entered into direct correspondence with Jefferson too during 1823, seeking to enlist his help likewise for the Greek cause and for steering the Revolution onto a genuinely republican path.[31] At the time of his death, in 1833, one panegyrist praised Koraís's achievement, not inappropriately, by exclaiming: "you spoke and wrote the language of Washington, Jefferson and Lafayette who are the genuine representatives of human perfection."[32]

The Greek and Spanish revolutions of the early 1820s renewed the basic three-way split in Western intellectual culture between defenders of the old order, moderate reformers, and Enlightenment radicals. Where Shelley was disgusted with his countrymen for permitting "their own oppressors [the Tory ministry] to follow its natural sympathy with the Turkish tyrant," Lafayette bitterly deplored the thoroughly reactionary stance of the British and French governments, decrying their efforts to reinforce and extend aristocracy and monarchy everywhere—in Spain, Brazil, and Latin America besides Greece.[33] The United States indeed could and should, he believed, be a much-needed global counterweight to monarchical Britain, and he continually entreated American leaders and publicists more actively to support the Greek insurgents. Lafayette's voice counted in the America of the 1820s in a way that no other foreigner's did. Not only the politically aware, noted Fenimore Cooper, but also housewives and schoolboys felt emotionally connected with him: "our admiration of his disinterestedness, of his sacrifices, and of his consistency, is just as strong as ever."[34] Lafayette's tour of the United States, in 1824–25, became "a constant and inexhaustible topic of conversation" and helped further boost his reputation.

The Greek Revolution, like the failed revolutionary movements in Spain, Venezuela, New Granada, and Italy, and the crushed 1825 Decembrist conspiracy in Russia, afforded ample grounds for disillusioned observers either side of the Atlantic to express cynicism. Lafayette strove indefatigably to sustain the transatlantic democratic republican revolutionary consciousness and especially promote the Greek and Spanish American causes in the United States. Using his personal prestige and popularity during his rousing 1824–25 celebratory tour of the United States, at the invitation of President Monroe, with whom he had been friends for nearly half a century, since 1777, he helped rally support for the Greeks by continually drawing parallels between America's fight for freedom in 1775–83 and Greece's heroic struggle since 1770. Public receptions and celebrations in 1824–25 to honor Lafayette for his outstanding role in the American Revolution, held at New York, Boston, New Haven, Providence, Baltimore, Washington, Yorktown, Richmond, Charleston, and New Orleans—besides Fayetteville, North Carolina, in March 1825—continually trumpeted the American Revolution's achievements, enabling him repeatedly to stress the parallel with resurgent Greece.[35]

Philhellenism was already the rage in America as it was in Europe but Lafayette's efforts increased the impetus. "I try to be useful to the Greek cause as much as I can," he told members of Congress, in Washington, and "assist them as far as United States policy toward Europe makes this possible."[36] His formal speech in the House of Representatives in which he pronounced himself "grateful to have been declared to have in every instance been faithful to those American principles of liberty, equality and true social order," his devotion to which would last to his dying breath, was followed by an unprecedented silence of deep reflection among the congressmen.[37] Many American observers agreed with Jefferson's ally, Gallatin, and with Everett and Webster, in urging the United States to intervene actively in the Greek struggle,[38] and many more regarded the Greek cause with more enthusiasm and fewer reservations than the revolutionary upsurge in Spanish America.[39] This was partly due to classical Greece's prestige but also to Bolívar's and other Spanish American leaders' freeing large numbers of blacks as part of their strategy against Spain, a policy that alienated many North Americans. Mexico led the way among the major Spanish American republics in abolishing black slavery (1829), and one reason Texas broke away from Mexico not long afterward, setting itself up as an independent republic, in 1836, was so that its eastern planter elite could reinstate black slavery. Greece presented no such complications for America's self-image.

Coinciding with the Greek Revolution, Lafayette's thirteen-month tour of the United States in 1824–25 marked the culmination of the surging transatlantic "internationalist ideology" portraying democratic revolution based on individual liberty, toleration, and human rights as the future of mankind with the United States as the global hub and pivot of that hope.[40] Even though, under government pressure, the French and English papers loudly scoffed at the outpouring of republican zeal expressed in America and, in Washington, the Holy Alliance powers boycotted all the diplomatic receptions laid on for Lafayette by the secretary of state (still John Quincy Adams, who became president only in March 1825), the innumerable newspaper articles Lafayette's triumphant American tour engendered either side of the Atlantic helped revive pro-republican sentiment in France and Europe more generally as well as in America (and Greece). The fanfares surrounding Lafayette's visit were all the more impressive in that they were not officially organized but "left to the good-will and grateful affection of the people" and seemingly encompassed all twenty-four states of the Union.[41] The tour remained among the most vivid recollections of Walt Whitman's childhood.[42] In New York, where the city council commissioned Samuel Morse, the inventor-artist, to paint Lafayette's portrait, an outdoor banquet for six thousand guests was mounted, in September 1824, amid a forest of flags and marquees at Battery Gardens, the southern tip of Manhattan.

At Philadelphia, "after a triumphal entry" accompanied by twenty thousand militia under arms and all the clergy of the city (over sixty preachers) "among the thousands who crowded around the venerable Frenchman," banqueters enthusiastically toasted "Greece—may Providence grant her a Washington to lead her armies and a Lafayette for a friend."[43] The same wish for a "Washington" to lead the Greeks to victory, and a "Lafayette" as an ally, and talk of providence, resounded at toasts elsewhere.[44] Hugely feted for his republican and revolutionary "principles," Lafayette everywhere reaffirmed his message conflating the American and the French revolutions into a unified platform renewed in the Greek and Spanish American freedom struggles. America and its constitution he projected to the world as a beacon of universal hope and "bien supérieure civilization politique."[45] Boosted by so much enthusiasm for the "esprit démocratique," Lafayette succeeded in publicly setting American liberty in direct symbolic opposition to Europe's monarchies as well as Ottoman rule before the American public in speech after speech. Such acclaim also helped rekindle enthusiasm for the United States, and the American model, in France and among the clandestine networks of Europe.[46] Prompting ovation after ovation, the publicity campaign filled the French ambassador with unease. Reporting the disconcerting spectacle to Louis XVIII's court, he styled Lafayette the "patriarch of Europe's revolutionaries."[47]

In June 1825 Lafayette attended the celebrations to mark the fiftieth anniversary of the Battle of Bunker Hill, in Boston, at the head of an immense crowd; having celebrated fifty years of the liberation of America, he provocatively toasted that evening the coming fifty years as that of the "liberation of Europe."[48] Lafayette's "journey along the coast," recalled Cooper afterward, "has been like the passage of a brilliant meteor."[49] On returning to France (on a Federal warship specially renamed USS *Brandywine* in his honor), the "Hero of Two Worlds" continued promoting the Greek cause, though his ability to do so, through speeches and banquets, at home was limited by the strict royal ban on political meetings. He cultivated Charles Fabvier (1782–1855), the Napoleonic officer leading the French volunteer unit that fought doggedly for the Greek insurgency through the later 1820s, the Neapolitan Santa-Rosa, and the American ambassador and opponent of slavery, Gallatin, whose activist pro-Greek attitude continued to clash with the conservative, rigidly non-interventionist stance of John Quincy Adams and his supporters. The expanded French-Greek Committee established in Paris, in February 1825, attracted enlighteners and democrats but also courtiers, conservatives, and the religiously devout to what became a contested ideological arena there too. For the Greek national revival could be projected as a triumph for religion, conservatism, and the blessings of the Holy Alliance just as much as it could for Christianity and the design of providence in the United States. Not everyone condemned the rebels' antipathy to Muslims and unrelenting anti-Semitism. Ironically, both Lafayette and the Counter-Enlightenment Catholic Romantic

Chateaubriand found themselves together exhorting the French to provide money, aid, and moral support for the French-Greek Committee dispatching weapons and supplies to Greece.[50]

Artists, poets, and other literary men figured among the most ardent supporters of the Greek cause. Among Lafayette's closest friends at the time was the Dutch Romantic artist Ary Scheffer (1795–1858), who had moved from Holland to Paris at an early age and, at this time, before his later religious conversion and shift to Counter-Enlightenment, was deeply committed to revolutionary politics, the Carbonari, and the Greek Revolution. Among Scheffer's first major romanticizing paintings was a full-length heroic portrait of Lafayette begun in 1818, exhibited at the Paris salon of 1819, and completed in 1822. Sent to America in 1824 to be hung in the rotunda of the United States' new capitol building (where it remained permanently), as a gift to the United States on the part of an "admirer of General Lafayette and American Liberty," this painting became the visual symbol of Lafayette's efforts to reactivate American revolutionary principles in American minds as part of his ongoing drive for the liberation and democratization of Greece, Spain, Spanish America, and the world.[51]

The artists' and poets' zeal for the Greek Revolution also illustrates a wider trend at this time—the tendency of the post-1815 Radical Enlightenment to evolve, in the face of general opposition, once again in a veiled fashion. Except in the United States (and even there it had to ally with the rhetoric of divine providence) and Britain, radicalism had to retreat from public discourse and newspapers into secret underground organizations; but it also flourished anew in a discreet arena of nostalgia, literature, and Romantic dissidence, a world of ex-patriots in exile and embittered, marginalized men of insight like Shelley, Foscolo, Thorild, Börne, Lamartine, Koraís, Michelet, Stendhal, Daumier, and Heinrich Heine. Heine, who moved to Paris in 1831, shared Stendhal's abhorrence of dishonest, hypocritical politicians but agreed that Lafayette stood out as an unusually reassuring figure—among the few statesmen who was neither a would-be Bonaparte nor a charlatan or thief. Disgusted with the repression of Restoration Germany, Heine projected Lafayette as the "purest character of the French Revolution," the most honorable, consistent defender of liberty, the living embodiment of France's republican revolutionary tradition.[52]

In his jottings of the 1820s Lafayette continually reverted to the themes of 1776 and 1789, especially the doctrine of Human Rights. Much as the democratic republican tendency either side of the Atlantic formed a single unity in his mind, so he perceived a menacing interconnectedness in the efforts of international royalty, aristocracy, and religious authority, backed by the strongest power, Britain, to disrupt and break that tendency. After war erupted between Argentina and imperial Brazil in 1825, he assured the president of Argentina, in October 1826, of his ardent sympathy for that republic in its latest armed clash with the leading proponent of ancien régime reaction in the New World during the 1820s, Brazil's emperor Dom Pedro I (1798–1834). "During my happy trip to the United States," he recalled, "I never ceased to remark that the entire American hemisphere has an interest in seeing the Brazilian throne disappear, since it is the natural foyer of monarchical and aristocratic intrigues on the part of all the cabinets of Europe."[53]

Dom Pedro was instrumental in securing Brazil's independence from Portugal, proclaimed on 7 September 1822, doing so with the help of Britain, a country anxious both to strengthen monarchy and aristocracy across the Atlantic and to exact special trade privileges for herself. In November 1823, encouraged by his court camarilla, the new emperor dissolved Brazil's constituent assembly and, not unlike Iturbide, emasculated the legislature. The New World would, quite possibly, be a bastion of "Holy Alliance" reaction after all. After suppressing the revolt in the north, in 1824, Dom Pedro went to war to prevent Brazil's rebellious southernmost province detaching and joining the Argentine republican federation. American opinion supported Argentina; British diplomacy intervened on behalf of monarchy to buttress Dom Pedro. Yet President Monroe, and other influential Americans, even Ambassador Gallatin, cautious and nervous about British and Holy Alliance policies in Latin America, remained only very tentatively willing to pronounce in favor of republican government.[54]

For the enlightened Greek fringe in the 1820s, the American republic represented the finest product of accumulated human wisdom. A resounding success in the New World, the American republic had no state church and was headed by an elected president presiding over a constitution that expressly ruled out dominance of society by a hereditary aristocracy. Yet among literate Greeks, there was also considerable skepticism, much as among literate Spaniards, as to whether anything resembling the American model was achievable in Greece. "It would be a stroke of good fortune," commented the editor of the newspaper *Geniki Ephemeris*, in 1825, if Greece were to be ruled not temporarily but permanently under such a constitution as that of the United States. "But to adopt America's constitution in Greece we would first have to transform the Greeks into Anglo-Americans."[55] An attempt to overcome the civil strife and disorder on the basis of reconciliation, compromise, and a new constitution was made via a national convention of all factions at Trizini in the spring of 1827. Kapdhístrias was elected modern Greece's first "president."

On paper the new constitution looked impressive: the executive was tightly constrained, a detailed Bill of Rights ensured the liberties and freedoms of the individual. Yet no sooner did he arrive in Greece than Kapdhístrias, backed by the British, French, and Russian governments, sided with the conservatives and sought to evade the checks and balances built into the constitution. In January 1828, with significant local support, he suspended the new Greek constitution altogether. Civil strife intensified. Church leaders divided, supporting different factions. In Greece's provisional capital, Nauplion, the rival commanders of the town's two main fortresses used their artillery against each other. A new National Assembly consisting of 236 delegates convened at Argos, in July 1829, but to general dismay failed to agree or restore order, or the 1827 constitution. The president, Kapdhístrias, was assassinated in Nauplion on 9 October 1831. Greece's political predicament grew only worse.

Under these circumstances, it was difficult for even the most idealistic foreign volunteers fighting in Greece not to experience disillusionment and aversion despite the continuing excitement in the West and an uninterrupted stream of fresh volunteers. Many of the first wave of French volunteers and Napoleonic veterans who had embarked in some numbers from Marseille, full of enthusiasm, in 1821–22 were already returning disillusioned and resentful by late 1822.[56] Dying of fever at Missalonghi, in April 1824, the international icon of Philhellenism, Byron, had succeeded in boosting European and American ardor for the Greek cause to new heights, but during his last weeks, severely depressed, suffered deep dismay and despair at the feuding between the insurgent groups. Likewise, Annibale Santorre, conte di Santarosa (1783–1825), a leader of the 1820–21 Piedmontese rising and enthusiast for the Spanish revolution of 1820–23, was profoundly dispirited on discovering the reality of the Greek revolution to be startlingly different from the heroic image fostered in the West; he died desperate and disillusioned near Navarino in May 1825.[57] The third wave, notably the Napoleonist Fabvier and his band of French and Italian volunteers, played a crucial role in the military operations from 1825, but he too had left Greece thoroughly disillusioned by 1829.[58] Among the most impressive American volunteers fighting in Greece were Captain Jonathan Peckham Miller (1797–1847) and Dr. Samuel Gridley Howe (1801–76), fresh from Harvard Medical School, both of whom were likewise bitterly disappointed. Arriving in 1825, fired by Byron's example, Howe spent five years (1824–29) in Greece both fighting and performing amputations and other surgical operations for the wounded, unpaid and feeding himself at his own expense, as well as sending back graphic letters that were published in the Boston papers. He was deeply unimpressed with the common Greek soldier, horrified by the disorderliness and acts of savagery he witnessed, and appalled by the primitive state of medical care.[59] Angered by the reluctance of America and other powers to assist the Greeks, he also assumed responsibility for distributing supplies paid for in America and France.

The chaotic struggle in Greece dragged on for an entire decade before the European powers finally intervened to impose an internationally agreed solution. The outcome was predictable. In accordance with the Holy Alliance's values and the Vienna Congress, France, Austria, and Russia, together with Britain, collectively resolved the crisis by applying their jointly sanctioned formula—the undisputed primacy in the world of monarchy, aristocracy, and ecclesiastical authority. These principles were rigorously applied to the new Greece (confined to Attica, the Peloponnese, and the Cycladic island group). In May 1832, the international Conference of London formally offered the allies' new throne to the seventeen-year-old son of King Ludwig I of Bavaria, Prince Otto. Surveying possible candidates, and anxious to prevent Greece's monarchy becoming either a Russian or French satellite, British ministers, with calculating discernment, in effect chose Greece's monarch for her while simultaneously stipulating the people must not be permitted to ratify the choice.[60]

Good care was taken to ensure that they were not consulted. It was thus in a surge of anti-democracy and revulsion against constitutions and radical ideas including American principles, and diametrically against American hopes for Greece, that the modern Greek monarchy was born. Arriving in his new kingdom on a fleet of twenty-five allied royal warships, King Otto "of Greece" and his entourage pointedly alighted in Nauplion Bay from a British frigate, symbolically setting popular sovereignty aside before the eyes of all humanity in the name of reaction, religion, and Counter-Enlightenment. The new Greek monarchy was inaugurated in 1833 surrounded by ecclesiastics and unaccompanied by any form of constitution or guarantee for minorities. The United States Congress and president did not bother to send a resident American ambassador to Greece until 1868.

CHAPTER 19

The Freedom-Fighters of the 1830s

The Revolutionary Culture of the Late Radical Enlightenment

Jefferson, Koraís, Foscolo, Jullien, and other aging radical veterans of the pre-1815 revolutionary era rested their indomitable faith in mankind's future on the Enlightenment's accumulated impact and universal diffusion, their trusting that the "light which has been shed on mankind by the art of printing has eminently changed the condition of the world." "Kings and the rabble of equal ignorance," held Jefferson, "have not yet received its rays; but it continues to spread. And, while printing is preserved, [the Enlightenment] can no more recede than the sun return on his course." Initial efforts to establish "self-government" might fail. Mankind's happier future had been set back in France, first by Robespierre, then Napoleon, and finally the Restoration, and in Mexico by Iturbide. "Yet I will not believe our labors are lost. I shall not die," averred Jefferson, "without a hope that light and liberty are on steady advance."[1] The French Revolution would eventually revive, and "all Europe, Russia except, has caught the spirit, and all will attain representative government, more or less perfect."[2] The Vienna Congress and Holy Alliance were defied, checked, and in the end inevitably thwarted if not fully defeated by an underground revolutionary culture, the late Radical Enlightenment, evolving into a broad international and transatlantic democratic opposition.

There was even a sense, it emerged around 1820, in which the Enlightenment could overawe its adversaries, popular, ecclesiastical, and aristocratic, without anyone striking a blow—and accomplishing this without armies, decrees, or constitutions; and here, especially, Jefferson proved prescient. During the 1820s, it was not just fading veterans like Jefferson, Lafayette, Koraís, and Jullien but especially younger, freshly inspired writers, poets, philosophers, scholars, and journalists such as Shelley, Stendhal, Lamartine, Ruge,

Michelet, Börne, Heine, Büchner, John Stuart Mill, Emerson, and Fenimore Cooper, a formidable and growing phalanx ardent to preserve the legacy of Paine, Condorcet, and Kościuszko, men more than ever convinced the "establishment of true republican principles, and their practice in the world," as Freneau had expressed it, "will work an astonishing change among mankind."[3] The thousands of political and literary exiles were highly dangerous to reactionary government because they nurtured and spread the culture of political resentment, sharing its doctrines with disaffected individuals staying at home and with not exiled, but barely tolerated, critics like the historian Jules Michelet (1798–1874), a passionate French sympathizer with the ideals of 1789 and future author of the classic *Histoire de la Révolution française* (7 vols.; 1847–53), seething with detestation for the restored Bourbon monarchy. Michelet showed scant regard for Louis XVIII and none at all for his successor, Charles X. A Paris University professor and disciple of Vico, this printer's son turned scholar burned throughout the 1820s with a deep republican ardor for the great Revolution's democratic principles and, directly coupled with this, eagerness to fight the Church.

Radical exiles, underground fugitives, and fuming critics led a growing but largely hidden home constituency of men bearing potentially explosive grudges. Censorship, the Restoration's broad impact, and the ideological reaction to it, in poetry, novels, painting, history, political thought, and social science, siphoned revolutionary impulses into allusion, sentiment, nostalgia, and visionary longing. Between 1815 and 1830, almost unnoticed behind the scenes, the cult of revolution and conspiratorial opposition, reworking memories of the revolutionary experience while suffusing journals, literature, drama, and poetry, as well as philosophy, permeated European intellectual life so profoundly that this resumed "revolution of the mind" registered appreciable advances despite the repression. Literature and art bolstered awareness of the revolutionary experience and its meaning. The challenge of reaction and Counter-Enlightenment weighed so unremittingly that it generated its own counterreaction in general culture. It appeared, as Hegel suggested, that a dialectical mechanism operated. If Romanticism also nurtured reactionary views, Romanticism was no less effective in boosting Revolution, and radical thought, and no less unforgiving. Confirmed literary "apostates" like Coleridge, Southey, and Wordsworth, who had broken with their former radical commitments and ties, and rejected the revolutionary cause, were fiercely rebuked for writings that "tainted the literature of the age," as Shelley put it, "with the hopelessness of the minds from which it flows."[4]

The 1830 revolutions in Europe are often misleadingly presented by historians as spontaneous initiatives of peoples, or classes, seeking national liberation and constitutional changes and opposing Restoration monarchy. Nationalist and Marxist historiography portrayed the revolutions as the actions of peoples or at least large social segments while playing down the primary role of clandestine organizations, political exiles, conspiratorial groups, and revolutionary reading societies acting against the majority tendency. But during these years such societies led the way. Often, the initiative for and especially the leadership, rhetoric, agendas, and general direction of the revolutionary movements, in east-central Europe and Germany, as in France and Italy, derived hardly at all from conventional thinking, class, popular culture, social impulse, or economic factors but predominantly from fringe groups of highly articulate revolutionary veterans and intellectuals, an unrepresentative mix of renegade nobles, defecting clergy, students, cashiered Napoleonist officers, artists, literary men and women, journalists, and professors.

Claiming social and economic pressures "caused" the revolutions has always been a dangerous oversimplification. But this does not mean social factors were not basic to the story, only that numerous social and economic pressures are relevant. Bad harvests occurred after as well as before 1815. Industry was changing the urban faces of Britain, Belgium, and very patchily parts of France, Germany, and the northeastern United States. More generally, population growth was everywhere intensifying social tensions and expanding pauperism and destitution. Louis XVIII's refusal to reemploy the officers of Napoleon's army, often risen from relatively low social strata to high positions and, from 1815, adrift and unemployed but unwilling to revert to inferior status, provided numerous recruits for the exiled, underground "grande armée" of Liberty and the Romantic cult of Revolution.[5] Increases in university enrollment in Germany during the 1820s and 1830s went unmatched by any growth of employment opportunities in German state bureaucracies, a situation that inevitably expanded the pool of highly qualified unemployed and frustrated graduates.[6]

Without the direction and guidance afforded by a coherent, philosophically grounded ideology and a highly motivated fringe of professional revolutionaries, the social factors generating distress and discontent could foment only inchoate protest, contradictory impulses, and aimless insurgency, just as easily captured by Counter-Enlightenment bigotry and authoritarian populism manipulating the credulous in the style of Robespierre as by republican egalitarianism. Not peoples, or classes, or gradual cultural processes, then, but the intelligentsia's disaffection with princely rule, bureaucracy, and religious sway chiefly generated the universal revolutionary credo of human rights and free expression, consciously drawing on the American revolutionary heritage of 1775 and French legacy of 1789. During these years, alienated students and writers renewed an Enlightenment radicalism which, owing to its relative sophistication and intellectual complexity, differed dramatically from the yearnings, dissatisfaction, and alienation of workers and peasants. This divergence was society's tragedy, being a main contributory factor in the collapse of the 1830 and 1848 revolutions.

Economic discontent was not so much impotent as readily diverted and mobilized to serve all sorts of conflicting interests. The real threat to the restored hegemony of royalty, aristocracy, and ecclesiastical primacy, Europe's regimes were acutely aware, derived not from the people but from clandestine underground opposition circles. The repressive Carlsbad Decrees, jointly announced by Austria and Prussia in September 1819, chiefly aimed to strengthen press control and tighten surveillance of universities and student societies. The resolutions of the princely Germanic Confederation of December 1835 likewise recognized that radical subversion was principally driven by a fringe of Akademiker (academics), student organizations,[7] and independent writers, most notoriously Ludwig Börne and the poet Heinrich Heine. Italy had been prepared for revolution by the secretive, underground lodges of the Carbonari and most of the notable personalities of the Risorgimento emerged originally from a Carbonarist milieu. In Russian Poland, clandestine student groups thrived especially in Warsaw, Vilnius, Cracow, and Lwow.[8] The Philomaths, a secret student group at Vilnius, dedicated to plotting revolution and emancipating the serfs, included a youth who became the greatest nineteenth-century Polish poet, Adam Mickiewicz (1798–1855). Son of a lawyer from the lesser nobility, who studied at Vilnius in the years 1815–19 and taught at a school at Kovno (Kaunas) from 1819 to 1823, he was imprisoned after an investigation into secret student societies that led to the arrest of several former members of the Vilnius Philomaths. From 1829, Mickiewicz lived in permanent exile abroad, chiefly Paris, where, from 1840, he occupied the newly established chair in Slavonic languages at the Collège de France, still expounding his strange political mythology combining veneration of Napoleonic France with exaltation of the Poles as *the* God-chosen people.[9] The mystical tonality and suffering Christ imagery permeating his poetry of Polish national awakening greatly extended his poetry's political resonance among wide sections of the populace.

America's example had been "silently operating on Europe for half a century" yet, disappointingly, averred Fenimore Cooper in 1827, American literature had not succeeded in impressing this "on our attention," leaving most observers—American and European—largely unaware of the extent and significance of America's impact.[10] Yet American writers were growing highly sensitive to the fact that the drama of the continuing transatlantic clash of principles inherent in the American Revolution remained unresolved. The international journalistic, literary, and artistic milieu of the day could not ignore the Revolution's earlier background and inheritance—the memory and principles of a revolutionary culture forged in America and impressed on the European consciousness with particular force and eloquence by Paine, Jefferson, Kościuszko, Condorcet, Brissot, and Lafayette, a vision of the democratic program of the American and French revolutions locked in conflict with an "aristocratic" *modérantisme* aspiring to capture a more restricted liberty for society's elites.

During the 1830s and 1840s, American intellectual and literary opinion still remained divided over the merits of the "mixed government" British model, of the ultimate meaning of "aristocratic" versus "democratic" republics and Enlightenment. Emerson and America's first female public intellectual, Margaret Fuller (1810–50), were two prominent literary Americans who both visited England and continental Europe, Emerson in the 1830s and 1840s, both concurring with Cooper that America, given her centrality in world political and cultural development since 1775, had offered less guidance and inspiration to others than she should have. Ever since first visiting Europe in 1833, Emerson had equated the inner struggle within American politics with Europe's ongoing battle between "aristocrats" and "democrats." Broadly his sympathies lay with the democratic side; still, at times he hesitated. An unrelenting devotee of late Enlightenment "reason," he disliked what he considered the crass materialism of American life. In a celebrated Harvard lecture of August 1837, "The American Scholar," he looked forward to a time "when the sluggard intellect of this continent will look from under its iron lids and fill the postponed expectation of the world with something better than the exertions of mechanical skill."[11] His projected "revolution of the mind" was that of the inner man, the rational soul, and this led him to suspicion of collective action and violent revolution and a hesitant, renewed respect for the British aristocracy. By contrast, Fuller, more conscious of the social and political inequality disfiguring Britain, and like many British and French radicals of the day dismayed by the misery and ignorance of the majority, viewed the splendor of the British Crown, empire, and aristocracy wholly negatively.[12]

The 1830 Revolutions: France

Political exiles, impassioned Romantics, student societies, and clandestine organizations steeped in rebellious literature, philosophy, and social theory, an underground political culture strikingly different from anything familiar to most Americans, were the spearhead of republicanism and democracy in Europe between 1815 and 1848. This key factor imparted to the 1830 and 1848 revolutions their distinctive world-historical character. But to precipitate any massive revolution powerful outside forces must supply a triggering mechanism and motive force sufficient to overthrow the apparatus of policing and repression. Deteriorating economic conditions for most and growing hardship had been in evidence for several years (1827–30) by the time the July rising of 1830, the first popular insurrection in the French capital since 1795, erupted. It broke out when France's unremittingly reactionary king, Charles X (reigned: 1824–30), refused any longer to tolerate the progressive element in the Chamber of Deputies. A discreet opposition, with Lafayette and Constant well to the fore, had by the mid-1820s regained a measure of national prominence. The tipping point was government's disastrous defeat in the elections of May 1830, largely due to the harsh conditions and the impact of a now barely trammeled press. Despite official pressure to elect conservative candidates, the elections produced a constitutionalist opposition majority of 274 over a mere 143 deputies still firmly supporting the Crown. Tightly boxed in, on 26 July the king, following the recommendations of his ultraroyalist minister Jules, third duke of Polignac (1780–1849) (whose mother had been a confidante of Marie-Antoinette), issued the Four Ordinances suspending the existing (very limited) constitution, in effect engineering a Rightist coup, "the great counter-revolution" about which onlookers had warned for some time.[13] Fundamental to this coup, the king tried to wholly abort press freedom, a hazardous step at a time when the resurgent enthusiasm for the achievements of the French Revolution and the anger of the Paris intelligentsia converged with added momentum from popular discontent fueled by high bread prices and growing unemployment.[14]

On 26 July, the Paris opposition editors, headed by the ambitious young journalist and historian Adolphe Thiers (1797–1877)—an admirer of Napoleon who, nevertheless, at that time preferred constitutional monarchy based on broad representation to Napoleonism or republicanism, and who in May, through his paper, had urged the electorate to vote for the opposition—published an open summons to the Paris populace. Appearing in four papers, signed by forty-four journalists sufficiently brave to risk imprisonment, Thiers's summons urged the people to protest en masse, refuse taxes, and denounce the king's actions as "tyranny." It precipitated a mass of inflammatory handbills and posters plastering the streets and cafés: Thiers's phalanx of literary men gathered in Paris sought to render the great French Revolution a success after all "by making representative government a reality."[15] The disturbances began in time-honored fashion at the Palais-Royal. On 27 July, troops entered the city to quell the protests while the police raided and shut down all the opposition papers. Parisians and the populace of Rouen, youths and workers especially, seizing whatever arms they could find, poured into the streets in impressive numbers. Fighting erupted and factories closed as firing spread across the city, but there was little hint of class warfare. Parisians of all classes, but especially students and working-class artisans from the Faubourg Saint-Antoine, with a conspicuous admixture of hundreds of former Napoleonic army officers and foreign political exiles, in all some seven or eight thousand combatants, converged to bar the king's soldiery.[16] Exiled Carbonari, Poles, Italians, and Spaniards joined in, as did Franz Liszt, Alexandre Dumas, and other writers, artists, and intellectuals, including Michelet, who later conceived these days as a pivotal moment in history, one of illumination and exaltation when a long and deep darkness finally dissipated.[17] There was also the odd American fighter, notably Samuel Gridley Howe, now back from Greece, whose bravery on this occasion greatly impressed Lafayette.[18]

Constructing barricades in the narrow streets to obstruct troop movements, a technique first adopted after the Bastille's fall and revived by the 1795 Germinal and Prairial risings, the people impeded the chief arm of royal power. The battle surged back and forth. "The admirable resistance of Paris," recorded Lafayette on 29 July, "still continues; there have been considerable losses on both sides, but despite the immense advantages of the royal guard and the king's other troops, the people continue the struggle with energy."[19] The Hôtel de Ville changed hands several times, expiring citizens crying out with their last breath: "Vive la Liberté!" Eventually, with several hundred dead, some royal troops defected, the loyalist hard core fell back, and the Louvre fell to the insurgents. As in July 1789, Lafayette was named National Guard commander by general acclaim. His first order of the day, issued late on 29 July, echoed his call of forty-one years before, ending with the stirring words; "Liberty will triumph, or we shall die together. *Vive la Liberté! Vive la patrie!* Lafayette."[20] By 30 July, practically all Paris was in their hands.

After three furious days known as the Trois Glorieuses, on 31 July, the repulsed and defeated royal troops pulled back completely. Thirty-eight years after breaking with the first Revolution, and being driven into exile, Lafayette appeared on the Paris Hôtel de Ville's balcony acknowledging the cheering crowds and the people's victory. Paris was theirs; and by the end of July the Bourbon authorities had been ejected from, or barricaded in, the town halls of Rouen, Arras, and other provincial cities. Shortly after midnight, on 31 July, King Charles evacuated Paris, retreating with his entourage to Versailles and then Rambouillet. A Counter-Enlightenment hero, who since 1789 had risked everything for unbending reaction and faith, in the end he failed even in this.

Having ruled in a most inept fashion, and seeing no way to regain control, on 2 August the elderly monarch abdicated—not just for himself but also on his son's behalf, permanently blighting French legitimacy according to ultraroyalists and the entire senior branch of the Bourbon dynasty.

At the moment of victory, the heroic Bostonian Dr. Howe designated the Trois Glorieuses "that wonderful event, the pride of France, the admiration of Europe and the world."[21] But general exaltation did not last long. It was almost instantly displaced by profound, shattering disillusionment resulting from the devastating split between constitutional monarchists and republicans, by the "loss of high hopes," as Michelet put it, by "moral cholera."[22] Concerting a united front against the Right, Lafayette, backed by a mix of constitutionalist and republican journalists, repeated what some saw as his old mistake of seeking to reconcile "moderation" with the radical Left, as in 1791–92, although once again this might have actually been the only realistic strategy at the time. Briefly, he joined forces with Thiers, Guizot, the centrist constitutional monarchists of the Chamber, and several ex-Napoleonist senior officers. The counsel of hard-core republican editors and leading voices, like Jullien, advising that a new national constitution should be debated and thrashed out first was ignored by a Lafayette still ambitious and eager for popularity and having the majority behind him, but not for assuming power. "Our republican faction," admitted Lafayette in mid-August, could have imposed their views on the rest, at any rate in Paris; but at that moment it seemed preferable to "reunite all the French under the regime of a constitutional throne, but one free and popular."[23] Rather than vigorously assume the lead, as he could have done, and attempt to become the "Washington of the French," Lafayette, now seventy-two, beyond promptly pronouncing the Bourbon dynasty ousted and no longer to reign, opted to align with the royalist moderates.[24] The surge of Parisian republican sentiment, representing a small minority in France as a whole, was disregarded.

Lafayette could have established the second French Republic in 1830, Fenimore Cooper advised the American public later, putting himself at its head, but tried instead to avoid reopening old wounds and divisions and prevent disorder and bloodshed through compromise. Mindful of the revolutionary wars that ravaged all Europe and that, since 1815, the Bourbons had largely disarmed the country, Lafayette knew France was in no position to resist the Holy Alliance and Britain, whose united forces would assuredly have crushed any openly republican French revolution, just as Louis XVIII crushed the 1820–23 Spanish revolution.[25] Nearly all French republicans in 1830 accepted that effectively freeing the people from royal tyranny, and spreading democracy, inevitably meant fighting a revolutionary war with Europe's princes.[26]

The revolutionary leadership, as in 1789, hence embraced a "liberal" monarchical compromise designed to avoid provoking international intervention, or any provincial Catholic backlash, and thus avoid civil war. But however motivated by anxiety to avoid strife and bloodshed, Lafayette looked spineless and his leadership misjudged to some, and he was scorned in republican circles. Lafayette's strategy swiftly unraveled because centrists, led by the banker Jacques Lafitte (1767–1844) and Casimir-Pierre Perier (another banker), opposing democracy, captured the initiative and steered a much too elitist, uncompromisingly "moderate" outcome.

Surrender to Lafitte's and Thiers's supporters meant France turned overnight into a constitutional monarchy with a highly restricted suffrage, lacking a *Declaration of the Rights of Man* such as Jullien and others recommended, a stilted constitutional monarchy retaining black slavery in the colonies and brusquely refusing to aid the other 1830 European revolutions, even in Belgium (where the British were determined the French should not interfere).[27] The "moderates," among them several former Napoleonic generals, selected as king the seemingly accommodating Orléanist prince Louis-Philippe d'Orléans (1773–1850). Arriving in Paris after being hurriedly endorsed by a vote in the old legislature (barely more than half of whom were present),[28] Louis-Philippe was proclaimed "King of the French" on 9 August 1830. He initially gave all the right signals, publicly embracing Lafayette, now France's prime revolutionary symbol, on the Hôtel de Ville balcony and proclaiming his (insincere) veneration for popular sovereignty, society's well-being, and the legacy of 1789.[29]

Briefly, the July Revolution, and soon the other 1830 revolutions, appeared to vindicate Lafayette's judgment and Jefferson's confidence that mankind was poised for vast strides forward. "It roused my utmost enthusiasm," later recalled the most influential English philosopher of the age, the Utilitarian John Stuart Mill (1806–73), "and gave me, as it were, a new existence." Mill went "at once to Paris, and was introduced to Lafayette."[30] Considering England's aristocracy the "great demoralizing agent in the country," Mill proclaimed himself a "radical and democrat for Europe" and especially "for England." "I thought the predominance of the aristocratic classes, the noble and the rich, in the English constitution, an evil worth any struggle to get rid of."[31] For radicals, Britain was as much entangled in the revolutionary upsurge, and in need of it, as the rest. There could be no more poignant vindication of Mill's and Jefferson's hopes than the letter Shelley's widow, Mary Shelley, daughter of Mary Wollstonecraft and William Godwin, sent Lafayette after the Trois Glorieuses. She *had* to address herself, she wrote, to the "hero of three revolutions," those of America, France in 1789, and France in

1830. Since 1815, royalist France under Bourbon legitimacy was the accomplice of Britain and Russia, the epitome of reaction, Counter-Enlightenment, and resurgent ecclesiastical privilege. Then, suddenly, all was transformed: "How has France redeemed herself in the eyes of the world—washing off the stains of her last attempt in the sublime achievements of this July." Shelley remained always loyal to his revolutionary creed (unlike the "apostates"— Wordsworth and Coleridge, who had defected during the new century's first decade to become foes of the revolutionary cause). Mary vowed to continue the fight for Shelley's republican ideals, congratulating Lafayette on her dead husband's behalf: "I rejoice that the cause to which Shelley's life was devoted, is crowned with triumph."[32] Events soon showed all such joyful expectations to be vastly premature.

Hesitation and disarray had enabled a conservative bankers' clique to capture the Revolution, change the ruling dynasty, and adopt a few cosmetic reforms. Louis-Philippe, the "Citizen King," announced that France would solidly eschew the democratic path and refrain from assisting republican revolutions abroad. Although some Italian "moderates" in exile briefly applauded, before long Louis-Philippe and his ministers were openly at war, observed John Stuart Mill in April 1831, with the very intellectuals who prepared and led the 1830 Revolution.[33] Louis-Philippe's France was not the France of 1789 or 1792 but a staunchly upper-middle-class "moderation" professing a "liberalism" Mill and other radicals despised as a complete sham supposedly acclaiming liberty, freedom of expression, and human rights but in fact entirely rejecting those very principles.[34] Bankers and rich industrialists, remarked onlookers, had striven for fifteen years to overthrow aristocratic dominance; yet, hardly was the July revolution achieved than they turned themselves into "a new aristocracy," lording over a restricted suffrage and a press subjected to a batch of stiff new censorship laws.[35]

Louis-Philippe's ministers claimed that English-style "mixed government" unquestionably offered the best and most judicious path forward. Far from prejudicing the common people's interests, constitutional monarchy bolstering a reformed "aristocracy" served the interests of all. This "liberal" doctrine of the "moderates," much in mode among the European middle classes of the 1830s, directly impinged on the continuing controversy in European and transatlantic culture and discourse about the real meaning of the American Revolution. No country was more prosperous than Britain, urged "moderates," and none more entirely under a wealthy, dominant, and universally respected aristocracy. Englishmen wholeheartedly identified with monarchy and aristocracy, acknowledging these to be the pillars of social stability. Yes, retorted Lafayette, "but the United States are a democracy; and is there less prosperity in democratic America than in aristocratic England?"[36] Did not America represent something of universal significance for mankind that England did not? In polite conversation in Europe, noted Fenimore Cooper in 1836, it remained standard practice at every turn to find fault with American democracy. In England, "votaries of monarchies regard all our acts with so much malevolence, and have so strong a desire to exaggerate all our faults," that anyone affirming the positive "influence of American example" in the world was immediately ridiculed.[37]

By publicly repudiating democracy, republicanism, cosmopolitanism, and "human rights," Louis-Philippe's ministers in effect also belittled and scorned the fighters at the Paris barricades and the revolutionaries of Germany, Italy, and Poland. Fruit of a people's revolution, the new French monarchy nevertheless quickly distanced and disassociated itself from all authentic republicans and revolutionaries.[38] Having done much to nurture a principled "moderation" based on the sacrosanctity of constitutional law and checks and balances, Constant died in December 1830; despite a magnificent state funeral, attended by vast crowds, his legacy was subsequently spurned by the regime he had helped create.[39] Börne, migrating to Paris from Frankfurt, intent on basking in the revived revolutionary scene, soon switched to a witheringly critical attitude. Furious at the Revolution's capture by a wealthy upper stratum of the bourgeoisie aspiring to become a new aristocracy of money, like Mill he took to depicting the July Revolution as pitifully threadbare and devoid of authentic republican, rights-oriented, democratic content. The one substantial deviation from an otherwise dispiriting general defection from meaningful reform was an initiative of the dour, anti-democratic Protestant historian François Guizot (1787–1874): as minister of education, early in the new reign, he brought in the epoch-making decree of 28 June 1833 establishing a comprehensive system of state primary education throughout France. Why Guizot, who explicitly rejected universal male suffrage and democracy, sought universal elementary education, an apparent startling contradiction, was never made clear.

Guizot called Louis-Philippe's rule a "middle-class" bourgeois government; but in reality, with its curbs on the press and allocating the right to vote to only 250,000 persons out of a population of thirty-five million, it was hardly that. Rather, Guizot's and Thiers's much-vaunted "liberalism" was anti-democratic to the core, an amalgam of "liberal" legal principles, laissez-faire economics, and a rigidly aristocratic conception of constitutional monarchy excluding even most of the middle class along with the working population from political rights, participation, and debate. The one redeeming feature was the progressive education policy.[40]

In key respects, Guizot's political ideal, noted De Tocqueville, directly contradicted the current American model.[41] The "United States are the model republic," acknowledged Guizot, "and the model democracy in the world."[42] But America's real triumph, he contended, was that it had contrived to circumvent the unrelenting struggle between aristocracy and democracy engulfing Europe, assuming the appearance of democracy while its leading figures still stemmed exclusively from the "natural and national aristocracy of the country," the principal planters and landowners and the big merchants of the cities. He was right, of course, about the American South and, partially, perhaps, about the rest. Independence and the American republic, in any case, were clearly not the accomplishment of social classes battling other classes but of all classes cooperating under the "most distinguished, the richest, the most enlightened who, more than once, had great difficulty in rallying the will and courage of the people." Requiring good officers for his untrained and untried troops, Washington was unbending, noted Guizot admiringly, in sticking to his principle: "appoint *gentlemen*, they are the most reliable and the most capable."[43] In short, the United States pretended to be but was not actually a "democratic republic" and precisely this was the reason it functioned so admirably. Since his narrow constitutionalism left the July monarchy defenseless before the charge that it purposely and undisguisedly opposed equality of rights and opportunity, and excluded the people, Guizot always avoided justifying the 1830 Orléanist revolution in terms of either the Revolution of 1789 or, despite his unbounded respect for Washington, even the "aristocratic" American Revolution.[44]

America and the Belgian Revolution

The July Revolution occurred at a crucial moment in world history when the post-Napoleonic reactionary wave faltered. In America, the first archetypal, self-made man of the people, Andrew Jackson (1767–1845), had just commenced his first presidency (1829–33). The son of poor Scottish Irish Presbyterian parents who had settled in the Carolinas, a frontier lawyer and military man with a fiery temper lacking the refinement and education of his aristocratic predecessors, he triumphed in the 1828 presidential election owing to his renown as a national hero, being the victor of the Battle of New Orleans (1815). He presented himself as the champion of those who despised elitism, the Electoral College, and the "corrupt bargain" that had decided the bitterly contested election of 1824. In that contest, Jackson had secured more votes than John Quincy Adams and two other candidates but failed to secure an overall majority. Citing a vague clause in the Constitution, the Electoral College had then opted not to declare Jackson president but left it instead to the House of Representatives to decide. The House proclaimed John Quincy president much to Jefferson's consternation: John Quincy's supporters "having nothing in them of the principles of '76, now look back to a single and splendid government of an aristocracy, founded on banking institutions, moneyed incorporations under the guise and cloak of their favored branches of manufactures, commerce and navigation, riding and ruling over the plundered ploughman and beggared yeomanry."[45]

If John Quincy Adams exuded the "aristocratic" American Revolution, it was hard to claim that Jackson genuinely represented the opposite. Jackson, the first truly populist candidate, projecting himself as the "voice of the people," subsequently won the 1828 election resoundingly. The presidential inauguration and White House inaugural ball in 1829 were the first at which the public at large was invited. In American domestic politics, the talk in and after 1828 was all about renewing American democracy, reviving the principles of 1776, and dismantling the old elite—possibly even abolishing the Electoral College. But the facade belied the reality. Jackson, a wealthy lawyer and gifted general who admired Napoleon, was actually a land speculator and plantation owner possessing over 150 slaves, with no interest whatever in the Enlightenment ideals motivating Jefferson, Madison, Lafayette, Paine, or even John Adams. Hardly the voice of the people he professed to be, what mattered to Jackson was the change in tone and image his inauguration introduced. The public were to an extent misled. Jackson's assumption of the presidency was indeed a pivotal moment, not because it marked a decisive step toward "democratization" but rather, as Fenimore Cooper, Emerson, and others dreaded, an unfortunate rerouting of American "democracy" toward a semiliterate populism enshrining commonplace prejudices.

Where Jefferson, Madison, and Paine conceived democracy and the principles of 1776 to be rooted in enlightened, highly motivated debate, reasoned argument, persuasion on the basis of evidence, and judgment of facts, most new electors, it transpired, had little time for any of this and were content to cheer the triumph of ordinary notions and Jackson. In this respect, the election marked a real turning point, a fundamental departure from around 1830 vividly illustrated by a change in the papers. "In America, while the contest was for great principles," as Fenimore Cooper described the shift, "the press aided in elevating the common character, in improving the common mind, and in maintaining the common interests; but since the contest has ceased, and the struggle had become one purely of selfishness and personal interests, it is employed, as a whole, in fast undermining its own work, and in preparing the nation for some terrible reverses, if not in calling down upon it, a just judgment of God." Native Americans, large numbers of whom were subsequently dispossessed of their lands and forcibly removed west of the Mississippi under Jackson's later notorious "Indian removal" program, were the most conspicuous victims of this retreat from basic human rights, republicanism, and enlightened values. But an even worse outcome in the long run, held Cooper, was the growing identification of "democracy" with uninformed popular opinion, empty speeches, crass chauvinism, and simplistic clichés about individualism and self-reliance.[46]

Resurgent populism helps explain what has been called the "superficiality" of American reaction to the 1830 revolutions—initial loud cheering followed by uncomprehending indifference to basic issues dividing the different revolutionary political factions. The initial American reaction to news of the July Revolution was one of excitement, banquets, orations, and processions, staged in New York, Philadelphia, Boston, Baltimore, New Orleans, and Washington. In his message to Congress of 7 December 1830, acknowledging the wave of national enthusiasm, Jackson celebrated "an event so auspicious to the dearest interests of mankind," declaring the "kindred feelings of Americans for the French in this revolutionary hour."[47] Although conservatives, like Adams in his last years, had been supportive of the Greek national rising, a new French Revolution possibly veering toward republicanism proved considerably more divisive. Where the democratic press positively gushed with approval, readily broadcasting what the New York *Morning Courier* called the "brave, the great, the noble acts of Frenchmen, in their efforts to preserve the liberty of the press, the rights of man and of human nature,"[48] and Monroe cheered the "late glorious revolution," anti-Jeffersonians were noticeably cool, even disapproving in their reaction.[49] Besides, republicanism and democracy had by no means triumphed in France and, before long, an exasperated Lafayette broke with the advisors around Louis-Philippe. On 25 December 1830, he was dismissed from his functions as commander of the Paris National Guard.

The July Revolution's initial éclat triggered a spectacular chain reaction across Europe, with tricolor flags and other emblems of the great French Revolution everywhere in evidence. Hardly was the July Revolution accomplished than disturbances erupted, in August and September, in Brussels, Liège, Namur, and other Belgian cities, followed by Germany, Switzerland, and Italy. The excitement fed off the long pent-up fervor of the secret societies and their preoccupation with "rights" but also, especially in Belgium and the Swiss confederacy, deep attraction to federalism and drawing on the American model and Constitution. For by removing France as a plausible or meaningful revolutionary example, the disillusioning compromise concocted in Paris enhanced the wider international revolution's *Américanisme*, its presenting itself to the world as a transatlantic human rights–based movement conjoining the principles of 1776 and 1789, of which Lafayette was the living symbol and figurehead. Brussels, Berlin, and other capitals were soon swept by popular demonstrations consciously emulating the July Revolution, indiscriminately conflating its liberal and radical slogans. When revolutionary demonstrations erupted at Leipzig, in the kingdom of Saxony, on 12 September 1830, the crowds yelled: "Vive la liberté, vive Lafayette!"[50]

The first Belgian revolution, of 1787–94, initiated by the Belgian "Franklin," Van der Noot, had come to nothing, ending in the triumph of aristocracy. In 1814–15, the Vienna Congress merged Belgium with the Northern Netherlands under the new monarchy of King Willem I. Historians long represented the 1830 Belgian revolution as an expression of nascent national feeling rebelling against Dutch rule, and this image impressed itself on later perceptions. But like so much else in the historiography of nineteenth-century nation-building, the "national" account is more myth than reality. Although language friction was certainly a factor this was mainly because the uppermost elites (whether Walloon or Flemish) in Belgian society had become used to using French, especially under Napoleon, whereas the new monarch rigidly insisted on the Dutch language as the sole language of administration, law, education, and the military throughout his Low Countries kingdom.[51] Actually, national feeling in Belgium hardly existed and the real circumstances were complex. Memories of the Belgian anti-Josephine Revolution of 1789–94, Catholic resentment of Protestant rule, worker dissatisfaction in the newly industrializing towns, and democratic republican enthusiasm for the July Revolution such as expressed by Louis De Potter and other radical journalists in Brussels and Liège all contributed. At first, during the last week of August 1830, the riots, chiefly in Brussels and Liège, seemed mainly directed against Belgian dignitaries and functionaries of the Great Netherlands state together with factory owners, machinery in a number of factories being attacked and smashed. The royal court at The Hague, though not the initial target, made every conceivable strategic mistake in reacting, most notably in its brutal attempt, with an inadequate force, to restore order using Dutch troops, the "Quatre Journées" (23–27 September 1830) leaving five hundred dead in the streets of the Belgian capital.[52] This only strengthened Belgian "unionisme," as Belgians called the temporary tactical alliance of Catholics, liberals, and radical enlighteners against the regime.[53]

The Belgian Revolution, initiated by journalists, students, and a few committed republicans, may have been devoid of national feeling but it was undoubtedly carried through by a broad public. Nevertheless, the Belgian Revolution, like all the 1830 and 1848 revolutions, cannot be correctly described as a people's revolution or even a revolution driven by the people. The bloodshed persuaded most orators and the crowds they addressed to opt for full secession from a detested foreign-imposed regime. But while workers, laborers, and the unemployed of the Belgian cities played the primary role in terms of street action and the sporadic violence,[54] the popular contribution proved notably hesitant, confused, and divided and always remained secondary in terms of direction and objectives. Catholic antipathy to a Protestant administration and to northern Dutch elites mixed with worker dissatisfaction and disparate local tendencies in both Francophone and Dutch-speaking Belgium.[55] Eventually, a dominant conservative Catholic wing, aiming for monarchy and reaction under ecclesiastical supervision with solid mass support—fiercely derided by Börne[56]—faced an anticlerical radical democratic tendency invigorated by the newly proclaimed freedom of the press. Belgium's democratic republicans, led by De Potter, the heirs of Jean-François Vonck (1743–92), who had led the anti-aristocratic opposition to the conservative revolution that gripped Belgium in 1789–90, came to be accommodated rather than silenced. Unlike the Orangist faction urging a strengthened autonomy within a larger Great Netherlands state, the radicals proved too strong to be wholly marginalized. They wrung enough concessions from their opponents to have a lasting impact on the shape of the new Belgian constitution and subsequent evolution of Belgium's representative institutions.[57]

The provisional government in Brussels declared Belgian independence on 4 October 1830 and arranged national elections for a constitutional convention named "the Congress," after the Belgian Congress of 1789 and the United States Congress. Undaunted by the fierce Dutch bombardment of Antwerp of late October, the new Belgian Congress was elected and convened the following month, confirming Belgium's independence on 18 November. As with the French National Assembly of 1789, journalists, academics, and intellectuals were disproportionately prominent in its proceedings while businessmen, financiers, and industrialists were chiefly conspicuous by their absence. This meant that Catholicism and the views of ordinary Belgians were less dominant than they would have been had professionals and journalists been less conspicuous. The relatively strong showing of the republican minority did not enable them to avert the two-chamber legislature based on a severely restricted electorate that the "moderates" and lawyers sought. The new constitution (proclaimed 7 February 1831) reserved considerable influence for the projected new monarch, and extensive influence and privileges for the Church, including control over education. Even so, De Potter's strategy of *unionisme* enabled the radicals to implant into the new constitution strands of the 1789 French *Declaration of the Rights of Man* along with features of the American model that subsequently proved of great importance. Solid civil liberties were instituted alongside separation of powers and a loudly proclaimed if initially partly bogus separation of church and state. In later decades, the secularizing articles of the constitution enabled Belgian secularists to claw back some of the clergy's early political, cultural, and educational ascendancy. Indeed, the 1831 Belgian constitution came to be widely acclaimed and, for compromisers and "moderates" especially, replaced the 1812 Cádiz Constitution as the best approximation to an ideal system built on strong civil rights and freedoms.[58]

Faced with the intransigence of the Orangist monarchy and continued Dutch incursions, the Belgian Congress appealed to Britain, France, and Prussia to recognize Belgium's independence and legitimize the new monarchy, determine its borders, and help choose the king. Britain was ready to be "principal midwife" but, as in Greece, only on the basis of conservatism, monarchy, and aristocracy along with Belgium's usefulness for obstructing future French expansion. Although many Walloon Belgians favored closer ties with France, Louis-Philippe, bowing to British pressure, in February 1831 declined the Belgian throne for his son. The alternative candidate who emerged, agreed on in Europe's throne rooms, was Prince Leopold of Saxe-Coburg (1790–1865), a reactionary uncle of Queen Victoria who had fought Napoleon as a Russian general. Leopold had already declined the Greek throne but accepted this offer, which was then ratified by the Belgian Congress. The new monarch swore allegiance to Belgium's monarchical-aristocratic constitution in the church of Saint Jacques-sur-Coudenberg in Brussels on 21 July 1831. A year later, in August 1832, he married Louise d'Orléans, daughter of Louis-Philippe, cementing the constitutional monarchist alliance facing Belgium's Orangists, radicals, democrats, secularists, and socialists.[59]

But Belgian success was not repeated elsewhere. By late August 1830, the unrest had reached Aachen, where modern industrial techniques had recently been adopted and workers were angry, and from there Hamburg, the Rhineland, and other parts of Germany and Switzerland. Though not shapeless or aimless, the popular dimension of the German and Swiss revolutionary movement of 1830 was highly fluid and conspicuously lacking in direction. Most disturbances expressed local social discontents rather than long-term, fundamental agendas.[60] Sporadically, most obviously in Switzerland, the disturbances nevertheless did register some solid, permanent gains. At Zurich, where the *Neue Zürcher Zeitung*, founded in 1821 by Paul Usteri (1768–1831), led the progressive papers in demanding press freedom, and soon other cantons, the longstanding struggle between the "aristocrats" and "democrats" for control of the Swiss federation intensified from November with lively demonstrations there and at Freiburg, Aarau, Schaffhausen, Basel, and Lausanne. With the Swiss "aristocrats" (town patricians), whom Börne judged "worse and more dangerous than the kings," battling to roll back the encroaching tide of republicanism and democracy, the conflict proved protracted and bitter. A longstanding tradition of democratic republican political symbolism and thought in Switzerland helped shape the revolutionary impulse and enhance the Swiss struggle's international dimension. Finally, during 1831, the oligarchies of no less than ten cantons, including Zurich, Berne, and Luzern, had to give ground and conceded heavily revised constitutions.

Swiss press freedom, secured in 1830, actually proved a major gain for all Europe, filling Börne with hope that a free flow of opinion and news in and from Switzerland would breach the repressive walls of censorship in Germany too. In the end, though, Zurich's only lasting contribution to the German revolutions of 1830 was as a reception center for fugitive exiles. The German refugees proved another decisive gain for Switzerland, though, contributing, among much else, to the emergence by 1833–34 of several new universities and colleges in Zurich and Berne of an emphatically secular and international stamp, thereby markedly lessening traditional theological influence in education.[61] Even so, the Swiss Revolution of 1830–31 was inconclusive, encountering determined popular as well as patrician resistance and leaving a legacy of strife, aggravated especially by tensions between urban and rural interests, promising further strife in the future. In 1833, the canton of Schwyz split in two—a conservative "Inner Schwyz" and a democratic outer canton.[62] In Basel, opinion divided over whether the city should accept equality of status for all or safeguard its traditional disproportionate representation in the cantonal assembly.

In Germany, the people expressed their frustration and discontent; but here the revolutionary movement was far less coherent even than in Belgium and Switzerland, and quickly fragmented in every direction. On 7 September 1830, crowds occupied the center of Brunswick attacking and burning down the early eighteenth-century Residenzschloss of the unpopular Duke Karl, who, in 1827, had suspended the former Brunswick constitution. In Leipzig, there were tumultuous scenes and the new machines of the publishing house Brockhaus were smashed by Luddite workers. In Hamburg, the popular movement dissipated into anti-Semitic rioting and hounding Jews. But the prime feature everywhere was the revolution's undirected, seemingly aimless character.[63] Börne, on exchanging Germany for Paris, in September 1830, and then seeing revolutions erupt in his homeland, briefly wondered whether the

Germans were ready for revolution after all but soon decided otherwise. Bitter at the popular movement's prejudices, anarchic character, and virulent anti-Semitism, Börne, in his *Briefe aus Paris* (1830–31), expressed even greater scorn for the chaotic, disjointed war of "freedom" against "tyranny" in Germany than in France and Belgium.

In late 1830 and 1831, Börne met numerous German revolutionaries in Paris, milling in throngs around Lafayette, Constant, Quiroga, and other renowned Revolutionshäupter (revolutionary leaders), captivated by the mystique of "Revolution" and the aura surrounding such republican celebrities. Ultimately, these seemed perplexed as to what they were aiming for and how to secure a meaningful revolutionary outcome.[64] Where the 1830 German revolutionary upsurge assumed a more coherent character, it was, as in 1792–93 and 1798–1806, principally the work of longstanding reading societies, intellectuals, writers, and journalists. In this respect, the 1830 German revolutions, like those in France and Belgium, hardly conformed to Hannah Arendt's picture of a revolutionary scenario in which "professional revolutionists" watched and analyzed without being able to "do much to advance and direct it."[65] The reality was exactly the opposite. Only where more structured political activity enabled committees of constitutional monarchists and democratic republicans to coordinate sustained, targeted pressure in state capitals did they briefly succeeded in twisting the arms of the Confederation's monarchs and princes sufficiently to extract substantial, meaningful freedoms.

Grand Duke Leopold of Baden (reigned: 1830–52) granted freedom of the press, in 1831, together with other legislative reforms. In Hesse-Cassel, the rioting forced the Grand Duke to concede a constitution, in January 1831, judged by some among the most progressive yet adopted, which massively widened the suffrage and, on paper, eroded privilege. This 160-article text—very reluctantly accepted by the Grand Duke—was principally drafted by a Marburg professor, the enlightened Austrian jurist Franz Sylvester Jordan (1792–1861).[66] Yet the Hesse Revolution too was fatally undermined by "moderation": its single-chamber legislature not only accorded an extensive share of power to the prince but assigned only thirty-two of its fifty members for election by the duchy's independent male householders, reserving eighteen seats for nobles, clergy, and members of the grand ducal household. Purportedly a landmark constitution, it was drenched with derision by Börne. Instead of advancing freedom, it entrenched nobility and monarchy, proclaimed press freedom but kept firm limits on the press, and declared equality of religious cults while retaining strict disabilities on the Jews.[67] In any case, the old order was not sufficiently eradicated for anything durable to emerge. From 1832, Elector Wilhelm II slowly subverted the constitution step by step until, by late 1834, he had succeeded in wholly marginalizing the Landtag (state parliament). With the legislature emasculated, Jordan was placed under police surveillance and, in 1839, imprisoned.

In the new post-1814 Kingdom of Hanover, under the king of England, disturbances erupted over the winter of 1830–31. Republican students and professors seized the city of Göttingen, where the Hanover state university, then academically the most progressive in Europe, was located.[68] Although the monarchy eventually suppressed the rioting, using regular troops, initial concessions included a revised, if still extremely limited, constitution strongly underlining the primacy of monarchy, nobility, and religion (September 1833). But this was meant only as an expedient to end the agitation. In Hanover, as elsewhere, practically all the gains on paper proved either temporary or illusory. The state government waited several years before formally nullifying the constitution in 1837; but when it did so, it brushed aside all objections: seven Göttingen University professors courageous enough to protest formally were peremptorily dismissed from their chairs, three expelled from the principality.

In Italy, the insurrections commenced in August 1830, the Carbonari and other societies having diffused reports of the July Revolution sent by Italian exiles from Paris, Brussels, and London. They culminated between November 1830 and March 1831. On 4 February 1831, unrest gripped Bologna and soon large parts of the Papal States. In the wake of the risings, incipient republican regimes appeared in Parma, in Modena, and in the northern part of the Papal States (Bologna and Ferrara), lasting some months. As in Germany, the chief feature of the Italian revolutionary upheavals of 1830–31 was a sharp divide between the popular movement in the towns and countryside and the secret cells of students and journalists and republican reading societies at the universities, reinforced by a network of former Napoleonist officers.[69] As elsewhere, the effusive displays of public indignation and frustration were hampered by lack of unity and limited perspectives as to how to reorganize institutions and society. Austrian troops, urgently summoned by the papacy and princes and helped by the disunity among the insurgents, eventually succeeded in suppressing all the revolutions.

The Polish Revolution (1830–31)

The longest-lasting, most tragic, and violent of the 1830 uprisings erupted four months after the Paris insurrection, in Russian Poland, in November. In east-central Europe, as well as at Petersburg, scores of politically conspiring secret student, officer, and professional societies and organizations had proliferated by the 1820s. Clandestine student groups thrived especially at the universities of Warsaw, Vilnius, Cracow, and Lwow.[70] An added ingredient in the explosive mix of Polish national sentiment was the (Napoleonic, anti-czarist) martial legacy of the roving Polish legions Bonaparte had recruited for his Grande Armée that had served in Spain as well as the Grand Duchy of Warsaw until 1814. Many habitual plotters in the Polish secret societies of the 1820s, including Piotr Wysocki, the leading instigator of the November rising in Warsaw, stemmed from this post-Napoleonic anti-Russian conspiratorial tradition.

Polish exiles abroad created a network of uprooted, liberty-loving refugees, the most tenacious and resolute of all the international coteries of conspiring republicans activating the world revolutionary scene before and after 1830, prominent among them, Mickiewicz and Chopin in Paris. Polish networks reached right across Europe as far as North and South America, as well as Siberia. By the 1820s, Polish revolutionary subversion had become a formidable underground opposition culture rooted in 1791 when the first Polish constitution had been proclaimed. A distinctly "moderate" exercise in constitutional monarchism that failed to accord full religious toleration or emancipate the serfs, the 1791 constitution nevertheless represented the first breach in the old aristocratic-monarchical system and became a national rallying point, after being ruthlessly suppressed by Russian forces sent in by the Empress Catherine. The Polish reform movement's leaders at that time, most importantly Tadeusz Kościuszko (1746–1817), one of the foremost military heroes of the American War of Independence—and most adamant supporters of black emancipation—were driven into exile.

Americans had not forgotten Kościuszko, whose renown as a symbol of the American and Polish fights for freedom lingered in the New World and even as far as Australia. In a sermon given in 1795, the Boston preacher Jedidiah Morse berated Britain for forcing war on revolutionary France and wrecking freedom there, while aiding Prussia and Russia in their despotic scheme to conquer and subjugate the Poles: "the blood of Kościuszko cries out against us."[71] Kościuszko fought for America's independence, Morse reminded Bostonians, and was "well known to many of our officers." "Confirmed in the principles of liberty," he fought as a disciple of Washington. The unfortunate prey of their "unprincipled neighbours," in the "memorable and happy Revolution of 1791," the Poles "effected without bloodshed or even tumult among the people" a revolution based on "principles highly favourable to their rights and liberties." Despotism had robbed Poland of her liberty, independence, and prosperity and all loyal Americans had suffered with them in this great tragedy for freedom.[72]

Driven from Poland, Kościuszko had returned to France, where in his youth he had read the *Histoire philosophique* and other radical philosophical works and acquired his democratic republican ideals, ideals diverging more than a little from those of Washington and of most Poles, converging rather with those of Jefferson. Ally of Jefferson (and William Short), and of Lafayette, with whom he had served at Albany and further north, in New York State, during the 1778 campaign,[73] Kościuszko had always remained especially focused on Russia's mounting repression of Poland. In early 1794, disgusted by the Montagnard Terror, he left Paris for Italy conspiring with other exiled Polish leaders to revive the faltering Polish cause, making known to his fellow conspirators scattered across Italy, France, and Germany, and within Poland itself, that he refused to fight for the nobility and the privileged. Fired by the ideals of 1776 and 1789 and equality before the law, he would combat despotism only on behalf of the people including Poland's serfs: if he was to lead, these conditions had to be publicly adopted by Poland's revolutionary movement.[74]

Kościuszko transferred his joint American-French radical perspective to the revived Polish Revolution and began democratizing the movement even though he had to make extensive concessions to the landowning nobility to win their, and any wider, support. This reborn Polish Revolution proclaimed its principles in Kościuszko's Manifesto of Polaniec of 7 May 1794, a one-page declaration that did not yet promise the end of serfdom but did hold out the hope that full emancipation would follow.[75] Kościuszko's manifesto granted outright freedom only for serfs joining his volunteer army. Other serfs were promised more if still restricted personal freedom, reduction of servile dues, and limited proprietary rights over the land they cultivated as well as the right of appeal to the royal courts against noble landowner abuses and oppression. Under Kościuszko's leadership, the 1794 Polish rising, commencing in Cracow, stirred all Europe and the United States. Their heroic struggle continued for many weeks. Overwhelmed by Russian troops, what survived in Poland and internationally was the legacy of valiant resistance, a new Polish national mythology.

Where foreigners had previously nurtured a basically negative view of Poland, as a land of religious intolerance and unchallenged aristocratic and ecclesiastical primacy, Kościuszko and the Russian repression permanently transformed the picture. The Polish Partition of 1793 by the three monarchs of Russia, Austria, and Prussia, who cynically divided what remained of the Polish "kingdom," provided a display of royal arrogance and despotism that, with its disregard for rights of every kind, shocked opinion everywhere. The brutality of the suppression generated a considerably more sympathetic image of Poland that lasted for the remainder of the revolutionary age. In the eyes of Europe and America, Poland was now the martyred republic, seething with brave freedom-fighters ready to lay down their lives for liberty and justice. "Unfortunate, afflicted brethren in the bonds of freedom," exclaimed Morse, at Boston, in 1795, "we weep with you!—Thy wounds, Kościuszko, are thy glory—Thy blood will accelerate the growth of 'the Tree of Liberty' through Europe and America—Thy rich reward is their esteem and admiration. May it comfort thee in thy prison [in Petersburg]."[76]

Eventually released from his dungeon owing to his status as an American hero, Kościuszko returned to the United States and, in 1797–98, resided for some months in Philadelphia at the heart of the American political and diplomatic scene, again seeing much of Jefferson, Rush, and other prominent figures. At this point the friendship of Jefferson and Kościuszko deepened and gained in ideological resonance.[77] Despite the deep rift between "Anglicans" and "American Jacobins" dividing the American political arena, the Federalists too were willing to eulogize Kościuszko and the Polish Revolution. Washington "sorely lamented" Poland's unhappy fate, he assured one Polish leader, in June 1798, and "if my vows, during the arduous contest could have availed, you would now have been as happy in the enjoyment of these desirable blessings [national liberty and the Rights of Man] under your own Vine and Fig tree, as the people of these United States may be under theirs."[78]

Infused with the memory of 1794, the November 1830 rising, which swiftly seized control of Warsaw and much of central Poland, was led by the "Patriotic Society" founded in 1821 to bring together conspiring officers and gentry with the Warsaw radical intelligentsia. The Patriotic Society functioned as a kind of revolutionary headquarters for the Left intellectuals leading the republican-democratic wing of the insurrection. At least two hundred leading conspirators of the society, mostly sons of nobles, belonged to just one contributing clandestine group organized at the Warsaw Cadet Infantry School by Piotr Wysocki (1797–1875).[79] Of the official list of 486 members of the Warsaw Patriotic Society, the social background of around one-third is known. Like the French Revolution's democratic wing in 1789–93, they were a mix of journalists, teachers, professors, students, and physicians with officials and army officers also strongly represented. There was the usual striking absence of businessmen, industrialists, artisans, laborers, and the less educated generally.[80]

By 1830, Polish resistance to Russian autocracy had a long tradition but, equally, an unfortunate record of being dragged backward (especially by sections of the nobility). While democratic republican elements aspired to lead, expressing their views during the rebellion, most conspicuously in the *Gazeta*

Polska and *Nowa Polska*, daily papers that advocated republicanism, a democratic franchise, ending all remnants of serfdom, and equal rights for Jews, the vast majority of Polish and Lithuanian insurgents, swayed by traditional piety, had little inclination to change the familiar forms of religious authority, monarchy, and deference to aristocracy. Since 1800, there had been no real successor to Kościuszko. With some reluctance, General Jozef Chlopicki, who had figured among Kościuszko's aides in 1794, was chosen by the Warsaw insurgents to be the Polish "Cincinnatus, a new Washington." Chlopicki, however, did not believe the rising could succeed. Eventually, he tried to dissolve the Patriotic Society and to negotiate with the czar, who, however, refused to make any concession.[81] Thrust aside in January 1831, Chlopicki was replaced with a new provisional government drawn from the Patriotic Society. Bolder and more determined, the new leadership, on 25 January, proclaimed the dethroning of Czar Nicholas and independence of the Polish people, who were pronounced free to offer the crown to whomever they deemed worthy. With a core of well-trained troops, an impressively large Polish national army was quickly formed. However, despite considerable pressure to do so from the intellectuals, the new regime, partly composed of nobles, refrained from issuing a general emancipation of the serfs.

The provisional executive in Warsaw, which declared the independence of Poland-Lithuania and convened the legislature (Sejm), in which the nobles remained prominent, was headed by a democratic egalitarian and fiercely anti-aristocratic intellectual, Joachim Lelewel (1786–1861), a history professor and linguist. Lelewel's public lectures on Polish history at Vilnius had been banned by the Russian authorities in 1824. Following investigation into subversive student secret societies at Vilnius later that year, Lelewel was among those interrogated and tried, one of five professors and twenty students expelled from Lithuania at that juncture for promoting forbidden ideas. Prevented from proclaiming the end of serfdom, during 1830–31 Lelewel strove nevertheless to steer the Polish uprising and legislature in a republican direction. Like Kościuszko in 1794, he called on Poland's Jews to support the Revolution, promising freedom from disabilities and integration into Polish society in return for their allegiance.

While part of the Patriotic Society was radical and democratic, this faction proved unable to surmount the split between radicals and "moderates" or dispense with the need to form a broader coalition with nobles and Catholics thereby preventing the emergence of any program of substantial reform.[82] Large numbers of Poles of all sorts nevertheless rallied to the flag. Bitter fighting with terrible and bloody battles followed. Only after a series of massive encounters that aroused admiration and much enthusiastic sympathy for

Poland among newspaper and journal readers all across Europe and America, after eleven months of struggle, in October 1831, were the vestiges of the Polish-Lithuanian rising finally crushed, marking the end of the 1830–31 revolutionary process throughout Europe.

By this time, Polish committees in exile had sprung up all over France, Britain, Belgium, and Germany to rally support and raise money for the rebels. In Paris arose both the Comité Franco-Polonais, chaired by Lafayette, and, remarkably, an American Polish committee chaired by Howe that included Fenimore Cooper and the painter and inventor Samuel F. B. Morse, a son of Pastor Jedidiah Morse, who, unlike his father, was a fierce anti-Federalist and stalwart champion of democratizing revolutionary values. This new international activist network set to work defying the efforts of German princes and the new French monarchy to curb the remitting of aid for Poland from Germany, France, and Belgium and public support for revolutions generally. As the Polish rebellion disintegrated, Lelewel escaped, crossing Germany in disguise, reaching France, where over 200 Polish rebels had already sought refuge and, by the late 1830s, over 1,000 Polish émigrés resided.[83] Pressured by the czar and Prussia, the French legislature, in April 1832, passed an "Alien Bill" authorizing immediate expulsion of hard-core political fugitives who, having left to fight in Switzerland, Germany, and Poland, had afterward returned to France. Despite the unfriendly anti-republican and anti-revolutionary atmosphere permeating Louis-Philippe's France (causing deep dismay and a high suicide rate among the Polish émigrés), Lelewel created a short-lived shadow Polish government-in-exile, the Komitet Narodowy Polski (Polish National Committee), staffed partly with refugee former members of the suppressed Warsaw Sejm.[84]

Colluding with Lafayette, Fenimore Cooper, and other enthusiasts for the Polish, Greek, and other revolutions, most notably Howe, Lelewel remained in France, intermittently forced into hiding, until 1833 when he was definitively expelled. Following his efforts in Greece and Paris, Howe later returned to America to become the most renowned of nineteenth-century champions of the movement to help the blind and disabled lead dignified lives. Declining invitations to move to Chile, or establish a Polish community in Missouri, Lelewel moved to Brussels where he spent the remainder of his life among the Polish, German, and Italian political fugitives editing journals and promoting republican and democratic causes. By the mid-1830s, Brussels had further consolidated its status as the principal focus of radical activism for all Europe. Among other organizations based there, the Demokratische Gesellschaft zur Einigung und Verbrüderung aller Völker (Democratic Society for the Union and Brotherhood of all Peoples) was founded in 1847 by Lelewel (along with Marx and Engels), among others.

Toasting the "Confederated Republican Europe of the Future!"

Suppression of the Polish November Rising marked the end of the 1830–31 revolutionary wave. But suppression alone was far from sufficient to reassure champions of the old order in Europe or the New World. In January 1831, answering a letter from Monroe, John Quincy Adams, who had long advocated American neutralism and scorned all moralistic and ideological republican diplomacy, contemplated the "present state of Europe" and especially the "influence it will exercise over this country [the United States]." The inevitable consequence of the revolutionary upsurge of 1830 would be to "strengthen the principle of democracy over all of Europe and America," which in turn would "proportionably diminish the securities of property." The old elites, he believed, were in deep trouble. The 1830 revolutions challenged America's social system and politics just as much as they challenged Europe's monarchical-aristocratic-ecclesiastical system. "Aristocracy" of property was, for the entire American revolutionary legacy he and his father represented, the cornerstone of a gentry republicanism backed by religion, tradition, and the hereditary principle. Although in "France, the alliance between political reform and religious infidelity is closer than in England," British radical agitation ultimately threatened American "aristocracy" of wealth even more. For in England, "abolition of tithes must overthrow the established Church and dissolve the connection between Church and state, and shake the pillars of the Christian religion," strengthening infidelity. Of course, it would only "shake the pillars": "if the gates of hell shall not prevail against [Christianity], neither will the revolutions of empires nor the convulsions of the people." However, secularism and anticlericalism were gaining ground and the demise of English "mixed government" must hugely menace America's East Coast oligarchy.[85]

Throughout his political career John Quincy had opposed Dutch, French, and American democratic republican movements. If the principle of aristocracy or British "mixed government" could not survive in logic or "popular sentiment" except "as forming part of one system with a hereditary peerage" and the British Crown, American "aristocracy" was equally dependent on entrenched structures of institutions and religion. "The fall of the Church in

England will exclude the bishops from the House of Peers, and the hereditary rights of the temporal peerage will not much longer withstand the consuming blaze of public opinion." Monarchy, aristocracy, and established churches, the core of the hereditary principle, "are equally obnoxious to democracy" and hence were all becoming weaker.[86] "Perhaps the only part of the doctrine of democracy that will find no favor" in the United States, he suggested, was Anglo-French abolitionism. Yet Anglo-French abolitionism too constituted a substantial threat for America viewed as an aristocratic republic. "The abolition of slavery will pass like a pestilence over all the British colonies in the West Indies," he predicted, and "may prove an earthquake upon this continent." Certainly, there was a hopeful side to this from a conservative standpoint: the "danger of abolition when brought home to the Southern states, may teach them the value of the Union—the only thing that can maintain their system of slavery." But even then, the "inevitable predominance" of democracy "impending over Europe will not end without producing bitter fruits in our own country."[87] The British reformers' victory, in 1832, did indeed soon produce legislation, a series of mid-1830s emancipation decrees, freeing the slaves of Jamaica, Barbados, Trinidad, and the other British islands.[88] The nervousness of the Southern states increased apace.

To the likes of Lafayette, Lelewel, Börne, Heine, De Potter, and Mazzini, it was obvious that the 1830 risings had accomplished relatively little of a lasting character and would continue to flounder and fragment uselessly unless the international revolutionary impulse achieved a more principled, structured, and disciplined form. In Germany, efforts to unify the revolutionary impulse following the 1830 revolutions culminated in the Hambacher Fest (Hambach Festival), the high point of pre-1848 German democratic republicanism, convened at a castle near Neustadt, in the Rhenish Palatinate, in May 1832.[89]

The Hambacher Fest was without doubt an extraordinary milestone in republican and democratic history. It was organized by a group of Rhineland journalists who, in February 1832, had founded a freedom of the press society, the Presse- und Vaterlandsverein (Press and Fatherland Society), an association that grew rapidly, acquiring a network of 116 branches with 5,000 members chiefly in southwestern Germany. Striving to mobilize the power of public opinion against that of the princes, for the "rebirth of Germany" and her "democratic reorganization," the association briefly became a vigorous movement.[90] Banned by the Bavarian authorities, the dissident journalists' organization replied by summoning a mass gathering using their network of societies to rally support over a large area. Their national freedom festival, from 27 May to 1 June, was staged on an unprecedented scale, with reportedly some 25,000 supporters attending, mostly workmen and students.[91] Polish exiles too figured prominently in the procession from Neustadt marketplace to the castle ruins and in the subsequent festivities. Börne figured among the revolutionary celebrities participating and was enthusiastically cheered by crowds sporting the odd Phrygian liberty cap and given to the occasional anti-Catholic outburst (it was a predominantly Protestant district).[92]

The principal organizers of the Hambacher Fest were Philipp Siebenpfeiffer (1789–1845), a well-known journalist, and Johann Georg August Wirth (1798–1848), a former leader of the Erlangen University student society and editor of the *Deutsche Tribune*, the main organ of the Presse- und Vaterlandsverein, appearing in Munich from July 1831, and then Homburg, but suppressed by the Bavarian authorities since March 1832. It was this paper which, in April, played the chief role in clandestinely inviting the societies and organizations to attend the Hambach freedom festival. Wirth publicly denounced Germany's princes as "traitors" to the people and designated press freedom the people's shield against arrogant, rapacious rulers, the eventual path to victory over tyranny. The gathering proclaimed democratic values, human rights, and a future united Germany, adopting as its symbol a tricolor in black, red, and gold, introducing into subversive German culture the colors later adopted by the Weimar Republic (and the present-day German flag).

The peroration Wirth delivered at the Hambacher Fest demonstrates that the essential goal was not in fact German nationhood, unification, and certainly not "moderation" or "liberalism"—at least not at that stage (Wirth drifted toward both "moderation" and a more nationalistic stance from around 1840). In 1832, Wirth demanded destruction of princely authority on the basis of "Freiheit, Aufklärung, Rationalität und Volkshoheit" (Freedom, Enlightenment, Rationality, and Sovereignty of the People).[93] He sought the overthrow of Germany's kings and princes not as a nationalist but to establish German democracy and republicanism together with fraternity of peoples, including active fraternal support for Polish, Italian, Hungarian, and Spanish liberty.[94] Stressing the Revolution's international character, he summoned the German people to rise against the Holy Alliance of Austria, Prussia, and Russia and their ally, Louis-Philippe's France, and fight for "Spain, Italy, Hungary and Poland" as well as Germany. The July Revolution, announced Wirth, had been shamefully captured by "liberal" vested interests, especially bankers, using Louis-Philippe to protect and extend their wealth and property at the expense of democracy and the people's happiness. France had embraced a monarchical compromise utterly disillusioning for all sincere Republikaner. No significant help for the German or the international Revolution could henceforth be expected from France. With France discredited,

Europe's revolutionaries should now look to themselves. Only the German people themselves could topple the repressive despotism Austria, Prussia, and Bavaria had imposed, and must do so as part of the wider revolutionary movement. Wirth ended his speech urging the crowds to give three rousing cheers for the peaceful, brotherly "conföderirte republikanische Europa" of the future![95]

In part a folk festival, accompanied by music and jollification, and in taverns over large beer mugs, there was doubtless less commitment to radical principles among the crowds than the intellectual leadership liked to assume.[96] The Bavarian court nevertheless sent in half the Bavarian army, 8,500 troops, to occupy the Hambach locality; they and the Austrian and Prussian authorities subsequently pursued everyone connected with organizing this seditious Fest.[97] Börne hurried back to Paris where he died in February 1837. Siebenpfeiffer, captured and imprisoned in June 1832, escaped, helped by friends, and spent the remainder of his life in Swiss exile. Wirth was caught in hiding and tried at Landau. By "republic," he declared, in a defiant eight-hour speech before the judges, he meant "the empire of reason, justice, humanity, freedom and happiness."[98] Condemned to a long spell of imprisonment, he escaped in 1836, first to France and then Switzerland, spending the rest of his life in exile apart from a brief return to Germany on the outbreak of the 1848 Revolution. Among other resonances, Hambach served as the pretext for conclusive suppression of the half freedom of expression, conceded in 1831, in Grand-Ducal Hesse.[99]

Protest and agitation against the post-Hambach repression and abrogation of the Hessian constitution continued sporadically, instigated especially by exiles abroad and students and professors at Heidelberg, Giessen, Göttingen, and Marburg. In 1834, the young dramatist Büchner created a considerable stir in Hesse with his *Hessischer Landbote* (Hessian Courier). This defiant clandestine pamphlet powerfully denounced Germany's princes and aristocrats, including the Grand Duke, while simultaneously echoing Börne's, Ruge's, and Heine's incisive literary critique of popular deference and acquiescence, deriding the "moderation" of middle-class German "liberalism" and feeble response to the defeat of the 1830 revolutionary surge. A network of protest and conspiracy developed, until, in April 1835, the police succeeded in breaking up the main network linking Marburg, Giessen, and Frankfurt. Büchner and other leaders escaped to Switzerland; several were imprisoned.[100]

On the surface, the defeat of the 1830 revolutions was an outright victory (outside Belgium, Baden, and Switzerland at least) for reactionaries, churchmen, and supporters of aristocracy. Veteran Freiheitsfreunde (Friends of Liberty), like Wirth, Börne, and Heine, frequently plunged in dejection, were left striving to preserve their revolutionary zeal teaching the "Marseillaise" to children, as Heine ironically described their plight, while rotting "at home, in prison, or in a garret in exile," like that in which Georg Forster, leader of the 1792–93 Rhenish revolution, had expired in Paris in 1794.[101] In southwest Germany, memories of 1830 and the Hambacher Fest helped keep alive a vigorous commitment to basic rights, democracy, and Revolution, especially in student networks and reading societies.[102] But, more generally, 1830 dejected radicals and had a powerfully disorienting effect on "moderates" who across Europe felt ever more torn between the need for constitutional, religious, and educational reform and fear of social unrest and radicalism.[103]

The revolutionary wave, meanwhile, had a deeply sobering effect on conservative opinion in Europe and in the United States. Below the surface, as John Quincy surmised, the princely-aristocratic system had been shaken to its foundations.[104] An obvious result of the failed 1830 revolutions, disconcerting for all conservatives, was the further expansion and spread of the networks of revolutionary émigrés in France, Belgium, Switzerland, England, and the United States. By 1848, the number of Polish exiles in France had risen to around 5,000 while at least 400 Polish exiles settled in America between 1834 and 1842.[105] In Europe, secret student, intellectual, and paramilitary groups positively burgeoned along with the literary and romantic cult of revolutionary liberty, republicanism, and democracy. Even more than in the 1820s, secret formations became the principal agent for propagating the democratic revolutionary consciousness. At the level of ideas and principle, the 1830 uprisings unquestionably further weakened the "Restoration" and the existing order. In France, it was undeniable that the fighters at the barricades had been cheated of what they fought for, but equally this was so obvious that they were unlikely to be so easily fobbed off again. Prominent republican-minded figures like Lafayette and the Napoleonic general Jean-Maximilien Lamarque (1770–1832) who had assisted with sending armed volunteers to Belgium and who both welcomed in the "liberal" regime, turned implacably against Louis-Philippe's "July monarchy" almost from the outset.

Loosely tied to the European international revolutionary movement during the 1820s and in 1830–32 was the continuing pro-democracy agitation in Britain. Despite the obstinate prevalence of a conservative mind-set in England, after 1815, growing radical opposition to the existing system drew in recruits from varied social backgrounds, and for many reasons. The British ruling classes, more obviously than in the past, maintained their power at home, observed Emerson, with a "standing army of police."[106] As always, the backbone of the agitation driven by an alliance of radicals and moderate "Whigs" were the journalists and intellectuals, leaders of suffrage reform societies, the most radical trumpeting the "American example," calling for democracy, and demanding a root and branch reform of what Bentham sarcastically called "our own matchless Constitution—matchless in rotten boroughs and sinecures!" Bentham's radicalism and internationalism, much more marked after 1815 than earlier (though during 1791–92 he had hoped for much from Brissot), were at their most outspoken and public during his last years, down to 1832. Originally, at the start of his career, highly critical of American republicanism and eager to "cut the throat" of pro-American, proto-democratic ideas in England, after 1815 he had gravitated to the opposite extreme and now regularly exalted democracy and the American Revolution.[107] At no time was America more of a guiding light for democratic critics of the English status quo than in the years 1830–32.[108]

The 1832 Reform Act was a partial triumph for British radicalism but in some ways yet another setback. The movement's narrow, parochial character and anti-intellectualism rendered it excessively vulnerable to "liberal" and "moderate" strategies aimed at restricting the suffrage to the propertied upper-middle classes. Hence the relative ease with which "moderates" captured the process and damped down the continuing agitation after 1832. "The last Reform-bill," noted Emerson, "took away political power from a mound, a ruin and a stone wall, whilst Birmingham and Manchester, whose mills paid for the wars of Europe, had no representative."[109] The Act gave representation to Birmingham and Manchester. But principally it was an object lesson showing how far there was still to go by proving that democratization could be successfully arrested halfway. The Great Reform Act expanded the British suffrage only slightly (from 14 to 18 percent of adult males), leaving the country heavily dominated by the hereditary elite allied to a select stratum of industrialists, financiers, and professionals.[110] The suffrage widened marginally, yet opposition agitation was effectively damped down. Only after subsiding for six years, from 1838, did the reform movement, now mainly in northern England as a more specifically working-class movement than in the past, regain some momentum with mass meetings and demonstrations renewing the call for universal suffrage and the secret ballot.

Yet, if not a few Englishmen felt the nation's majority had been "betrayed" and supported the drive for universal suffrage from the late 1830s, only a minute fringe shared the broad, internationalist approach of a Bentham or George Julian Harney (1817–97), a journalist credited with a more detailed knowledge of Europe's revolutionary underground than any other British republican. Otherwise, the revived English ferment remained generally antagonistic to the wider revolutionary movement, circumscribed by narrow aims, insularity, and short-termism. None of this, though, prevented Chartist meetings demanding parliamentary reform from sometimes growing extremely disorderly. During several weeks as a nineteen-year-old seaman in Liverpool, in August 1839, Melville was so shocked and dismayed by this that, despite his sympathy for the poor and downtrodden, it prejudiced him against radicalism and mass movements for the rest of his life.[111]

Apparent conservative triumph in 1830–31 failed, in consequence, to restore anything resembling political stability in Europe. In France, the new regime, despite temporarily markedly easing press restrictions, doubling the suffrage, adopting the tricolor of the Revolution, and downgrading the status of the old nobility and clergy, lost popular support at a stunning rate.[112] Spreading awareness of political realities rapidly discredited and undermined the regime, as was hardly surprising given that under Louis-Philippe approximately ten times more people in Paris could read newspapers than were eligible to vote.[113] Admittedly, Louis-Philippe's regime remained relatively generous to the thousands of Polish, German, and Italian refugees who crowded into France between 1831 and the late 1830s, indeed assisted efforts to provide shelter and financial aid; but the regime assisted the influx of political refugees proclaiming Catholic charity toward fellow Catholics in distress rather than any kind of political commitment.[114] To an impressive state funeral laid on, in May 1832, for a conservative banker and pillar of the monarchy who died in the recent cholera epidemic, the Paris democratic republicans replied, on 5 June 1832, by staging an impressive counterprocession to mark the funeral of the republican-minded General Lamarque, who had expired in the same epidemic. Thousands gathered, workers and students supplemented by an impressive array of Polish, German, Spanish, and Italian exiles waving their respective national revolutionary *tricoleurs* (Lamarque had spoken out strongly in 1830–31 on behalf of the Italian and Polish revolutions).

Lafayette presided. In his public address, he proclaimed the revolutionary triumph of human rights and freedom of expression in 1789 and 1830. The crowds cheered but then, despite his appeals for calm, became frenzied, getting out of hand. Shots rang out, the crowds dispersed, and what afterward became known as the "June rebellion" erupted, street fighting witnessed from close quarters by Victor Hugo, then still in his conservative mode who absentmindedly wandered into the cross fire. By the evening of 5 June, a force of 4,000 insurgents had occupied the Bastille area and neighboring parts of central and eastern Paris. The recently purged National Guard forced the insurgents back to their bastion, the cloister of Saint-Méry. In the ensuing battle around 800 people were killed. With the firm backing of Thiers, some

La Liberté guidant le peuple by Eugène Delacroix (1830). Photo credit: © Musée du Louvre, Dist. RMN-Grand Palais / Philippe Fuzeau / Art Resource, NY.

1,500 insurgents were afterward arrested including several organizers of the 5 June *journée* who were subsequently tried and imprisoned.[115] Altogether 82 prisoners were condemned to deportation or imprisonment. Available statistics taken from the archives, though incomplete, clearly show that most of the revolutionary mass were not working men but small traders, shopkeepers, master artisans, students, and teachers.[116]

The press laws began to be tightened again. For caricaturing the king as Gargantua consuming the wealth of the nation, the republican opposition artist Honoré Daumier (1808–91) was imprisoned for six months from the late summer of 1832 until February 1833. Inevitably, the policy of repression bred opposition especially since economic circumstances were harsh, which in turn provoked further repression. Curbing the press and forbidding public meetings rapidly further radicalized the democratic republican opposition in France by giving rise to a batch of clandestine militant new secret societies, first and foremost the paramilitary Société des Droits de l'Homme (Society of the Rights of Man), founded by students early in 1832, with several cells or "sections" plotting revolutionary action, the insurrectionary Société des Saisons, and the Amis du Peuple, a society devoted to the memory of Marat and the leveling ideology of the Montagne.[117] In 1833, while urging the legislature to take stronger action against these clandestine republican clubs, Guizot estimated the membership of the Droits de l'Homme to have reached around three thousand.[118]

Having secured power through a revolutionary uprising and initially paraded the Revolution's emblems and rhetoric of liberty, Louis-Philippe and his ministers ever more unequivocally repudiated free expression, popular sovereignty, and the Revolution. At one point, early in the reign, Guizot ventured to rebuke the king for joining in the singing of the "Marseillaise." "Do not concern yourself, Minister," replied Louis-Philippe, "I stopped saying the words long ago!"[119] Having purchased Delacroix's painting *La Liberté guidant le Peuple* when first publicly displayed, in May 1831, originally intending it to remain on view in the throne room of the Palais du Luxembourg to commemorate how the new dynasty had gained the throne and power, king

"Enfoncé Lafayette! [Lafayette crushed!]" (1834), political cartoon by Honoré Daumier (1808–79). King Louis-Philippe hypocritically pretends to weep at the funeral of Lafayette with a disconsolate populace in the background. Photo credit: Special Collections & College Archives, Skillman Library, Lafayette College.

and ministers, disconcerted by its unmistakably republican message, completed their thoroughgoing repudiation of the concept of liberty being conquered by the people by removing their country's most sensational modern picture (today displayed in the Louvre) from view. It was stored unseen in a Louvre basement until, in 1832, it was returned to the artist.

Thiers, now again minister of the interior, and (ironically) responsible for enforcing new press restrictions as well as a system licensing street sellers of newspapers to restrict sales of republican material, on 10 April 1834, after concentrating 40,000 troops in Paris, unveiled his law suppressing all opposition political associations stipulating harsh penalties for illegal convening in groups. Around 150 leading activists of the Société des Droits de l'Homme were arrested and its paper was outlawed. Altogether, some 2,000 arrests for conspiracy against "state security" occurred in Paris and Lyon in the spring of 1834. In response, from April 1834, further disturbances swept the country commencing with a violent rising of discontented Lyon silk workers largely instigated by the Droits de l'Homme, followed by unrest in Paris, Grenoble, and Saint-Étienne. When Lafayette died in May 1834, the government imposed special crowd restrictions to minimize the scale of the event. It took until early 1835 before the regime regained a sufficiently firm grip to enforce the press restrictions (further tightened by additional measures in September 1835) and stop publication of political cartoons like those with which the republican artist Daumier and another key opposition journalist and caricaturist, Charles Philippon (1800–1861), persisted in attempting to flagellate the regime.[120] During the mid- and late 1830s, opposition largely disappeared from the streets and from the printed page, although the police repression failed to prevent a spectacular assassination attempt against the king, at a parade, on 28 July 1835, planned by a Corsican Napoleonist, misfit, and anarchist, Giuseppe Fieschi, using a specially designed volley gun comprising twenty-five barrels primed to fire simultaneously (which killed nineteen members of the royal entourage but missed the king).

CHAPTER 20

The Revolutions of 1848: Democratic Republicanism versus Socialism

Fractures within the Revolution

Contrasting with the American public's response to the 1830 revolutions, which had been predominantly enthusiastic, the ambiguity and divided character of America's response to the massive new revolutionary wave that swept Europe in 1848–49 proved a turning point. In and after 1848, mainstream American opinion, on both sides of Congress, increasingly detached itself from the radical current and repudiated the international democratic republican tendency.

Already early on, in April 1848, an incipient rift permeated American reaction to the 1848 revolutions. Americans championing abolition, democratization, black emancipation, secularism, and women's rights, and sympathetic to the problems of recent immigrants,[1] proved broadly enthusiastic and supportive, but by the late spring these trends were losing ground. Women's rights, only weakly backed in early nineteenth-century America, far less so than abolitionism, gained a temporary boost from the initial fervor of 1848 but soon lost momentum. Even so, where the British press, except for a few Chartist papers, waxed uniformly hostile and scornful, the American press was more obviously divided, and in a quandary, the growing hostility to the revolutionary movements being driven in particular by the rise of socialism.

The great revolutionary wave of 1848 began not in France but Switzerland and neighboring parts of Germany, erupting in late 1847 in the Swiss cantons and the Grand Duchy of Baden, before convulsing all Europe. Conflict between Swiss patrician oligarchies and *démocrates* had been a notable feature of European political consciousness since the Genevan revolution against the local patrician oligarchy in 1782. Nearly all the twenty-five sovereign Swiss cantons were deeply divided over religion, pitting Protestant against Catholic, and oligarchy—still strongly entrenched in most cantons—against democrats. The steady growth of Switzerland's population since 1800 by around 40 percent to 2.4 million inhabitants, in 1847, and diversification of the economy had narrowed the basis of patrician rule and more closely identified it than in the past with commercial, industrial, and banking interests. The introduction of new industrial machinery, while causing less dislocation and deprivation than elsewhere, had added enough extra tension to render the whole system unstable. Since 1830, more and more concessions to democracy, immigrants, and new groups had to be made. Responding to these changes, and especially the secularizing tendency in the newspapers, universities, colleges, and schools, which infuriated traditionalists and greatly antagonized both the Catholic and Protestant clergy who saw their influence dwindling, seven conservative Catholic cantons (Lucerne, Fribourg, Valais, Uri, Schwyz, Unterwalden, and Zug), incited by a hard-line conservative coalition backed by the Austrian chancellor, Metternich, attempted to oust the "democrats" and secularists where they predominated by a coup and secede.

The democrats, now prevalent in the major cities, had simply grown too preponderant for Switzerland's religious and political patrician and clerical old guard. Sharp divisions destabilized Berne, Zurich, Basel, and Geneva. A brief civil war broke out in November 1847 that ended with the capitulation of Lucerne (24 November) and surrender of the confederate cantons (the Sonderbund) to the democratic republican bloc. Like the early achievements of the new European revolutionary upsurge elsewhere, the 1847 Swiss revolution met with undivided approval and applause in the United States. After being threatened by Austria and the great powers in December 1847, and needing to conciliate cantonal sovereignty with democracy within a sturdier federal framework, delegates of the Swiss cantons drafted a new national constitution, eventually finalized on 12 September 1848.

The Swiss revolution of 1847–48 was the European historical development that most closely shadowed the American Revolution and Constitution. At this point, the Swiss adopted both federalism and bicameralism, leaving only a limited sovereignty to the cantons insofar as this did not impinge on the newly defined powers of the federal authority.[2] Separation of powers was proclaimed, resulting in a separate federal court of justice to direct the judiciary and a federal council, under a revolving presidency, to serve as the executive. With the precedent of the American Congress in mind,[3] a two-chamber Swiss legislature was agreed on, featuring a lower house, or Nationalrat, with 111 deputies each representing 20,000 inhabitants, and a small (at first indirectly) elected senate or upper house. Federal elections to choose deputies for the lower house were based on universal male suffrage, with every male citizen over twenty enjoying the right to vote. In this way, the Swiss revolution of 1848 gave crucial new vitality to the still widespread European perception that the United States had initiated the essential spirit and forms of the modern age and remained the chief model and pointer to the world's democratic and egalitarian future.

The swift triumph of the Swiss democrats immediately sent unsettling ripples into France, Italy, and Germany. At a "democratic" banquet in Lille, on 7 November 1847, one of the most active and eloquent republican opposition leaders, Alexandre August Ledru-Rollin (1807–74), loudly denounced "aristocrats" and "bad priests" everywhere, toasting the Swiss and Italian "radicals" while vigorously extolling the great French Revolution and the "Rights of Man," "proclaimed in principle by two glorious revolutions [i.e., 1789 and 1830] but artfully evaded in their application." Renegades and miscreants had insidiously wrested the great Revolution and its achievements from the people so that these "today are nothing but a glorious and bitter memory."[4] At Dijon, a fortnight later, he repeated this rhetoric exalting popular sovereignty and the designation "radical" and declaring a war of "liberty" against "tyranny," a fight to the death between the "oppressed" and the "oppressor" with a view to finally securing the triumph of liberty, freedom of expression, *le suffrage universel*, and democracy.[5]

Southern Italy became the second major revolutionary scenario of 1848. On 12 January, the people of Palermo and Messina rose in rebellion against their tyrant, King Ferdinand II of Naples and Sicily, who had come to the throne in 1830, the same year as Louis-Philippe, and had been resorting since 1837 to harsh repression and police surveillance to thwart the growing demand for a constitution. The rising was timed by its instigators to coincide with Ferdinand's birthday and was incited for several days beforehand by means of clandestine posters and handbills. Royal forces were mobilized but rapidly defeated all across Sicily, and a provisional representative republic destined to last sixteen months established. It was not until May 1849 that Ferdinand, refusing all concessions and systematically bombarding his subjects into submission, finally suppressed the remnants of the Sicilian revolution.

Margaret Fuller, the most perceptive American observer of the Italian revolutionary scene in 1848–49, had already arrived there, in March 1847, and discovered much about the Italians and their literature. Early on, she felt something massive was brewing and that Americans generally were far too little conscious of, and involved in, the escalating struggle between liberty and despotism, democracy and Counter-Enlightenment. She scorned the "shallow, thoughtless, worthless" American travelers, often businessmen she encountered in Europe who seemed to her to look only to their own concerns and tastes; she especially mocked the "conceited American, instinctively bristling and proud of—he knows not what. He does not see, not he, that the history of humanity for many centuries is likely to have produced results it requires some training, some devotion, to appreciate and profit by."[6] But besides the shallow, unseeing observer there was also the "thinking American" conscious of the cultural richness of the Old World and intuitively grasping the significance of the American Revolution in its Italian and broader context, appreciating that America's destiny was to be the "advance-guard of humanity, the herald of all progress" and how often, sadly, America had "betrayed this high commission."[7] "Thinking Americans," writers, and artists, Fuller felt, should rouse themselves and strive harder on an individual level to assist Italy's revolutionary upsurge, the struggle for democracy and republicanism, as should the United States government on a national level. "Ah! America, with all thy rich boons, thou has a heavy account to render for the talent given; see in every way that thou be not found wanting."[8] She did not believe the United States was repaying its debt to Europe or adequately esteemed the energy and skills of the untold thousands of immigrants she had received from the Old World.

From Sicily, the revolutionary turmoil spread northward. On 18 March, starting with a street brawl between Austrian soldiers and local civilians, a furious five-day battle erupted in Milan that ended with the (temporary) total expulsion of the Austrians from the Milanese and all northeastern Italy. In February began the agitation in Rome that eventually developed into one of the most prolonged and hardest-fought revolutionary episodes in Europe, leading to a full-scale popular revolt in November 1848 and the flight of the pope. On 22 March 1848, the city of Venice proclaimed the—in the event brief—rebirth of the "Venetian Republic" and established a provisional government. One of its first major public manifestations brought huge crowds to congregate before the American consulate shouting, "Long live the United States! Long live our sister republic!" Daniele Manin (1804–57), chief organizer of the local revolutionary movement, released from prison (to which he had been sentenced for giving expression to popular discontent with Austrian rule) and made president of the new Venetian Republic, sent an official letter to the United States government. While the "ocean divides us," he claimed that Venice and America were nevertheless now united by special bonds of sympathy and devotion to republican freedom: "liberty, like the electric current traversing the seas, will bring us your examples, and maintain the communion of thought and feeling, which is far more precious than that of interest. We have much to learn from you; and, though your elders in civilization, we blush not to acknowledge it."[9]

In France, too, the mood grew heated owing to the stirring news from Switzerland and Italy. By 1847, the French democratic republican opposition had focused its rhetoric and publicity efforts on a remarkable series of political banquets (designed to circumvent the laws against political gatherings). The "banquet" campaign regularly invoking the early "banquets" of 1829 at Grenoble and Lyon when Lafayette had first exploited this method of stoking up opposition[10] now roused France's major cities and electrified Paris, prominently featuring such leading opposition orators as Ledru-Rollin, Alphonse de Lamartine (1790–1869), and the socialist Louis Blanc (1811–82). Lamartine, among the most eloquent speakers at these banquets, predicting the immanence of revolution and overthrow of the July monarchy, was a poet, *littérateur*, and friend of Heine, and a former royalist and champion of the Bourbon Restoration, who since 1833 had been a deputy in the legislature. Only since 1842–43 had he become a convert to Left democratic republicanism. But he now used his conspicuous gifts to champion the classic radical stance: democracy and universal male suffrage with general emancipation (like Ledru-Rollin urging abolition of slavery), pacifism between democratic peoples, secularism, anticolonialism, and admiration of the great Revolution's "heroic" democratic republicans—headed by Condorcet and Brissot.

While there were significant differences between Lamartine, Ledru-Rollin, and Blanc, there was sufficient consensus to enable them temporarily to unify the now competing movements of democratic republicanism and socialism. Blanc aimed to end social distress by creating workshops, workers' and producers' associations organized by the state, doing so via a democratic revolution and in alliance with the democratic republicans. For this, rival socialist theorists who were mostly less disposed to cooperate with the democratic republicans loudly derided him, Pierre-Joseph Proudhon (1809–65) styling him the "pygmy of democracy."[11] The intellectual gulf between Radical Enlightenment and early socialism in its various streams had long been perceptible before 1848; it was soon to grow wider and more bitter. The 1848 revolutions were, for the first time, to show how profoundly the tension within this duality, democratic republicanism and socialism, was to affect the future of France and all humanity.

Where the democratic republicans wholeheartedly embraced the Enlightenment and especially its radical tendency, the socialists, the economic Left, did not. The two groups differed in both their approach to philosophy and economics and their historical perspectives, though both rejected Christianity, Lamartine, like Shelley and Heine, thinking of himself as a Spinozist pantheist.[12] In 1847, the same year that Michelet and Louis Blanc published the first parts of their major histories of the great Revolution of 1789–99, Lamartine published his best-selling eight-volume *Histoire des Girondins*, the most immediately influential and widely read history of the Revolution of the age. It became a key source for charting readers' and reviewers' ideological orientation in French politics and internationally. The later renowned American poet and essayist Walt Whitman (1819–92), who spent most of the 1840s working on newspapers in and around New York, reviewed the work that August, acclaiming both Lamartine and Lamartine's view of the French Revolution with enthusiasm: "in the overthrow of the despotism of that period we hail a glorious work, for which whole hecatombs of royal carcasses were a cheap price indeed!"[13] For Whitman, Margaret Fuller, and other progressive American writers of the time, as well as for the French democratic republicans,[14] Lamartine's history confirmed that while "human thought had been renewed in the century of philosophy," as Lamartine termed the eighteenth century, in the mid-nineteenth it still remained for "l'esprit philosophique" to "transform the social world." The ideas of the *philosophes* remained mankind's best guide.[15] Lamartine, like Ledru-Rollin, summoned the French to renew their Revolution on the model of 1792–93, this time venerating the "true spirit" of the great Revolution, rejecting Robespierre and the *ultra-radicaux* of the Montagne and their heirs, Babeuf, Buonarotti, and the nondemocratic socialists.

The French 1848 Revolution began on 22 February, with an open challenge to the monarchy—a Paris march in the rain organized by the left-wing press, featuring a column of unemployed and poor, many women and hundreds of students raucously singing the "Marseillaise." Disorderly scuffles turned into violent clashes, bringing armed rebels into the streets who, over the next few days, seized sections of the capital and began building barricades in the time-honored manner of 1789 and 1830. Louis-Philippe's National Guard was called out, but the militia first hesitated, then refused fully to support the now utterly discredited monarchy. On the second day of the Revolution, Heine, very sick at the time, became entangled in turmoil when trying to return to hospital from home. Declining to storm barricades or push back the crowds, defecting National Guardsmen yelled "Vive la Réforme!" A belated attempt to crush the barricades by opening fire on them with regular troops was hampered by the National Guard and too half-hearted to have much effect.

Exulting revolutionaries stormed the Hôtel de Ville and Tuileries Palace, which crowds of working people then ransacked and pillaged, disporting themselves with particular glee in the throne room, "a magnificent sight, though a savage one," remarked the New York writer George Duyckinck (1828–63). "Out go gilded tables, and statues of King and Queen, and paintings," recorded another American eyewitness. "Above and below the whole building is swarming. From cellar grating they pass up mouldy-topped bottles of wine; and sitting on fragments of royal furniture and on national drums, they drink—confusion to the royal runaway. Salutes are firing from palace roof and a drunken Marseillaise is breaking out from the wine vaults below."[16] Louis-Philippe's throne was carried to the Place de la Bastille in triumph, where it was ceremonially burned. Fleeing Paris hurriedly, Louis-Philippe abdicated on 24 February, departed for the Normandy coast on 25 February, and, on 2 March, under the alias "Mr. Smith," sailed for England.

Amid wild enthusiasm, a provisional government headed by Lamartine, Ledru-Rollin, Louis Blanc, and the parliamentary republican leadership was proclaimed from the Hôtel de Ville in Paris on the same day that the king abdicated. They resoundingly adopted "Liberté, Égalité, Fraternité" as the Revolution's official motto and announced plans to hold elections and prepare a democratic constitution for France, and "on the morrow," noted the anonymous American eyewitness, "the proclamations, the self-made soldiers standing guard at the Palace gates, the printed words *République Française*, upon door of church and of Caserne, dissipated illusion and brought the truth home."[17] The Second French Republic had come into existence. It was the creation of the people, certainly, but the people led by a particular clique with an outlook that was anything but representative of conventional or typical attitudes. "Literary men," concluded Whitman, on 8 April 1848, at the time one of the editors of the New Orleans paper *The Crescent*, "seem to have been not only the prime starters of this French Revolution [of 1848]—but to be recognized as the ones from whom liberalism is to take body and form in a new Government there."[18] Lamartine, considered by many the "executioner" of monarchy and "accoucheur" of the Second Republic,[19] was in fact just the democratic republican intellectuals' spokesman, the mouthpiece of a Leftist segment rejecting monarchy and aristocracy.

On 8 March the republican regime issued a manifesto announcing that the newborn Republic harbored no aggressive intentions against Europe's (already nervous) princes and aimed to focus all its efforts on France's domestic scene. But while disavowing—as Lamartine instructed all French representatives abroad—all ambition to spread republicanism and democracy by force, the new regime at the same time advised Europe's kings that it would defend France's republican heritage with vigor and "protect" republican movements in exile, being the reliable intellectual ally and support of all progressivist movements everywhere seeking to secure for their societies those republican principles that now prevailed in France.[20] Fiercely criticized by those wanting a more aggressive interventionist policy though this relatively prudent universalist stance was, it was no idle boast. Before long, legions of Polish, Italian, and German volunteers were being organized, in particular by Ledru-Rollin, for intervention in their respective countries, with the French republican government assisting by providing financial support and weapons.[21] In particular, noted Marx in his *Neue Rheinisches Zeitung*, there was the force of Belgian workers Ledru-Rollin made ready in Paris to attempt a republican invasion of their country, a force joined by a stream of democrats arriving from Brussels that Marx accused Lamartine of subsequently betraying to the Belgian authorities.[22]

Parisians enthusiastically acclaimed the Republic, at first keeping perfect order. On 4 March, when the public funeral for those killed at the barricades took place, vast crowds, some said four hundred thousand people, lined the streets from where the Bastille formerly stood to the Madeleine, with admirable dignity and decorum without hardly a police officer or guardsman in sight. But the provisional republican government's edicts, it quickly became plain, would not unify revolutionary sentiment for long. "Tumult does not cease upon the Square of the Hotel de Ville," added the anonymous American eyewitness; "you can scarcely crowd your way through the company of unfed Parisians clamorous for more quick help than these edicts promise."[23] During March and subsequent months, Proudhon penned a series of articles predicting the Revolution was heading for disaster by assigning insufficient priority to the economic challenge, pauperism, and deprivation, concentrating instead, in his view excessively and misleadingly, like the great Revolution, on political and legal emancipation and democratization.[24] The dilemma had become ominously familiar to all serious thinkers and observers. However one examined it, rising economic discontent and lack of harmony between radicals and socialists threatened to destabilize the Republic and disrupt the Revolution in France and throughout Europe.

The European Chain Reaction

Radicals were democrats also concerned with "removing the injustice—for injustice it is," as John Stuart Mill expressed it, "whether admitting of a complete remedy or not—involved in the fact that some are born to riches and the vast majority to poverty." Yet, equally, they felt apprehensive about the democracy they proclaimed, dreading, "so long as education continues to be so wretchedly imperfect," the ignorance and "especially the selfishness and brutality of the mass." Radical enlighteners "repudiated with the greatest energy that tyranny of society over the individual which most Socialistic systems are supposed to involve"; they refused to deprive individuals of their natural economic freedom. But they also "looked forward to a time when society will no longer be divided into the idle and the industrious; when the rule that they who do not work shall not eat, will be applied not to paupers only, but impartially to all." The social problem of the future "we considered to be, how to unite the greatest individual liberty of action, with a common ownership in the raw material of the globe, and an equal participation of all in the benefits of combined labor."[25]

It took months before the full implications of the intellectual and cultural collision between Radical Enlightenment and socialism became generally evident and understood. Initially, sympathetic onlookers welcoming the Revolution found cause only for satisfaction. Duyckinck dispatched detailed reports to his still more influential brother, Evert Duyckinck (1816–78), editor of the magazine the *Literary World* and leader of the literary Young America group pressing for a new American democratic consciousness and a more engaged literature. The Duyckinck brothers were effectively the leaders of a prorevolutionary New York intellectual literary coterie. "It is a proud thing now to be an American in Europe," wrote George, concluding his twenty-page description of the Paris insurrection, "for our country leads the world."[26] "I did not think," exclaimed Margaret Fuller when the exciting news reached Rome, recalling her visit to Louis-Philippe's Paris the previous year, "as I looked with such disgust on the empire of sham he had established in France, and saw the soul of the people imprisoned and held fast as in an iron vice, that it would burst its chains so soon. Whatever be the result, France has done gloriously."[27]

Fuller was confident that this time the Revolution would be obliged, without delay or evasion, head-on to confront the social and economic challenge. To her it also seemed vital that the American people should learn some valuable preventive wisdom from this dramatic change: "you may learn the true meaning of the words *Fraternity, Equality*; you may, despite the apes of the past who strive to tutor you, learn the needs of a true democracy."[28] "The drama has been one where the people have acted sublimely; and where monarchy has appeared ridiculous," commented Bancroft, the American ambassador to Britain. "It has had no martyrs, no sympathy, and no respect." If the effect throughout Europe was enormous, the effect in England too was distinctly menacing to the old order: "here [in London] there is consternation. The high aristocracy dread the future." Riots occurred in "Edinburgh, Glasgow, Manchester, and London, but civil force as yet has suppressed them: and the fashionable doctrine is that riots save a rebellion."[29]

The February Revolution in France, historians often note, caused intense excitement also in Germany and Austria. Actually, though, revolutionary unrest in southern Germany, if falling short of outright revolution, began earlier, in the autumn of 1847. The news first from Switzerland and then France electrified students, professors, and members of the clandestine revolutionary societies while provoking a more mixed, reserved, and hesitant reaction among the general population. Popular response remained confused and everywhere remained deeply divided. As in 1830, much of the urban and rural agitation remained strictly local in aims, backward-looking, communitarian, and, in much of central Europe, violently anti-Semitic.[30] This was counterbalanced by the more coherent, structured rebellion emanating from intellectual and professional circles whose societies and organizations fixed the Revolution's aims and general agenda. The best organized and most energized group was certainly the professional ex-patriot German opposition to monarchy and aristocracy. On 24 March, the French Republic's provisional government, very differently from Louis-Philippe in 1830, allocated sixty thousand francs to assist German exiles in Paris aspiring to bolster the Revolution in Germany. On 30 March, no less than 1,500 members of the Paris Société démocratique allemande (German Democratic Society) left Paris by train bound for Alsace and southwest Germany, bearing arms, supplies, and bundles of revolutionary literature.[31]

In fixing revolutionary priorities and strategies what chiefly counted, once again, was not some spontaneously arising mood but rather reading societies and meetings in taverns, and eventually large halls, dominated by well-known radical orators and publicists. Early on, a key gathering convening in an inn at Offenburg, on the Rhine opposite Strasbourg, had produced the democratic manifesto known as the *Offenburger Programm* (12 September 1847), a thirteen-point democratic agenda drawn up in crowded meetings presided over by a renegade Bavarian noble, Gustav von Struve (1805–70), and the radical republican Friedrich Hecker (1811–81), who afterward migrated to America. Von Struve had in recent years been imprisoned several times for short spells for expressing democratic sentiments in his paper, the *Mannheimer Journal*. The *Offenburger Programm* called for freedom to gather, freedom of the press and of conscience, abolition of all noble privilege, equal voting rights, progressive taxation, restrictions on policing, educational reform, people's militias with officers swearing allegiance not to princes but to the *Programm* and to the people as represented in the assembly of the German Confederation.[32] It made no pronouncement about nationality.

But if the revolutionary process of 1848 in central Europe did not begin with the declaration of the Second Republic in France it certainly was intensified by it as were its own internal divisions.[33] At Cologne, both the democrats and the socialists sprang into frenetic action and into strife with the "moderates." Almost from the first, the Baden revolution, like the wider German Revolution as a whole, had split between democratic radicals backing the *Programm* and "liberals" demanding "moderation" based on compromises with princely authority and aristocracy together with a more "nationalist" approach. This split between radical enlighteners and "moderates" came to be popularly termed the fight between "Ganze" (fully committed) and "Halbe" (half-hearted).[34] Throughout late 1847 and 1848–49, Mainz, Speyer, Trier, Mannheim, and other southwestern German towns were hotbeds of furious ideological strife that were typically undifferentiated and socially indistinct in the sense that shopkeepers, off-duty soldiers, students, peasants, and members of societies randomly abounded on both sides, rendering social difference no guide to the factional splits. Allegiance and ideological dividing lines were principally indicated by symbols, badges, slogans, and pamphlets.

Admittedly, democratic radicalism was more prevalent in southwest Germany than other German regions; but this too had little relation to social strata though it had some to local cultural traditions. Massive political rallies in Mannheim and Karlsruhe in the Grand Duchy, in February 1848, obliged the Grand Duke of Baden to concede full freedom of the press and, on 1 March, a new constitution. Over the next months, and through 1849, revolutionary ferment engulfed Frankfurt, Berlin, and Dresden as well as Baden, Württemberg, the Palatinate, and Bavaria. Struve was widely proclaimed a "man of the deed," fighting for Germany's "liberation from tyranny and servitude." Innkeepers and other storekeepers, even far beyond the boundaries of Baden, often affixed portraits of Struve and Hecker to their walls, provoking a sharply divided response. Calls to remove a portrait of Hecker hanging beside one of the Bavarian king in a bookstore in Speyer precipitated a fight between passersby and off-duty soldiers on 17 July 1848, instigated by army officers who were afterward warmly praised by some for defending the king's honor. The many brawls between off-duty soldiers and civilian democrats might suggest that the Prussian and other armies at least were solidly behind the princes, but even here there were many examples of insubordination, indiscipline, and soldiers shouting out cheers for the republic and for Hecker and Struve.[35]

As the insurgency spread across the states of western Germany, profound social and ideological divisions became manifest at every level. The revolution in Mainz, doubtless aided by memories of the 1792–93 Rhenish revolution that had been based on Mainz, was unusual in producing a vigorous "cross-class" republican solidarity—in which women too were conspicuously active—reflected in the close collaboration of the revolutionized city government, the papers, the Democratic Club, and the local Gymnastics Society that seemingly effectively combined democratic and socialist goals.[36] Rallying round the black-red-and-gold flag of Hambach, and expressing Protestant-Catholic-Jewish solidarity, Mainz radicals, and many others in the Rhineland, often regarded the United States as the key model for Germany's future.[37] Very different was the situation in Cologne. There vigorous artisan, master craftsman, journeyman, and salaried worker resentment of industrial and commercial capitalists was successfully mobilized into a socially heterogeneous embryonic socialist movement that by the autumn of 1848 had come directly under Karl Marx's leadership. But the group used its energy purely to conduct the local economic fight while condemning the city's democratic committees and refusing to play any part in the drive for wider republican goals.[38]

In March 1848, a full-scale revolution, led by university students, overwhelmed the capital of the Habsburg Empire.[39] Censorship and police surveillance ended. On 13 March, freedom of the press was proclaimed in Vienna and bookshop owners carried out their stocks of forbidden texts for display. A few days later, Berlin too erupted in revolt. Most of the public, however, remained in a state of profound consternation and confusion. In German-speaking lands, there was widespread sporadic and mostly uncoordinated peasant and artisan unrest, illustrating the considerable gap between "the people" and the radicals leading the Revolution, who were predominantly journalists and intellectuals.[40] The rifts between "Ganze" and "Halbe," republican democrats and "liberals," and between republicans and socialists, undermining the Revolution came more and more into the open. In April, "liberals" in the southwest managed to get the journalist, democrat, and radical leader Joseph Fickler (1808–65) arrested, to which Hecker and Struve responded by organizing an armed republican rising of eight hundred students and motley tradesmen, artisans, and professionals that attempted to seize Karlsruhe. This diminutive republican army, armed with scythes and a few guns, was crushed at Kandern on 20 April by a military force mostly of reinforcements sent from Bavaria and other neighboring states.[41]

The Second French Republic's Collapse

The Second French Republic's executive—Ledru-Rollin, Lamartine, Crémieux, the Jewish defender of human rights heading the new ministry of justice, Garnier-Pagès, a hero of the barricades and future historian of the Revolution, as mayor of Paris, and François Arago (1786–1853), the mathematician, astronomer, and director of the Paris Observatory, now heading the

Second Republic's armed forces—plowed ahead with their program. Besides establishing freedom of expression and persuading the Republic's legislature to move swiftly to abolish slavery in the colonies with compensation to the owners, they proceeded to social reform on several fronts, in particular police and prison reform and improving conditions for the army's and navy's lower ranks, including abolition of flogging. The new government also issued its fateful declaration that the Republic committed itself "to guarantee the right to work to all the citizens."[42] A journalist and wine dealer, Marc Caussidière (1808–61), a leader of the Lyon rising of April 1834 afterward imprisoned, and a commander at the barricades in 1848 who had led the group that conquered the Paris police headquarters, became Paris prefect of police. He founded a new republican police force of 2,700, called Montagnards, consisting of his own revolutionary comrades, a force well paid and picturesquely attired, many of whom had been members of the secret societies, political suspects, and often themselves prisoners.

Sending out new department heads from Paris, Ledru-Rollin and his colleagues did everything possible to sway provincial opinion in a republican and democratic direction. Emmanuel Arago (1812–96), the astronomer's idealistic son, took charge in Lyon where he abolished the religious orders, imposed a swinging property tax, and established the "right to work," proceeding with such vigor that his name became a byword for republican zeal. Nevertheless, from February onward, the leadership striving to establish the Republic on radical foundations, Ledru-Rollin, Lamartine, Blanc, Crémieux, and Arago, found their initially considerable popularity waning rapidly as difficulties mounted and populist blocs encroached more and more on their following.

Crucially important was the French republican regime's outright rejection of the legacy of Robespierre and the Montagne, its decree abolishing the death penalty for political offenses, its repudiation of the Terror, and guarantees of freedom of expression. Buoyed by the new freedom of the press, every possible viewpoint flourished. No less than 479 newspapers were established in Paris between February and December 1848 while the entire city was plastered in wall placards.[43] The names of many renowned papers of the first revolution reappeared, including *Le Pere Duchêne* and *Le Vieux Cordelier*. There were several women's papers. But this abundantly flourishing free press hardly worked in favor of the provisional government for long; initial praise soon turned into a deluge of criticism. Heine was among those eulogizing Lamartine to begin with only to despise him in print a few weeks later.[44] Like the Girondins of 1792–93, the democratic republicans tried to use the press and the theaters to bolster their position and win over more of the public. Ledru-Rollin's ministry zealously reorganized and fostered the press, theaters, and arts, seeking to build up the republican papers in the provinces. With many of the wealthy having left Paris and other main cities, the theaters were in some straits. The government allocated funds so that tickets could be sent to the Town Hall and other official bodies for free distribution among the poorer citizenry, much as during the great Revolution. Among the Republic's keenest supporters was the novelist George Sand (1804–76), the lover of Chopin, Blanc, and Alfred de Musset among others, now no longer young but a passionate republican and sympathizer with the proletariat who rushed to Paris from the country the moment the Revolution broke out. Ensconced in the Interior Ministry, she devoted herself to publicity on the Revolution's behalf with an uninterrupted stream of fiery articles in the *Bulletin de la République*.[45]

Parisians enthusiastically embraced the new liberty of association. Hundreds of clubs representing every possible point of view came into being; and if this was enlivening and fascinating, it was also divisive and deeply disconcerting. As everywhere during the 1848 revolutions, the French Revolution almost immediately began fragmenting into rival blocs with democratic republicans facing intense resistance from social conservatives and Catholics and also multiple populist authoritarian blocs. Those attracting working people and striving to unseat the radicals comprised three main populist tendencies: neo–Montagnards, socialists, and Bonapartists. Political clubs mushroomed everywhere, including that of Louis Auguste Blanqui (1805–81), the Société républicaine centrale, among the best known and most given to attacking the provisional government from a proletarian standpoint, counting several thousand members. The main rival to Blanqui's club was that of Armand Barbès, a socialist less hostile to Lamartine and Ledru-Rollin leading the Club de la Révolution.

The French provisional government's executive faced a daunting task. There was plenty of talent at hand. Victor Hugo had now discarded his earlier conservatism but declined Lamartine's invitation to take up the education ministry. The post went to Hippolyte Carnot (1801–88), son of the notorious Carnot of the 1790s Directory who, unlike his father, was a zealous radical republican as well as enthusiast for literature and philosophy. Carnot introduced an impressive batch of educational reforms, including agricultural schools, public libraries, public lecture courses, and a course for women at the Collège de France. The leadership fought hard for universal free education for children up to fourteen but found themselves obdurately obstructed by the Church, which refused to relinquish control of France's educational establishment having regained it with the Restoration and consolidated it under Louis-Philippe. Carnot made no attempt to hide the fact his new schools would be centers of secularism and republicanism and France's schoolmasters the Republic's agents entrusted with actively reeducating the public as well as France's young and steering the electorate away from traditional values. "Let us make new men as well as new institutions" figured among his slogans.[46]

Too radical for most Frenchmen as well as most Americans and British, the new democratic republican leadership found themselves opposed also by the socialist organizations. Proudhon, antagonistic to Blanc as well as Lamartine, adopted an extreme position, denouncing democracy and elections outright as obstructive, doctrinaire, and retrograde.[47] Blanqui admired Arago as a scientist but despised him as a republican and social theorist. The basic split in the Revolution appeared already in March when serious discord arose between the democratic republicans and the Paris clubs over whether an immediate appeal to the people on the basis of universal male suffrage should be made and a Constituent Convention elected to draw up the new constitution. In the view of socialist militants and neo-Montagnards sweeping economic reforms were requisite without waiting for the assent of the majority of France's population, which was mostly more conservative and traditional than that of Paris. Socialists urged a long, indefinite postponement of elections and pushing ahead on the economic front without waiting for majority approval. Democratic radicals, though apprehensive too about the response of provincial France, insisted reform could proceed only on the basis of the people's will and consent, conceding only a short postponement.

The principle of "universel et direct" male suffrage was proclaimed on 5 March 1848. France had formally joined the United States as the world's second democratic republic. When a large demonstration of some one hundred thousand, organized by Blanqui at the Hôtel de Ville, demanded elections for the Constitutional Assembly be put off until 31 May to enable republicans and socialists to promote their program in the provinces first, Lamartine (who had secretly brought up troops) and his colleagues refused to yield.[48] The regime opted to push ahead with the elections on 23 April after only a two-month interval since the monarchy's overthrow. In her *Bulletin* article of 15 April, George Sand appealed to the people not to "undo the work of the Revolution." "If social justice fails to win out in the elections," if the interests of just certain strata of society succeed in diverting the trust of the people, the "elections, which should be the salvation of the Republic, will be its downfall."[49] She was right: with universal male suffrage in place for the first time since 1792–93, a majority of the French nation unhesitatingly reaffirmed their loyalty to Church, monarchism, and conservatism, rejecting both democratic republicanism and socialism outright. The elections of late April resulted in a majority of the new legislature consisting of Catholic and monarchist deputies with minimal sympathy for the Revolution and none for the Republic. The French National Convention that convened in early May in effect was chosen by conservative peasants and provincial townsmen strongly predisposed against both republicanism and the Parisian workers.

A high proportion, over 80 percent of the nearly nine million electors registered to vote, actually voted in the elections of 23 April, a level of electoral participation that had no precedent during the first French Revolution. But though elected on a democratic suffrage vastly wider than that of the pre-1848 legislature, the rooted biases of the less educated proved an insuperable barrier to the radical tendency. While around 500 of the 900 deputies elected claimed to be "moderate republicans," distinguishing themselves from the around 250 to 300 out-and-out monarchist legitimists and reactionaries, many or most of these "republicans" were in fact conservative very half-hearted democrats largely opposed to social reform and anticlericalism. To their dismay, the combined radical republican and revolutionary socialist Left could count on at most around 70 to 80 deputies in the new National Assembly. Paradoxically, the birth of French democracy and comprehensive adoption of adult male suffrage had resulted in empowering the Catholic vote with the ironic consequence that there were now many more nobles, landowners, and especially clergy in the new legislature than in any of Louis-Philippe's assemblies. This dramatic turnaround, fortifying the Right, effectively undermined the reform program, secularism, and the Republic.[50]

The Revolution and radicalism conceived as an essentially democratic impulse based on Enlightenment philosophy, aimed at freeing and improving the individual and society, for all practical purposes disintegrated under the impact of the elections of 23 April 1848. Electoral defeat proved a tremendous psychological blow to radicals and socialists alike. Such a sweeping, crushing setback led the anarchist-socialist Proudhon to announce that the "proletariat must emancipate itself without the help of the government"; the Left's great mistake had been to rely on political means trusting in the illusory principle of universal suffrage. The contentious belief that rescuing working people from exploitation and degradation must forge ahead in spite of, and even against, the will of the great majority, in disregard of the democratic process, powerfully obtruded against this dispiriting, disillusioning background. Improving the lot of the poor had become a separate fight from that for freedom of expression and the drive for equal rights.

Catastrophic defeat at the polls drained the lifeblood from radical republicanism but boosted several confrontational forms of socialism—Marxism, non-Marxist communism, and militant anarcho-socialism as well as anti-authoritarian, libertarian socialism of the type preached by Charles Fourier (1772–1837). Fourierism was a variety of communitarian socialism influential in both France and America during the 1840s due to its libertarianism, stress on social harmony, and rejection of class warfare. Fourier's utopian socialism held that deprivation and poverty are the chief source of misery in the world and that men can only achieve freedom and satisfaction through work collaboration, social harmony, shares in businesses, and forming urban-rural communes based on collective dwelling and work quarters he called *phalanstères*. Fourier's socialism aspired to eliminate poverty (not inequality) and foster harmonious collaboration in place of strife and exploitation by setting up work cooperatives, called "phalanxes," with a hierarchy of precedence and wages.[51] To a degree it was espoused by the Republic. Widely influential at first, before long, Fourierism and the Republic's "national workshops" lost their fleeting prestige and the workshops were clearly failing. While one hundred thousand or more working men had enrolled in them by May 1848, they were far from being the socialist cooperatives some had dreamed of. Rather, they degenerated into unedifying unemployment centers where bodies of men gathered daily to receive their two francs per day but where few serious work projects materialized. Paying these men their welfare handouts meant higher taxes and enraged the peasantry and the conservative bloc.

France was now hopelessly divided. But for the moment there was no change at the top. The new executive, appointed on 9 May, once more comprised Lamartine, Arago, Ledru-Rollin, Blanc, Crémieux, and Garnier-Pagès, and again excluded all their socialist ideological rivals from power. But their position was so debilitated that the new government lasted only six weeks. To Blanqui's disgust, the democratic republicans refused to act unconstitutionally and resort to outright force against the conservative opposition. On 15 May, a rowdy procession from the Bastille to the Place de la Concorde, around twenty thousand strong, accompanied by Polish, Irish, and Italian delegations, turned into a full-scale revolt against the National Assembly, setting siege to the Convention and the Hôtel de Ville where an insurrectionary government was proclaimed by Blanqui, Louis Blanc, Barbès, Raspail Aloysius Huber, a fiery Alsatian and longstanding professional conspirator, and supposedly also Ledru-Rollin. The event turned into an attempted socialist coup with Blanqui, Barbès, Raspail, and the rest defying and trying to intimidate the National Assembly and proclaiming a new provisional government from the Hôtel de Ville.

The National Guard hesitated and divided, as did the radical republicans. Ledru-Rollin rejected the insurrection. Lamartine and the Convention's executive were supported by enough of the National Guard to forcibly oust the insurgents from their strongholds. The proletariat, as Marx construed matters, failing in its attempted coup, "only delivered its energetic leaders to the jailors of the bourgeoisie."[52] Blanqui, Huber, Barbès, and Raspail were arrested and imprisoned; the outcome was a further appreciable strengthening of the conservatives in the Assembly.[53] Radical republicans and socialists blamed each other for the debacle. Blanqui, throughout the most resolute of the socialist leaders seeking to disrupt the republican regime, subsequently styled Arago, Ledru-Rollin, and the rest of the provisional leadership of May 1848 "mournful sinister" men responsible for the Republic's fatal predicament and demise since the "reaction only did its job when it slaughtered democracy. The crime was perpetrated by the traitors [i.e., the radicals] whom the trusting population accepted as their guides and who delivered the population to the reactionaries."[54]

Undone by 15 May, the democratic republican revolutionary consensus in France collapsed utterly with the subsequent canceling of the Republic's earlier decision to maintain the system of national workshops. To live up to its principles, the Revolution had to combat poverty, misery, and lack of work. But it had now ceased even attempting to do that. The Revolution's final collapse ensued in June when the eastern proletarian and industrial quarters of Paris rose in open armed revolt against the Convention. France's predominantly right-wing legislature had ordered the workshops closed on ideological grounds and as a cost-cutting step. With this, Paris descended briefly into the first full-scale class war of modern times.

Several leaders of the Parisian socialist leaders and clubs, including Blanqui—albeit not Barbès—organized a massive revolutionary *journée* to block suspension of the workshops. On 24 June, crowds of workers poured into the streets with Blanqui conspicuously to the fore, some armed. Hundreds of barricades went up. Ordered to remove the barricades, the National Guard tried to scatter the crowds, provoking bitter fighting that lasted three days and left over a thousand dead and many wounded. As this ugly confrontation escalated, key republican leaders such as Ledru-Rollin, Crémieux, and Caussidière refused to take sides and receded into the background.[55] It was impossible for them, or onlookers like Heine and many like him, to approve of the brutal way the insurgents were suppressed; but neither could genuine radicals approve of the strategy and attitudes of the populists and socialists. The disorder, violence, and slaughter of the "June Days" (23–26 June 1848), which reportedly left 3,600 dead and 1,600 behind bars and was followed by the deportation of around 11,000 insurgent prisoners to Algeria, left a legacy of hatred and bitterness that was never fully to be dispelled.

The catastrophe of the June Days has often unfairly been blamed on a republicanism and revolutionary tradition refusing to join the socialists.[56] But the cause of the ferocious strife setting the poorest against the rest, and leading to the breakdown of the Republic, in the process overthrowing the new freedom of the press and expression, was not a property-loving provincial bourgeoisie fighting the Parisian proletariat but a socialist revolt against a weak republican regime refusing to act unconstitutionally in the face of a conservative election victory. Blanc and others wavered; but in the end he and most radical and Left republicans realized they had to back the Republic against the insurgents. Proudhon sympathized with the insurgents but even he wanted a peaceful compromise, not internecine war.[57] Many onlookers in Paris of all stripes, including Proudhon, were profoundly shocked by the brutal violence and effusion of blood. The real tragedy lay not in the refusal of a democratic and radical republican leadership to endorse the growing frustration and radicalism of the workers but the provinces' and the Convention's unyielding monarchism and conservatism, and the anti-republican, pro-clergy bias of the electorate, especially that of the bulk of the rural population. Most Frenchmen rejected both the radicals and the socialists, seeing the solution to France's political crisis in the dictatorial populism of Louis-Napoleon.[58]

The veritable conflict, as radicals understood it, was not class war of the kind Blanqui, Barbès, Proudhon, and Marx fomented but a war against Counter-Enlightenment, ignorance, conservative bias, and religious authority stiffened by the Convention's large ecclesiastical bloc denouncing republican radicals who were a blend of workers, bourgeois, and especially intellectuals. "Socialism," Ledru-Rollin and Crémieux rightly insisted, like John Stuart Mill, was not the overriding issue both Right and Left interminably alleged. Proclaiming the "right to work," Ledru-Rollin reminded audiences, is not "socialism" but an authentic democratic republican principle. To those insisting the "right to work" *is* "socialism," Ledru-Rollin retorted that it was democratic republicanism applied, a right in the authentic spirit of the great Revolution of 1789–93.[59] At a banquet held on 22 September 1848 to commemorate the anniversary of the proclaiming of the First French Republic on 22 September 1792, he repeatedly decried the use of the now ubiquitous term "socialism" to characterize the campaign for improved social institutions and as a means to discredit elections and democracy among the public. For this was deliberately to obscure the real character of the 1789–93 Revolution and divide the Republic's supporters, undermining the Republic.[60]

More broadly, if 1848 represents in history the "revolution of the intellectuals," their defeat, in June, represented the great "disillusionment of the intellectuals," except among hard-core socialists who declared the whole debacle entirely predictable. An unprecedented gulf had now opened up between Europe's (and soon also America's) intellectuals and the people. Faith in democracy and the people, hence in democratic republicanism, rapidly withered. Everywhere popular elements had acted in a violent but contradictory and inchoate manner. Intellectuals had led but failed to carry through the Revolution. Large segments of the population remained either inert or else willing to assist Napoleon's ambitious heir, Louis-Napoleon, the Prussian monarch, Metternich, the Sicilian tyrant Ferdinand II, and the pope crush whatever remained of the Revolution. Heine felt deeply dismayed by the collapse in both France and Germany.[61] The consequence was withdrawal into isolation and defeat, as with Lamartine and Ledru-Rollin, or, as with Wagner and Bakunin (both active in the Dresden revolution of March 1849), banishment to Switzerland and Siberia, respectively, conclusive estrangement from any further thought of accomplishing a great social and political transformation via the mechanism of general revolution.

The swing to right-wing populism in France gathered impetus, in December 1848, when Louis-Napoleon, nephew of Bonaparte, exploiting the quasi-American "presidency" adopted by the Second Republic at the urging of those invoking the American example as their guide, to the dismay of the republicans and socialists was elected France's president. With this, the Second French Republic was aborted in essence, and the hopes of American democratic republicans shifted from France to focus elsewhere. Louis-Napoleon, having captured the organs of government, extinguished the Republic altogether with his coup of December 1851 and the oppressive system with which he replaced it. "The European reaction after 1848," concluded John Stuart Mill, "and the success of an unprincipled usurper [Louis-Napoleon] . . . put an end, as it seemed, to all present hope of freedom or social improvement in France and the Continent."[62]

Among the intellectuals who had made the Revolution, the profoundly sobering result was all too often withdrawal from society, politics, and the actual world into a state of yet more extreme intellectual and artistic alienation, an estrangement—at its profoundest in Schopenhauer—into profound pessimism and disengagement from all schemes to ameliorate man and society. This was to repudiate the Enlightenment itself, a process in which the increasingly hostile and rejectionist attitudes toward the revolutionary legacy manifested in America played a part.[63] Only a few stuck to the radical republican creed, and those who did entered into another sort of intellectual isolation, of a more resolute and, from a political standpoint, perhaps more impressive kind. Mill, in his *Considerations on Representative Government* (1861), rethought and reworked the dilemmas of the 1830 and 1848 democratic republican revolutions in search of a more differentiated and refined representative democracy that recognized all minorities and subgroups as well as the majority through the mechanism of proportional representation.

If democratic enlightened republican democracy was to overcome the "mediocrity" of the early nineteenth-century democratic model, in Mill's view, it had to devise a mechanism to bring to the fore those personages most outstanding in a given society in terms of moral and intellectual stature.[64] But it was far from easy to see how this was to be accomplished.

CHAPTER 21

American Reaction (1848–52)

1848 and America's Domestic Political Crisis

News of the 1848 revolutions exerted a significant impact on America, but a mixed one. Later in the year, Melville commented: "with the utmost delight, these tidings were welcomed by many; yet others heard them with boding concern."[1] Furthermore, America's initially enthusiastic but soon increasingly cool response mattered. Ignoring international pleas to help bolster stability and monarchy, the United States was actually the first, and only, power promptly to recognize the Second French Republic.

Within days of Louis-Philippe's overthrow, the American minister in Paris, Richard Rush (1780–1859), son of Founding Father Benjamin Rush, unabashedly broke ranks with the rest of the international diplomatic community, ignoring strenuous British objections. Appearing at the Paris Hôtel de Ville in his official capacity, on 28 February 1848, he announced publicly that America gladly embraced the Second French Republic among the states of the world.

Openly clashing with the British minister in Paris, but with the concurrence of his staff and other prominent Americans visiting France at the time, on his own initiative and motivated by his republican sympathies, Rush warmly congratulated the new republic on its proclaimed principles. Apart from the United States, only Switzerland also acclaimed the new republic; all the rest of the diplomatic community adhered rigidly to the Holy Alliance's boycott of republican regimes. In Paris, a delegation of around 250 Americans currently residing there followed Rush to the Hôtel de Ville, making a group visit to congratulate France on her renewed Revolution and to present an address that "would have been much stronger," noted a New England clergyman in Paris, whose letter was quoted in the *New York Daily Tribune* in early April, "but a Southern member of the committee objected to certain expressions about the right of all to liberty."[2]

News of the democratic republican upsurge in Europe caused great excitement in the New World. At first mainly viewed as simply fresh confirmation of the legitimacy of "democracy" and popular sovereignty, by early April the New York press was already stressing that, in the renewed revolution, social and economic ideas enjoyed a prominence they had not had in 1789–99 or 1830. It was a shift bound before long to disturb a good many. So central were social ideas in the "earthquake which has shaken the European thrones," observed one American correspondent in Paris, in March 1848, "that I should not hesitate to aver that Fourier is to this Revolution what Voltaire and Rousseau were to the first,"[3] a remarkable if not fully accurate prediction. Fourierism, ardently championed by Horace Greeley (1811–72), the influential Leftist editor of the *New York Daily Tribune*, already possessed a small but growing foothold in the United States, the oldest Fourierist collectivist commune in America, Utopia, Ohio, dating from 1844.

At the same time many longstanding political controversies, questions of universal male suffrage, recent immigrants' rights, and democratic procedure, were still not fully resolved in the United States even if they had progressed much further than in Europe. In America, universal white male suffrage had only recently, during the 1820s, come close to being secured and remained still bitterly controversial in some quarters, most notoriously Rhode Island where the old landed and mercantile elite tenaciously clung to their former privileges. In Rhode Island until the early 1840s, pre-revolutionary property qualifications restricting the white male suffrage remained intact, so that only around 40 percent to half of the adult male white population were eligible to vote. A vociferous protest movement arose led by Thomas Wilson Dorr (1805–54), a Harvard graduate and lawyer from Providence who sat in the state's lower house and who, though from a Federalist family, had come to view the Lockean principle of basing participation on property as insidious. Idealistic and uncompromising, his protest movement, for a time backed by most of the state militia, expressly sought only universal adult male white suffrage, excluding blacks as well as women, although they did also demand free universal public education.[4]

Dorr's efforts led to the so-called Dorr War, three years of highly disruptive controversy and agitation in the state (1841–43). For six weeks, in May and June 1842, the Rhode Island disturbances gave rise to two rival, irreconcilable state governments that briefly stood in armed confrontation, one grounded on Dorr's "People's constitution" proclaiming universal white male suffrage, the other championing the "old charter" dating back to colonial times—unashamedly oligarchic and anchoring power in property. Each vying Rhode Island state regime declared the other illegitimate. Although Dorr's unbending attachment to principle, naïveté, and refusal to compromise eventually led to most of his supporters abandoning him out of fear of the mounting threat of violence, instability, and disorder, the episode proved deeply disturbing to democrats not only locally but throughout the United States. For despite their invoking the principles of '76, the anti-Lockean democratic foundational principles of the American Revolution, Dorr and his faction found themselves widely condemned in the press and in legislatures in North and South alike as enemies of society, pernicious agitators mounting an armed challenge to an elected state government. They were not entirely defeated. In November 1842 the victorious Rhode Island political elite compromised to the extent of agreeing to a new state constitution widening adult male suffrage so that that only a minimal taxpayer property qualification remained, with free blacks being permitted to qualify; however, the property restrictions on officeholding and exclusion of resident foreign-born whites (mainly Irish) from voting rights remained. Moreover, on returning from his refuge outside the state, following adoption of the new constitution, Dorr himself was tried for high treason and sentenced to life imprisonment, though this caused such outrage among democrats that he served only one year until, in 1845, when a new Democratic legislature was voted in and he was released.[5]

Although the armed confrontation of 1842 was confined to Rhode Island, the disturbing questions as to whether a citizen majority could alter a manifestly undemocratic state constitution, overruling its defenders with claims that the majority possesses the revolutionary right to use force to install a "republican" government where its will was being thwarted, together with the issues of the federal government's and Supreme Court's role in arbitrating such disputes, had a much wider relevance, as did the bitter controversy over political rights for recent immigrants, Irish, Polish, Italian, and German and for the free black community.[6] Rhode Island's political elite opted for compromise; but the American press nevertheless remained sharply divided over the Dorrite insurrection. Pro-oligarchy papers denounced Dorr in violent terms; democratic papers in Boston and New York eulogized him as a people's hero endorsing the Rhode Island "People's Party," and heaping scorn on the "Algerines," Rhode island's local elite. Although the state's suffragists had no economic platform and were not challenging the social dominance of the state's political elite, and (despite Dorr's own wishes) eschewed black voting rights, Southern slave-owning landowners warned Northern conservatives that to save themselves from a rampant democratic surge of Dorrism (and behind that socialism) they must more tightly ally politically with their aristocratic Southern counterparts.[7]

In pockets of the North and most of the South the principle of "democracy" itself hence still remained a fraught question, even in America; and if democracy's legitimacy and desirability were no longer broadly challenged (at least not openly) there, the principle and language of democracy continued to be sweepingly rejected by the entirety of Europe's political establishment. Across the Atlantic, the Chartist protest movement in Britain, vigorously praised by America's democratic press, now again brought the issue of "democracy" powerfully to the fore. But British upper- and middle-class society vehemently rebuffed Chartist pretensions. Equally, while a growing ambivalence in English working-class attitudes toward monarchy, the court, and deeply entrenched inequality was definitely detectable and a minority of the working class exhibited an openly oppositional attitude, sympathy for the Continental democratic revolutions in British society remained generally remarkably limited. In 1848, and for decades after, both radical republicans and European-style socialists were spurned by Tories and run-of-the-mill "Liberals" alike as "unacceptable outsiders in British politics."[8]

Owing to the country's deeply conservative, anti-revolutionary temper, in England the resounding initial success of the 1848 revolutions caused near universal despondency. "Here [in Britain]," noted the American ambassador George Bancroft (1800–1891), "the aristocracy are overwhelmed with gloom. In the court circle I alone am the one to speak and think of the French Republic with hope, with subdued exultation, with trust."[9] By March, the English papers identified recent French developments as "a social revolution" and this, it was reported in New York, "has caused the greatest fear and distrust in all the journals": the English papers "rave about Communism and charge the French people with ignorance of the very elements of political economy."[10] *The Times* "denounced and discredited the French Republic of 1848," noted Ralph Waldo Emerson later, "and checked every sympathy with it, in England, until it had enrolled 200,000 special constables to watch the Chartists and make them ridiculous."[11] Despite initial consternation, the eventual fiasco of the revolutionary upsurge of 1848–49, when it came, was pronounced by the London press and British upper classes entirely predictable as well as thoroughly desirable.

In the spring of 1848, mainstream American reaction hence still contrasted vividly with British opinion, just as during the early and mid-1790s and in 1830. In fact, initial American enthusiasm was almost unbounded. On 18 March, the prominent literary critic Evert Duyckinck (1816–78), editor of the *Literary World*, reported to his brother, in France, that New York was positively electrified by the new French revolution: "a walk in Broadway to-day is a thing for excitement, the news of the Revolution in Paris having imparted to everyone that vivacity of eye, quickness of intelligence and general exhilaration which great public events extend to private ones. I have heard one rather quiet man say he would give a thousand dollars to have been there."[12] Horace Greeley, at the *New York Daily Tribune*, a committed democrat, once an apprentice print worker himself, assured readers that the "emancipation of Europe had now begun in earnest" and would "thrill the hearts of Milan, of Venice, of Rome and of Naples," moving them too to defy despotism.[13] Rush's initiative "makes us feel proud of our own country," insisted the *Brooklyn Daily Eagle*, "and contrasts with the timorous and conservative course of our patrician senate."[14]

Rush was warmly complimented on his diplomatically disruptive initiative by President James Polk, eleventh president of the United States (1845–49), who unhesitatingly lauded his defying the whole of the European court system and diplomatic corps. Polk congratulated the French for basing their "future government on liberal institutions similar to our own." Rush's report to Congress stressed the respect for property and lack of violence, the "moderation and magnanimity" of the new French Republic so far, a point echoed generally in the press and taken by Democratic papers like the *Brooklyn Daily Eagle* to show "clearly what we have endeavored before to point out, that, instead of the excesses reported by the English journals there have never been accomplished, in the world's wide history, a series of changes so stupendous, in a period so brief, with so little manifestation of popular violence."[15] Until the summer of 1848, the vehement antipathy to the European revolutionary movement voiced by some conservatives only marginally reflected American opinion more generally.

In America, newspapers competed to publish the latest and most detailed news from the revolutionary stage of Europe. "One's blood rushes and grows hot within him the more he learns or thinks of this news from the continent of Europe!" noted the now twenty-nine-year-old poet and essayist Walt Whitman, in March 1848, in a paper he coedited in New Orleans, where the news likewise evoked a momentous ferment. "Is it not glorious?" exclaimed Whitman, an ardent democrat and egalitarian: "this time, the advent of Human Rights, though amid unavoidable agitation, is also amid comparative peace."[16] Europe was now following the United States, it seemed, not only in espousing the principle of "human rights" but in throwing off the yoke of the old political elites as Jefferson, the "Columbus of our democratic faith," had done when defeating America's aristocratic, Anglophile Federalists in 1800.[17] Among the greatest American poets of the nineteenth century, Whitman eulogized the leaders of the 1848 French Revolution, especially Lamartine, whose revolutionary performance was a "stronger argument against kings than all the philosophy of the most scholastic radicals. For where is there—where has there ever been— such a king! Lamartine has a wondrous union of physical and moral courage, to begin with; the first of which the masses must always admire, and the other clinches the respect of every intellectual person."[18] He repeatedly compared him to Washington in his effort to represent the Second French Republic as seconding the ideals of the American Revolution.

A vast public rally held in New York's City Hall Park on 3 April 1848 was attended by many thousands, some estimated one hundred thousand, including numerous recent immigrants, Irish, Italians, Germans, and Poles eager to celebrate Europe's revolutions, human rights, equality, and democracy. New York's mayor presided over an afternoon of speeches and then singing, including a grand chorus of the "Marseillaise" sung by a vast throng, accompanied by a brass band, in the evening followed by illuminations, candlelight processions, and fireworks ignited from City Hall. Besides New York, New Orleans, and Boston, exhilaration, public mass gatherings, celebrations, flowery orations, and grand banquets seized Philadelphia, Baltimore, and Washington, the revolutions being celebrated with passionate applause for republican liberty, equality, and democracy.[19] Receding little by little, the banquets and eulogies persisted for over a year.

So captivated were American writers by the great European drama, realizing that it was also a profound American drama, that several key literary figures of the day—Emerson, Melville, and Margaret Fuller—either already in Europe, or soon hastening thither, turned their attention not just to investigating and learning more but to immersing themselves in the democratic revolution, for a time making the revolutions central to their own creative activity. Whitman, Hawthorne, and Thoreau stayed in America but likewise felt pulled in, all becoming in their respective ways preoccupied with the Revolution and its significance for mankind, democracy, and the United States, all wondering whether the excited response in America would bring forth much-needed reforms there too.

But if English initial reaction diverged markedly from the early American response, the two reactions began to converge during the summer of 1848 and there were signs of this even earlier. Before long, like the Dorrite agitation of 1841–43, only on a vaster scale, the 1848 European revolutions impacted on American domestic culture and politics in a way that proved highly divisive. To no small extent this was because the meaning of "democracy" and popular sovereignty remained vague and contested, with conservatives still seeking ways to champion the primacy of the traditionally privileged elites on the basis of popular consent. But there were also additional factors. This time

America's reaction to Europe's revolutionary turmoil more directly involved the ferociously contentious questions of slavery and socialism. Melville, before leaving for Europe, met regularly with the circle at Evert Duyckinck's New York apartment where the talk was all of revolution, democracy, and human emancipation; but unlike them, he oscillated between enthusiasm and aversion, subtly satirizing all their effusiveness in his novel *Mardi* (1849), albeit, like them, avidly perusing European developments in the newspapers.[20]

If President Polk endorsed Rush's initiative and, according to the *Brooklyn Daily Eagle*, "caught the popular feeling" and "uttered forth the popular voice,"[21] Congress, restrained by conservative voices, hesitated and advised waiting to see how things turned out. Following a clash over an antislavery amendment initiated by a New Hampshire senator urging colleagues additionally to congratulate French republicans for their decree of 27 April 1848 ending slavery in the French Caribbean, both houses procrastinated.[22] Congress viewed the democratic upsurge in France with increasingly mixed feelings due to the growing sense of America being a "House Divided," as Abraham Lincoln had expressed it as early as 1842–43. This was by no means just because of the slavery issue.[23] The antithesis between "free society" and "slave society" in Congress had indisputably become conjoined to the wider rift between two increasingly divergent worldviews, democratic and aristocratic, with the North being glorified "as the home of progress, opportunity and freedom" and the South of aristocracy, slavery, and traditional values. The antislavery campaign in this way became inseparably linked to the general question of "democracy" in North and South and other emancipationist causes such as voting rights for free blacks and recent immigrants, women's rights, and correcting the one-sidedness, or as some termed it, "slavery," of American marriage law.[24] Although very few women were prepared to brave charges of being immodest, unwomanly, and encouraging immorality to the extent of publicly championing women's rights, a few intrepid females did, most obviously Margaret Fuller, for whom women's emancipation followed from black emancipation as a "natural following out of principles."[25] So limited had progress been toward securing black voting rights on a basis equal to that of whites that even as late as 1860 it was to be only in the New England states, a part of the country containing only a tiny fraction of the more than two million blacks in the Union, that free blacks enjoyed civil rights equivalent to those of white male voters.

Slavery had recently become even more explosive and tightly linked to wider issues of civil rights, the balance of power in Congress, and the republican character of the Union through the United States' further vast territorial expansion due to the recent war with Mexico. That conflict, erupting in May 1846, arose from unsettled earlier disputes over Spanish and, since 1825,

Mexican territory in Texas, New Mexico, and further west. Resulting expansionist claims, questioned by some Americans but vigorously supported in the South, helped Polk, who was strongly committed to acquiring Texas and much additional territory from Mexico, win the presidential election of 1844. A Tennessee lawyer, son of a slave-owning farmer, and protégé of Jackson, he was known to some as "Young Hickory" for being under "Old Hickory's" tutelage and supporting Jacksonian chauvinism, exceptionalism, and expansionism. As president, Polk declared war on Mexico with congressional approval.

Inflicting shattering military defeats on the Mexicans, the United States army eventually besieged and, in September 1847, captured Mexico City. The invasion of Mexico dragged on until March 1848, backed by considerable popular enthusiasm and much invoking of divine providence as justification. But chauvinism, religious sanction, and lack of republican self-criticism prevailed conspicuously more in Southern than in Northern states where attitudes were more mixed and included a dose of fierce dissent, stoked not least by worries over the slavery issue. Not only Fenimore Cooper (now in more conservative mode) but even such avowed republican democrats as Walt Whitman glowed with satisfaction in the conviction that the expansion of American territory and power equated with "the increase of human happiness and liberty."[26] Domestic American opposition to the war often emanated less from republican idealism than staunch New England conservatism, the aged John Quincy Adams being among the leading opponents of Polk's venture. Nevertheless, several spokesmen, most notably the now elderly Albert Gallatin, loudly objected on the basis of republican principle. "Your mission," he reminded Americans, in his pamphlet *Peace with Mexico* (1847), "was to be a model for all other governments and for all other less-favoured nations."[27] This strand of internal opposition to the war—and the critiques of claims of "divine providence" to justify American expansionism—sufficed to hearten at least a few distraught Spanish American republicans with the distant hope that, however improbable for the moment, North American rejection of Anglo-Saxon "exceptionalism" and of invocations of divine providence and what later came to be called Manifest Destiny could still, one day, surge up sufficiently to become the basis once again for a genuine democratic republican vision—one of a pan-American federation of sister republics.[28]

In August 1846, a proposal known as the Wilmot Proviso presented by a Pennsylvanian Democrat, David Wilmot, echoing the 1787 Northwest Ordinance, proposed banning the extension of slavery to all the new territories acquired from defeated Mexico. The proviso passed in the House of Representatives but was stopped in the Senate, causing an uproar that further contributed to turning the slavery debate into a generalized national political confrontation.[29] Southern representatives expected the territorial gains from the Mexican war appreciably to increase the number of slave states, while Northern qualms and opposition grew on the same expectation. Under the Treaty of Guadalupe Hidalgo (2 February 1848), Mexico was obliged to surrender half its territory to the United States—Texas, Colorado, New Mexico, Arizona, Nevada, California, and parts of Oklahoma, Wyoming, and Kansas— for fifteen million dollars without there being any ban on the extension of slavery (which had been abolished in Mexico including pre-independence Texas in 1829). In Europe and Latin America the Mexican war and its outcome, viewed as blatantly arrogant expansionism, permanently compromised America's democratic republican reputation, image, and credentials.

The fast-changing and increasingly embattled relationship between slave and non-slave states in Congress was additionally aggravated by several highly politicized Supreme Court cases that temporarily weakened Article IV (section 2) of the Constitution, affecting enforcement of the 1793 Fugitive Slave Act.[30] At this point, a formidable alliance emerged between Southern congressmen defending slavery and conservative Northern leaders headed by Daniel Webster (1782–1852), an affluent New Hampshire lawyer who had become one of the Senate's most influential figures. Webster was a key political figure of the age, being the first prominent spokesman to shift the focus of American conservatism, as he had begun to do already during America's Greek furor in 1823–24, from the old Federalist overt elitism and aristocratism to a populist and supposedly "democratic" format. An ex-Federalist veteran opponent of Jefferson and Madison who had helped devise the new legal doctrine of strong corporate rights, Webster continued aggressively championing banking and commercial interests while at the same time seeking to coax the masses over to conservative attitudes by combining defense of the monied interest with ardent rhetoric and pleas for universal white voting rights and mass participation in politics, a blend he presented as the American Revolution's true legacy. Exalting the Union and a form of American patriotism that eschewed criticism of slavery and the South, he loudly deplored all socially egalitarian republican tendencies, whether in America or Europe. "Mr. Webster," remarked Ambassador George Bancroft, disapprovingly in April 1848, "condemns the Revolution in toto, as the work of communists and anarchists."[31]

Southern pro-slavery sentiment combining with Webster's Northern elite anti-republican, anti-democratic, anti-abolitionist, and anti-socialist conservatism eventually secured the so-called Compromise of 1850 between the states, a set of agreements including the soon notorious new Fugitive Slave Law of 18 September 1850. This revived the law of 1793, unambiguously affirming the responsibility of all states of the Union to cooperate in the seizure and return to their "owners" of slaves escaping to the North or West, obliged them to proceed solely on the basis of slave owners' sworn testimonies, stipulating heavy fines for federal and state officials refusing compliance with its provisions. Although Vermont and Wisconsin refused to assent, Massachusetts and other non-slave states did acquiesce.[32] The Compromise of 1850 and new Fugitive Slave Law inflamed feeling in the North in a way that no other issue did. "Who would have believed it, if foretold," declared Emerson, "that a hundred guns would be fired in Boston on the passage of the Fugitive Slave Bill?"[33] Bostonians placed compromise with the South above equal rights and the democratic republican principles of '76. A fugitive who has "run the gauntlet of a thousand miles for his freedom," protested Emerson in an oration given at Concord, Massachusetts, in May 1851, "the statute says, you men of Massachusetts shall hunt, and catch, and send back again to the dog-hutch he fled from." "The last year," he averred, "has forced us all into politics, and made it a paramount duty to seek what it is often a duty to shun."[34]

This forcing "of us all into politics" coincided with 1848 and its immediate aftermath. The alliance between Northern conservatism and the South, or what Emerson termed "Mr. Webster's treachery," was hailed by Northern conservatives, including many New England clergymen, as the "great action of his life." The prevailing mood among the clergy, professionals, and the business elite in the North generally seemed so despicable to zealots for the principles of '76 that one could not "open a newspaper, without being disgusted by new records of shame." "There is infamy in the air," declared Emerson, rebuking both the state legislature and the city of Boston, where it was once said "no fugitive slave can be arrested" but which had now shamefully submitted to the new Fugitive Slave Law: the "Boston of the American Revolution . . . spoiled by prosperity, must bow its ancient honor in the dust, and make us irretrievably ashamed." City and suburbs all were involved in this abject surrender, he lamented, "presidents of colleges, and professors, saints and brokers, insurers, lawyers, importers, manufacturers;—not an unpleasing sentiment, not a liberal recollection, not so much as a snatch of an old song for freedom, dares intrude on their passive obedience . . . the college, the churches, the schools, the very shops and factories are discredited; real estate, every kind of wealth, every branch of industry, every avenue to power, suffers injury, and the value of life is reduced."[35]

Abolition of slavery in the French colonies, Martinique, Guadeloupe, and Cayenne, on 4 March 1848, was among the Second French Republic's earliest decrees. Although not all members of the new government wanted immediate emancipation without waiting for the convening of the future Constituent Assembly elected in April, the staunchly republican new navy minister, François

Arago (1786–1853), under whose responsibility the colonies fell, pushed ahead regardless. Monarchy's overthrow provoked ferment among the blacks and half castes in the French Caribbean, especially on Martinique where there were armed clashes in May, rendering it unwise and impracticable to delay emancipation or try to stage its implementation. The Republic's decree, issued in the Caribbean in mid-April, came into effect from the end of May,[36] stipulating that all the slaves must be freed within two months and outlining future measures to broaden civic rights, agriculture, and education in the colonies and provide state subsidies for schools, clinics, and law courts. The entire Caribbean was stirred. In early July, insurrection erupted among the twenty-five thousand slaves on Saint-Croix loudly invoking the Martinique emancipation. On 3 July, the Danish governor, on his own initiative (afterward ratified by the Danish Crown), proclaimed the end of slavery in the Danish islands. By mid-1848 black slavery survived in the Caribbean only in Surinam, Puerto Rico, and Cuba.

In Congress, France soon drew criticism from conservative detractors deploring the new Revolution in various respects. Over a third of the Senate, including a substantial minority from non-slave states, signed motions citing the new republic's inadequate respect for property, religion, and social order. One proposed addition to the original draft resolution to congratulate the French Republic attached wording admonishing the French legislature and people to adhere to "moderation, humanity, regard for order, and veneration of Christianity."[37]

Another factor dampening American zeal for equal rights was the effect of Ireland's great Potato Famine (1845–52) and the pervasive effect of the growing Irish, Italian, and German immigration in stirring, in many parts of the United States and for the first time on a large scale outside Pennsylvania, strong feelings of "Nativist," anti-foreigner resentment. Although the influx of Italians in the 1840s was still on a modest scale compared to that of the late nineteenth century, in 1844 anti-Catholic, anti-Italian, and anti-Irish riots erupted in Philadelphia.[38] In Rhode Island, by 1848, the most vocal opposition to the state's post-1845 status quo emanated from disgruntled Irish immigrant workers. Beside controversy over voting rights, the growing influx heightened tension between Protestantism and Catholicism and aggravated disputes over public interdenominational "common schools" and the place of religious schools in America.[39] Catholics resented having to send their children to "common schools" that were essentially "Protestant" in tone and character. Philadelphia schools, complained Catholics, and schools in many other parts, though paid for by all and, under the Pennsylvania and other state constitutions, purportedly guaranteeing religious liberty, actually favored Protestantism and actively fomented antipathy to Catholicism.

Official impartiality and non-sectarianism, Irish, Italian, Polish, and German Catholic immigrants complained, was bogus.[40] Radicals and secularists would have preferred solving the problem by removing Bible and religious instruction from their hegemony in the common schools; but this was unacceptable to Protestants *and* Catholics. The only way forward was a dual system with more specifically Catholic and Protestant schools, a solution that favored expanded confessionalization, preoccupation with theology, and the influence of the clergy, further weakening the non-theological and non-denominational base of American education.

Conservative Populism versus "Socialism"

America's most far-reaching reservations regarding the 1848–49 republics, though, concerned socialism. American papers were quick to stress the prominence of the controversies and disputes surrounding socialism. Only very few followed Greeley's *New York Daily Tribune* in complimenting the French "Associationists," as Americans then called the Fourier socialists. "Joint stock association is becoming the common principle of business," Greeley on 4 April 1848 reported one American observer in Paris as confirming, "and everywhere firms are giving their workmen shares in the concern."[41] The Second French Republic, steered by Ledru-Rollin, Arago, Lamartine, Crémieux, and Blanc, aimed to draw workmen into owning shares in businesses by means of "associationism" and to assist the unemployed and impoverished by guaranteeing work for all. Americans resenting the boost imparted to American abolitionism emanating from France, and to further democratization, women's rights, and public education and especially to labor unrest, seized on all of these as supposedly apt targets for scorn but especially fiercely decried socialism and the newly created French "National Workshops." These workshops, which Greeley, unlike most other American paper editors, presented sympathetically, attracted sizable numbers of unemployed and destitute in France and much attention in America. Greeley and a few others urged Americans to emulate the French example also in this respect.[42]

The rise of socialism and "associationism" as transatlantic phenomena during the 1840s became the chief spur to the growing (and lasting) alienation of most Americans from European democratic republicanism, again largely for domestic reasons. After some improvement in the mid-1840s, from 1846 down to 1849, renewed adverse price and subsistence trends in the United States had aggravated social tensions in the major cities. In New York, unrest commencing among the bricklayers, plasterers, and shoemakers culminated in the so-called working men's "insurgency" of 1850, a wave of strikes that convulsed the city that year in which immigrant workers in various trades participated. Besides garment workers, particularly prominent were the cabinetmakers and confectioners, mostly German craft associations, organized by the socialist leader Wilhelm Weitling (1808–71) and his Central Committee of the Trades, an organization representing 4,500 workers belonging to seventeen different trade unions.[43] In early adulthood a garment worker in Leipzig, Dresden, and Vienna, Weitling had acquired socialist leanings through reading and then activism in Parisian street battles during the late 1830s. His first book *Die Menschheit, wie sie ist und wie sie sein sollte* (Humanity as it is and should be), of 1838, combines passionate pleas for ending gross wealth inequality with a call to revolutionary action and renewal of the (radical, democratic) Aufklärung. He urged jettisoning all former notions about politics and society in favor of a brotherhood of all men and permanently erasing national and religious divisions. Capital should be reorganized into public funds vested in national banks, operated solely for the benefit of families and society.

Most workingmen, remarks Weitling in the first chapter, criticizing the typical artisan and early socialist tendency to focus on immediate economic concerns, searched for the causes of economic deprivation in their immediate circumstances instead of seeking them where they really lay—in princely authority and arrogance: "Ihr sucht immer die Ursache eurer Noth in eurer nächsten Umgebung, während sie in Pallästen, auf Thronen und weichen Teppichen ruht" (You constantly search for the cause of your distress in your immediate surroundings whereas it lies in palaces, thrones and on soft carpets).[44] Partly inspired by Moses Hess, the first theorist of German communism, Weitling ardently admired Babeuf and Buonarotti, and was the first in Europe and America to fuse a clear communist vision with calls for mass revolutionary action.[45] Tried and imprisoned in Zurich for sedition and blasphemy in 1845 (stating Jesus was a communist and Mary's illegitimate son), and subsequently deported from Switzerland, Weitling returned first to Paris where, during 1846–47, he gained prominence in the socialist movement there,[46] and then, in late 1847, transferred to New York where his reputation among the German immigrants preceded him. He at once began organizing workers' associations (as well as introducing improvements to sewing machines).

Weitling's New York workers' associations, a new development in American society, became a spur to America's growing reaction against unwelcome European influences and growing denunciation of revolutionary democratic republicanism. Mass gatherings of striking New York workers in May and June 1850 resulted by July and August in serious riots with the crowds, often recent immigrant workers, assailed by squads of baton-wielding police. Of the New York newspaper editors earlier sympathetic to the 1848 revolutionary wave, only Greeley, who initiated a publicity campaign to end the picket lines and ugly clashes, while calling for workers' cooperative workshops and associations, stuck with the demonstrators. The rest all turned against Greeley and the strikers, along with the unions and associationism.[47] Weitling continued organizing workmen in groups, centralizing his associations through the Allgemeiner Arbeiterbund (General Workingmen's League), a central organ representing some four thousand trade union members established in the autumn of 1850 by a General Workmen's Convention in Philadelphia attended by forty-four delegates.[48]

Weitling, working class himself and committed to promoting the working-class interest to which he devoted his life, nevertheless rejected the new dogma of class warfare, quarreling over this with Marx and Engels, former allies who, after 1848, consistently denounced and impeded his efforts.[49] Very different was another recent immigrant and socialist pioneer, Joseph Weydemeyer (1818–66), a former Prussian officer dishonorably discharged for radical views. In the years 1845–48, Weydemeyer edited several socialist periodicals in Germany, working closely with Marx and Engels, helping spread the new communist message. With the Revolution's demise, he fled to Switzerland and then, in November 1851, New York where he started *Die Revolution*, a Marxist paper preaching class warfare that encountered such hostility from other German-speaking immigrants it ceased publication after a week. Nevertheless, in 1851–53 Weydemeyer was a key figure in establishing Marxism as an intellectual and organizational movement in New York.[50] Vainly seeking to establish his brand of socialism in other cities, Weydemeyer spent his last years in St. Louis.

Besides big-city labor unrest, another Northern element impelling the great reversal of values and attitudes driven by America's multilayered 1847–52 domestic crisis was a temporary but massive resurgence of friction between anti-renters and big landlords, again most conspicuously in rural New York State. Resurgent anti-renter insurrection was the chief factor that pushed Fenimore Cooper to now abandon the democratic radicalism he had so conspicuously and eloquently championed in the 1820s and 1830s, moving him to adopt a conservative pro-gentry stance from the mid-1840s onward.[51] Friction had increased as a result of a campaign to recoup unpaid rents on the now 750,000-acre Rensselaerswyck estate left in arrears following the death, in 1839, of Stephen van Rensselaer III whose leniency regarding rent arrears had been legendary.[52] Mobilizing for local political action against landlords pushing for rent arrears, anti-renter leagues collected funds and organized rent boycotts as well as initiated collective legal actions over a considerable area.

By 1844–45, the anti-renters' campaign of intimidation as well as rent strikes had led to several violent incidents, including the killing of a deputy sheriff, prompting a soon powerful backlash. Temporarily, in the New York State spring elections of 1845 and 1846, anti-renters achieved breakthroughs in five counties and subsequently exacted measures in the state legislature weakening the big proprietors in both rent disputes and state politics. The radical wing of the movement to "emancipate" the anti-renters, headed by the Irish firebrand Thomas Ainge Devyr, editor of the *Albany Freeholder*, insistently called for sweeping measures to break up big landholdings and limit the size of future land acquisitions to 160 acres. Son of a baker, Devyr was a staunch Paineite and enlightener in the tradition of 1776 (in America), 1792 (in France), and 1798 (in Ireland).[53] In his booklet *Our Natural Rights* (1835), originally published in Ireland but reprinted at Williamsburg in 1842, Devyr styled Britain a country where "aristocracy are possessed of all power in making the laws" and Ireland an exploited land languishing in "the deplorable state of slavery to which that country was reduced by the despotism of England." Britain and Ireland, he fully conceded, had "evinced no rational idea of freedom" prior to the American Revolution: he did not doubt that it was America's revolutionary struggle that "served to give them a knowledge of its nature and importance."

Proclaiming the American Revolution the most decisive event in the history of the modern struggle for liberty universally, in Ireland and Scotland no less than America, he maintained that the pre-1775 flight of impoverished Irish and Scots Highlanders to the American colonies, under pressure from unfeeling landlords exacting excessive rents, had been a major factor in generating the momentum needed to break free of the tyranny imposed by "our Lords and Gentlemen" in America. He saw impoverished and expropriated Irish and Scots fleeing Britain as having contributed in a major way to the entire global process of American-inspired anti-aristocratic republican emancipation and democracy starting in the United States itself.[54]

Between 1844 and 1848, anti-rentism, with the agrarianism of Fourier attached to its coattails, gained ground impressively. But in the years 1848–50, bolstered by a growing conservative backlash, the New York landlords reversed the tide through a vigorous campaign of repression, eviction notices, and legal targeting of rent boycotters. Anti-renters, especially the "men who enjoy most of the hatred of the Aristocracy," as Greeley styled Devyr and his set, had also ardently backed the antislavery campaign. They were now tarred by their foes as instigators of the dangerous new "democratic" agitation breeding subversion, irreligion, and "socialism" now threatening to subvert all America. To conservatives, abolitionism, anti-rentism, secularism, and socialism, including Fourierism, had all come to be ideologically closely connected.[55] As evictions soared, the anti-renters increasingly divided into anti-socialist "moderates" and uncompromising radicals headed by Devyr.[56] The landlords had some success in encouraging tenants to buy out their interest in particular farms, thereby gradually weakening their adversaries. Owing to evictions, ending tenancy arrangements, and the chorus decrying "socialism," support for the anti-renter campaign steadily contracted in the years 1848–50. By 1851, the anti-renter revolt was dead and Devyr's *Albany Freeholder* had closed down.

During the late 1840s, for the first time in America, the alleged menace of "socialism" came to be widely invoked for political and social purposes. Populist vilification of "socialism" and new immigrants became a potent weapon against striking workers, anti-renters, Catholicism, Jews, and, in the South, abolitionism. On 4 April 1848, the *Savannah Republican* admonished readers that the "greatest danger" threatening the Second French Republic was the eagerness of its "directors to do too much" and "rush into Socialism," and that "still more cruel absurdity of immediately emancipating the slaves of all the Colonies of France."[57] From April 1848, reports of continuing outbreaks of violent mob rule evoking the threat of anarchy served step-by-step to blacken the image of the 1848 Revolution and the Second French Republic in the majority of American eyes. There was a growing impulse to align the American public behind English rejectionist opinion, viewing France with its republican and socialist tendencies as a kind of "anti-Britain" incorrigibly rebelling against religion, morality, and proper attitudes, including sound economics. The "threat of socialism" began being deployed as an instrument for prodding American opinion more energetically to condemn the entire democratic republican revolutionary program and consciousness. Bit by bit American reaction came to scorn 1848 along with immigrants, "philosophists," Enlightenment, Chartism, women's rights, Paineism, and "equality."

Within months the Second French Republic descended from democratic euphoria to disillusionment and civil strife and, from the autumn of 1848, triumphant conservative and clerical reaction. Only Greeley's *New York Daily Tribune* and the *New York Globe*, representing a minute enclave of opinion, had anything positive to say about the French republican Left striving to combine pursuit of social and economic fairness and commercial regulation with civil and political rights.[58] Intellectual and emotional retreat from their earlier publicly declared sympathy for the Revolution, observers of American intellectual life noted, led to a dramatic volte-face among such prominent figures as Rush, George Bancroft, Fenimore Cooper, Henry Wadsworth Longfellow, and Charles Sumner, a prominent Massachusetts advocate of civil rights and antislavery senator. Unlike Emerson, they all retreated in step with the growing hostility to the revolutions evinced by the propertied elite, which at Boston, according to Bancroft, was by April 1848 already "frightened out of its wits."[59] At Boston, New York, and Philadelphia, the sway of money, property, and commerce was felt to be under immediate threat. That strand of American ideology, since the 1790s summoning Americans to differentiate sharply between their own revolutionary achievement and that of others, was in these circumstances powerfully bolstered. According to the now potent "exceptionalist" myth, foreign revolutions, whether in France, Italy, Latin America, Canada, or wherever, were inherently different, anarchic, backward, and inferior.

Briefly, the mounting wave of condemnation of the Second French Republic in American conservative and Southern papers was countered by pro-Revolution zeal in Northern progressive papers and antislavery journals. But the 1848 Swiss and Dutch constitutions turned out to be the only successful, enduring outcome from the upheavals. The balance of opinion, ominously for the future, shifted noticeably along with a growing tendency to distance the political and constitutional dimensions of the 1848 Revolution (apart from slavery) from the European revolutionary movements' social and economic concerns. Insistence on segregating the constitutional from the social became ever more pronounced, as did disgust at the persistent unrest and reports that extreme Leftist groups were active in Paris. Suspicion grew that the mob that ransacked the Tuileries was using the power of the street to direct the new Republic toward far-reaching economic goals—raise wages, reduce rents and unemployment, and even perhaps forcibly appropriate the railways. A powerful anti-revolutionary bias, initially especially marked at Boston, viewing the 1848 Revolution as the harbinger of class strife and socialism, in this way became politically tied to the pro-slavery interest.

The myth gained ground that "liberty" and "democracy" were peculiarly and particularly American. At the heart of this reworked conservative ideology was the belief that "habits, essentially necessary to the continuance of such a government, must be formed by practice, and that each step in the road of improvement must be made, as in a school, by slow degrees and under a peculiar arrangement." It was a thesis according to which "no people can become fit for a republican government" without sufficient maturity, "without a long preparation, under political institutions so managed as to be made more and more liberal or popular" with the passage of time, as it was expressed by Theodore Dwight (1796–1866), a nephew of the reactionary Yale president Timothy Dwight. Theodore Dwight was a school reformer, travel writer, and champion of Garibaldi and the Risorgimento who detested his uncle's narrow conservatism. "In support of this new doctrine," he noted sarcastically, "we are referred to our own history; and indeed we there find that our ancestors, in England first and in America afterwards, advanced, from time to time; and we can trace at least some of the steps made between the days of Magna Carta and our own." Since nearly all the revolutions apart from the American had distressingly collapsed in one way or another, those of Latin America uniformly failing to produce democratic or libertarian outcomes, the almost unrelieved catalogue of failure outside the Anglo-Saxon world could readily be attributed to other peoples' lack of the requisite qualities and of the long preparation characteristic of Americans, who had derived much from the stability and supposed superiority of British institutions, a point as dear to the American as the British gentry. "We therefore, reasonably, as many think, come to the conclusion, that we have pursued the right course and they"—foreigners, continental Europeans, and French Canadians—"a wrong one."[60] For the French, Italians, Germans, Spaniards, Poles, Greeks, and Ibero-Americans, let alone Asians and Africans, it would require centuries to catch up.

Those propagating such views, significantly, included some of the most highly articulate and educated, among them Ambassadors Rush in Paris and Bancroft in London. Other notable gentleman-scholars like Walter H. Prescott and Francis Parkman were also busy constructing the new patriotic narrative of American history in which American freedom and constitutionalism were the achievement of white Anglo-Saxon Protestants while the predicated inherent political and cultural inferiority of the black, Mexican, French Canadian, and Amerindian, as well as Catholic and Jew, also accounted for their social and cultural marginality and subordination.[61] This current of imputed ethnic, cultural, and religious superiority liked to emphasize "manifest destiny" and white Anglo-Saxon Protestant roots, and gently accommodated—even if it was not quite willing to "justify"—marginalization of the Native American, enslavement of blacks, seizure of territory from Mexicans, and prejudice against new immigrants, especially anti-Irish sentiment, anti-Italianism, and anti-Semitism.[62]

Rush remained eager for international constitutional reform, but despite his efforts to draw French attention to American federalism and the *Federalist Papers*, France's republican leaders, to his intense disappointment, persisted in ignoring federalism, bicameralism, division of powers, and Anglo-American constitutionalism generally.[63] Bancroft, long prominent in the world of books, research, and universities, and among the leading American scholars of his time, is a particularly notable case. A torchbearer of the American Enlightenment and Unitarian conception of progress (though also a key supporter of Jacksonianism and architect of the attack on Mexico), he hailed from Worcester, Massachusetts, where his father had been a Unitarian minister, stalwart revolutionary, and author of a popular biography of Washington. If chauvinistic and triumphalist at times, none could question his dedication to the American revolutionary tradition which in his historical writing he characterized above all as one of "moderation."[64] None could deny his cosmopolitanism: he had studied at Harvard, Heidelberg, Göttingen, and Berlin, knew French and Italian as well as German literature, and had acquired Hebrew, Arabic, and New Testament Greek. He had met Goethe, Hegel, Lamartine, Schleiermacher, Wilhelm von Humboldt, Byron, Constant, and Manzoni. Despite his Jacksonian proclivities, Bancroft energetically opposed slavery and urged a general renewal of American revolutionary values.

When the 1848 revolutions first erupted, Bancroft rejoiced to find that the American Revolution was proving an inspiring example. Initially, he regretted only that there was not more enthusiasm for the European revolutions in America. "Has the echo of American Democracy which you now hear from France, and Austria, and Prussia and all Old Germany, no power to stir up the American people to new achievements?"[65] He was still delighted, in April 1848, that Lamartine, Crémieux, and other members of the Republic's provisional government were devising a constitution that would express the French national character while also "studying ours," Crémieux having "ordered everything he could find: manuscripts and commentaries" while Lamartine was "diligently inquiring about us." "The moderation of the people," he agreed with Rush, "is marvelous, and will be rewarded."[66] But as the scene turned uglier, Bancroft's zeal rapidly waned; increasingly he began insisting on the special, unique virtues of America. "Our own country," he observed in September 1848, "furnishes the only example of a people contented with its government. I love the principles of popular power that lies at the bottom of our institutions and I love the Union."[67]

Bancroft's and Rush's early fervor for Europe's 1848 rapidly transmogrified into its exact opposite. The French, Germans, and Italians, unlike the Swiss and Belgians, failed to venerate or replicate the basic format of American liberty and constitutionalism. Mistakenly, they adhered to their own more centralized republican vision. "They have made a very poor constitution," Bancroft assured Congress, in February 1849, referring to the new French Republic's founding document finalized only months later with universal male suffrage as its primary characteristic; "and how this impatient people are to get on with it surpasses my skill to divine."[68] The constitutional convention had indeed rejected De Tocqueville's proposal that France emulate America by adopting a two-chamber legislature. But Rush's claiming the French had comprehensively ignored the American model was not wholly accurate. For the most obviously disastrous feature of the 1848 French constitution was precisely its popularly elected, excessively powerful, one-man presidency, an executive directly copied from American example and practice pushed through—in particular by Lamartine and De Tocqueville—against those of more genuinely republican tendency desiring the French president to be elected by the legislature.[69] This overt piece of *Américanisme* proved calamitous and was to be bitterly rued.

Subtle and skeptical, Melville's aversion to the revolutions and the initial American enthusiasm they engendered was more reserved and complex. No less than Whitman, Hawthorne, Emerson, Fuller, Bancroft, Dwight, and other American commentators on 1848, Melville remained deeply engrossed in the revolutions and their meaning for humanity.[70] The events of 1848 profoundly affected him too, but in his case intensifying a sense of revulsion, of a fatal deadlock between the warring classes, that overcame him during his 1849 visit to France when, revolted by the unruly crowd behavior around him, he mostly kept to museums and restaurants, eschewing the crowds.[71] His ambitious but unsuccessful novel *Mardi* (1849) seethed with negative reflections on the 1848 Revolution, marking an important turning point in his literary output—prompting his quest for a deeper, more meaningful creativity and, simultaneously, the waning of his former popularity. For Melville, revolution now signified what he called in his moving story *Billy Budd* "the enemy's red meteor of unbridled and unbounded revolt," a terrible negative pitting the crowd's ungovernable ignorance, bigotry, and faithlessness against the uprightness of the exceptional individual who stands against it. The message of *Billy Budd* (unfinished and never published during his lifetime) is that revolution means crowd irrationality, violence, and death, decimating the good along with the bad to everyone's loss.[72] For Melville, worldly salvation became individual, not collective. His late post-1848 writing in this respect reflected a growing rejection of the masses as irredeemably unpredictable and disorderly that, by 1849, dominated the entire American reaction to the 1848 revolutions (and the great French Revolution). Melville's post-1849 loss of popularity that blighted the rest of his life was in no way due to this shift in political perspective, though: its cause was just his writing's growing strangeness and obscurity.

However, sections of the intelligentsia, Walt Whitman among them, strongly resisted these trends and a few, while rejecting socialism and communism, continued strongly to sympathize with the 1848 Revolution's democratic radicalism.[73] Several spirited American commentators on the 1848–50 upheavals

proclaimed in no uncertain terms that the United States was shamefully failing to fulfill its destined role in mankind's affairs. "And what shall we say of
our own position," demanded Dwight in 1851, "and the part we have taken
in the affairs of Italy?" There was no excuse for self-congratulation in being
a people "whose agents abroad and whose statesmen at home have generally
shown extreme ignorance and indifference towards the character and claims of
Italians, and too often, have used their official influence against them." Aware,
upright Americans, contended Dwight, should openly express "indignation
at the discredit thus brought upon our country, and the utter perversion of
our true principles and policy, to the irreparable injury of men and nations,
whom our ancestors would have loved and honoured, for the noble part they
have taken on the theatre of the world."[74] In this way, an unprecedented gulf
opened up between the American public and a Left-leaning intellectual fringe
expressing bitter, sweeping criticism of the United States. The rift was to
prove an enduring one both at home and among Americans abroad.

Emerson, arriving in England for a lecture tour in October 1847, was prevented by engagements from proceeding to Paris until the late spring of 1848.
While in England, he criticized the aristocratic character of society, huge inequality of wealth, and barriers to meritocratic self-advancement, echoing the
usual criticism of American, European, and British radicals.[75] The Britain of
1848 was no model to the world. His three-week stay in Paris began on 7 May,
just as the crisis point was reached in efforts to hold the new French Revolution together. The challenge confronting Lamartine and the radicals was
how to prevent the legacy of the Brissotins and Jeffersonian American heritage
from being pulverized between the two powerfully divergent mutually hostile
blocs—on one side "moderation" (i.e., social conservatism) pursuing political
rights without measures of social reform, and, on the other, socialism, pursuing economic and social reform without much concern for democratic politics, liberty of the press, institutions, education, and the individual. Plainly,
French socialists in 1848 were not greatly interested in freedom of expression,
education, or secularization. Rather, Fourier, Proudhon, Blanqui, Blanc, and
Barbès disdained the *philosophes* and all they stood for. To them, cultivating
an independent-minded, freethinking population exercising political rights
within a democratic framework along with human rights, full toleration, and
liberty of expression and to criticize was an essentially secondary affair largely
irrelevant to their schemes to capture and transform the economic system.

In Paris, Emerson attended a lively socialist meeting in the Club de la Révolution, with the flamboyant Armand Barbès presiding. The scene was dominated by students, journalists, literary people, artists, and intellectuals, noted
Emerson, with hardly any genuine workingmen present. The composition of

the new socialist movement in fact scarcely differed from that of the radical revolutionary intelligentsia of the past. Only now these men had switched priorities and goals, adopting an economically and socially oriented but also narrower standpoint. The passionate debates he witnessed at the clubs upset Emerson's delicate New England equanimity. For months he had been imbibing and had half accepted the outright disdain for the European revolutionary upsurge propagated by the British press. Though it bothered him already in England that the "frame of society is aristocratic, the taste of the people is loyal," the drama of revolutionary polarization and the passion and deep earnestness he encountered in Paris still came as a shock.[76] "It is easy to see," he remarked, "that France is far nearer to socialism than England and it would be easy to convert Paris into a phalanstery."[77] He felt drawn to the "generous ideas of the socialists, the magnificence of their theories, and the enthusiasm with which they have been urged." "All winter I have been admiring the English and disparaging the French. Now in these weeks I have been correcting my prejudice and the French rise many entire degrees."[78] On 13 and 14 May, he attended meetings at the Club des Droits de l'Homme, on the very eve of the great demonstrations that so fatally split the Revolution. Afterward, he wrote to his wife of the "deep sincerity of the speakers who are agitating social not political questions, and who are studying how to secure a fair share of bread to every man, and to get God's justice done through the land."[79]

By this time, though, polarization had progressed to a point where it had become impossible to heal the divisions within the Revolution or steer republicanism along a middle path between socialism and the democratic republicans. Emerson sympathized with both sides—democratic republicans and socialists. But those who chiefly benefited from the rift were the provincial men of reaction. Emerson felt his democratic idealism trapped in a quandary, not knowing which way to turn. Rethinking his democratic creed in the months after the May rising, he concluded that a writer like himself, ardently seeking the truth, could not unequivocally opt for either socialism *or* democratic radicalism. He withdrew into a defiant "armed neutrality."[80] The scholar's and poet's aloofness from the fray became Emerson's new creed: "the scholar" must recoil less from socialist leaders and their theories than the crassness and unruliness of their following and the divisive effect of socialist teaching; while he must equally loathe the "oppression and hopeless selfishness of the rich." "I have mended my opinions of French and English very materially this year in the two capitals," he assured Fuller, and would "heartily wish to add now your knowledge of the Southerner, the dwellers of the land of *si* [i.e., Italy]."[81]

In Italy, the revolutionary turmoil persisted and the republicans fought on for many more months. It thrilled Margaret Fuller that, by late 1848, progressive

Italians had now discarded "moderation" in the face of the repeated betrayals by the princes, aristocracy, and the pope—and finally of "the imbecile Louis Bonaparte." "The work is done; the Revolution in Italy is now radical, nor can it stop till Italy becomes independent and united as a republic."[82] Describing the eventual collapse of the Italian Revolution, Fuller, like Ledru-Rollin, Sand, and other democratic leaders, routinely employed what had long been standard political vocabulary, using "moderates" to distinguish those preferring constitutional monarchy, aristocracy, and church hierarchy from "radicals" fighting for republicanism, secularism, and democracy. This was current usage in the early and mid-nineteenth century but one later historians rather confusingly abandoned for the Marxist habit of labeling socialists "the radicals" and Left republicans opposing the militant socialists and authoritarian populists "moderates." This distorted usage came to prevail despite the glaring contradiction involved in explaining how and why the "bourgeoisie fell back into royalism," as Marx himself expressed it, when the February Revolution had, according to Marxists, brought bourgeois rule to its apogee.[83] Marx claimed the bourgeoisie overthrew monarchy and aristocracy in 1848 but then, presumably changing its mind, "fell back into royalism" a thesis hard to make sense of.

Italian exiles were among the largest contingents in Belgium, Switzerland, France, England, and the New World. The most renowned of all the Italian revolutionaries, Giuseppe Garibaldi (1807–82), having joined both Young Italy (Giovine Italia) and the Carbonari, by 1833, and participated in a failed insurrection in Piedmont, in 1834, spent the entire period between 1834 and 1848 in exile, mostly in Brazil and Uruguay. The young Giuseppe Mazzini (1805–72), later to become the foremost republican political and social commentator of Risorgimento Italy, joined the Carbonari in 1829 and was among the many captured Carbonarists imprisoned by the Piedmontese ducal government in the autumn of 1830. Released some months later, he went into exile abroad from March 1831 at Marseilles, a noted center of Carbonarist intrigue, where he founded the soon fast-growing Young Italy movement with its manifesto rejecting the constitutional monarchist format of the 1812 Cádiz Constitution in favor of a purer, more centralized, and democratic republicanism.

Son of a Genoa university professor, and a lover of literature, Mazzini was an eager student of philosophy, particularly Vico, Condorcet, Rousseau, and Herder. Exceptional intellectual attainments gained him preeminence during the 1830s within the Italian republican exile networks in France and Switzerland of a very different kind from that of Garibaldi, with whom he collaborated closely in 1848–49. Directing these networks, he continued the secretive methods and clandestine correspondence of the Carbonari while discarding their nomenclature and antiquated ritual. Different though they were, Mazzini and

Garibaldi were undoubtedly both more typical of the international democratic revolutionary Left of the 1830s than the early socialists. Often described as a "nationalist," Mazzini was more especially a democratic republican patriot desiring the entire nation to be equalized legally and politically, and equally represented by the legislature. Later, residing in England, he admired the stability of English institutions but always spurned monarchy and especially the hegemony of aristocracy prevailing in Britain.

Mazzini's fervent republican creed (and knowledge of the United States) derived mainly from the enlightened journals he studied in France. Attempts to discredit democratic republicanism with the perversity of the Robespierre regime he compared to judging Christianity by tarring it with the St. Bartholomew Day's massacre or the cruelty of the Inquisition. It was certainly not Robespierre or the Terror that inspired the radicalism of 1830 and 1848. A dedicated democratic republican, in fact Mazzini dreaded the populist authoritarianism that undermined the French Revolution and such as Emerson feared was undermining the legacy of the American: "Give the suffrage to a people unfitted for it, governed by hateful reactionary passions, they will sell it, or will make a bad use of it; they will introduce instability into every part of the state; they will render impossible those great combined views, those thoughts for the future, which make the life of a nation powerful and progressive." Certainly, Mazzini, like other radicals, aspired to lessen economic inequalities; but, like Ruge and the radical tendency more generally, he profoundly disagreed with Marx, rejecting class and economic warfare as the prime motors of history. Mazzini loved Switzerland but firmly rejected federalism whether in its Swiss or American manifestations (which tended to estrange him from older Carbonarists more inclined to venerate the American model). The Roman Republic, proclaimed by Mazzini and Garibaldi in February 1849, was among the last and most stirring episodes of the revolutionary sequence. Short-lived though it proved, it won a special, resounding place in the history of the Risorgimento, Italy's national rebirth.

The Italian people, now radicalized, were showing themselves capable, believed Fuller, of rising up and performing grandiose feats. Unfortunately, Americans were doing little to assist: "How I wish my country would show some noble sympathy when an experience so like her own is going on." Americans no longer appeared willing to remember their own past or even offer the financial collections made for Greece and Poland in the 1820s and 1830s: "It would make me proud to have my country show a religious faith in the progress of ideas, and make some small sacrifice of its own great resources in aid of a sister cause, now." But her pleas published in Greeley's *New York Daily Tribune* for American help, volunteers, and intervention had little effect. To her distress, the American envoy in Rome had no desire to emulate Rush and Bancroft. Americans in Italy, she felt, "talk about the corrupt and degenerate state of Italy as they do about that of our slaves at home," ruinously adopting "that mode of reasoning which affirms that because men are degraded by bad institutions, they are not fit for better."[84] How much more inspiring and satisfactory would it have been had America "acted nobly and all that is most truly American in America" had intervened to "sustain the sickened hopes of European democracy."[85]

In a bid to secure the increasingly confident conservative Catholic bloc, dominant in rural France, Louis-Napoleon, in the spring of 1849, with great fanfares, dispatched an expeditionary military force to champion the papacy in central Italy. Despite the fact that the new French constitution strictly forbade any such intervention against the liberty of another people, its clear purpose was to overthrow the recently formed Roman Republic, crush the republican fighters, and restore reaction and the papal government. Establishing his personal dictatorship and fully suppressing democratic republicanism in France, Louis-Napoleon grasped, required Catholic support and that of the peasantry, and there was no better way to consolidate his grip in France than by assisting the pope to quash Mazzini's and Garibaldi's revolutionary republican government in Rome.[86] Republicans everywhere viewed the French intervention as the betrayal of betrayals. Nothing could be more contrary to the republican spirit of 1789–93 than Louis-Napoleon's populism, Italian intervention, and plea for Catholic support. Louis-Napoleon aimed to reinstate autocratic papal rule under French protection or, as Dwight styled it, seal the "disgrace of one republic and the overthrow of another, with the destruction, or at least the long delay of religious liberty and the restoration of popery. Louis-Napoleon no doubt looks to the sovereigns for a reward, as he has made France disgrace republicanism at home by suppressing it in a much purer form, among a superior race, and in a much more important position, abroad."[87]

Democrats and republicans everywhere were plunged into despondency. Italian patriots and republicans could draw comfort only from the brief heroic defense of the Roman barricades, and the heroic national myth Mazzini and Garibaldi forged.[88] All her private hopes, averred a distraught Fuller, had "fallen with the hopes of Italy."[89] Everywhere in Italy, the struggle ended, as in Vienna and Prague, and later Hungary, with the triumph of the Right. By his intervention, Louis-Napoleon effectively buried democratic republicanism itself. The defeat in Rome was resounding and also final. Yet, where republicans and democrats in France, Italy, and the wider world were impotently furious at the French Republic's overthrowing the Roman Republic and restoring papal rule, this development baffled but did not particularly antagonize Americans.

If the Second "Republic" under Louis-Napoleon disgraced itself in the eyes of republicans and democrats, Italy was betrayed scarcely less ignominiously by American opinion, contended Fuller. It distressed her to hear compatriots, whether in Europe or at home, voice the "same arguments against the emancipation of Italy, that are used against the emancipation of our blacks; the same arguments in favor of the spoliation of Poland, as for the [American] conquest of Mexico. I find the cause of tyranny and wrong everywhere the same,—and lo! My country! The darkest offender, because with the least excuse, forsworn to the high calling with which she was called, no champion of the rights of men, but a robber and a jailer; the scourge hid behind her banner, her eyes fixed not upon the stars, but on the possession of other men."[90]

In the French legislature, resistance to Louis-Napoleon, especially opposition to the expedition to Rome, led by Ledru-Rollin, was tenacious but, given the paucity of deputies of republican disposition, easily stifled. When his attempt to impeach the would-be dictator in June 1849 failed, his supporters incited demonstrations (13 June) that were then suppressed by force, obliging Ledru-Rollin to flee to London where, alongside Mazzini, he joined the executive of the international revolutionary committee based there. In subsequent months, Louis Blanc, Victor Hugo, and many other writers and intellectuals, including Théophile Thoré (1807–69), the great nineteenth-century historian and critic of Dutch Golden Age art, departed into foreign exile. Month by month, populist acclaim grew as the new dictator's grip tightened. The shattering abasement of democracy, freedom of expression, and revolutionary values was completed with the introduction of additional press and electoral restrictions, together with curbs on gathering and petitioning, introduced in May 1850.

The most "immediate peril of the Republic," suggested Horace Greeley, contemplating Louis-Napoleon's May 1850 amendments to the French constitution, was degradation of the French electorate. France's new president, he noted while in Paris in June 1851 during a European trip, was enforcing "arbitrary disfranchisement of nearly half the electorate," imposing "severe restrictions on the press, withdrawal of the right to gather for deliberation and debate, and the transfer of the state's patronage into the hands of his supporters." If the republicans were "to attempt holding a convention to elect a candidate for president, their meetings would be promptly suppressed by the police and the bayonet."[91] Greeley was not yet completely disheartened, though; among other hopeful signs, he found no less than three thousand Americans in Paris alone (according to official sources), most "residing here for months if not for years. It gives me pleasure to state that, contrary to what I have often heard of the bearing of our countrymen in Europe [notably from Fuller], a large majority of these, so far as I can judge from meeting a good many and learning the sentiments of more, are warmly and openly on the side of the Republic and opposed to the machinations of the motley host who seek its overthrow."[92]

It was but a small further step, however, for Louis-Napoleon to launch his culminating coup d'état in December 1851. After a good deal of firing and loss of life in the streets, the republicans were finally crushed totally. Having extinguished the Second Republic in all but name, the new dictator erased its name too, in December 1852, proclaiming himself Napoleon III, "Emperor of the French" and "protector of the Church." Those republicans remaining in office on the Republic's dissolution refusing to swear an oath of loyalty to the new "emperor" were stripped of their posts and driven abroad or into political isolation within France, among them Jules Michelet, now deprived of his professorship (for the second time) and his position as head of the historical section of the National Archives.[93]

America's "Forty-Eighters"

Within Europe, the political refugees of 1848–49 driven from France, Italy, Germany, and Austria mostly fled to Belgium, Britain, and Switzerland. The historian Jakob Burckhardt (1818–97) eyed the large influx of defeated revolutionaries to Zurich and his native Basel with a mixture of pessimism, suspicion, and unease. The greatest number of political refugees, though, migrated to the United States accompanied across the Atlantic during these years by exceptionally large numbers of other migrants: several hundred thousand entered the United States from Germany alone during the five-year period between 1848 and 1853. The exodus of refugees of every sort from German-speaking lands occurred on such a massive scale that this social-cultural reverse "revolution" in Europe, depleting the continent's revolutionary underground, helped preclude any chance of another revolutionary upsurge in Europe for many decades while injecting a whole new cultural and social dimension into American society and politics. "The unprecedented influx of republican-minded non-English-speaking political refugees entering the United States," among them an estimated 4,000 front-line "Forty-Eighters" (as they came to be known), radicals who had directly participated in the revolutions, continued unabated until the mid-1850s.[94] The sheer scale of this intellectual and political hemorrhage of revolutionary activism was not the least of the reasons why Europe lapsed for decades into quiescence after 1849.

"The 'demagogues' of the last four years," commented one contemporary in America, in 1852, "are in exile; the energetic portion of their adherents have followed them, going to the republic when the republic would not come to them. Those who remain behind have lapsed into their former state of contented servitude."[95] The exiles and revolutionary refugees driven from German lands, in 1848–53, including several former members of the 1849 Frankfurt Parliament and other short-lived local revolutionary governments, settled in countless places across the United States. Notable concentrations outside New York and Philadelphia were at Milwaukee, Chicago, and St. Louis. The most important and striking feature of these networks of Forty-Eighters in America was their rapidly fragmenting into competing democratic republican and socialist blocs. In Germany as well as France, socialism had emerged strongly during the 1840s and begun to rival democratic republicanism, so that even before the 1848 Revolution, in those parts of Germany where censorship weakened or broke down, a few journals, like the Trier paper, *Die Trier'sche Zeitung*, had already shifted from republican radicalism to socialism.[96] During the revolutionary months in Germany and Austria, socialists and democratic republicans had increasingly diverged. It is unsurprising, therefore, that one specifically American consequence of the dividing of the revolutionary movement of 1848–49 was a permanent rift between those focused on social reform and those seeking a wider emancipation—the splintering of the Forty-Eighters shortly after arriving in America, with the thousands of political refugees migrating to the United States replicating the polarizing division that had helped destroy the revolutionary republics in Germany, Austria, and France.

But both rival factions faced the problem that dispersal of the new German immigration was so wide that it proved difficult to establish a successful politically progressive German press in the many states, including Indiana and Ohio, where this was attempted. At a less politically engaged level, the new wave of German immigration included many farmers, manufacturers, and businessmen.[97] In Missouri and Wisconsin, two of the states where the impact of the German influx was greatest, whole rural enclaves were established. German farmers along the Missouri River settled as a group, working their farms themselves without slaves. Together with the large German population in St. Louis they formed a locally effective antislavery, pro-Unionist bloc that developed a separate identity and consciousness from the mostly pro-Confederate majority of white Missouri society. German newspapers in St. Louis, like the *Missouri Radikale*, the *Anzeiger*, and the *Westliche Post*, helped entrench an antislavery, pro-Unionist attitude that led to fighting between the rival white communities on the outbreak of the Civil War (1862–65) and the swift securing of St. Louis for the Union.

Most Forty-Eighter political activists and publicists, though, journalists, teachers, physicians, artists, musicians, and literary people of one sort or another were an ousted leadership without a sufficient following of skilled artisans or educated workers to enable them organize effectively. A leading early propagator and popularizer of Marxism alongside Weydemeyer was Carl Douai (1819–88), who had studied at Leipzig and Dorpat and been imprisoned for revolutionary writings. In America, Douai was expelled from Texas, in 1856, and Boston in 1860; he finally settled in New York, briefly as editor of the New York *Demokrat*. Among Forty-Eighter professors was a Marburg philosopher, Karl Theodor Bayrhoffer (1812–88), known for spreading radical views among students until suspended in 1846 for "blasphemy and incitement against the [Hessian] government."[98] Forty-Eighters, as distinct from the wider German, Irish, and Italian immigration and as a segment of American society, typically called on Americans to become more actively involved in the work of freeing Europe from oppression but with relatively little success. Briefly, some idealistically dreamed of the United States—much as Anarcharsis Cloots, during the Great French Revolution, had thought of France—as the headquarters of the world's liberation movements, the focal point and political guide of the future world's league of free republics.

One curious network of non-socialist utopian radicals was headed by the Philadelphia teacher Theodor Poesche (1824–99), a philosophy student who had been a leader of the 1848 rising in Halle, and a Pennsylvania German, Charles Goepp (1827–1907), who together fused democratic republicanism with American expansionism and racism to form a bizarre new ideology. Exalting America's mission in the world as the prime agent of humanity's emancipation, Poesche and Goepp convened a "congress of Germans" at Philadelphia in January 1852 that launched the so-called American Revolutionary League for Europe. Despising "moderate liberalism" lacking genuine republican content, and all nationalism, they urged every people, "upon throwing off the yoke of its tyrants," to seek "admission into the league of states already free, that is, into the American Union; so that these states may become the nucleus of the political organization of the human family, and the starting-point of the World's Republic."[99] These two afterward convened another congress at Wheeling, West Virginia, in September 1852, relaunching their organization as the People's League of the Old and New World. Undaunted by dwindling support, they later produced a jointly written book, *The New Rome, or, The United States of the World* (New York, 1853), offering an unprepossessing vision of America's future world domination that included outright annexation of Canada, Mexico, Central America, Cuba, Haiti, and the Dominican Republic.[100]

French Canadians, contended Poesche and Goepp, preferred annexation to the United States to remaining under Britain while the same allegedly held true for Canadian English speakers, given Canada now boasted over three times as many Irish and Scots as English Canadians—by their figures 318,000 as against 94,000. Distant countries Brazil and beyond would gradually become "infederated."[101] The "flame of American liberty" born of the American Revolution they construed as a process of continuing "revolution" but also of future domination of the world: "the revolution which rose in and with America, must for ever return to it; and America which began in revolution, must live in it, and end with it. When the dominion of nationality is crushed and the sovereignty of the individual is attained everywhere and everyhow, the missions of the revolution and of America will both be accomplished."[102] Their "crucible in which European, Asiatic and African nationalities and peculiarities are smelted into unity," this "New Rome" they purportedly based on universal and equal "rights" and constitutionality without taint of group chauvinism or ethnic superiority.[103] But Poesche and Goepp's utopia turned out to be purely the accomplishment of Anglo-Saxons and Germans. They claimed to approve of racial mixing; but the fruits of miscegenation were unfortunately lost when a "higher order of beings" is "deteriorated by admixture with a lower," by "cohabitation of the male of the lower race with the female of the higher," resulting in the "ovum of the latter being thus tainted."[104] Blatant racism vitiated their conflation of universal rights with American individualism producing a curious new strain of imperialism tied to rejection of exceptionalism and aristocracy.

Forty-Eighters settled among numerous local pools of German and other recent immigrants that were neither large enough to sustain radical movements nor small enough to appear insignificant. By the early 1850s these dominated whole quarters of a few large cities and sometimes—as at Louisville, Kentucky, where by 1850 there were no less than 7,357 Germans among 12,500 recent immigrants (over 3,000 of whom were Irish) in a total population of only 43,000—amounted to a sizable slice of the population of small towns.[105] Such obtrusive segments of small towns with few recent immigrants in surrounding areas were especially exposed to prejudice. Much the most paradoxical and least edifying dimension of American reaction to 1848 was the ensuing upsurge of anti-intellectual "Nativism" and anti-foreignism. Characteristic was the hostile local reaction to the personage who more than any other represented an authentic post-1848 radical republican enlightenment, rejecting socialism, "moderation," racism, and imperialism—the journalist Karl Peter Heinzen (1809–80), an unbending champion of free thought and free expression who settled in Louisville in 1853. As a student Heinzen had been expelled from Bonn University for sedition and, in 1844, after publishing a pamphlet attacking the Prussian bureaucracy, had been stripped of his job and forced to flee to Switzerland. During wandering years prior to the 1848 revolutions, while at Brussels, he became embroiled in controversy in verbal debate and the *Deutsche Brüsseler Zeitung* with Marx and Engels, who both rejected his American-style federalist republicanism and plea for democracy.[106]

After participating in the 1848 Baden Revolution, while combating "moderates" and socialists equally, Heinzen had failed to get elected as a delegate for Hamburg in the Frankfurt Parliament. On the Revolution's collapse, he fled first to Switzerland from where he was expelled and then, in 1850, to the United States where he edited various short-lived newspapers in several cities, including Cincinnati, Louisville, New York, and, finally, Boston. A leading abolitionist and resolute atheist, his last paper, the *Pionier*, was among the few German-language papers in America consistently advocating women's rights. Spurning authoritarian socialism and, like Weitling, repudiating the doctrine of class warfare and communism, Heinzen plied a lifelong campaign against Marxism. Partly with Louis-Napoleon in mind, he equally denounced the wide powers of the American presidency,[107] viewing this institution, not unlike Franklin, Paine, and Jefferson, as a borrowing from the old British constitution. To him, America's president was just a "British monarch" renamed. Like Franklin and Paine, he also queried the Senate, even going so far as to recommend abolition. Given the subordinate character of the Swiss executive and its frequent plebiscites and more active citizen involvement, Heinzen viewed Switzerland as, in some respects, a better example of "American" federal democracy than the United States. Only the United States, though, could prod the world toward democracy and societies based on respect for the rights of man. The global democratic republican Revolution would triumph in the end, Heinzen was convinced, with minimal violence through revolutionary mass action, but only when enlightenment of the people had freed them from the mental shackles of deference to monarchy, aristocracy, nationalism, populism, socialism, theology, and religious authority.[108]

Among Heinzen's chief projects was his launching the "Louisville Platform" together with a group of other German radicals at Louisville in February 1854. Designed to create a major new reform movement, their goal was to right what they considered the defects of the American Constitution—especially the overmighty presidency—and strengthen its "republican" character, as well as end the "political and moral cancer" of slavery and oppression of women. Heinzen sought an alliance between German non-socialist democratic radicalism and "all true republicans" of America to reform politics and the party system and end the cliques controlling the parties, restoring the latter to authentic democratic principles. The twelve main points of the Louisville Platform included abolition of slavery, equal rights for women, terminating religious tests and all state support for religion, and protection of

American Reaction (1848–52) / **599**

the laboring classes from capitalists with the state mediating "as arbiter of all contending interests," fixing maximum working hours and minimum wages. Other main objectives were free trade on the basis of genuine reciprocity, subsidized justice without fees paid by individuals, rescinding the temperance laws as encroaching on individual liberty, and control of the electorate over their representatives.[109]

The abject failure of the Louisville Platform became in a way the supreme irony of mid-nineteenth-century American reaction to the 1848 revolutions, symbolizing the end of democratic republicanism in any meaningful sense as a transatlantic force emanating from America. Already a hotbed of anti-German immigrant and anti–Forty Eighter sentiment well before 1854, Louisville developed into one of the most fervent centers of the mid-1850s Know-Nothing movement, a national anti-Catholic and anti-foreigner political faction with representation in Washington that used the excuse of the papacy's siding with Europe's monarchs against the 1848 revolutions to mobilize prejudice against Catholics, especially recent immigrants, and claim Catholicism was the "ally of tyranny." The Know-Nothing movement, it was especially ironic, powerfully fused anti-immigrant prejudice with negative reaction to Forty-Eighter radicalism and the Louisville Platform.

Many so-called "Native Americans" (i.e., third- and fourth-generation whites) became deeply upset, as one historian put it, "over Germans telling Americans what was wrong with their country."[110] Hatred of the Germans in Louisville culminated, in August 1855, in an unprecedented eruption of ugly violence directed against immigrants. Sadly, far from growing, during the 1850s and 1860s, authentic democratic Radical Enlightenment republicanism receded noticeably on both sides of the Atlantic. Many were disillusioned; others doggedly fought on, Whitman among them.[111] A failure to all outward appearances, Heinzen ended his days in Boston forgotten and in grinding poverty, still editing, assisted only by his wife.

"Exceptionalism," Populism, and the Radical Enlightenment's Demise

The "Palmer Thesis" placing a common "Atlantic Revolution" at the origin of democratic modernity needs vindicating, vigorous reaffirmation, and broadening beyond where Palmer himself took it. The "expanding blaze," the partly imagined and partly real transformation of Europe, the Americas, and the wider world away from the hierarchies of the ancien régime into the supposed era of emancipation, equality, and justice for all, commenced in earnest in 1775–76 with the rise of the principles of '76. The American Revolution, divided within, became an ideological arena presenting the two rival sides of the Enlightenment coin, moderate and radical, and it is this, we have argued, that accounts for "revolution in the principles of government" and transforming also of the principles of society and the moral order, with which "America's founders adorned an otherwise parochial struggle for national independence."[1]

Contrary to more established views, the wider impact was enduring and immense. *Américanisme* rendered democratic republicanism a decisive factor in French radical Enlightenment thought before the outbreak of the French Revolution. Condorcet's egalitarian republican ideology contending that the "right to contribute, either directly or by representatives, in the making of the laws," as he put it in 1786, "and in all enactments made in the name of society," was a "necessary consequence of the natural and original equality of man" he derived in the years immediately prior to 1789 directly from the American Revolution, adapting its basic principles to help chart the direction of the subsequent French Revolution while continually reaffirming the centrality of this crucial transatlantic link for France and all Europe.[2]

No one understood this better than Jefferson, who, in his last major letter, written in June 1826 on his deathbed, stalwartly refused to abandon the

Enlightenment fervor, the ideals to which he and Condorcet had devoted their lives, reiterating one last time his heartfelt expectation that America's Revolution would finally prove a "signal" to the world "arousing men to burst the chains under which monkish ignorance and superstition had persuaded them to bind themselves, and to assume the blessings and security of self-government," to restore the "unbounded exercise of reason and freedom of opinion," open all eyes "to the rights of man," and promote the "general spread of the light of science" in a manner proving finally that the "mass of mankind has not been born with saddles on their backs."[3] There was nothing of the Protestant Reformation whatever in any of this, or of Catholic tradition.

Were Condorcet and Jefferson right in closely linking the futures of America and Europe, as well as the rest of the world, on the basis of democracy, liberty, and universal and equal human rights? It remains in an important sense still too early to tell. In any case, theirs was a creed and sentiment the intellectually aware of today have little choice but to adopt and endorse. The divided political culture of the American Revolution, produced by circumstances and social forces, we see, was throughout framed and expressed in terms of Enlightenment thought and controversy. The strand of the American Revolution that for the first time entrenched universal and equal rights, democratic republicanism, and the unrelenting secularism at the heart of Western and global debate was that dimension forged by the radical enlighteners—Jefferson, Franklin, Paine, Monroe, and sporadically Madison in the front rank but with many impressive representatives—Young, Allen, Cannon, Barlow, Coram, Leib, Palmer, Fellows, and Freneau among them—forming a large phalanx behind them. Unsurprisingly, given the depth of the resulting split, the Founding Fathers proved unable to resolve the internal conflict within the Revolution or the clash between the two fundamentally incompatible Enlightenment tendencies that they inherited from Europe and expanded in the Americas. Hence, they could not establish an uncontested path to representative government and basic freedoms evident and acceptable to all.

Those leaders of the French Revolution during its positive phase, from 1789 to June 1793, concerned with promoting democratic republicanism and freedom of expression and the press, underpinned by universal and equal rights, stressed not just the American origins of the democratic French Revolution and its essential ideological principles but also the power of those universal principles to encompass the Western world: just as "the American Revolution gave birth to ours," as Brissot put it in 1789, "ours will without doubt revolutionize the whole of Europe" including Britain, which will "blush to have a defective constitution" when "it sees the French create one exempt from the English Constitution's defects."[4] The fact that some radicals advancing the Revolution's democratizing republican tendency, like Young, Cannon, and Paine, were outsiders and newcomers on the American political scene while others, like Jefferson and Madison, belonged to the old landowning elites does not of itself invalidate Hannah Arendt's principal distinction between the American and French revolutions—her claim that the first was based on "experience" and was purely political while the second rested on intellectual theories[5] and partly for this reason fatally tried to solve the social question, the issue of poverty, by political means.[6] However, recognizing the radical democratizing tendency's decisive, central role in both revolutions does finally invalidate the highly influential analytical framework she forged. Giving due weight to the split between radical and moderate within the American Revolution means weakening her distinctions to the point that they lose all their old plausibility and force. If the revolutionary new concept of universal and equal rights was equally central to the American upheaval and the French so, likewise, were moderate Enlightenment ideas attempting to build on Locke and property, to combine a limited enlightened toleration and restricted suffrages with the core of the old monarchical-aristocratic-ecclesiastical system and Protestant theology. What for Arendt was the fundamental modern contrast, or contradiction, was in reality the basic modern parallelism. The contrast Arendt drew between a French Revolution deemed fundamentally flawed—for her the starting point of the road that led to the Bolshevik Revolution—and a "republican" American Revolution she described sympathetically[7]—is left entirely erased once the Terror, debased Rousseauisme, and Robespierriste populist streak is properly characterized and separated from the French Revolution's republican democratizing principles.

The early impact of the American Revolution's radical dimension on the Western world was almost a secular enlightened version of a religious revelation. To Europe's revolutionaries, "child-like," as Melville expressed it, in *Mardi* (1849), "standing among the old-robed kings and emperors of the Archipelago," Vivenza (the United States), "this republican land" where "all men are born free and equal," towered like a "young Messiah, to whose discourse the bearded rabbis bowed."[8] Until 1848, the American Revolution exerted an immense transatlantic impact, remaining for decades a key inspiration of democratic republican movements and dissidents everywhere. Those the American Revolution attracted and fascinated with its new vision of the human future, however, were never the established elites, or the kings, aristocrats, or clergy, and rarely the common people either, but rather predominantly society's estranged, inquiring, and critical intellectual fringe. In the 1770s, intellectual radicals emerged for the first time as the principal revolutionary vanguard throughout the transatlantic world and retained this role throughout the entire revolutionary era down to the overwhelming disillusionment of the 1850s and 1860s.

Many historians have supposed that universal and equal human rights grew out of and were closely related to the "rights" culture of early eighteenth-century Natural Law and the thought-world of Locke. It has long been assumed that there exists a basic continuity between the legacy of the 1688 Glorious Revolution and the modern democratizing revolutionary tendency that began in the 1770s. This turns out to be an error rooted in failure to understand and accept the basic division of the Enlightenment into "moderate" and "radical" wings first introduced into the historiography by Leo Strauss in the 1920s. In reality, there was no connection between the inalienable rights of 1776 and the highly stratified "rights" of pre-1770 rights discourse and Locke.[9] It is equally erroneous to suppose universal and equal rights grew out of any broad social impulse, or cultural turn, such as might have been introduced by reading novels. The revolutionary new concept of rights introduced by the American Revolution, and shared by the American and French revolutions, far from being tied to broad cultural trends in society, nowhere existed before the 1770s. Any "account of Human Rights" that envisages their "invention" as dependent upon something like "cultural change" or "sympathy" is assuredly well "wide of the mark." Universal and equal human rights were everywhere profoundly and relentlessly divisive from the 1770s onward—and on the whole generally rejected.[10] Nor is it in the least true that the sources for Anglo-American and French revolutionary universal and equal rights "have remained hard to isolate."[11] It is simply that these sources have nothing to do with reading novels, culture, tradition, with pre-1770 Natural Law or with Locke; but they are not hard to identify: their origin was the philosophical revolution carried through by the Radical Enlightenment.

Scholarly controversy over the "Radical Enlightenment" has markedly escalated in recent years. Defined as an intellectual *and* sociocultural movement that first assumed its basic features in the 1650s and 1660s, it has become the focus of extraordinary disagreement among historians and philosophers. Combining a philosophical revolution—strict separation of philosophy from theology and the advent of a one-substance immanent naturalism—with the rise of democratic republicanism based on equality, the Radical Enlightenment subsequently evolved in stages, for some two centuries, becoming the most widespread and comprehensive international opposition culture, or counterculture, in the West. Eliminating miracles, Revelation, and divine providence, and proclaiming scientific and philosophical "reason" the exclusive criterion for determining truth, this Enlightenment tendency tied its attack on religious authority to a democratizing republicanism striving to reconceive and reorganize the entire moral and political order. "Radical Enlightenment" fought to ameliorate human existence generally and emancipate oppressed sections of society not by changing the economic order, like the socialists (who gradually displaced this current from the 1830s onward), but by changing the way men think, persevering with their efforts through successive defeats throughout the revolutionary era from the 1770s down to the 1848 revolutions. Radical Enlightenment—whether European or American—battled to replace credulity, "ignorance," "superstition," and "fanaticism" with a fundamentally new conception of the individual as a free, educated, and enlightened citizen participating on an equal basis in society, debate, opinion-making, and politics. Vehemently condemned from the outset, Radical Enlightenment remains fiercely contested today.

Despite slavery, inadequate education, restricted electoral suffrages, aristocratic interpretations of bicameral constitutional arrangements, compulsory taxes to bolster churches, religious tests for office, and many other characteristically conservative features deemed blatant defects by radical enlighteners, the Revolution of '76 was also long presumed to have ushered in a new age in mankind's history and rendered the United States the prime model for the transatlantic Western world. Yet, well before 1848, a basic change in perspectives set in: it became obvious that the American Revolution had neither fully fulfilled its own promises nor become a viable model elsewhere except in the case of a handful of small European countries such as Switzerland, Norway, and Belgium. By 1815, with Napoleon defeated, monarchy, aristocracy, and ecclesiastical authority were visibly reviving their pre-1789 hegemony practically everywhere outside the United States. For all enlighteners, moderate and radical, the post-1815 situation proved vastly and bitterly disillusioning in Europe and Latin America alike while colonizing powers exploited Asia and Africa even more ruthlessly than in the past.

To all appearances, the winner on the post-1815 world stage, Jefferson and Adams both confessed, was not revolution, democracy, republicanism, or the United States as a new model society but rather old-style European aristocracy, Counter-Enlightenment, ecclesiastical authority, monarchical forms, colonial oppression, and slavery. Had the Enlightenment been permanently reversed? "Is the Nineteenth Century to be a contrast to the Eighteenth? Is it to extinguish all the Lights of its Predecessor? Are the Sorbonne, the Inquisition, the Index expurgatorius, and the Knights Errant of St Ignatius Loyola to be revived and restored to all their salutary Powers," demanded

Adams with evident sarcasm, "of supporting and propagating the mild Spirit of Christianity? The Proceedings of the Allies [i.e., Britain, Austria, Prussia, and Russia] and their Congress at Vienna, the Accounts from Spain, France etc., the Chateaubriands and the Genlis, indicate which Way the Wind blows. The Priests are at their Old Work again."[12] Pessimism largely replaced the earlier optimism but without entirely eradicating it.

Most American statesmen and congressmen—and, in the background, most Americans—in the end rejected the push for universal and equal rights, and the impulse to secularize and fully democratize their society. Not only did the "moderate Enlightenment" stream prove stronger than the radical fringe among America's ruling elites and the American people and those of Europe, but in America radicalism was further undercut by the "Second Great Awakening," the great Evangelical revivalist movement commencing around 1790 led by preachers and congregations of the Baptist and Methodist churches. These new religious voices and popular movements firmly rejected the skepticism, deism, and stress on philosophical reason of moderate and radical Enlightenment alike, insisting rather on faith and fundamentalist piety. "Second Awakening" Evangelical preachers often became political allies of Adams, Hamilton, and Jay, being no less anxious than they to block Jeffersonian democratic republicanism and "infidelity," which they too denounced as the foreign-inspired work of "philosophists" plunged in irreligion, propagating un-American "Jacobin" influence and menacing what they considered the American Revolution's authentic democratic and Christian legacy. Radical "philosophists" were charged with trying to purloin America as they were alleged to have perverted France.

After 1800, American Radical Enlightenment was heavily "defeated in its pure form," concluded Henry May, but survived residually in the continuing intellectual battle for the "soul of America." Analyzing American library acquisitions between 1800 and 1810 revealed that "writers of the radical Enlightenment" continued to be read "more than one might have guessed."[13] Condorcet, Raynal, Paine, and Godwin still figured prominently with Volney gaining "sharply." "Transformed and watered down," the radical tendency receded to the intellectual and artistic fringes but, nevertheless, in the political realm—especially the ubiquitous rhetoric surrounding "democracy"— and through the expansion of Unitarianism, exerted "major effects on the culture, including the religious culture, of all nineteenth-century America."[14] Parallel phenomena occurred in Europe and Latin America.

The grandiose reactionary pretensions but very incomplete success of the post-1815 Restoration guaranteed that the radical tendency persisted through the early nineteenth century as a vigorous political underground and counterculture. Too many social groups had been pushed down or short-changed for an immense transatlantic pool of resentment and discontent not to accumulate, a pool that only needed the merest opening to agitate afresh and give the radical tendency new opportunities to proclaim democratic republican values, as occurred with the revolutions of 1830 and 1848. These failed by and large but again left a solidly meaningful if receding legacy. In Europe and the Caribbean, as John Quincy Adams predicted, in 1831, the progressive disintegration of the aristocratic-monarchical-ecclesiastical world order so grandly reaffirmed by the Holy Alliance, in 1814, meant a renewed thrust toward democratization and black emancipation with vast and unavoidable consequences for Europe and the entire world, including the United States.

The swift collapse of the revolutions of 1848–49, and the transatlantic reaction to them, effectively broke the revolutionary cycle, ending the basic parallelism of transatlantic developments. "The events of 1848 in America," notes one historian, show that the "continuity with the American Revolution had been broken by a crisis over slavery and expansionism," while "in France and throughout Europe, continuity with the French Revolution and its 'universal' impact ended with the red, 'ugly revolution' of 1848, the (seeming) specter of communism."[15] In America, Enlightenment and the emancipation process were in the end heavily disrupted by surges of intolerant, overbearing populism—De Tocqueville's and Mill's "dangers" of direct democracy and the "tyranny of the majority"—repressing and running counter to the fundamental values of democratic republicanism. After 1850, America's path abutted much less closely on Europe and the rest of the world until the United States' entry into World War II.

The astounding enthusiasm shown by Americans of every hue for the supposedly heroic achievements of the Hungarian national leader Lajos (Louis) Kossuth (1802–94), the man who had headed the Hungarian Revolution of 1848–49 with energy, charisma, and stirring oratory, has often been cited as contrary evidence, clear proof of continued American support and fervor for the 1848 revolutions stretching into the 1850s, evidence that Americans still zealously identified with democratic and republican values internationally. The Hungarian Revolution was among the last of the 1848 revolutions to erupt (March 1848) and last to be crushed (August 1849), overwhelmed only by combined Russian and Austrian imperial forces after bitter fighting a month after the quashing of the Roman Republic by the future Napoleon III. So euphoric was American exaltation of Kossuth and the Hungarian rising and, seemingly, the 1848 revolutions' wider message of "democracy," universal liberty, and national independence, that many have supposed that American enthusiasm for the "revolution" must have resoundingly revived after all.

Bordering on hysteria, the "Kossuth furor" or "Kossuth craze" raged in America for months. Unlike the other revolutionary leaders of 1848–49, Kossuth toured the United States in person following the collapse of the revolutions. Released from his Turkish prison two years after his capture (due to the intercession of the American secretary of state)[16] and unable to return to the restored Austro-Hungarian monarchy, the figure who for a year had been "virtual dictator" of Hungary, presiding over a Hungarian diet dominated by Magyar nobles until August 1849, embarked on a fateful tour of the West. He had presided over a revolutionary regime that introduced a broader suffrage than was adopted in Britain in 1832 but that was still one that excluded most peasants and laborers, and all Hungarian Jews, that failed to eliminate serfdom fully, and that preserved noble political privilege.[17] He commenced his tour in England where he was ecstatically received by both middle classes and working-class Chartists as an uplifting "national leader" who for once, unlike the despised radicals of 1789, 1830, and 1848, uninhibitedly praised Britain's aristocracy and monarchy, publicly disavowing democratic republicanism.

Next, he crossed the Atlantic, invited—much to the unease and dissatisfaction of the Austrian Habsburg envoy in Washington—by the American government, landing on 4 December 1851 to the deafening accompaniment of repeated artillery salutes fired from New York's shore batteries. He received a rousing reception and popular applause such as no one had received before. It was impossible to hear the official speech of welcome honoring Hungary's hero, delivered by New York's mayor, because the thousands crammed into the building hosting the event refused to stop cheering.[18] Yet, examined more closely, Kossuth's 1851–52 American visit was an unmitigated democratic fiasco. The Kossuth "furor," notwithstanding the public's love of his exciting oratory, illustrated not the depth but the shallowness, non-comprehension, and disillusionment of prevailing perceptions of the 1848 revolutions and accompanying controversies, non-comprehension profoundly symptomatic of the withering of the spirit of '76.

Part of Kossuth's unparalleled appeal lay in being the only revolutionary hero not to have been discredited, or fallen from grace in some way, in American eyes. Lamartine (in 1848) and Mazzini and Garibaldi (in 1849) too had been international celebrities. Their renown, exploits, and good looks appealed to the romantic sensibilities of the age. For months, articles about and portraits of Lamartine circulated, eulogizing his leadership, insight, and "moderation." Much interest focused on his *History of the Girondists* (1847), a publishing success in America as in France that fixed Lamartine's reputation as a key interpreter of the Revolution and helped reinvigorate democratic republicanism as a political creed by demonstrating the immense gulf between Brissotins and the Montagne in ideas and attitudes, and close affinities between the pre-1793 French Revolution and the American. But with his resounding defeat in France in June 1848, Lamartine's stock plummeted irretrievably. His reputation never recovered. In the American consciousness of the 1850s Kossuth alone, released from Turkish confinement by American pressure, stood as an upright, indomitable, heroic figure striding the Atlantic. His portrait proliferated everywhere.

Kossuth's procession down Broadway drew immense cheering crowds bordering on frenzy, but the speeches were just froth with no substance; genuine enthusiasts for the revolutions began murmuring that the United States should have exerted itself more energetically to support the suppressed movements against despotism and repression. Hungarian banners and posters hung on every building down Broadway, but some read: "His Visit Reminds us of Our Neglected Duty to Freedom and the People of Europe!"[19] Aside from an insipid residual endorsement of movements for national independence from foreign oppressors, the Kossuth furor demonstrated only that there was, beyond restricted circles, remarkably little understanding or sympathy in the United States for core revolutionary principles. Lauded in Britain for his "moderate" and pragmatic "liberalism" compatible with monarchy and aristocracy, and rejection of socialism,[20] in America Kossuth's voice became that of national self-congratulation, expressing a vapid, preposterous triumphalism that entirely failed to reaffirm America's revolutionary legacy, made no effort to promote emancipation or extend human rights, and remained silent about the outbreaks of anti-Semitic violence and curtailed rights of Slovaks, Rumanians, Serbs, and other sizable minorities within the borders of the inflated greater Hungary Kossuth and the Magyar leadership styled their national homeland.

Although earlier he had criticized the Magyar nobility and called for an end to serfdom, during the 1848–49 upheaval Kossuth did his utmost to preserve the nobility's political and social ascendancy and prevent Hungary's ethnic minorities gaining control of their own particular regions.[21] Few questioned him about the startling gaps in the Hungarian Revolution's emancipating and libertarian credentials or his unquestioningly pro-aristocratic stance. Aware that speaking out in favor of abolition would cost him backing in the South, Kossuth not only defended aristocracy and cosseted monarchy but also pointedly avoided pronouncing on slavery, the question most profoundly troubling America, or indeed any aspect of American politics.[22] On 12 December 1851, his mostly unruffled American progress received a jolt in a crowded New York ballroom when he was confronted by a black delegation that congratulated him for everywhere promoting "the great principle" that he upheld with such distinction—that "a man has a right to the full exercise of his faculties in the land of his birth." At a loss for words, Kossuth made no reply, indeed was furious at being thus confronted, realizing it was a deliberate attempt to get him to pronounce on human rights, on equality, and by implication on serfdom and America's blacks.[23] Before long, Kossuth's evasiveness on rights, equality, serfdom, and race began to alienate abolitionists and members of ethnic minorities previously avid to applaud him.[24] The vapidity of his revolutionary creed especially irritated those numerous Forty-Eighters convinced "all nationality is fiction" who thoroughly scorned the threadbare doctrine that to fight for liberty is to fight for nationality.[25]

Even so, Kossuth's nationalist creed represented a threat to Austria's multinational empire. The Habsburg court protested repeatedly about the effusive receptions laid on for Kossuth by American officials and dignitaries. The cabinet in Washington replied unapologetically, turning the incident into one of the few mid-nineteenth-century diplomatic tiffs involving the United States. America's secretary of state rebuked the Habsburgs for protesting to a republican people in the name of monarchy: as a republic the United States had every right to encourage national independence movements. This American spokesman was none other than Daniel Webster, leading proponent of the reactionary, pro-elite imperialistic "new nationalism" in America, hero of the new bigotry striving to reinforce religious values in politics by claiming the American presidency, laws, and Congress were obliged to foster religion to uphold the moral order, a figure detesting equality and detested by all radicals and abolitionists. Abjuring democracy and black emancipation while rebuking the Viennese court, Webster nonetheless unreservedly admired (and wrote about) Kossuth as a fighter for nation and independence.[26]

Despite signs of a residual lively democratic republicanism voiced by the Young America Movement committed to "progress" in the North, zeal for the spread of democracy, ending slavery, and social amelioration, support for democratic and libertarian causes tied to European democratic republicanism, receded into a highly reductive, empty rhetoric. Instead of embracing humanity either side of the Atlantic, and pursuing identical democratic, republican goals, Americans began viewing the world more in terms of their own unrivaled example being specific to the United States, something the rest remained incapable of replicating. Hence, the most regressive, damaging aspect of the rupture between democratic republicanism and socialism, and the rejectionist American response to 1848, was the growing shift toward a culture of "exceptionalism."

Europe's 1848 revolutions came to be construed by most Americans not as a failed struggle for the ideals America shared but, even by leading scholars, as an abject failure that merely confirmed for all to see the alleged national and cultural shortcomings of the French, Italians, and Germans. If allowing in the Forty-Eighters reflected America's uniquely progressive status,[27] for the most part American liberty, independence, democracy, and prosperity and the "American dream" mutated into properties supposedly ingrained in the United States owing to a God-given mix of special endowments originating in the remote English past. Beyond America, such values were just a distant, unrealizable utopia and the Forty-Eighters entirely irrelevant.

American public sentiment had evolved since the 1790s from a force for into a barrier against human rights, democracy, and freedom of expression, culminating in the Know-Nothing movement and anti-foreigner bigotry of the 1850s. This forsaking of former values driven by prejudice and loathing of "socialism" and religious "infidelity" soon became part of a new parallelism—the clearly corresponding shift at work also in Britain, France, Italy, and Germany.[28] The transition within American society preceded—but was quickly soon accompanied by—a comparable Old World estrangement from democratic republican values, including from the American Revolution and from American "democracy." European politicians and intellectuals no longer showed much interest in democracy, republicanism, or equal rights, and no longer cited the United States as a model or inspiration to follow. In Britain, waning enthusiasm for the American example was accompanied by an upsurge of upper-middle-class complacency helped by the rapid receding of Chartism and limited broadening of the suffrage arising from the 1832 Great Reform Bill. During the 1850s, it became clear that 1848 marked a watershed beyond which a decisively weakened radicalism could no longer challenge the established social, political, and imperial order or foster a vigorous democratic intellectual counterculture.[29] Philosophic radicalism in the British Parliament and public sphere receded just as noticeably as in America during the 1850s and 1860s, as the campaign for universal suffrage, shorter parliaments, and redistribution of seats, vigorous since 1775 and kept up throughout the years down to 1848, inexorably retreated.[30]

If America went its own way, in Europe the lingering but superficial compromises with republicanism and democracy were almost entirely an obvious sham—most of all in Napoleon III's France and Bismarck's Germany—and everywhere created many painfully unresolved problems and tensions for the future. Despite appearances, the developments of the 1840s, 1850s, and 1860s pushed authentic democratic republican ideas and values more and more into the background, while causing the radical strand of the revolutionary tradition of '76 to be all but forgotten. That the authentic legacy of transatlantic democratic revolution was jointly American and European, that the American and French revolutions had pursued the same goals, and that their joint values had flourished equally, albeit in the face of tremendous opposition either side of the Atlantic, came to be buried in obscurity. After 1848, Enlightenment values were everywhere displaced by a vestigial "liberalism" suffused in imperialism, nationalism, "exceptionalism," populist monarchism, and rival forms of undemocratic socialism including Marxism.

Greatly to the relief of the only recently tottering monarchies and aristocracies, democratic republicanism, the backbone of the revolutionary challenge to their primacy, during the aftermath of 1848–49 suddenly proved—unexpectedly but increasingly—an enfeebled, spent force politically and socially but also psychologically and intellectually. So disillusioned and sunk in gloom were the leading intellectuals exalted by 1848 as they had been by 1830—Lamartine, Ledru-Rollin, Heine, Mazzini, and the rest, and Michelet most of all—that they sank into a dismal mood from which the old democratic republicanism seemed barely retrievable or even irretrievable. In the mid-1840s Michelet had interrupted his *History of France*, plunging into his fiercely anti-Orléanist *History of the Revolution*, fervently hoping to re-animate France with the old republican spirit; by late 1848, his resolve had been replaced by total disillusionment.[31] The radical impulse he represented was rapidly marginalized intellectually, culturally, and politically during the 1850s and 1860s. As Louis-Napoleon, crowned Emperor Napoleon III, consolidated repressive dictatorship in France, hard-line activists of the *parti républicain* were forced underground or abroad, congregating in Brussels and Liège, in parts of Switzerland, or with Victor Hugo's group of exiles in the Channel Islands, a marginalized, lingering vestige of radical republican sentiment.[32] Establishing their own periodicals or publishing in the Belgian and Swiss liberal press, a motley collection of exiled professors, journalists, and writers struggled vainly to keep their fading message alive. In 1861, King Victor Emmanuel II of Sardinia, steered by Count Cavour, became the first king of modern Italy: to loud acclaim he demonstrated that monarchy, aristocracy, and the Church had definitively defeated democracy and republicanism in the Italian peninsula too. Meanwhile, Bismarck's deft reactionary strategy together with the huge exodus of Forty-Eighters from Germany to America ensured that all echoes of revolutionary republicanism after 1848–49 in German lands were effectively muffled if not entirely emasculated under the heel of the militaristic new post-1870 imperial Germany.

By the 1850s, the radical impulse subsided either side of the Atlantic. But in the United States a particular confluence of factors in 1847–52 gave conservatives

"The (Modern) Deluge." Depicts the failure of the 1848 revolutions with "republican liberty" a broken stump; the British "balanced" constitution is the only one afloat. Photo credit: Yale Center for British Art, Paul Mellon Collection.

added scope to denounce efforts to promote equal rights and condemn schemes to reduce economic injustice as "foreign," "un-American" intrusion, as "socialism" and unwelcome penetration by alien immigrants.[33] If, for radicals, the United States, from 1848, represented the supreme example of a majority "tyranny" unresponsive to minority rights driving alienation of the intellectuals, for American conservatives the neutered rhetoric "democracy" stripped of association with economic and social "regulation," equal rights, secular moral values, cosmopolitanism, and egalitarianism could now safely be bandied on all sides. Where during the 1790s American elite reaction to the first French Revolution had generated a powerful and explicitly anti-democratic discourse, American opinion, conservative and liberal, after the 1848–49 French Revolution no longer needed explicitly to champion "aristocracy" or reject "democracy": it simply reaffirmed American "democracy" in national context, vigorously contrasting it with the failure and supposed inadequacy of French, Italian, German, and other European efforts to secure a stable constitutional outcome.[34]

America's international appeal among progressives was dimmed further by the fact that Canada and other more recently colonized parts of the globe, Australia and New Zealand especially, gained new social momentum in the 1840s and 1850s. Growing impressively, these new immigrant societies introduced democratizing reforms that—prior to the American Civil War— seemed more convincingly to promote democratic progress and equal human rights than the caste-ridden societies of Europe and the American South, despite the highly questionable treatment of Native Americans and Chinese immigrants in Canada and of the Aborigines in Australia.[35] Canada, Australia, and New Zealand were now replicating the relative openness, opportunities for new immigrants, and mass electoral politics characteristic of the dynamic North and West of the United States, without needing to present America as a predecessor or model of social and political organization. In Britain and Canada diminished admiration for the United States resulted also from prolongation of the unresolved Oregon dispute.[36] Although the Oregon treaty of 1846 finally fixed the main line of the border dividing the United States from Canada in the Pacific northwest, disagreement over the border on the Pacific coast persisted until 1872.

The United States ceased to represent a universal model. Worse, prejudice and bigotry rooted in anti-Enlightenment sentiment deploying nationalistic rhetoric, an appeal to conservative values, and the pretext of "exceptionalism" had by the 1850s largely ousted the spirit of '76. Nativist reaction against European radicalism and the rise of the Know-Nothing movement, following on from the Mexican War together with revulsion against socialism, effectively ended America's role as the reputed pioneer of democratic republican modernity. The most influential newspaper editor in Kentucky in the 1850s, George D. Prentice (1802–70), was known not for Enlightenment or democratic idealism but rabble-rousing nationalistic chauvinism and support for the Know-Nothings.[37] If Know-Nothingism had its heartland in the rough interior, observers of the 1852 and 1854 elections were astounded by the strength of Know-Nothingism also in New England and the Middle Atlantic states, most of all Massachusetts where, as elsewhere, it was strongly spiced with anti-Irish sentiment.[38] Among the worst of the displays of bigotry directed at recent immigrants that shocked the immigrant communities were the August 1855 riots in Louisville, resulting in rows of immigrant houses being burned down and around twenty recently arrived Germans and Irish being shot or beaten to death.[39]

All considered, the United States of the 1850s was not an internationally inspiring spectacle. "Our progress in degeneracy," concluded Abraham

Lincoln, in a letter written in August 1855, "appears to me to be pretty rapid." In 1776, the United States had begun by declaring that "all men are created equal." Yet the United States Constitution of 1787 accommodated black slavery and nothing was subsequently done to correct that wrong.[40] "When the Know-Nothings get control," declared Lincoln with exasperation, America's national creed would read: "all men are created equal, except negroes, and foreigners and Catholics." When it came to that, he added, "I shall prefer emigrating to some country where they make no pretense of loving liberty—to Russia for instance, where despotism can be taken pure, and without the base alloy of hypocrisy."[41]

Notes

Introduction

1. Quoted in Keane, *Tom Paine*, 510.
2. Price, *Observations*, 1–2; Reich, *British Friends*, 93–95, 100.
3. Price, *Observations*, 2; Schama, *Patriots and Liberators*, 65, 323.
4. Price, *Observations*, 2–3.
5. Paine to Condorcet, Bonneville, and Lanthenas, Paris, June 1791, in Paine, *Complete Writings*, 2:1317.
6. Peterson, *Thomas Jefferson*, 1008; Grant, *John Adams*, 450; Wills, *Inventing America*, 359–60.
7. Paine, *Complete Writings*, 2:956; Goetzmann, *Beyond the Revolution*, 3, 5.
8. Dickinson, "Counter-revolution," 354–64; Smyth, "The 1798 Rebellion," 12–13.
9. Pagden, *The Enlightenment*, 265.
10. Palmer, *Age of the Democratic Revolution*, 2:5.
11. Goggi, "Ancora su Diderot-Raynal e Filangieri," 126–27; Israel, *Democratic Enlightenment*, 368–70.
12. Pace, *Benjamin Franklin*, 147, 151; Gabrieli, "Impact," 189.
13. Filangieri, *La scienza*, 1:139–41, 149, 2:chap. 8, 3:chap. 47; Gabrieli, "Impact," 175, 177–84; Grab, "Italian Enlightenment," 36–37.
14. Filangieri, *La scienza*, 1:104–22.
15. Gabrieli, "Impact," 177, 182; Pace, *Benjamin Franklin*, 149–52.
16. Pace, *Benjamin Franklin*, 153–54, 160–61; Belissa, "Leçons de républicanisme," 73–83.
17. Miranda, *New Democracy*, 42.
18. Cérutti, *Bréviaire philosophique*, 25.
19. Filangieri, *La scienza*, 4:248–49; Gabrieli, "Impact, 183.
20. Salfi, *L'Italie au dix-neuvième siècle*, 11–12; Morelli, "The United States Constitution," 102; Staloff, *Hamilton, Adams, Jefferson*, 3.
21. Quoted in Stewart, *Nature's God*, 7.
22. Fea, "John Adams and Religion," 188–90, 192, 197.
23. Bailyn, *Faces*, 204; Valsania, *Limits*, 13–14; Bernstein, *Founding Fathers*, 26–29; Belissa, "Leçons de républicanisme," 63–64.
24. Grant, *John Adams*, 37, 119–20, 254; Jacoby, *Freethinkers*, 30, 43–44; Staloff, "John Adams," 40.
25. Peterson, *Thomas Jefferson*, 50–56; Luebke, "Origins," 344–45; Jayne, *Jefferson's Declaration*, 19.
26. Adams, *Memoirs*, 8:270–72; Sloan, "Thomas Jefferson," 484; Allen, *Our Declaration*, 179–81; Blasi, Freeman, and Kruse, *Citizen's Share*, 31.

27. Dixon, "Henry F. May and the Revival," 255; Staloff, *Hamilton, Adams, Jefferson*, 3–4.
28. Valsania, *Limits*, 17; Israel, *Democratic Enlightenment*, 3–7.
29. May, *Enlightenment in America*, 24, 88, 100–101, 153–54, 360–62.
30. Meyer, *Democratic Enlightenment*, vii.
31. Ellis, "Habits of Mind," 153; Dixon, "Henry F. May and the Revival," 259–60, 263–64.
32. Dixon, "Henry F. May and the Revival," 279–80.
33. The remark was made by Rufus King (1755–1827); see Nelson, *Royalist Revolution*, 2.
34. Nash, *Unknown American Revolution*, xv–xxviii; Cotlar, *Tom Paine's America*, 3–11; Stewart, *Nature's God*, 3–7; Wood, "Radicalism of Thomas Jefferson"; Bernstein, "Nature's God," 66–69.
35. Himmelfarb, *Roads to Modernity*, 20.
36. Israel, *Revolutionary Ideas*, 695–708.
37. Kloppenberg, *Toward Democracy*, 16, 151–52, 155–58, 162–63, 166–72, 273.
38. Ibid., 561, 563, 569–74, 584–85.
39. For a short account of this distinction, see Israel, *Revolution of the Mind*, 13–21.
40. Israel, *Revolutionary Ideas*, 103–11, 130–33, 152–60, 207–10.
41. Ibid., 2–4, 104, 695.
42. May, *Enlightenment in America*, 225.
43. Palmer, *An Enquiry*, 34–35.
44. Meyer, "Uniqueness," 172; Cotlar, *Tom Paine's America*, 211–14.
45. Bouton, *Taming Democracy*, 261.
46. Price, *Observations*, 83–84; Démeunier, *L'Amérique indépendante*, 1:46; Davis, *Problem of Slavery*, 399–400; Foner, *Story*, 32.
47. Price, *Observations*, 85; Foner, *Story*, 9.
48. Condorcet, *Bibliothèque de l'Homme Public*, series II (1791), 3:71–72.
49. Adams to Jefferson, 16 July 1814, in *Adams-Jefferson Letters*, 2:435–36; Staloff, "John Adams," 36.
50. Adams to Jefferson, 2 February 1816, in *Adams-Jefferson Letters*, 2:463.
51. Appleby, "New Republican Synthesis," 594; Sloan, "Thomas Jefferson," 472–73.
52. Adams to Jefferson, 16 July 1814, in *Adams-Jefferson Letters*, 2:435.
53. Jefferson to Adams, 11 January 1816, in *Adams-Jefferson Letters*, 2:459–60.
54. Adams to Jefferson, 2 February 1816, in *Adams-Jefferson Letters*, 2:462–63.
55. Fenimore Cooper, *The Bravo*, 146.
56. Ibid., 91; Connell, "Darker Aspects," 17.
57. Goetzmann, *Beyond the Revolution*, 157–58; Wood, *Empire of Liberty*, 118, 224, 320.
58. Arendt, *On Revolution*, 16, 49; Rana, *Two Faces*, 20–21.
59. Newman, *Europe's American Revolution*, xii.
60. Lefer, *Founding Conservatives*, 3–5; Allen, *Our Declaration*, 100, 267–69.

Chapter 1: First Rumblings

1. Adams to Jefferson, 24 August 1815, in *Adams-Jefferson Letters*, 2:455; Stewart, *Nature's God*, 17.

2. Gould, *Among the Powers*, 42; Saunt, *West of the Revolution*, 21.
3. Conway, "British Governments, Colonial Consumers," 721–22, 730.
4. Saunt, *West of the Revolution*, 192–206.
5. Young, "Ebenezer Mackintosh," 16; Nash, *Unknown American Revolution*, 48–51.
6. Ferling, *Whirlwind*, 26; Beeman, *Varieties*, 261.
7. Middlekauff, *Glorious Cause*, 89–92; Raphael, *People's History*, 18–19; Leamon, *Revolution Downeast*, 42–43; Beeman, *Varieties*, 252–54.
8. Nash, *Unknown American Revolution*, 45–50; Young, "Ebenezer Mackintosh," 24–29.
9. Middlekauff, *Glorious Cause*, 180–86, 208, 232; Maier, *Resistance to Revolution*, 115–22; Wood, *Radicalism*, 35, 117; Leamon, *Revolution Downeast*, 47, 50; Nash, *Unknown American Revolution*, 90, 99–100, 104.
10. Hume to W. Strahan, Edinburgh, 11 March 1771, in Hume, *Letters*, 2:237.
11. Chastellux, *De la félicité publique*, 2:163; Sonenscher, *Before the Deluge*, 301.
12. Rush, *Autobiography*, 139; Rakove, "Constitutionalism," 106–7.
13. Bourke, *Empire and Revolution*, 323; Beeman, *Our Lives, Our Fortunes*, 22–23.
14. Adams, *Diary and Autobiography*, 21–22.
15. Bailyn, *Ideological Origins*, 118–19; Dickinson, "'The Friends of America,'" 14; Countryman, *American Revolution*, 98, 113; Raphael, "Democratic Moment," 124.
16. Ward, *The War*, 15; Butler, *Awash in a Sea*, 202–4, 209.
17. Ward, *The War*, 15.
18. Maier, *Resistance to Revolution*, 85.
19. Ibid., 224–25.
20. Stewart, *Nature's God*, 18–21, 135–36, 205–6, 292; see also Maier, *Resistance to Revolution*, 116–17, 137–38; Leamon, *Revolution Downeast*, 50–51, 60; Countryman, *American Revolution*, 92, 129–30.
21. Smith, *Freedoms We Lost*, 99–100, 106–8.
22. Franklin, *Papers*, 21:235; Franklin, "Rules," 77.
23. Fenton, *Religious Liberties*, 20, 34; Waldman, *Founding Faith*, 50–51; Kloppenberg, *Toward Democracy*, 301–2.
24. Bonwick, *American Revolution*, 79, 90; Dickinson, "'The Friends of America,'" 15; Clark, *Language of Liberty*, 261; Marshall, "British North America," 373; Taylor, *American Revolutions*, 84–85.
25. Havard and Vidal, *Histoire*, 684; Bourke, *Empire and Revolution*, 465.
26. Raphael, "Blacksmith Timothy Bigelow," 41–42; Raphael, *People's History*, 48–52.
27. Raphael, "Blacksmith Timothy Bigelow," 45.
28. Raphael, *People's History*, 41–43; Papas, *Renegade Revolutionary*, 103.
29. Jefferson, *A Summary View*, 5; Halliday, *Understanding Thomas Jefferson*, 124–25.
30. Jefferson, *A Summary View*, 5; Pocock, *Virtue, Commerce, and History*, 84; Allen, *Our Declaration*, 50.
31. Jefferson, *A Summary View*, 6–8.
32. Houston, *Algernon Sidney*, 4, 7–8, 257–58, 261–66.
33. Adams, *Novanglus*, 26–34; Pocock, *Machiavellian Moment*, 531, 546.
34. Adams, *Novanglus*, 91; Bonwick, *American Revolution*, 2–4, 134; Nelson, *Royalist Revolution*, 159–60.
35. Adams, *Novanglus*, 12, 27; Bailyn, *Ideological Origins*, 81, 83; Grant, *John Adams*, 144–45.

36. Adams, *Novanglus*, 29.
37. Alden, *History*, 165; Dickinson, "'The Friends of America,'" 17.
38. Clark, "Burke's Reflections," 75, 88; Bromwich, *Intellectual Life of Edmund Burke*, 234–35, 239–41, 270, 326–27; Ferling, *Independence*, 49.

Chapter 2: A Republican Revolution

1. Leamon, *Revolution Downeast*, 60–66.
2. Kammen, *Colonial New York*, 342, 363–65, 367.
3. Adams, *Gouverneur Morris*, 43–46, 56; Lefer, *Founding Conservatives*, 46–52.
4. Fay, *L'Esprit révolutionnaire*, 53; Spieler, "France," 59; Ferling, *Independence*, 109.
5. Countryman, *American Revolution*, 101–2, 133–36.
6. Ramsay, *History*, 1:195, 197.
7. Lefer, *Founding Conservatives*, 72–76; Ferling, *Independence*, 135–36; Beeman, *Our Lives, Our Fortunes*, 251–53.
8. Leamon, *Revolution Downeast*, 66–73; Allen, *Our Declaration*, 53–54; Slaughter, *Independence*, 427–28.
9. Maier, *American Scripture*, 10–12; Gould, *Among the Powers*, 4; Fowler, *American Crisis*, 46.
10. Jasanoff, *Liberty's Exiles*, 29.
11. Countryman, *American Revolution*, 115–16.
12. Blackburn, *Overthrow*, 103–4, 112; Taylor, *Internal Enemy*, 23–27.
13. Taylor, *Internal Enemy*, 24; Popkin, *You Are All Free*, 250, 253–54, 275.
14. Taylor, *Internal Enemy*, 23–24; Gilbert, *Black Patriots*, 15–30; Beeman, *Our Lives, Our Fortunes*, 291–92.
15. O'Shaughnessy, *Empire Divided*, 142–43.
16. Ferling, *Independence*, 193–94; Gilbert, *Black Patriots*, 17–21; Horne, *Counter-Revolution*, 234–35; Rossignol, "Black Declaration," 112–14.
17. Franklin, *Papers*, 29:590–91; Parkinson, *Common Cause*, 153–72.
18. Horne, *Counter-Revolution*, 222–23, 240.
19. Raphael, *People's History*, 320–22; Nash, *Unknown American Revolution*, 161–63; Papas, *Renegade Revolutionary*, 154–57.
20. Bonwick, *American Revolution*, 131; Nash, *Unknown American Revolution*, 391–94.
21. Smith, *Correspondence*, 196.
22. Jefferson, *A Summary View*, 16; Sluiter, "Declaration of Independence," 19; Ferling, *Independence*, 307.
23. Taylor, *Indentured to Liberty*, 22–25.
24. Conway, "Continental European Soldiers," 87, 94–95, 99.
25. Taylor, *Indentured to Liberty*, 110–11.
26. Krebs, "Deutsches Museum," 2, 4–5; Delinière, "Polémique."
27. Lessing, *Philosophical and Theological Writings*, 209; Baumgarten, *Benjamin Franklin*, 23–24.
28. Israel, *Democratic Enlightenment*, 274–78, 541–43; see also Palmer, *Age of the Democratic Revolution*, 1:260.
29. Losfeld, *Philanthropisme*, 172–63, 177.
30. Nash and Gao Hodges, *Friends of Liberty*, 29–35.

31. Lafayette to Mme. Lafayette, 19 June 1777, in Lafayette, *Mémoires*, 1:93–94.

32. Franklin to Washington, Paris, 4 September 1777, in Franklin, *The Works*, 7:186.

33. Paine, *Age of Reason*, 63; Ferling, *Independence*, 218–21; Beeman, *Our Lives, Our Fortunes*, 312–18.

34. Rush, *Letters*, 2:1008; Keane, *Tom Paine*, 107, 112, 120, 459; Sher, *Enlightenment and the Book*, 511–31.

35. Nelson, *Thomas Paine*, 79–80; Foner, *Tom Paine*, 74, 84; Beeman, *Our Lives, Our Fortunes*, 321.

36. Pocock, *Virtue, Commerce, and History*, 167; Wood, *Americanization*, 155; Lepore, "World of Paine," 87.

37. Ramsay, *History*, 1:315; Rosenfeld, *Common Sense*, 154; Nelson, *Royalist Revolution*, 111–12.

38. Keane, *Tom Paine*, 109–10; Nash, *Unknown American Revolution*, 189; Ferling, *Independence*, 222–23; Cotlar, "Conclusion," 288; Rosenfeld, *Common Sense*, 136–37.

39. Paine, *Le Sens-Commun*, title page and pp. 6–8.

40. Raynal, *Revolution in America*, 120; Nelson, *Royalist Revolution*, 111, 148.

41. Foner, *Story*, 16; Rosenfeld, *Common Sense*, 155.

42. Israel, *Democratic Enlightenment*, 456.

43. Raynal, *Revolution in America*, 119–20; Rush, *Autobiography*, 114–15; May, *Enlightenment in America*, 162.

44. Raynal, *Revolution in America*, 79–90; Démeunier, *L'Amerique indépendente*, 1:27; Bailyn, *Faces*, 68–71.

45. Ferguson, *American Enlightenment*, 110.

46. Papas, *Renegade Revolutionary*, 129; Slaughter, *Independence*, 429.

47. Gordon, *History*, 2:275; Countryman, *American Revolution*, 105–7.

48. Lefer, *Founding Conservatives*, 96–97; Rakove, *Revolutionaries*, 93–95.

49. Paine, *Common Sense*, 84–88, 99; Ferling, *Independence*, 219–21.

50. Bailyn, *Ideological Origins*, 285–86; Cotlar, *Tom Paine's America*, 2, 127.

51. Wilentz, *Politicians and the Egalitarians*, 75–77; Kloppenberg, *Toward Democracy*, 322–23.

52. Inglis, *True Interest of America*, vii; Rosenfeld, *Common Sense*, 156; Jasanoff, *Liberty's Exiles*, 29–30, 148.

53. "Candidus" [William Smith], *Plain Truth*, 2–3, 37.

54. Paine, *The American Crisis*, 9; Rosenfeld, *Common Sense*, 5–6.

55. Bailyn, *Ideological Origins*, 288–89; Foner, *Story*, 16–18; Nash, *Unknown American Revolution*, 190, 202–3.

56. Huston, *Land and Freedom*, 13–22.

57. Adams, *Gouverneur Morris*, 3–4.

58. Paine, *Complete Writings*, 2:915–16; Nelson, *Thomas Paine*, 95–96; Bernstein, *Founding Fathers*, 51; McCullough, *John Adams*, 97, 101; Cotlar, "Languages of Democracy," 16.

59. Adams, *Thoughts on Government*, 13–15; Ferguson, *American Enlightenment*, 117–18; Nelson, *Royalist Revolution*, 114.

60. Adams, *Thoughts on Government*, 4–5, 7; Lutz, "Relative Influence," 193, 195; Casalini, "L'Esprit," 325.

61. Adams, *Thoughts on Government*, 21; Siemers, "John Adams's Political Thought," 103, 110–12; Beeman, *Varieties*, 15–16, 279.

62. Paine, *Common Sense*, 98; Dragonetti, *Treatise on Virtues*, 17, 31, 33, 89; Keane, *Tom Paine*, 122.

63. Paine, *Common Sense*, 96, 109; Countryman, *American Revolution*, 122–23; Cotlar, *Tom Paine's America*, 38, 44; Wilentz, *Politicians and the Egalitarians*, 77.

64. Papas, *Renegade Revolutionary*, 99–103.

65. Lutz, "Relative Influence," 193, 195.

66. Paine, *Common Sense*, 54; Paine, *The American Crisis*, 4; Keane, *Tom Paine*, 133; Carpanetto and Ricuperati, *Italy*, 257; Wootton, *Republicanism, Liberty*, 26–27.

67. Dragonetti, *Treatise on Virtues*, preface; Paine, *Political Writings*, 28; Wootton, *Republicanism, Liberty*, 36–37.

68. Lutz, "Relative Influence," 193.

69. Dragonetti, *Treatise on Virtues*, 33, 39, 40–41; Robbins, "Lifelong Education," 135; Wootton, *Republicanism, Liberty*, 38; Keane, *Tom Paine*, 122.

70. Dawson, *Gods of Revolution*, 44–45; Wootton, "Helvétius," 326–28.

71. Dragonetti, *Treatise on Virtues*, 179; Paine, *Common Sense*, 72–80; Taylor, "Down with the Crown," 53.

72. Dragonetti, *Treatise on Virtues*, 2; *Histoire philosophique*, 9:374–75; May, *Enlightenment in America*, 162; Ferguson, *American Enlightenment*, 117.

73. Paine, *Common Sense*, 63; *Histoire philosophique*, 9:374–75; Israel, *Democratic Enlightenment*, 436–38; see also Fowler, *American Crisis*, 28; Osterhammel, *Transformation*, 515.

74. Paine, *Common Sense*, 100; Cotlar, *Tom Paine's America*, 149; Stuurman, *Invention of Humanity*, 261–3, 328.

75. Paine, *The American Crisis*, 17; Countryman, *American Revolution*, 105.

76. Watt, "Fictions," 157–61.

77. Paine, *Common Sense*, 85; Ferling, *Independence*, 219–20.

78. Paine, *Common Sense*, 68; Bailyn, *Ideological Origins*, 285–86.

79. Paine, *Common Sense*, 71; Keane, *Tom Paine*, 114–16; Nelson, *Thomas Paine*, 84–86.

80. Paine, *Common Sense*, 86; Keane, *Tom Paine*, 189–91.

81. Ryerson, *The Revolution*, 223–26; Bonwick, *American Revolution*, 92; Ferling, *Independence*, 278; Nelson, *Royalist Revolution*, 111.

82. Keane, *Tom Paine*, 134–35; Raphael, "Democratic Moment," 128–29.

83. Ferling, *Whirlwind*, 151–52, 225; Wilentz, *Rise of American Democracy*, 24.

84. Bonwick, *American Revolution*, 128–29; Nash, *Unknown American Revolution*, 187–88.

85. Paine, *Common Sense*, 84–85; Ferling, *Independence*, 218–19, 222–23; Rosenfeld, *Common Sense*, 155–58.

86. Ryerson, *The Revolution*, 74–75, 91, 103, 105; Bouton, *Taming Democracy*, 46–51.

87. Lefer, *Founding Conservatives*, 105–20; Bonwick, *American Revolution*, 93–95; Armitage, *Declaration*, 95; Grant, *John Adams*, 173–74.

88. Coelho, *Timothy Matlack*, 57.

89. Bernstein, *Thomas Jefferson*, 33–34; Sluiter, "Declaration of Independence," 18, 23.

90. Nash, "Philadelphia's Radical Caucus," 79.

91. Rush to Lee, Philadelphia, 23 July 1776, in Rush, *Letters*, 1:103; Rosenfeld, *Common Sense*, 159–60.

92. Rush, *Letters*, 1:108; Bouton, *Taming Democracy*, 64.

93. Brissot, *Examen critique*, 112; Wilentz, *Rise of American Democracy*, 14; Cotlar, "Languages of Democracy," 17.

94. Appleby, "America as a Model," 276; Nash, *Unknown American Revolution*, 272; Bennett, *A Few Lawless Vagabonds*, 132–33; Bouton, *Taming Democracy*, 5.
95. Rush, *Letters*, 1:105–7; Ryerson, *The Revolution*, 187; Beeman, *Varieties*, 248–49.
96. Rush, *Letters*, 1:336.
97. Rush to John Adams, 21 November 1805, in Rush, *Letters*, 2:908.
98. Wills, *Inventing America*, 32–33; Nash, "Philadelphia's Radical Caucus," 69.
99. Douglas, *Rebels and Democrats*, 263–64; Nash, "Philadelphia's Radical Caucus," 69–70.
100. Lefer, *Founding Conservatives*, 136.
101. Rush, *Letters*, 1:107, 336; Foner, *Tom Paine*, 125–26.
102. Rush, *Letters*, 2:1009; Grundfest, *George Clymer*, 105–6, 109.
103. Walters, *Revolutionary Deists*, 89–90; Stewart, *Nature's God*, 18, 63–67, 133–38, 142.
104. Stewart, *Nature's God*, 18–24; Nash, "Philadelphia's Radical Caucus," 70, 72; Bellesiles, *Revolutionary Outlaws*, 15, 136, 139–40; Bennett, *A Few Lawless Vagabonds*, 18, 128, 132, 219.
105. Coelho, *Timothy Matlack*, 65; Stewart, *Nature's God*, 21–22.
106. Nash, *Unknown American Revolution*, 269; Grundfest, *George Clymer*, 105; Bonwick, *American Revolution*, 130; Blasi, Freeman, and Kruse, *Citizen's Share*, 19.
107. Bouton, *Taming Democracy*, 52–56.
108. Nash, *Unknown American Revolution*, 273–74; Wright, *Franklin*, 250; Ward, *Politics of Liberty*, 407.
109. Keane, *Tom Paine*, 152; Wright, *Franklin*, 250–51; Rosenfeld, *Common Sense*, 165, 171–72.
110. Démeunier, *L'Amérique indépendante*, 3:22; Middlekauff, *Glorious Cause*, 618–19.
111. Rush, *Letters*, 1:336; Grant, *John Adams*, 234–35; Frost, *Perfect Freedom*, 65, 80; Nash, "Philadelphia's Radical Caucus," 79.
112. Mably, *Collection*, 8:366–71, 385–86; Israel, *Democratic Enlightenment*, 471.
113. Démeunier, *L'Amérique indépendante*, 1:46, 3:23; Price, *Observations*, 48; Frost, *Perfect Freedom*, 65.
114. Frost, *Perfect Freedom*, 74–75; Rosenfeld, *Common Sense*, 171–72.
115. Ryerson, *The Revolution*, 221–23, 227–29; Coelho, *Timothy Matlack*, 49, 52.
116. Pinto, *Letters*, 35.
117. Rush, *Letters*, 1:109, 111, 114; Ellis, *Revolutionary Summer*, 44, 193–97.
118. Ellis, *Revolutionary Summer*, 184–87, 216–19.
119. Nelson, *Thomas Paine*, 87; Beeman, *Our Lives, Our Fortunes*, 367–68, 375; Armitage, *Declaration*, 73.
120. Conway, "Continental European Soldiers," 94–95.
121. Fowler, *American Crisis*, 41–43; Wright, *Franklin*, 326–27.
122. Ellis, *Revolutionary Summer*, 42–43, 45–46, 87, 107; Parkinson, *Common Cause*, 329–30.
123. Ramsay, *History*, 2:384–86; Ferling, *Whirlwind*, 194–95, 208.
124. Havard and Vidal, *Histoire*, 685–86; Eccles, *French in North America*, 259–60.
125. Havard and Vidal, *Histoire*, 686–87.
126. Démeunier, *L'Amérique indépendante*, 1:91, 142; Bromwich, *Intellectual Life of Edmund Burke*, 292, 305.
127. Ramsay, *History*, 2:588–89.
128. Fowler, *American Crisis*, 15–18; Bernstein, *Founding Fathers*, 67–69.

129. Démeunier, *L'Amérique indépendante*, 1:91, 142; Wood, *Empire of Liberty*, 14–17.
130. Guyatt, *Providence*, 128–29; Waldman, *Founding Faith*, 69–71.
131. *Archivo Miranda*, 1:394–95.

Chapter 3: Revolutionary Constitutionalism and the Federal Union (1776–90)

1. Turgot to Price, Paris, 22 March 1778, in Price, *Observations*, 92–93, 103, 113; Appleby, "America as a Model," 273–75; Lutz, *Origins*, 49, 104–5, 107; Grab, "Italian Enlightenment," 42, 44.
2. Allen, *An animadversary address*, 6.
3. McGarvie, *One Nation under Law*, 145.
4. Ellis, *Founding Brothers*, 13–15.
5. De Bolla, *Architecture of Concepts*, 141–42, 245–46.
6. *Justification de la résistance*, 13.
7. D'Holbach, *Système social*, 296; Doyle, *Aristocracy*, 141; Lutz, *Origins*, 107.
8. Romani, *National Character*, 192.
9. Edwards, "Contradictions," 42–43; Wood, *Empire of Liberty*, 530; McGarvie, *One Nation under Law*, 141.
10. Rakove, *Revolutionaries*, 188–89; Nash, *Unknown American Revolution*, 241–42; Cotlar, "Languages of Democracy," 17–18.
11. Lefer, *Founding Conservatives*, 164; Adams, *Gouverneur Morris*, 77–87; Nelson, *Royalist Revolution*, 166–67.
12. D'Holbach, *Système social*, 297.
13. Paine, *Letter to George Washington*, 183; Kaye, *Thomas Paine*, 53, 94; Romani, *National Character*, 186–87.
14. Palmer, *An Enquiry*, 16–17.
15. D'Holbach, *Système social*, 293–302.
16. Ibid., 302.
17. *Histoire philosophique*, 9:209–10; Brissot, *New Travels*, 100; Démeunier, *L'Amérique indépendente*, 1:153–56; Israel, "Radical Enlightenment's Critique," 57; Cotlar, *Tom Paine's America*, 141.
18. Nadelhaft, *Disorders*, 81, 111–14, 125; Brissot, *New Travels*, 100.
19. Brissot, *New Travels*, 19, 50–51; Dahl, *Political Equality*, 1; Mirabeau, *Considérations*, 19.
20. Mirabeau, *Considérations*, 50–51; Démeunier, *L'Amérique indépendante*, 1:154; Barlow, *Advice*, 1:114–15; Higonnet, *Sister Republics*, 230.
21. Wood, *Empire of Liberty*, 530.
22. *Histoire philosophique*, 9:381.
23. Ibid.; Diderot, *Oeuvres complètes*, 15:547.
24. Price, *Observations*, 89.
25. Ibid., 69, 84–85; Bonwick, *American Revolution*, 53.
26. Price, *Observations*, 68–69; Démeunier, *L'Amérique indépendante*, 2:141–42, 156; Cotlar, "Languages of Democracy," 20.
27. Chastellux, *Discours*, 36–37, 81–83.
28. Price, *Observations*, 71–73.

29. Ibid., 71; Reich, *British Friends*, 100.
30. Price, *Observations*, 72.
31. Mirabeau, *Considérations*, 1–4; Desprat, *Mirabeau*, 295–97.
32. Lafayette to Adams, Paris, 8 March 1784, in Adams, *Papers*, 16:75–76; Ziesche, "Thomas Paine," 127; Meleney, *Public Life*, 90–91; Cotlar, "Conclusion," 282–83.
33. Démeunier, *L'Amérique indépendente*, 1:163–75; Mirabeau, *Considérations*, 3; Israel, *Revolutionary Ideas*, 46.
34. Meleney, *Public Life*, 90–91.
35. Brissot, *New Travels*, 88; Démeunier, *L'Amérique indépendente*, 1:170–75; Palmer, *Age of the Democratic Revolution*, 1:267, 270–71; Doyle, *Aristocracy*, 124–25.
36. Keane, *Tom Paine*, 254; Wood, *Radicalism*, 207, 241; Fowler, *American Crisis*, 206–7.
37. Miranda, *Diario*, 63; Démeunier, *L'Amérique indépendente*, 1:163–67; Ziesche, "Thomas Paine," 126–27.
38. Mirabeau, *Considérations*, 19, 33–36; Wood, *Radicalism*, 241–42.
39. Mirabeau, *Considérations*, 2–3, 14.
40. Huston, *Land Freedom*, 17–22, 29; Bayly, *Birth of the Modern World*, 115.
41. Miranda, *Diario*, 153–54; *Archivo Miranda*, 1:314; Rodríguez, *Revolución Americana*, 211; Racine, *Francisco de Miranda*, 59–60.
42. Wood, *Radicalism*, 230–31; Higonnet, *Sister Republics*, 166; Loft, *Passion, Politics*, 13–14, 99–100, 221.
43. Cotlar, "Languages of Democracy," 18.
44. *The Federalist* no. 4 (Jay, 7 November 1787), 13 and *The Federalist* no. 15 (Hamilton, 1 December 1787), 65; Wood, *Empire of Liberty*, 15.
45. *The Federalist* no. 6 (Hamilton, 14 November 1787), 22–23.
46. Raphael, *People's History*, 34–38; Papas, *Renegade Revolutionary*, 219–20; Bennett, *A Few Lawless Vagabonds*, 145–50.
47. Allen, *An animadversary address*, 4.
48. Bennett, *A Few Lawless Vagabonds*, 14, 129–33; Stewart, *Nature's God*, 19–20, 23.
49. Bellesiles, *Revolutionary Outlaws*, 140.
50. Allen, *An animadversary address*, 7, 9–13; *The Federalist* no. 7 (Hamilton, 17 November 1787), 27.
51. *The Federalist* no. 7 (Hamilton, 17 November 1787), 28; *The Federalist* no. 9 (Hamilton, 21 November 1787), 35.
52. *The Federalist* no. 67 (Hamilton, 11 March 1788), 327.
53. Kloppenberg, *Toward Democracy*, 392, 425–26, 788n60.
54. Cole, "American Bicameralism," 85–86.
55. *The Federalist* no. 9 (Hamilton, 21 November 1787), 37–38.
56. Ibid., 37–39; Levy, "Montesquieu's Constitutional Legacies," 122.
57. Mably, *Collection*, 8:364, 366–67.
58. Ibid., 364, 366, 371, 386–87; Démeunier, *L'Amérique indépendente*, 1:49–50; Richards, *Shays's Rebellion*, 70.
59. *The Federalist* no. 10 (Madison, 22 November 1787), 40.
60. Ibid., 41, 46; Middlekauff, *Glorious Cause*, 658.
61. *The Federalist* no. 20 (Madison with Hamilton, 11 December 1787), 93; Venturi, *Pagine repubblicane*, 144.
62. *The Federalist* no. 20 (Madison with Hamilton, 11 December 1787), 91.
63. Ibid., 92–93; *The Federalist* no. 54 (Madison, 12 February 1788), 89–93, 268.

64. *The Federalist* no. 39 (Madison, 16 January 1788), 185.
65. *The Federalist* no. 45 (Madison, 26 January 1788), 227.
66. Labunski, *James Madison*, 103–4.
67. Wood, *Empire of Liberty*, 581; McGarvie, *One Nation under Law*, 144.
68. Lambert, *Founding Fathers*, 229–33.
69. Ibid., 233–39; Frost, *Perfect Freedom*, 105, 110; Ferguson, *American Enlightenment*, 78–79; Billias, *American Constitutionalism*, 79–80.
70. Lambert, *Founding Fathers*, 235; Bauszus, "Religious Aspects," 336.
71. McGarvie, *One Nation under Law*, 148–50.
72. Priestley, *Autobiography*, 117.
73. Price, *Observations*, 21–22.
74. Jayne, *Jefferson's Declaration*, 163–65.
75. Palmer, *An Enquiry*, 27; Holifield, *Theology*, 163.
76. Lambert, *Founding Fathers*, 220; Bauszus, "Religious Aspects," 337; Walzer, *Paradox of Liberation*, 136–38, 160n9.
77. Miranda, *Diario*, 153–54; *Archivo Miranda*, 1:314; Racine, *Francisco de Miranda*, 59–60.
78. Démeunier, *L'Amérique indépendante*, 1:44, 2:190; Lambert, *Founding Fathers*, 220, 249.
79. Miranda, *Diario*, 153–54; Sehat, *Myth*, 26–27, 55; Fea, "John Adams and Religion," 194–95.
80. Price, *Observations*, 48; Démeunier, *L'Amérique indépendante*, 3:123–24; Sehat, *Myth*, 28, 54.
81. Sehat, *Myth*, 55; McGarvie, *One Nation under Law*, 154–55.
82. Démeunier, *L'Amérique indépendante*, 1:44, 2:190–91, 3:62–63, 74; Nadelhaft, *Disorders*, 38.
83. Price, *Observations*, 49.
84. Sehat, *Myth*, 22–23.
85. Chastellux, *Discours*, 83–84; Foner, *Tom Paine*, 259.
86. Chastellux, *Discours*, 47; Sehat, *Myth*, 59, 62.
87. Frost, *Perfect Freedom*, 133–34.

Chapter 4: Schooling Republicans

1. Paine, *Letter Addressed to the Abbé Raynal*, 49; Wood, *Radicalism*, 191.
2. Ellis, *After the Revolution*, 56–58, 169–70; Cotlar, *Tom Paine's America*, 35.
3. Post, "Jeffersonian Revisions"; Kloppenberg, *Toward Democracy*, 151–52.
4. Post, "Jeffersonian Revisions," 301–4.
5. Israel, *Democratic Enlightenment*, 428; Israel, *Enlightenment Contested*, 604–5.
6. Fenimore Cooper, *American Democrat*, 89–90.
7. Rush, *Letters*, 1:532, 2:865; Nash, *Unknown American Revolution*, 453; Davidson, *How Revolutionary Were the Bourgeois Revolutions?* 56, 62.
8. Wilentz, *Rise of American Democracy*, 10.
9. Pulliam, *History of Education*, 48–49; Tyack, *Turning Points*, 86–87; Urban and Wagoner, *American Education*, 76–77.
10. Loft, *Passion, Politics*, 121–22.
11. Brissot, *New Travels*, 297.

12. Rush to Price, Philadelphia, 2 June 1787, in Rush, *Letters*, 1:419.
13. Palmer, *An Enquiry*, 23.
14. Price, *Observations*, 50–51.
15. Smith, *Wealth of Nations*, 2:165–66; Wood, *Empire of Liberty*, 24, 230–31; Israel, *Democratic Enlightenment*, 237–43.
16. McDaniel, *Adam Ferguson*, 191–92, 204–5.
17. Grant, *John Adams*, 225–26.
18. Ibid., 65; Cotlar, *Tom Paine's America*, 177–78; Wood, *Empire of Liberty*, 470–72.
19. Priestley, *Essay*, 186; Turgot to Price, 22 March 1778, in Price, *Observations*, 92, 99–100, 113.
20. Miranda, *Diario*, 152; Zeuske, *Francisco de Miranda*, 78–80; Racine, *Francisco de Miranda*, 60.
21. Miranda, *New Democracy*, 58.
22. Ibid., 164.
23. Ibid., 166.
24. Coram, *Political Inquiries*, 78–80; May, *Enlightenment in America*, 235.
25. Priestley, *Essay*, 211.
26. Barlow, "To His Fellow Citizens," 2:1121.
27. Ibid.
28. Barlow, *Advice*, 1:95.
29. Foner, *Tom Paine*, 264–65; Wilentz, *Chants Democratic*, 184–93.
30. Skidmore, *Rights of Man to Property*, 32, 58, 62.
31. Freneau, "On some of the Principles."
32. See "Principes et maximes politiques de M. de Mirabeau," in Condorcet, *Bibliothèque de l'Homme Public*, series II (1791), 11:55, 59; Cérutti, *Mémoire*, 49.
33. Chastellux, *De la félicité publique*, 2:78.
34. Loft, *Passion, Politics*, 144–46.
35. Freneau, "On some of the Principles," 2.
36. Wood, *Empire of Liberty*, 472–73.
37. McGarvie, *One Nation under Law*, 62.
38. Price, *Observations*, 50–51.
39. Staloff, "Politics," 128; Burstein and Isenberg, *Madison and Jefferson*, 67–68; Ferling, *Jefferson and Hamilton*, 57–58; Meacham, *Thomas Jefferson*, 469.
40. Jefferson to Adams, 28 October 1813, in *Adams-Jefferson Letters*, 2:390; Staloff, "Politics," 128–29; Urban and Wagoner, *American Education*, 72–74.
41. Douglas, *Rebels and Democrats*, 307–8; Staloff, "Politics," 129–30.
42. Jefferson to Adams, 28 October 1813, in *Adams-Jefferson Letters*, 2:390; Peterson, *Thomas Jefferson*, 146–49; Berkowitz, *Virtue and the Making*, 166.
43. Jefferson to Adams, 28 October 1813, in *Adams-Jefferson Letters*, 2:289–90; Peterson, *Thomas Jefferson*, 147–49, 960.
44. Bernstein, " 'Nature's God,' " 67–68; Holmes, *Faiths*, 85–87; Schachtman, *Gentlemen Scientists*, 128.
45. Robson, *Educating Republicans*, 106–8; Rakove, *Revolutionaries*, 306–7.
46. Spurlin, *Rousseau in America*, 64–65; Wood, *Empire of Liberty*, 558, 560; Ferling, *Jefferson and Hamilton*, 58.
47. Pulliam, *History of Education*, 49–50; Wood, *Empire of Liberty*, 473; Peterson, *Thomas Jefferson*, 147, 150.

626 / *Notes to Chapter 4*

48. Coram, *Political Inquiries*, 77, 80–81; Cotlar, *Tom Paine's America*, 116–19.
49. Coram, *Political Inquiries*, 11–16; Ferguson, *American Enlightenment*, 153–54.
50. Coram, *Political Inquiries*, 78; Cotlar, *Tom Paine's America*, 118; McGarvie, *One Nation under Law*, 77.
51. Coram, *Political Inquiries*, 15; May, *Enlightenment in America*, 235–36; Cotlar, "Robert Coram," 347–48.
52. Coram, *Political Inquiries*, 60–61.
53. Ibid., 87–90, 92.
54. Ibid., 89.
55. Ibid., 74–75.
56. Ibid., 78; Foner, *Democratic-Republican Societies*, 14–15.
57. Quoted in Slack, *Liberty's First Crisis*, 188.
58. Cooper, *Some Information*, 78.
59. Skidmore, *Rights of Man to Property*, 16, 18.
60. Pulliam, *History of Education*, 49–50; Urban and Wagoner, *American Education*, 75.
61. Cole, *Great American University*, 15; Wood, *Empire of Liberty*, 472.
62. Franklin, *Papers*, 4:74, 112–13, 325, 469; Cole, *Great American University*, 14, 87.
63. Tyack, *Turning Points*, 75–77; Urban and Wagoner, *American Education*, 70.
64. Franklin, *Papers*, 5:20n, 190, 331; Tyack, *Turning Points*, 74–76.
65. Ibid., 4:468–69; Frost, *Perfect Freedom*, 49–50, 65–66; Wright, *Franklin*, 41–42, 358.
66. May, *Enlightenment in America*, 81–83, 85–86.
67. Staloff, "Politics," 134, 137–38; Walters, *Benjamin Franklin and His Gods*, 22; Lambert, *Founding Fathers*, 188, 243.
68. Jefferson to Priestley, Philadelphia, 18 January 1800, in Jefferson, *Writings*, 1070–71; Bernstein, *Founding Fathers*, 89; Holmes, *Faiths*, 85–86.
69. McGarvie, *One Nation under Law*, 158–59; Cole, *Great American University*, 21, 73; Burstein and Isenberg, *Madison and Jefferson*, 569; Meacham, *Thomas Jefferson*, 468–72.
70. Bernstein, *Thomas Jefferson*, 175; Burstein and Isenberg, *Madison and Jefferson*, 585.
71. Bernstein, *Thomas Jefferson*, 175–76.
72. Malone, *Public Life*, 259–61; Slack, *Liberty's First Crisis*, 238–39.
73. Quoted in Malone, *Public Life*, 261.
74. Volokh, "Thomas Cooper," 372–73, 380.
75. May, *Enlightenment in America*, 185–86; Stewart, *Nature's God*, 65, 67, 435; Wilentz, *Politicians and the Egalitarians*, 35, 96.
76. Wells, "Timothy Dwight's American 'Dunciad,'" 177, 187; Holifield, *Theology*, 352–54.
77. Kuklick, *Churchmen and Philosophers*, 95–96; Morgan, "Ezra Stiles," 116–17; Buel, *Joel Barlow*, 278, 315.
78. Dwight, *Nature and Danger*, 50, 81; McGarvie, *One Nation under Law*, 161–62.
79. Dwight, *Nature and Danger*, 89.
80. Ibid., 90, 95.
81. Wells, "Timothy Dwight's American 'Dunciad,'" 185.
82. Quoted in Taylor, *American Revolutions*, 444.
83. Ellis, *After the Revolution*, 114–15, 139–40; McGarvie, *Law and Religion*, 42, 45, 159.
84. Holifield, *Theology*, 175; Meacham, *American Gospel*, 67–68.
85. May, *Enlightenment in America*, 270; Kuklick, *Churchmen and Philosophers*, 68, 72–74.

86. Miranda, *New Democracy*, 169–70.
87. Brissot, *New Travels*, 97–98.
88. Quoted in Loft, *Passion, Politics*, 144.
89. Brissot, *New Travels*, 95, 97; Robson, *Educating Republicans*, 131–32.
90. Brissot, *New Travels*, 90; Wood, *Radicalism*, 240.
91. Dwight, *Nature and Danger*, 95; McGarvie, *Law and Religion*, 42–43, 62.
92. Holifield, *Theology*, 199.
93. Lundberg and May, "The Enlightened Reader," 269–71; Morgan, "Ezra Stiles," 109, 117.
94. Stewart, *Nature's God*, 28–29; May, *Enlightenment in America*, 172, 186, 192–93, 246–27.
95. Koch, *Religion*, 184, 261; Foner, *Story*, 19–20; Kaye, *Thomas Paine*, 5, 99.
96. Sheehan, *James Madison*, 63–81, 145, 150.
97. May, *Enlightenment in America*, 241; Buel, *Joel Barlow*, 92, 238.
98. Rosenfeld, *American Aurora*, 235; Kaye, *Thomas Paine*, 111.
99. Lundberg and May, "The Enlightened Reader," 271.
100. Cole, "American Bicameralism," 83; Bernstein, *Thomas Jefferson*, 9–10, 109.
101. Wood, *Empire of Liberty*, 554–59.
102. Spencer, *Bloomsbury Encyclopaedia*, 1:357–58.
103. Monette, *Rendez-vous manqué*, 88–90; Spencer, *Bloomsbury Encyclopaedia*, 1:356.
104. Miranda, *New Democracy*, 43.
105. Quoted in Sumrell, "John Trumbull: Art and Politics."
106. Andrew, *Patrons*, 185; May, *Divided Heart*, 175.
107. Peterson, *Thomas Jefferson*, 858–59; Pulliam, *History of Education*, 48.
108. Paine, *Letter Addressed to the Abbé Raynal*, 50–51.

Chapter 5: Benjamin Franklin

1. Luchet, *Les Contemporains de 1789*, 2:34–35.
2. Franklin, *Autobiography*, 62–63.
3. Ibid., 69; Walters, *Benjamin Franklin and His Gods*, 26.
4. Franklin, *Papers*, 1:57–58; Walters, *Revolutionary Deists*, 62–65; Stewart, *Nature's God*, 184–85; Lyons, *The Society*, 30–31.
5. Franklin, *Autobiography*, 96, 113–14; Morgan, *Benjamin Franklin*, 17–18; Walters, *Revolutionary Deists*, 62–63.
6. Anderson, *Radical Enlightenments*, 9–12, 167–72.
7. Walters, *Benjamin Franklin and His Gods*, 104–5.
8. Franklin, *Autobiography*, 116–18; Anderson, *Radical Enlightenments*, 13, 210, 218; Nash, *Unknown American Revolution*, 96.
9. Ferling, *Independence*, 144.
10. Franklin to James Parker, Philadelphia, 20 March 1751, in Franklin, *Papers*, 4:118–19.
11. Franklin, *Autobiography*, 242–43.
12. Wood, *Americanization*, 112; Lyons, *The Society*, 131.
13. Wood, *Americanization*, 116.
14. Priestley, *Autobiography*, 116–17; Walters, *Benjamin Franklin and His Gods*, 3; Fruchtman, "Unrespectable and Reluctant Radical," 5.

15. Dickinson, "'The Friends of America,'" 6, 9–10; Lyons, *The Society*, 29–30; Page, *John Jebb*, 171–72.

16. Wilson, *Diderot*, 572–73.

17. Franklin, "Rules," 78.

18. Hume to Smith, 13 February 1774, in Smith, *Correspondence*, 171; Rakove, *Revolutionaries*, 254–55.

19. Bourke, *Empire and Revolution*, 493–94; Fruchtman, "Unrespectable and Reluctant Radical," 11–16.

20. Ferling, *Independence*, 144.

21. Middlekauff, *Benjamin Franklin*, 208–9; Jasanoff, *Liberty's Exiles*, 64.

22. Middlekauff, *Glorious Cause*, 318; Foner, *Tom Paine*, 72; Beeman, *Our Lives, Our Fortunes*, 309–20; Keane, *Tom Paine*, 84; Nelson, *Thomas Paine*, 49–50, 52.

23. Ziesche, "Thomas Paine," 124.

24. [Petit], *Observations*, 64–69, 75; *Histoire philosophique*, 9:41.

25. Smith, "To the People of Pennsylvania," *Pennsylvania Gazette* Letter II (13 March 1776); Keane, *Tom Paine*, 130–31; Nelson, *Thomas Paine*, 94.

26. Smith, "To the People of Pennsylvania," *Pennsylvania Gazette* Letter VII (10 April 1776).

27. Keane, *Tom Paine*, 130–31; Kaye, *Thomas Paine*, 51–52.

28. Rush, *Letters*, 1:137, 148; Foner, *Tom Paine*, 136–38; Keane, *Tom Paine*, 191–92.

29. Rush to Lee, Philadelphia, 24 October 1779, in Rush, *Letters*, 1:244; Rosenfeld, *Common Sense*, 174–75.

30. Paine, *Complete Writings*, 2:280.

31. Sehat, *Myth*, 16.

32. Rush, *Letters*, 1:111; Armitage, *Declaration*, 81.

33. Condorcet, *Writings on the United States*, 97.

34. Badinter and Badinter, *Condorcet*, 156–57; Wood, *Americanization*, 174–77, 208–9.

35. Israel, *Revolutionary Ideas*, 14–29, 36–49; Jonathan Israel, "Response to Jeremy Popkin," *H France Forum* 15, no. 67 (May 2015): 4–6.

36. Dawson, *Gods of Revolution*, 46; Staloff, *Hamilton, Adams, Jefferson*, 175; Moravia, *Il tramonto*, 81.

37. Condorcet, *Réflexions sur l'esclavage des nègres*, 251.

38. Badinter and Badinter, *Condorcet*, 159; Marchione, "Philip Mazzei," 8–9; Tortarolo, "Philip Mazzei," 59–60; Venturi, *Pagine repubblicane*, 105–6; Gabrieli, "Impact"; Levine, "Idea of America," 27.

39. Condorcet, *Esquisse*, 274–75; Foner, *Tom Paine*, 236.

40. Mirabeau, *Considérations*, 91; Oldfield, *Transatlantic Abolitionism*, 20–21.

41. Billias, *American Constitutionalism*, 79, 85; Israel, *Revolutionary Ideas*.

42. Price, *Observations*, 123; Moravia, *Il tramonto*, 80.

43. Franklin, *Papers*, 29:47.

44. Grimm, *Correspondance Littéraire*, 10:74.

45. Adams, *Diary and Autobiography*, 69; Staloff, *Hamilton, Adams, Jefferson*, 173; Schiff, *Dr. Franklin*, 133–34.

46. Bentham to Samuel Bentham, London, 27 October 1778, in Bentham, *Correspondence*, 2:183; see also Jourdan, "Alien Origins," 190.

47. Franklin, *Papers*, 26:9–10; Rakove, *Revolutionaries*, 258–59.

48. Franklin, *Papers*, 26:8–9.

49. Ibid., 30:44–45.

50. Kroes-Ligtenberg, *Dr. Wybo Fijnje*, 80; Kaplan, "Founding Fathers," 432–33.
51. Franklin, *Papers*, 26:20–21, 132–33, 27:116–17, 186, 352–53.
52. Condorcet, *Writings on the United States*, 97.
53. Franklin, *Papers*, 26:252.
54. Ibid., 26:199–202.
55. Ibid., 1:287–318, 2:218; Rahe, *Republics*, 330; Rosenfeld, *Common Sense*, 151, 192.
56. Appleby, "America as a Model," 267.
57. [Franklin], *Science du Bonhomme Richard*, 69.
58. Ibid., 59–60; Rosenfeld, *Common Sense*, 185.
59. [Franklin], *Science du Bonhomme Richard*, 82–83, 90–91.
60. Ansart, "From Voltaire to Raynal," 81, 86–89; Pocock, *Barbarism*, 4:319–27.
61. Moravia, *Il tramonto*, 78–79; Wright, *Franklin*, 252–53, 355.
62. Franklin, *Papers*, 29:185–86, 30:6; Wekhrlin, *Chronologen* 6 (1779): 31–33; Wright, *Franklin*, 281; Auricchio, *The Marquis*, 81.
63. Smith, *Correspondence*, 408–9; Brands, *First American*, 579–80.
64. Grimm, *Correspondance Littéraire*, 10:285.
65. Rosenfeld, *American Aurora*, 318, 320; Wright, *Franklin*, 321.
66. Schiff, *Dr. Franklin*, 83; Dunn, *Sister Revolutions*, 143; Billias, *American Constitutionalism*, 67–70; Olson, "Franklin on National Character," 121.
67. Davidson, *How Revolutionary Were the Bourgeois Revolutions?* 61–62; Wood, *Empire of Liberty*, 712–14.
68. Condorcet, *Writings on the United States*, 98.
69. Meyer, *Democratic Enlightenment*, 75–76; Wood, *Americanization*, 182; Schiff, *Dr. Franklin*, 82, 114–15.
70. Grimm, *Correspondance Littéraire*, 11:360; Olson, "Franklin on National Character," 129–30.
71. Middlekauff, *Benjamin Franklin*, 195–99; Stewart, *Nature's God*, 286–87; Unger, *John Quincy Adams*, 334–37.
72. Franklin, *Papers*, 29:9; Wekhrlin, *Chronologen* 2 (1779): 272 .
73. Franklin, *Papers*, 28:288–89; Sloan, "Thomas Jefferson," 474.
74. Franklin, *Papers*, 28:570–71.
75. Fowler, *American Crisis*, 118–22; Ellis, *First Family*, 98–100.
76. Grant, *John Adams*, 287–89; Peterson, *Thomas Jefferson*, 298; Unger, *John Quincy Adams*, 55–56.
77. Rosenfeld, *American Aurora*, 313; Moravia, *Il tramonto*, 73–76.
78. Rakove, *Revolutionaries*, 257.
79. Bellesiles, *Revolutionary Outlaws*, 137–39; Bennett, *Few Lawless Vagabonds*, 130–33.
80. Carter, *"One Grand Pursuit,"* 15.
81. Ziesche, "Thomas Paine," 123; Adams, *Gouverneur Morris*, 145–46.
82. Wilentz, *Rise of American Democracy*, 25.
83. Wright, *Franklin*, 250; Wood, *Americanization*, 219–20; Morgan, *Benjamin Franklin*, 311–12.
84. Appleby, "America as a Model," 276; Kloppenberg, *Toward Democracy*, 358.
85. Franklin, *Writings*, 10:54.
86. Middlekauff, *Glorious Cause*, 618–21; Bonwick, *American Revolution*, 153–54; Wright, *Franklin*, 251–52; Frost, *Perfect Freedom*, 69, 74; Morgan, *Benjamin Franklin*, 239–40, 310–11, 313.

87. Jefferson to William Smith, Philadelphia, 19 February 1791, in Jefferson, *Writings*, 973–74.
88. Dunn, *Sister Revolutions*, 69, 72–73; McCullough, *John Adams*, 420; Nelson, *Royalist Revolution*, 158–59, 237n20.
89. Polasky, *Revolution in Brussels*, 134–38.
90. Gorman, *America and Belgium*, 184–87; Polasky, *Revolutions without Borders*, 41–42.
91. Grimm, *Correspondance Littéraire*, 15:163.
92. Ibid., 15:102–3.
93. Condorcet, *Writings on the United States*, 95, 128–29; Badinter and Badinter, *Condorcet*, 311.
94. *Archives Parlementaires* 17 (17 July 1790): 178–79.
95. Chastellux, *Chronique de Paris*, series 2, 234 (21 July 1790): 933; *Feuille villageois*, series 1, no. 10 (2 December 1790): 187; Badinter and Badinter, *Condorcet*, 337; Vincent, "Les Américains," 483–86.
96. [Bonneville], *Bouche de fer* 1 (1790): 110–11; Godard, *Exposé*, 203–4; Luchet, *Les Contemporains de 1789*, 2:34; Israel, *Revolutionary Ideas*, 137–38.
97. Wood, *Empire*, 51, 589, 713; Stewart, *Nature's God*, 185–87.
98. Maréchal, *Dictionnaire*, 115.
99. British Library Pamphlets: Printed Fr 371/8: "Extrait du Journal de la Société de 1789," 7–9, 15; Badinter and Badinter, *Condorcet*, 288.
100. Cruise O'Brien, *Long Affair*, 88–92, 96–100; Fleming, *Great Divide*, 140.
101. Maclay, *Journal*, 350, 379; Wood, *Americanization*, 231, 233; Wilentz, *Rise of American Democracy*, 38; Nelson, *Thomas Paine*, 192–93.
102. Maclay, *Journal*, 408; May, *Enlightenment in America*, 213; Lyons, *The Society*, 167–68.
103. Wood, *Americanization*, 246; Wright, *Franklin*, 356–57.
104. Wright, *Franklin*, 8–9; Wood, *Americanization*, 4–9; Wood, *Empire of Liberty*, 712–14.
105. Nash, "Philadelphia's Radical Caucus," 79.
106. Franklin to David Hartley, Philadelphia, 4 December 1789, in Franklin, *Writings*, 10:72; Ferling, *Jefferson and Hamilton*, 246.
107. Brookhiser, *Alexander Hamilton*, 160–61.
108. Emerson, "The American Scholar," 23–25.
109. Ibid., 24; Dolan, *Emerson's Liberalism*, 41, 47.

Chapter 6: Black Emancipation

1. *Waarschouwing der reede* (Knuttel 21041), 8.
2. Raphael, *People's History*, 388; Wood, *Empire of Liberty*, 509; Steckel, "African American Population," 439.
3. Raphael, *People's History*, 311.
4. Millar, *Observations*, 223, 237, 241–42; Losurdo, *Contre-histoire*, 20.
5. Israel, *Democratic Enlightenment*, 229; Sher, *Enlightenment and the Book*, 397.
6. Davis, *Problem of Slavery*, 274–76, 306–8; Waldstreicher, *Slavery's Constitution*, 46–48, 54.
7. Halliday, *Understanding Thomas Jefferson*, 148–49; Nash and Gao Hodges, *Friends of Liberty*, 116–23; Stewart, *Madison's Gift*, 316–17; Waldstreicher, *Slavery's Constitution*, 46–47, 134–41.

8. Papas, *Renegade Revolutionary*, 157–58.
9. Walsh, "African American Population," 194; Steckel, "African American Population," 436, 454.
10. Slaughter, *Independence*, 423–24; Papas, *Renegade Revolutionary*, 154–55.
11. Gilbert, *Black Patriots*, 64, 99–101, 107, 109; Raphael, *People's History*, 358–64; Parkinson, *Common Cause*, 175–76.
12. Gilbert, *Black Patriots*, 98–105; Nash and Gao Hodges, *Friends of Liberty*, 18; Raphael, *People's History*, 359–62.
13. Gilbert, *Black Patriots*, 86, 91; Papas, *Renegade Revolutionary*, 156–57, 164; Slaughter, *Independence*, 422.
14. Walsh, "African American Population," 194; Steckel, "African American Population," 435.
15. Gilbert, *Black Patriots*, 116, 119; Gould, *Among the Powers*, 148; Rossignol, "Black Declaration," 114–15.
16. Taylor, *Internal Enemy*, 27; Taylor, *American Revolutions*, 240–41.
17. Gould, *Among the Powers*, 150–51.
18. Fowler, *American Crisis*, 199–200; Rossignol, "Black Declaration," 115–16.
19. Coelho, *Timothy Matlack*, 135–37; Keane, *Tom Paine*, 194–96; Nash, *Unknown American Revolution*, 323–27.
20. Sluiter, "Declaration of Independence," 27.
21. Lagrave, *Fleury Mesplet*, 24; Wood, *Americanization*, 227; Kaye, *Thomas Paine*, 36.
22. Kaye, *Thomas Paine*, 147. I was alerted to the tendency of historians to paper over this gap in Paine's campaign for universal rights by Jonathan Clarke, to whom I am indebted for this.
23. Rush, *Letters*, 2:939.
24. Adams, *Gouverneur Morris*, 157–59.
25. Gilbert, *Black Patriots*, 53–54, 516.
26. Wekhrlin, *Graue Ungeheuer* 1 (1784): 250–52, 255; Davis, *Problem of Slavery*, 313–14.
27. Badinter and Badinter, *Condorcet*, 172, 175.
28. Condorcet, *Réflexions sur l'esclavage des nègres*, 15.
29. Ibid., 5, 50; Badinter and Badinter, *Condorcet*, 172–73.
30. Condorcet, *Réflexions sur l'esclavage des nègres*, 15; Popkin, *You Are All Free*, 333, 341.
31. For Brissot, see Brissot, *Examen critique* (1786): 96–98, 100–127.
32. Ibid., 96–97.
33. Ibid., 103–4.
34. Condorcet, *Réflexions sur l'esclavage des nègres*, 22–23; Badinter and Badinter, *Condorcet*, 174.
35. Badinter and Badinter, *Condorcet*, 292–93.
36. Franklin to Condorcet, London, 20 March 1774, in Franklin, *Papers*, 21:152.
37. Condorcet, *Réflexions sur l'esclavage des nègres*, 46–47.
38. Brissot, *New Travels*, 237; De Luna, "Dean Street Style," 170, 173; Gilbert, *Black Patriots*, 245–47.
39. Rush to Price, Philadelphia, 15 October 1785, in Rush, *Letters*, 1:371.
40. Brissot, *New Travels*, 218–19, 233; Oldfield, *Transatlantic Abolitionism*, 69–70.
41. Brissot, *New Travels*, 232.
42. Anderson, *Radical Enlightenments*, 15, 207–13; Allen, *Our Declaration*, 241.

43. Wood, *Americanization*, 227; Sluiter, "Declaration of Independence," 28; Grayling, *Towards the Light*, 169–70.
44. Franklin, *The Works*, 12:158–59; see also Wood, *Empire of Liberty*, 524–55; Gilbert, *Black Patriots*, 250–52.
45. Meleney, *Public Life*, 186–87.
46. Maclay, *Journal* 196 (15 February 1790); Parkinson, *Common Cause*, 635–38.
47. Condorcet, *Réflexions sur l'esclavage des nègres*, 50; Israel, *Democratic Enlightenment*, 416.
48. Condorcet, *Political Writings*, 151–52.
49. Wekhrlin, *Graue Ungeheuer* 1 (1784): 250–52, 255; Israel, *Democratic Enlightenment*, 473.
50. Hirschfeld, *George Washington*, 203; Fergus, *Revolutionary Emancipation*, 48–51.
51. O'Neill, *Burke-Wollstonecraft Debate*, 85–86; Losurdo, *Contre-histoire*, 39, 158–59; Israel, "Radical Enlightenment's Critique," 51.
52. Price, *Observations*, 83–84; Foner, *Story*, 32; Levine, "Idea of America," 28.
53. Condorcet, *Réflexions sur l'esclavage des nègres*, 249; Chastellux, *Discours*, 90–91; Brissot and Clavière, *De la France*, 324.
54. Loft, *Passion, Politics*, 215–17.
55. Condorcet, *Political Writings*, 152.
56. Démeunier, *L'Esprit*, 2:152, 155.
57. Brissot, *New Travels*, 227; De Luna, "Dean Street Style," 174–75.
58. *Histoire philosophique*, 9:28, 118.
59. Mably, *Collection*, 8:385.
60. Keane, *Tom Paine*, 196; Nash and Soderlund, *Freedom*, 103; Berlin, *Long Emancipation*, 68–69.
61. Steckel, "African American Population," 438.
62. Brissot, *New Travels*, 229; Nash and Soderlund, *Freedom*, 111.
63. Steckel, "African American Population," 438.
64. Ibid.; Condorcet, *Réflexions sur l'esclavage des nègres*, 308; Nash and Soderlund, *Freedom*, 7; Nash and Gao Hodges, *Friends of Liberty*, 148–49; Raphael, *People's History*, 355.
65. Gigantino, "The Whole North," 411–12, 435; Wilentz, *Rise of American Democracy*, 82, 218.
66. Brissot, *New Travels*, 227–28; Losurdo, *Contre-histoire*, 26–27; Gigantino, "The Whole North," 433.
67. Adams, *Gouverneur Morris*, 78–81.
68. Cotlar, *Tom Paine's America*, 225n32.
69. Zilversmit, *First Emancipation*, 120–21, 123–24, 201–2; Bellesiles, *Revolutionary Outlaws*, 140; Wood, *Empire of Liberty*, 519–20; Raphael, *People's History*, 359, 372.
70. Zilversmit, *First Emancipation*, 192–93; Steckel, "African American Population," 438.
71. Adams, *Gouverneur Morris*, 81–84; Wilentz, *Chants Democratic*, 36, 186; Wood, *Empire of Liberty*, 520; Raphael, *People's History*, 372.
72. Démeunier, *L'Esprit*, 2:231; Mirabeau, *Considérations*, 198; Brissot, *New Travels*, 227.
73. Brissot, *New Travels*, 227–28; Loft, *Passion, Politics*, 17.
74. Loft, *Passion, Politics*, 17.
75. Cloquet, *Recollections*, 150–55; Hirschfeld, *George Washington*, 126; Gilbert, *Black Patriots*, 246; Nash, *Unknown American Revolution*, 432–33; Kramer, "Lafayette and the Historians," 385.

76. Washington to Lafayette, Mount Vernon, 10 May 1786, quoted in Hirschfeld, *George Washington*, 127.
77. Nash, *Unknown American Revolution*, 433; Hirschfeld, *George Washington*, 203–5.
78. Paine, *Letter to George Washington*, 183; Rosenfeld, *American Aurora*, 33; Keane, *Tom Paine*, 429–32; Nelson, *Thomas Paine*, 292–94.
79. Steckel, "African American Population," 438.
80. Nash and Gao Hodges, *Friends of Liberty*, 115–16; Matthewson, "Jefferson and Haiti," 212.
81. Wood, *Empire of Liberty*, 122–23, 362; Countryman, *American Revolution*, 181, 209; Hirschfeld, *George Washington*, 180; Gould, *Among the Powers*, 158.
82. Edwards, "Contradictions," 50; Egerton, "Race and Slavery," 75. The ordinance also prohibited primogeniture and sold off lands cheaply to landless whites. Blasi, Freeman, and Kruse, *Citizen's Share*, 30.
83. Waldstreicher, *Slavery's Constitution*, 87–88.
84. Wood, *Empire of Liberty*, 362.
85. Waldstreicher, *Slavery's Constitution*, 96–97; Nash, *Unknown American Revolution*, 168, 415.
86. Taylor, *Internal Enemy*, 86; Ketcham, *Anti-Federalist Papers*,162; Gilbert, *Black Patriots*, 53; Horne, *Counter-Revolution*, 200.
87. Ketcham, *Anti-Federalist Papers*, 161–63.
88. Stewart, *Madison's Gift*, 316.
89. Foner, *Story*, 35–36; Gilbert, *Black Patriots*, 55; Waldstreicher, *Slavery's Constitution*, 3–5, 88.
90. Barman, *Brazil*, 31.
91. Madison, *The Federalist* no. 54 (February 1788): 266.
92. Blackburn, *Overthrow*, 123–25; Taylor, *Internal Enemy*, 35; Stewart, *Madison's Gift*, 297–98, 316; Edwards, "Contradictions," 49

Chapter 7: Expropriating the Native Americans

1. Israel, *Radical Enlightenment*, 179–80; Israel, *Democratic Enlightenment*, 480–83; Lavaert, "Radical Enlightenment," 55–59.
2. Israel, *Enlightenment Contested*, 599–601; Rosenfeld, *Common Sense*, 107–9.
3. Jefferson to Adams, 11 June 1812, in Jefferson, *Writings*, 1263.
4. Brissot, *Examen critique*, 100, 104; Cotlar, "Robert Coram," 345–46; Wills, *Inventing America*, 304; Ellis, *American Sphinx*, 119; for Freneau, see Spencer, *Bloomsbury Encyclopaedia*, 1:459.
5. Wolloch, "Barbarian Tribes," 527.
6. Keane, *Tom Paine*, 147–50, 221; Kaye, *Thomas Paine*, 54; Nelson, *Thomas Paine*, 113, 117.
7. Nash, *Unknown American Revolution*, 248.
8. Ibid., 174–75; Bennett, *Few Lawless Vagabonds*, 87; Hoffman, "Simon Girty," 227.
9. Jasanoff, *Liberty's Exiles*, 191.
10. Kloppenberg, *Toward Democracy*, 296–97.
11. Gould, *Persistence*, 211; Jasanoff, *Liberty's Exiles*, 38–40, 195.
12. Papas, *Renegade Revolutionary*, 177–78.

13. Kammen, *Colonial New York*, 373.
14. Jasanoff, *Liberty's Exiles*, xi–xii, 66.
15. Alden, *History*, 320–21; Nash, *Unknown American Revolution*, 252–53; Parkinson, *Common Cause*, 351.
16. Higonnet, *Sister Republics*, 180, 200; Nash, *Unknown American Revolution*, 251–56; Fowler, *American Crisis*, 118; Parkinson, *Common Cause*, 433–38.
17. Desserud, "Nova Scotia," 89–111.
18. Leamon, *Revolution Downeast*, 94, 130; Clarke, *Siege of Fort Cumberland*, 96.
19. Leamon, *Revolution Downeast*, 96–97, 130; Kolodny, "History," 14.
20. Hoffman, "Simon Girty," 222–23.
21. Quoted in Peterson, *Thomas Jefferson*, 169, 177.
22. Kammen, *Colonial New York*, 373.
23. Hyde, *Empires*, 234; Ferguson, *American Enlightenment*, 165–66; Nash, *Unknown American Revolution*, 248, 254, 440.
24. Jasanoff, *Liberty's Exiles*, 196–97.
25. Countryman, *American Revolution*, 232–33; Ferling, *Jefferson and Hamilton*, 143, 148.
26. Madison, *The Federalist* no. 42 (January 1788): 206.
27. Hawkins, *Collected Works*, 9.
28. Weisberger, *America Afire*, 143; Hyde, *Empires*, 233.
29. Wood, *Empire of Liberty*, 129–30; Peterson, *Thomas Jefferson*, 450–51.
30. Dunbar-Ortiz, *Indigenous Peoples' History*, 81.
31. Hoffman, "Simon Girty," 236–37; Merritt, "Native Peoples," 241–42.
32. Lakomäki, "'Our Line,'" 601.
33. McInnis, "Population of Canada," 376.
34. Hyde, *Empires*, 236–37, 250, 252; Stewart, *Madison's Gift*, 249; Lakomäki, "'Our Line,'" 614–17.
35. Dunbar-Ortiz, *Indigenous Peoples' History*, 84–87, 93, 98; Jasanoff, *Liberty's Exiles*, 198, 330.
36. Wilentz, *Rise of American Democracy*, 148–53; Lakomäki, "'Our Line,'" 617–19.
37. Leamon, *Revolution Downeast*, 218–19; Kolodny, "History," 15–16; Pawling, *Wabanaki Homeland*, 15–17.
38. McDonnell, *Politics of War*, 248–49; Fowler, *American Crisis*, 119; Papas, *Renegade Revolutionary*, 179.
39. Dunbar-Ortiz, *Indigenous Peoples' History*, 88–89; Calloway, "Declaring Independence," 191–93.
40. Parmenter, "Dragging Canoe," 117, 125–26.
41. Peterson, *Thomas Jefferson*, 193, 258–59; Hoffman, "Simon Girty," 226.
42. Parmenter, "Dragging Canoe," 117–18; Calloway, "Declaring Independence," 185–86.
43. Parmenter, "Dragging Canoe," 117, 128–33; Merritt, "Native Peoples," 246.
44. Calloway, "Declaring Independence," 195–96; Dunbar-Ortiz, *Indigenous Peoples' History*, 89–90.
45. Hawkins, *Collected Works*, 9; Nash, *Unknown American Revolution*, 386–87, 437–38.
46. Jefferson to Adams, 11 June 1812, in Jefferson, *Writings*, 1263.
47. Ibid., 1264.
48. Hawkins, *Collected Works*, 11; Dunbar-Ortiz, *Indigenous Peoples' History*, 98–99.

49. Dunbar-Ortiz, *Indigenous Peoples' History*, 78–79.
50. Wood, *Radicalism*, 357–58; Sayre, "Jefferson and Native Americans," 65–66.
51. Jefferson to Hawkins, 18 February 1803, in Jefferson, *Writings*, 1114–16.
52. Jefferson to Hawkins, 18 February 1803, in Jefferson, *Writings*, 1115.
53. Jefferson, *Writings*, 520; Sayre, "Jefferson and Native Americans," 65–66, 70.
54. Jefferson, *Writings*, 520–21; Bernstein, *Thomas Jefferson*, 144–45; Sayre, "Jefferson and Native Americans," 66, 70.
55. Jefferson, *Writings*, 521.
56. Jefferson to Hawkins, 18 February 1803, in Jefferson, *Writings*, 1115.
57. Staloff, *Hamilton, Adams, Jefferson*, 339–40; Peterson, *Thomas Jefferson*, 471–74; Hyde, *Empires*, 236.
58. Mandell, *Tribe, Race, History*, 7, 45, 84.

Chapter 8: Whites Dispossessed

1. Foner, *Tom Paine*, 145–46, 150–52, 161–62; Keane, *Tom Paine*, 192.
2. Rush, *Letters*, 1:337; Smith, *Freedoms We Lost*, 178–79.
3. Alexander, "Fort Wilson Incident," 599–600; Nelson, *Thomas Paine*, 156–57; Keane, *Tom Paine*, 187–92.
4. Ryerson, *The Revolution*, 242–43.
5. Wood, *Radicalism*, 366.
6. Ibid.; Smith, *Freedoms We Lost*, 189–90, 204.
7. Foner, *Tom Paine*, 164–66; Raphael, *People's History*, 123.
8. Rush to Adams, Philadelphia, 12 October 1779, in Rush, *Letters*, 1:240.
9. Alexander, "Fort Wilson Incident," 596; Middlekauff, *Glorious Cause*, 615–16.
10. Adams, *The Works*, 9:499; Alexander, "Fort Wilson Incident," 589.
11. Alexander, "Fort Wilson Incident," 602; Nash, *Unknown American Revolution*, 318.
12. Martin, *A Narrative*, 82–83, 87–88; Taylor, *Liberty Men*, 13–14, 34, 47, 59.
13. Smith, *Freedoms We Lost*, 194.
14. Huston, *Land and Freedom*, 34.
15. Taylor, "Agrarian Independence," 237; Kornblith and Murrin, "Making and Unmaking," 52–53.
16. Huston, *Land and Freedom*, 14–15, 18; Taylor, "Agrarian Independence," 225–27.
17. Huston, *Land and Freedom*, 36.
18. Nash, *Unknown American Revolution*, 343; Papas, *Renegade Revolutionary*, 154; Taylor, *American Revolutions*, 241–42.
19. Humphrey, "Conflicting Independence," 168–70.
20. Martin, *A Narrative*, 243–44; Raphael, *People's History*, 129; Mead, "'Adventures, Dangers,'" 128–29.
21. Paine, *Letter to George Washington*, 1; Kaye, *Thomas Paine*, 88.
22. Taylor, *Liberty Men*, 37, 39–43.
23. Martin, *A Narrative*, 243, 262; Mead, "'Adventures, Dangers,'" 130–31; Mandell, *Tribe, Race, History*, 83–84; Taylor, "Agrarian Independence," 223.
24. Maier, "Reason and Revolution," 231.
25. Humphrey, "William Prendergast," 83; Kammen, *Colonial New York*, 300–303, 337, 342–43.

26. Quoted in Taylor, *American Revolutions*, 72.
27. Nash, *Unknown American Revolution*, 246; Lefer, *Founding Conservatives*, 165.
28. Hirschfield, *George Washington*, 75.
29. Peterson, *Thomas Jefferson*, 523–34.
30. Humphrey, "William Prendergast," 94–96; Walters, *Revolutionary Deists*, 91–93.
31. Adams, *Gouverneur Morris*, 33, 142–44; Nash, *Unknown American Revolution*, 100, 202.
32. Huston, *Land and Freedom*, 30–31; Wilentz, *Chants Democratic*, 67–8
33. Rosenfeld, *American Aurora*, 462, 466; Rana, *Two Faces*, 100–101.
34. Wilentz, *Rise of American Democracy*, 30–31.
35. Richards, *Shays's Rebellion*, 26, 54; Raphael, *People's History*, 389–90; Nobles, "Satan, Smith," 216–17.
36. Hamilton, *The Federalist* no. 6 (November 1786): 21; Szatmary, *Shays' Rebellion*, 64, 66, 99; Rosenfeld, *American Aurora*, 466; Chernow, *Alexander Hamilton*, 225.
37. Nobles, "Satan, Smith," 220–21; Wilentz, *Rise of American Democracy*, 30–31.
38. Whiting, *Some Brief Remarks*, 133; Riley, "Doctor William Whiting," 122–23.
39. Huston, *Land and Freedom*, 12; McDonnell, *Politics of War*, 523–24; Richards, *Shays's Rebellion*, 83.
40. Richards, *Shays's Rebellion*, 55, 68–69, 107.
41. Rosenfeld, *American Aurora*, 461; Casalini, "L'*Esprit*," 334.
42. Taylor, *Liberty Men*, 16–18, 120.
43. Leamon, *Revolution Downeast*, 197–200.
44. Richards, *Shays's Rebellion*, 63, 74, 84, 89.
45. Ibid., 74–76; Edwards, "Contradictions," 46–47; Taylor, *American Revolutions*, 366–67.
46. Adams to Jefferson, London, 30 November 1786, in *Adams-Jefferson Letters* 1:156, 165; see also McCullough, *John Adams*, 368–69; Grant, *John Adams*, 329–30; Meacham, *Thomas Jefferson*, 206.
47. Richards, *Shays's Rebellion*, 76–79; Middlekauff, *Glorious Cause*, 600–601.
48. Whiting, *Some Brief Remarks*, 133; Nobles, "Satan, Smith," 219.
49. Whiting, *Some Brief Remarks*, 134–35, 144; Riley, "Doctor William Whiting," 123.
50. Taylor, "Agrarian Independence," 228; Himmelfarb, *Roads to Modernity*, 195; Ellis, *American Sphinx*, 117–18.
51. Richards, *Shays's Rebellion*, 34, 120; Bennett, *Few Lawless Vagabonds*, 225–26; Stewart, *Nature's God*, 432.
52. Whiting, *Some Brief Remarks*, 132; Andrew, *Imperial Republics*, 14–15, 91; Richards, *Shays's Rebellion*, 34, 81, 113, 120.
53. Wood, *Empire of Liberty*, 111; Richards, *Shays's Rebellion*, 109–11; Brookhiser, *Alexander Hamilton*, 60–61.
54. Whiting, *Some Brief Remarks*, 131, 146–47; Szatmary, *Shays' Rebellion*, 17, 97.
55. Whiting, *Some Brief Remarks*, 142; Riley, "Doctor William Whiting," 122–23.
56. Whiting, *Some Brief Remarks*, 148–49; Riley, "Doctor William Whiting," 130.
57. Whiting, *Some Brief Remarks*, 145, 149; Szatmary, *Shays' Rebellion*, 33; Patterson, "Federalist Reaction," 115–18; Lienesch, "Reinterpreting Rebellion," 169.
58. Jefferson, *Writings*, 671, 911; Wills, *Inventing America*, 143–44.
59. Ferling, *Jefferson and Hamilton*, 168–69.
60. Richards, *Shays's Rebellion*, 119–20, 132, 137–40; Lefer, *Founding Conservatives*, 293–94; Andrew, *Imperial Republics*, 91–92; Patterson, "Federalist Reaction," 117.

61. Hamilton, *The Federalist* no. 21 (December 1787): 95; Lienesch, "Reinterpreting Rebellion," 173–74, 176–81.
62. Wilentz, *Rise of American Democracy*, 31–32; Kloppenberg, *Toward Democracy*, 368–69.
63. Riley, "Doctor William Whiting," 130; Nobles, "Satan, Smith," 228–29.
64. Berkin, *Bill of Rights*, 21, 55, 79.
65. Quoting Ezra Ripley in ibid., 55.
66. Verhoeven, *Americomania*, 8–9.
67. Condorcet, *Writings on the United States*, 43.
68. Ibid., 43–45.
69. Ibid., 46.
70. Jefferson to William Smith, Paris, 13 November 1787, in Jefferson, *Writings*, 911.
71. Humphrey, "Conflicting Independence," 176; Taylor, "Agrarian Independence," 235–36.

Chapter 9: Canada

1. *Histoire philosophique*, 9:369.
2. Wood, *Empire of Liberty*, 7.
3. Bennett, *Few Lawless Vagabonds*, 86–88; Beeman, *Our Lives, Our Fortunes*, 221–22, 297–98.
4. McInnis, "Population of Canada," 373; Lanctot, *Canada*, 31.
5. Clarke, *Siege of Fort Cumberland*, 3–4.
6. Bonwick, *American Revolution*, 79, 90; Pocock, *Barbarism*, 4:318; Jasanoff, *Liberty's Exiles*, 61, 202; Marshall, "British North America," 380.
7. Pinto, *Seconde lettre* (Knuttel 19124), 8, 23.
8. Ibid., 34; Marshall, "British North America," 374.
9. Clark, "Burke's Reflections," 75; McInnis, "Population of Canada," 375; Israel, *Revolutionary Ideas*, 546.
10. Ferling, *Independence*, 280; Bennett, *Few Lawless Vagabonds*, 88.
11. Quoted in Mapp, *Faiths*, 75.
12. Monette, *Rendez-vous manqué*, 112–13, 161.
13. Rush, *Letters*, 1:95.
14. Eamon, "Extensive Collection," 7–8; Bennett, *Few Lawless Vagabonds*, 53–54.
15. Lagrave, *Fleury Mesplet*, 22, 64–65; Eamon, "Extensive Collection," 9–10.
16. Monette, *Rendez-vous manqué*, 93–94; Lanctot, *Canada*, 27–29.
17. *Lettre adressé aux habitants de la Province de Québec*, 162–63; Oury, *Mgr Briand*, 186–87; Andrès, *Conquête des lettres*, 163; Fenton, *Religious Liberties*, 24–27.
18. *Lettre adressé aux habitants de la Province de Québec*, 155.
19. Ibid., 157.
20. Monette, *Rendez-vous manqué*, 163–67.
21. Oury, *Mgr Briand*, 149; Neatby, *Quebec*, 25.
22. Monette, *Rendez-vous manqué*, 148–49, 167; Oury, *Mgr Briand*, 177–79, 188, 197; Lanctot, *Canada*, 257–58.
23. Lagrave, *Fleury Mesplet*, 35–38, 79; Suhonen, "Le Canadien," 103–6; Andrès, *Conquête des lettres*, 154.

24. Monette, *Rendez-vous manqué*, 121, 148, 150, 152; Oury, *Mgr Briand*, 188–91.
25. Monette, *Rendez-vous manqué*, 152–57; Fenton, *Religious Liberties*, 27; Jasanoff, *Liberty's Exiles*, 61.
26. Neatby, *Quebec*, 146; Andrès, *Conquête des lettres*, 164; Lanctot, *Canada*, 36–37, 60; Lagrave, *Fleury Mesplet*, 46.
27. Monette, *Rendez-vous manqué*, 196–97.
28. Lanctot, *Canada*, 116; Renwick, "Benjamin Franklin and Canada," 44.
29. Ferling, *Independence*, 215–16; Ellis, *Revolutionary Summer*, 50–51, 235n31; Beeman, *Our Lives, Our Fortunes*, 299–300.
30. Beeman, *Our Lives, Our Fortunes*, 299; Clarke, *Siege of Fort Cumberland*, 21, 23–24.
31. Monette, *Rendez-vous manqué*, 307–8.
32. Franklin, *Papers*, 22:380–84; Wood, *Americanization*, 91; Ferling, *Independence*, 280.
33. Franklin, *Papers*, 22:383, 385; Renwick, "Benjamin Franklin and Canada," 41.
34. Pochard to Franklin, Montreal, 11 October 1776, in Franklin, *Papers*, 22:656.
35. Monette, *Rendez-vous manqué*, 151; Oury, *Mgr Briand*, 190–91.
36. Oury, *Mgr Briand*, 193–95; Neatby, *Quebec*, 240; Wood, *Americanization*, 73–74.
37. *Apocalypse de Chiokoyhikoy*, 1–5; Israel, *Democratic Enlightenment*, 500.
38. Smith, "To the People of Pennsylvania," *Pennsylvania Gazette* Letter III (20 March 1776).
39. Franklin, *Papers*, 22:414.
40. Ibid., 22:422.
41. Morgan, *Benjamin Franklin*, 231; Neatby, *Quebec*, 152–53.
42. Franklin, *Papers*, 22:425; Ferling, *Whirlwind*, 154.
43. Franklin, *Papers*, 22:425.
44. Smith to Strahan, 10 June 1776, in Smith, *Correspondence*, 200.
45. Andrès, *Conquête des lettres*, 145; Eamon, "Extensive Collection," 9–10.
46. Rush to Lee, Philadelphia, 23 July 1776, in Rush, *Letters*, 1:103.
47. Pochard to Franklin, Montreal, 11 October 1776, in Franklin, *Papers*, 22:655.
48. Clarke, *Siege of Fort Cumberland*, 93, 104, 115, 131, 138.
49. Ibid., 128, 165, 194–95, 197, 202.
50. Thomas Walker to Franklin, Boston, 25 October 1777, in Franklin, *Papers*, 23:112.
51. Smith, *Correspondence*, 382–83.
52. Lanctot, *Canada*, 178–79, 214; Ellis, *Founding Brothers*, 132–33; Bennett, *Few Lawless Vagabonds*, 165.
53. Condorcet, *Tolérance aux pieds du Trône*, 184.
54. Cerisier, *Réplique*, 27–28; Israel, *Democratic Enlightenment*, 524–25.
55. Turgot to Price, 22 March 1778, in Mirabeau, *Considérations*, 197; Popkin, *News*, 175; Popkin, "From Dutch Republican," 537.
56. Franklin, *Papers*, 28:334, 340, 603; Bellesiles, *Revolutionary Outlaws*, 194; Bernier, *Lafayette*, 108; Adams, *Gouverneur Morris*, 97–98.
57. Franklin to Vergennes, Passy, 25 February 1779, in Franklin, *Papers*, 28:604–5; Desserud, "Nova Scotia," 101; Bernier, *Lafayette*, 112–13; Ferling, *Whirlwind*, 237.
58. Lafayette to Washington, Flemmingtown, 9 February 1778, in Lafayette, *Mémoires*, 1:154; Andrès, *Conquête des lettres*, 150; Mézière, *Observation*, 534.
59. Lafayette to the United States Congress, Cadiz, 5 February 1783, in Lafayette, *Mémoires*, 2:55, 57–58.
60. Paine, *Complete Writings*, 2:258.

61. Palmer, *Age of the Democratic Revolution*, 2:515–16.
62. Condorcet, *Bibliothèque de l'Homme Public*, series II (1791), 6:184–85.
63. Jasanoff, *Liberty's Exiles*, 203–4; Thomas, *Philosophic Radicals*, 373; Taylor, *Civil War*, 36–37, 41.
64. Jasanoff, *Liberty's Exiles*, 207; Taylor, *Civil War*, 37–38.
65. Ducharme, "Closing the Last Chapter," 418–19.
66. Suhonen, "Le Canadien," 115; Elkins and McKitrick, *Age of Federalism*, 333, 349, 371–72.
67. Mézière, *Observation*, 534, 539.
68. Lagrave, *Fleury Mesplet*, 412; Lagrave, "Thomas Paine," 62.
69. Andrès, "Sur les utopies," 22–24; Wood, *Empire of Liberty*, 186.
70. McInnis, "Population of Canada," 373, 377.
71. Hyde, *Empires*, 236–37; Stagg, *War of 1812*, 20–21.
72. Taylor, *Civil War*, 354–55.
73. Adams to Jefferson, 16 July 1814, in *Adams-Jefferson Letters*, 2:436.
74. Wood, *Empire of Liberty*, 676–79; Stagg, *War of 1812*, 6, 8.
75. McInnis, "Population of Canada," 385–86.
76. Taylor, *Civil War*, 184–85.
77. Stagg, *War of 1812*, 64–65; Taylor, *Civil War*, 164–65.
78. Stagg, *War of 1812*, 9–12; Martin, "Canada," 536.
79. Ouellet, *Louis Joseph Papineau*, 5, 9.
80. Ibid., 10–11.
81. Schofield, *Utility and Democracy*, 204, 218.
82. Thomas, *Philosophic Radicals*, 374, 377.
83. Andrès, "De l'Utopie," 131, 134–37.
84. *Hansard Parliamentary Sittings* ser. 3, vol. 36, Debate: 6 March 1837, "Affairs of Canada," 1336.
85. Ducharme, "Closing the Last Chapter," 421–23; Thomas, *Philosophic Radicals*, 396–403.
86. Ouellet, *Louis Joseph Papineau*, 16.
87. Andrès, "De l'Utopie," 121; Martin, "Canada," 530, 537–38; Ducharme, "Closing the Last Chapter," 421.
88. Armitage, *Declaration*, 125–26.
89. Ducharme, "Closing the Last Chapter," 429; Bloom, *Restless Revolutionaries*, 168–69.
90. Thomas, *Philosophic Radicals*, 403.

Chapter 10: John Adams's "American Revolution"

1. Grant, *John Adams*, 203, 213.
2. Fea, "John Adams and Religion," 191–92; Staloff, "John Adams," 51–58.
3. Grant, *John Adams*, 205.
4. Schulte Nordholt, *Dutch Republic*, 60–62.
5. Houston, *Algernon Sidney*, 226–28, 244–45, 250–51.
6. Morison, *History of the Constitution of Massachusetts*, 18; Arendt, *On Revolution*, 164–65; Zilversmit, *First Emancipation*, 112; Levy, "Montesquieu's Constitutional Legacies," 132; Bernstein, *Founding Fathers*, 50–51.

7. Ellis, *Founding Brothers*, 207.
8. Wilentz, *Rise of American Democracy*, 187–88.
9. Ellis, *First Family*, 80–81, 135, 154; Wilentz, *Rise of American Democracy*, 27, 75–77.
10. Philp, *Reforming Ideas*, 121, 186; Higonnet, *Sister Republics*, 199–201, 227; Levy, "Montesquieu's Constitutional Legacies," 132; Casalini, "L'*Esprit*," 332–33.
11. Morison, *History of the Constitution of Massachusetts*, 16–18; Higonnet, *Sister Republics*, 181, 195; Sheehan, *James Madison*, 18; Ferling, *Independence*, 265–66; Nelson, *Royalist Revolution*, 173–74.
12. Arendt, *On Revolution*, 150–52; Wood, *Americanization*, 219; Richards, *Shays's Rebellion*, 71–74.
13. Ward, *Politics of Liberty*, 180–81, 422–24; Grant, *John Adams*, 221–26.
14. Rosenfeld, *American Aurora*, 391.
15. Postma, "John Adams," 91.
16. Franklin, *Papers*, 21:412n9; Ramsay, *History*, 2:535; Gould, *Among the Powers*, 83–85; Te Brake, "Dutch Republic," 205.
17. Schulte Nordholt, *Dutch Republic*; Te Brake, "Dutch Republic," 205–6.
18. Jameson, "St. Eustatius," 686; Hartog, *History*, 40.
19. Van der Capellen, *Aan het Volk*, 63.
20. Schutte, *Nederlandse Patriotten*, 5–6, 60–64.
21. Schulte Nordholt, *Dutch Republic*, 71–72.
22. Franklin, *The Works*, 8:145.
23. Schulte Nordholt, *Dutch Republic*, 76; Polasky, *Revolutions without Borders*, 33.
24. Quoted in Schama, *Patriots and Liberators*, 62.
25. Hutson, "John Adams," 420; Te Brake, "Dutch Republic," 208–10.
26. Adams, *Papers*, 12:242.
27. Ibid., 12:242; Gorman, *America and Belgium*, 95.
28. Adams to Robert Livingston, The Hague, 14 May 1782, in Adams, *Papers*, 15:50; see also Popkin, "From Dutch Republican," 536–37.
29. Klein, *Patriots republikanisme*, 96–97; Schutte, *Nederlandse Patriotten*, 43, 194.
30. Cerisier, *Observations impartiales*, 15–16; a point made earlier by Chastellux and later reiterated in his *Voeux d'un Gallophile* (1785) by the Dutch German cosmopolitan revolutionary Anarcharsis Cloots (1755–94); see Mortier, *Anarcharsis Cloots*, 93, 102.
31. Cerisier, *Politique Hollandois* 6 (1783): 196, 205.
32. Cerisier, *Politique Hollandois* 5 (1783): 51–53.
33. Schutte, *Nederlandse Patriotten*, 64–75, 118.
34. [Bernard], *L'Afrique hollandoise*, 6, 9, 42; Van Goor, *Nederlandse koloniën*, 116–17.
35. Schutte, "Johannes Hermanus Redelinghuys," 49–50.
36. [Bernard], *L'Afrique hollandoise*, 5; Schutte, *Nederlandse Patriotten*, 78–81.
37. [Bernard], *L'Afrique hollandoise*, 9.
38. Cerisier, *Réplique*, 31–33; Cerisier, *Politique Hollandois* 5 (March 1783): 52–53.
39. Cerisier, *Observations impartiales*, 15.
40. *Histoire philosophique*, 1:215–16; see also [Bernard], *L'Afrique hollandoise*, 9.
41. *Histoire philosophique*, 1:312–13.
42. Cerisier, *Politique Hollandois*, 1 (1781): 174; [Bernard], *L'Afrique hollandoise*, 2–4.
43. *Justification de la résistance*, 59.
44. Cerisier, *Observations impartiales*, 47.

45. Ibid., 15–16.

46. Cerisier, *Tableau*, 10:338–39; Rosendaal, *Nederlandse Revolutie*, 133.

47. Nijenhuis, *Joodse philosophe*, 9.

48. Pinto, *Letters on the American Troubles*, 34–35, 40–41.

49. Ibid., 41–42; Nijenhuis, *Joodse philosophe*.

50. Ramsay, *History*, 2:535; Jameson, "St. Eustatius," 695.

51. Ramsay, *History*, 2:535–37; Gould, *Among the Powers*, 89–90; Taylor, *American Revolutions*, 291.

52. Jameson, "St. Eustatius," 695; Bourke, *Empire and Revolution*, 435–36.

53. Ramsay, *History*, 2:536–37; Bromwich, *Intellectual Life of Edmund Burke*, 427–29.

54. Jameson, "St. Eustatius," 695; Bourke, *Empire and Revolution*, 436.

55. Goslinga, *Dutch in the Caribbean*, 147–50.

56. Van Goor, *Nederlandse koloniën*, 179, 181.

57. Schutte, "Johannes Hermanus Redelinghuys," 57, 59.

58. Adams, *Papers*, 12:242 .

59. Postma, "John Adams," 86; Kroes-Ligtenberg, *Dr. Wybo Fijnje*, 86; Popkin, *News*, 152–54.

60. Gorman, *America and Belgium*, 39; McCullough, *John Adams*, 249; Klein, *Patriots republikanisme*, 290.

61. Rosenfeld, *American Aurora*, 299; Te Brake, "Dutch Republic," 207.

62. Wright, *Franklin*, 303–5; McCullough, *John Adams*, 213–14.

63. Popkin, *News*, 152–53; Van Vliet, *Elie Luzac*, 369, 530n68.

64. Van der Capellen, *Aan het Volk*, 46; Israel, *Democratic Enlightenment*, 795.

65. Van der Kemp, *Het gedrag van Israel en Rehabeam ten spiegel van volk en vorst* (Leiden, 1782); Schulte Nordholt, *Dutch Republic*, 121; Jourdan, *La Révolution*, 358.

66. Adams to Robert Livingston, 14 May 1782, in Adams, *Papers*, 15:50; Popkin, "From Dutch Republican," 538; Jourdan, "Alien Origins," 190.

67. Popkin, *News*, 175; Polasky, *Revolutions without Borders*, 113.

68. Adams to Cerisier, The Hague, 22 February 1784, in Adams, *Papers*, vol. 16.

69. Pinto, *Lettre de Mr**** (Knuttel 19122), 14–15.

70. Ibid., 14.

71. Pinto, *Seconde lettre* (Knuttel 19124), 7–8.

72. D'Holbach, *Système social*, 301.

73. *Discours d'un bon Hollandois à ses compatriotes*, 34; Nijenhuis, *Joodse philosophe*, 30–31.

74. Pinto, *Réponse* (Knuttel 19126), 42–44.

75. Ibid., 42.

76. Pinto, *Lettre de Mr**** (Knuttel 19122), 15, 18–19.

77. Nijenhuis, *Joodse philosophe*, 37.

78. *Observations d'un homme impartial* (Knuttel 19123), 56.

79. *Discours d'un bon Hollandois à ses compatriotes*, 18.

80. Cerisier, *Tableau*, 3:iii–iv, vi; Cerisier, *Observations impartiales*, 10, 58–60.

81. Adams, *The Works*, 7:399; Kaplan, "Founding Fathers," 424; Grant, *John Adams*, 259–60; Polasky, *Revolutions without Borders*, 34.

82. Dohm, "Briefe," *Deutsches Museum* 1 (January–June 1777): 186–88; Krebs, "Deutsches Museum," 7–8.

83. Schulte Nordholt, *Dutch Republic*, 127.

84. Franklin, *Papers*, 31:47; Palmer, *Age of the Democratic Revolution*, 1:325–26; Kossmann, *Politieke Theorie*, 249; Desportes, "Giuseppe Ceracchi," 143–44.
85. Quoted in Van der Cappelen, *Aan het Volk*, 7; see also Van Vliet, *Elie Luzac*, 384; Prak, *Republikeinse veelheid*, 191; Jongenelen, *Van Smaad tot erger*, 41.
86. Van der Cappelen, *Aan het Volk*, 23.
87. Ibid., 36; Palmer, *Age of the Democratic Revolution*, 1:330; Velema, "Vrijheid als volkssouvereiniteit," 294–95.
88. Van der Cappelen, *Aan het Volk*, 59; Kossmann, *Politieke Theorie*, 252; Rosendaal, *Nederlandse Revolutie*, 180–81.
89. Kossmann, *Politieke Theorie*, 250; Postma, "John Adams," 95; Schulte Nordholt, *Dutch Republic*, 193.
90. Adams, *Papers*, 12:242–43; Siemers, "John Adams's Political Thought," 110–11.
91. Popkin, "From Dutch Republican," 539; Velema, "Vrijheid als volkssouvereiniteit," 298–300, 302.
92. Kroes-Ligtenberg, *Dr. Wybo Fijnje*, 85; Israel, *Democratic Enlightenment*, 890; Rosendaal, *Bataven!* 248, 446–47.
93. Schulte Nordholt, *Dutch Republic*, 203.
94. Postma, "John Adams," 87; Popkin, *News*, 153.
95. Van Vliet, *Elie Luzac*, 530n68.
96. Popkin, *News*, 158–59; Altena, *Gerrit Paape*, 188; Polasky, *Revolutions without Borders*, 30–31.
97. Schulte Nordholt, *Dutch Republic*, 194; Prak, *Republikeinse veelheid*, 192.
98. Anes, *Siglo de Las Luces*, 276–79.
99. Klein, *Patriots republikanisme*, 119; Rosenfeld, *American Aurora*, 431–32; Grant, *John Adams*, 261.
100. Staloff, *Hamilton, Adams, Jefferson*, 202.
101. Quoted in Ellis, *First Family*, 87, 99.
102. Quoted in Grant, *John Adams*, 288; Hutson, "John Adams," 414–15; Ellis, *First Family*, 98.
103. Schulte Nordholt, *Dutch Republic*, 259–61.
104. Ellis, *Revolutionary Summer*, 214.
105. Adams to Jefferson, 14 September 1813, in *Adams-Jefferson Letters*, 2:374–75.
106. Franklin to Price, Passy, 6 February 1780, in Franklin, *Papers*, 31:452–53; Reich, *British Friends*, 97, 101.
107. McCullough, *John Adams*, 343–45; Page, "Liberty," 222.
108. Popkin, *News*, 177; Postma, "John Adams," 97.
109. Popkin, *News*, 182–84; Popkin, "Dutch Patriots," 556.
110. Schulte Nordholt, *Dutch Republic*, 274; Van Vliet, *Elie Luzac*, 371.
111. Altena, *Gerrit Paape*, 188; Postma, "John Adams," 98.
112. Altena, *Gerrit Paape*, 205, 716; Israel, *Democratic Enlightenment*, 889.
113. Popkin, "Dutch Patriots," 556; Altena, *Gerrit Paape*, 205, 213, 215.
114. Popkin, "Dutch Patriots," 555; Prak, *Republikeinse veelheid*, 193–97; Israel, *Democratic Enlightenment*, 883.
115. Israel, *Dutch Republic*, 1107.
116. Adams to Jefferson, 13 July 1813, in *Adams-Jefferson Letters*, 2:356; Appleby, "New Republican Synthesis," 580, 582.

117. Adams to Jefferson, London, 28 October 1787, in *Adams-Jefferson Letters*, 1:203–4.
118. Klein, *Patriots republikanisme*, 34.
119. Nelson, *Royalist Revolution*, 170.
120. Jefferson to William Stephens Smith, 13 November 1787, in *Jefferson Papers*, 12:356.
121. Klein, *Patriots republikanisme*, 157–58; Kaplan, "Founding Fathers," 423–25.
122. Nelson, *Royalist Revolution*, 144.
123. Bernier, *Lafayette*, 215.
124. Altena, *Gerrit Paape*, 247–69; Jongenelen, *Van Smaad tot erger*, 53–55.
125. Rosendaal, *Bataven!* 39–50; Altena, *Gerrit Paape*, 251–52.
126. Jefferson to Adams, Paris, 28 September 1787, in *Adams-Jefferson Letters*, 1:199–200; Kaplan, "Founding Fathers," 433.
127. Adams to Jefferson, London, 28 October 1787, in *Adams-Jefferson Letters*, 1:204.
128. Schutte, "Johannes Hermanus Redelinghuys," 53.
129. Adams to Jefferson, London, 28 October 1787, in *Adams-Jefferson Letters*, 1:204.
130. Adams, *Papers*, 15:49–50; Grant, *John Adams*, 275, 335; Jourdan, *La Révolution*, 369.
131. Desportes, "Giuseppe Ceracchi," 143–44.
132. Adams to Jefferson, London, 10 November 1787, in *Adams-Jefferson Letters*, 1:210.
133. Burke to Gilbert Elliott, 17 October 1787, in Burke, *Correspondence*, 5:354; Palmer, *Age of the Democratic Revolution*, 1:339.
134. Jefferson to Abigail Adams, Paris, 4 October 1787, in *Adams-Jefferson Letters*, 1:201.
135. Sloan, "Thomas Jefferson," 475; Kaplan, "Founding Fathers," 426–27.
136. Postma, "John Adams," 99.
137. Adams, *Writings*, 1:332, 337.
138. Ibid., 1:338; Palmer, "Two Americans," 401–2.
139. John Quincy Adams to Randolph, The Hague, 24 June 1795, in Adams, *Writings*, 1:363.

Chapter 11: Jefferson's French Revolution

1. Steele, *Thomas Jefferson*, 94–96.
2. Hickey, *War of 1812*, 20.
3. Wills, *Inventing America*, 173–75; Jayne, *Jefferson's Declaration*, 2; Valsania, *Limits*, 28–29.
4. Wills, *Inventing America*, 201–2.
5. Staloff, "Politics," 136.
6. Raphael, *Founding Myths*, 127, 134, 359n32.
7. Meyer, *Democratic Enlightenment*, 121; Stewart, *Nature's God*, 24–26.
8. King-Hele, *Doctor of Revolution*, 14, 60–61; Jayne, *Jefferson's Declaration*, 19–40; Stewart, *Nature's God*, 35, 171.
9. Wills, *Inventing America*, 177–80; Jayne, *Jefferson's Declaration*, 19; Valsania, *Limits*, 28–29; Schachtman, *Gentlemen Scientists*, 12–14.
10. King-Hele, *Doctor of Revolution*, 96–97.
11. See, for example, Leask, "The Undivulged Event," 63–65; Israel, *Enlightenment Contested*, 184–87.

12. Jayne, *Jefferson's Declaration*, 37–38, 40; Walters, *Revolutionary Deists*, 170–73; Peterson, *Thomas Jefferson*, 50–51; Valsania, *Limits*, 80; Stewart, *Nature's God*, 197–99, 311–12.

13. Jayne, *Jefferson's Declaration*, 21; Valsania, *Limits*, 49; De Bolla, *Architecture of Concepts*, 132–35.

14. Rakove, *Revolutionaries*, 173–75; Wood, *Radicalism*, 181.

15. Gottschalk, *American Heretics*, 197–98.

16. Jefferson, *Autobiography*, 36.

17. Démeunier, *L'Amérique indépendante*, 3:15–16.

18. Hunt, *Inventing Human Rights*, 25, 121, 126; Peterson, *Thomas Jefferson*, 89; Raphael, *Founding Myths*, 127; Wood, *Empire of Liberty*, 66.

19. Jefferson, *Political Writings*, 31–32; Staloff, *Hamilton, Adams Jefferson*, 255–57; Clark, *Language of Liberty*, 138; Rakove, *Revolutionaries*, 305; Ferling, *Jefferson and Hamilton*, 56.

20. Rush to Jefferson, Philadelphia, 2 August 1800, in Rush, *Letters*, 2:820; Bailyn, *Faces*, 192.

21. Sehat, *Myth*, 36–38; Meacham, *American Gospel*, 10–11; Lambert, *Founding Fathers*, 209; Ferling, *Jefferson and Hamilton*, 57; Holmes, *Faiths*, 86–88; McGarvie, *Law and Religion*, 17–18.

22. Jefferson to William Smith, Philadelphia, 19 February 1791, in Jefferson, *Writings*, 974.

23. Peterson, *Thomas Jefferson*, 333.

24. Loveland, *Emblem*, 11–12; Bernier, *Lafayette*, 211–12.

25. Badinter and Badinter, *Condorcet*, 195, 217n3, 346, 465; Sheehan, *James Madison*, 148.

26. Israel, *Democratic Enlightenment*, 439–41.

27. *Le Bon Sens* (1772), a short incisive atheistic book, today is usually attributed to d'Holbach albeit with participation by Diderot. Rosenfeld, *Common Sense*, 122–25; Israel, *Democratic Enlightenment*, 786–87.

28. Jefferson to Adams, 8 April 1816, in *Adams-Jefferson Letters*, 2:467.

29. Israel, *Democratic Enlightenment*, 863–72; Scurr, "Varieties," 61, 65.

30. Ferling, *Jefferson and Hamilton*, 165; Fleming, *Great Divide*, 59.

31. Jefferson, *Autobiography*, 71–72; Paine, *Letter to George Washington*, 177–78; Tortarolo, "Philip Mazzei," 64; Fleming, *Great Divide*, 37–38.

32. Peterson, *Thomas Jefferson*, 360; Philp, *Reforming Ideas*, 190; Ferling, *Jefferson and Hamilton*, 195; Stewart, *Madison's Gift*, 128–29.

33. Jefferson to Mason, Philadelphia, 4 February 1791, in Jefferson, *Writings*, 971–72; Ferling, *Jefferson and Hamilton*, 245; Cruise O'Brien, *Long Affair*, 113.

34. Philp, *Reforming Ideas*, 198–201; Steele, *Thomas Jefferson*, 95.

35. Peterson, *Thomas Jefferson*, 371–74, 378; Ellis, *American Sphinx*, 129; Philp, *Reforming Ideas*, 198–99.

36. Peterson, *Thomas Jefferson*, 372–74; Tortarolo, "Philip Mazzei," 60–61, 64; Kloppenberg, *Toward Democracy*, 488.

37. Jefferson to Price, Paris, 8 January 1789, in Jefferson, *Writings*, 938–39.

38. Condorcet, *Writings on the United States*, 28.

39. Ibid., 26–28.

40. Condorcet, *Sentiments d'un républicain*, 4–5, 8, 18–19.

41. Condorcet, *Seconde lettre d'un citoyen des États-Unis*, 21–22.

42. Jefferson to Madison, 18 June 1789, in *Republic*, 1:616–17; Jefferson to Madison, 28 August 1789, in Jefferson, *Papers*, 15:366.

43. Jefferson, *Writings*, 87, 94; Bernier, *Lafayette*, 227–28; Peterson, *Thomas Jefferson*, 380–81.

44. Jefferson, *Writings*, 954–56; Staloff, *Hamilton, Adams, Jefferson*, 306; Ferling, *Jefferson and Hamilton*, 169.

45. Condorcet, *Writings on the United States*, 25.

46. The idea that this was inessential to Condorcet's program at that time lacks all justification; see Scurr, "Varieties," 60; Israel, *Revolutionary Ideas*, 28–29, 35, 70.

47. Jefferson, *Writings*, 92.

48. Jefferson to Madison, 18 June 1789, in *Republic*, 1:616; Baker, "Political Languages," 631; Tackett, *Becoming*, 23.

49. Jefferson, *Papers*, 15:196; Kloppenberg, *Toward Democracy*, 486.

50. Jefferson to Trumbull, Paris, 18 June 1789, in Jefferson, *Papers*, 15:199.

51. Jefferson to Jay, Paris, Paris, 24 June 1789, in Jefferson, *Papers*, 15:205.

52. Ziesche, "Exporting American Revolutions," 435; Wilentz, *Rise of American Democracy*, 33–34.

53. Morris, *A Diary of the French Revolution*, 1:121.

54. Ibid.; see also Ziesche, "Exporting American Revolutions," 427–32; Kloppenberg, *Toward Democracy*, 487.

55. *Archives Parlementaires* 8 (23 June 1789): 144–45.

56. Ibid., 145.

57. Ibid., 143.

58. Ibid., 145–47.

59. Jefferson to Jay, Paris, 24 June 1789, in Jefferson, *Papers*, 15:208.

60. Jefferson to Jay, Paris, 29 June 1789, in Jefferson, *Papers*, 15:221–22.

61. *Archives Parlementaires* 8 (27 June 1789): 165–66; *Archives Parlementaires* 8 (30 June 1789): 171–72.

62. Tønnesson, "Démocratie directe," 298.

63. Badinter and Badinter, *Condorcet*, 276–77.

64. Slavin, *French Revolution*, 62; Lemny, *Jean-Louis Carra*, 158–59; Badinter and Badinter, *Condorcet*, 267.

65. Monnier, *Républicanisme*, 97–98.

66. Sabatier, *Journal politique* 1 (1790): 47; McMahon, *Enemies*, 65.

67. Slavin, *French Revolution*, 57–58; Philp, *Reforming Ideas*, 197.

68. Jefferson to Paine, 11 July 1789, in Jefferson, *Papers*, 15:268; Hunt, *Inventing Human Rights*, 129.

69. Jefferson, *Papers*, 15:230–32; Zuckert, "Two Paths," 252; Ferling, *Jefferson and Hamilton*, 170.

70. Peterson, *Thomas Jefferson*, 335; Loft, *Passion, Politics*, 228; Dunn, *Sister Revolutions*, 13; Andress, *1789: The Threshold*, 345; Bernier, *Lafayette*, 262.

71. Jefferson to Jay, Paris, 19 July 1789, in Jefferson, *Papers*, 15:285.

72. Ibid.; Nelson, *Thomas Paine*, 189.

73. Jefferson to Paine, 11 July 1789, in Jefferson, *Papers*, 15:266–67.

74. *Archives Parlementaires* 8 (8 July 1789): 208–10.

75. Jefferson to Paine, 11 July 1789, in Jefferson, *Papers*, 15:266–67; Gorsas, *Courrier* 1, no. 9 (15 July 1789): 131.

76. Jefferson, *Papers*, 15:273; Peterson, *Thomas Jefferson*, 379.
77. Jefferson to Paine, Paris, 11 July 1789, in Jefferson, *Papers*, 15:268; Fleming, *Great Divide*, 62.
78. Gorsas, *Courrier* 1, no. 11 (17 July 1789): 161.
79. Desmoulins, *Vieux Cordelier*, 115; Malouet, *Mémoires*, 1:326.
80. Peterson, *Thomas Jefferson*, 380; Cruise O'Brien, *Long Affair*, 80–81.
81. Hammersley, *French Revolutionaries*, 36–37, 60; Ozouf, "Révolution," 213.
82. Gorsas, *Courrier* 1, no. 9 (15 July 1789): 142.
83. Bernier, *Lafayette*, 243–44.
84. Villette, *Lettres*, 4.
85. Gaulmier, *Grand témoin*, 89–90; Peterson, *Thomas Jefferson*, 379.
86. Morellet, *Mémoires*, 1:381; Mortier, *Le Cœur*, 458.
87. Garat, *Mémoires*, 2:315, 354, 365–66; Pellerin, "Naigeon," 32; Mortier, *Le Cœur*, 457–59.
88. Morellet, *Mémoires*, 1:387–88; Rials, *Déclaration*, 125.
89. Lucas, "Crowd and Politics," 274.
90. Bailly, *Œuvres posthumes*, xii–xiii, xxxi, xlii–xliii; Mounier, *De l'influence*, 103–4.
91. Monnier, "L'Évolution," 50–51; Geffroy, "Louise de Kéralio-Robert," 113; Hammersley, *French Revolutionaries*, 18–19.
92. Villette, *Lettres*, 6.
93. Price to Jefferson, Hackney, 3 August 1789, in Jefferson, *Papers*, 15:329.
94. Jefferson, *Papers*, 15:329; Israel, *Revolutionary Ideas*, 71, 741; Fleming, *Great Divide*, 91–92.
95. Fleming, *Great Divide*, 92.
96. Burke, *Reflections*, 92.
97. Ibid., 93–94; Bourke, *Empire and Revolution*, 718.
98. Condorcet, *Writings on the United States*, 30.
99. Jefferson to Madison, Paris, 27 August 1789, in Jefferson, *Papers*, 15:366; Elkins and McKitrick, *Age of Federalism*, 315.
100. Jefferson, *Writings*, 95; Bernier, *Lafayette*, 231.
101. Rials, *Déclaration*, 621–24.
102. [Prudhomme and Tournon], *Révolutions de Paris* 6 (16/22 August 1789): 36; Rials, *Déclaration*, 219, 226, 238–39, 242–43, 246; Israel, *Revolutionary Ideas*, 77–84.
103. *Archives Parlementaires* 8, no. 439 (19 August 1789); Mirabeau, *Courier* 22 (21 August 1789): 2; Hunt, *Inventing Human Rights*, 16, 21, 220.
104. Dumont, *Souvenirs sur Mirabeau*, 97; Israel, *Revolutionary Ideas*, 84–85.
105. Carra, *L'Orateur*, 2:37–39, 73.
106. Jefferson, *Writings*, 97; Kloppenberg, *Toward Democracy*, 488–89.
107. Jefferson, *Papers*, 15:355; Meacham, *Thomas Jefferson*, 223.
108. Jefferson to Jay, 19 September 1789, in Jefferson, *Papers*, 15:459; Halliday, *Understanding Thomas Jefferson*, 107, 113.
109. Jefferson, *Writings*, 95–96; Luttrell, *Mirabeau*, 149–50; Bernier, *Lafayette*, 246–48.
110. Roederer, *Spirit of the Revolution*, 71; Israel, *Revolutionary Ideas*, 87–88, 141–42; Scurr, "Varieties," 63; Innes and Philp, "Synergies," 196.
111. Jefferson to Jay, 19 September 1789, in Jefferson, *Papers*, 15:458–59; Andress, *1789: The Threshold*, 326.
112. Quoted in Petersen, *Thomas Jefferson*, 381; see also Ellis, *American Sphinx*, 128–30.

113. Nash and Gao Hodges, *Friends of Liberty*, 121.
114. Jefferson to Jay, Paris, 27 August 1789, in Jefferson, *Papers*, 15:360; Andress, *1789: The Threshold*, 327.
115. Loft, *Passion, Politics*, 208; Nash and Gao Hodges, *Friends of Liberty*, 120–21; Brown, *Toussaint's Clause*, 6; Raphael, *Founding Myths*, 136–37.
116. Walzer, *Paradox of Liberation*, 144–45.
117. Kloppenberg, *Toward Democracy*, 517–20, 534; Israel, *Revolutionary Ideas*, 396–419, 478, 509–11.
118. Ferling, *Jefferson and Hamilton*, 206.
119. Jefferson, *Writings*, 99.
120. Franklin, *Writings*, 10:68–69.
121. Quoted in Chernow, *Alexander Hamilton*, 318.
122. Morris, *Diary of the French Revolution*, 1:381–82.
123. Morris to Washington, Paris, 22 November 1790, in ibid., 2:68–69.
124. Kates, "From Liberalism to Radicalism," 572–75.
125. Desmoulins, *Jean-Pierre Brissot Démasqué*, 23–24, 26, 30, 33–34.
126. Cruise O'Brien, *Long Affair*, 138; Fleming, *Great Divide*, 142–46.
127. Morris, *Diary of the French Revolution*, 2:362.
128. Jefferson to Morris, Philadelphia, 23 January 1792, in ibid., 2:396–97; Cruise O'Brien, *Long Affair*, 126.
129. Morris, *Diary of the French Revolution*, 2:472–79; Fleming, *Great Divide*, 142.
130. Chernow, *Alexander Hamilton*, 440–46; Cruise O'Brien, *Long Affair*, 143–44.
131. Morris to Washington, Paris, 30 September 1791, in Morris, *Diary of the French Revolution*, 2:275.
132. Morris, *Diary of the French Revolution*, 2:366, 387.
133. Jefferson to Short, Philadelphia, 3 January 1793, in Jefferson, *Writings*, 1004; Stewart, *Madison's Gift*, 148; Wilentz, *Politicians and the Egalitarians*, 91; Fleming, *Great Divide*, 142.
134. Condorcet, *Réflexions sur la Révolution*, 15, 19.
135. Jefferson, *Writings*, 93, 1007.
136. Israel, *Revolutionary Ideas*, 343–44, 512–13, 697–98.
137. Ibid., 269–73; Jonathan Israel, "Conspiracy Fiction," HNN History News network, 15 July 2014.
138. Jefferson to Short, Philadelphia, 3 January 1793, in Jefferson, *Writings*, 1003–4; Kloppenberg, *Toward Democracy*, 564–65; Cruise O'Brien, *Long Affair*, 136–39.
139. Chernow, *Alexander Hamilton*, 318–20, 434, 439–42; Federici, *Political Philosophy of Alexander Hamilton*, 43–46, 223–26.
140. Jefferson to Short, Philadelphia, 3 January 1793, in Jefferson, *Writings*, 1004–5; Elkins and McKitrick, *Age of Federalism*, 317.
141. Wilentz, *Politicians and the Egalitarians*, 92; Cruise O'Brien, *Long Affair*, 310; Steele, *Thomas Jefferson*, 95, 99, 101.
142. Paine to Danton, Paris, 6 May 1793, in Paine, *Complete Writings*, 2:1336–37.
143. Jefferson to Démeunier, Monticello, 29 April 1795, in Jefferson, *Writings*, 1027–28; Cruise O'Brien, *Long Affair*, 219; Steele, *Thomas Jefferson*, 220; Fleming, *Great Divide*, 219.
144. Chinard, *Volney et l'Amérique*, 38–40.
145. Jefferson to Adams, 4 September 1823, in *Adams-Jefferson Letters*, 2:596.

146. Jefferson to Short, Monticello, 31 October 1819, in Jefferson, *Writings*, 1432; Jefferson to Adams, Monticello, 4 September 1823, in *Adams-Jefferson Letters*, 2:596; Israel, *Revolutionary Ideas*, 373, 532, 534–35, 554.
147. Keane, *Tom Paine*, 415.
148. Jefferson to Mme. De Stael, 24 May 1813, in Jefferson, *Writings*, 1271.

Chapter 12: A Tragic Case

1. Lock, *Edmund Burke*, 1:294; Page, *John Jebb*, 225.
2. Hayton, "Williamite Revolution," 186.
3. Gibbons, *Edmund Burke*, 8–9, 152; Lock, *Edmund Burke*, 2:566–67; Bromwich, *Intellectual Life of Edmund Burke*, 313; Bourke, *Empire and Revolution*, 12, 179.
4. Brown, *Irish Enlightenment*, 81–85; Marshall, *John Locke*, 39.
5. Molyneux, *Case of Ireland*, 3; Israel, *Enlightenment Contested*, 613.
6. Hayton, "Williamite Revolution," 210; McLoughlin, *Contesting Ireland*, 43–44.
7. Chastellux, *De la félicité publique*, 2:191.
8. Gordon, *History of the Irish Rebellion*, xx–xxi; Cullan, "The Politics," 37.
9. Mossner, *Life of David Hume*, 495.
10. Bailyn, *Ideological Origins*, 132–33; Page, "'Liberty,'" 221; Schofield, *Utility and Democracy*, 80, 137, 153, 159, 170, 217.
11. Watt, "Fictions," 171–72.
12. Page, "'Liberty,'" 218.
13. Ibid., 218–20; Clark, *Language of Liberty*, 314, 345; Gould, *Persistence*, 167, 171, 177.
14. Page, "'Liberty,'" 219–20; Page, *John Jebb*, 212–15.
15. Gillen, "Varieties," 179–80; Dickinson, *Liberty*, 240–44.
16. Gordon, *History of the Irish Rebellion*, 3; Smyth, *Revolution*, 12–13; Cullan, "The Politics," 21.
17. McBride, *Scripture Politics*, 118–19.
18. Ibid., 169–70; Dunne, *Theobald Wolfe Tone*, 44–46; Bartlett, "Burden," 13, 15; Brown, *Irish Enlightenment*, 423.
19. Coupland, *American Revolution*, 64–65; Burke, *Works*, 9:136; Bourke, *Empire and Revolution*, 393–94.
20. Burke, *On Empire, Liberty*, 424; Pakenham, *The Year*, 26; Bourke, *Empire and Revolution*, 392–95.
21. Smith, *Wealth of Nations*, 2:547; Winch, "Commercial Realities," 297, 300.
22. Phillipson, *Adam Smith*, 235–36; McDaniel, *Adam Ferguson*, 114.
23. Burke, *On Empire, Liberty*, 102–3; Lock, *Edmund Burke*, 2:567.
24. Clark, *Language of Liberty*, 104; Noland, *Benjamin Franklin*, 148, 157.
25. Franklin, *The Works*, 7:557; Coupland, *American Revolution*, 107.
26. Coupland, *American Revolution*, 96–97.
27. Gillen, "Varieties," 164, 177.
28. Gordon, *History of the Irish Rebellion*, 3; Brown, *Irish Enlightenment*, 423–24.
29. Gordon, *History of the Irish Rebellion*, 34; Brown, *Irish Enlightenment*, 424–30.
30. Bourke, *Empire and Revolution*, 390–92.

31. Quoted in Tesch, "Presbyterian Radicalism," 43. Bartlett was much in error in claiming that "Ireland remained resolutely loyal [to Britain] during the American War of Independence" ("Burden," 11).
32. Bernier, *Lafayette*, 109–10, 235.
33. Tesch, "Presbyterian Radicalism," 43–45.
34. Burke, *On Empire, Liberty*, 415–16; Wells, *Insurrection*, 1–2; Gillen, "Constructing Democratic Thought," 151–52.
35. Bourke, *Empire and Revolution*, 400–401.
36. Smith to Lord Carlisle, 8 November 1779, in Smith, *Correspondence*, 243.
37. Arnold, *Edmund Burke: Irish Affairs*, 125–26; Bourke, *Empire and Revolution*, 390, 397–99.
38. Coupland, *American Revolution*, 121.
39. Arnold, *Edmund Burke: Irish Affairs*, 129.
40. Walpole, *Letters*, 10:408; McBride, *Scripture Politics*, 123–26.
41. Lafayette to Franklin, 2 November 1779, in Franklin, *Papers*, 31:25.
42. Arnold, *Edmund Burke: Irish Affairs*, 129–30; Brown, *Irish Enlightenment*, 370.
43. Tone, *An Address*, 25.
44. Brown, *Irish Enlightenment*, 363–68.
45. Page, *John Jebb*, 254; Cullan, "The Politics," 21; Gillen, "Varieties," 167.
46. Wells, *Insurrection*, 6–7.
47. Gordon, *History of the Irish Rebellion*, 1; Brown, *Irish Enlightenment*, 375–78, 381.
48. Brown, *Irish Enlightenment*, 374–76.
49. Burke, *On Empire, Liberty*, 438; Bromwich, *Intellectual Life of Edmund Burke*, 323–24.
50. Moore, *Memoirs*, 151; Gordon, *History of the Irish Rebellion*, 2.
51. Gordon, *History of the Irish Rebellion*, 2; Hampshire-Monk, "British Radicalism and the Anti-Jacobins," 664.
52. Gordon, *History of the Irish Rebellion*, 2; MacDermot, *Theobald Wolfe Tone*, 12.
53. Gillen, "Varieties," 174.
54. Page, *John Jebb*, 214; Brown, *Irish Enlightenment*, 346–48.
55. Brown, *Irish Enlightenment*, 346, 381, 401–4.
56. See the review of Brissot's work on America in the *Bibliothèque de l'Homme Public*, series II (1791), 5:250–60.
57. MacDermot, *Theobald Wolfe Tone*, 47–48, 54, 56; Elliott, *Partners in Revolution*, 22–27; Gillen, "Constructing Democratic Thought," 153.
58. Stewart, *Deeper Silence*, 146–48.
59. Drennan, *The Drennan Letters*, 54; Clark, *Language of Liberty*, 286, 288; Gillen, "Varieties," 164.
60. Drennan, *The Drennan Letters*, 60; Dunne, *Theobald Wolfe Tone*, 23–24, 64n4.
61. Gordon, *History of the Irish Rebellion*, 6; Wells, *Insurrection*, 125; Pakenham, *The Year*, 151, 250, 286.
62. Burke, *On Empire, Liberty*, 427, 437–38; Gibbons, *Edmund Burke*, 163.
63. Dickson, "Paine and Ireland," 139.
64. Moore, *Memoirs*, 156–57; Cullan, "Radicals," 181–82.
65. Ó Muirí, "Newry," 108–9; Cotlar, *Tom Paine's America*, 34.

66. Gillen, "Constructing Democratic Thought," 150; Stewart, *Deeper Silence*, 179–84; for an analysis in terms of "empiricism" versus "rationalism," see Brown, *Irish Enlightenment*, 400–401.
67. Priestley, *Letters*, iv; Bourke, *Empire and Revolution*, 724, 747.
68. Andrew, *Patrons*, 180; McBride, *Scripture Politics*, 109.
69. Lock, *Edmund Burke*, 1:294.
70. Andrew, *Patrons*, 174.
71. Priestley, *Letters*, viii.
72. Paine, *Rights of Man*, 178–79.
73. Ó Muirí, "Newry," 105, 120; Elliott, *Partners in Revolution*, 29, 31.
74. Armstrong, *The Liberty Tree*, vi, 9, 17.
75. Gillen, "Varieties," 178–80; Burke, *On Empire, Liberty*, 431.
76. Burke, *On Empire, Liberty*, 425.
77. Ibid., 427–28; Andrews, *British Periodical Press*, 188.
78. Barlow, *Conspiracy of Kings*, 16.
79. Ibid., 5, 10; Mulford, "Joel Barlow," 175.
80. Ó Muirí, "Newry," 114.
81. Roe, *Wordsworth*, 81–82; Erdman, *Commerce*, 305.
82. The account of the toasts in Girey-Dupré, *Patriote français* 1199 (21 November 1792): 588 and Alger, "British Colony," 673, 678 is incomplete; for a fuller contemporary account, see *Journal de Perlet* 2, no. 61 (21 November 1792): 485–87.
83. Moore, *Memoirs*, 126–28; Nelson, *Thomas Paine*, 249; Foner, *Tom Paine*, 253.
84. Dunne, *Theobald Wolfe Tone*, 26.
85. Drennan, *Drennan Letters*, 49; Keane, *Tom Paine*, 333; Foner, *Tom Paine*, 253; Gillen, "Varieties," 165; Cotlar, *Tom Paine's America*, 43, 79; Elliott, *Partners in Revolution*, 26–27.
86. Dickson, "Paine and Ireland," 140.
87. Ibid., 136–37.
88. Stewart, *Deeper Silence*, 154, 184; McBride, *Scripture Politics*, 173, 183; Tesch, "Presbyterian Radicalism," 46–48.
89. Durey, "Irish Deism," 57–58.
90. Drennan, *The Drennan Letters*, 54; Gibbons, *Edmund Burke*, 233–36.
91. Drennan, *The Drennan Letters*, 63; Cullan, "Internal Politics," 181; Brown, *Irish Enlightenment*, 424.
92. Gordon, *History of the Irish Rebellion*, 6; Wells, *Insurrection*, 53–55.
93. Cullan, "Radicals," 181.
94. Burke, *Correspondence*, 9:112–15.
95. Wells, *Insurrection*, 10; Durey, "Irish Deism," 61–62; Andrews, *British Periodical Press*, 105.
96. Dickson, "Paine and Ireland," 144, 148.
97. McKenna, *Essay on Parliamentary Reform*, 12–13.
98. Ibid., 13, 23, 25, 36.
99. Ibid., 35.
100. Callender, *Political Progress*, 77; Andrews, *British Periodical Press*, 194.
101. Callender, *Political Progress*, advertisement to the 1794 edition.
102. Zamoyski, *Holy Madness*, 106; Cullan, "Internal Politics," 188–93; Gibbons, "Republicanism," 237.

103. Elliott, "Wolfe Tone," 53–54.
104. Tone, *An Address*, 18.
105. Palmer, *Age of the Democratic Revolution*, 2:265–67; Buel, *Joel Barlow*, 207.
106. Elliott, *Partners in Revolution*, 81; Kleinman, "Tone and the French Expeditions," 92.
107. Tone, *An Address*, 11; Gibbons, "Republicanism," 213–14.
108. Hampshire-Monk, "British Radicalism and the Anti-Jacobins," 664.
109. Tone, *An Address*, 18; Dunne, *Theobald Wolfe Tone*, 50–52; Bartlett, "Burden," 15.
110. Gillen, "Varieties," 163.
111. Tone, *An Address*, 2–3; Hampshire-Monk, "British Radicalism and the Anti-Jacobins," 662–3.
112. Tone, *An Address*, 26; Kleinman, "Tone and the French Expeditions," 97–98.
113. Tone, *An Address*, 20.
114. Elliott, "Wolfe Tone," 53, 55.
115. Schama, *Patriots and Liberators*, 278; Pakenham, *The Year*, 18–19; Elliott, *Partners in Revolution*, 104, 110–14.
116. Tone, *Writings*, 2:77–78; Rutjes, *Door gelijkheid gegrepen*, 90.
117. Tone, *Writings*, 2:78; Wells, *Insurrection*, 115.
118. Tone, *Writings*, 2:61, 78; Dunne, *Theobald Wolfe Tone*, 30–35, 40.
119. Tone, *Writings*, 2:118; Smyth, "The 1798 Rebellion," 12.
120. Tone, *Writings*, 2:95–96.
121. Lock, *Edmund Burke*, 2:565–66; Smyth, "Act of Union," 147; Bourke, *Empire and Revolution*, 880–86.
122. Tone, *Writings*, 2:118; Schama, *Patriots and Liberators*, 278.
123. Wells, *Insurrection*, 111.
124. Navickas, *Loyalism*, 116, 129.
125. Rosenfeld, *American Aurora*, 217.
126. Durey, "United Irishmen," 96–97.
127. O'Donnell, "Military Committee," 129–34.
128. Cleary, "Wexford in 1798," 102–4.
129. Brown, *Irish Enlightenment*, 405–6.
130. Dunne, *Theobald Wolfe Tone*, 23–24; Pakenham, *The Year*, 171–72, 217; Clark, *Language of Liberty*, 287–89.
131. Elliott, *Partners in Revolution*, 81.
132. Rosenfeld, *American Aurora*, 527.
133. Wells, *Insurrection*, 160; Elliott, *Partners in Revolution*, 30–31, 224–25, 227.
134. Kleinman, "Tone and the French Expeditions," 83, 95.
135. Cleary, "Wexford in 1798," 105.
136. O'Donnell, "Military Committee," 136.
137. Cullan, "Radicals," 162–63.
138. Rosenfeld, *American Aurora*, 571, 577; Pakenham, *The Year*, 344–45.
139. Lafayette, *Mémoires*, 5:74; Navickas, *Loyalism*, 80–81.
140. Durey, "Irish Deism," 62.
141. Rosenfeld, *American Aurora*, 231, 596.
142. Durey, "United Irishmen," 104–6; Wells, *Insurrection*, 161.
143. Durey, "Marquess Cornwallis," 132.
144. Smyth, "The 1798 Rebellion," 6–17; Foot, *Red Shelley*, 20–21.

145. Gillen, "Constructing Democratic Thought," 159.
146. O'Donnell, "Military Committee," 137–42.
147. Wells, *Insurrection*, 252, 263.

Chapter 13: America's "Conservative Turn"

1. Wilentz, *Rise of American Democracy*, 53–75.
2. Merrill and Wilentz, *The Key*, 268.
3. Wood, "Is There a 'James Madison Problem'?" 426–27; Stewart, *Madison's Gift*, 135–37, 148; Allen, *Moral Minority*, 103, 109–10.
4. Matthews, *Radical Politics of Thomas Jefferson*, 106–9; Sheehan, *James Madison*, 62.
5. Burstein and Isenberg, *Madison and Jefferson*, 214–15, 221–23, 232.
6. Sheehan, "Politics of Public Opinion," 615, 618, 621–22, 627; Sheehan, *James Madison*, 158, 161.
7. Madison to Jefferson, New York, 27 June 1791, in Jefferson, *Papers*, 20:581; Spellberg, *Thomas Jefferson's Qur'an*, 201–3; Burstein and Isenberg, *Madison and Jefferson*, 225–28.
8. Jefferson, *Papers*, 20:692–93.
9. Jefferson, *Writings*, 997–98; Weisberger, *America Afire*, 70–71; Burstein and Isenberg, *Madison and Jefferson*, 232–35; Stewart, *Madison's Gift*, 138–40.
10. Link, *Democratic-Republican Societies*, 58n; May, *Enlightenment in America*, 236–37, 326; Holmes, *Faiths*, 45.
11. Freneau, "On some of the Principles."
12. Adams, *Gouverneur Morris*, 198, 227–29, 232, 234–35; Lefer, *Founding Conservatives*, 329; Kloppenberg, *Toward Democracy*, 487.
13. Maclay, *Journal*, 382.
14. Ibid., 407, 26 February 1791.
15. McNamara, "Alexander Hamilton," 190–91; Federici, *Political Philosophy of Alexander Hamilton*, 6, 8–10.
16. Washington to Louis XVI, Philadelphia, 14 March 1792, in Jefferson, *Papers*, 23:281; Jefferson, *Political Writings*, 101; Adams, *Gouverneur Morris*, 229–30.
17. Lafayette, *Mémoires*, 3:422–26; Adams, *Gouverneur Morris*, 227, 233.
18. Nash and Gao Hodges, *Friends of Liberty*, 168–69, 219.
19. Jefferson to Lafayette, 16 June 1792, in Jefferson, *Political Writings*, 990–91. Jefferson had written to George Mason in similar terms, earlier, in February 1791; see pp. 971–72.
20. De Francesco, "Federalist Obsession," 243–46, 250–51.
21. Kloppenberg, *Toward Democracy*, 510–11, 533. Kloppenberg's mistake, as I see it, in identifying Condorcet and Brissot as "moderates," and Robespierre as "radical," undermines his entire construct distinguishing moderate from radical Enlightenment.
22. Foner, *Democratic-Republican Societies*, 17; White, *Encountering Revolution*, 91.
23. McNamara, "Alexander Hamilton," 191; Federici, *Political Philosophy of Alexander Hamilton*, 223–26.
24. May, *Enlightenment in America*, 252; Sharp, "France and the United States," 204; Wood, *Empire of Liberty*, 176–83.
25. Zamoyski, *Holy Madness*, 196; Sharp, "France and the United States," 204–5.

26. Paine, *Letter to George Washington*, 697; Stewart, *Madison's Gift*, 147–49; Kloppenberg, *Toward Democracy*, 510.
27. Jefferson, *Writings*, 689–90.
28. White, *Encountering Revolution*, 106–8; Stewart, *Madison's Gift*, 149–51.
29. Peterson, *Thomas Jefferson*, 481–86; Davis, *Revolutions*, 39.
30. White, *Encountering Revolution*, 88–91.
31. Paine, *Letter to George Washington*, 704; Staloff, *Hamilton, Adams, Jefferson*, 106–7; Elkins and McKitrick, *Age of Federalism*, 317–22.
32. Paine, *Letter to George Washington*, 706–7.
33. De Francesco, "Federalist Obsession," 249; Brookhiser, *Alexander Hamilton*, 104, 110, 122–23; Adams, *Gouverneur Morris*, 257–58.
34. Brookhiser, *Alexander Hamilton*, 122–25; Ferling, *Jefferson and Hamilton*, 272.
35. Davis, *Revolutions*, 32–33; Unger, *John Quincy Adams*, 92–93; Gilje, *Road to Mobocracy*, 102–3; Furstenberg, *When the United States Spoke French*, 336–38.
36. Cotlar, "Languages of Democracy," 22; Kloppenberg, *Toward Democracy*, 569.
37. Foner, *Democratic-Republican Societies*, 9, 22–23; Wilentz, *Rise of American Democracy*, 40–41, 56–57; Elkins and McKitrick, *Age of Federalism*, 453–55; Wood, *Empire of Liberty*, 162–63, 718.
38. Foner, *Democratic-Republican Societies*, 22–23; Wilentz, *Rise of American Democracy*, 58–59.
39. Israel, *Revolutionary Ideas*, 320–44.
40. Link, *Democratic-Republican Societies*, 6; Foner, *Democratic-Republican Societies*, 6–9, 411, 422; Spencer, *Bloomsbury Encyclopaedia*, 2:632–33.
41. Elkins and McKitrick, *Age of Federalism*, 458–59; Slack, *Liberty's First Crisis*, 42–46.
42. Quoted in Link, *Democratic-Republican Societies*, 11; Foner, *Democratic-Republican Societies*, 7.
43. Foner, *Democratic-Republican Societies*, 7; Burstein and Isenberg, *Madison and Jefferson*, 275.
44. Link, *Democratic-Republican Societies*, 57–59; Sharp, *American Politics*, 69–70, 85–86; Pasley, "Thomas Greenleaf," 364–65.
45. Adams to Jefferson, Quincy, 30 June 1813, in *Adams-Jefferson Letters*, 2:346–47; Hazen, *Contemporary American Opinion*, 186; McCullough, *John Adams*, 445–46; Sharp, "France and the United States," 210.
46. Foner, *Democratic-Republican Societies*, 12.
47. Cotlar, *Tom Paine's America*, 50–51; Wood, *Empire of Liberty*, 309, 311.
48. Coram, *Political Inquiries*, 68, 78; Cotlar, *Tom Paine's America*, 116–20.
49. Link, *Democratic-Republican Societies*, 15; Buel, *Securing the Revolution*, 127–29; Sharp, "France and the United States," 211; Cotlar, *Tom Paine's America*, 190.
50. Slaughter, *Whiskey Rebellion*, 194; Ellis, *American Sphinx*, 182–83; Cotlar, *Tom Paine's America*, 190–91.
51. Sharp, *American Politics*, 98–100; Taylor, *American Revolutions*, 413–14.
52. Bouton, *Taming Democracy*, 218–19; Ferling, *Jefferson and Hamilton*, 265–67; Cotlar, *Tom Paine's America*, 186–88.
53. Bouton, *Taming Democracy*, 226, 235–37, 241; Rana, *Two Faces*, 101–2; Kloppenberg, *Toward Democracy*, 566–67.
54. Bouton, "William Findlay, David Bradford," 234, 245–46, 249; Chernow, *Alexander Hamilton*, 470.

55. Chernow, *Alexander Hamilton*, 471, 473–77; Wilentz, *Rise of American Democracy*, 64–65.
56. Slaughter, *Whiskey Rebellion*, 200, 202, 268; Wilentz, *Chants Democratic*, 68; Burstein and Isenberg, *Madison and Jefferson*, 289–92.
57. Bouton, "William Findlay, David Bradford," 240; Miller, *Federalist Era*, 160–62; Buel, *Securing the Revolution*, 128–29.
58. Brookhiser, *Alexander Hamilton*, 117–21; Burstein and Isenberg, *Madison and Jefferson*, 289–90.
59. Madison, *Writings*, 6:220; Wood, *Empire of Liberty*, 134, 196–97.
60. Bache, *Philadelphia Aurora* 1224 (8 November 1794): 2; Staloff, *Hamilton, Adams, Jefferson*, 120–21.
61. John Quincy Adams to John Adams, The Hague, 12 September 1795, in John Quincy Adams, *Writings*, 1:410.
62. Jefferson to Madison, Monticello, 28 December 1794, in Jefferson, *Writings*, 1015; Ellis, *American Sphinx*, 181–83; Meacham, *Thomas Jefferson*, 288–89; Cotlar, *Tom Paine's America*, 165, 186–87, 190–91.
63. Navickas, *Loyalism*, 40.
64. May, *Enlightenment in America*, 218; Durey, "Thomas Paine's Apostles," 193; Sheps, "American Revolution," 308.
65. Malone, *Public Life*, 133; Rosenfeld, *American Aurora*, 43; Ferling, *Jefferson and Hamilton*, 299.
66. McDowell, *Ireland*, 3112; Sher, *Enlightenment and the Book*, 576–78.
67. Vincent, "Thomas Paine et la république," 183; Durey, "Thomas Paine's Apostles," 197–98, 211.
68. Sher, *Enlightenment and the Book*, 576–78.
69. Carey, *Collected Wisdom*, 14; Wood, *Empire of Liberty*, 252.
70. Munck, "Troubled Reception," 171; Durey, "Thomas Paine's Apostles," 194–95.
71. Weisberger, *America Afire*, 206–7, 212, 237; Wood, *Empire of Liberty*, 258–61.
72. Bourke, *Empire and Revolution*, 769.
73. Jefferson, *Papers*, 26:715; Wood, *Empire of Liberty*, 724; Bloom, *Restless Revolutionaries*, 169.
74. Priestley, *Autobiography*, 133; Foner, *Democratic-Republican Societies*, 182, 423.
75. Jefferson, *Papers*, 26:716; Malone, *Public Life*, 4, 12–13, 80–81.
76. Cooper, *Some Information*, 48.
77. Ibid., 52–53.
78. Ibid., 78; Miranda, *New Democracy*, 72; Verhoeven, *Americomania*, 177.
79. Morse, *Sermon* (19 February 1795): 31, 35–36.
80. Ibid., 29–30.
81. Quoted in ibid., 15.
82. Ibid., 11.
83. Ibid., 14; Nash, "American Clergy," 393.
84. Gilje, *Road to Mobocracy*, 102–3, 107.
85. Wilentz, *Chants Democratic*, 78–79; Lepore, "World of Paine," 93.
86. Webster, "Revolution in France," 21.
87. Richards, *Shays's Rebellion*, 80–82.
88. Webster, " Revolution in France," 34.
89. Ellis, *After the Revolution*, 164.

90. Webster, "Revolution in France," 21; May, *Enlightenment in America*, 195–96.

91. Ellis, *After the Revolution*, 198–99; Wood, *Empire of Liberty*, 203; Dunn, *Sister Revolutions*, 40.

92. Sharp, "France and the United States," 204–11; Cotlar, *Tom Paine's America*, 190–192.

93. Webster, "Revolution in France," 35; Spurlin, *Rousseau in America*, 106–7, 111.

94. Webster, "Revolution in France," 35; Cotlar, *Tom Paine's America*, 89–90.

95. Webster, "Revolution in France," 36.

96. Buel, *Joel Barlow*, 238.

97. Brookhiser, *Alexander Hamilton*, 138; McNamara, "Alexander Hamilton," 192–95.

98. Webster, "Revolution in France," 23–29.

99. Ibid., 32.

100. Ellis, *After the Revolution*, 205–7; Ingrams, *Life and Adventures*, 31–32.

101. Miller, *Federalist Era*, 264–65; Buel, *Securing the Revolution*, 168–70; May, *Enlightenment in America*, 261; Nash, "American Clergy," 393; Davis, *Revolutions*, 30–31.

102. Richards, *Shays's Rebellion*, 114–15; Szatmary, *Shays' Rebellion*, 13–14, 60, 64–69.

103. Richards, *Shays's Rebellion*, 111–15; Guyatt, *Providence*, 150–52, 154–56, 170; Waldman, *Founding Faith*, 165.

104. Riordan, "'O Dear, What Can the Matter Be?'" 193–94.

105. Ibid., 209, 211 221–22, 227.

106. *La Décade philosophique* 5, no. 32 (August 1797): 302–3.

107. Peterson, *Thomas Jefferson*, 576, 580; Ingrams, *Life and Adventures*, 22–23.

108. Bauszus, "Religious Aspects," 340–42.

109. Sharp, *American Politics*, 167, 171; Buel, *Joel Barlow*, 222.

110. May, *Enlightenment in America*, 260–62; Jacoby, *Freethinkers*, 48–49; Wood, *Empire of Liberty*, 244–46, 602–3, 722.

111. Cotlar, *Tom Paine's America*, 200–203; Nash, *Unknown American Revolution*, 424–26; McGarvie, *One Nation under Law*, 79, 161–62, 168–69, 172.

112. Madison to Jefferson, 5 May 1798, in *Republic of Letters*, 2:1046.

113. Jefferson, *Writings*, 1076–77; Buel, *Securing the Revolution*, 170–71, 226; Newman, *Fries's Rebellion*, 66–67; Wood, *Empire of Liberty*, 244.

114. Kuklick, *History*, 50; Holifield, *Theology*, 175; Spencer, *Bloomsbury Encyclopaedia*, 1:362.

115. Butler, *Awash in a Sea*, 219; Guyatt, *Providence*, 156; Buel, *Securing the Revolution*, 170–75; Wilentz, *Politicians and the Egalitarians*, 106, 136.

116. Palmer, *Posthumous Pieces*, 26.

117. Wilentz, *Politicians and the Egalitarians*, 101, 106.

118. Ferling, *Jefferson and Hamilton*, 299–300; Federici, *Political Philosophy of Alexander Hamilton*, 88, 177; Furstenberg, *When the United States Spoke French*, 371–73.

119. Chernow, *Alexander Hamilton*, 571–72; Federici, *Political Philosophy of Alexander Hamilton*, 176–77; see also Jacoby, *Freethinkers*, 45, 239; Wood, *Empire of Liberty*, 258–60.

120. Chernow, *Alexander Hamilton*, 17–18, 570, 599–600.

121. Burstein and Isenberg, *Madison and Jefferson*, 336, 616; Rana, *Two Faces*, 369n37; Slack, *Liberty's First Crisis*, 82–83, 191; Mayers, *Dissenting Voices*, 23–26, 30.

122. Weisberger, *America Afire*, 211–13; Labunski, *James Madison*, 257; Brookhiser, *Alexander Hamilton*, 141–44; Bird, "Reassessing Responses," 519–20, 530–32, 543–44; Slack, *Liberty's First Crisis*, 173–74.

123. Sharp, *American Politics*, 218; Grant, *John Adams*, 405–8; Sheehan, *James Madison*, 28.

124. Elkins and McKitrick, *Age of Federalism*, 709–11; Slack, *Liberty's First Crisis*, 15–16, 156–62.

125. McCullough, *John Adams*, 494, 536; Rosenfeld, *American Aurora*, 198, 526–27, 532–33; Meacham, *Thomas Jefferson*, 317; Cotlar, *Tom Paine's America*, 241n89.

126. Rosenfeld, *American Aurora*, 169–70, 175, 207; Slack, *Liberty's First Crisis*, 121–23.

127. Pasley, "Thomas Greenleaf," 369–71; Chernow, *Alexander Hamilton*, 575–77.

128. McCullough, *John Adams*, 536–37; Buel, *Joel Barlow*, 232; Ferling, *Adams vs. Jefferson*, 136–37, 140.

129. Malone, *Public Life*, 109, 112, 116; Volokh, "Thomas Cooper," 375–76; Slack, *Liberty's First Crisis*, 190–91.

130. Wood, *Empire of Liberty*, 257, 261; Verhoeven, *Americomania*, 300–301.

131. Madison, *Writings*, 6:320–21; Burstein and Isenberg, *Madison and Jefferson*, 333.

132. Wood, *Empire of Liberty*, 260; Nash and Gao Hodges, *Friends of Liberty*, 161–62, 170; Slack, *Liberty's First Crisis*, 191.

133. Volney, *Œuvres*, 2:27; Chinard, *Volney et l'Amérique*, 83, 92, 100; Gaulmier, *Grand témoin*, 271–72; Furstenberg, *When the United States Spoke French*, 355–59.

134. Volney, *Œuvres*, 2:22–23; Buel, *Joel Barlow*, 259; Serna, "In Search," 260–61.

135. Williams, "Morgan John Rhys and Volney's *Ruins*," 58–59.

136. Serna, "In Search," 262; Jacoby, *Freethinkers*, 115; Cotlar, *Tom Paine's America*, 241n89.

137. Volney, *Ruins*, v–vi.

138. Buel, *Joel Barlow*, 259–60.

139. May, *Enlightenment in America*, 265–66; Sharp, "France and the United States," 213–14.

140. Rosenfeld, *American Aurora*, 216; Brookhiser, *Alexander Hamilton*, 107.

141. Knudsen, *Justus Möser*, 184–86; see also Armitage, *Declaration*, 68; Kloppenberg, *Toward Democracy*, 547, 573.

142. Whaley, *Germany*, 593.

143. Newman, *Fries's Rebellion*, 3, 7, 159–64; Rosenfeld, *American Aurora*, 613, 622, 781–72; McCullough, *John Adams*, 540–41; Weisberger, *America Afire*, 195, 237.

144. Bouton, *Taming Democracy*, 245–47, 252; Chernow, *Alexander Hamilton*, 578–79.

145. Rosenfeld, *American Aurora*, 613; Newman, *Fries's Rebellion*, 158–61.

146. Bouton, "William Findlay, David Bradford," 250; Weisberger, *America Afire*, 195, 237.

147. Sheps, "American Revolution," 291; Jacoby, *Freethinkers*, 55.

148. Rosenfeld, *American Aurora*, 44–45.

149. Burke, "Piecing Together," 298.

150. Walters, *Revolutionary Deists*, 221–22.

151. Foner, *Story*, 43, 301; Ellis, *American Sphinx*, 221; Burstein and Isenberg, *Madison and Jefferson*, 342, 363, 396, 408.

152. Rahe, *Republics*, 686; Sharp, *American Politics*, 239–41; Brookhiser, *Alexander Hamilton*, 143–44, 214; Chernow, *Alexander Hamilton*, 510–11, 598–600; Federici, *Political Philosophy of Alexander Hamilton*, 43, 210–11, 244.

153. Rosenfeld, *American Aurora*, 729–30; Chernow, *Alexander Hamilton*, 601.

154. Allen, *Moral Minority*, 42–44; Holmes, *Faiths*, 140–41, 160, 162.
155. Adams to Jefferson, 3 September 1816, in *Adams-Jefferson Letters*, 2:488.
156. Allen, *Moral Minority*, xiii–xiv; Meacham, *American Gospel*, 74–75.
157. Grant, *John Adams*, 435; Peterson, *Thomas Jefferson*, 625.
158. Rosenfeld, *American Aurora*, 733–34.
159. Ferling, *Adams vs. Jefferson*, 143–44; Cotlar, "Robert Coram," 350.
160. Rosenfeld, *American Aurora*, 751, 753; Spencer, *Bloomsbury Encyclopaedia*, 1:346–47; Burke, "Piecing Together," 298; Slack, *Liberty's First Crisis*, 147–48.
161. Sharp, *American Politics*, 218–20; Elkins and McKitrick, *Age of Federalism*, 704–5.
162. Innes and Philp, "Synergies," 198–99; Chernow, *Alexander Hamilton*, 606–9.
163. Jefferson, *Writings*, 1062; Rahe, *Republics*, 687.
164. Jefferson to Priestley, Washington, 21 March 1801, in Jefferson, *Writings*, 1085–87; Meacham, *Thomas Jefferson*, 355–57.
165. Cotlar, "Languages of Democracy," 14; Waldman, *Founding Faith*, 170–71, 175.
166. Appleby, *Inventing the Revolution*, 28–32, 52–53.
167. Palmer, *An Enquiry*, 4.

Chapter 14: America and the Haitian Revolution

1. *Il est encore des Aristocrates* (British Library London: R-328/11), 6–7.
2. Jacques-Pierre Brissot de Warville, *Mémoire aux Etats-généraux sur la nécessité de rendre, dès ce moment, la presse libre et surtout pour les journaux politiques* (Paris, 1789) 2:96–97; Garrigus, "Opportunist or Patriot?" 11; Hunt, *Inventing Human Rights*, 163.
3. Destutt de Tracy, *Premiers écrits*, 72.
4. Charles de Secondat, Baron de Montesquieu, *De L'Esprit des Lois*, part 3, book 7, in *Oeuvres complètes*, ed. D. Oster (Paris, 1964), 620; Ghachem, "Montesquieu in the Caribbean," 195–97; Ehrard, "Audace théorique," 35–38; Israel, *Democratic Enlightenment*, 423–24.
5. Condorcet, *Bibliothèque de l'Homme Public*, series I (1790), 7:12–16; *Le Conservateur des Principes des Républicains* 2, no. 7 (20 Messidor Year II): 3–8; Israel, *Revolutionary Ideas*, 335–36, 698.
6. De Bolla, *Architecture of Concepts*, 143–67.
7. Paine to Short, 2 November 1791, in Paine, *Writings*, 2:1321.
8. Garrigus, "Opportunist or Patriot?" 7; Klooster, *Revolutions*, 98–99; Régent, "From Individual to Collective Emancipation," 170–71.
9. Popkin, *You Are All Free*, 45–46.
10. Régent, *France et ses esclaves*, 242–43; Popkin, *You Are All Free*, 87; Curran, *Anatomy*, 206.
11. Raimond, *Réflexions*, 35–36.
12. Malouet, *Mémoires*, 2:195.
13. Blackburn, *Overthrow*, 197–99, 228–29; Régent, *France et ses esclaves*, 243–45.
14. Girey-Duré, *Patriote français* 1278 (10 February 1793): 164–65.
15. Wood, *Empire of Liberty*, 534; White, *Encountering Revolution*, 28–30.
16. Quoted in White, *Encountering Revolution*, 1–2.

17. Egerton, "Race and Slavery," 75; White, *Encountering Revolution*, 7–10.
18. White, *Encountering Revolution*, 66–73.
19. Rush, *Letters*, 2:658–59.
20. Ibid., 2:738.
21. Popkin, *You Are All Free*, 210–11, 234–35, 248–49; Garrigus, "Opportunist or Patriot?" 11; Hunt, *Inventing Human Rights*, 165.
22. Popkin, *You Are All Free*, 250–51.
23. Toussaint Louverture to Laveaux, 18 May and 7 July 1794, and 7 July 1795, in Toussaint Louverture, *Lettres*, 156, 166, 168, 218.
24. Popkin, *You Are All Free*, 276; Fenton, *Religious Liberties*, 110–11.
25. Raimond, *Réflexions*, 8, 10; Brown, *Toussaint's Clause*, 96.
26. [Momoro?], *Coup d'œil sur la question*, British Library R-328/12, 4–5, 12.
27. Buck-Morss, "Hegel and Haiti," 830–31.
28. [Momoro?], *Coup d'œil sur la question*, British Library R-328/12, 8.
29. McPhee, *Robespierre*, 173.
30. Toussaint Louverture to Laveaux, 18 May and 28 June 1794, 30 January and 17 August 1796, in Toussaint Louverture, *Lettres*, 157–58, 163, 298, 360.
31. Toussaint Louverture to Laveaux, 7 July and 9 September 1794, in Toussaint Louverture, *Lettres*, 165, 176.
32. White, *Encountering Revolution*, 1.
33. Toussaint Louverture to Laveaux, 6 February 1794, in Toussaint Louverture, *Lettres*, 202.
34. Klooster, "Rising Expectations," 66–67; Jordaan, *Slavernij en vrijheid*, 212.
35. Toussaint Louverture to Laveaux, 23 May 1797, in Toussaint Louverture, *Lettres*, 367.
36. Fenton, *Religious Liberties*, 111–13.
37. White, *Encountering Revolution*, 118–19.
38. Toussaint Louverture, *Lettres*, 337–38, 340–41, 346.
39. Toussaint Louverture to Laveaux, 22 February 1796, in Toussaint Louverture, *Lettres*, 305.
40. Oldfield, *Transatlantic Abolitionism*, 122.
41. Toussaint Louverture to Laveaux, 12 September 1797, in Toussaint Louverture, *Lettres*, 369.
42. Toussaint Louverture to Laveaux, 1 June 1798, in Toussaint Louverture, *Lettres*, 374; Buck-Morss, "Hegel and Haiti," 834.
43. Toussaint Louverture to Laveaux, 1 June 1798, in Toussaint Louverture, *Lettres*, 372–74.
44. Brown, *Toussaint's Clause*, 149, 219.
45. Toussaint Louverture to Laveaux, 5 June 1798, in Toussaint Louverture, *Lettres*, 377.
46. Buck-Morss, "Hegel and Haiti," 833–34.
47. Unger, *John Quincy Adams*, 117–19, 131; Chernow, *Alexander Hamilton*, 619–20.
48. Matthewson, "Jefferson and Haiti," 213; White, *Encountering Revolution*, 125, 156–61; Brown, *Toussaint's Clause*, 145–46, 156–57.
49. Peterson, *Thomas Jefferson*, 748–49.
50. Régent, *France et ses esclaves*, 256–57; Keane, *Tom Paine*, 439.

51. Welch, *Liberty*, 37–38; Bredin, *Sieyès*, 463–64.
52. Gaulmier, *Grand témoin*, 234–6; Forsyth, *Reason*, 8–9; Harris, *Antoine d'Estutt de Tracy*, 28; Jainchill, *Reimagining Politics*, 198–200.
53. Lafayette, *Mémoires*, 5:245–46; Wood, "Benjamin Constant," 8.
54. Lafayette, *Mémoires*, 5:245.
55. Bredin, *Sieyès*, 454, 459, 461, 466.
56. Brown, *Toussaint's Clause*, 123–24, 185.
57. Toussaint Louverture to Laveaux, 17 June and 22 August 1795, in Toussaint Louverture, *Lettres*, 208–9, 236.
58. Jefferson to Monroe, 24 November 1801, in Jefferson, *Writings*, 1098.
59. Brown, *Toussaint's Clause*, 174–75.
60. Davis, *Problem of Slavery*, 30, 150.
61. Lafayette to Jefferson, 20 June 1801, in Lafayette, *Mémoires*, 6:253; Cloquet, *Recollections*, 5.
62. Nash and Gao Hodges, *Friends of Liberty*, 171–72.
63. Gaulmier, *Grand témoin*, 248, 254–56.
64. Gueniffey, *Bonaparte*, 596–98, 657.
65. Gaulmier, *Grand témoin*, 256–57; Furstenberg, *When the United States Spoke French*, 387–90, 392.
66. Quoted in Brown, *Toussaint's Clause*, 211.
67. Jefferson, *Writings*, 1105; Matthewson, "Jefferson and Haiti," 245–46.
68. Brown, *Toussaint's Clause*, 211; Burstein and Isenberg, *Madison and Jefferson*, 375–77, 379–80.
69. Gueniffey, *Bonaparte*, 658; Roberts, *Napoleon the Great*, 300–302.
70. Matthewson, "Jefferson and Haiti," 209; Roberts, *Napoleon the Great*, 300.
71. Brown, *Toussaint's Clause*, 200–203.
72. Roberts, *Napoleon the Great*, 300–301.
73. Matthewson, "Jefferson and Haiti," 229–30; Peterson, *Thomas Jefferson*, 750; Brown, *Toussaint's Clause*, 216–17.
74. Régent, *France et ses esclaves*, 265–66; Brown, *Toussaint's Clause*, 225.
75. Brown, *Toussaint's Clause*, 219–20; Oldfield, *Transatlantic Abolitionism*, 165–66; Curran, *Anatomy*, 208–9.
76. Popkin, *You Are All Free*, 380.
77. Kukla, *A Wilderness*, 224–25; Régent, *France et ses esclaves*, 268–69; Curran, *Anatomy*, 209–10.
78. Paine to Jefferson, 1 January 1805, in Paine, *Complete Writings*, 2:1454.
79. Popkin, *You Are All Free*, 379; Furstenberg, *When the United States Spoke French*, 387, 390.
80. Roberts, *Napoleon the Great*, 303.
81. White, *Encountering Revolution*, 164; Brown, *Toussaint's Clause*, 237–38.
82. Nash and Gao Hodges, *Friends of Liberty*, 176–77; Wood, *Empire of Liberty*, 368–69; Matthewson, "Jefferson and Haiti," 211.
83. Egerton, "Race and Slavery," 75–76.
84. White, *Encountering Revolution*, 177–79.
85. Brown, *Toussaint's Clause*, 148.
86. Ibid., 268, 272, 276.

87. Popkin, *You Are All Free*, 379–80; Matthewson, "Jefferson and Haiti," 232–36.
88. Lafayette to Jefferson, 4 July 1812, in Lafayette, *Mémoires*, 3:287.
89. Vincent, "Thomas Paine et la 'républicanisation,'" 132–33; Keane, *Tom Paine*, 506–7.
90. Nash and Gao Hodges, *Friends of Liberty*, 210.

Chapter 15: Louisiana and the Principles of '76

1. Jefferson to Washington, 8 May 1791, in Jefferson, *Writings*, 977; see also Jefferson, *Writings*, 1451.
2. Jefferson to Washington, 8 May 1791, in Jefferson, *Writings*, 977.
3. Ellis, *American Sphinx*, 151, 257; Bourke, *Empire and Revolution*, 809; Weisberger, *America Afire*, 68–69.
4. Jefferson to Paine, 19 June 1792, in Jefferson, *Writings*, 992; Wilentz, *Politicians and the Egalitarians*, 74.
5. Whatmore, "French and North American Revolutions," 223–25; Sharp, "France and the United States," 204–5, 211.
6. Elkins and McKitrick, *Age of Federalism*, 333, 349–50; Kukla, *A Wilderness*, 158–59, 164–65.
7. Robespierre, *Lettres [. . .] à ses comméttans* 1, no. 4 (19 January 1793): 232.
8. Newman, "Paine, Jefferson," 74–76.
9. Quoted in Kaye, *Thomas Paine*, 104–5; see also Cotlar, *Tom Paine's America*, 77, 184–88, 223.
10. Jefferson to Madison, 9 June 1793, in Jefferson, *Writings*, 1012.
11. De Francesco, "Federalist Obsession," 249; Buel, *Joel Barlow*, 194.
12. Paine, *Letter to George Washington*, 701; Foner, *Tom Paine*, 244; Nelson, *Thomas Paine*, 283–86.
13. Quoted in Macleod, "Thomas Paine and Jeffersonian America," 214.
14. Unger, *Last Founding Father*, 122–24, 126; Nelson, *Thomas Paine*, 286–89.
15. Slaughter, *Whiskey Rebellion*, 194, 227.
16. Paine, *Letter to George Washington*, 691, 696, Ellis, *Founding Brothers*, 126; Miller, *Federalist Era*, 194.
17. Guizot, *Démocratie*, 27–29, 37–39; Fawcett, *Liberalism*, 48–54.
18. Foner, *Tom Paine*, 256, 258; Cotlar, "Robert Coram," 337; Macleod, "Thomas Paine and Jeffersonian America," 209–10.
19. Palmer, *An Enquiry*, 11.
20. Ibid., 15; Stewart, *Nature's God*, 217–18.
21. Paine, *Complete Writings*, 2:931, 1436.
22. Ibid.
23. Jacoby, *Freethinkers*, 60; Nelson, *Thomas Paine*, 312; Munck, "Troubled Reception," 179.
24. Miller, *Federalist Era*, 265; Appleby, *Inheriting the Revolution*, 199; Buel, *Securing the Revolution*, 170.
25. Lepore, "World of Paine," 92; Elkins and McKitrick, *Age of Federalism*, 329.
26. Palmer, *Principles*, 158; Fischer, "Religion Governed by Terror," 13–15; Durey, "Irish Deism," 67.

27. Aldridge, *Man of Reason*, 283; Lause, "The 'Unwashed Infidelity,'" 392–93; Kaye, *Thomas Paine*, 127, 144.
28. Fellows, "Memoir," in Palmer, *Posthumous Pieces*, 9–10; Walters, *Revolutionary Deists*, 181, 187, 191; Buel, *Joel Barlow*, 230, 237.
29. Palmer, *Principles*, 135; Walters, *American Deists*, 182.
30. Jefferson, *Writings*, 1451; Stewart, *Nature's God*, 35.
31. Wood, *Empire of Liberty*, 579; Bouton, *Taming Democracy*, 258–59.
32. Sharp, "France and the United States," 213.
33. Webster, *Oration*, 1227.
34. Ibid., 1226–27.
35. Durey, "Irish Deism," 71.
36. Newman, "Paine, Jefferson," 77–78.
37. Macleod, "Thomas Paine and Jeffersonian America," 215.
38. Chernow, *Alexander Hamilton*, 571–72; Brookhiser, *Alexander Hamilton*, 138–39; Federici, *Political Philosophy of Alexander Hamilton*, 177, 227.
39. Durey, "Thomas Paine's Apostles"; Sheehan, *James Madison*, 115–18, 120, 122.
40. Paine, *Complete Writings*, 2:914–15.
41. Bernstein, *Thomas Jefferson*, 135–37.
42. Wilentz, *Politicians and the Egalitarians*, 7, 118–21.
43. Paine, *Complete Writings*, 2:919.
44. Ibid., 2:920.
45. Taylor, *American Revolutions*, 428–29.
46. Paine, *Complete Writings*, 2:918.
47. Stagg, *War of 1812*, 54; Taylor, *Civil War*, 280.
48. Durey, "Irish Deism," 67–68; Fischer, "Religion Governed by Terror," 17.
49. Rush, *Letters*, 2:900; Wilentz, *Rise of American Democracy*, 105–7.
50. Rush, *Letters*, 2:664, 996; Wood, *Empire of Liberty*, 426–27, 429; Wilentz, *Rise of American Democracy*, 122–23, 245.
51. Bouton, *Taming Democracy*, 260–61; Cotlar, *Tom Paine's America*, 211; Taylor, *American Revolutions*, 429.
52. De Tocqueville, *De la Démocratie*, 20.
53. Cotlar, *Tom Paine's America*, 212–13.
54. McCullough, *John Adams*, 537; Rosenfeld, *American Aurora*, 799; Slack, *Liberty's First Crisis*, 234, 240–41.
55. Rosenfeld, *American Aurora*, 612; Wilentz, *Politicians and the Egalitarians*, 114.
56. Meacham, *Thomas Jefferson*, 357–59, 378–79; Slack, *Liberty's First Crisis*, 240–42.
57. Peterson, *Thomas Jefferson*, 569–70, 706–8; Ellis, *American Sphinx*, 258–62.
58. Jefferson to Madison, 8 June 1797, in *Republic of Letters*, 2:981.
59. Paine, *Complete Writings*, 2:909–10.
60. Ibid., 2:912.
61. Keane, *Tom Paine*, 456; Nelson, *Thomas Paine*, 306–7.
62. Keane, *Tom Paine*, 456; Wilson, "Thomas Jefferson's Portrait," 245.
63. Ferling, *Adams vs. Jefferson*, 205.
64. Wilson, "Thomas Jefferson's Portrait," 247.
65. Ibid., 236.
66. Walters, *Revolutionary Deists*, 114
67. Rush, *Letters*, 2:1009; Kaye, *Thomas Paine*, 108; Keane, *Tom Paine*, 478–79.

68. Sam Adams to Paine, Boston, 30 November 1802, in Paine, *Age of Reason*, 201–2.
69. Keane, *Tom Paine*, 475–78; Nelson, *Thomas Paine*, 312–13.
70. Keane, *Tom Paine*, 524–25; Buel, *Joel Barlow*, 277; Lepore, "World of Paine," 94–95.
71. Foner, *Tom Paine*, 23–24; Buel, *Joel Barlow*, 278–80; Durey, "Irish Deism," 67–68.
72. Paine, *Complete Writings*, 2:910–12.
73. Kates, "From Liberalism to Radicalism," 575, 578–79; Macleod, "Thomas Paine and Jeffersonian America," 212, 218; Philp, "Revolutionaries in Paris," 138, 151, 153.
74. Nash, *Unknown American Revolution*, 423–24; Cotlar, "Conclusion," 281.
75. Macleod, "Thomas Paine and Jeffersonian America," 215; Richards, *Shays's Rebellion*, 68–69; Newman, *Fries's Rebellion*, 6–8; Bouton, *Taming Democracy*, 261.
76. Webster, *American Minerva* 1 (9 December 1793): 1.
77. Ellis, *American Sphinx*, 244; Wood, *Empire of Liberty*, 368.
78. Paine to Jefferson, 25 December 1802, in Paine, *Complete Writings*, 2:1432; Vincent, "Thomas Paine et la 'républicanisation,'" 127; Nelson, *Thomas Paine*, 309–10.
79. Rush, *Letters*, 2:66; Keane, *Tom Paine*, 473–74.
80. Brissot, *New Travels*, 422.
81. Kukla, *A Wilderness*, 149–52.
82. McFarlane, "American Revolution," 36; Peterson, *Thomas Jefferson*, 811–14.
83. Blasi, Freeman, and Kruse, *Citizen's Share*, 30–31, 36; Unger, *John Quincy Adams*, 126.
84. Vernet, *Strangers*, 3.
85. Paine to Jefferson, 2 August 1803 and 25 January 1805, in Paine, *Complete Writings*, 2:1441, 1457.
86. Burstein and Isenberg, *Madison and Jefferson*, 395–96.
87. Vernet, *Strangers*, 34–36, 60, 149, 156.
88. Ibid., 43–45; Unger, *John Quincy Adams*, 132.
89. Ellis, *American Sphinx*, 250–51; Burstein and Isenberg, *Madison and Jefferson*, 395–96.
90. Unger, *John Quincy Adams*, 128, 132; Vernet, *Strangers*, 31, 153.
91. Hyde, *Empires*, 6–8.
92. Vernet, *Strangers*, 32–33, 110; Unger, *Last Founding Father*, 175–76.
93. Jefferson, *Writings*, 513; Ellis, *American Sphinx*, 249–50.
94. Vernet, *Strangers*, 67–69, 70–71.
95. Ibid., 72, 155.
96. Paine, "To the French Inhabitants of Louisiana," in Paine, *Complete Writings*, 2:964–68.
97. Vincent, "Thomas Paine et la 'républicanisation,'" 132–33; Nelson, *Thomas Paine*, 310–11.
98. Paine to Jefferson, New York, 25 January 1805, in Paine, *Complete Writings*, 2:1456; Vernet, *Strangers*, 85.
99. Paine to Jefferson, New York, 25 January 1805, in Paine, *Complete Writings*, 2:1461.
100. Paine, "To the French Inhabitants of Louisiana," in Paine, *Complete Writings*, 2:964–95, 968.
101. Keane, *Tom Paine*, 488–89, 508–9; Lynch, "Limits," 193–94; Macleod, "Thomas Paine and Jeffersonian America," 219.

102. Paine to Jefferson, New York, 25 January 1805, in Paine, *Complete Writings*, 2:1457–58, 1464.
103. Ibid., 2:1458.
104. Popkin, *You Are All Free*, 311–14, 318; Matthewson, "Jefferson and Haiti," 216.
105. Lachance, "The 1809 Immigration," 110n5; White, *Encountering Revolution*, 181.
106. Lachance, "The 1809 Immigration," 110.
107. Paine to Jefferson, 2 August 1803, in Paine, *Complete Writings*, 2:1441.
108. Fenton, *Religious Liberties*, 31–33.
109. Vincent, "Thomas Paine et la 'républicanisation,'" 126–27; Foner, *Story*, 78; Lynch, "Limits," 194.
110. Buel, *Joel Barlow*, 271–72; Vincent, "Thomas Paine et la 'républicanisation,'" 130; Nash and Gao Hodges, *Friends of Liberty*, 178, 234; Macleod, "Thomas Paine and Jeffersonian America," 219–20; Lynch, "Limits," 194–95.
111. Jefferson, *Writings*, 519.
112. Taylor, *Internal Enemy*, 103, 432, 464n47; Blackburn, *Overthrow*, 284–85.
113. Davis, *Problem of Slavery*, 168–69; Ellis, *American Sphinx*, 315–21; Egerton, "Race and Slavery," 75.
114. Blackburn, *Overthrow*, 126–27; Waldstreicher, *Slavery's Constitution*, 66–67.
115. Ellis, *Founding Brothers*, 239–40.
116. Jefferson to Gallatin, 26 December 1820, in Jefferson, *Writings*, 1448–49.
117. Egerton, "Race and Slavery," 73, 75, 80.
118. Matthewson, "Jefferson and Haiti," 217–18, 223, 229, 243–44; Macleod, "Thomas Paine and Jeffersonian America," 220; Ferling, *Jefferson and Hamilton*, 353–55; Nash and Gao Hodges, *Friends of Liberty*, 177–78.
119. Vernet, *Strangers*, 157–58.
120. Steckel, "African American Population," 439; Vernet, *Strangers*, 3.
121. Hammond, "Slavery, Settlement, and Empire" 204–5; Wilentz, *Politicians and the Egalitarians*, 102–3; Wilentz, *Rise of American Democracy*, 219–20, 844n3; Nash and Hodges, *Friends of Liberty*, 177–78; Mayers, *Dissenting Voices*, 21–22.
122. Kukla, *A Wilderness*, 312; Lachance, "The 1809 Immigration," 116–17.
123. Hammond, "Slavery, Settlement, and Empire," 193.
124. Lachance, "The 1809 Immigration," 115, 117.
125. White, *Encountering Revolution*, 192–93.
126. Blackburn, *Overthrow*, 284; Lachance, "The 1809 Immigration," 110–11; Steckel, "African American Population," 439.
127. Steckel, "African American Population," 439; Hammond, "Slavery, Settlement, and Empire," 196; White, *Encountering Revolution*, 181–83.
128. Sarrans, *Lafayette et la Révolution*, 2:136–38.
129. Lachance, "The 1809 Immigration," 139.
130. Steckel, "African American Population," 439.
131. Jefferson to Adams, 10 December 1819, in *Adams-Jefferson Letters*, 2:549; Stewart, *Madison's Gift*, 320; Oldfield, *Transatlantic Abolitionism*, 252–53.
132. Jefferson to John Holmes, 22 April 1820, in Jefferson, *Writings*, 1434; Meacham, *Thomas Jefferson*, 474–75; Burstein and Isenberg, *Madison and Jefferson*, 576–77.
133. Jefferson to Gallatin, 26 December 1820, in Jefferson, *Writings*, 1450.
134. Jefferson, *Writings*, 1448–49; Ellis, *American Sphinx*, 316–18; Gutzman, *James Madison*, 338–39.

135. Steckel, "African American Population," 439; Ferling, *Jefferson and Hamilton*, 354.
136. Taylor, *Internal Enemy*, 407–8; Wood, *Empire of Liberty*, 526–27; Stewart, *Madison's Gift*, 318–20.
137. Taylor, *Internal Enemy*, 400–403; Peterson, *Thomas Jefferson*, 996–97; Stewart, *Madison's Gift*, 320–21.
138. Aldridge, *Man of Reason*, 282.
139. Paine to Jefferson, 23 September 1803, in Paine, *Complete Writings*, 2:1448.
140. Foner, *Tom Paine*, 258–59; Keane, *Tom Paine*, 463–64.
141. Foner, *Tom Paine*, 261; Keane, *Tom Paine*, 495–96, 513, 519; Macleod, "Thomas Paine and Jeffersonian America," 222.
142. Newman, "Paine, Jefferson," 71; Wilentz, *Politicians and the Egalitarians*, 69.
143. Buel, *Joel Barlow*, 276–77; Peterson, *Thomas Jefferson*, 859; Israel, "Radical Enlightenment's Critique," 59.
144. Buel, *Joel Barlow*, 238–39.
145. May, *Enlightenment in America*, 311–12; Buel, *Joel Barlow*, 281–83.
146. Wood, *Empire of Liberty*, 737.
147. Jefferson to Barlow, 24 February 1806, in Jefferson, *Writings*, 1160.
148. May, *Enlightenment in America*, 312; Peterson, *Thomas Jefferson*, 859–60.
149. Buel, *Joel Barlow*, 341–42, 346, 356.
150. Quoted in ibid., 360.
151. Palmer, *Principles*, 160; Walters, *American Deists*, 263–64; Jacoby, *Freethinkers*, 55.
152. Palmer, *Principles*, 160–61; Wilentz, *Chants Democratic*, 83.
153. Palmer, *Principles*, 161; Walters, *American Deists*, 276–77; Gilmartin, *Print Politics*, 3–4.
154. Freneau, "On some of the Principles."
155. May, *Enlightenment in America*, 326; Walters, *Revolutionary Deists*, 221–22; Peterson, *Thomas Jefferson*, 508.
156. Meyer, "Uniqueness," 172; Newman, "Paine, Jefferson," 79–81.
157. Nash, *Unknown American Revolution*, 454–55; Cotlar, "Robert Coram," 345.
158. Lambert, *Founding Fathers*, 238–39, 244.
159. May, *Enlightenment in America*, 241, 175–76; Frost, *Perfect Freedom*, 80–81; Robson, *Educating Republicans*, 176, 213; Kaye, *Thomas Paine*, 108–10.
160. Walters, *American Deists*, 43; Walters, *Revolutionary Deists*, 272.
161. Stewart, *Nature's God*, 423; Holifield, *Theology in America*, 163–70.
162. Lambert, *Founding Fathers*, 177–78, 228–30; Peterson, *Thomas Jefferson*, 957–60; Stewart, *Nature's God*, 409–12.
163. May, *Enlightenment in America*, 351; Holifield, *Theology in America*, 217; Kuklick, *Churchmen and Philosophers*, 85.
164. Brissot, *New Travels*, 87, 90.
165. Holifield, *Theology in America*, 199–200; Holmes, *Faiths*, 82, 88.
166. Brissot, *New Travels*, 87, 90; Jacoby, *Freethinkers*, 49.
167. Wilentz, *Chants Democratic*, 153–54.
168. Palmer, *An Enquiry*, 7; Palmer, *Principles*, 9.
169. Foner, *Tom Paine*, 263–64; Munck, "Troubled Reception," 178–79; Macleod, "Thomas Paine and Jeffersonian America," 222.
170. Kaye, *Thomas Paine*, 127; Keane, *Tom Paine*, 519, 522.

171. Foner, *Tom Paine*, 264; Kaye, *Thomas Paine*, 139–45; Honeck, *We Are the Revolutionists*, 89; Schmidt, *Village Atheists*, 11.
172. Whatmore, "French and North American Revolutions," 224–26, 229–30.
173. Lause, "The 'Unwashed Infidelity,' " 403; Crook, "Whiggery and America," 192.
174. Freneau, "On some of the Principles."

Chapter 16: A Revolutionary Era

1. Lafayette to Jefferson, 8 October 1804, in Lafayette, *Mémoires*, 5:260–61; Sarrans, *Lafayette et la Révolution*, 1:126.
2. Lafayette, *Mémoires*, 5:261.
3. Constant, *Écrits politiques*, 297.
4. Jefferson to Lafayette, Monticello, 14 February 1815, in Jefferson, *Writings*, 1361.
5. Mirow, *Florida's First Constitution*, 25.
6. Varela, "Discurso preliminar," xxxiii, xxxviii.
7. Chastellux, *De la félicité publique*, 2:92.
8. *Observations d'un homme impartial* (Knuttel 19123), 56.
9. Cabarrús, "Discurso sobre la libertad de comercio," 290.
10. Ibid., 291.
11. Kennedy, *Orders from France*, 315–16.
12. Quoted in Taylor, *American Revolutions*, 272.
13. Quoted in Fitz, *Our Sister Republics*, 25.
14. Laviña, "Participación de pardos," 166–67, 181; Rodríguez, *Independence*, 55.
15. Carr, *Spain, 1808–1939*, 113.
16. Durán López, "Construcción," 76–77.
17. Blanco White, *Life*, 1:140; Blaquiere, *Historical Review*, 133; Aymes, "Mise en cause," 111.
18. Hocquellet, *Résistance et révolution*, 277; Fuentes, *José Marchena*, 222–58.
19. Fernández Sebastián, " 'Voice of the People,' " 230–31.
20. Aymes, "Mise en cause," 112–15; Fernández Sebastián, " 'Voice of the People,' " 230–32.
21. Blaquiere, *Historical Review*, 24.
22. Aymes, "Mise en cause," 113.
23. Rodríguez López-Brea, *Don Luis de Borbón*, 211, 218.
24. Ibid., 187–88, 192, 210–11; Fernández Sebastián, " 'Voice of the People,' " 230; Varela Suanzes-Carpegna, "Image of the British System," 194, 201–4.
25. Hocquellet, *Résistance et révolution*, 264–82; Durán López, "Construcción," 85.
26. Dérozier, *Manuel José Quintana*, 619–28, 634; Fernández Sebastián, " 'Voice of the People,' " 230; Durán López, "Construcción," 69.
27. Elliott, *Empires*, 378.
28. Schofield, *Utility and Democracy*, 212, 287.
29. Elliott, *Empires*, 378–79.
30. Dérozier, *Manuel José Quintana*, 635–40.
31. *Proyecto de Constitución política de la monarquía española* (Cadiz, 17 August 1811), 15–16; Herr, "Constitution of 1812," 84–85.

32. *Proyecto de Constitución política de la monarquía española*, 12, 22; Herr, "Constitution of 1812," 86.
33. Fernández Sarasola, "Portée des droits," 92, 99.
34. Herr, "Constitution of 1812," 86; Fernández Sarasola, "Portée des droits," 103.
35. Suárez, *Crisis política*, 56–59; Suárez, *Cortes de Cádiz*, 114–19.
36. Flórez Estrada, *Representación*, 37–38; Herr, "Constitution of 1812," 88; Varela Suanzes-Carpegna, "Image of the British System," 203–5.
37. Suárez, *Cortes de Cádiz*, 116–20, 127.
38. Ibid., 153–56.
39. Mirow, *Florida's First Constitution*, 75–76; Elliott, *Empires*, 385.
40. Blaquiere, *Historical Review*, 54; Mirow, *Florida's First Constitution*, 272, 294–95.
41. Bethencourt, *The Inquisition*, 421.
42. Rodríguez López-Brea, *Don Luis de Borbón*, 215–16; Murphy, *Blanco White*, 89–90; Herr, "Constitution of 1812," 90.
43. Jefferson to Dupont de Nemours, 24 April 1816, in Jefferson, *Writings*, 1387–88.
44. Herr, "Constitution of 1812," 90.
45. Ibid., 91–92.
46. Saavedra, *Memorias*, 134, 149, 202; Weber, *Bárbaros*, 159; Morales Padrón, "México," 356–57.
47. Morales Padrón, "México," 357.
48. Saavedra, *Memorias*, 134; Israel, *Democratic Enlightenment*, 520–21; Weber, *Bárbaros*, 35.
49. Morelli, "Quito frente a la crisis," 431–33; Israel, *Democratic Enlightenment*, 397, 399, 517–18.
50. Rocafuerte, *Ensayo Político*, 31; Walter, "Revolution, Independence," 109.
51. Bushnell, *Simón Bolívar*, 9–12; Israel, *Democratic Enlightenment*, 503.
52. Saavedra, *Memorias*, 134; Ruiz Martínez, *Librería*, 25–26; McFarlane, "American Revolution," 41–42.
53. Morales Padrón, "México," 357.
54. Viceroy Flórez to Gálvez, Cartagena, 11 July 1781, Archivo General de Indias (Seville) section, Santa Fe 578/1.
55. Thibaud, "Salus populi," 341; Jordaan, *Slavernij en vrijheid*, 181.
56. Chassin, "Opinion publique," 259n.
57. Irisarri, *Semanario Republicano* 3 (21 August 1813): 20–21; McFarlane, "American Revolution," 44–45; Minchom, *People of Quito*, 242–43.
58. Morelli, "Quito frente a la crisis," 420–21.
59. Andrien, "Soberanía y revolución," 327–29, 333.
60. Chassin, "Opinion publique," 260–61.
61. Ibid., 261–63; Chiaramonte, *Ilustración en el Rio de la Plata*, 67–68.
62. Leal Curiel, "Juntismo caraqueño," 404–7; Quintero, "Movimiento," 392–95.
63. Walter, "Revolution, Independence," 109–10; Osterhammel, *Transformation*, 476.
64. Leal Curiel, "Juntismo caraqueño," 399–400; Thibaud, "Salus populi," 360–62.
65. Laviña, "Participación de pardos," 168–69.
66. Irisarri, *Semanario Republicano* 2 (14 August 1813), 10–12.
67. Blanco White, *Life*, 3:328.
68. García de Sena, *Independencia*, 33.
69. Bastin, Echeverri, and Campo, "Translation and the Emancipation," 59–61; Billias, *American Constitutionalism*, 115, 123.

70. Aldridge, *Early American Literature*, 233.
71. Ibid., 221, 224–26.
72. Bastin, Echeverri, and Campo, "Translation and the Emancipation," 60–61; Brewer-Carías, *Constituciones de Venezuela*, 1:126–27.
73. Irisarri, *Semanario Republicano* 7 (18 September 1813): 49–50.
74. Irisarri, *Semanario Republicano* 1 (7 August 1813): 2–4.
75. Irisarri, *Semanario Republicano* 2 (14 August 1813): 9–14; Walter, "Revolution, Independence," 120.
76. Irisarri, *Semanario Republicano* 8 (25 September 1813): 53.
77. Ibid., 63–64, 70.
78. Irisarri, *Semanario Republicano* 12 (28 October 1813): 89.
79. Breña, "Ideas, acontecimientos," 141; Gleijeses, "Limits of Sympathy," 481.
80. Roscio, *Triumfo de la libertad*, 11, 25, 28, 71–72; Ruiz Barrionuevo, "Juan Germán Roscio," 182–83, 189.
81. Ruiz Barrionuevo, "Juan Germán Roscio," 182–83; Aldridge, *Early American Literature*.
82. Billias, *American Constitutionalism*, 125–27.
83. Brewer-Carías, *Constituciones de Venezuela*, 1:117, 555–56.
84. Ibid., 1:560.
85. Bailyn, *Atlantic History*, 106; Brewer-Carías, *Constituciones de Venezuela*, 1:113, 563.
86. Martínez Garnica, "Experiencia," 372; Vanegas, "Actualización," 379.
87. Rodríguez, *Independence*, 70–71; Martínez Garnica, "Experiencia," 372–73; Vanegas, "Actualización," 378.
88. Martínez Garnica, "Experiencia," 375; Vanegas, "Actualización," 387.
89. Martínez Garnica, "Experiencia," 379–80.
90. Ortiz and Martínez Delgado, *El Periodismo*, xxiii–xxxiii.
91. Ibid., 29–30.
92. Ibid., 123–26.
93. Restrepo, *Historia de la Revolución*, 5:27.
94. Rodríguez, *Independence*, 150–57.
95. Restrepo, *Historia de la Revolución*, 5:27–28.
96. Andrien, "Soberanía y revolución," 331–34.
97. Rocafuerte, *Ensayo Político*, 8.
98. Fernández Sebastián, "'Voice of the People,'" 230–32.
99. Rocafuerte, *Ideas necesarias*, 9–10.
100. Ibid., 3–4.
101. Ibid., 78.
102. Rocafuerte, *Ensayo Político*, 31.
103. Rocafuerte, *Ideas necesarias*, 2–3.
104. Ibid., 11–12; see also Rocafuerte, *Ensayo Político*, 73; Aldridge, *Early American Literature*, 232.
105. Rocafuerte, *Ideas necesarias*, 8, 45–46, 61–62; see also Rocafuerte, *Ensayo Político*, 22, 37.
106. Rocafuerte, *Ensayo Político*, 31.
107. Rocafuerte, *Ideas necesarias*, 4, 6.
108. Ibid., 7–8; Aguilar Rivera, *Ausentes del universo*, 76–79.
109. Rocafuerte, *Ideas necesarias*, 17.

110. Ibid., 66, 71–72, 74, 77–78.
111. Ibid., 8–9; Rocafuerte, *Ensayo Político*, 19; Aguilar Rivera, *Ausentes del universo*, 74.
112. Rocafuerte, *Ensayo Político*, 6–7, 36.
113. Bushnell, *Simón Bolívar*, 15.
114. Ibid.,, 4, 96–97.
115. Brewer-Carías, *Constituciones de Venezuela*, 1:119–20.
116. Murphy, *Blanco White*, 78–79, 83.
117. Rodríguez, *Independence*, 117; Klooster, *Revolutions*, 138.
118. Rodríguez, *Independence*, 117–18; Adelman, *Sovereignty*, 214.
119. Elliott, *Empires*, 386–87.
120. Jefferson to Lafayette, Monticello, 3 November 1813, in Lafayette, *Mémoires*, 5:291–92; Breña, "Ideas, acontencimientos," 142–44.
121. Restrepo, *Historia de la Revolución*, 5:26, 110–11, 137, 139.
122. Ibid., v, 52, 78; Hamnett, "Popular Insurrection," 309–12.
123. Carr, *Spain, 1808–1939*, 120–21; Rodríguez, *Independence*, 105, 171.
124. Restrepo, *Historia de la Revolución*, 5:62–63; Suárez, *Cortes de Cádiz*, 197–98; Durán López, "Construcción," 93.
125. Bethencourt, *The Inquisition*, 421–22.
126. Carr, *Spain, 1808–1939*, 122–23; Schofield, *Utility and Democracy*, 208–9, 287.
127. [Jullien], *Revue Encyclopédique* 3 (July 1819): 345–51; Klooster, *Revolutions*, 139; Fitz, *Our Sister Republics*, 162–63.
128. Hamnett, "Popular Insurrection," 314, 316, 318–19; Adelman, *Sovereignty*, 275.
129. Schofield, *Utility and Democracy*, 208–10.
130. Klooster, *Revolutions*, 140; Blanchard, *Slavery and Abolition*, 9–10, 196; Lombardi, *Decline and Abolition*, 41.
131. Elliott, *Empires*, 393–94.
132. Gleijeses, "Limits of Sympathy," 483; Fitz, *Our Sister Republics*, 161–64.
133. Johnson, "United States–British Rivalry," 356.
134. Adams to Jefferson, 28 January 1818, in *Adams-Jefferson Letters*, 2:523; Bernier, *Lafayette*, 299.
135. Jefferson to Adams, Monticello, 17 May 1818, in *Adams-Jefferson Letters*, 2:524.
136. Lombardi, *Decline and Abolition*, 42; Blanchard, *Slavery and Abolition*, 195–96.
137. Quoted in Johnson, "United States–British Rivalry," 346.

Chapter 17: Reaction, Radicalism, and Américanisme under "the Restoration" (1814–30)

1. Quoted in Foot, *Red Shelley*, 46.
2. Johnson, "United States–British Rivalry," 350–53; Jarrett, *Congress of Vienna*, 314, 337–38; Schroeder, *Transformation*, 634–35.
3. Jefferson to Lafayette, 14 May 1817, in Jefferson, *Writings*, 1408.
4. Ibid., 1408–9.
5. Ibid., 1409.
6. Lafayette, *Mémoires*, 6:161, 232.
7. Shelley, *Poetical Works*, 4:40.
8. Ibid.; Angeloni, *Dell' Italia uscente*, 2:9–10; Thomas, *Philosophic Radicals*, 372–80.

9. Fenimore Cooper, *Gleanings in Europe*, xxii–xxiii.
10. Robinson, *Fight for Freedom*, 165–70; Beckles, "Struggle of Blacks," 71, 96.
11. Angeloni, *Dell' Italia uscente*, 1:83–84.
12. Bentham, *Three Tracts*, 10; Billias, *American Constitutionalism*, 143–44; Schroeder, *Transformation*, 430.
13. Van der Burg, *Nederland*, 258; Op de Beeck, *Verlies van België*, 77–97.
14. Jefferson to Madison, 12 May 1822, in *Republic*, 3:1840.
15. Jennings, *French Anti-Slavery*, 5–10.
16. Fuentes, *José Marchena*, 222–58, 262–70.
17. [Jullien], *Revue Encyclopédique* 9 (January 1821): 192 ; Wood, "Benjamin Constant," 14–15.
18. Shelley, *Poetical Works*, 4:41; McMahon, *Enemies*, 157–59.
19. Berlin, *Crooked Timber*, 137; Aprile, *La Révolution inachevée*, 15; Claudes, "Joseph de Maistre," 92, 95–99.
20. Stendhal, *Scarlet and Black*, 44.
21. [Jullien], *Revue Encyclopédique* 40 (October 1828): 8–9, 26.
22. Finch, *French Literature*, 71–72.
23. Bethencourt, *The Inquisition*, 421.
24. Flórez Estrada, *Representación*, 82–83; Petiteau, "La Restauration," 31–32; Duprat, "Le sacre de Charles X," 69–76.
25. McMahon, *Enemies*, 158–59, 165.
26. Rodríguez, *Independence*, 105, 171.
27. Flórez Estrada, *Representación*, 22.
28. Ibid., 20–21, 38–39, 41.
29. Aprile, *Siècle des exilés*, 83–84; Isabella, *Risorgimento*, 22–30.
30. [Jullien], *Revue Encyclopédique* 3 (1819): 494.
31. Kennedy, *Orders from France*, 344; Bruyère-Ostells, *Grande Armée*, 29–30.
32. Op de Beeck, *Verlies van België*, 7–16, 70–72.
33. Angeloni, *Dell' Italia uscente*, 2:3–4; Morandi, "Giuseppe Compagnoni," 260–61; Morelli, "The United States Constitution," 100, 102.
34. Salfi, *L'Italie au dix-neuvième siècle*, 91, 111–12.
35. Hobsbawm, *Age of Revolution*, 145; Zamoyski, *Holy Madness*, 183–85.
36. Davis, "Spanish Constitution of 1812," 2.
37. [Jullien], *Revue Encyclopédique* 1 (1819): 281–82.
38. Flórez Estrada, *Representación*, 32–37, 80–84.
39. Ibid., 57; Dérozier, *Manuel José Quintana*, 687–89.
40. Ruge, "Self-Critique," 246.
41. Finch, *French Literature*, 63.
42. Ruge, "Self-Critique," 245–46; Salfi, *L'Italie au dix-neuvième siècle*, 14–15, 42–44; Aaslestad, *Place and Politics*, 282–92, 313–20.
43. Ruge, "Self-Critique," 246–47.
44. Ibid., 259.
45. Jager, "After Atheism," 622; Roberts, *Shelley*, 30.
46. Roberts, *Shelley*, 44–45.
47. Hoagwood, *Skepticism and Ideology*, 174–76; Jager, "After Atheism," 613, 619–20; Roberts, *Shelley*, 83–85.
48. Roberts, *Shelley*, 44–45.

49. Shelley, *A Philosophical View*.
50. Shelley, *Poetical Works*, 4:41.
51. Hoagwood, *Skepticism and Ideology*, 144–45, 179–80; Foot, *Red Shelley*, 63.
52. Shelley, *Poetical Works*, 4:40–41; Hoagwood, *Skepticism and Ideology*, 179–80.
53. Dérozier, *Manuel José Quintana*, 687–88.
54. Butrón Prida, "Liberté, Nation," 177, 183, 189.
55. Blaquiere, *Historical Review*, 17, 54; Carr, *Spain, 1808–1939*, 130–31.
56. Blaquiere, *Historical Review*, 17.
57. Ibid., 54.
58. Fuentes, *José Marchena*, 280–83.
59. Ibid., 281.
60. Dérozier, *Manuel José Quintana*, 693, 700.
61. *Consejos que dirige á las Cortes y al pueblo español Jeremías Bentham: Traducidos del ingles por José Joaquín de Mora* (Madrid, 1820), 3.
62. Jarrett, *Congress of Vienna*, 309–10.
63. Blaquiere, *Historical Review*, 6; Fuentes, *José Marchena*, 292–97; Busaall, "Constitution," 111; Isabella, *Risorgimento*, 34–35.
64. Fuentes, *José Marchena*, 297–98.
65. [Jullien], *Revue Encyclopédique* 10 (April 1821): 200.
66. D. Holohan, introduction to d'Holbach, *Christianity Unveiled* (Kingston, Surrey, 2008), x.
67. Bethencourt, *The Inquisition*, 10–15.
68. Anna, "Independence," 83.
69. Foot, *Red Shelley*, 209; Paquette, *Imperial Portugal*, 112.
70. Shelley, *Poetical Works*, 4:40–41.
71. Davis, "Spanish Constitution of 1812," 2; Paquette, *Imperial Portugal*, 108–9.
72. Morelli, "The United States Constitution," 100, 102; Butrón Prida, "Liberté, Nation," 186–88.
73. Salfi, *L'Italie au dix-neuvième siècle*, 71–74; Schroeder, *Transformation*, 608, 610–11; Bruyère-Ostells, *Grande Armée*, 81–82, 100.
74. Wilcken, *Empire Adrift*, 79, 83.
75. Leite, *A Insurreição Pernambucana*, 21–23; Paquette, *Imperial Portugal*, 104.
76. Wilcken, *Empire Adrift*, 196.
77. Jefferson to Lafayette, 14 June 1817, in Jefferson, *Writings*, 1409.
78. Leite, *A Insurreição Pernambucana*, 38–39, 44–45; Wilcken, *Empire Adrift*, 192–98; Fitz, *Our Sister Republics*, 68–70.
79. Wilcken, *Empire Adrift*, 197–98; Schultz, *Tropical Versailles*, 244.
80. Barman, *Brazil*, 279n136.
81. Ibid., 120–22, 278; Schultz, *Tropical Versailles*, 280.
82. Murphy, *Blanco White*, 111–12; Busaall, "Constitution," 122–23.
83. Dérozier, *Manuel José Quintana*, 718–25; Fuentes, *José Marchena*, 284–86.
84. Bentham, *Three Tracts*, 3–4, 9–10.
85. De Champs, *Enlightenment and Utility*, 179.
86. Bentham, *Three Tracts*, 4–6, 47.
87. Blanco White, *Life*, 1:375; Murphy, *Blanco White*, 111.
88. [Jullien], *Revue Encyclopédique* 10 (April 1821): 170.
89. Lafayette, *Mémoires*, 6:161.

90. Jefferson to Adams, 12 September 1821, in *Adams-Jefferson Letters*, 2:574; Isabella, *Risorgimento*, 33–34.
91. Adams to Jefferson, 18 September 1823, in *Adams-Jefferson Letters*, 2:598.
92. Jefferson to Adams, 4 September 1823, in *Adams-Jefferson Letters*, 2:597.
93. Bethencourt, *The Inquisition*, 423.
94. Caron, "Mouvements insurrectionnels," 57.
95. Anna, "Independence," 84, 86, 89–90; Aguilar Rivera, *Ausentes del universo*, 70–71.
96. Anna, "Independence," 87–88.
97. Rocafuerte, *Ensayo Político*, 7.
98. Anna, "Independence," 93.
99. Quoted in Unger, *John Quincy Adams*, 217.
100. Duprat, "Le sacre de Charles X," 70–71.
101. Lafayette, *Mémoires*, 6:158.
102. Adams to Jefferson, 15 August 1823, in *Adams-Jefferson Letters*, 2:594–95.
103. Jefferson to Adams, 4 September 1823, in *Adams-Jefferson Letters*, 2:596.
104. Fitz, *Our Sister Republics*, 187–90; Unger, *John Quincy Adams*, 216.
105. Peterson, *Thomas Jefferson*, 937, 1001–2; Unger, *John Quincy Adams*, 217.
106. Unger, *Last Founding Father*, 316.
107. Paquette, *Imperial Portugal*, 189.
108. Unger, *John Quincy Adams*, 216–17; Osterhammel, *Transformation*, 100.
109. Gleijeses, "Limits of Sympathy," 489; Jarrett, *Congress of Vienna*, 342–43.
110. Rémond, *Les États-Unis*, 2:602.
111. Angeloni, *Dell' Italia uscente*, 2:8–10.
112. Rémond, *Les États-Unis*, 2:570–77, 626–28.
113. Ibid., 1:288–96.
114. Ibid., 1:300–302, 306.
115. Grove Jones, *An Examination*, iii–iv.
116. Ibid., 46–47.
117. Rémond, *Les États-Unis*, 1:421–27.
118. [Jullien], *Revue Encyclopédique* 10 (April 1821): 381; Sehat, *Myth*, 54–55.
119. [Jullien], *Revue Encyclopédique* 5 (January 1820): 7, 15–16; Palmer, *From Jacobin to Liberal*, 181; Isabella, *Risorgimento*, 43–44.
120. Wood, *Radicalism*, 294.
121. Jefferson to Adams, 12 September 1821, in *Adams-Jefferson Letters*, 2:575.
122. Palmer, *From Jacobin to Liberal*, 180.
123. Stelling-Michaud, "Sismondi," 157, 160; De Luca, "Benjamin Constant," 111; Tillet, "La place ambiguë de Jean-Louis de Lolme," 204–5.
124. Stelling-Michaud, "Sismondi," 154–55; De Luca, "Benjamin Constant," 110–12.
125. Schoorl, *Jean-Baptiste Say*, 161–62.
126. Sismondi, "L'Amérique," 34; Palmer, *From Jacobin to Liberal*, 192–93.
127. Steckel, "African American Population," 435.
128. Ibid.
129. Sismondi, " L'Amérique," 34–36; [Jullien], *Revue Encyclopédique* 34 (April 1827): 54.
130. Isabella, *Risorgimento*, 43; Auricchio, *The Marquis*, 301.
131. Fenimore Cooper, *American Democrat*, 138.
132. Rémond, *Les États-Unis*, 1:296; Goetzmann, *Beyond the Revolution*, 157–58.
133. Fenimore Cooper, *American Democrat*, 78–79.

134. Dekker and Johnston, "Introduction," 23.
135. Goetzmann, *Beyond the Revolution*, 159–60.
136. Dekker and Johnston, "Introduction," 8; Jaume, *Tocqueville*, 143–44.
137. Fenimore Cooper, *American Democrat*, 122.
138. Ibid., 128–34, 171–73.
139. Ibid., 185.
140. Emerson, *Political Writings*, 120; Fawcett, *Liberalism*, 32.
141. Fenimore Cooper, *American Democrat*, 128.
142. Ibid., 130, 132.
143. Ibid., 180–86; Wood, *Empire of Liberty*, 732.

Chapter 18: The Greek Revolution (1770–1830)

1. Rosen, *Bentham, Byron*, 248–49.
2. Schroeder, *Transformation*, 615; Osterhammel, *Transformation*, 137.
3. Shelley, *Poetical Works*, 4:41; Gourgouris, *Dream Nation*, 127; Foot, *Red Shelley*, 209; Zamoyski, *Holy Madness*, 234–38.
4. Kitromilides, *Enlightenment*, 43–49; Israel, *Enlightenment Contested*, 322–24.
5. Kitromilides, *Enlightenment*, 130–35; Gourgouris, *Dream Nation*, 72–73; Israel, *Democratic Enlightenment*, 617–18.
6. Kitromilides, *Enlightenment*, 135–39.
7. Brewer, *Greek War*, 17; Gourgouris, *Dream Nation*, 84–85; Zamoyski, *Holy Madness*, 122–23.
8. Israel, *Revolutionary Ideas*, 654, 659–61; Brewer, *Greek War*, 17–19; Kitromilides, *Enlightenment*, 214.
9. [Jullien], *Revue Encyclopédique* 1 (January 1819): 175–76, 384–85, 542–43; 3 (July 1819): 371–72; and 4 (October 1819): 197, 574; Brewer, *Greek War*, 14–15.
10. [Jullien], *Revue Encyclopédique* 5 (January 1820): 427–30 and 9 (January 1821): 20.
11. [Jullien], *Revue Encyclopédique* 5 (January 1820): 425–26.
12. Shelley, *Poetical Works*, 4:40–41.
13. Jarrett, *Congress of Vienna*, 297–99, 306–7.
14. Rosen, *Bentham, Byron*, 80–83; Koliopoulos and Veremis, *Greece*, 39.
15. Fleming, *Greece*, 16–17.
16. Koliopoulos and Veremis, *Greece*, 36.
17. Kitromilides, "Adamantios Korais," 220–21; Fleming, *Greece*, 18.
18. Kors, *Encyclopedia of the Enlightenment*, 2:159.
19. Mackridge, "Koraís and the Greek Language," 127, 133.
20. Kitromilides, *Enlightenment*, 277.
21. Evrigenis, "Enlightenment Emancipation, and National Identity," 99.
22. Kitromilides, *Enlightenment*, 263, 272, 277, 284.
23. Mourdoukoutas, "Koraís and the Idea of Progress," 235; Kitromilides, *Enlightenment*, 184.
24. Gourgouris, *Dream Nation*, 91.
25. Kitromilides, *Enlightenment*, 188.
26. Ibid., 179–80.
27. Bartlett, *Daniel Webster*, 101–3; Mayers, *Dissenting Voices*, 65–74.

28. Brewer, *Greek War*, 24; Kitromilides, "Adamantios Koraís," 214; Mayers, *Dissenting Voices*, 72–76.
29. Flemming, *Greece*, 15; Showalter, *Civil Wars*, 26.
30. Adams to Jefferson, 29 December 1823, in *Adams-Jefferson Letters*, 2:602.
31. Kitromilides, *Enlightenment*, 285; Mayers, *Dissenting Voices*, 64.
32. Quoted in Kitromilides, *Enlightenment*, 290.
33. Lafayette, *Mémoires*, 6:245, 257; Shelley, *Poetical Works*, 4:41.
34. Fenimore Cooper, *Notions of the Americans*, 1:39; Kramer, "America's Lafayette," 228, 231.
35. Lafayette, *Mémoires*, 6:167–68, 173–74, 223; Unger, *Last Founding Father*, 28–30, 334–35.
36. Lafayette, *Mémoires*, 6:185; Bruyère-Ostells, *Grande Armée*, 127.
37. Fenimore Cooper, *Notions of the Americans*, 2:142–43.
38. Loveland, *Emblem*, 106–7, 114–15; Mayers, *Dissenting Voices*, 59–60.
39. Gleijeses, "Limits of Sympathy," 481.
40. Isabella, *Risorgimento*, 34–35, 43–44.
41. Fenimore Cooper, *Notions of the Americans*, 1:201; Neely, "Politics," 151, 157; Bernier, *Lafayette*, 343.
42. Whitman, *Complete Poetry and Collected Prose*.
43. Fenimore Cooper, *Notions of the Americans*, 2:136–37, 179–83; Kramer, *Lafayette*, 107.
44. Loveland, *Emblem*, 115.
45. Lafayette, *Mémoires*, 6:190; Wood, *Empire of Liberty*, 700–701; McCullough, *John Adams*, 637.
46. Isabella, *Risorgimento*, 43.
47. Bernier, *Lafayette*, 341–42; Auricchio, *The Marquis*, 300–301.
48. Bernier, *Lafayette*, 345–46.
49. Fenimore Cooper, *Notions of the Americans*, 1:109; Kramer, "Lafayette and the Historians," 392; Loveland, *Emblem*, 113–14.
50. Neely, "Politics," 162, 164–66, 169; Kramer, *Lafayette*, 104.
51. Lafayette, *Mémoires*, 6:181; Neely, "Politics," 170–71; Kramer, *Lafayette*, 111–12.
52. Kramer, *Lafayette*, 113.
53. Lafayette, *Mémoires*, 6:23; Neely, "Politics," 163, 166.
54. Barman, *Brazil*, 110–11, 118–25; Johnson, "United States–British Rivalry," 358.
55. Quoted in Koliopoulos and Veremis, *Greece*, 39.
56. Bruyère-Ostells, *Grande Armée*, 117.
57. Isabella, *Risorgimento*, 86.
58. Bruyère-Ostells, *Grande Armée*, 119–26.
59. Brewer, *Greek War*, 242–43, 339; Showalter, *Civil Wars*, 23–28; Mayers, *Dissenting Voices*, 59.
60. Brewer, *Greek War*, 350; Hobsbawm, *Age of Revolution*, 132–33; Mayers, *Dissenting Voices*, 76.

Chapter 19: The Freedom-Fighters of the 1830s

1. Jefferson to Adams, 12 September 1821, in *Adams-Jefferson Letters*, 2:575.
2. Jefferson to Adams, 4 September 1823, in *Adams-Jefferson Letters*, 2:596.

3. Palmer, *From Jacobin to Liberal*, 138–39; Foot, *Red Shelley*, 46, 202–3.
4. Foot, *Red Shelley*, 196.
5. Bruyère-Ostells, *Grande Armée*, 26–29.
6. Sperber, *Rhineland Radicals*, 70–71; Wende, *Radikalismus*, 22–23.
7. Wende, *Radikalismus*, 21, 28.
8. Kieniewicz, "Revolutionary Nobleman," 276.
9. Zamoyski, *Holy Madness*, 327–28.
10. Fenimore Cooper, *Notions of the Americans*, 2:122.
11. Emerson, "The American Scholar," 11; Ellis, *After the Revolution*, 219–20; Dolan, *Emerson's Liberalism*, 14, 20, 40–41, 55, 68, 70; Koch, "Revolution," 129–30.
12. Reynolds, *European Revolutions*, 59–62.
13. Bury and Tombs, *Thiers*, 27; Zamoyski, *Holy Madness*, 257–58; Vincent, *Benjamin Constant*, 200.
14. Caron, "Mouvements insurrectionnels," 52–55.
15. Bury and Tombs, *Thiers*, 19–20, 29–31.
16. Lafayette, *Mémoires*, 6:417, 423; Bruyère-Ostells, *Grande Armée*, 207–9.
17. Gossman, "Jules Michelet"; Gossman, "Michelet and the French Revolution," 645.
18. Curtis, "American Opinion," 253.
19. Lafayette, *Mémoires*, 6:385.
20. Ibid.; Fureix, "Les trois Glorieuses," 64.
21. Quoted in Curtis, "American Opinion," 253.
22. Fureix, "Les trois Glorieuses," 63.
23. Palmer, *From Jacobin to Liberal*, 143–44; Furet, *Revolutionary France*, 322–26, 388; Zamoyski, *Holy Madness*, 259; Bruyère-Ostells, *Grande Armée*, 223.
24. Sarrans, *Lafayette et la Révolution*, 1:248; Bernier, *Lafayette*, 358–59; Aprile, *La Révolution inachevée*, 56–64.
25. Fenimore Cooper, *Gleanings in Europe*, 67–69.
26. Ibid.; Darriulat, *Les Patriotes*, 20–21, 24.
27. Bury and Tombs, *Thiers*, 33–37; Pilbeam, *The 1830 Revolution*, 152–53.
28. Lafayette, *Mémoires*, 6:423–25; Pilbeam, *The 1830 Revolution*, 65–66.
29. Lafayette, *Mémoires*, 6:684–85; Fureix, "Introduction," 19; Bruyère-Ostells, *Grande Armée*, 228–29; Fawcett, *Liberalism*, 49.
30. Mill, *Autobiography*, 132.
31. Ibid., 131.
32. Kramer, *Lafayette*, 115; Foot, *Red Shelley*, 196–97.
33. Thomas, *Philosophic Radicals*, 175; Isabella, *Risorgimento*, 149.
34. Furet, *Revolutionary France*, 309–11; Wood, "Benjamin Constant," 17–19; Vincent, *Benjamin Constant*, 200–201, 208–10.
35. Marx, "Eighteenth Brumaire," 258; Börne, *Briefe aus Paris*, 1:139–41; Wood, "Benjamin Constant," 18.
36. Lafayette, *Mémoires*, 6:621.
37. Fenimore Cooper, *Gleanings in Europe*, 255–56.
38. Fureix, "Les trois Glorieuses," 70; Pilbeam, *The 1830 Revolution*, 5–6.
39. Börne, *Briefe aus Paris*, 1:173; Wood, "Benjamin Constant," 17–19.
40. Guizot, *Démocratie*, 10–13; Furet, *Revolutionary France*, 361, 364.
41. Guizot, *Démocratie*, 28–29; Pilbeam, *The 1830 Revolution*, 5.

42. Guizot, *Démocratie*, 36.
43. Ibid., 37–39.
44. Jaume, *Tocqueville*, 256–58, 261.
45. Peterson, *Thomas Jefferson*, 1002–3; Wood, *Radicalism*, 367.
46. Fenimore Cooper, *American Democrat*, 181–83, 186.
47. Quoted in Curtis, "American Opinion," 250.
48. Ibid.
49. Ibid., 252.
50. Aprile, "Des cantons suisses," 87; Caron, "Mouvements insurrectionnels," 58–59; Wegert, *German Radicals*, 117.
51. Op de Beeck, *Verlies van België*, 88–90.
52. Kossmann, *Low Countries*, 152–55.
53. Op de Beeck, *Verlies van België*, 98–102.
54. Witte, "Belgique," 137.
55. Ibid., 138–39; Kossmann, *Low Countries*, 154–56.
56. Börne, *Briefe aus Paris*, 2:1–3.
57. Witte, "Belgique," 139–40.
58. Fureix, "Introduction," 29; Billias, *American Constitutionalism*, 156; Caron, "De la Belgique," 74–75.
59. Witte, "Belgique," 142; Dubois, *L'Invention de la Belgique*, 186, 238.
60. Aprile, "Des cantons suisses," 85–88; Wegert, *German Radicals*, 108–10, 112; Nipperdey, *Germany*, 324–27.
61. Börne, *Briefe aus Paris*, 1:160, 175–76; Ohles, *Germany's Rude Awakening*, 96–97; Maissen, *Geschichte der Schweiz*, 186–87.
62. Maissen, *Geschichte der Schweiz*, 189–90.
63. Wegert, *German Radicals*, 116–17.
64. Börne, "Ninth Letter" (Paris, 6 October 1830) in *Briefe aus Paris*, 1:83–86.
65. Arendt, *On Revolution*, 263.
66. Ramm, *Germany*, 161–62, 164; Wegert, *German Radicals*, 110–11; Nipperdey, *Germany*, 324.
67. Börne, *Briefe aus Paris*, 2:14–16; Ohles, *Germany's Rude Awakening*, 12, 25–27; Nipperdey, *Germany*, 324–25, 330.
68. Wegert, *German Radicals*, 131–43.
69. Caron, "Marges latines," 99; Bruyère-Ostells, *Grande Armée*, 256–60.
70. Kieniewicz, "Revolutionary Nobleman," 276.
71. Morse, *Sermon* (19 February 1795): 17; Davis, *Revolutions*, 30.
72. Morse, *Sermon* (19 February 1795): 23n24.
73. Nash and Gao Hodges, *Friends of Liberty*, 2, 87–88.
74. Billias, *American Constitutionalism*, 167; Nash and Gao Hodges, *Friends of Liberty*, 107.
75. Nash and Gao Hodges, *Friends of Liberty*, 100–101, 106–9.
76. Morse, *Sermon* (19 February 1795): 23–24.
77. Nash and Gao Hodges, *Friends of Liberty*, 156–60.
78. Cienciala, "American Founding Fathers and Poland," 118.
79. Kieniewicz, "Revolutionary Nobleman," 276–81.
80. Ibid., 279, 282; Baranska, "Pologne," 147.

81. Zamoyski, *Holy Madness*, 272–74.
82. Jędruch, *Constitutions*, 222–23; Baranska, "Pologne," 148–49.
83. Lewalski, "Lelewel's Third Exile," 33.
84. Ibid., 34–35.
85. Adams, *Memoirs*, 8:269–70; Mayers, *Dissenting Voices*, 61.
86. Adams, *Memoirs*, 8:269; Unger, *John Quincy Adams*, 217.
87. Adams, *Memoirs*, 8:270.
88. Ibid.; Beckles, "Struggle of Blacks," 67.
89. Wende, *Radikalismus*, 13, 23–25.
90. Nipperdey, *Germany*, 326–27.
91. Ibid.; Wende, *Radikalismus*, 23.
92. Heuberger, *Ludwig Börne*, 20.
93. Görisch and Mayer, *Untersuchungsberichte*, 42, 276–77, 280–81, 358; Wende, *Radikalismus*, 41–44.
94. Wirth, "Rede von Johann Georg August Wirth," 31–33.
95. Ibid., 34.
96. Wegert, *German Radicals*, 153–56; Sperber, *Rhineland Radicals*, 112, 152, 175, 217–18.
97. Sperber, *Rhineland Radicals*, 112.
98. Wegert, *German Radicals*, 147–48; Wende, *Radikalismus*, 23–25.
99. Görisch and Mayer, *Untersuchungsberichte*, 11; Ohles, *Germany's Rude Awakening*, 37–41, 44.
100. Görisch and Mayer, *Untersuchungsberichte*, 331, 335–45, 357; Nipperdey, *Germany*, 330.
101. Heine, *Zur Geschichte*, 244.
102. Görisch and Meyer, *Untersuchungsberichte*, 42–43, 276–84.
103. Sheehan, "The German States," 262–63.
104. Ibid., 263–64.
105. Lewalski, "Lelewel's Third Exile," 33, 38.
106. Emerson, *Complete Works*, 5:97.
107. Elazar, "Liberty," 418, 425, 429, 438; Thomas, *Philosophic Radicals*, 19, 21, 28–29, 125, 408.
108. Crook, "Whiggery and America," 191.
109. Emerson, *Complete Works*, 5:97.
110. Schofield, *Utility and Democracy*, 336; Osterhammel, *Transformation*, 603.
111. Reynolds, *European Revolutions*, 30–31; Melville, *Mardi*, 417–18.
112. Pilbeam, *The 1830 Revolution*, 150–51, 180–84; Merriman, "Contested Freedoms," 179–80; Aprile, *La Révolution inachevée*, 74–77.
113. Merriman, "Contested Freedoms," 181; Furet, *Revolutionary France*, 361–64.
114. Bury and Tombs, *Thiers*, 52–55; Aprile, *Siècle des exilés*, 83, 87.
115. Lafayette, *Mémoires*, 6:664–65, 666–71; Bury and Tombs, *Thiers*, 47–48; Caron, "Mouvements insurrectionnels," 59.
116. Aprile, *La Révolution inachevée*, 127; Vigier, *Paris*, 89–92.
117. Aprile, *La Révolution inachevée*, 105–8.
118. Pilbeam, *The 1830 Revolution*, 162.
119. Ibid., 84; Merriman, "Contested Freedoms," 179.
120. Aprile, *La Révolution inachevée*, 76, 78–81; Darriulat, *Les Patriotes*, 55.

Chapter 20: The Revolutions of 1848

1. Handlin, "The American Scene," 34; Wood, *Empire of Liberty*, 506–7; Foner, *Story*, 71–73, 81.
2. Maissen, *Geschichte der Schweiz*, 202; Billias, *American Constitutionalism*, 192.
3. Maissen, *Geschichte der Schweiz*, 200–201; Hobsbawm, *Age of Revolution*, 364.
4. Ledru-Rollin, *Discours politiques*, 1:328, 338; Vigier, *Paris*, 549n.
5. Ledru-Rollin, *Discours politiques*, 1:340–43, 348–49; Rapport, *1848*, 39, 56–57; Darriulat, *Les Patriotes*, 161.
6. Fuller, *At Home and Abroad*, 251; Chevigny, *The Woman*, 431, 436–37.
7. Fuller, *At Home and Abroad*, 254, 387; Allen, "Political and Social Criticism," 565–66.
8. Fuller, *At Home and Abroad*, 249.
9. Marraro, *American Opinion*, 36–37; Blanchard, *Margaret Fuller*, 285–86.
10. Ledru-Rollin, *Discours politiques*, 1:370–71; Rapport, *1848*, 38; Vigier, *Paris*, 548–50.
11. Haubtmann, *Proudhon*, 543, 587–88, 712; Vincent, *Pierre-Joseph Proudhon*, 156–57; Jennings, *Revolution*, 98–99.
12. Lamartine, *Histoire*, 1:16–17; Fortescue, *Alphonse de Lamartine*, 44, 64, 99.
13. Whitman, *The Journalism*, 2:307–8.
14. Reynolds, *European Revolutions*, 20; Jennings, *Revolution*, 265.
15. Lamartine, *Histoire*, 1:17–19.
16. Mitchell, *Battle Summer*, 55.
17. Ibid.
18. Quoted in Reynolds, *European Revolutions*, 134.
19. Mitchell, *Battle Summer*, 68.
20. Darriulat, *Les Patriotes*, 171–75, 193.
21. Darriulat, *Les Patriotes*, 193–94.
22. Aprile, *La Révolution inachevée*, 285–86.
23. Mitchell, *Battle Summer*, 95.
24. Vincent, *Pierre-Joseph Proudhon*, 169–75.
25. Mill, *Autobiography*, 174.
26. Reynolds, *European Revolutions*, 9.
27. Fuller, *At Home and Abroad*, 305; Chevigny, *The Woman*, 445–46.
28. Chevigny, *The Woman*, 446.
29. Bancroft, *Letters*, 2:31–32.
30. Bayly, *Birth of the Modern World*, 156–57.
31. Fortescue, *Alphonse de Lamartine*, 221.
32. Gunkel, "Halbe gegen Ganze," 44; Nipperdey, *Germany*, 346; Ramm, *Germany*, 170.
33. Sperber, *Rhineland Radicals*, 146–51.
34. Gunkel, "Halbe gegen Ganze," 44–45; Zamoyski, *Holy Madness*, 342, 408; Rapport, *1848*, 118–19.
35. Sperber, *Rhineland Radicals*, 243–45, 247.
36. Ibid., 232–33, 249–50.
37. Ibid., 249, 267, 491.
38. Ibid., 226–32; Wegert, *German Radicals*, 247, 267.
39. Robertson, *Revolutions*, 206–17.

40. Wegert, *German Radicals*, 229–55.
41. Sheehan, "The German States," 269–74; Rapport, *1848*, 120–21.
42. Aprile, *La Révolution inachevée*, 277–78.
43. Ibid., 290–92.
44. Sammons, *Heinrich Heine*, 299, 301.
45. Jack, *George Sand*, 297–99.
46. Furet, *Revolutionary France*, 401, 419.
47. Vincent, *Pierre-Joseph Proudhon*, 168–69, 175.
48. Aprile, *La Révolution inachevée*, 298–99.
49. Jack, *George Sand*, 300.
50. Lévêque, "Revolutionary Crisis," 102; Aprile, *La Révolution inachevée*, 300–303.
51. Woodcock, *Pierre-Joseph Proudhon*, 125.
52. Marx, "Class Struggles," 160; Fortescue, *Alphonse de Lamartine*, 239.
53. Rapport, *1848*, 186–88; Fortescue, *Alphonse de Lamartine*, 176–77.
54. Emerson, *Letters*, 4:72–73; Chouraqui, "At the Crossroads," 20–21.
55. Robertson, *Revolutions*, 89–94; Rapport, *1848*, 202–4; Vincent, *Pierre-Joseph Proudhon*, 180–86.
56. Higonnet, *Sister Republics*, 278–79; Jourdan, *La Révolution*, 398–99.
57. Robertson, *Revolutions*, 87–96; Furet, *Revolutionary France*, 404–6; Vincent, *Pierre-Joseph Proudhon*, 181–82; Fortescue, *Alphonse de Lamartine*, 183–87.
58. Lévêque, "Revolutionary Crisis," 103.
59. Ledru-Rollin, *Discours politiques*, 2:90–93, 96, 102; Jennings, *Revolution*, 57.
60. Ledru-Rollin, *Discours politiques*, 2:105–10.
61. Sammons, *Heinrich Heine*, 301–2.
62. Mill, *Autobiography*, 179; Kloppenberg, *Toward Democracy*, 653–54.
63. Burrow, *Crisis of Reason*, 1–2, 27–30; Jacobitti, *Revolutionary Humanism*, 9, 36, 39–41, 49.
64. Berkowitz, *Virtue and the Making*, 161.

Chapter 21: American Reaction (1848–52)

1. Parker, *Melville*, 1:589.
2. *New York Daily Tribune* 8, no. 308 (4 April 1848): 1.
3. Ibid.
4. Wilentz, *Rise of American Democracy*, 539–45; Kloppenberg, *Toward Democracy*, 637–38.
5. Chaput, "Proslavery and Antislavery Politics," 663; Wilentz, *Rise of American Democracy*, 542–44; Coleman, "The Dorr War."
6. Honeck, *We Are the Revolutionists*, 143–46.
7. Wiecek, "'A Peculiar Conservatism,'" 239; Chaput, "Proslavery and Antislavery Politics," 659–70; Wilentz, *Rise of American Democracy*, 542–45.
8. Taylor, "Down with the Crown," 50–51, 95.
9. Bancroft, *Letters*, 2:92.
10. *New York Daily Tribune* 8, no. 308 (4 April 1848): 1.
11. Emerson, *Complete Works*, 5:264; Koch, "Revolution," 132.
12. Parker, *Melville*, 1:588; Reynolds, *European Revolutions*, 9–10.

13. Reynolds, *European Revolutions*, 11.
14. *Brooklyn Daily Eagle*, 6 April 1848, 2.
15. Ibid.
16. Reynolds, *European Revolutions*, 14; Jacoby, *Freethinkers*, 214–15.
17. Smith, "Fortunate Banner," 30–31.
18. Quoted in Reynolds, *European Revolutions*, 20, 135–36.
19. Gazley, *American Opinion*, 22, 26.
20. Reynolds, *European Revolutions*, 11–12; Erkilla, "Melville, Whitman," 257–59.
21. *Brooklyn Daily Eagle*, 6 April 1848, 2.
22. Fortescue, *Alphonse de Lamartine*, 211–12; Curtis, "American Opinion," 255–56; Curti, "The Impact," 209; Rohrs, "American Critics," 362–63.
23. Petranovich and Holbreich, "Valley of the Dry Bones," 209, 220n9.
24. Foner, *Story*, 82–83, 86–90; Kloppenberg, *Toward Democracy*, 672–76.
25. Quoted in Stuurman, *Invention of Humanity*, 378.
26. Quoted in Mayers, *Dissenting Voices*, 109.
27. Ibid., 118.
28. Sanders, *Vanguard*, 75–76; Guyatt, *Providence*, 218–19, 221; Mayers, *Dissenting Voices*, 118, 120–23.
29. Mayers, *Dissenting Voices*, 126–27.
30. Wood, *Empire of Liberty*, 538, 599; Jacoby, *Freethinkers*, 379n9.
31. Quoted in Bancroft, *Letters*, 2:91; see also Wood, *Empire of Liberty*, 201–2; Wilentz, *Rise of American Democracy*, 321, 485–86, 644.
32. Bartlett, *Daniel Webster*, 249, 252–53; Berlin, *Long Emancipation*, 149–50.
33. Emerson, *Political Writings*, 139; Lee, *Slavery, Philosophy*, 179, 192.
34. Emerson, *Political Writings*, 135; Handlin, "The American Scene," 38–39.
35. Emerson, *Political Writings*, 138–39; Lee, *Slavery, Philosophy*, 191–93; Koch, "Revolution," 134.
36. Blackburn, *Overthrow*, 496–98; Rohrs, "American Critics," 367.
37. Rohrs, "American Critics," 365.
38. Hutcheson, "Louisville Riots," 162.
39. Ibid., 150–51; Frost, *Perfect Freedom*, 154; Sehat, *Myth*, 155, 158.
40. Frost, *Perfect Freedom*, 154–58; Meacham, *American Gospel*, 135–36.
41. *New York Daily Tribune* 8, no. 308 (4 April 1848): 1.
42. Wilentz, *Chants Democratic*, 381.
43. Ibid., 368, 373, 377.
44. Weitling, *Die Menschheit*, chapter 1; Wilentz, *Chants Democratic*, 355–56.
45. Haubtmann, *Proudhon*, 444–45.
46. Ibid., 632, 637.
47. Foner, *Story*, 63; Wilentz, *Chants Democratic*, 338, 369.
48. Lause, *Young America*, 31.
49. Dobert, "The Radicals," 178–79; Rapport, *1848*, 213; Wilentz, *Chants Democratic*, 368–69.
50. Zucker, *Forty-Eighters*, 354; Sperber, *Rhineland Radicals*, 123; Wilentz, *Chants Democratic*, 385–86.
51. Goetzmann, *Beyond the Revolution*, 159–60.
52. Smith, "Fortunate Banner," 32; Wilentz, *Rise of American Democracy*, 591–93.
53. Huston, *Land and Freedom*, 152–55; Wilentz, *Chants Democratic*, 340, 369.

54. Devyr, *Our Natural Rights*, 14; McDowell, *Ireland*, 239.
55. Foner, *Story*, 63; Zilversmit, *First Emancipation*, 218–19; Huston, *Land and Freedom*, 183, 188.
56. Huston, *Land and Freedom*, 166–67.
57. Rohrs, "American Critics," 371; Curtis, "American Opinion," 258.
58. Curti, "Impact," 211.
59. Bancroft, *Letters*, 2:91.
60. Dwight, *Roman Republic of 1849*, 22–23; Osterhammel, *Transformation*, 546.
61. Foner, *Story*, 77–78, 98.
62. Ibid., 77; Blanchard, *Margaret Fuller*, 286, 301.
63. Rohrs, "American Critics," 373.
64. Ibid., 375; Goetzmann, *Beyond the Revolution*, 252.
65. Bancroft, *Letters*, 2:33; Rapport, *1848*, 331–32; Billias, *American Constitutionalism*, 178, 182–83.
66. Bancroft, *Letters*, 2:92.
67. Ibid., 2:37.
68. Gazley, *American Opinion*, 18, 27; Rohrs, "American Critics," 374; Reynolds, *European Revolutions*, 15.
69. Jennings, *Revolution*, 94–95; Billias, *American Constitutionalism*, 180–83.
70. Reynolds, *European Revolutions*, 24–25; Goldner, *Herman Melville*.
71. Goldner, *Herman Melville*, 20, 128–29; Davis, *Revolutions*, 180.
72. Arendt, *On Revolution*, 76–82; Erkilla, "Melville, Whitman," 258, 270–71.
73. Reynolds, *European Revolutions*, 50–51.
74. Dwight, *Roman Republic of 1849*, ix; Fuller, *These Sad But Glorious Days*, 257–58, 276.
75. Taylor, "Down with the Crown," 51.
76. Emerson, *Complete Works*, 5:172; Reynolds, *European Revolutions*, 32–33.
77. Emerson, *Letters*, 4:77; Koch, "Revolution," 132.
78. Emerson, *Letters*, 4:76; Rusk, *Life of Ralph Waldo Emerson*, 346–53.
79. Emerson, *Letters*, 4:73–74; Reynolds, *European Revolutions*, 34.
80. Reynolds, *European Revolutions*, 36.
81. Emerson, *Letters*, 4:79.
82. Fuller, *At Home and Abroad*, 381.
83. Davidson, *How Revolutionary Were the Bourgeois Revolutions?* 144.
84. Fuller, *These Sad But Glorious Days*, 259; Gemme, "Domesticating Foreign Struggles," 77.
85. Fuller, *These Sad But Glorious Days*, 259, 276–77; Koch, "Revolution," 131.
86. Mack Smith, *Mazzini*, 69, 85.
87. Dwight, *Roman Republic of 1849*, 12; Fuller, *At Home and Abroad*, 380.
88. Mack Smith, *Mazzini*, 65–69.
89. Blanchard, *Margaret Fuller*, 312–14.
90. Fuller, *At Home and Abroad*, 255; Marraro, *American Opinion*, 76–86; Connell, "Darker Aspects," 18.
91. Greeley, *Glances at Europe*, 142.
92. Ibid., 143.
93. Gossman, "Jules Michelet," 594; Creyghton, "Vaderfiguren," 26.
94. Poesche and Goepp, *The New Rome*, 25–26.

95. Ibid., 96; Gossman, *Basel*, 228–30, 234.
96. Sperber, *Rhineland Radicals*, 123.
97. Zucker, *Forty-Eighters*, 270.
98. Ibid., 275.
99. Poesche and Goepp, *The New Rome*, 99–100; Zucker, *Forty-Eighters*, 162, 326.
100. Poesche and Goepp, *The New Rome*, 11–19; Dobert, "The Radicals," 162.
101. Poesche and Goepp, *The New Rome*, 15.
102. Ibid., 71.
103. Ibid., 47.
104. Ibid., 56–57, 95.
105. Hutcheson, "Louisville Riots," 151–52.
106. Dobert, "The Radicals," 169–70; Mastellone, *Mazzini and Marx*, 137.
107. Sperber, *Rhineland Radicals*, 492; Honeck, *We Are the Revolutionists*, 137–39.
108. Dobert, "The Radicals," 171–72; Curti, "Impact," 215.
109. Dobert, "The Radicals," 173–74; Honeck, *We Are the Revolutionists*, 29, 32, 43.
110. Hutcheson, "Louisville Riots," 152–53.
111. Kloppenberg, *Toward Democracy*, 707–8.

Conclusion

1. Stewart, *Nature's God*, 429.
2. Condorcet, "De l'influence de la Révolution de l'Amérique," 4.
3. Jefferson to R. C. Weightman, Monticello, 24 June 1826, in Jefferson, *Writings*, 1517; see also Rahe, *Republics*, 336–37; Armitage, *Declaration*, 2.
4. Brissot, *Mémoire aux États-Généraux*, 70–71; Israel, *Revolutionary Ideas*, 41.
5. King, *Arendt and America*, 85, 225–27, 245.
6. Arendt, *On Revolution*, 54–56, 61; King, *Arendt and America*, 23, 96, 220–21, 227–28, 245.
7. Arendt, *On Revolution*, 62–68; King, *Arendt and America*, 248–50.
8. Melville, *Mardi*, 412; Reynolds, *European Revolutions*, 14, 49–50; Erkkila, "Melville, Whitman," 6–7.
9. Israel, "Philosophy, Religion," 115–22; De Bolla, *Architecture of Concepts*, 74–76.
10. De Bolla, *Architecture of Concepts*, 12n3, 48n1, 56n17, 245.
11. Moyn, *Last Utopia*, 24.
12. Adams to Jefferson, 13 November 1815, in *Adams-Jefferson Letters*, 2:456–57.
13. Lundberg and May, "The Enlightened Reader," 270.
14. May, *Enlightenment in America*, 176; Cotlar, *Tom Paine's America*, 213–14.
15. Goldner, *Herman Melville*, 45, 119.
16. Bartlett, *Daniel Webster*, 261.
17. Deák, *Lawful Revolution: Louis Kossuth*, 71, 84–85, 97–98.
18. Spencer, *Louis Kossuth*, 6–7; Deák, *Lawful Revolution: Louis Kossuth*, 303–4; Taylor, *Decline of British Radicalism*, 209–10.
19. Spencer, *Louis Kossuth*, 8.
20. Taylor, *Decline of British Radicalism*, 208–9.
21. Deák, *Lawful Revolution: Louis Kossuth*, 71, 86, 98.
22. Ibid., 305.

23. Spencer, *Louis Kossuth*, 78–80; Zamoyski, *Holy Madness*, 380; Rapport, *1848*, 173–74.
24. Spencer, *Louis Kossuth*, 76–80; Wilentz, *Rise of American Democracy*, 662.
25. Spencer, *Louis Kossuth*, 111.
26. Bartlett, *Daniel Webster*, 262–63; Sehat, *Myth*, 67, 164.
27. Osterhammel, *Transformation*, 546.
28. Marx, "Eighteenth Brumaire," 286–88.
29. Bayly, *Birth of the Modern World*, 117.
30. Taylor, *Decline of British Radicalism*, 338.
31. Gossman, "Michelet and the French Revolution," 639, 645.
32. Nord, *Republican Moment*, 192–93.
33. Cotlar, *Tom Paine's America*, 213–14; Dobert, "The Radicals," 159; Nash, *Unknown American Revolution*, 455; Burrow, *Crisis of Reason*, 4–5, 154–55.
34. Smith, "Fortunate Banner," 36–37.
35. Bayly, *Birth of the Modern World*, 116.
36. Crook, "Whiggery and America," 197, 199–201.
37. Hutcheson, "Louisville Riots," 166–68.
38. Wilentz, *Rise of American Democracy*, 684–86.
39. Hutcheson, "Louisville Riots," 161.
40. Armitage, *Declaration*, 26, 92–93, 96–97.
41. Quoted in Hutcheson, "Louisville Riots," 172.

Bibliography

Abbreviations

AHR   *American Historical Review*
AHRF   *Annales historiques de la Révolution française*
AmQu   *American Quarterly*
BMGN   *Bijdragen en Mededelingen betreffende de Geschiedenis der
        Nederlanden*
HEI   *History of European Ideas*
JER   *Journal of the Early Republic*
JHI   *Journal of the History of Ideas*
PAPhS   *Proceedings of the American Philosophical Society*
WMQ   *William and Mary Quarterly*

Primary Sources

Adams, John. *Novanglus, or, A History of the Dispute with America*. Boston, 1774.
———. *Thoughts on Government applicable to the present State of the American Colonies*. Philadelphia, 1776.
———. *The Works*, ed. Charles Francis Adams. 10 vols. Boston, 1856.
———. *Papers of John Adams*, ed. R. J. Taylor. 16 vols. Cambridge, MA, 1977–2012.
———. *Diary and Autobiography*. In *The Portable John Adams*, ed. J. P. Diggins. New York, 2004.
Adams, John Quincy. *The Memoirs*, ed. Charles Francis Adams. 12 vols. Philadelphia, 1874–77.
———. *The Writings of John Quincy Adams*, ed. W. Chauncey Ford. 7 vols. New York, 1913–17.
The Adams-Jefferson Letters: The Complete Correspondence between Thomas Jefferson and Abigail and John Adams, ed. L. J. Cappon. 2 vols. Chapel Hill, NC, 1959.
Allen, Ethan. *An animadversary address to the inhabitants of the state of Vermont; with remarks on a proclamation, under the hand of His Excellency George Clinton, Esq; governor of the state of New-York*. Hartford, CT, 1778.
American Political Writing during the Founding Era, 1760–1805, ed. Charles S. Hyneman and Donald Lutz. 2 vols. Indianapolis, 1983.
Andrès, Bernard, ed. *La Conquête des lettres au Québec (1759–99): Anthologie*. Montreal, 2007.

Angeloni, Luigi. *Dell' Italia uscente il settembre de 1818*. 2 vols. Paris, 1818.

Apocalypse de Chiokoyhikoy, chef des Iroquois. "Philadelphie" [Montreal], 1777.

Archives Parlementaires, Series 1. 1787–94, ed. M. J. Mavidal et al. 102 vols. Paris, 1879–2005.

Archivo [del General Francisco de] Miranda, ed. V. Dávila. 14 vols. Caracas, 1929–33.

Bailly, Jean-Sylvain. *Œuvres posthumes*. Paris, 1810.

Bancroft, George. *The Life and Letters of George Bancroft*, ed. M. A. DeWolfe Howe. 2 vols. New York, 1908.

Barlow, Joel. *An Oration Delivered at the North Church in Hartford at the meeting of the Connecticut Society of Cincinnati*. 4 July 1787. In Joel Barlow, *The Works*, 1:1–20. Gainesville, FL, 1970.

———. *A Letter to the National Convention of France on the Defects of the Constitution of 1791*. London, 1792.

———. *The Conspiracy of Kings; A Poem: Addressed to the Inhabitants of Europe, From Another Quarter of the World*. London, 1792.

———. *Advice to the Privileged Orders in the Several States of Europe* (1792). New York, 1796.

———. "To His Fellow Citizens of the United States." 1801. In *American Political Writing*, ed. Hyneman and Lutz, 2:1099–1125.

Bentham, Jeremy. *Three Tracts relative to Spanish and Portuguese Affairs*. London, 1821.

———. *The Correspondence of Jeremy Bentham*, ed. T. L. S. Sprigge, Stephen Conway, et al. 12 vols. London, 1968–2006.

[Bernard, François]. *L'Afrique hollandoise, ou, Tableau historique et politique de l'état originaire de la colonie du Cap de Bonne-Espérance comparé avec l'état actuel de cette colonie*. [Leiden?], 1783.

Blanc, Louis. *Histoire de la Révolution française*. 2nd ed. 12 vols. Paris, 1864–70.

Blanco White, Joseph. *The Life of the Rev. Joseph Blanco White, written by himself*. 3 vols. London, 1845.

Blaquiere, Edward. *An Historical Review of the Spanish Revolution*. London, 1822.

Bolingbroke, Henry. *Political Writings*. Cambridge Texts in the History of Political Thought. Cambridge, 1997.

Bolívar, Simon. *El Libertador: Writings of Simon Bolívar*, ed. F. H. Fornoff. Oxford, 2003.

Bonneville, Nicolas de. *La bouche de fer*. Paris, 1790–91.

Börne, Ludwig. *Briefe aus Paris, 1830–31*. 2 vols. Hamburg, 1832.

[Brissot de Warville, Jacques-Pierre]. *Recherches philosophiques sur le droit de propriété considéré dans la nature*. N.p., 1780. Repr., Paris, n.d.

———. *Correspondance universelle sur ce qui intéresse Le Bonheur de l'Homme et de la société*. "London" [Neuchâtel], 1783.

———. *Le Philadelphien à Genève, ou, Lettres d'un Américain sur la dernière Révolution de Genève*. "Dublin" [Amsterdam?], 1783.

———. *Tableau de la situation actuelle des Anglois dans les Indes Orientales*. Paris, 1784.

———. *Examen critique des voyages dans l'Amérique septentrionale, de M. le marquis de Chastellux*. "Londres" [Paris?], 1786.

———. *New Travels in the United States of America*. 1788, ed. D. Echeverria. Cambridge, MA, 1964.

———. *Mémoire aux États-Généraux sur la nécessité de rendre, dès ce moment, la presse libre et surtout pour les journaux politiques*. Paris, 1789.

————. *Le Patriote français: Journal libre, impartial et national*, ed. Brissot. April 1789–June 1793.

[Brissot de Warville, Jacques-Pierre] with Étienne Clavière. *De la France et des États-Unis, ou, De l'importance de la Révolution de l'Amérique pour le bonheur de la France.* "Londres," 1787.

Burke, Edmund. *A Vindication of Natural Society.* 1756. In *The Works of the Right Honourable Edmund Burke*, 1:1–80. London, 1815.

————. *Reflections on the Revolution in France.* 1790. New York, 1987.

————. *The Works.* 16 vols. London, 1826–27.

————. *The Correspondence of Edmund Burke*, ed. R. B. McDowell. 9 vols. Cambridge, 1958–70.

————. *Pre-Revolutionary Writings.* Cambridge, 1993.

————. *On Empire, Liberty, and Reform: Speeches and Letters*, ed. D. Bromwich. New Haven, CT, 2000.

Cabarrús, Francisco. "Discurso sobre la libertad de comercio concedido por S.M. a la América." In *Memorias de la Sociedad Económica de Madrid*, 3:282–94. Madrid, 1787.

Callender, James Thomson. *The Political Progress of Britain, or, An Impartial History of Abuses in the Government of the British Empire.* Philadelphia, 1794.

"Candidus." [William Smith?] *Plain Truth: Addressed to the Inhabitants of America, containing Remarks on a late Pamphlet, intitled "Common Sense."* 2nd ed. Philadelphia, 1776.

Capellen, Joan Derk Van der. *Aan het Volk van Nederland.* 1781, ed. H . L. Zwitzer. Amsterdam, 1987.

Carey, James [Timothy Telltruth]. *The Collected Wisdom of the Ages, The Most Stupendous Fabric of Human Invention, the English Constitution.* Philadelphia, 1799.

Carra, Jean-Louis. *L'Orateur des États-Généraux, pour 1789.* 2 vols. Paris, 1789.

Cerisier, Antoine-Marie. *Observations impartiales d'un vrai Hollandois pour servir de réponse au discours d'un soi-disant bon Hollandois à ses compatriotes.* N.p., 1778.

————. *Réplique au second discours d'un soi-disant bon Hollandois . . . par l'auteur de la réponse au premier discours.* Knuttel 19248. Leiden, 1779.

————. *Tableau de l'histoire générale des Provinces-Unies.* 10 vols. Utrecht, 1777–84.

————. *Le Politique Hollandois.* Leiden, 6 vols. 1781–84.

Cérutti, Joseph-Antoine. *Mémoire pour le peuple françois.* [Paris?], 1788.

————. *Bréviaire philosophique, ou, Histoire du Judaïsme, du Christianisme et du Déisme.* N.p. [Paris], 1791.

Chastellux, François Jean, marquis de. *De la félicité publique.* 2 vols. Amsterdam, 1772.

————. *Discours sur les avantages et désavantages qui résultent pour l'Europe de la découverte de l'Amérique.* "Londres" [Paris?], 1787.

————. *Le Chronique de Paris.* Journal appearing August 1789–August 1793, ed. Louis-Pierre Manuel, Rabaut Saint-Étienne, Anarcharsis Cloots, et al.

Cloots, Anarcharsis. *De Algemeene Republiek of Aanspraak van de ombrengers der dwingelanden.* Dunkirk, 1792.

Cloquet, Jules. *Recollections of the Private Life of General Lafayette.* London, 1835.

Condorcet, Jean-Antoine-Nicolas de Caritat, marquis de. *La Tolérance aux pieds du Trône, par Monsieur de . . . Avocat au Parlement de . . .* "Londres" [Paris], 1778.

————. *Réflexions sur l'esclavage des nègres.* 1781, ed. Jean-Marc Simonet. http://classiques.uqac.ca/.

———. "De l'influence de la Révolution de l'Amérique sur l'Europe." 1786. In *Œuvres de Condorcet*, ed. A. Condorcet O' Connor and M. F. Arago, 8:1–113. Paris, 1847–49.

———. *Quatre Lettres d'un Bourgeois de New-Haven sur l'unité de la législation.* In Ph. Mazzei, *Recherches historiques et politiques sur les États-Unis,* 1:281–87. Colle, 1788.

———. *Sentiments d'un républicain; sur les Assemblées Provinciales et les États-Généraux.* "Philadelphie" [Paris], 1788.

———. *Seconde lettre d'un citoyen des États-Unis à un Français.* N.p., n.d. [Paris, 1788].

———. "La Politique naturelle." In *Bibliothèque de l'Homme Public,* 6:62–225. Paris, 1790.

———. *Bibliothèque de l'Homme Public.* Journal. Paris, 1790–92.

———. *Réflexions sur la Révolution de 1688, et celle du 10 août 1792.* N.p., n.d. [Paris, 1792].

———. *Œuvres completes,* ed. L. S. Caritat et al. 21 vols. Brunswick and Paris, 1804.

———. *Esquisse d'un tableau historique des progrès de l'esprit humain,* ed. A. Pons. Paris, 1988.

———. *Tableau historique des progrès de l'esprit humain,* ed. J. P. Schandeler and P. Crepel. Paris, 2004.

———. *Writings on the United States,* ed. Guillaume Ansart. University Park, PA, 2012.

Constant, Benjamin. *De la Terreur.* 1796. In *Œuvres politiques,* ed. C. H. Louandre, 337–60. Paris, 1874.

———. *Écrits politiques,* ed. M. Gauchet. Paris, 1997.

Cooper, James Fenimore. *Notions of the Americans.* 1828. New ed. 2 vols. Philadelphia, 1838.

———. *The Bravo.* 1831. New York, 1963.

———. *The American Democrat.* 1838. New ed., London, 1989.

———. *Gleanings in Europe.* Oxford, 1928.

Cooper, Thomas. *Some Information respecting America.* London, 1794.

Coppens, Bernard, ed. *Chronique des Révolutions Belgique et Liégeoise, 1789–1790.* Beauvechain, 1992.

Coram, Robert. *Political Inquiries: To which is Added a Plan for the General Establishment of Schools throughout the United States.* Wilmington, DE, 1791.

De La Hodde, Lucien. *History of the Secret Societies of the Republican Party of France from 1830 to 1848.* Philadelphia, 1848.

Démeunier, Jean-Nicolas. *L'Esprit des usages et des coutumes des différents peuples.* 3 vols. "Londres" [Paris], 1776.

———. *L'Amérique indépendante, ou, Les différentes constitutions des treize provinces qui se sont érigées en républiques, sous le nom d'États-Unis de l'Amérique.* 3 vols. Ghent, 1790.

Desmoulins, Camille. *Jean-Pierre Brissot Démasqué.* Paris, 1793.

———. *Le Vieux Cordelier,* ed. P. Pachet. Journal. 1793–94. Paris, 2010.

Destutt de Tracy, Antoine. *Premiers écrits: Sur l'éducation et l'instruction publique,* ed. Claude Jolly. Paris, 2011.

Deutsches Museum, ed. H. Ch. Boie and Christian Wilhelm von Dohm. Journal. Leipzig, 1776–88.

Devyr, Thomas Ainge. *Our Natural Rights: A Pamphlet for the People.* 1835. Repr., Williamsburg, VA, 1842.

Diderot, Denis. *Oeuvres completes,* ed. R. Lewinter. 15 vols. Paris, 1969–73.

———. *Political Writings.* Trans. and ed. J. H. Mason and Robert Wokler. Cambridge, 1992.

Discours d'un bon Hollandois à ses compatriotes, sur différents objets intéressants. N.p., 1778. Knuttel 19189.

Dohm, Christian Wilhelm von. *Exposé de la Révolution de Liège en 1789.* Liège, 1790.

Dragonetti, Giacinto. *A Treatise on Virtues and Rewards.* London, 1769.

Drennan, William. *The Drennan Letters,* ed. D. A. Chart. Belfast, 1931.

Dumont, Étienne. *Souvenirs sur Mirabeau,* ed. J. Benetruy. Paris, 1951.

Dwight, Timothy. *The Nature and Danger of Infidel Philosophy, exhibited in two discourses, addressed to the candidates for the Baccalaureate, in Yale College.* New Haven, CT, 1797.

Emerson, Ralph Waldo. "The American Scholar." 1837. In R. W. Emerson, *Political Writings,* ed. Sacks. Cambridge, 2008.

———. *The Complete Works of Ralph Waldo Emerson,* ed. E. W. Emerson. 12 vols. Boston, 1903–4.

———. *The Letters,* ed. R. L. Rusk. 6 vols. New York, 1939.

———. *Political Writings,* ed. K. S. Sacks. Cambridge, 2008.

Essays on Education in the Early Republic, ed. Frederick Rudolph. Cambridge, MA, 1965.

Estala, Pedro. *Cartas de un Español a un anglómano.* Madrid, 1805.

———. *El Imparcial, o Gazeta política y literaria.* Madrid, 2010.

The Federalist by Alexander Hamilton, James Madison, and John Jay, ed. T. Ball. Cambridge, 2003.

[Feller, Francois Xavier De, S.J.] *Journal historique et littéraire.* Luxembourg-Liège, 1773–94.

Ferguson, Adam. *Remarks on a Pamphlet Lately Published by Dr Price.* London, 1776.

La Feuille villageoise, ed. Joseph-Antoine Cérutti et al. Paris, 1790–94.

Filangieri, Gaetano. *La scienza della legislazione,* ed. A. Trampus. 7 vols. Venice, 2003–4.

Finestrad, Joaquín de. *El Vasallo instruido en el estado del Nuevo Reino de Granada y en sus respectivas obligaciones.* 1789. Bogotá, 2000.

Flórez Estrada, Álvaro. *Representación hecha a S.M.C. el señor Don Fernando VII.* London, 1818.

Franklin, Benjamin. "Rules by Which a Great Empire May Be Reduced to a Small One." 1773. In *Fart Proudly: Writings of Benjamin Franklin You Never Read in School,* ed. Carl Japikse. 1990. New ed., Columbus, OH, 2003.

———. *The Works of Benjamin Franklin,* ed. John Bigelow. 12 vols. New York, 1904.

———. *The Writings,* ed. Albert Henry Smyth. 10 vols. New York, 1907.

———. *The Papers,* ed. L. W. Labaree et al. 37 vols. New Haven, CT, 1959–.

———. *The Autobiography,* ed. L. W. Labaree. New Haven, CT, 1964.

[Franklin, Benjamin]. *La Science du Bonhomme Richard, ou moyen de payer les impôts.* 2nd ed. "à Philadelphie" [Paris?], 1778.

Freneau, Philip. "On some of the Principles of American Republicanism." *The Time-Piece; and Literary Companion* (New York), 5 May 1797.

Fuller [Ossoli], Margaret. *At Home and Abroad, or, Things and Thoughts in Europe,* ed. A. M. Fuller. Boston, 1856.

———. *These Sad But Glorious Days: Dispatches from Europe, 1846–1850,* ed. L. J. Reynolds. New Haven, CT, 1991.

Garat, Dominique-Joseph. *Mémoires historiques sur la vie de M. Suard, sur ses écrits et sur le XVIIIe siècle.* 2 vols. Paris, 1820.

García de Sena, Manuel. *La Independencia de la Costa Firme justificada por Thomas Paine Treinta Años ha.* Philadelphia, 1811.

Godard, Jacques. *Exposé des travaux de l'Assemblée-Générale des Représentans de la Commune de Paris, depuis le 25 juillet 1789, jusqu'au mois d'octobre 1790, époque de . . . par ordre de l'Assemblée.* Paris, 1790.

Godwin, William. *History of the Internal Affairs of the United Provinces from the Year 1780, to the Commencement of Hostilities in June 1787.* London, 1787.

Gordon, James. *The History of the Irish Rebellion, in the Year 1798, etc. Containing an impartial Account of the Proceedings of the Irish Revolutionists.* London, 1803.

Gordon, William. *The History of the Rise, Progress and Establishment of the Independence of the United States of America.* 2 vols. London, 1788.

Gorsas, Antoine-Joseph. *Le Courrier de Paris dans les 83 départemens.* Later titled *Le Courrier des LXXXIII départemens.* Paris, 1790–91.

Greeley, Horace. *Glances at Europe in a Series of Letters from Great Britain, France, Italy, Switzerland etc.* New York, 1851.

Grimm, Friedrich Melchior. *Correspondance Littéraire, Philosophique et Critique.* 15 vols. New ed., Paris, 1829–31.

Grove Jones, Leslie. *An Examination of the Principles of Legitimacy.* 1817. London, 1827.

Guizot, François. *De la Démocratie en France.* Paris, 1849.

Hawkins, Benjamin. *The Collected Works,* ed. Thomas Foster. Tuscaloosa, AL, 2003.

Heine, Heinrich. *Zur Geschichte der Religion und Philosophie in Deutschland.* In Heine, *Sämmtliche Werke v,* 15–294. Hamburg, 1861.

———. *On the History of Religion and Philosophy in Germany.* Cambridge, 2007.

Histoire philosophique et politique des établissemens et du commerce des Européens dans les Deux Indes [attributed to the abbé de Raynal]. 10 vols. Geneva, 1780.

Holbach, Baron d', Paul-Henri Thiry. *La Politique naturelle, ou, Discours sur les vrais principes du gouvernement.* 1773. Repr., Paris, 1998.

———. *Système social, ou, Principes naturels de la morale et de la politique.* 1773. Paris, 1994.

Hume, David. *Letters,* ed. J. Y. T. Greig. 2 vols. Oxford, 1969.

Il est encore des Aristocrates, ou, Réponse à l'infâme Auteur d'un Écrit intitulé Découverte d'un Conspiration contre les intérêts de la France. N.p., n.d. [Paris, 1791?].

Inglis, Charles. *The True Interest of America Impartially Stated, in certain Strictures on a Pamphlet entitled "Common Sense."* Philadelphia, 1776.

Irisarri, Antonio José. *Semanario Republicano de Chile.* Nos. 1–12. Santiago, 1813.

Jebb, John. *The Works: Theological, Medical, Political and Miscellaneous.* 3 vols. London, 1787.

Jefferson, Thomas. *A Summary View of the Rights of British America.* Philadelphia, 1774.

———. *Autobiography.* In *Writings,* ed. Peterson, 3–101.

———. *Justification de la résistance des colonies Américaines aux oppressions du gouvernement britannique.* "Londres" [Amsterdam?], 1776. Knuttel 19120.

———. *Writings,* ed. M. D. Peterson. New York, 1984.

———. *The Papers of Thomas Jefferson,* ed. J. P. Boyd, Ch. Cullen, et al. 42 vols. Princeton, 1950–.

———. *The Political Writings,* ed. M. D. Peterson. Monticello, VA, 1993.

———. *The Republic of Letters: The Correspondence between Thomas Jefferson and James Madison, 1776–1826,* ed. James Morton Smith. 3 vols. New York, 1995.

Ketcham, R., ed. *The Anti-Federalist Papers and the Constitutional Convention Debates.* New York, 1986.

Lafayette, Gilbert du Motier, marquis de. *Mémoires, Correspondance et Manuscrits.* 6 vols. Paris, 1837–38.

Lamartine, Alphonse de. *Histoire des Girondins.* 4 vols. Paris, 1847.

Ledru-Rollin, Alexandre Auguste. *Discours politiques et écrits divers.* 2 vols. Paris, 1879.

Lessing, Ephraim Gotthold. *Philosophical and Theological Writings.* Trans. H. B. Nisbet. Cambridge, 2005.

Lettre adressé aux habitants de la Province de Québec, ci-devant le Canada. Philadelphia, 1774.

Lettres du Congrès continental aux habitants de la province de Québec. [Philadelphia?], 1774.

Luchet, Jean-Pierre-Louis de. *Les Contemporains de 1789 et 1790, ou, les Opinions débattues pendant la première législature.* 2 vols. Paris, 1790.

Mably, Gabriel Bonnot de. *Observations sur le gouvernement et les lois des États-Unis d'Amérique.* 1783. In *Collection complète des œuvres de l'Abbé de Mably.* 15 vols. Paris l'An III de la République [1794–95].

Maclay, William. *Journal of William Maclay, United States Senator from Pennsylvania, 1789–1791,* ed. E. S. Maclay. New York, 1890.

Madison, James. *The Writings of James Madison comprising his Public Papers and his Private Correspondence,* ed. G. Hunt. 9 vols. New York, 1900–1910.

Malouet, Pierre-Victor. *Mémoires.* 2 vols. Paris, 1868.

Maréchal, Pierre-Sylvain De. *Dictionnaire des athées anciens et modernes.* Brussels, 1883.

Marmontel, Jean-François. *Mémoires,* ed. M. Touneaux. 3 vols. Paris, 1891.

Martin, Joseph Plumb. *A Narrative of a Revolutionary Soldier.* 2001. New ed., New York, 2010.

Marx, Karl. "The Eighteenth Brumaire of Louis Bonaparte." In Karl Marx and Frederick Engels, *Selected Works in Two Volumes,* 2:247–344. 5th printing. Moscow, 1962.

———. "Class Struggles in France, 1848–1850." In Karl Marx and Frederick Engels, *Selected Works in Two Volumes,* 1:118–242. 5th printing. Moscow, 1962.

McKenna, Theobald. *An Essay on Parliamentary Reform and on the Evils likely to ensue from a Republican Constitution in Ireland.* Dublin, 1793.

Melville, Herman. *Mardi, and a Voyage Thither.* London 1849.

———. *Journal of a Visit to London and the Continent, 1849–1850.* Cambridge, MA, 1948.

Merrill, Michael, and Sean Wilentz, eds. *The Key of Liberty: The Life and Democratic Writings of William Manning, "A Laborer," 1747–1814.* Cambridge, MA, 1993.

Mézière, Henri-Antoine. *Observation sur l'état actuel du Canada et sur les dispositions de ses habitans.* 1793. In *Conquête des lettres au Québec,* ed. Andrès, no. 65.

Mill, John Stuart. *The Autobiography.* New York, 1961.

Millar, John. *Observations Concerning the Distinction of Ranks in Society.* London, 1771.

Mirabeau, Gabriel-Honoré de. *Avis aux Hessois et autres peuples de l'Allemagne, vendus par leurs princes à l'Angleterre.* 1777. In Mirabeau, *Essai sur le Despotisme,* 309–18. 3rd ed. Paris, 1792.

———. *Considérations sur l'Ordre de Cincinnatus.* "Londres" [Amsterdam], 1784.

———. *Aux Bataves sur le Stadhouderat.* N.p. [Paris?], 1788.

Miranda, Francisco de. *Diario de viaje a Estados Unidos.* 1783–84. Santiago, Chile, 1998.

———. *The New Democracy in America: Travels in the United States,* ed. J. S. Ezell. Norman, OK, 1963.

Mitchell, Donald Grant. *The Battle Summer: Being Transcripts from Personal Observation in Paris during the Year 1848.* New York, 1850.

Molyneux, W. *The Case of Ireland Being Bound by Acts of Parliament in England, Stated.* 1698. Gloucester, 2009.

[Momoro, Antoine-François]. *Coup d'œil sur la question de la traite et l'esclavage des noirs.* N.p., n.d. [Paris].

Monette, Pierre. *Rendez-vous manqué avec la révolution américaine: Les adresses aux habitants de la province de Québec diffusées à l'occasion de l'invasion américaine de 1775–1776.* Montreal, 2007.

Moore, Thomas. *Memoirs of Captain Rock, The Celebrated Irish Chieftain.* London, 1824.

Morellet, André. *Mémoires sur le dix-huitième siècle et sur la révolution française.* 2 vols. Paris, 1822.

Morris, Gouverneur. *A Diary of the French Revolution*, ed. B. Cary Davenport. 2 vols. Boston, 1939.

Morse, Jedidiah. *A Sermon delivered at Charleston . . . Massachusetts, February 19, 1795 Being the Day Recommended by George Washington, President of the United States of America, for Public Thanksgiving and Prayer.* Boston, 1795.

———. *A Sermon Delivered at the New North Church in Boston . . . May 9th 1798, Being the Day recommended by John Adams, president of the United States of America, for Solemn Humiliation, Fasting and Prayer.* Boston, 1798.

———. *A Sermon Exhibiting the Present Dangers, and Consequent Duties of the Citizens of the United States of America, April 25 1799.* Hartford, CT, 1799.

Mounier, Jean-Joseph. *Considérations sur les gouvernements et principalement sur celui qui convient la France.* Versailles, 1789.

———. *De l'influence attribuée aux philosophes, aux franc-maçons et aux Illuminés sur la Révolution de la France.* Tübingen, 1801.

Nassy, David de Ishac Cohen. *Lettre-politico-théologico-morale sur les Juifs.* Paramaribo, 1798.

Necker, Jacques. *De l'importance des opinions religieuses.* "Londres" [Paris], 1788.

———. *De la Révolution françoise.* 4 vols. N.p., 1796.

Nuix, Juan. *Reflexiones imparciales sobre la humanidad de los españoles en las Indias, contra los pretendidos filósofos y políticos.* Madrid, 1782.

*Observations d'un homme impartial sur la lettre de Mr. ***** [Isaac de Pinto] à Mr. S. B. docteur en médecine à Kingston, dans la Jamaïque au sujet des troubles qui agitent toute l'Amérique Septentrionale.* Knuttel 19123. The Hague, 1776.

Paape, Gerrit. *De Hollandsche wijsgeer in Braband.* 4 vols. Antwerp-Dordrecht, 1788–90.

———. *De Hollandsche wijsgeer in Vrankrijk.* Dordrecht, 1790.

———. *De Zaak der verdrukte Hollandsche Patriotten voor de vierschaar der Menschlijkheid gebragt.* Dunkirk, 1790.

———. *De onverbloemde geschiedenis van het Bataafsch Patriottismus.* Delft, 1798.

Pagano, Francesco. *Saggi politici de' principi, progressi e decadenza della società.* Naples, 1791–92.

Paine, Thomas. *Common Sense.* 1776, ed. Isaac Kramnick. Penguin Classics, 1986.

———. *Le Sens-Commun, adressé aux habitans de l'Amérique . . . Traduit de l'Anglois.* Rotterdam, 1776.

———. *The American Crisis.* Nos. 1–3. Philadelphia, 1777.

———. *Rights of Man.* 1791–92, ed. E. Foner. New York, 1985.

———. *A Letter Addressed to the Abbé Raynal, on the Affairs of North America, in which the mistakes in the Abbé's Account of the Revolution of America are Corrected.* 1782. New ed., London, 1793.

————. *The Age of Reason*. 1794–95, ed. Kerry Walters. Peterborough, Ontario, 2011.

————. *Letter to George Washington*. 30 July 1796. In Paine, *Complete Writings*, 2:691–723.

————. *The Complete Writings*, ed. Philip Foner. 2 vols. New York, 1945.

————. *Political Writings*, ed. Bruce Kuklick. Cambridge, 1989.

Palmer, Elihu. *An Enquiry relative to the Moral and Political Improvement of the Human Species*. New York, 1797.

————. *Principles of Nature, or, A Development of the Moral Causes of Happiness and Misery among the Human Species*. New York, 1801.

————. *Posthumous Pieces, being Three Chapters of an Unfinished Work Intended to have been entitled "The Political World."* London, 1824.

Pétion, Jerôme. *Avis aux François sur le salut de la Patrie*. Paris, 1788.

[Petit, Émilien]. *Observations sur plusieurs assertions, extraites littéralement de l'Histoire philosophique des Deux Indes*. Amsterdam, 1776.

Pinto, Isaac de. *Letters on the American Troubles*. London, 1776.

————. *Lettre de Mr*** [I. de Pinto] à Mr. S. B. . . . au sujet des troubles qui agitent actuellement toute l'Amérique Septentrionale*. Knuttel 19122. The Hague, 1776.

————. *Réponse de Mr. I. de Pinto aux observations d'un homme impartial, sur sa lettre à Mr S. B. docteur en médicine à Kingston dans la Jamaïque*. Knuttel 19126. The Hague, 1776.

————. *Seconde lettre de Mr. de Pinto à l'occasion des troubles des colonies, contenant des réflexions politiques*. Knuttel 19124. The Hague, 1776.

Poesche, Theodore, and Charles Goepp. *The New Rome, or, The United States of the World*. New York, 1853.

Price, Richard. *Observations on the Importance of the American Revolution and the Means of Making It a Benefit to the World*. London, 1785.

————. *Political Writings*, ed. D. O. Thomas. Cambridge, 1991.

Priestley, Joseph. *Autobiography*. Bath, 1970.

————. *An Essay on the First Principles of Government and on the Nature of Political, Civil and Religious Liberty*. Dublin, 1768.

————. *Letters to the Right Honourable Edmund Burke occasioned by his Reflections on the Revolution in France*. 2nd ed. Birmingham, 1791.

[Prudhomme, Louis-Marie, and A. Tournon]. *Révolutions de Paris*. Paris, 1789–90.

Raimond, Julien. *Réflexions sur les véritables causes des troubles et des désastres de nos colonies, notamment sur ceux de Saint-Domingue*. Paris, 1793.

Ramsay, David. *The History of the American Revolution*, ed. L. H. Cohen. 2 vols. Indianapolis, 1989.

Raynal, Guillaume Thomas François. *The Revolution of America*. London, 1781.

Rehberg, August Wilhelm. *Untersuchingen über die französische Revolution*. 2 vols. Hanover, 1793.

Restrepo, José Manuel. *Historia de la Revolución de la Republica de Colombia*. 5 vols. Paris, 1827.

Riem, Andreas. "On Enlightenment." In *What Is Enlightenment?* ed. James Schmidt. Berkeley, CA, 1996.

Rivarol, Antoine de. *De la philosophie moderne*. Hamburg, 1797. 2nd ed. N.p., 1799.

Robertson, William. *The History of America*. 4th ed. London, 1783.

Rocafuerte, Vincente. *Ideas necesarias a todo pueblo americano independiente: Que Quiera ser Libre*. Philadelphia, 1821.

————. *Ensayo Político: El Sistema Colombiano popular, electivo*. New York, 1823.

Roederer, Pierre Louis. *De la philosophie moderne, et de la part qu'elle a eue à la Révolution française*. Paris, 1799.

———. *The Spirit of the Revolution of 1789 and Other Writings*, trans. M. Forsyth. Aldershot, 1989.

Roscio, Juan German. *El Triumfo de la libertad sobre el despotismo*. Philadelphia, 1817.

Ruge, Arnold. "A Self-Critique of Liberalism." 1843. In *The Young Hegelians: An Anthology*, ed. L. S. Stepelevich, 237–59. Atlantic Highlands, NJ, 1983.

Rush, Benjamin. *The Autobiography of Benjamin Rush*, ed. G. W. Corner. Princeton, 1948.

———. *Letters*, ed. L. H. Butterfield. 2 vols. Princeton, 1951.

———. "Plan for the Establishment of Public Schools." 1786. In *Essays on Education in the Early Republic*, ed. Frederick Rudolph, 1–23. Cambridge, MA, 1965.

Saavedra y Sangronis, Don Francisco Arias de. *Memorias inéditas de un ministro ilustrado*. Seville, 1992.

Sabatier de Castres, M. *Journal politique national des États-Généraux et de la Révolution de 1789*. Paris, 1789.

Salfi, Francesco Severio. *L'Italie au dix-neuvième siècle*. Paris, 1821.

Sarrans, Bernard. *Lafayette et la Révolution de 1830*. 2 vols. Paris, 1832.

Shelley, Percy Bysshe. *The Poetical Works*, ed. H. Buxton Forman. 5 vols. London, 1892.

———. *A Philosophical Review of Reform*, ed. T. W. Rolleston. Oxford, 1920.

Sismondi, J. C. I. de. "L'Amérique." *Revue Encyclopédique* 33 (January 1827): 17–40.

Skidmore, Thomas. *The Rights of Man to Property! Being a Proposition to make it equal among Adults of the present Generation*. New York, 1829.

Smith, Adam. *An Inquiry into the Nature and Causes of the Wealth of Nations*, ed. J. E. Thorold Rogers. 22 vols. 2nd ed. Oxford, 1880.

———. *The Correspondence of Adam Smith*, ed. E. Campbell Mossner and I. S. Ross. Oxford, 1977.

Smith, William. "To the People of Pennsylvania." *Pennsylvania Gazette*, March–April 1776.

Stendhal. *Scarlet and Black*, trans. Margaret Shaw. Penguin Classics, 1953.

Thompson, Zadock. *History of Vermont, Natural, Civil and Statistical*. 3 vols. Burlington, 1842.

Tocqueville, Alexis de. *De la Démocratie en Amérique*, ed. H. G. Nicholas. London, 1961.

Tone, Theobald Wolfe. *An Address to the People of Ireland*. Belfast, 1796.

———. *The Writings, 1763–98*, ed. T. W. Moody, R. B. McDowell, and C. J. Woods. 3 vols. Oxford, 2009.

Toussaint Louverture, François-Dominique. *Lettres à la France (1794–1798)*, ed. M. Baggio and R. Augustin. Bruyères-le-Châtel, 2011.

Varela y Ulloa, Pedro de. "Discurso preliminar" to Nuix, *Reflexiones imparciales*.

Vereul, Abraham. *Redevoering over de gelijkheid der menschen*. Amsterdam, 1795.

Villette, Charles. *Lettres choisies sur les principaux événements de la Révolution*. Paris, 1792.

Volney, Constantin François. *Ruins of Empires and the Laws of Nature*. New York, 1850.

———. *Œuvres*. 2 vols. Paris, 1989.

Vreede, Pieter. *Zakboek van Neerlands Volk, voor Patriotten, Antipatriotten, Aristokraten en Prinsgezinden*. Dordrecht, 1785.

Waarschouwing der Reede, tegen het geschrift getytelt Vriend-Broederlyke Vermaaning en Raadgeeving aan de Hessische en andere Duitsche Hulpbenden. Amsterdam, 1777. Knuttel 21041.

Walpole, Sir Horace. *The Letters*, ed. P. Toynbee. 16 vols. Oxford, 1903–5.

Webster, Noah. "Revolution in France (1794)." In *Collection of Papers on Political, Literary and Moral Subjects*. New York, 1843.

———. "An Oration on the Anniversary of the Declaration of Independence." 1802. In *American Political Writing*, ed. Hyneman and Lutz, 2:1220–40.

Weitling, Wilhelm. *Die Menschheit wie sie ist und wie sie sein sollte*. 1838. 2nd ed. Berne, 1845.

Wekhrlin, Wilhelm Ludwig. *Chronologen*. 12 vols. Frankfurt-Nuremberg, 1779–84.

———. *Das graue Ungeheuer*. 31 vols. Nuremberg, 1784–87.

Whiting, William. *Some Brief Remarks on the Present State of Public Affairs* (1786) and letters in *Proceedings of the American Antiquarian Society* 66 (1956): 131–61.

Whitman, Walt. *Complete Prose Works*. Philadelphia, 1892.

———. *Complete Poetry and Collected Prose*, ed. J. Kaplan. New York, 1982.

———. *The Journalism*, ed. H. Bergman. 2 vols. New York, 1998.

Wirth, J. G. A. *Die politische Reform Deutschlands: Noch ein dringendes Wort an die deutschen Volksfreunde*. Strasbourg, 1832.

———. "Rede von Johann Georg August Wirth auf dem Hambacher Fest 1832." In J. G. A. Wirth, *Das Nationalfest der Deutschen zu Hambach*, 31–41. Neustadt an der Haardt, 1832.

Secondary Sources

Aaslestad, Katherine. *Place and Politics: Local Identity, Civic Culture, and German Nationalism in North Germany during the Revolutionary Era*. Leiden, 2005.

Acomb, F. *Mallet Du Pan (1749–1800): A Career in Political Journalism*. Durham, NC, 1973.

Adams, W. H. *Gouverneur Morris: An Independent Life*. New Haven, CT, 2003.

Adelman, J. *Sovereignty and Revolution in the Iberian Atlantic*. Princeton, 2006.

Aguilar Rivera, José Antonio. *Ausentes del universo: Reflexiones sobre el pensamiento político hispanoamericano en la era de la construcción nacional, 1821–1850*. Mexico City, 2012.

Albertone, Manuela. "Democratic Republicanism: Historical Reflections on the Idea of Republic in the 18th Century." *HEI* 33 (2007): 108–30.

———. "Thomas Jefferson and French Economic Thought: A Mutual Exchange of Ideas." In *Rethinking*, ed. Albertone and De Francesco, 123–46.

Albertone, Manuela, and Antonio De Francesco, eds. *Rethinking the Atlantic World: Europe and America in the Age of Democratic Revolutions*. Basingstoke, 2009.

Alden, J. R. *A History of the American Revolution*. New York, 1969.

Aldridge, A. O. *Man of Reason: The Life of Thomas Paine*. Philadelphia, 1959.

———. *Early American Literature: A Comparative Approach*. Princeton, 1982.

Alexander, J. K. "The Fort Wilson Incident of 1779." *WMQ*, 3rd ser., 31 (1974): 589–612.

Alger, J. G. "The British Colony in Paris, 1792–3." *English Historical Review* 13 (1898): 672–94.

Allen, Brooke. *Moral Minority: Our Skeptical Founding Fathers*. Chicago, 2006.

Allen, Danielle. *Our Declaration: A Reading of the Declaration of Independence*. New York, 2014.

Allen, Margaret. "The Political and Social Criticism of Margaret Fuller." *South Atlantic Quarterly* 72 (1973): 560–73.

Altena, Peter. "'O Ondankbaar vaderland': Gerrit Paape en de 'vebeterende' balling-schap." *De Achttiende Eeuw* 38 (2006): 168–80.

———. *Gerrit Paape (1752–1803): Levens en werken*. Nijmegen, 2012.

Anderson, Douglas. *The Radical Enlightenments of Benjamin Franklin*. Baltimore, 1997.

Andrès, Bernard. "De l'Utopie aux répercussions de la Révolution de Juillet 1830 au Qué-bec." In *Utopies en Canada: 1545–1845*, ed. Andrès and Desjardins, 119–43.

———. "Sur les utopies québécoises, des Lumières aux Révolutions continentales." In *Utopies en Canada: 1545–1845*, ed. Andrès and Desjardins, 11–34.

Andrès, Bernard, and Nancy Desjardins, eds. *Utopies en Canada: 1545–1845*. Montreal, 2001.

Andress, David. *1789: The Threshold of the Modern Age*. London, 2008.

Andrew, E. G. *Patrons of Enlightenment*. Toronto, 2006.

———. *Imperial Republics: Revolution, War and Territorial Expansion*. Toronto, 2011.

Andrews, Stuart. *The British Periodical Press and the French Revolution, 1789–99*. London, 2000.

Andrien, K. J. "Soberanía y revolución en el reino de Quito, 1809–1810." In *En el umbral de las revoluciones*, ed. Breña, 313–34.

Anes, Gonzalo. *El Siglo de Las Luces*. Madrid, 1994.

Anna, Timothy. "The Independence of Mexico and Central America." In *The Independence of Latin America*, ed. Leslie Bethel, 49–92. Cambridge, 1987.

Ansart, G. "From Voltaire to Raynal and Diderot's *Histoire des Deux Indes*." In *America through European Eyes*, ed. A. Craiutu and J. C. Isaacs, 71–89. University Park, PA, 2009.

Appleby, Joyce. "America as a Model for the Radical French Reformers of 1789." *WMQ* 28 (1971): 267–86.

———. "The New Republican Synthesis and the Changing Political Ideas of John Ad-ams." *AmQu* 25 (1973): 578–95.

———. "Republicanism and Ideology." *AmQu* 37 (1985): 461–73.

———. *Inheriting the Revolution: The First Generation of Americans*. Cambridge, MA, 2000.

Aprile, S. *La Révolution inachevée, 1815–1870*. Paris, 2010.

———. *Le Siècle des exilés: Bannis et proscrits de 1789 à la Commune*. Paris, 2010.

———. "Des cantons suisses aux États allemands." In *La Liberté guidant les peuples*, ed. Aprile, Caron, and Fureix, 81–90.

Aprile, S., Jean-Claude Caron, and E. Fureix, eds. *La Liberté guidant les peuples: Les Révo-lutions de 1830 en Europe*. Seyssel, 2013.

Apt, Léon. *Louis-Philippe de Ségur: An Intellectual in a Revolutionary Age*. The Hague, 1969.

Arana, Marie. *Bolívar: American Liberator*. New York, 2013.

Arendt, Hannah. *On Revolution*. New York, 1963.

Armitage, David. *The Declaration of Independence: A Global History*. Cambridge, MA, 2007.

Armstrong, Murray. *The Liberty Tree: The Stirring Story of Thomas Muir and Scotland's First Fight for Democracy*. Edinburgh, 2014.

Arnaud, Claude. *Chamfort: A Biography*. Chicago, 1992.

Arnold, M., ed. *Edmund Burke: Irish Affairs*. London, 1988.

Astigarraga, Jesús, ed. *The Spanish Enlightenment Revisited*. Oxford, 2015.

Auricchio, Laura. *The Marquis: Lafayette Reconsidered*. New York, 2014.

Ávila, Alfredo, and P. Pérez Herrero, eds. *La Experiencias de 1808 en Iberoamérica*. Madrid, 2008.

Aymes, Jean-René. "La Mise en cause des élites et, en particulier, des 'philosophes' et des 'savants' pendant la Guerre de l'Independence." In *Las Élites y la Revolución de España (1808–1814)*, ed. A. Alberola and E. Larriba, 107–25. San Vicente del Raspeig, 2010.

Baczko, Bronislaw. *Politiques de la Révolution française*. Paris, 2008.

Badinter, E., and R. Badinter. *Condorcet: Un intellectuel en politique*. Paris, 1988.

Bailyn, Bernard. *Faces of Revolution: Personalities and Themes in the Struggle for American Independence*. New York, 1990.

——. *The Ideological Origins of the American Revolution*. 1967. New ed., Cambridge, MA, 1992.

——. *Atlantic History: Concepts and Contours*. Cambridge, MA, 2005.

Baker, Keith Michael. *Condorcet: From Natural Philosophy to Social Mathematics*. Chicago, 1975.

——. "The Idea of a Declaration of Rights." In *The French Idea of Freedom: Origins of the Declaration of the Rights of Man and of the Citizen*, ed. Dale Van Kley, 154–96. Stanford, CA, 1994.

——. "Political Languages of the French Revolution." In *The Cambridge History of Eighteenth-Century Political Thought*, ed. Mark Goldie and Robert Wokler. Cambridge, 2006.

Baranska, Anna. "Pologne: Une insurrection sans révolution?" In *La Liberté guidant les peuples*, ed. Aprile, Caron, and Fureix, 143–52.

Barman, R. J. *Brazil: The Forging of a Nation, 1798–1852*. Stanford, CA, 1988.

Bartlett, I. A. *Daniel Webster*. New York, 1978.

Bartlett, Thomas. "The Burden of the Present: Theobald Wolfe Tone, Republican and Separatist." In *The United Irishmen: Republicanism, Radicalism and Rebellion*, ed.D. Dickson, D. Keogh, and K. Whelan, 1–15. Dublin, 1993.

Bastin, G. L., Álvaro Echeverri, and Ángela Campo, eds. "Translation and the Emancipation of Hispanic America." In *Translation, Resistance, Activism*, ed. M. Tymoczko, 42–64. Amherst, MA, 2010.

Baumgarten, Eduard. *Benjamin Franklin: Der Lehrmeister de Amerianischen Revolution*. Frankfurt, 1936.

Baumstark, M. "The End of Empire and the Death of Religion: A Reconsideration of Hume's Later Political Thought." In *Philosophy and Religion in Enlightenment Britain*, ed. R. Savage, 231–77. Oxford, 2012.

Bauszus, D. D. "The Religious Aspects of the Founding of America." In *Religion, Politics and Law*, ed. B. Labuschagne, 335–62. Leiden, 2009.

Bayly, C. A. *The Birth of the Modern World, 1780–1914*. Oxford, 2004.

Beckles, H. M. "The Struggle of Blacks and Free-coloureds for Freedom in Barbados, 1800–1833." In *Freedom Road*, ed. J. Millette. 1988. 2nd ed. Kingston, Jamaica, 2007.

Beeman, Richard. *The Varieties of Political Experience in Eighteenth-Century America*. University Park, PA, 2006.

——. *Plain Honest Men: The Challenge of the American Constitution*. New York, 2009.

——. *Our Lives, Our Fortunes and Our Sacred Honor: The Forging of American Independence, 1774–1776*. Philadelphia, 2013.

Belissa, Marc. "Les leçons de républicanisme de Thomas Paine." *AHRF* 363 (2011): 59–84.

Bellesiles, M. A. *Revolutionary Outlaws: Ethan Allen and the Struggle for Independence on the Early American Frontier.* Charlottesville, VA, 1993.

Bennett, David. *A Few Lawless Vagabonds: Ethan Allen, the Republic of Vermont, and the American Revolution.* Philadelphia, 2014.

Bennett, Noland J. *Benjamin Franklin in Scotland and Ireland.* Philadelphia, 1938.

Berkin, Carol. *The Bill of Rights: The Fight to Secure America's Liberties.* New York, 2015.

Berkowitz, Peter. *Virtue and the Making of Modern Liberalism.* Princeton, 1999.

Berlin, Ira. *The Long Emancipation: The Demise of Slavery in the United States.* Cambridge, MA, 2015.

Berlin, Isaiah. *The Crooked Timber of Humanity.* 1990. 2nd ed. Princeton, 2013.

Bernier, Olivier. *Lafayette: Hero of Two Worlds.* New ed. Paris, 1988.

Bernstein, J. A. "Nature's God as *Deus sive Natura*: Spinoza, Jefferson, and the Historical Transmission of the Theological-Political Question." In *Resistance to Tyrants*, ed. Gish and Klinghard, 65–81.

Bernstein, R. B. *Thomas Jefferson.* Oxford, 2003.

———. *The Founding Fathers Reconsidered.* New York, 2009.

Bethencourt, Francisco. *The Inquisition: A Global History, 1478–1834.* Cambridge, 1995.

Billias, George Athan. *American Constitutionalism Heard around the World, 1776–1989: A Global Perspective.* New York, 2009.

Bird, Wendell. "Reassessing Responses to the Virginia and Kentucky Resolutions." *JER* 35 (2015): 519–51.

Blackburn, R. *The Overthrow of Colonial Slavery (1776–1848).* New York, 1998.

Blanchard, Paula. *Margaret Fuller: From Transcendentalism to Revolution.* New York, 1978.

Blanchard, Peter. *Slavery and Abolition in Early Republican Peru.* Wilmington, DE, 1992.

Blasi, J. R., R. B. Freeman, and D. L. Kruse. *The Citizen's Share: Putting Ownership Back into Democracy.* New Haven, CT, 2013.

Bloom, Clive. *Restless Revolutionaries: A History of Britain's Fight for a Republic.* 2007. New ed., Brimscombe Port Stroud, Gloucestershire, 2010.

Bonwick, Colin. *The American Revolution.* Basingstoke, 1991.

Bourke, Richard. *Empire and Revolution: The Political Life of Edmund Burke.* Princeton, 2015.

Bouton, Terry. *Taming Democracy: "The People," the Founders, and the Troubled Ending of the American Revolution.* Oxford, 2007.

———. "William Findley, David Bradford, and the Pennsylvania Regulation of 1794." In *Revolutionary Founders*, ed. Young, Nash, and Raphael, 233–51.

Bowersock, G. W. "The March of Reason: When Liberalism Came to Greece: An Unknown Story." *The New Republic*, 14 July 2014, 42.

Brands, H. W. *The First American: The Life and Times of Benjamin Franklin.* New York, 2000. Repr., 2002.

Bredin, Jean-Denis. *Sieyès: La clé de la Révolution française.* Paris, 1988.

Breña, Roberto. "Ideas, acontecimientos y prácticas políticas en las revoluciones hispánicas." In *Experiencias*, ed. Ávila and Pérez Herrero.

———, ed. *En el umbral de la revoluciones hispánicas: El bienio, 1808–1810.* Mexico City, 2010.

Brewer, David. *The Greek War of Independence: The Struggle for Freedom and from Ottoman Oppression.* London, 2011.

Brewer-Carías, Allan. *Constituciones de Venezuela.* 2 vols. San Cristóbal-Madrid, 1985.

Bromwich, D. *The Intellectual Life of Edmund Burke: From the Sublime and Beautiful to American Independence*. Cambridge, MA, 2014.

Brookhiser, R. *Alexander Hamilton: American*. New York, 1999.

Brown, A. W. *Margaret Fuller*. New York, 1964.

Brown, Gordon S. *Toussaint's Clause: The Founding Fathers and the Haitian Revolution*. Jackson, MI, 2005.

Brown, Michael. *The Irish Enlightenment*. Cambridge, MA, 2016.

Bruyère-Ostells, Walter. *La Grande Armée de la Liberté*. Paris, 2009.

Buck-Morss, Susan. "Hegel and Haiti." *Critical Inquiry* 26:4 (2000): 821–65.

Buel, Richard. *Securing the Revolution: Ideology in American Politics, 1789–1815*. Ithaca, NY, 1972.

———. *Joel Barlow: American Citizen in a Revolutionary World*. Baltimore, 2011.

Burke, Martin. "Piecing Together a Shattered Past: The Historical Writings of the United Irish Exiles in America." In *The United Irishmen: Republicanism, Radicalism and Rebellion*, ed. D. Dickson, D. Keogh, and K. Whelan, 297–307. Dublin, 1993.

Burns, J. H. "Jeremy Bentham from Radical Enlightenment to Philosophic Radicalism." *Bentham Newsletter* 8 (June 1984): 4–14.

Burrow, J. W. *The Crisis of Reason: European Thought, 1848–1914*. New Haven, CT, 2000.

Burstein, A., and N. Isenberg. *Madison and Jefferson*. New York, 2010.

Bury, J. P. T., and R. P. Tombs. *Thiers, 1797–1877: A Political Life*. London, 1986.

Busaall, Jean-Baptiste. "Constitution et 'gouvernement des modernes' dans l'Espagne du Trienio liberal (1820–1823)." In *Guerre d'Indépendance*, ed. Luis, 111–24.

Bushnell, David. *Simón Bolívar: Liberation and Disappointment*. New York, 2004.

Butler, Jon. *Awash in a Sea of Faith: Christianizing the American People*. Cambridge, MA, 1990.

Butrón Prida, Gonzalo. "Liberté, Nation et Constitution: Le modèle révolutionnaire espagnol en Italie au début des années 1820." In *Guerre d'Indépendance*, ed. Luis, 177–91.

Calloway, C. G. "Declaring Independence and Rebuilding a Nation: Dragging Canoe and the Chickamauga Revolution." In *Revolutionary Founders*, ed. Young, Nash, and Raphael, 185–98.

———. *The Victory with No Name: The Native American Defeat of the First American Army*. Oxford, 2015.

Capaldi, N. *John Stuart Mill: A Biography*. Cambridge, 2004.

Caron, Jean-Claude. "Mouvements insurrectionnnels et internationale libérale dans les années 1820." In *La Liberté guidant les peuples*, ed. Aprile, Caron, and Fureix, 43–60.

———. "De la Belgique à la Pologne: Des révolutions-soeurs?" In *La Liberté guidant les peuples*, ed. Aprile, Caron, and Fureix, 72–80.

———. "Les marges latines de la Révolution: De l'Italie centrale à l'Espagne." In *La Liberté guidant les peuples*, ed. Aprile, Caron, and Fureix, 96–101.

Carpanetto, Dino, and Giuseppe Ricuperati. *Italy in the Age of Reason, 1685–1789*. London, 1987.

Carr, Raymond. *Spain, 1808–1939*. Oxford, 1966.

Carter, Edward C. *"One Grand Pursuit": A Brief History of the American Philosophical Society's First 250 Years, 1743–1993*. Philadelphia, 1993.

Casalini, Brunella. "L'*Esprit* di Montesquieu negli Stati Uniti durante la seconda metà del XVIII secolo." In *Montesquieu e I suoi interpreti*, ed. Domenico Felice, 1:325–55. Pisa, 2005.

Chaput, E. J. " Proslavery and Antislavery Politics in Rhode Island's 1842 Dorr Rebellion." *New England Quarterly* 85:4 (2012): 658–94.

Chassin, Joëlle. "Opinion publique et opinion populaire au Pérou." In *L'avènement*, ed. Fernández Sebastián and Chassin, 257–70.

Chernow, Ron. *Alexander Hamilton*. New York, 2004.

Chevigny, B. G. "Growing out of New England: The Emergence of Margaret Fuller's Radicalism." *Women's Studies: An Inter-disciplinary Journal* 5 (1977): 65–100.

———. *The Woman and the Myth: Margaret Fuller's Life and Writings*. New York, 1976.

Chiaramonte, José Carlos. *La Ilustración en el Río de la Plata: Cultura eclesiástica y cultura laica durante el Virreinato*. Buenos Aires, 2007.

Chinard, Gilbert. *Volney et l'Amérique d'après des documents inédits*. Baltimore, 1923.

Chouraqui, Frank. "At the Crossroads of History: Blanqui at the Castle of the Bull." In Louis-Auguste Blanqui, *Eternity by the Stars: An Astronomical Hypothesis*, 1–62. New York, 2013.

Cienciala, A. M. "The American Founding Fathers and Poland." In *The American and European Revolutions, 1776–1848: Sociopolitical and Ideological Aspects*, ed. J. Pelenski, 111–24. Iowa City, 1980.

Claes, Gregory. *Thomas Paine, Social and Political Thought*. Boston, 1989.

Clark, J. C. D. *The Language of Liberty, 1660–1832: Political Discourse and Social Dynamics in the Anglo-American World*. Cambridge, 1994.

———. "Edmund Burke's Reflections on the Revolution in America 1777." In *Imaginative Whig*, ed. I. Crowe, 71–92. Columbia, MO, 2005.

Clarke, Ernest. *The Siege of Fort Cumberland, 1776: An Episode in the American Revolution*. Montreal, 1999.

Claudes, Pierre. "Joseph de Maistre face à la Restauration." In *Repenser la Restauration*, ed. Mollier, Reid, and Yon, 87–102.

Cleary, Brian. "Wexford in 1798: A Republic before Its Time." In *The Great Irish Rebellion of 1798*, ed. Cathal Poirteir, 101–14.

Coelho, Chris. *Timothy Matlack: Scribe of the Declaration of Independence*. Jefferson, NC, 2013.

Cole, Jonathan. *The Great American University: Its Rise to Preeminence*. New York, 2009.

Cole, Nicholas P. "American Bicameralism and the Legacy of the Roman Senate." *Classical Receptions Journal* 7:1 (2015): 79–90.

Coleman, Aaron. "'A Second Bounaparty?' A Reexamination of Alexander Hamilton during the Franco-American Crisis, 1796–1801." *JER* 28 (2008): 183–214.

Coleman, Peter J. "The Dorr War and the Emergence of the Leviathan State." *Reviews in American History* 4:4 (1976): 533–38.

Colley, Linda. *Britons: Forging the Nation, 1707–1837*. New Haven, CT, 1992.

Connell, W. J. "Darker Aspects of Italian American Prehistory." In *Anti-Italianism: Essays on a Prejudice*, ed. W. J. Connell and F. Gardaphe, 11–22. New York, 2010.

Conway, Stephen. "Continental European Soldiers in British Imperial Service, c. 1776–1792." *English Historical Review* 129 (2014): 79–106.

———. "British Governments, Colonial Consumers and Continental European Goods in the British Atlantic Empire, 1773–1775." *Historical Journal* 58:3 (2015): 711–32.

Copulsky, J. E. "The Last Prophet: Spinoza and the Political Theology of Moses Hess." *Religion and Culture Web Forum*. March 2008.

Cotlar, Seth. "Robert Coram and the American Revolution's Legacy of Economic Populism." In *Revolutionary Founders*, ed. Young, Nash, and Raphael, 337–53.

———. *Tom Paine's America: The Rise and Fall of Transatlantic Radicalism in the Early Republic.* Charlottesville, VA, 2011.

———. "Languages of Democracy in America from the Revolution to the Election of 1800." In *Re-Imagining Democracy*, ed. Innes and Philp, 13–27.

———. "Conclusion: Thomas Paine in the Atlantic Historical Imagination." In *Paine and Jefferson*, ed. Newman and Onuf, 277–96.

Countryman, Edward. *The American Revolution.* 1985. Rev. ed., New York, 2003.

Coupland, Reginald. *The American Revolution and the British Empire.* London, 1930.

Craiutu, Aurelian. *A Virtue for Courageous Minds: Moderation in French Political Thought, 1748–1830.* Princeton, 2012.

Creyghton, C. M. H. G. "Vaderfiguren in de historiografische canon: De casus Jules Michelet." *Tijdschrift voor Geschiedenis* 127 (2014): 21–40.

Crook, Paul. "Whiggery and America: Accommodating the Radical Threat." In *Radicalism and Revolution in Britain, 1775–1848*, ed. M. T. Davis, 191–206. Basingstoke, 2000.

Cruise O'Brien, Conor. *The Long Affair: Thomas Jefferson and the French Revolution, 1785–1800.* Chicago, 1996.

Cullan, Fintan. "Radicals and Reactionaries: Portraits of the 1790's in Ireland." In *Revolution, Counter-revolution and Union*, ed. Smyth, 161–94.

Cullan, Louis M. "The Internal Politics of the United Irishmen." In *The United Irishmen: Republicanism, Radicalism and Rebellion*, ed. D. Dickson, D. Keogh, and K. Whelan, 176–96. Dublin, 1993.

———. "The Politics of Crisis and Rebellion, 1792–1798." In *Revolution, Counter-revolution and Union*, ed. Smyth, 21–38.

Curran, Andrew. *The Anatomy of Blackness: Science and Slavery in an Age of Enlightenment.* Baltimore, 2011.

Curti, M. "The Impact of the Revolutions of 1848 on American Thought." *PAPhS* 93 (1949): 209–15.

Curtis, E. N. "American Opinion of the French Nineteenth-Century Revolutions." *AHR* 29 (1924): 249–70.

Dahl, Robert A. *On Political Equality.* New Haven, CT, 2007.

Darriulat, Philippe. *Les Patriotes: La Gauche républicaine et la nation, 1830–1870.* Paris, 2001.

Davidson, Neil. *How Revolutionary Were the Bourgeois Revolutions?* Chicago, 2012.

Davis, David Brion. *Revolutions, Reflections on American Equality and Foreign Liberations.* Cambridge, MA, 1990.

———. *The Problem of Slavery in the Age of Revolution, 1770–1823.* New York, 1999.

Davis, John. "The Spanish Constitution of 1812 and the Mediterranean Revolutions (1820–25)." *Bulletin for Spanish and Portuguese Historical Studies* 37:2 (2013): article 7.

Davis, M. T., ed. *Radicalism and Revolution in Britain, 1775–1848.* Basingstoke, 2000.

Davis, M. T., and P. A. Pickering, eds. *Unrespectable Radicals? Popular Politics in the Age of Reform.* Aldershot, 2008.

Davis, Roger. "José Manuel Restrepo and the Emergence of Colombian Political Culture." *Platte Valley Review* 17 (1989): 5–13.

Dawson, Christopher. *The Gods of Revolution.* New York, 1972.

Deák, Istvan. *The Lawful Revolution: Louis Kossuth and the Hungarians, 1848–1849*. New York, 1979.

De Bolla, Peter. *The Architecture of Concepts: The Historical Formation of Human Rights*. New York, 2013.

De Champs, Emmanuelle. *Enlightenment and Utility: Bentham in French, Bentham in France*. Cambridge, 2015.

De Dijn, A. "A Pragmatic Conservatism: Montesquieu and the Framing of the Belgian Constitution (1830–1831)." *HEI* 28 (2002): 227–46.

De Francesco, Antonio. "Federalist Obsession and Jacobin Conspiracy: France and the United States in a Time of Revolution." In *Rethinking*, ed. Albertone and De Francesco, 239–56.

Dekker, George, and L. Johnston. "Introduction: The Novelist as Political Theorist." In James Fenimore Cooper, *The American Democrat*, 7–55. London, 1969.

Delinière, Jean. "Polémique à propos d'un poème à la gloire de la liberté de l'Amérique." In *Révolution américaine*, ed. Krebs and Moes, 53–62.

De Luca, Stefano. "Benjamin Constant and the Terror." In *The Cambridge Companion to Constant*, ed. H. Rosenblatt, 92–114. Cambridge, 2009.

De Luna, F. "The Dean Street Style of Revolution: J. P. Brissot, jeune philosophe." *French Historical Studies* 17:1 (1991): 159–90.

Del Vento, Christian. "Il democratismo di Ugo Foscolo." In *Studi per Umberto Carpi: Un salute da allievi e colleghi pisani*, ed. M. Santragata and A. Stussi, 357–74. Pisa, 2000.

Dérozier, Albert. *Manuel José Quintana y el nacimiento del liberalismo en España*. Madrid, 1978.

Deseure, Brecht. " 'Ouvrez l'histoire': Revolutionaire geschiedenispolitiek in de Zuidelijke Nederlanden (1792–1799)." *BMGN* 125 (2010): 25–47.

Desportes, Ulysse. "Giuseppe Ceracchi in America and His Busts of George Washington." *Art Quarterly* 26 (1963): 140–79.

Desprat, Jean-Paul. *Mirabeau*. Paris, 2008.

Desserud, Donald. "Nova Scotia and the American Revolution." In *Making Adjustments: Change and Continuity in Planter Nova Scotia, 1759–1800*, ed. M. Conrad, 89–112. Fredericton, New Brunswick, 1991.

Dhondt, Luc. "De conservatieve Brabantse ontwenteling van 1789 en het proces van revolutie en contrarevolutie in de Zuidelijke Nederlanden tussen 1780 en 1830." *Tijdschrift voor Geschiedenis* 102 (1989): 422–50.

Dickinson, H. T. *Liberty and Property: Political Ideology in Eighteenth-Century Britain*. London, 1977.

———. "Counter-revolution in Britain in the 1790s." *Tijdschrift voor Geschiedenis* 102 (1989): 354–67.

———. " 'The Friends of America': British Sympathy with the American Revolution." In *Radicalism*, ed. Davis, 1–29.

Dickson, David. "Paine and Ireland." In *The United Irishmen: Republicanism, Radicalism and Rebellion*, ed. D. Dickson, D. Keogh, and K. Whelan, 135–50. Dublin, 1993.

Dixon, John M. "Henry F. May and the Revival of the American Enlightenment." *WMQ* 71 (2014): 255–80.

Dobert, Eitel Wolf. "The Radicals." In *The Forty-Eighters*, ed. Zucker, 157–81.

Dolan, Neal. *Emerson's Liberalism*. London, 2009.

Douglas, Elisha. *Rebels and Democrats: The Struggle for Equal Political Rights and Majority Rule during the American Revolution*. Chapel Hill, NC, 1955.

Dowe, Dieter, Heinz-Gerhard Haupt, D. Langewiesche, and Jonathan Sperber, eds. *Europe in 1848: Revolution and Reform*. New York, 2000.

Doyle, William. *Oxford History of the French Revolution*. Oxford, 1989.

———. *Aristocracy and Its Enemies in the Age of Revolution*. Oxford, 2009.

Droixhe, Daniel. "Raynal à Liège." In *Lectures de Raynal: L'Histoire des deux Indes en Europe et en Amérique au XVIIIe siècle*, ed. H. J. Lüsebrink and M. Tietz, 205–33. Oxford, 1991.

Dubois, Sébastien. *L'Invention de la Belgique: Génèse d'un État-Nation, 1648–1830*. Brussels, 2005.

Ducharme, Michel. "Closing the Last Chapter of the Atlantic Revolution." *Humanities Association Review* 27 (1976): 413–30.

Dunbar-Ortiz, Roxanne. *An Indigenous Peoples' History of the United States*. Boston, 2014.

Dunn, Susan. *Sister Revolutions: French Lightning, American Light*. New York, 1999.

Dunne, Tom. *Theobald Wolfe Tone, Colonial Outsider: An Analysis of His Political Philosophy*. Cork, 1982.

Duprat, A. "Le sacre de Charles X: Justification et critique." In *Repenser la Restauration*, ed. Mollier, Reid, and Yon, 69–84.

Durán López, Fernando. "La Construcción de la opinión pública en España, 1808–1809." In *En el umbral de la revoluciones*, ed. Breña, 67–94.

Durey, Michael. "Thomas Paine's Apostles: Radical Emigrés and the Triumph of Jeffersonian Republicanism." *WMQ* 44 (1987), reprinted in *Thomas Paine*, ed. Kuklick, 187–214.

———. "Irish Deism and Jefferson's Republic: Denis Driscol in Ireland and America, 1793–1810." *Eire-Ireland: A Journal of Irish Studies* 25:4 (1990): 56–76.

———. "Marquess Cornwallis and the Fate of the Irish Prisoners in the Aftermath of the 1798 Rebellion." In *Revolution, Counter-revolution and Union*, ed. Smyth, 128–45.

———. "The United Irishmen and the Politics of Banishment, 1798–1807." In *Radicalism and Revolution in Britain, 1775–1848*, ed. M. T. Davis, 96–109. London, 2000.

———. "William Maume: United Irishman and Informer in Two Hemispheres." *Eighteenth-Century Ireland/Iris an dá chultúr* 18 (2003): 118–40.

Dwight, Theodore. *The Roman Republic of 1849; with accounts of the Inquisition and the Siege of Rome*. New York, 1851.

Dynner, Glenn. *Yankel's Tavern: Jews, Liquor and Life in the Kingdom of Poland*. New York, 2014.

Dziewanowski, M. K. "Tadeusz Kosciuszko, Kazimierz Pulaski, and the American War of Independence." In *The American and European Revolutions, 1776–1848: Sociopolitical and Ideological Aspects*, ed. J. Pelenski, 125–46. Iowa City, 1980.

Eamon, Michael. "An Extensive Collection of Useful and Entertaining Books." *Journal of the Canadian Historical Association/Revue de la Société historique du Canada* 23, no. 1 (2012): 1–38.

Eccles, W. J. *The French in North America, 1500–1783*. Markham, Ontario, 1998.

Edelstein, D. "A Response to Jonathan Israel." In *Self-Evident Truths? Human Rights and the Enlightenment: The Oxford Amnesty Lectures*, ed. Kate Tunstall, 127–35. London, 2012.

Edwards, Laura. "The Contradictions of Democracy in American Institutions and Practices." In *Re-Imagining Democracy*, ed. Innes and Philp, 40–54.

Egerton, D. R. "Race and Slavery in the Era of Thomas Jefferson." In *The Cambridge Companion to Thomas Jefferson*, ed. Shuffelton, 73–82.

Ehrard, Jean. "Audace théorique, prudence pratique: Montesquieu et l'esclavage colonial." In Olivier Pétré-Grenouilleau, *Abolir l'esclavage: Un réformisme à l'épreuve (France, Portugal, Suisse, XVIIIe–XIXe siècles)*, 27–40. Rennes, 2008.

Elazar, Yiftah. "Liberty as Caricature: Bentham's Antidote to Republicanism." *JHI* 76:3 (2015): 417–39.

Elkins, Stanley, and E. McKitrick. *The Age of Federalism: The Early American Republic, 1788–1800.* New York, 1993.

Elliott, J. I. *Empires of the Atlantic World: Britain and Spain in America, 1492–1830.* New Haven, CT, 2006.

Elliott, Marianne. *Partners in Revolution: The United Irishmen and France.* New Haven, CT, 1982.

———. "Wolfe Tone and the Republican Ideal." In *The Great Irish Rebellion of 1798*, ed. Cathal Pointeir, 49–57. Cork, 1998.

Ellis, Joseph J. "Habits of Mind and an American Enlightenment." *AmQu* 38, special issue "An American Enlightenment" (1976): 150–64.

———. *American Sphinx: The Character of Thomas Jefferson.* New York, 1998.

———. *Founding Brothers: The Revolutionary Generation.* New York, 2000.

———. *Passionate Sage: The Character and Legacy of John Adams.* 1993. New ed., New York, 2001.

———. *After the Revolution: Profiles of Early American Culture.* 1979. New ed., New York, 2002.

———. *First Family: Abigail and John Adams.* New York, 2010.

———. *Revolutionary Summer: The Birth of American Independence.* New York, 2013.

Erdman, D. V. *Commerce des Lumières: John Oswald and the British in Paris, 1790–93.* Columbia, MO, 1986.

Erkilla, B. "Melville, Whitman, and the Tribulations of Democracy." In *A Companion to American Literature and Culture*, ed. P. Lauter, 250–83. Hoboken, NJ, 2010.

Evrigenis, Ioannis. "Enlightenment, Emancipation and National Identity: Koraís and the Ancients." In *Adamantios Koraís and the European Enlightenment*, ed. P. Kitromilides, 91–108. Oxford, 2010.

Fawcett, Edward. *Liberalism: The Life of an Idea.* Princeton, 2014.

Fay, Bernard. "L'Esprit révolutionnaire en France et aux États-Unis à la fin du dix-huitième siècle." In *Bibliographie Critique des Ouvrages Français relatifs aux États-Unis, 1770–1800.* Paris, 1925.

Fea, John. "John Adams and Religion." In *A Companion to John Adams and John Quincy Adams*, ed. D. Waldstreicher, 184–98. Oxford, 2013.

Federici, M. P. *The Political Philosophy of Alexander Hamilton.* Baltimore, 2012.

Fenton, Elizabeth. *Religious Liberties: Anti-Catholicism and Liberal Democracy in Nineteenth-Century U.S. Literature and Culture.* New York, 2011.

Fergus, Claudius K. *Revolutionary Emancipation: Slavery and Abolitionism in the British West Indies.* Baton Rouge, 2013.

Ferguson, R. A. *The American Enlightenment, 1750–1820.* Cambridge, MA, 1994.

Ferling, John. *Adams vs. Jefferson: The Tumultuous Election of 1800.* Oxford, 2004.

———. *Independence: The Struggle to Set America Free.* New York, 2011.

———. *Jefferson and Hamilton: The Rivalry That Forged a Nation.* New York, 2013.

———. *Whirlwind: The American Revolution and the War That Won It.* New York, 2015.

Fernández Sarasola, Ignacio. "La Portée des droits individuels dans la constitution espagnole de 1812." In *Guerre d'Indépendence*, ed. Luis, 91–109.

Fernández Sebastián, Javier. "From the 'Voice of the People' to the Freedom of the Press." In *The Spanish Enlightenment Revisited*, ed. J. Astigarraga, 213–33. Oxford, 2015.

Fernández Sebastián, Javier, and J. Chassin, eds. *L'avènement de l'opinion publique: Europe et Amérique, XVIIIe–XIXe siècles*. Paris, 2004.

Ferrone, Vincenzo. *The Enlightenment: History of an Idea*. Princeton, 2015.

Finch, Alison. *French Literature: A Cultural History*. Cambridge. 2010.

Fischer, Kirsten. "Religion Governed by Terror: A Deist Critique of Fearful Christianity in the Early American Republic." *Revue française d'Études Américaines* 125 (2010): 13–36.

Fisher, J. R., Allan J. Kuethe, and Anthony McFarlane, eds. *Reform and Insurrection in Bourbon New Granada and Peru*. Baton Rouge, 1990.

Fitz, Caitlin. *Our Sister Republics: The United States in an Age of Revolutions*. New York, 2016.

Fleming, K. E. *Greece: A Jewish History*. Princeton, 2008.

Fleming, Thomas. *The Great Divide: The Conflict between Washington and Jefferson That Defined a Nation*. Cambridge, MA, 2015.

Foner, Eric. *The Story of American Freedom*. Basingstoke, 1999.

———. *Tom Paine and Revolutionary America*. 1976. Rev. ed., New York, 2005.

Foner, Philip S. *The Democratic-Republican Societies, 1790–1800: A Documentary Sourcebook of Constitutions, Declarations, Addresses, Resolutions and Toasts*. Westport, CT, 1977.

Fontana, A., et al., eds. *Venise et la Révolution française: Les 470 dépêches des ambassadeurs de Venise au Doge, 1786–1795*. Paris, 1997.

Foot, Paul. *Red Shelley*. 1984. New ed., London, 2004.

Forsyth, M. *Reason and Revolution: The Political Thought of the Abbé Sieyès*. Leicester, 1987.

Fortescue, W. *Alphonse de Lamartine: A Political Biography*. London, 1983.

Fowler, William M. *American Crisis: George Washington and the Dangerous Two Years after Yorktown, 1781–1783*. New York, 2011.

Frost, J. William. *A Perfect Freedom: Religious Liberty in Pennsylvania*. 1990. New ed., University Park, PA, 1993.

Fruchtman, Jack. "Unrespectable and Reluctant Radical: Benjamin Franklin as a Revolutionary." In *Unrespectable Radicals?* ed. Davis and Pickering, 5–19.

Fuentes, Juan Francisco. *José Marchena, biografía política e intelectual*. Barcelona, 1989.

Fureix, E. "Introduction" to *La Liberté guidant les peuples*, ed. Aprile, Caron, and Fureix, 9–32.

———. "Les trois Glorieuses: Jeu d'échelles et inscription transnationale." In *La Liberté guidant les peuples*, ed. Aprile, Caron, and Fureix, 61–71.

Furet, François. *Revolutionary France, 1770–1880*. 1988. Repr., Oxford, 1995.

Furstenberg, François. *When the United States Spoke French: Five Refugees Who Shaped a Nation*. New York, 2014.

Gabrieli, Vittorio. "The Impact of American Political Ideas in 18th Century Italy." In *American Constitution, ed.* Noether, 175–89.

Garrigus, J. D. "Opportunist or Patriot? Julien Raimond (1744–1801) and the Haitian Revolution." *Slavery and Abolition* 28 (2007): 1–21.

Gaulmier, Jean. *Un grand témoin de la Révolution et de l'empire, Volney*. Paris, 1959.

Gazley, J. G. *American Opinion of German Unification, 1848–1871*. New York, 1926.

Geffroy, A. "Louise de Kéralio-Robert, pionnière du républicanisme sexiste." *AHRF* 344 (2006): 107–24.

Gemme, Paola. "Domesticating Foreign Struggles: American Narratives of Italian Revolutions and the Debate on Slavery in the Antebellum Era." *Prospects* 27 (2002): 77–101.

Ghachem, Malick W. "Montesquieu in the Caribbean: The Colonial Enlightenment between 'Code Noir' and 'Code Civil.'" *Historical Reflections / Réflexions Historiques* 25:2 (1999): 183–210.

Gibbons, Luke. "Republicanism and Radical Memory: The O'Connors, O'Carolan and the United Irishmen." In *Revolution, Counter-Revolution and Union*, ed. Smyth, 211–37.

———. *Edmund Burke and Ireland*. Cambridge, 2003.

Gigantino, James. "The Whole North Is Not Abolitionized: Slavery's Slow Death in New Jersey, 1830–1860." *JER* 34 (2014): 411–37.

Gilbert, Alan. *Black Patriots and Loyalists Fighting for Emancipation in the War of Independence*. Chicago, 2012.

Gilje, Paul. *The Road to Mobocracy: Popular Disorder in New York City, 1763–1834*. Chapel Hill, NC, 1987.

Gillen, Ultàn. "Varieties of Enlightenment: The Enlightenment and Irish Political Culture in the Age of Revolutions." In *Peripheries of the Enlightenment. SVEC* 2008:01, ed. R. Butterwick, S. Davies, and G. Sanchez Espinosa. Oxford, 2008.

———. "Constructing Democratic Thought in Ireland in the Age of Revolution, 1775–1800." In *Re-Imagining Democracy*, ed. Innes and Philp, 149–61.

Gilmartin, K. *Print Politics: The Press and Radical Opposition in Early Nineteenth-Century England*. Cambridge, 1996.

Gish, Dustin, and Daniel Klinghard, eds. *Resistance to Tyrants: Reason, Religion and Republicanism at the American Founding*. Lanham, MD, 2013.

Gleijeses, Piero. "The Limits of Sympathy: The United States and the Independence of Spanish America." *Journal of Latin American Studies* 24 (1992): 481–505.

Goetzmann, W. H. *Beyond the Revolution: A History of American Thought from Paine to Pragmatism*. New York, 2009.

Goggi, Gianluigi. "Ancora su Diderot-Raynal e Filangieri e su altre fonti della *Scienza della legislazione*." *La Rassegna della letteratura italiana* 84 (1980): 112–60.

Goldner, Loren. *Herman Melville: Between Charlemagne and the Antemosaic Cosmic Man*. New York, 2006.

Goor, J. van. *De Nederlandse koloniën: Geschiedenis van de Nederlandse expansie, 1600–1975*. Bilthoven, 1997.

Görisch, Joseph, and Thomas Mayer. *Untersuchungsberichte zur republikanischen Bewegung in Hessen, 1831–1834*. Frankfurt am Main, 1982.

Gorman, Thomas. *America and Belgium: A Study of the Influence of the United States upon the Belgian Revolution of 1789–90*. London, 1925.

Goslinga, Cornelius C. *The Dutch in the Caribbean and on the Wild Coast, 1580–1680*. Gainesville, FL, 1971.

Gossman, Lionel. "Jules Michelet and Romantic Historiography." In *Scribner's European Writers*, ed. Jacques Barzun and George Stade, 5:571–606. New York, 1985.

————. "Jules Michelet and the French Revolution." In *The Transformation of Political Culture, 1789–1848*, ed. F. Furet and Mona Ozouf, vol. 3 of *The French Revolution and the Creation of Modern Political Culture*, 639–63. Oxford, 1989.

————. *Basel in the Age of Burckhardt: A Study in Unseasonable Ideas*. Chicago, 2000.

Gotschel, W. "Heine's Spinoza." *Idealistic Studies* 33 (2003): 203–17.

Gottschalk, P. *American Heretics: Catholics, Jews, Muslims, and the History of Religious Intolerance*. New York, 2013.

Gould, Eliga. *The Persistence of Empire: British Political Culture in the Age of the American Revolution*. Chapel Hill, NC, 2000.

————. *Among the Powers of the Earth: The American Revolution and the Making of a New World Empire*. Cambridge, MA, 2012.

Gourgouris, S. *Dream Nation: Enlightenment, Colonization and the Institution of Modern Greece*. Stanford, CA, 1996.

Grab, Alexander. "The Italian Enlightenment and the American Revolution." In *American Constitution*, ed. Noether, 35–53.

Grant, James. *John Adams, Party of One*. New York, 2005.

Grayling, A. C. *Towards the Light*. London, 2007.

Grundfest, J. *George Clymer: Philadelphia Revolutionary*. New York, 1983.

Grunert, Frank, ed. *Concepts of (Radical) Enlightenment: Jonathan Israel in Discussion*. Halle, 2014.

Gueniffey, Patrice. *Bonaparte, 1769–1802*. Paris, 2013.

Gunkel, Christoph. "Halbe gegen Ganze: Der Grundkonflikt zwischen Liberalen und Radikalen zeigt sich zuerst in Baden." *Spiegel Geschichte* 3 (2014): 43–49.

Gutzman, Kevin. *James Madison and the Making of America*. New York, 2013.

Guyatt, Nicholas. *Providence and the Invention of the United States, 1607–1876*. Cambridge, 2007.

Haines, M. R., and R. H. Steckel, eds. *A Population History of North America*. Cambridge, 2000.

Halliday, E. M. *Understanding Thomas Jefferson*. New York, 2001.

Hammersley, Rachel. *French Revolutionaries and English Republicans: The Cordeliers Club, 1790–1794*. Rochester, NY, 2005.

Hammond, John Craig. "Slavery, Settlement, and Empire: The Expansion and Growth of Slavery in the Interior of the North American Continent, 1770–1820." *JER* (2012): 175–206.

Hamnett, Brian. "Popular Insurrection and Royalist Reaction: Colombian Regions, 1810–1823." In *Reform and Insurrection in Bourbon New Granada and Peru*, ed. Fisher, Kuette, and McFarlane, 292–326.

Hampshire-Monk, I. "British Radicalism and the Anti-Jacobins." In *The Cambridge History of Eighteenth-Century Political Thought*, ed. Mark Goldie and Robert Wokler, 660–87. Cambridge, 2006.

Handlin, Oscar. "The American Scene." In *The Forty-Eighters*, ed. Zucker, 26–40.

Harris, Jean-Pierre. *Antoine d'Estutt de Tracy: L'éblouissement des Lumières*. Précy-sous-Thil, 2008.

Hartog, Johannes. *History of St. Eustatius*. Aruba, 1976.

Haubtmann, Pierre. *Proudhon: Sa vie et sa pensée (1809–1849)*. Paris, 1982.

Havard, Gilles, and C. Vidal. *Histoire de l'Amérique française*. 2003. New ed., Paris, 2006.

Hayton, D. W. "The Williamite Revolution in Ireland." In *Anglo-Dutch Moment*, ed. Israel, 185–213.

Hazen, Charles D. *Contemporary American Opinion of the French Revolution*. Baltimore, 1897.

Heirwegh, Jean-Jacques. "La fin de l'Ancien Régime et les révolutions." In *La Belgique autrichienne, 1713–1794: Les Pays-Bas méridionaux sous les Habsbourg d'Autriche*, ed. H. Hasquin, 467–504. Brussels, 1987.

Herr, Richard. "The Constitution of 1812 and the Spanish Road to Parliamentary Monarchy." In *Revolution and the Meanings of Freedom*, ed. Woloch, 65–102.

Heuberger, Georg. *Ludwig Börne: Ein Frankfurter Jude kämpft für die Freiheit*. Frankfurt, 1996.

Hickey, Donald. *The War of 1812: A Forgotten Conflict*. Urbana-Champaign, IL, 2012.

Higonnet, Patrice. *Sister Republics: The Origins of French and American Republicanism*. Cambridge, 1988.

Himmelfarb, Gertrude. *The Roads to Modernity: The British, French and American Enlightenments*. New York, 2004.

Hirschfeld, Fritz. *George Washington and Slavery: A Documentary Portrayal*. Columbia, MO, 1997.

Hoagwood, T. A. *Skepticism and Ideology: Shelley's Political Prose and Its Philosophical Context*. Iowa City, 1988.

Hobsbawm, Eric. *The Age of Revolution, 1789–1848*. 1962. New ed., London, 2010.

Hocquellet, Richard. *Résistance et révolution durant l'occupation napoléonienne en Espagne, 1808–1812*. Paris, 2001.

———. "L'invention de la modernité par la presse." In *L'avènement*, ed. Fernández Sebastian and Chassin, 163–80.

Hoffman, Philip. "Simon Girty: His War on the Frontier." In *Human Tradition*, ed. Rhoden and Steele, 221–40.

Holifield, E. Brooks. *Theology in America: Christian Thought from the Age of Puritans to the Civil War*. New Haven, CT, 2003.

Holmes, David L. *The Faiths of the Founding Fathers*. Oxford, 2006.

Honeck, Mischa. *We Are the Revolutionists: German-Speaking Immigrants and American Abolitionists after 1848*. Athens, GA, 2011.

Horne, Gerald. *The Counter-Revolution of 1776: Slave Resistance and the Origins of the United States of America*. New York, 2014.

Houston, Alan C. *Algernon Sidney and the Republican Heritage in England and America*. Princeton, 2014.

Houtman-De Smedt, H. "Het prinsbisdom Luik, 1581–1787." In *De Lage Landen van 1500 tot 1780*, ed. Ivo Schöffer et al., 409–24. 1978. Amsterdam, 1991.

Howe, John R. "Republican Thought and the Political Violence of the 1790s." *AmQu* 19 (1967): 147–65.

Humphrey, Th. J. "William Prendergast and the Revolution in the Hudson River Valley." In *Human Tradition*, ed. Rhoden and Steele, 81–98.

———. "Conflicting Independence: Land Tenancy and the American Revolution." *JER* 28 (2008): 159–82.

Hunt, Lynn. *Inventing Human Rights: A History*. New York, 2007.

Huston, Reeve. *Land and Freedom: Rural Society, Popular Protest, and Party Politics in Antebellum New York*. New York, 2000.

Hutcheson, Wallace. "The Louisville Riots of August 1855." *Register of the Kentucky Historical Society* (April 1971): 150–72.

Hutson, J. H. "John Adams and the Birth of Dutch-American Friendship, 1780–82." *BMGN* 97 (1982): 409–22.

Hyde, Anne. *Empires, Nations and Families: A New History of the North American West, 1800–1860*. New York, 2011.

Ingrams, Richard. *The Life and Adventures of William Cobbett*. London, 2005.

Innes, Joanna, and Mark Philp, eds. *Re-Imagining Democracy in the Age of Revolutions: America, France, Britain, Ireland, 1750–1850*. Oxford, 2013.

———. "Synergies." In *Re-Imagining Democracy*, ed. Innes and Philp, 189–212.

Isabella, Maurizio. *Risorgimento in Exile: Italian Émigrés and the Liberal International in the Post-Napoleonic Era*. Oxford, 2009.

Israel, Jonathan. *The Dutch Republic: Its Rise, Greatness, and Fall, 1477–1806*. Oxford, 1995.

———. *Radical Enlightenment: Philosophy and the Making of Modernity, 1650–1750*. Oxford, 2001.

———. *Enlightenment Contested: Philosophy, Modernity, and the Emancipation of Man, 1670–1752*. Oxford, 2006.

———. *A Revolution of the Mind: Radical Enlightenment and the Intellectual Origins of Modern Democracy*. Princeton, 2010.

———. "Radical Enlightenment and Revolt in Ibero-America (1770–1809)." In *Religiosidad y Clero en América Latina*, ed. Peer Schmidt et al., 37–53. Cologne, 2011.

———. *Democratic Enlightenment: Philosophy, Revolution, and Human Rights, 1750–1790*. Oxford, 2012.

———. "Philosophy, Religion and the Controversy about Basic Human Rights in 1789." In *Self-Evident Truths? Human Rights and the Enlightenment*, ed. Kate E. Tunstall, 111–25. New York, 2012.

———. "The Radical Enlightenment's Critique of the American Revolution." In *Resistance to Tyrants*, ed. Gish and Klinghard, 43–63.

———. *Revolutionary Ideas: An Intellectual History of the French Revolution from "The Rights of Man" to Robespierre*. Princeton, 2014.

———. "Democratic Republicanism and One Substance Philosophy: On the Connection of Two Disparate Concepts." In *Concepts of (Radical) Enlightenment*, ed. Frank Grunert, 14–43, 112–17. IZEA Kleine Schriften 5/2014. Halle, 2014.

———. "'Radical Enlightenment': Peripheral, Substantial or the Main Face of the Trans-Atlantic Enlightenment (1650–1850)." *Diametros* 40 (2014): 73–98.

———. "'Les Lumières radicales' comme théorie générale de la modernité démocratique séculière, et ses critiques." In *Lumières radicales et histoire politique: Un débat*, ed. Marta García Alonso, 387–436. Paris, 2017.

Israel, Jonathan, ed. *The Anglo-Dutch Moment: Essays on the Glorious Revolution and Its World Impact*. Cambridge, 1991.

Israel, Jonathan, and Martin Mulsow, eds. *Radikalaufklärung*. Berlin, 2014.

Jack, Belinda. *George Sand: A Woman's Life Writ Large*. New York, 2000.

Jacobitti, Edmund. *Revolutionary Humanism and Historicism in Modern Italy*. New Haven, CT, 1981.

Jacobs, Erik. "'Het Volk zal over de constitutie beslissen': De strijd om de publieke opinie van 1797." *De Achttiende Eeuw* 44 (2012): 85–100.

Jacoby, Susan. *Freethinkers: A History of American Secularism*. New York, 2004.

Jager, Colin. "After Atheism." *Studies in Romanticism* 49 (2010): 611–31.

Jaher, F. C. *The Jews and the Nation: Revolution, Emancipation, State Formation and the Liberal Paradigm in America and France*. Princeton, 2002.

Jainchill, A. *Reimagining Politics after the Terror*. Ithaca, NY, 2008.

Jameson, J. Franklin. "St. Eustatius in the American Revolution." *AHR* 8 (1903): 683–708.

Jarrett, Mark. *The Congress of Vienna: War and Great Power Diplomacy after Napoleon*. New York, 2014.

Jasanoff, M. *Liberty's Exiles: American Loyalists in the Revolutionary World*. New York, 2012.

Jaume, Lucien. *Tocqueville: The Aristocratic Sources of Liberty*. Princeton, 2013.

Jayne, Allen. *Jefferson's Declaration of Independence: Origins, Philosophy and Theology*. Lexington, 1998.

Jennings, Jeremy. *Revolution and the Republic: A History of Political Thought in France since the Eighteenth Century*. Oxford, 2013.

Jennings, L. C. *French Anti-Slavery: The Movement for the Abolition of Slavery in France, 1802–1848*. Cambridge, 2000.

Johnson, John J. "United States–British Rivalry in Latin America, 1815–1830: A Reassessment." *Jahrbuch für Geschichte von Staat, Wirtschaft und Gesellschaft Lateinamerikas* 22 (1985): 341–90.

Jongenelen, Ton. *Van Smaad tot erger: Amsterdamse boekverboden, 1747–1794*. Amsterdam, 1998.

Jordaan, Han. *Slavernij en vrijheid op Curaçao*. Zutphen, 2013.

Jourdan, Annie. *La Révolution, une exception française?* Paris, 2004.

———. "The 'Alien Origins' of the French Revolution: American, Scottish, Genevan, and Dutch Influences." *Proceedings of the Western Society for French History* 35 (2007): 185–205.

Kaiser, Thomas E. "Politics and Political Economy in the Thought of the Idéologues." *History of Political Economy* 12, issue 2 (1980): 141–60.

Kammen, Michael. *Colonial New York: A History*. Oxford, 1996.

Kaplan, L. S. "The Founding Fathers and the Two Confederations." *BMGN* 97 (1982): 423–38.

Kates, Gary. "From Liberalism to Radicalism: Tom Paine's Rights of Man." *JHI* 50 (1989): 569–87.

Kaye, Harvey J. *Thomas Paine and the Promise of America*. New York, 2006.

Keane, John. *Tom Paine: A Political Life*. New York, 2003.

Kennedy, R. G. *Orders from France: The Americans and the French in a Revolutionary World, 1780–1820*. New York, 1989.

Kieniewicz, Stefan. "The Revolutionary Nobleman: An East European Variant of the Liberation Struggle in the Restoration Era." In *The American and European Revolutions, 1776–1848: Sociopolitical and Ideological Aspects*, ed. J. Pelenski, 268–86. Iowa City, 1980.

King, Richard H. *Arendt and America*. Chicago, 2015.

King-Hele, Desmond. *Doctor of Revolution: The Life and Genius of Erasmus Darwin*. London, 1977.

Kitromilides, P. M. "The Enlightenment and the Greek Cultural Tradition." *HEI* 36 (2002): 39–46.

———. "Adamantios Koraís and the Dilemmas of Liberal Nationalism." In *Adamantios Koraís and the European Enlightenment*, ed. P. Kitromilides, 213–23. Oxford, 2010.

———. "Itineraries in the World of the Enlightenment." In *Adamantios Koraís and the European Enlightenment*, ed. P. Kitromilides, 1–33. Oxford, 2010.

———. *Enlightenment and Revolution: The Making of Modern Greece*. Cambridge, MA, 2013.

Klein, S. R. E. *Patriots republikanisme: Politieke cultuur in Nederland (1766–1787)*. Amsterdam, 1995.

Kleinman, S. "Tone and the French Expeditions to Ireland, 1796–1798." In *Republics at War, 1776–1840: Revolutions, Conflicts, and Geopolitics in Europe and the Atlantic World*, ed. Pierre Serna, A. De Francesco, and J. A. Miller, 83–103. London, 2013.

Klooster, Wim. *Revolutions in the Atlantic World: A Comparative History*. New York, 2009.

———. "The Rising Expectations of Free and Enslaved Blacks in the Greater Caribbean." In *Curaçao in the Age of Revolutions, 1795–1800*, ed. W. Klooster and Gert Oostindie, 57–74. Leiden, 2011.

Kloppenberg, J. T. *Toward Democracy: The Struggle for Self-Rule in European and American Thought*. New York, 2016.

Knigge, Adolph Freiherr. *Ausgewählte Werke in zehn Bänden*, ed. W. Fenner. 10 vols. Hanover, 1991–96.

Knudsen, J. B. *Justus Möser and the German Enlightenment*. Cambridge, 1986.

Koch, Daniel R. *Ralph Waldo Emerson in Europe: Class, Race and Revolution in the Making of an American Thinker*. London, 2012.

———. "Revolution." In *Ralph Waldo Emerson in Context*, ed. Wesley T. Mott, 127–35. Cambridge, 2013.

Koch, G. Adolf. *Religion of the American Enlightenment*. 1933. New ed., New York, 1968.

Koliopoulos, J. S., and Th. Veremis. *Greece: A History since 1821*. Hoboken, NJ, 2009.

Kolodny, Annette. "A History of the Penobscot Nation." In Joseph Nicolar, *The Life and Traditions of the Red Man*, 1–92. Durham, NC, 2007.

Kornblith, G. J., and J. M. Murrin. "The Making and Unmaking of the American Ruling Class." In *Beyond the American Revolution*, ed. Young, 27–79.

Kors, Alan. *Encyclopedia of the Enlightenment*. 4 vols. Oxford, 2003.

Kossmann, E. H. *The Low Countries, 1780–1940*. Oxford, 1978.

———. *De Lage Landen, 1780–1980*. 2 vols. Amsterdam, 1986.

———. *Politieke Theorie en geschiedenis: Verspreide opstellen en voordrachten*. Amsterdam, 1987.

Krabbendam, Hans. "From New Netherland to 'New Zeeland.'" *BMGN* 128 (2013): 62–70.

Kramer, Lloyd. "America's Lafayette and Lafayette's America." *WMQ*, 3rd ser., 38 (1981): 228–41.

———. "Lafayette and the Historians." *Historical Reflections/Réflexions historiques* 11 (1984): 373–401.

———. *Lafayette in Two Worlds*. Chapel Hill, NC, 1996.

Krebs, Roland. "Le 'Deutsches Museum' et l'Indépendance américaine." In *La Révolution américaine*, ed. Krebs and Moes, 1–21.

Krebs, Roland, and J. Moes, eds. *La Révolution américaine vue par les périodiques de langue allemande, 1773–1783*. Paris, 1992.

Kroes-Ligtenberg, Christina. *Dr. Wybo Fijnje (1750–1809): Belevenissen van een journalist in de Patriottentijd*. Assen, 1957.

Kukla, Jon. *A Wilderness So Immense: The Louisiana Purchase and the Destiny of America*. New York, 2003.

Kuklick, Bruce. *Churchmen and Philosophers: From Jonathan Edwards to John Dewey.* New Haven, CT, 1985.

———. *A History of Philosophy in America, 1720–2000.* Oxford, 2001.

———, ed. *Thomas Paine.* Aldershot, 2006.

Labunski, R. *James Madison and the Struggle for the Bill of Rights.* Oxford, 2006.

Lachance, P. F. "The 1809 Immigration of Saint-Domingue Refugees to New Orleans." *Louisiana History* 29 (1988): 109–41.

Lagrave, Jean-Paul de. *Fleury-Mesplet (1734–1794): Diffuseur des Lumières au Québec.* Montreal, 1985.

———. "Thomas Paine et les Condorcet." In *Thomas Paine ou La République sans frontières,* ed. B. Vincent, 57–64. Nancy, 1993.

Lakomäki, S. "'Our Line: The Shawnees, the United States, and Competing Borders on the Great Lakes 'Borderlands,' 1795–1832." *JER* 34 (2014): 598–624.

Lambert, F. *The Founding Fathers and the Place of Religion in America.* Princeton, 2003.

Lanctot, Gustave. *Canada and the American Revolution, 1774–1783.* Cambridge, MA, 1967.

Langley, Lester D. *The Americas in the Age of Revolution, 1750–1850.* New Haven, CT, 1996.

Larriba, Elisabel. "Estudio preliminar." In Estala, *El Imparcial,* 11–81.

Lause, M. A. "The 'Unwashed Infidelity': Thomas Paine and Early New York City Labor History." *Labor History* 27 (1986): 385–409.

———. *Young America: Land, Labor, and the Republican Community.* Urbana, IL, 2005.

Lavaert, Sonja. "Radical Enlightenment, Enlightened Subversion, and Spinoza." *Philosophica* 89 (2014): 49–102.

Laviña, Javier. "La participación de negros y pardos en el proceso de 1808." In *Las Experiencias de 1808 en Iberoamérica,* ed. P. Pérez Herrera. Madrid, 2008.

Leal Curiel, C. "El juntismo caraqueño de 1808: Tres lecturas de una misma fidelidad." In *Experiencias,* ed. Ávila and Pérez Herrero, 399–415.

Leamon, J. S. *Revolution Downeast: The War for American Independence in Maine.* Amherst, MA, 1993.

Leask, Ian. "The Undivulged Event in Toland's *Christianity Not Mysterious.*" In *Atheism and Deism Revalued: Heterodox Religious Identities in Britain, 1650–1800,* ed. Wayne Hudson, Diego Lucci, and J. R. Wigelsworth, 63–80. Farnham, 2014.

Lee, Maurice. *Slavery, Philosophy and American Literature.* Cambridge, 2005.

Lefer, David. *The Founding Conservatives: How a Group of Unsung Heroes Saved the American Revolution.* New York, 2013.

Leiby, A. C. *The Revolutionary War in the Hackensack Valley: The Jersey Dutch and the Neutral Ground, 1775–1783.* New Brunswick, NJ, 1962.

Lemny, Stefan. *Jean-Louis Carra (1742–1793), parcours d'un révolutionnaire.* Paris-Montreal, 2000.

Lempérière, A. "L'opinion publique au Mexique: Le concept et ses usages." In *L'avènement,* ed. Fernández Sebastián and Chassin, 211–26.

Lepore, Jill. "A World of Paine." In *Revolutionary Founders,* ed. Young, Nash, and Raphael, 87–96.

Lerner, Ralph. *Revolutions Revisited: Two Faces of the Politics of Enlightenment.* Chapel Hill, NC, 1994.

Lévêque, Pierre. "The Revolutionary Crisis of 1848/51 in France." In *Europe in 1848,* ed. Dowe et al., 91–119.

Levine, Alan. "The Idea of America in the History of European Political Thought: 1492 to 9/11." In *America through European Eyes*, ed. A. Craiutu and J. C. Isaac, 17–42. University Park, PA, 2009.

Levy, Jacob. "Montesquieu's Constitutional Legacies." In *Montesquieu and His Legacy*, ed. R. E. Kingston, 115–38. Albany, NY, 2008.

Lewalski, K. W. "Lelewel's Third Exile." *Polish Review* 23 (1978): 31–39.

Lienesch, Michael. "Reinterpreting Rebellion: The Influence of Shays's Rebellion in American Political Thought." In *In Debt to Shays: The Bicentennial of an Agrarian Insurrection*, ed. R. A. Gross, 161–82. Charlottesville, VA, 1993.

Link, E. P. *Democratic-Republican Societies, 1790–1800*. New York, 1942.

Livesey, James. *Making Democracy in the French Revolution*. Cambridge, 2001.

Lock, F. P. *Edmund Burke*. 2 vols. Oxford, 1998, 2006.

Loft, Leonore. *Passion, Politics and Philosophie: Rediscovering J.-P. Brissot*. Westport, CT, 2002.

Lok, Mattijs. "The Establishment of the Orange Monarchy in 1813–15: A National Myth." *The Low Countries: Arts and Sciences in Flanders and the Netherlands* 21 (2013): 208–17.

Lombardi, J. V. *The Decline and Abolition of Negro Slavery in Venezuela, 1820–1854*. Westport, CT, 1971.

Losfeld, Christophe. *Philanthropisme, Libéralisme et Révolution: Le "Braunschweigisches Journal" et le "Schleswigsches Journal" (1788–1793)*. Tübingen, 2002.

Losurdo, Domenico. *Contre-histoire du libéralisme*. Paris, 2013.

Loveland, Anne C. *Emblem of Liberty: The Image of Lafayette in the American Mind*. Baton Rouge, 1971.

Lubinski, R. *James Madison and the Struggle for the Bill of Rights*. Oxford, 2006.

Lucas, Colin. "The Crowd and Politics." In *Political Culture*, ed. Lucas, *The Political Culture of the French Revolution*, vol. 2 of *The French Revolution and Modern Political Culture*. Oxford, 1988.

Luebke, F. C. "The Origins of Thomas Jefferson's Anti-Clericalism." *Church History* 32 (1963): 344–56.

Luis, Jean-Philippe, ed. *La Guerre d'Independence espagnole et le libéralisme au XIX siècle*. Madrid, 2011.

Lundberg, David, and Henry May. "The Enlightened Reader in America." *AmQu* 28 (1976): 262–93.

Luttrell, B. *Mirabeau*. Carbondale, IL, 1990.

Lutz, Donald. "The Relative Influence of European Writers on Late Eighteenth-Century American Political Thought." *American Political Science Review* 78 (1984): 189–97.

———. *The Origins of the American Constitution*. Baton Rouge, 1987.

Lynch, J. V. "The Limits of Revolutionary Radicalism: Tom Paine and Slavery." *Pennsylvania Magazine of History and Biography* 123 (1999): 177–99.

Lyons, Jonathan. *The Society of Useful Knowledge: How Benjamin Franklin and Friends Brought the Enlightenment to America*. New York, 2013.

MacDermot, Frank. *Theobald Wolfe Tone: A Biographical Study*. London, 1939.

Mackridge, Peter, "Koraís and the Greek Language Question." In *Adamantios Koraís and the European Enlightenment*, ed. P. Kitromilides, 127–49. Oxford, 2010.

Mack Smith, Denis. *Mazzini*. New Haven, CT, 1994.

Macleod, Emma. "Thomas Paine and Jeffersonian America." In *Paine and Jefferson*, ed. Newman and Onuf, 209–28.

Maier, Pauline. "Reason and Revolution: The Radicalism of Dr. Thomas Young." *AmQu* 28, special issue, "An American Enlightenment" (1976): 229–49.

———. *From Resistance to Revolution: Colonial Radicals and the Development of American Opposition to Britain, 1765–1776*. 1972. New ed., New York, 1991.

———. *American Scripture: Making the Declaration of Independence*. New York, 1997.

Maissen, Thomas. *Geschichte der Schweiz*. Baden, 2010.

Malone, Dumas. *The Public Life of Thomas Cooper, 1783–1839*. Charleston, 1961.

Mandell, D. R. *Tribe, Race, History: Native Americans in Southern New England, 1780–1880*. Baltimore, 2008.

Mapp, Alf. *The Faiths of the Founders: What America's Founders Really Believed*. Lanham, MD, 2003.

Marchione, Margherita. "Philip Mazzei and the American Revolution." In *The United States and Italy*, ed. H. S. Nelli, 3–12. New York, 1977.

Marden, John Lardas. *Secularism in Antebellum America*. Chicago, 2011.

Marraro, Howard R. *American Opinion on the Unification of Italy, 1846–1861*. New York, 1932.

Marshall, John. *John Locke, Toleration and Early Enlightenment Culture*. Cambridge, 2006.

Marshall, Peter. "British North America, 1760–1815." In *The Oxford History of the British Empire*, vol. 2, *The Eighteenth Century*, ed. Marshall, 372–93. Oxford, 1998.

Martin, G. "Canada from 1815." In *The Oxford History of the British Empire*, vol. 3, *The Nineteenth Century*, ed. A. Porter, 522–45. Oxford, 2001.

Martínez Delgado, L., and S. C. Ortiz. *El Periodismo en la Nueva Granada, 1810–11*. Bogotá, 1960.

Martínez Garnica, A. "La Experiencia del Nuevo Reino de Granada." In *Experiencias*, ed. Ávila and Pérez Herrero, 365–80.

Maspero-Clerc, Hélène. "Une 'Gazette anglo-française' pendant la Guerre de l'Amérique: Le *Courrier de l'Europe* (1776–1788)." *AHRF* 48 (1976): 572–94.

Mastellone, Salvo. *Mazzini and Marx: Thoughts upon Democracy in Europe*. Westport, CT, 2003.

———. *La nascità della democrazia in Europa: Carlyle, Harney, Mill, Engels, Mazzini, Schapper: Addresses, Appeals, Manifestos (1836–1855)*. Florence, 2009.

Mathewes, Ch., and Christopher McKnight, eds. *Prophecies of Godlessness: Predictions of America's Immanent Secularization from the Puritans to the Present Day*. New York, 2008.

Matthews, Richard K. *The Radical Politics of Thomas Jefferson: A Revisionist View*. Lawrence, KS, 1984.

Matthewson, Tim. "Jefferson and Haiti." *Journal of Southern History* 61 (1995): 209–48.

May, H. F. *The Enlightenment in America*. 1976. New ed., New York, 1978.

———. *The Divided Heart: Essays on Protestantism and the Enlightenment in America*. Oxford, 1991.

Mayers, David. *Dissenting Voices in America's Rise to Power*. Cambridge, 2007.

McBride, I. R. *Scripture Politics: Ulster Presbyterians and Irish Radicalism in the Late Eighteenth Century*. Oxford, 1998.

McCullough, David. *John Adams*. New York, 2001.

McDaniel, Iain. *Adam Ferguson in the Scottish Enlightenment*. Cambridge, MA, 2013.

McDonnell, M. A. *The Politics of War: Race, Class, and Conflict in Revolutionary Virginia*. Chapel Hill, NC, 2007.

McDowell, R. B. *Ireland in the Age of Imperialism and Revolution, 1760–1801.* 1979. New ed., Oxford, 1991.

McFarlane, Anthony. "The American Revolution and the Spanish Monarchy." In *Europe's American Revolution*, ed. Newman, 26–50.

McGarvie, M. D. *One Nation under Law: America's Early National Struggles to Separate Church and State.* DeKalb, IL, 2005.

———. *Law and Religion in American History: Public Values and Private Conscience.* New York, 2016.

McInnis, Marvin. "The Population of Canada in the Nineteenth Century." In *A Population History of North America*, ed. Haines and Steckel, 371–432.

McLoughlin, T. *Contesting Ireland: Irish Voices against England in the Eighteenth Century.* Dublin, 1999.

McMahon, Darrin M. *Enemies of the Enlightenment: The French Counter-Enlightenment and the Making of Modernity.* New York, 2001.

McNamara, Peter. "Alexander Hamilton, Religion and American Conservatism." In *Resistance to Tyrants*, ed. Gish and Klinghard, 183–97.

McPhee, Peter. *Robespierre: A Revolutionary Life.* New Haven, CT, 2012.

Meacham, Jon. *American Gospel: God, the Founding Fathers, and the Making of a Nation.* New York, 2006.

———. *Thomas Jefferson: The Art of Power.* New York, 2013.

Mead, Philip. "'Adventures, Dangers and Suffering': The Betrayals of Private Joseph Plumb Martin, Continental Soldier." In *Revolutionary Founders*, ed. Young, Nash, and Raphael, 117–34.

Meleney, J. C. *The Public Life of Aedanus Burke.* Columbia, SC, 1989.

Merriman, John. "Contested Freedoms in the French Revolutions, 1830–1871." In *Revolution and the Meanings of Freedom*, ed. Woloch, 173–91.

Merritt, Jane T. "Native Peoples in the Revolutionary War." In *The Oxford Handbook of the American Revolution*, ed. E. G. Gray and J. Kamensky, 234–49. Oxford, 2013.

Meyer, Donald. *The Democratic Enlightenment.* New York, 1976.

———. "The Uniqueness of the American Enlightenment." *AmQu* 28 (1976): 165–86.

Middlekauff, R. *The Glorious Cause: The American Revolution, 1763–1789.* New York, 1982.

———. *Benjamin Franklin and His Enemies.* Berkeley, CA, 1996.

Miller, J. C. *The Federalist Era, 1789–1801.* New York, 1960.

Minchom, Martin. *The People of Quito, 1690–1810.* Boulder, CO, 1994.

Mirow, M. C. *Florida's First Constitution: The Constitution of Cádiz.* Durham, NC, 2012.

Mollier, Jean-Yves, M. Reid, and Jean-Claude Yon, eds. *Repenser la Restauration.* Paris, 2005.

Monnier, R. "L'Évolution du personnel politique de la section Marat et la rupture de Germinal An 11." *AHRF* 263 (1986): 50–73.

———. *Républicanisme, Patriotisme et Révolution française.* Paris, 2005.

Morales Padrón, F. "México y la independencia de Hispanoamérica en 1781 según un comisionado regio: Francisco de Saavedra." *Revista de Indias* 29 (1969): 335–58.

Morandi, Carlo. "Giuseppe Compagnoni e la storia dell'America." *Annali della R. Scuola Normale Superiore di Pisa: Lettere, Storia e Filosofia*, series II, vol. 8:3 (1939): 252–61.

Morange, Claude. "Opinion publique: Ambivalence d'un concept (Espagne: 1750–1823)." In *L'avènement*, ed. Fernández Sebastián and Chassin, 181–210.

Moravia, Sergio. *Il tramonto dell'Illuminismo: Filosofia e politica nella società francese (1770–1810)*. Bari, 1986.

Morelli, Emilia. "The United States Constitution Viewed by Nineteenth-Century Italian Democrats." In *American Constitution*, ed. Noether, 99–118.

Morelli, F. "Quito frente a la crisis de 1808." In *Experiencias*, ed. Ávila and Pérez Herrero, 417–40.

Morgan, E. S. "Ezra Stiles and Timothy Dwight." *Proceedings of the Massachusetts Historical Society* 72 (1957/60): 101–17.

———. *American Slavery, American Freedom: The Ordeal of Colonial Virginia*. 1975. New ed., New York, 2005.

———. *Benjamin Franklin*. New Haven, CT, 2002.

Morison, Samuel Eliot. *A History of the Constitution of Massachusetts*. Boston, 1917.

Mortier, Roland. *Le Cœur et la raison: Receuil d'études sur le dix-huitième siècle*. Oxford, 1990.

———. *Anacharsis Cloots ou l'utopie foudroyée*. Paris, 1995.

Mossner, E. C. *The Life of David Hume*. 1954. 3rd rev. ed., Oxford, 2001.

Mott, Wesley T. *Ralph Waldo Emerson in Context*. Cambridge, 2014.

Mourdoukoutas, Y. "Koraís and the Idea of Progress." In *Adamantios Koraís and the European Enlightenment*, ed. P. Kitromilides, 225–44. Oxford, 2010.

Moyn, Samuel. *The Last Utopia: Human Rights in History*. Cambridge, MA, 2010.

Muglioni, Jacques. *Auguste Comte: Un philosophe pour notre temps*. Paris, 1995.

Mulford, Carla. "Joel Barlow, Edmund Burke, and Fears of Masonic Conspiracy in 1792." In *Secret Texts: The Literature of Secret Societies*, ed. M. M. Roberts and H. Ormsby-Lennon, 169–87. New York, 1995.

———. "Benjamin Franklin, Virtue's Ethics, and 'Political Truth.'" In *Resistance to Tyrants*, ed. Gish and Klinghard, 85–104.

Munck, Thomas. "The Troubled Reception of Thomas Paine in France, Germany, the Netherlands and Scandinavia." In *Paine and Jefferson*, ed. Newman and Onuf, 161–82.

Murphy, Martin. *Blanco White: Self-Banished Spaniard*. New Haven, CT, 1989.

Nadelhaft, J. J. *The Disorders of War: The Revolution in South Carolina*. Orono, ME, 1981.

Nash, Gary. "The American Clergy and the French Revolution." *WMQ*, 3rd ser., no. 3 (1965): 392–412.

———. *The Unknown American Revolution*. London, 2006.

———. "Philadelphia's Radical Caucus That Propelled Pennsylvania to Independence and Democracy." In *Revolutionary Founders*, ed. Young, Nash, and Raphael, 67–85.

Nash, Gary, and G. R. Gao Hodges. *Friends of Liberty: Thomas Jefferson, Tadeusz Kosciuszko and Agrippa Hull*. New York, 2008.

Nash, Gary, and Jean R. Soderlund. *Freedom by Degrees: Emancipation in Pennsylvania and Its Aftermath*. Oxford, 1991.

Navickas, K. *Loyalism and Radicalism in Lancashire, 1798–1815*. Oxford, 2009.

Neatby, Hilda. *Quebec: The Revolutionary Age, 1760–1791*. Toronto, 1966.

Neely, S. "The Politics of Liberty in the Old World and New: Lafayette's Return to America in 1824." *JER* 6 (1986): 151–71.

Nelson, Craig. *Thomas Paine: His Life, His Time and the Birth of Modern Nations*. London, 2006.

Nelson, Eric. *The Royalist Revolution: Monarchy and the American Founding.* Cambridge, MA, 2014.

Nesbitt, Nick. *Universal Emancipation: The Haitian Revolution and the Radical Enlightenment.* Charlottesville, VA, 2008.

Newman, P. D. *Fries's Rebellion: The Enduring Struggle for the American Revolution.* Philadelphia, 2004.

Newman, Simon, ed. *Europe's American Revolution.* Basingstoke, 2006.

———. "Paine, Jefferson and Revolutionary Radicalism in Early National America." In *Paine and Jefferson,* ed. Newman and Onuf, 71–94.

Newman, Simon, and P. S. Onuf, eds. *Paine and Jefferson in the Age of Revolution.* Charlottesville, VA, 2013.

Nijenhuis, I. J. A. *Een joodse philosophe, Isaac de Pinto (1717–1787).* Amsterdam, 1992.

Nipperdey, Thomas. *Germany from Napoleon to Bismarck.* Princeton, 1996.

Nobles, Gregory. "Satan, Smith, Shattuck, and Shays." In *Revolutionary Founders,* ed. Young, Nash, and Raphael, 215–31.

Noether, E. P., ed. *The American Constitution as a Symbol and Reality for Italy.* Lewiston, NY, 1989.

Nord, Philip. *The Republican Moment: Struggles for Democracy in Nineteenth-Century France.* Cambridge, MA, 1998.

O'Donnell, R. "The Military Committee and the United Irishmen, 1798–1803." In *Unrespectable Radicals,* ed. Davis and Pickering, 125–45.

Ohles, Frederick. *Germany's Rude Awakening: Censorship in the Land of the Brothers Grimm.* Kent, OH, 1992.

Oldfield, J. R. *Transatlantic Abolitionism in the Age of Revolution: An International History of Anti-Slavery, c. 1787–1820.* Cambridge, 2013.

Olson, Lester. "Franklin on National Character and the Great Seal of the United States." In *The Cambridge Companion to Benjamin Franklin,* ed. C. Mulford, 117–31. New York, 2008.

Ó Muirí, R. "Newry and the French Revolution, 1792." *Seanchas Ardmhacha: Journal of the Armagh Diocesan Historical Society* 13 (1989): 102–20.

O'Neill, D. *The Burke-Wollstonecraft Debate.* University Park, PA, 2007.

Op de Beeck, Johan. *Het Verlies van België: De strijd tussen de Nederlandse koning en de Belgische revolutionairen in 1830.* Amsterdam, 2015.

O'Shaughnessy, A. J. *An Empire Divided: The American Revolution and the British Caribbean.* Philadelphia, 2000.

Osterhammel, Jurgen. *The Transformation of the World: A Global History of the Nineteenth Century.* Princeton, 2014.

Ouellet, Fernand. *Louis Joseph Papineau: Un être divisé.* Ottawa, 1960.

Oury, Guy Marie. *Mgr Briand: Évêque de Québec et les problèmes de son époque.* Sablé-sur-Sarthe, 1983.

Ozouf, Mona. "La Révolution française et l'idée de l'homme nouveau." In *Political Culture of the French Revolution,* ed. Colin Lucas, vol. 2 of *The French Revolution and the Creation of Modern Political Culture,* 213–32. Oxford, 1988.

Pace, Antonio. *Benjamin Franklin and Italy.* Philadelphia, 1958.

Pagden, Anthony. *The Enlightenment and Why It Still Matters.* Oxford, 2013.

Page, Anthony. "'Liberty Has an Asylum': John Jebb, British Radicalism and the American Revolution." *History* 87 (2002): 204–26.

————. *John Jebb and the Enlightenment Origins of British Radicalism.* Westport, CT, 2003.

Pakenham, Thomas. *The Year of Liberty: The Great Irish Rebellion of 1798.* New York, 1998.

Palmer, R. R. *The Age of the Democratic Revolution: A Political History of Europe and America, 1760–1800.* 2 vols. Princeton, 1959.

————. "Two Americans in Two Dutch Republics: The Adamses, Father and Son." *BMGN* 97 (1982): 393–408.

————. *From Jacobin to Liberal: Marc-Antoine Jullien, 1775–1848.* Princeton, 1993.

Papas, Phillip. *Renegade Revolutionary: The Life of General Charles Lee.* New York, 2014.

Parker, Hershel. *Herman Melville: A Biography.* 2 vols. Baltimore, 1997–2003.

Parkinson, R. G. *The Common Cause: Creating Race and Nation in the American Revolution.* Chapel Hill, NC, 2016.

Parmegiani, S. *Ugo Foscolo and English Culture.* London, 2011.

Parmenter, J. W. "Dragging Canoe (Tsi'yu-gunsi'ni): Chickamauga Cherokee Patriot." In *Human Tradition,* ed. Rhoden and Steele, 113–37.

Pasley, Jeffrey. "Thomas Greenleaf: Printers and the Struggle for Democratic Politics and Freedom of the Press." In *Revolutionary Founders,* ed. Young, Nash, and Raphael, 355–73.

Patterson, S. E. "The Federalist Reaction to Shays' Rebellion." In *In Debt to Shays: The Bicentennial of an Agrarian Rebellion,* ed. R. A. Gross, 101–18. Charlottesville, VA, 1993.

Pawling, Micah. *Wabanaki Homeland and the New State of Maine.* Amherst, MA, 2007.

Pellerin, Pascale. "Naigeon: Une certaine image de Diderot sous la Révolution." *Recherches sur Diderot et sur l'Encyclopédie* 29 (2000): 32.

Perrone, Sean. "John Stroughton and the *Divina Pastora* Prize Case, 1816–1819." *JER* 28 (2008): 215–41.

Peterson, M. D. *Thomas Jefferson and the New Nation: A Biography.* New York, 1970.

Petiteau, N. "La Restauration face aux vétérans de l'Empire." In *Repenser la Restauration,* ed. Mollier, Reid, and Yon.

Petranovich, D., and M. Holbreich. "In the Valley of the Dry Bones: Abraham Lincoln's Biblical Oratory and the Coming of the Civil War." In *Resistance to Tyrants,* ed. Gish and Klinghard, 201–21.

Phillipson, N. "Adam Smith as Civic Moralist." In *Wealth and Virtue: The Shaping of Political Economy in the Scottish Enlightenment,* ed. I. Hont and M. Ignatieff, 179–202. Cambridge, 2002.

————. *Adam Smith: An Enlightened Life.* Penguin, 2010.

Philp, Mark. "Revolutionaries in Paris: Paine, Jefferson, and Democracy." In *Paine and Jefferson,* ed. Newman and Onuf, 137–60.

————. *Reforming Ideas in Britain: Politics and Language in the Shadow of the French Revolution.* Cambridge, 2014.

Pilbeam, Pam. *The 1830 Revolution in France.* New York, 1991.

Piquet, Jean-Daniel. *L'émancipation des Noirs dans la Révolution française (1789–1795).* Paris, 2002.

Pocock, J. G. A. *The Machiavellian Moment: Florentine Political Thought and the Atlantic Republican Tradition.* 1975. New ed., Princeton, 2003.

————. *Virtue, Commerce, and History: Essays on Political Thought and History, Chiefly in the Eighteenth Century.* Cambridge, 1985.

————. *Barbarism and Religion.* 6 vols. Cambridge, 1999–2015.

Poirteir, Cathal, ed. *The Great Irish Rebellion of 1798*. Dublin, 1998.

Polasky, Janet L. *Revolution in Brussels, 1787–1793*. Hanover, NH, 1987.

———. "The Success of a Counter-Revolution in Revolutionary Europe: The Brabant Revolution of 1789." *Tijdschrift voor Geschiedenis* 103 (1989): 413–21.

———. *Revolutions without Borders: The Call to Liberty in the Atlantic World*. New Haven, CT, 2015.

Popkin, J. "From Dutch Republican to French Monarchist: Antoine-Marie Cerisier and the Age of Revolution." *Tijdschrift voor Geschiedenis* 102 (1989): 534–44.

———. *News and Politics in the Age of Revolution: Jean Luzac's "Gazette de Leyde."* Ithaca, NY, 1989.

———. "Dutch Patriots, French Journalists and Declarations of Rights." *Historical Journal* 38 (1995): 553–65.

———. *You Are All Free: The Haitian Revolution and the Abolition of Slavery*. Cambridge, 2010.

Post, D. M. "Jeffersonian Revisions of Locke's Education, Property Rights, and Liberty." In *The American Enlightenment*, ed. Frank Shuffelton, 295–317. Rochester, NY, 1993.

Postma, Jan. "John Adams en zijn Leidse vrienden." *Leids Jaarboekje* (2011): 81–108.

Prak, Maarten. *Republikeinse veelheid, democratisch enkelvoud: Sociale verandering in het Revolutietijvak, 's-Hertogenbosch, 1770–1820*. Nijmegen, 1999.

Pulliam, John D. *History of Education*. 5th ed. New York, 1991.

Quintero, Inés. "El Movimiento juntista de 1808 en la provincial de Caracas." In *Experiencias*, ed. Ávila and Pérez Herrero, 381–98.

Racine, K. *Francisco de Miranda: A Transatlantic Life in the Age of Revolution*. Wilmington, DE, 2003.

Rahe, Paul. *Republics Ancient and Modern: Classical Republicanism and the American Revolution*. Chapel Hill, NC, 1992.

Rakove, Jack. *Revolutionaries: A New History of the Invention of America*. Boston, 2011.

———. "Constitutionalism: The Happiest Revolutionary Script." In *Scripting Revolution: A Historical Approach to the Comparative Study of Revolutions*, ed. Keith Michael Baker and D. Edelstein, 103–17. Stanford, CA, 2015.

Ramm, Agatha. *Germany, 1789–1919: A Political History*. London, 1967.

Rana, Aziz. *The Two Faces of American Freedom*. Cambridge, MA, 2010.

Raphael, Ray. *A People's History of the American Revolution*. New York, 2002.

———. "Blacksmith Timothy Bigelow and the Massachusetts Revolution of 1774." In *Revolutionary Founders*, ed. Young, Nash, and Raphael, 35–52.

———. "The Democratic Moment: The Revolution and Popular Politics." In *The Oxford Handbook of the American Revolution*, ed. E. G. Gray and J. Kamensky, 121–38. Oxford, 2013.

———. *Founding Myths: Stories That Hide Our Patriotic Past*. New York, 2014.

Raphael, Ray, and Marie Raphael. *The Spirit of '74: How the American Revolution Began*. New York, 2015.

Rapport, M. *1848: Year of Revolution*. 2008. New ed., New York, 2010.

Ravitch, N. "The Abbé Fauchet: Romantic Religion during the French Revolution." *Journal of the American Academy of Religion* 42 (1974): 247–62.

Régent, Frédéric. *La France et ses esclaves*. Paris, 2007.

———. "From Individual to Collective Emancipation: War and the Republic in the Caribbean during the French Revolution." In *Republics at War, 1776–1840: Revolutions,*

Conflicts, and Geopolitics in Europe and the Atlantic World, ed. Pierre Serna, A. De Francesco, and J. A. Miller, 165–86. London, 2013.

Reich, Jerome R. *British Friends of the American Revolution.* London, 1997.

Rémond, René. *Les États-Unis devant l'opinion française, 1815–1852.* 2 vols. Paris, 1962.

Renwick, W. R. "Benjamin Franklin and Canada." In *The Empire Club of Canada Addresses.* Toronto, 1923.

Reynolds, L. J. *European Revolutions and the American Literary Renaissance.* New Haven, CT, 1988.

Rhoden, N. L. "William Smith: Philadelphia Minister and Moderate." In *Human Tradition*, ed. Rhoden and Steele, 61–80.

Rhoden, N. L., and I. K. Steele, eds. *The Human Tradition in the American Revolution.* Wilmington, DE, 2000.

Rials, Stéphane. *La Déclaration des droits de l'homme et du citoyen.* Paris, 1988.

Richards, Leonard. *Shays's Rebellion: The American Revolution's Final Battle.* Philadelphia, 2002.

Riley, Stephen. "Doctor William Whiting and Shays' Rebellion." *Proceedings of the American Antiquarian Society* 66 (1956): 119–31.

Riordan, Liam. "'O Dear, What Can the Matter Be?' The Urban Early Republic and the Politics of Popular Song in Benjamin Carr's *Federal Overture.*" *JER* 31 (2011): 179–227.

Robbins, Caroline. "The Lifelong Education of Thomas Paine (1737–1809)." *PAPhS* 127, no. 3 (1983): 135–42.

Roberts, Andrew. *Napoleon the Great.* London, 2014.

Roberts, Hugh. *Shelley and the Chaos of History: A New Politics of Poetry.* University Park, PA, 1997.

Robertson, Priscilla Smith. *Revolutions of 1848: A Social History.* 1952. New ed., Princeton, 1968.

Robinson, C. *Fight for Freedom: The Destruction of Slavery in Jamaica.* Kingston, 2007.

Robson, D. W. *Educating Republicans: The College in the Era of the American Revolution, 1750–1800.* Westport, CT, 1985.

Rodríguez, Jaime E. *The Independence of Spanish America.* Cambridge, 1998.

Rodríguez, Mario. *La Revolución Americana de 1776 y el mundo hispánico.* Madrid, 1976.

Rodríguez López-Brea, Carlos. *Don Luis de Borbón, el cardenal de los liberales (1777–1823).* Toledo, 2002.

Roe, Nicholas. *Wordsworth and Coleridge: The Radical Years.* Oxford, 1988.

Roegiers, J., and N. C. F. Van Sas. "Revolutie in Noord en Zuid (1780–1830)." In *Geschiedenis van de Nederlanden*, ed. J. C. H. Blom and E. Lamberts, 219–49. Rijswijk, 1993.

Rohrs, R. C. "American Critics of the French Revolution of 1848." *JER* 14 (1944): 359–77.

Romani, R. *National Character and Public Spirit in Britain and France, 1750–1914.* Cambridge, 2002.

Rosen, Fred. *Bentham, Byron and Greece.* Oxford, 1992.

Rosendaal, Joost. *Bataven! Nederlandse vluchtelingen in Frankrijk, 1787–1795.* Nijmegen, 2003.

———. *De Nederlandse Revolutie: Vrijheid, volk en vaderland, 1783–99.* Nijmegen, 2005.

Rosenfeld, R. N. *American Aurora: A Democratic-Republican Returns.* New York, 1997.

Rosenfeld, Sophia. "Tom Paine's Common Sense and Ours." *WMQ*, 3rd ser., 65:4 (2008): 633–68.

———. *Common Sense: A Political History.* Cambridge, MA, 2011.

Rossignol, Marie-Jeanne. "A 'Black Declaration of Independence'? War, Republic, and Race in the United States of America, 1775–1787." In *Republics at War, 1776–1840: Revolutions, Conflicts and Geopolitics in Europe and the Atlantic World*, ed. Pierre Serna, A. De Francesco, and J. A. Miller, 107–30. London, 2013.

Ruiz Barrionuevo, Carmen. "Juan Germán Roscio y el pensamiento antiliberal." *Philologia Hispalensis* 25 (2011): 181–200.

Ruiz Martínez, Eduardo. *La librería de Nariño y los Derechos del Hombre*. Bogotá, 1990.

Rusk, Ralph L. *The Life of Ralph Waldo Emerson*. New York, 1949.

Rutjes, Mart. "De Staatsregeling van 1798 als maatschappelijk verdrag." *De Achttiende Eeuw* 44 (2012): 73–84.

Ryerson, Richard A. *The Revolution Is Now Begun: The Radical Committees of Philadelphia, 1765–1776*. Philadelphia, 1978.

Saillant, John. "The American Enlightenment in Africa: Jefferson's Colonization and Black Virginians' Migration to Liberia, 1776–1840." *Eighteenth-Century Studies* 31 (1998): 261–82.

Sammons, J. L. *Heinrich Heine: A Modern Biography*. Princeton, 1979.

Sánchez-Blanco, Francisco. *El Absolutismo y las Luces en el reinado de Carlos III*. Madrid, 2002.

Sanders, James S. *The Vanguard of the Atlantic World: Creating Modernity, Nation, and Democracy in Nineteenth-Century Latin America*. Durham, NC, 2014.

Saunt, Claudio. *West of the Revolution: An Uncommon History of 1776*. New York, 2014.

Sayre, G. M. "Jefferson and Native Americans." In *The Cambridge Companion to Thomas Jefferson*, ed. Shuffelton, 61–72.

Schachtman, T. *Gentlemen Scientists and Revolutionaries: The Founding Fathers in the Age of Enlightenment*. New York, 2014.

Schama, S. *Patriots and Liberators: Revolution in the Netherlands, 1789–1813*. London, 1977.

Schiff, Stacy. *Dr. Franklin Goes to France: How America Was Born in Monarchical Europe*. London, 2005.

Schmidt, Leigh Eric. *Village Atheists: How America's Unbelievers Made Their Way in a Godly Nation*. Princeton, 2016.

Schofield, Philip. *Utility and Democracy: The Political Thought of Jeremy Bentham*. Oxford, 2006.

Schoorl, E. *Jean-Baptiste Say: Revolutionary, Entrepreneur, Economist*. London, 2013.

Schroeder, Paul. *The Transformation of European Politics, 1763–1848*. Oxford, 1994.

Schulte Nordholt, Jan Willem. *The Dutch Republic and American Independence*. Chapel Hill, NC, 1982.

Schultz, Kirsten. *Tropical Versailles: Empire, Monarchy and the Portuguese Royal Court in Rio de Janeiro, 1808–1821*. New York, 2001.

Schutte, G. J. "Johannes Hermanus Redelinghuys: Een revolutionair Kapenaar." *South African Historical Journal* 3 (1971): 49–62.

———. *De Nederlandse Patriotten en de koloniën (1770–1800)*. Groningen, 1974.

Scurr, Ruth. "Varieties of Democracy in the French Revolution." In *Re-Imagining Democracy*, ed. Innes and Philp, 57–68.

Sehat, David. *The Myth of American Religious Freedom*. Oxford, 2011.

Selbin, Eric. "Revolution in the Real World." In *Theorizing Revolutions*, ed. John Foran, 123–36. London, 1997.

Serna, Pierre. "In Search of the Atlantic Republic: 1660–1776–1799 in the Mirror." In *Rethinking the Atlantic World*, ed. Albertone and De Francesco, 256–75.

Sewell, William H. "Ideologies and Social Revolutions: Reflections on the French Case." *Journal of Modern History* 57 (1985): 57–85.

Sharp, J. R. *American Politics in the Early Republic: The New Nation in Crisis*. New Haven, CT, 1993.

————. "France and the United States at the End of the Eighteenth Century." In *Rethinking*, ed. Albertone and De Francesco, 203–18.

Sheehan, C. A. "The Politics of Public Opinion." *WMQ*, 3rd ser., 49 (1992): 609–27.

————. *James Madison and the Spirit of Republican Self-Government*. Cambridge, 2009.

Sheehan, James. "The German States and the European Revolution." In *Revolution and the Meanings of Freedom*, ed. Woloch, 246–79.

Sheps, Arthur. "The American Revolution and the Transformation of English Republicanism." *Historical Reflections/Réflexions historiques* 11 (1975), reprinted in *Thomas Paine*, ed. Kuklick, 285–310.

Sher, R. B. *The Enlightenment and the Book*. Chicago, 2006.

Showalter, E. *The Civil Wars of Julia Ward Howe*. New York, 2016.

Shuffelton, Frank, ed. *The Cambridge Companion to Thomas Jefferson*. Cambridge, 2009.

Siemers, D. J. "John Adams's Political Thought." In *A Companion to John Adams and John Quincy Adams*, ed. D. Waldstreicher, 102–24. Oxford, 2013.

Slack, Charles. *Liberty's First Crisis: Adams, Jefferson and the Misfits Who Saved Free Speech*. New York, 2015.

Slaughter, Thomas P. *The Whiskey Rebellion: Frontier Epilogue to the American Revolution*. New York, 1986.

————. *Independence: The Tangled Roots of the American Revolution*. New York, 2014.

Slavin, M. *The French Revolution in Miniature: Section Droits-de-l'Homme, 1789–1795*. Princeton, 1984.

Sloan, H. E. "Thomas Jefferson and the John Adams Family." In *A Companion to John Adams and John Quincy Adams*, ed. D. Waldstreicher, 472–86. Oxford, 2013.

Smith, Barbara C. *The Freedoms We Lost: Consent and Resistance in Revolutionary America*. New York, 2010.

Smith, George H. *The System of Liberty: Themes in the History of Classical Liberalism*. Cambridge, 2013.

Smyth, Jim. "The 1798 Rebellion in Its Eighteenth-Century Contexts." In *Revolution, Counter-revolution and Union*, ed. Smyth, 1–20.

————. "The Act of Union and 'Public Opinion.'" In *Revolution, Counter-revolution and Union*, ed. Smyth, 146–60.

————, ed. *Revolution, Counter-revolution and Union: Ireland in the 1790s*. Cambridge, 2000.

Sonenscher, Michael. *Before the Deluge: Public Debt, Inequality, and the Intellectual Origins of the French Revolution*. Princeton, 2007.

Spellberg, Denise. *Thomas Jefferson's Qur'an: Islam and the Founders*. New York, 2013.

Spencer, D. S. *Louis Kossuth and Young America: A Study of Sectionalism and Foreign Policy, 1848–1852*. Columbia, MO, 1977.

Spencer, M. G., ed. *The Bloomsbury Encyclopaedia of the American Enlightenment*. 2 vols. New York, 2015.

Sperber, Jonathan. *Rhineland Radicals: The Democratic Movement and the Revolution of 1848–1849*. Princeton, 1991.

Spieler, Miranda. "France in the Atlantic World." In *The Blackwell Companion to the French Revolution*, ed. P. McPhee, 57–73. Oxford, 2012.

Spini, Giorgio. "The Perception of America in Italian Consciousness, 1776–1865." In *The United States and Italy*, ed. H. S. Nelli, 49–59. New York, 1977.

Spitz, Jean-Fabian. "Républicanisme et libéralisme dans le moment révolutionnaire." *AHRF* 358 (2009): 19–45.

Spurlin, P. M. *Rousseau in America, 1760–1809*. Tuscaloosa, AL, 1969.

Stagg, J. C. A. *The War of 1812: Conflict for a Continent*. Cambridge, 2012.

Staloff, Darren. *Hamilton, Adams, Jefferson: The Politics of Enlightenment and the American Founding*. New York, 2005.

———."The Politics of Pedagogy: Thomas Jefferson and the Education of a Democratic Citizenry." In *The Cambridge Companion to Thomas Jefferson*, ed. Shuffelton, 127–42.

———. "John Adams and the Enlightenment." In *A Companion to John Adams and John Quincy Adams*, ed. D. Waldstreicher, 36–59. Oxford, 2013.

Staum, Martin S. *Cabanis: Enlightenment and Medical Philosophy in the French Revolution*. Princeton, 1980.

———. "The Enlightenment Transformed: The Institute Prize Contests." *Eighteenth-Century Studies* 19, no. 2 (1985–86): 153–79.

Steckel, R. H. "The African American Population of the United States, 1790–1920." In *A Population History of North America*, ed. Haines and Steckel, 433–81.

Steele, Brian. *Thomas Jefferson and American Nationhood*. New York, 2012.

Steell, Willis. *Benjamin Franklin of Paris (1776–1785)*. New York, 1938.

Stelling-Michaud, Sven. "Sismondi face aux réalités politiques de son temps." In *Sismondi européen* (Actes du Colloque international tenu à Genève, 1973), 153–60. Geneva-Paris, 1976.

Stewart, A. T. Q. *A Deeper Silence: The Hidden Roots of the United Irish Movement*. London, 1993.

Stewart, D. O. *Madison's Gift: Five Partnerships That Built America*. New York, 2015.

Stewart, Matthew. *Nature's God: The Heretical Origins of the American Republic*. New York, 2014.

Stuurman, Siep. *The Invention of Humanity: Equality and Cultural Difference in World History*. Cambridge, MA, 2017.

Suárez, Federico. *Las Cortes de Cádiz*. Madrid, 1982.

———. *La crisis política del Antiguo Régimen en España (1800–1840)*. 3rd ed. Madrid, 1988.

Suhonen, K. "Le Canadien entre chimère et bonheur." In *Utopies en Canada, 1545–1845*, ed. Andrès and Desjardins, 103–18.

Sumrell, Morgan. "John Trumbull: Art and Politics in the Revolution." *Journal of the American Revolution* (January 2013).

Szatmary, D. P. *Shays' Rebellion: The Making of an Agrarian Insurrection*. Amherst, MA, 1980.

Tackett, Timothy. *Becoming a Revolutionary: The Deputies of the French National Assembly and the Emergence of a Revolutionary Culture (1789–1790)*. Princeton, 1996.

Taylor, Alan. *Liberty Men and Great Proprietors: The Revolutionary Settlement on the Maine Frontier, 1760–1820*. Chapel Hill, NC, 1990.

———. "Agrarian Independence: Northern Land Rioters after the Revolution." In *Beyond the American Revolution*, ed. Young, 221–45.

———. *The Civil War of 1812: American Citizens, British Subjects, Irish Rebels, and Indian Allies*. New York, 2010.

———. *The Internal Enemy: Slavery and the War in Virginia, 1772–1832*. New York, 2014.

———. *American Revolutions: A Continental History, 1750–1804*. New York, 2016.

Taylor, Antony. "Down with the Crown." In *British Anti-Monarchism and Debates about Royalty since 1790*. London, 1999.

Taylor, Miles. *The Decline of British Radicalism, 1847–1860*. Oxford, 1995.

Taylor, Peter K. *Indentured to Liberty: Peasant Life and the Hessian Military State, 1688–1815*. Ithaca, NY, 1994.

Te Brake, Wayne. *Regents and Rebels*. Cambridge, MA, 1989.

———. "The Dutch Republic and the Creation of the United States." In *Four Centuries of Dutch-American Relations, 1609–2009*, ed. H. Krabbendam, 204–15. Albany, NY, 2009.

Tesch, Pieter. "Presbyterian Radicalism." In *The United Irishmen: Republicanism, Radicalism and Rebellion*, ed. D. Dickson, D. Keogh, and K. Whelan, 33–49. Dublin, 1993.

Thibaud, Clement. "Salus populi: Imaginando la reasunción de la soberanía en Caracas, 1808–1810." In *En el umbral de las revoluciones*, ed. Breña, 335–63.

Thomas, D. O. Introduction to Richard Price, *Political Writings*. Cambridge, 1991.

Thomas, William. *The Philosophic Radicals*. Oxford, 1979.

Tillet, Edouard. "La place ambiguë de Jean-Louis de Lolme dans la diffusion du modèle anglais de l'Ancien régime à la Révolution française." In *Genève, lieu d'Angleterre, Geneva an English Enclave*, ed. V. Cossy, B. Kapossy, and R. Whatmore, 199–240. Geneva, 2009.

Tønnesson, Kare D. "La démocratie directe sous la Révolution française: Le cas des districts et sections de Paris." In *The Political Culture of the French Revolution*, ed. Colin Lucas, vol. 2 of *The French Revolution and the Creation of Modern Political Culture*. Oxford, 1988.

Tortarolo, Eduardo. "Philip Mazzei and the Liberty of the New Nation." In *American Constitution*, ed. Noether, 55–68.

Tyack, David B. *Turning Points in American Educational History*. Waltham, MA, 1967.

Unger, H. G. *The Last Founding Father: James Monroe and a Nation's Call to Greatness*. Philadelphia, 2009.

———. *John Quincy Adams*. Boston, 2012.

Urban, Wayne, and J. Wagoner. *American Education: A History*. New York, 1996.

Valsania, M. *The Limits of Optimism: Thomas Jefferson's Dualistic Enlightenment*. Charlottesville, VA, 2011.

Van den Bossche, G. *Enlightened Innovation and the Ancient Constitution (1787–1790)*. Brussels, 2001.

Van der Burg, M. *Nederland onder Franse invloed (1799–1813)*. Amsterdam, 2009.

Vanegas, Isidro. "De la actualización del poder monárquico al preludio de su disolución: Nueva Granada, 1808–1809." In *En el umbral de las revoluciones*, ed. Breña, 365–97.

Van Vliet, R. *Elie Luzac (1781–1796): Boekverkoper van de Verlichting*. Nijmegen, 2005.

Vanysacker, D. "Verlicht ultramontaan: Een contradictio in terminis?" *De Achttiende Eeuw* 32 (2000): 97–115.

Varela Suanzes-Carpegna. "The Image of the British System of Government in Spain (1759–1814)." In *Spanish Enlightenment Revisited*, ed. Astigarraga, 193–212.

Velema, W. R. E. "Vrijheid als volkssouvereiniteit (1780–1795)." In *Vrijheid: Een geschiedenis van de vijftiende tot de twintigste eeuw*, ed. E. O. G. Haitsma Mulier and W. R. E. Velema, 287–303. Amsterdam, 1999.

Venturi, Franco. *Pagine repubblicane.* Turin, 2004.

Verhoeven, W. *Americomania and the French Revolution Debate in Britain, 1789–1802.* Cambridge, 2013.

Vernet, Julien. *Strangers on Their Soil: Opposition to United States' Governance in Louisiana's Orleans Territory, 1803–1809.* Jackson, MS, 2013.

Vigier, Philippe. *Paris pendant la Monarchie de Juillet (1830–1848).* Paris, 1991.

Vincent, Bernard. "Les Américains à Paris et leur image sous la Révolution." *Revue de Littérature Comparée,* no. 251 (1989): 479–95.

———. "Thomas Paine et la 'républicanisation' de la Louisiane." In *Thomas Paine ou La République sans frontières,* ed. B. Vincent, 125–35. Nancy, 1993.

———. "Thomas Paine et la république comme l'instrument du paix." In *Thomas Paine ou La République sans frontières,* ed. B. Vincent. Nancy, 1993.

Vincent, K. S. *Pierre-Joseph Proudhon and the Rise of French Republican Socialism.* New York, 1984.

———. *Benjamin Constant and the Birth of French Liberalism.* New York, 2011.

Volokh, Eugene. "Thomas Cooper, Early American Public Intellectual." *New York Journal of Law and Liberty* 4 (2009): 372–81.

Wahnich, Sophie. "Identité et Altérité: Thomas Paine dans la Révolution Française." In *Thomas Paine ou la République sans frontières,* ed. B. Vincent, 65–77. Nancy, 1993.

Waldman, Steven. *Founding Faith: How Our Founding Fathers Forged a Radical New Approach to Religious Liberty.* New York, 2008.

Waldstreicher, David. *Slavery's Constitution: From Revolution to Ratification.* New York, 2009.

Walicki, Andrzej. "The Problem of Revolution in Polish Thought, 1831–49." In *The American and European Revolutions, 1776–1848,* 287–319. Iowa City, 1980.

Walsh, L. S. "The African American Population of the Colonial United States." In *A Population History of North America,* ed. Haines and Steckel, 191–239.

Walter, R. J. "Revolution, Independence, and Liberty in Latin America." In *Revolution and the Meanings of Freedom,* ed. Woloch, 103–37.

Walters, Kerry. *The American Deists.* Lawrence, KS, 1992.

———. *Benjamin Franklin and His Gods.* Urbana, IL, 1999.

———. *Revolutionary Deists: Early America's Rational Infidels.* New York, 2011.

Walzer, Michael. *The Paradox of Liberation: Secular Revolutions and Religious Counterrevolutions.* New Haven, CT, 2015.

Ward, Christopher. *The War of the Revolution.* New York, 1952.

Ward, Lee. *The Politics of Liberty in England and Revolutionary America.* 2004. New ed., Cambridge, 2010.

Watt, James. "Fictions of Commercial Empire, 1774–1782." In *India and Europe in the Global Eighteenth Century,* ed. S. Davies, D. S. Roberts, and G. Sánchez Espinosa, 157–73. Oxford, 2014.

Weber, D. J. *Bárbaros: Spaniards and Their Savages in the Age of Enlightenment.* New Haven, CT, 2005.

Wegert, Karl H. *German Radicals Confront the Common People: Revolutionary Politics and Popular Politics, 1789–1849.* Mainz, 1992.

Weisberger, Bernard. *America Afire: Jefferson, Adams and the First Contested Election.* New York, 2000.

Welch, Cheryl. *Liberty and Utility: The French Idéologues and the Transformation of Liberalism.* New York, 1984.

Wells, Colin. "Timothy Dwight's American 'Dunciad: The Triumph of Infidelity' and the Universalist Controversy." *Early American Literature* 33 (1998): 173–91.

Wells, Roger. *Insurrection: The British Experience, 1795–1803.* Gloucester, 1983.

Wende, Peter. *Radikalismus im Vormärz.* Wiesbaden, 1975.

Whaley, Joachim. *Germany and the Holy Roman Empire*, vol. 2, *The Peace of Westphalia to the Dissolution of the Reich, 1648–1806.* Oxford, 2012.

Whatmore, Richard. *Republicanism and the French Revolution: An Intellectual History of Jean-Baptiste Say's Political Economy.* Oxford, 2000.

———. "The French and North American Revolutions in Comparative Perspective." In *Rethinking*, ed. Albertone and De Francesco, 210–38.

White, Ashli. *Encountering Revolution: Haiti and the Making of the Early Republic.* Baltimore, 2010.

Wickham-Crowley, T. P. "Structural Theories of Revolution." In *Theorizing Revolutions*, ed. John Foran, 38–72. London, 1997.

Wiecek, W. M. "'A Peculiar Conservatism' and the Dorr Rebellion." *American Journal of Legal History* 22:3 (1978): 237–53.

Wilcken, Patrick. *Empire Adrift: The Portuguese Court in Rio de Janeiro, 1808–1821.* London, 2004.

Wilentz, Sean. *Chants Democratic: New York City and the Rise of the American Working Class, 1788–1850.* New York, 1984.

———. *The Rise of American Democracy: Jefferson to Lincoln.* New York, 2005.

———. *The Politicians and the Egalitarians.* New York, 2016.

Williams, G. A. "Morgan John Rhys and Volney's *Ruins of Empires.*" *Bulletin of the Board of Celtic Studies* 20 (1962): 58–73.

Wills, Gary. *Inventing America: Jefferson's Declaration of Independence.* New York, 1979.

Wilson, Arthur M. *Diderot.* Oxford, 1972.

Wilson, Gaye. "Thomas Jefferson's Portrait of Thomas Paine." In *Paine and Jefferson*, ed. Newman and Onuf, 229–51.

Winch, D. "Commercial Realities, Republican Principles." In *Republicanism: A Shared European Heritage*, ed. Martin Van Gelderen and Quentin Skinner, 2:293–310. Cambridge, 2002.

Winterer, Caroline. *American Enlightenments: Pursuing Happiness in the Age of Reason.* New Haven, CT, 2016.

Witte, E. "Belgique, débats et controverses historiographiques sur une révolution originaire." In *La Liberté guidant les peuples*, ed. Aprile, Caron, and Fureix, 113–43.

Wolloch, Nathaniel. "Barbarian Tribes, American Indians and Cultural Transmission: Changing Perspectives from the Enlightenment to Tocqueville." *History of Political Thought* 34:3 (2013): 507–39.

Woloch, Isser, ed. *Revolution and the Meanings of Freedom in the Nineteenth Century.* Stanford, CA, 1996.

Wood, Dennis. "Benjamin Constant: Life and Work." In *The Cambridge Companion to Benjamin Constant*, ed. H. Rosenblatt, 3–19. Cambridge, 2009.

Wood, Gordon S. *The Radicalism of the American Revolution.* 1991. New ed., New York, 1993.

———. *The American Revolution: A History.* New York, 2002.

———. *The Americanization of Benjamin Franklin.* New York, 2004.

———. "Is There a 'James Madison Problem'?" In *Liberty and American Experience in the Eighteenth Century*, ed. D. Womersley, 426–47. Indianapolis, 2006.

————. *Empire of Liberty: A History of the Early Republic, 1789–1815.* Oxford, 2009.

————. "The Radicalism of Thomas Jefferson and Thomas Paine Considered." In *Paine and Jefferson*, ed. Newman and Onuf, 13–25.

Woodcock, George. *Pierre-Joseph Proudhon: A Biography.* 1956. New ed., Abingdon, 2010.

Wootton, David. *Republicanism, Liberty and Commercial Society, 1649–1776.* Stanford, CA, 1994.

————. "Helvétius: From Radical Enlightenment to Revolution." *Political Theory* 28:3 (2000): 307–33.

————. "Liberty, Metaphor, and Mechanism: 'Checks and Balances' and the Origins of Modern Constitutionalism." In *Liberty and American Experience in the Eighteenth Century*, ed. D. Womersley, 209–74. Indianapolis, 2006.

Wright, Edmund. *Franklin of Philadelphia.* Cambridge, MA, 1986.

Young, A. F., ed. *Beyond the American Revolution: Explorations in the History of American Radicalism.* DeKalb, IL, 1993.

————. "Ebenezer Mackintosh: Boston's Captain General of the Liberty Tree." In *Revolutionary Founders*, ed. Young, Nash, and Raphael, 15–33.

Young, A. F., G. B. Nash, and R. Raphael, eds. *Revolutionary Founders: Rebels, Radicals and Reformers in the Making of the Nation.* New York, 2011.

Zamoyski, Adam. *Holy Madness: Romantics, Patriots and Revolutionaries, 1776–1871.* London, 1999.

Zaunstock, Holger. *Das Milieu des Verdachts.* Berlin, 2010.

Zeuske, M. *Francisco de Miranda und die Entdeckung Europas.* Münster, 1995.

Ziesche, Philipp. "Exporting American Revolutions: Gouverneur Morris, Thomas Jefferson, and the National Struggle for Universal Rights in Revolutionary France." *JER* 26 (2006): 419–47.

————. "Thomas Paine and Benjamin Franklin's French Circle." In *Paine and Jefferson*, ed. Newman and Onuf, 121–36.

Zilversmit, Arthur. *The First Emancipation: The Abolition of Slavery in the North.* Chicago, 1967.

Zucker, A. E., ed. *The Forty-Eighters: Political Refugees of the German Revolution of 1848.* New York, 1950.

Zuckert, Michael. "Two Paths from Revolution: Jefferson, Paine, and the Radicalization of Enlightenment Thought." In *Paine and Jefferson*, ed. Newman and Onuf, 252–76.

Zurbuchen, Simone. "Religion and Society." In *The Cambridge History of Eighteenth-Century Philosophy*, ed. Knud Haakonssen, 2:779–813. Cambridge, 2006.

Index

492–93, 575, 581, 584; *The American Dem-ocrat* (1838), 460, 493; *The Bravo* (1831), 22–23; *The Last of the Mohicans* (1826), 486
Cooper, Thomas (1759–1839), Manchester radical, 86, 88, 93, 101, 104, 109, 190, 339, 553
Cooperstown (New York), 492
Coram, Robert, Anglo-American revolutionary, 3, 17, 93, 100, 109, 158, 334, 391, 417, 601; *Political Inquiries* (1791), 100–101
Corfu and Ionian Islands, 378, 497–500
Cork (Ireland), 306–7; *Cork Gazette*, 306, 313
Cornwallis, Lord Charles (1738–1805), British commander at Yorktown, 68–69, 129, 143, 315–16
Coro (Venezuela), 371, 439–40, 450
Cortes, Spanish parliament in Madrid, 474, 479–80, 482. *See also* Cádiz Cortes
Council of Nicaea (AD 325), 25
Counter-Enlightenment, 21, 346, 349, 432, 452, 458, 462, 467, 469, 476, 483, 500, 508, 513–14, 549, 565
Creek Native American Confederacy, 26, 161, 168–70
Crémieux, Adolphe (1796–1880), French-Jewish republican leader, 559, 563, 586
Cromwell, Oliver (1599–1658), Lord Protector of England (1653–58), 77, 125, 188, 324, 418
Cruz de Malta, Madrid revolutionary club (1820–23), 474, 479
Cuba, 402, 410, 435, 440, 578
"cultural turn," the, 13
Curaçao (Dutch Caribbean), 214, 224, 229, 371–72, 374

Danish West Indies, 578
Darwin, Erasmus (1731–1802), grandfather of Charles Darwin, 6, 247, 289
Daumier, Honoré (1808–79), French caricaturist, 508, 544–46
Declaration of Human Rights (December 1948), by the United Nations, 5
Declaration of Independence (1776), 5, 11, 14, 49, 51, 58, 61, 76, 91, 107, 124, 141, 148, 200, 210, 226, 230, 247–49, 256, 271, 333, 358, 398, 440, 448, 462

Declaration of the Rights of Man and the Citizen (1789), 205, 255, 261–62, 270–71, 361, 368, 376, 445, 497, 520, 528
deism and anticlerical irreligion, political significance, 16, 85–86, 109
Deistical Society of New York, 18, 391, 417; *The Temple of Reason* (paper founded in 1800), 395
Delacroix, Eugène (1798–1863), French artist, 544, 545–46; *La Liberté Guidant le Peuple* (1830), 544, 545–46
Delaware, 58, 69, 94, 100–101, 151, 334; church-state linkage, 88
Delaware Indians (Ohio), 164–67
Démeunier, Jean Nicolas (1751–1814), writer on American state constitutions, 50, 68, 77, 87, 150, 251, 260, 270, 322
democratic societies, in America (1793–96), 331–35, 338, 387, 395
Democratic Society of Washington County (Pennsylvania), 335–37
De Potter, Louis (1786–1859), Belgian radical, 467, 526–28, 538
Desmoulins, Camille (1760–94), French revolutionary, 261, 263–64, 267
Dessalines, General Jean-Jacques (1758–1806), Haitian dictator, 383, 406
Devèze, Jean (1753–1829), French yellow fever expert, 368
Devyr, Thomas Ainge (1805–87), Irish-American radical, 582–83; *Our Natural Rights* (1835), 582
Dickinson, John (1732–1808), fifth "president" of Pennsylvania (1782–85), 33, 39, 51, 56–60, 64–65, 175
Dickinson Sergeant, Jonathan (1746–93), American radical, 333–34, 337
Diderot, Denis (1713–1808), 7, 29, 49, 52, 62, 117, 121–22, 126, 145, 233, 251, 341, 392, 438, 474; equality, 62–63, 75–76, 78, 223, 471; general will, 121–22; right of revolutionary resistance, 219–23; *Encyclopédie*, 96–97, 392, 419; *Histoire philosophique des Deux Indes* (1770) (see *Histoire philosophique des Deux Indes*)
Dohm, Christian Wilhelm (1751–1820), radical enlightener, 45, 146, 229–31

Franklin (*continued*)
204–5; early life, 113–14; education reform, 102–3; England, 114–18; France (1776–85), 45–46, 77, 113, 119, 121, 134, 216–17; Francophilia, 116, 124, 128–29; icon of American Revolution in Europe, 128–29, 131, 134–38, 209, 334, 347, 358, 475, 486–87; icon of American Revolution in Spanish America, 445, 449; Ireland, 293–95, 297, 301; lifestyle at Passy and Auteuil (Paris), 123–24, 128–29; and Paine, 47–49, 118–19, 123, 128, 385; irreligion of, 86, 109–10, 114–15, 137–38; and Pennsylvania's democratic constitution of 1776, 56, 59–61, 125–26, 128, 132–34; political radicalization, 59–62, 103, 117–18, 124–26, 128, 138; as sixth "president" of Pennsylvania (1785–8), 121, 132; *Autobiography*, 113–15; *Bonhomme Richard* (1777), 125–28, 216, 486
Franklin, William (1730–1814), son of Benjamin, last royal governor of New Jersey (1763–76), 65, 118
Franco-American Alliance (February 1778), 67–68, 123–24, 129–31, 201, 211–12, 216–18, 235, 296, 328, 350, 386
"Freiheit, Aufklärung, Rationalität und Volkshoheit" [Freedom, Enlightenment, Rationality and Sovereignty of the People], slogan of the Hambacher Fest, (1832), 538–41, 558
French Revolution (1789–99), 254–80, 471, 517, 549; abolition of slavery (1793–94), 367–69, 373; American enthusiasm for, 331–34, 333–36, 341–42, 346–47; *Assemblée Nationale* (National Assembly) in 1789, 128, 136–37, 257, 259–63, 268, 273, 277, 282, 329, 358, 527; "aristocratic" versus "democratic" republicanism, 4, 11, 15, 17–18, 34, 268–71, 278, 327, 386, 480; Bastille, 146, 265–67, 269, 301–2, 501, 518; black emancipation, 146–47, 260, 274–75, 361–84, 559; Brissotins (Girondins), 147, 204, 279, 329, 331, 369, 387, 489, 534, 552, 559, 588; Constitution of 1791 (constitutional monarchist), 325–27, 432, 523; Constitution of 1795 (bicameral), 446–47; debt to American Revolution, 1–4, 11, 122, 270–71, 279, 300,

328, 341; "democratization," 282, 353, 503, 554, 561; ending the French Monarchy (1792), 279–81, 303–4; equal population bloc representation, 431–33, 444, 478, 480; Federalist critique of, 239, 257–58, 268, 273–74, 277–79, 324, 341–46, 349–50; Feuillant "aristocratism," 258, 270, 272–73, 327, 365; inspired by radical *philosophes*, 259–60, 268–69, 552–53; newspapers and press freedom, 260, 267, 271, 559; parallelism with American Revolution, 17–18, 34, 38, 110–11, 137, 269, 278–80, 282–83, 326, 328, 341, 344–46, 384, 386–87, 399, 413, 514, 516, 602; *Robespierrisme*, Montagnard regime, 18, 279–83, 327–28, 330, 369, 387, 394, 503, 532, 545, 552, 559; "September massacres" (1792), 282; Terror, the (1793–94), 17, 20, 205, 328, 338, 448, 503, 591; unicameralism versus bicameralism, 136, 239, 480; viewed as proof that republicanism requires an enlightened population, 442
French Revolution of 1830 (July Revolution), 22–23, 517–20, 525, 530, 538 549; "June rebellion" (1832), 543–44
French Revolution of 1848: American and British reactions contrasted, 570–72; February uprising, 551–54; "democratic" banquets, 549, 551; April 1848 democratic elections, 561–62; influence of American institutions and concepts, 566, 585–87; "June Days" (23–26 June 1848), 564; National Assembly, 562–64; "national workshops," 563–64, 579; provinces less radical than Paris, 260–67, 519–20, 561–62, 565; radical-socialist split, 562–65, 588–89; Second Republic (1848–51), 53–54, 560–66, 568, 583, 593–94; Second Republic's democratic constitution, 561, 586; slavery abolished in French Caribbean, 574, 577–78; socialism, 551, 555, 560–63, 565, 574, 579, 588
French and Indian War. *See* Seven Years' War
Freneau, Philip (1752–1832), American revolutionary poet, v, 1, 3, 17, 88–89, 93, 96–97, 101, 109, 158; democratic republican ideology, v, 324, 334, 356, 391, 399, 418, 513, 601
Fugitive Slave Act (February, 1793), 576

752 / *Index*